ENCYCLOPEDIA OF

FAMILY HEAL+H

ENCYCLOPEDIA OF

FAMILY HEAL+H

Editors

Martha Craft-Rosenberg

The University of Iowa

Shelley-Rae Pehler

St. Ambrose University

1

Los Angeles | London | New Delhi
Singapore | Washington DC

Los Angeles | London | New Delhi
Singapore | Washington DC

FOR INFORMATION:

SAGE Publications, Inc.
2455 Teller Road
Thousand Oaks, California 91320
E-mail: order@sagepub.com

SAGE Publications Ltd.
1 Oliver's Yard
55 City Road
London, EC1Y 1SP
United Kingdom

SAGE Publications India Pvt. Ltd.
B 1/I 1 Mohan Cooperative Industrial Area
Mathura Road, New Delhi 110 044
India

SAGE Publications Asia-Pacific Pte. Ltd.
33 Pekin Street #02-01
Far East Square
Singapore 048763

Publisher: Rolf A. Janke
Assistant to the Publisher: Michele Thompson
Acquisitions Editor: Jim Brace-Thompson
Developmental Editor: Carole Maurer
Reference Systems Manager: Leticia Gutierrez
Reference Systems Coordinator: Laura Notton
Production Editor: Kate Schroeder
Copy Editors: Colleen B. Brennan, Patrice Sutton
Typesetter: Hurix Systems Pvt. Ltd.
Proofreaders: Sally Scott, Olivia Weber-Stenis,
Sandy Zilka
Cover Designer: Bryan Fishman

Printed in the United States of America.

Library of Congress Cataloging-in-Publication Data

Encyclopedia of family health / edited by Martha Craft-Rosenberg, Shelley-Rae Pehler.

p. cm.
"A Sage reference publication."

Includes bibliographical references and index.

ISBN 978-1-4129-6918-5 (cloth : alk. paper)

1. Family medicine–Encyclopedias.
2. Families–Health and hygiene–Encyclopedias.
I. Craft-Rosenberg, Martha. II. Pehler, Shelley-Rae.
[DNLM: 1. Family Health–Encyclopedias–English.
2. Health Promotion–Encyclopedias–English. WA 13]

RA418.5.F3E43 2011

610–dc22   2010030639

11 12 13 14 15 10 9 8 7 6 5 4 3 2 1

DISCLAIMER: All information contained in the *Encyclopedia of Family Health* is intended only for informational and educational purposes. The information is not intended to diagnose medical problems, prescribe remedies for illness, or treat disease. We recommend that you always seek the advice of a health care professional with respect to any medical condition, illness or disease.

Contents

.

List of Entries

Abortion Experienced by Childbearing Couples
Access to Health Care: Child Health
Access to Health Care: Elderly
Access to Health Care: Uninsured
Acute Care/Hospitalization of Family Members
Acute Health Problems and Interventions for the
  Childrearing Family
Acute Health Problems and Interventions for the
  Midlife Family
Addition of Family Members Through Marriage
Adolescent Counseling
Adoption Experiences for Infertile Couples
Adult Child Returning Home
Adult Child With Disability: Planning for by
  Parents
Adult Children Living at Home
Adult With Disability Living at Home
Adults With Childhood-Acquired Conditions
Advance Directives and the Family
Advocacy for Families
Affect Management and the Family
African American Families: Perspectives of
  Health
Aging and Shifting Roles in Families
Alcohol Addictions in the Family
Allergies and the Family
Alzheimer's Disease: An Overview of Family
  Issues in
Alzheimer's Disease: Caregiver Burden
Alzheimer's Disease and Communication
American Indian Families: Perspectives of Health
Americans with Disabilities Act and the Family
Animal-Assisted Therapy and the Family
Anorexia and Family Dynamics
Asian Families: Perspectives of Health
Assessing Family Health
Assisted Living Placement
Asthma Family Issues: Prevention and Control
Asynchronous Development Between Partners

Attention Deficit/Hyperactivity Disorder: Family
  Involvement and Management
Attention Deficit/Hyperactivity Disorder and the
  Family
Autism Spectrum Disorder and the Family

Babysitting and the Family
Bereavement and Perinatal Loss in Childbearing
  Families
Biopsychosocial Theoretical Perspectives of
  Family Systems
Bipolar Disorders and the Family
Birth Defects and the Family
Birth Order of Children in Families
Blindness and the Family
Buddhism's Influence on Health in the Family
Bulimia and Family Dynamics
Bullying and the Family

Cancer in the Family
Cancer Survivorship and the Family
Caregivers of Adults With Developmental
  Disabilities
Caregiving: Adults With Developmental
  Disabilities
Caregiving: Elderly
Caregiving: Infants
Caregiving: Partners/Spouses
Case Management for Chronic Illness/Disability
  and the Family
Cerebral Palsy and the Family
Changes in Family Structure
Changes in Family Structure, Roles
Changing Family and Health Demographics
Changing Views of Marriage, Home
  Responsibilities, and Caregiving
Child Beginning School
Child Emotional Abuse and the Family
Child Neglect and the Family

Reader's Guide

The Reader's Guide is provided to assist readers in locating entries on related topics. It provides a view of the scope of topics presented in entries to ensure a careful and systematic reading of related topics. It also classifies entries into 11 general topical categories to increase reader speed in locating topics of interest. Please note that entries may be listed under more than one topic.

At-Risk Conditions and At-Risk Situations

Alcohol Addictions in the Family
Bullying and the Family
Child Emotional Abuse and the Family
Child Neglect and the Family
Child Physical Abuse and the Family
Child Sexual Abuse and the Family
Cigarettes, Smoking, and Secondhand Smoke and Family Health
Community Violence Exposure and Family Health
Conflict in Family Life, Role and Management of
Death From Unnatural Causes: Drug Overdose
Death From Unnatural Causes: Homicides, Drive-By Shootings
Death From Unnatural Causes: Injuries
Death From Unnatural Causes: Poisoning
Dietary and Exercise Patterns in Families
Drinking by Underage Family Members
Drug Addictions in the Family
Early Periodic Screening, Diagnosis, and Treatment Program for Low-Income Children
Economic Downturn and Families
Elder Emotional Abuse and the Family
Elder Neglect and the Family
Elder Physical Abuse and the Family
Elder Sexual Abuse and the Family
Foster Care for Minors
Gambling Addictions in the Family
Home Environments and their Relationship to Safety
Incest in Families
Lead Poisoning and the Family
Rape and the Family
Refugees and Family Health
Risk Perception Based on Family Health History
Shaken Baby Syndrome in Childbearing Families
Sibling Physical Abuse
Spouse/Domestic Partner Physical Abuse
Suicide in the Family
Verbal Abuse in Families
War and Families

Education of Health Care Providers

Education of Child Life Providers in Family Health
Education of Health Care Providers: WHO Family Health Nurses
Education of Medical Health Care Providers in Family Health
Education of Nursing Health Care Providers in Family Health
Education of Occupational Health Providers in Family Health
Education of Physical Therapists in Family Health
Education of Recreational Therapy Providers in Family Health

Factors Influencing Family Health

African American Families: Perspectives of Health
American Indian Families: Perspectives of Health
Asian Families: Perspectives of Health
Buddhism's Influence on Health in the Family
Christianity's Influence on Health in the Family
Coping Management Styles in Families

Cultural Attitudes Toward Help-Seeking and
Beliefs About Illness in Families
Ethnic/Racial Influences in Families
Factors Influencing Family Health Values, Beliefs,
and Priorities
Families: The Basic Unit of Societies
Family Self-Management
Hinduism's Influence on Health in the
Family
Hispanic/Latino Families: Perspectives of Health
History of Families
Influence of Close Relationships on Health
Islam's Influence on Health in the Family
Judaism's Influence on Health in the Family
Poverty, Children in, and Health Care
Recreation in Family Health
Religious/Spiritual Influences on Health in the
Family
Resilience in Families With Health Challenges
Rituals, Routines, and Their Influence on Health
in Families
Sibling Conflict
Socioeconomic Status of Families
Stress Management Theory and Techniques in
Families

Families Experiencing Acute Physical and Mental Illness

Acute Health Problems and Interventions for the
Childrearing Family
Acute Health Problems and Interventions for the
Midlife Family
Affect Management and the Family
Birth Defects and the Family
Communicable Disease: Adult and Elderly
Communicable Disease: Children
Cord Blood Banking and the Childbearing
Family
Developmental Care of Preterm Infants and the
Childbearing Family
Families Experiencing a Child's Illness
Life-Threatening Illness and the Family
Men's Health
Prenatal Surgery and the Family
Sexually Transmitted Diseases and the Family
Sport-Related Accidents and Injuries and the
Family
Sudden Infant Death Syndrome in Childrearing
Families
Women's Health

Families Experiencing Chronic Physical and Mental Health Conditions

Adult With Disability Living at Home
Allergies and the Family
Alzheimer's Disease: An Overview of Family
Issues in
Alzheimer's Disease: Caregiver Burden
Alzheimer's Disease and Communication
Anorexia and Family Dynamics
Asthma Family Issues: Prevention and Control
Attention Deficit/Hyperactivity Disorder: Family
Involvement and Management
Attention Deficit/Hyperactivity Disorder and the
Family
Bipolar Disorders and the Family
Blindness and the Family
Bulimia and Family Dynamics
Cancer in the Family
Cancer Survivorship and the Family
Cerebral Palsy and the Family
Chronic Health Problems and Interventions for
the Childrearing Family
Chronic Health Problems and Interventions for
the Elderly Family
Chronic Health Problems and Interventions for
the Midlife Family
Chronic Illness and Family Management Styles
Cocaine Exposure and the Neonate
Deaf and Hearing Families
Depression in the Family
Diabetes, Type 1, and the Family
Diabetes, Type 2, and the Family
Disabilities and Family Management
Families Experiencing Chronic Physical and
Mental Health Conditions
Family Adherence to Health Care Regimen
Family Emotional Climate and Mental Health
Family Pediatric Adherence to Health Care
Regimen
Fetal Alcohol Exposure and Family Health
Food Allergies and Family Experiences
Health Management in Families
Heart Disease and the Family
HIV/AIDS and Influence on Family Structure and
Roles
Hypertension and the Family
Intellectual Disability in the Family
Learning Disabilities in the Family
Life Span: Care Coordination for Chronic Illness/
Disabilities and the Family

About the Editors

Martha Craft-Rosenberg joined the College of Nursing faculty at the University of Iowa in 1980 after a 15-year practice career with children and families. She currently serves as Emeritus Professor in the Parent, Child, and Family Area of Study. She is an elected fellow of the American Academy of Nursing.

An active researcher, Craft-Rosenberg has focused her studies on siblings of ill children, families of critically ill patients, and nursing standardized languages. Her language classification research includes nursing intervention classification since 1987 and diagnoses classification for a decade as principal investigator for the Nursing Diagnosis Extension and Classification team.

The author of 70 articles and 4 book chapters, and author or editor of 10 books, Craft-Rosenberg's funded research on children and families has garnered awards from the American Association for Critical Care Nursing and the Midwest Nursing Research Society. She is the first editor of the book *Nursing Interventions for Infants and Children,* which was awarded the *American Journal of Nursing* and *Pediatric Nursing* Book of the Year Award in 2000. Her most recent book, based on work from the American Academy of Nursing Child Family Expert Panel, was published in 2006.

Craft-Rosenberg recently completed a term as president of NANDA International and served as director of the Institute for Nursing Knowledge at the University of Iowa College of Nursing. She served 1 year as interim dean after having served 17 years as a department head and forming a new Parent Child Family Area of Study and initiating a doctoral program in Child-Family Nursing. In addition, she taught at both undergraduate and graduate levels. She served as the major advisor for 44 thesis/dissertation research topics.

After she retired, Craft-Rosenberg assumed a consulting position with the University of Iowa College of Nursing.

Shelley-Rae Pehler, PhD, RN, completed her PhD from the College of Nursing at the University of Iowa in 2006. She joined the Department of Nursing at St. Ambrose University in 2005, where she is currently serving as Associate Professor. Prior to her doctoral studies, Pehler was an active clinician and advanced practice nurse caring for children and families. She was one of the first counselors in the RTS: Resolve Through Sharing program at Lutheran Hospital in La Crosse, Wisconsin, a grief support program for families who have lost a child through miscarriage, stillbirth, or neonatal death. She continued interest in grief support of children and families as she chaired a Pediatric Bereavement Committee, also at Lutheran Hospital. Her research interests include spirituality in children and teens. Pehler has been involved in the development of the Nursing Outcome Classification (NOC), serving as a member of the NOC team, and currently is serving as chair to the Physiologic Focus Group section. Pehler has 6 publications and 12 presentations, which have included discussions of her research in the area of children and adolescent spirituality, self-esteem in children, and pediatric growth and development. While in graduate school, she received a T-32 Training in Nursing Effectiveness Grant and an F-31 National Research Science Award from the National Institute of Nursing Research.

Contributors

Marie Abraham
Institute for Patient- and Family-Centered Care

S. Heath Ackley
University of Washington

Susan A. Albrecht
University of Pittsburgh

Melissa A. Alderfer
Children's Hospital of Philadelphia, University of Pennsylvania

Harlene Anderson
Our Lady of the Lake University

Keith A. Anderson
The Ohio State University

Denise B. Angst
Advocate Health Care

Christine M. Aramburu Alegría
University of Nevada, Reno

Carolyn Arcand
University of Massachusetts Boston

Sally Baddock
Otago Polytechnic, New Zealand

Don Bailey
Research Triangle Institute International

Susan Balandin
Molde University College, Norway

Dennis A. Balcom
Private Practice

Margaret Barnes
University of the Sunshine Coast, Australia

Barbara Beacham
University of Pennsylvania

Rosina M. Becerra
University of California, Los Angeles

Dorothy S. Becvar
Saint Louis University

Cynthia J. Bell
Indiana University

Linda G. Bell
Indiana University–Purdue University Indianapolis

Didem Bernard
U.S. Agency for Healthcare Research and Quality

Diane Berry
University of North Carolina at Chapel Hill

Stephanie Cosner Berzin
Boston College

Cecily Lynn Betz
University of Southern California

Donald W. Black
The University of Iowa

Deborah Blizzard
Rochester Institute of Technology

John Blosnich
West Virginia University

Mitzi Boilanger
Riley Hospital for Children, Clarian Health

Rebecca M. Bolen
The University of Tennessee

Georg Bollig
Universitetet i Bergen, Norway

Barbara L. Bonner
University of Oklahoma

Robert M. Bossarte
University of Rochester

Michel Boudreaux
University of Minnesota

Sharon Bowland
University of Louisville

Dalia Brahmi
Albert Einstein College of Medicine

Linda Brannon
McNeese State University

Bonnie Braun
University of Maryland

Moriah Brier
Memorial Sloan Kettering Cancer Center, New York

Angela D. Broadus
University of Nevada, Reno

Tricia A. Brodbeck
University of California, Riverside

Alvin C. Bronstein
Rocky Mountain Poison Center

Marion E. Broome
Indiana University

Sean E. Brotherson
North Dakota State University

Suzanne Brown
Case Western Reserve University

Kathleen C. Buckwalter
The University of Iowa

Lisa Burkhart
Loyola University Chicago

Joe Burrage, Jr.
Indiana University

Cori Bussolari
University of San Francisco

Jorie M. Butler
University of Utah

Jane Caflisch
City University of New York

Samantha Callan
Conservative Party, UK

Lynn Clark Callister
Brigham Young University

Christine Calmes
VA Capitol Healthcare Network MIRECC

Laura K. Campbell
Medical University of South Carolina

Alice Campbell Reay
Dudley and Walsall Mental Health Partnership Trust

Nicole Campione-Barr
University of Missouri

Jane M. Carrington
University of Colorado Denver

John P. Caughlin
University of Illinois at Urbana-Champaign

Julie Cerel
University of Kentucky

I. Joyce Chang
University of Central Missouri

Subrata Chattopadhyay
West Bengal University of Health Sciences, India

Claudia Chaufan
University of California, San Francisco

Barry Chiswick
University of Illinois at Chicago

Jin Young Choi
Sam Houston State University

Becky J. Christian
University of Alabama at Birmingham

Marilyn Coleman
University of Missouri

Terri Combs-Orme
The University of Tennessee

Elaine P. Congress
Fordham University

Ann E. Cornell
University of Rochester

Amy C. Cory
Valparaiso University, Indiana

Steven S. Coughlin
Environmental Epidemiology Service, Washington, D.C.

Julia Muennich Cowell
Rush University

Martha Craft-Rosenberg
The University of Iowa

W. E. Craighead
Emory University

Cheryl Lee Crisp
Riley Hospital, Indianapolis

Donna Miles Curry
Wright State University

Holly Dabelko-Schoeny
The Ohio State University

Constance Dallas
University of Illinois at Chicago

Judith C. Daniluk
University of British Columbia, Canada

Maryanne Davidson
Yale University

Jonathan C. Davis
Samford University

Janet A. Deatrick
University of Pennsylvania

Sharon A. Denham
Ohio University

Janet DesGeorges
University of Colorado

Mary Amanda Dew
University of Pittsburgh

Ada Diaconu-Muresan
University of Nevada, Reno

Heather E. Dillaway
Wayne State University

M. Robin DiMatteo
University of California, Riverside

Chamlong Disayavanish
Chiang Mai University, Thailand

Lisa Dixon
University of Maryland

Jan Dougherty
Banner Alzheimer's Institute, Phoenix

Amy Drapalski
VA Maryland Healthcare System

Howard Dubowitz
University of Maryland

Naomi Nichele Duke
University of Minnesota

Marie-Anne Durand
University of London, UK

Carmel B. Dyer
University of Texas

Julia Eggert
Clemson University

W. Suzanne Eidson-Ton
University of California, Davis

Shelly Eisbach
Johns Hopkins University

Deborah Ellis
Wayne State University

Glyn Elwyn
Cardiff University, UK

Janet Enslein
St. Ambrose University

Sharon Lindhorst Everhardt
Delta College

Robin S. Everhart
Bradley/Hasbro Research Center, Brown Medical Center

Heidi Harriman Ewen
Miami University, Ohio

William S. Fals-Stewart
University of Rochester

Melissa Spezia Faulkner
University of Arizona

Michele A. Faulkner
Creighton University

Suzanne Feetham
University of Wisconsin–Milwaukee, Children's National Medical Center, University of Illinois at Chicago

Noelle Fields
The Ohio State University

Barbara H. Fiese
University of Illinois at Urbana-Champaign

Gordon E. Finley
Florida International University

Kathleen Fitzpatrick
Stanford University

P. Maria Flavin
University of Pittsburgh

Kathleen Flecky
Creighton University

Paula Fomby
University of Colorado Denver

Karen Forrest Keenan
University of Aberdeen, UK

Roxie L. Foster
University of Colorado Denver

Nathan S. Fox
Mount Sinai School of Medicine

Peter Fraenkel
City College of the City University of New York

Cynthia Franklin
University of Texas at Austin

Debbie Fraser
Athabasca University, Canada

Cynthia Ann Frosch
University of Texas at Dallas

Eric Frost
Université de Sherbrooke, Canada

Tamas Fulop
Université de Sherbrooke, Canada

Michael E. Galbraith
University of Colorado Denver

Maribeth Gallagher
Hospice of the Valley

Lawrence Ganong
University of Missouri

Linda Garand
University of Pittsburgh

Joseph E. Gaugler
University of Minnesota

Kerstin Gerst
University of Texas

Ellen Giarelli
University of Pennsylvania

Roseann Giarrusso
California State University, Los Angeles

Stephen R. Gillaspy
University of Oklahoma

Laura N. Gitlin
Thomas Jefferson University

Mitch Golant
Cancer Support Online Community

Jacqueline Lytle Gonzalez
Miami Children's Hospital

Judith Goodell
University of San Francisco

Joan S. Grant
University of Alabama at Birmingham

Lacey Teneal Greathead
University of Miami

Kimberly Greder
Iowa State University

Robert-Jay Green
Alliant International University

Mary Ruth Griffin
University of Charleston

Terry Griffin
Rush University Medical Center

Victor Groza
Case Western Reserve University

Mary P. Guerrera
University of Connecticut

Elaine M. Gustafson
Yale University

Barbara Habermann
Indiana University

Nora Hager
University of Missouri

Geri R. Hall
Banner Alzheimer's Institute, Phoenix

Barbara U. Hamilton
University of Colorado Denver

Shirley May Harmon Hanson
Oregon Health & Science University

Carl Haub
Population Reference Bureau, Washington, D.C.

Nancy Havil
University of North Carolina

Bert Hayslip, Jr.
University of North Texas

Bronwyn Hemsley
University of Queensland, Australia

Laura Mendoza Hernandez
Miami Children's Hospital

Dalice L. Hertzberg
University of Colorado Denver

Brian J. Higginbotham
Utah State University

Jennifer M. Hill
Oregon State Hospital

Andreas Hoff
University of Oxford, UK

Bonnie Holaday
Clemson University

M. Cay Holbrook
University of British Columbia, Canada

Mary L. Houston
Baylor University

Amy Houtrow
University of California, San Francisco

Jidong Huang
University of Illinois at Chicago

Angela J. Huebner
Virginia Polytechnic Institute and State University

Daniel Hughes
Quittie Glen Center for Mental Health, Pennsylvania

Robert E. Hurd
Cincinnati Veterans Affairs Medical Center

Alfreda P. Iglehart
University of California, Los Angeles

Evan Imber-Black
Ackerman Institute for the Family, New York

Melissa Dodd Inglese
Children's Memorial Hermann Hospital, Houston

Jessica Jablonski
Richard Stockton College of New Jersey

Robert M. Jacobson
Mayo Clinic

Tyler Jamison
University of Missouri

Parastoo Jangouk
Kennedy Krieger Institute, Baltimore

Yun-Hee Jeon
University of Sydney

Jason Aaron Jones
Alliant International University, California and Mexico City

Vanya Jones
Johns Hopkins Bloomberg School of Public Health

Allan M. Josephson
University of Louisville

Tess Judge-Ellis
The University of Iowa

Evangelos C. Karademas
University of Crete, Greece

Jennifer K. Kauder
Poweshiek County Mental Health Center, Iowa

David J. Kavanagh
Queensland University of Technology, Australia

Melissa Keene
Northwestern University

Victoria Floriani Keeton
University of California, San Francisco

Rick D. Kellerman
University of Kansas

Michael S. Kelly
Loyola University Chicago

Norman Lee Keltner
University of Alabama at Birmingham

Judith Kendall
Oregon Health & Science University

Christine Kennedy
University of California, San Francisco

Lisa Zaynab Killinger
Palmer College of Chiropractic

Il-Ho Kim
University of Toronto, Canada

Yeoun Soo Kim-Godwin
University of North Carolina Wilmington

Patricia A. Kinne
University of Louisville

Mumbe Kithakye
Oklahoma State University

Dorte Kjaer
Randers Hospital, Denmark

George J. Knafl
*University of North Carolina
at Chapel Hill*

Kathleen A. Knafl
*University of North Carolina
at Chapel Hill*

Stan Knapp
Brigham Young University

Kathie Kobler
*Advocate Lutheran General
Hospital, Illinois*

Emily Koert
*University of British Columbia,
Canada*

Marilyn J. Krajicek
*University of Colorado
Denver*

Miriam Aroni Krinsky
*ABA Youth At Risk
Commission, University of
California, Los Angeles*

Jeffrey Todd Kullgren
University of Pennsylvania

Anahid Kulwicki
*Florida International
University*

Jane M. Kurz
Temple University

Wendy K. K. Lam
University of Rochester

Wendy G. Lane
University of Maryland

Suzanne Lareau
*University of Colorado
Denver*

Dana Lassri
*Ben-Gurion University of the
Negev, Israel*

gretchen Lawhon
*Children's Regional Hospital at
Cooper University*

David Lester
*Richard Stockton College
of New Jersey*

Linda Ann Lewandowski
Wayne State University

M. Kay Libbus
University of Missouri

Howard A. Liddle
University of Miami

Russell F. Lim
*University of California,
Davis*

Rana Limbo
*Gundersen Lutheran Medical
Foundation, Inc., Wisconsin*

Darlene M. Lindahl
University of Minnesota

Megan F. Liu
The University of Iowa

James Lock
Stanford University

Bruce Lott
*Brigham Young University,
Retired*

Sana Loue
*Case Western Reserve
University*

Carol Loveland-Cherry
University of Michigan

Courtney Lupia Blasi
*University of Colorado
Denver*

Barbara Mandleco
Brigham Young University

Elizabeth Frost Maring
University of Maryland

Gillian Marit
University of Guelph, Canada

Beth Marks
*University of Illinois at
Chicago*

Sara Martino
*Richard Stockton College of
New Jersey*

Donna D. McAlpine
University of Minnesota

Graham McCaulley
University of Missouri

Betsy M. McDowell
Newberry College

James P. McHale
*University of South Florida
St. Petersburg*

Linda McKie
*Glasgow Caledonian
University, UK*

Susan M. McLennon
Indiana University

Diane McNaughton
Rush University

Cynthia Mears
Northwestern University

William P. Meehan III
Children's Hospital Boston

Natthani Meemon
University of Central Florida

Suzanne Mellon
Saint Anselm College

Lyle J. Micheli
Children's Hospital Boston

Elizabeth Miller
*University of California,
Davis*

Laura E. Miller
The University of Tennessee

Lou Ann Montgomery
The University of Iowa

Amanda Sheffield Morris
Oklahoma State University

Margaret P. Moss
University of Minnesota

Kim T. Mueser
Dartmouth College

Carles Muntaner
University of Toronto, Canada

Anjana Muralidharan
Emory University

Harvey J. Murff
Vanderbilt University

Colleen I. Murray
University of Nevada, Reno

Ian Murray
University of Stirling, UK

Wendy M. Nehring
East Tennessee State University

Alice W. Newton
Children's Hospital Boston

Katherina Nikzad-Terhune
University of Kentucky

Ashley N. Nolan
*University of Massachusetts
    Lowell*

M. Lelinneth Beloy Novilla
Brigham Young University

Ruth A. O'Brien
University of Colorado Denver

Thomas Olkowski
Private Practice

Alessandra Padula
*Università degli Studi
    dell'Aquila, Italy*

Kyle S. Page
University of North Texas

Jane Peace
*University of Wisconsin–
    Madison*

Geraldine S. Pearson
University of Connecticut

Julie K. Philbrook
*Hennepin County Medical
    Center*

Sabrina Pickens
*University of Texas at
    Houston*

Carl Pickhardt
Private Practice, Author

Laura Pickler
*University of Colorado
    Denver*

Makeba Pinder
University of Texas at Austin

Martin Pinquart
*Philipps University, Marburg,
    Germany*

Carol Ann Podgorski
University of Rochester

Vincent H. K. Poon
Tyndale Seminary, Canada

Eileen Jones Porter
University of Missouri

Samuel F. Posner
*Centers for Disease Control
    and Prevention*

Michèle Preyde
University of Guelph, Canada

Christine Proulx
University of Missouri

Linda Quan
University of Washington

Oliver Quarrell
*Sheffield Children's Hospital,
    UK*

Carol Quayle
*Mercy Health and Aged Care,
    Australia*

Jill Radtke
University of Pittsburgh

Minna Raivio
*Memory Research and
    Treatment Centers,
    Lahti, Finland,
    Department of Health,
    Helsinki, Finland*

Ann M. Rhodes
The University of Iowa

Nancy Ellen Richeson
University of Southern Maine

Roberta Riportella
*University of Wisconsin–
    Madison*

Karen A. Roberto
*Virginia Polytechnic Institute
    and State University*

Carole A. Robinson
*University of British Columbia,
    Canada*

John C. Robinson
University of Charleston

Rosemarie Rodriguez
University of Miami

Brian Rothberg
*University of Colorado
    Denver*

Jennifer Rowe
*University of the Sunshine
    Coast, Australia*

Polly Ryan
*University of Wisconsin–
    Milwaukee*

Rajiv Samant
*Ottawa Hospital Cancer
    Centre, Canada*

Katherine Sanchez
University of Texas at Austin

Yoshie Sano
*Washington State University
    Vancouver*

Marilyn Sass-Lehrer
Gallaudet University

Edward J. Saunders
The University of Iowa

Teresa A. Savage
Northwestern University

Kathleen J. Sawin
Children's Hospital of

*Wisconsin, University
of Wisconsin–Milwaukee*

Anju Purohit Sawni
*Wayne State University,
Children's Hospital of
Michigan*

John Scanzoni
University of Florida

Maximilian D. Schmeiser
*University of Wisconsin–
Madison*

Janet U. Schneiderman
*University of Southern
California*

Lisa S. Segre
The University of Iowa

Barbara H. Settles
University of Delaware

Nina G. Shah
Epidemiologist

Golan Shahar
*Ben-Gurion University
of the Negev, Israel*

Jenelle R. Shanley
University of Oklahoma

Constance Hoenk Shapiro
University of Illinois

Martha C. Shaw
The University of Iowa

Linda Shields
Curtin University, Australia

William J. Sieber
*University of California,
San Diego*

Leigh Ann Simmons
Duke University

Paul D. Simmons
University of Louisville

Nancy L. Sin
*University of California,
Riverside*

Douglas A. Singh
Indiana University South Bend

Anita Sinicrope Maier
*Philadelphia Educational
Network for Eating
Disorders*

Jasmina Sisirak
*University of Illinois at
Chicago*

Kathryn Smith
*Childrens Hospital
Los Angeles*

Kelly Smith
The University of Iowa

Julia A. Snethen
*University of Wisconsin–
Milwaukee*

Linley Snyder
University of Missouri

Elena McKeogh Spearing
Private Practice

Janet K. Pringle Specht
The University of Iowa

Mary Virginia Sprang
University of Kentucky

Amy R. Stanley
*University of Massachusetts
Lowell*

Marlys Staudt
The University of Tennessee

Richard Albert Stein
Princeton University

Deborah Stiffler
Indiana University

Elizabeth A. Stormshak
University of Oregon

Wilma Powell Stuart
Shannon Medical Center

Monica H. Swahn
Georgia State University

Martha K. Swartz
Yale University

Jane H.-C. Tang
Immaculata University

Jennifer L. Tanner
Rutgers University

Bonita E. Taylor
HealthCare Chaplaincy

Donald H. Taylor
Duke University

Sandra Taylor, Jr.
*University of Tasmania,
Australia*

Heide S. Temples
Clemson University

Sanna J. Thompson
University of Texas at Austin

Sally E. Thorne
*University of British Columbia,
Canada*

Leanne Togher
*University of Sydney,
Australia*

Ellen Tsai
Queen's University, Canada

Tara Tucker
*University of Ottawa,
Canada*

Judith M. Tuerck
*Oregon State Public Health
Laboratory*

Prudence Twigg
Indiana University

Paul N. Van de Water
*Center on Budget and Policy
Priorities, Washington,
D.C.*

Marcia Van Riper
*University of North Carolina
at Chapel Hill*

Beth Vaughan-Cole
Brigham Young University

Judith A. Vessey
Boston College

Ruvanee P. Vilhauer
Felician College

Augusta M. Villanueva
Drexel University

Kathryn R. Wagner
*Kennedy Krieger Institute,
   Baltimore*

Froma Walsh
University of Chicago

Thomas T. H. Wan
University of Central Florida

Sharon M. Wasco
*University of Massachusetts
   Lowell*

Janice G. Weber
*The University of Louisiana at
   Lafayette*

Karin Weber-Gasparoni
The University of Iowa

Stevan Weine
*University of Illinois at
   Chicago*

Christian E. Weller
*University of Massachusetts
   Boston*

James M. White
*University of British Columbia,
   Canada*

Sarah W. Whitton
University of Cincinnati

Sharon Wallace Williams
*University of North Carolina
   at Chapel Hill*

Lucia D. Wocial
*Clarian Health, Indiana
   University*

Danuta Wojnar
Seattle University

Alan D. Woolf
Harvard University

Kynna Wright
*University of California,
   Los Angeles*

Jin-Shang Wu
*National Cheng Kung
   University, Taiwan*

Guohua Xia
*University of California,
   Davis*

Glen L. Xiong
*University of California,
   Davis*

Daniel J. Yoo
Emory University

Arlene R. Young
*Simon Fraser University,
   Canada*

Talia Zaider
*Memorial Sloan Kettering
   Cancer Center, New York*

Michelle Zeager
Harvard University

Denis Zilaff
Sacramento County

David J. Zucker
Shalom Park, Denver

Introduction

Even though discussions of health conditions (e.g., diabetes) occurring in families are common, the relationship of these conditions to family context and to the family unit is too often left unstated. A major reference is needed to provide that relationship. The concept of the *Encyclopedia of Family Health* originated from this need to provide a compilation of knowledge on health and families for all learners, practitioners, researchers, theorists, and educators across the disciplines of health-related sciences as well as to the general public. The purpose of the encyclopedia is to provide knowledge for readers with diverse interests. Some readers are just beginning an interest in families. In contrast, some readers will be seeking an update on their existing knowledge. The direct aim of this encyclopedia is to increase family health knowledge. The indirect aim is to improve the health of families.

The specification of content to be included in this *Encyclopedia of Family Health* was a combined effort among Sage Publications, the Editorial Board, the two editors, and the contributors. First, staff members from Sage identified health issues occurring in the literature related to family health that might be included as headwords in the encyclopedia. Next, these potential headwords were reviewed by members of the Editorial Board, and modifications were made. Members of the Editorial Board represent the disciplines of family medicine, nursing, child psychiatry, and social work. They live in the United States and Australia. Final decisions on content were made by the editors. Importantly, each topic, or headword, specifies a relationship to family. Encyclopedia contributors were asked to provide their working definition or perspective of *family* for their entries.

The editors searched electronic databases to identify the experts who are actively contributing to family health knowledge through the conduct of research, education, practice, and policy development. The contributors to the *Encyclopedia of Family Health* are nationally and internationally recognized authorities. Even though the encyclopedia content reflects a U.S. perspective, the editors recruited writers from around the world, with the exception of contributors for topics that are central to the United States (e.g., health care reform, Medicare, Medicaid). These contributors provide a global perspective of family health issues. The editors searched for expertise, wherever it might dwell.

It is with great appreciation we acknowledge these entry contributors. The individuals who have written for this encyclopedia are experts in theory, research, practice, and education. We find it exciting to see the breadth and depth of theory and research that contributors are utilizing to improve to knowledge in family health.

The future of family health, like all disciplines, rests with the leaders. Those with a commitment to families will find continued excitement and challenges throughout their careers. Those in practice encounter the complexity of family communication, reciprocity, and relationships on a daily basis. Wise practitioners will observe and listen carefully to enlarge perspectives and to increase skills. Educators will use creativity to explicate family dynamics with an awareness of the paucity of family knowledge we have compared to that needed. Theorists and researchers will continue to struggle to keep up with the changing nature of families in their attempts to assist all of us committed to family health.

After 2 years of locating and interacting with the contributors to this encyclopedia, we feel a sense of awe and wonder at the global talent in place to improve the health of families. For this reason, we are confident that remaining challenges will be addressed and that our knowledge will continue to grow.

All of us are from families, and most adults are responsible for families. The intent of this encyclopedia is to help anyone with questions related to health and questions related to families who may be at any point in family life and the family health continuum. Students and practitioners in the health sciences will find specific help from this readily accessible information that they will use throughout their careers. This encyclopedia is a unique source for the public and for health care professionals.

As you begin to explore the encyclopedia content, we recommend that you begin with the entries on "Defining Family" by Barbara H. Settles, "Family Health Perspectives" by M. Lelinneth Beloy Novilla, and "Families: The Basic Unit of Societies" by Linda McKie and Samantha Callan to provide a background for further reading. Next, we recommend that you review the Reader's Guide to examine the scope and organization of content available to you in the encyclopedia. Use this guide often to increase the breadth of your knowledge and to increase your efficiency in accessing the knowledge.

We hope that you learn and that you enjoy.

Acknowledgments

The conceptualization of the *Encyclopedia of Family Health* began with the vision of Martha Craft-Rosenberg and Jim Brace-Thompson, the Sage Acquisition Editor. Guidance for the process of developing the encyclopedia was provided by the Developmental Editor, Carole Maurer, and Systems Coordinator, Laura Notton. Kate Schroeder was our Production Editor, who helped us see new options for presenting content. All of these individuals represent the epitome of professionalism in both their competence and their ability to provide encouragement and helpful suggestions even during the most difficult periods in this 2-year process. We feel privileged to have worked with them, and we will miss them.

Members of the Editorial Board provided a balance of constructive criticism and assistance throughout the process. Board members were always accessible to the editors at any time of the day or night to provide opinions, answer questions, and give us contributor suggestions. Some Editorial Board members even took advantage of professional meetings to recruit. Their support was invaluable to this project.

The individuals we invited to contribute are passionate, committed, and hard working. It was common for us to receive e-mail messages sent in the middle of the night from the United States and several countries. All contributors were patient with the editing process and responded rapidly to e-mail messages from both encyclopedia and Sage editors. Their talent and their willingness to work through the process with the editors were incredible. They are the reason you have this strong resource for your use.

On a more personal note, we wish to thank our husbands, Guy Rosenberg and Adrian Pehler, who became accustomed to seeing their wives from a side or back view during the hours of computer work. Their understanding and support made the long hours comfortable and possible.

Martha Craft-Rosenberg
Shelley-Rae Pehler

The Relationship of Family to Health: Historical Overview

The purpose of this historical overview is to describe the evolving definitions and constructs of family and our understanding of the relationship of family to health. Historical exemplars of the evolving science of family and health are described.

Scholars and researchers have reported on the relationship of family and health from the time of Florence Nightingale. Although the findings have varied based on the discipline lens of the scholars, there are consistent findings reported and also persistent deficits in our knowledge due to conceptual and measurement issues.

Health as a Function of the Family

Findings across the decades of research and scholarship support the significant relationship and importance of the family to the health of the family, individual family members, and communities. The family is described as the primary unit for health and as the most important social context in which health and illness occur and illness is resolved. Some report that one of the primary purposes, if not *the* primary purpose of family, is to ensure the health and well-being of its members (Friedman, Bowden, & Jones, 2003) and that health is a criterion for family life (Grzywacz & Ganong, 2009). The family is seen as a dynamic system that helps to maintain health, offers support to family members, affects health decisions, and attaches meaning to illness (Pardeck & Yuen, 2001; Rolland, 1987; Wright & Bell, 2009). The health of the family and family members is considered a function of the family the same as other functions such as biological reproduction, emotional development, and socialization (Friedman et al., 2003; Litman, 1974). The ability of families to meet their primary functions rests, at least in part, on the health of individual family members (Doherty & Campbell, 1988). For example, the state of family members' physical and mental health determines if and how family functions are met. These functions include the ability for employment, consistent monitoring of the behavior of children, and providing a safe environment for family members. Health is also reported as essential to effective family interactions and relationships. In 1976, the World Health Organization (WHO) reported that family is not only the basic unit of human social organization, but it is one of the most accessible for preventive and therapeutic intervention. WHO also noted that the health of the family is more than the sum of the health of individual family members.

A distinction has been made between the health of individual family members and the health of the family. In 1976, WHO reported that the health of a family goes beyond the physical and mental conditions of its members to the extent that it provides a social environment for the natural development and fulfillment of all who live within it. Importantly, WHO recognized that health is the interaction between social variables and family health; these social variables include ethnicity, socioeconomic status, employment, migration, and social and cultural norms and mores. This distinction between health and family health is considered a landmark in the recognition that multiple factors interact to affect health and that the health of family members is different from the health of the family.

Definitions of Health, Family Health, and Familial Health

How health, family health, and familial health are defined directs the actions and relationship of health professionals and families. The 1948 World Health Organization definition of health as "a state of complete physical, mental and social well being and not merely the absence of disease or infirmity" remains a global standard. It was a major conceptual advance in that it expanded the definition of health to psychological and social dimensions. A dilemma in these ensuing years has been a need for an operational definition of health and that the lack of such a definition continues to limit our understanding of the relationship of family to the health of its members and to the family system (Grzywacz & Ganong, 2009; Saracci, 1997). One effort to attempt to address this gap in the understanding of the relationship of the family to health was led by WHO in 1976. WHO established a workgroup, the WHO Consultation Family Unit and Health, to better describe the role of the family and health (WHO, 1976). The goal of the workgroup was to identify statistical indices of family and health by examining the family research and policy across four approaches: demographic, epidemiological (medical), social, and economic. The 1976 report resulted in recommendations and priorities for research, but the workgroup members were not able to identify specific indices of family health because of the complexity of measurement and because "family health is more than the sum of the health of individual family members" (p. 13). Through their work, they differentiated family health from familial health. The report recommended that family health, as an established concept, should apply to the sum of the states of health of the individual family members. Family health is measured by the ability of the family to meet its functions and not by the health of individual family members. Mauksch (1974) and Pardeck and Yuen (2001) further reported that family health is demonstrated by the development of, and continuous interaction among, the physical, mental, emotional, social, economic, cultural, and spiritual dimensions of the family, which results in the holistic well-being of the family and its members.

In contrast, familial health was proposed to indicate the functioning of the family for the promotion of the health and well-being of individual family members and the family system. To measure familial health requires the recognition that the level of health may be different across family members, ranging from demonstrated illnesses and conditions to the absence of observable illness to the actual positive health measured by development, function, and physiological measures (WHO, 1976). These are distinctions that can guide the research and scholarship on families.

Historical Evolution of Science of Family and Health

From the time of Nightingale, nurses have been encouraged to consider family members as important for nursing care (Whall & Fawcett, 1991). In a detailed case study in 1945, physician Henry Richardson acknowledged the importance of the family and emphasized the need to connect activities within the home and across family members to the care of individual patients. From the 1950s to the present, sociologists have been major contributors to our understanding of families and health, with their systematic focus on the role of the family with ill individual family members and their beginning study of the impact of illness on family (Litman, 1974; Vincent, 1963). Researchers examined intergenerational health care and the family, including patterns of decision making and the role of the family in health and illness behavior (Hill, 1958). Similar to current research, sociologists reported that families were unable and unwilling to care for sick family members in the home (Parsons & Fox, 1952). During this time, Sussman (1953) reported that existing techniques for measuring the interrelationship of family behavior to the etiology of disability and chronic illness were too limited to clearly advance our understanding of the important relationship between family and health. Litman and Venters (1979) noted that although much was known about health and health care of the populations, far less was known about the family as the unit of health. Importantly, this research began to examine the reciprocal nature of illness on the family and the effect of the family on health and illness of family members. It was also noted that mothers were the primary source of family data, resulting in the research being the mothers' perceptions of the family and its members. Wakefield and colleagues, in a state of the science review, further delineated the conceptual and methodological issues in research of families (Wakefield, Allen, & Washchuck, 1979). They noted that the research focused on the internal family processes and gave limited attention to the interdependence of individual family members and the family to the larger social and physical environment. They reported that such a focus inferred the cause-and-effect relationship of family and health was internal to the family.

Beginning in the 1980s, more clinician family scholars such as Campbell (1986), Doherty (1993), Doherty and Campbell (1988), Feetham (1984, 1999), Feetham and Thomson (2006), Friedman (1981, 1998), Friedman et al. (2003), Gilliss and Knafl (1999), Grzywacz and Ganong (2009), McCubbin (1999), McDaniel, Campbell, Hepworth, and Lorenz (2003), Ransom (1986), Ross and Mirowsky (2002), and Wright and Bell (2009) advanced our understanding of the relationship of family to health through review articles synthesizing the state of the science. The reviews focused on two primary areas: family roles in health and illness and the effects of health and illness on individual family members and the family as an interdependent, interactive system. The outcomes of this research further demonstrate the importance of the family to the health of the individual family members and to the family system.

Roles of Family in Health of Family Members

One family role is in the health promotion and risk reduction for the family and its members (Roth & Simanello, 2004). The WHO (1976) cites the family as the primary social agent in the promotion of health and well-being. Families are known to have a significant effect on behaviors that influence individual health; these include exercise, diet, and substance use (alcohol, cigarette smoking, and drugs; McDaniel et al., 2003). The family creates the environment in which the family members develop their behavioral patterns that promote health or result in risk for illness and injury. During the past decades, genomics has contributed to our knowledge of the mechanisms of and prevention of disease (Feetham & Thomson, 2006). This research has also strengthened our

understanding of the relationship of the biological family to the health of individual family members and the intergenerational family (Rolland & Williams, 2005). Family is the convergence of sociocultural and genetic influences. The intergenerational family influences how individual family members and the family respond to genetic information and the risk of disease, including behaviors to reduce their risk (Feetham & Thomson, 2006; Rolland & Williams, 2005).

The family is known to have a role in psychosocial factors and disease risk. Building from the knowledge that psychosocial factors can affect an individual's susceptibility to disease, research has shown that the family is an important source of support of family members and also a source of stress (Fisher, 2006). For decades, researchers have demonstrated that the family can be related to the onset of illness and affect the trajectory of illness (Coyne et al., 2001). The family is also reported as an important influence or buffer between the family member with an illness and the larger system, including the health care system (Weihs, Enright, & Simmens, 2008). Some researchers have reported a relationship to depression or stress and a decrease in cellular immunity. For example, Meyer and Haggerty (1962) demonstrated that chronic stress in families was related to the incidence of strep infections and days of school missed in children. Similarly, in a study of 500 families, a relationship between family stress and the increased utilization of health care was shown (Roghmann & Haggerty, 1973).

Families are also known to play a critical role in appraising both physical and mental health. While mothers are recognized as the gatekeeper of family members' access to the health care system, the mother's health care use is more of a predictor of the child's access to care than the child's health status. In addition to the role of the family as health appraiser, patterns of health service utilization are related to family structure and health beliefs.

Family Responses to Health and Illness in Family Members

Family responses to illness in family members and the role of the family in adaptation to illness and recovery provide further evidence of the importance of family and the health of family members (Deatrick, Alderfer, Knafl, & Knafl, 2006). Research focused on family responses to specific illnesses has resulted in a body of literature reporting that the interactions within the family system affect the health outcomes of family members (Fisher, 2006; Svavarsdottir, McCubbin, & Kane, 2000). The progression of disease and disability can be linked to relationship of family members (Coyne et al., 2001; Holder, 1997; Reiss, 1990). Grzywacz and Ganong (2009) note that we determine the health of the family by how they respond to changes in the physical and mental health status of family members and how they function to prevent health problems. Because of the research design and measures, we know more about the negative outcomes of acute and chronic illness on the family than the strengths and resources demonstrated by families. The family as caregiver has been examined from childhood to family members with acute and chronic illness across the age continuum (Gilliss & Knafl, 1999).

Summary: What Do We Know About Family and Health?

The interdependence and importance of health and the family are accepted in theory and supported by research. Although our knowledge of this relationship has increased, it has also been limited in that research continues to focus more on measures of the negative outcomes (e.g., depression) of illness and injury on the family and family members. The research also continues to focus more on the responses of individual family members than on the responses of the family as a unit. Because the focus has been on the individual as the unit of measure and on conducting research of families with physical and/or mental pathology, less knowledge has been generated about health and how the family functions. A classic exception is the synthesis by McCubbin (1999) of research of normative family transitions and health outcomes. If research of families would build on the premise that health is a criterion of family, Grzywacz and Ganong (2009) suggest that such research should result in knowledge and strategies for protecting and promoting health across the life span while distinguishing the interdependence of activities of family to health of the family and individual family members. A limitation of this science is the lack of translation into the education of health professionals

and practice in health care systems. As important is that the knowledge of the significance of family to the health of the family and family members has not translated into policy. This limitation is due in part to the conceptual and methodological limitations of the research but more importantly because there is not sufficient recognition of the need to build the process of informing policy into programs of research and scholarship (Feetham, 1999; Feetham & Meister, 1999; Healthy People 2010, n.d.). As a result, the family is not seen as the context of care, and the health care system continues to focus on the health and illness of individuals and not the health of families as a system (Feetham, 1999; Feetham & Meister, 1999; Pardeck & Yuen, 2001).

Suzanne Feetham, PhD, RN, FAAN

References

Bell, J. (2000). Editor's choice: Selected bibliography on research with families. *Journal of Family Nursing, 6,* 400–404.

Campbell, T. L. (1986). Family's impact on health: A critical review and annotated bibliography. *Family Systems Medicine, 4*(2/3), 135–328.

Coyne, J. C., Rohrbaugh, M. J., Shoham, V., Sonnega, J. S., Nicklas, J. M., & Cranford, J. A. (2001). Prognostic importance of marital quality for survival of congestive heart failure. *American Journal of Cardiology, 88,* 526–529.

Deatrick, J., Alderfer, M., Knafl, G., & Knafl, K. (2006). Identifying patterns of managing chronic conditions. In R. Crane & E. Marshall (Eds.), *Families and health: Interdisciplinary perspectives* (pp. 62–80). Thousand Oaks, CA: Sage.

Doherty, W. J. (1993). Health and family interaction: What we know. In G. E. Hendershot & F. B. LeClere (Eds.), *Family health: From data to policy* (pp. 98–101). Minneapolis, MN: National Council on Family Relations.

Doherty, W. J., & Campbell, T. (1988). *Families and health.* Newbury Park, CA: Sage.

Feetham, S. (1984). Family research in nursing. In H. H. Werley & J. Fitzpatrick (Eds.), *Annual Review of Nursing Research* (Vol. 2, pp. 3–25). New York: Springer.

Feetham, S. L. (1999). Families and health in the urban environment. *International Journal of Child & Family Welfare, 4*(3), 197–227.

Feetham, S. L., & Meister, S. B. (1999). Nursing research of families: State of the science and correspondence with policy. In A. S. Hinshaw, S. L. Feetham, & J. L. F. Shaver (Eds.), *Handbook of clinical nursing research* (pp. 251–272). Thousand Oaks, CA: Sage.

Feetham, S. L., & Thomson, E. J. (2006). Keeping the individual and family in focus. In S. M. Miller, S. H. McDaniel, J. S. Rolland, & S. L. Feetham (Eds.), *Individuals, families, and the new era of genetics: Biopsychosocial perspectives* (pp. 3–35). New York: Norton.

Fisher, L. (2006). Research on the family and chronic disease among adults: Major trends and directions. *Families, Systems, & Health, 24*(4), 373–380.

Friedman, M. M. (1981). *Family nursing: Theory and assessment.* New York: Appleton-Century-Crofts.

Friedman, M. M. (1998). *Family nursing: Research, theory, and practice* (4th ed.). Stamford, CT: Appleton & Lange.

Friedman, M., Bowden, V. R., & Jones, E. G. (2003). *Family nursing: Research, theory, and practice* (5th ed.). Upper Saddle River, NJ: Prentice Hall.

Gilliss, C. L., & Knafl, K. (1999). Nursing care of families in non-normative transitions. In A. S. Hinshaw, S. L. Feetham, & J. L. F. Shaver (Eds.), *Handbook of clinical nursing research* (pp. 231–249). Thousand Oaks, CA: Sage.

Grzywacz, J. G., & Ganong, L. (2009). Issues in families and health research. *Family Relations, 58*(4), 373–378.

Healthy People 2010. (n.d.). *Intimate partner violence and Healthy People 2010* [Fact sheet]. Retrieved from endabuse.org/userfiles/file/HealthCare/healthy_people_2010.pdf

Hill, R. (1958). Sociology of marriage and family behavior: A trend report, 1945–56. *Current Sociology, 7,* 1–33.

Holder, B. (1997). Family support and survival among African-American end-stage renal disease patients. *Advances in Renal Replacement Therapy, 1,* 13–21.

Litman, T. J. (1974). The family as a basic unit in health and medical care: A social-behavioral overview. *Social Science and Medicine, 18,* 495–519.

Litman, T. J., & Venters, M. (1979). Research on health care and the family: A methodological overview. *Social Science and Medicine, 13,* 379–385.

Mauksch, H. O. (1974). A social science basis for conceptualizing family health. *Social Science and Medicine, 8*(9/10), 521–528.

McCubbin, M. (1999). Normative family transitions and health outcomes. In A. S. Hinshaw, S. L. Feetham, &

J. L. F. Shaver (Eds.), *Handbook of clinical nursing research* (pp. 201–230). Thousand Oaks, CA: Sage.

McDaniel, S. H., Campbell, T. L., Hepworth, J., & Lorenz, A. (2003). How families affect illness: Research on the family's influence on health. In *Family-oriented primary care* (2nd ed., pp. 16–25). New York: Springer.

Meyer, R. J., & Haggerty, R. J. (1962). Streptococcal infections in families factors altering individual susceptibility. *Pediatrics, 29,* 539–549.

Pardeck, J. T., & Yuen, F. Y. (2001). Family health: An emerging paradigm for social workers. *Journal of Health & Social Policy, 13*(3), 59–74.

Parsons, T., & Fox, R. (1952). Illness, therapy and the modem urban American family. *Journal of Social Issues, 8*(4), 31–44.

Ransom, D. C. (1986). Research on the family in health, illness and care—State of the art families systems and medicine. *Family Systems Medicine, 4,* 329–335.

Reiss, D. (1990). Patient, family, and staff responses to end-stage renal disease. *American Journal of Kidney Diseases, 15,* 194–200.

Richardson, H. P. (1945). *Patients have families.* New York: Commonwealth Fund.

Roghmann, K. J., & Haggerty, R. G. (1973). Daily stress, illness and use of health service in young families. *Pediatric Research, 7,* 520–526.

Rolland, J. S. (1987). Chronic illness and the life cycle: A conceptual framework. *Family Process, 26,* 203–221.

Rolland, J. S., & Williams, J. K. (2005). Toward a biopsychosocial model for 21st-century genetics. *Family Process, 44,* 3–24.

Ross, C. E., & Mirowsky, J. (2002). Family relationships, social support and subjective life expectancy. *Journal of Health and Social Behavior, 43,* 469–489.

Roth, P., & Simanello, M. A. (2004). Family health promotion during transitions. In P. J. Bomar (Ed.), *Promoting health in families: Applying family research and theory to nursing practice* (3rd ed., pp. 477–506). Philadelphia: Saunders.

Saracci, R. (1997). The World Health Organization needs to reconsider its definition of health. *BMJ, 314,* 1409–1410.

Sussman, M. B. (1953). The help pattern in the middle class family. *Sociological Review, 18,* 22–28.

Svavarsdottir, E. K., McCubbin, M. A., & Kane, J. H. (2000). Well-being of parents of young children with asthma. *Research in Nursing and Health, 23,* 346–358.

Vincent, C. (1963, March). The family in health and illness: Some neglected areas. *Annals of the American*

Academy of Political and Social Science, 346, 109–116.

Wakefield, R. A., Allen, C., & Washchuck, C. (Eds.). (1979). *Family research: A source book, analysis and guide to federal funding* (Vol. 1). Westport CT: Greenwood Press.

Weihs, K. L., Enright T. M., & Simmens, S. J. (2008). Close relationships and emotional processing predict decreased mortality in women with breast cancer: Preliminary evidence. *Psychosomatic Medicine, 70*(1), 117–124.

Whall, A. L., & Fawcett, J. (1991). The family as a focal phenomenon in nursing. In *Family theory*

development in nursing state of the science and the art (pp. 7–29). Philadelphia: F. A. Davis.

World Health Organization. (1948). *WHO definition of health: Preamble to the Constitution of the World Health Organization.* Retrieved from http://www.who .int/about/definition/en/print.html

World Health Organization. (1976). *Statistical indices of family health report of a WHO study group* (WHO Tech. Rep. No. 587). Geneva, Switzerland: Author.

Wright, L. M., & Bell, J. M. (2009). *Beliefs and illness: A model for healing.* Calgary, Alberta, Canada: 4th Floor Press.

Abortion Experienced by Childbearing Couples

Primary care providers are uniquely situated to provide abortion care and counsel women and families about their options regarding the termination of a pregnancy. They provide continuity of care throughout the life cycle, are well trained in counseling, and are situated in both urban and rural areas. The Guttmacher Institute estimates that approximately 48% of the 1.2 million unintended pregnancies in the United States end in abortion. Abortion is a common procedure with 45% of reproductive age women having at least one abortion in their lifetime, and 88% of women who obtain abortions are less than 13 weeks pregnant according to Rachel Jones and associates. Women often present to their primary care clinicians for pregnancy tests, and when faced with an unplanned pregnancy, they seek information from a trusted source. Women also seek abortion care when they are faced with fetal anomalies or health issues during pregnancy. Professionalism requires health care providers to provide accurate information about abortion to their patients. This requires knowing some background and information about referral sources even if the clinician does not provide abortion as part of his or her practice.

Abortion is part of options counseling for any woman who presents with a positive pregnancy test. Although women frequently consult friends and family about their decision to terminate a pregnancy, ultimately the decision is the woman's alone. The context in which women experience abortion is important to their experience, so it is important to ask women about support systems in place. If a partner or other family members are aware of a woman's decision to terminate a pregnancy, clinicians can involve them to help normalize the experience.

Abortion is safe in the United States due to its legality following the 1973 *Roe v. Wade* Supreme Court decision. Globally, however, unsafe and illegal abortions persist and the World Health Organization estimates 68,000 deaths and millions of complications from unsafe abortions each year. Laws and regulations about abortion vary from state to state and are available from the Guttmacher Institute. The most common restrictions that states impose are parental notification or consent for minors' counseling, waiting periods, and limitations on the use of public funding such as Medicaid for abortion services. This entry describes the abortion method options and discusses health care for the woman after the abortion procedure.

Medication Abortion

Sometimes called the *abortion pill,* or *medical abortion,* medication abortion is the use of medications to terminate a pregnancy. This method is generally used by women who are no more than 9 weeks pregnant (63 days since the last menstrual period) and can be done by a family physician in an office setting. In the United States, the Food and Drug Administration (FDA) approved mifepristone, previously known as RU-486 in Europe, for use through clinicians' offices in 2000. The clinician must register with the U.S. distributor of mifepristone and sign a prescriber's agreement prior to offering this service to patients.

Medication abortion involves two medications: mifepristone and misoprostol that are taken at various intervals depending on the protocol. Mifepristone is an antiprogesterone, which causes the pregnancy to detach from the uterus. Misoprostol is a prostaglandin analogue, which causes uterine contractions that result in expulsion of the pregnancy. The process is similar to a miscarriage and is accompanied by cramping and bleeding generally within 24 hours after the misoprostol is taken. Several protocols are available for the use of these medications; one evidence-based approach recommends taking 200 mg of mifepristone orally on Day 1 given by the clinician followed by 800 mcg of misoprostol buccally on Day 2 (24 hours later) at the patient's home.

The success rate of a medication abortion is between 95% and 98%, with greater efficacy the earlier the gestational age according to Beverly Winikoff and colleagues. Aspiration abortion is necessary for the few failures in medication abortion; this possibility should be included in the patient counseling and informed consent. Vaginal bleeding following medication abortion can continue for 9 to 16 days and occasionally spotting may persist for up to a month as stated by Irving M. Spitz. Cramping pain caused by the misoprostol can be treated with analgesics and other supportive care commonly used for menstrual cramping. Despite these side effects, women who choose medication abortion site the lack of instrumentation and privacy as reasons why they prefer this method.

Patients are generally seen 1 to 2 weeks after the mifepristone was taken in the office for a follow-up visit. Completion of the process is usually obvious from the patient's history of bleeding and cramping and diminished signs and symptoms of pregnancy. Wesley Clark and colleagues note that the success of the medication abortion can be followed by ultrasound or declining serum human chorionic gonadotropin (hCG) levels.

Aspiration Abortion

Aspiration or *surgical abortion* is a method that uses a vacuum aspirator to gently suction the contents of the uterus through a plastic cannula. The vacuum source consists of either a handheld portable device, known as a manual vacuum aspirator (MVA) or an electrical pump, known as an electrical vacuum aspirator (EVA). This procedure can also be done in a family physician's office as part of comprehensive reproductive health care. Unlike medication abortion, aspiration abortion requires the insertion of instruments inside the uterus. The procedure takes about 5 to 10 minutes and can be done using local anesthesia in which lidocaine is used to perform a paracervical block while the patient is awake. This process enables the clinician to reassure the patient during the procedure and requires counseling skills well suited to a family physician. In dedicated abortion clinics, women are also offered intravenous sedation if they prefer to be unconscious during the procedure.

First-trimester aspiration abortions are extremely safe; the mortality rate for abortions performed at less than 8 weeks gestation is 0.3 per 100,000 procedures, most of which are related to anesthesia as reported by H. Lawson and colleagues. The possible but rare complications include cervical laceration, hemorrhage, infection, incomplete abortion, uterine perforation, and hematometria. Unlike medication abortion, the woman is done with the abortion at the end of the clinic visit, and for women who choose this option, they are often anxious to be done with the experience that day. Ultrasound and/or bimanual exam are used to assess gestational age prior to the procedure and examination of the pregnancy tissue is used to confirm completion.

Second-Trimester Abortion

Although 88% of all abortions are in the first trimester, women may have compelling reasons to obtain abortions later. Often, this is due to a delay in the diagnosis of pregnancy, severe fetal anomalies, medical conditions that put the mother's health at risk, and delays in accessing abortion care due to financial or other barriers. This situation is especially true for adolescents in states where there are parental consent laws, which lead to delayed procedures due to concerns about confidentiality and difficulty navigating the health system. Family physicians that provide genetic screening as part of prenatal care will likely have to discuss the option of a second-trimester abortion with a patient who discovers a severe fetal anomaly or develops a serious health problem.

Postabortion Care

Postabortion care is well suited to clinicians who form continuous relationships with patients and families. It involves discussing any feelings surrounding the abortion and reassuring the woman that abortion is a safe procedure that will not impact future fertility. Women often hear myths about abortion negatively impacting their physical and mental health, and depending on the level of support from their families and friends, women have a wide range of experiences. If desired, women and their partners can be referred to Exhale, a free after-abortion counseling service available in English and Spanish by telephone. In addition to emotional support, postabortion care involves contraception counseling. Most forms of contraception can be given immediately after the abortion such as immediate postabortion IUD insertions.

Dalia Brahmi

See also Contraception in Childbearing Couples; Genetic Conditions, Experience of Families During Prediagnosis and Diagnosis Phases of; Teen Pregnancy; Women's Health

Further Readings

Clark, W., Panton, T., Hann, L., & Gold, M. (2007). Medication abortion applying routine sequential measurements of serum hCG and sonography only when indicated. *Contraception, 75*(2), 131–135.

Jones, R., Zolna, M. R. S., Henshaw, S. K., & Finer, L. B. (2008). Abortion in the United States: Incidence and access to services, 2005. *Perspectives on Sexual and Reproductive Health, 40*(1), 6–16.

Lawson, H., Frye, A., Atrash, H. K., Smith, J. C., Shulman, H. B., & Ramick, M. (1994). Abortion mortality, United States, 1972 through 1987. *American Journal of Obstetrics and Gynecology, 171*(5), 1365–1372.

Spitz, I. (1998). Early pregnancy termination with mifepristone and misoprostol in the United States. *New England Journal of Medicine, 338*(18), 1241–1247.

Winikoff, B., Dzuba, I. G., Creinin, M. D., Crowden, W. A., Goldberg, A. B., Gonzales, J., et al. (2008). Two distinct oral routes of misoprostol in mifepristone medical abortion. *Obstetrics and Gynecology, 112*(6), 1303–1310.

Websites

Guttmacher Institute: http://www.guttmacher.org
Exhale: http://www.4exhale.org

ACCESS TO HEALTH CARE: CHILD HEALTH

Health care for children includes well child care, episodic illness care, specialty care, oral health care, developmental care, and mental health care. While access to care is often operationally defined by the health insurance policies held by parents, there are a number of other variables that affect access, including geography, physical and temporal factors, the availability of providers within the community, the cultural competency of providers, philosophical similarities and differences between people seeking health care and providers, and the ability to pay for care. This discussion focuses on the types of care needed by children in order to achieve optimal health and the variables affecting access.

All children should receive health care in the context of a medical or health care home, a model of delivering care that is accessible, comprehensive, family centered, and coordinated. This model provides the child with a primary care provider, well child preventive care (including developmental screening), episodic illness care, and referrals to needed specialists and community agencies and programs. This home serves as the central repository of records related to the child's health and provides a point from which all other care is coordinated. This model does not suggest that all care can be provided by a single primary care provider, as children, especially those with chronic and/or serious health conditions, may need specialist care and community-based supports and services. It does require, however, that the primary care provider coordinates care with specialists to ensure that it is comprehensive and coordinated. Guidelines for preventive care are readily available to the medical home practice; knowledge of community-based programs and resources is crucial, as well as an adequate specialty care provider network to which one can refer.

In addition to primary care, some children will need access to high-quality *pediatric* specialty care. Specialists who focus primarily on adults are often not prepared to care for the full range of pediatric conditions, even within their specialty. For instance, when children have a cardiac condition, care should be provided by a pediatric cardiologist in order to ensure an adequate breadth of knowledge, rather than a cardiologist who provides care primarily to adults. Pediatric specialists are often affiliated with children's hospitals, which facilitate access to other necessary support services.

Oral health problems are one of the leading causes of school days missed and pain in children; therefore, access to health care includes preventive and restorative oral health care. Likewise, with growing concerns regarding the escalating numbers of children diagnosed with autism and other developmental and learning disabilities, access to developmental screening within the medical home and referral to appropriate developmental, mental health, and learning specialists are important to optimize child health and well-being.

A number of variables affect access to health care, not the least of which is the ability to pay for care. A variety of funding options exist to help families afford care including employer-sponsored health insurance, Medicaid, the State Children's Health Insurance Program (SCHIP), State Title V Programs for Children with Special Health Care Needs, and developmental disability and mental health service systems. In addition, different locales may have locally funded health insurance programs or access to low-cost health care through county hospitals and clinics or safety net providers, such as free clinics. Despite these resources, there are still a number of children who remain uninsured because they do not have access to commercial insurance, cannot afford it, or do not know about or qualify for publicly funded programs.

This situation is a particular problem for children who are not legal residents or citizens and therefore may not be eligible for publicly funded programs.

Access to providers, in particular certain pediatric specialists, can be a challenge in some communities. There is a nationwide shortage of certain pediatric providers, such as pediatric neurologists and others who may be unwilling to accept Medicaid or SCHIP due to low reimbursement rates. In smaller communities, particularly rural areas, there may be a population base inadequate to support specialists, necessitating travel to larger communities to seek services. Certain geographic features, for instance, mountain ranges that are impassable during winter months, may also affect access and necessitate travel to distant cities to receive needed care. Accessibility also includes offices that are open when families need to use them. For working families, it may be important to have access to providers in the evenings or on weekends, particularly for those families who do not get paid by employers when taking time off from work. Similarly, for parents of children with special health care needs, it is important to find primary care providers comfortable taking care of a child with complex issues, and offices must be accessible for wheelchairs and other devices used by the child. Some communities may lack primary care providers as well, especially in rural or remote areas.

Accessibility also includes access to care that feels comfortable in a cultural context. In addition to access to providers and office staff that speak the primary languages of the families they serve, it is also important to be aware of cultural influences on health care and demonstrate respect for cultural differences. Likewise, care should be philosophically accessible, so that providers and parents share philosophies of care to work as partners toward optimizing the health of the child.

Access to health care is important to the health and development of children. Various provider and environmental factors affect access, and should be considered in the broader context of child health.

Kathryn Smith

See also Health Care or Medical Home; Medicaid and Family Health

Further Readings

American Academy of Pediatrics. (2009, May). *Bright futures*. Retrieved May 1, 2009, from http://brightfutures.aap.org

American Academy of Pediatrics. (2009, May). *National Center for Medical Home Implementation*. Retrieved May 1, 2009, from http://www.medicalhomeinfo.org

Centers for Medicare and Medicaid Services. (2009, May). *Children's health insurance program*. Retrieved May 1, 2009, from http://www.cms.hhs.gov/home/chip.asp

Centers for Medicare and Medicaid Services. (2009, May). *Medicaid*. Retrieved May 1, 2009, from http://www.cms.hhs.gov/home/medicaid.asp

Health Resources and Services Administration, Maternal and Child Health Bureau. (2009, May). Title V block grant to states. Retrieved May 1, 2009 from http://mchb.hrsa.gov/programs

Websites

Centers for Medicare and Medicaid Services, *Children's Health Insurance Program:* http://www.cms.hhs.gov/home/chip.asp

Centers for Medicare and Medicaid Services, *Medicaid:* http://www.cms.hhs.gov/home/medicaid.asp

ACCESS TO HEALTH CARE: ELDERLY

Across the globe, the population of adults over the age of 65 is increasing. Baby boomers, born between 1946 and 1964 (who begin turning age 65 in 2011), will accelerate this growth. One of the greatest barriers to health care access in the United States is lack of adequate insurance coverage. The Medicare public insurance safety net system was put in place to ensure that older Americans had coverage because of their restricted employment opportunities and the high cost of individual health insurance policies for people with preexisting conditions. As such, the barriers to health care among elderly adults are less about insurance and more about functional health status, proximity to physicians and specialists, and a shortage of specialists in geriatric medicine. This entry focuses on the barriers to health care services and factors for family consideration regarding health care decisions.

Health Status

Studies using representative samples of adults aged 65 and older have found that the majority have a primary care physician. Those who report having a primary care physician receive more frequent and higher-quality preventive care services. The leading illnesses and causes of mortality among older adults regardless of gender, race, or ethnicity include cardiovascular diseases and cancer. The risk for these chronic illnesses increases with age but can be prevented or modified with behavioral interventions. As these illnesses progress, quality of life and functional ability decline. Other illnesses that contribute to functional impairment include arthritis and chronic obstructive pulmonary disease. Older adults who have chronic health conditions and functional impairments may be dependent on others for assistance and have a harder time scheduling appointments and procuring transportation to physician appointments. Some older people living in the community have access to various services through their place of residence. Such services may include meal preparation, laundry and cleaning services, help with medications, and in-home health care (nurse visits and physical therapy). Availability of such services varies based on location but is commonly found in both rural and urban settings.

Rural and Urban Areas

Older adults living in rural areas often have difficulties obtaining health care. Hospitals and care clinics are more widely dispersed and require the older individual to travel to obtain care. Additionally, rural hospitals have fewer physicians and may not have any specialists. As a result, rural elders often present with more serious chronic health conditions due to a lack of preventive care and delays in scheduling or obtaining appointments. Research has shown that rural elders who experienced cardiovascular incidents were less likely than those treated in urban hospitals to receive recommended treatments and had significantly higher mortality rates from all causes than those in urban hospitals. Rural elders often have higher rates of certain cancers due to exposure to farm chemicals. Additionally, rural residents on average tend to be older, lower income, and suffer from higher rates of chronic illness than their urban counterparts.

Many rural hospitals and home-based health care providers are dependent on Medicare revenues. Therefore, the network of providers that serves rural Americans is fragile due to its dependence on Medicare moneys and the high percentage of Medicare beneficiaries residing in rural areas.

Specialists

The vast majority of older adults receive their health care from a primary care physician. Often, the primary care physician has training in family or internal medicine. However, aging related health conditions often require medical management from physicians and health care professionals with specialized training. For example, individuals with cardiovascular disease require assessment, interventions, and treatment from cardiologists and vascular surgeons. Access to specialists may be more difficult due to tight office and procedural schedules, need for physician referral, and the relative numbers of such specialists in a given region. Physicians with specialized training in geriatric medicine will be in increased demand, and at present, there are an inadequate number of faculty members to educate and train future geriatricians and nurses. Research has shown that geriatricians currently provide the most benefit to the aging population by serving the most vulnerable older adults. This, however, will not be sustainable in the coming years, and colleges of medicine are striving to create geriatric training programs that are comparable to those of other medical specialties to meet demand.

Family Considerations

Most older adults have access to a primary care physician if they are covered under Medicare. Adults who are approaching the age of qualification for Medicare and family who may be in a position to provide care for them need to be informed about the types of Medicare coverage and gaps in coverage (also known as the *donut hole*). Supplemental insurance policies and the Patient Protection and Affordable Care Act are poised to address gaps in coverage. Educating oneself on one's own or a family member's health conditions is essential to asking the right questions about appropriate management, treatment, and physician referrals to specialists. If specialist care may be needed, caregivers may need to consider travel time and expenses for such visits and procedures, particularly if the caregiver is also in the workforce. Scheduling appointments and coordinating care may be cumbersome when balancing work-family-caregiving duties. Rural elders who may need to travel considerable distances for specialist care may need to plan for a multiday stay and coordination of allied health care specialist needs (i.e., oxygen delivery).

Heidi Harriman Ewen

See also Caregiving: Elderly; Case Management for Chronic Illness/Disability and the Family; Health System Options for Families; Managed Care; Medicare and Family Health; Types of Family Provider Relationships

Further Readings

Cohen, R. A., Bloom, B., Simpson, G., & Parsons, P. E. (1997). Access to health care (Pt. 3: Older adults). *Vital Health Stat 10*(198), 1–32.

Federal Interagency Forum on Aging-Related Statistics. (2008, March). *Older Americans 2008: Key indicators of well-being*. Washington, DC: U.S. Government Printing Office.

Okoro, C. A., Strine, T. W., Young, S. L., Balluz, L. S., & Mokdad, A. H. (2005). Access to health care among older adults and receipt of preventive services: Results from the behavioral risk factor surveillance system. *Preventive Medicine, 40*(3), 337–343.

Warshaw, G. A., Bragg, E. J., Fried, L. P., & Hall, W. J. (2008). Which patients benefit the most from a geriatrician's care? Consensus among directors of geriatrics academic programs. *Journal of the American Geriatrics Society, 56*(10), 1796–1801.

ACCESS TO HEALTH CARE: UNINSURED

Fundamentally, *access* means the ability of a person to obtain needed medical services from hospitals, physicians, and other sources. Health insurance plays a critical role in access to medical care because insurance is the major source of payment to the providers of medical services. At least theoretically, the consumers of medical services will be responsible to pay out of pocket unless they have insurance coverage to pay for those services. A person's ability to obtain needed medical care by using health insurance assumes these three factors: (1) The services that an insured person is seeking are available, (2) those services can be obtained at the time the need arises, and (3) the providers are willing to accept the amount of payment in return for the services they provide. Clearly, factors other than health insurance are necessary to access needed medical care. In other words, a person may have insurance and yet not be able to obtain medical care when needed. Conversely, a person may not have health insurance and yet be able to obtain certain medical services. Nevertheless, because of limitations on the availability of medical care to the uninsured, health insurance is the primary mechanism for obtaining medical services. This entry discusses the avenues for obtaining health insurance and options for uninsured individuals and families who wish to receive health care services.

How Health Insurance Is Obtained

There are three main avenues for obtaining health insurance. Employers are the most important source for obtaining health insurance in the United States. In most cases, they pay the bulk of the cost of health insurance; the employee generally pays a fraction of the cost. The U.S. government also runs several types of health insurance programs for U.S. citizens and residents who qualify for these programs. For example, on reaching the age of 65 years, a person becomes eligible for the Medicare program. There are special programs for the very poor, children in low-income households,

veterans, American Indians, and U.S. military personnel and their families. There is a lot of variation in these programs. In some cases, the cost of insurance is fully paid through taxes. In other cases, the beneficiary may have to pay part of the cost of insurance. In other situations the government delivers health care through its own facilities, such as hospitals and clinics operated by the Veterans Health Administration or the Department of Defense. Last, a person or family can buy health insurance directly from an insurance company.

The Uninsured

The uninsured are those who either are unable to or for some reason do not obtain health insurance through one of the sources just mentioned. It is almost impossible to get an accurate count of the number of uninsured. This situation exists because some people are uninsured only part of the time and others, especially many single young adults, have decided that they do not need health insurance because they are in good health. Then, there are the illegal immigrants who are neither citizens nor legal residents and do not have health insurance. The U.S. Census Bureau estimated that in 2008, the number of people without health insurance coverage was 46.3 million or 15.4% of the population. Compared to uninsured rates for whites, the uninsured rates are higher among African Americans and Asians; they are even higher among Hispanics. The uninsured are often poor or low-income. Between 2007 and 2008, the number of people covered by employment-based health insurance declined from 177.4 million to 176.3 million while the number covered by government health insurance climbed from 83.0 million to 87.4 million.

Access to Health Care

The uninsured receive medical care through a variety of sources and pay about one third of the cost of their care out of pocket. The remaining services are delivered on the basis of uncompensated care. For these services, the providers do not receive any direct payment. More than half of the uninsured do not have a usual source of health care such as a primary care physician or clinic. The National

Health Interview Survey conducted by the U.S. Census Bureau showed that from 2005 to 2006, 53% of the uninsured did not have a usual source of health care compared to a little less than 10% of the insured population. Hence, compared to the insured, health care received by the uninsured is likely to be uneven and sporadic.

Hospitals and physicians, as well as a variety of safety net providers, deliver care to the uninsured. Safety net providers are those who are legally obligated to deliver medical services to persons who cannot afford them.

Inpatient Hospitals

The bulk of uncompensated care costs are incurred in hospitals. Although public and non-profit hospitals are legally required to provide uncompensated care because they receive direct or indirect government subsidies, for-profit hospitals also provide their fair share of uncompensated care to the uninsured.

Hospital Emergency Departments

Various estimates suggest that at least 50% of the cases treated in the nation's emergency departments are for conditions that could be seen in other less acute care settings, such as urgent care centers and physicians' private offices. The Emergency Medical Treatment and Labor Act of 1986 requires an evaluation of every patient, necessary stabilizing treatment, and admission to the hospital when necessary, regardless of ability to pay. Hence, emergency departments function as a safety net for the uninsured, who account for nearly one fifth of the total visits to emergency departments.

Clinics for the Underserved

Since the 1960s, the federal government has been supporting community health centers, migrant health centers for transient agricultural workers, rural health centers in isolated rural areas, and community mental health centers. These clinics deliver primary care, dental care, and mental health services in medically underserved geographic areas. These areas are so designated because they may have high infant mortality, high poverty, and/or high elderly population. The centers are required by law to provide medical services to anyone seeking care, regardless of insurance status or ability to pay. About 40% of the patients served in these clinics are uninsured. The federally funded Health Care for the Homeless (HCH) program operates almost 200 HCH clinics across the country for homeless populations. Together, community, migrant, and homeless centers operate over 8,000 delivery sites. In addition, a volunteer workforce of doctors, dentists, nurses, therapists, pharmacists, nurse practitioners, technicians, and other health care professionals see patients in approximately 1,200 free clinics nationwide. These clinics are funded by churches, hospitals, private donations, and government grants.

Charity Care by Private Physicians

Many physicians provide free or reduced-cost care to uninsured patients in their private practices. However, financial pressures have contributed to a decline in charity care. Based on national surveys of physicians, the Center for Studying Health System Change reported that the percentage of physicians providing free or reduced-cost care decreased to 68.2% in 2004 to 2005 from 71.5% in 2000 to 2001.

Local Health Departments

Across the nation, state and local governments operate health departments that provide basic health care services. For example, many health departments provide services such as physical exams, screening tests, and immunizations for children. Almost all health departments provide services related to family planning, sexually transmitted diseases, tuberculosis control, and nutritional counseling.

The uninsured in America receive medical care through a variety of sources, but the care they receive is not uniformly sustained or coordinated over time as it would be for those who have a regular source of primary care. There is wide variation in access to medical care among uninsured individuals living in different communities; one main reason is the safety net capacity and where the safety net providers are located.

Douglas A. Singh

See also Access to Health Care: Child Health; Community Services Supporting Health; Costs of Medical Care and Existing National, State, and Private Pay Avenues for Families; Employment/Unemployment and Family Health Insurance Coverage; Factors Influencing Access to Health Care for Families; Socioeconomic Status of Families

Further Readings

Agency for Healthcare Research and Quality. (2009, July 15). *New data say uninsured account for nearly one-fifth of emergency room visits.* Retrieved January 31, 2010, from http://ahrq.hhs.gov/news/press/pr2009/hhsuninserpr.htm

Cunningham, P. J., & May, J. H. (2006). *A growing hole in the safety net: Physician charity care declines again.* Washington, DC: Center for Studying Health System Change.

Hadley, J., Holahan, J., Coughlin, T., & Miller, D. (2008). Covering the uninsured in 2008: Current costs, sources of payment, and incremental costs. *Health Affairs, 27*(5), w399–w415.

ACUTE CARE/HOSPITALIZATION OF FAMILY MEMBERS

Acute illness is an altered health state of a severity and immediacy whereby ill individuals recognize that they are ill, must accept the "sick role," and seek appropriate help. For most minor acute illnesses, individuals can care for themselves or remain in their home and be cared for by a family member. This situation is particularly true for children who are dependent on their family to provide this critical function. For some, the acuity of the illness or altered health state requires the individual to be hospitalized to receive a level of health care that the individual or family cannot provide. This entry discusses the history and impact of hospitalization of a family member for acute illness and the implications of this event for family health care.

History

Prior to World War II, hospitals had strict visitation policies, limiting family members by length of visit, day of the week, and even who in the family was allowed to visit. This was particularly traumatic for children. René Spitz coined the term *hospitalism* to define the negative psychological and physiological effects of separation from family members during hospitalization. The family members of hospitalized children were allowed to visit only once a week for a few hours. These children suffered depression and withdrawal. With the advent of family-centered care in the 1970s, the importance of family presence and participation in care is now recognized. Historically, the *family* was defined as limited to blood relatives or those with formal legal arrangements, such as marriage. Modern family health care recognizes that the family consists of whoever the family says it does. However, this broad-minded definition is not always shared by formal health care institutions as some continue to restrict visitation by nontraditional family members.

Impact of Hospitalization on the Family

The impact on the family of hospitalization of a family member for acute illness can be conceptualized using the family resiliency model. In this systems model, the illness is the stressor to which the family must respond with the outcome or goal of adaptation. The model recognizes the interrelationship of many variables such as appraisal, coping, and resources to determine the outcome.

The impact of the hospitalization of the family member varies depending on the nature of the illness or on which member of the family is hospitalized. First, the nature of the illness or reason for hospitalization presents stress for the family. Research has shown that characteristics such as timing; sources, or cause, of the illness; stigma; and demands of the illness influence the degree of stress perceived by the family. Demands on the family such as medical bills and loss of income related to the hospitalization affect family economic functioning. The hospitalized family member's role in his or her family clearly influences the family's response. If the primary breadwinner was hospitalized and/or if the hospitalized family member is the primary caregiver for the children in the family, the impact will be felt on that area of socialization.

Family Interventions and Desired Outcomes

While the family resiliency model provides an excellent framework to research and understand the dynamics of this situation, a comparable framework is the three-pronged crisis intervention model developed by Donna Aguilera. The crisis intervention model is a practical approach that is easy for health professionals to remember and use. The model recognizes that the goal of all family units is to attain equilibrium, and equilibrium is attained when three factors are in balance. These balancing factors include (realistic) perception of the event, (adequate) coping behaviors, and (adequate) situational supports. Hospitalization can be a situational crisis for many families. Based on assessment of the family for these three balancing factors, interventions are focused on supplementing or strengthening each factor as indicated. Interventions may include clarifying aspects of the hospitalization (perception), supporting the family in problem solving and providing information (coping) and referrals to other health care professionals, such as social workers (situational support).

Interventions can also be conceptualized as meeting the needs of the family. Much research has been done over the past several decades about the needs of family members of a hospitalized individual. Often, what is perceived as what the family needs is not the case. Health providers working with families should be cautioned about making assumptions about family members; rather, providers need to verify with the family members what they need. Family needs can be summarized in five categories: information, assurance, proximity, comfort, and support. Family members need information about the diagnosis and prognosis of their ill family member. Information for the family members should include specific facts about the patient's progress, rationale for care being provided, and care provided in terms that are understandable. Family members' questions should be answered honestly. Health care team members should identify who they are and their role when meeting family members. Family members need assurance that there is hope and that the hospital personnel care about their family member. They need proximity. That is, they need to be close by either being at the bedside or have visiting hours and a close area to wait. Family members cope through information seeking and also desire to have some control. Many families need to have directions as to what they can do at the bedside to participate in the patient's care. It is important for the health care providers in acute care settings to acknowledge the role of the family and their importance in meeting the needs of all family members. When the nonhospitalized family members' needs are met and they are coping and adaptive, they are better able to support the acutely ill family member.

Donna Miles Curry

See also Acute Care/Hospitalization of Family Members; Acute Health Problems and Interventions for the Childrearing Family; Acute Health Problems and Interventions for the Midlife Family; Chronic Illness and Family Management Styles; Critical Theory and Family Health; Families Experiencing a Child's Illness; Hospitalization and Family Presence; Resuscitation, Family Presence During

Further Readings

Aguilera, D. (1998). *Crisis intervention: Theory and methodology* (8th ed.). Philadelphia: Elsevier.

Institute for Family-Centered Care. *Bibliographies/ supporting evidence.* Retrieved January 2, 2009, from http://www.familycenteredcare.org/index.html

Woolley, N. (1990). Crisis theory: A paradigm of effective intervention with families of critically ill people. *Journal of Advanced Nursing, 15,* 1402–1408.

ACUTE HEALTH PROBLEMS AND INTERVENTIONS FOR THE CHILDREARING FAMILY

Changes in the health of a child can be a stressful time for both the children and their families. This entry discusses potential problems encountered by families with an ill child and establishes a foundation for planning interventions with these children and their caregivers. Interventions may teach coping skills, provide education, or identify needed support to reduce stress responses associated with the child's illness. The interventions may be used in the home, clinic, or the hospital setting.

Concerns of the Childrearing Family During Period of Acute Illness

Childrearing years can be challenging for parents, and changes in the health of the child are known to create additional stressors for all members of the family. Health issues result in over 2 million acute care hospital admissions of children and adolescents each year in the United States. The most common reasons for the admissions are pneumonia, asthma, acute bronchitis, dehydration, and appendicitis. Threats to a child's health can trigger responses that may extend across years and may reshape the dynamics of the family. Parents, as the nurturers and caregivers of the child, must suddenly depend on others to meet the needs of the acutely ill child. Children and families can be stressed by the highly disruptive, strange environment; fear an unknown outcome; and experience a loss of control. Children's anxiety related to the illness and associated treatments, if not addressed, may manifest in both short-term and extended behavioral changes, such as sleep disturbances, crying, separation anxiety, or emotional withdrawal. Parents are seldom prepared to assist their child during this period. They may fear their child will experience pain and may feel powerless to prevent their suffering. The needs of siblings may also be compromised by rapid unexpected changes in their daily routines, isolation from their family members, and fears for the safety of the ill child. There is existing evidence that interventions for stress reduction enhance coping skills and improve health care outcomes. Such interventions must be tailored to the unique needs of the family with consideration of the social support, cultural influences, language needs, and cognitive abilities of the family.

Stress and Coping

Findings based on the work of Richard Lazarus and Susan Folkman show that no single event triggers stress; stress is a subjective response created by the person and his or her appraisal of the environment. People respond to the trigger based on their coping abilities. A stress appraisal response can be influenced by past experiences as well as by the uncertainty of the health threat. The child and adult cognitively assess their coping resources for the threat and determine the level of risk. While such a simple explanation fails to adequately explain such a complex process, increases in parental stress and child stress have been repeatedly measured in response to acute health changes. Interventions focus on changing the appraisal of the environment to reduce perceptions of risk. Reducing uncertainty may be a targeted outcome of the intervention as well as teaching coping skills to be used in the presence of the threat.

Background

It is not possible during a period of acute illness to isolate the reciprocal influences of either the child or the family on one another. As recently as the 1970s, it was common practice to approach the child as an individual and not to allow parents to collaborate in the child's care. Over the past 3 decades family-centered care (FCC) has evolved in acute health care settings. FCC redefines the *patient-client* from a single individual to a complex integrated family unit. This shift moves the child's caregiver from a visitor status to being integrated into collaborative care planning with the health care team. It is with the understanding that the individual cannot be separated from the interdependent complex group known as *family* that the health care provider must plan interventions. Interventions within the context of the family use knowledge with roots in developmental theory, family system theory, stress and coping theories, and cognitive-behavioral theories.

Overview of the Current Literature

Although tremendous strides have been made in health care to encourage the presence of families, presence and collaborative participation are not yet in balance. Family participation improves care outcomes, develops skills, enhances coping, and facilitates an easier transition to home care. Interventions with the acutely ill child and his or her family have been approached from a wide range of disciplines with interventions using primarily two approaches: cognitive-behavioral and education or resource support. Theoretical frameworks for interventions are interdisciplinary with foundations in coping theories as well as nursing, psychology, public health, and sociology.

Family-Centered Care

The concept of *family-centered care* may differ among health care professionals and families. The term may be used to mean *parental participation* in some facilities; however, parents may not be the primary caregiver of the child. Additionally, sibling needs may be overlooked. As a result of the variance in defining the commonly referenced concept of family-centered care, there are resentments on the part of some parents that health care staff have simply transitioned their work to the parents rather than encouraged active collaboration. Caregivers describe a paternalistic attitude on the part of health care providers that stifles effective planning and participation. Role negotiation for how parents will participate in the care of their acutely ill child has largely been absent. Recurrent perceptions of power shifts between parents and health care professionals have been identified with parents experiencing power losses for parental decisions and health care staff assuming gatekeeper roles for levels of parental participation. Such power imbalances further compromise communication.

The onset of acute illness or injury often provides parents little warning and may have long-term implications for the family unit. Of particular concern is the presence of a higher risk for post-traumatic stress disorder (PTSD) in parents and children who have experienced an acute health threat. PTSD is a prolonged psychological response to the perceived or actual threat. Effects of PTSD have been described secondary to acute hospitalization associated with neonatal or pediatric intensive care, burn care, wound care, cardiac surgery, or traumatic injury. PTSD symptoms may be present when hospitalization is caused by trauma even if the injuries are mild. Interventions to reduce stress such as effective pain management may also reduce the risk of PTSD.

There are a limited number of studies of the needs of siblings during the acute illness period. Most work has been focused in areas of neonatal intensive care and cancer care. Siblings have described both a disruption from "normal" for the family during the period of acute illness or procedures and changes in parenting styles as well as internal disruption of their sense of self and role in the family. Treatment and prognosis information, as well as involvement in the daily activity, are desired by siblings of acutely ill children.

Cognitive-Behavioral Approaches

Interventions to teach parents skills to provide support to their child during procedures using such behaviors as distracting, soothing, and relaxing techniques have been effective for improving responses to stress. Although there are endorsements from the American Academy of Pediatrics and the Emergency Nurses Association encouraging practitioners to allow parental presence to be a choice during complex invasive procedures and/or emergency resuscitation, many health care facilities have not embraced the practice. Lower levels of depression and anxiety have been found in parents who were allowed to remain with their child during invasive procedures. In situations of failed emergency resuscitation, parental observation has been found to assist with later grief.

Preparation

Interventions with families of acutely ill children have used parental education for preparation for surgery and invasive procedures, the care of premature infants, and critical care information. Parental and child preparation for scheduled surgery uses such techniques as modeling by recreating the environment or allowing the child and parent to visit the actual setting, discussing anticipated activities, and teaching coping skills such as distraction and soothing behaviors. The child using the coping skills taught prior to surgery may need parental support during periods of increased stress to be effective. Parental presence during induction of anesthesia remains a controversial topic. Findings of the benefit of anxiety reduction from parental presence during anesthesia induction remain mixed.

Pain Management

Pain management in children continues to be inconsistent in many health care settings particularly in emergent situations. Uncontrolled procedural and postoperative pain for both the child and his or her parent can create sustained traumatic reactions. In addition to pharmacologic interventions and the use of sucrose for infant pain, studies in pain management have also focused on the role of distraction to reduce both the child's distress and reported pain. As families began to participate in the care of the hospitalized child, training of parents evolved to provide distraction during painful procedures. Differences in responses of children to parents or health care professionals as pain distracters have not been fully explored. While both groups may provide distraction, parental participation provides an added value of potentially reducing the anxiety of an isolated parent.

Many pediatric acute procedures have transitioned to an outpatient setting, which removes families from prolonged contact with health care providers. The short contact period with parents for the provision of information, training, and opportunities to reduce stress create new opportunities for interventions. Lisa Butler and others trained parents in the use of interventions with self-hypnosis to reduce anxiety in the child during an acute outpatient procedure. The active participation of the parents served to reduce parental anxiety and feelings of helplessness while reducing distress for the child. Another approach includes parents and children in pain measurement through the use of a temporary tattoo of a pediatric pain scale. Although the tattoo approach is still in early stages of evaluation, it reflects a growing focus on the importance of transitioning effective measures of distress from the acute setting to the home setting.

Therapeutic animal visits provide distraction as yet another approach to pain management. Animals are being used in animal therapy programs in acute care settings across the country and are described by both children and their parents as providing a pain distraction. Music has also been used with children to create a distracting environment including in some surgical suites.

Education Support

The care of a premature infant or a critical child can be particularly frightening for parents. COPE (Creating Opportunities for Parent Empowerment) provides a structured education process for parents to diminish parental stress and anxiety. A tested, structured program ensures parent education is consistent between health care providers. Additional benefits from such interventions are earlier transitions to the home setting.

The Community Pathways program in North Carolina provided an interdisciplinary early intervention program for families of hospitalized children up to 3 years of age. The program was structured on family support models, which targeted improved outcomes for the child through diminished stress levels of the family. It was partnered with community agencies to ensure a smooth transition from acute care settings to the home settings. Community Pathways staff participated in rounds in both the critical care unit and the pediatric units to assess and identify intervention needs.

Rapid Response Activation

Many acute care hospitals now have special teams of health care professionals called Rapid Response Teams (RRTs) who respond to urgent changes in patients' conditions. In a limited number of hospitals, families of pediatric patients have been educated to access urgently needed care by calling for the RRT without initially asking for a member of the health care team to confirm the need. Initial concerns from the hospital staff were that the use of the RRT would be abused, a concern that has not been supported by the actual practice. Parents are educated in the use of the RRT system and become proactive partners with the staff in the delivery of care to their child, a significant opportunity to allow parents to participate in protecting their child from harm.

Desired Family Health Outcomes

Goals of interventions with families and children are to achieve effective coping skills, which will avoid prolonged distress related to changes in the health of the child and to ensure a safe transition between levels of care. Reduction of stress for the family allows improved skills to focus on needed information related to the child's care. Through active family participation, the family members become comfortable with assisting with the care needs of the child as well as with practicing coping behaviors to avoid distress. Parents who fear for their child's safety may perceive their child as more vulnerable than other children. Perceived vulnerability of a child, real or imagined, may contribute to developmental delays and increased cost for health care due to recurrent health care visits. It is expected that the needed skills will be developed collaboratively to to help the child achieve the highest possible developmental level and to enhance the daily life of the family.

A Foundation for Future Interventions

The Role of Play

The design of interventions with children must consider the role of play in their daily lives. Play is an integral component of development and can be used to communicate feelings of the child and to encourage family participation. Therapeutic play interventions may be as simple as encouraging children to make signs communicating displeasure with invasive procedures or ensuring an adolescent has access to the Internet for distraction during treatments. Clowns, with the support of parents, are an integral part of some pediatric settings to both distract and empower children. Play activities are important components of preparation and distraction interventions.

Role Negotiation for Family-Centered Care

Intervention planning with the childrearing family is a dynamic process dependent on the give and take of information between the child, the family members, and the health care team. As such, the intervention must be flexible and easily modified. Interventions may include concepts related to physiologic threats, social needs, and/or cognitive needs. As health care technology continues a rapid evolution, time spent with families continues to grow shorter and diminishes the opportunity for ongoing assessments. Structured interview tools, such as Lorraine Wright and Maureen Leahey's 15-minute family interview, provide targeted information quickly to allow the health care practitioner to identify unique family needs. In brief encounters, Wright's single question for a family to probe a specific priority need may also be used to center interventions on the area creating the greatest stress for the family. Structured approaches for data collection permit a collaborative, nonhierarchal relationship to develop between the nurse and the family and removes assumptions related to family need.

Unique Needs of the Family

Most interventions have focused on parents and most specifically on birth parents. Yet across the country, children are cared for by many other caregivers including grandparents, aunts, uncles, and sometimes siblings. Effective interventions will include the most influential individuals in the child's daily life as well as anticipated caregivers after discharge.

Cultural influences on expectations of the family during periods of acute illness must be considered in planning interventions. The U.S. Census Bureau reports that by the year 2050 nearly one third of the residents of the United States will be Hispanic. Interventions with all families must ensure an understanding of cultural influences on the family during periods of acute illness. Bilingual interventions for those generations of the family who may understand English as a second language should also be evaluated.

The Institute of Medicine reports that 90 million people in the United States are unable to comprehend and act on health care information. Teaching materials must be tailored to the unique needs of the individual family. Routine provision of information in writing, posters, and other written means of communication cannot ensure patient understanding and must be used with caution as a sole source of interventions with families.

In summary, acutely ill children and their parents experience lower stress and improved coping responses when interventions reduce the uncertainty of the illness threat and provide some control of the environment. Interventions are planned with a consideration of unique cultural and learning needs of the family. Interventions to reduce stress and anxiety may reduce the risk of prolonged stress reactions for both the child and the family.

Wilma Powell Stuart

See also Acute Care/Hospitalization of Family Members; Chronic Health Problems and Interventions for the Childrearing Family; Families Experiencing a Child's Illness; Hospitalization and Family Presence; Partnering With Families: Family-Centered Care; Resuscitation, Family Presence During; Stress Management Theory and Techniques in Families

Further Readings

Broome, M., & Stuart, W. (2006). Interventions with families of an acutely or critically ill child. In D. R. Crane & E. Marshall (Eds.), *Handbook of families & health* (pp. 451–466). Thousand Oaks, CA: Sage.

Corlett, J., & Twycross, A. (2006). Negotiation of parental roles within family-centred care: A review of the research. *Journal of Clinical Nursing, 15,* 1308–1316.

Dingeman, R., Mitchell, E., Meyer, E., & Curley, M. (2007). Parent presence during complex invasive procedures and cardiopulmonary resuscitation: A systematic review of the literature. *Pediatrics, 120*(4), 842–854.

Duhamel, F., Dupuis, F., & Wright, L. (2009). Families' and nurses' responses to the "One question question": Reflections for clinical practice, education, and research in family nursing. *Journal of Family Nursing, 15*(4), 461–485.

Franck, L., Allen, A., & Oulton, K. (2007). Making pain assessment more accessible to children and parents: Can greater involvement improve the quality of care? *Clinical Journal of Pain, 23*(4), 331–338.

Freund, P., Boone, H., Barlow, J., & Lim, C. (2005). Healthcare and early intervention collaborative supports for families and young children. *Infants & Young Children, 18*(1), 25–36.

Gold, J., Kant, A., & Kim, S. (2008). The impact of unintentional pediatric trauma: A review of pain, acute stress and posttraumatic stress. *Journal of Pediatric Nursing, 23*(2), 81–91.

Kleiber, C., Montgomery, L., & Craft-Rosenberg, M. (1995). Information needs of the siblings of critically ill children. *Children's Health Care, 24*(1), 47–60.

Melnyk, B., Alpert-Gillis, L., Feinstein, N., Crean, H., Johnson, J., Fairbanks, E., Small, L., et al. (2004). Creating opportunities for parent empowerment: Program effects on the mental health/coping outcomes of critically ill young children and their mothers. *Pediatrics, 113*(6), e597–e607.

Acute Health Problems and Interventions for the Midlife Family

Midlife can be defined in various ways, including by chronological age, by life stage, or by developmental age. Despite the various definitions, it is often in midlife when an individual may assume the role of caregiver for an ill family member or may become ill him- or herself. This entry discusses health counseling and education for patients and families during the midlife stage, including the issues associated with becoming a caretaker and interventions for the entire family.

Health Counseling and Education

Due to increasing service demands, insurance pressures, and rising health care costs, individuals tend to spend less time in recuperation under direct supervision of medical care professionals following major medical events. Hospital stays are shorter and time for health counseling and education of patients and families is limited. Appropriate information must be relayed successfully in a timely fashion to safely discharge patients back to the family and ensure adequate follow-up care. Often, additional information can be passed on by home health nurses, but home visits are also overburdened with numerous tasks to be accomplished in short periods of time. Whether at home or in the hospital, the health professional must obtain the patient's medical information, provide health counseling and education, and address patient and family concerns. Even though time for intervention care planning will often be brief, it is vital for the health care professional to convey an individualized care plan goal for both the patient and family that can be met. This is not always easy because there may be ambiguity surrounding the diagnosis, the course of the illness, or the outcome of treatment. It is the health care professional's task to communicate clearly the patient's condition and needs while helping the family assess resources and transition into the caregiving role. Since the role of family caregiver is increasing in the patient recovery process and will likely continue to increase, the health care professional must also consider the unique needs of caregivers and their families in the development of any intervention strategy. Health counseling and education will need to be modified based on the developmental needs of the patient and family members.

The Definition of Family

The definition of *family* significantly impacts individuals as they come into contact with health care systems by determining who is included on health insurance policies or who has access to medical records. The medical establishment's definition of who is family often does not resemble the patient's.

To provide thorough family care, the health professional must view the individual's definition of family as primary. Since families may occur in many forms and have diverse cultural and ethnic orientations, it is helpful to view family simply as a complex social system composed of a network of individuals who influence each other's lives. Biological or legal ties may or may not be present. Based on this definition, it can be assumed that all people regardless of age or circumstances are members of some type of family.

Encouraging involvement of an individual's family in the recovery process is important because the health or illness of an individual is a family matter. The family provides for the well-being of its individuals on multiple levels, externally and internally. Family provides physical care and maintenance in the form of food, clothing, shelter, intellectual development, and medical care. The family also socializes individuals by influencing their internal drives, such as values, beliefs, attitudes, hopes, and aspirations. The family has the ability to either facilitate or repress the growth of its members in any of these areas. If illness does occur, how the family interprets the symptoms often will influence the decision to seek care. Following treatment, the family influences how members comply with treatment regimens. Once an individual has overcome the illness and is returning to health, the family influences recovery by the caregiving and support it gives. For instance, the family can influence lifestyle choices that may prevent illness or increase its likelihood. Because of its importance to the individual, the family has the potential to play important roles at all levels of health care and illness prevention.

Midlife Description

To successfully provide meaningful health counseling and education to individuals at midlife, it is important to have a general description of the life stage. The definition of *midlife* varies greatly concerning the actual age of start and ending. It also varies from country to country due to different life expectancies and historically has changed as individuals in modern societies now expect to live into their 70s or even 80s. Middle adulthood can be defined by the chronological, biological, or developmental ages in an individual's life. If defined strictly by chronological age, it starts at 35 and ends at 50; if it is related to biological changes and childrearing, then the ranges would be 40 to 60 or 45 to 65. Generally, an individual's own concept of what constitutes a young adult versus an older or old adult determines this range. The developmental age of an individual is marked not by a specific number range but instead by a specific life challenge. All stages of human development including middle adulthood have specific developmental tasks associated with them. Understanding the developmental stage of an individual can help a health professional gain an understanding of the motivations most likely driving the individual. It will also aid in the development of strategies for the patient and family to enhance quality of life.

Erik Erickson, a noted psychologist of developmental theory, defined middle adulthood as a time when a person chooses between generativity and stagnation. With generativity, individuals in midlife seek to continue to work creatively and productively on the life they have achieved (career and family) but the meaningfulness of this work becomes very important. Midlife is a time for passing along values and norms. Care for the next generation also becomes a concern. This care often extends from family and friends out into the larger community and is marked by the individual freely giving time, energy, and resources without expectations of specific compensation. It is important that adults in midlife gain a sense of accomplishment and balance in this stage of development. Stagnation can result in self-absorption with little connection to others and lack of meaning for life. Overextension is also a potential problem where individuals take no time for their needs because they are so busy.

Assuming the Role of Caregiver in Midlife

Taking on the responsibility of the role of caregiver is not an easy adjustment for an individual at any life stage. Therefore, understanding the consequences of assuming the role for an ill family member in midlife is important. Prevalence of caregiving for ill family members peaks in midlife and often conflicts with demands of family, self-need, and paid employment. This places caregivers in the life circumstance of having to fulfill multiple-role responsibilities. This circumstance is becoming more common, and the likelihood of having to serve in a caregiving role numerous times during one's lifetime is expected to increase. This expectation is related to demographic trends toward longer lives, women delaying childbirth, couples having fewer children or none, higher rates of divorce, lower rates of marriage and remarriage, and higher rates of women's employment. The number of people living alone in modern societies is also expanding rapidly. Consequently, caregiving responsibilities are expected to fall on fewer shoulders in the not so distant future. This will significantly impact individuals in midlife due to their unique characteristics.

Due to the wide age range characteristic of individuals in midlife along with many couples delaying childbirth, it is possible for midlife families to have children with ages ranging from infancy to adulthood. This is also a unique time in history when children are likely to have living grandparents and even great-grandparents. Caregiving responsibilities for the elderly are also expected to increase dramatically as large portions of the United States become increasingly aged. This generational pull experienced by midlife caregivers in the position of caring for both dependent children and sick parents or grandparents simultaneously has earned them the nickname *sandwich generation*. These individuals find they must balance their own needs with those of their offspring and their aging parents. The balance often occurs at the expense of the caregiver's personal well-being and resources. In addition, most contemporary work environments are not organized to facilitate employees' fulfillment of family responsibilities.

In some cases, the need to relocate to seek better career and work opportunities can also result in limited resources and isolation from extended family and social support systems. It is understandable that caregiving can lead to increased distress and burden and has been associated with poor personal health particularly if the caregiver must provide high levels of intense personal care. Individuals should be encouraged to elicit additional support before burnout and exhaustion from overextension incapacitate the caregiver. Balance is crucial. Caregiving can provide much satisfaction to a family member by offering an opportunity to experience increased purpose in life and personal growth thus successfully fulfilling the developmental needs of individuals in midlife.

Helping Individuals in Midlife Avoid Overextension

Because midlife caregivers are a valuable asset to the medical community, they need to be educated and counseled about their own health vulnerabilities to prevent health issues related to the stress of caregiving. Some common problems that can develop when the family is under stress are sleep problems, decline in school or work performance, and increased escapism activities, such as drinking or drug use. Lack of sleep can become a serious issue for caregivers as they attempt to juggle the multidimensional needs of self, family, and work. Inadequate sleep can trigger irritability and fatigue and lead to difficulty in coping, which can lead to more stress. In addition, typical midlife hormonal changes can also result in a lack of sleep. Other health issues associated with midlife are osteoporosis, obesity, and heart disease risks. A healthy lifestyle is the key to reducing stress and risk of illness. Appropriate nutrition, vitamin supplementation, and moderate exercise during midlife can produce important physical and psychological gains, improve quality of life, and minimize physiological changes in aging, by optimizing body composition. Abstinence from tobacco smoking and reduced alcohol consumption are also essential. The entire family needs to be alert to the increased risk of illness and distress associated with stress-related problems and incorporate preventive activities, which will reduce its members' stress load, such as family movies, card playing, and a day or even a few hours off. The health care professional also should be able to suggest individual or family oriented health promotion programs available in the area.

Interventions for the Family

A care intervention is any direct care treatment aimed at enhancing health status or assisting patients and their families achieve a desired health outcome. Care interventions for the family need to begin in the hospital and continue into the recovery setting. Care in the acute hospital environment can become very demanding and complex. Health care professionals are challenged to successfully meet all the patient's physical, mental, and emotional needs and keep family members involved and up to date. A helpful tool to suggest to the family would be the use of an independent journal in which family members and the patient can communicate medical interventions and changes in condition, in addition to personal thoughts, ideas, or reactions.

Once individuals are released from the hospital, the development of any intervention strategy for a family will depend on a number of factors, including desired health outcomes, diagnosis characteristics, feasibility of implementation, and acceptability of the intervention to the patient. An additional consideration for the health professional will include the cultural background of the family, since race and ethnicity can impact the concept of health and health-oriented activities. Because the United States is becoming increasingly diverse, it is necessary to consider what language is primarily spoken in the home, family education level, and the likelihood of participation in family-based health programs. In the development of any care intervention strategy, the health care professional must not make any generalizations or assumptions about a family's likelihood of participation. Clear communication and development of a mutual sense of cooperation and trust between the care professional and the family and the family caregivers is critical to developing the best intervention approach for the entire family.

Following a severe health event in the life of one of its members, family stress will be high and coping strategies by the family will be low, so integrating new knowledge and skills will be difficult. Repeating information several times in different ways and asking for feedback is important to determine comprehension. Any intervention program should focus on the posthospitalization period, include both ill individuals and the family, include written instructions and resources for additional information, focus on reducing stress and encouraging coping efforts, address safety issues, include strategies for both physical and psychological adaptation, and outline the recovery process.

The health care professional needs to encourage a proactive care approach, which will help the family prepare for potential areas of trouble instead of only reacting to each situation that requires a change in the family's routine. Determining the role and tasks fulfilled by the ill family member and helping the family plan for who will step in and fill these during the recovery time is important. The health care professional can facilitate this planning process by asking family members open-ended questions, such as what the person typically did around the house or what the person most liked to do for the family. Also, determining care needs for the ill family member is necessary. The health care professional can help by providing an outline that includes safety, personal care, follow-up care, appointment transportation, and personal property maintenance needs. Encouraging the family to write ideas and important information down during the initial brainstorming meeting will help facilitate planning. The health care professional also needs to help the family identify potential external resources of help and support.

Because acute health problems typically have a rapid onset, family members are generally caught off guard and unprepared. The health care professional should keep in mind that the event represents a new and unwanted circumstance to which the family must now adapt. A care intervention strategy developed in the post-hospital setting for the family following an acute health event should explain the differences between an acute versus a chronic health problem. It may be helpful for caregivers to understand they can expect to provide care for a finite amount of time since acute conditions generally have a short duration, and barring unforeseen complications, family routines typically disrupted during times of emergency may be able to eventually resume. Any health problem, however, can disrupt the family's homeostasis and can cause family members, especially during the adaptation period, to be less sensitive and loving toward each other. This adaptation period, may also occur during the critical recovery time when the activity of caregiving may be the most time and energy intensive. It is important to relay to the family that even temporary inattentiveness to an ill family member's needs may be harmful if the lack of attention occurs when that individual is particularly vulnerable during recovery.

Frustration and feelings of powerlessness can be helped in part by encouraging all family members to put forth their own ideas and suggestions. Family members need to believe they can freely express their preferences, make choices, and ultimately feel as though they have contributed to the care and recovery process. Any plan for health care must be clearly understood by the family and mutually agreed on by all members. Whatever goals that are set in place to provide care for the family must be concrete and realistic, compatible with the family's developmental stage, and acceptable to family members. Collaborating with other disciplines is important during discharge planning from a health care facility to home or an extended care facility because it increases the likelihood of a comprehensive approach to the family's health care needs and ensures better continuity of care. The health care professionals also must always be aware of the limits of their area of expertise and make referrals when appropriate.

Finally, evaluation of the success of the family's care plan will be necessary for reassessment and modification. This reassessment process allows for adjustments to be made to the overall care plan to ensure that the family's needs are being met. Obtaining family members' perspectives of the intervention process and the care plan will help the health care professional and family make necessary adjustments to better accomplish the goal of the health care professional to promote, support, and provide for the well-being and health of the entire family.

Mary Ruth Griffin

See also Acute Care/Hospitalization of Family Members; Aging and Shifting Roles in Families; Changes in Family Structure, Roles; Dietary and Exercise Patterns in Families; Family Conflict Related to Caregiving; Managing Work and Family Responsibilities in the Age of Increased Technology; Partnering With Families: Family-Centered Care; Problem Solving in the Context of Health and Illness; Stress Management Theory and Techniques in Families

Further Readings

Bonanno, G. A. (2004). Loss, trauma and human resilience: Have we underestimated the human capacity to thrive after extremely aversive events? *American Psychologist, 59,* 20–28.

Cowen, P. S., & Moorhead, S. (2006). *Current issues in nursing* (7th ed.). St. Louis, MO: Elsevier Mosby.

Danielson, C. B., Hamel-Bissell, B., & Winstead-Fry, P. (1993). *Families, health and illness: Perspective on coping & intervention.* St. Louis, MO: Elsevier Mosby.

Friedman, M. M. (1998). *Family nursing: Research, theory, and practice* (4th ed.). Stamford, Connecticut: Appleton & Lange.

Gingerich, B. S., & Ondeck D. A. (1994). *Discharge planning for home health care: A multidisciplinary approach.* Gaithersburg, MD: Aspen.

Jenkins, C. D. (2003). *Building better health: A handbook of behavioral change.* Washington, DC: Pan American Health Organization.

Katz, A. H., Hedrick, H. L., Isenberg, D. H., Thompson, L. M., Goodrich, T., & Kutscher, A. H. (1992). *Self-help: Concepts and applications.* Philadelphia: Charles Press.

Marks, N. F. (1998). Does it hurt to care? Caregiving, work-family conflict, and midlife well-being. *Journal of Marriage and the Family, 60,* 951–966.

NANDA International. (2003). *Nursing diagnoses: Definitions and classification 2003–2004.* Philadelphia: Author.

Pierret, C. R. (2006, September). The "sandwich generation": Women caring for parents and children. *Monthly Labor Review, 129,* 3–9.

Potter, P. A., & Perry, A. G. (2009). *Fundamentals of Nursing* (7th ed.). St. Louis, MO: Elsevier Mosby.

Spillman, B. C., & Pezzin, L. E. (2000). Potential and active family caregivers: Changing networks and the "sandwich generation." *Milbank Quarterly, 78*(2), 347–374.

ADDITION OF FAMILY MEMBERS THROUGH MARRIAGE

Marriage can add an assortment of new family members. Through marriage, parents-in-law are gained, extended family networks are enlarged, and increasingly steprelationships are formalized. Additional familial relations and associated interactions can add a strain or a protective factor to a marriage. Ultimately, in terms of family well-being and individual health, the quality of new family relationships is more critical than quantity or proximity. Prominent explanatory frameworks in this line of research include attachment, family development, role, stress, and systems theories as well as Bronfenbrenner's social ecology model and the life course perspective.

According to the National Vital Statistics System, in the United States during the first decade of 2000, over 2 million marriages occurred each year; approximately half were remarriages for one of the spouses. These unions introduce new grandparents, parents, brothers, sisters, sons, daughters, uncles, aunts, and cousins into family systems. Some individuals may even consider pet animals to be part of their family. In light of the extant literature, in this entry the focus is on individual and family outcomes associated with parents-in-law, stepchildren, and stepsibling relationships.

Parents-in-Law

Parents-in-law can be a source of support and stress. Individuals who have the approval of parents-in-law at the time of marriage are more likely to feel supported and accept influence. In Western societies, adaptive in-law relationships are generally characterized by mutual appreciation, respect, and appropriate boundaries. In the clinical literature, newlywed couples are encouraged to become autonomous together and to avoid parental enmeshment (emotional or financial). When in-laws are viewed as meddling or controlling, marriages may be strained and loyalty conflicts can ensue. Similarly, when one spouse feels that the needs, preferences, and requests of parents-in-law are valued more than his or her own, marital dissatisfaction and conflict may increase.

Stepchildren

The prevalence of remarriage and unwed child birthing equates to an increasing number of unions that create stepfamilies. Compared to childless women, remarrying women who already have children at the time of remarriage are statistically more likely to experience second marriage disruption. Outcomes for children in stepfamily households tend to fall between those of single-and married-parent families. Children in stepfamilies are, on average, slightly lower on a variety of outcomes (e.g., academic, self-esteem) when compared to families with both biological parents. However, remarriage may have a buffering effect for children whose biological parents did not model healthy relationship processes. There is some evidence to suggest that the relationship quality of parental remarriage may be more influential on adult children's own relationship attitudes, behaviors, and quality than their parents' first marriage.

The overlapping distributions of child outcomes, when comparing family types, indicate that family dynamics rather than family structures account for the majority of variance in outcomes. Child adjustment and couple satisfaction are enhanced when there is respectful communication, realistic expectations, empathy, an understanding of child development, a focus on strengthening dyadic relationships versus blending the entire family, and when the biological parent is the primary disciplinarian. Unlike traditional nuclear families where marriage predates parent–child relationships and the couple relationship is the key predictor of family dissolution, the quality of the parent–stepchild relationship is central to the long-term viability of a marriage that already includes children.

Relationships With Stepsiblings

Approximately 17% of all U.S. children under age 18 live in a *blended family* that is defined as a household where a stepparent, stepsibling, or half sibling is present. An estimated 75% of children residing with a remarried parent have at least one sibling, and for one third of them, this includes either a stepsibling or a half sibling. Stepsibling relationships have not been extensively researched. The little that is known suggests they are less close than siblings in other family types, and relationship quality may deteriorate over time. In terms of gender differences, boys in stepfamilies appear to be more negative, while girls tend to offer more support to siblings, comparatively. Depending on the age of children, efforts to force friendships and blend the entire family may have an adverse effect.

Options to Enhance Relationships

Some married couples may never meet their new family members (e.g., uncle-in-law); others may have more interactions than they would prefer; and in some cultures or families, the additional family members may share the same dwelling (e.g., stepsiblings). Relationship education can be used to assist individuals before, during, and after the addition of family members through marriage. Also known as couple or marriage education, *relationship education* is a generic title for educational programs that teach relational skills and information about adaptive family processes. The desired outcome is for participants to be more prepared and better equipped to deal with common problems, resolve differences, and cultivate a healthy environment where personal and family development can thrive. Topics in most relationship education courses include communication skills, stress management, financial issues, and conflict resolution. Online and face-to-face relationship education courses that target specific groups and include group-specific content are becoming increasingly common (e.g., stepfamily education, courses for committed nonwed expectant parents). Individual and family therapy is also considered a viable intervention for maladjusted families.

Brian J. Higginbotham

See also Changes in Family Structure; Coparenting: Children; Divorce and Child Custody; Parenting; Psychoeducational Interventions for Families; Remarriage and Stepfamilies

Further Readings

Bramlett, M. D., & Mosher, W. D. (2002). Cohabitation, marriage, divorce, and remarriage in the United States. *Vital and Health Statistics, 23*(22), 1–32.

Ganong, L. H., & Coleman, M. (2004). *Stepfamily relationships: Development, dynamics, and interventions.* New York: Kluwer.

Kreider, R. M. (2007). *Living arrangements of children: 2004* (Current Population Reports, pp. 70–114). Washington, DC: U.S. Census Bureau.

Pryor, J. (Ed). (2008). *International handbook of stepfamilies: Policy and practice in legal, research and clinical spheres.* Hoboken, NJ: Wiley.

ADOLESCENT COUNSELING

Adolescent well-being is integral to the health of family. *Family* describes a social and support network that is responsible for orienting youth to a sense of self, meaning, and value, nurturing strengths and offering unconditional love and providing guidance on moral and culturally appropriate behavior. In this respect, the family presents a context of care for the adolescent and the adolescent's health reflects and directly impacts family interaction and function.

Effective counseling for adolescents includes a careful process of assessment and evaluation, a model for open lines of communication, and the provision for referral in cases where individuals or families need specialized treatment and therapy. Most of the causes of poor health during adolescence are due to behavior-related problems that have great potential for being improved with good physical and mental health counseling. This entry discusses the importance of understanding development when counseling adolescents, the critical roles for family in youth development, a framework for interviewing and assessing adolescents, and three contexts for counseling teens and emerging adults.

Developmental Context for Adolescence

It has been more than 100 years since G. Stanley Hall introduced the concept of adolescence as a distinct developmental category. Although the definition of *adolescence* differs across countries and cultures, there is recognition of the period between childhood and adulthood as one of significant physical and emotional change. Adolescence is characterized by wide variation in biological and psychological growth, and each adolescent responds to this transitioning in unique and personal ways. Although the developmental period is sometimes described with words such as *storm* and *stress*, most adolescents cope well and ultimately thrive during this time.

Adolescence is divided into three phases: (1) early (10–13 years, marked by rapid physical changes with the onset of puberty), (2) middle (14–16 years, marked by the rise in importance of peer group values), and (3) late (17–mid-20s, marked by years of college or work after high school, increased decision-making capacity, and transition from full family financial dependence to limited monetary support and a goal of economic independence). During adolescence, youth may express a spectrum of concerns including the following: gaining privacy, navigating rules such as curfew, finding friends and being popular, surviving peer pressure, body image, sexual and gender identity, academic pressures, family–sibling conflict, mood changes, and economic, family, and career prospects for the future. Parents and family members also identify a number of concerns about their adolescents including normal development, acting-out and risk-taking behaviors, mood swings, peer influences, limit setting, the impact of stress on development, academic success, and achieving happiness.

Adolescent Health, Critical Roles for Family

Urie Bronfenbrenner's developmental model identifies contexts of care for the young person including the microsystem, mesosystem, exosystem, and macrosystem. The microsystem is comprised of family, school, peer, and neighborhood structures directly impacting the youth. The mesosystem describes relationships between structures in the microsystem such as consistency and level of involvement within family and school and within family and peer circles. Threats to the microsystem in the form of less supportive relationships and inadequate bonding result in increased adolescent vulnerability and poor social development. Youth may attempt to fill the resulting emotional void with risk and self-damaging behaviors, such as substance use, violence involvement, and seeking inappropriate romantic relationships and/or pregnancy. The final levels in the developmental model (exosystem, macrosystem) describe contexts indirectly affecting adolescent development and behavior, such as the legal and social welfare systems, and define broad belief and value systems unique to a culture.

The family carries great responsibility in supporting the adolescent by encouraging the development of individual assets and holding high expectations for success. Contexts for success include (a) identifying a positive sense of self-worth, (b) forming healthy relationships, and (c) achieving personal goals, developing lifelong learning habits, envisioning a promising future, and acquiring skills to participate in the larger economy.

The family is necessary for youth achievement of competencies: social, emotional, cognitive, behavioral, and moral. Social competence involves the ability of the adolescent to take in information, to respond appropriately, and to incorporate effective problem-solving strategies. The adolescent's abilities to manage internal feelings and to handle relationships are central to the development of emotional competence. Family contribution to the development of adolescent cognitive competence involves modeling frameworks for self-talk, belief in self-efficacy, and capacities for positive self-awareness and decision making. Behavioral competence develops through examples set by caregivers where meaning is given to participation in positive activities and actions focused on helping others, and there is practice in anticipating and avoiding negative situations. Moral competence comes from caregiver expression and fostering of empathy and ethical behavior.

A Framework for Adolescent Counseling

Drawing from the disciplines of youth development and positive psychology, counseling can be instrumental in fostering developmental milestones during adolescence by (a) helping adolescents tap into thought processes that lead to healthy functioning, (b) viewing each adolescent as a resource rather than a focus for remediation, and (c) fostering positive connections for young people to family and other prosocial adults. Young people respond best to counseling approaches that resist attributions of deficit and embrace a perspective that assigns them value and sees them as capable of excellence and in possession of great capacity for contribution. The process of counseling acknowledges the existence of adversities and developmental challenges that may affect youth in various ways. Ultimately, the goal is to help the adolescent find his or her innate health through strategies that facilitate empathy, education, and engagement.

Interactions With Adolescent and Family

The ability to engage adolescents in healthy decision making is directly linked to the formation of an effective relationship. Activities that contribute to the development of effective partnerships recognize the critical importance of establishing trust with the young person. Interactions that focus on lecturing and the use of abstract terms that the youth may not be able to grasp, moralizing, or reinforcing the adolescent's sense of shame can be devastating. Instead, effective counseling reduces anxiety by opening lines of communication and helping the adolescent focus when decisions have to be made; creates a nonjudgmental, safe environment for the youth to discuss hopes and fears; gives accurate information; and clarifies a youth's feelings and choices.

Beginning with a care framework that envisions the adolescent embedded within a family context is important. It is helpful to understand the style of parenting. Research has shown that authoritative parenting, parenting that is warm and caring, firm and involved, and consistent in rule and limit setting, contributes to better adolescent competence, physical health, and psychological well-being. Whenever possible, involving family and caregivers, eliciting their input and insight, is critical. While adolescence is a developmental stage in which the young person is moving toward independence, when queried, most adolescents identify their parents as their primary support system.

Health providers and youth advocates must be familiar with federal, state, and local laws and regulations concerning consent and confidentiality for minors. Adolescents must clearly understand that one-on-one conversations with a provider are built on a standard of privacy. However, there are limitations to keeping information private, which exclude any information indicating the young person is contemplating self-harm, planning to hurt another person, or being abused or neglected by an adult. In instances where damaging behaviors are occurring and there is concern for the safety of the adolescent outside of the office, such as an ongoing risk for driving under the influence, the provider should make clear to the adolescent her or his concern for safety and begin work with the young person to identify immediate sources of help. It is important to enlist the adolescent's agreement before disclosures outside of the above noted exclusions to privacy (personal threat to self or others, abuse or neglect) take place. The expectations and limitations of confidentiality should also be reviewed with family and caregivers.

In cases where adolescent–parent conflict is a focus of concern during the visit, interviewing the parent and adolescent individually, after initial introductions, is recommended. During these interactions, the provider may problem solve with the adolescent and the caregiver on how to allow for open communication about the source of conflict and generate solutions in the office setting, deemed neutral ground at the outset of the visit. In such cases, interviewing the caregiver first is paramount. This allays adolescent fears that what they initially tell the provider will be divulged in the separate conversation with the caregiver.

Providers and advocates must be aware of and sensitive to potential hidden or underlying concerns that are not readily apparent at the outset of a visit. For example, physical complaints may be a manifestation of a social concern, such as chronic headaches heralding a youth's fear of parental divorce. It is important to recognize that a parent's presenting concern may not be the most pressing issue for the adolescent at that time. For example, a parent may relate apprehension about new sibling conflict; however, on further review with the adolescent, sibling conflict may underscore symptoms of depression or anxiety, which often manifest as irritability.

The tone of the visit should be guided by the adolescent's developmental stage. Jean Piaget's theory of cognitive development identifies four increasingly advanced stages of mental awareness and psychological understanding that youth traverse on their way to adult insight and judgment. The period of adolescence includes the third and fourth stages of cognitive development: concrete operational (7–11 years) and formal operational (beginning at 11–15 years and continuing into adulthood). The progression from concrete operational to formal operational thought signals the youth's transition from an inability to problem solve using abstract concepts and a lack of understanding of hypothetical risk to processing information with a framework of future orientation and a recognition of the theoretical and potential impact of behaviors.

Aspects of cognitive, emotional, and social development must be assessed to allow for tailoring of information to the young person's ability to receive and engage. For example, early adolescence is often marked by thinking patterns in which the adolescent focuses on short-term cause and effect of behavior. Better understanding of relationships and consideration for other viewpoints is characteristic of middle adolescence. More abstract reasoning and the ability to understand complex relationships and long-term consequences mark later adolescence. It is important to realize that cognitive age does not exactly equate with chronologic (numeric) age.

Preventive Health Counseling

Behavioral Screening and Anticipatory Guidance

Provision of behavioral screening and anticipatory guidance is recommended for all adolescents based on its potential for benefit and low risk for harm. Critical topics to cover include normal development, attention to hygiene and self-care, achieving and maintaining healthy relationships with food and physical activity, violence and injury prevention, making responsible and safe choices about sexual behavior, avoidance of substances, and practice in setting short- and long-term personal and career-oriented goals. In general, screening and anticipatory guidance for sensitive topics are conducted with the adolescent alone; however, the adolescent should always be given the choice to have a parent or caregiver present. Screening and counseling are best facilitated by beginning with less sensitive areas first, such as interests and activities, with progression to more sensitive topics as the adolescent and provider develop increased rapport. An adaptation of Eric Cohen's mnemonic (HEADSS) in facilitating comprehensive screening and preventive counseling is HEADDSSS, which stands for home, education, activities (social, sports, work), diet (nutrient intake, dieting behaviors or eating patterns, weight concerns or changes), drugs, safety (risk for intentional and unintentional injury, risk for abuse), sexuality, and symptoms of depression or being suicidal. An alternate approach offered by Kenneth Ginsburg begins with questions about the adolescent's strengths before proceeding to environmental context and risk potential, SSHADESS, which stands for strengths or interests, school, home, activities, drugs and/or substance use, emotions or depression, sexuality, and safety.

Identifying caregiver and family strengths may also facilitate adolescent competence. Interactions encouraging consistent caregiver monitoring and role modeling of healthy behaviors are essential. Parents or caregivers need counseling on normal adolescent development including review of progressive physical, emotional, cognitive, and social changes and of how to keep open lines of communication with the adolescent.

Mental Health Counseling

Health Realization

Health realization is credited with establishing a standard of mental health by circumventing stress physiology. It offers a mechanism for young people to maintain health and to heal in cases of abuse or negative life circumstance. The model incorporates three operative principles: (1) mind (a universal energy that produces life and is the source of innate health), (2) consciousness (an awareness of one's life), and (3) thought (the power to create one's experience of reality). It teaches the individual to understand feelings and emotions as indicative of the quality of one's thinking. Memory may produce an abundance of low-energy, low-quality thinking that is based on insecurities and learned patterns. The adolescent can change reactions to circumstances through awareness that people create their own experiences by responding to the low-quality thinking. Practically, youth are taught to (1) recognize low-value, intrusive thoughts; (2) detach from these thoughts by refusing to relive or entertain them; and (3) shift consciousness to better-quality, resourceful thinking. Evidence exists for the utility of health realization in altering trajectories for substance use, delinquency, and violence perpetration. Family may facilitate the health realization process by offering positive reinforcement for desired behaviors, responding to mistakes with encouragement, and redirecting youth to their innate health when outside influences distract from achieving resourceful, responsive thoughts.

Cognitive-Behavioral Therapy

Cognitive and behavioral therapies (often combined into cognitive-behavioral therapy) for adolescents include skills-based counseling that facilitates identification of damaging thought patterns, evaluation of these patterns, and generation of alternative explanations that are less global and personal, thus avoiding statements such as "I am useless." In contrast to health realization, cognitive therapies teach youth to challenge the accuracy and content of negative thoughts and to alter perceptions of situations. Behavioral therapies focus on assisting adolescents in learning to give up self-defeating attitudes and responses. Family and group counseling may accompany the individual skills-based interventions. Family counseling allows members to work toward easing household conflict. Group counseling gives youth the opportunity to gain perspective about individual problems, realizing he or she is not alone.

Counseling for Behavior Change

Stages of Change

Although historic evidence for the effectiveness of behavior change counseling originates from the adult literature, adolescent advocates recognize its value in helping youth to achieve health goals. It is based on the transtheoretical model or stages of change theory. The model begins with the tenet that interventions to facilitate behavior change must be tailored to an individual's readiness for that change. Five stages describe an individual's progress toward achieving change: (1) precontemplation (not yet considering change), (2) contemplation (thinking about change but still ambivalent), (3) preparation (strategizing, making plans for change), (4) action (implementing change plans), and (5) maintenance (supporting and sustaining change behavior). Originally developed for tobacco prevention and cessation, the five As may be used in assessing an adolescent's readiness for change: *ask*—recognize the presence of the problem, *advise*—give a clear message on the need to change behavior, *assess*—inquire about the adolescent's willingness to change behavior, *assist*—set goals for the next steps in moving toward change, and *arrange*—schedule follow-up, maintaining a connection with the adolescent to convey a belief in the adolescent's ability to make healthy choices.

Motivational Interviewing

Motivational interviewing is a patient-centered, office-based counseling technique that builds on the intrinsic desire to make necessary behavior change(s). It is particularly useful for youth who are in the precontemplation and contemplation stages of change. Motivational interviewing comprises three elements: (1) collaboration (forming a partnership with the adolescent, positioning the adolescent as the expert in his or her experiences, values, and goals), (2) evocation (using open-ended questions and reflections to help the adolescent in identifying his or her internal desire for change and to resolve any conflicts with values, goals, and beliefs), and (3) autonomy (affirming the adolescent's responsibility in deciding if, how, and when change will occur). Four principles help to operationalize steps in the office setting: (1) express empathy, (2) develop discrepancy by recognizing inconsistencies between the youth's current status and identified goals or values, (3) roll with resistance by recognizing that expressions of ambivalence about behavior change are normal and avoid disputes with the adolescent, and (4) support of the adolescent with expressions of optimism in his or her ability to be successful at each encounter. Past successes and failures in behavior change are used as learning opportunities, helping the adolescent to identify a range of effective strategies for achieving goals. Although it does take time to implement motivational interviewing, it may be more effective in producing behavior change in adolescents than the traditional provision of brief office advice that focuses on risks for shock value.

In sum, resourceful and constructive counseling for adolescents helps to facilitate well-being by fostering cognitive and psychological assets to help the adolescent and family navigate developmental challenges and milestones.

Naomi Nichele Duke

See also Cigarettes, Smoking, and Secondhand Smoke and Family Health; College Transition for Families; Conflict in Family Life, Role and Management of; Developmental Transitions in Families; Family Emotional Climate and Mental Health; Parenting; Role of Families in Health Promotion; Suicide in the Family; Teen Pregnancy; Youth Violence Prevention in the Family

Further Readings

Bronfenbrenner, U., & Evans, G. W. (2000). Developmental science in the 21st Century: Emerging questions, theoretical models, research designs and empirical findings. *Social Development, 9*(1), 115–125.

Evans, D. L., Foa, E. B., Gur, R. E., Hendin, H., O'Brien, C. P., Seligman, M. E. P., et al. (Eds.). (2005). *Treating and preventing adolescent mental health disorders: What we know and what we don't know.* New York: Oxford University Press.

Ginsburg, K. R. (2007). Viewing our patients through a positive lens. *Contemporary Pediatrics, 24,* 65–75.

Goldenring, J. M., & Cohen, E. (1988). Getting into adolescent heads. *Contemporary Pediatrics, 5*(2), 75–90.

Hagan, J. F., Shaw, J. S., & Duncan, P. (Eds.). (2007). *Bright futures guidelines for health supervision of infants, children, and adolescents* (3rd ed.). Elk Grove Village, IL: American Academy of Pediatrics.

Kelley, T. M. (2003). Health realization: A principle-based psychology of positive youth development. *Child & Youth Care Forum, 32*(1), 47–72.

Klein, J. D., & Camenga, D. R. (2004). Tobacco prevention and cessation in pediatric patients. *Pediatrics in Review, 25*(1), 16–24.

Miller, W. R., & Rollnick, S. (2002). *Motivational interviewing: Preparing people for change* (2nd ed.). New York: Guilford.

Neinstein, L. S., Gordon, C. M., Katzman, D. K., Rosen, D. S., & Woods, E. R. (Eds.). (2009). *Adolescent health care: A practical guide* (5th ed.). Philadelphia: Lippincott, Williams & Wilkins.

Rew, L. (2005). *Adolescent health: A multidisciplinary approach to theory, research, and intervention.* Thousand Oaks, CA: Sage.

Websites

Jean Piaget Society: http://www.piaget.org

ADOPTION EXPERIENCES FOR INFERTILE COUPLES

According to the American Society for Reproductive Medicine (ASRM), 12% of the American population of reproductive age, approximately 7.3 million women and their partners, are estimated to be faced with infertility. Infertility is defined as the inability to obtain and sustain a pregnancy after 12 months of regular, unprotected intercourse for women under 35 and after 6 months for women 35 and over. Those facing fertility challenges and committed to having their own biological offspring often turn to assisted reproductive technologies (e.g., fertility drugs, in vitro fertilization, donor sperm and/or eggs, surrogacy) to build their families. Fertility treatments can extend over several years and are often financially prohibitive. Judith C. Daniluk contends that the medical treatment process is fraught with anxiety and stress, as couples live through the emotional roller coaster of hope and disappointment with each menstrual and unsuccessful treatment cycle.

For approximately 50% of those who seek fertility treatment, assisted reproductive technology is unsuccessful in helping them achieve their reproductive goals. Daniluk and Joss Hurtig-Mitchell maintain that following failed treatment, couples are faced with constructing their lives without children or pursuing other parenting options, such as third-party reproduction (donated eggs, sperm, or embryos, or surrogacy) or adoption. In either case, Linda P. Salzer argues couples must separate their desire for a genetically related child and additionally, in the case of women, their desire for the experience of pregnancy and childbirth from their desire to become parents. For some, the ethical, religious, social, or financial implications of third-party reproductive options make adoption a more desirable and acceptable parenting option. This entry discusses adoption after infertility with the couple as the family unit and their psychosocial experience as the focal point. It also offers ways in which health professionals can provide family support during and after the adoption process to ensure optimal functioning and adjustment.

Adoption and the Psychosocial Experience of the Infertile Couple

The decision to adopt involves ongoing negotiation between the couple, sometimes with one member feeling more strongly in favor of and more comfortable with adoption. Salzer contends that there are common fears that serve as roadblocks in the decision to pursue adoption. For example, couples often fear that they will not be able to fully love a child to whom they do not share biological ties. They sometimes worry that the child will later reject them in favor of his or her birth parents and that the child may develop psychological problems in the future. According to Daniluk and Hurtig-Mitchell, for couples who have endured years of fertility treatments and adoption processes, expectations of their "ideal" child and what parenthood will look like may need to be adapted and reintegrated in a more realistic picture. During this stage, health professionals can provide accurate and supportive psychoeducation to dispel myths and normalize common concerns about the adoptive process.

There is evidence that infertile couples who become parents through adoption demonstrate better psychosocial adjustment than those who remain involuntarily childless, suggesting that adoption can be an important factor in mediating the emotional impact of infertility. However, as studies such as Daniluk and Hurtig-Mitchell's demonstrate, the adoption process is very complex and challenging, even more so for infertile couples whose emotional, financial, and social resources are often depleted after years of pursuing fertility treatments. In particular, from Lynne Cudmore's research, it was found that the invasiveness of the application process and home study can trigger feelings of inadequacy and exposure similar to what couples experienced while undergoing fertility treatments. Long waiting periods and the uncertainty of whether a birth mother will elect to place her child in their home or in the case of international adoption, not knowing whether a country will allow the couple to finalize the adoption and return to their home country with their adopted son or daughter further exacerbate the stress and uncertainty of the adoption process. During this time, couples feel very much out of control in terms of their future parental status. They are unable to move forward with other life plans and goals until they know whether their future lives will include being parents. Daniluk and Hurtig-Mitchell found that hopeful adoptive couples often feel powerless and frustrated for what they perceive as a dismissal of their needs and emotional well-being and their lack of rights in the adoptive experience. Health professionals can play an important role in helping couples cope with the emotional impact of the adoption process.

Once a couple has been selected by a birth mother, the couple often must manage challenging negotiations with the birth parents and birth family members about the degree of openness and involvement members of the birth family will have

in the child's life. After the child has been placed in the couple's home, the transition to adoptive parenthood involves a complex array of emotions including the joy of finally becoming parents, sadness for the birth mother and birth family's loss, and feelings of isolation and lack of support from adoptive personnel and others in their social worlds who perceive adoption to be a less desirable form of family building than biological parenthood. Follow-up care by health care professionals is necessary to assist in optimal functioning and adjustment.

Salzer suggests that there are three important developmental tasks of adoptive families: (1) to resolve any remaining feelings about infertility, (2) to maintain a balance between accepting the difference in adoptive parenting and rejecting the difference, and (3) to learn how to deal with others' misinformed beliefs and myths around the adoptive parenting experience. Health professionals can be instrumental in helping families succeed in these tasks.

Conclusion

Ultimately, the majority of couples are surprised that they grow to love and develop strong and deep attachment to a child who is not their biological child. For the majority of couples who pursue adoption after infertility, it is possible to move beyond the loss of biological childlessness to build healthy, satisfying, and meaningful lives as adoptive parents.

Emily Koert and Judith C. Daniluk

See also Childlessness; Family Experiencing Transitions; Parental Attachment; Parenting

Further Readings

Cudmore, L. (2005). Becoming parents in the context of loss. *Sexual and Relationship Therapy, 20,* 299–308.

Daniluk, J. C. (2001). *The infertility survival guide: Everything you need to know to cope with the challenges while maintaining your sanity, dignity, and relationships.* Oakland, CA: Harbinger.

Daniluk, J. C., & Hurtig-Mitchell, J. (2003). Themes of hope and healing: Infertile couples, experiences of adoption. *Journal of Counseling and Development, 81,* 389–399.

Salzer, L. P. (1999). Adoption after infertility. In
    L. Hammer-Burns & S. N. Covington (Eds.),
    *Infertility counseling: A comprehensive handbook
    for clinicians* (pp. 391–409). New York: Parthenon.

Websites

American Society for Reproductive Medicine:
    http://www.asrm.org

ADULT CHILD RETURNING HOME

An adult child returning to the parental home represents a reversal event in the progress a young adult child is expected to make toward independence during the transition to adulthood. Historically, home-returning has been linked with the fluctuating economy. Returns to the parental home became increasingly common in the late 20th century as the economy tightened and strained opportunities for gaining self-sufficiency in the early adult years. Both family resources and lack of opportunities available that will lead to self-sufficiency contribute to the likelihood that an adult child will return or re-return to the parental home. The return of *boomerang kids* has different effects on families. Available resources to support semiautonomy can ease the financial and emotional demands of providing an extended period of care to adult children. Family health can be maintained and enhanced through an adult child's return to the parental home when the family members make progress in family and individual developmental tasks, respectively.

Trends in numbers of adult children returning home are linked to variation in economic strength. Historically, the number of boomerang kids rises when the economy weakens. According to the U.S. Census Bureau, in the 1970s, less than 8% of adult children ages 25 to 34 lived with parents. By 2000, over 10% of 25- to 34-year-olds were living in the family home. The Pew Research Center reports that in 2009, an estimated 13% of all parents with grown children said one of their adult sons or daughters had moved back home in the past year; among parents of ages 45 to 54, some 19% reported their grown children had moved back home.

Approximately half of adult children who live with their parents are employed full- or part-time, a quarter are unemployed, and the remaining are students.

A number of family factors contribute to adult children's likelihood of returning home. Two-parent, intact family households are less likely to experience an adult child returning home. Adult children are more likely to return when they depart from divorced and stepfamilies. Higher parent income, education, and occupation all reduce the likelihood of a return to the parental home after initial departure. A history of living near the poverty line or receiving public economic assistance contributes to an increased likelihood of a return to the family home. Parents' expectations that an adult child will progress toward autonomy also influence the likelihood of a complete launch into self-sufficiency without a return home.

Family factors indirectly influence home-returning through the *exit destinations* of adult children. Exit destinations are the roles and situations that adult children move into when they initially leave the parental home. Leaving home for roles or living situations that increase earning power decreases chances that an adult child will return home. Leaving home for college reflects progress toward increased earning power. Because children from more economically advantaged families are more likely to leave home to go to college, and college affords greater opportunity for establishing oneself financially, they are less likely to return home. In contrast, adult children from less economically advantaged families return home at a greater rate due to constraints associated with lower educational attainment. Leaving home for marriage also decreases the likelihood of a return to the parental home. Because marriage reflects an increase in the earning potential of a household, married young adults are less likely to return home. Unmarried status significantly increases the risk of returning home. The end of a cohabiting relationship also predicts home returns.

The notion of boomerang kids reflects the popularized and negative notion that returning adult children burden aging parents. Research does not support this generalized conclusion. Rather, family health will be affected by an adult child's return home depending on the established relationship quality between the parents and the adult child, the net balance of investments in the adult child and the adult child's contribution to the family, and the ability of the family and individual family members to make developmental progress.

The timing of an adult child's return home may contribute to the effect that the event has on the family. At each stage of the life span, families and individuals are challenged with tasks that are specific to a life stage. The contemporary launching phase of the family life span involves parents providing support for the semiautonomy of their adult children until they are independent and self-sufficient. A return to the parental nest during this family stage may be considered normative and within the scope of family goals. For families that have launched all of their children to independence and have moved beyond the launching phase, the return of an adult child may be non-normative and present a more significant interruption in family functioning.

The availability of family resources plays a key role in determining the extent to which an adult child returning home introduces burden and stress to the family system. Families that have the financial and emotional resources to support an adult child living at home will fare better than those families with fewer resources. When a family can support a return to the family home, this support can provide tremendous financial relief to the young person. It may also provide nonnegligible income to the parents; however, it is most often the case that young adults do not contribute significant financial resources to the family household.

The extent to which the family can support individual family members' progress in their own developmental tasks when an adult child returns home will also influence the impact of the event on family health. First, parent–adult child relations are expected to become more mutually supportive and less hierarchical. Parents are expected to reorganize their life goals and priorities as a function of reduced demands for daily parenting and caretaking. And young adults, whether living in the parental home or not, are expected to make progress toward self-sufficiency. An adult child returning home does not necessarily undermine a family's ability to provide support for this maturation. To the extent that family support for family and individual development and adaptation are compromised, an adult child returning home represents a risk to family health.

Jennifer L. Tanner

See also Adult Children Living at Home; Aging and Shifting Roles in Families; Changes in Family Structure; Developmental Transitions in Families; Economic Downturn and Families; Last Child Leaving Home

Further Readings

Mitchell, B. A. (2006). *The boomerang age: Transitions to adulthood in families.* Piscataway, NJ: Aldine Transaction.

U.S. Census Bureau. (2009). *America's families and living arrangements: 2008* (Table A1). Retrieved from http://www.census.gov/population/www/socdemo/hh-fam/cps2008.html

Wang, W., & Morin, R. (2009, November 24). *Home for the holidays . . . and every other day.* Washington, DC: Pew Research Center. Retrieved from http://pewsocialtrends.org

Adult Child With Disability: Planning for by Parents

Parents whose children with disabilities enter adulthood face a number of challenges in responding to their children's ongoing individual and service needs in planning for the future. Their adult children's ongoing service needs include housing and community placement, job training and employment, the development of social and intimate relationships, ongoing and acute health concerns, recreational activities and interests, and transportation. Parents face the uncomfortable but likely inevitable issue of ensuring that their children continue to receive services and care in the event that parents are no longer able to provide due to their own deteriorating health status or death. Some of the difficult issues that parents face as their children age are related to (a) housing arrangements—where will they live and under what circumstances; (b) financial assistance—methods to ensure their children have the financial security needed and are not at risk for losing benefits; (c) exploitation—safeguards that can be established to ensure that their adult children are protected from at-risk situations, such as physical, sexual, and emotional abuse as well as from financial exploitation and intimidation and bullying situations; and (d) quality of life—services and supports needed to facilitate the achievement of life goals related to their needs, interests, and preferences. These issues are not exhaustive but reflect some of the very significant concerns families continue to have for adult children with disabilities that reflect the need for ongoing family involvement.

Data from a recent National Organization on Disability/Harris Associates survey provided a lifestyle profile of adults with disabilities. Survey findings indicated significant differences between adults with and without disabilities related to education, employment, income levels, and quality of life outcomes. High school completion was less frequent for students with disabilities compared to students without disabilities: 6 of 10 students with disabilities graduated from high school, as compared to 8 of 10 without disabilities. Percentages of students enrolled in postsecondary education were significantly different as well: 78% for students without disabilities compared to 37% for students with disabilities. These percentages were similar for part-time and full-time employment rates as well: 78% for individuals without disabilities and 33% for individuals with disabilities. Poverty rates have been reported as 3 times greater for individuals with disabilities (26%) compared to individuals without disabilities (9%). In light of these differences, quality-of-life measures showed the same pattern with lower levels reported by individuals with disabilities compared to individuals without disabilities.

Key to promoting adult children with disabilities' achievement of their goals in the life domains of health, training or education, recreation, employment, social relationships, and community life is to ensure that the formalized process of transition planning begins during the secondary school years. This process of transition planning begins in the systems of care education, rehabilitation, social service, disabilities, employment, and health care for those between the ages of 14 and 16 years. It is important that parents fully understand the services and supports available for their transition-age youth as it will provide the foundation for emerging adulthood and beyond.

As youth with disabilities transition to adulthood, their parents may have clashes with the service agencies providing care when their children reach the *age of majority*. This legal concept refers to the transfer of rights and responsibilities, according to state law, to make legal decisions as an adult. According to age of majority, the youth is no longer considered a minor. Examples of age-of-majority rights and responsibilities include decision making pertaining to health care and to high school and college educational planning and to voting. Beginning between late adolescence and early adulthood, depending on the laws of the state (ages 18 to 21 years), legal rights and protection are conferred on the individual, not the family. If the individual's disability negatively impacts decision-making capabilities, then the legal authority to make decisions must be obtained by the parents or guardians from the legal system. This process is referred to as *conservatorship,* meaning that the power for making decisions for the individual with disabilities, known as the *conservatee,* is conferred to the parents and/or advocate. Conservatorship appointments made by judges may vary as to type depending on the scope of the conservator's authority to make decisions on behalf of the conservatee, the individual with a disability. The authority given to the conservator to make decisions on behalf of the conservatee may be limited to health care decisions or as broad as to include health care, personal care, housing, and finances.

Upon reaching the age of majority, service providers will confer directly with the legally designated adult unless the parents or guardians have obtained a conservatorship that covers decision making on behalf of their adult child. This alteration in the family's role as the advocate and decision maker can conflict with parental expectations and family beliefs and values. Families will likely be involved as conservators or advocates when decisions are made concerning their adult child's future planning, particularly when the individual has an intellectual disability.

The adult child, depending on individualized needs for services and programs, and if circumstances warrant it, the conservator, will be assigned a service coordinator who will be responsible for ensuring the individual has access to the services and programs provided by that agency. These agencies include Vocational Rehabilitation, Social Security Administration, the state's Medicaid program, Independent Living Centers, the state's disability program, Housing and Urban Development Section 8 program, and federal and state advocacy and civil rights and protection programs, such as the Protection and Advocacy Program. Depending on the service system or as requested by the consumer and/or conservator, periodic reviews will be conducted of the individual's plan of services to ensure his or her needs are met, which may require revision(s) to the plan.

Families may want to set up a Special Needs Trust (SNT) for supplemental expenses and additional care for the benefit of the adult child with a disability. SNT is a legal mechanism by which families can allocate additional assets into the trust for later use by their adult child. A third-party trustee oversees and manages the SNT. For example, funds in the SNT might be used for attendant care not covered by a government program—a computer or personal needs, such as getting a haircut or purchasing books. The SNT is tightly regulated and is designed in a manner to prevent jeopardizing the adult's eligibility for public assistance. SNT funds are not considered countable assets and are not subject to creditor claims or seizures. The SNT is a financial tool that enables families to provide extended supplemental financial support in response to their adult children's ongoing and changing personal needs.

The long-term care for the adult child with a disability is an emotional and financial challenge for families. Although long-term publicly financed programs exist to provide the type of ongoing assistance adults with disabilities require, the role of families is critical to ensuring these services and programs are appropriate, comprehensively coordinated, and responsive to the individual's needs.

Cecily Lynn Betz

See also Access to Health Care: Child Health; Adult With Disability Living at Home; Adults With Childhood-Acquired Conditions; Chronic Health Problems and Interventions for the Midlife Family; Chronic Illness and Family Management Styles; College Transition for Families; Developmental Transitions in Families; Disabilities and Family Management; Educating the Family Regarding Chronic Physical Illness; Families Experiencing Chronic Physical and Mental Health Conditions

Further Readings

Betz, C. L., & Nehring, W. M. (2007). *Promoting health care transition planning for adolescents with special health care needs and disabilities.* Towson, MD: Brookes.

California Courts Self-Help Centers. (n.d.). *Handbook for conservators.* Retrieved March 31, 2010, from http://www.courtinfo.ca.gov/selfhelp/seniors/handbook.htm

Family Village. (2007). *Planning the future for children with special needs.* Retrieved March 31, 2010, from http://www.cfp.net/enewsletter/Jan2007.html#3

National Center on Secondary Education and Transition. (2002, May). *Age of majority: Preparing your child to make their own choices.* Minneapolis, MN: Author. Retrieved April 5, 2010, from http://www.ncset.org/publications/parent/NCSETParent_May02.pdf

National Organization on Disability & Harris Associates. (2004). *2004 Survey of Americans with disabilities.* Washington, DC: Author. Retrieved from http://nod.org/research_publications/nod_harris_survey

Websites

National Organization on Disablity: http://nod.org

Adult Children Living at Home

The U.S. Census Bureau estimates that 51% of adult children 18 to 24 years of age and 11% of adult children 25 to 34 years of age are living at home. As defined by the Census Bureau, these figures include adults who are living in the homes of their parent(s) and unmarried college students who are living in dormitories. With societal shifts that have led to changes in the age of marriage, educational attainment, and employment opportunities, there have been significant changes in the transition out of the parental home. This change has considerable implications for adult children and their parents. This entry describes the historical shifts that led to these changes; impacts for families in the financial, emotional, and social domains; and the relevance of this trend to family health.

Since the 1960s, census data suggest a rise in the number of adult children living at home, with a peak in these numbers in the early 1980s. This rise, however, is in part reflective of rising college enrollment due to the inclusion of residential college students in the statistics. Some argue that adult children have always lived at home and that there has been only a slight increase in children returning home in recent years. Although the magnitude of the shift in living arrangements is debatable, it is clear that a new stage of development supporting this shift has emerged in the last 50 years. Jeffrey Arnett describes this stage occurring between the ages of 18 and 25 as *emerging adulthood*. During this period, youth are no longer adolescents, but they have not moved into adulthood; this stage is characterized by identity exploration, role experimentation, and optimism for the future. Shifts in education, marriage, and job opportunities delay the move into traditional role markers of adulthood, creating a different environment for today's young adults and impacting their residential mobility.

When adult children live at home, there are influences for the adult child and family in the financial, emotional, and social domains. The primary motivation for living at home often relates to the financial relief it provides for the young person. As a young adult completes education, seeks employment, and establishes a career, the financial support of family is beneficial. However, the support does not come without additional strain for the family. Adult children living at home may create a financial burden for the family, as financial contributions are much higher for young adults living at home than those living independently. Arrangements where the adult child pays rent or provides specific housework in exchange for room and board mitigate these stressors. Youth from poor families face particular issues, as their families have even less resources for support and little government assistance exists for adult children living at home.

The emotional impact of adult children living at home can be both positive and negative for the family. It can lead to more positive parent–child relationships, particularly when the adult child plays a supportive function for the parent or takes responsibility for the household. This role has especially been noted when the child cares for elderly parents or grandparents. Additionally, having the ability to spend significant time together as adults can improve the parent–child dyad. The parent–child relationship may, however, become strained with this living arrangement. Negative emotions

may be exacerbated when children expect the parent to take care of them, when they are financially dependent, or when the home has previously had high conflict. If the adult child is financially independent, is employed, and contributes to household tasks, fewer emotional issues arise.

The trend of adult children living at home has implications for the social domain for both parent and child. For the adult child, there may be difficulties in meeting parental expectations, particularly if they have previously lived independently. Strain on friendships and dating relationships is also common. Parents of adult children living at home also face a social impact. They have increased caregiving responsibilities at a time when many expected an empty nest. Parents face additional social obligations that they assumed they would no longer be experiencing. The living arrangement may also have implications for the parents' marriage, particularly if the parent–child relationship is strained. To ameliorate potentially negative social stressors, adult children and their parents should maintain separate social lives and create defined boundaries.

Given that adult children are living at home and that societal shifts make this trend likely to continue, this issue requires attention when considering family health. In the mental health arena, it becomes particularly salient as it impacts family well-being and emotional health. It also creates the potential for more integration of adult children into individual health treatment planning and decisions and the potential for additional resources and support around caregiving. It may have implications for health insurance, as this age group is one of the largest and fastest growing segments of the uninsured. Adult children living at home may be seen as resources for their families, but may also add financial and emotional stress that affects health at the individual and family levels. Working with families to encourage shared financial responsibility, define supportive roles for adult children, and create social boundaries can reduce these negative influences. These changes must be integrated into the approach for health care delivery and treatment, as these trends have considerable impact on the lives of young people and the parents with whom they live.

Stephanie Cosner Berzin

See also Adult Child Returning Home; Aging and Shifting Roles in Families; Changing Views of Marriage, Home Responsibilities, and Caregiving; Changes in Family

Structure, Roles; Developmental Transitions in Families; Economic Downturn and Families; Family Experiencing Transitions; Last Child Leaving Home

Further Readings

Arnett, J. J. (2004). *Emerging adulthood: The winding road from the late teens through the twenties.* New York: Oxford University Press.

Goldscheider, F., & Goldscheider, C. (1999). *The changing transition to adulthood: Leaving and returning home.* Thousand Oaks, CA: Sage.

Settersten, R. A., Jr., Furstenberg, F. F., & Rumbaut, R. G. (2005). *On the frontier of adulthood: Theory, research, and public policy.* Chicago: University of Chicago Press.

ADULT WITH DISABILITY LIVING AT HOME

More people are surviving catastrophic trauma and disease and are living longer than ever before, often with a variety of disabilities. In the 2008 American Community Survey (ACS), more than 10% of adults ages 21 to 64 years reported disabilities. This rises to 40% of adults ages 65 years and older. According to the Family Caregiver Alliance, about 44 million family members provide unpaid care to relatives in the United States, accounting for 80% of long-term care.

The term *disability* represents a broad spectrum of abilities and functional limitations that vary based on the cause(s) of the condition, the individual's cultural and psychological makeup, and the level of accessibility and support in the environment. Adults with disabilities experience functional impairments, which often affect their abilities to fulfill their roles within the family as well as to work and contribute to the community. From the ACS, it was found that of adults aged 21 to 64 years with a disability only 40% are employed and 25% are living in poverty. Depending on the degree of impairment, the adult with a disability may require assistance with self-care from family members or from paid care providers, which can be intrusive to the family. Some adults with severe physical, but not cognitive, disabilities can direct their own care, even if they are unable to physically care for themselves. Some

conditions in adults, such as amputation, rheumatoid arthritis, paraplegia, and mild cerebral palsy, cause some activity limitations and adaptations but may have little or no effect on the adult's role in the family.

Families' responses to disability are variable, and are based on prior experience, values, expectations, culture, and family dynamics. The presence of disability can affect the family in many ways—financial, emotional, physical, psychological—and impact relationships and intimacy, work productivity of the adult and the caregiver, communication, and reproduction.

The family position of the adult with a disability influences family coping; for example, if the father is unable to fulfill typical roles, such as wage earner or parent, other family roles must be altered to fill in the gap. Women are most often the caregivers in the family, but they may also have disabilities. Children may be required to assist in caring for the adult, taking on responsibilities that may be beyond their abilities. After a brief discussion of the current literature, this entry focuses on the services, supports, and interventions available to families who have an adult with a disability living in the home.

Overview of Current Literature

Disability arises from many causes, from congenital and genetic conditions, injury, and disease to the consequences of aging. The type, severity, course, and trajectory of the disabling condition affect both the individuals' and the families' coping. Cognitive disabilities, such as dementia or traumatic brain injury, are generally the most difficult for family adjustment. The level of physical and mental impairment influences family coping due to the scope of caregiving necessary. If the adult with a disability is completely dependent for care, family stress is increased. In adults with tetraplegic spinal cord injury (paralysis of all four limbs and of the head), family members were found to experience reduced quality of life and a higher than expected rate of physical disease and depression. Some researchers suggest that family caregivers who observe suffering in a close relative also suffer emotionally and physically.

A disabling condition with a predictable course is less stressful than one that is unpredictable. Conditions may be stable and unchanging, such as a traumatic amputation or cerebral palsy; progressive, such as dementia; or relapsing and remitting, such as multiple sclerosis. Disabling conditions that progress to death, such as multiple sclerosis or amyotrophic lateral sclerosis, present profound stress in family members and the individual.

The sudden onset of a permanently disabling disease or trauma creates a crisis. Relationships are altered, and intimate relationships are strained, often never to return to pre-injury levels. Family members, especially the partner of the adult with a disability, must grieve the loss of the relationship and the prior lifestyle and adapt to the changes.

Culture and ethnicity influence how families respond to disability and its effect on family roles. In some cultures, stigma can play an important role, as cultural beliefs vary as to the cause and meaning of disability. Some cultures value the family as a whole more than the individual, and thus, the family may be more comfortable caring for a family member with a disability. Interdependence may be valued above independence.

Services and Supports Available to Families

Home care agencies provide direct personal care and home therapies as well as medical supplies. Other companies provide durable medical equipment, such as wheelchairs, respiratory equipment, and oxygen. Medicaid and Medicare insurance coverage may limit access to health care as some providers may choose to not honor public insurance; most adults with disabilities are covered by either Medicaid or Medicare. Accessible transportation may be inconvenient and difficult to obtain. Day programs offer adults with cognitive disabilities a chance to socialize and to take part in activities outside of the family. Organizations such as the Brain Injury Association of America and Alzheimer's Association offer information and training for adults with disabilities and for caregivers. Researching, contacting, arranging for services, and coordinating these agencies can be time consuming.

Interventions/Outcomes

One of the most effective interventions for families is respite care, which gives family caregivers time off. Family members can benefit from emotional support in the form of friends, other family caregivers, or professionals. Families with an extensive formal and informal support network cope the most successfully with an adult family member with a disability. Some medical practices now have case managers who assist individuals and families with arranging for services. Independent Living Centers (ILCs) exist in most communities and provide a variety of services, including financial management, self-care, and mobility. ILCs offer information to the adult with a disability to promote independence and reduce the strain on the family.

Dalice L. Hertzberg

See also Adult Child With Disability: Planning for by Parents; Adults With Childhood-Acquired Conditions; Alzheimer's Disease: Caregiver Burden; Americans with Disabilities Act and the Family; Caregiving: Partners/Spouses; Case Management for Chronic Illness/Disability and the Family; Disabilities and Family Management; Rehabilitation Act

Further Readings

Banks, M. E. (2003). Disability in the family: A life span perspective. *Cultural Diversity and Ethnic Minority Psychology, 9*(4), 367–384.

Devins, G. M., Gupta, A., Cameron, J., Woodend, K., Mah, K., & Gladman, D. (2009). Cultural syndromes and age moderate the emotional impact of illness intrusiveness in rheumatoid arthritis. *Rehabilitation Psychology, 541*(1), 33–44.

Erickson, W., Lee, C., von Schrader, S. (2010, March 17). *Disability statistics from the 2008 American Community Survey (ACS).* Ithaca, NY: Cornell University Rehabilitation Research and Training Center on Disability Demographics and Statistics (StatsRRTC). Retrieved March 23, 2010, from http://www.disabilitystatistics.org

Feigin, R., Barnetz, Z., & Davidson-Arad, B. (2008). Quality of life in family members coping with chronic illness in a relative: An exploratory study. *Families, Systems, & Health, 26*(3), 267–281.

Hui, S. A., Elliott, T. R., Shewchuk, R., & Rivera, P. (2007). Communal behaviors and psychological adjustment of family caregivers and persons with spinal cord injury. *Rehabilitation Psychology, 52*(1), 113–119.

Martire, L. M., Lustig, A. P., Schulz, R., Miller, G. E., & Helgeson, V. S. (2004). Is it beneficial to involve a family member? A meta-analysis of psychosocial interventions for chronic illness. *Health Psychology, 23*(6), 599–611.

Monin, J. K., & Schulz, R. (2009). Interpersonal effects of suffering in older adult caregiving relationships. *Psychology and Aging, 24*(3), 681–695.

Websites

Disability.Gov: http://www.disability.gov

Family Caregiver Alliance: http://www.caregiver.org/caregiver/jsp/home.jsp

Minnesota Governor's Council on Developmental Disabilities, *Parallels in time*: http://www.mnddc.org/parallels/index.html

National Council on Independent Living: http://www.ncil.org

ADULTS WITH CHILDHOOD-ACQUIRED CONDITIONS

Only in the last half century have children with once uniformly fatal diseases, such as leukemia, sickle cell anemia, and cystic fibrosis, begun surviving into adulthood. Advances in medical treatment and care are responsible for extended life expectancy, improved quality of life, and the ability of many people diagnosed with these conditions to plan careers, get married, and have families of their own. However, adults with childhood-acquired conditions still face a number of medical and psychosocial issues that continue to impact not only the individual but also the entire family. These include ongoing and progression of symptoms over time, complications, and long-term effects from the disease and its treatment, the possibility of early death, barriers to following lifesaving medical treatment regimens, fertility issues and concerns of disease transmission to offspring, and the impact of lifelong illness on all domains of life and family relationships. This entry focuses on the transition from childhood to adulthood, the transition from pediatric to adult health care, and coping with chronic illness.

Transition From Childhood to Adulthood

Parents are tasked with the responsibility of ensuring a successful transition for children with chronic and life-threatening illnesses through adolescence with the goal of not only surviving but also thriving well into adulthood. *Adolescence,* broadly defined as the second decade of life, is a time of change for all children as they develop their identities and gain independence from parents and caregivers as they move toward young adulthood. Adolescence can be particularly challenging for individuals with childhood-acquired illnesses, as typical development may be complicated by various aspects of the disease and treatment. Also, adolescents with chronic illnesses, like all individuals at this age, seek to detach from parental authority and earn approval from peers. They may go to great lengths to appear normal to others in an effort to be accepted. At this stage of development, the brain has not yet fully developed its capacity for anticipating future consequences of behavior. Consequently, adolescents with chronic and life-threatening illnesses may not consider the impact that substance use and adherence to treatment regimens will have on their disease in the future. The risk for disease progression and even death can increase during this stage of development as a result of poor health behaviors. Adults with childhood-acquired conditions whose adherence to treatment in youth was poor often experience advanced stages of disease earlier in life.

Transition From Pediatric To Adult Health Care

At some point during adolescence or young adulthood, people with childhood-acquired conditions discontinue care with their pediatric medical specialists. This disrupted continuity of care can lead to serious consequences unless an organized, coordinated approach to easing the transition from pediatric to adult health care is taken. For example, adults who underwent treatment for childhood cancer may not be contacted for routine exams and lab tests that can identify common long-term effects of chemotherapy, such as heart disease and second cancers. Ideally, the transition from pediatric to adult care begins by early adolescence and occurs gradually over a number of years with the assistance of medical personnel, nurse coordinators, psychologists, and social workers who will help the child take on increasing responsibility for their condition under parental supervision.

Depending on the condition, the end goal may be facilitating transition to an adult specialist, for example, from pediatric to adult endocrinology in the case of diabetes. Alternatively, an individual may be followed by a general practitioner once they are discharged from a pediatric clinic. Currently, there is no universally accepted model or approach at this time; however, the role of the primary care provider is of utmost importance in coordinating services and ensuring that all health prevention and treatment needs are being met. Long before the transition to adult care occurs, treatment providers should begin addressing issues that are common to all young people, such as sexuality, fertility, substance use, driving, independent living, financial and medical insurance issues, and vocational and educational opportunities as they relate to the specific childhood-acquired condition. With an appropriate level of knowledge and self-care skills, adults with childhood-acquired conditions can experience a smooth transition from pediatric to adult health care.

Coping and Emotional Adjustment

While the majority of adults with childhood-acquired conditions adjust well to the stress associated with chronic illness, some will demonstrate clinically concerning emotional and behavioral problems. For example, certain groups of adults who were treated for childhood cancers appear to be at risk for developing anxiety, depression, and even thoughts of suicide. Emotional distress related to illness may further reduce quality of life and worsen the experience and impact of symptoms such as chronic pain regardless of diagnosis. Resources aimed at assisting adults in coping with childhood-acquired conditions, such as online support groups, are difficult to come by, and few mental health professionals have specialized knowledge to target the unique problems in this population.

Conclusion

Adults with childhood-acquired conditions have encountered and continue to face a number of unique challenges that medical professionals are only beginning to understand and address. Research on this group is in its infancy given that children with serious illnesses only began surviving into adulthood in recent history.

Laura K. Campbell

See also Adult Child With Disability: Planning for by Parents; Adult With Disability Living at Home; Case Management for Chronic Illness/Disability and the Family; Cystic Fibrosis and the Family; Developmental Transitions in Families; Diabetes, Type 1, and the Family; Health Care Transition Planning; Life Span: Care Coordination for Chronic Illness/Disabilities and the Family; Sickle Cell Disease and the Family

Further Readings

Freed, G. L., & Hudson, E. J. (2006). Transitioning children with chronic diseases to adult care: Current knowledge, practices, and directions. *Journal of Pediatrics, 148*, 824–827.

Okumura, M. J., Kerr, E. A., Cabana, M. D., David, M. M., Demonner, S., & Heisler, M. (2010). Physician views on barriers to primary care for young adults with childhood-onset chronic disease. *Pediatrics, 125*, e748–e754.

Rosen, D. S., Blum, R. W., Britto, M., Sawyer, S. M., & Siegel, D. M. (2003). Transition to adult health care for adolescents and young adults with chronic conditions: Position paper of the Society of Adolescent Medicine. *Journal of Adolescent Health, 33*, 309–311.

Websites

American Diabetes Association: http://www.diabetes.org
Childhood Cancer Survivor Study: http://ccss.stjude.org
Cystic Fibrosis Foundation: http://www.ccf.org

ADVANCE DIRECTIVES AND THE FAMILY

The ability of medical technology to prolong life has grown tremendously in recent years. These advances, coupled with highly publicized legal cases involving patients who could not speak for themselves, have raised many questions about how we should care for people at the end of their lives. In its simplest form, an advance directive (AD) is a written statement that details a person's wishes for health care. The document may state choices for certain types of treatments or name someone, a surrogate, to speak on the person's behalf. People have the right to do this, guaranteed by federal legislation. The intent of such documents is to help health care professionals, family, and friends make decisions about a person's health care and treatments should that person become seriously ill or unable to speak for him- or herself.

History

As early as the 1960s, advocates for consumer rights and hospice care promoted the concept of a living will to help patients who were terminally ill avoid futile life-sustaining treatment. The case of Karen Ann Quinlan, a 21-year-old woman in a persistent vegetative state, captured wide media attention. In 1976, the New Jersey Supreme Court granted Ms. Quinlan's parents, who believed it was maintaining their daughter's life, the right to withdraw a ventilator from their daughter. With the help of a feeding tube, Ms. Quinlan lived until 1985.

The parents of Nancy Beth Cruzan, who also lived in a persistent vegetative state following a serious car accident, asked to have her feeding tube removed so that her life would not be artificially prolonged. Without a court order, the hospital caring for Nancy refused to honor the Cruzans' request. The request went all the way to the U.S. Supreme Court. In 1990, the Court ruled that individual states could establish standards by which surrogates request limits on life-sustaining treatment. The Cruzan case established the criteria of "clear and convincing evidence" and contributed in part to the development of federal legislation that was meant to encourage people to make their wishes known to their loved ones to ensure their values would be respected at the end of life.

The Patient Self-Determination Act (PSDA) is federal legislation. Through regulations, the PSDA dictates policies for states and institutions. It was designed to protect a person's right to participate in health care decisions while they are capable of expressing their preferences. Under the PSDA, institutions are required, among other things, to maintain in writing the policies and procedures that inform individuals of their rights, provide for placement in the medical record of an AD, and provide for education of staff and the community on topics related to AD. At the time of admission to any health care facility, patients must be given the opportunity to give a copy of their AD to their health care provider, receive information about completing an AD, and receive assistance in completing one if they so desire.

Nearly 20 years after the PSDA, less than 25% of admitted patients have completed an AD. Since first being introduced, ADs have evolved, sometimes becoming very detailed and specific and only addressing some hypothetical medical scenario. States vary in their legal recognition of the document and have specific requirements before they become active.

Advance Directives and the Law

While laws differ from state to state, in general, a person's expressed wishes will be honored. The two most common forms of an AD are a living will (LW) and a durable power of attorney for health care (DPOAHC). The term *living will* may be used interchangeably with *advance directive*, but in fact, an LW is one type of AD. An LW is a document that states a person's wishes regarding wanted and unwanted treatments in the event that person has a terminal illness and/or becomes permanently unconscious and is not able to make his or her own decisions. A DPOAHC is a different document that allows more flexibility. The DPOAHC names a specific individual to make decisions for a person if he or she is not able to express their wishes, even if he or she does not have a terminal illness.

It is possible for a person to complete these documents by using standard forms found in a stationery store or from sources on the Internet, as long as the state's requirements for witnessing the document are followed. Both documents require the person to sign them, date them, and be witnessed, preferably by someone who knows the person well. Specific medical treatment preferences, for example, artificial nutrition and hydration, kidney dialysis, or being placed on a ventilator, should be discussed with a trained health care provider. AD documents alone are not effective in improving end-of-life care. AD documents are most effective when they serve as part of an overall advance care planning process. Additionally, because in legal terms an LW is not the same as a DPOAHC, individuals must be clear about which document they are completing.

Advance Care Planning

People are living longer, but they are also living with chronic illnesses and disabilities. The potential exists for substantial burden of suffering at the end of life. Often, in the context of aggressive life-prolonging treatment, the majority of deaths occur in hospitals or extended-care nursing facilities, yet many people would prefer to die at home. There is evidence that completing an AD document in and of itself is not as helpful to others as having a conversation about end-of-life preferences as part of an overall care plan. Efforts are under way to shift the focus from a single event when a formal document is completed to a discussion that happens over time.

Because they have knowledge of how their loved one would make a decision, families and surrogates who have participated with a loved one in conversations about values and goals of treatment rather than discussions about specific treatment options, for example, a ventilator or kidney dialysis, are more likely to make decisions consistent with a person's wishes. Early advance care planning is ideal because a person's capacity to make decisions may diminish over time, and he or she may suddenly lose the ability to participate. Advance care planning should be routine community and clinical practice, and plans should be periodically revisited to reflect a person's changes in values and perceptions at different stages and circumstances of life.

Effective and respectful advance care planning requires recognition that both overtreatment and undertreatment may be concerns of persons contemplating future care. Advance care planning that focuses on designation of a proxy decision maker and elicitation of goals and values rather than attempts to elicit treatment-specific preferences is more effective. Interventions to facilitate discussion might include workbooks and other aids that help elicit a person's values and goals over time and that will engage surrogates in the process. Effective advance care planning requires two types of conversations: those with friends and family *and* those with health care professionals.

Lucia D. Wocial

See also Acute Care/Hospitalization of Family Members; Adult Child With Disability: Planning for by Parents; Assisted Living Placement; Case Management for Chronic Illness/Disability and the Family; Communication in Families Related to Health and Illness; Decision Making in the Context of Health and Illness; Health Care Transition Planning; Hospice Care; Life Span: Care Coordination for Chronic Illness/Disabilities and the Family; Long-Term Care Facilities for Families; Palliative Care and the Family

Websites

American Bar Association, *Consumer's toolkit for health care advance planning*: http://www.abanet.org/aging/toolkit

Caring Connections, *Advanced Directives*: http://www.caringinfo.org/stateaddownload

U.S. Department of Health and Human Services, *Literature review on Advance Directives*: http://aspe.hhs.gov/daltcp/reports/2007/advdirlr.htm

ADVOCACY FOR FAMILIES

Advocacy is a central task of nursing and many health professions. Advocacy is an action that fosters change. Conceptually, advocacy is an action related to the need for change. Figure 1 illustrates a model of the advocacy process. The first step of the advocacy process is a needs assessment to identify a family's capacity for managing the problem. At this point, families may demonstrate competence sufficient for managing a problem. If support is needed, the assessment includes environmental factors that may contribute to the problem as well as the family's capacity for change. Once the assessment is completed, the plan is developed with families, spelling out actions for the advocate and family. The advocacy action takes many forms that are based on the needs. Finally, the outcome is measured, and evaluation steps determine the competence of families for future problem solving.

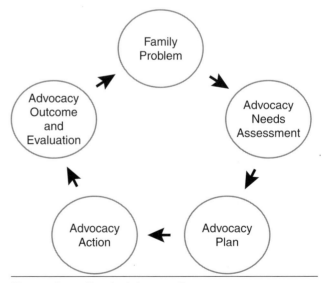

Figure 1   Family Advocacy Process

Practitioners advocate by protecting clients from harm due to unethical, incompetent, or illegal practice. Advocacy is action taken to influence the outcome. Thus, advocacy requires that a cause, idea, or policy is adopted and then actively supported. Advocacy in the acute care setting has been described as a process to guard legal rights and protect patient values while championing social justice. In public health, advocacy is often on the population level. For example, advocates in public health and school health promote health behavior, such as physical activity and healthy diet for children and families. They then work with institutions to limit unhealthy food, provide healthy food, and build physical activity skill. The advocate may use strategies to publicize the need for change to gain widespread support. Thus, advocacy outcomes reflect actions where health professionals, families, and institutional representatives must work together through the interventions to build collective capacity.

There are three constituencies in advocacy situations: the advocate, the recipient of the advocate's actions, and the adversary. Advocacy can be used for influencing public policy or resource allocation. For example, health care reformists advocate for access to health care for children through the State Children's Health Insurance Program (SCHIP) funded by the federal government. SCHIP enhances access to care for a wide socioeconomic range of children by providing payment to providers. Considering the constituencies involved in this effort, the policy advocates take the cause of access to care for children (the recipients) and face the opponents for governmental funding of health care for children through SCHIP. While it is simplistic to say that opponents of SCHIP are not supportive of health care for children, it can be said that they are against governmental support.

Positive advocacy outcomes require cooperation. For example, the Maternal and Child Health Bureau (MCHB) provides data from national surveys to describe the proportion of children with special health care needs who meet the MCHB's six core outcomes. The core outcomes include partnership in decision making between families and providers, the provision of coordinated, ongoing care that is comprehensive and based in a health care home. Further, families are assured of having adequate private and/or public insurance

coverage to pay for services. Children with special health care needs are assured of regular screening for special needs and community service systems that are accessible. Finally, children with special health care needs are assured of transitions into adulthood that include adequate care as adults. These core outcomes were determined through collaboration of different professional groups, community and family groups, and the MCHB. The MCHB conducted a survey of 52,445 children with special health care needs to identify the proportion of children meeting the six core outcomes. The results indicate a success rate of 6% to 74%. The success rate is only 6% for the outcome ensuring transition into adulthood with adequate care as an adult. These results point to the need for cooperation across families, health care providers, insurance companies, and organizations providing for continuity of care. The three constituencies in this proposed advocacy situation would be the advocate (person or group) who adopts the cause of meeting the MCHB recommended guidelines, the recipient of the advocate's actions (the population of children with special health care needs), and the adversary (represented as the disjointed health care system).

Homeless families represent a population that benefits from advocacy. Homeless families often lack resources that are connected to belonging to a community. For example, they may use emergency department services rather than a health care home. Their children are often moved from school to school as shelter opportunities change. In these instances, homeless families are trying to adapt to life challenges and, in fact, are seeking health care, albeit the most expensive, and are trying to keep their children in school. Yet the health care system and the educational system operate separately. Advocacy groups suggest that an interagency collaborative for agencies that provide primary care can enhance continuity of care by offering a health care home. Further, the interagency collaborative can promote "housing first" programs that offer more stable housing for families thus giving children a residence associated with a particular school. In this example, the advocates are the interagency collaborative coordinating services that benefit homeless families. The advocacy recipients are the families who are homeless, and the adversary is represented by the inflexible system members, such as schools, and homeless services that are competing for financial resources and autonomy rather than collaborating to share scarce resources.

Policy Practice Implications

Families across the health and wellness continuum face many situations in which they would benefit from advocacy. The advocate identifies scarce resources and works systems and families to use resources to guard legal rights and protect client values while championing social justice.

Julia Muennich Cowell

See also Factors Influencing Access to Health Care for Families; Health System Options for Families; Welfare Benefits and Family Health

Further Readings

McPherson, M., Weissman, G., Strickland, B., van Dyck, P., Blumberg, S., & Newacheck, P. (2004). Implementing community-based systems of services for children and youth with special health care needs: How well are we doing? *Pediatrics, 113*(5), 1538–1544.

Westbrook, L., & Schultz, P. (2000). From theory to practice: Community health nursing in a public health neighborhood team. *Advances in Nursing Science, 23*(2), 50–61.

Affect Management and the Family

Affect management (AM) refers to the need for children to learn to regulate their emotions in order to function in a flexible, adaptive manner in the face of the stimulations and stresses of their life. *Affect* refers to the nonverbal expression of one's emotions in facial expressions, voice prosody, gestures, and movements. When children are able to manage their emotions, they have developed a thermostat whereby their emotions are now able to be regulated.

The family is the primary—and most effective—setting for the development of AM. Children raised in orphanages manifest very poor AM.

Understanding the family environment is crucial in understanding how to provide interventions that are helpful in facilitating AM. This entry focuses on the development of AM and parental factors that influence such development.

The Development of Affect Management

From birth, infants begin the ongoing process of learning to regulate various bodily systems. Immediately, the infant begins the process able to regulate homeostatic, sleep, eating, and other basic physiological systems. Shortly afterward, older infants and toddlers begin to regulate emotions and behavior, which is quickly followed by emerging cognitive abilities. The task of the early preschool years is to develop these early regulatory abilities, with AM being one of the most important. AM is central to what has become known as a child's emotional intelligence—considered to be at least as important in one's long-term success in life as cognitive intelligence.

The early stages in the development of AM consist in the dyadic regulation of the child's various systems by the parents. When a child is in distress and begins to experience an intense negative emotion, whether it be anger, fear, or sadness, the child will learn to regulate that emotion and its affective expression when the child's parent is near him or her, accepts his or her experience of the negative emotion, and responds to the situation with confidence while remaining regulated him- or herself. The parent's AM in the presence of the child's intense emotional experience is the primary way that young children begin to develop their own AM abilities. The coregulation of the child's emotional experiences is the foundation for the child to begin to autoregulate emotions, as demonstrated in the child's AM skills.

Children who manifest attachment security in relationship with their parents are likely to demonstrate good AM skills. Children who have insecure attachments—and especially disorganized attachments—with their parents are at risk for poor AM skills. With attachment security, children develop a sense of safety in their lives, with the confidence that their parents will respond in a timely and sensitive manner to their expressions of distress. They have confidence that any threat to self will be managed with the parents' active presence and support. Confidence that parents will assist them in dealing with intense emotions enables the child to develop AM skills, first with the parents' assistance and then alone.

Parental Factors for Facilitating Affect Management in the Child

The most important factor in assisting the child to develop AM skills is for the parent to habitually manifest the same skills, especially in times of distress for the child and/or the parent. If the child's emotional distress is caused by the parent's poor AM, the child is much less likely to develop AM of his or her emotions. The nonverbal expression of affect is very contagious. Screaming at a child to stop screaming at the parent is probably the least effective way of helping the child to learn AM. Modeling for the child good AM is probably the most effective means of accomplishing this goal. Similarly, if the child's emotional distress triggers emotional distress in the parent (which is often associated with the parent's having features of an unresolved attachment history him- or herself), then the parent will not be in position to facilitate the child's AM skills.

While it is important for the parent to remain fairly relaxed and flexible in responding to his or her child who is showing poor AM, it is often not helpful for the parent to be too calm and rational in his or her response. If children are manifesting anger by being agitated and screaming, parents are likely to increase AM if they become more animated, matching the rhythm and intensity of their child's voice, *without* being angry. This situation enables children to have confidence that parents understand the strength and nature of their anger, parents accept their state of distress, and parents will assist them in attaining AM of the situation. This interaction and teaching are much more experiential and nonverbal than rational and verbal.

Parents differentiate between the child's affective expressions of emotions and behaviors. While setting limits on specific behaviors (e.g., hitting, name calling, stealing), parents do not set limits on the affect expression itself. This affect is accepted and understood with empathy. If a child is being disciplined, it is for behavior, not for any related expressions of affect. If the child is not permitted to express affect, then the child is not likely to be able to identify it and regulate it. When children have confidence that parents really understand them, the children are more likely to let the affect go and accept the parental authority.

The parent assists the child in AM for positive emotions as well. Parents provide this assistance by being careful not to provide the child with a series of exciting, stimulating events. The parent needs to provide opportunities for quiet times, to provide a natural cycle of active and quiet activities, and to remember the child's need for soothing transitional and bedtime routines and rituals. Activities that are calming and soothing for a child must not serve as rewards for desirable behaviors. They need to be provided unconditionally because they assist the child in overall emotional development, including affect management skills.

Conclusions

Affect management is a developmental skill, central to one's emotional intelligence that develops primarily within the family context. Dyadic regulation of affect precedes the autoregulation of affect. Such regulation develops best in circumstances of attachment security. Professionals who are offering treatment in facilitating the child's AM need to assess and then incorporate the relational family context into the interventions. Once the dyadic regulation of AM is established, the cognitive-behavioral interventions can be introduced if needed.

Daniel Hughes

See also Child Emotional Abuse and the Family; Parental Attachment; Parenting

Further Readings

Feldman, R., Greenbaum, C. W., Yirmiya, N. (1999). Mother–infant affect synchrony as an antecedent of the emergence of self-control. *Developmental Psychology, 35,* 223–231.

Sroufe, L. A. (1995). *Emotional development: The organization of emotional life in the early years.* Cambridge, UK: Cambridge University Press.

Sroufe, L. A., Egeland, B., Carlson, E. A., & Collins, W. A. (2005). *The development of the person.* New York: Guilford.

AFRICAN AMERICAN FAMILIES: PERSPECTIVES OF HEALTH

Health care professionals and researchers know that African American families, similar to families of other racial or ethnic groups, are involved in providing and/or managing health for ill or disabled family members. It is also widely accepted that African American family members influence and are influenced by the health of their ill or disabled family members. The family helps to define the illness and/or health-related experience, navigate the medical system, and make medical choices. The family's involvement in these tasks can improve the health of the ill or disabled family member. Conversely, involvement in these health-related tasks can affect the physical, emotional, financial, and spiritual health of the family.

African American families are embedded in racial, cultural, and environmental contexts that can influence attributions of health-related symptoms, decision making, access and choice of healthy foods, and access and choice of medical interventions and health care in general. While families throughout the life course influence or are influenced by the health of family members, this entry focuses on African American families and health-related influences when a middle-aged and/or older family member has a chronic illness or disability.

For many chronic illnesses and disabilities, including diabetes, cancer, strokes, dementia, and HIV/AIDS, African American adults experience some of the highest disability and mortality rates. Further complicating health and health care interactions are experiences of racial prejudice in the history, cultural memory, and present experiences of many African Americans and other people of color. As a result of these and other structural and personal experiences, African Americans often express distrust toward the health care system.

This distrust can affect health care experiences and interactions. For example, when adults have a serious or life-threatening chronic illness or disability, such as cancer or stroke-related disability, the individual and family often face a staggering amount of medical information, clinical encounters, and decisions that need to be made. Therefore, effective communication between these seriously ill adults, their families, and health care providers (HCPs) is critical for effective management of the disease. However, African Americans and other racial and ethnic minorities report less informed decision making, more unmet communication needs, and poorer satisfaction with health care and health-related quality of life compared to majority groups.

Perhaps as a result of such experiences, researchers document that African Americans rely more heavily than whites on informal social networks to meet their disease management needs and more often employ a family-centered decision-making process. These informal family networks can be invaluable sources in the transfer of health-related information and how individuals and family members identify and manage chronic disease or disability over time.

Researchers also document that family cohesion and strong cultural values and beliefs about helping and giving support encourage cohesiveness among African American families. However, in a note of caution, it was found that in one recent study family members who reported the highest levels of cultural beliefs had the poorest health outcomes. While family cohesion has been historically connected with better disease and/or disability outcomes for families and the ill or disabled family member, the opposite is true for family conflict and disagreements. In general, the following family characteristics have demonstrated consistently negative relationships with disease and disability outcomes: low family cohesion, high family conflict, hostile family affiliative tone, and lack of clear communication. It is important for physicians and other HCPs to understand that family functioning is a key component in providing comprehensive care for individuals with serious illnesses and their family members.

The use of formal supports, in terms of home health, support groups, long-term care facilities, and hospice, is currently equivocal. Historically, African American families' interactions with community-based formal support systems have been fewer than for white Americans. However, in a study to examine four racial/ethnic groups, no differences were found in formal support use for African Americans when compared with whites and Hispanics. This differs from most studies that show significantly lower use of hospice when

African American families have a seriously ill family member. In terms of spiritual support, African American families continue to report talking with and including their pastors in the decision-making process. Also reported is God as a part of the support system and as "the way through" when coping and managing health-related needs and crises within the family.

In summary, health care management for African Americans and other groups often extends beyond the individual to include the family and HCPs. Researchers and HCPs refer to this as a *health care triad,* or *partnership,* and recognize the involvement of all entities as optimal for provision of medical care for seriously ill older adults. Further, recommendations of the National Institute of Neurological Disorders and Stroke, Institute of Medicine, American Medical Association, and the Critical Care Medicine Task Force state that health care, including palliative care, needs to expand to include family-centered outcomes. This expansion of strategies and interventions to include the family are especially important for ill or disabled African American adults who more often than whites include family members in the decision-making process.

It is critical that HCPs acknowledge patient rights and Health Insurance Portability and Accountability Act guidelines and understand that ill and disabled African Americans also vary in their openness about disease outcomes and the level of involvement they desire from their families. It is also critical to remember that while race- and/or culture-specific findings from any group can inform and guide health-related interactions, they can also be used to apply stereotypes and thus do harm. Therefore, physicians, other HCPs, and researchers are reminded to use race- and culture-specific knowledge as a guide and not as truth applicable to all members within the racial and/or cultural group.

Theoretical frameworks including Family Systems Illness Model (Rolland, 1994; Clipp, 2005), Bowles and Kington's (1998) conceptualization of how African American families function in the context of health, Dilworth-Anderson and Anderson's (1994) contextual approach to research on caregiving, Fisher and colleagues' (2000, 2004) family structure and organization model, Andersen and colleagues' (1973, 1995)

health services use model, Engel's biopsychosocial approach (perhaps with the addition of a spiritual component), and Pearlin and colleagues' stress and coping model (1990) can also guide HCPs' and researchers' conceptualizations and understanding of African American families and health outcomes.

Sharon Wallace Williams

See also Access to Health Care: Elderly; Access to Health Care: Uninsured; Advance Directives and the Family; Alzheimer's Disease: An Overview of Family Issues in; Alzheimer's Disease: Caregiver Burden

Further Readings

Dilworth-Anderson, P., Brummett, B. H., Goodwin, P., Williams, S. W., Williams, R. B., & Siegler, I. C. (2005). Effects of race on cultural justifications for caregiving. *Journal of Gerontology: Social Sciences, 59,* S138–S145.

Pinquart, M., & Sorenson, S. (2005a). Ethnic differences in stressors, resources, and psychological outcomes of family caregiving: A meta analysis. *Gerontologist, 45,* 90–106.

Rabow, M. W., Hauser, J. M., & Adams, J. (2004). Supporting family caregivers at the end of life: "They don't know what they don't know." *Journal of the American Medical Association, 291,* 483–491.

Rolland, J. S. (1987). Chronic illness and the life cycle: A conceptual framework. *Family Process, 26,* 203–221.

Williams, S. W., Hanson, L. C., Boyd, C., Green, M., Goldmon, M., Wright, G., et al. (2008). Communication, decision making and cancer: What African Americans want physicians to know. *Journal of Palliative Medicine, 11,* 1221–1226.

AGING AND SHIFTING ROLES IN FAMILIES

Social roles are behaviors with prescribed functions and norms that help to characterize individuals and their positions within families and social systems. Victoria Hilkevitch Bedford and Rosemary Bleiszner's definition of *family* is used in this discussion: "A family is a set of relationships determined by biology, adoption, marriage . . . and social designation, and existing even in the absence of affective involvement . . . (or) even after the death of certain members" (2000, p. 160). Family is considered the context of care in this entry.

Throughout the life span, individuals tend to shed old roles and assume new ones as they age and as the environment around them changes. While gaining new roles can be fulfilling for older adults and their family members, these changes can also induce stress and strain both within and among roles. The manner in which individuals adjust to these changes is influenced by a number of variables including coping resources, health, wealth, gender, race and ethnicity, and family composition. While these variables contribute to a wide diversity in family structure and roles, several trends have emerged that offer some insight into the shifts that have occurred and, in all likelihood, will continue to occur in society.

Due to advances in science, health, and medical technology, life expectancy in the United States has increased from 47 years to over 77 years during the past century. This increase in life expectancy has lengthened the time window in which role changes can occur for older adults and their family members. Both opportunities and challenges accompany these shifts in roles and are most evident in three specific roles and activities associated with aging: retirement, grandparenting, and caregiving.

Retirement

While 65 has long been considered the accepted age for retirement, many now find that they are working into their 70s and 80s—some due to financial necessity, others by their own choosing. This prolonged productivity into old age may change social role expectations, increase the perceived value of older adults in the workplace, and add to self-esteem and self-worth for older adults. While delaying retirement may have benefits for some, others may experience more troubling effects. For some older adults, continuing to assume a work role may prevent them from fully engaging in other important roles, such as active grandparent, spousal caregiver, or relaxed retiree. Research has shown that role conflict and strain can occur when work interferes with the fulfillment of these important and often highly cherished and anticipated roles. Available research is mixed on the health effects of retirement, including the influence

of retirement on mental or physical health and life satisfaction. Interventions such as those designed to enhance retirement planning and individuals' social support in preparation for this transition may prove helpful.

Grandparenting

As the life span has increased, there have also been shifts in the grandparent role. In the past, grandparenting has traditionally been a relatively brief role due to the truncating effects of morbidity and mortality. Many older adults are now finding that the grandparent role has expanded in terms of both longevity and scope. For example, a growing number of grandparents are actively involved in raising their grandchildren due to socioeconomic stressors and other factors affecting adult children. Research has shown that grandparents raising grandchildren is an important role for older adults, adding to self-identity and worth and providing opportunities for generativity and enhanced ego integrity in later life. For other older adults, the expansion into a "grandparent as parent role" and the resulting ambiguities can introduce new sources of stress as grandparents help to raise their grandchildren. This shifting role also influences other roles and relationships within the family system, including grandparents' relationships with their grandchildren, their adult children, and their spouses. It is important to note that grandparents raising grandchildren are at greater risk for depressive symptoms than noncaregivers; however, national organizations, such as the American Association of Retired Persons, have developed substantial resources for individuals in this situation.

Caregiving

Finally, for those family members who provide care to older relatives, a longer life span means that many individuals are assuming the caregiver role more frequently and for longer periods of time. With longer life has come an increase in the number of years that individuals live with chronic health care conditions and disabilities. The leading causes of death have shifted from infectious disease and acute illness to chronic disease, such as heart disease, cancer, stroke, and diabetes. These trends in disability have required a growing number of family members (such as older adult spouses or adult children) to step into the often challenging role of a caregiver. Research has shown that caregiving is a complex role associated with a wide array of potentially negative outcomes, such as depressed immune system response, emotional and psychological distress, and subjective health impairments. In contrast, the caregiver role is fulfilling and provides a sense of filial responsibility and emotional gain for some family members. Psychosocial interventions, particularly multicomponent approaches that often combine individual consultation with family sessions and ongoing "ad hoc" support over the course of illness, have proven effective in alleviating some of the negative outcomes related to caregiving.

It has been projected that by 2030 the average life span will be 10 years longer and that one in every five people in the United States will be age 65 and older. The transformations that have taken place in the past in terms of aging and shifting family roles provide some indication on how projected societal changes might affect family roles in the future. For instance, modifications in income maintenance programs including Social Security and private pensions may render the retirement role a thing of the past. The expectation that grandparents should assist in raising grandchildren may become more and more common as parents have fewer opportunities to leave the workforce to care for their young children. While the caregiver role is currently becoming a part of reality for more and more families, there is some evidence that advances in policy such as paying family caregivers and technology use of personal health care records may significantly alter this role in the future. Family systems are dynamic organisms and these projected changes in the aging structure of society will call on family members to continue to shift roles. Such shifts will undoubtedly result in various opportunities and challenges.

*Joseph E. Gaugler, Holly Dabelko-Schoeny,
and Keith A. Anderson*

Author's note: The senior author of this contribution thanks the 2 co-authors (Dr. Dabelko-Schoeny and Dr. Anderson) for their efforts in assembling this entry.

See also Caregiving: Elderly; Changes in Family Structure; Changes in Family Structure, Roles; Family

Experiencing Transitions; Grandparenting; Grandparents Parenting; Retirement

Further Readings

Bedford, V. H., & Blieszner, R. (2000). Personal relationships in later life families. In R. M. Milardo & S. Duck (Eds.), *Families as relationships* (pp. 157–174). New York: Wiley.

Centers for Disease Control and Prevention & Merck Company Foundation. (2007). *The state of aging and health in America.* Whitehouse Station, NJ: Merck Company Foundation.

National Institute on Aging. (2007). *The health & retirement study.* Bethesda, MD: U.S. Department of Health and Human Services, U.S. Department of State.

National Institute on Aging (2007). *Why population aging matters: A global perspective.* Bethesda, MD: U.S. Department of Health and Human Services, U.S. Department of State.

Topa, G., Moriano, J. A., Depolo, M., Alcover, C.-M., & Morales, J. F. (2009). Antecedents and consequences of retirement planning and decision-making: A meta-analysis and model. *Journal of Vocational Behavior, 75,* 38–55.

Websites

American Association of Retired Persons, *GrandCare Toolkit:* http://www.aarp.org/family/grandparenting/articles/grandcare_toolkit.html

ALCOHOL ADDICTIONS IN THE FAMILY

Alcohol addiction in the family is considered present when at least one family member suffers from an alcohol use disorder. It is now well recognized that alcohol addiction affects not only the afflicted individual but also the health and well-being of others in the family system of the alcoholic individual. Indeed, some of the most deleterious effects of alcohol misuse are saved for family members who often do not even drink, including spouses and children. Alcoholism and family functioning are linked via complex genetic, psychological, and social pathways. Several family problems may co-occur with or be exacerbated by alcoholism, including poor communication and problem solving, inconsistency and unpredictability, high conflict and low relationship satisfaction, intimate partner violence, economic vulnerability, and poor psychosocial adjustment of children. Family-involved treatments have been shown to be highly effective, in terms of both drinking reduction and improvements in family adjustment. This entry discusses the prevalence of alcoholism, its effects on family relationships, and treatments to improve family functioning.

Prevalence

Among the most prevalent disorders in the general population, alcoholism is estimated to affect about 14 million Americans, or 1 in every 13 adults. The National Institute on Alcohol Abuse and Alcoholism reports that in 2002, about 30% of those dependent on alcohol in the past year were women and about 53% were between the ages of 18 and 29 years old. Over half of American men and women are reported to have a close relative with a drinking problem. Approximately 1 in 4 children younger than 18 years in the United States is exposed to alcoholism in the family.

Couple Relationships

Couples in which one partner abuses alcohol usually have distressed relationships and markedly poor communication and problem-solving abilities; verbal or physical abuse is also prevalent. About 60% of married or cohabiting patients entering treatment for alcoholism report intimate partner violence in the past year. Risk for separation or divorce increases greatly when one partner is alcoholic. The negative effects of alcoholism on partner interactions, such as lying to conceal excessive drinking or related job problems, create relationship problems and broader family stress. Each partner is also at heightened risk for other emotional problems, such as depression and anxiety. These reciprocally causal problems create a vicious cycle, where the family stressors create a context for continued drinking (or relapse if drinking has previously ceased), and drinking fuels family problems.

Children of Alcoholic Parents

A substantial body of research indicates children of alcoholics (COAs) are at significantly increased risk for developing a variety of physical, emotional, behavioral, and social problems. Compared to children of parents who do not misuse alcohol, COAs exhibit elevated levels of physical illness as well as internalizing (e.g., depression, anxiety, mood disorders) and externalizing (e.g., aggression and antisocial behaviors) problems. They are also more likely than others to become substance users themselves. Developmental factors influence the nature of effects of parental alcoholism, with highest risks occuring prenatal (e.g., fetal alcohol syndrome) and for young children. Adolescent children are most vulnerable to engaging in alcohol and substance use themselves. Evidence suggests that preadolescent children, while likely to manifest elevated symptoms, are also most likely to respond to protective factors within the family.

Family Dysfunction Factors

Parenting by individuals with alcohol use disorders may be dysfunctional compared with parents who do not abuse alcohol. Negative interactions within the vicious cycle of the partners may spill over into interactions with children. Studies have found that parental alcohol abusers engage in inadequate and inconsistent parenting, low monitoring and limit setting, negative parent–child interactions, and increased likelihood of child abuse and neglect—all of which are linked to poor child adjustment. It is also well established that children who witness interparental conflict and violent episodes, compared to those not so exposed, are more likely to (a) experience feelings of fear and insecurity, (b) engage in acting-out behaviors, and (c) be overly aggressive in their interactions with others. The life stress created in the broader family environment from the vicious cycle of alcoholism and poor relationship communication and problem solving serves to further increase children's risks for maladjustment.

Family-Involved Treatment

The substance abuse treatment community has been encouraged to address the current dysfunction that can emerge from alcohol addiction in the family. Although individual-based treatments for parental substance abuse have shown some benefits, they are less effective at promoting family and child well-being. Evidence suggests involvement, when possible, of the alcoholic's partner in treatment can have even greater positive influences on family functioning. Involving children in treatment may also be beneficial. However, the majority of custodial parents who enter substance abuse treatment are reluctant to involve their children in mental health services and, except in extenuating circumstances, cannot be required to do so. Thus, interventions for substance-abusing parents that do not directly involve children but nonetheless serve to improve the family environment as a whole may hold the most potential for promoting family health.

From this vantage, one of the most consistently effective family-involved approaches to alcohol addiction is behavioral couple's therapy (BCT). BCT requires engagement of the intimate partner in treatment along with the alcoholic partner, concurrently targeting both drinking behavior and the couple's relationship. BCT has been found to increase abstinence and reduce heavy drinking, reduce conflict and violence in the family, improve parenting, and promote the emotional and behavioral functioning of children in the home.

Wendy K. K. Lam and William S. Fals-Stewart

See also Drinking by Underage Family Members; Drug Addictions in the Family; Parenting; Spouse/Domestic Partner Physical Abuse

Further Readings

Fals-Stewart, W., O'Farrell, T. J., Birchler, G. R., Cordova, J., & Kelley, M. L. (2005). Behavioral couples therapy for alcoholism and drug abuse: Where we've been, where we are, and where we're going. *Journal of Cognitive Psychotherapy, 19,* 231–249.

Grant, B. F., Dawson, D. A., Stinson, F. S., Chou, S. P., Dufour, M. C., & Pickering, R. P. (2004). The 12-month prevalence and trends in DSM-IV alcohol abuse and dependence: United States, 1991–1992 and 2001–2002. *Drug and Alcohol Dependence, 74(3),* 223–234.

O'Farrell, T. J., & Fals-Stewart, W. (2006). *Behavioral couples therapy for alcoholism and drug abuse.* New York: Guilford.

National Institute on Alcohol Abuse and Alcoholism (2005, March). *Module 10J: Alcohol and the family.* Retrieved March 28, 2009, from http://pubs.niaaa.nih.gov/publications/Social/Module10JFamilies/Module10J.html

ALLERGIES AND THE FAMILY

Allergy is a hypersensitivity to an allergen, a normally harmless substance. In an allergic subject, an allergen may cause an untoward reaction when it comes into contact with the skin or the eyes, is inhaled, eaten, or injected. When individuals with allergies come into contact with specific allergens, their immune systems identify these allergens as dangerous invaders, and their immune systems overreact. It triggers the release of histamines and other chemicals, whose task is to expel allergens from the body. The symptoms of an allergic reaction are precisely the results of the body's attempts to turn away the allergen: These symptoms may affect the eyes, nose, lungs, throat, ears, sinuses, skin, and/or mucous membranes.

Managing allergy can be very challenging for a patient and his or her family, but by making healthy behaviors the norm, allergy attacks can be prevented or controlled. The entry focuses on the measures that can be taken in the family to identify allergens and to prevent and control allergy symptoms.

Managing Allergies

In the United States, as many as 40 to 50 million people suffer from allergies, according to the National Institute of Allergy and Infectious Diseases, and S. J. Arbes and colleagues report that 54.6% of all inhabitants test positive to one or more allergens. Current research suggests that the prevalence of allergic diseases has increased since the 1960s, becoming a major public health concern. Allergies may affect the nervous, respiratory, digestive, integumentary, and genito-urinary system. The most common symptoms are itching in the eyes, redness, swelling, and watering; sneezing, coughing, shortness of breath, wheezing, and chest tightness; bloating, nausea, vomiting, and diarrhea; skin rashes and swelling; and pain associated with urination and urinary frequency. Many factors may predispose a subject to allergies: genetics, birth-related factors (for instance, preterm birth or birth in a high-pollen season), environmental factors (continuous exposure to high pollen quantities, industrial pollution, dust, insects, and/or other allergens or poor sanitation).

When clinicians diagnose allergy, they take into consideration many clinical features (e.g., the symptoms, family history for atopic disorder), evaluate results of physical exams and tests, and rule out other diagnoses. For this reason, it is essential that the individual with allergies (if a child, his or her parents, guardians, or caregivers) provide the health professional with detailed information about the symptoms and other events that may be linked with them (e.g., specific illnesses, presence of pets, dust mites, molds, cockroaches, pollen, insect bites or stings, ingestion of specific food and/or beverage, assumption of medications).

Strategies to cope with allergies include identifying the allergens that cause allergic reaction, avoiding contact with these allergens, and consulting a health care provider in order to make an action plan, which can help in preventing or reducing symptoms. The action plan may include suggestions for healthy behaviors (such as wearing a bracelet that alerts people about the subject's allergies) and prescriptions for medications. Allergy medications may comprise antihistamines, decongestants, bronchodilators, mast cells stabilizers, corticosteroids, leukotriene modifiers, and epinephrine as emergency medication. If the symptoms of a chronic allergy are severe, an allergist/immunologist may recommend immunotherapy. In allergen immunotherapy, the individual with allergies receives increasingly larger doses of an allergen, with the aim of reducing or suppressing his or her immune response to it. The administration may be sublingual or subcutaneous.

Allergy attacks can be very serious. Anaphylactic shock is a life-threatening allergic reaction, whose symptoms include swelling of the tongue and breathing tubes and consequent difficulty breathing, low blood pressure, and loss of consciousness. As serious allergy attacks require immediate emergency treatment, patients need to be able to prevent or at least control allergy symptoms as much as possible.

Improvement of Indoor Air

An important aspect of allergy prevention and control is the improvement of indoor air quality in the patient's home. This goal can be achieved by the following:

1. Running the air conditioning when the pollen count is high and opening windows only after midmorning

2. Changing the air filter in the air conditioner and the air furnace once a month

3. Using polyester-fill pillows and hypoallergenic blankets and washing them in hot water once a week

4. Removing upholstered furniture and carpets

5. Washing bedding and curtains in hot water weekly

6. Reducing the number of dust-collecting objects (e.g., books, nonwashable stuffed animals, knickknacks, houseplants)

7. Using a vacuum cleaner with a high-efficiency particulate filter once a week

8. Avoiding humidifiers; repairing water leaks in faucets, pipes, and ductwork; and using clothes dryers and exhaust fans to limit exposure to mold and damp

9. Avoiding wood fires or ensuring that the doors of wood-burning stoves fit tightly

10. Finding another home for warm-blooded pets and selecting low-dander pets in order to control animal dander

11. Sealing holes in walls, floors, and cabinets; storing food in airtight containers; and covering trash cans to limit exposure to cockroaches

Other Measures Aimed at Preventing and Controlling Allergies

Moreover, to prevent and control allergies, individuals with allergies can assist themselves by the following:

1. Identifying food that causes allergic reactions to avoid or limit its ingestion—in the majority of cases, foods responsible for allergic reactions include wheat, eggs, peanuts, tree nuts, soy, fish and shellfish, some fruits

2. Identifying beverages that cause allergic reactions to avoid or limit their ingestion—in the majority of cases, beverages responsible for allergic reactions include wine, some fruit juices, milk

3. Avoiding or limiting contact with nickel-containing metals (present in jewelry, clothing, money, and articles such as kitchen utensils and paper clips)

4. Avoiding or limiting exposure to pollen

5. Avoiding raking leaves, mowing lawns, working with peat, mulch, hay, or dead wood

6. Avoiding or limiting contact with and exposure to latex

7. Limiting assumption of medications such as paracetamol, aspirin, beta blockers, penicillins, cephalosporins

8. Undergoing allergen immunotherapy, for the purpose of achieving clinical tolerance of the allergens that cause symptoms

9. Taking medication as prescribed

Alessandra Padula

See also Asthma Family Issues: Prevention and Control; Chronic Health Problems and Interventions for the Childrearing Family; Food Allergies and Family Experiences; Genetic Family Histories; Immunizations and Vaccinations

Further Readings

Arbes, S. J., Jr., Gergen, P. J., Elliott, L., & Zeldin, D. C. (2005). Prevalences of positive skin test responses to 10 common allergens in the U.S. population: Results from the Third National Health and Nutrition Examination Survey. *Journal of Allergy and Clinical Immunology, 116*(2), 377–383.

Greenberger, G. (2006). Drug allergy. *Journal of Allergy and Clinical Immunology, 117*(2), S464–S470.

Grimshaw, K. E. C., Allen, K., Edwards, C. A., Beyer, K., Boulay, A., van der Aa, L. B., et al. (2009). Infant feeding and allergy prevention: A review of current knowledge and recommendations. A EuroPrevall state of the art paper. *Allergy, 64*(10), 1407–1416.

Hogan, D. J. (2009, July). Contact dermatitis, allergic. *eMedicine Dermatology*. Retrieved April 3, 2010, from http://emedicine.medscape.com/article/1049216-overview

Kelkar, P. S., & Li, J. T. C. (2001). Cephalosporins allergy. *New England Journal of Medicine, 345*, 804–809.

Primeau, M. N., & Adkinson, N. F. (2001). Recent advances in the diagnosis of drug allergy. *Current Opinion in Allergy and Clinical Immunology, 1*(4), 337–341.

Toogood, J. H. (1987). Beta-blocker therapy and the risk of anaphylaxis. *Canadian Medical Association Journal, 136*(9), 929–933.

U.S. Department of Health and Human Services, National Institutes of Health (2003, April). *Airborne allergens: Something in the air* (NIH Publication No. 03–7045). Washington, DC: National Institute of Allergy and Infectious Diseases. Retrieved April 3, 2010, from http://www3.niaid.nih.gov

ALZHEIMER'S DISEASE: AN OVERVIEW OF FAMILY ISSUES IN

Alzheimer's disease and related disorders (ADRD) are progressive, irreversible conditions that cause degeneration to the cerebral cortex. The degeneration causes a condition known as *dementia*. Dementia is characterized by changes in memory, thinking ability, reasoning, personality, visuospatial perception, capacity for language, and a loss of functional abilities. There are many conditions that cause irreversible brain degeneration, yet of all of the dementing illnesses, Alzheimer's is the most common, causing 60% to 80% of all dementias.

After a brief history of dementia care, this entry focuses on family care of the person with ADRD. Then, this entry describes desired outcomes for the person with ADRD and the family and treatment. Lastly, the relevance of ADRD to family health care is discussed.

History of Dementia Care

While there are references to behavioral changes as early as ancient or classic Greek literature, dementia was thought to be a normal change of aging. It was not until 1906 that Alois Alzheimer first identified Alzheimer's disease as a rare form of "senile dementia" occurring in younger adults. Over the years, research has shown that the disease can affect adults of any age yet increases in prevalence with aging. At age 55, from 9% to 17% of people will have developed ADRD while roughly half of people age 85 have developed dementia.

Prior to the 1960s, people with ADRD were admitted to mental health institutions (MHI) where they lived relatively brief lives. In the 1960s, states began closing their MHIs with the theory that people with mental illness could be best managed in community day programs. People with ADRD become dependent in meeting basic personal needs and thus were placed in nursing homes. In 1965, the Medicaid program as part of the Title XIX Social Security Amendment Act was passed to pay for care of impoverished dependent people, which included people with ADRD in nursing homes. The Medicaid budget soared, and federal policy clarified that families must bear primary responsibility for elder care. Today, families are the primary source of care in ADRD as there is limited public funding for "custodial care."

Families Providing Care

For the purposes of this chapter, *family* is loosely defined as the person with dementia, his or her spouse, and immediate and distant relatives; however, family may also be broadened in meaning to include others in a household or those who are providing unpaid (informal) care. Examples of other family might include same-sex partners, roommates, in-laws, or close friends who provide care. In cases of ADRD, it is very important to find out whether there are advance directives with someone appointed to have a durable power of attorney (DPOA) that allows that person to assist with health care and/or financial decisions. The DPOA person need not be the care partner but is the primary contact who health professionals may speak with when providing services.

The Challenges of Families Providing Care

While most ADRDs last 7 to 10 years, about one third needs care longer than 10 years. As the

disease progresses, the person experiences declining cognition, including memory changes, language loss, loss of judgment, and inability to abstract or make decisions in addition to a slow, insidious functional decline. In addition to these losses, personality symptoms appear including increasing self-absorption, changes in insight, decreased inhibitions, declining ability to tolerate stimulus, and decreased ability to plan. Confounding care are noncognitive behavioral symptoms including confusion, behavioral outbursts, and/or periods of social inaccessibility resulting in nighttime agitation, wandering, aggression, and/or psychosis.

In early and moderate dementia, all symptoms are expressed in changes of behavior. The family is confronted with a person who is increasingly self-absorbed, has "hair trigger" emotions, anger, and limited insight into their losses. People with ADRD are often aware of their illness but not of the impact of the losses. An example of this is when the person must give up driving. Despite multiple accidents and mishaps, the person may stubbornly insist on driving and become angry or combative when the family takes the keys.

Due to functional decline, people with dementia need increasing assistance from care partners; however, the noncognitive behavioral symptoms may render such persons resistant by, for example, refusing to surrender the car, checkbook, or guns or refusing to bathe. As a general rule, families begin the dementia journey as consultants, progress to giving direction, then supervising before taking on hands-on care provision 24 hours daily. The symptoms of dementia progress unevenly; thus, family must continually reassess how much assistance must be provided throughout each day.

Use of Evidence in Providing Care

There are thousands of studies of families providing care ranging from descriptions of mood states to educational programs, support systems, respite programs, and interventions such as music, art, and exercise to enhance communications between care partners (see Table 1). For clinicians, there are several issues that must be considered when evaluating evidence-based care suggestions. First, one must be concerned with the "fit" of the intervention with the stage of illness and culture of the people served. An example might be trying to

Table I   Family Research in Alzheimer's Disease

Type of Study	Variables Measured	Findings
Development of assessments of mood states of caregivers including burden, depression, mastery, worrying, and positive experiences	New assessment scales to be used to evaluate the efficacy of programs and the effects (on the care partner) of specific interventions for person with dementia	Establish psychometric properties for scales and usefulness in measuring mood states.
Description/evaluation of care partner responses to caring for the person in various situations and cultures	Measures of burden, depression, and positive mood states	Caring for a person with dementia is stressful, can produce physical and mental burden and depression, yet caregivers find positive aspects to care. Caregivers of non-Anglo cultures perceive the stress of caregiving differently than Anglo cultures.
Evaluation of specific activities for the person with dementia including day programs, music, individualized activity programs, reminiscence, exercise, music, group therapy, cognitive exercises, and the arts	Mood and noncognitive symptoms Level of function, short and long term Mental status tests Caregiver burden and response, satisfaction Need for psychotropic medications	While not all findings are statistically significant, most activity programs demonstrate some efficacy over the status quo.
Evaluation of educational and support programs for caregivers	Measures of burden, depression, mood state, mastery, potential for endurance, and positive mood states	Educational programs and structured support programs decrease burden and improve sense of mastery.

teach creative writing to people who are dependent in basic activities of daily living.

A second concern is the measures used to determine efficacy of interventions. Some studies evaluate psychosocial interventions by evaluating their effect on daily function or effect on mental status tests, yet the affective effects may be overlooked. Finally, the methods (what was done during the study) should be scrutinized to evaluate whether other unintentional things were done that might have affected the outcome.

Family Care by Stage

Because dementing illnesses last so long and change dramatically over time, it is important to discuss care by stage. Few professionals agree on a standardized staging system. While some clinicians rely on a subjective observation of "mild, moderate, and severe," others use the Global Deterioration Scale (GDS) and its functional cousin, the Functional Assessment Staging Scale (FAST). For this entry, ADRD is condensed into four stages:

1. Mild cognitive impairment (MCI)—Mild memory loss, no functional loss

2. Confused—Loss of instrumental activities of daily living (ADL), unless living alone

3. Dementia—Loss of basic ADLs

4. Advanced dementia—No purposeful mobility

Mild Cognitive Impairment Stage

The person with mild cognitive impairment (MCI) is aware of changes in their mental abilities, most often their recent memory. The person may experience problems with depression and shifts in the balance of power in marital and family relationships. If employed, there may be problems at work. During MCI it is important to help families understand change in cognitive function. Families must be encouraged to accomplish six things during this stage:

1. Discuss the symptoms with the person in order to clarify and agree to move on to the second task.

2. Seek a baseline diagnosis.

3. Obtain treatment (if indicated) with cholinesterase inhibitors and/or for depression.

4. Assist with preparation of advance directives including standby durable powers of attorney (DPOA) for health care, finances, and mental health (where applicable). If employed, pursue disability status.

5. Practice health promotion measures that have shown to slow progression of the disease, including exercise, socialization, intellectual activity, a low-fat diet, and controlling comorbidities.

6. Decide when to disclose the illness to employers, family, and friends.

In some areas, there are support groups, classes, and activities for people with MCI. Check with the Alzheimer's Association or nearest Area Agency on Aging for local availability of support groups for MCI. There are online and published resources for MCI including *Alzheimer's From the Inside Out,* written by a man with Alzheimer's disease to help families to understand the lived experience of dementia (Taylor, 2006).

Confused Stage

The confused stage starts when the person needs supervision or assistance to perform complex activities. Early in this stage, the family and person struggle with issues of autonomy versus protection. Employment, managing financial responsibilities, driving, shopping, and being able to manage the telephone in a crisis are typical early losses. It is the family's responsibility to monitor and stop the person from driving and managing money, often a source of conflict both with the person with dementia and between caring family members and friends.

As the disease progresses, additional problems arise: loss of reading comprehension, loss of sense of risk or danger, and loss of time sense. Families compensate by introducing clocks, calendars, and lists to prompt the person for activities such as medications, yet these are soon useless, and the person must rely on family for cuing. The losses also lead to problems of taking medications appropriately as the person may forget to take them, misread directions, or take multiple doses due to forgetting the previous dose. Families must supervise medication administration as soon as functional losses become apparent. The loss of sense of risk increases the difficulty in convincing the person of the hazards of continued driving or dealing with unscrupulous individuals.

At this stage, the person with dementia is generally aware of losses. Family members recognize the changes, each at different points in the illness. This precipitates conflicts about changes and how to proceed with care. All begin the grieving process at their own pace and style. Support groups and educational programs can help members clarify the person's needs and basic techniques of care. There are four nationally recognized evidence-based dementia educational models: the Savvy Caregiver program, the REACH program, the progressively lowered stress threshold model, and the New York University Spouse Caregiver Intervention. Each provides families with disease information and the basics of providing care.

The family's responsibilities expand in the confused stage to include the following tasks:

1. Acknowledge losses and seek formal diagnosis with a plan for care and additional disease information.

2. Identify selves as care partners.

3. Finalize legal and financial plans including advance directives.

4. Develop respite mechanisms, including increased help in the home, outings with friends, or early participation in early dementia day programming.

5. Develop understanding of what triggers noncognitive behavioral symptoms and how to structure the environment.

6. Modify communication techniques to avoid confrontations.

7. Provide emotional support to allay fear of abandonment.

8. Stop the patient from driving. Remove guns, power tools, and hazards.

9. Plan daily schedule and activities.

10. Arrange care for people with dementia who live alone.

11. Assume increased responsibility for paying bills, managing money, shopping, household chores, cooking, social outings, and administering medications.

12. Inform family members who are not directly involved with day-to-day issues and plan to inform friends.

None of the above are easily accomplished. The family may deny the illness, fearing abandonment by friends. The person with dementia often complains his or her family is controlling. There may be role reversal.

With the exception of support groups and educational programs, there are few services or providers who can help families. Some chapters of support charities, such as the Alzheimer's Association and the Alzheimer's Foundation, have care managers to assist families on an intermittent basis.

Families develop conflicts among members, especially when separated by distance. Old conflicts resurface. Visiting or distant family members may not recognize the changes in the person, attributing it to dysfunction between the care partner and person with dementia. The visiting or distant family member may have little information regarding dementia and may insist the person keep driving, advise nontraditional measures for care, or be concerned about stigma or preservation of assets and inheritances. Research indicates the conflicts emerge as a way for members to develop enough energy to cope; interventions to resolve conflicts led to family failure as there was no coping energy.

Dementia Stage

The dementia stage begins when the person forgets, refuses, or is less proficient at personal cleanliness. Losses progress to include oral care, grooming, selecting clothing, dressing, bowel and bladder control, and the ability to walk and program basic purposeful movements, such as trying to sit or stand on command. The functional losses are compounded by the presence of noncognitive symptoms, declines in verbal communications, and altered visual perception. Family members are not consistently recognized and the primary care partner may seem like a pleasant stranger. Television, mirror images, and family pictures may seem alive to the person and are often mistaken for hallucinations.

The person withdraws from social activities and fatigues rapidly when in groups, becoming upset when her or his care partner is out of sight yet is increasingly resistant to intimacy. The person experiences retrogenesis, a reversal of developmental stages in coping and understanding. In the dementia stage, the family is overwhelmed with the sheer volume of things to be done including the following:

1. Provide increased personal care and activities to an often resistant person.

2. Modify communication patterns to increase effectiveness.

3. Maintain responsibility for the "patient story," informing all new acquaintances of the person's history.

4. Coordinate health care and services balanced with the need to maintain care the recipient will trust.

5. Deal with "cling" and the care partner's need for basic privacy.

6. Provide cuing and monitor for safety 24 hours daily.

7. Watch for behavioral triggers (fatigue, change of routine, inappropriate stimuli, excessive demand, lack of activities, family conflict, illness, pain, and/or medication reaction) and structure the person's environment to control it for them.

8. Monitor the person's health.

9. Administer all medications.

10. Communicate with family and health providers.

11. Begin to consider long-term care needs including evaluating care sites.

12. Care for your own health and depression.

13. Find social support from extended family, professionals, and laypersons.

14. Grieve.

There are increased conflicts with the care recipient over personal care: desire for autonomy and increased self-absorption. The person with dementia often refuses services, lacking insight into the breadth and challenges of the caregiving role. Care partners must continually reevaluate their abilities to provide 24-hours-daily care. Family may not recognize the extent of the caregiving burden, and interactions may be complicated by the following:

1. Feelings of stigma

2. Need for privacy

3. Differing stages of family understanding and grief and/or denial

4. Beliefs about long-term care use and what the person with dementia needs

5. Competing demands with other responsibilities

6. Long-standing conflicts that existed before the illness and power struggles within the family

7. Conflicts about treatment decisions and "medical breakthroughs"

8. Concerns about preservation of assets

Advanced Dementia Stage

Advanced dementia typically begins when the person requires total assistance for all basic activities of daily living, such as dressing, bathing, mobility, toileting, and feeding. The demands on family are more than one person can handle. Round-the-clock responsibilities increase as the diurnal rhythms reverse. All needs are unspoken. The person with advanced dementia can no longer walk and is at high risk for falls when trying to stand. There is a loss of bowel and bladder continence and difficulty executing conscious body movements.

Severe losses in memory and verbal communication hinder the person's abilities to interpret and interact with others, producing anxiety and withdrawal. Families learn that while traditional communication methods have been altered, the person with advanced dementia still communicates with those who try alternative methods to maximize communication. The role of the family in the end stage includes the following:

1. Learn to focus on facial expressions, vocalizations, body language, and overall reactions to a situation to gain insight as to how the person is feeling.

2. Identify unmet needs through behavioral cues, including hunger, pain, and elimination.

3. Provide all aspects of personal care including monitoring for and treating decubiti, contractures, joint spasticity, and positioning.

4. Take steps to maintain physical and emotional comfort using anticipatory measures such as round-the-clock scheduled pain medication.

5. Provide a balance of sensory stimulating and calming experiences to prevent boredom, provide pleasurable distraction, and enhance quality of life.

6. Reinforce choices from advance directives.

7. Request hospice services.

8. Coordinate care services, even if placed in a residential setting.

9. Advocate for the person, helping others to realize that the person is "still in there."

10. Update others on the person's condition.

11. Provide frequent rest opportunities and monitor nighttime wakening.

12. Provide careful, almost continual feeding and monitor for aspiration.

Researchers have found that failure to recognize ADRD as terminal illnesses contributes to more aggressive and burdensome treatments and underutilization of hospice care during the last days of life. Advance directives address treatment decisions, such as CPR, hospitalizations, respirators, antibiotics, and feeding tubes. In cases where a person has not clarified such choices, it is essential that the proxy decision maker serve as an advocate to honor and communicate the values and wishes believed to represent what the person would prefer regarding comfort measures and aggressive medical interventions. The Alzheimer's Association provides a free brochure called *End-of-Life Decisions: Honoring the Wishes of the Person With Alzheimer's Disease* that provides detailed information concerning health care decisions and hospice care.

Medicare offers a hospice benefit for dementia. In addition to providing direct patient services at home by an interdisciplinary team, hospice care also offers valuable education, social support, and predeath bereavement services for family and friends and care partners. Studies suggest hospice services improve pain management, avoid hospitalizations, and receive high ratings in service satisfaction by family members. Criteria for hospice eligibility are as follows:

1. Life expectancy of 6 months or less or

2. Inability of person to walk, bathe, or dress independently

3. Urinary and fecal incontinence

4. Unstable comorbid conditions, such as heart disease, cancer, or renal failure

5. Person speaks few intelligible words

6. One or more of the following has occurred in the past year:

   ○ Aspiration pneumonia
   ○ Upper urinary tract infection
   ○ Recurring fever after antibiotics
   ○ Pressure ulcers (multiple stages 3–4)
   ○ Weight loss
   ○ Cerebral vascular accident (stroke)

The above criteria are not empirically based and were created for Alzheimer's-type dementia. Clinicians need to recognize variability that exists in end-of-life presentations depending on the type of dementia and comorbidities when considering a referral to hospice care.

Desired Outcomes

Because the disease lasts so long, is eventually terminal, and has no meaningful medical treatment to slow or cure it, the desired outcomes are general. For the person with ADRD, the outcomes focus on maintaining a high quality of life through the following:

1. The person will be safe and personal care needs met.

2. Disease progress will be minimized though the use of daily exercise, Mediterranean-type diet, adequate rest, social and cognitively stimulating activities, promotion of health, use of dementia-specific medications as appropriate, and maintaining good management of concomitant medical conditions.

3. Functional capabilities will be maintained and assisted or supported as appropriate.

4. The person will communicate verbally and nonverbally to express unmet needs.

5. Noncognitive behavioral symptoms and medications will be minimized through prevention and good management.

6. The person will be free from pain.

7. The person will be assessed and treated for concomitant conditions and complications of immobility.

8. The person's end of life care preferences will be met, as appropriate by the DPOA empowered to make decision.

The outcomes for the family focus on physical well-being, maintenance of mental health, and preserving family integrity are the following:

1. Family will be free of stress-related illnesses and depression.

2. Family will assess and intervene when safety is threatened while protecting themselves from injury.

3. Family will express satisfaction with their role.

4. Family will seek help and information appropriately.

5. Family will inform others of the person's condition and how they might contribute to the care.

6. Family will recognize when they can no longer provide direct physical care and either find help or seek an institutional setting that will meet the person's needs.

7. The family will remain intact.

Treatments

The vast majority of treatment for ADRD is environmental: adjusting the environment to be simpler and quieter while adapting activities to meet the person's declining cognition. Evidence on use of nonpharmacological measures including exercise and activities is shown to be far more effective than use of medications.

Relevance to Family Health Care

Alzheimer's disease and related disorders affect the entire family. The 5.3 million people today with ADRD are cared for primarily by 10.9 million families. The number of cases of ADRD in 40 years is projected to increase from 11 to 16 million people. It is estimated that one in three families have a member with ADRD. If the family caregiving network collapses due to death or illness of the care partner and/or family disintegration, the cost to society will be staggering in terms of Medicaid dollars to pay for long-term care. Continued research is needed to support this fragile system.

*Geri R. Hall, Maribeth Gallagher,
and Jan Dougherty*

See also Advance Directives and the Family; Alzheimer's Disease: Caregiver Burden; Caregiving: Partners/ Spouses; Alzheimer's Disease and Communication; Case Management for Chronic Illness/Disability and the Family; Decision Making in the Context of Health and Illness; Elder Neglect and the Family; Elder Physical Abuse and the Family; Elder Sexual Abuse and the Family; Palliative Care and the Family

Further Readings

Alzheimer's Association. (2010). *Alzheimer's facts and figures*. Retrieved March 5, 2010, from http://www.alz. org/documents_custom/report_alzfactsfigures2010.pdf

Alzheimer's Association. (2006). *End-of-life decisions: Honoring the wishes of the person with Alzheimer's disease*. Retrieved January 17, 2009, from http:// www.alz.org/national/documents/brochure_ endoflifedecisions.pdf

Hall, G. (2008). *The progressively lowered stress threshold (PLST) model*. Rosalyn Carter Institute. Retrieved January 20, 2009, from http://www.raisingbar. eventwebsitebuilder.com/f/Hall_Power_Point_1.pdf

Reisberg, B. (1988). Functional assessment staging (FAST). *Psychopharmacology Bulletin, 24*, 653–659.

Taylor, R. (2006). *Alzheimer's from the inside out*. Baltimore: Health Professions Press.

Websites

Alzheimer's Association: http://www.alz.org
Alzheimer's Foundation: http://www.alzfdn.org

ALZHEIMER'S DISEASE: CAREGIVER BURDEN

Caregiver burden in the context of Alzheimer's disease (AD) and other forms of dementia refers to both (a) the objective sets of tasks or forms of assistance provided by family member's to ill people and (b) the feelings of psychological strain that are often associated with providing such care. Caregiver burden can result in negative health outcomes, including the development or exacerbation of physical and/or psychiatric symptoms and illnesses in the family member(s) providing care. This entry describes these family caregivers and their role in providing care and assistance to persons with AD. Health outcomes linked to caregiver burden are discussed, and selected assessment instruments are identified to guide health care providers when evaluating various aspects of family AD caregiver burden. A range of interventions that have been developed and tested for family AD caregivers is discussed. The entry concludes with a brief discussion of health care policy issues relevant to the health and wellness of these important individuals, so they can continue to provide long-term care and assistance to a growing population of older adults with AD.

The Alzheimer's Disease Family Caregiver

Of the 22.4 million households providing long-term care and support to a family member, 5 million provide care to someone with AD. A family member, such as a spouse or adult child, who has assumed unpaid responsibility for an individual with AD is defined as a family AD caregiver. Typically, family AD caregiving responsibilities fall on the shoulders of one family member (the primary caregiver), but some AD caregivers receive assistance from other family members or friends.

Most often, the spouse becomes the primary family caregiver for an individual with AD. Because AD usually affects older adults, spousal caregivers are generally older adults with their own health concerns. Daughters are the second largest group of AD caregivers, with daughters-in-law being the third largest group. Many daughter and daughter-in-law caregivers are married and raising children of their own. These AD caregivers are described as members of the *sandwich generation* since they juggle multiple roles and responsibilities. Sons typically assist with the financial, legal, and business aspects of caregiving. Grandchildren often assist with supervising the older adult with AD.

The Alzheimer's Disease Family Caregiver Role

AD is associated with progressive cognitive (thinking) and behavioral impairments. Family caregivers must contend with their loved one's worsening memory, judgment, functional abilities, and language skills. The affected individual may experience changes in personality and lose the ability to recognize family members or perform activities of daily living. In addition to physical caregiving tasks, such as bathing and dressing, changes in the affected family member's mental abilities, personality, and need for supervision and assistance can be difficult for family caregivers to cope with on an emotional level. The course of the illness is unpredictable, as is the speed of decline. The only certainty is that the progressive nature of AD will lead to an increasing need for supportive care and eventual death of the affected person.

Early in the disease process, family caregivers must come to terms with the diagnosis of dementia, anticipate their family member's future care needs, and ensure the health and safety of their family member while also providing emotional support to that person. Spouses who may have long provided daily support and advice to their spouses may experience significant emotional upheaval as their "normal" care for their loved ones transitions to what is required in the face of increasing limitations in thinking and functional abilities.

The progressive impairment of cognition and physical function and the development of a wide range of behavioral symptoms constitute daily burdens for family caregivers. Caregivers must be increasingly vigilant since persons with AD may wander from home or inadvertently injure themselves. Efforts to assist the affected family member often lead to increasing levels of confusion and agitation in the person when family caregivers lack the necessary skills to manage these behaviors effectively. In the final stages of the disease, persons with AD need to be fed, bathed, toileted, and dressed. Eventually, providing care to a person with AD becomes an all-consuming, 24-hour-a-day job. AD caregiving responsibilities vary and may extend for 10 years or longer.

In addition to the stress or burden of providing physical and emotional care to the person with AD, family caregivers describe adverse effects on a number of other facets of their lives. The progressive and inexorable losses typically associated with AD and the emotional and behavioral changes that accompany these losses can result in a total transformation of the affected person. This transformation, in turn, reshapes the caregiver's relationship with the affected person such that the patterns of actions and interactions are sharply different from those that previously existed. Even though the affected person's physical appearance may not have dramatically changed, caregivers describe grieving the loss of their family members with AD since they no longer recognize them as the person they once knew.

As the disease progresses and time demands become increasingly intense, caregivers have less time for their own interests and social activities. Friends may visit less frequently because of the behavioral problems exhibited by the person with AD, and caregivers become increasingly reluctant to take the family member to public places where they may become confused or upset. Finally, a caregiver's financial resources may become seriously strained as respite care or home care services may be too expensive for individuals on fixed incomes or trying to raise a family. These caregiving strains can have a cumulative impact over time. Thus, the notion of caregiver burden—referring to both the objective tasks that must be performed as well as psychological responses to caregiving and the family member with AD—has emerged as an important concept in AD caregiver research. These elements of objective and subjective caregiver burden are also important to health care professionals: To the extent that these professionals can carefully identify the areas of burden that are greatest for a given family caregiver, they may be better able to assist the caregiver in locating appropriate health care resources to ensure that they are able to continue providing long-term care to the family member with AD in the loving environment of their home.

Health Outcomes of the Alzheimer's Disease Family Caregiver Role

The burdens associated with caring for a family member with AD at home can have detrimental effects on the physical or emotional health of family caregivers. These physical and psychological effects of family AD caregiving can persist even beyond the death of the person with AD. Caregivers' psychological health appears to be the most strongly affected. Studies consistently report high levels of depressive and anxiety symptoms among family AD caregivers, with 40% to 70% having clinically significant levels of depressive symptoms and from 30% to 40% meeting diagnostic criteria for major depression. Depressed AD caregivers often have coexisting anxiety disorders, substance abuse or dependence, and chronic disease. Family caregivers use more prescription medications for mental health problems, such as depression or anxiety, than family caregivers of persons with other conditions.

The impact of providing care to a family member with AD can also lead to increased physical health care needs for the family caregiver. Studies show that family AD caregivers have more physical health symptoms, a higher incidence of chronic health conditions, high rates of self-reported poor health, increased blood pressure and insulin levels, impaired immune function, and may be at risk for cardiovascular disease. Researchers also know that elderly (aged 66–96 years) family caregivers (all types, not just AD caregivers) who experience high levels of burden have a 63% higher mortality rate than noncaregivers of the same age. Many caregivers have physical health problems that began before their caregiving responsibilities, and given these responsibilities, they become less likely to see the need for health care for themselves or to engage in preventive health behaviors, including physical exams, routine cancer screening, and immunizations. In fact, the primary reason given by spousal family AD caregivers for institutionalization of their spouses is feeling "worn out," with one third reporting ill health as a consequence of the caregiving role.

While AD caregiving is a burdensome role with negative health outcomes for many family caregivers, benefits can include feeling positive about being able to help a disabled spouse or feeling appreciated by the family member with AD. Family caregivers who have strong support systems and effective coping skills may be able to manage the burden of caring for a family member with AD with the help of others. Family caregivers who have few breaks from caregiving responsibilities and/or have preexisting illnesses may be more vulnerable to the physical and emotional effects of the AD caregiving role.

Caregiver Burden Assessment

There are numerous instruments available to measure both the objective elements of caregiving, including events and activities that describe the daily caregiving experience, and the subjective component of serving as a family caregiver or the emotional reactions of the caregiver, such as worry and frustration. The instruments vary in how long they take to complete and whether they were developed specifically for AD caregiving or for caregiving in general. While these instruments are not without flaws, they all have contributed in some way to assessing various components of caregiver burden. Such measures are useful for health care providers who want to assess the extent to which caregivers are experiencing difficulties in managing their caregiving responsibilities. Results might provide a springboard for discussion of other caregiving options, either within the family or through other institutional sources. These measures are also particularly helpful when health care professionals want to measure the effects of interventions designed to alleviate burden levels in family AD caregivers.

By far the most widely used measure of caregiver burden is the Burden Interview (BI), developed by Steven Zarit and colleagues. The BI is a brief measure that examines burden associated with functional and behavioral impairments in the home care situation. While not dementia-specific, it focuses on both the positive and negative affective response of the caregiver to the consequences of caregiving. Major strengths of the BI include the broad scope of stimuli or situations considered to be sources of AD caregiver burden and its ease of administration. It can be used with both spousal and adult child caregivers.

Rhonda Montgomery and colleagues were the first to clearly distinguish between objective and subjective aspects of family caregiver burden. Their measure is also not specific to AD but includes general items measuring changes or constraints on the caregiver's lifestyle (to tap objective burden) and items measuring attitudes and emotional responses of the caregiver (to evaluate subjective burden). Because many items in this measure were derived from the BI, it has similar strengths and weaknesses. Later, Peter Vitaliano and associates developed a Screen for Caregiver Burden (SCB) to assess objective and subjective burden specifically among spousal caregivers of persons with AD. It was designed to be used either as a substitute for, or as a complement to, more lengthy approaches of measuring caregiver burden. The SCB measures several domains of caregiver burden including the affected person's behaviors, disruptions in family and social life, and caregiver affective responses. The SCB yields two scores: objective burden and subjective burden.

The Caregiver Reactions Assessment (CRA) was developed by Barbara Given and associates to measure four general areas specific to AD caregiver burden: (1) finances, (2) positive and negative reactions, (3) impact on schedule, and (4) perceived impact on caregiver health. The CRA is based on a model whereby caregiver characteristics (such as health and relationships) and patient characteristics (such as memory problems, communication issues, and need for assistance) combine to determine involvement in care (activities of daily living), which in turn lead to caregiver reactions. The CRA conceptualized family members' responses to their caregiving role as reactions rather than burdens in that these feelings may be both positive and negative and may vacillate over time. While not widely used, the CRA may be appropriate when health care professionals are interested in measuring changes in the AD caregiver's reaction to the caregiving situation over time.

Another popular measure of AD caregiver burden is the Caregiver Burden Inventory (CBI) developed by Mark Novak and Carol Guest. Concepts measured in the CBI include time-dependent burden, developmental burden, physical burden, social burden, and emotional burden. The CBI items include both affective response and task-related sources of caregiving burden. The CBI is a relatively short measure of caregiver burden that is a practical tool for assessing, responding to, and designing therapeutic interventions with family AD caregivers.

Interventions for Alzheimer's Disease Family Caregivers

A number of interventions have been designed to help caregivers with the burdens of providing care to a family member with AD. Educational interventions typically provide information about dementia and resources for dementia care (such as day care and respite programs) in one session. Dementia-specific therapies are targeted primarily to the person with AD and include cognitive stimulation and reminiscence, or life review, to provide meaningful activities for the person. Supportive interventions for caregivers typically last longer than one session and include telephone or Internet-based information and opportunities for discussion about dementia, dementia caregiving, and community-based resources for dementia care. Although these interventions may be useful in some respects, research has consistently shown them to have little to no effect on burden or depression levels of family caregivers.

In contrast, interventions focused more specifically on the AD family caregiver's use of coping strategies and behavioral management techniques have more consistently positive effects. Over a series of multiple sessions, coping strategies taught and reinforced in caregiver interventions include stress management, problem appraisal, and problem solving techniques, in combination with education about dementia. Behavioral management interventions also involve multiple sessions aimed at teaching behavioral management theory and specific techniques for managing problematic behaviors in the family member with AD. Both coping interventions and behavioral management interventions appear to reduce caregiver depression, but only behavioral management interventions positively impact burden levels. These interventions' beneficial effects appear to be strongest when they are delivered individually rather than in group setting.

Information and problem-solving needs of caregivers evolve over time, just as the disease progresses in the affected family member. Thus, multicomponent AD caregiver interventions must meet the specific needs of the family caregiver(s) at various stages of the disease (AD). Early in family members' caregiving career, it is important to provide information about AD and community-based resources, ways to respond to new and complex caregiving demands, and a variety of practical caregiving strategies. This approach may also be an optimal time to strengthen caregivers' coping resources, as they learn about their loved one's condition. Later in the disease process, the focus of the intervention may need to shift to instruction and support in the use of behavioral management techniques while continuing to strengthen their coping resources and locate health care resources. The intervention is individualized to meet the caregiving demands of the family member with AD at specific points along the disease trajectory and can be used by anyone involved in that person's care. It is important to teach family caregivers how to interpret the emotional and behavioral cues of persons with AD and to understand the sequence of events that often lead to burdensome behavioral responses, such as arguing, irritability, or wandering, in the person with AD.

Health Care Policy

As longevity is extended and the size of the older adult population increases, there will be a corresponding increase in the number of people suffering from AD. People with AD require high levels of caregiving, and society benefits greatly from the willingness and ability of family caregivers to provide such care. The value of this unpaid labor force of family members is estimated to be at least $306 billion annually, nearly double the combined costs of home health care ($43 billion) and nursing home care ($115 billion). Although family AD caregiving may help to contain health care costs to society, it often results in serious costs to the primary caregivers. These costs to their physical, emotional, social, and financial health and well-being were enumerated earlier.

The nature of caregiving will become more complex as increasing life expectancies tax the ability of family members to provide care. The challenge for public health systems is to design and implement evidence-based interventions to address specific needs of individual family caregivers at different points along the AD caregiving trajectory. From a public health perspective, it is important to establish a well-developed and coordinated system of community and institutional long-term care, along with a reasonable payment method that combines public and private funding. Many families wish to retain caregiving responsibilities, and they can do so when taught behavioral management techniques and effective coping mechanisms combined with the temporary respite provided through day care programs and in-home health care services. Such programs must also address the transportation challenges experienced by persons with AD and their caregivers. Linking AD caregivers to available health care and community services can promote health and well-being in these families.

Linda Garand and Mary Amanda Dew

See also Aging and Shifting Roles in Families; Alzheimer's Disease: An Overview of Family Issues in; Alzheimer's Disease and Communication; Caregiving: Elderly; Caregiving: Partners/Spouses; Elder Care Options for Families: Long-Term Care

Further Readings

Administration on Aging. (2007). *A profile of older Americans: 2005.* Washington, DC: Department of Health and Human Services.

Alzheimer's Association. (2007). *Alzheimer's Disease Facts and Figures, 2007.* Retrieved January 20, 2009, from http://www.alz.org/nationoal/document/Report_2007FatsAndFigures.pdf

DiBartolo, M. C. (2000). Caregiver burden: Instruments, challenges, and nursing implications for individuals with Alzheimer's disease and their caregivers. *Journal of Gerontological Nursing 26*(6), 46–53.

Family Caregiver Alliance. (2006a). *Caregiver assessment: Principles, guidelines and strategies for change* (Report from a National Consensus Development Conference: Vol. 1). San Francisco: Author.

Family Caregiver Alliance (2006b). *Caregiver health.* Retrieved January 20, 2009, from http://caregiver.org/caregiver/jsp/conent_node.jsp?nodeid=1822#13#13

National Institute on Aging. (2008, September). *Alzheimer's disease: Unraveling the mystery* (NIH Publication No. 08–3782). Washington, DC: U.S. Department of Health and Human Services.

Schulz, R. (2000). *Handbook on dementia caregiving.* New York: Springer.

Selwood, A., Johnston, J., Katona, C., Lyketsos, C., & Livingston, G. (2007). Systematic review of the effect of psychological interventions on family caregivers of people with dementia. *Journal of Affective Disorders, 101*(1), 75–89.

ALZHEIMER'S DISEASE AND COMMUNICATION

Alzheimer's disease (AD) is a progressive neurodegenerative disorder affecting over 5 million Americans according to statistics provided by the Alzheimer's Association for the year 2009. Characterized by memory loss, personality changes, behavioral symptoms, and functional decline, AD is a deficit in communication at all levels ranging from cellular to interpersonal communications. A simplified discussion of the concepts follows.

Cellular Communication

A key concept in AD, *cellular communication* occurs when stimulated neurons produce an electrical charge that travels across synapses by producing neurotransmitters. Each neuron has up to 15,000 synapses. In AD, researchers see the presence of *neurofibrillary tangles*, which are abnormal collections of tau protein found within neurons. Tau normally binds to microtubules, which support the neuron. In AD, tau disengages and forms large clumps. This causes the microtubules to disintegrate, and the neuron transport system collapses. This situation produces a loss of connections within cells and cell death—probably related to both beta-amyloid and tau accumulations. In addition, there is a loss of neurotransmitters that enable communication between cells. Neurons that are unconnected and unable to communicate with other neurons die. Thus, the loss of communications within and between the cells causes cell death.

Amyloid plaques, large insoluble deposits of beta-amyloid, are found between neurons along with proteins and cell remnants. Initially thought to be the cause of the disease, it is now understood that amyloid plaques are the result.

The decreased production of the neurotransmitter acetylcholine is the basis for the Food and Drug Administration (FDA)–approved medications for treatment, the acetyl cholinesterase inhibitors (AChI). These drugs delay the destruction of the acetylcholine at the synapse, enhancing intercellular communication. The three commonly used medications are donepezil, rivastigmine, and galantamine. A second class of medication has been approved, an N-methyl-D-aspartate (NMDA) receptor agonist, memantine. It targets the neurotransmitter glutamate that is associated with learning and memory. Abnormal glutamatergic activity in the brain may lead to AD symptoms; thus, the NMDA receptor agonist may help to improve abnormal glutamatergic activity.

Systemic Communication

Alzheimer's disease progresses by destroying selective neurons in large numbers thus impairing communication, cell metabolism, and repair. As the neurons degenerate, more synapses (points of communication) are destroyed and brain structures begin to atrophy, impairing function.

Initially, the disease attacks the hippocampus, which is associated with sorting and organizing memory storage to other areas of the brain. The entorhinal cortex and related structures are also involved. These structures are involved with pre-memory processing (familiarity), sense of direction, and a neural map of the spatial environment.

The AD spreads to the amygdala that governs emotion and fear and triggers responses to danger (fight or flight responses). Visual perception is affected quite early including the ability to recognize familiar places and faces. These structures are associated with the limbic system, which is associated with emotion and motivation. With additional progression, association of environmental stimuli, language, and reasoning functions are also affected. AD finally spreads throughout the brain causing diffuse atrophy (wasting).

Electroencephalography (EEG) shows slowing of the electrical activity in the brain. This slows processing of information and of formulating communication. By impairing processing speed, people with dementia are unable to keep up with the cadence of a normal conversation.

As the damage occurs to each of the brain's systems, the ability for structures to communicate with each other is progressively impaired. Moreover, the damaged structures limit memory, ability to perceive environmental stimuli, behavioral responses, and the ability to understand and process language thereby limiting the person's ability to receive information from the environment and communicate her or his thoughts with others. Impaired intersystem communication also leads to progressively impaired coping.

The alterations in ability to perceive produce intolerance to competing stimuli and noise. People with these deficits become highly sensitive to noise and will fatigue easily as uncoding stimuli takes more cognitive effort than in nondemented people.

People with AD are progressively isolated from the world around them, yet the process is not fully understood as even in the last days of life moments of lucidity can occur where a person may express understanding of his or her circumstances. A primary concern in providing care to people with AD is maintaining communication through nonverbal means and spoken language.

Interpersonal Communication

Human communication is a complex interaction between individuals and others in their environment. The person must be able to sense and perceive in order to receive messages, comprehend and remember information, and respond through nonverbal and verbal language. Language is a set of agreed-on symbols to express thoughts, objects, and concepts to the particular group. Humans must be able to send and receive these symbols to be fully understood.

Verbal Language

There are two primary language centers in the brain, Wernicke's and Broca's areas. Wernicke's area is in the posterior section of the superior temporal gyrus, encircling the auditory cortex in the dominant hemisphere. It is responsible for language comprehension and for speech that has a natural-sounding rhythm and a relatively normal syntax. Wernicke's area is affected quite early in AD.

Affected later in AD, Broca's area is located in the posterior inferior frontal gyrus and is associated with language production. Damage to the Broca's area results in halting, nonfluent aphasia. People who exhibit difficulty in the production of speech (agrammatical speech production) also show inability to use nonverbal (syntactic) information, such

as speed, gestures, voice intensity, rhythm, and facial expressions to determine the meaning of sentences. Broca's area plays a role in interpreting motor action of others and speech-related gestures. As a person loses verbal language abilities from damage to the Wernicke's and Broca's areas, one might wonder if nonverbal languages, such as sign language, might be effective. Newer studies of Broca's area would suggest this is not possible. At this writing, there are no studies of users of sign language with AD or studies of using computers to facilitate communication.

Clinical presentation of loss of language varies enormously between people with AD; however, it often follows a trajectory. It should be assumed by the practitioner that there is overlapping of losses especially as the disease worsens, including the following:

1. Loss of ability to write (this does not include signing one's name, which is automatic and does not require thought)

2. Loss of reading comprehension

3. Loss of ability to use spoken language coupled with declines in auditory comprehension and processing speed

As verbal abilities fade, the person is increasingly dependent on nonverbal communication; thus, body language, intonation, and gestures made by others are increasingly important but may also be impaired.

Evidence-Based Practice

Problems with communication are often expressed and studied in terms of "acting out" behaviors and linked with *uncertainty* as the person and caregiver struggle to understand each other. The caregiver's attribution of the person's pleasure and displeasure to the response and the caregiver's actual response to it lead to uncertainty. People with AD are more likely to respond positively when the caregiver's speech is perceived to have positive psychosocial qualities including demonstrating respect, caring, not controlling, and indicating feelings that the person was competent.

While there is limited research on effective communication techniques for people with AD, the promising programs assume a restorative rather than behavioral approach, such as use of interdisciplinary teams, speech pathologists, or occupational therapy. Most approaches focus on training caregivers in communications techniques.

Enhancing communication in the person with AD using psychotherapeutic techniques has been tried. After conducting six sessions of psychodynamic interpersonal therapy, however, there was no overall improvement in people with AD.

Increasing concern is being raised about the construct of *personhood* in the literature, both as a framework for future research and in the writings of people with dementia. All too often, communication issues are addressed as if all responses are the result of neuropathology. Richard Taylor especially invites readers to regard him and other people with dementia as "whole people." A few programs have been developed to enhance communications for people with dementia:

1. A Memory Club for people with early stage dementia and their caregivers provides information and support and opportunities to discuss issues regarding AD. The program has been "rated positively" by participants.

2. A program that uses storytelling to encourage people with dementia to take part in associated conversations helps them to remember and talk of past experiences. Increases in spontaneous conversation and group interactions were noted.

3. A program was designed to help elders with early stage dementia, and their caregivers participate in five aspects of decision making: information received, being listened to, expressing an opinion, time allowed for reflection on the decisions, and the possibility of changing their mind.

4. An evidence-based program for speech and language pathologists has been developed to evaluate the person with dementia and then train the caregiver afterward.

Most specialized training programs for communication skills work only with caregivers. There are still discussions regarding whether or not to disclose the diagnosis to the person with AD. Until there is generalized agreement about whether people with dementia have insight into their conditions,

communications programs that include the person with AD will be limited. More studies are needed of dyadic interventions where caregivers and people with dementia work together to bridge communication gaps.

Best Practices

While there are few evidence-based communication interventions, there is broad agreement on best practices. The following is a compilation of suggestions for successful communication with people affected by AD:

- Approach the person with respect. Avoid "talking down" to them or using childlike voice tones.
- Avoid complex explanations.
- Discuss the illness with the person, reinforcing that AD is "just an illness."
- Ask yes and no questions.
- Touching a hand may enhance attention as well as demonstrate you care.
- Gently leading and cuing the person through the (verbal) request may be helpful.
- Showing and touching physical objects and/or pictures may help with memory and assist with conversation.
- Exercise forgiveness and don't correct mistakes.
- Tense situations can be defused by agreeing with the person who has AD, apologizing to the person with AD when he or she is upset, and pleading ignorance.
- Always begin communication by eliminating any possible background distractions, such as the TV or background conversations.
- Make sure glasses, hearing aids (with batteries), and dentures are in place.
- Allow ample time for the person to communicate. Try not to finish the person's sentences.
- Remain still and with the person while you are talking. This will make it easier to follow the conversation and demonstrates a sincere empathetic approach.
- When the person has difficulty finding a word, consider asking him or her to explain in a different way or try giving clues. You may also try to guess the meaning and ask if you are correct.
- Ask the person to show you what he or she is referring to. Pointing to an object may also help get the message across.

- Try to avoid allowing your own stress and exasperation to show as it will increase tension.
- Incorporate information in your conversation that tells the person where he or she is, what is happening around him or her, and who the person is with and use descriptors with names to enhance security and orientation.

Geri R. Hall

See also Alzheimer's Disease: An Overview of Family Issues in; Alzheimer's Disease: Caregiver Burden; Elder Neglect and the Family; Elder Physical Abuse and the Family; Elder Sexual Abuse and the Family; Palliative Care and the Family

Further Readings

Alzheimer's Association (2007). *FDA-approved treatments for Alzheimer's disease*. Retrieved January 20, 2009, from www.alz.org/national/documents/topicsheet_treatments.pdf

O'Conner, D., Phinney, A., Smith, A., Small, J., Purves, B., Perry, J., et al. (2007). Personhood in dementia care: Developing a research agenda to broaden the vision. *Dementia, 6*(1), 121–142.

Petersen, R. (Ed.). (2002). *Mayo Clinic on Alzheimer's disease*. Philadelphia: Mason Crest.

Taylor, R. (2006). *Alzheimer's from the inside out*. New York: Health Professions Press.

U.S. Department of Health and Human Services. (2007). *Journey to discovery: 2005–2006 Progress report on Alzheimer's disease*. Washington, DC: Author.

Websites

Alzheimer's Association: http://www.alz.org
Alzheimer's Foundation: http://www.alzfdn.org

AMERICAN INDIAN FAMILIES: PERSPECTIVES OF HEALTH

The definition of *family health* has been somewhat elusive in the nursing, medical, and health literature. Sharon Denham offered one definition of family health as a set of complex interactions across members and households within their social context. Here, family health is described as it pertains to American Indian members, households, and social contexts. Heterogeneous tribes make up the United States' American Indian population, making it important to note that there will be no *one* American Indian perspective on what family health means. However, there are many shared beliefs, practices, and cultural threads connecting perspectives across tribes, regions, and nationally. For most of America's tribes, a concept of family health will be largely familiar. Many tribes embrace a perspective called variously, *Mitakuye Oyasin,* or "we are all related." This traditional perspective binds members to a duty to care for and watch out for each other, including the health of its members. This looking out for one another is especially important in one's extended family. Not only are households loosely related and crossed, but they are also often assigned to formal clan groups with attendant roles and responsibilities for one another. A larger proportion of American Indians care for their families' health outside of formal care than do those in the dominant culture.

Definitions

American Indian

American Indian is the term used in this entry to describe those persons who are members of federally recognized U.S. tribes indigenous to North America. There are 564 of these tribes in the United States on 310 reservations in the 48 contiguous states and Alaska according to the Bureau of Indian Affairs. American Indians are politically distinct from all other U.S. citizens in that they hold dual citizenship, tribal and United States. This adds another layer to their realities, or social context, as members of sovereign nations within a nation.

Family

American Indians have traditionally been described as collectivist societies where it is the group that is more important than the individuals making up the group. Extended family is the basic social, economic, and organizing unit for American Indians. This creates an interdependence including care for all those within the unit. In contrast, an individualist perspective is embraced by the West making family health a relatively new term and innovative way of seeing health. In the United States, there are certain shared concepts of family along with legal definitions as to next of kin and degrees of relationship. Under these rules, in the health setting, usually one's parents, spouse, sibling, or adult children may enter into decisions and plans for care of the patient. In Indian country, U.S. definitions and lines of family may not coincide in scope, concept, roles, or relationships with those generally held. Even with the dominant culture's evolving inclusive understanding of a family and by extension family health, this evolution may still not be inclusive of certain American Indian concepts and beliefs. For example, the ancestors may play into the family concept on a regular basis. There are referrals to grandfather rocks and ancestor uncles who appear to members as deer or references to grandmother moon. Each of these concepts is an example that has been accepted by various tribes. And these "family" members are teachers, protectors, and providers to the individual, family, or clan.

Lines of Relationship

The lines of relationship within an American Indian family vary greatly by region and tribe. In one Southwest pueblo, for example, there are seven possible lines of relationship. A patient may belong to the mother's clan, be a child of the father's clan, have a ceremonial father and relationship to his kiva—the medicine and priest society on the pueblo, have relationship to his or her spouse's family, and belong to adoptive and nonrelative categories. Often, nonblood relatives may be addressed as brother, grandfather, and so forth. These are culturally defined relations. These variations on the family must be taken into account when dealing with the family as patient. The clans themselves can have family determinations, such as the elder brother clan or the younger brother, and so on. In some tribes, it is the paternal aunt, for example, who makes health decisions for the patient. This relative is not considered a legal next of kin in the West. Understanding who the decision makers are, who the family is, and what social roles are is

critical to keeping the pattern of health for the individual and her or his lines of kinship intact.

Family Involvement

Many American Indian societies are matrilineal and many are *matrilocal,* meaning they are located intentionally around a mother's home. The "old mother" will be in the central home with daughters and family around that home. Some tribes have members bury the umbilical cords of the newborns around the mother's house to keep them near, or some tribes members' may keep them in medicine pouches around their necks. Frequently, grandparents are the teachers, caretakers, and family companions to the young children in their extended family. In Navajo tradition, good thinking and forward thinking are taught by the elder women, where family, relatives, and neighbors live in harmony. Often, elder women are in charge of the prayers and spiritual life deemed integral to family health and well-being. Men are often involved in the wider society's spiritual and health well-being.

Family Health

Health in American Indian reality is more than physical or even mental in scope. Generally, health itself is a holistic concept incorporating spiritual, physical, mental, and emotional domains. Therefore, health for the individual necessarily includes family in maintaining multiple-domain health. Missteps across those relationships themselves can have repercussions on who becomes ill, why they become ill, and what must be done to achieve health again. That is, breaks with family members may be a cause of illness. Traditional American Indians may not necessarily believe in germ theory or genetics as roots of illnesses. Therefore, ceremony, prayer, and community "doings" all represent healing that families engage in to get or keep the affected person well. Examples of healing ceremonies may be sweats, specific dances, and "wiping of the tears" ceremonies. Among Navajo, it is incumbent on the family members to keep a positive attitude for and about the affected individual and to use traditional ways and help from relatives. But collectivism can potentially negatively impact health. For example, if a woman has the role of feeding her extended family but she has diabetes, she may not change the household food for the many to accommodate only herself.

Family health for American Indian societies is a known concept but diverges from the mainstream in what is considered to be family and their expectations, roles, and behaviors, which may be largely unfamiliar to the West. Understanding tribally specific social context is imperative to work with the families and clans in achieving optimum health.

Margaret P. Moss

See also African American Families: Perspectives of Health; Hispanic/Latino Families: Perspectives of Health; Cultural Attitudes Toward Help Seeking and Beliefs About Illness in Families

Further Readings

Benally, K. R. (1999). Thinking good: The teachings of Navajo grandmothers. In M. M. Schweitzer (Ed.), *American Indian grandmothers*. Albuquerque: University of New Mexico Press.

Caresse, J., & Rhodes, L. (2000). Bridging cultural differences in medical practice: The case of discussing negative information with Navajo patients. *Journal of General Internal Medicine, 15*(2), 92–96.

Cushing, F. H. (1985). Outlines of Zuni creation myths. In D. H. Thomas (Ed.), *The ethnographic American Southwest: A sourcebook—Southwestern society in myth, clan, and kinship*. New York: Garland.

Deloria, V., & Lytle, C. M. (1998). *The nations within: The past and future of American Indian sovereignty*. Austin: University of Texas Press.

Denham, S. (1999). Part 1: The definition and practice of family health. *Journal of Family Nursing, 5*(2), 133–159.

Ross, A., Ross, A. C., & Emaciyapi, E. (1989). *Mitakuye Oyasin: We are all related*. Denver, CO: Wicóni Wasté.

AMERICANS WITH DISABILITIES ACT AND THE FAMILY

The Americans with Disabilities Act (ADA) was signed into law in 1990 by President George H. Bush to ensure individuals with disabilities had the same rights and protections as individuals without disabilities. One or more family members who have a disability may experience discrimination or violations of their civil rights because of their disability. For example, an individual with a disability who applies for a job may not be hired even though highly qualified for the position—based on the employer's concern for the costs of instituting workplace accommodations. In another situation, an adult daughter may be unable to take her elderly mother shopping at a local retail store—aisles are not wide enough to accommodate her mother's wheelchair. A young mother is unable to take her child who uses a wheelchair to the park—it is not accessible. As these situations illustrate, individuals with disabilities and their families in community, workplace, and educational settings encounter challenges that require legal protections to eliminate potential or actual discrimination and/or infringements of their civil rights.

The Americans with Disabilities Act extended rights and protections to individuals with disabilities for the purpose of creating "a clear and comprehensive national mandate for the elimination of discrimination against individuals with disabilities." According to the ADA, a person is considered to have a disability based on one of three criteria: (1) currently has a physical or mental impairment that significantly impairs one or more major life activities, (2) has a past history of having had an impairment affecting one or more major life activities, or (3) is regarded as having an impairment affecting one or more major life activities although the individual does not consider himself or herself as having a disability, such as with a person who has Type 1 diabetes, cancer, or moderate to severe burns.

This law builds on the previous legislation of the Rehabilitation Act of 1972 and the Civil Rights Act of 1964 to extend additional civil rights and protections to individuals with disabilities as formerly these rights were limited in their full application of civil rights and protections. The ADA extends federal civil rights protections to individuals with disabilities specified in the five titles of the law: employment (Title I), public services and transportation (Title II), public accommodations (Title III), telecommunications (Title IV), and miscellaneous (Title V).

The ADA Title I provisions related to employment address issues pertaining to the hiring, wages, job benefits, on-the-job training, and social activities sponsored by employers. These regulations apply to private employers with 15 or more employees, state and local governments, and labor unions. Title II transportation provisions pertain to the publicly funded bus and rail transportation. Public accommodation (Title III) refers to physical accessibility of buildings as seen with the use of ramps, altered height of counters and restroom facilities, the use of doors, and use of levers rather than knobs. Additionally, businesses are expected to provide auxiliary aids as needed, such as large-print materials or assistance with selection of retail items. Physical accessibility is predicated on the philosophy of "universal design" meaning "designing all products, buildings, and exterior spaces to be usable by all people to the greatest extent possible." Telecommunication provisions (Title IV) refer to the use of relay services for individuals with hearing and speech limitations and the use of close captioning on television. Finally, other provisions (Title V) of the ADA refer to administrative and legal issues, such as attorney fees and federal outreach and disability exceptions, such as illegal drug use.

In 2008, President George W. Bush signed into law the Americans with Disabilities Act Amendments Act (ADAAA) of 2008. The purpose of the ADAAA was to clarify and extend legal protections that had been adversely affected by Supreme Court rulings between 1999 and 2002. The definition of major life functions was expanded to include other activities that the Equal Employment Opportunity Commission (EEOC) had not previously recognized such as communicating and reading and bodily functions associated with body systems (i.e., gastrointestinal, endocrine, and respiratory). If a disabling condition that is temporary or in remission substantially limits major life activity, it is now eligible. An individual whose disability is considered as being merely "regarded as" is not entitled to accommodations.

The ADA provides individuals with disabilities with needed protections and civil rights to ensure that they are not excluded from participating fully in the community, enjoy the same rights as individuals without disabilities, and are not discriminated against based on their disability. It is important for families to be aware of the rights and protections afforded to individuals with disabilities by the ADA, so when circumstances arise, they can be effective advocates for their family member, especially for one who is dependent, such as a child or elderly parent. Childbearing and childrearing families have significant responsibilities to teach their children about their rights and protections guaranteed by the ADA. Additionally, it is important for families to teach their children self-advocacy skills, so they learn to become their own advocates for the rights and protections of the ADA and other federal, state, and municipal laws and regulations.

Cecily Lynn Betz

See also Adult Child With Disability: Planning for by Parents; Adult With Disability Living at Home; Adults With Childhood-Acquired Conditions; Chronic Health Problems and Interventions for the Midlife Family; Developmental Transitions in Families; Disabilities and Family Management; Educating the Family Regarding Serious Mental Illness; Families Experiencing Chronic Physical and Mental Health Conditions

Further Readings

American Cancer Society. (2008). *Cancer patients are not protected under the ADA*. Retrieved February 5, 2009, from http://csn.cancer.org/node/162685

Moore, E. (2008). *Changes to the Americans with Disabilities Act*. Retrieved February 9, 2009, from http://autoimmunedisease.suite101.com/article.cfm/changes_to_the_american_with_disabilities_act

U.S. Equal Employment Opportunity Commission. (2008). *Notice concerning the Americans with Disabilities Act (ADA) Amendments Act of 2008*. Retrieved February 9, 2009, from http://www.eeoc.gov/ada/amendments_notice.html

Websites

Center for Universal Design, College of Design, North Carolina State University: http://www.design.ncsu.edu/cud

Center for an Accessible Society: http://www.accessiblesociety.org/topics/universaldesign

U.S. Department of Justice, *Americans with Disabilities Act of 1990, as amended*: http://www.ada.gov/pubs/ada.htm

ANIMAL-ASSISTED THERAPY AND THE FAMILY

The purpose of this entry is to emphasize how animal-assisted therapy (AAT) within health care organizations can contribute to the health and happiness of people with disabilities and illness. A review of the literature highlights how AAT can intervene to treat a variety of diseases, disabilities, and conditions across the life span and an overview of risk management concerns are addressed. Recommendations from the literature on AAT interventions are also highlighted.

Human–Animal Bond

The relationship between humans and animals dates back thousands of years. According to the American Veterinary Medical Association, in 2007, more than half of all households in the United States had a pet, with more than 43 million people owning dogs and more than 37 million people owning cats. According to the University of Minnesota, the relationships humans had with their animals 100 years ago were different. Dogs were used to herd, pull, hunt, track, or protect. Cats were kept outside to hunt and kill rodents. Today, dogs and cats are kept in the house with 60% to 80% of our pets sleeping in our bedrooms, mostly on our beds—indicating the closeness of our relationships with our animals. Families with pets report higher domestic happiness, are more affectionate, and spend more time with each other than families without pets. Animals are part of our families. Therefore, it is not a surprise that animals can help us heal wounds and enhance our health.

History of Animal-Assisted Therapy

In 1964, Boris Levinson, an American child psychiatrist, coined the term *pet therapy*, which is considered the birth of AAT. Levinson, entirely by accident, discovered that a nonverbal child he was treating improved his ability to communicate when his dog was present during therapy sessions. Early researchers included Sam and Elizabeth Corson, who expanded on Levinson's work with adolescents and adults at Ohio State University Psychiatric Hospital. Their project involved patients choosing a dog from the local kennel to interact with each day. The outcomes included an increase in the patient's self-respect and socialization with staff. In 1981, an Australian nursing home staff introduced a former guide dog to the residents. The residents demonstrated increased happiness, alertness, responsiveness, and optimism. In addition, residents who interacted with the dogs showed more self-reliance, responsibility, and motivation. Today, AAT is being conducted in a variety of settings including hospitals, rehabilitation facilities, schools, prisons, senior centers, and nursing homes.

What Is Animal-Assisted Therapy?

The Delta Society, a nonprofit organization that brings together individuals who love animals and people, defines AAT as a goal-directed intervention in which an animal that meets specific criteria is an integral part of the treatment process. AAT is directed and/or delivered by a health or human service professional with specialized expertise and within the scope of practice of his or her profession. AAT is designed to promote improvement in human physical, social, emotional, and/or cognitive functioning. AAT is provided in a variety of settings and may be group or individual in nature. The Delta Society recommends that the term *pet therapy* be avoided pointing out that the term was used decades ago to refer to animal behavior training programs and therefore is misleading.

Therapy animals, as described by the Delta Society, are animals that have been trained to provide people with contact to animals. The therapy animals are typically the personal pets of their handlers and work with their handlers to provide services to others. The Delta Society, Therapy Dogs Incorporated, and Therapy Dogs International are three organizations that train and register therapy animals. In addition, the Delta Society licenses instructors and team evaluators.

Risk Management Concerns

Animal-assisted therapy is an intervention that holds promise but is not without risk, both to the participants and the animals. Families and health care staff need to be aware of the following physical and psychological risks and be prepared to deal with them:

Injury. Animals may bite and scratch, and people may trip over animals underfoot.

Infectious disease. Proper veterinary care is a must; there are several zoonotic diseases that can be a problem if one is not careful.

Sanitation. Individuals may be allergic to pet dander, and animals may have "accidents" on the floor.

Abuse of the animal. Individuals could take out feelings of aggression on the animal.

Perceived rejection. Feelings of worthlessness may emerge if an animal ignores the person who wishes to interact with it and seems to be paying attention to everyone else.

Isolation. It is possible for people to further isolate themselves if they are able to spend unlimited time with the animals in their home or a health care facility. They may do so at the expense of relationships with people.

These are some of the concerns one may face when introducing AAT into health care facilities. However, risks can be minimized by focusing on prevention and planning. A thoughtful approach to risk management will help ensure a safe and enjoyable experience for all who participate.

Animal-Assisted Therapy Interventions

Animal-assisted therapy interventions are designed to assist the person in need and are often broken down into three categories: contact with animals, caring for animals, and animals used with psychotherapy. Intervention strategies are chosen depending on the specific needs of each individual.

Examples of interventions that concentrate on contact with animals might be visits with an AAT team (registered therapy animal and handler) implemented to increase the quality of one's life, decrease loneliness, or provide a sense of overall well-being. Another intervention strategy—designed by Linda Buettner, a recreational therapist—is called Pet Encounters. Pet Encounters is a holistic intervention for people with disabilities intended to work on the physical, cognitive,

and emotional domains. Participants move from station to station working with an AAT team at each station. The stations include walking, fetching, grooming, and thinking. The walking station encourages physical activity, agility, mobility, leg strength, and balance. The fetching station promotes upper extremity strength, balance, and fine motor skills. The grooming station centers on nurturing; the participants brush and groom the animals. In addition, feelings-based questions are asked about the animal–human bond. Lastly, the thinking station is designed for those participants who need cognitive stimulation. A series of stimulating questions are asked, tailored to the level of functioning. Participants can move from station to station or focus in one area, depending on the individual's needs. Moreover, caring for animals can be part of an organization's therapeutic milieu. Animals can live in health care agency units and be cared for by individuals. Another approach for residential agencies might be using farm animals and developing interventions facilitating their care. Additionally, animals can be used in conjunction with psychotherapy. The presence of a therapy animal may encourage communication through the animal and calm the participant.

Entrance Criteria for AAT Interventions

Prior to admittance into AAT interventions, participants typically need to have an interest in or past history with animals, for example, current or past pet ownership. In addition, the participants must have no known allergies or fears of the animal and no known infectious diseases. Lastly, the participant must be interested in the AAT intervention.

Components of the Interventions

Janelle Nimer and Brad Lundahl in a meta-analysis pointed out that dogs are most often used in AAT and have the best results; no studies involving cats were found. AAT interventions are best delivered in a one-to-one manner when dealing with emotional issues. People with disabilities benefited more from AAT on medical outcomes, while nondisabled participants did better on behavioral or well-being outcomes. When comparing AAT interventions with other interventions, the

AAT interventions decrease behavior problems and increase pleasure and social interaction. Little is known about the optimal frequency and the cumulative effect of AAT over time.

Animal-Assisted Therapy and Children

In a review of the literature in AAT and health care settings, researchers found that young children consistently benefited from AAT across all outcomes that were studied, perhaps because animals are nonjudgmental, empathetic, and nurturing thus resulting in an acceptance of the animal's presence. Autistic children's behaviors improved, immigrant children learned language more rapidly, aggression was reduced, stress decreased, self-esteem increased, reading improved, and motor skills were enhanced simply from the presence of dogs in a classroom.

In addition, hospital-based AAT programs have reported an accepting attitude toward hospitalization and an increase in well-being. For children hospitalized due to cancer, AAT programs contributed to a decrease in distress, adaption to hospitalization, and an increase in well-being for both the children and parents. These results could be due to the animals' capacity to listen without judgment, making the atmosphere safe to experience and express emotions.

Animal-Assisted Therapy and Survivors of Trauma

The effects of trauma can enter into all aspects of a person's life, affecting one's sense of self, one's work, one's relationships—the effects are everywhere. Trauma could stem from childhood sexual assault, physical or emotional abuse, accidents, war, and/or disasters. An animal's empathetic and nurturing disposition can detect human need for unconditional love and acceptance. Entering into a relationship with an animal within the context of a family pet or within an organized intervention within a health care agency can help facilitate trust and help an individual cope with his or her pain. Relationships heal, including the relationships we have with animals. Within the context of the family, animals can provide unconditional love and acceptance, security, empathy, nonthreatening touch, and joy for individuals healing from

the effects of trauma. Therefore, for those with affinity toward animals, engaging in a relationship with an animal might be beneficial when healing from trauma.

Animal-Assisted Therapy and Healthy Lifestyles

Developing a healthy lifestyle is a concern for children, adolescents, and adults in the United States. This concern is based on high rates of sedentary lifestyles and the risks these lifestyles have on developing chronic diseases and health conditions, including coronary heart disease, Type 2 diabetes, some cancers, high blood pressure, and cholesterol. An ingredient in developing a healthier lifestyle includes increasing physical activity.

Dogs love to walk and play; they take great joy in these activities and in turn provide their human handlers with similar reactions. People enjoy their antics, and instead of considering physical activity a chore, joyfully engage. Kushner and colleagues suggest that another role animals play in our health is social support, which is an important predictor for adaption and maintenance of changing behavior. Animals support, encourage, and motivate us toward health.

Research suggests that people with dogs report a more active lifestyle by spending time walking and playing with their pets. For those people who are in need of physical activity, participating in AAT programs within the health care setting in activities such as playing fetch and walking can provide the motivation to increase mobility, balance, agility, upper extremity strength, and motor skills.

Animal-Assisted Therapy and Communication

Animals can serve as a catalyst for communication, as discovered by Levinson, the pioneer of AAT. However, despite this historical significance, little research has been conducted on the effects of AAT on communication. Animals can help people recall memories, socialize, and communicate with others. They stimulate laughter, provide entertainment, and help us express ourselves in meaningful ways. Additionally, animals serve as empathetic listeners. Many people experience communication as risky; they may encounter rejection, criticism, judgment, and unsolicited advice. By comparison, animals listen attentively, giving empathetic non-verbal feedback.

Specific speech and communication disorders, such as hearing disorders and deafness, cleft lip and palate, developmental disabilities, brain injury, and stroke, may make it difficult to communicate. Specific AAT interventions within health care settings can be designed to encourage communication. For example, playing fetch, grooming, walking, or engaging in cognitive activities provides many opportunities to talk, share stories, recall memories, gain confidence, and express feelings, serving as a catalyst for communication.

Animal-Assisted Therapy and Pain

Pain needs to be managed in a way that is medically sound and agreeable to the patient and doctor. While analgesics are the mainstay of many pain management regimes, use of complementary or alternative approaches to care, such as AAT within health care settings, may permit fewer analgesics or lower doses of them thereby reducing side effects and minimizing the risks of adverse events that arise from multiple medications, an important consideration for many who live with comorbid illnesses requiring different types of medications. AAT can provide social support and relaxation and encourage the engagement in meaningful activity thus assisting people in coping with or diverting their attention from their pain.

Animal-Assisted Therapy and Aging

AAT interventions in health care settings for older adults are growing in popularity. For older adults for whom animals have been an important part of their families and their lives, this bond can be used to improve the physical, emotional, cognitive, and social skills needed to enhance one's quality of life. In addition, AAT can assist with conditions, diseases, and disabilities experienced by elders, such as stroke, dementia, arthritis, osteoporosis, heart disease, cancer, and Type 2 diabetes.

Physical health can be enhanced by walking and playing with an animal. Being able to connect with and bond to an animal, express feelings with an animal, and nurture an animal helps older adults connect emotionally thus decreasing feelings of loneliness or alienation.

Cognitive activities promote the stimulation of the brain through problem solving, decision making, attention, and judgment. Connecting to animals increases the ability to socialize with residents, visitors, staff, and family members. The presence of animals increases social behaviors, such as smiles, laughs, touches, and talking.

Nancy Edwards and Alan Beck developed an innovative AAT program by installing an aquarium in a facility dining hall to increase nutrition and socialization. The presence of the aquarium increased alertness and attentiveness and calmed residents thus increasing food intake. In addition, the residents were observed to be more social during mealtimes. Other outcomes from AAT interventions include the decrease in depression, apathy, and agitation and an increase in engagement; all affect the quality of life.

Animal-Assisted Therapy: Training the Family Pet

Training one's family pet to be a therapy animal can be a rewarding experience. While each organization that trains therapy animals has different criteria there are some basic requirements. Most organizations require that the animal be a year old, have updated rabies and vaccinations, fecal check, and yearly examinations. The animals must be in good health and well groomed—nails trimmed and filed. Generally, the animals have basic obedience skills and will undergo training and evaluation before being registered as therapy animals. Some organizations have a minimal age for membership, for example, Therapy Dogs Inc. requires that the member be 16 years old. Membership in an organization includes liability insurance, a big benefit for people interested in this type of work. Delta Society registers dogs, cats, rabbits, and horses, while Therapy Dogs Inc. and Therapy Dogs International register only dogs.

Conclusion

This entry provides an overview of how AAT within health care organizations can intervene to assist family members in need. Research has provided evidence that supports the use of animals to treat a variety of conditions, diseases, and disabilities. Documentation supports the use of AAT to increase health and happiness, promoting well-being. Risk management concerns demonstrate the need for prevention and planning. Sharing one's joy of animals with others by training and registering one's animal to provide therapy is one way to bond with one's animal, be of service to others, and connect with the community in meaningful ways. Animals have the power to heal; the human–animal bond is real and contributes to satisfaction with life.

Case Scenario: AAT in Action

Mrs. White was an 80-year-old widow, a wife, mother, grandmother, and great-grandmother. She was a nurse for 30 years at the local hospital. She was diagnosed with dementia of the Alzheimer's type 10 years ago and was admitted to a memory impaired unit approximately 2 years ago. She was in the later stages of the disease and was experiencing depression and lacked motivation, staying in her room talking to her stuffed animals. Mrs. White's family informed the staff that she loved animals, sharing that the family used to breed golden retrievers. This resulted in enrolling Mrs. White into the AAT program. The small group met every day from 9:00 a.m. to 10:00 a.m. The early morning time frame was chosen to stimulate and engage Mrs. White first thing in the morning. The intervention consisted of talking to the dog, the handler, and others in the group; engaging in activities with the dog; feeding the dog treats and water; and grooming the dog. At times, the participants would walk the dog. After 3 weeks of daily intervention, Mrs. White's depression began to decrease; she talked often about the dogs to staff members, residents, and her family. She began to participate in other activities that were meaningful, like the weekly cooking group. The AAT was able to meet her needs for engagement in meaningful activity, connection, nurturance, and love.

Nancy Ellen Richeson

See also Adolescent Counseling; Autism Spectrum Disorder and the Family; Disabilities and Family Management; Education of Recreational Therapy Providers in Family Health; Long-Term Care Facilities for Families

Further Readings

Buettner, L. (2009). Pet encounters: Animal-assisted therapy for frail older adults. *Activity Directors' Quarterly, 9*(2), 29–45.

Connor, K. (2001). Animal-assisted therapy: An in-depth look. *Dimensions of Critical Care Nursing, 20,* 20–27.

Gagnon, J., Bouchard, F., Landry, M., Belles-Isles, M., Fortier, M., & Fillion, L. (2004). Implementing a hospital-based animal therapy program for children with cancer: A descriptive study. *Canadian Oncology Nursing Journal, 14*(1), 217–230.

Kushner, R. F., Blatner, D. J., Jewell, D. E., & Rudloff, K. (2006). The PPET study: People and pets exercising together. *Obesity, 14*(10), 1762–1770.

Martin, F., & Farnum, J. (2002). Animal-assisted therapy for children with pervasive developmental disorders. *Western Journal of Nursing Research, 24*(6), 657–670.

Websites

Delta Society: https://www.deltasociety.org

Therapy Dogs Incorporated: http://www.therapydogs.com

Therapy Dogs International: http://www.tdi-dog.org

ANOREXIA AND FAMILY DYNAMICS

Families have been viewed as an essential part of the etiology and treatment of anorexia nervosa, an eating disorder where the person is obsessed with food and being thin, since its initial descriptions in the medical literature. Early literature on family relationships and anorexia nervosa suggested that families caused and perpetuated the disorder. Consistent with the view of families as iatrogenic, or at the least not central to therapy, the focus on treatment development focused on individual therapy (e.g., the work of Hilde Bruch) and self-empowerment models for almost 100 years. However, in the 1970s, the seminal work of Salvador Minuchin and colleagues introduced the model of structural family therapy, which focused on the family as potentially helpful in resolving anorexia nervosa. Therapy was particularly focused on strengthening boundaries between family generations (e.g., strengthening the parent relationship) by disrupting maladaptive communication patterns between members. Minuchin described the family processes in anorexia nervosa families in the context of what he called *psychosomatic families*. Family processes in psychosomatic families were characterized as enmeshed, conflict avoidant, overprotective, and rigid. Although the theoretical concept of psychosomatic families has not been supported by research, the perspective that family interventions were potentially helpful to their children with eating disorders was a fundamental shift from viewing families as pathological, causative mechanisms in the development of anorexia nervosa. Open trials and case reports of Minuchin and colleagues' work indicated that family therapy was effective, particularly compared to previous evaluations of individual approaches. Other models of family therapy emerged following Minuchin's initial work, most notably the Milan Systems group and the work of Mara Selvinni-Palazzoli and narrative family therapy. Taken together, these clinical studies established family therapy as a useful therapy for children and adolescents suffering from anorexia nervosa.

Early family therapy work focused on extension of techniques for use with eating disorder– specific symptoms and modifications that have come to be identified as systems, strategic, structural, and narrative models. While therapists from each of these therapeutic modalities reported on the successful or unsuccessful use of these techniques with eating disorders, research evaluating family characteristics and factors has failed to support the notion that specific familial patterns or identifying features lead to anorexia nervosa. In the absence of a specific theoretical rationale for interventions, more general family functioning models have been employed that have increasingly adopted a nonpathologizing stance with an eye toward improving resources and coping within the family. In addition, while family therapy models for anorexia nervosa treatment exist, few have been subjected to more rigorous scientific evaluation through randomized clinical trials—the majority of information about treatment response coming from case reports and open clinical trials. Although these open trials indicated positive response, recovery rates were far from optimal, and they combined individual, family, and hospitalization programs, which might have been used simultaneously, clouding evaluation of outcome. These observations by Christopher

Dare and colleagues led to the development of an increasingly behavioral approach to family work, integrated with structural, strategic, systemic, and narrative components.

The model of family therapy developed by Dare and colleagues has been manualized as family-based therapy (FBT). FBT was developed to empower parents to directly assist in weight restoration of their child with anorexia nervosa. Approaching parents as critical members of a treatment team, empowering them to develop their own skills in shaping eating and weight-related behaviors and to enforce appropriate nutrition was a significant departure from previous models of therapy. In addition to these factors, FBT employs an agnostic theoretical stance to the causal nature of the disorder: Parents are not viewed as causal or pathological, although they are viewed as having a responsibility to assist their child in overcoming the illness. This nonjudging, nonpathologizing, and active stance seeks to motivate parents to take charge of their child's illness while continuing to reinforce developmentally appropriate behaviors that might remain untouched by the illness.

FBT has been evaluated in several research studies and is the only therapy to have been evaluated in randomized clinical trials. Initial studies comparing FBT to individual therapy found that FBT was specifically useful for patients who had fewer than 3 years of illness and were under 18 years of age with gains maintained at 5-year follow-up. A form of family therapy very similar to FBT (conjoint) was compared to individual psychotherapy: Although both the individual and family groups showed positive outcome, FBT was effective at inducing more rapid and sustained weight gain with no difference in measures of psychological change. Other studies were performed to evaluate separated versus conjoint FBT. In separated family therapy, the affected child and parents were seen separately, by the same therapist, with individual sessions providing supportive therapy and parent sessions empowering parents as in the conjoint version of FBT. Results indicated that families with greater levels of criticism benefited from a separated family therapy approach. A dose study of FBT showed that, in general, 10 sessions of FBT provided over 6 months was comparable to 20 sessions of FBT provided over 12 months. However, nonintact families and an affected child with higher levels of obsessive and compulsive features did better in a longer FBT dosing schedule. Improvements were maintained at 4-year open follow-up with no additional benefit detected from having had the higher dose of FBT.

Although FBT is the most systematically evaluated treatment for anorexia nervosa, the treatment studies conducted to date are not definitive because of small sample sizes and other methodological limitations. Nonetheless, it appears families play an important role in helping adolescents with anorexia nervosa recover from their illness. Little data supports a particular familial pathological process for causing or maintaining anorexia nervosa.

James Lock and Kathleen Fitzpatrick

See also Bulimia and Family Dynamics; Family Therapy; Nutrition and Nutrition Promotion for Families; Obesity, Weight Problems, and Healthy Weight for Families; Outpatient Mental Health Care for Families; Parenting

Further Readings

Bulik, C. M., Berkman, N., Brownley, K. A., Sedway, J. A., & Lohr, K. N. (2007). Anorexia nervosa: a systematic review of randomized clinical trials. *International Journal of Eating Disorders, 40,* 310–320.

Bruch, H. (1973). *Eating disorders: Obesity, anorexia nervosa, and the person within.* New York: Basic Books.

Dare, C., & Eisler, I. (1997). Family therapy for anorexia nervosa. In D. M. Garner & P. Garfinkel (Eds.), *Handbook of treatment for eating disorders* (pp. 307–324). New York: Guilford.

Lock, J., Le Grange, D., Agras, W. S., & Dare, C. (2001). *Treatment manual for anorexia nervosa: A family-based approach.* New York: Guilford.

Minuchin, S., Rosman, B., & Baker, I. (1978). *Psychosomatic families: Anorexia nervosa in context.* Cambridge, MA: Harvard University Press.

ASIAN FAMILIES: PERSPECTIVES OF HEALTH

The terms *Asian* and *Asian American* refer to people having origins in any of the original peoples of the Far East, Southeast Asia, or the Indian subcontinent, for example, people from China, India, Japan, Cambodia, Korea, Pakistan, Thailand, and Vietnam. Asians represent a large—and the fastest-growing—ethnic group of the U.S. population. According to the 2000 U.S. Census, Asians constitute approximately 11.9 million or 4.2% of the U.S. population, an increase of 72% or 5 million people from 1990 to 2000. The Census Bureau projects that by 2050 the Asian population will grow to approximately 37.6 million and account for 9.3% of the nation's population. It is important to understand the perspectives and values of the Asian culture and how the cultural values intersect with health care among Asian families.

Asian populations are extremely heterogeneous and the most diverse groups in the United States. They represent nearly 50 countries and ethnic groups, each with distinct languages, cultures, traditions, histories, and politico-economic environments. Asians speak over 100 different languages and dialects. Asian groups differ in their reasons for immigration to and length of residence in the United States. The variation also extends to educational and socioeconomic levels. Following an introduction to the Asian population, this entry discusses the health concerns, perspectives and cultural values about health, and recommendations for promoting health among Asian Americans.

Asian Profile

Based on the 2000 Census, the five largest Asian groups in descending order are Chinese, Filipino, Asian Indian, Vietnamese, and Korean. Combined, they account for 80% of the Asian population. About one half of the Asian population live in the West. While Asians reside in every state, more than half of the population lives in just three states: California, New York, and Hawaii. The cities with the largest Asian populations are New York, Los Angeles, San Jose, San Francisco, and Honolulu. The majority of Asian Americans (69%) are foreign born, except for Japanese, of whom only 40% are foreign born compared with about 75% of Asian Indians, Vietnamese, Koreans, Pakistanis, and Thai. This situation may explain why the majority of Asian Americans (79%) aged 5 and over speak a language other than English at home, and about 40% speak English less than "very well."

Asian populations are more likely to be married and their households to be family households compared with the non-Hispanic white population. Language fluency among Asian groups varies. According to the 2007 Census, Vietnamese have the highest percentage, 62%, of persons 5 years and older who do not speak English at home; the rate is 50% among Chinese. In regard to educational attainment, Asians have a larger proportion of college graduates. Fifty percent of Asians in comparison to 28% of the total U.S. population have received a bachelor's degree. A larger proportion of Asians are employed in management, professional, and related occupations. With regard to economics, Asians households have the highest median incomes. In 2007, the median income of Asian households was $66,103, which is 120% higher than the median for non-Hispanic white households. However, 10% of Asians in comparison to 8.2% of non-Hispanic whites lived at the federally defined poverty level, while 2.2% of Asians compared to 1.3% of Caucasians lived on public assistance. The overall insurance coverage for Asian Americans was 83.9% compared to 89.6% of the non-Hispanic white population.

Because of their visible appearance of success in the education and socioeconomic spheres, Asian Americans have historically been portrayed as the *model minority,* an intelligent, hardworking, passive, and compliant group that enjoys a high socioeconomic status, are well educated, and are healthy. Many have the misconception that Asian Americans need no government or social services. The stereotype of the model minority is misleading and dangerous because it fails to recognize the enormous diversity within the Asian group, disguises the needs of Asian subgroups, and results in lack of action to address those needs and problems experienced by subgroups within the Asian population. Subsequently, it leads to health disparities and negative health outcomes for Asian populations.

Health Concerns

Asian Americans represent both extremes of health and socioeconomic indices. The U.S. Department of Health and Human Services Office of Minority Health notes the various health disparities among Asian American populations. Even though Asian women have the highest life expectancy of any ethnic group, Asian Americans experience multiple health disparities including higher rates of tuberculosis and hepatitis B than other racial or ethnic groups in the United States. Asian Americans account for over half of deaths resulting from chronic hepatitis B infection in the United States. Cancer and cardiovascular disease are two leading causes of death for Asian Americans. Although cancer is the leading cause of death for Asians in the United States, they have the lowest rate of hospice use. Also, Asian American women have the lowest cancer screenings rate and are usually diagnosed at a later stage compared to other racial or ethnic groups. Asian-Pacific Islander men are twice as likely to die from stomach cancer compared to the non-Hispanic white population, and Asian-Pacific Islander women are 2.6 times as likely to die from the same disease. Chinese have the higher rates of nasopharyngeal cancer than any other racial or ethnic group. The cervical cancer rate is five times higher among Vietnamese women than among Caucasian women. There is also a particularly high rate of coronary artery disease among Asian Indians. Asian Americans are at high risk for cancer, heart disease, stroke, unintentional injuries and accidents, and diabetes as well as chronic obstructive pulmonary disease, hepatitis B, HIV/AIDS, smoking, tuberculosis, and liver disease.

Asian Americans also experience disparities in mental health. For instance, Asian women aged 65 years and older have the highest suicide rate in the United States compared to women of other ethnic groups of the same age. Also, Asian American adolescent girls have the highest rates of depressive symptoms compared to girls of other racial or ethnic groups. In addition, the post-traumatic stress disorder (PTSD) rate is reported high among Southeast Asian refugees in the United States. Despite the prevalence of mental health problems, mental health services remain inadequate for Asian Americans.

In addition, Asian Americans contend with numerous factors that may threaten their health. For example, Asian Americans face cultural and language barriers that may discourage or prevent them from using health services available to them. Asian Americans with limited English proficiency may have difficulties understanding the American health care system and communicating with health care providers. Also, Asian Americans have perceptions and practices concerning health and illness that differ from those of the general population. They believe that their care providers do not understand their culture and values and have reported less confidence about their care compared to the overall population. Factors contributing to poor health outcomes also include infrequent medical visits due to the fear of deportation or stigma associated with certain conditions or illness, lack of social support, geographic proximity, and lack of health insurance.

Culture and Value on Health

Unlike Western culture in which individualism is supported, Asian cultures in general are more collectivist, which tends to downplay individual needs and place the goals and interests of the family or the group first. Shared or deferred decision making within families are norms. In contrast with the common American health care practice where the individual patient is the decision maker, many Asian families assign medical decision-making duties to a family member, such as an elder or the oldest son.

The strong sense of familial collectivism also places great emphasis on harmonious interpersonal relationships. Harmony must be preserved and conflict avoided as conflict may disrupt group relationships and bring shame to the family. For this reason, Asian families are less likely to question the decision made by a family member assuming the decision was made for the overall good of the family. They are also less likely to question the decisions made by physicians because of the respect for authority and avoidance of conflict. Asian families are usually uncomfortable about sharing bad news with the group because it may disrupt the harmony of the group. They may be more likely to endure pain or suffering (e.g., family violence or sexual abuse) and not seek help to avoid bringing inconvenience to others or shame to the family, also known as *saving face*. The feeling of shame or saving face presents a significant barrier for Asian families seeking help.

As a collectivist culture, Asian families place great reliance of health care on their social networks and community resources. The difference in perceptions on the etiology of disease may also lead the Asian family to seek initial care in the family or social unit, such as a traditional healer, acupuncturist, or member of the clergy rather than seeking help through the Western medicine system. Access to the Western medicine system and interaction with Western health care professionals may be delayed until emergency care is required.

Traditional beliefs about caring for parents and the elderly, or *filial piety,* are important concepts in Asian culture that promote group values over individual needs. People are obligated to take care of their parents and family when they are in old age or sick. They must respect the elders and ensure that they are well taken care of or the families feel great shame and guilt. This familial expectation for taking care of family members, or fulfilling the duty of filial piety, creates a dilemma if family cannot arrange home-based care for their elders and must place them in an institution. On the other hand, the strong sense of duty and responsibility for the family may result in reluctance or underutilization of professional services or support. This value also may result in a reluctance to tell the true diagnosis and prognosis to the elder patient as the family members have the obligation to protect their loves ones from hearing the bad news or making difficult decisions.

Health Outcome

Many demographic characters, socioeconomic, environmental, and cultural factors, have affected the health status of Asian Americans. To improve the quality of health of Asian Americans, the disparities must be eliminated. Healthy People 2010, the national prevention agenda which targets reducing disparities, has selected six health areas for emphasis. These six target areas were selected because they reflect areas of disparity that are known to affect multiple racial and ethnic minority groups. These key health areas are infant mortality, child and adult immunizations, diabetes, cardiovascular disease, HIV/AIDS, and cancer.

Intervention Programs

Health disparities are major public health problems threatening the health of Asian populations. There is a need for health advocates and providers, policymakers, and community leaders to work together to improve the health and well-being of Asian Americans. Recommendations regarding interventions to eliminate health disparities include public policies, community-based programs, and culturally appropriate care. The Asian and Pacific Islander American Health Forum (APIAHF), in a report on Asian American and Pacific Islander (AAPI) Health Agenda, listed five domains that must be addressed to attain optimal health and well-being for this population: (1) guaranteed affordable health care, (2) guaranteed access to high-quality care, (3) health equity, (4) healthy communities, (5) leadership, civic engagement, and political will. These areas should be considered in developing policies to eliminate racial and ethnic disparities.

Another approach for reducing or eliminating health disparities is through community effort. Studies have identified the inadequacy of community services to support Asian Americans. Community must be strengthened in its capacity to provide adequate health care services, and a community health program must be developed that promotes health. The Centers for Disease Control and Prevention (CDC) suggested three steps. First, join with others to promote community-wide health activities and campaigns. Second, form coalitions with civic, professional, religious, and education organizations to advocate health policies, programs, and services. Third, support policies that promote health care access for all.

Culturally appropriate care must be provided to reduce or eliminate health disparities. The primary recommendation for culturally competent care is for increased sensitivity of the health care providers. Education and training are two strategies that promote understanding and appreciation of Asian cultures. Health care providers must be aware of their own biases and assumption about Asians to establish rapport with them. They need to be open-minded and immerse themselves in Asian cultures to gain more understanding about Asian cultural traditions. The strength of family bonds in the Asian culture is well recognized, and thus, it may be necessary to include family and/or community members to obtain consent and adherence to treatments. Also, the health care provider should be nonjudgmental, supportive, and able to coordinate health care with traditional healers according to the Asian cultures and their traditional health practices. Interpreter services should be made available and accessible if needed. Organizational and administrative assistance to help in obtaining social services for limited English proficiency Asians may be needed. Asian American health care providers need to be recruited and retained. The Office of Minority Health has issued the National Standards on Culturally and Linguistically Appropriate Services (CLAS) that provide directions, recommendations, and standards for health care organizations to follow. Individual health care providers should also use those standards to make their practices more culturally accessible.

Conclusion

Asians are one of the fastest growing and most ethnically diverse minority groups in the United States. Asian Americans have been described as the model minority because of their achievements in the socioeconomic and educational spheres. The stereotype of model minority is misleading and overlooks the health disparities that are experienced by the Asian American subgroups. Health advocates and providers, policymakers, and community leaders must work together to eliminate the health disparities and improve the health and well-being of Asian Americans. Public policies to address the health needs, community services to support the underserved, and culturally competent health care providers are needed to adequately serve the Asian Americans.

Jane H.-C. Tang

See also Advocacy for Families; Assessing Family Health; Buddhism's Influence on Health in the Family; Cultural Attitudes Toward Help Seeking and Beliefs About Illness in Families; Ethnic/Racial Influences in Families; Family Health Perspectives; Hinduism's Influence on Health in the Family

Further Readings

Esperat, M. C., Inouye, J., Gonzalez, E. W. Owen, D. C., & Feng, D. (2004). Health disparities among Asian Americans and Pacific Islanders. *Annual Review of Nursing Research, 22,* 135–159.

Inouye, J. (2006). Narrowing the health disparities gap: Asians and Pacific Islanders and nursing. In P. S. Cowen & S. Moorhead (Eds.), *Current issues in nursing* (pp. 578–585). St. Louis, MO: Mosby Elsevier.

McLaughlin, L. A., & Braun, K. L. (1998). Asian and Pacific Islander cultural values: Considerations for health care decision making. *Health & Social Work*, 23(2), 116–126.

Ngo-Metzger, Q., Massagli, M. P., Clarridge, B. R., Manocchia, M., Davids, R., B., Lezzoni, L. I., & Phillips, R. S. (2003). Linguistic and cultural barriers to care: Perspectives of Chinese and Vietnamese immigrants. *Journal of General Internal Medicine, 18*, 44–52.

Weil, J. M., & Lee, H. H. (2004). Cultural considerations in understanding family violence among Asian American Pacific Islander Families. *Journal of Community Health Nursing, 21*(4), 217–227.

Weir, R. C., Tseng, W., Yen, I. H., & Gaballero, J. (2009). Primary health-care delivery gaps among medically underserved Asian American and Pacific Islander populations. *Public Health Report, 124*(6), 831–840.

Yick, A. G., & Oomen-Early, J. (2008). A 16-year examination of domestic violence among Asians and Asian Americans in the empirical knowledge base: A content analysis. *Journal of Interpersonal Violence, 23*(8), 1075–1094.

U.S. Census Bureau. (2004). *We the people: Asians in the United States*. Retrieved April 30, 2010, from http://www.census.gov/prod/2004pubs/censr-17.pdf

U.S. Census Bureau. (2008). *Income, poverty, and health insurance coverage in the United States: 2007*. Retrieved April 30, 2010, from http://www.census.gov/prod/2008pubs/p60–235.pdf

Websites

Asian & Pacific Islander American Health Forum (APIAH): http://www.apiahf.org

National Library of Medicine (NLM), National Institutes of Health, Asian-American Health: http://asianamericanhealth.nlm.nih.gov/intr01.html

U.S. Department of Health and Human Services, Health Resources and Services Administration (HRSA): http://www.hrsa.gov/culturalcompetence

U.S. Department of Health and Human Services, Office of Minority Health: http://www.cdc.gov/omhd/Populations/AsianAm/AsianAm.htm#Disparities

ASSESSING FAMILY HEALTH

The purpose of this entry is to briefly define and discuss the concepts of family health and wellness, present some basic issues to consider when planning to assess family health, and finally introduce some common models and measures of family health assessment.

Defining Family Health and Wellness

Health and Wellness in Individuals

Health can be defined in many ways. The most common conceptualizations of health indicate that it is the condition of being sound in body, mind, and spirit and free from physical disease or pain. Broader, more positive definitions of health move toward the construct of wellness. For example, the World Health Organization in its 1948 Constitution defined health as a state of complete physical, mental, and social well-being, not merely the absence of disease or infirmity.

It is important to note that these definitions of health go beyond a physical or bodily state. Health and well-being in mental and psychological domains, such as emotional and intellectual functioning; social domains including interpersonal relationships and community ties; and spiritual domains, such as religion and meaning in life, are also included. The concept of *wellness* goes even further and captures a sense of happiness and personal satisfaction with one's quality of life.

While most definitions of health and wellness characterize these constructs as outcomes or states of being, they can also be thought of as processes. For example, health can be defined as the process of adaptation to one's environment. At a biological level, this might mean an immune response after exposure to a virus. At a behavioral level, this might mean managing one's diet and exercising to promote well-being and remain disease free. Similarly, wellness can be defined as an active process. The National Wellness Association defines wellness as the process of becoming aware of and making choices toward a more successful existence.

Defining Family Health and Wellness

At a basic level, families are organized systems that aim to foster the development and well-being of their members by meeting everyone's basic needs. Families and the larger community are mutually dependent in serving economic, educational, religious, and social functions. With this information as background, for the purpose of this entry, family health and wellness are defined as the ability of the family to promote the physical, emotional, intellectual, social, and spiritual well-being of itself as a unit and its members. This definition encompasses the family's ability to work as a single unit to accomplish family tasks and foster the development, resilience, and quality of life of the family system and its members. Healthy families are those that can appropriately rise to challenges and successfully cope with stressful experiences that threaten the family system or individual family members.

It should be noted that healthy family functioning does not suppose the absence of problems within the family or its members, and the presence of problems within a family or its members is not an indicator of unhealthy family functioning. There are other biopsychosocial factors that influence individual family members and the family system aside from family health and wellness. Further, healthy families do not adhere to a single structure, pattern, or style. Many different types of families are healthy and adaptive. Also, healthy families may or may not be functioning at an optimal level. Even healthy, well-functioning families may have some areas of weakness or difficulties from time to time, yet they are capable of appropriately meeting their needs. Finally, family health and wellness must be considered within the context of culture; the life-cycle stage of the family as a unit, for example, being newlyweds or having an empty nest; the developmental stage or age of its members; and the specific context, situation, or event the family is confronting. A certain family pattern may be considered functional in one context but not another or adaptive for one member but not another. For all of these reasons, assessment of family health and wellness is a challenging endeavor.

Issues to Consider When Assessing Family Health

Families are more complex and multifaceted than individuals and therefore are more difficult to assess. When setting out to assess the health of a family, there are many issues to consider. First, it is important to define the purpose of the assessment and have a plan for how the information will be used. Second, the specific aspects of family functioning to be assessed need to be identified. Many different domains of family functioning may

contribute to health and wellness and different family models stress different aspects of family functioning. Third, there are various methods that can be used to assess family functioning ranging from individual family member self-reports to observations of the family in specific situations Choices need to be made regarding which method will be used. Each of these issues should be considered when setting out to assess family health.

Purpose of the Assessment

When planning an assessment of family health and wellness, the reason for obtaining the information should be clear and at the forefront of one's mind. A clear conceptualization of why the information is wanted will help guide all other decisions about the content, context, and format of the assessment. For example, a researcher interested in developing a family-based intervention to reduce obesity in childhood might conduct a study comparing the interactional patterns of families with obese children to families with healthy-weight children during mealtimes. Videotaping family meals and coding aspects of the interactions may be most appropriate in this case. A clinician desiring to help a married couple successfully adapt to the transition of having a first child may examine the couple's relationship quality and perspectives on parenting. Here, self-report measures completed by each individual might be most useful. With a clear idea of the purpose of the assessment, other aspects of the assessment process may more easily fall into place.

Domains of Family Health and Wellness

There are many different aspects or domains of family functioning. In fact, no theories or models of family functioning reduce family health to a single dimension, nor do they recommend using a single indicator to assess health. To capture important components of the functioning of the family, most family assessments target the structure and organization of the family such as roles, leadership, and alliance formation; the affective environment of the family including the expression of feelings and conflict; the problem-solving ability of the family; the cohesiveness or the involvement and closeness of the family; and the communication patterns within the family.

There are many different models of family functioning and different models emphasize different constructs or approach them differently. Each model has associated assessment techniques, and these are presented in the next section of this entry. When constructing an assessment of family health or wellness, it is important to choose measures that capture the constructs believed to be most relevant to the specific purposes of the evaluation.

Method of Assessment

The method of the assessment is also an important consideration. Family members may report on their family through self-report questionnaires, they may be interviewed individually or as a family unit, or they may be observed and their interactions coded. There are typically low associations between self-report assessments and direct observational coding of similar domains of family functioning, so each method provides a different window into family functioning. The different methods each have certain benefits and limitations. For example, asking a family to engage in a certain type of interaction and coding their behavior is much more rigorous than having a family member complete a questionnaire about their family. The coding of an interaction by a trained observer is less likely than self-report measures to be influenced by the family's desire to present themselves as positively as possible. On the other hand, observation coding may be more intrusive and time consuming for the family and costly for the assessor as it requires highly trained observers and video equipment. In the next section of this entry, both observational and self-report measures are discussed, and assessors need to consider the benefits and limitations of each method when deciding which is best for their purpose.

Assessing Family Health and Wellness

Most measures of family health and wellness can be traced back to specific models of family functioning and are best understood within those models. A series of theories are presented below along with forms of assessment associated with each theory. While this is not an exhaustive list of assessment approaches, these models and measures were selected because they are well researched and well articulated, and the measures are commonly used in either research or clinical contexts.

The Beavers Systems Model and Assessment Approaches

The Beavers systems model of family functioning defines family health and functioning along two dimensions: competence and style. *Competence* refers to how well the family organizes and manages itself. Highly competent families establish strong, clear generational boundaries and include adults who are able to negotiate and share leadership. They are also capable of open and direct communication, fostering confidence and self-esteem, and resolving or accepting differences among family members. Highly competent families are also optimistic, flexible, and display a broad range of emotions. Style refers to the orientation of the family on the continuum of internally focused (centripetal) to externally focused (centrifugal). Centripetal families are more self-contained and seek satisfaction from within the family, distrust the world outside of the family, downplay negative or hostile feelings within the family, and pull together. Centrifugal families, on the other hand, tend to seek satisfaction from outside the family, are more comfortable expressing negative or angry feelings, and tend to push apart as individuals. Families at either extreme on this continuum are considered to be less wellfunctioning. Families with optimal health and wellness flexibly blend these two styles.

Two assessment devices have emerged from the Beavers systems model: (1) the Beavers Interactional Scales and (2) the Self-Report Family Inventory (SFI). The Beavers Interactional Scales are observational methods with one scale assessing family competence (the Beavers Interactional Competence Scale or BICS) and one scale assessing family style (the Beavers Interactional Style Scale or BISS). On the BICS, family interactions are coded on a 10-point scale with lower scores indicative of greater family health. The specific aspects of family functioning assessed include structure (overt power, parental coalitions, closeness); family mythology; goal-directed negotiation; autonomy (clarity of expression, responsibility, permeability); family affect (range of feelings, mood and tone, unresolvable conflict, empathy); and global health or pathology. On the BISS, family style is coded on a 5-point scale with lower scores indicative of centripetal style and higher scores indicative of centrifugal style. The specific domains assessed include meeting dependency needs, managing conflict, use of space, appearance to outsiders, professed closeness, managing assertion, expression of feelings, and global style. The Self-Report Family Inventory is a 36-item questionnaire on which family members (aged 11 and older) indicate the extent to which each item fits their family (1=fits our family well; 5=does not fit our family). The items assess general family health—competence, cohesion (a proxy for style) as well as conflict, leadership, and emotional expressiveness within the family.

The developers of this model designed the assessment tools for training, research, and clinical purposes. The observational techniques require a significant investment of time for families and money and personnel resources for those using the tools—carefully trained personnel are required. For these reasons, the observational measures are typically used in training and research as opposed to clinical settings. The authors note, however, that scores on the SFI are highly associated with scores on the observational measures and that the SFI is widely available and easy to administer and score. It has also been translated into many languages, has been used in many countries, and reportedly is sensitive to modest changes in family functioning.

The Circumplex Model of Marital and Family Systems and Assessment Approaches

Developed by David H. Olson and colleagues, the circumplex model of marital and family systems characterizes families on two orthogonal dimensions: cohesion and flexibility. *Cohesion* refers to emotional bonds between family members. Families can range from being disengaged (very low cohesion) to being enmeshed (very high cohesion). *Flexibility* refers to the amount of change that occurs in a family's leadership, role relationships, and relationship rules. Flexibility is characterized on a continuum ranging from rigid (very low flexibility) to chaotic (very high flexibility). Families on the extremes of these dimensions are considered unbalanced or unhealthy and those falling toward the midrange are considered balanced or

well functioning. Families with healthy levels of cohesion strike a balance between separateness and togetherness and are able to be both connected to their families and independent from them. Families with healthy levels of flexibility are able to balance stability and change in roles, leadership, and rules. A third component of the model—*communication*—is considered a facilitating dimension. Communication allows the family to maintain its balance and effectively adapt its functioning to meet its changing needs. Open communication patterns are present in balanced families.

Where a family falls on the dimensions of cohesion and flexibility is expected to change predictably across the family life course. For example, families with young children are expected to be more connected and structured than families with adolescents. Additionally, under times of family-level stress, such as the birth of a new baby or the diagnosis of a family member with a chronic illness, a family is expected to change along the dimensions of cohesion and flexibility. An unhealthy family, however, may remain entrenched in its dysfunctional family pattern when confronted with a stressor or become even more poorly functioning.

A clinician-rated observational measure and a series of self-report inventories have been created to assess the constructs represented in the circumplex model. The Clinical Rating Scale is designed to be used by clinicians or researchers to organize and rate material emerging from clinical interviews and observations of families. Cohesion and flexibility are rated on 10-point scales with 1 corresponding to disengaged or rigid patterns and 10 corresponding to enmeshed or chaotic patterns. Communication is rated on a 6-point scale with higher scores indicating better communication skills. The Family Adaptability and Cohesion Evaluation Scale IV (FACES IV) and its companion scales, Family Communication (FCS) and Family Satisfaction (FSS), are the current self-report questionnaires of the circumplex model (for ages 12 and older). The FACES IV is a 42-item questionnaire that includes six subscales: adaptability and cohesion (assessing the midranges of flexibility and cohesion) and rigid, chaotic, disengaged, and enmeshed (assessing the extremes of each dimension). Both the FCS and FSS include 10 items. For all three of these measures, the respondent rates the extent to which each item characterizes his or her family on a 5-point scale (1=strongly disagree to 5=strongly agree).

The circumplex model and the tools to assess its central constructs have changed across time and continue to evolve to best meet the goal of bridging gaps between research, theory, and practice. While there is strong empirical and clinical evidence of the importance of the constructs of this model (i.e., cohesion, flexibility, and communication) to the effective functioning and health of families, previous versions of the self-report FACES instrument were not capable of capturing the curvilinear relationships between cohesion and flexibility and family adjustment. The FACES IV was created to better capture the extremes of functioning. More research is needed to evaluate this measure. Strengths of this model and its assessment tools include a clear emphasis on using the instruments to guide clinical intervention.

The McMaster Model of Family Functioning and Assessment Approaches

The McMaster Model of Family Functioning specifies six domains of functioning proposed to have the greatest impact on the ability of the family to meet basic needs (food, money, transportation, shelter), developmental needs of family members and the family unit, and emerging needs (crises that arise for the family such as job loss, illness, etc.). These six dimensions are problem solving, communication, roles, affective responsiveness, affective involvement, and behavioral control. Effective, healthy families are believed to solve most problems efficiently and easily, approach problems systematically and have few, if any, unresolved problems. Communication within these families is clear, directed at the person to which it is intended, consistent across verbal and nonverbal modalities, and fulfills instrumental and affective goals. In healthy families, family roles, the repetitive patterns of behavior by which a family comes to function, are appropriately assigned and allocated so as to not overburden any one member. Additionally, accountability (responsibility and checks and balances) for roles is clear. Healthy families also express a full range of emotions that are appropriate to the situation in terms of intensity and duration (affective

responsiveness) and show an active interest and investment in one another (affective involvement). Further, the standards for behavioral control within healthy families are reasonable, and there is opportunity for negotiation and change dependent upon the situation.

The McMaster Clinical Rating Scale (MCRS) and the self-report Family Assessment Device (FAD) have been created to assess family health across the six dimensions described above. The MCRS is for use by clinicians well trained in the McMaster model. The clinician may conduct his or her own interview with the family or follow the guidelines of the McMaster structured interview of family functioning (McSIFF) to explore each of the dimensions that make up the model. The family is coded on each of the six dimensions using a scale of 1=severely dysfunctional, 5=nonclinical, 7=superior. The FAD is a 60-item self-report questionnaire designed for use with all family members (aged 12 and older). Respondents indicate on 5-point Likert-type scales the extent to which each item describes their families. Seven subscale scores are created, one for each of the six dimensions mentioned above and a general functioning subscale.

While the MCRS and accompanying McSIFF have been used primarily for training purposes, they are also valuable for clinical and research endeavors. The FAD has been shown to be psychometrically sound. It was designed to be completed by all family members and their scores averaged. Cut scores have been developed to classify family functioning on each of the dimensions and "unhealthy" families have been defined as those scoring above the cut score on four or more of the dimensions. The FAD is widely used and has been translated into approximately 20 different languages.

The Mealtime Interaction Coding System (MICS) was not developed by the McMaster group but is strongly based upon the model. This observational coding system involves videotaping a family within their home during mealtime and then rating the family interactions in regard to task accomplishment, communication, roles, affect management, interpersonal involvement, and behavioral control. The MICS has been used primarily with families of young children but has proved valuable in understanding general family dynamics.

The Process Model of Family Functioning and Assessment Approaches

The Process Model of Family Functioning proposes seven interdependent aspects of family functioning vital to the ability of the family to meet basic and developmental needs and effectively meet crises. Central to these seven constructs is *task accomplishment,* the process by which the family confronts problems, achieves goals, and fulfills needs. To accomplish tasks appropriately, the family members must have defined roles and adequately enact these roles (*role performance*). Communication is essential within the family to achieve mutual understanding regarding roles and to express emotion (*affect expression*). The degree and quality of family members' interests in one another (*involvement*) also impacts task accomplishment. *Control* refers to the management style of the family and the ways in which family members influence one another. Finally, the *values and norms* of the family and their culture provide the context within which all of these processes must be considered. This model strives to define ways in which families operate and considers various levels within families (i.e., individuals, interpersonal relationships, and the family unit) as well as the influence of larger social systems and the family's history.

A clinical rating scale associated with the process model of family functioning is reportedly under development, but the self-report Family Assessment Measure (FAM-III) is the primary measure of the constructs proposed in this model. This self-report questionnaire for family members ages 10 and older includes three sections: (1) the general (family) scale, (2) the dyadic scale, and (3) the self-rating scale. The general (family) scale includes 50 items and the dyadic and self-rating scales each include 42 items. The dyadic section is to be completed by each member of the family regarding his or her relationship with each other member of the family. Each section of the measure provides scores for each of the seven dimensions of the model. The general scale also produces defensiveness and social desirability scores. Respondents indicate the extent to which they agree with each statement on a 4-point scale; raw scores can be converted to T-scores with scores above 60 indicating problem areas. A brief version of the FAM with 14 items per section is also available.

The psychometric properties of the FAM-III are reportedly solid and the measure has been used successfully in both clinical and research contexts. The full instrument can take considerable time to administer if all sections are used and multiple dyadic relationships are assessed; however, it does have the ability to carefully pinpoint where family members perceive difficulties, be they at the level of the family, specific dyadic relationships, or within individual family members.

The Social Climate of the Family and the Family Environment Scale

Based on a general social ecology framework in which the family is conceptualized as an important environment that impacts and is impacted by individuals within the family, Rudolf Moos and Bernice Moos developed a model of the social climate of families. From data gathered through structured interviews with members of a variety of types of families, three social climate dimensions were distilled with corresponding areas of emphasis: interpersonal relationships (cohesion, expressiveness, conflict); personal growth (independence, achievement orientation, intellectual-cultural orientation, active-recreational orientation, moral-religious emphasis); and family structure (organization, control). The Family Environment Scale was designed to assess these three broad constructs and the 10 specific areas of emphasis. The 90-item scale uses a true-false response set and results in 10 subscale scores. An abbreviated 27-item version of the scale called the Family Relationship Index includes only the cohesion, expressiveness, and conflict subscales. There has been much debate regarding the factor structure of this measure and reports of low internal consistency of the individual subscales; however, it remains widely used in research endeavors.

Family Stress Theory and Assessment Approaches

Various stress and coping models, such as Hill's ABC-X model, McCubbin and Patterson's double ABC-X model of family stress, and Patterson's family adjustment and adaptation model can be described under the umbrella term *family stress theory*. These models all identify three basic elements: (1) a stressor, (2) family resources, and

(3) family perceptions and meaning. The *stressor* is defined as an environmental influence that threatens the family's well-being. *Family resources* are strengths of individual members and the family system across psychological, cognitive, social, interpersonal, and/or material realms. Resources may be preexisting thus reducing vulnerability to stressors or may develop in response to stress. *Family perceptions and meaning* is the third component of these models and refers to the family's conceptualization of the stressor and the members' perceptions of the resources they have to cope with it. During a crisis, healthy families cope by fitting their resources to the demands of the stressor, seeking more resources as needed, removing some of the demands, and/or changing their perceptions of their circumstances. Families are hypothesized to go through repeated cycles of stable adjustment, crisis, and adaptation. Some cycles occur naturally as part of the family life cycle and others arise in response to atypical stressors.

Various self-report instruments have been developed to assess aspects of family stress theory and just a few of these will be mentioned here as examples. The McCubbin research group has created the Family Inventory of Life Events and Changes to assess family stressors. This 71-item self-report instrument assesses a range of family transitions and strains occurring over the past year and provides three subscale scores: finance and business strains, work–family transitions and strains, and illness and family care strains. The McCubbin group has also created a measure of family resources called the Family Inventory of Resources for Management. This 69-item self-report scale assesses family member's perceptions of the family's internal and external resources and provides an assessment of family strengths, social support and financial well-being. Another relevant measure is the Family Inventory of Resources and Stressors by Lawrence. This 104-item inventory has 70 items related to family resources and 34 items related to family stressors. Seven subscales assess resources in the following domains: basic life resources, such as housing, finances, and health care; personal resources including, for example, emotional functioning and problem solving; parent–child resources, such as structure within the family, rules, control, and cooperation; social support resources from outside the family; partner relationship resources; child education resources, such as academic performance,

attendance, and parent–school cooperation; and adult employment resources including employment status and job satisfaction. Two stressor scales assess emotional stressors, such as depression, anxiety, and substance abuse, and family and community stressors including family conflict, neighborhood safety, and cultural barriers.

Typically, these stressor and resource measures are created to be specific to a certain event such as confronting a chronic illness in a child or specific subgroups of families, for example, low-income or multiproblem families, but they may have great value across stressful events and family types if used and evaluated more broadly.

Family Resilience Models and Assessment Approaches

Family resilience refers to the ability of the family to rebound from crises and successfully overcome life challenges. This model, championed by the McCubbins and Froma Walsh, is focused upon strengthening families so that they are better able to deal with adversity. While there is some variation in constructs specified in different models of family resilience, important components include the following: (a) a family belief system that includes a positive outlook, transcendence (values and purpose), spirituality, and the ability to find meaning in adversity; (b) functional organizational patterns characterized by flexibility, connectedness, and adequate social support and financial resources; (c) strong communication patterns characterized by clarity, open sharing of emotions, and collaborative problem solving; and (d) minimal demands, chronic stressors, and vulnerabilities within the family.

No single assessment system has been created to assess all of these components of resilience; however, some self-report instruments are emerging to assess aspects of resilience or related constructs. For example, the McCubbin research team has developed the Family Hardiness Index which is a 20-item scale measuring an individual's perceptions of his or her family's internal strength and durability in the face of adversity and the sense of control over the outcomes of life events and hardships. Four subscales, commitment, challenge, control, and confidence, are calculated. The Inventory of Family Protective Factors developed by Deborah Gardner and colleagues reportedly assesses the primary protective factors that contribute to family resilience. The brief 16-item scale assesses stressors, adaptive appraisals, social support, and compensating experiences. To further the assessment of family health and wellness, additional carefully developed, comprehensive measures of family resilience are needed.

Summary and Conclusions

This overview of methods and measures of family health and wellness is provided as an introduction to this topic area. In this entry, an emphasis was placed on measures of the family unit as a whole as opposed to measures of specific subsystems within the family or dyadic relationships. Useful measures exist that target these aspects of families. All of the measures reviewed also apply to family health and wellness generally. Specific family measures have been developed within certain contexts and may be of interest for specific assessment needs.

Family assessment is a challenging endeavor yet vital in the pursuit of increasing our knowledge about family health and wellness. When attempting to assess family health and wellness, one is presented with many options. It is important that the purpose of the assessment is kept clearly in mind, that a model of family functioning relevant to the issue at hand is chosen, and that measures based on that model are used. It is also important to consider what format the assessment will take, for example, observational coding or self-report questionnaires, and the psychometric properties of the method (internal consistency, test-retest reliability, inter-rater reliability, validity). Finally, the results of the assessment should be used appropriately to further promote the health and wellness of the family.

Melissa A. Alderfer

See also Communication in Families Related to Health and Illness; Coping Management Styles in Families; Developmental Transitions in Families; Quantitative Methods and Data Analysis in Family Health Research; Theoretical Perspectives Related to the Family

Further Readings

Alderfer, M. A., Fiese, B., Gold, J., Cutuli, J. J., Holmbeck, G., Goldbeck, L., et al. (2008). Evidence-based assessment in pediatric psychology: Family measures. *Journal of Pediatric Psychology, 33,* 1046–1061.

Beavers, R. W., & Hampson, R. B. (1990). *Successful families: Assessment and intervention.* New York: Norton.

Craddock, A. E. (2001). Family system and family functioning: Circumplex model and FACES IV. *Journal of Family Studies, 7,* 29–39.

Gardner, D. L., Huber, C. H., Steiner, R., Vazquez, L. A., & Savage, T. A. (2008). The development and validation of the Inventory of Family Protective Factors: A brief assessment for family counseling. *The Family Journal: Counseling and Therapy for Couples and Families, 16,* 107–117.

Hofferth, S. L., & Casper, L. M. (2007). *Handbook of measurement issues in family research.* Mahwah, NJ: Erlbaum.

Lawrence, E. C. (2006). Guidelines for a family assessment protocol. In L. Combrinck-Graham (Ed.), *Children in a family context* (2nd ed., pp. 51–70). New York: Guilford.

McCubbin, H. I., Thompson, E. A., Thompson, A. I., & Futrell, J. A. (1999). *Resiliency in families: Vol. 4.* Thousand Oaks, CA: Sage.

Moos, R., & Moos, B. (1994). *Family environment scale manual* (3rd ed.). Palo Alto, CA: Consulting Psychologists Press.

Moos, R. H. (1990). Conceptual and empirical approaches to developing family-based assessment procedures: Resolving the case of the Family Environment Scale. *Family Process, 29,* 199–208.

Olson, D. H., Gorall, D. M., & Tiesel, J. W. (2006). *FACES IV package.* Minneapolis, MN: Life Innovations.

Skinner, H., Steinhauer, P., & Sitarenios, G. (2000). Family Assessment Measure (FAM) and process model of family functioning. *Journal of Family Therapy, 22,* 190–210.

Walsh, F. (2003). *Normal family processes: Growing diversity and complexity* (3rd ed.). New York: Guilford.

Walsh, F. (2006). *Strengthening family resilience* (2nd ed.). New York: Guilford.

ASSISTED LIVING PLACEMENT

Assisted living (AL) is defined by Medicare as "a general term for living arrangements in which some services are available to residents who still live independently within the assisted living complex" (U.S. Department of Health and Human Services, n.d., "Nursing Homes"). In this regard, assisted living refers to a type of residential environment as well as the specific services received by the client. Assisted living is sometimes marketed as an alternative to nursing homes, but it is more widely recognized as a residential option that bridges home care with the intensive, skilled care provided in a nursing facility. Examples of services provided in a typical AL include a range of instrumental activities of daily living assistance, such as housekeeping, medication reminders or management, laundry, meal preparation, and to a lesser extent personal activities of daily living help, such as bathing. It is important to note that the considerable heterogeneity in state certification standards, client-centered purchasing options, size, and case mix in assisted living facilities make it difficult to actually define assisted living. For these reasons, the informed selection of an AL facility is a challenge for many families.

Assisted living use can occur across the life span. However, limited research exists on populations other than the older adult. For this reason, the focus of this entry is on AL for older adults. Specifically, this entry examines family structure in AL, types of family involvement in AL, predictors of family involvement in AL, and family outcomes related to the AL entry.

A review of national and regionally representative studies by Joseph E. Gaugler and Robert L. Kane found that the typical AL resident is generally widowed, does not live with a spouse, and often has a proximate family member within an hour's drive. In general, residents are greater than 85 years old and have more cognitive disabilities when compared to physical disabilities. Approximately 45% of residents suffer from moderate to severe cognitive impairment, and approximately 20% require assistance with 3 or more activities of daily living. These findings suggest the presence of disability among AL residents and that families may be in a position to provide some degree of care as needed.

Gaugler and Kane also note that available studies of AL often examine family visits or frequency of family contact with residents. Families tend to visit their relatives in AL once a week or more, generally providing socioemotional aid, such as talking, holding hands, reminiscing, and engaging in social activities with the resident. Instrumental care, including laundry, cleaning, organizing room/apartment, food and beverage preparation and

storage, financial support, and transportation is provided 1 to 3 times per month by family members, on average. Personal care, such as activity of daily living assistance, is provided much less frequently.

Various qualitative studies have also examined family involvement in AL. An important facet of many of these efforts is that they identify themes not explored in quantitative studies, including the need to consider family–resident relationships prior to AL entry, the importance of environmental characteristics in facilitating family involvement, the role of the AL resident herself or himself in influencing family involvement (in contrast to the passive "care recipient" role of quantitative research), and the relevance of families during key transition points during the AL experience, such as entry, exit, and end of life.

Several studies have compared family involvement in AL with more traditional nursing home environments. Several analyses have found that family members of AL residents engage in greater instrumental assistance, monitoring of AL residents' well-being, and overall family interaction when compared to family members of nursing home residents. Other studies have identified empirical correlates or predictors of greater family involvement in AL, including family proximity and residents who are women. Other factors such as resident race or ethnicity, length of stay, cognitive status, and facility–level factors have varying directional effects across studies.

Few studies examine family outcomes in AL. Most analyses suggest that residents indicate greater satisfaction with AL than their family members do. Family members of residents in AL report less "burden" (or the financial, social, emotional, and physical load of family care) than those providing at-home care to disabled relatives but more burden than those family members providing assistance to nursing home residents. Several qualitative studies suggest that family members experience an array of positive and negative feelings after a relative's move to AL. As in other qualitative studies in AL, the importance of preadmission relationships between family members and residents as well as the ongoing family–resident relationship dynamic following AL entry appears critical when examining how family members adapt emotionally and psychologically to the AL experience.

Family involvement in AL continues to receive research attention as the need and popularity of these residential long-term care arrangements grow. Future qualitative and empirical inquiry on family involvement in AL should address several gaps to enhance our understanding of family integration in residential long-term care. These include an emphasis on more complex models of family involvement that incorporate residents' contributions to family care in AL, an awareness of diverse ways families remain involved in residents' lives following AL entry, a greater understanding of how heterogeneous environments and family structures influence family involvement, and analyses of key transition points. These transition points include deciding on an AL, entry, acclimation, and exit. Undertaking this ambitious research agenda will result in a better understanding of how the AL experience influences critical family outcomes and how clinical interventions could improve the social, psychological, and emotional well-being of family members.

Joseph E. Gaugler and Darlene M. Lindahl

See also Aging and Shifting Roles in Families; Alzheimer's Disease: An Overview of Family Issues in; Alzheimer's Disease: Caregiver Burden; Caregiving: Elderly; Elder Care Options for Families: Long-Term Care; Health Care or Medical Home; Long-Term Care Facilities for Families; Respite Care

Further Readings

Beel-Bates, C. A., Ziemba, R., & Algase, A. L. (2007). Public policy: Families' perceptions of services in assisted living residence: Role of RNs and implications for policy. *Journal of Gerontological Nursing, 33,* 5–12.

Castle, N. G., & Sonon, K. E. (2007). The search and selection of assisted living facilities by elders and family. *Medical Care, 45,* 729–738.

Gaugler, J., & Kane, R. (2001). Informal help in the assisted living setting: A 1-year analysis. *Family Relations, 50,* 335–347.

Gaugler, J. E., & Kane, R. L. Families and assisted living. (2007). *Gerontologist, 47*(Suppl. 1), 83–89.

Kane, R. A. (2001). Long-term care and a good quality of life: Bringing them closer together. *Gerontologist, 41,* 293–304.

U.S. Department of Health and Human Services. (n.d.). *Nursing homes: Alternatives to nursing home care.*

Retrieved July 6, 2010, from http://www.medicare.gov/Nursing/Alternatives/Other.asp

Websites

Medicare, *Nursing homes:* http://www.medicare.gov/Nursing/Alternatives/Other.asp

ASTHMA FAMILY ISSUES: PREVENTION AND CONTROL

Asthma is a chronic condition that affects the airways of the lungs. In patients with asthma, certain triggers can cause inflammation and swelling of the airway lining, tightness of the chest muscles, and production of thick mucus. All these processes reduce airflow in and out of the lungs, making breathing difficult and causing wheezing and coughing. Managing asthma can be very challenging for individuals with asthma and their families, but by making healthy behaviors the norm, exacerbations can be prevented or controlled. This entry focuses on the measures that can be taken by the family in order to prevent and control asthma symptoms.

Managing Asthma

In the United States, more than 22 million people are currently diagnosed with asthma, and 4,000 people die every year from asthma-related diseases and disorders. Current research suggests that the prevalence of childhood asthma has increased since the 1980s. Therefore, the Centers for Disease Control and Prevention (CDC) has begun to conduct interventions to prevent or treat asthma. A successful program educated parents about managing asthma in young children, and the first step was teaching them to keep asthma diaries.

When clinicians diagnose asthma, they take into consideration many clinical features (e.g., the symptoms, history of atopic disorder, affected individual and family's history of asthma or atopic disorder); evaluate the results of physical exams, X-rays, and/or lung function tests; and rule out other diagnoses. For this reason, it is essential that the affected individual (if a child, his or her parents, guardians, or caregivers) provide the doctor with detailed information about the patient's symptoms and other events that may be linked with them (specific illnesses, stressful events, reactivity to allergens).

An asthma diary records the symptoms (episodes of shortness of breath, wheezing, chest tightness); their severity, frequency and duration; events caused by shortness of breath (such as disturbed sleep or decreased productivity at school or at home); specific illnesses (for instance, colds or flu) and their severity, frequency, and duration; anything that seems to increase asthma symptoms (presence of pets, dust mites, molds, cockroaches, pollen, smoke, irritants); stressful events, which may have caused a physical or psychological imbalance in the patient.

Preventing Asthma Attacks

Asthma attacks, also known as "flare-ups," are acute exacerbations of asthma, the onset of which may be sudden. Individuals with asthma experience a sense of constriction in the chest, shortness of breath, wheezing, chest tightness, rapid heart and respiratory rate, cyanosis, numbness in the limbs, and even loss of consciousness. Asthma attacks can be life threatening, and therefore, patients need to be able to prevent or at least control them as much as possible.

The first step in controlling asthma is establishing a partnership between clinician and patient to create an individualized action plan aimed at monitoring and managing symptoms. In this action plan, the doctor lists long-term control medications (which prevent the airway inflammation that causes asthma symptoms) and quick-relief inhalers (which contain a short-acting bronchodilator that opens up the airways).

Parents and other family members can have an important role in stimulating the compliance of the patient to the treatment prescribed. For instance, a young child who has to use a nebulizer will be more cooperative if the nebulizer mask is shaped like a cartoon character and if the treatment time can be spent watching a DVD.

Moreover, the individuals with asthma and their families should single out the specific triggers that exacerbate asthma. Although the primary triggers are colds or exercise, it is estimated that 75% to 85% of people with asthma have some type of allergy, which can aggravate the condition.

Improvement of Indoor Air

An important aspect of asthma prevention and control is the improvement of the indoor air quality in the patient's home. This goal can be reached by the following:

1. Limiting use of products and materials that emit strong odors and irritants (e.g., aerosol household cleaning products, aerosol pesticides, scented room fresheners, hair sprays, strong perfumes, talcum powder, chalk dust, paint fumes, sawdust)

2. Running the air conditioning when the pollen count is high and opening windows only after midmorning

3. Running the air conditioning when there is a high level of pollution and opening windows very early in the morning

4. Changing the air filter in the air conditioner and the air furnace once a month

5. Using polyester-fill pillows and hypoallergenic blankets and washing them in hot water once a week

6. Removing upholstered furniture and carpets Washing bedding and curtains in hot water weekly

7. Reducing the number of dust-collecting objects (e.g., books, nonwashable stuffed animals, knickknacks, houseplants)

8. Using a vacuum cleaner with a high-efficiency particulate filter once a week

9. Avoiding humidifiers, repairing water leaks in faucets, pipes, and ductwork, and using clothes dryers and exhaust fans to limit exposure to mold and damp

10. Avoiding wood fires or ensuring that the doors of wood-burning stoves fit tightly

11. Using an exhaust fan when cooking on a gas stove to limit nitrogen dioxide production

12. Finding another home for warm-blooded pets and selecting low-dander pets to control animal dander

13. Sealing holes in walls, floors, and cabinets and storing food in airtight containers and

covering trash cans to limit exposure to cockroaches

14. Avoiding smoking (including secondhand smoke) and choosing smoke-free environments in restaurants, theaters, and hotel rooms

Other Measures Aimed at Preventing and Controlling Asthma

Moreover, to prevent and control asthma, the family should support individual family members with asthma by the following actions:

1. Avoiding or limiting exposure to fossil fuel air pollution (e.g., ground-level ozone, particulates, nitrogen dioxide, sulfur dioxide), scheduling outdoor activities for times when pollutants are low

2. Avoiding or limiting exposure to pollen as well as to extremes of temperature and/or humidity

3. Avoiding raking leaves, mowing lawns, working with peat, mulch, hay, or dead wood

4. Avoiding or limiting ingestion of food and wine that contain sulfites and/or salicylates

5. Limiting exposure to latex, sulfites, or chloramines (the latter are generated by chlorinated swimming pools)

6. Limiting assumption of medications such as paracetamol, aspirin, beta blockers, penicillin

7. Limiting participation in endurance sports (e.g., long-distance running, soccer, ice hockey) but being active by practicing swimming, leisurely biking, and walking

8. Undergoing allergen immunotherapy through the use of repeated allergen injections for the purpose of achieving clinical tolerance of the allergens that cause symptoms

9. Retraining breathing habits, for instance, playing a wind instrument, or practicing the Buteyko method

10. Taking medication as prescribed

Alessandra Padula

See also Allergies and the Family; Chronic Health Problems and Interventions for the Childrearing Family; Chronic Illness and Family Management Styles; Cigarettes, Smoking, and Secondhand Smoke and Family Health; Exercise Promotion and Fitness

Further Readings

Akinbami, L. J. (2006, December 12). The state of childhood asthma, United States, 1980–2005. *Advance Data*, (*381*), 1–24.

National Asthma Education and Prevention Program Expert Panel. (2007). *Expert panel report 3 (EPR-3): Guidelines for the diagnosis and management of asthma—Summary report 2007*. National Institutes of Health: National Heart, Lung, and Blood Institute. Retrieved March 15, 2010, from http://www.nhlbi.nih.gov/guidelines/asthma/asthsumm.htm

National Heart, Lung, and Blood Institute. (2007). *Expert guidelines for the diagnosis and management of asthma*. National Institutes of Health: National Heart, Lung, and Blood Institute. Retrieved March 15, 2010, from http://www.nhlbi.nih.gov/guidelines/asthma

ASYNCHRONOUS DEVELOPMENT BETWEEN PARTNERS

In the context of this encyclopedia, asynchronous development between partners contains two hidden assumptions that must be made explicit at the outset: (1) asynchrony is presumed to exacerbate stress that in turn is known to serve as a generalized risk factor for a host of medical, social, and emotional illnesses; and (2) asynchronous development presumes a change over time—both historical-social time and partnered time. Asynchronous development is also considered to be a risk factor for divorce in contemporary society. This entry examines changes in family parenting roles, gendered educational attainment, and the implications of both for life satisfaction, stress, and health.

Paternal and Maternal Roles

In their classic book published more than a half century ago, Talcott Parsons and Robert Bales theorized that roles of fathers were assigned by society and assumed the *instrumental* role while mothers were assigned and assumed the *socioemotional*, or *nurturant-expressive*, roles within the family system. Fathers were expected to be breadwinners and mothers nurturing homemakers and caregivers for children. For the decade of the 1950s when this book was written, it likely was an accurate theoretical formulation for the modal American family.

However, social expectations for both mothers and fathers have changed substantially over the following half century beginning with the sexual and women's revolutions of the 1960s and continuing to the present. The broad thrust of these changes in social norms has been the demand that fathers add to their instrumental role components of the nurturant-expressive role previously assigned to mothers. In a synchronous fashion, mothers were expected to add an instrumental component to their previous nurturant and social-emotional assignment.

While changing social mores dictate what is "supposed" to change, the most highly involved component of the father's role—breadwinning—has remained an expectation from the 1950s to the present. Gordon Finley and Seth Schwartz used a retrospective design with 1,989 undergraduates who rated their fathers on a 5-point scale indicating how involved their fathers were in 20 different domains of their lives. In this study, young adult children continued to rank breadwinning as the most highly involved paternal domain. There was, however, clear evidence that fathers were involved in nurturant and expressive functions as well.

Historical Changes in Gendered Educational Attainment

In tandem with the family role norm changes noted above, differential educational attainment also can lead to asynchronous development. Data from the U.S. Department of Education Institute of Education Sciences chronicle this asynchronous transformation. Earlier in our nation's history, males received substantially more degrees in higher education than did females until gender equality was attained for bachelor's degrees in 1981, for master's degrees in 1985, and for doctoral degrees in 2006. Following each of these years, where males and females attained educational equality, accelerating trends and projections indicate that females currently receive and are projected to continue to receive more degrees in higher education than are males.

These demographic projections are of substantial social and economic significance. In the early years of our nation, men dominated education and consequently the higher social and economic status positions in society. Since highly educated women were a minority, men who wanted to marry often were required to "marry down"—educationally speaking. In the parlance of social exchange theory, men traded education and economic status for spouses with physical attractiveness, personality, companionship, or motherly characteristics for their children. This educational differential contributed to the differential roles assigned to men and women by Parsons and Bales.

The current changes in educational preparation pose intriguing uncertainties. That is, now that today's cohorts of younger women have markedly higher levels of education than do men, the impact of this asynchrony of marriage, family formation, and divorce as well as for role assignments within the family is unknown. There currently is a minority of well-educated males available for the majority of well-educated females. Thus, the current educational asynchronies present substantial issues for marriage, family formation, parenting role assignments, and divorce for today's younger generation of well-educated women and men who are educated less well.

Asynchrony, Stress, and Health

Some researchers predict that gender relations will be more stressful and health impairing in the future than they have been in the past. While the stress of asynchrony experienced by women under the "traditional" Parsons and Bales model led to the women's movement beginning in the 1960s, this perceived stress later was replaced by educational, social, and economic synchrony. However, the attained synchrony subsequently was replaced by asynchronous educational and economic transformations favoring women.

The current educational asynchrony likely will increase stress for both genders for two reasons. First, men now are in the less educated position and thus most likely to experience educational, occupational, and income stress. Second, there generally is a lag in social expectations in the hearts and minds of both sexes. When educational and economic realities are inconsistent with these lagged expectations, stress and conflict tend to be exacerbated. The current educational asynchrony combined with lagged social expectations from earlier eras likely will lead to lower rates of marriage, higher rates of cohabitation, and higher rates of divorce.

Gordon E. Finley

See also Affect Management and the Family; Changes in Family Structure, Roles; Changing Views of Marriage, Home Responsibilities, and Caregiving; Roles and Functions of Families: Divorce

Further Readings

Finley, G. E., & Schwartz, S. J. (2006). Parsons and Bales revisited: Young adult children's characterization of the fathering role. *Psychology of Men & Masculinity, 7*(1), 42–55.

Parsons, T., & Bales, R. F. (1955). *Family, socialization and interaction process. Glencoe,* IL: Free Press.

U.S. Department of Education Institute of Education Sciences. (n.d.). *Degrees conferred by degree-granting institutions, by level of degree and sex of student: Selected years, 1869–70 through 2016–17.* Retrieved from http://nces.ed.gov/programs/digest/d07/tables/dt07_258.asp

ATTENTION DEFICIT/ HYPERACTIVITY DISORDER: FAMILY INVOLVEMENT AND MANAGEMENT

Attention deficit/hyperactivity disorder (ADHD) is a broad term that is used to describe a cluster of symptoms that comprise a neurodevelopmental disorder in which the child struggles to control impulses, manage behavior, and listen to directions. Steven Pliszka notes that it is not considered a disorder that can be directly attributed to other medical or psychiatric conditions, and it tends to cause impairment in social and academic functioning, especially if untreated. ADHD is included in this encyclopedia because it is one of the most commonly occurring pediatric disorders and likely to be treated by a primary care provider. It can also be treated in a variety of other health care settings including child guidance clinics and other outpatient mental health treatment environments. Treatment may include medication management, psychosocial interventions, or a combination of both that involves parental figures, other family members, and other individuals involved with the child. These individuals can also include school personnel, community activity leaders, and child care providers. ADHD, in some variant of symptoms, continues into adulthood and influences functioning throughout the life span.

The core symptoms of ADHD include inattention, which usually persists into adulthood; hyperactivity, which tends to decrease around ages 9 to 11 years; and impulsivity, which may begin to remit from around ages 12 to 14 years. ADHD is rarely a simple disorder and needs to be assessed carefully before treatment begins.

This entry begins with historical and current literature contexts. Next, the entry discusses desired family health outcomes, assessment, and treatment interventions. This entry concludes with a brief description of ADHD's relevance to family health care.

Historical Context

First identified by George Still in 1902, children with ADHD were predominantly seen as "hyperactive" while a small number of children were viewed as not being able to focus attention. This identified subset of children then led to identifying attention deficit disorder (ADD) to describe children without behavioral hyperactivity who showed predominant inattention. Both ADHD and ADD were eventually folded into one diagnosis in the American Psychiatric Association's *Diagnostic and Statistical Manual of Mental Disorders* (2000, 4th ed., text revision); these diagnostic categories, in the *DSM-IV-TR,* are listed as 314.01: attention-deficit/hyperactivity disorder, combined type; and 314.00: attention-deficit/hyperactivity disorder, predominantly inattentive type. In the revised edition of *DSM-V*, it is speculated that this may change. Currently, the onset of symptoms must be prior to age 7; under new guidelines, this would increase to age 12. Discontinuation of subtypes is being considered, and children with autism spectrum or pervasive developmental disorder (PDD) diagnoses could receive the diagnosis of ADHD. Currently, autism and PDD are excluded from ADHD diagnoses.

Overview of Current Literature

Research has shown that ADHD is a brain-based disorder. However, it is complicated by a variety of other issues and comorbid disorders that can cloud the practitioner's ability to make a clear diagnosis and treatment plan. Over the life span, ADHD can move from behavior hyperactivity to disruptive behavior, learning problems, poor social skills, and oppositional defiant behaviors and in adolescence, to school difficulties, substance abuse, mood and conduct disorders, and complex learning disabilities. Untreated, ADHD predisposes youth to substance use, involvement in the juvenile justice system, and poor adult functioning.

Nongenetic risk factors have also been identified as contributing to ADHD. These include traumatic brain injury, low birth weight and traumatic perinatal events, maternal smoking during pregnancy, and environmental deprivation in infancy. Some researchers suggest that all of these issues combine with the genetic risks to produce the disorder in a child. ADHD is frequently comorbid with other psychiatric conditions. It is estimated by Thomas Spencer, Joseph Biederman, and Timothy Wilens that 50% to 90% of children diagnosed with ADHD will also meet criteria for another psychiatric diagnosis. These diagnoses include oppositional behavior, conduct disorder, depression, anxiety, and tic disorders. Comorbid learning and language disorders can include receptive and expressive language disorders, poor motor control, difficulty with math skills, and language processing deficits. All of these psychiatric and academic comorbidities require an intensive intervention strategy carefully aimed at improved functioning at home and school through symptom change.

Desired Family Health Outcomes

In defining ADHD, it is essential to consider the functioning of all family members living in the household of the affected individual. This is especially important given that many children diagnosed with ADHD have one or both biological parents who also show symptoms of ADHD. ADHD is heritable and tends to run in families. This situation has implications for the entire family since the symptoms of ADHD can adversely affect all family members. Untreated, the disorder can adversely influence adult functioning with regards to education, work, and personal relationships. As health care is provided to the child with ADHD, it is essential to carefully ask parents about their own possible symptoms and how this influences the family. If the child is struggling with behavior at home and school, then the family is essential in planning therapeutic interventions that address the difficulties in these systems.

The other risk issue that can influence family functioning is the presence of other comorbid disorders in addition to ADHD. Psychiatric disorders, in general, adversely influence family functioning and need to be diagnosed and treated.

Assessment

Assessment of ADHD must include information from a variety of sources. The referrant, the reason behind the initial referral for care, the length of time there has been a problem, and the circumstances around the symptoms of ADHD must be assessed. Prenatal, perinatal, postnatal, and maternal or caregiver functioning should be evaluated. Temperament, milestones, and unusual patterns of behavior are considered. Family history issues include who lives in the household, history of out-of-home placement, exposure to trauma, substance abuse (current and past) in caregivers, legal issues, and stability of the family. School assessment includes progress in school, presence or absence of learning disabilities, peer relationships, academic functioning, and whether or not the child receives special education services.

In considering ADHD, the practitioner needs a comprehensive physical health history of the child that documents lead exposure, general health, presence or absence of past cardiac problems in the child or an immediate relative, sleeping and eating patterns, history of infections, and exposure to toxins.

Once the diagnosis is being considered and the child meets criteria for ADHD, further support for this can be obtained from parent and teacher scales. Vital signs, including blood pressure, pulse, height, and weight at baseline, before treatment with any medication, are necessary.

Assessment Tools

Several standardized rating instruments are useful in assessing the presence of ADHD. The Vanderbilt ADHD Diagnostic Teacher Rating Scale and the Vanderbilt ADHD Diagnostic Parent Rating Scale are available free online from the National Initiative for Children's Healthcare Quality website and cover the subscales of inattention and hyperactivity-impulsivity. These tools also assess for oppositional and conduct disorder tendencies. School functioning is assessed through Academic Performance and Behavioral Performance. Readily available and easily scored, these tools are used in many pediatric primary care settings.

Other rating instruments for ADHD include the Conners Rating Scale (revised), a parent, teacher, and youth self-report form. It is an excellent tool for comprehensive assessment of ADHD and related problems and looks at ADHD variants as well as problems involving conduct disorder and oppositional defiant behaviors. This tool is available for purchase. The Child Behavior Checklist (CBCL), developed by Thomas Achenbach, is widely used to assess internalizing, externalizing, and total problems. It includes a parent form, caregiver or teacher form, and youth self-report form. It must also be purchased.

While standardized assessment tools compose one aspect of assessing for symptoms of ADHD, they should not be used in isolation. Multidimensional evaluation of the child and family, including clinical interviews, observation of the child, and a rating instrument for ADHD are the best ways of making the diagnosis.

Treatment Interventions

Pharmacological

Treating this disorder with stimulant medication began in the 1930s and continues today as the standard of care in managing children and adolescents with ADHD and ADD. This disorder, if correctly diagnosed, has a high positive response rate to treatment with stimulants.

Children and adolescents with ADHD can show a dramatic difference in behavior control, ability to pay attention, and academic performance if given the correct type and dose of medication. The most effective treatment involves a multidimensional approach that combines medication with parent management training and school interventions. Because youngsters with ADHD have an increased chance of being diagnosed with learning disabilities, it is essential to their academic progress that ADHD be identified and treated early in their school years.

Choosing the best medication to treat ADHD depends on a number of issues. The symptoms, including patterns, timing, and intensity; the home, school, and community issues influencing behavior; and the presence or absence of comorbidities have to be considered. Side effects must be evaluated as medication is initiated. Decrease in appetite and subsequent weight loss can be a concerning side effect with the stimulant class of medication. Children beginning stimulant treatment should be weighed at baseline and then at each appointment with the practitioner.

The family culture and viewpoint around medication management must be carefully assessed. The risks, benefits, and side effects must be reviewed in the family's predominant language. Review should occur more than once, preferably at each follow-up appointment. Parents and those with custody of the child must consent to the use of medication, and the child, if over the age of 7, must assent to this. Practitioners usually begin with a low dose trial of a long acting stimulant from the methylphenidate or dexedrine family. The risk of substance abuse in all family members must be carefully assessed. Stimulants have a high abuse potential and significant street value if sold illegally.

Other types of medication can be used to treat ADHD and include alpha agonists, atomoxetine (a norepinephrine reuptake inhibitor), and lisdexamfetamine (a stimulant prodrug that cannot be abused due to its water solubility). The predominant side effects of atomoxetine include stomach distress, and practitioners should obtain baseline liver function tests and monitor this. Bupropion has been used with moderate effect to treat older children and adolescents who have ADHD and comorbid depression and/or smoke cigarettes. Seizure potential is increased with this medication and should be explained to the individual as a risk factor. Both bupropion and atomoxetine take from 3 to 4 weeks to achieve maximum symptom effectiveness.

EKGs are not routinely required but should be ordered if there is any family history of sudden death due to cardiac issues. There is no evidence to suggest that height is adversely affected by use of stimulants to treat ADHD. The predominant side effect is decrease in normal developmental weight gain associated with anorexia, which must be monitored. Difficulty falling asleep may also be a side effect and can be initially treated with sleep hygiene instructions, regulation of the stimulant dose, or sleep medication, such as low dose catapres, which induces sleep. Long acting tenex is being used to treat hyperactivity and has no effect on inattention. It is also useful with children with appetite suppression who could receive this medication and a lower dose of their stimulant. The goal is improved appetite using both agents. All agents require regular monitoring of blood pressure.

Some children complain of feeling odd or weird when taking stimulants, as if their personality is dulled. Decreasing the dose or changing agents can influence this complaint. Parents can also note personality changes and differences and should be encouraged to watch for this.

Psychosocial

While the majority of children with simple ADHD will respond to medication management, there is a subset that will require medication *and* psychosocial interventions. A multimodal approach should involve intensive and repeated parent and child education about the disorder, the way it presents, and its influence on functioning at home and school. Families might benefit from a community support group for parents of children with ADHD. One such support group is Children and Adults with Attention Deficit/Hyperactivity Disorder (CHADD).

Specific interventions include parent management training, social skill training for the child, and family or individual psychotherapy. For the adolescent who struggles with ADHD, vocational counseling will be important. Duration and type of treatment are dependent on the symptoms, response to care, and effectiveness of medication management. It is essential that practitioners pay attention to the comorbid symptoms that might signal the presence of another psychiatric disorder. Families are reassured if the target symptoms and likely treatment response are clearly outlined for them at the beginning of treatment.

Specific suggestions for parents include limiting behavior demands to when the medication is most effective, taking time-outs, offering consistent rules, and encouraging open communication about the problematic behavior. It is essential that the child or adolescent with ADHD have a regular, consistent routine that offers play, sleep, and meals in a predictable manner.

The concepts of teach and reward are especially applicable to children with ADHD. Their behavior can result in a negative cycle of punishment that spirals downward and creates family stress and discord. If parents have untreated ADHD, this is even more of a risk as they struggle with regulation of their own behavior.

Communication with schools is essential for parents of the child with ADHD. Parents can advocate for the identification of comorbid learning issues and subsequent special education services if warranted. Parents need to be supported as they request testing and assessment, which is their parental right under federal law.

While some parents might not want to share with school personnel that their child is taking a medication for ADHD, all are encouraged to be open with the teacher about this, especially as the teacher can assist in ascertaining effectiveness of the medication and dose. Long acting preparations can be given before school, and there should be no need for children to receive medication in the middle of the day, unless determined by the practitioner.

Relevance to Family Health Care

ADHD in a child or adolescent influences the entire family. If the goal is improved mental and physical health, then treating ADHD is essential. This could be as simple as using the primary care provider to prescribe stimulant medication or as complex as a psychiatric provider arranging day treatment services and advocating for special education needs. Each child is different and requires a careful assessment that will ascertain the level of intervention needed to maximize functioning. Untreated ADHD puts the adolescent and adult at risk for substance abuse, vocational difficulties, automobile accidents, and legal problems. Treatment of this common psychiatric disorder is essential to individual and family health.

Geraldine S. Pearson

See also Attention Deficit/Hyperactivity Disorder: Family Involvement and Management; Conflict in Family Life, Role and Management of; Disabilities and Family Management; Families Experiencing Chronic Physical and Mental Health Conditions; Learning Disabilities in the Family; Psychiatric Medication for Families

Further Readings

American Psychiatric Association. (2000). *Diagnostic and statistical manual of mental disorders* (4th ed., text rev.). Washington, DC: Author.

Biederman, J. (2005). Attention-deficit/hyperactivity disorder: A selective overview. *Biological Psychiatry, 57,* 1215–1220.

Biederman, J., Faraone, S. V., Spencer, T., Wilens, T., Norman, D., Lapey, K. A., et al. (1993). Patterns of psychiatric comorbidity, cognition, and psychosocial functioning in adults with attention deficit hyperactivity disorder. *American Journal of Psychiatry, 150*(12), 1792–1798.

Connor, D. F., & Meltzer, B. M. (2006). *Pediatric Psychopharmacology Fast Facts.* New York: W. W. Norton.

Daughton, J. M., & Kratochvil, C. J. (2009). Review of ADHD pharmacotherapies: Advantages, disadvantages and clinical pearls. *Journal of the American Academy of Child and Adolescent Psychiatry, 48*(3), 240–248.

Daviss, W. B. (2008). A review of co-morbid depression in pediatric ADHD: Etiologies, phenomenology, and treatment. *Journal of Child and Adolescent Psychopharmacology, 18,* 565–571.

Galanter, C. A., Carlson, G. A., Jensen, P. S., Greenhill, L. L., Davies, M., Li, W., et al. (2003). Response to methylphenidate in children with ADHD and manic symptoms in the Multimodal Treatment Study of Children with Attention Deficit Hyperactivity Disorder Titration Trial. *Journal of Adolescent Psychopharmacology, 13,* 123–136.

Kunwar, A., Dewan, M., & Faraone, S. V. (2007). Treating common psychiatric disorders associated with attention deficit/hyperactivity disorder. *Expert Opinion in Pharmacotherapy, 8,* 555–562.

Leary, A., Collett, B., & Myers, K. (2010). Rating Scales. In M. K. Dulcan (Ed.), *Dulcan's textbook of child and adolescent psychiatry* (pp. 89–110). Washington, DC: American Psychiatric.

Martin, A., Scahill, L., Charney, D. S., & Leckman, J. F. (2003). *Pediatric Psychopharmacology.* New York: Oxford University Press.

Pliszka, S. R. (2010). Attention-Deficit/Hyperactivity. In M. K. Dulcan (Ed.), *Dulcan's textbook of child and adolescent psychiatry* (pp. 205–221). Washington, DC: American Psychiatric.

Spencer, T., Biederman, J., & Wilens, T. (1999). Attention-deficit/hyperactivity disorder and comorbidity. *Pediatric Clinics of North America, 46,* 915–927.

Waxmonsky, J. (2003). Assessment and treatment of attention deficit hyperactivity disorder in children with comorbid psychiatric illness. *Current Opinions in Pediatrics, 15,* 476–482.

Wilens, T. E., Faraone, S. V., Biederman, J., & Gunawardene, S. (2003). Does stimulant therapy of attention-deficit/hyperactivity disorder beget later substance abuse? A meta-analytic review of the literature. *Pediatrics, 111*(1), 179–185.

Websites

Children and Adults with Attention Deficit/Hyperactivity Disorder (CHADD): http://www.chadd.org

National Initiative for Children's Healthcare Quality: http://www.nichq.org

ATTENTION DEFICIT/ HYPERACTIVITY DISORDER AND THE FAMILY

Attention deficit/hyperactivity disorder (ADHD) is a neurobiological disorder theorized to be a result of impaired adaptive functioning related to defects in the neurotransmitters (primarily dopamine) in the frontal lobe of the brain that affects executive functioning. Executive functions are best described as a collection of brain processes that are responsible for planning, organizing, inhibiting inappropriate actions, and initiating self-directed actions that are used to self-regulate behaviors, cognitions, and emotions. Executive functions help us inhibit stimulating and interesting activities in favor of doing what needs to be done to adapt to our surroundings and needs.

People with ADHD struggle to inhibit their responses to rewarding stimuli and often cannot initiate self-directed actions, even when the stakes of not doing so are high. Because of this defect in executive functioning, they often find everyday activities, such as chores or homework, boring and difficult to perform because there are no tangible rewards for completing them, and these activities are not inherently stimulating to them. ADHD is not a defect in knowing what to do; it is a defect in doing what one knows needs to be done. It is about performance, not skills or knowledge. The five executive functions that most impact life for children and adults with ADHD are perception of time, inhibition of responses, working memory, internalization of speech, and self-regulation or control. After some background information, this entry focuses on how ADHD symptoms manifest in everyday life, their effects on the family, and the importance of support and mental health interventions for all members of the family as well as the family as a unit.

Background

The symptom cluster now known as ADHD has been recognized for over 100 years. Previous diagnostic terms have included brain-injured child syndrome (late 1800s), volitional inhibition (1902), minimal brain damage (1908), minimal brain dysfunction (1930s), hyperkinetic reaction (1950s), hyperactive child syndrome (1960s), ADD (1980), and ADHD—with and without hyperactivity (1987). In 1994, researchers and clinicians decided that the best description of this group of symptoms was attention deficit/hyperactivity disorder (ADHD) with three subtypes: ADHD, predominantly inattentive type; ADHD, predominantly hyperactive-impulsive type; and ADHD, combined type.

The etiology of ADHD is primarily genetic with several genes having demonstrated statistical significance of association with the disorder: dopamine 4 and 5 receptors, the dopamine transporter gene, dopamine-hydroxylase gene, the serotonin transporter gene, the serotonin 1B receptor, and synaptsomal associated protein 25 gene. Only about 7% of ADHD cases have been linked to other causes such as head injury, infections, and lead poisoning. There is no evidence that poor parenting causes ADHD.

Since this disorder is primarily genetic in origin, most families with children with ADHD also have parents, more than one child, or other relatives with ADHD, adding to the complexity of familial relationships and needs. Interventions need to be made at the family level, so all its members and the functioning of the family as a whole can be addressed. Currently, however, this is rarely done in clinical practice.

ADHD is generally considered a chronic disorder. However, there has been speculation recently that some children with ADHD may have a gene variant affecting dopamine receptors. This gene is called the dopamine receptor D4 gene (DRD4). Having this particular gene variant seems to be linked with better outcomes and may explain why some children seem to improve as they age. Most children with ADHD, however, continue to experience symptoms into adulthood, with many learning to adapt to the symptoms of the disorder as they get older.

Symptom Characteristics and Real Life

Children and adults with ADHD have core problems that they live with every day, with some days being better than other days. Looking at these difficulties, it is easy to understand why these children do so poorly academically and socially and why parenting demands can often exceed parents' abilities. Adding to the mix that one or both parents may also have ADHD makes parenting, family organization, and family needs even more daunting. These core problems are the following:

1. Poor sustained attention and vigilance on things that are not rewarding or stimulating

2. Poor delay of gratification and impulsiveness

3. Poor behavioral regulation

4. Poorly regulated activity that is often described as hyperactivity

5. Diminished rule-governed behavior and disinhibition

6. Increased variability of task performance (can do something well one day but can't do it the next)

7. Aggression, low motivation, learning difficulties

8. Risk for emotional and social problems

9. Academic and occupational underachievement

10. Interpersonal difficulties and family disruption

Effects on the Family

Families play a vital role in the care of children and adolescents with ADHD. Although various neurochemical and genetic factors form the basis of the etiological theories of ADHD, certain psychosocial factors, such as parent–child interactions, degree of family stability, and environmental supports, are believed to contribute to the exacerbation or remission of symptoms. Because of this, ADHD is thought of as an environmentally dependent disorder, with symptoms increasing and decreasing in relation to environmental demands and expectations. The family environment is paramount.

Raising a child with ADHD is a long-term process that is marked by frequent disruptions brought about by the variability in symptoms and performance that are characteristic of the disorder. Because of these characteristics, families are at an increased risk for interpersonal conflict, separation and divorce, decreased parenting self-esteem, higher levels of depression and anxiety, and a heightened sense of social isolation. There is now evidence that ADHD predicts increased stress within families and depression in mothers. Increasing family stability and using family-based interventions for helping family members cope with the difficulties of living with ADHD is important in order to optimize the outcomes for both the child and the family. A comprehensive family approach must be the treatment focus for the families affected by this disorder.

It is important not to overlook the nonaffected siblings when offering family support strategies. Siblings experience many losses when they have a sibling with ADHD: missing out on having a normal relationship with a brother or sister, parents being so overwhelmed in the care of child with ADHD that they do not have the time or energy for the nonaffected siblings, loss of having a "normal" family, and loss of happy family outings.

Siblings often talk about their ambivalent feelings, sometimes termed as if they are in a "sandwich" position. They feel caught in the middle between wanting to be loyal to the person with ADHD, while at the same time feeling resentful of the burdens it causes the family. Siblings, both younger and older than the ADHD child, are often expected to help take care of their brother or sister by befriending, playing with, and supervising him or her. The quality and burden of caregiving responsibilities are influenced by a variety of factors, including the quality of interactions in the family, degree of affection, reciprocity, and parental availability and involvement.

Clearly, no social phenomenon, especially one as complex as family life, is either all negative or all positive but involves a mix of both positive and negative effects. Siblings have also talked about the positive effects of having a brother or sister with ADHD. These include building a stronger sense of self, character development, developing a strong sense of empathy and sensitivity to others, assertiveness, maturity, resilience, and family cohesion when the family pulls together during periods of crisis. Offering support and interventions at the family level can increase the likelihood that all members of the family will benefit.

Conclusion

Increasing family stability and using family-based interventions for helping family members cope with the difficulties of living with ADHD is important in order to optimize the outcomes for both the child and the family. Children with ADHD who are raised in stable family environments and have well-adjusted parents have less negative adolescent outcomes. It is in the area of family environment that clinicians and social or behavioral researchers can have the greatest impact in changing the downward spiral that many of these families experience as children grow older.

Judith Kendall

See also Attention Deficit/Hyperactivity Disorder: Family Involvement and Management; Disabilities and Family Management; Family Conflict Related to Caregiving; Family Emotional Climate and Mental Health; Families Experiencing Chronic Physical and Mental Health Conditions; Family Self-Management; Learning Disabilities in the Family; Mental Health Assessment for Families; Psychiatric Medication for Families

Further Readings

Barkely, R. (2000). *Taking charge of ADHD: The complete authoritative guide for parents.* New York: Guilford.

Barkely, R. (2005). *ADHD and the nature of self-control.* New York: Guilford.

Barkely, R. (2006). *Attention deficit hyperactivity disorder: Handbook for diagnosis and treatment.* New York: Guilford.

Kendall, J. (1998). Outlasting disruption: The process of reinvestment in families with ADHD children. *Qualitative Health Research, 8*(6), 839–857.

Kendall, J. (1999). Sibling accounts of ADHD. *Family Process, 38,* 117–136.

Kendall, J., & Shelton, K. (2003). A typology of management style in families with children with ADHD. *Journal of Family Nursing, 9*(3), 257–280.

Websites

ADHD Family Online: http://www.adhdfamilyonline .com

Children and Adults with Attention Deficit/Hyperactivity Disorder: http://www.chadd.org

Autism Spectrum Disorder and the Family

Autism spectrum disorder (ASD) is a neurodevelopmental disorder characterized by impairments in socialization, limitations in communication, and the presence of restricted and repetitive behaviors and/or interests. ASDs are a spectrum of disorders because the symptoms can occur in a variety of combinations and present with varying degrees of severity.

Each child with ASD is unique and requires intervention tailored to meet his or her needs. To achieve the best possible outcomes for children with ASD, care needs to involve the child and the family, and intervention needs to include minimizing stressors associated with caring for a child with ASD and maximizing support available to families. Following an introduction to ASD, this entry focuses on caring for an autistic child in the context of the family and highlights several specific stressors commonly encountered by families. Emphasis is on the importance of alleviating these stressors and providing family support to ensure optimal family functioning.

History

In 1943, Leo Kanner described the presentation of children later labeled as *autistic*. He highlighted the "aloneness" these children experience. This social impairment, coupled with communication difficulties and the display of unusual behavior, has come to characterize ASD.

The Centers for Disease Control and Prevention report that in 2007, 1 in 150 children in the United States was living with an ASD. ASD is not, however, unique to the United States. Current international initiatives aim to explore the worldwide prevalence rates of ASD. The rate of autism in boys is four times higher than in girls.

Unlike conditions where a precise cause is clear, the etiology of ASD is unknown. Growing evidence supports the idea that ASD is a disorder with diverse etiologies, primarily involving interaction between genetic susceptibility and environmental influences.

Effects on the Family

Having a child with ASD influences the family unit significantly. Experts around the world agree that parents should collaborate with a treatment team in the design and implementation of a package of services for their children. Parents thus play a large role in obtaining and implementing services for their children. By identifying family strengths and weaknesses at the start of therapy and attempting to alleviate stressors and capitalize on family strengths, providers can best help children with ASD. The following sections explore several commonly encountered issues, which include obtaining a diagnosis, advocating for services, appreciating the financial burden, and attending to siblings.

Obtaining a Diagnosis

Despite improvements in early screening for ASD, the lengthy evaluation process required for formal diagnosis can result in parental anxiety and frustration. Many evaluation centers have long waiting lists. As parents wait, they must cope with their child's behavior and learning problems alone. When a child is suspected to have ASD, prior to formal evaluation, parents should be directed to resources that can begin to help them. Health care providers, schoolteachers, and therapists can provide preliminary information on ASD even if the child has not received a formal diagnosis. This can alleviate stress associated with lack of information, misinformation, and the feeling that "nothing can be done" until the child sees an evaluation team.

Advocating for Services

Following formal diagnosis, parents often find themselves overwhelmed by the number of appointments, secondary evaluations, and decisions they need to make to establish a treatment program. The early years of therapy can be intense, and there are hundreds of available treatment options to evaluate. Establishing a network of providers is a priority and may involve traveling long distances if the family lives in a rural area. Identifying a medical home (one provider to coordinate the child's overall care) is critical to ensuring that families can access resources. Having a central provider to advocate for the child and family can alleviate the burden that often falls on a single family member (commonly, the mother). Reinforcing the sense of partnership and collaboration can minimize confusion, and ease parental fears about navigating a lifelong illness.

Appreciating the Financial Burden

Families of children with ASD quickly realize the tremendous time commitment required to care for their child. This frequently involves a parent quitting a job or reducing the number of work hours. Reports indicate that compared to families of children with other health care needs, families of children with special health care needs and autism have greater financial, employment, and time burdens. Many treatments for ASD (some still lacking scientific evidence of efficacy) encourage parents to try special diets and purchase expensive vitamins or supplements. The intense therapy required to improve skills in children with ASD is also expensive and insurance coverage varies by policy and state. Parents need guidance as to whether the benefit of a suggested treatment is worth the price they must pay to provide it.

Attending to Siblings

Parents often express concern for siblings in the family. Caring for the child with ASD is tiring and time consuming. Additionally, the nature of ASD itself limits the ability of siblings to interact with their brother or sister the way friends might relate to their siblings. Open communication with each child is important to ensure that he or she understands the social and emotional limitations associated with ASD. Ensuring one-on-one time with each parent is critical to balancing out the amount of time that is spent with the autistic child. Parents need to be sensitive to sibling needs and work to ensure that they have a role in helping the family care for the child with ASD.

Conclusion

Given the increasing international attention to ASD, it is important for those working with these families to be aware of issues they encounter. This entry provided an introduction to several key issues that can become a source of stress for families. This stress can then lead to poor family functioning and the deterioration of family health. ASD is a lifelong illness requiring lifelong support. A well-informed professional can ensure that families of children with ASD undergo assessment for these common sources of stress and can then mobilize resources early in the process of care.

Melissa Dodd Inglese

See also Access to Health Care: Child Health; Family Experiencing Transitions; Partnering With Families: Family-Centered Care; Stress Management Theory and Techniques in Families

Further Readings

Kogan, M. D., Strickland, B. B., Blumberg, S. J., Singh, G. K., Perrin, J. M., & van Dyck, P. C. (2008).

A national profile of the health care experiences and family impact of autism spectrum disorder among children in the United States, 2005–2006. *Pediatrics, 122*(6), e1149–e1158. Retrieved January 14, 2009, from http://pediatrics.aappublications.org/cgi/content/full/122/6/e1149

Volkmar, F. R., Rhea, P., Klin, A., & Cohen, D. (Eds.). (2005). *Handbook of autism and pervasive developmental disorders: Assessment, interventions, and policy* (3rd ed., Vol. 2). Hoboken, NJ: John Wiley & Sons.

Websites

Autism Speaks: http://www.autismspeaks.org
National Autistic Society: http://www.nas.org.uk

B

BABYSITTING AND THE FAMILY

Babysitting is the practice of caring for a child or children on a short-term, temporary basis for the parents or guardians of the child. Babysitting is different from child care or nanny care, both of which are ongoing and consistent and have an educational expectation. The primary purpose of babysitting is to keep children safe. Babysitting is not regulated by a legal entity as are child care programs. To help ensure that the child or children have a satisfying and safe experience, the parent or guardian should select a sitter who is responsible, has basic skills, and is willing to follow directions and enforce family policy. This entry describes the characteristics of a desirable babysitter and presents information on preparing for the babysitter.

Characteristics of a Desirable Babysitter

When choosing a babysitter, families should determine that the babysitter has the necessary age-appropriate knowledge and skills to care for their children. They should discuss with the babysitter their expectations and review the skills and knowledge they desire. The babysitter should enjoy being with the age of the children under their care. Selecting a babysitter who enjoys his or her work will allow both the parents and children to have a good experience, and the individual should also be sufficiently mature to handle common emergencies. Babysitters should have basic first aid training and cardiopulmonary resuscitation (CPR) knowledge and skills. A babysitter may be asked to undergo first aid and CPR training, such as the American Red Cross program or a program offered in the school system. The babysitter should possess knowledge of basic safety practices. These practices include placing infants on their backs to sleep, knowing an appropriate fire evacuation route, choosing appropriate toys for the child's age, not opening the door to strangers, serving age-appropriate foods and preparing them accordingly, and never leaving the child alone in the house or car. Babysitters should demonstrate that they understand the importance of proper hand hygiene (i.e., when and how to wash their hands and the children's). When applicable, they should demonstrate appropriate diapering and bathing procedures.

Preparing for the Babysitter

Prior to finalizing arrangements with a babysitter, parents or guardians should check the babysitter's references and training. Ideally, the sitter will spend time with the family before babysitting so that the babysitter can meet the children and learn their routines. During this introductory time, the family can take the opportunity to observe the "chemistry" between the babysitter and the children. Giving the babysitter a tour of the house including the quickest fire escape route, location of emergency supplies, and areas in the home that might be a potential hazard help the babysitter be better prepared for an emergency. Parents or guardians should develop a list of people to contact in case of problems or an emergency. This list needs to be posted in an easily accessible place for the babysitter. The listing of contact people and their phone numbers should include the parents' or guardians' full names, home address, and phone number in case the sitter needs to call 911, the child's or children's doctor, the police department, the fire department, and the names and phone numbers of nearby neighbors. Parents and guardians must also provide the name, address, and phone number where they can be reached and the time when the babysitter can expect them to return.

With the babysitter and the children present, parents or guardians can review the following family policies and guidelines so that there is no misunderstanding between parent or guardian, babysitter, and child: mealtime routines and the types of snacks that are permissible, appropriate telephone and cell use, computer and Internet use, TV and DVD viewing, and bedtime routines and expectations. If the children have allergies or special health care needs, then parents or guardians must explain in detail the conditions, appropriate response, and instructions on any medications to be given. Parents or guardians need to actually demonstrate how to give medications and request a return demonstration to ensure the babysitter knows how and can actually do it correctly. If at all possible, parents should try to give medications before leaving so that they do not need to be given by the babysitter. Also, parents or guardians should communicate clearly with the babysitter their policy regarding the children's friends visiting while the parents or guardians are away—who is allowed to visit and for how long.

Most states do not regulate when a child is old enough to stay home alone or to babysit other children. Guidelines developed by state child protective services are available on the Child Welfare Information Gateway's website.

Marilyn J. Krajicek and Barbara U. Hamilton

See also Caregiving: Infants; Grandparenting; Injury Prevention for Infants and Children Family Members; Kinship Care; Parenting; Selecting Child Care for Children

Further Readings

American Academy of Pediatrics. (2010). *Baby-sitting reminders*. Retrieved from http://www.healthychildren.org/English/safety-prevention/at-home/Pages/Babysitting-Reminders.aspx

Child Welfare Information Gateway. (2007). *Leaving your child home alone*. Retrieved from http://www.childwelfare.gov/pubs/factsheets/homealone.cfm

National Child Care Information Center. (2006). *Child care terminology*. Retrieved from http://nccic.acf.hhs.gov/poptopics/terminology.html#babysitting#babysitting

Parker, W. (2010). *Choosing the right babysitter*. Retrieved from http://fatherhood.about.com/od/parentingadvice/a/babysitting.htm

Websites

Child Welfare Information Gateway: http://www.childwelfare.gov

BEREAVEMENT AND PERINATAL LOSS IN CHILDBEARING FAMILIES

Perinatal loss refers to the death of a baby during pregnancy, at birth, or shortly after birth. A baby's death affects the parents, siblings, and extended family and friends. The grief they feel is not related to how long the pregnancy lasted or how long the baby lived. Instead, the intensity of the grief depends on what this pregnancy or baby meant to those left behind. Health care interventions are centered on the provision of individualized, supportive care that acknowledges the baby's brief life in ways meaningful to the family.

Types of perinatal loss include miscarriage, ectopic pregnancy, stillbirth, and newborn death. Miscarriage, the ending of a pregnancy prior to 20 weeks gestation, occurs more than a million times each year in the United States. Ectopic pregnancies, when the baby grows outside the uterus, occur in 1 out of every 60 pregnancies, according to the American Pregnancy Association. The National Center for Health Statistics reports that stillborn babies of 20 weeks gestation or older die at or before birth more than 26,000 times a year in the United States, and newborn death of live-born babies within the first 28 days of life occurs 18,000 times per year. Due to the prevalence of perinatal death, all health care providers will, within the context of their work, come in contact with families affected by such a loss.

Historical Context

In the early to mid-1900s, giving birth in hospitals became more common than home births. Fathers were not allowed in the delivery room, and a baby's death was often treated as a situation to be quickly forgotten. In the late 1960s, hospital policies started to change as care centered on the family and its needs, and preferences became commonplace. While health care providers are now attuned to providing compassionate, comprehensive care for families facing a perinatal death, society as a whole still struggles with how to best support those who experience perinatal loss. Many parents who experience a miscarriage or stillbirth find their grief is not fully recognized or validated.

Overview of Current Literature and Interventions

Upon diagnosis of the baby's death, usually by ultrasound, parents experience a myriad of emotions as their hopes are shattered. Simultaneously, parents must assimilate the necessary medical information while feeling the emotional pain of their loss. Through prenatal testing, some parents will learn their baby has a life-limiting condition that will result in death shortly after birth. Their grief will be affected by needing to make decisions regarding their baby's care. In all diagnostic situations, professionals must be mindful of respecting the parents' feelings while effectively answering their questions.

When perinatal death is diagnosed, the baby's gestational age will determine next steps in medical management. For early miscarriages, the mother may be advised to wait until labor naturally begins, or a dilation and curettage (D&C) may be performed. With a later miscarriage or stillbirth, labor will be medically induced in the hospital. Parents report it is helpful to receive both verbal and written information on what to expect during this time.

Health care providers establish relationships with the family, learning what would be most important as they anticipate the baby's delivery, thus facilitating creation of a supportive plan of care. Researchers have noted that parents value being provided with options such as viewing and spending time with their baby's body, collecting mementos, taking photographs, and participating in ritual. Asking parents about their religious or cultural values and beliefs allows professionals to deliver care within a meaningful context for the family. The inclusion of siblings, grandparents, friends, and extended family in the plan of care, according to the parents' wishes, helps to establish a supportive community.

Health care interventions should be centered on allowing families to experience and acknowledge their baby's life in ways that are most helpful to them. Care continues after the baby's death and families leave the hospital. Parents report the value of bereavement follow-up support, whether by phone, written information, or participation in memorial services or support groups. Grief does not end in a few days or months, as parents continue to find ways to honor the baby's short life.

Desired Family and Individual Health Outcomes

Many families experiencing the death of a baby feel alone because others are likely to view the baby's death as less significant than the death of an older person. Others may say, "Well, at least you never knew it," or "You'll get pregnant again." Instead, parents report needing to hear "I'm sorry" or "Please tell me more about your baby." Bereaved families value acknowledgement of the loss as they strive to live with their heartbreak. Eventually, most parents move through their grief to find meaning and connection to their baby's living and dying.

Recommendations for Health Care Providers

When a baby dies, parents and health care providers are reminded that parenthood can be tragic as well as joyful. A specific model for educating professionals about perinatal loss began in 1981 when Resolve Through Sharing was founded. Using this model, those who care for bereaved families learn there are no words to take away the sorrow. Yet developing relationships and being present with families provide comfort to both parents and health care providers, which can affect a family's emotional health for a lifetime.

Rana Limbo and Kathie Kobler

See also Childbirth by Childbearing Couples: Reported Meanings; Death and the Grieving Process in Families; Death Rituals in Families; Sibling Death/Loss

Further Readings

American College of Obstetricians and Gynecologists. (1995). *Early pregnancy loss* (Tech. Bulletin No. 212). Danvers, MA: Author.

Gold, K. J., Dalton, V. K., & Schwenk, T. L. (2007). Hospital care for parents after perinatal death. *Obstetrics & Gynecology, 109*(5), 1156–1166.

Kobler, K., Limbo, R., & Kavanaugh, K. (2007). Meaningful moments: The use of ritual in perinatal and pediatric death. *American Journal of Maternal Child Nursing, 32*(5), 288–295.

Limbo, R., & Wheeler, S. (2003). *When a baby dies: A handbook for healing and helping*. La Crosse, WI: Gundersen Lutheran Medical Foundation. (Original work published 1986)

MacDorman, M. F., & Kimeyer, S. (2009). Fetal and perinatal mortality, United States, 2005. *National Vital Statistics Reports, 57*(8). Retrieved April 15, 2010, from http://www.cdc.gov/nchs/data/nvsr/nvsr57/nvsr57_08.pdf

Mathews, T. J., & MacDorman, M. F. (2008). Infant mortality statistics from the 2005 period linked birth/infant death data set. *National Vital Statistics Reports, 57*(2). Retrieved April 15, 2010, from http://www.cdc.gov/nchs/products/nvsr.htm#v0157

Munson, D., & Leuthner, S. (2007). Palliative care for the family carrying a fetus with a life-limiting condition. *Pediatric Clinics of North America, 54*(5), 787–798.

Websites

American Pregnancy Association: http://www.americanpregnancy.org

Bereavement Services: http://www.bereavementservices.org

BIOPSYCHOSOCIAL THEORETICAL PERSPECTIVES OF FAMILY SYSTEMS

Substantial evidence linking family functioning to its members' well-being and health outcomes has accumulated over the past several decades. Five essential health functions of the family include (1) development of members' sense of personal identity and self-worth as a foundation for mental health, (2) socialization of family members to value and maintain practices that optimize health, (3) emotional sustenance and guidance during life cycle transitions, (4) education about when and how to use the health care system, and (5) care provision and management for chronically ill, disabled, and aging family members. This entry provides an overview of the family as a *biopsychosocial system* and illustrates how such knowledge may be used by health professionals to assess how well a family is meeting its health functions.

The Concept of Family

Health and human service professionals working with families need a broad conceptual perspective that recognizes diverse compositions, including the traditional two-parent nuclear family, single-parent families, blended families, childless couples, and gay or lesbian families. Based on general systems theory, a family is defined as two or more individuals who identify themselves as family and who manifest interdependence in interaction with each other and their environment in meeting basic needs for survival, affection, and meaning. As an interdependent system, the family is comprised of both subsystems and suprasystems. When the family is the focal system of interest, the suprasystems are the sociocultural group, neighborhood, community, state, or country in which the family is embedded, and the subsystems are sets of family relationships, such as husband–wife dyad (or partner dyad in case of gay or lesbian families), parent–child dyad, sibling–sibling dyad, or the individual members themselves. While components within a system may be described by their attributes, it is the relationship between the components that holds the system together. Because of these relationships, a system behaves as a coherent whole. The latter principle is foundational to understanding the issues that a family may experience in optimizing the health potential of its members.

Theoretical Perspectives of Family Health

No single theory is sufficient to address the complex dynamics that influence the family's competence to fulfill its health functions. The literature on family functioning identifies role competency, communication processes, and adaptability as core variables that influence a family's ability to fulfill its health functions. Four theoretical perspectives that provide health professionals with foundational knowledge to assess these core variables are family structural-functional theory, family developmental theory, family interactional theory, and family stress theory. A brief overview of each of these family theories is presented with emphasis on how each contributes to an understanding of the family's competence to optimize health for its members.

Family Structural-Functional Theory

The structural-functional perspective of the family originated in the disciplines of sociology and anthropology. The family is viewed as the basic social unit responsible for reproduction and socialization of members to the norms and values that lay the foundation for becoming responsible and participating citizens of the society. While the latter denotes the primary functions of the family, structure refers to how the family is organized. Family structure has been defined differently by various theorists; however, the allocated roles and power among family members are commonly accepted indicators of family structure. The degree of role complementarity that exists is a critical issue. Discrepancies in role expectations of family members tend to give rise to tension and conflict that, if left unresolved, may impede the family's ability to fulfill its societal expectations.

Difficulty in performance of one's role is defined as role insufficiency. With the birth of a child, parents are challenged to learn role behaviors for meeting the needs of the newborn. Likewise, the terminal illness or disability of a family member who has been the major economic support for the family may wreak havoc in the ability of the family to fulfill its functions for its members as well as for society. Understanding how the addition of a new family member or illness has altered family roles can facilitate interventions to assist families to redistribute role responsibilities using support networks and community resources as appropriate. Attention to power associated with selected family roles is also important in identifying who in the family has the authority for deciding when and for what reasons members use the health care system. While a strength of the structural-functional perspective is the emphasis on family functioning within the larger social context, a major weakness of this approach is the tendency to view family functioning at one moment in time rather than as a social system that changes over time.

Family Developmental Theory

Family developmental theory, which has its roots in developmental psychology, views the family system as undergoing a series of developmental life cycles revolving around the addition and exiting of members, for example, birth of baby, entry of child to school, or transition of older family member to assisted living or nursing home. The concept of family development tasks refers to specific role responsibilities that must be met during each life cycle stage to successively meet the health and developmental needs of its members. Role behaviors expected of parents of infants will differ from those expected of parents with children who are in their adolescent years. Thus, flexibility in role functioning over time enables the family to deal more effectively with developmental transitions.

The increasing diversity of family types has resulted in variations in the traditional family life cycle and associated developmental tasks. While a single-parent or lesbian family may experience the same life cycle changes as the traditional two-parent nuclear family, the absence of a second parent to share childrearing responsibilities or, in the case of the lesbian family, the added complexity of gender role modeling for children, may result in added stressors in meeting developmental tasks. Research suggests that families who are at most risk of experiencing difficulty in meeting developmental tasks are those who are (a) experiencing a greater number of concurrent life cycle changes, (b) facing role transitions of greater magnitude (e.g., blended families or families with children with special health care needs), (c) have a social support network that is small and nonsupportive, and (d) live in a community that has few available services to assist them with the transitions confronting them.

Family Interactional Theory

Family interactional theory emphasizes the internal processes within the family, specifically the way family members relate to one another and the meanings about self that members acquire through their interactions with one another. The underpinnings of this approach come from the discipline of social psychology and its emphasis on *symbolic interactionism*. Thus, in examining family processes, the *how* of interactions is viewed as more relevant than the *what*—that is, the content of the exchange. Communication patterns among family members, verbal and nonverbal, are considered primary modes for conveying meaning about self and other, particularly as it relates to self-identity, worth, and a sense of belonging—factors critical to a member's evolving mental health.

The concept of *differentiation* is particularly relevant to the interactional framework. Differentiation is the process whereby family members evolve a definition of *I* within the family group. The sensitivity of family interactions to each member's needs and the encouragement of personal responsibility for feelings and behavior serve to foster autonomy and the development of a sense of I. Thus, the extent to which families are able to maintain age-appropriate interpersonal boundaries is crucial to effective fulfillment of its affective function. Boundaries among family members may be described as lying along a continuum from disengaged (rigid and unresponsive to changing personal needs) to clear (respectful and age-appropriate) to enmeshed (diffuse and dependent). In addition to observing communication patterns among family members, attention to how the family uses physical space also provides information about how it strives to maintain interpersonal boundaries. Provision for individual privacy and personal possessions fosters the experiencing of self as separate and distinct from others.

While internal interactions among family members may facilitate or impede members' sense of self-worth and overall mental health functioning, families also vary in their extent of openness to environmental interchange and change. The interrelationships that develop between the family and its social networks, neighborhoods, communities, institutions, and culture are key factors in how well the family is able to meet its health responsibilities. Families that maintain relatively closed external boundaries may send their children to school but fail to become actively involved in school or other community activities that have the potential to enhance overall family functioning. A healthy family generally has some clearly defined boundaries but enough flexibility to be able to capitalize on its social network and other external resources as appropriate.

Another critical concept inherent to the family interactional perspective is *equifinality*, referring to the progressive complexity of interaction patterns found within the family and between the family and its environment over time. Families vary in their extent of openness to environmental interchange and change. When events within the family or environment trigger a change in the family's customary mode of functioning, family processes in the form of positive or negative feedback are activated. Negative feedback is directed toward maintaining constancy or the status quo, whereas positive feedback processes accommodate change and adaptation. Attention to the feedback processes that a family uses to manage change can assist the health professional to identify difficulties that it may be experiencing in meeting its members' developmental transitions.

Family Stress Theory

While family developmental theory focuses attention on the normative role transitions that occur within all families, family stress theory is concerned with nonnormative change in family functioning. The origins of contemporary family stress theory evolved out of research on war-induced separations and reunions in families during World War II. According to family stress theory, unexpected or unplanned events may be perceived as stressful and lead to disruptive changes in the family system if it is unable to manage the hardships associated with the event. Typically, stressors arising within the family (illness, divorce, death) tend to have the potential to be more disruptive than stressors that occur outside the family, such as natural disasters. However, the extent to which any given event is perceived as stressful depends on the family's appraisal of the event as potentially threatening, its past experience with stressors, and its resources (internal and external to the family) for dealing with change.

The concept of resiliency has been used to help explain why some families respond positively to challenges and others do not. Salient factors in family resiliency include overall positive outlook, shared values, role flexibility and role complementarity, clear communication patterns and open emotional expression, collaborative decision making and problem solving, routines and rituals that promote close family relationships and coherence, and strong support networks. Families that are unable to effectively deal with stressors as they arise may be more prone to experiencing increased disruption and crisis when confronted with new stressors due to unresolved past emotions and the perpetuation of ineffective behaviors.

Emerging Evidence on Genetic and Genomic Basis of Health and Illness

As illustrated in the overview of predominant family theories, biological factors contributing to health and illness within families are rarely addressed explicitly. The structural-functional approach emphasizes the reproductive function of the family, which lends itself to preconceptual consideration of genetic risk factors as well as maternal exposure to environmental hazards that may influence fetal outcomes. Furthermore, since one of the fundamental developmental tasks of families is to protect and nurture the health and development of its members, attention to biological, lifestyle choices (sleep, diet, exercise, smoking, alcohol and drug misuse) and environmental factors (home, community, workplace) that may negatively impact members' health is implied.

However, emerging evidence from genetic and genomic research suggests that the mechanisms contributing to disease processes within families can be complex and an increasing challenge, which health and human service professionals need to be prepared to address. A person's genetic makeup has been linked to a wide variety of child and adult conditions, including Tay Sachs, phenylketonuria, sickle cell disease, fragile X syndrome, Marfan's syndrome, Duchenne muscular dystrophy, Huntington's disease, cardiomyopathy and cardiovascular disorders, diabetes, breast cancer, osteoporosis, colorectal cancer, prostate cancer, and schizophrenia. Genomics, however, has shown that the development of many of these conditions is not the result of a single gene expression but a pattern of interconnections between a person's genotype, lifestyle, and external environmental factors. Although one's genotype may not be readily altered, the genomics or interaction among genes and other factors can be changed. Professionals working with families need to be able to effectively use knowledge of genetics and genomics to assist families with risk assessment, risk reduction, and disease prevention.

Application of Theoretical Perspectives to Assessment of Family Health

The integration of theoretical perspectives about the family as a biopsychosocial system provides direction to the collection, organization, and interpretation of data on the extent to which a family is able to fulfill its health functions. The conclusions reached from one's assessment is an evaluation that the family is functioning more or less optimally in meeting its health responsibilities, as opposed to an evaluation of the health status of a particular family member. A guide for the collection of data to assess how well a given family is able to fulfill each of its five health responsibilities follows.

Development of Personal Identity and Self-Worth

The family plays a key role in promoting the mental health of family members by providing opportunities for each to achieve a satisfactory sense of personal identity and self-worth. These areas are relevant to assessing how well the family is meeting this function: (a) family interactions are affirming and nonjudgmental, (b) interpersonal boundaries between parents and children or siblings are age-appropriate, (c) family interactions promote a sense of attachment without over-involvement or over-closeness, (d) verbal and nonverbal exchanges among family members are congruent, (e) family members are free to express their feelings or differences of views, (f) family exchanges include all members where appropriate, with no one member repeatedly ignored or excluded, and (g) family rituals and routines support the development of affection and a sense of shared meaning.

Socialization of Family Members to Value and Maintain Health

Values about health and practices to reduce risks to one's health are first learned within the context of the family. The latter reflect the family's culture as well as the knowledge and beliefs it holds about how to maintain health. Salient indicators to consider in assessing the family's capacity to meet this responsibility are (a) placement of health within the family's hierarchy of values, (b) lifestyle choices that facilitate or impede health, (c) family history (genogram) of risks for particular disease conditions, and (d) knowledge about actions family members can take to minimize predisposing health risks.

Emotional Sustenance and Guidance During Life Cycle Transitions

As noted earlier, the family is responsible for nurturing members' attainment of developmental tasks across life cycle transitions, including preparing them to be responsible members of society. Pertinent areas to consider in assessing how well the family is meeting this function are (a) knowledge about developmental needs of its members, (b) role competence to meet changing developmental needs of family members, (c) role flexibility to adapt members' changing developmental stages or unplanned events, and (d) openness to using social network and community resources to assist with life cycle transitions.

Education on Use of Health Care Services

While the family is instrumental in helping members to acquire values about health and how to maintain health, it also socializes members about how and when to use professional health care services. Key indicators that help to assess how well the family is meeting this function include (a) cultural definitions of health and illness, (b) use of folk remedies or complementary healing modalities, (c) decision-making processes about when to seek professional health care services, (d) ability to articulate health care concerns and questions in interactions with professionals, (e) resources (transportation, insurance) for accessing health care services, and (f) health care services available in the community.

Provision of Care for Ill or Disabled Family Members

Illness, disability, or functional dependence of individual members can be major stressors for a family. Yet families continue to play a major role in providing or managing care for ill or impaired family members. Salient areas to assess how the family is coping with this responsibility are (a) competence to address demands associated with a member's illness or disability, (b) flexibility to shift roles as needed, (c) social network resources to help alleviate the strain produced by care demands, (d) resources for accessing community services to assist with caring for an ill or aging family member, and (e) ability to balance the needs of other family members along with caregiving responsibilities.

Conclusion

Theoretical perspectives of the family as a biopsychosocial system have been presented as a foundation for the collection of data to assess how well a family is able to fulfill its health functions. Assessment of current family functioning is the first step in planning interventions to assist a family to more effectively address its health functions. The reader is encouraged to pursue additional reading about potential nursing interventions for working with families to promote health and the well-being of its members.

Ruth A. O'Brien

See also Critical Theory and Family Health; Defining Family: An Overview of Family Definitions From a Historical Perspective; Factors Influencing Family Health Values, Beliefs, and Priorities; Families: The Basic Unit of Societies; Family Emotional Climate and Mental Health; Family Health Perspectives; Genetic

Research Findings and Family Health; Psychological Theories Related to Family Health; Sociological Theories of Families

Further Readings

Boss, P. (2002). *Family stress management: A contextual approach* (2nd ed.). Thousand Oaks, CA: Sage.

Hanson, S. M. H., Gedaly-Duff, V., & Kaakinen, J. R. (2005). *Family health care nursing: Theory, practice, and research* (3rd ed.). Philadelphia: F. A. Davis.

Skolnick, A. S., & Skolnick, J. H. (2009). *Family in transition* (15th ed.). Boston: Pearson Education.

Wright, L. M., & Leahey, M. (2005). *Nurses and families: A guide to family assessment and intervention* (4th ed.). Philadelphia: F. A. Davis.

BIPOLAR DISORDERS AND THE FAMILY

Bipolar disorder is a debilitating illness with a large cost to individuals, families, and society. Lifetime prevalence estimates are 1.0% for bipolar I and 1.1% for bipolar II and 2.4% for subthreshold bipolar disorder, according to Kathleen Merikangas and colleagues. The lifetime risk of suicide in individuals diagnosed with bipolar disorder far exceeds the population norm. Bipolar disorder is highly comorbid with many disorders including substance abuse disorders, impulse control disorders, and anxiety disorders. Amid the burdens of the disorder, the family plays a significant role in the course and treatment of bipolar disorder. *Family* is here defined as individuals who live with and are related to the bipolar disorder individual (either biologically or adoptively). For example, family could include the bipolar disorder individual's spouse and children or his or her parents and siblings. Family members do not necessarily need to be in a caregiving role to affect the course of bipolar disorder illness.

Relatives of bipolar disorder individuals are more likely to suffer from the disorder than would be expected by predictions based on the population statistics. Across multiple studies, 10.7% of first-degree relatives of individuals with bipolar disorder had bipolar disorder, compared to a rate of 1.0% among relatives of nonbipolar disorder

controls. First-degree relatives also have an increased rate of major depression, 15.9%, more than double the rate in relatives of controls, according to Frederick K. Goodwin and Kay Redfield Jamison. Children of bipolar disorder parents are more likely to suffer from some psychological disorder and much more likely to suffer specifically from a mood disorder.

Several family environmental variables impact the course of bipolar disorder. One of the most robust findings regarding the effects of the family on the course of bipolar disorder is in the expressed emotion (EE) literature. EE measures the presence or absence of a critical, hostile, or emotionally overinvolved attitude of a family member toward a bipolar disorder individual. High-EE families contain family members who display critical or hostile ("He is too lazy to get a job") or emotionally overinvolved ("I worry about her mood swings constantly") attitudes toward the bipolar disorder individual. Bipolar disorder individuals in high-EE families are at greater risk for relapse and recurrence than bipolar disorder individuals in low-EE families.

High- and low-EE relatives tend to differ on the types of attributions they make regarding bipolar disorder illness. High-EE relatives tend to attribute the bipolar disorder individual's symptoms to internal, personal, and controllable causes; low-EE relatives, on the other hand, tend to attribute the bipolar disorder individual's symptoms to external, universal, and uncontrollable causes, such as illness.

Although there is clear evidence that family variables affect the course of bipolar disorder, the relationship is bidirectional. Bipolar disorder can impact interpersonal relationships within a family and contribute to the development of high EE. Significant deficits in interpersonal skills have been found among individuals with bipolar disorder, including deficits in processing of facial emotions and theory of mind. These deficits, as well as mood state and severity of symptoms, contribute to poorer interpersonal functioning by bipolar disorder individuals and, transitively, affect the family; for example, depressive episodes and more severe symptoms among bipolar disorder individuals have been associated with poorer family functioning.

The interpersonal stressors that the bipolar disorder individual places on the family may contribute to the development of high-EE attitudes held by family members. This view is supported by evidence that high-EE attitudes tend to decrease as bipolar disorder individual symptoms improve. However, relatives who are the most critical tend to remain the most critical over time. Thus, high-EE attitudes develop in part in reaction to the bipolar disorder individual and in part are a stable trait in the high-EE relative.

The current consensus in the literature is that family attitudes and symptoms of the affected individual influence each other via bidirectional, transactional processes over time. This is supported by studies examining patterns of interaction in families with a bipolar disorder individual. For example, bipolar disorder individuals' interactions with high-EE relatives are characterized by coercive bipolar disorder individual–relative exchanges that quickly escalate in intensity and hostility, while bipolar disorder individuals are less likely to respond to low-EE relatives with negative statements.

Because family attitudes and bipolar disorder symptoms mutually influence each other, treatments designed to intervene in this cycle can aim to improve the functioning of both the bipolar disorder individual and the family. David Miklowitz's family focused therapy (FFT) for bipolar disorder is one intervention designed to meet this goal. FFT is a 21-session family-based intervention involving family psychoeducation, communication skills training, and problem-solving skills training. FFT aims to reduce negative family communication and increase positive family communication via psychoeducation and skills training.

Several clinical trials have demonstrated the efficacy of this intervention, combined with pharmacotherapy, in relapse prevention and enhancement of long-term outcomes in bipolar disorder adults, including longer periods of stability without relapse, greater improvement in symptoms of depression and mania, and increased medication adherence. High EE moderates the effects of FFT in bipolar disorder adults; in a trial of FFT versus a control condition (crisis management), bipolar disorder individuals in high-EE families who received FFT experienced the most improvement in depressive symptoms. Family-based interventions may also be useful in the treatment of bipolar disorder adolescents.

Families with a bipolar disorder individual spend nearly 3 times as much on health care as families without serious mental illness. Direct lifetime mental health care costs have been estimated as $75K, of which nearly half is spent on medications. Costs vary greatly depending on the chronicity and severity of the illness and responsiveness to treatment. There is evidence that family-based interventions for bipolar disorder can reduce hospitalization rates thereby reducing cost to the family. Further research is needed to determine the extent to which the 21-session FFT or other family-based interventions might reduce this heavy cost burden.

The family is an important factor in the course and treatment of bipolar disorder. The relationship between the family and individuals with bipolar disorder is bidirectional and transactional. The combination of medications and family-based interventions, such as FFT, are effective.

W. E. Craighead, Anjana Muralidharan,
and Daniel J. Yoo

See also Depression in the Family; Families Experiencing Chronic Physical and Mental Health Conditions; Family Emotional Climate and Mental Health; Outpatient Mental Health Care for Families; Psychoeducational Interventions for Families

Further Readings

Begley, C. E., Annegers, J. F., Swann, A. C., Lewis, C., Coan, S., Schnapp, W. B., et al. (2001). The lifetime cost of bipolar disorder in the US: An estimate for new cases in 1998. *Pharmacoeconomics, 19,* 483–495.

Butzlaff, R., & Hooley, J. (1998). Expressed emotion and psychiatric relapse: A meta-analysis. *Archives of General Psychiatry, 55,* 547–552.

Chatterton, M. L., Ke, X., Lewis, B. E., Rajagopalan, K., & Lazarus, A. (2008). Impact of bipolar disorder on the family: Utilization and cost of health care resources. *Pharmacy and Therapeutics, 33,* 15–34.

Goodwin, F. K., & Jamison, K. R. (2007). *Manic-depressive illness: Bipolar disorders and recurrent depression* (2nd ed.). New York: Oxford University Press.

Hooley, J. M., & Gotlib, I. H. (2000). A diathesis-stress conceptualization of expressed emotion and clinical outcome. *Applied and Preventive Psychology, 9,* 131–151.

Merikangas, K. R., Akiskal, H. S., Angst, J., Greenberg, P. E., Hirschfeld, R. M. A., & Petukhova, M., et al. (2007).

Lifetime and 12-month prevalence of bipolar spectrum disorder in the National Comorbidity Survey replication. *Archives of General Psychiatry, 64,* 543–552.

Miklowitz, D. (2004). The role of family systems in severe and recurrent psychiatric disorders: A developmental psychopathology view. *Development and Psychopathology, 16*(3), 667–688.

Miklowitz, D., & Johnson, S. L. (2008). Bipolar disorders. In W. E. Craighead, D. J. Miklowitz, & L. W. Craighead (Eds.), *Psychopathology: History, diagnosis, and empirical foundations* (pp. 366–401). New York: Wiley.

Simoneau, T. L., Miklowitz, D. J., & Saleem, R. (1998). Expressed emotion and interactional patterns in the families of bipolar patients. *Journal of Abnormal Psychology, 107,* 497–507.

BIRTH DEFECTS AND THE FAMILY

Birth defects are a major contributor to the rate of deaths among newborns (infant mortality). In the 1940s, rubella infection during pregnancy was found to have devastating effects on the fetus, from fetal death to hearing impairment, cataracts, and heart defects. Twenty years later, the perception of the placenta as a barrier against drugs changed. Women taking thalidomide during early pregnancy gave birth to children with severe limb deformities. Thus, the placenta did not protect the fetus against environmental factors (e.g., teratogens), such as infectious agents and chemical agents (drugs). Furthermore, birth defects with a genetic origin could be inherited from parents via the fetus. In the early 1990s, folic acid supplementation was found to reduce the occurrence of neural tube defects and other kinds of birth defects.

This entry reviews the etiology and diagnosis of birth defects affecting one person but having an impact on the family as well. Interventions, treatment programs, and future plans are also illuminated.

Definitions and Epidemiology of Birth Defects

Birth defects can be divided into structural and functional defects present at birth and with physical or mental disabilities or death as the result. *Structural defects* can be minor, severe, or lethal. *Minor birth defects* (tortio-collis) don't require immediate surgery or medical treatment to maintain life, as both severe and lethal defects do (heart defects, cleft lip with or without cleft palate, neural tube defects). *Functional defects* are related to the functionality of body parts or systems, and they may lead to developmental disabilities. This can be chromosome abnormalities (Down syndrome), sensory problems (loss of vision or hearing), metabolic disorders (phenylketonuria [PKU]), or degenerative disorders (muscular dystrophy). The disorders may be detectable before or at birth, but the metabolic and some sensory disorders can be detected only at birth or later, and the degenerative disorders deteriorate the health bit by bit. Structural and functional defects may be inherited with familial clustering of heart anomalies, midline abnormalities, cystic fibrosis, and neural tube defects. A carrier gene test could be relevant for single gene disorders (cystic fibrosis).

For 70% of all birth defects, the etiology is multifactorial or without known cause. The rest are due to genetics, chromosomal deletions, or different environmental or prenatal exposure factors, such as teratogens: infections (rubella, toxoplasmosis, cytomegalovirus), drugs, alcohol and cigarettes, pesticides, radiation, maternal diseases, or high or very low prepregnancy maternal body mass index (BMI). Organs are most vulnerable to teratogens during the development in early pregnancy, and the most severe structural defects (neural tube defects, heart defects, cleft lip and palate) occur in this period.

According to the March of Dimes, an estimated 6% of all births globally are children born with a serious birth defect (nearly 8 million) partly or totally with a genetic origin. Further, hundreds of thousands more are born with birth defects after prenatal exposure to teratogens. Every year, more than 3 million babies die within the first 5 years of life. The occurrence of birth defects is higher in low- and middle-income countries, maybe due to malnutrition, infections, consanguineous pairs, or unawareness of the etiology. European and American studies report frequencies of birth defects per year: heart defects (0.6–1 per 100), cleft lip and/or palate (1–6.3 per 700), Down syndrome (1–1.4 per 800), and spina bifida (1–1.3 per 2,500).

Desired Health Outcome for the Family and the Child

The desired health outcome for the family and the child with a birth defect would be a life that could meet the needs and wishes for the individual and the family. The possibility of a prenatal diagnostic gives the family the opportunity to prepare, the unborn or newborn child to be operated on, or the family to choose an abortion if the fetus has severe birth defects.

Interventions and Treatment Programs

Family planning reduces the number of unplanned pregnancies, thus eliminating unintended exposure to teratogens and minimizing the amount of very young or old mothers. The safety and health of both mother and family should be optimized, preferably before pregnancy: a maternal BMI within the normal range, healthy food and exercise habits, folic acid supplementation (0.4 mg/day), and no alcohol drinking or cigarette smoking. Prescribed or recommended drug use should be limited to what is the safest and most effective. For epilepsy, that means valproate; polytherapy should be avoided. For depression, paroxetin should be avoided. Certain other drugs should also be avoided: thalidomide, lithium, isotretionin, tetracycline, anticancer drugs, angiotensin-converting enzyme (ACE) inhibitors (enalapril, captopril), androgens and testosterone by-products, and illegal drugs (cocaine, marijuana, ecstacy). Use of other drugs should be discussed with the physician before pregnancy. Maternal diseases should be well regulated, including diabetes mellitus, epilepsy, depression, and hypertension. Precautions to avoid infections should be taken, including vaccination against rubella (German measles) at least 1 to 3 months before pregnancy if the woman hasn't had the infection. Other infections such as toxoplasmosis or cytomegalovirus should be avoided.

Counseling of the woman or family could include (a) a preconception diagnostic (before pregnancy)—a genetic test—if the parents or a sibling has birth defects; (b) a prenatal diagnostic (in early pregnancy)—counseling by the physician; an estimate for the child's risk of having Down syndrome, other chromosome anomalies, or open birth defects examined by a blood test (double test); and an ultrasound examination; (c) neonatal diagnostic (after birth)—a physical examination of the newborn and a blood test (PKU test) taken before discharge from the maternity unit to identify birth defects or metabolic disorders (phenylketonuria).

Relevance to Broader Issues of Family Health Care

To reduce the occurrence of birth defects, it is essential to focus on health and social care for the woman, family, and child before, during, and after pregnancy. The woman or family should be educated to be aware of the different teratogenic and genetic factors that could be minimized, optimized, or even changed before pregnancy. Physicians or health caregivers may assist the family. Several studies of birth defects are ongoing, and published work from these must be followed carefully to make good recommendations and guidelines.

Dorte Kjaer

See also Fetal Alcohol Exposure and Family Health; Health Needs of Childbearing Families; Newborn Screening for Families; Preconceptual Counseling for Childbearing Couples; Prediction of Genetic Health Problems in Family Members; Prenatal Surgery and the Family

Further Readings

March of Dimes. (n.d.). *The March of Dimes global report on birth defects: The hidden toll of dying and disabled children.* Retrieved from http://www.marchofdimes.com/professionals/871_18587.asp

Websites

Centers for Disease Control and Prevention, National Center on Birth Defects and Developmental Disabilities: http://www.cdc.gov/ncbddd/index.html
Eurocat, European Surveillance of Congenital Anomalies: http://www.bio-medical.co.uk/eurocatlive

Birth Order of Children in Families

The effect of birth order on personality, behavior, and achievements has been a controversial issue, with popular books describing the precise personality traits for firstborns, middle borns, and last borns, while scholars disagree about whether there is empirical evidence for differences. Recently, Frank Sulloway reviewed the research and concluded that whereas firstborns identify with power and authority and are assertive, dominant, and ambitious, younger siblings are more likely to question the status quo and become revolutionaries.

Birth order effects are complicated by the sex of the children, the number of children, and the age differences between them. There are also potential differences between one's actual birth order in the family and psychological birth order based on such factors as the death of siblings and the presence of stepsiblings and half siblings. In addition, differences in the patterns of behavior observed in firstborns and later borns may appear only in the presence of their parents; that is, the differences may be context specific.

The first theorist to stress the importance of birth order was Alfred Adler. Adler noted how the firstborn is "dethroned" by the birth of the next sibling, often becomes a surrogate parent, emphasizes the importance of law and order, and becomes a power-hungry conservative. If firstborns fail to regain favorite status with their parents, they may rebel. Second borns try to catch up with their older sibling and try harder at life's tasks. They find it hard to follow other leaders. The last born is never dethroned and so may become lazy and spoiled, often experiencing a feeling of inferiority.

Although Sigmund Freud did not devote a great deal of attention to birth order, later psychoanalysts have. Walter Toman, an Austrian psychoanalyst, proposed that matching birth order between spouses, along with the number and sex of a person's siblings, determined the success of marriages, and his study of data from Austria confirmed this.

Although siblings share a common family environment experience, including similar social and financial resources, each sibling also has a unique experience based on when they entered the family. For example, firstborns may receive greater frequency of discipline than later born children. Parents may have higher expectations for older children and require them to take on more responsibility around the house, take care of younger siblings, and act as a role model. Parents tend to perceive the behavioral, emotional, and physical changes of firstborns during the onset of adolescence more negatively as compared to how they perceive those changes in middle-born or last-born children.

Middle borns typically have the least positive views of their families of origin and are the least likely to offer help to their families as compared to firstborns and last borns. Middle borns are also the least likely to report being either a mother's or father's favorite child in the family, and they perceive their parents as being less emotionally and financially supportive as compared to the perceptions of firstborn and last-born children.

Birth order differences can appear at a young age. Only children and firstborns are more sociable at age 2, while later borns are less sociable. Firstborn children are less depressed and anxious than later borns and have higher self-esteem. One possible explanation for these early differences could be that mothers spend less time engaging in social interaction and affection with later-born infants as compared to firstborns.

Sulloway has suggested several sources for these differences by birth order: (1) differences in parental investment, which favor, in different ways, the firstborns and last borns; (2) sibling dominance hierarchies; (3) the tendency for siblings to strive to be different from one another; (4) the social stereotypes for siblings of different birth orders (which lead to shaping behavior to conform to the stereotypes); and (5) the adoption of different roles within the family by the siblings (as when a firstborn becomes a surrogate parent).

Andrew Schwebel and Mark Fine presented a cognitive-behavioral family model that suggests siblings may develop unique cognitions about relationships based on their unique experience within their family. For example, firstborns are more likely to identify themselves as taking the "responsible" role within the family, middle borns the "popular" role, and last borns the "spoiled" role.

Birth order may also impact other interpersonal relationships. In one study, middle borns had the most positive views of friends and were the least likely to cheat on their sexual partners as compared to firstborns and last borns. Research has shown that firstborns report a significantly greater number of irrational beliefs about romantic relationships than last borns, while a study in the Netherlands found that later borns had higher scores on measures of reactive, possessive, and anxious jealousy even when controlling for personality differences, attachment style, and gender.

Studies of the birth order of people with personality dispositions or psychiatric problems are often methodologically unsound since the proportions of firstborns and second borns (and also later borns) in the general population are not identical. Comparisons of the personalities of those with differing birth order are more meaningful, and Daniel Eckstein has provided a summary of 151 articles published between 1960 and 1999 that reported statistically significant birth order personality differences.

Despite the difficulties of controlling for all of the potentially confounding variables in birth order research, it is important for clinicians to recognize the impact of birth order within a family. It is helpful to identify the significance that family members themselves attribute to birth order and how it relates to the current problems that have led the family to seek treatment.

David Lester and Jessica Jablonski

See also Educating the Family Regarding Serious Mental Illness; Family Experiencing Transitions; Family Therapy; Sibling Conflict; Sibling Death/Loss; Sibling Physical Abuse

Further Readings

Eckstein, D. (2000). Empirical studies indicating significant birth-order-related personality differences. *Journal of Individual Psychology, 56*, 481–494.

Hoopes, M. M., & Harper, J. M. (1987). *Birth order roles and sibling patterns in individual family therapy.* Rockville, MD: Aspen.

Schwebel, A. I., & Fine, M.A. (1992). Cognitive-behavioral family therapy. *Journal of Family Psychotherapy, 3*, 73–91.

Sulloway, F. J. (1996). *Born to rebel.* New York: Pantheon Books.

Toman, W. (1976). *Family constellation.* New York: Springer.

BLINDNESS AND THE FAMILY

Legal blindness is defined as a visual acuity of 20/200 in the better eye after correction and/or a visual field of no greater than 20 degrees. This level of visual impairment is required to access certain benefits and resources, but from a functional standpoint, a visual impairment can be defined using different acuity levels. For example, most state requirements for obtaining an unrestricted driver's license set the visual acuity cutoff as 20/40 or 20/50.

The term *blind* is routinely used to refer to individuals who meet the definition of legal blindness; however, most people who are blind have some level of usable vision. Individuals who have decreased sight but are still able to use vision to help accomplish daily tasks are considered to have *low vision.*

Visual impairments can be categorized into three distinct types. Some visual impairments result in decreased overall acuity, others result in decreases of central or peripheral visual fields, and some visual impairment is the result of an inability of the brain to interpret visual input.

This entry begins with a brief discussion of the prevalence of blindness and the issues faced by families with a child or adult member who is blind. Lastly, the entry presents sources of support for the person who is blind.

Prevalence

The global prevalence of blindness varies widely depending on economic, social, and medical services. Blindness among children is considered a low-incidence disability (0.03% of children in developed countries, 0.1% in developed countries). It is estimated that approximately 50% of children with congenital visual impairments also have additional disabilities.

Blindness among adults, especially among older adults, is considered a high-incidence disability (approximately 3.5%). Many adults with age-related visual impairments also have other health concerns that may or may not be related to the cause of their visual impairment.

Regardless of the age of onset of a visual impairment, the cause of the visual impairment, or the association of additional health complications, a visual impairment will have an impact on family life.

The Family and Child Who Is Blind

Some causes of visual impairments are hereditary, but it is likely that most parents do not have a warning that their child will have a visual impairment prior to the birth of their baby. This may have implications for adjustment and daily life. The low-incidence nature of this disability may create challenges for parents since their experience with blindness may be unique in their community. It is therefore important to connect parents and family members as soon as possible to resources that can provide support. In the preschool and school-age years, the core group of skills developed by all children is also important for children with visual impairments. In addition, there are skills that are specifically needed by children who are blind or visually impaired, and the family plays a critical role in this development. In the school years, these disability-specific skills are called the *expanded core curriculum*. Development of these skills begins in early childhood. Areas of the expanded core curriculum are the following:

Orientation and mobility

Social interaction skills

Independent living skills

Recreation and leisure skills

Career education, use of or assistive technology

Sensory efficiency

Self-determination

The Family and Adult With Acquired Visual Impairment

Visual impairment among adults is relatively common. Most adult causes of visual impairment are age-related and are characterized by gradual loss of vision. These age-related causes of visual impairment mostly occur during the later working years or after retirement. Individuals with age-related vision loss and their family members often find themselves addressing the following issues:

Accessibility. Individuals with visual impairments address accessibility issues by making environmental modifications and learning new skills that allow a different approach to barriers to accessibility.

Involvement. Some people report that loss of vision results in loss of involvement in ordinary activities, at least temporarily, while adjusting to the visual impairment. Families often find creative ways of maintaining and encouraging ongoing involvement.

Safety. Safety is a primary concern for family members of individuals who are blind or visually impaired. Safety issues relate directly to a person's ability and confidence in his or her use of special skills.

Emotional Support. Adults with decreasing vision can experience emotional distress. The issue of visual impairment can be frightening and confusing, and emotional support from family members is critical.

Independence. Adults with age-related visual impairments may find that independence is challenged, especially when related to daily activities that involve driving. Levels of independence can be increased through instruction in compensatory skills.

Maintenance of Traditionally Defined Roles. A common complaint from adults with visual impairments is the loss of a sense of place within a family. It may take some time to acquire skills and adjust to differences in routine, but families can find ways to maintain and nurture changing dynamics.

Literacy. People with visual impairments use a wide range of literacy tools including print (with or without enlargement or the use of optical devices), braille, and audio sources. Children with visual impairments learn to read at the same pace and with the same efficiency as their sighted peers. Adults with acquired blindness may have more difficulty and fewer opportunities to learn braille and may feel more efficient using auditory information (e.g., audiobooks) and live readers.

Professional Support

There are several sources of support related to needs associated with visual impairment. Medical issues are addressed by ophthalmologists and by optometrists. Low vision specialists are helpful in determining optical devices and assistive technology that can be helpful. Children with visual impairments should have the support in school of a teacher of students with visual impairments, and adults are often supported by rehabilitation teachers who provide help in learning adaptive skills. In addition, both children and adults will benefit from instruction by an orientation and mobility specialist who will help them learn how to move safely and efficiently throughout the environment.

M. Cay Holbrook

See also Adult With Disability Living at Home; Americans with Disabilities Act and the Family; Disabilities and Family Management; Family Transitions and Ambiguous Loss

Further Readings

Duffy, M. A. (2002). *Making life more livable: Simple adaptations for living at home after vision loss.* New York: AFB Press.
Holbrook, M. C. (Ed.). (2006). *Children with visual impairments: A parent's guide.* Bethesda, MD: Woodbine House.
Ponchillia, P. E., & Ponchillia, S. V. (1996). *Foundations of rehabilitation teaching with persons who are blind or visually impaired.* New York: AFB Press.

BUDDHISM'S INFLUENCE ON HEALTH IN THE FAMILY

Family relationships, dynamics, and social supports are significantly related to the health and wellness of an individual. Positive relationships support health functioning, and negative relationships contribute to stress and adverse health outcomes.

Marriage is the family relationship that is mainly associated with physical and mental health; divorce and remarriage are two common and stressful transitions in the family life cycle. A family with an emphasis on religion, discipline, and parenthood tends to create a happy family atmosphere.

Many studies indicate that the Buddhist doctrine can be effectively applied to promote health among the family members. In many good Buddhist families, parents and children spend some time together reciting religious verses, practicing loving kindness and meditation. This establishes and maintains a friendly and peaceful environment in the family.

History

Due to the Buddha's compassion and concern for maintenance of happiness through marriage, he laid down specific instructions for the guidance of husband and wife as follows: A husband serves his wife by (a) honoring her in accordance with her status as his wife, (b) not disparaging her, (c) being faithful to her and not committing adultery, (d) handing over authority of household concerns, and (e) giving her occasional gifts of ornaments and clothing. In turn, a wife honors her husband by (a) keeping the household affairs tidy and well managed, (b) being helpful to the relatives and friends of both sides of the family, (c) being faithful to him and not committing adultery, (d) safeguarding any wealth or property that has been acquired, and (e) being diligent in all her work.

Health Effect in Family

Hence, a happy and sustainable relationship between the couple in the family can be accomplished by responding to each other with love, warmth, and sympathy as taught by the Buddha. On the contrary, a poor relationship between husband and wife can result in separation, divorce, and remarriage. The process of divorce varies for individual family members and puts them at risk for more physical and mental problems. Children's reactions to parental divorce vary according to age and gender. There are short-term and long-term effects for children and adolescents. Many people remarry and form a stepfamily after divorce. This can be stressful for adults and children. Research in psychoimmunology has shown that stress can decrease immunity and make individuals more susceptible to a host of different diseases.

Buddhist Teaching for Parents and Children

There is evidence suggesting that the family is one of the most proximal influences on child behavior and mental disorder. The Buddha's teaching for parents and children can be adopted as an intervention to promote health in the family. The parents should show their love for children by (a) cautioning and protecting them from evil, (b) nurturing and training them in goodness or virtue, (c) providing an education, (d) arranging a suitable spouse for them, and (e) handing over the inheritance to them at the proper time. In turn, a child administers to his parents by (a) looking after them in turn for their support, (b) helping them in their work, (c) continuing the family line and tradition, (d) behaving as is proper for an heir, and (e) performing meritorious acts and dedicating the merits to them when they have passed away.

Five Precepts as a Standard of Living

The Buddha advocated that the Five Precepts, or moralities (sila in the Pali text), are considered as a moral standard of a human being. The Five Precepts consist of the following: (1) to abstain from killing any sentient being, (2) to abstain from stealing others' properties, (3) to abstain from committing sexual misconduct, (4) to abstain from telling lies, and (5) to abstain from intoxicants causing heedlessness. If the family members observe the Five Precepts, they will be free from aggression, violence, delinquency, crime, promiscuity, sexual misconduct, AIDS, sexually transmitted diseases, corruption, alcohol and drug abuses, and other negative outcomes.

Training of Mental and Spiritual Health

In Buddhism, there are two kinds of mental training, namely, (1) concentration meditation (*samadhi* in the Pali text) and (2) insight meditation (*vipassana* in the Pali text). The purpose of concentration meditation is to develop calmness and tranquility of the mind, while the goal of insight meditation is to cultivate wisdom that leads to the cessation of suffering. The cause of suffering is craving and attachment to one's self or ego, which arise from deep-rooted unconscious defilements. According to the Buddhist's viewpoint, what is called *spiritual disease,* the opposite of spiritual health, is related to these unconscious defilements, which can be eradicated only through the practice of insight meditation.

Conclusion

The layperson's duties to his or her associates, as taught by the Buddha, for example, the duties of children to the parents and vice versa, can bring happiness, peace, pleasant interpersonal relations, and cohesiveness among the family members. This kind of atmosphere is conducive to the enhancement of positive health in a family. The practice of Five Precepts, concentration meditation, and insight meditation are closely related to the holistic model of health, which encompasses the physical, mental, social, and spiritual aspects of health.

Meditation is now included in complementary and alternative medicine as well as in body-mind medicine. For example, meditation is used to reduce stress, blood pressure, adrenal levels, heart rates, and skin temperature and to alter hormone levels and elevate mood.

Chamlong Disayavanish

See also Asian Families: Perspectives of Health; Factors Influencing Family Health Values, Beliefs, and Priorities; Family Health Perspectives

Further Readings

Bray, J. H., & Campbell, T. L. (2007). The family's influence on health. In R. E. Kakel (Ed.), *Textbook of family medicine* (7th ed., pp. 25–41). Philadelphia: Saunders Elsevier.

Edlin, G., Golany, E., & Brown, K. M. (1999). *Health and wellness* (6th ed.). Boston: Jones & Bartlett.

Phraphomkhunaphon (Payutto, P. A.). (1998). *A constitution for living: Buddhist principles for a fruitful and harmonious life* (1st impression). Bangkok, Thailand: Office of National Buddhism Press.

Sri Dhammananda, K. (1997). *Human life and problems* (1st ed.). Kuala Lumpur, Malaysia: Missionary Society.

Bulimia and Family Dynamics

Eating disorders are potentially life-threatening illnesses with physical, emotional, genetic, and societal components. Anorexia nervosa has the highest death rate of any mental illness—estimated at up to 20% over time. Cardiac arrest, kidney failure, and suicide comprise some of the most common causes of death in both anorexia and bulimia. Although these two illnesses may sometimes exhibit different symptoms, personality traits, and family dynamics, the similarities often outnumber the differences. It is not unusual for anorexia to evolve into bulimia or binge eating disorder and evolve back to anorexia during the course of the illness.

This entry begins with a discussion of the effects of eating disorders on families. Next, the common types of eating disordered families are presented. Lastly, treatments for eating disorders are addressed.

Implications for Family

Bulimia and anorexia are, in reality, family disorders affecting not only the persons with the illness but also everyone in their lives. Those who could be considered family may be parents, siblings, grandparents, spouses, in-laws, or any other significant group of people who hold importance in the sufferer's life. The system as a whole will be affected as the illness interrupts the family's usual schedules, daily routines, social involvements, and established roles. The identified patient often becomes the sole focus of attention and concern. Communication becomes guarded and distant. Afraid of saying the wrong thing or prompting a confrontation, family members may harbor unspoken feelings of resentment and guilt. Frustration, anger, and silence may permeate the entire household. As attempts by the family to correct "the problem" may prove unsuccessful, the sufferer may be seen as uncooperative, manipulative, demanding, and willful. It becomes difficult to separate the illness from the person, and the family is baffled at the changes they witness in the person they love. If the family was "functional" before the illness, dysfunction may present itself in many areas when the status quo is shattered and anxiety and worry surface concerning the patient's well-being. If there were preexisting dysfunctions in the family, such as alcoholism; mental illness; or emotional, physical, sexual, or drug abuse, they may be magnified with the chaos and uncertainties that present themselves as a result of the family trying to adjust to new rules and functioning in the face of illness.

The range of emotions experienced by the family may include fear of stigma, guilt, shame, anger, despair, bewilderment, and worry. Families often find themselves increasingly isolated and alone as extended family and friends, who often do not understand the complex nature of the illness, try to simplify the problem and place judgment on the parents for not "taking control" of the situation by simply getting their loved one to eat or stop bulimic symptoms, such as bingeing, vomiting, and excessive exercising or laxative, diuretic, and diet pill abuse. Partners face confusion on how to respond to the symptoms and still be supportive. They often feel torn between taking a tough custodial stand or expressing unconditional love. In addition, feelings of hopelessness and helplessness are driven in the entire family by the fear of impending loss or death.

The issues are complex and multifaceted, and the illness may indeed serve a purpose in the family. The purpose may encompass several and various needs such as to distract from a bad marriage, divorce, or addiction; to numb mourning from a loss or anesthetize the effects of abuse; or to gain attention from an emotionally distant parent. The need to be cared for, to receive affection and approval, and for recognition of pain through the expression of symptoms may be an unconscious drive for the illness. Being ill often justifies receiving attention where it has been devoid in the past. The sufferer often appears to assume a position of power and control in the family as it is evidenced that no one can "take away" the sufferer's dangerous behaviors. Consequently, siblings may resent the status of power and the attention the ill member is receiving and feel that their needs are being neglected.

Family Types

It is generally regarded that there are three common family types of the eating disordered family. These family types are labeled as *overprotective, perfect,* and *chaotic.* In the perfect family, appearance and reputation are of the utmost importance. There are often rigid rules of behavior and achievement with a denial that family problems exist. The achievements of family members rule supreme, and often, they are the most salient defining factor of each individual. Emphasis is placed on diet, food, weight, and physical appearance, leading the person with the disorder to believe that if she or he is not meeting the family standards, then she or he is somehow flawed and vulnerable to rejection.

The overprotective family may exhibit extreme discomfort with separation and individuation issues. Parents often show disapproval, hurt, and anger in attempts to separate. The need for autonomy and independence is seen as a lack of attachment and allegiance to the family, and the ill persons often feel that if they try to break away, they will be hurting the family. Parents in this type of family tend to be very involved in their children's lives (even through adulthood) and do things for them and complete tasks for them rather than teach or encourage them to do them independently. Risk taking is discouraged. They do not regard making mistakes and an occasional failure as teaching tools but rather as tragedies that must be avoided at any cost. This can lead to emotional immaturity and create a lack of feelings of confidence and competence.

Chaotic families are often unstructured and unstable. Rules may be inconsistent, and children may not know what to expect at any given time. Addictive behaviors and emotional, physical, and sexual abuse may be more prevalent. Parents may also suffer with depression, anxiety, obsessive-compulsiveness, or bipolar disorder and are not always emotionally available. The eating disordered child often takes on adult roles prematurely and may become a caretaker for other family members, which can lead to anxiety, resentment, and fearfulness. Anger may be expressed more often than in other families, and it may be excessive, violent, or inappropriate in nature. When lack of impulse control and poor conflict resolution are modeled, the person with bulimia is left with no resources for her or his own recovery. With the lack of predictability in this type of family, bulimia becomes an escape, provides a false sense of security and safety, and is, perhaps, the only outlet for emotional expression.

Treatment

Eating disorders require help from professionals specializing in eating disorders who have had extensive training in etiology, emotional and medical issues, family dynamics, and treatment of these complex problems. Professionals should include therapists, nutritionists, medical doctors, and psychiatrists. A team approach is required so that each specialist is up-to-date on treatment and goals for recovery. Services should be offered with compassion, nonjudgment, support, and understanding for both the patient and the family.

In treatment, communication in the family must be evaluated, and poor, indirect, critical, and aggressive communication must be addressed. If there is no safe outlet for feelings, teaching assertiveness and open communication skills can immensely improve family functioning. Attitudinal and behavioral changes should be encouraged. Separation and individuation issues, abuse issues, and the lack of conflict resolution and effective problem solving need to be worked on to create a better environment for recovery to occur. Family therapy can provide systemic changes that will potentially lead to a more satisfying life for all.

Anita Sinicrope Maier

See also Alcohol Addictions in the Family; Anorexia and Family Dynamics; Educating the Family Regarding Serious Mental Illness; Families Experiencing Chronic Physical and Mental Health Conditions; Family Emotional Climate and Mental Health; Family Therapy

Further Readings

LeGrange, D., & Lock, J. (2005). *Help your teenager beat an eating disorder.* New York: Guilford Press.

Maine, M. (2004). *Father hunger: Fathers, daughters and the pursuit of thinness.* Carlsbad, CA: Gurze Books.

Sherman, R., & Thompson, R. (1990). *Bulimia: A guide for family and friends.* New York: Lexington Books.

Siegel, M., Brisman, J., & Weinshel, M. (1997). *Surviving an eating disorder: Strategies for families and friends.* New York: HarperCollins.

Sinicrope Maier, A. (2009). Family therapy with eating disorders: Creating an alliance for change. In M. Maine, W. Davis, & J. Shure, (Eds.), *Effective clinical practice in the treatment of eating disorders: The heart of the matter.* New York: Routledge.

BULLYING AND THE FAMILY

Bullying is defined as dynamic and repetitive patterns of verbal, nonverbal, or virtual (cyber) behaviors directed by one or more individuals toward another individual that are intended to deliberately inflict psychological or physical abuse and where a real or perceived power differential exists.

Bullying occurs among children, within families, and in the workplace. It has the potential to significantly disrupt the health of individuals and, by extension, their families. Optimal outcomes are achieved when bullying is prevented. If bullying has occurred, interventions that minimize its impact need to be tailored to a recipient's specific situation. Following a brief discussion of bullying, prevention strategies within the family and community context are presented.

Historical Context

Bullying has existed since the dawn of civilization. Nonhuman primates, in order to survive within social groups, began sorting themselves into hierarchies while jockeying for dominant positions. Bullying among humans is tied to the rise of Western civilization; hierarchical governments, individualism, and personal recognition became valued over community harmony. Scholarly reports from the 18th to the 20th centuries denote bullying as a despicable behavior although family and community norms did not reflect this sentiment. If bullying was reported, the "whistleblower" often was marginalized by peers and authorities. From the late 20th century, as the long-term effects of bullying were recognized, greater emphasis was placed on recognition and intervention.

Overview of Current Literature

Bullies (instigators), victims (recipients), and victim-bullies (provocative recipients) come from all ethnic or racial groups, socioeconomic backgrounds, and either gender. Females more often engage in relational bullying (e.g., ostracism, spreading rumors); males are more physical, with equal participation in cyber bullying. The interplay of two parameters—the instigator's intent and the recipient's response—determine the type of bullying that occurs. *Subjective bullying* occurs when the recipient perceives that he or she is being bullied despite the absence of a power differential and/or intent to harm. *Objective bullying* occurs in the presence of a power differential and where the instigator(s) is successful in intimidating the recipient repeatedly.

Targets for bullying generally have dissimilar characteristics from those of the group norm. Different physical features, behaviors and mannerisms, and family traits are risk factors. Children with insecure parent–child attachment patterns or who are perceived as vulnerable by their parents also are at greater risk. In competitive schools and workplaces, successful individuals may be targeted by peers or supervisors as they are considered a threat. Finally, others are targeted for no identifiable reason. The presence of risk factors, however, does not mean bullying will occur. Personal resiliency and community norms demonstrating little tolerance for bullying serve as protective factors.

Recipients of bullying tend to have lower sociometric status within their referent group. Passive recipients are likely to be neglected (neither liked nor disliked) by others. They frequently demonstrate internalizing of problems (e.g., anxiety, depression), become submissive and insecure, restrict activities, and do not readily defend themselves when feeling threatened. A smaller group are *provocative recipients*, also called victim-bullies, and are rejected (highly disliked) by others. They often demonstrate externalizing manifestations including aggression, conduct problems, and engagement in other forms of violence. All recipients may manifest loneliness, diminished self-esteem, worsening attendance and performance at school or work, and increased psychosomatic complaints. For all recipients, a downward cycle of poor interactions with their harassers further exacerbates the bullying and concomitant victimization. Associated stresses result in a lower quality of personal and family life.

Children are more likely to bully if they come from a family where there is a lack of parental warmth, involvement, and/or supervision; parents are either overly permissive or use harsh, physical discipline; or parents engage in bullying themselves. These children are easily frustrated, impulsive, lack empathy, and view violence positively.

Adult bullies may have begun bullying in childhood or, having been bullied as a child, are now in family structures or professional positions where they can bully others.

Desired Family Health Outcomes and Interventions

Individuals of all ages must be educated about bullying through media campaigns and other venues. For schoolyard bullying, primary prevention consists of incorporating into school curricula programs that include teaching social competence and conflict resolution, creating a safe environment, and establishing and enforcing codes of conduct. Bullying should be discussed during children's and adults' primary health care visits. Parenting classes assist in creating an emotionally healthy milieu for all family members. Positive role modeling by adults throughout the community is requisite.

Secondary and tertiary prevention interventions, designed to detect bullying either at its earliest stages or after frank bullying and attendant suffering has ensued, are tailored to the targeted individual and, as appropriate, their family members, friends, and school or workplace authorities. General principles include providing specific strategies for deflecting future attacks (e.g., personal empowerment, help-seeking, modifying bystander behavior). Individuals are assisted in recognizing attributes that place them at risk for bullying, understanding the consequences of their choices, and modifying their behaviors accordingly. Knowing the warning signs of bullying by parents and professionals is paramount, as bullied individuals are often reluctant to confide in others.

Intervening with bullies is difficult. For those individuals who do not realize the impact of their behavior on others, creating awareness and offering suggestions for behavioral change may be effective. However, many bullies are gratified with the consequences of their behaviors. In such cases, bullies must be held accountable through consistent discipline with escalating, nonhostile consequences. Professional counseling is advised.

Conclusion

Because bullying is endemic, virtually all families have felt its sting. Bullying and its consequences diminish any family member's well-being and, by extension, the entire family. Early intervention is critical but especially for children as bullying can influence their developmental outcomes. Preventing bullying from developing or curtailing it in its infancy is associated with the best outcomes for families and their larger community.

Judith A. Vessey

See also Community Violence Exposure and Family Health; Psychoeducational Interventions for Families; Psychological Theories Related to Family Health; Sociological Theories of Families; Youth Violence Prevention in the Family

Further Readings

Hawker, D. S., & Boulton, M. J. (2000). Twenty years' research on peer victimization and psychosocial maladjustment: A meta-analytic review of cross-sectional studies. *Journal of Child Psychology and Psychiatry, 41,* 441–455.

Nansel, T. R., Overpeck M., Pilla, R. S., Ruan, W. J., Simons-Morton, B., & Scheidt, P. (2001). Bullying behaviors among U.S. youth: Prevalence and association with psychosocial adjustment. *JAMA: Journal of the American Medical Association, 16,* 2094–2100.

Olweus, D., Block, J., & Radke-Yarrow, M. (1993). *Development of antisocial and prosocial behavior: Research, theories, and issues.* Orlando, FL: Academic Press.

Websites

Stop Bullying Now: http://www.stopbullyingnow.hrsa.gov

CANCER IN THE FAMILY

The implications of cancer affect the entire family. The following discussion first reviews the influence cancer has on families and describes challenges relating to family communication patterns and prevention efforts. Resources for families facing cancer are provided at the conclusion of this entry.

The Centers for Disease Control and Prevention (CDC) estimate that there are 1.4 million cancer diagnoses in the United States every year, and the American Cancer Society (ACS) reports that people living in the United States have lifetime odds of about 1 in 2 of developing some kind of cancer. These odds mean that most families must deal with cancer at some point. Cancer is a frequent cause of death; according to the CDC, approximately 550,000 deaths in the United States are attributable to cancer each year. At the same time, improved detection and treatment have significantly increased the life expectancy for many people who are diagnosed with cancer, meaning that families often must deal with cancer as an ongoing challenge.

The effects of cancer on the family can happen in very direct ways; for example, if a breast cancer patient subsequently tests positive for a gene associated with breast cancer, such as BRCA1, this means that other family members are at greater risk for also developing breast cancer. Family implications happen indirectly as well; for example, people with cancer often need support and suffer individual setbacks that reverberate throughout the family, including the example of job loss. Cancer can also isolate the patient from other family members when extended hospitalization is required.

Cancer Prevention and Families

Individuals' orientation toward cancer prevention is influenced by family life. Healthy dietary choices, for instance, are at least somewhat interdependent among family members. Children are typically dependent on their parents for diet patterns. Even adult family members who want to make healthy choices can have their efforts complicated by other family members who follow less restricted regimens. In addition, cancer prevention behaviors can be a topic of conflict among family members; for instance, family members who smoke are sometimes criticized by family members who do not smoke.

Controversy also exists regarding the vaccine intended to prevent infection with the human papillomavirus (HPV). Because HPV causes most cases of cervical cancer, physicians now routinely recommend the vaccine to 11- and 12-year-old girls, but some parents oppose the vaccine because they believe preventing the sexually transmitted disease associated with HPV will implicitly encourage promiscuity. Parental decisions in such instances greatly influence the child's risk for cancer.

Families are additionally influential in determining whether individuals participate in screening. Other family members' attitudes about various screenings can be important; for instance, one spouse's willingness to accompany the other spouse during a colonoscopy can encourage screening.

Challenges for Families Dealing With Cancer

Families face a myriad of difficulties when a member has cancer. Certainly, the physical ailments and limitations associated with cancer are challenging for families. Family members often provide various types of support to the patient, including emotional support and tangible support, such as rides to treatment. Family members sometimes become directly involved with the physical care of people with cancer; for instance, when cancers require major surgery to remove tumors, the need for proper wound care often extends for a considerable time after the hospital stay. People with cancer often rely on their family to help them with their post-procedure care.

No matter how effectively a family supports a patient, some people with cancer die, and deaths in the family affect the entire family. Family members, including spouses, siblings, parents, and children, suffer from the loss of a loved one due to cancer, regardless of whether it was expected. Individuals may grieve for many years or even for a lifetime.

Whereas dealing with illness and death are prominent stressors involved in coping with cancer, there are a number of less obvious ones. Even when cancer is successfully treated, the various treatments can have serious physical and psychological side effects. Surgery, chemotherapy, and radiation can all lead to fatigue, which affects ability to relate to family members. Cancer treatment is also associated with nausea, loss of appetite, reduced immunity, and the inability to control certain bodily functions. Many people with cancer report experiencing "chemo brain," which refers to difficulties with memory, concentration, planning, and other cognitive functioning. Such unseen symptoms are often frustrating for people with cancer and families alike, and can last for years after treatment.

Some courses of cancer and the associated treatments lead to long-term changes in the patient's body. Cancer and its treatments can affect the body in many ways, including patients' physical abilities, physical attractiveness, sexuality, and fertility.

Such changes can have psychosocial implications for entire families; for instance, even a young wife who survives cancer with a good prognosis may have to alter her sense of identity and her family's planned course if she becomes infertile. Her husband needs to adjust as well if he planned on having more biological children with his spouse.

Cancer also can be very hard on relationships within families. In marriage, there is a myth that it is common for spouses to leave people with cancer, but this has not been found to happen more often than divorce among similar couples who have not had cancer. The myth that people with cancer are frequently abandoned by their spouses may stem from salient instances when a spouse leaves during a patient's treatment; it seems particularly devastating for people with cancer to have to simultaneously deal with divorce, especially because it comes at a time when most people with cancer turn to their family for greater support.

Even though cancer itself does not appear to markedly increase the odds of divorce, it is still a major challenge for family relationships. People with cancer whose immune systems have been compromised often have restrictions on making physical contact. Small children, who frequently have colds and other viruses, may not understand why a sick family member cannot touch or hold them. Such barriers to touch and physical closeness can adversely influence children's ability to bond with an ill adult in the family, such as a grandparent with cancer. Couples who have a child with cancer often face difficulties in supporting each other, supporting the child, and making treatment decisions. Adult children often are in the position of making treatment and end-of-life decisions for elderly parents with cancer. This situation can be difficult for families, particularly when adult siblings do not agree on the proper course of action. The various challenges to family relationships are not inevitably associated with adverse outcomes; nor are they permanent. For instance, some married couples have reported that coping together with cancer has made their relationship closer.

In addition to the aforementioned psychosocial implications for families, cancer can have devastating financial effects on families. All but the least serious cancer treatments cause interruptions in work for patients, and some patients even lose their jobs during treatment. Family members' support obligations may also interfere with their work. A cancer diagnosis can stimulate a family to begin worrying about potential estate planning issues, including what might happen to young children if the patient is the sole caregiver. Even if a family member survives treatment and has a good prognosis, it can affect that person's ability to obtain health insurance in the future, which leaves open the possibility of subsequent financial disaster.

Finally, once families have coped with all the physical, psychosocial, and financial consequences of cancer, they typically must live with the possibility that the cancer could come back. The uncertainty about the future and need for heightened vigilance about the cancer survivor's health can remain for years after treatment has ended.

Disease Characteristics

The discussion to this point has treated cancer as if it is a unitary disease and experience, but there are actually many different cancers with various characteristics. The impact that cancer has on a family depends on factors such as the stage of the cancer, the prognosis, and the particular type of cancer (e.g., skin, breast, or lung). According to 2008 statistics from the ACS, for example, melanoma of the skin has a 92% 5-year survival rate, whereas only 5% of people diagnosed with cancer of the pancreas live that long.

Outcomes associated with cancer also vary considerably in terms of treatment course. Even two people with ostensibly the same type of cancer may have quite different treatment regimens, depending on the exact progression, idiosyncratic factors, and sometimes even the physicians' specialties. For instance, men with prostate cancer are more likely to end up having surgery if they consult with a surgeon. The various treatment options can, in turn, influence relationships within the family; for example, a husband with diminished erectile functioning due to prostate surgery would face different marital issues than would a man whose prostate cancer treatment was able to preserve sexual functioning.

Various cancers also have different meanings for patients' identities. Common side effects of prostate cancer treatments, including impotence and incontinence, have implications for a husband's masculine identity that are specific to that type of cancer.

Also, certain types of cancers are more stigmatized than others. Lung cancers, which are the leading cause of death among cancers in the United States, are among the most stigmatized of all cancers because people often assume that lung cancer patients caused their own disease by smoking. The stigma of lung cancer is so strong that lung cancer patients who were never smokers often report that others blame them for their disease. This stigma influences family dynamics in complex ways. When other family members perceive that lung cancer patients have not changed their smoking behavior, they are less likely to help the patient manage their illness, perhaps because they believe the continued smoking makes the patient particularly blameworthy. Clearly this has an impact on the relationship between the cancer patient and those individuals who withdraw support, but it can also adversely affect relationships among other family members; for example, those family members who remain close to the patient may be angry with those who withdraw. Withholding support while a family member struggles with lung cancer also can complicate the family's grieving process if those who withdrew support feel guilty about their behavior. Additionally, other family members of lung cancer victims are often smokers themselves, which can lead to family conflict over the issue of continued smoking upon the death of a family member from smoking.

Family Communication and Cancer

Communication is the means through which other family members support the patient and each other, make decisions about treatment options, and collaborate on plans for dealing with various courses the disease may take. Many scholars have suggested that the complexities involved with having a family member coping with cancer means that families should try to be as open as possible in their communication. There is good reason to believe that open communication is important in many cases. For instance, people with cancer need support from other family members, and often the only way they can access that is by disclosing about the issues they face.

Despite the intuitive appeal of simple prescriptions for open communication, complete openness may not be desirable or always lead to optimal outcomes. Nearly all married people with cancer report avoiding at least some topics pertaining to cancer with their spouses. Other family members, such as parents and siblings, report avoiding topics with the patient as well.

There are a number of different reasons why people with cancer and their families avoid talking with each other. Sometimes they avoid communicating to protect themselves or the other person from worrying. Other times individuals believe that talking about certain issues could hurt their relationship or that talking would not be fruitful anyway. People sometimes feel constrained from talking because they believe that others do not want to talk.

People with cancer and their families often believe that they have good justifications for avoiding, though some scholars consider such reasons to be mere excuses for not being open. Some of the reasoning involved in avoiding suggests some real dilemmas that people must face when deciding whether to talk. For instance, wives of prostate cancer patients might want to discuss potential side effects but may wish to protect their husband, thinking that talking about the possibility of impotence may make him more self-conscious and concerned. A husband who would like to talk about physical changes in his wife due to breast cancer may believe that talking about those changes will highlight them and make the wife feel worse rather than better. The existence of such dilemmas hints that any blanket statements about being completely open are likely to be overly simplistic. There are risks in discussing some topics.

Indeed, research suggests that the most communicatively competent families are able to talk when they really need to talk, because they feel it is important or because the health of other family members may be at risk, but do not talk with unfettered openness. Instead they pick and choose when, where, and how to discuss important issues. Moreover, when they choose to avoid a topic, their reason for doing so influences whether the outcomes are functional and satisfying. People who avoid communication because they think talking about a topic is futile or because they feel others do not want them to talk tend to be particularly distressed by the need to avoid certain topics. Yet people who avoid communication even though they believe they *could* talk about an issue and others would be willing to

listen tend to be untroubled by avoidance. At least with respect to psychosocial dynamics within families dealing with cancer, it may be more important to believe one could talk about a topic than it is to actually talk about that topic. If individuals' reasons for avoiding topics influence positive outcomes, health professionals should keep this in mind when working with families and interventions.

Laura E. Miller and John P. Caughlin

See also Communication in Families Related to Health and Illness; Genetic Conditions, Communication in Families; Genetic Research Findings and Disease Management for Families; Resources for Families During Life-Threatening Illnesses

Further Readings

Badr, H., & Taylor, C. L. C. (2006). Social constraints and spousal communication in lung cancer. *Psycho-Oncology, 15,* 673–683.

Barsevick, A. M., Montgomery, S. V., Ruth, K., Ross, E. A., Egleston, B. L., Bingler, R., et al. (2008). Intention to communicate BRCA1/BRCA2 genetic test results to the family. *Journal of Family Psychology, 22,* 303–312.

Donovan-Kicken, E., & Caughlin, J. P. (2010). A multiple goals perspective on topic avoidance and relationship satisfaction in the context of breast cancer. *Communication Monographs, 77*(2), 231–256.

Gilbar, O., & Ben-Zur, H. (2002). *Cancer and the family caregiver: Distress and coping.* Springfield, IL: Charles C Thomas.

Goldsmith, D. J., Miller, L. E., & Caughlin, J. P. (2008). Openness and avoidance in couples communicating about cancer. *Communication Yearbook, 31,* 62–115.

Weihs, K., & Politi, M. (2006). Family development in the face of cancer. In D. R. Crane & E. S. Marshall (Eds.), *Handbook of families and health* (pp. 3–18). Thousand Oaks, CA: Sage.

Websites

American Cancer Society: http://www.cancer.org

Cancer.com: http://www.cancer.com

Cancer Network: http://www.cancernetwork.com

Centers for Disease Control and Prevention: http://www.cdc.gov/cancer

National Cancer Institute: http://www.cancer.gov

Prevent Cancer Foundation: http://www.preventcancer.org

CANCER SURVIVORSHIP AND THE FAMILY

A *cancer survivor* is defined as a person living with, through, and beyond cancer. However, cancer is a disease that affects not just the patient but the entire family, and the needs of the family will only grow over time. The National Cancer Institute estimates that the number of people diagnosed with the disease annually will double in the next 50 years from 1.4 to 2.6 million. Early diagnosis, enhanced patient care, and survival rates for cancer patients have improved significantly over the past 10 years. In fact, 5-year survival rates are increasing. The majority of those diagnosed with cancer (approaching 70%) can expect to be alive in 5 years.

Despite these laudable gains, the pressure on family caregivers of these patients (and especially the *primary* family caregiver, or the individual who is directly involved with providing care, most often the spouse or partner) is increasing. As a consequence, there is a growing need to address the long-term well-being of primary caregivers and arm them with coping strategies that enhance their capacity to provide vital supportive care to their loved ones while avoiding burnout.

Factors That Lead to Increased Burden on Caregivers

Advances in screening leading to earlier diagnosis, coupled with refinements in treatment, have increased survival rates significantly. Cancer patients are living longer and fuller lives. Indeed, increasingly cancer is viewed as a chronic illness rather than a universally fatal one.

However, as a consequence of these positive medical outcomes, family members can face added responsibilities and heightened burden in caring for a loved one with cancer. This is particularly relevant in the United States, as the National Cancer Institute estimates that 85% of cancer patients are treated in the community (oncology practices, cancer centers, or hospitals) rather than in comprehensive cancer centers. Moreover, newer oral medications and targeted therapies increase the likelihood that treatment will occur outside of the hospital or in an outpatient setting. The utilization of community-based medical facilities and shorter hospital stays, due to a greater demand on doctors and nurses, also contribute to the growing burden on family caregivers. Today, primary caregivers are likely to provide more complex care for longer periods of time and to be increasingly stressed by their growing and difficult role.

The Three Phases of Caregiving

A caregiver's burden is linked to one of three specific phases in the cancer experience. During the initial or acute phase, the family—caregiver(s) and patient—is under siege. They act as a unit to adjust to the diagnosis.

The chronic phase follows. Primary treatment has been administered, and the patient is dismissed from the hospital. Caregivers are left to take on additional responsibilities; some are complex, such as supporting outpatient treatment protocols, whereas others may be simple but tedious, such as additional housework, errands, and new transportation routines.

The final phase is resolution, when the family begins the survivorship or bereavement process.

Caregiving Is Stressful

Depending on the stage of the disease and treatment, cancer requires long-term treatment and presents numerous physical and psychological demands on individuals with cancer and their caregivers. Diminishing functional ability, organ function, appearance, career, family and social role, and self-image of the person with cancer directly impact the caregiver.

Most research analyzes caregiving along a continuum of physical, emotional, social, and/or economic demands based on the specific needs of the patient. The demands are not sequential and may burden the caregiver all at once or selectively, depending on the most pressing needs of the patient.

In this discussion, the psychosocial stressors are emphasized. The November 2007 Institute of Medicine report titled *Cancer Care for the Whole Patient* emphasizes that health is determined not just by biological processes but by people's emotions, behaviors, and social relationships. Quality health care must encompass psychosocial problems and provide services to enable people to better manage their illnesses and underlying health.

Psychosocial Stressors for Cancer Patients and Their Families

For many cancer patients as well as their caregivers, the most significant psychosocial stressors that accompany diagnosis are unwanted aloneness, loss of control, and loss of hope. Unwanted aloneness occurs at the time of diagnosis. Not only do people with cancer and their loved ones experience themselves as different from others in their social network, but also the sense of isolation may create gaps in intimacy between people with cancer and their loved ones. Consequently, the cancer patients and their caregivers may find it much more difficult to easily share feelings with each other.

Loss of control is often reflected in feelings of helplessness, especially when the person with cancer and family members are unsure of the right course of treatment. This is particularly true when they are faced with treatment decisions that are complicated or confusing. Loss of hope may occur as a result of the debilitating effects of treatment (fatigue, pain, nausea), an uncertain prognosis, having to face new treatment decisions, or upsetting news.

Caregivers' challenges parallel those of people with cancer. Understandably, much attention is focused on the family member who is ill, but all too often caregivers have no outlet for their emotions and concerns. Instead, their emotions are often suppressed—especially fear, anger, and sadness—and resentment can arise toward the loved one with cancer. Caregivers sometimes feel that life now revolves around their loved one's illness and that they are emotionally invisible except to the extent that they take care of the person who is ill, thus increasing their loneliness, burden, and stress.

Long-Term Physiological Effects of Caregiving

A longitudinal study involving cancer patients and their spouses showed that whereas patient distress diminished over time, caregiver stress did not. Researchers found a critical chemical pathway through which the human immune system is weakened by chronic stress. This study reinforced earlier research showing that long-term caregivers suffer from impaired immunity for as long as 3 years after their caregiving role has ended, suggesting that people who care for those with chronic illnesses such as cancer are at an increased risk for developing their own serious health problems.

Understanding Compassion Fatigue or Burnout

Caring for a person with cancer can be so stressful that the medical community now refers to this overwhelmed state as the "caregiver syndrome" and "compassion fatigue." Burnout—the feeling of having reached the limits of one's ability to cope—is a very real possibility. Burnout has both emotional and physical symptoms. The emotional symptoms may emerge as frustration, anger, emptiness, insecurity, resentfulness, or depression. Physical symptoms can include headaches, insomnia, backaches, lethargy, lingering colds, gastrointestinal upsets, or cardiovascular problems.

In one study, the number of caregivers seeking treatment for depression (29%) and anxiety (31%) nearly equaled that of cancer patients/survivors (34% report being treated for depression and 37% for anxiety) during their cancer experience.

One of the contributing factors may be the discrepancy between how cancer patients view caregivers' emotional states as compared to how caregivers would evaluate it themselves. In May 2007 and again in October 2007, the Cancer Support Community (an international program of free psychological and emotional support for cancer patients and their families), in conjunction with KRC Research (a market and opinion research firm), conducted a national online survey of a total of 185 cancer patients/survivors and 93 caregivers to define specific stressors and concerns caregivers face. Findings suggest that caregiver stress deserves much more attention than it has been receiving until now.

Sixty percent of individuals with cancer interviewed for this study stated their spouse or partner was their primary caregiver, and nearly three quarters (73%) reported receiving daily assistance from a caregiver. Twenty-two percent of caregivers reported being in this role for more than 4 years, and 60% were caring for loved ones with advanced or metastatic cancer. All respondents agreed caregivers provide support in a variety of ways that are invaluable to the well-being of the cancer patient.

Nearly half the cancer patients/survivors (49%) believed their caregivers felt regular distress during their cancer experience. But surprisingly, 45% did not believe their caregivers suffered any regular distress at all. In stark contrast, 80% of the caregivers said they personally experienced regular distress throughout their loved one's cancer experience.

This gap provides some insight into why caregivers are just as likely to report being treated for depression and anxiety as are cancer patients/survivors.

Managing Caregiver Stress to Avoid Burnout

Often in the rush and anxiety to care for someone with cancer, caregivers who are on the front lines battling cancer alongside their diagnosed loved ones can be overlooked. They may get lost in the maze of very real needs and demands. Consequently, it is critical for caregivers to make their own well-being a priority. Although managing their own stress may seem less important than the immediate needs of their loved one who is ill, it is not. Caregivers should be reminded of the directions given in an airplane in case of a loss of oxygen. Passengers are always asked to fasten their own masks before helping their children. The situation is the same when caring for someone with cancer. It is hard to be available if the caregiver is worn out and suffering.

To be helpful to their loved ones, caregivers need to know how to cope with their own stress. This knowledge will help them become a strengthened ally, using a process of providing aid and comfort through self-care and knowledge. There are many methods to become a strengthened ally and revitalize one's energy. They are as follows:

Support. Caregivers should be encouraged to join a support group. The Cancer Support Community teaches that sharing one's feelings and concerns with others in a safe, supportive group setting helps to normalize them. Moreover, research shows that talking to people who share one's problems reduces stress and alleviates isolation.

Education. Information is power. Understanding the course of the disease, the possibility of relapse, the recommended treatments, and the side effects of medications can help caregivers plan for the near and distant future.

Journaling. In a journal or diary, caregivers can dialogue with themselves to vent frustrations and problem-solve without causing conflict. Research indicates that writing about one's deepest thoughts and feelings regarding a stressful or traumatic event reduces anxiety and depression while enhancing well-being.

Friendships. Social support is a key component of lowering distress. Caregivers should be encouraged to continue contacts with friends and family despite their loved one's illness.

Routines. Retaining as much control over the routines of life as is reasonable helps to provide some order in the face of uncertainty. In that way, although there are obvious pressures and stresses, work provides an opportunity to be productive in a familiar environment. Also, the friendships and camaraderie of work colleagues may help ease some of the aloneness.

Hobbies. It is important for caregivers to maintain favorite pastimes that bring pleasure.

The Future. Caregivers need to realize that they have a future. Caregivers are separate persons from their ill loved one, and it is essential that caregivers find ways to enjoy their own life. Caregivers should be encouraged to attend classes, start a hobby, go to a movie, or make new friends.

"Let Go." Caregivers should allow themselves to feel replenished by others' gestures—a card or a kind word sent by e-mail. Music, religious services, yoga, or a video can also help caregivers recharge their batteries.

Seek Respite. Caregivers must realize that they can't do it all; they should reach out to others (including professional caregivers) to do some caring in their stead.

Physical Health. Caregivers can be at risk, so it is important for them to eat well, get enough sleep, and tend to any physical ailments that arise.

The Relaxation Response. Biofeedback, meditation, yoga, listening to music, running, hiking, gardening, even washing the car can relieve stress. By focusing on breathing, caregivers can trigger the mind–body connection.

Manage Frustration. A short fuse can be a sign of burnout. Caregivers may need more emotional support, such as a support group or private therapist.

Self-Care and Setting Limits. Caregivers need to identify when they are feeling overwhelmed and be firm in delineating what they can and cannot do. Being a strengthened ally means having the ability to derive simple pleasures in the face of uncertainty.

It means sharing fears and struggles with a trusted friend. It can also mean having faith in one's loved one's ability to cope.

Mitch Golant

See also Cancer in the Family; Caregiving: Partners/Spouses; Changing Views of Marriage, Home Responsibilities, and Caregiving; Clarifying Family as Context of Care and Family as Focus of Care in Family Health; Families Experiencing Chronic Physical and Mental Health Conditions; Family Conflict Related to Caregiving

Further Readings

Adler, N. E., & Page, A. K., Institute of Medicine (IOM). (2007). *Cancer care for the whole patient: Meeting psychosocial health needs.* Washington, DC: National Academies Press.

Bucher, J. A., & Zabora, J. R. (2010). Building problem-solving skills through COPE education of family caregivers. In J. C. Holland, W. S. Breitbart, P. B. Jacobsen, M. S. Lederberg, M. J. Loscalzo, & R. McCorkle (Eds.), *Psycho-oncology* (2nd ed., pp. 469–472). New York: Oxford University Press.

Golant, M., & Haskins, N. (2008). "Other cancer survivors": The impact on family and caregivers. *Cancer Journal, 14,* 420–424.

Hewitt, M., Greenfield, S., & Stovall, E. (Eds.). (2005). *From cancer patient to cancer survivor: Lost in transition.* Washington, DC: National Academies Press.

Holland, J. C., Breitbart, W. S., Jacobsen, P. B., Lederberg, M. S., Loscalzo, M. J., & McCorkle, R. (Eds.). (2010). *Psycho-oncology* (2nd ed.). New York: Oxford University Press.

Websites

Cancer Support Community:
http://www.cancersupportcommunity.org

CAREGIVERS OF ADULTS WITH DEVELOPMENTAL DISABILITIES

Family carers often provide care and support to adult sons or daughters with developmental disabilities in hospitals. Given the lifelong nature of developmental disabilities, the life course narrative for many carers of adults with developmental disabilities unfolds to an enduring responsibility and devotion in providing support in the hospital. Adults with developmental disabilities are more likely to enter hospitals more frequently as they age, and to stay for longer periods, than other adults. Therefore, as they age, demands upon family carers to provide support in hospitals are also likely to increase. Given that carers have reported providing care in hospitals to be stressful, and that concerns over the health of a loved one can affect quality of life in older people, it is possible that continued or increasing responsibilities over the care of the hospitalized adult may negatively impact the older carer's quality of life. This entry reviews the roles, needs, and experiences of family carers supporting adults with developmental disabilities and associated complex communication needs in hospitals; discusses the implications of family carers' roles and the continued reliance upon them; and considers options for improved support to caregivers of adults with developmental disabilities.

Increased support for family carers of adults with disabilities is vital for two reasons: (1) These carers are aging, and there is a need to reduce the impact of caring on those who will eventually need more support, either to continue providing care or else to transfer their roles to hospital staff or paid carers within disability organizations; and (2) adults with developmental disabilities will continue to require hospital care, and potentially more frequently, after older carers are no longer able to provide care as a result of age-related functional decline, illness, or death. If carers are not supported in passing on their expertise to others before they are no longer able to provide care in the hospital, there is a risk that a substantial gap will eventuate in the care provided to adults with developmental disabilities during their hospital stays.

Reasons for Providing Care in Hospitals

Recent research into the experience of family carers in hospitals highlights several reasons why they view their presence at the hospital as vital in the care of adults with developmental disabilities and complex communication needs.

Communication

The primary reason for caring in hospitals stems from the patient's difficulty in communicating with hospital staff directly. Communication is essential in the provision of effective nursing care, and nurses encounter difficulties in communicating with and caring for patients with developmental disabilities. This can also have serious consequences, as patients with communication difficulty have a threefold increased risk of preventable and harmful patient safety incidents in the hospital. Hospital staff, who are unfamiliar communication partners to the adult with disabilities, may lack knowledge and experience in ways to communicate with adults with little or no speech. Although these adults rely upon augmentative and alternative communication (AAC)—including communication boards, speech generating devices, sign or gesture systems—many do not take their AAC systems with them to the hospital. There are several reasons for this situation, including fear that the AAC system will be lost or damaged, that they may not be able to use it lying in bed, or that nursing staff would not know how to communicate with them using the system. Without an effective means of communicating with hospital staff, carers view their roles in the hospital as protecting the adult patient from potential harm. Nurses have also reported difficulty in communicating with adults who have little or no speech and reliance upon carers to avoid compromising nursing care.

Time Efficiency in Care

Although members of a busy hospital staff do not necessarily expect carers to stay at the hospital and provide care, they report appreciating greatly any help in meeting the patient's care requirements. In effect, nurses in hospitals are "time poor," and patients with high support needs require extra time in provision of basic care. This dilemma creates a tension that is relieved by the presence and help of a carer. In being an "extra pair of hands" to assist nursing staff in care, carers might help to reduce the time demands associated with caring for people who are dependent upon others for all aspects of daily care needs, including mobility, eating, drinking, toileting, and showering. However, assistance from carers may also lead nurses to allocate their time to other patients, resulting in the carers working in isolation and taking responsibility for the bulk of the care to the patient.

Expertise in Care

Adults with developmental disabilities and complex communication needs often have high individual support requirements, including provision of modified food or drinks, positioning supports, and adaptive techniques or equipment. In attempting to convey these requirements and care techniques to hospital staff, carers often provide written information and demonstrate care strategies in situ. However, it is often difficult for hospital staff to glean the necessary information from folders of written notes, and there is a tendency to rely upon the carers for verbal instructions and demonstration. Relying upon verbal information is also problematic, as detailed information is not included in the nurse handover and there is a need to repeat explanations of care techniques to each staff member. Some carers report that, over time, hospital staff members come to rely upon them and so will often wait for the carer to arrive at the hospital to provide basic care.

The Impact of Providing Care in Hospitals

Family carers often step in to protect the person from adverse events and to provide care to that person in the hospital, and they do so repeatedly as their son or daughter gets older and enters the hospital more frequently. Some carers report feeling they have no choice but to provide care, as there are reportedly few other sources of support for their son or daughter in the hospital. The extent to which paid care staff of disability organizations are also called upon to provide hospital care in the absence of a family carer or to help in their roles is not yet known.

Family carers report that once they are notified that their son or daughter has been admitted to the hospital, they "drop everything," putting their own lives, work, and other responsibilities on hold, or else juggling responsibilities, in order to attend to their son or daughter in the hospital for long periods. These carers report that providing care in the hospital is exhausting both emotionally and physically. This may be related to (a) the *comprehensive* nature of their roles in care, including direct care, advocacy, information, communication, and emotional support; (b) the constant nature of providing care and *vigilance against* adverse events; (c) the absence of support throughout their hospital care experience while competing work or family responsibilities continue or are waiting their attention; (d) ongoing concern over the health of the family member who has been hospitalized; and (e) any continuing care responsibility following the patient's discharge from the hospital. Carers, who report feeling anxious when away from the hospital for fear that hospital staff will not be able to communicate with the patient, tend to remain at the hospital for long periods to monitor and supervise the care provided by nurses. Older carers also hold fears for the future when they will no longer be able to provide care in the hospital to their adult son or daughter with disabilities. It is apparent that these carers need additional support in providing care in the hospital and in handing over their expertise to hospital staff.

Improving Support in Hospitals

It is important for health service providers to have a good understanding of the experiences and needs of family carers of adults with developmental disabilities in hospitals, particularly as these carers get older. Additional, or indeed alternative, strategies to those provided to parents of children in hospitals may be needed to make better use of their expertise in care, advocacy, and communication with the adult with developmental disabilities, and to respect the adult's growing need for autonomy. This section describes the kinds of support carers, hospital and disability staff, and people with developmental disabilities suggested would improve the hospital care experience.

Practical Support

Family carers appreciate the provision of refreshments or meals in recognition of their roles in providing care on the ward. Providing the carer with a place to rest or accommodation at the hospital may support them in taking a break from care. However, hospital staff may need to make clear that the provision of practical support does not imply that the carers need to maintain a constant presence on the ward or take responsibility for all aspects of care.

Emotional Support

Providing care for a loved one in hospitals can be emotionally and physically exhausting for carers. Family carers recognize that hospital staff are busy, and therefore they do not always ask for help or support on the ward. These carers have reported feeling isolated through replacing the nurse in care and therefore not seeing nursing staff very often, or through their relative being in a single room and away from other patients and relatives. Their anxiety when away from the hospital may lead them to stay at the bedside 24 hours a day, taking only short breaks when other visitors arrive. Therefore, it is important that hospital staff be aware of any emotional impact of caring and that they offer support and encouragement to the carers. Encouraging carers to take a break in care might not be sufficient to support their emotional needs if the carer is also anxious when away from the bedside. Nursing staff might also need to provide reassurance that while the carer is away, the hospital staff will provide care to the adult with disabilities.

Increasing Collaboration in Care

Family carers often encounter barriers to providing care, primarily through lack of formal recognition of their role and lack of access to information in hospitals. They may feel disempowered and excluded by policy from formal avenues for information transfer. They need more support and access to facilities to maintain caring roles during hospital admissions and more efficient, formal, and effective ways of passing on their expertise and information about care to hospital staff.

Occupational Support

Occupational support was also seen as potentially valuable in raising awareness of the needs of the carer in being recognized, accepted, and valued as a care partner on the ward. Occupational support recognizes the role of the family carer as a volunteer or unpaid carer in the hospital setting and may include orientation to the working relationships between hospital staff, meetings between staff and carers, discussion about the use of equipment on the ward, and occupational health and safety information or training. To prevent strain injuries associated with caring and risks associated with infection control, carers providing direct care may need training on occupational health and safety measures in line with existing hospital policies. The concept of training new family carers of adults is not a novel one, but older carers who have a good deal of expertise in providing care may also need information and training in relation to using unfamiliar hospital equipment in the setting and context of the hospital ward.

Support in Exchange of Knowledge and Expertise

Family carers might need support in letting go of their care responsibilities in the hospital, particularly if they have reached the stage where they can no longer provide care because of their advancing age. Clearly, as they get older and less able to provide care in hospitals, it is important to develop policies and practices to facilitate the transfer of expertise and care responsibility to hospital staff and address the barriers to hospital staff communicating directly with patients with disabilities and complex communication needs in the hospital. Therefore, carers need to be included in information transfer on the ward and asked about care techniques and, rather than being relied upon to provide care, be encouraged to hand over care to hospital staff.

Information Support

Information resources available for family carers typically do not include information about providing care in hospitals, as it might be assumed nursing staff would provide this care. Written information is helpful in preparing people for admission to the hospital and might also be helpful for carers preparing to take up roles in the hospital setting. Providing preadmission information to people preparing to enter the hospital is also helpful in significantly reducing anxiety in patients and their carers. To date there are no information resources designed to guide carers in providing care to adults with developmental disabilities during hospitalization. Such information might be useful in helping these carers to negotiate their

roles with hospital staff and provide clear information to the carer on relevant hospital policies surrounding care on the ward.

Implications for Policy

If family carers are to be valued and supported in their roles during the hospitalization of adults with lifelong or long-standing disabilities, it is important that hospitals and disability service providers develop policies and procedures that support them in their roles. New hospital policies should reflect the important role family carers play in passing on information, advocacy, and communication support, as well as the need to acknowledge their expertise and facilitate their involvement as collaborative care partners; increase the capacity of hospital staff to provide care to adults with developmental disabilities; improve direct communication between the patient with developmental disabilities and hospital staff, such as through supporting the use of AAC systems; and increase collaborative links between hospital and disability services to ensure continuity of support to family carers across settings. Such policies might support carers in the process of transferring their roles in direct care to health care providers in preparation for the future when the family carer is no longer able to provide care. Policies on the care of adults with developmental disabilities in the hospital are also needed to include a focus on the use of adaptive equipment, including communication devices and wheelchairs, preadmission planning procedures, involvement of paid carers, and improvements in discharge planning. The process for developing such policies should include not only the family carer but also the adult with developmental disabilities and complex communication needs.

Family carers are a valuable resource in the provision of care and support to adults with developmental disabilities in the hospital. However, it is important to consider the support needs of family carers, particularly as they get older. It is important that these carers are included in a collaborative approach toward planning for the future care of these adults in the hospital. Family carers may benefit from improved support for their roles in care and encouragement to impart their knowledge and expertise to hospital staff effectively. In collaborating more closely with family carers, hospital staff may develop competency in caring for, and communicating with, patients with developmental disabilities and complex communication needs.

Bronwyn Hemsley, Susan Balandin,
and Leanne Togher

See also Acute Care/Hospitalization of Family Members; Adult Child With Disability: Planning for by Parents; Family Caregiving: Caring for Children, Adults, and Elders With Developmental Disabilities; Hospitalization and Family Presence; Life Span: Care Coordination for Chronic Illness/Disabilities and the Family

Further Readings

Balandin, S., Hemsley, B., Sigafoos, J., & Green, V. (2007). Communication with nurses: The experiences of 10 individuals with cerebral palsy and complex communication needs. *Applied Nursing Research, 20,* 56–62.

Bartlett, G., Blais, R., Tamblyn, R., & Clermont, R. J. (2008). Impact of patient communication problems on the risk of preventable adverse events in acute care settings. *Canadian Medical Association Journal, 178*(12), 1555–1562.

Bigby, C. (2000). Moving on without parents: Planning, transitions and sources of support for older adults with intellectual disabilities. Baltimore: Paul H. Brookes.

Gabriel, Z., & Bowling, A. (2004). Quality of life in old age from the perspectives of older people. In A. Walker & C. H. Hennessy (Eds.), *Growing older: Quality of life in old age* (pp. 14–34). New York: Open University Press.

Hemsley, B., Balandin, S., & Togher, L. (2008). Family caregivers discuss roles and needs in supporting adults with cerebral palsy and complex communication needs in the hospital setting. *Journal of Developmental and Physical Disabilities, 20,* 257–274.

Hemsley, B., Balandin, S., & Togher, L. (2008). Professionals' views on the roles and needs of family carers of adults with cerebral palsy and complex communication needs in hospital. *Journal of Intellectual & Developmental Disabilities, 33*(2), 127–136.

Hemsley, B., Balandin, S., & Togher, L. (2008). "We need to be the centrepiece": Adults with cerebral palsy and complex communication needs discuss the roles and needs of family carers in hospital. *Disability & Rehabilitation, 30*(23), 1759–1771.

Nolan, M., Lundh, U., Grant, G., & Keady, J. (Eds.). (2003). *Partnerships in family care: Understanding the caregiving career.* Maidenhead, UK: Open University Press.

CAREGIVING: ADULTS WITH DEVELOPMENTAL DISABILITIES

Families of individuals with developmental disabilities (DD) and support persons have a pivotal role in meeting the care and support needs of adults with DD as they age. Ensuring health-related services and support for people with DD requires an understanding of health issues and available resources.

Aging With a Disability

Individuals with DD living in community settings increasingly enjoy similar life spans as the general population. For individuals with a variety of syndromes and conditions—including Down syndrome, severe intellectual disability, cerebral palsy, multiple disabilities, conditions requiring wheelchairs and assistance with feeding or dressing—life expectancies are lower. Additionally, although many health concerns are similar to those of nondisabled peers, persons with DD have health issues related to the convergence of biological factors associated with their disability and the combination of aging with a lifelong disability, access to adequate health care, and lifestyle and environmental issues. With longer life spans, people with DD are experiencing earlier age-related changes in health, function, and psychosocial status—suggestive of premature aging. Adults with DD have increased morbidity and mortality for several conditions. Thyroid disease, psychotropic drug polypharmacy, and deaths due to pneumonia, bowel obstruction, and intestinal perforation have a higher prevalence.

Persons with specific syndromes and conditions (Down syndrome, fragile X, Prader-Willi, cerebral palsy, epilepsy) have an increased predisposition to certain health issues. Adults with Down syndrome have a higher prevalence (15%–40%) of early-onset Alzheimer's disease occurring 15 to 20 years earlier compared to the general population and may experience hypothyroidism and sleep apnea more frequently. Adults with fragile X may have heart problems (mitral valve prolapse), musculoskeletal disorders, earlier menopause, epilepsy, or visual problems. Persons with Prader-Willi have high rates of cardiovascular disease and diabetes. With age, people with cerebral palsy may experience reduced mobility, bone demineralization, fractures, decreased muscle tone, increased pain, difficulty eating or swallowing, respiratory problems, or bowel and bladder concerns. Long-term use of psychotropic and antiseizure medications, along with limited physical activity and poor diets, increases the risk of developing osteoporosis and constipation. Depression is more prevalent among people with DD and is frequently underassessed, underdiagnosed, and untreated.

Resources to Address Aging Issues

As people with DD age and need more assistance with activities of daily living, maintaining a household or employment may be difficult. A need may exist for caregivers to access assistive technologies, environmental and vocational accommodations, therapeutic and nursing services, and respite care. More than three quarters of adults with DD live with families. As people with DD live longer, parents may experience extended caregiving at a time in life when they are experiencing their own health care issues and are potentially in need of support for themselves. Few family support services are available for families, and they also face long waiting lists for residential services. Currently, many service delivery systems and communities cannot meet the needs of adults with DD, who will likely need day and residential services as they age and no longer have parental support.

Assistive Technology and Environmental Interventions

As individuals with DD experience functional changes, a need exists for assistive technology (AT) and environmental interventions (EIs) to maintain function and ease of caregiver assistance. Personalized devices and technological advances can help individuals with DD maintain or increase their independence, productivity, and quality of life. AT and EI innovations can reduce the need for caregiver support, prevent chronic conditions, and decrease risk of nursing home admission. See Table 1 for examples of AT and EIs.

Advances in microelectronics, computer science, communications, bioengineering, and health and rehabilitation sciences have led to the development of a range of physical and cognitive aids to assist people at work, home, recreational, and other community settings. Individuals with DD lag behind other disability groups in their use of AT and EIs because of lack of awareness, poor assessment of need and fit of mobility devices, limited training and money to pay for and use equipment, and reluctance to use devices. In the United States, the Technology-Related Assistance for Individuals with Disabilities Act of 1988 and 1994 amendments provide financial and technical assistance, information, training, and public awareness activities of AT and EI devices and services for individuals with disabilities of all ages.

Providing Care

Health promotion and disease prevention is critical as people live longer. Although a need exists for routine screenings, surveillance and early detection of chronic health conditions are poor. Many people with DD experience barriers in obtaining screenings. These screenings may include breast, pelvic, and prostate examinations; blood

---

Table 1   Examples of Assistive Technology (AT) and Environmental Interventions (EIs)

- Activities of daily living (robotics, personal digital assistants, eating devices, handrails)
- Cognitive support (cognitive prosthetics for planning, execution, attention, and memory)
- Communication and learning aids for educational and employment settings (augmentative communication devices)
- Community participation (navigational and communication devices, recreational aids)
- Health and safety monitoring (tele-health, alert systems)
- Home environmental control (automatic doors, electronic aids for daily living, voice-operated lighting, ramps)
- Information technology (computers)
- Mobility (wheelchairs), vision (glasses), and hearing (hearing aids)

pressure and cholesterol checks; urinalysis; and bowel analysis, which can reduce the onset of chronic conditions. Physical barriers to health facilities may restrict access for people who have physical and sensory impairments. Fear of examinations and procedures may also prevent people from obtaining care. Another major obstacle to effective health care is case complexity. Because people with DD often encounter a variety of medical specialists, dentists, mental health providers, and other health professionals without sufficient guidance, coordination among health care providers, patients, and families is critical.

Although community-based services are increasingly providing health promotion activities for persons with DD, guidelines pertaining to the types of exercises and nutritional requirements are limited. For example, for people with cerebral palsy, exercise prescriptions need to consider the potential for muscle overuse resulting in pain, injury, and fatigue. Adults with Down syndrome are prone to osteoporosis and more likely to require calcium and vitamin D supplements. Limited education and training in dealing with multiple conditions, interacting medicines, and unique aspects of various DD among many health care professionals provide an opportunity for families and support persons to advocate for obtaining health care services for individuals with DD. Promoting positive lifestyle behaviors throughout the life span can enhance health status and engagement in community life.

Beth Marks and Jasmina Sisirak

See also Adult Child With Disability: Planning for by Parents; Disabilities and Family Management; Health Care Transition Planning

Further Readings

Braddock, D., Hemp, R., Rizzolo, M. C. (2008). *The state of the states in developmental disabilities: 2008* (7th ed.). Boulder: University of Colorado, Department of Psychiatry & Coleman Institute for Cognitive Disabilities.

Fujiura, G. T. (2003). Continuum of intellectual disability: Demographic evidence for the "forgotten generation." *Mental Retardation, 41*(6), 420–429.

Marks, B. A., Brown, A., Hahn, J. E., & Heller, T. (2003). Nursing care resources for individuals with intellectual and developmental disabilities across the life span. *Nursing Clinics of North America, 38*(2), 373–393.

Marks, B., Sisirak, J., Hsieh, K. (2008). Health services, health promotion, and health literacy: Report from the State of the Science in Aging with Developmental Disabilities Conference. *Disability and Health Journal, 1*(3), 136–142.

Prasher, V. P., & Janicki, M. P. (2002). *Physical health of adults with intellectual disabilities.* Malden, MA: Wiley-Blackwell.

Websites

The Arc of the United States: http://www.thearc.org

Rehabilitation Research and Training Center on Aging with Developmental Disabilities: http://www.rrtcadd.org

CAREGIVING: ELDERLY

Most elderly people with different stages of incapacities want to be cared for in their own homes. Often caregivers are spouses of the same age, with their own health concerns or incapacities. These elderly couples may be supported by siblings and their spouses, other relatives or friends, neighbors, or in-home care. Because the number of elderly people is rapidly growing in every country, it is important to create sufficient home support for elderly people with growing incapacities to maintain their quality of life. If home support is not sufficient, the need for long-term care beds in hospitals or institutions grows. Insufficient or improperly allocated home support is an expensive way to care for elderly people with growing incapacities. In this entry, the focus is on the common diseases leading to incapacity and need for help for elderly individuals, the family context as perceived by the caregivers, the cultural context, the service implementation, and the health and social care policies.

Historical Context

In past history, families from different generations were more likely to live together. Elderly people might be taken care of at home until the end of life, usually by women of the family. Doctors and nurses were not always available, and diseases, incapacities, and deaths were considered a normal part of the life course.

During recent decades, rapid increases in diagnostic and treatment possibilities have changed circumstances. As the standard of living increases with better nutrition and hygiene, many novel advances in medicine have benefited most the oldest old—people over 90 years of age. Nowadays the fastest growing part of the population in many countries is the oldest old. Many people might be in good health and lead active lives 20 to 30 years after retirement. However, as one's age increases, the possibilities for diseases and incapacities, along with need for help, become more immediate.

Main Diseases Causing Need for Services Among the Elderly

The most common primary causes of death for the elderly are strokes, coronary artery disease, different cancers, and dementias. The medical and surgical treatment of cardiovascular disorders, including strokes and myocardial infarctions, has advanced, and the prevention of these diseases is taken seriously in middle-aged people. In some countries, schoolchildren are screened for high cholesterol, and their parents are given nutritional advice, if needed. The treatment of different cancers has also met important advances. When focusing on elderly people, who might have survived cancer or cardiovascular disorders already, an important reason for the need for help is a memory disorder—dementias in different stages. Elderly, home-dwelling people with health issues other than memory disorders are better able to care for themselves than those with dementia, whose psychological and behavioral disorders may very soon lead to the need for help. Dementia is the most important disease leading to the need for permanent institutionalization and thus creates a challenging economic burden for societies. For example, in Finland, more than 90% of elderly people living in institutions suffer from dementia.

Alzheimer's Disease—A Challenge for Support Services

The most common dementive disease is Alzheimer's disease, which accounts for 70% of dementias. The prevalence of Alzheimer's disease is estimated to be about 22% to 35% among elderly persons over 85 years of age. The definition and diagnostics of dementive diseases are quite exact today. However, the treatment possibilities and practices vary according to different health and social care systems and countries. Treatment exists for some symptoms of Alzheimer's disease, and the psychological and behavioral disorders can also be managed with medical and nonmedical means with a specialist's guidance. Nevertheless, many elderly persons go undiagnosed. These persons may say that they need help "just because they are getting old," without recognizing the underlying cause. It is common for people with Alzheimer's disease to fail to recognize their cognitive problems themselves, and even their loved ones may think that is it normal for the affected person not to handle practical routines because of increased age. This situation may create problems in families, or with relatives, neighbors, friends, and health and social care workers. Home care providers especially should be alert to these persons, who need not only home help but also a precise diagnosis and treatment of their underlying dementia.

Cultural Context

Practices in handling the support system for caregivers vary according to country. In most Western countries, families have the possibility to use communal or private services in addition to the help they give as caregivers. However, in countries where it is customary for women to work outside the home, such services may not be available to the same extent. Depending on cultural background and personal attitudes, families may need different support from the service system. Cultural issues have numerous effects on caregiving. Regardless of the way of thinking, families often need support also after the death of the care recipient. The caregiver and other family members sustain many emotional losses through caregiving and experience a situation called "dual dying": Their loved one with dementia seems to die emotionally before physical death occurs. The permanent transfer from home to an institution may also be regarded as a severe loss for the caregiver, contributing to depression, anxiety, and a need for emotional support.

Overview of Current Literature

Caregiving in families is the most common way to take care of elderly persons. Communal services are frequently offered to these families, but the services are typically not used until a crisis has reached the family. Depending on the culture and caregiving habits, spouse-caregivers may feel they have a moral commitment to their spouse and a duty not to entrust their spouse to any other person. Many elderly people do not want a "stranger" to come to their home, or they may have had previous disappointments with the services. Families need more information about the services available—many times they are so involved in the caregiving that they do not have enough strength to check out and evaluate all available services. Even if services are available, it might be complicated for caregivers to access them and to know which services might require admission documentation from a doctor to implement the service. It could be too stressful for family members to make numerous inquiries to various places to determine whether the services are appropriate for the person's specific dementia and behavioral disorders. Many families are in need of greater flexibility from the service system, with services tailored to respect their autonomy, privacy, and dignity. Many times the care recipient's reluctance to have home support is the reason for not using the services available. Unmet service needs are an ongoing issue in the caregiving of elderly people. In a large-scale study of dementia families in the United States, early community-based service utilization was found to be cost-effective and to delay institutionalization. Unmet needs are associated with an increase in nursing home placements and deaths and loss of follow-ups.

Medicolegal and Ethical Issues

Cognitive decline and dementia are critical threats to the autonomy of elderly people. Dementive diseases deteriorate a person's ability to handle financial affairs and to make other critical decisions that influence his or her life. Caregivers may find these financial and legal problems challenging; for example, a spouse may take responsibility for the couple's investments for the first time in his or her life. Caregivers may need advice from professionals on how to appraise the financial capacity of a person with dementia and determine whether a financial power of attorney or legal guardianship is needed. Some countries allow for the making of enduring powers of attorney in advance, when a person is still healthy, which is then carried out when the person is considered incapable of making financial or other decisions.

Telling the truth to the patient about his or her dementia is of specific value. Although some patients and caregivers may have depression, most of them appreciate hearing the diagnosis and prognosis from the doctor after the examinations. They appreciate also that the doctor takes the initiative to bring these issues into the discussion, even though they might be difficult to hear. End-of-life issues are of special importance to elderly persons, and a professional can start the discussion regarding their preferences for dying as well as give them guidance regarding their possible advance directives.

Focus of Care

Both the care recipient and the caregiver should be the focus when considering an elderly person's service needs and quality of life. Caregiving is emotionally difficult work, and these care recipients–caregiver couples need not only physical help but also listening and training in coping strategies to handle their situation. Unsolved psychological and behavioral disorders of dementia are main reasons for the permanent institutionalization of elderly persons. When planning services, it is important that the family is asked about their own personal needs.

Desired Family Health Outcomes and Intervention Programs

Regular Evaluation

Elderly persons often appreciate a precise diagnosis and treatment of their diseases. They value health care providers' listening to their thoughts when planning their treatments and support services. Regular health care provider (in the United States, often geriatric nurse practitioner) appointments—consisting of a thorough health investigation with laboratory tests; an examination of the person's current medications, including the possibility of inappropriate medications; and nutritional and physical exercise recommendations—are needed. Memory tests should be considered to determine if an elderly person shows weakening in cognitive levels. Professionals should also routinely ask loved ones whether they have noticed a change in the person's cognitive level.

Nutrition

Improvement in nutritional status of the elderly is a remarkable health outcome that can be achieved by obtaining proper information through media and from health care professionals. Many elderly people, especially those with diseases causing incapacities, may suffer from low protein intake and deficiency of vitamin D. If the diet is not healthy enough, deficiencies from other vitamins may also exist. This may cause frailty due to muscle weakness in elderly people, which may contribute to falls and bone fractures.

Muscle Strength

Muscle strength decreases during aging. Many diseases with possible incapacities may lead to an inactive lifestyle, which can enhance muscle weakening and result in walking difficulties. Exercise is recommended to the elderly for continuing an active lifestyle. Special fitness centers for the elderly may offer a comfortable environment to improve balance and strength.

Loneliness Prevention

Loneliness is a risk factor of functional decline among elderly. Warm family relationships can create a positive emotional environment, which may make it easier for an elderly person to seek and receive care from loved ones during times of illness. Also, feeling needed can protect elderly persons, for example, against depression. Social events for the elderly are one way to prevent loneliness.

Further Intervention Needs

In a Finnish large-scale study of 1,943 caregivers of persons with Alzheimer's disease, Minna Raivio and colleagues found that the services most wanted by the caregivers were physiotherapy for the person with dementia, financial support from the community, housecleaning, and home respite for a few hours. Health providers may trust that the families know their needs best, and they can offer the means to make their caregiving easier. Depression and anxiety of the caregiver should be noticed as early as possible, and the family should be given the social, psychological, or medical support they need. Such support can also increase the elderly person's quality of life and delay institutionalization.

Sometimes health providers face the situation in which a caregiver is reluctant to place his or her loved one in a nursing home unless the professionals regard this solution as necessary for the safety of the loved one. Caregivers may need support from the professionals in such situations to make difficult decisions that will benefit the care recipient.

Conclusion

Elderly persons need thorough interventions to support their wish to live at home even with their diseases. Through cooperation among health care, social, psychological, nutritional, legal, and economic professionals and the family (the care recipient and the caregiver), the oldest olds' own personal way of living can be maintained and their quality of life increased. Because dementia is a primary reason for the need for services in this age group, persons suffering from dementia should be a specific focus of professionals working with these individuals. Dementia also causes strain for the caregivers, is a main reason for long-term hospitalization, and results in economic burden worldwide. Tailored support services offered to families as soon as the diagnosis has been made may make it possible to delay institutionalization and prevent financial hardship while increasing quality of life for oldest old individuals.

Minna Raivio

See also Access to Health Care: Elderly; Advance Directives and the Family; Alzheimer's Disease: An Overview of Family Issues in; Alzheimer's Disease: Caregiver Burden; Social Support Systems for the Family

Further Readings

Brodaty, H., Thomson, C., Thompson, C., & Fine, M. (2005). Why caregivers of people with dementia and memory loss don't use services. *International Journal of Geriatric Psychiatry, 20*(6), 537–546.

Eloniemi-Sulkava, U., Saarenheimo, M., Laakkonen, M. L., Pietilä, M., Savikko, N., Kautiainen, H., et al. (2009). Family care as collaboration: Effectiveness of a multicomponent support program for elderly couples with dementia. Randomized controlled intervention study. *Journal of the American Geriatric Society, 57*(12), 2200–2208.

Gaugler, J. E., Kane, R. L., Kane, R. A., & Newcomer, R. (2005). Early community-based service utilization and its effects on institutionalization in dementia caregiving. *Gerontologist, 45*(2), 177–185.

Laakkonen, M. L., Raivio, M. M., Eloniemi-Sulkava, U., Saarenheimo, M., Pietilä, M., Tilvis, R. S., et al. (2008). How do elderly spouse care givers of people with Alzheimer disease experience the disclosure of dementia diagnosis and subsequent care? *Journal of Medical Ethics, 34*(6), 427–430.

Lamura, G., Mnich, E., Nolan, M., Wojszel, B., Krevers, B., Mestheneos, L., et al. (2008). Family carers' experiences using support services in Europe: Empirical evidence from the EUROFAMCARE study. *Gerontologist, 48*(6), 752–771.

Lawrence, V., Murray, J., Samsi, K., & Banerjee, S. (2008). Attitudes and support needs of black Caribbean, south Asian and white British carers of people with dementia in the UK. *British Journal of Psychiatry, 193*(3), 240–246.

Noro, A., Finne-Soveri, H., Björkgren, M., & Vähäkangas, P. (Eds.). (2005). Quality and productivity in institutional care for elderly residents—benchmarking with the RAI [in Finnish]. Helsinki, Finland: National Research and Development Centre for Welfare and Health (STAKES).

Ott, C. H., Sanders, S., & Kelber, S. T. (2007). Grief and personal growth experience of spouses and adult-child caregivers of individuals with Alzheimer's disease and related dementias. *Gerontologist, 47*(6), 798–809.

Raivio, M. (2007). *Pitfalls in the treatment of persons with dementia.* Unpublished dissertation, Helsinki University, Finland. https://oa.doria.fi/bitstream/handle/10024/28143/pitfalls.pdf?sequence=1

Raivio, M., Eloniemi-Sulkava, U., Laakkonen, M. L., Saarenheimo, M., Pietilä, M., Tilvis, R., et al. (2007). How do officially organized services meet the needs of elderly caregivers and their spouses with Alzheimer's disease? *American Journal of Alzheimer's Disease and Other Dementias, 22*(5), 360–368.

Saarenheimo, M. (2007). Exploring the borderlines of family caregiving in Finland. In I. Paoletti (Ed.), *Family caregiving for older disabled people: Relational and institutional issues.* Hauppage, NY: Nova Science Publishers.

Schneider, J., Murray, J., Banerjee, S., & Mann, A. (1999). EUROCARE: A cross-national study of co-resident spouse carers for people with Alzheimer's disease: I—Factors associated with carer burden. *International Journal of Geriatric Psychiatry, 14*(8), 651–661.

Viramo, P., & Sulkava, R. (2006). Epidemiology of the memory disorders and dementia. In T. Erkinjuntti, K. Alhainen, J. Rinne, & H. Soininen (Eds.), *Memory disorders and dementia* [in Finnish] (pp. 23–39). Helsinki, Finland: Finnish Medical Association Duodecim.

Whitlatch C. (2008). Informal caregivers: Communication and decision making. *American Journal of Nursing, 108*(9 Suppl), 73–77.

CAREGIVING: INFANTS

A good early start in life is essential for the health and well-being of infants and has influence through childhood and into adult years. Around the globe, infant mortality and illness are high in some countries, whereas in others, infants enjoy relatively good survival and health in the first year of life. The ability to promote infant health and well-being through care is central to good outcomes as examination of World Health Organization data demonstrates. Regardless of the diverse situations of families with an infant, there are universal care principles that promote optimal growth and development during the first year of life. The purpose of this entry's discussion is to identify these and to set out their essential features.

The Context of Infant Care

In the mid-20th century, pediatrician and psychoanalyst Donald Winnicott made the comment that there is always a *"baby and someone."* The premise of this statement underpins every aspect of infant care. An infant depends on ongoing and secure care given by one or more primary caregivers. In the vast majority of families, this caregiver is the mother. A woman's confidence in her ability or self-efficacy in mothering is related to her ability to care for her infant. Therefore, the health and well-being of the mother is integral to the infant's well-being.

In practical terms, the attachment of mother and infant (or other primary caregiver) is a process that is central to, and a foundation for, infant care. Attachment describes the relationship or way of relating between an infant and his or her mother or other primary caregiver over time. With secure attachment relations, a synchrony develops wherein the infant indicates her or his needs and is responsive to the caregiver, who in turn engages in a responsive repertoire of caregiving. Recent evidence suggests that it is not only psychosocial well-being that is influenced by secure attachment but also an infant's neurological development.

Infant Feeding

Feeding is the single most significant aspect of care influencing the health and well-being of the infant. The benefits of breast-feeding are well recognized, with research suggesting that breast-feeding infers a wide range of health benefits for the infant (e.g., protection against bacterial and viral infection, reduced incidence of allergy). For women, breast-feeding aids uterine involution in the postnatal period, with longer-term benefits, including a reduced risk of ovarian and breast cancer and increased maternal confidence. Attachment and the parent–child relationship are enhanced when an infant is breast-fed.

A number of factors may influence a woman's ability to breast-feed her baby. Appropriate support and access to information are important for a successful start. Providing a healthy environment that promotes, protects, and supports breast-feeding—through, for example, the implementation of the Baby Friendly Hospital Initiative—has demonstrated positive effects on the initiation of breast-feeding.

Current recommendations suggest that breast-feeding exclusively for 6 months and the introduction of appropriate food together with breast-feeding into the infant's second year will optimize health benefits. Breast-feeding is essential for child survival in families living in circumstances where access to clean water is limited.

Infant Sleep and Settling

Settling an infant and creating a safe and nurturing sleep environment are essential aspects of everyday infant care. The sleep cycle of a newborn and young infant is immature and shorter than that of older children. The total hours of sleep also changes through infancy and childhood, and a range of biorhythms develop to help the growing child self-regulate. These are natural, neurobiological developments.

Care practice influences the quality of an infant's rest and sleep and, by association, health and well-being. Care that is infant-led and sensitive to the infant's needs is required, that is, where the infant's needs for sleep and activity are recognized and responded to. This involves, for example, recognizing and responding to the difference between an infant's need for stimulation and activity, the need for the removal of intense stimulation, the need for attention to such cares as feeding or providing comfort, and the need for settling to allow sleep.

The infant sleep environment has attracted considerable attention in recent decades. Co-sleeping, that is, an arrangement where the infant sleeps near parents on either a shared or separate sleeping surface, was, historically, the universal environment for an infant to sleep in. Today this continues to be the environment for the majority of the world's population, although there is some divergence from this pattern in a number of developed countries in particular, where infants may be placed in a solitary environment for sleep. Evidence suggests that there is no advantage for an infant sleeping away from the company of caregivers; however, there are some conditions that promote a safe sleep environment. A separate sleep surface, next to that of the parents, is recommended, and not on the same surface, particularly if parent responsiveness might be affected by alcohol or drugs (legal or illicit). The environment needs to have adequate ventilation and good air quality that is smoke free. For safety, the surface needs to be firm and one where the baby will not become stuck between surfaces, be caught up in loose bedding, or be at risk of falling. Finally, young infants are best placed on their back to sleep.

Growth and Development

Infant care also involves everyday practices that promote the infant's cognitive and psychosocial health and development. Caregiving involves parents talking to, singing to, reading to, and stimulating their infants. Language development, for example, is a social act, or put another way, interactive. Infants' prelingual language development is supported when parents repeat words and point to objects and name them. Recent evidence also points to the impact of reading to babies, from an early age—an activity that appears to influence brain development and enhance later literacy skills, which, in turn, facilitate academic and vocational opportunities and thus psychosocial well-being. Reading also engages the infant closely with their caregivers, influencing attachment through the opportunity the setting affords for close, responsive interaction.

Conclusion

The infant cares that have been considered in this entry take place in everyday family life. Infant care is also a community responsibility, and a number of societies seek to prevent illness and promote infant health through regular health screening, where infant growth and development are tracked across a range of physical, cognitive, motor skills, and psychosocial landmarks. These landmarks or milestones tend to have wide ranges and require specific assessment tools—for example, growth charts for males or females, and for primarily breast-fed versus artificially fed infants. Other community-based infant care includes immunization, globally considered to be an important illness prevention program.

To care for infants, parents need support, good information, and commitment. Support needs to be built on an understanding of the resources available to the family to provide a safe and nurturing environment for their infant. Support helps mothers and other primary carers to make informed choices, within their life context, in order to care for their infant.

Jennifer Rowe and Margaret Barnes

See also Developmental Care of Preterm Infants and the Childbearing Family; Health Needs of Childbearing Families; Maternal Lactation; Parental Attachment; Parenting

Further Readings

Barnes, M., & Rowe, J. (Eds.). (2008). *Child youth and family health: Strengthening communities*. Sydney, Australia: Elsevier.

McKenna, J., & McDade, T. (2005). Why babies should never sleep alone: A review of the co-sleeping controversy in relation to SIDS, bedsharing and breast feeding. *Paediatric Respiratory Reviews, 6,* 134–152.

Neuman, S., & Dickinson, D. (Eds.). (2003). *Handbook of early literacy research*. New York: Guilford Press.

Winnicott, D. W. (1957). *The child and the outside world: Studies in developing relationships*. London: Tavistock.

World Health Organization. (2003). *Global strategy for infant and young child feeding*. Geneva, Switzerland: Author.

Websites

Baby Friendly Hospital Initiative USA: http://www.babyfriendlyusa.org/eng/index.html

CAREGIVING: PARTNERS/SPOUSES

It is estimated that in the United States 5.8 million informal helpers provide care to an older adult (65+ years) who needs assistance with everyday activities. Spouses are usually the first in line to assume caregiving responsibility. If the spouse is not able to care for the frail elderly, often the adult children take the caregiver role. According to the 1999 National Long-Term Care Survey and Informal Caregiver Survey, about 99% of the spousal/partner caregivers are married to the care recipient, and about 73% of them are wives. Spousal caregivers provide, on average, 41 hours of support per week, including 38 hours with personal care, such as help with eating, dressing, bathing, and toileting. Almost half of them have provided care for more than 4 years. Love is the main caring motive for many spouses, whereas obligation and duty are more prevalent motives of adult children.

Caregiving can be characterized as a process: In the case of a progressive chronic illness, such as dementia, the onset of spousal caregiving is a gradual process. There are two other transitions of caregiving: institutional placement of the relative, which is experienced by a minority of caregivers, and bereavement, which is the ultimate end of the caregiving career. Results are inconsistent regarding whether spousal caregivers are more or less likely than adult children to place the care recipient in a nursing home. This entry focuses on the health consequences of the caregiving partner/spouse and interventions to assist the caregiving partner/spouse.

Health Consequences of Spousal Caregiving

Studies that compare caregivers and noncaregivers show that carers are more stressed and depressed and have lower levels of subjective well-being, physical health, and self-efficacy than noncaregivers. However, there is large interindividual variability in effects of caregiving, and caregiver status by itself explains, on average, less than 8% of the variance of psychological health. For example, spousal caregivers of patients with dementia are more distressed than spousal caregivers of physically frail older adults, and behavior problems of dementia patients—such as irritability, impulsivity, and paranoid delusions—are the strongest stressors for caregivers.

On average, spousal caregivers experience higher levels of depression and of physical and financial strain than adult children. As spouses are most likely to live with the care recipient, they tend to provide more support and find less relief from the caregiver role than adult children and children-in-law. The vulnerability of spouse caregivers may also stem from the greater likelihood of having health problems associated with older adulthood, such as chronic illnesses and diminished physical capacity. In addition, because married couples are likely to have similar risks for bad health outcomes as a result of selection, lifestyle factors, and access to health care, having a disabled spouse increases the risk of poor health, even if no care is provided.

Caregiving may also affect the quality of the couple relationship. Spousal caregivers show, on average, less reciprocity and fewer shared pleasures and report lower levels of couple satisfaction than spousal noncaregivers. Potentially harmful caregiver behaviors—such as screaming and yelling, insulting, and threatening to send to a nursing home—may emerge when the disabled spouse has great needs for care and when caregiver is at risk for clinical depression. However, maintaining a close marital relationship may protect the psychological well-being of spousal caregivers.

Husbands and wives as caregivers differ with regard to psychological and physical health: Wives show higher levels of caregiver burden and depression and lower levels of subjective well-being and physical health than husbands. This is, in part, based on the fact that they help with more caregiving tasks and assist with more personal care.

Not all factors associated with caregiving are negative to all caregivers. Caregiving may also make caregivers feel more useful, needed, and proud of their abilities to meet caregiving demands. Such positive appraisals of the caregiving experience are reported by up to 90% of the caregivers and are as frequently experienced by spouses and by adult children.

Help for the Caregivers

Given the high levels of psychological distress in spouses and other caregivers, several forms of interventions have been developed and evaluated. Interventions most often focus on (a) reduction of the level of objective stressors (e.g., reducing symptoms of the care recipient or the amount of support provided), (b) reduction of psychological distress (e.g., caregiver burden and depression), (c) increasing resources of the caregiver (e.g., coping abilities, self-efficacy, availability of social support), and (d) delay of institutionalization. Psychoeducational interventions are the most often applied interventions for caregivers. They focus on the structured presentation of information about illness of the care recipient and caregiving-related issues. These interventions have the strongest effect on caregiver knowledge about the illness of the care recipient and sources of support. However, the strongest effects on caregiver depression and caregiver burden are found for cognitive-behavioral therapy, which focuses on identifying and modifying caregiving-related beliefs, developing a new behavioral repertoire to deal with caregiving demands, and fostering positive activities. Respite care, which is a planned, temporary relief for the caregiver through the provision of substitute care (e.g., center-based day care program or in-home respite) has small effects on caregiver burden and depression, but delays the institutionalization of the care recipient. Unstructured support groups have, on average, very low effects on any outcome variables. The forms of interventions can also be combined. Spousal caregivers tend to profit less from these interventions than adult children, probably because of more risk factors for distress, such as shrinking social networks, lower income, and health problems.

Martin Pinquart

See also Alzheimer's Disease: Caregiver Burden; Caregiving: Elderly; Elder Care Options for Families: Long-Term Care; Elder Physical Abuse and the Family

Further Readings

Beach, S. R., Schulz, R., Williamson, G. M., Miller, S., Weiner, M. F., & Lance, C. E. (2005). Risk factors for potentially harmful informal caregiver behavior. *Journal of the American Geriatrics Society, 53,* 255–261.

Pinquart, M., & Sörensen, S. (2005). Caregiving stress and psychological health of caregivers. In K. V. Oxington (Ed.), *Psychology of stress* (pp. 165–206). New York: Nova Science Publishers.

Wolff, J. L., & Kasper, J. D. (2006). Caregiving of frail elders: Updating a national profile. *The Gerontologist, 46,* 344–356.

CASE MANAGEMENT FOR CHRONIC ILLNESS/DISABILITY AND THE FAMILY

When a family faces a chronic illness or disability in one of its members, numerous challenges often present themselves and affect all areas of family life. Work or school attendance can be compromised by the condition or the need for ongoing health care. Unanticipated or burdensome health care expenses can compromise a family's financial situation. Usual caregiving roles may be disrupted if a caregiver is ill and other members of the family need to assume new responsibilities. In addition, each family member must adapt to the diagnosis and medical needs of the ill or disabled person and deal with their own sadness or worry. A significant challenge faced by many families is the need to learn about service systems and advocate for, and access care needed for, the affected family member. Case management is a collaborative process that includes the patient, the family, and the case manager used to assist individuals and families in identifying needs and coordinating and accessing the health and related services necessary to optimize the health and well-being of the chronically ill or disabled member of the family.

Case management, care coordination, service coordination, and care management are all terms used to describe a process whereby an individual, typically employed by a health care or service organization, assists a patient, family member, or family to develop a plan to meet the needs of the family member with the chronic illness or disability, in order to achieve optimal health and related goals. Case management is often provided as part of hospital discharge planning, health insurance company benefits and utilization management, or public systems designed to provide services for specific populations, such as those with developmental disabilities. In addition, hospitals and clinics designed to serve those with chronic conditions or disabilities may also provide case management. For instance, a university hospital program for individuals with hemophilia may include case management carried out by a nurse or social worker to coordinate and enhance the care of individuals served in the program. A children's hospital that has a special care center devoted to the care of children with cystic fibrosis may provide case management as part of the service delivery. Typically, case management is provided when the condition is complex and/or long term, the patient population is vulnerable, and the care required is complex, expensive, difficult to access, and/or fragmented.

An example of an ideal candidate for case management is a child, newly diagnosed with autism, whose family is challenged by lack of health insurance and now must provide for their child by locating needed services and learning to utilize a new and unfamiliar service system. Case management might be provided by the developmental disability system service coordinator, the nurse in the child's special education setting, or the social worker in the hospital-based neurology program where the child was diagnosed. The case management might focus on accessing needed therapy services, identifying an appropriate school placement, or providing support for the family. More important than who provides case management is the communication that must take place between the case manager, patient, family, and all providers of care, and the utilization of a comprehensive process for carrying out case management.

Typically, case management begins with the assessment of client and family strengths and needs related to the condition, as well as other circumstances in the patient's or family's life that may influence the patient's health and well-being. After an assessment of needs is completed, the case manager, the patient, and family discuss goals for care and desired outcomes. The next step is identification of services and resources that will lead to achievement of the desired goals and outcomes. Finally, responsibility is defined for each of the action steps to be carried out. For instance, a goal might be return to employment for a person seriously injured in an accident. Services or resources needed to achieve this goal might include vocational rehabilitation, adaptive equipment, or modifications to a work environment. An action step might include contact with the local vocational rehabilitation agency to determine eligibility and to begin an application process. By patient, family, and case manager agreement, it may be decided that the case manager will take responsibility for completion of this task. Periodic reassessment of the plan is necessary to monitor achievement of goals and to modify the plan as needed.

Benefits of case management include support for the affected individual and family, achievement of health and related goals, improved knowledge of the service system, and enhanced access to services. In addition, coordination of services minimizes gaps in care and duplication of efforts and helps to maintain the cost-effectiveness of services.

In summary, case management is a frequently used tool to assist patients with chronic illnesses or disabilities and their families to learn about, access, and coordinate needed health and related services. Case management may be provided in a variety of settings, by individuals with various types of professional backgrounds. Some patients may have more than one case manager representing different agencies or service settings, necessitating careful communication and coordination among the case managers. As they learn more about the condition or disability and the service systems, some families may choose to serve as their own case managers, either alone or in partnership with a health care or related provider. Additional support should continue to be available during times of crisis or when there is a need for respite.

Kathryn Smith

See also Access to Health Care: Child Health; Access to Health Care: Elderly; Adult With Disability Living at Home; Chronic Health Problems and Interventions for the Childbearing Family; Chronic Health Problems and Interventions for the Elderly Family; Chronic Health Problems and Interventions for the Midlife Family; Chronic Illness and Family Management Styles; Disabilities and Family Management

Further Readings

Cohen, E., & Cesta, T. G. (2004). *Nursing case management*. Philadelphia: Elsevier Science.

Websites

The Case Manager: http://www.elsevier.com/wps/find/journaldescription.cws_home/623112/description#description
Professional Case Management (the Official Journal of the Case Management Society of America): http://journals.lww.com/professionalcasemanagementjournal/pages/default.aspx

CEREBRAL PALSY AND THE FAMILY

The term *cerebral palsy* (CP) is not so much a diagnosis as it is a description of conditions that affect movement and muscle coordination. Specific areas of the brain, such as the cerebrum and connections between the cortex and cerebellum, are affected, usually during fetal development, the perinatal period, or infancy. CP affects each person differently. Some individuals with CP have normal cognition and are able to function well in their everyday lives with minimal support. Others have severe to profound cognitive and physical disabilities and will require total care for their entire lives. Still others with profound physical disabilities may not have any cognitive delays. Much depends on the exact cause of the injury, the size of the injury, and the area of the brain where the injury occurred. Any part of the body that functions in movement and/or muscle coordination can be affected.

Four types of CP have been described: athetoid, ataxic, spastic, and mixed. The most common type is *spastic diplegia*, which involves muscle spasticity in the lower extremities causing difficulty in movement. Individuals may or may not be able to walk. However, spasticity is not always limited to the lower extremities. Other individuals may have spastic quadriplegia, which involves all four extremities, or monoplegia, which affects a single spastic extremity. Those individuals with athetoid CP have random movements of all extremities and have very little control over their gross motor abilities. Their movement patterns are uncoordinated and frequently involuntary. Individuals with ataxic CP experience low muscle tone and typically have problems with balance, coordination, and depth perception. Individuals with mixed CP experience problems consistent with more than one type of CP.

The long-term effect of CP on the family is directly related to type of CP and the degree of involvement for the person with CP. Many families feel guilty about what may or may not have happened to lead to their child's disability. Other parents will suffer chronic sorrow whenever their child is not able to perform a developmental task on time or when a younger, typically developing friend or sibling advances beyond the abilities of the child with CP.

Children with mild CP develop much the same as their typically developing peers. They achieve many of the same milestones with some delays related to movement and muscle coordination. Early intervention services are imperative to make sure these children achieve these early milestones and do not suffer further developmental delays. These children often do very well in school and function much the same as their peers. These children require frequent medical appointments to assess their growth and development, but few interventions are needed.

As the degree of disability increases, so do the problems faced by the individual and family. Child care issues for children with more severe forms of CP arise from an increased incidence of seizures, feeding difficulties, sleep issues, and behavior problems. These children require much more intense medical management, therapy services, and occasional psychological or psychiatric interventions. Individuals who are cognitively intact but who are trapped in a body that they have no control over often become frustrated and may be aggressive or take out their frustrations on the people who are closest to them.

Assistive technology can be very beneficial to individuals with CP and their families. Augmentative and alternative communication (AAC) methods can provide a voice to the individual who thinks clearly but is unable to speak. Computers, iPods, and cell phones provide communication with the outside world in a way that the individual is not judged merely on his or her appearance. Power wheelchairs, feeding devices, and adaptive vehicles help to promote independence. Environmental controls can provide the individual with a way to have some control over the environment that he or she might not have otherwise. Companion animals and personal caregivers also help to provide greater independence and success in the outside world.

The family burden is greatest for those families who have a child who has suffered significant cognitive damage as well as suffering from movement and muscle coordination. These individuals require continual care to meet all of their basic human needs. Many remain infantile in their responses to others and cannot provide any assistance to the person providing direct care to them. Oftentimes, the primary caregiver is forced to give up full-time employment to take care of the child because finding appropriate care providers is extremely difficult. These families face financial difficulties, marital stress, depression, and a different life path than the one they envisioned when they began contemplating having a family. Having a child with a significant disability often leads to isolation for those persons closest to him or her. Medical issues, care provider issues, and a lack of understanding of the stress the family is undergoing often create a chasm between the family and their friends and extended family, thus eliminating a great resource for support.

It is important that families be connected with the appropriate supports early and that they begin to consider long-term outcomes and access services to provide for eventual independent living for those individuals for whom it is appropriate. Even parents and siblings of the most profoundly affected individuals need to consider "Who will care for ____, when something happens to me?"

An interdisciplinary health care team is essential in assisting families with all of the transitions facing the individual with CP throughout life. Most individuals with CP will reach adulthood, so it is important to work with a health care team that understands the medical and social needs of individuals with CP. Education for families, individuals with CP, and their health care providers is essential if the person is to succeed in the world of typically developing individuals. CP is no longer considered a death sentence. With the appropriate interventions and assistive technology, individuals with specific movement and coordination disorders can live life to the fullest extent possible.

Cheryl Lee Crisp

See also Adult Child With Disability: Planning for by Parents; Chronic Health Problems and Interventions for the Childrearing Family; Disabilities and Family Management; Family Caregiving: Caring for Children, Adults, and Elders With Developmental Disabilities

Further Readings

Hinchliffe, A. (2007). *Children with cerebral palsy: A manual for therapists, parents and community workers* (2nd ed.). Thousand Oaks, CA: Sage.

Martin, S. (2006). *Teaching motor skills to children with cerebral palsy and similar movement disorders.* Bethesda, MD: Woodbine House.

Miller, F. (2005). *Cerebral palsy.* New York: Springer.

Miller, F. (2006). *Cerebral palsy: A complete guide for caregiving.* Baltimore: Johns Hopkins University Press.

CHANGES IN FAMILY STRUCTURE

Family structure refers to the organization of individuals who are related by blood, marriage, adoption, or strong social bonds into a household. In the United States, family structure has been through two dramatic shifts in the past 160 years. The first shift occurred between 1850 and 1950 and saw the decline of the vertically extended household that included grandparents, parents, and children in the same dwelling and the rise of the nuclear family household, which included married biological parents and full siblings only. Since then, family structure has transitioned into a plurality of forms. Factors that contribute to family structure change since 1950 include delayed marriage, divorce, remarriage, cohabitation, nonmarital fertility, family formation among gay and lesbian couples, and population aging. These changes in family structure require resilience in families experiencing them and increased complexities for interacting with the health care system. Health professionals also need to adapt to these new structures as they partner with families to promote family health.

Delayed Marriage

According to the U.S. Census Bureau, at the turn of the 20th century, the median age at first marriage was about 22 years for women and 26 years for men. Over the next half-century, the age at first marriage *declined* for women and men and reached a low point of about 20 years for women and 22.5 years for men in 1956. This decline and the nearly universal entry into marriage in the late 1940s and 1950s have been attributed to a postwar economic recovery that facilitated early family formation. Since then, the age at marriage has increased steadily. In 2005, the median ages at marriage for women and men were 25.3 years and 27.1 years, respectively. The rising age at marriage has coincided with the development of more reliable and accessible contraceptive methods, women's increased educational attainment and labor force participation, and a cultural shift in attitudes toward greater tolerance for premarital sex and cohabitation.

While age at marriage has risen, the probability that an adult will *ever* marry has held steady overall. Over the past century, about 90% of women in the United States eventually married, according to Andrew J. Cherlin, a family sociologist. However, not everyone is equally likely to marry: Among women born since 1960, college-educated and white women are more likely to eventually marry than are African American women or women with less than a college education. Racial differences are especially striking. Among African American women in the United States, just over 6 out of 10 women born since 1960 are expected to eventually marry, compared to over 9 out of 10 white women in the same birth cohort, according to data from the 1995 Current Population Survey. Social scientists have long been interested in investigating differences in the likelihood of marriage by race, ethnicity, and social class and have debated the relative influence of welfare policy, patterns of economic restructuring and male unemployment, the decoupling of childbearing from marriage, and cultural attitudes about the symbolic and practical significance of marriage.

Divorce

Divorce is the legal dissolution of a marriage. In the United States, 1 in 10 marriages ended in divorced in 1890, a rate that caused considerable public alarm at the time. Divorce rates rose incrementally through the 20th century and escalated during the 1960s and 1970s, peaking in 1980. Since then, divorce rates have declined, but they remain high compared to those in other developed countries. Today, nearly half of first marriages for men and women under age 45 are expected to end in divorce within 15 years, according to the National Center for Health Statistics (NCHS). As with marriage, the risk of divorce is not equally distributed in the population. Hispanic and white women experience similar rates of divorce, while divorce rates are highest for African American women (with 55% of unions ending within 15 years) and lowest for Asian women (23% of unions end within 15 years). Divorce rates are highest in the first five years of marriage, and women who marry in their teen years, who have a high school education or less, or who have low family incomes are more likely to divorce than are their counterparts.

The mid-century escalation of divorce rates is attributed largely to the liberalization of divorce laws and pent-up demand for divorce. The sustained, relatively high level of divorce in the U.S. population has been explained by women's increasing economic independence, by the rise of an individualist approach to marriage, and by the declining social stigma attached to divorce.

Remarriage

Remarriage following a divorce or the death of a spouse is frequent in the United States. Recent estimates from the NCHS show that in a given year, about 40% of all marriages are second or higher-order unions. Three quarters of women and a larger share of men remarry within 10 years of a divorce. Gender differences in remarriage rates have been attributed to divergence in the opportunities men and women have to repartner in the marriage market, as well as different economic, emotional, and familial motivations to remarry. Increasingly, remarriage is preceded by cohabitation, and some couples who repartner opt to remain in a long-term cohabiting relationship rather than to transition to marriage.

Second and higher-order unions are more likely to end in divorce than are first marriages, with 39% of women's second marriages ending in divorce after 10 years, compared to 33% of women's first marriages. Explanations for the higher dissolution rate include the demands that arise from the complexity of blended family structures, including role ambiguity, financial arrangements, and competing interests among family members. In addition, individuals who remarry may be distinctive from those in first marriages in ways that make union dissolution more likely.

Cohabitation

Cohabitation is usually defined as an arrangement by which unmarried romantic partners live together in the same household. The partners may be of the same or opposite sex, but the majority of family structure research on the topic has focused on heterosexual unions. Changes in the prevalence and role of cohabitation in union formation have dramatically altered the face of family structure over the past 30 years. For baby boomers who married in the 1960s and 1970s, fewer than 7% of couples lived together before marriage, according to a study by demographers Larry Bumpass and James Sweet. In contrast, NCHS data show that 40% of all women under 45 in 2002 had cohabited. In the United States, cohabitation functions as a short-term arrangement that eventually dissolves or transitions to marriage. Nationally, half of couples separate within 5 years, and 70% of cohabiting couples who remain together marry within 5 years. Few couples remain in a cohabiting union indefinitely.

Increasingly, cohabitation has become a setting for childbearing and childrearing. Nearly 2 out of every 10 children born in the United States are born to cohabiting parents, and two fifths of children are expected to spend some time in a household with a cohabiting union before age 12, either with both biological parents or a biological parent and a stepparent-like figure. Cohabiting parents are more common in nonwhite and low-income families. Compared to marriage, cohabitation remains a relatively unstable family form with high rates of union dissolution. In a sample of urban, mostly low-income families, a quarter of couples who were cohabiting when they had a child together broke up before the child's first birthday, in contrast to 6% of similar married couples.

Public opinion data indicate that Americans are increasingly accepting of cohabitation as a precursor to marriage but express ambivalence about cohabitation as a context for family formation. In a 2002 national survey, two thirds of Americans agreed with or felt neutral about the statement "It is all right for a couple to live together without intending to get married." But in the same survey, 70% of Americans agreed with the statement "People who want children ought to get married."

Nonmarital Childbearing

Historically, the majority of children who lived with only one parent came to that status after a parental death or divorce. Increasingly, however, children of single parents are born to never-married mothers. Two out of every 10 children born in the United States are born to an unmarried, noncohabiting mother, according to recent NCHS data. Childbearing outside of the teen years represents an increasing share of all nonmarital births, with 77% of such births occurring to women who were age 20 or older in 2007. In contrast, only half of nonmarital births were to older women in 1970. About half of nonmarital births outside of cohabitation are planned, and planned nonmarital births are more common among women in their 30s, Hispanic women, and women with a college degree compared to other women. The rise in nonmarital childbearing is attributable to delays in marriage, increasing public tolerance for children outside of marriage, and changes in contraceptive use and effectiveness. Although the composition of the pool of unmarried mothers is changing, nonmarital fertility is associated with lower odds of ever marrying or forming a cohabiting union, and families headed by unmarried mothers are more likely than other family types to be characterized by low income and compromised outcomes for children's health and development.

Gay and Lesbian Families

Gay and lesbian couples are increasingly likely to live together and raise children. In the United States in August 2009, only six states had legalized gay marriage. More states permit civil unions, domestic partnerships, or other types of recognition, but vary in the provision of associated benefits. In some ways, the public debate in the United States over gay marriage encapsulates a distinctly American tendency to valorize marriage over other family arrangements. In European countries, for example, gay and lesbian activists are less likely to embrace legal access to marriage as an end goal because civil unions are viewed as an equivalent alternative to marriage in public discourse.

Children in gay and lesbian unions may be biologically related to one partner (conceived either in an earlier heterosexual union or through sperm donation or in vitro fertilization) or adopted by both partners. A summary of current research concluded that children in gay and lesbian families are similar to children raised by heterosexual parents in terms of psychological and emotional adjustment and physical health. As in heterosexual families, children in gay and lesbian families fare better in two-parent households characterized by warmth and support. Depending on the legal status of the relationship between children and a nonbiological parent, health care–related issues like health insurance coverage, hospital visitation, and treatment decisions are potentially complicated.

Population Aging

Life expectancy has increased dramatically over the last century. The average 65-year-old in 2002 could expect to live another 18 years, according to life table estimates based on NCHS data. Women live about 3 years longer than men on average and are therefore more likely to experience the death of a spouse, and are less likely than widowed men to remarry. Increasingly, adult children and health care systems have collaborated to promote independent, community-based living for older adults as an alternative to nursing home care or extended kin coresidence. Such programs include efforts to encourage elderly adults to follow prescribed regimens for medication and physicians' care.

Conclusion

Family structure has changed dramatically in the past 60 years. A variety of family forms have emerged in response to demographic change, economic transformation, and an evolution in social norms and attitudes about family composition and the life course. The plurality of family forms in the United States today poses dramatic challenges to population health and the health care system. The overrepresentation of low income in some family forms increases the likelihood of accumulating health disadvantages for adults and children, while divorce and the creation of blended families introduce complexities pertaining to health insurance coverage and health care access within families. Undoubtedly, family forms will continue to evolve as marriage becomes a smaller share of the life course, introducing further challenges and opportunities to health care practitioners and researchers.

Paula Fomby

See also Assessing Family Health; Changes in Family Structure, Roles; Changing Family and Health Demographics; Defining Family: An Overview of Family Definitions From a Historical Perspective; Family Experiencing Transitions; Remarriage and Stepfamilies; Same-Sex Partner Rights

Further Readings

Bramlett, M. D., & Mosher, W. D. (2002). Cohabitation, marriage, divorce, and remarriage in the United States. *Vital Health Statistics Report, 23*(22). Hyattsville, MD: National Center for Health Statistics.

Casper, L. M., & Bianchi, S. M. (2002). *Continuity and change in the American family.* Thousand Oaks, CA: Sage.

Cherlin, A. J. (2009). *The marriage-go-round: The state of marriage and the family in America today.* New York: Knopf.

Manning, W. D. (2001). Childbearing in cohabiting unions: Racial and ethnic differences. *Family Planning Perspectives, 33,* 217.

McLanahan, S., & Sandefur, G. (1994). *Growing up with a single parent: What hurts, what helps.* Cambridge, MA: Harvard University Press.

CHANGES IN FAMILY STRUCTURE, ROLES

Family roles refers to the established patterns of behavior of family. Traditionally, family roles have been relatively clear with three primary roles within a family: the wage earner role, the domestic care role, and the nurturance/socialization role. In a traditionally structured family, the father is typically the breadwinner, the mother is the domestic caregiver, and both participate in the nurturance/socialization of their children. However, the traditional nuclear family has been declining and diverse types of families, including single-parent, stepparent, blended, unmarried partners, same-sex partners, and grandparent families, have become common. Although a family may be traditional in structure, it is most likely nontraditional in family roles. For example, as dual career families are increasingly common, traditional gender stereotyping is diminishing and contemporary male gender roles are enmeshed in parenthood and family. This entry explores the roles of family with regard to the current literature, health outcomes, and methods for enhancing family health outcomes.

Overview of Current Literature

The traditional nuclear family has been declining noticeably. According to the U.S. Census Bureau's Current Population Survey (CPS) report, *Americans' Families and Living Arrangements of 2009,* the largest proportional of families are married couples without children under age 18 (42.1%); nuclear families (married with children under 18) represented only 31% of the total U.S. families, followed by single-parent families (mother only or father only) with children (14%), families living with other relatives (including grandparents) (11.1%), and unmarried parent couple families (1.8%). The same report indicated that nationally 59% of children in married couple households had both parents in the labor force, and only 22.6% of married-couple family groups with children under 15 had a stay-at-home mother.

The roles of families today are multiple and complex, both in scope and nature. As life in today's society has become more complex, many people in the family hold a number of roles requiring intense role demand, role ambiguity, role incongruity, or role conflict. In particular, in studies of families, role overload appears to be a significant source of role strain among females. Previous research reported women spent more hours than men in child care and domestic responsibilities after a full day of work outside the home. For example, Arlie Hochschild reported in her book *The Second Shift* that American women put in 15 hours more each week than their husbands on all types of work.

Family Roles and Family Health Outcomes

Role strain and role enhancement are two perspectives central to role theory and predict different outcomes for family members occupying multiple roles. A role strain perspective suggests that multiple roles can make family members feel overburdened, thereby having a detrimental effect on mental and physical well-being. In contrast, the role enhancement perspective proposes that multiple roles improve mental well-being by providing emotional gratification. For example, a positive employment experience of women may make their caretakers' roles easier through role spillover effect. However, neither role strain nor role enhancement perspective fully explains the health outcomes of a family. A third perspective, role balance perspective, considers that the health effects depend on the balance between role satisfaction and role stress within and between key roles of a family member. Role balance reflects the tendency to become fully engaged in the performance of every role in the total role system, to approach every typical role and role partner with an attitude of attentiveness and care.

Enhancing Family Health Outcomes

A family's role strain may be managed in several ways of role sharing, role negotiating or role bargaining, and role reversals. The stereotypical jobs belonging to husband or wife have no relevance in the role-sharing marriage, and efforts toward the achievement of a role-sharing family often result in a compromise between contemporary and traditional experiences. Family researchers have found advantages of coparenting, including marital satisfaction. A role-sharing family expands the concept to include the children, as well as others considered family members in the family decision-making process and domestic care responsibilities, and many modern family functions have role-sharing characteristics.

Redefining or restructuring of the family role is a method of resolving conflict, and role negotiation or role bargaining permits mutual acceptance of role expectation. Related to role negotiation, role reversal can be an option for couples trying to cope with full-time employment while balancing home and child care demands. It is reported that role reversals can provide an opportunity to promote health and personal growth when the woman deliberately assumes the role of primary breadwinner and the man deliberately assumes the role of child and/or home caretaker.

Family roles are developed in response to multiple cultural, socioeconomic, and developmental factors. The increases in diverse types of families lead to changes in roles for family members, resulting in role stress or role strain. For example, single parents, unmarried parents, and grandparents are facing various sources of role stress from the absence of one partner or the lack of boundaries in parenting. Additionally, family structure transitions (i.e., divorce, separation, and remarriage) could cause parental stress. These nontraditional family structures involve adding new roles and dropping other roles of family members. Role modeling and/or role enhancement will benefit the families who experience role ambiguity or role conflict from their role transition.

Yeoun Soo Kim-Godwin

See also Aging and Shifting Roles in Families; Changes in Family Structure; Changing Family and Health Demographics; Coparenting: Children; Grandparents Parenting

Further Readings

Cooper, C., McLanahan, S., Meadows, S., & Brooks-Gunn, J. (2009). Family structure transitions and maternal parenting stress. *Journal of Marriage and Family, 71*(3), 558–574.

Hochschild, A. (1989). *The second shift: Working parents and the revolution at home.* New York: Viking.

Perron, K., Wright, S., & Jackson, Z. (2009). Traditional and nontraditional gender roles and work–family interface for men and women. *Journal of Career Development, 36*(1), 8–24.

U.S. Census Bureau. (2010). *Families and living arrangements: 2009 Current Population Survey (CPS) Reports.* Retrieved from http://www.census.gov/population/www/socdemo/hh-fam.html

CHANGING FAMILY AND HEALTH DEMOGRAPHICS

During the latter half of the 20th century, family demographics underwent numerous profound changes, and these changes were global in nature. Given the importance of the family in contemporary society, it is necessary that the potential impact of these changes be understood. In industrialized countries, the one-earner family became the two-earner family, birthrates fell to historically low levels, the proportion of births outside of marriage rose rapidly, and marriage became less common or much delayed. In both industrialized and developing countries, a significant quantitative development was the overall decrease in the birthrate and the consequent shrinking of family size. In developing countries, many countries reacted to rapid population growth by adopting policies to reduce traditionally high birthrates, with significant effects on family formation.

The Size of Families

In the mid-20th century, women in developing countries typically averaged five to eight children in their lifetimes. In many developing countries, governments sought to influence the number of children per family by educating couples regarding family planning and by providing reproductive health services. Some of these programs worked well and quickly, but others took quite some time to be effective. Nonetheless, birthrates in many developing countries have decreased to the point where women average 1.8 children in their lifetimes in Thailand, 2.0 in Brazil and Tunisia, 2.5 in Bangladesh, and 3.8 in Zimbabwe, according to the Population Reference Bureau. All of those declines are large changes from the past. Not only do smaller families slow population growth, easing strain on national budgets, but they also facilitate a healthier and better educated society. Parents are better able to raise their expectations for their children to have a better life than they themselves did. It does not always work that way, of course. Some developing countries with reduced family sizes are mired in desperate poverty.

Family size and formation in industrialized countries have also undergone wholesale changes. Currently, a family size of two is considered large in Europe, North America, and other developed countries. A variety of factors, often differing by country, have intervened to place childbearing farther down on many couples' list of priorities than ever before. A poor economy and a lack of effective child support, along with a change in values, have resulted in births delayed or not realized at all. By way of example, in Germany, Italy, and Japan, women are averaging only about 1.4 children in their lifetimes. Countries have been slow to consider or to take steps to facilitate both childbearing and childrearing in the current economy and for couples in two-career families. These measures have met with some success, but even where birthrates have risen slightly, they are still considered low.

Delaying Family Formation

There has also been something of a revolution in the timing of family formation itself: an increase in the age at first marriage and a greater acceptability of births outside formal marriage. According to the U.S. Census Bureau, in 1960, in the United States, 11% of females ages 25 to 29 had never been married. By 2008, that proportion had risen to 45%. In 1960, the median age at first marriage for women was 20.3 years and, for men, 22.8 years. By 2008, that had risen to 25.9 for women and 27.6 for men. Such a social change is significant in that it can provide time for the additional education often required in today's labor market. The rise in the frequency of divorce has also had an effect on family stability and the increase in blended families containing siblings from previous marriages. And, in 1960, slightly less than 9% of women in the United States remained divorced at ages 45 to 54, a proportion that rose to about 18% by 2008.

Healthier Families

In terms of health, life expectancy at birth has risen to unprecedented heights in industrialized countries. Working lives are being extended, and parents are surviving to much older ages, requiring long-term health care and a longer period of support from their offspring. In the United States, life expectancy at birth was but 47 years in 1900. As World War II approached, it had risen to 63 years and, at present, stands at 78 years. Such a dramatic change was by no means restricted to industrialized countries. The Population Reference Bureau reports that currently, life expectancy is 64 years in India, 75 years in Mexico, and 80 in South Korea.

Along with that, there has been a sharp decrease in infant mortality throughout the world. To fully appreciate this, consider that the Soviet dictator, Joseph Stalin, born in 1879, was the only survivor of four children, an occurrence that was not unusual at the time. In the United States, the infant mortality rate in 1915 was about 100 infants dying in the first year of life per 1,000 births, or 10%. Today, that rate is about 6 per 1,000 births, and rates in other industrialized countries are even lower. In developing countries, the rate is now about 50 infant deaths per 1,000 births, but that is down from 175 in the mid-20th century. As a result, parents generally expect their children to live to adulthood, a factor that can ultimately contribute to declining birthrates and smaller families in developing countries. It was also the rapid decrease in infant mortality and mortality at all ages in developing countries—without a similar decrease in the birthrate—that resulted in the population "explosion" of the 20th century, whereby world population grew from 1.6 billion in 1900 to 6.1 billion in 2000.

In recent years, there have been marked improvements in family health measures, in part motivated by the UN Millennium Development Goals, which set specific targets for many health indicators. For example, in Pakistan, the proportion of pregnant women receiving prenatal care from a health professional rose from 27% in the early 1990s to 62% by 2006–2007. In Ghana, the number of children who had received all recommended vaccinations rose from 19% in 1988 to 79% in 2008.

Conclusion

Families today are smaller, healthier, and better educated. Whereas that has been true for some time in industrialized countries, a similar transformation is under way in developing countries. At the same time, starting a family is no longer viewed as a foregone conclusion in wealthier countries and is often being delayed. With longer lives, multiple generations spend more time in family relationships, with all the rewards and responsibilities that brings.

Carl Haub

See also Aging and Shifting Roles in Families; Childbirth by Childbearing Couples: Reported Meanings; Childlessness; Defining Family: An Overview of Family Definitions From a Historical Perspective

Further Readings

Haub, C., & Kent, M. (2009). *2009 world population data sheet*. Washington, DC: Population Reference Bureau.

U.S. Census Bureau. (1975). *Historical statistics of the United States: Colonial times to 1970*. Washington, DC: Author.

Websites

Demographic and Health Surveys: http://measuredhs.com
Population Reference Bureau: http://www.prb.org
STATcompiler: http://www.statcompiler.com
U.S. Census Bureau: http://www.census.gov
U.S. National Center for Health Statistics: http://www.cdc.gov/nchs

CHANGING VIEWS OF MARRIAGE, HOME RESPONSIBILITIES, AND CAREGIVING

Within recent literature on families in the United States, social science researchers outline changes in marriage, caregiving, and home responsibilities, for families are typically defined via these relationships and activities over time. This entry documents whether people's views toward marriage, caregiving, and home responsibilities have changed. Changing views of marriage with increased responsibilities and caregiving demands can challenge the emotional and physical health of families.

Marriage

Marriage is no longer viewed as a cultural, social, or economic necessity. Increasing numbers of individuals select alternative pathways to coupling, such as cohabitation or living apart while having an intimate relationship. Despite growing alternatives, however, individuals still value marriage, as most adults choose to marry at some point. Even after divorce, most adults remarry; this highlights the importance individuals place on marriage. Thus, marriage is not devalued as much as other types of relationships have become more acceptable.

In addition, the way people enter into and exit marriage has also changed. A trend toward delayed marriage can be explained by the greater opportunities for women in the workforce, increased numbers of individuals seeking college degrees, effective birth control, and a revived interest in feminist ideologies. Contemporary adults are likely to have premarital sex and cohabitate before marriage as well. Additionally, since the 1980s, approximately one out of every two marriages ends in divorce in an average year, partially because no-fault divorce laws have made it easier to secure these exits. Further, Anthony Giddens suggests that we concentrate on the quality of relationships more today than ever before and how these relationships affect us individually. This does not mean that people have devalued the importance of emotional connectedness between married partners; it is simply that individuals expect more out of marital unions for themselves than they have in the past. Overall, adults may spend as much of their adult lives outside of marriage as inside. Giddens urges us to remember, however, that changing purposes of marriage, delayed marriage, and high divorce rates do not signify our desires to avoid marriage and other intimate relationships; rather, we have just altered our trajectories of "coupling" and "uncoupling" in contemporary times.

Caregiving

Views of children (and parenting, by default) have changed over recent generations as well. Because of declining mortality rates, the advent of birth control, parents' increased labor force participation, and the increased costs of raising children in contemporary times, fertility rates have declined. With fewer children, It is assumed that stronger emotional bonds exist between parents and children.

It is also still assumed that women are the primary caregivers for children. Since the 1950s, the stay-at-home mother has been a mainstay in U.S. culture. This narrow image has prevailed even as women's labor force participation, divorce, cohabitation, single-headed households, and nonmarital births increase. Stay-at-home mothering ideology is currently defined through "intensive mothering." In her work on mothering ideology, Sharon Hays suggests that there are three main tenets of intensive mothering, to which all women must adhere if they are to be viewed as "good" mothers: (1) Child care is primarily the responsibility of the mother, (2) child care should be child-centered, and (3) children should be protected from the outside world (and remain separate from the world of paid work). Intensive mothering is also considered a constant responsibility—at least in a child's early years. Even though most mothers work outside the home in recent decades, these views persevere, making maternal guilt prevalent. The burden on parents to find care for children while they are at paid work is also great; debates exist about whether public day care is damaging to children, and what "appropriate" day care is when parents are not present. There are also cultural debates about how involved fathers should be in day-to-day caregiving. In his study of fathers' involvement in childrearing, Nicholas Townsend found that men are increasingly willing to put family before career;

yet, for now, involvement in child care remains optional for fathers and mandatory for mothers.

Finally, we should not forget that large-scale demographic changes are allowing grandparents to have long-term relationships with their grandchildren, and some grandparents are heavily involved in caregiving. Additionally, middle-aged women are often caring for two generations simultaneously: young children and aging parents. Public recognition of elderly caregiving is new, and views vary about its importance alongside parenting. Burgeoning social science research now exists on the "carework" that families do, both for the young and old, and the (still gendered) nature of this caregiving.

Home Responsibilities

When social scientists write about home responsibilities in contemporary times, they are usually referring simply to either caregiving or household tasks (e.g., cleaning, cooking, laundry, general upkeep of the home). Researchers focus on the division of household labor and find that women still overwhelmingly have responsibility for household tasks. Men are helping with household labor more than ever before, though, suggesting a slow change in how couples view household tasks. Longitudinal studies also illustrate the amount of time spent on household tasks has declined considerably over the past several decades. Research indicates that families are increasingly purchasing services (e.g., restaurant meals, housecleaning, laundry services, and home repair) rather than engaging in these activities themselves. Some upkeep activities (e.g., ironing, dusting, mopping) have been virtually eliminated from our daily routines as well, either through advances in technology or higher tolerance for dirtier homes and wrinkled clothing. Thus, views about which home responsibilities really must get done (and which can be ignored) are changing with advances in technology, the speed-up of paid work, and the constant time crunch within which families find themselves.

Debates exist about whether families are "falling apart" due to a decline in "family values," or whether families are changing out of necessity in response to other, large-scale societal shifts in paid work, law, demographics, and U.S. culture. Most social science research documents the latter argument: Views and experiences of marriage, caregiving, and home responsibilities are changing out of necessity as families adapt to their changing world.

Heather E. Dillaway and
Sharon Lindhorst Everhardt

See also Changes in Family Structure; Defining Family: An Overview of Family Definitions From a Historical Perspective; Divorce: Effect on Children or the Family; Family Caregiving: Caring for Children, Adults, and Elders With Developmental Disabilities; Grandparenting; History of Families; Remarriage and Stepfamilies

Further Readings

Baca Zinn, M., Eitzen, D. S., & Wells, B. (2010). *Diversity in families* (9th ed.). Boston: Allyn & Bacon.

Coontz, S. (1998). *The way we really are: Coming to terms with America's changing families.* New York: Basic Books.

Giddens, A. (2009). The global revolution in family and personal life. In A. Skolnick & J. Skolnick (Eds.), *Family in transition* (15th ed., pp. 25–31). Boston: Allyn & Bacon.

Hays, S. (1996). *The cultural contradictions of motherhood.* New Haven, CT: Yale University Press.

Townsend, N. W. (2002). *The package deal: Marriage, work, and fatherhood in men's lives.* Philadelphia: Temple University Press.

CHILD BEGINNING SCHOOL

Entry into school is a common life transition for young children that represents a significant developmental step and the beginning of a formal learning process. A child beginning school encompasses several important components of a young person's development and care. First, school entry involves a major social transition for a child, with extension from the circle of family and kin into the larger world of peers and other adults. Second, beginning school typically moves a child from a learning environment that is more informal and open to an atmosphere that is more structured and focused on formalized learning processes. Third, a child's entry into school signifies a step toward developmental maturity and integration of all aspects of a child's development. Fourth, school entry indicates a child's inclusion in the broader community as a developing citizen and interest in that child's overall physical, cognitive, social, and emotional well-being and development.

In the world of early childhood care and education, the preparation of children to enter school successfully and perform well in their learning environments has become a subject of significant interest and concern. The term *school readiness* is generally used to describe the process of ensuring children are prepared by parents and society for a successful school experience. Clearly defined, school readiness embraces the combination of knowledge, skills, and behaviors that a child should learn and be able to do as they enter the school environment. Expectations for children in these areas are generally applied in a manner that is both age appropriate and developmentally appropriate. Areas of a child's growth and well-being that receive attention in school readiness include physical abilities and motor development; social and emotional development; motivation and desire for learning; cognitive development and practical knowledge; creativity and imagination; and language and literacy development.

Children and Schooling

Health care and education overlap and share concerns with the well-being of individuals over the entire life span and attentiveness to dimensions of health across all areas of a person's life, including physical, cognitive, social, emotional, and other aspects of development and well-being. Young children are dependent on adults for their care and guidance toward healthy development and preparation for school. Up to a quarter of children under the age of 6 live in poverty, and nearly half of all children face one or more risk factors associated with gaps in school readiness. Thus, the involvement of young children in formal educational opportunities is designed to facilitate growth and ensure successful development.

Parents are the first teachers of children and play an instrumental role in preparing children for successful entry into school. Most human societies have provided children with a variety of formal and informal learning opportunities from a young age that are guided by adults. Today, increased global competition in education is encouraging children to enter school more prepared and ready to learn than ever before.

Historically, formalized education was often limited to individuals with greater economic resources, while other children may have been taught through at-home instruction, religious instruction, or apprenticeships in a variety of trades. Over time, the emergence of stable communities and governments fostered the development of public education, in which a majority of children in the community or state were initiated into schooling experiences at younger ages.

Young children generally enter formal education in a school setting at between 5 and 7 years of age. A variety of educational environments may provide formal schooling, including public schools, private or religious schools, and home-based or cooperative schools. Historically, the "kindergarten" concept was adopted from its use in Germany as a transitional schooling experience in the year leading into primary school, and variations on this educational practice are used worldwide. Children may enter learning and care environments, including child care, nursery school, and preschool, at ages in years ranging from 1 to 6 depending on community programs, state practices, and parental preferences for their children.

In early childhood education and care, the focus of attention is on the developing child between birth and 6 years. In addition, attention is given to collaboration of parents, other caregivers, and community systems in supporting and guiding the child's well-being.

Benefits of Successful Entry Into School

Contemporary research on child development has shown that a young child's brain is primed for learning and that interactions with the surrounding environment are central to all aspects of a child's healthy development. Further, a child's school achievement has been linked strongly to other areas of well-being such as life satisfaction, quality of relationships with peers and adults, and engagement in risk behaviors.

Approaches to school readiness in young children have expanded to emphasize a holistic emphasis on the whole child and all aspects of a child's healthy development, rather than a narrow focus on a specific set of knowledge or skills needed to function in a school environment. At the same time, young children are encouraged to participate in learning experiences that will enable a successful transition into school. Elements of a child's preparation and knowledge might include understanding of the alphabet and basic numbers, self-care skills, ability to interact with peers and follow adult instructions, and desire to participate in learning activities.

Children who do not make a successful school transition may struggle over time with academic performance and achievement, quality relationships with peers, display of prosocial behaviors, educational attainment, and job success. Programs that provide support to children in the early years indicate success in preparing children for school, building collaboration between early education and health care, and assisting children and families toward healthy development. The greatest benefits of early childhood programs that target children and families prior to kindergarten or formal schooling tend to accrue for those children who are most disadvantaged. Costs associated with children who are not prepared for school and ready to learn include delayed treatment for health or developmental concerns, educational costs for special services or behavioral health, and future concerns about delinquency or limited productivity. Young children are most likely to exhibit healthy development and enter school ready to learn as families, schools, and communities work together to provide an atmosphere intended to support the well-being of children across all aspects of growth and development.

Sean E. Brotherson

See also Developmental Transitions in Families; Family Experiencing Transitions; Family Interventions Across the Life Span; Learning Disabilities in the Family; Parenting; Poverty, Children in, and Health Care; Systems Supporting Family Health

Further Readings

Booth, A., & Crouter, A. C. (2008). *Disparities in school readiness: How families contribute to transitions into school.* New York: Erlbaum.

Dockett, S., & Perry, B. (1999). Starting school: What do the children say? *Early Childhood Development and Care, 159,* 107–119.

Pianta, R. C., Cox, M. J., & Snow, K. L. (Eds.). (2007). *School readiness and the transition to kindergarten in the era of accountability.* Baltimore: Paul H. Brookes.

Power, T. J., DuPaul, G. J., Shapiro, E. S., & Kazak, A. E. (2003). *Promoting children's health: Integrating school, family, and community.* New York: Guilford Press.

CHILD EMOTIONAL ABUSE AND THE FAMILY

Emotional abuse of children is defined as a form of child maltreatment that causes psychological harm. In this type of abuse, children receive the repeated message, either verbal or nonverbal, from a family member in a position of power, that they are worthless, unloved, unwanted, or bad. Emotional abuse is willfully causing a child to suffer through verbally negative comments and rejecting behavior. Emotional abuse frequently occurs within the context of other types of abuse, including neglect, physical abuse, and sexual abuse. Emotional abuse has existed throughout history, as long as humans have come together in family units.

More specifically, emotional abuse is defined as nonphysical mistreatment and can involve screaming, yelling, name calling, and being subjected to extreme hostility of negativity. Some define child emotional abuse as exposure to parental or relationship violence and discord. This broadens the definition to include both direct and indirect sources. In child emotional abuse, the focus of care is on both the individual child experiencing the emotional abuse and the family where this abuse is occurring. Family is defined in this entry as individuals with both biological and nonbiological relationships who live in the same dwelling and form a familial unit.

Emotional abuse is seldom the focus of child welfare system interventions. It is difficult to delineate from suboptimal parenting and, although perceived as less physically dangerous than physical or sexual abuse, is still very adverse to a child's emotional and mental health. The Brassard and

Donovan scale has categorized emotional abuse into four types: spurning, terrorizing, isolating, and exploiting/corrupting. Many children have experienced more than one type of emotional abuse; many also experience this abuse repeatedly over long periods of time. Emotional abuse is seldom the only form of abuse experienced by a child and may be accompanied by other forms of maltreatment, including neglect, physical abuse, or sexual abuse. Emotional abuse is dangerous to the mental health and well-being of children and requires intervention to be identified and then stopped.

The desired individual and family outcome when emotional abuse of a child occurs involves stopping the cycle of abuse and ending the emotional abuse. This requires a complex intervention model in which the individuals perpetrating the abuse define it as such and begin to alter their behavior and communication patterns. Treatment interventions could involve removal of the offending individual, family treatment, individual treatment, and parent management training.

Emotional abuse is best prevented by provision of parent support and identification of parenting risk factors that might predispose parents to emotionally abusing their children. Adult risk factors for this behavior include a personal history of abuse during their own childhood, substance abuse, untreated mental health disorders, and psychosocial stresses involving financial resources, housing, and lack of emotional support. A "difficult" temperament of the child might predispose the child to being emotionally abused. A lack of goodness of fit between parent and child might also predispose the child to emotional abuse. Research suggests that children with high levels of emotional reactivity involving anger, sadness, and fear, along with behavior dysregulation, might be more at risk for developing psychopathology when exposed to harsh parenting or emotional abuse. Research around vulnerability, resilience, and long-term effects of emotional abuse is ongoing. To date, it strongly suggests formal intervention is necessary in order to change the cycle of abuse.

Emotional abuse is a damaging experience for a child and has long-term implications for functioning and development of psychiatric psychopathology. Decreasing or eliminating child emotional abuse has a positive cascade effect on the child's functioning, mental health, and self-esteem; this should be the goal of interventions aimed at eliminating this damaging behavior of parental figures.

Geraldine S. Pearson

See also Affect Management and the Family; Child Neglect and the Family; Child Physical Abuse and the Family; Child Sexual Abuse and the Family; Elder Emotional Abuse and the Family; Elder Neglect and the Family; Elder Physical Abuse and the Family; Elder Sexual Abuse and the Family; Family Therapy; Marriage and Family Therapy for Families; Spouse/Domestic Partner Physical Abuse

Further Readings

Brassard, M. R., & Donovan, K. L. (2006). Defining psychological maltreatment. In M. M. Feerick, J. F. Knutson, P. K. Trickett, & S. M. Flanzer (Eds.), *Child abuse and neglect: Definitions, classifications, and a framework for research* (pp. 151–197). Baltimore: Paul H. Brookes.

Cummings, E. M., El-Sheikh, M., Kouros, C. D., & Buckhalt, J. A. (2009). Children and violence: The role of children's regulation in the marital aggression-child adjustment link. *Clinical Child and Family Psychological Review, 12,* 3–15.

Finkelhor, D., Ormrod, R. K., & Turner, H. (2007). Re-victimization patterns in a national longitudinal sample of children and youth. *Child Abuse & Neglect, 31,* 479–502.

Trickett, P. K., Mennen, F. E., Kim, K., & Sang, J. (2009). Emotional abuse in a sample of multiply maltreated, urban young adolescents: Issues of definition and identification. *Child Abuse & Neglect, 33,* 27–35.

CHILD NEGLECT AND THE FAMILY

Child neglect, the most widespread form of childhood maltreatment, pertains to caregivers' failure to either satisfy the child's needs or prevent harm to the child. It is classified as either mild, moderate, or severe. Neglect may be *physical* (failure to provide food, clothing, or shelter, despite financially capability; lack of supervision), *emotional* (failure to provide psychological care, chronic inattention to the child, exposure to domestic violence or drugs/alcohol), *medical* (failure to provide necessary medical care), *educational* (failure to educate, permitting chronic nonattendance, ignoring special educational needs), and *exposing newborns to drugs* (substance abuse during pregnancy). Because child neglect involves acts of omission (rather than commission), its signs tend to be less visible, although its detriments are vast.

Neglect occurs in a familial context of dysfunctional parenting. However, it results from interactions between individual, familial, and environmental factors. Examining neglect from this socioecological perspective enables the development of unique comprehensive prevention/intervention programs, based on the family's weaknesses and strengths.

Herein, issues concerning neglect are discussed, including history, risk factors, effects on the child, family assessment, and intervention.

History

In 1962, C. Henry Kempe's publication "The Battered-Child Syndrome" brought childhood maltreatment into public attention. Since then, however, child neglect has been the least acknowledged form of maltreatment (with the exception of physical neglect, which is easier to identify) by both professionals and the general public. This "neglect of neglect" began to wane at the late 1980s, owing to findings as to child neglect's devastating consequences. Nevertheless, the many definitions of neglect have derailed systematic research. Importantly, child neglect accounts for almost 70% of all reported maltreatment cases, affecting 30 out of every 1,000 children in the United States, with physical neglect being the commonly reported type.

Risk Factors

Environmental risk factors associated with neglect are poverty, social isolation, and the absence of social support, as well as neighborhood characteristics, such as violence and cultural health disparities. Familial factors include constant family chaos, chronic daily stress, major stressful life events (i.e., unemployment/financial diffiulties, housing/marital problems, illness or death), communication deficits (especially lack of positive interactions), domestic violence, and single parenthood.

Parental characteristics include history of childhood maltreatment, unstable personality and/or mental illness, lack of required cognitive resources or educational abilities, poor parenting skills (inconsistent discipline), and young age. Unawareness or denying neglect, along with substance abuse, is associated with neglect recurrence.

Risk factors concerning the child are age (being under 3 years); being born prematurely, with low birth weight, or with birth anomalies/disabilities (physical/developmental); and having an irritable/difficult temperament.

The Effects of Neglect

Child neglect puts children in danger for severe injuries, lack of hygiene, malnutrition, and exposure to toxins, all causing numerous diseases, along with other health complications resulting from medical neglect. Additionally, neglect is known to be the largest cause of fatalities due to maltreatment. Some cases of failure to thrive—a condition that occurs mostly among toddlers and is likely to have long-term consequences—may be the result of child neglect.

Impairments in brain development, causing dysfunctional physical, mental, and emotional growth, have also been associated with neglect. Thus, neglect may lead to a significantly smaller brain (an indication of fewer neuronal pathways available for learning) as well as to chronic "hyperarousal" (constant anticipating to threats), contributing to intellectual disadvantage. Related cognitive developmental deficits include developmental delays in expressive and receptive language and poor academic performance. Additionally, neglect can lead to insecure/anxious or disorganized attachment to primary caregivers, in turn causing impaired social cognition.

Neglect is also associated with variety of mental disorders, such as depression, anxiety, attention deficit/hyperactivity disorder, conduct disorders, and self-abusive or other pathological behaviors (tics, eating/sleeping abnormalities, aggressiveness, low self-esteem, stealing). Adults with histories of neglect are at risk for delinquency, experience stress, abuse alcohol/drugs, and are more likely to be diagnosed with personality disorders.

Assessment and Intervention

Child Protective Services (CPS) is the state authority responsible for evaluating potential neglect cases and intervening when required. Nevertheless, the entire community (especially health/educational services) has the obligation to report suspected neglect to CPS or law enforcement. After receiving a report, CPS evaluates the need for an investigation and performs an initial assessment of the child's safety and the risk for future neglect. Next, a comprehensive assessment is conducted as to the family strengths, needs, and risk factors, laying the ground for intervention planning. Specific desirable outcomes are determined, along with the changes, strategies, and services (in home or out of home) necessary to accomplish them.

The intervention focuses on empowering the family strengths, respecting cultural diversity, and creating alliance. Multiple strategies can be employed, including necessary services provision (pediatric or mental care and concrete resources), family-centered intervention techniques, and individual cognitive-behavioral therapy for parents. After a predetermined time frame, an evaluation of outcome is made, resulting in a decision regarding the need for further intervention.

Another empirically supported intervention is the ecological-behavioral model SafeCare, which was found to improve home safety and child health care by using behavioral methods addressing deficits in the family ecology.

Project STEEP, developed at the University of Minnesota, was found to promote sensitivity to, and understanding of, children's needs and improving the life-management skills of newborns' mothers. The intervention includes parent education, home visitations, and group support taking place prior to the child's birth, targeted to inform mothers about child development, so as to develop adequate bonding with their child. An additional intervention model, using home visitations (during and after pregnancy) is David Olds's Nurse Family Partnership model, found to improve parental attitudes and behaviors.

An empirically supported intervention was developed by Dante Cicchetti, a world leader in the study of child maltreatment, and his colleagues. This program focuses on promoting secure attachment through infant/toddler–parent psychotherapy and has been found to be more successful than standard community-based intervention in promoting secure attachment relationships among 12-month-old maltreated infants, as well as among children of depressed mothers.

Conclusion

Despite growing awareness of child neglect, a large proportion of the cases remain unreported and consequently untreated. Young children have difficulties conveying complex emotions and thoughts, including those related to their neglect experience; therefore, it is crucial that professionals working with children be sensitive to markers of neglect, so as to mobilize successful familial intervention.

Golan Shahar and Dana Lassri

See also Child Emotional Abuse and the Family; Child Physical Abuse and the Family; Child Sexual Abuse and the Family; Verbal Abuse in Families

Further Readings

Chaffin, M., & Friedrich, B. (2004). Evidence-based treatments in child abuse and neglect. *Mark Children and Youth Services Review, 26,* 1097–1113.

Cicchetti, D., & Toth, S. L. (2005). Child maltreatment. *Annual Review Clinical Psychology, 1,* 409–438.

DePanfilis, D. (2006). *Child neglect: A guide for prevention, assessment, and intervention.* U.S. Department of Health and Human Services Child Abuse and Neglect User Manual Series. Retrieved October 31, 2009, from http://www.childwelfare.gov/pubs/usermanuals/neglect/neglect.pdf

Hildyard, K. L., & Wolfe, D. A. (2002). Child neglect: Developmental issues and outcomes. *Child Abuse & Neglect, 26,* 679–695.

Websites

Nurse-Family Partnership: http://www.nursefamilypartnership.org

Steps Towards Effective, Enjoyable Parenting: http://www.cehd.umn.edu/ceed/profdev/inpersontrainings/steepsib.htm

CHILD PHYSICAL ABUSE AND THE FAMILY

Child physical abuse is defined as an inflicted act by a parent or caregiver that injures a child or places that child at risk of injury. Child abuse often reflects poor family health and functioning. Children who are physically abused are at risk for developing long-term mental health problems, such as depression and substance abuse and are at increased risk for poor physical health. They are also at increased risk of maltreating their own children, perpetuating a "cycle of violence."

Efforts to prevent maltreatment may benefit children through improved cognitive, emotional, and social development. They also have the potential to improve family functioning through improved parental health and parent–child communication, decreased use of public assistance, and decreased criminal justice involvement.

Following a brief historical context and an introduction to types of physical abuse, this entry reviews potential risk factors for abuse, focusing on family-level risk. It includes a review of interventions for families in which abuse has occurred. The entry ends by discussing interventions to prevent maltreatment.

Historical Context

Child abuse is not a new problem; it has existed since the beginning of recorded history. Until the late 19th century, child abuse was sometimes accepted, usually denied, and rarely addressed. The 1874 case of Mary Ellen led to the first modern recognition of the state's role in protecting children. As there were no laws protecting children, the New York Society for the Prevention of Cruelty to Animals intervened to remove Mary Ellen from her abusive mother. This led to the founding of the New York Society for the Prevention of Cruelty to Children. These two organizations later merged to become the American Humane Association.

Laws to protect maltreated children were first enacted in the United States in 1964. Within the following years, laws were passed in every state. In 1974, Congress passed the Child Abuse Prevention and Treatment Act, which created a minimum definition for child maltreatment. Mandatory reporting requirements were added in 1978. Today, numerous organizations in the United States and abroad exist to protect maltreated children and to help prevent this problem.

Types of Physical Abuse

Child physical abuse encompasses a variety of types of injuries. Bruises may result from pinching, punching, kicking, or hitting with an object. Bruises in the shape of an object, in pairs (e.g., from grabbing), or in unusual locations (e.g., genitals, back) are suspicious for abuse. In not-yet mobile infants, any bruising should prompt further assessment. Abusive burns commonly involve contact with a hot object (e.g., cigarette) or immersion in hot liquid (e.g., a child's body forcefully placed in bathwater). Characteristics of inflicted immersion burns include a stocking or glove appearance with clear lines of demarcation between burned and healthy skin, and sparing of flexoral creases where skin touches skin. Most fractures in children are not inflicted. However, fractures in nonambulatory infants are more likely to be the result of abuse. In the absence of significant trauma (e.g., motor vehicle crash), fractures of the ribs, spine, sternum, scapulae, and ends of long bones (metaphyses) in young children are suspicious. Abusive head injury may include contact injuries, for example, when a child's head is slammed against an object. It may also include noncontact injuries, such as those that result from violent shaking.

Distinguishing inflicted from noninflicted injury requires a detailed history, a careful developmental assessment, and a thorough physical examination. Laboratory tests and x-rays may be needed to assess injuries further.

Family Risk and Protective Factors for Physical Abuse

Any discussion of the causes, treatment, and prevention of physical abuse would be incomplete without examining the family context. The "ecological" framework of child maltreatment posits that abusive behavior involves complex interactions between the child, parent, community, and society. Therefore, the role of the family cannot be considered in isolation. Child characteristics such as chronic illness or a "difficult" temperament may contribute to maltreatment by increasing parental stress. Depression and substance abuse may increase parental risk for abusing their children. Additionally, there is a strong association between intimate partner violence and child abuse. Family stressors, including poverty, unemployment, negative life events, and social isolation, also increase maltreatment risk. Clearly, environmental factors in the community (e.g., dangerous neighborhood) and the larger society (e.g., social policies) can impair parents' ability to adequately care for their children.

Even when risk factors are present, maltreatment may not occur. Protective characteristics may buffer risk. For example, strong social networks may provide material, informational, and emotional support that reduces the stress of raising children. A parent's sense of competence in parenting may also offset the challenges posed by risk factors.

Interventions for Families of Maltreated Children

Reporting of suspected child physical abuse to Child Protective Services (CPS) is mandated by law throughout the United States. A report typically leads to an investigation to determine whether abuse has occurred. This is the most common gateway for maltreating families to receive services to prevent further maltreatment.

Services provided vary according to the needs of individual families, the appropriate identification of needs, and the community resources available. Services may include individual and/or family counseling, case management, family support services, respite care, parenting education, housing assistance, substance abuse treatment, day care, and home visits. Promising programs include early childhood education (e.g., Head Start) and "differential response," in which CPS agencies replace an adversarial investigation with an assessment of family needs and referral to appropriate resources.

Family Interventions to Prevent Maltreatment

Prevention programs have been developed for community-based and health care settings. The most promising community-based interventions include home visitation and parent training programs. Both vary widely in the nature of services offered.

Home visitation may be provided by nurses or paraprofessionals. Studies have found that some of these programs are effective, particularly when nurses are used. In addition to helping prevent maltreatment, there may be other positive outcomes concerning child health, safety and cognitive development, and parenting.

Parent training programs aim to improve parents' comfort and competence with parenting. Programs often focus on emotional communication and positive parent–child interaction skills, as well as constructive approaches to reduce negative behavior. Examples include the Triple P program, Sure Start, and Family Connections. Studies of parenting programs have demonstrated improved maternal psychosocial health and child-rearing attitudes.

Several health care–based prevention programs appear promising. One is a newborn nursery-based shaken baby syndrome prevention program. This includes education about the dangers of shaking and how to cope with a crying infant. Another promising program is *SEEK*—a pediatric primary care-based intervention that trains clinicians to screen for risk factors (e.g., maternal depression and substance abuse), conduct brief assessments, and make referrals to community resources.

Wendy G. Lane and Howard Dubowitz

See also Child Emotional Abuse and the Family; Child Neglect and the Family; Child Sexual Abuse and the Family; Shaken Baby Syndrome in Childbearing Families; Spouse/Domestic Partner Physical Abuse; Systems Supporting Family Health; Youth Violence Prevention in the Family

Further Readings

Barlow, J., Coren, E., & Stewart-Brown, S. S. B. (2003). Parent-training programmes for improving maternal psychosocial health. *Cochrane Database of Systematic Reviews*, Issue 4, Art. No. CD002020.

Diaz, M. S., Smith, K., de Guehery, K., Mazur, P., Li, V., & Shaffer, M. (2005). Preventing abusive head trauma among infants and young children: A hospital-based parent education program. *Pediatrics, 115*, 470–477.

Dubowitz, H., Feigelman, S., Lane, W., & Kim J. (2009). Pediatric primary care to help prevent child maltreatment: The Safe Environment for Every Kid (SEEK) model. *Pediatrics, 123*, 858–864.

Paxson, C., & Haskins, R. (Eds.). (2009). Preventing child maltreatment [Special issue]. *Future of Children, 19*(2).

Prinz, R. J., Sanders, M. R., Shapiro, C. J., Whitaker, D. J., & Lutzker, J. R. (2009). Population-based prevention of child maltreatment: The U.S. Triple P system population trial. *Prevention Science, 10*(1), 1–12.

CHILD SEXUAL ABUSE AND THE FAMILY

Broadly defined, child sexual abuse refers to any exploitation of a child or adolescent for another person's sexual gratification. Sexual abuse has varying effects on families. Family is defined as the individuals with whom the child resides and may include biological parents, adoptive parents, foster parents, or any sort of kinship placement such as grandparents, aunts, or uncles. A variety of behaviors and actions are considered sexual abuse, including fondling, oral-genital stimulation, digital/object penetration, and vaginal and anal intercourse, or noncontact activities such as exposing oneself to a child, masturbating in front of a child, exhibitionism, voyeurism, and involving children in pornography. Sexual abuse is perpetrated by family members, acquaintances of the child, and, much less frequently, strangers. This entry discusses the prevalence, history, and current literature of child sexual abuse, as well as treatment and prognosis for those who have been sexually abused.

Prevalence

The exact prevalence of childhood sexual abuse is unknown; current estimates report 1 in 4 girls and 1 in 7 boys will experience unwanted sexual involvement before 18 years of age. Several risk factors may increase the likelihood of abuse: (1) gender, with girls being at higher risk, (2) children with disabilities, (3) children who do not live with their natural parents, and (4) children in dysfunctional families who experience problems such as domestic violence, mental illness of parents, substance abuse, or multiple partners in the home. In 2006, approximately 9% of nearly 1,000,000 substantiated maltreated cases (children's cases that were investigated and determined that sexual abuse had occurred) were classified as sexual abuse in the United States, according to the U.S. Department of Health and Human Services, Administration on Children, Youth and Families.

History

Prior to the 1970s, child sexual abuse was seen as a rare occurrence causing little harm to the child, and when it did occur, it was believed to be the child's or mother's fault. The mid-1970s saw a shift in the understanding of how sexual abuse impacts children, and the 1980s saw an increase of knowledge regarding the extent to which sexual abuse occurs and its negative impact on children. Today sexual abuse is seen as a serious childhood event that can have a long-lasting impact on children and their families.

Current Literature

The impact of sexual abuse on children is related to many factors: (a) child's age, (b) child's preabuse adjustment, (c) child's coping strategies and attributions of the abuse, (d) family response and coping strategies, (e) reporting factors, (f) abuse characteristics, including frequency, duration, intensity, level of force, and (g) relationship of the perpetrator to the child. Sexual abuse that involves penetration and force, and occurs longer in duration or frequency, increases the potential for children developing significant difficulties. Such difficulties may include trauma symptoms, such as reexperiencing traumatic events, avoidance of reminders/places, and hyperarousal; anxiety symptoms, including separation anxiety and fear of places or people; depressive symptoms, such as sadness, irritability, and withdrawal; behavioral problems, including enuresis, encopresis, and tantrums; and conduct problems, such as inappropriate sexual behaviors, truancy, running away, and substance use. A comprehensive assessment provides information on the child's presenting problems, factors impacting recovery, and proper intervention(s).

Family members (defined as those with whom the child lives or who often care for the child) react to sexual abuse in different ways. They may be divided as to who to believe, especially if the alleged perpetrator was a trusted member of the family, such as the case with stepfathers or live-in boyfriends. Families may feel ashamed and not want anyone else to know. However, families who believe the allegations, respond quickly to children's disclosure of abuse, and provide positive support increase children's likelihood of successfully coping with their traumatic experience.

Evidence-Based Treatment

Evidence-based treatment for children and adolescents (trauma-focused cognitive-behavioral therapy) targets the reduction of children's cognitive and behavioral reactions, helps them cope more effectively, and increases their positive adjustment in the future. Techniques used in treatment include (a) psychoeducation, (b) relaxation and coping skills, (c) exposure to trauma, and (d) addressing misconceptions of the abuse, such as self-blame.

Psychoeducation involves discussing the nature of abuse, personal safety, and appropriate relationships. Children develop skills to properly identify their emotions, learn relaxation techniques to use when they become anxious or upset, and employ cognitive coping approaches to decrease anxious or fearful reactions to reminders of their abuse. Children process their thoughts and emotional reactions by talking, writing, or drawing about their abuse experiences. Discussing their thoughts and emotions helps children to reduce automatic negative responses to reminders of their trauma (e.g., avoidance) and replace their misconceptions of the abuse (e.g., it was their fault) or of themselves (e.g., they are a bad person).

In cases of child sexual abuse by a family member, the child and nonoffending family members may be seen in individual or family therapy. The offending family member may be seen separately and later be reunified with the family. Treatment involving nonoffending parents and caregivers further promotes children's positive adjustment. It is important that the therapist assess at the onset of services the stance of family members in regard to the abuse, as family members who do not believe the child can be problematic for treatment success. The caregivers' portion of treatment includes discussing what the child is learning in treatment, which allows them to encourage children's use of acquired skills outside of session. Parent sessions also focus on reducing parents' distress due to the abuse and provide them with techniques to address any behavioral concerns with the child. Involving family members in treatment provides children with a sense of support, security, and acceptance.

Prognosis

Children who have been sexually abused are at a greater risk of developing long-term difficulties compared to nonabused peers. This risk is minimized with family support and appropriate therapeutic intervention. Children who do not receive needed psychological services are at risk of developing long-term difficulties, including depression, substance abuse, and interpersonal difficulties.

Jenelle R. Shanley and Barbara L. Bonner

See also Child Emotional Abuse and the Family; Child Neglect and the Family; Child Physical Abuse and the Family; Sibling Physical Abuse; Spouse/Domestic Partner Physical Abuse; Verbal Abuse in Families

Further Readings

Cohen, J. A., Mannarino, A. P., & Deblinger, E. (2006). *Treating trauma and traumatic grief in children and adolescents.* New York: Guilford Press.

Myers, J. E. B., Berliner, L., Briere, J., Hendrix, C. T., Jenny, C., & Reid, T. A. (Eds.). (2002). *The APSAC handbook on child maltreatment* (2nd ed.). Thousand Oaks, CA: Sage.

U.S. Department of Health and Human Services, Administration on Children, Youth and Families (2008). *11 years of reporting: Child maltreatment 2006.* Washington, DC: U.S. Government Printing Office.

CHILDBIRTH BY CHILDBEARING COUPLES: REPORTED MEANINGS

Giving birth is a pivotal life event representing the shift from being a couple to being a family. Paternal and maternal perspectives of this significant experience may differ, but both serve to enrich the experience of beginning a family.

Maternal Birth Experience

There are decades of studies documenting the maternal birth experience, including those of culturally diverse women. Two national surveys of childbearing women conducted in the United States provide important data about maternal perspectives. Listening to the voices of childbearing women as they share their birth experiences is imperative. Women often describe the experience of giving birth in paradoxical terms, indicating that birth is a bittersweet experience. This description is confirmed in the national surveys, which reported that women articulated conflicting emotions, feeling both "confident and overwhelmed," "powerful and weak." Based on two decades of research with

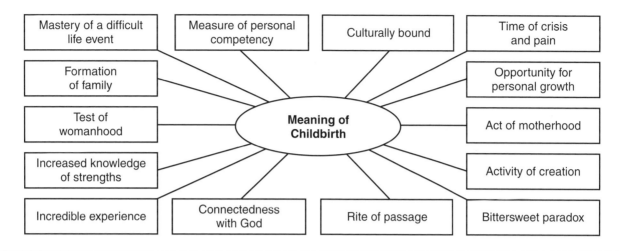

Mastery of a difficult life event	Measure of personal competency	Culturally bound	Time of crisis and pain
Formation of family			Opportunity for personal growth
Test of womanhood	Meaning of Childbirth		Act of motherhood
Increased knowledge of strengths			Activity of creation
Incredible experience	Connectedness with God	Rite of passage	Bittersweet paradox

Figure 1   Maternal Meaning of Childbirth Model

childbearing women, a model has been generated that identifies the multidimensional facets of the maternal meaning of giving birth (Figure 1).

Dimensions include mastery of a difficult life event, an incredible experience, a time of crisis and pain, a bittersweet paradox, an opportunity for personal growth with an increased knowledge of strengths, a test of womanhood, an activity of creation, an act of motherhood, a rite of passage, a culturally bound experience, an experience fostering connectedness with God, and symbolic of the formation of a family.

In interviews with childbearing women by the author, one woman spoke of "the excitement to have the baby here with my husband right by my side—we were a great team" (unpublished data). Another woman explained, "When the baby was born, I started to cry because I felt many things I can't describe. When you have a baby, you feel very beautiful, gentle. You feel scared, but it's beautiful. It's difficult to express. When you are in labor you feel a lot of pain, but it's all taken away when the baby is born. You feel happy and well—so much so that the pain is alleviated" (unpublished data).

Paternal Birth Experience

Laboring for relevance was the major theme identified in classic work on the paternal experience of giving birth. Processes including grappling with the reality of the pregnancy and the child, struggling for recognition as a parent, and making the transition to involved fatherhood.

Expectant fathers may assume a variety of roles, including that of coach and advocate (directing the labor and birth) or teammate working under the direction of professionals; the majority of fathers prefer to serve as witnesses to the event. One mother said, "I loved that my husband could be involved in every step. He was with me during labor and helped me walk the hospital halls. He was with me in the birthing room and helped me push" (unpublished data). A study conducted in the United Kingdom with first-time fathers focused on the paternal meaning of the experience. They found birth to be intense and unpredictable and identified the need for paternal support during labor and birth.

A review of the literature by Lucia Genesoni and Maria Anna Tallandini found that some fathers perceive birth to be traumatic, being concerned about potential maternal/newborn harm, seeing their partner experiencing pain, feeling helpless, having a lack of knowledge, and being fearful of technological interventions. One first-time father said, "I felt helpless during labor knowing I couldn't take away the pain and make it better. I don't like seeing my wife in pain. I don't like seeing her cry. I don't like seeing tears in her eyes and trickling down her cheeks. I remember looking at her and wishing I could take that pain upon myself" (Callister, Matsumura, & Vehvilainen-Julkunen, 2003, p. 16). In contrast, the same father described, "The overwhelming feelings that come over you once you see this baby come into the world and knowing that you created this baby. Feelings of love, joy, and happiness come from this experience" (Callister et al., 2003, p. 18).

The majority of studies that have been performed are qualitative and descriptive, with white, socially advantaged first-time fathers. Further research is needed with culturally and socioeconomically diverse fathers. Interventions such as mentoring by experienced fathers, father-facilitators in childbirth education classes, and separate father classes are interventions for further study. In addition, studies documenting the paternal birth experience and the transition to fatherhood are needed. One such example is the conduct of a large national survey, *Listening to Fathers*.

Lynn Clark Callister

See also Access to Health Care: Child Health; Caregiving: Infants; Parenting

Further Readings

Callister, L. C. (2003). Making meaning: Women's birth narratives. *Journal of Obstetric, Gynecologic, and Neonatal Nursing, 33*(4), 508–518.

Callister, L. C., & Khalaf, I. (2009). Culturally diverse women giving birth: Their stories. In H. Selin (Ed.), *Childbirth across cultures* (pp. 33–39). New York: Springer.

Callister, L. C., Matsumura, G., & Vehvilainen-Julkunen, K. (2003, January). He's having a baby: The paternal childbirth experience. *Marriage and Families*, pp. 14–20.

Chapman, L. L. (1992). Expectant fathers' roles during labor and birth. *Journal of Obstetric, Gynecologic, and Neonatal Nursing, 21*(2), 114–120.

Clifton, A. K. (2008). And father came too . . . *Midwifery, 18*(1), 57–66.

DeClercq, E. R., Sakala, C., Corry, M. P., & Applebaum, S. (2006). *Listening to mothers, II: Report of the second national U.S. Survey of Women's Childbearing Experiences*. New York: Childbirth Connection.

Genesoni, L., & Tallandini, M. A. (2009). Men's psychological transition to fatherhood: An analysis of the literature, 1989–2008. *Birth, 36*(4), 305–317.

Hanson, S., Hunter, L. P., Bormann, J. R., & Sobo, E. J. (2009). Paternal fears of childbirth: A literature review. *Journal of Perinatal Education, 18*(4), 12–20.

Jordan, P. L. (1990). Laboring for relevance: The male experience of expectant and new fathers. *Nursing Research, 39*, 11–16.

Nuzum, R., & Nuzum, R. (2009). Rowen's birth story: His and her versions. *Journal of Perinatal Education, 18*(3), 4–9.

Websites

Childbirth Connection: http://www.childbirthconnection.org

CHILDLESSNESS

Childlessness, which refers to the reproductive state of never having had children, is of concern to individuals and couples as they make decisions about whether to have children. Historically, people gave birth to or adopted children with the expectation that those offspring would contribute to the work and economic livelihood of the family. In more recent times, as birth control and pregnancy termination became more available, whether and when to have children has become a significant family health choice for most people of reproductive age.

Childlessness can be grouped into several categories. The first category is those individuals who consider themselves to be voluntarily childless: women who never have had children and who desire to remain in that category.

The second category of childlessness belongs to those individuals who are involuntarily childless. Research on individuals in this category refers to medically infertile heterosexual married couples from whom data have been collected in numerous studies. A population that has been excluded from data collection are persons with what is identified as "social factor infertility," namely, those same-sex couples who will need a third party to enable them to become parents.

A final category, identified as temporary childlessness, is those individuals of reproductive age but temporarily not planning to conceive. Of this category, some will choose to become parents, some will encounter fertility problems, and some will make the conscious decision not to have children.

Voluntary Childlessness

The most comprehensive data on voluntary childlessness come from the National Survey on Family Growth (NSFG), which has collected data from married men and women since 1973. These data indicate that voluntary childlessness has fluctuated over a 20-year period in the United States, with women ending their reproductive years recently with the highest rates of childlessness in the past 30 years. Increases in voluntary childlessness show that percentages approximately doubled from 1995 to 2002 for women in the top age groups surveyed (ages 30–34; 35–39; and 40–44). Overall, 5.7% of ever-married women of reproductive age in 2002 were voluntarily childless—a figure that has nearly tripled since 1976. Data on demographic characteristics of these women show that they are generally Caucasian, born in the United States, high on educational attainment, employed, have a relatively high total family income, and reside in metropolitan areas.

For those women who are voluntarily or involuntarily childless, their status as nonmothers is a way of life that many of them are called upon to explain or defend. Many voluntarily childless women see their choice as one that should require no explanation, as an increasing number of their age-mates are also making the conscious decision to remain childfree. However, for infertile individuals, the expectation of an explanation for why they are childless can be medically complex and emotionally painful.

Involuntary Childlessness

Infertility is a term used to describe the condition wherein the woman has not been able to get pregnant after 1 year of unprotected intercourse. Women who are able to become pregnant and who experience a loss of the pregnancy are also said to be infertile. About 12% of women (7.3 million) in the United States aged 15–44 had difficulty getting pregnant or carrying a pregnancy to term in 2002, according to the National Center for Health Statistics of the Centers for Disease Control and Prevention. However, a woman's incapacity to become pregnant does not necessarily mean that she is the person with the infertility problem. In only about one third of cases is infertility due to the woman. In another one third of cases, infertility is due to the man. The remaining cases are a mixture of male and female factors or unknown factors.

Infertility can result from problems that interfere with any of the complex chain of events necessary for a pregnancy to occur: First, a woman must release an egg from one of her ovaries. Next, the egg must go through a fallopian tube toward the uterus. Next, a man's sperm must join with the egg along the way. And, finally, the fertilized egg must attach to the inside of the uterus.

The causes of infertility in men most often relate to problems making sperm or problems with the sperm's ability to reach the egg and fertilize it. The number and quality of sperm can be affected negatively by use of alcohol, drugs, environmental toxins, smoking tobacco, sexually transmitted diseases, certain medicines, radiation and chemotherapy treatment for cancer, and age.

In women, problems in ovulation account for most cases of infertility. Without ovulation, there are no eggs to be fertilized. Other causes of infertility problems include blocked fallopian tubes and physical problems with the uterus, including uterine fibroids. Factors that can negatively affect a woman's fertility include poor diet, athletic training, being overweight or underweight, tobacco smoking, use of alcohol or drugs, sexually transmitted diseases, radiation and chemotherapy treatment for cancer, and health problems that cause hormone changes. Age—more a factor for women than for men—can affect women's ability to have children.

More and more women are waiting until their 30s and 40s to have children. In the United States, about 20% of women now have their first child after age 35. About one third of couples in which the woman is over 35 have fertility problems. Aging decreases a woman's chance of having a baby in the following ways: The ability of the woman's ovaries to release eggs ready for fertilization declines with age; the health of a woman's eggs declines with age; as a woman ages, she is more likely to have health problems that can interfere with fertility; and as a woman ages, her risk of having a miscarriage increases.

Finding the cause of a couple's infertility problem can be a lengthy and emotionally draining process. For males, the physician usually begins by testing his semen to look at the number, shape, and movement of the sperm. Testing of male hormone levels also may be a part of the diagnostic workup. For the woman, doctors will check to see whether she is ovulating by doing blood tests and an ultrasound of the ovaries. Further diagnostic tests are done to check for physical problems of the uterus and fallopian tubes, including scarring, adhesions, and disease.

Infertility can be treated with medication, surgery, artificial insemination, or assisted reproductive technology (ART). In many cases, these treatments are combined. About two thirds of couples who are treated by specialists for their infertility are able to have a baby. In addition to using medications to stimulate ovulation in female patients, infertility clinics also use assisted reproductive technology to help infertile couples conceive. ART involves removing eggs from a woman's body, mixing them with sperm in the laboratory and putting the embryos back into the woman's body.

ART procedures sometimes involve the use of donor eggs from another woman, donor sperm, or previously frozen embryos. Donor eggs can be used for women who cannot produce healthy eggs. Also, donor eggs or donor sperm are sometimes used when the woman or man has a genetic disease that can be passed on to the baby.

Additional choices for infertile couples include the use of gestational surrogates to carry the baby to term when the couple wants one or both parents to be genetically related to the baby. For infertile couples for whom genetic ties are not important, adoption, either domestic or international, is an option.

Not all involuntarily childless individuals are married and asked to complete large-scale surveys and questionnaires on their interest in parenthood. An increasing number of single women are seeking to become parents, either as a single parent or as a cohabiting partner. Lesbian and gay couples, who need reproductive support in order to become parents, can choose from options including artificial insemination, ART, a gestational surrogate, or adoption. In the case of same-sex couples, the parent not giving birth to the child will need to take legal measures to formally adopt the baby after its birth.

Temporary Childlessness

The temporarily childless category includes a diverse group of individuals who vary with age, with success of birth control, with increasing understanding of the joys and responsibilities of parenthood, with pressures from peers and parents, with

economic fluctuations, and with increasing tolerance in society of the conscious choice some couples make to remain childfree. This category is likely to be a combination of the involuntarily childless (single persons hoping ultimately to become parents, individuals with fertility problems, or individuals with social factor infertility seeking assisted routes to parenthood), and those who intend ultimately to become parents.

Challenges of Childlessness

A major challenge in our society is to provide individuals with knowledge of good health care and access to reproductive health and education services that will enable them to make timely choices about whether to have children. Individuals of reproductive age need to be aware of those behaviors that can negatively impact their fertility, including the consequences of a woman waiting to become pregnant past the mid-30s, when her likelihood of infertility increases.

Access to infertility services tends to be less available for rural couples, same-sex couples, low-income couples, and couples having no health insurance or whose insurance lacks coverage for infertility diagnosis and treatment. For those couples hoping to pursue adoption (either domestic or international), financial considerations present constraints, as do laws in some states that prevent same-sex couples from adopting children.

Social and emotional challenges associated with the three categories of childlessness will differ depending upon the extent to which choice is involved. The decision to be childless, influenced by reliable birth control and by the increasing options women see for themselves besides motherhood, has enabled a growing number of women and their partners to sidestep parenthood as they craft fulfilling lives.

Contrast the emotional satisfaction of this group with those individuals who are childless involuntarily. Often feeling stigmatized, surrounded by a fertile society where most people either use birth control or take parenthood for granted, involuntarily childless people struggle, both emotionally and financially, to succeed in achieving the one thing they want to make their lives complete: a child. In addition to putting their lives on hold while medical treatments, adoption paperwork, and even psychotherapy become interwoven in their quest for parenthood, these individuals yearn for the day when they, too, can celebrate their status as new parents. Some will succeed in this life quest, whereas others will reconcile to filling their lives with relationships and experiences that do not include parenthood.

The last category, the temporarily childless, is more in limbo than the other two. Believing it is simply a matter of time before making the choice about whether or not to have children, these individuals are looking toward their futures with every belief they can make whatever choices about childbearing they opt to pursue. In truth, some will decide in favor of voluntarily childlessness; others will, with regret, find themselves involuntarily childless; and still others will have the luxury of time to remain in their temporarily childless state a few more years before realizing that "childlessness" is best if it is a conscious choice rather than an imposition of age, societal expectations, or reproductive medical conditions.

Constance Hoenk Shapiro

See also Bereavement and Perinatal Loss in Childbearing Families; Family Transitions and Ambiguous Loss; Men's Health; Preconceptual Counseling for Childbearing Couples; Stress Management Theory and Techniques in Families; Women's Health

Further Readings

National Center for Health Statistics. (1973, 1976, 1982, 1988, 1995, 2002). *National Survey of Family Growth,* Cycles I, II, III, IV, ICPSR version [Data files]. Hyattsville, MD: Author.

Websites

American Congress of Obstetricians and Gynecologists: http://www.acog.org

American Society for Reproductive Medicine: http://www.asrm.org

National Center for Health Statistics, National Survey of Family Growth: http://www.cdc.gov/nchs/nsfg.htm

National Women's Health Information Center: http://www.womenshealth.gov

Resolve: The National Infertility Association: http://www.resolve.org

CHILDPROOFING MEDICATIONS AND DANGEROUS AGENTS

Accidental injury, including accidental ingestion, is the number one cause of death among children in the United States. National statistics indicate that more than 2 million children ingest medications or dangerous agents each year in the United States alone. Because accidental ingestions are preventable, deliberate action is necessary to reduce their occurrence.

Childproofing is a process of identifying and subsequently reducing or eliminating environmental threats to young children. Toddlers and preschoolers are at risk because of their innate curiosity and their tendency to learn about their environment by tasting it. Young children's stature also places them at risk because ground-level objects and cabinet doors and drawers are at their eye level, inviting exploration. In a 2005 article, Robin Wilkerson and colleagues noted that although young children may be able to say the word *poison*, they don't have the cognitive maturity to associate the word with danger. These authors cautioned that children with cognitive impairment are, therefore, at additional risk for ingestion of dangerous substances.

This entry focuses on childproofing to prevent accidental ingestion of medications and dangerous agents. Because the process of childproofing requires vigilant adult caregivers, this topic is explored within the context of the family. Following a historical overview, this discussion includes categories of risk and recommendations for childproofing discussions with families at health care encounters.

Historical Overview

The history of poison prevention in the United States was detailed in 2005 by the U.S. Consumer Product Safety Commission (CPSC). That document is the source for this historical overview. The first poison control center was established in Chicago in 1953. By 1957, the number of local centers had grown to require formation of the National Clearinghouse for Poison Control Centers, charged with collating data across centers to produce better poison prevention guidelines. Currently, cases reported to local poison control centers are collected within the Toxic Exposure Surveillance System, a database maintained by the American Association of Poison Control Centers. Reports of poisoning cases treated in hospital emergency departments are collated in the CPSC's National Electronic Injury Surveillance System.

Child-resistant packaging has contributed significantly to decreased ingestions in recent decades. The movement began in the 1960s with the leadership of concerned U.S. Food and Drug Administration (FDA) officials. Research conducted in the United States and Canada at that time documented dramatic decreases in childhood ingestions when medication bottles were equipped with caps that required pushing and turning instead of the traditional screw caps or snap caps. This research led to Public Law 91-601, the Poison Prevention Packaging Act (PPPA), enacted in 1970. The PPPA regulates child-resistant/adult-friendly packaging for medications and a wide variety of other household products.

Risk Categories

Agents at risk for ingestion can be categorized as pharmaceutical and nonpharmaceutical substances. Within these categories, agents commonly ingested by children include medications and dietary supplements, cosmetics and personal care products, cleaning products, pesticides and other chemicals, alcohol, hydrocarbons, plants, and button batteries. *Essentially, children should ingest nothing besides age-appropriate food and beverages.* When one considers the number of dangerous agents that may be within a young child's reach and that ingestion can occur in seconds, childproofing becomes a crucial task for preventing accidental ingestion.

Pharmaceutical Agents

Analgesics such as acetaminophen and nonsteroidal anti-inflammatory drugs formulated for children are frequent sources of accidental ingestion. Because they are commonly administered in the home to young children who have fever or pain, the drugs come in flavor-enhanced preparations to improve tolerance. Even if parents avoid suggesting the drug "tastes like candy," children are encouraged to swallow it and are often praised for doing

so. Unfortunately, small children cannot distinguish between appropriate (parent-administered) and inappropriate (child-administered) ingestion and may consume a large quantity of medication if they manage to reach and open the container. Research has documented that liver damage can occur at acetaminophen doses of 150 mg/kg, and a recent study by Sa'ed Zyoud and colleagues also linked acetaminophen poisoning to kidney damage.

Analgesics are only one example of medications associated with fatal poisonings. Cough and cold medications are frequently cited dangers, as are all prescription medications. Although prescription medications have child-resistant packaging, adults with hand arthritis can invert the push-and-turn cap to form a screw cap, thus negating the cap's safety feature. For this reason, visits to the home of older individuals require additional caution. Older adults may keep medications in colorful and easily opened plastic pill containers and may also have dropped small pills on the floor when filling the containers.

Dietary supplements such as vitamins can also be dangerous for young children, especially when the product contains iron. As noted by the WebMD website, doses of iron greater than 10 mg/kg of body weight can be toxic.

Nonpharmaceutical Agents

Nondrug agents are numerous and widely available to children (Table 1). Something as seemingly benign as mouthwash can be toxic in large quantities because of the ethanol base, and a child may consume a large quantity because of the pleasant taste. Button batteries are another risk that may go unrecognized. The National Capital Poison Center notes that battery ingestion often results from batteries intended for hearing aids and that the peak incidence is in children under 2 years of age. When these tiny batteries adhere to tissue in the esophagus or stomach rather than passing through the gastrointestinal system, chemical burns can result in serious or fatal injuries. Clearly, childproofing involves identifying risks in every aspect of the young child's environment.

Desired Family Health Outcomes

The goal of childproofing is to prevent accidental ingestion of harmful agents. Ideally, families are armed with the motivation, knowledge, and resources to identify and reduce ingestion risks and to respond to ingestion emergencies.

Recommendations for Anticipatory Guidance

The American Academy of Pediatrics recommends initiating injury prevention counseling in the first months of well child care. Research has shown that children are at greater risk for accidental ingestion when they live in poverty. The increased risk might relate not only to environmental factors, such as poor home repair, but also to transient living conditions and reduced access to health care. Thus, health care providers must seize every opportunity to provide written fact sheets and other materials that can assist families in identifying and reducing risks. One such resource is a Mr. Yuk sticker, a bright green cartoon face bearing the national, toll-free number for the National Poison Control Center: 1-800-222-1222. Calls placed to the hotline are automatically routed to the nearest poison center. This and other key resources are listed in Table 2.

Importantly, syrup of ipecac to induce vomiting is no longer the treatment of choice for accidental ingestion. The American Academy of Pediatrics does not recommend home use of ipecac for accidental ingestion. Instead, the National Poison Control Center should be called.

Almost every reference to childproofing includes the recommendation to keep medications and dangerous agents in a locked cabinet. In reality, few people have locked cabinets in their homes, and it would take a great number of locked cabinets to secure all potentially dangerous agents. Parents can, however, survey the hazards readily accessible in the child's environment and move risky agents to the least accessible areas and install child locks. Child locks are widely available and can be very effective in reducing access. Ideally, no dangerous agents should be stored in base cabinets or in cabinets accessible to a climbing child. In combination with

Table 1   Nonpharmaceutical Agents Associated With Accidental Ingestion

Risk Location	Commonly Ingested Agents
Kitchen	Soaps and detergents (e.g., dishwasher detergent)
	Disinfectants (e.g., bleach and disinfectant wipes)
	Cleaning products (e.g., furniture polish, window cleaner, oven cleaner)
	Lamp oil
	Air freshener
	Alcoholic beverages
Bathroom/Bedroom	Cosmetics
	Perfumes and aftershave products
	Hair products (e.g., hairspray, shampoo, conditioner, depilatories)
	Nail polish remover
	Mouthwash
	Drain and toilet bowl cleaners
	Aerosol tub and shower cleaning products
	Button batteries, such as those for hearing aids
Garage	Gasoline, kerosene
	Pesticides
	Fertilizers
	Windshield wiper fluid
	Antifreeze
	Abrasive hand soap
	Paint, paint thinner
House and Garden	Plants (e.g., pepper plant, peace lily, philodendron, holly, poinsettia, pokeweed)

Table 2   Childproofing Resources

Resource	Available at
Mr. Yuk stickers	http://www.upmc.com/Services/poisoncenter/Pages/educational-materials.aspx#stickers
Brochure: *Everyone's Guide to Everyday Poisons*	http://www.upmc.com/Services/poisoncenter/Pages/educational-materials.aspx#everyones
WebMD webpage: *Tips to Prevent Poisoning in the Home*	http://www.webmd.com/parenting/prevent-poisoning-home
Nationwide Poison Control Center	1-800-222-1222
National Battery Ingestion Hotline	1-202-625-3333

parental vigilance and supervision, childproofing is a safety essential. Accidental ingestion is a *preventable* cause of childhood morbidity and mortality.

Roxie L. Foster

See also Acute Health Problems and Interventions for the Childrearing Family; Assessing Family Health; Factors Influencing Access to Health Care for Families; Factors Influencing Family Health Values, Beliefs, and Priorities; First Aid and the Family; Injury Prevention for Infants and Children Family Members

Further Readings

National Institutes of Health Office of Dietary Supplements. (2007). *Dietary supplement fact sheet: Iron.* Retrieved from http://ods.od.nih.gov/factsheets/iron.asp#h8

U.S. Consumer Product Safety Commission. (2005). *Poison prevention packaging: A guide for healthcare professionals.* Retrieved from http://www.cpsc.gov/cpscpub/pubs/384.pdf

Wilkerson, R., Horthington, L., & Fisher, W. (2005). Ingestion of toxic substances by infants and children. What we don't know can hurt. *Critical Care Nurse, 25*(40), 35–44.

Zyoud, S. H., Awang, R., Sulaiman, S. A. S., & Al-Jabi, S. W. (2010, April 28). Assessing the impact of vomiting episodes on outcome after acetaminophen poisoning. *Basic & Clinical Pharmacology & Toxicology.* Advance online publication.

Websites

American Association of Poison Control Centers: http://www.aapcc.org

National Capital Poison Center: http://www.poison.org

CHILDREN'S HEALTH: DENTAL DEVELOPMENT

Knowledge of the different stages of tooth development is critically important to ensure an adequate treatment plan for health care consumers, as well as to understand the occurrence of dental anomalies. In many cases, it is difficult to accurately discuss dental anomalies without pinpointing the stage of tooth development in which they manifest. Teeth are formed by tissues originating from both ectoderm and mesoderm tissues. Tooth development is organized by the following stages: initiation, proliferation, histodifferentiation, morphodifferentiation, apposition, calcification, and eruption (see Figure 1, next page). This entry first describes these stages and then discusses dental anomalies and primary prevention for healthy dentition.

Tooth Developmental Stages

Initiation

Initiation is first noticed in the 6-week-old fetus where the basal layer of its oral epithelium demonstrates areas of increased activity and enlargement that will eventually give rise to the dental lamina. Shortly after the dental lamina differentiates, 20 tooth buds begin to appear on the dental lamina, predicting the location of the future primary teeth. These tooth buds are somewhat round; this stage is known as *bud stage*. In addition to developing 20 primary teeth, each unit develops a dental lamina ultimately responsible for future permanent teeth development.

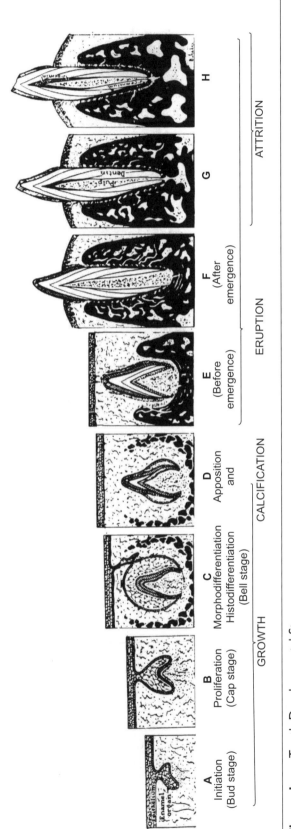

Figure 1   Tooth Developmental Stages

Source: Reproduced by permission from Schour, I., & Massler, M. (1940). Studies in tooth development: The growth pattern of human teeth. *JADA, 27*(11), 1778–1793. Copyright © 1940 American Dental Association. All rights reserved. Reprinted by permission.

Proliferation

Proliferation is a further multiplication of cells and expansion of the tooth bud, resulting in tooth germ formation. As the tooth germ proliferates, it produces a cap-like appearance. This phase is termed *cap stage*. The tooth germ continues its evolution and has all necessary elements for the development of the complete tooth: (a) dental organ, (b) dental papilla, and (c) dental sac. The dental organ produces the enamel, the dental papilla generates the dentin and pulp, and the dental sac generates the cementum and periodontal ligament.

Histodifferentiation

Histodifferentiation is marked by histological differences of tooth germ cells that begin to specialize. The cap continues to develop and grows deeper into the mesoderm, adopting a bell appearance. This development phase is called *bell stage*. The tissue within the bell is the tissue that gives rise to the dental papilla. The dental organ is now surrounded by basement membrane and divided into an inner and outer dental epithelium. Ultimately, the dental organ becomes enamel. Condensation of the tissue (mesoderm) adjacent to the outside of the bell is responsible for the dental sac. Ultimately, the dental sac gives rise to cementum (covering of the tooth's root) and to periodontal ligament (attachment between tooth and bone). During the latter portion of the bell stage, the dental lamina continues to shrink and eventually disintegrates. As the dental lamina disappears, the succedaneous tooth bud is formed from it.

Morphodifferentiation

Morphodifferentiation is the stage during which the specialized cells arrange themselves to give each tooth its final size and shape and prepare the tooth for the development of enamel, dentin, pulp, cementum, and periodontal ligament. This phase is called *advanced bell stage*. Ameloblasts and odontoblasts begin their formation and are responsible for the formation of dentin and enamel, respectively. The primary tooth bud becomes a free internal organ.

Apposition

Apposition occurs when the tooth network or tissue matrix is formed. The growth is appositional, additive, and regular, explaining the layered appearance of the enamel and dentin.

Calcification

Calcification occurs with an influx of mineral salts within the previously developed tissue matrix. Enamel consists of about 96% inorganic material (calcium and phosphate) and about 4% organic material and water. Enamel and dentin calcification consists of a very sensitive process that occurs over a long period beginning at the cusp tip or the incisal edge of the tooth. The enamel of all 20 primary teeth is usually completed by the age of 1 year. With the exception of third molars, all permanent teeth show some hard tissue formation by age 3.

Eruption

Before addressing eruption, it is necessary to discuss root development, as the two are correlated. Upon tooth crown completion, inner and outer epithelia fold over the cementoenamel junction area, starting the root development stage. The enamel organ proliferates a structure known as *Hertwig's sheath*, which is responsible for the root's size and shape and tooth eruption. The root is usually about one half to two thirds of its final length at the time the tooth erupts into the oral cavity through the mucous membrane cover of the alveolar process. The length of time for root completion after eruption of primary teeth is 18 months, whereas for permanent teeth it is 3 years.

The eruption process is completed when the tooth meets its opposing tooth in the opposite arch. The time interval between crown completion and eruption to full occlusion in permanent teeth is approximately 5 years. The first primary tooth to erupt is the mandibular primary incisor; by age 3 years, all 20 primary teeth have erupted. By 6 years, the first permanent molars erupt. Then deciduous teeth exfoliate one by one to be replaced by 32 permanent teeth at or around age 18 years. Some factors, such as race and sex, influence permanent tooth eruption. Permanent tooth eruption occurs slightly earlier in African Americans compared with Caucasians and earlier in females compared with males.

Dental Anomalies

Tooth malformations are more common in permanent teeth and can be related to variations in number, size, shape, or structure. Disturbance of the epithelial-mesenchymal interactions (central mechanism regulating tooth development) can disturb tooth development. Trauma and infection of primary teeth may cause malformations of their succedaneous permanent teeth, while tooth germ division or joining of adjacent germs may cause variations in tooth number or shape.

Some nutrients are essential during tooth development and maintenance. Deficiencies in calcium, phosphorus, and vitamin D are related to less mineralized tooth structures, and deficiencies in vitamin A can reduce the amount of enamel formation. Lack of fluoride can increase demineralization when an erupted tooth is exposed to organic acids and delay remineralization; conversely its excess during tooth development can lead to fluorosis.

Primary Prevention for Healthy Dentition

Oral health is integral to general health. Children with untreated caries are at increased risk for pain, emergency room visits, premature tooth loss, failure to thrive, developing new carious lesions in both primary and permanent dentitions, and eating, sleeping, and learning difficulties. Ideally, oral health promotion should initiate prenatally. Pregnant women should optimize nutrition by consuming adequate amounts of vitamins A, C, D, calcium, and phosphorus, especially during the third trimester when enamel undergoes maturation. Lack of these essential vitamins and minerals can lead to enamel hypoplasia, a defect that predisposes children to caries early in life. Frequent infections (i.e., periodontal disease) during pregnancy also increase the risk for preterm and low birth weight infants, who consequently are more susceptible to enamel hypoplasia. Because caries is a transmissible infectious disease, it can spread from parent/caregiver to child. Therefore, it is important to educate pregnant women and parents/caregivers of infants and toddlers to keep their own teeth healthy and free of caries by visiting the dentist regularly, flossing, brushing twice daily with fluoride toothpaste, using antimicrobial agents, avoiding high consumption of sugary drinks and foods, and eliminating saliva-sharing activities (i.e., sharing utensils, toothbrushes, orally cleansing a pacifier) to prevent spreading high levels of caries-causing bacteria to their children.

Primary prevention of dental disease also involves establishing a dental home for children within 6 months after the eruption of their first primary tooth or no later than 12 months of age. Early dental intervention aims timely delivery of family education on caries etiology/process, appropriate oral hygiene and feeding/dietary habits for caries prevention, delivery of anticipatory guidance, consideration of appropriate fluoride management (i.e., use of fluoride toothpaste, consumption of fluoridated community water), early identification of children at high risk for caries, and tailored preventive programs. Early prevention, identification, and intervention of oral health problems are cost-effective and lead to satisfactory outcomes.

Karin Weber-Gasparoni

See also Early Periodic Screening, Diagnosis, and Treatment Program for Low-Income Children; Nutrition and Nutrition Promotion for Families

Further Readings

American Academy of Pediatric Dentistry. (n.d.) *Dental Growth and Development*. Retrieved from http://www.aapd.org/media/Policies_Guidelines/RS_DentGrowthandDev.pdf

Berkowitz, B. K. B., Holland, G. R., & Moxham, B. J. (2002). Early tooth development. In *Oral anatomy, histology and embryology* (3rd ed., pp. 290–303). London: Mosby.

Ten Cate, A. R. (1998). Development of the tooth and its supporting tissues. In *Oral histology* (5th ed., pp. 78–103). St. Louis, MO: Mosby.

Websites

American Dental Association: http://www.ada.org

Chiropractic Care for Families

The Association of Chiropractic Colleges, representing all accredited chiropractic colleges, defines chiropractic as "a health care discipline which emphasizes the inherent recuperative power of the body to heal itself without the use of drugs or surgery." The association describes chiropractic practice as focusing on "the relationship between structure (primarily the spine) and function (as coordinated by the nervous system) and how that relationship affects the preservation and restoration of health."

By contrast, the World Health Organization (WHO) defines chiropractic as "a health care profession concerned with the diagnosis, treatment and prevention of disorders of the neuromusculoskeletal system and the effects of these disorders on general health" (p. 3). The WHO emphasizes manual techniques, including joint adjustment, manipulation, or both.

Chiropractic is the largest "alternative" health care profession and is also the third largest doctoral-level health profession in the United States, after medical doctors and dentists. There are approximately 70,000 practicing chiropractors in the United States.

The term *chiropractic* was coined by the profession's founder Daniel David Palmer to emphasize "hands-on healing." Chiropractic care is known for this hands-on approach, with the chiropractic adjustment (sometimes referred to in the scientific literature as "spinal manipulation") at its core. Chiropractic providers personalize care to suit both patient needs and doctor skills and preferences. Chiropractic techniques vary from provider to provider, just as surgical techniques vary from surgeon to surgeon. Some chiropractors take a traditional approach, utilizing manual maneuvers to "adjust" or "manipulate" the bones of the spine and extremities with a high-velocity thrust. Other chiropractors use instruments developed specifically to control or vary the force or increase the accuracy of the adjustment/manipulation.

This entry begins with a discussion of the uses of chiropractic care. Next, chiropractic education, with a focus on family care, is discussed, as well as the scientific evidence for the effectiveness of chiropractic care. Lastly, desired outcomes and the role of chiropractic care in family health care are discussed.

Uses of Chiropractic Care

Chiropractors care for a variety of primarily musculoskeletal problems, but the vast majority of visits are from patients seeking care for low back or neck pain, other joint pain, and headaches. The most commonly sought treatment for back pain, aside from traditional medical care, is chiropractic care.

Chiropractors do not prescribe medicine, but most chiropractors do emphasize to their patients the importance of healthy lifestyles and behaviors for the prevention or resolution of health concerns. This holistic view of health makes chiropractic a popular choice among people who prefer a more natural approach to health care. So, although most chiropractic patients initially seek care with a complaint of back pain, many established chiropractic patients continue to see their chiropractor for wellness or prevention.

The Job Analysis of Chiropractic indicates that a typical chiropractic practice sees patients of all ages. Slightly less than 20% of chiropractic patients are under the age of 18 years, nearly half of patients are from 18 to 50 years old, and approximately one third of chiropractic patients are over 50 years of age.

Chiropractic Education With a Focus on Family Care

There are 16 accredited chiropractic colleges in the United States. Chiropractic students receive about the same number of total hours of education as medical students, although chiropractors obtain less hours of education in clinical settings. Most students entering chiropractic programs possess either a baccalaureate degree or graduate-level training emphasizing basic sciences, biology, and chemistry. Chiropractic College consists of another 3 to 4 years of intensive training, after which Doctors of Chiropractic (DCs) can apply for a license to practice. A four-part series of National Board Examinations is also taken as part of the overall licensure process.

Chiropractic education includes many courses to prepare the chiropractor for family care. Required courses include pediatrics, geriatrics, obstetrics and gynecology, clinical psychology, and men's and women's health topics. Whereas in some other health professional training programs these courses are optional, all chiropractic students must complete training in each of these topics prior to graduation.

Scientific Evidence on Chiropractic Care for Family Health Issues

There is sound scientific evidence for the safety and effectiveness of chiropractic's primary treatment technique, the chiropractic adjustment, for common musculoskeletal problems such as low back and neck pain. Chiropractic is one of the few recommended treatments, according to national evidence-based guidelines, for low back pain. The risk of a serious complication following chiropractic care is exceedingly low, according to the numerous studies on this topic. Regarding patient satisfaction with chiropractic care, patients seeing chiropractors for back pain tend to be significantly more satisfied than patients cared for by medical professionals.

There is a growing evidence base on the effectiveness of chiropractic care for various nonmusculoskeletal disorders, such as infantile colic, asthma, and hypertension. Special populations, such as pregnant women, may also seek chiro-practic care not only to address musculoskeletal pain but also in hopes of experiencing a less painful or shorter delivery. Virtually hundreds of published case studies report the positive outcomes observed in chiropractic practice for health issues beyond pain in the spine and joints. The scientific literature base on nonmusculoskeletal concerns also consists of pilot studies and small-scale clinical trials.

Chiropractic research infrastructure has grown, matured, and improved immensely over the past 20 years, with an exponential growth in research funding from such sources as the National Institute of Health, the National Center for Complementary and Alternative Medicine, and the Health Resources and Services Administration.

Desired Outcomes of Chiropractic Care

The majority of chiropractic studies focus on the outcome of pain reduction. Other important outcomes in chiropractic care are functional improvement and return to normal activities of daily living. Additionally, some studies report on reduced medication use, hospitalizations, and medical visits, particularly in older adults. From a patient's perspective, all of these outcomes are important, as they relate to an improvement in overall wellness and quality of life.

Chiropractic for Families

DCs recognize the value and responsibility of working in cooperation with other health care practitioners when in the best interest of the patient and have become increasingly integrated into the health care mainstream. Collaboration between chiropractors and other health professionals is increasing, and referrals to chiropractors are becoming more common. In the areas of training, practice, and research, chiropractic is playing an increasingly important role in the global health care market.

Lisa Zaynab Killinger

See also Complementary and Alternative Medicine; Home Remedies; Integrative Medicine and Health Care Settings

Further Readings

Carey, T. S., Garrett, J., Jackman, A., McLaughlin, C., Fryer, J., & Smucker, D. (1995). The outcomes and costs of care for acute low back pain among patients seen by primary care practitioners, chiropractors, and orthopedic surgeons. *New England Journal of Medicine, 333,* 913–917.

Cherkin, D. C., & Mootz, R. D. (1997). *Chiropractic in the United States: Training, practice, and research.* Rockville, MD: Agency for Health Care Policy & Research.

Christensen, M. G., & Kollasch, M. W. (2005). *Job Analysis of Chiropractic 2005: A project report, survey analysis, and summary of chiropractic practice in the United States.* Greeley, CO: National Board of Chiropractic Examiners.

Eisenberg, D. M., Davis, R. B., Ettner, S. L., Appel, S., Wilkey, S., Van Rompay, M., et al. (1998). Trends in alternative medicine use in the United States, 1990–1997: Results of a follow-up national survey. *Journal of the American Medical Association, 280,* 1569–1575.

Killinger, L. Z. (2004). Chiropractic care of aging patients: A review of the training, role, and scope of chiropractic in the care of an aging society. *Clinics in Geriatric Medicine, 20,* 223–235.

Mootz, R. D., Hansen, D. T., Breen, A., Killinger, L. Z., & Nelson, C. (2006). Health services research related to chiropractic: Review and recommendations for research prioritization by the chiropractic profession [Position paper for U.S. Health Resources and Services Administration]. *Journal of Manipulative and Physiological Therapeutics, 29,* 707–725.

World Health Organization. (2005). *WHO guidelines on basic training and safety in chiropractic.* Geneva, Switzerland: Author. Retrieved from http://whqlibdoc.who.int/publications/2006/9241593717_eng.pdf

Websites

Association of Chiropractic Colleges:
    http://www.chirocolleges.org

CHRISTIANITY'S INFLUENCE ON HEALTH IN THE FAMILY

Family health has been of central importance to theology from the beginning of the Christian witness and through more than 2,000 years, as the Christian faith increasingly diversified into numerous denominations. During these years controversial positions have arisen on certain family health–related topics. While some controversies have been resolved, others have not. Remaining controversies in the context of family health appear to center on behavior related to sexuality. Specifically, these controversies include birth control decisions and options, views on abortion, and choices on the use of condoms to prevent HIV/AIDS and other sexually transmitted diseases. These controversies will continue to be negotiated in the upcoming years, and providing interventions that bring health and strength to those hurting from disease or injury in families is a continuing challenge not always successfully met. The primeval family was portrayed as healthy and long-lived. But illness and disease afflicted them as well as sibling rivalry and domestic violence. The need for interventions to ensure family health and stability endures through the ages.

Perhaps the most effective influence of Christianity on family health is seen in its norms for Christian living that contribute to health and longevity. Five principles help to frame issues of family health. *Monogamy*, the first principle of marriage, was construed as one man and one woman bound together for life, thus rejecting polygamy and polygyny. *Mutuality* of mind and spirit emphasized compatibility in values and beliefs, thus encouraging factors that cultivate compatibility and the value of continuity in relationship. *Fidelity* is a virtue cultivated to control the promiscuous nature of the sexual impulse and to deepen commitments that make for *permanence* in marriage. Divorce was condemned or prohibited on pain of religious sanctions, which tended to cause couples to stay married despite dysfunctional relations. *Agape love* is the fifth but perhaps the most important principle in family health. Some speak of *erape*, a special combination of sexual love and sacrificial living, toward one another, to bring together the special love attributed to God and commanded of believers with the self-giving required in healthy, long-term commitments.

Living by these principles helps create an environment for nourishing children to maturity and for assisting the growth and strength of each member of the family. The importance of the family is focused in the fact that the family uniquely expresses and represents God's care for each person within a community of love and concern.

Stories of Jesus's healings also buttress Christian support for family health. Christian theology supports evidence-based medicine, and family medicine embodies the commitments of health care professionals. But ministries dedicated to "faith healing" often insist that belief in miracles is an article of faith. Christian Scientists extended the mind–body connection to include false thinking as the source of illness. Jehovah's Witnesses also tend to contrast faith with healing as in their rejection of blood products.

Jesus's ministry went beyond stories of miraculous healings. His saying that "you will do greater things than these" (John 14:12) has inspired many people in science, medicine, nursing, and religion to seek an integrated approach to health and wellness that involves research and discovery into personal, social, spiritual, and psychological factors involved in health or illness.

Jesus's concern for justice has motivated some of the great social reform movements of the world led by people like Mohandas Gandhi, Nelson Mandela, Martin Luther King, Jr., Mother Teresa, Florence Nightingale, and Harriet Tubman. In both writings and actions, such people have brought light to the social debate and inspired noble actions toward better health and a more equitable justice.

The two grand insights of Christianity are first, that God is, and second, that God loves and wills the health and well-being of all creation. God is Creator, Redeemer, and Sustainer of all that is. People have capacities to carry on the work of the Creator. The notion that people are "made in the image of God" (Gen. 1:28) indicates spiritual and intellectual capacities, not a physical likeness. People are able to live by internal values, beliefs, and commitments and expand their knowledge of persons and the world.

Christian anthropology also gives depth and encouragement to healthy living. The body is a temple of the holy spirit, thus making care for the body a spiritual duty. The believer lives by values and actions in an ongoing venture with God in an effort to redeem people from the destructive powers of evil.

Human life is a matter of psychosomatic wholeness. Personal development and growth—both physical and spiritual—are matters of the interactions of mind, spirit, and body. Each influences the other for good or ill as is seen by the impact of environmental toxins on the body.

These and other powerful religious insights have influenced or motivated efforts to combine the spread of Christianity with medical science in order to bring health and wholeness to people worldwide. The first hospitals were monasteries and convents, which later became centers of learning and devotion. The most pervasive and powerful of all religious mandates is that love is to be shared among all people so that health and wholeness can be experienced. Health care is a concrete expression of God's love and care for people.

Paul D. Simmons

See also Buddhism's Influence on Health in the Family; Factors Influencing Family Health Values, Beliefs, and Priorities; Hinduism's Influence on Health in the Family; Judaism's Influence on Health in the Family

Further Readings

Aquinas, T. (1947). *Summa theologica* (Fathers of the English Dominican Province, Eds.; 2 vols.). New York: Bensiger Brothers.

Latourette, K. S. (1953). *A history of Christianity.* New York: Harper & Brothers.

Nelson, J. B. (1978). *Embodiment: An approach to sexuality and Christian theology.* Minneapolis, MN: Augsburg Publishing.

Troeltsch, E. (1960). *The social teaching of the Christian churches* (O. Wyon, Trans.). New York: Harper Torchbooks.

CHRONIC HEALTH PROBLEMS AND INTERVENTIONS FOR THE CHILDREARING FAMILY

There is a growing prevalence of children who have chronic health conditions. In the United States alone, the number of children with chronic health problems—and the challenges that they and their families encounter—has been on the incline for the past several decades. The diagnosis of a chronic illness is devastating to a parent. The challenges are substantial for the childrearing family who has a child with chronic health problems. The Social Security Administration indicates that the number of children who receive social security income (SSI) has increased threefold to 1 million in 2005 from 275,000 in 1986. In 1960, only a small percentage of U.S. children, 1.8%, had limiting conditions. From among the many childhood illnesses that contribute to chronic health care conditions, James Perrin and colleagues note the leading conditions include (a) obesity, which affects 18% of children (increased from 5% 1971–1974), (b) asthma, which has doubled since the 1980s with prevalence now at 9%, and (c) attention deficit/hyperactivity disorder (ADHD) affecting 6% of school-age children.

According to the 2007 National Health Interview Survey (NHIS), 7% of children had a health condition that limited routine daily activities. A few conditions have decreased over time, including lead encephalopathy and human immunodeficiency virus type 1 infection. Some conditions—including cystic fibrosis, leukemia, and congenital heart disease—which in prior years had high fatality rates have been on the rise due to enhanced survival rates.

This entry focuses on children with chronic health problems and their families the challenges and implications of the child's condition, and the desired outcomes and interventions for coping.

Child With Chronic Health Problems

Throughout the literature a child with a chronic condition or a chronic health problem is defined as an individual between the ages of birth and 17 years of age requiring special health care needs.

Chronic conditions continue over a long period of time, with the terms *chronic condition, chronic illness,* and *chronic health problem* being used interchangeably. The chronic health problem for a child will vary in condition, condition symptoms, treatments, interventions, and limitations. Children who are affected by chronic health problems suffer from limitations constituting self-care, particularly in the areas of mobility, communication, sight, hearing, or learning. They may have both special health care needs and chronic disabilities stemming from chronic illness existing either solely or in combination with other health problems; often the chronic health problems continue into adulthood.

Family of a Child With Chronic Health Problems

A childrearing family is defined as a group of individuals in society, living together and traditionally and having at least one of the following: (a) a child, (b) a parent, or (c) a head of household/guardian assuming responsibilities for the family's childrearing needs inclusive of, but not limited to, its health care needs. Families devote substantial amounts of time balancing their financial and psychosocial needs, devoting time to their children's health care. Families' time is overwhelmingly consumed. For example, they may administer medications and therapies, procure and maintain equipment, and provide or arrange transportation to medical appointments. Additionally, they also organize complex coordination of care such as making appointments and ensuring that medical multidisciplinary providers are updated on the child's medical progress. The National Survey of Children with Special Health Care Needs (NS-CSHCN) 2005–2006 reports that families devote an excessive amount of time to their child's health care management. Therefore, congruent with the severity, complexity, and chronicity of the child's health problem is the amount of time the family spends on the child's care.

Obesity, asthma, and ADHD are the most prevalent childhood chronic health problems meriting global and local initiatives for the childrearing family, demanding interventions with outcomes addressing the childrearing families' chronic health care needs. Asthma, allergies, ADHD, cancer, cerebral palsy, cystic fibrosis, congenital heart diseases, diabetes, depression, developmental delays, hearing loss, human immunodeficiency virus (HIV/AIDS), juvenile rheumatoid arthritis, obesity, and seizures have also been identified as having characteristics that carry with them medical longevity and health care chronicity.

Challenges of Managing Chronic Health Problems

Children with chronic health problems face many challenges including limitations of activity (7.3%), absenteeism from school, and lack of health insurance (8.9%), according to the Centers for Disease Control and Prevention (CDC). Disparities have continued to emerge within obesity, asthma, and ADHD. Hispanic, non-Hispanic black, and Native American children are more susceptible to obesity. African American, Native American, and Puerto Rican children are more prone to asthma. Males are more at risk for asthma than females. Children who have fair to poor health are more likely to have ADHD. Generally, families with lower income are more likely to be affected by a chronic health problem.

Contributing Factors and Implications of Childhood Chronic Conditions

There are multifactorial reasons behind the etiology that contributes to chronic conditions in children, including their dietary habits, social awareness and genetic predisposition, perinatal risk factors, television and media, decreased physical activity, and other exposures from the environment. Families are challenged to overcome the persistent threats to "normal" life when confronted with a chronic illness. Chronic illness also contributes to a rise in health care expenses as these children grow to adulthood. For example, the following health issues often continue to adulthood: (a) Obesity increases the risk of adult chronic health problems, such as cardiovascular disease, hyperlipidemia, hypertension, and Type 2 diabetes mellitus; (b) asthma is known to manifest into chronic obstructive pulmonary diseases, such as adulthood asthma; and (c) ADHD is associated with limitations in education linked with a risk for accidents and criminal behaviors.

Desired Health Outcomes for the Childrearing Family

With the complexity of any chronic health problem comes a multitude of challenges that impact the childrearing family. Numerous multidisciplinary studies have been conducted to address how family structure, dynamics, family finances, and most importantly, coping are affected. There appears to be a growing consensus that the ability to balance the special health care needs of a child with a chronic health problem can be extremely overwhelming, hence creating (a) confusion, with loss of hope for having an "ideal child"; (b) neglected family members other than the ill child; (c) loss of opportunities or work, with increasing financial burden as families struggle to keep up with rising insurance costs and health insurance out of pocket or dependency on federal aid or supplementation; and (d) fatigue and stress on the families' functionality. Prioritization of the families' overall social needs and health focus is mainly delegated to the ill child while all others' personal social needs and health tend to be neglected. According to family-based studies, due to these family tendencies, parents are more likely to report or experience headaches, depression, anxiety, marital stress, and financial stress. To give the ill child the multifaceted care he or she needs, parents not only give of themselves but also overextend themselves to provide and, many times, exhaust all of their internal and external resources. To be able to cope effectively and maintain a holistic balance to stay in full circle of their family and children's needs, parents need to be empowered with health, knowledge, resources, time, and interventions, as depicted in Figure 1 (above) and Table 1.

The following evidence-based factors are interdependent and are strong predictors of wellness for a childrearing family experiencing a chronic health problem:

1. Health, the condition of being sound in body, mind, and spirit, provides strength and endurance in dealing with the complexity of the chronic issue along with assisting to maintain a positive outlook for the development of coping mechanisms. The World Health Organization (WHO) defines health as a state of total mental, physical, and social well-being and not only the absence of disease or illness.

Figure 1   Success Factors for Wellness on a Continuum for the Childrearing Family With a Chronic Health Problem

2. Knowledge includes guidance, advice, and education on all issues surrounding the chronic health problem.

3. Resources may be sought internally within the family support systems, such as income, savings, health insurance, family, neighbors, or friends, or externally provided by federal aid, parent-to-parent support groups, spiritual support from a local church, psychological outreach programs, respite services, babysitting, and many others.

4. Much time is needed to provide the complex, quality care inherent in chronic health problems and allow uninterrupted delivery of care to all members. Families become fully consumed with the daily complex health care requirements surrounding the chronic health problem, further placing the family and child at risk for poor coping outcomes.

Interventions for Coping With Chronic Health Problems

A childrearing family with a chronic health problem attains the desired health outcomes with strategies that assist with coping and preventing the disruption, disturbance, and depletion of the wellness on a continuum of success factors (health, knowledge, resources, and time) as depicted in Figure 1. Table 1 identifies interventions for how

Table 1   Family Copying Interventions for the Childrearing Family Dealing With a Chronic Health Problem

Risk Outcomes for Poor Coping	*Interventions to Enhance Coping*
Confusion, loss of hope for having an "ideal" child	• Seek advice from counseling services, spiritual advisors, or chaplains as needed. • Focus on the "normals" of the child and the positives and not on their limitations or inabilities. • Entrust and allow others to step in by telling them exactly what you want to be done for you. • Build partnerships with those you trust. • Learn to delegate: You cannot do everything. • Build partnerships with the health care team. • Seek assistance and how-tos on coordination of care. • Provide support to other parents dealing with the same chronic health problems.
Neglected family members other than ill child (i.e., sibling, spouse)	• Accept regression or attention-seeking behaviors. • Be truthful with all aspects of medical implications of the chronic health problem. • Apply the same rules from before the illness to post-illness to all members. • Allow visits and participation of care for the ill child. • Include the "here and now" happenings with the siblings. • Communicate therapeutically by using age-appropriate language. • Attend family members' outside activities (e.g., school functions, sports-related activities, choir/band, etc.). • Keep promises, most importantly, keeping them realistic and attainable. • Include the family member in family decision making, when applicable. • Reserve alone time regularly with the family member (eat meals together, take walks, have a conversation on something other than the chronic health problem). • Touch base to see "how they are doing" at least once per day.
Loss of opportunities/work (e.g. financial burden)	• Recognize financial disarray. • Allow religious affiliations and/or family support systems to provide assistance as needed. • Become informed of special programs through the media, Internet, camps, and other parents. • Obtain financial counseling as needed. • Seek assistance from multidisciplinary health care team and guidance from community outreach programs. • Apply for federal, state, and local funding as applicable. • Keep abreast of legislative changes. • Keep informed. • Educate lifelines of support systems (neighbors, family, school counselors, nurses, teachers) of financial situation and need for assistance.

(Continued)

Table 1 (Continued)

Fatigue and stress	• Keep a schedule and a routine.
	• Keep a list of specific "tasks" and delegate from the list to a trusted individual when needed.
	• Seek continuity of care from health care advocates.
	• Take time out for respite alone or with family.
	• Allow for restful full night sleep, daily.
	• Eat a balanced diet.
	• Provide yourself with energy enhancers (e.g., exercise, diversion, regular rest/sleep, prayer, meditation, hobbies, etc.).

Sources: Adapted from Fisher (2001); Hatzmann et al. (2008); Nuutila & Salanterä (2006); U.S. Department of Health and Human Services, Health Resources and Services Administration, Maternal and Child Health Bureau (2008).

to best cope with the risk outcomes of chronic health problems in childrearing families.

*Jacqueline Lytle Gonzalez and
Laura Mendoza Hernandez*

See also Asthma Family Issues: Prevention and Control; Attention Deficit/Hyperactivity Disorder and the Family; Case Management for Chronic Illness/Disability and the Family; Cerebral Palsy and the Family; Costs of Medical Care and Existing National, State, and Private Pay Avenues for Families; Cystic Fibrosis and the Family; Obesity, Weight Problems, and Healthy Weight for Families

Further Readings

Bloom, B., Cohen, R. A., & Freeman, G. (2009, January). *Summary health statistics for U.S. children: National Health Interview Survey, 2007* (DHHS Publication No. 2009–1567 Series 10, No. 239). Hyattsville, MD: National Center for Health Statistics. Retrieved from http://www.cdc.gov/nchs/data/series/sr_10/sr10_239.pdf

Cohen, M. H. (1993). The unknown and unknowable: Managing sustained uncertainty. *Western Journal of Nursing Research, 15,* 77–96.

Eddy, L. L., & Engel, J. M. (2008). The impact of child disability type on the family. *Rehabilitation Nursing, 33*(3), 98–103.

Fisher, H. R. (2001). The needs of parents with chronically sick children: A literature review. *Journal of Advanced Nursing, 36*(4), 600–607.

Hatzmann, J., Heymans, H. S., Ferrer-i-Carbonell, A., Van Praag, B. M., & Grootenhuis, M. A. (2008). Hidden consequences of success in pediatrics: Parental health-related quality of life-results from the Care Project. *Pediatrics, 122*(5), 1030–1038.

Msall, M. E., Avery, R. C., Tremont, M. R., Lima, J. C., Rogers, M. L., & Hogan, D. P. (2003). Functional disability and school activity limitations in 41300 school-age children: Relationship to medical impairments. *Pediatrics, 111*(3), 548–543.

National Center for Health Statistics. (2009). *FastStats: Child health.* Washington, DC: U.S. Government Printing Office. Retrieved from http://www.cdc.gov/nchs/fastats/children.htm

Nuutila, L., & Salanterä, S. (2006). Children with a long-term illness: Parents' experiences of care. *Journal of Pediatric Nursing, 21*(2), 153–160.

Perrin, E. C., Lewkowicz, C., & Young, M. H. (2000). Shared vision: Concordance among fathers, mothers, and pediatricians about unmet needs of children with chronic health conditions. *Journal of the American Academy of Pediatrics, 105*(1), 277–285.

Perrin, J. M., Bloom, S. R., & Gortmaker, S. L. (2007). The increase of childhood chronic conditions in the United States. *Journal of the American Medical Association, 27*(24), 2755–2759.

Svavarsdottir, E. K. (2005). Hardiness in families of young children with asthma. *Journal of Advanced Nursing, 50*(4), 381–90.

U.S. Department of Health and Human Services, Health Resources and Services Administration, Maternal and Child Health Bureau (2008). *The National Survey of Children with Special Health Care Needs chartbook 2005–2006.* Rockville, MD: Author. Retrieved June 30, 2009, from http://mchb.hrsa.gov/cshcn05/NF/6family/intro.htm

Websites

World Health Organization: http://www.who.int

CHRONIC HEALTH PROBLEMS AND INTERVENTIONS FOR THE ELDERLY FAMILY

A *chronic health problem* is defined as any ongoing condition, illness, or disease that lasts over a year, has the potential to impair health or physical function, and requires ongoing medical attention. While chronic health problems include specific illnesses, they also encompass nonspecific syndromes, which usually involve multiple causes and organ systems. Examples include frailty, delirium, frequent falling, and dizziness. Compared to other age groups, elders are disproportionately affected by chronic conditions. The most common health problems in this cohort include arthritis, hypertension, heart disease, diabetes, lung disease, stroke, cancer, and visual and hearing impairments.

Chronic health problems typically affect more than the person with the condition. The relationship between chronic illness and family relationships is recursive in that illnesses and families affect each other. For this reason, interventions described here target older adult families from the perspectives of care recipient, intermediary, and caregiver.

Overview of Current Literature

As noted by Anderson and Horvath in 2004, approximately 84% of persons age 65 and older have been diagnosed with at least one chronic condition, and 62% have two or more chronic diseases. Prevalence rates do not differ by gender or income. The rate of chronic illness is higher among white populations (46%) than African American populations (37%) or other racial groups (32%), but African Americans are 1.5 times more likely than whites to report functional impairment. Activities of daily living (ADLs), which include tasks such as bathing, dressing, feeding, toileting, and ambulation, are commonly used as markers of function. The Administration on Aging reported that among Medicare recipients who lived at home in 2007, more than 25% were impaired in one or two ADLs. According to the Federal Interagency Forum on Aging, 8% reported impairment in three to six ADLs. Another manifestation of chronic illness is pain. More than 25% of community-dwelling elders live with chronic pain, which often contributes to decreased function, appetite, and sleep, as well as increased social isolation, depression, and anxiety.

The National Alliance for Caregiving (NAC) estimates that there are 43.5 million caregivers in the United States, often family members who provide unpaid care to an adult over age 50. The average ages of caregiver and care recipient are 50 and 77, respectively. The mean duration of caregiving is 5 years, during which time three quarters of caregivers remain in the workforce. Seventeen percent of caregivers provide more than 40 hours of care per week. Factors that contribute to caregiver stress include caring for someone with complex diseases such as Alzheimer's disease; the perception that the individual had no choice in becoming a caregiver; high perceived burden; and living more than an hour away from the care recipient.

The Burden of Chronic Illness

The NAC also reports that of older care recipients, 58% live in their own homes and 47% live alone, which increases the need for help. Asking for help, however, is often perceived as stressful. While some elders feel guilty about imposing on family members, approximately 40% reported that they often fail to get sufficient support to manage their conditions. Chronic illness also imposes economic stress. The median income for an American aged 65 and over is about $15,000, and the average annual out-of-pocket health care cost is approximately $2,600. Functional limitations and pain often lead chronically ill elders to relinquish leisure activities and related social interaction. Many also grapple with difficult decisions regarding moving to a setting that can better accommodate their needs, such as a single-story home, a handicapped-accessible dwelling, assisted living, or a nursing home. Such moves typically involve losing independence, a family home and possessions, and social connections. Each stressor alone is significant, and the cumulative effects of stressors—including chronic illness, pain, depression, and isolation—are known to increase suicide risk among older adults.

Emotional stress is among the greatest burdens family caregivers experience. Caregiving can strain family relationships. Caregivers often become frustrated when the care recipient fails to comply with the proper disease management regimen, will not ask for help, becomes too dependent, does not appear appreciative, seems critical, or is not proactive with medical providers. Family caregivers report feelings of anger and helplessness along with guilt about not being able to do more. According to the NAC survey, 43% of caregivers reported moderate or high emotional stress and more than a fifth reported exhaustion. More than half reported having less time for family and friends. Between 40% and 70% of caregivers develop clinically significant depressive symptoms. The incidence of depression and anxiety increases with hours of care provided per week.

The NAC report indicated that 16% of caregivers described their health as fair or poor. Caregivers generally report poorer self-care than noncaregivers, which may contribute to the increased physical ailments they experience in the form of headaches, acid reflux, and pain, and to their increased rates of obesity, hypertension, high cholesterol, and diabetes. Elderly spouse caregivers have higher mortality rates than noncaregivers.

The value of services family caregivers provide is estimated to be $306 billion annually. Caregiving families have median incomes that are more than 15% lower than noncaregiving families. According to NAC, 23% of caregivers reported moderate or high financial hardship.

Desired Outcomes

Although the priorities of older adults and family members sometimes differ with respect to preferred outcomes, both typically agree that interventions that maximize quality of life and minimize disruption for all are most desirable. Such interventions include those that promote preservation of each family member's capacity to carry out respective roles and responsibilities and to prevent further exacerbation of illness, including further decline and increased risk of developing other medical conditions. The quality of relationships among the elderly, family members, and health care providers has been shown to contribute to overall health outcomes. Hence, patients and families also desire positive relationships with trusted health care providers along with high- quality care.

A predominant value inherent in these outcomes is recognition that families and providers strongly encourage the inclusion of the elder's wishes in planning for care. Quality of life includes more than ratings of physical health. Current quality of life markers also include social, emotional, and economic health, which encompass respect, dignity, independence, freedom, and opportunities for challenging and stimulating activities. According to elders, factors that most diminish quality of life are those rooted in fear, including fear of being alone; fear of conflict in family relationships; and fear of disability, crime, poverty, substandard housing, and disregard for wishes.

From a family perspective, a desired outcome includes efforts that minimize the stress that family members experience while tending to the needs of an older adult. A key factor in determining how a family will approach caring for an aging family member is the history of their respective relationships. Studies have shown repeatedly that health outcomes for the aging individual and family are related to the quality of their relationship prior to the illness and to the family member's motivation for providing care and support. Families that function well and have less conflict tend to have better outcomes. In addition, family members who are motivated to provide care by feelings of affection associated with close, secure bonds, tend to experience more favorable outcomes than those who are motivated by a sense of obligation or anticipation of personal gain.

Outcomes for the affected individual improve when families are involved in their care. Studies have shown that family support contributes to better self-management behaviors, increased self-efficacy, and decreased depressive symptoms on the part of the affected individual. Improvements in disease-specific health outcomes, including better glycemic control, improved blood pressure control, fewer cardiac events, and better joint function, have also been reported.

Interventions to Improve Health and Function

Prevention

The first-line approach in the management of chronic conditions is prevention, which commonly includes a combination of lifestyle changes and preventive screenings. Prevention strategies associated with the incidence of most chronic illnesses include avoiding tobacco, maintaining a healthy body weight, and exercise. Screenings for conditions such as breast and colon cancer, hypertension, elevated blood lipids, and osteoporosis are recommended as a way to identify disease before symptoms appear.

Clinical Guidelines

Once an elderly individual has been diagnosed with a chronic condition, the focus of care is on disease management and prevention of further symptoms. Interventions include regular medical care, adherence to prescribed medication regimens, health-promoting lifestyle behaviors, and active participation in illness management. The National Guideline Clearinghouse provides detailed information on clinical practice guidelines for many chronic conditions. The American Geriatrics Society, however, cautions that such guidelines are generally not developed with considerations for elders with more than one chronic illness and that there is little evidence currently available about how best to apply disease management guidelines for the very old with multiple health conditions. In addition to guidelines, other interventions developed by health plans and providers include nurse and disease educator visits, health navigator programs, and peer support programs, all designed to encourage self-care.

Evidence-Based Interventions

The most inexpensive interventions toward illness prevention in older adults are vaccinations for influenza and pneumonia. Other interventions involve promoting positive health behaviors. The U.S. Administration on Aging maintains a current registry of evidence-based programs that promote behaviors that can prevent or minimize the negative effects of chronic illness; these behaviors include physical activity, nutrition, smoking cessation, fall prevention, and medication management. The chronic disease self-management paradigm developed at Stanford University is one such program. This approach of using a manual has been adapted to many chronic health conditions. The curriculum addresses topics such as techniques to deal with frustration, fatigue, pain, and isolation; appropriate exercise; proper use of medications; communicating effectively with family, friends, and health

professionals; nutrition; and how to evaluate new treatments.

Evidence-based approaches for depression treatment include models consisting of coordinated care that combines primary care, care management, medication monitoring, and skills development either in problem solving or socialization. Examples include Improving Mood, Promoting Access to Collaborative Treatment for Late-Life Depression (IMPACT) and Program to Encourage Active, Rewarding Lives for Seniors (PEARLS).

Other interventions aim to improve the relationship between older patients and their physicians. Government websites, including *NIH Senior*, provide materials to educate patients and families about how to prepare for visits and communicate effectively with doctors.

Aging Services

A widely available resource for older Americans is the Aging Services Network (ASN), which consists of 56 state units on aging, 655 area agencies on aging, 250 tribal organizations, 29,000 community-based organizations, more than 500,000 volunteers, and numerous nonprofit organizations. The ASN mission is to provide services that enable elders to remain at home, thereby preserving their independence and dignity. Aging service providers coordinate and support multiple home and community-based services, including information and referral, home-delivered and congregate meals, transportation, employment services, senior centers, and adult day care. The network serves 8 million elders and more than 600,000 caregivers annually.

Opportunities and Challenges

Without question families are the backbone of support for chronically ill elders. Interventions that support caregivers are critical to sustaining this valuable resource. The current structure, however, is threatened by many factors. The baby boom cohort differs from previous generations in that their families are more geographically dispersed, they tended to have smaller families, and more couples were childless. Another threat to the stability of community-based care is the shortage of available, trained home care providers. A combination of low wages, high injury rates, and poor job satisfaction all contribute to vacancy rates that are projected to grow as the boomer cohort ages. One market that is growing in response to gaps in informal care is telemedicine. Advances in technology allow in-home monitoring of the older adult's health status and safety from remote locations.

One positive trend has been the increase in planning by older families for future care needs. While purchasing long-term care insurance remains unpopular, the recent proliferation of housing options that provide supportive services in less restrictive settings are testaments to this trend. With this trend, however, comes another. As elders begin to move across levels of care with changes in health status, the number of transitions that families can anticipate will increase. Transitions, often accompanied by changes in routines, social networks, and loss of function, may also necessitate changing physicians and transferring medical records, both of which can affect continuity of care, especially when chronic illnesses are involved.

Carol Ann Podgorski and Ann E. Cornell

See also Access to Health Care: Elderly; Caregiving: Elderly; Chronic Health Problems and Interventions for the Childrearing Family; Chronic Health Problems and Interventions for the Midlife Family; Chronic Illness and Family Management Styles

Further Readings

Administration on Aging. (2009). *A profile of older Americans: 2009. Disability and activity limitations.* Retrieved June 30, 2010, from http://www.aoa.gov/AoARoot/Aging_Statistics/Profile/2009/16.aspx

Anderson, G., & Horvath, J. (2004). The growing burden of chronic disease in America. *Public Health Reports, 119,* 264–270.

Federal Interagency Forum on Aging-Related Statistics. *Older Americans 2010: Key indicators of well-being.* Bethesda, MD: Author. Available from http://www.agingstats.gov

McDaniel, S. H., Doherty, W. J., & Hepworth, J. (1992). *Medical family therapy: A biopsychosocial approach to families with health problems.* New York: Basic Books.

National Alliance for Caregiving. (2009). *Caregiving in the U.S.: A focused look at those caring for the 50+.* Retrieved from http://www.caregiving.org/data/2009CaregivingAARP_Full_Report.pdf

Rosland, A.-M. (2009, August). *Sharing the care: The role of family in chronic illness.* California HealthCare Foundation. Retrieved from http://www.chcf.org/publications/2009/08/sharing-the-care-the-role-of-family-in-chronic-illness

Warshaw, G. (2006). Chronic conditions in later life [Special issue]. *Generations, 30*(3).

Websites

Family Caregiver Alliance: http://www.caregiver.org/caregiver/jsp/home.jsp

National Alliance for Caregiving: http://www.caregiving.org

National Guideline Clearinghouse: http://www.guideline.gov

Stanford University Chronic Disease Self-Management Program: http://patienteducation.stanford.edu/programs/cdsmp.html

U.S. Department of Health and Human Services, Administration on Aging: http://www.aoa.gov

CHRONIC HEALTH PROBLEMS AND INTERVENTIONS FOR THE MIDLIFE FAMILY

A midlife family typically consists of parents (or partners) in their 40s or 50s and children who are probably grown and may have already left home. Yet, many people decide to start a family in their midlife. At midlife most persons still lead busy lives and have many obligations (e.g., at work). They usually feel confident that they are fit and healthy, but in fact the majority of chronic health problems occur during this period of life. Coronary artery disease, such as hypertension and cardiac infarction, respiratory disease, cancer, diabetes, and other chronic illnesses often are detected during midlife and seriously affect the patient and, consequently, the family, which in turn can affect the ill family member's adaptation to illness.

Therefore, several comprehensive intervention programs, which are designed to address family difficulties after the emergence of a chronic illness and also help family members adapt to the new situation and regain their balance and efficiency, have been developed. In this entry, the aims and goals, the types and basic components, as well as the efficiency of interventions targeting the patient and at least one other member of the midlife family (usually the partner) are discussed.

Psychosocial Interventions

The emergence of a chronic illness can cause great troubles in the emotional life and the organizational patterns of the family (e.g., changes in family goals, disruption of routines). These problems in turn may result in lasting distress and significant difficulties in family relationships. On the other hand, family can play a key role regarding the adaptation of the ill family member to illness (e.g., by facilitating adherence to medical advice, promoting rehabilitation and functioning) and thus corroborate quality of life and well-being of the ill family member. However, psychosocial interventions for midlife families can help both the patient and the family adapt to chronic illness. The majority of the interventions for families are modified versions of patient-focused programs. They typically have the form of support groups, psychoeducational programs, and cognitive-behavioral skills training. Their overall aim is to help families (a) effectively adapt to the new situation and (b) become able to assist their ill family member by means of identifying the problems and limits imposed by the illness and managing them in a proper and health-promoting way. An additional important aim is (c) to help family members "keep illness in its place." That is, be able to accept and come to terms with illness, balance living needs with care management responsibilities, develop positive but realistic expectations, manage the more controllable aspects of the illness experience, and continue setting and achieving goals in order to meet the developmental needs of all family members.

To this end, interventions for midlife families include the following goals: (a) identify the needs, the limitations, and the strengths of each family; (b) provide information regarding the patient's medical condition, its treatment and prognosis, the emerging problems and limitations, and the challenges that the family is probably going to face; (c) provide training in skills necessary for managing the illness-related stress, providing care to the patient, communicating in an effective way, and using available resources, such as support from friends and health professionals.

In general, psychosocial interventions for families are characterized by flexibility so as to meet the specific needs of each family and fit into the family's cultural, social, and educational background. The interventions may be delivered by medical and mental health professionals, as well as lay persons (e.g., other patients or other family members with experience in coping with illness) depending on the content and the goals of each program. Normally, intervention programs are based on a combination of strategies and methods for delivering help, ranging from regular psychological sessions to home visits and use of technological innovations.

Intervention Methods and Components

A midlife family intervention program for coping with chronic illness typically has multiple components and goals, although a program may also focus on a sole objective, such as providing information. The most common intervention types and components are described in this section.

Providing Information

One of the first needs of the family members after the emergence of a severe or chronic illness is to comprehend the new reality and develop a rather common perspective of it. In this regard, it is essential for health professionals to provide the family with information in a gradual manner. In the early phases of the illness, family members need information about the illness per se and the problems it might cause, the challenges they are faced with, possible emotional reactions, and the changes that may be necessary for the family in order to keep illness in its place. In later phases, family members need information about the possible course of the disease and the appropriate treatment, methods of helping the ill family member adapt to illness, ways to communicate appropriately with health professionals, and available community resources. Information can be provided verbally or through videotapes or written material.

Psychoeducation

Psychoeducation probably represents the most common type of family intervention for chronic illness. There are a variety of psychoeducational programs, all of which are aimed at providing information and promoting adaptive thinking and behavior. Psychoeducation typically involves strategies and techniques coming from self-management programs and cognitive-behavioral therapy, such as learning new skills (e.g., stress management, time management, and problem solving); understanding the interaction between cognitions, emotions, and behavior; cognitive restructuring; and behavior modification. Skills are normally taught by (a) presenting their rationale, (b) demonstrating their function, (c) encouraging a rehearsal among family members, (d) resolving possible difficulties and misunderstandings, and (e) discussing the ways of using these skills in everyday life. Psychoeducation can be provided in an array of formats ranging from written material, Intranet resources, or computer-based lessons to full lectures or discussions and psychotherapeutic or counseling interventions.

Group Counseling

The specific characteristics of group work—that is, high accessibility, low cost, and considerable effectiveness—as well as the long experience in this form of intervention have rendered group counseling an increasingly important aspect of interventions for families coping with chronic illness. There are several such programs, including multifamily psychoeducation groups, group therapy, and family therapy. Furthermore, a number of rather supplementary multifamily interventions have been developed, such as peer intervention groups and special-interest groups (i.e., intervention efforts focusing on specific subjects, such as spouse/marital problems, illness-related issues, vocational rehabilitation, caregiving, and parenting).

Crisis Intervention

To the extent that an illness represents a state of emergency, specific strategies aimed at dealing with crisis are also needed. Crisis intervention is a problem-solving focused method. It specifically aims at resolving specific problems and managing the most stressful aspects of the situation. It includes strategies like the strengthening of the ability to recognize and manage the emotional impact of the illness, the enhancement of coping skills, the increase of positive affect and self-efficacy, and the enhancement of the ability to anticipate problems and plan appropriate actions for dealing with them. Crisis intervention programs are brief and are frequently offered in single-session therapies.

Improving Communication

Resolving preexisting or illness-related communication problems among family members and providing training in communication skills represent a central target for many midlife family programs. Marital or family relationships often deteriorate, while children may react in maladaptive ways due to the chaos imposed by illness. Consequently, a serious conflict may surface. In this regard, the improvement of the communication patterns among family members may be the suitable way of dealing with and/or preventing such problems. A first objective of the relevant programs is to help family members feel free to discuss their thoughts and emotions about the current situation. Fears about the illness prognosis or about the future of the family, worries about not providing the proper care for the patient, and concerns regarding the burden illness imposes on the family are further issues that need to be addressed. Communication training consists of several skills, including (but not limited to) exploring and expressing positive and negative emotions, active listening, assertiveness, confronting fear and anxiety through open communication, and exploring and challenging the dysfunctional beliefs of the family members about the illness experience and the role of each member, which can impede family communication.

Enhancing Treatment and Rehabilitation for the Ill Family Member

Family plays a crucial role in rehabilitation of the family member. Therefore, a special objective of several intervention programs is to help families develop effective skills for helping the patient. Paul Power and Arthur Dell Orto have described four ways of assisting families toward this aim: (1) becoming aware of what the patient is emotionally going through; (2) involving the patient in family household and social activities, as well as preventing family from placing the patient in a "sick role"; (3) providing specific help regarding patient's needs, as well as treatment goals (e.g., regarding transportation, adherence to medical advice); and (4) becoming aware of and changing the dysfunctional personal attitudes and emotions toward the patient and the other family members.

Innovative Technological Types of Intervention

Besides the intervention strategies already presented, several more have been developed in order to make interventions more easily accessed, effective, and cost-saving. For instance, since the mid-1990s several technological innovations have been used, including informational telephone services, telephone-based support groups, computer-assisted home monitoring, and computerized health promotion. The overall aim of these techniques is to provide the patient and the family with education on specific issues (e.g., what to do in a crisis) and decision-making support, as well as to facilitate communication with health professionals and peers. The use of technological innovations is frequently combined with home visits from health professionals or with family and multifamily counseling.

The Effectiveness of Family Interventions

As the public health importance of family interventions for chronic illness and the public interest in these interventions are growing, it is essential to examine the efficiency of such treatment efforts. The question arising is whether psychosocial interventions involving the ill family member and the family members (or at least one of them) are better in terms of enhancing the family and the patient's well-being and functioning compared to typical medical or psychological interventions focused solely on the ill individual. Overall, existing reviews conclude that family interventions are indeed helpful and probably more effective than usual care as far as the mental health of both the ill family member and the family, the use of adaptive illness-related behaviors, and the improvement of the physical health and survival rates for the patient are concerned. Although there is some evidence that psychoeducational programs are more

effective, family interventions in general appear to be a promising approach for the well-being of the patient and the family.

Evangelos C. Karademas

See also Caregiving: Partners/Spouses; Chronic Health Problems and Interventions for the Elderly Family; Chronic Illness and Family Management Styles; Educating the Family Regarding Chronic Physical Illness; Families Experiencing Chronic Physical and Mental Health Conditions; Life-Threatening Illness and the Family; Psychoeducational Interventions for Families

Further Readings

Akamatsu, T. J., Stephens, M. A. P., Hobfoll, S. E., & Crowther, J. H. (1992). *Family health psychology.* Washington, DC: Taylor & Francis.

Campbell, T. L., & Patterson, J. M. (1995). The effectiveness of family interventions in the treatment of physical illness. *Journal of Marriage and Family Therapy, 21,* 545–584.

Elliott, T. R., & Shewchuk, R. M. (2005). Family adaptation in illness, disease, and disability. In T. Boll, J. M. Raczynski, & L. C. Leviton (Eds.), *Handbook of clinical health psychology* (Vol. 2, pp. 379–403). Washington, DC: American Psychological Association.

Martire, L. M., Lustig, A. P., Schulz, R., Miller, G. E., & Helgeson, V. S. (2004). Is it beneficial to involve a family member? A meta-analysis of psychosocial interventions for chronic illness. *Health Psychology, 23,* 599–611.

Power, P. W., & Dell Orto, A. E., (2004). *Families living with chronic illness and disability. Interventions, challenges and opportunities.* New York: Springer.

Websites

National Health System, Great Britain: http://www.nhs.uk

The Rosalynn Carter Institute for Caregiving: http://rosalynncarter.org

U.S. Department of Health and Human Services: http://www.hhs.gov

U.S. Department of Health and Human Services, National Guideline Clearinghouse: http://www.guideline.gov

Chronic Illness and Family Management Styles

Chronic illness during childhood influences both the child and the family. How the family views the illness, deals with the challenges it presents, and incorporates illness management into their daily lives can either promote healthy functioning or create additional stress and burden on the family unit. The family management styles (FMS) framework identifies the way a family responds to a childhood chronic illness, concentrating on the active, behavioral responses that define the management of the illness. The five family management styles—thriving, accommodating, enduring, struggling, and floundering—identify different types of family responses to childhood chronic illness. Knowledge of the management style a family uses can help health care providers and others who deal with chronically ill children and their families better guide and intervene to assist the families in dealing with the children and their illnesses. This entry reviews the development of the FMS framework, provides an explanation of the five styles identified, and discusses clinical relevancy.

Background

The FMS framework defines areas parents of children with a chronic illness have identified as important to consider when managing the illness. The framework, refined by working more than 20 years with families of children with chronic conditions, by Kathleen Knafl, Janet Deatrick, and Agatha Gallo and others, recognizes the common challenges parents encounter and identifies styles the parents may be using in their daily management of the child's condition. Maintaining the health of the child with a chronic illness is crucial to both the family and the child. Since the child's condition affects the family and family well-being, awareness of the way the family is managing the chronic illness provides crucial information about the family and the process they use to manage the chronic condition.

Within the context of childhood chronic illness and family management, family refers to those individuals who live in the household with the child and are thought of as family. Most definitions of chronic illness recognize a health condition that has a time component (duration of the disease) and requires management over time to monitor symptoms and control the disease. Although the child with a chronic illness is the impetus for examination of the family management style, the FMS framework examines and refers to the family as a unit, not a collection of individuals. Family management is defined by Lynne Schilling, Margaret Grey, and Kathleen Knafl as the active, daily, and flexible process in which youth and their parent(s)/guardian(s) share responsibility and decision making for achieving disease control, health, and well-being through a wide range of illness-related activities.

Family Management Styles

Five unique family management styles—thriving, accommodating, enduring, struggling, and floundering—have been identified by Knafl and Deatrick. Each style is characterized by a unique combination of beliefs and attitudes surrounding the child, the illness, management of the illness, and consequences of the illness. The following overview of each style is a summarization of the style from Knafl, Breitmayer, Gallo, and Zoeller (see Further Readings).

Thriving

Normalcy is the overriding theme within the thriving management style. The parents view the child as normal, the illness is viewed as manageable, and life goes on. Parents are confident of their ability to manage the child's illness, are proactive in their approach to management, and learn from prior experience to avoid problems or deal with them quickly when they occur. The child views himself or herself as equally healthy or healthier than peers and has normalized his or her perspective of the illness. No evidence of major negative consequences is presented, and family members seem to frame the illness in terms of positive outcomes, such as the added emotional closeness among family members.

Accommodating

A more negative view of the situation of identifying trouble managing the child's chronic illness differentiates the accommodating style from the thriving style, although this style is also marked by normalcy as the dominant theme. Difficult aspects of illness management are identified by family members. They view the child's life and future opportunities as compromised. The child is seen as a tragic figure or the illness is viewed as ominous, with its seriousness and the potential for future complications highlighted. The child views himself or herself as less healthy than peers and may describe the illness as a source of continual worry in his or her life. The family incorporates illness management into their daily routine, and parents perceive themselves as competent caregivers. An accommodating parenting philosophy is common, with parents being proactive with illness management. These parents, while proactive, may be more focused on following doctors' orders—carefully monitoring the child's symptoms, treatment regimen, and behavior—in order to provide health care providers with an accurate assessment of current issues to guide future treatment decisions instead of deciding themselves. Although there are few negative consequences for the family as a result of the childhood illness, parents may have a sense of dread regarding the child's illness trajectory.

Enduring

Difficulty is the overriding theme in the enduring family management style. Family members view their situation negatively and describe the tremendous effort invested by the members in illness management. The child with the chronic illness is seen as a tragic figure whose life has been irreparably compromised by the illness. Parents are bothered by people treating their child differently, feel guilt regarding the illness, and feel sorry for the child. The child may perceive himself or herself as less healthy than peers. A sheltering parenting philosophy is apparent, with an emphasis on protecting the child from possible harm. Restrictions are placed on the child, and the importance of teaching the child to recognize and accept the limitations imposed by the illness is stressed. If an accommodating parenting philosophy is identified, parents in the enduring style describe how difficult it is to make their accommodative goals a reality. Although confident in their ability to manage the illness, parents explain the tremendous effort required to adhere to the treatment regimen. The illness is seen as a difficult and significant responsibility, and illness management is perceived as a burden. Parents talk about the illness all the time and are constantly aware of how difficult it is to manage the daily changes that occur because of the illness. Illness has a major negative effect on family life and is an ever-present concern. Having a child with a chronic illness is perceived as an inherently difficult situation, and the family has no ability to envision ways to make illness management less burdensome. The future is sometimes viewed with a sense of dread.

Struggling

Parental conflict around differing views of the illness situation and differing expectations of one another is the overriding theme in the struggling style. The parent is aware that a less difficult family life is possible but holds his or her spouse responsible for not realizing this vision. Mothers typically view the situation more negatively than do fathers. Either they view the illness as an ominous situation and are fearful of future complications or they see it as a hateful restriction that significantly decreases the quality of their own lives. Mothers feel they receive little support from their spouses, that their spouses are insufficiently involved in the illness management and are unappreciative or critical of the efforts the mothers make to adhere to the treatment regimen. If the child is viewed to be deficient in self-care ability, mothers identify this as an additional source of conflict in the family. In contrast to the mothers' ominous, fearful view, fathers have a "life goes on" attitude and view the child as normal. Fathers express confidence in their ability to provide care for the child but provide little evidence of providing care and are critical of the way their spouse manages the situation. The child emphasizes the extent to which the illness intrudes in his or her own life and describes the illness as an ongoing source of worry. Family life is negatively impacted by the lack of agreement between parents and the conflict associated with the lack of mutuality. Although neither parent is pleased with the way things are, there is little agreement about how the situation could be improved. The illness is constantly in the foreground of the family life.

Floundering

The floundering style is identified by confusion, with negative themes dominating the parents' perspectives. Ironically, the child does not share these negative views. Parents view the child as a tragic figure or as a problem child whose illness and academic or behavioral problems, when added to the illness, create difficult parenting situations. The illness is described as ominous or as a hateful situation. Parents express uncertainty about how to best manage the illness and have an inconsistent or absent parenting philosophy. They also state ambiguous parenting goals containing conflicting statements, such as they might want to be accommodating but also espouse a protective stance. This situation creates tension and confusion. Illness management is seen as difficult, and the illness is not effectively managed. Aspects of the treatment regimen are not adhered to, and efforts to manage the illness more effectively are often unsuccessful. Illness management is viewed as a burden. Parents feel inadequate, focus on their feelings of inadequacy, and have conflicts with the child over treatment regimens. Illness management is handled in a reactive manner, and an inability to integrate prior experiences into current illness management strategies is apparent. This strategy results in illness problems being managed once they are serious; there is little recognition of the benefits of early interventions. The child describes minimal involvement in the management of the illness and little awareness of the requirements of the treatment regimen. Some children see the illness as an intrusion on their lives and have worries about the future, whereas others minimize the impact of the illness. The illness has negative consequences on family life, and there is little evidence of the family working together as a unit to problem solve. In general these families view the illness as a very negative situation that they are incapable of managing effectively.

Improving Family Management of Childhood Chronic Illness

The FMS framework provides a description of a range of management styles a family develops when confronted with the chronic illness of a child.

Understanding the way the family is managing the chronic illness of their child provides baseline information for health care providers regarding the family's approach to illness management and the effect the illness has on the family. According to Melissa Alderfer, this information can assist health care providers to better understand the family's situation in order to best plan, implement, and evaluate family-based interventions. To be most effective, interventions may be tailored by the management style a family uses. For example, an intervention that assumes the parents work well together might not be successful in a family using a floundering management style. Initial interventions to creating a common view of the illness and working through ways they can work together to manage the illness may produce better results. The ability to identify the management style a family is using becomes a useful tool in developing family-based interventions.

The Family Management Measure (FaMM) is a 53-item questionnaire that measures the core factors that comprise family management (Child's Daily Life, Condition Management Ability, Condition Management Effort, Family Life Difficulty, Parental Mutuality, and View of Condition Impact). Work is now under way to quantitatively develop FMS based upon the new FaMM questionnaire. The FMS framework and the FaMM have increased our knowledge of how the family responds to childhood chronic illness. Future work will test interventions based on family management styles that may assist families in developing styles that enhance child outcomes and family life.

Janet A. Deatrick and Barbara Beacham

See also Assessing Family Health; Chronic Health Problems and Interventions for the Childrearing Family; Communication in Families Related to Health and Illness; Conflict in Family Life, Role and Management of; Coping Management Styles in Families; Parenting

Further Readings

Alderfer, M. A. (2006). Use of family management styles in family intervention research. *Journal of Pediatric Oncology Nursing, 23*(1), 32–35.

Gallo, A. M. (1990). Family management style in juvenile diabetes: A case illustration. *Journal of Pediatric Nursing, 5*(1), 23–32.

Knafl, K. A., Breitmayer, B., Gallo, A., & Zoeller, L. (1996). Family response to childhood chronic illness: Description of management styles. *Journal of Pediatric Nursing, 11*(5), 315–326.

Knafl, K. A., & Deatrick, J. A. (2003). Further refinement of the family management style framework. *Journal of Family Nursing, 9*(3), 232–256.

Knafl, K. A., & Deatrick, J. A. (2006). Family management style and the challenge of moving from conceptualization to measurement. *Journal of Pediatric Oncology Nursing, 23*(1), 12–18.

Knafl, K. A., Deatrick, J. A., & Gallo, A. M. (2008). The interplay of concepts, data, and methods in the development of the family management style framework. *Journal of Family Nursing, 14*(4), 412–428.

Knafl, K., Deatrick, J. A., Gallo, A., Dixon, J., Grey, M., Knafl, G., et al. (2009, May 18). Assessment of the psychometric properties of the Family Management Measure. *Journal of Pediatric Psychology.* Advance online publication.

Ogle, S. K. (2006). Clinical application of family management styles to families of children with cancer. *Journal of Pediatric Oncology Nursing, 23*(1), 28–31.

Schilling, L. S., Grey, M., & Knafl, K. A. (2002). The concept of self-management of type 1 diabetes in children and adolescents: An evolutionary concept analysis. *Journal of Advanced Nursing, 37,* 87–99.

Websites

Family Management Measure (FaMM): http://nursing.unc.edu/research/famm

Cigarettes, Smoking, and Secondhand Smoke and Family Health

Smoking cigarettes and the associated exposure to secondhand smoke can negatively affect all family members. The purpose of this entry is to describe the impact of smoking cigarettes and exposure to secondhand smoke across different roles within the family and steps health care providers can take to intervene. Tobacco use is widely recognized as the most preventable cause of illness and death in the United States. Cigarette use is a known cause of numerous diseases, including multiple cancers, heart disease, stroke, complications of pregnancy, and chronic obstructive pulmonary disease (COPD), and is a risk factor for six of the world's eight leading causes of death. Approximately 21% of adult Americans smoke, representing 45 million current smokers. Worldwide, almost 1 billion men and approximately 250 million women smoke. Smoking results in significant costs to society, with smoking-attributable health care expenditures estimated at $96 billion per year in direct medical expenses and $97 billion in lost productivity.

Pregnancy and Postpartum

Smoking during pregnancy is the greatest preventable risk factor for pregnancy-related morbidity and mortality in the United States, resulting in adverse health outcomes for both mother and fetus. Adverse fetal outcomes include stillbirths, spontaneous abortions, decreased fetal growth, premature births, low birth weight, placental abruption, and sudden infant death syndrome (SIDS). Estimates suggest 20% or more of low birth weight births could be prevented by eliminating smoking during pregnancy. This behavior has also been linked to cognitive, emotional, and behavioral problems in children.

During pregnancy, many mothers are motivated to quit, providing an opportunity for health care professionals to intervene and capitalize on the existing motivation. Ceasing smoking prior to conception or early in the pregnancy is most beneficial, but quitting at any time results in increased health benefits. During the postpartum period, smoking mothers are less likely to breast-feed their children. Compared to mothers who do not smoke, mothers who smoke typically breast-feed for a shorter time, have reduced milk volume, and have milk that contains less fat. Unfortunately, many women who quit smoking during pregnancy relapse during the postpartum period. This highlights the need for health care providers to continue to provide education and smoking cessation interventions to mothers during the postpartum period.

Youth

Although smoking is traditionally viewed as an adult issue, it represents a significant pediatric concern.

Youth experiment or begin smoking for a variety of reasons, including social and parental norms, advertising, movies and popular media, peer influence, parental smoking, weight control, and curiosity. Ninety percent of adults who ever smoked daily report their first cigarette use was before the age of 21. Estimates suggest that each day in the United States, approximately 4,000 children and adolescents under the age of 18 smoke their first cigarette, and 1,200 children and adolescents become daily cigarette smokers. In 2006, it was estimated that 2.6 million U.S. adolescents aged 12 to 17 were current cigarette smokers. In general, youth are more likely than nonsmokers to think they can quit at any time and greatly underestimate the addictive properties of nicotine. Estimates suggest more than 80% of youth aged 11 to 19 years are thinking about quitting, and more than 70% have made a quit attempt. Unfortunately, only about 4% of adolescent smokers successfully quit each year, with failed quit attempts higher for youth than for adult smokers. Although youth who enroll in tobacco cessation programs are twice as likely to quit, most youth neither plan attempts to quit nor seek assistance in quitting. Because tobacco use often begins in adolescence, it is important that health care providers deliver tobacco prevention and cessation messages to youth and their parents.

Because youth have more frequent preventive and acute-care visits than do adults, parents may interact with pediatric health care providers more often than with their own primary care physicians. Indeed, many parents may not have access to health insurance and therefore may not have a primary care physician. Thus pediatric outpatient medical appointments serve as frequent opportunities to intervene with smoking parents to aid in improving the health of the family. Although it is recommended that interventions be offered to every patient who uses tobacco, pediatricians intervene with parents who smoke at a low rate. National surveys of practitioners and parents indicate that less than 50% of parents are even questioned about their smoking. Studies have demonstrated that tobacco use interventions provided to parents in pediatric clinics increase parents' interest in stopping smoking, as well as quit attempts and parent quit rates. Furthermore, research indicates that providing parents with information on the harms of secondhand smoke reduces childhood exposure and may decrease parental smoking rates.

Older Smokers and Smokers With Medical Conditions

It is never too late to benefit from quitting smoking. It has been estimated that more than 4 million Americans over age 65 smoke, and more than 18 million over the age of 45 smoke. By quitting smoking, all smokers, no matter the age, can reduce their risk of death from coronary heart disease, COPD, and lung cancer, and decrease their risk of osteoporosis. Quitting can also promote more rapid recovery from illnesses that are exacerbated by smoking and can improve cerebral circulation. Given the role that smoking plays in exacerbating conditions such as cancer, cardiac disease, COPD, diabetes, and asthma, it is important for health care professionals to address smoking with individuals who have these conditions. One setting that provides for a "teachable moment" is when smokers are hospitalized. Hospitalized smokers may be more motivated to quit for two primary reasons: (1) The illness resulting in the hospitalization may have been caused or exacerbated by smoking and demonstrates the smokers' vulnerability to the health risks of smoking; and (2) all hospitals accredited by the Joint Commission must now be smoke-free. Because of these factors, health care providers should view hospitalizations as opportunities to provide smoking cessation services.

Secondhand Smoke

Although the direct effects of smoking on the individual smoker are frequently cited, exposure to secondhand smoke also represents a significant health risk. Secondhand smoke is classified as a "known human carcinogen" by the U.S. Environmental Protection Agency (EPA) and causes more cases of cancer than all of the federally regulated environmental carcinogens combined. Tobacco smoke contains more than 4,000 chemical compounds; more than 60 of these are known, or suspected, to cause cancer. Each year in the United States, secondhand smoke is responsible for significant health consequence in nonsmoking adults. It is estimated that secondhand smoke exposure for nonsmoking adults causes more than 45,000 deaths from heart disease, more than 3,000 lung cancer deaths, and high rates of breathing problems (such as cough, mucus, chest discomfort, and reduced lung function). In children younger than 18 months, exposure to secondhand smoke results in increased lung infections (such as pneumonia and bronchitis), increased hospitalizations, and increased risk of SIDS. Secondhand smoke exposure also results in increased number and severity of asthma attacks, middle ear infections, and acute respiratory problems in children.

There is no safe level of exposure to secondhand smoke. Preventing all smoking in indoor spaces is the only way to completely protect nonsmokers from exposure to secondhand smoke indoors. Four places are of particular concern when addressing exposure to secondhand smoke: at work, in public places, at home, and in the car. For adults, a significant source of secondhand smoke exposure exists in the workplace. Both adults and children are at risk for exposure to secondhand smoke in public places, such as restaurants, shopping centers, and public transportation. Although some businesses appear to be concerned with the effects of banning smoking on their businesses, there is no evidence that going smoke-free is bad for business. Parents' making their home a smoke-free home is one of the most important things they can do for the health of their family. It has been estimated that 21 million children, or 35%, live in homes where residents or visitors smoke in the home on a regular basis. Secondhand smoke exposure in cars is a significant concern given the amount of time people spend in cars and how quickly hazardous levels of smoke can build up. In recognition of this issue, some states have laws that ban smoking in the car if passengers are under the age of 17 years.

Chronic Disease Model

It is estimated that more than 70% of smokers today report that they want to quit, and approximately 44% report that they try to quit each year. Despite this desire and efforts to quit, the majority of quit attempts are unaided and unsuccessful. In 2005, of the 19 million adults who attempted to quit, only 4% to 7% were likely to be successful. Therefore, tobacco dependence can be viewed as a chronic disease, with only a minority of tobacco users achieving permanent abstinence in an initial quit attempt. Most users smoke for many years and cycle through periods of remission and relapse. Viewing tobacco dependence from a chronic disease model recognizes the long-term nature of smoking and allows for health care providers to better understand the relapsing nature of the condition. A chronic disease model also emphasizes the importance of continued patient education, counseling, and advice over time.

Assessing and Brief Intervention

It is imperative that health care providers begin to ask about and identify tobacco use, and provide at least brief intervention to every tobacco user at health care visits. Health care providers can make a difference with as little as a 3-minute intervention. Even if smokers are not willing to make a quit attempt, brief interventions can enhance motivation and increase the likelihood of future quit attempts.

The Public Health Service publication, *Treating Tobacco Use and Dependence Clinical Practice Guideline: 2008 Update*, provides guidelines for the provision of effective interventions for smoking. These guidelines specifically recommend offering interventions to parents to promote smoking cessation and limit children's exposure to secondhand smoke. The guidelines recommend that health care providers follow the "Five A's": (1) *Ask*—systematically identify all tobacco users at every visit; (2) *Advise*—strongly urge all tobacco users to quit; (3) *Assess*—determine readiness to make a quit attempt; (4) *Assist*—aid the patient in quitting; and (5) *Arrange*—schedule follow-up contact. It is recommended that health care providers implement A1 to A3 with each tobacco user, regardless of the smokers' willingness to quit. For those individuals not interested in quitting, the guidelines recommend practitioners provide brief motivational interventions focused on the "Five R's": (1) *Relevance*—why quitting is personally relevant; (2) *Risks*—identify potential negative consequences; (3) *Rewards*—identify potential benefits of stopping; (4) *Roadblocks*—identify barriers to quitting; and (5) *Repetition*—motivational intervention should be repeated at every time.

Smoking Cessation Treatment

Effective smoking cessation interventions now exist for smokers. In addition to counseling, medication should be offered to all smokers trying to quit, except when contraindicated or for specific populations for which there is insufficient evidence of effectiveness (i.e., pregnant women, smokeless tobacco users, light smokers, and adolescents). There is a relationship between the intensity of the counseling intervention and the effectiveness of the intervention. Intensive interventions are more effective than less intensive interventions and should be used whenever possible. Person-to-person counseling delivered for four or more sessions appears especially effective in increasing smoking cessation. Additionally, proactive telephone counseling, group counseling, and individual counseling formats have all been found to be effective. The most effective components in smoking cessation counseling appear to be active problem-solving skills, social support, and support from the health care provider.

Stephen R. Gillaspy

See also Asthma Family Issues: Prevention and Control; Cancer in the Family; Pediatric Primary Care for the Family; Role of Families in Health Promotion; Women's Health

Further Readings

Fiore, M. C., Jaén, C. R., Baker, T. B., Bailey, W. C., Benowitz, N. L., Curry, S. J., et al. (2008, May). *Treating tobacco use and dependence: 2008 update* [Clinical practice guideline]. Rockville, MD: U.S. Department of Health and Human Services, Public Health Service.

U.S. Department of Health and Human Services. (2006). *The health consequences of involuntary exposure to tobacco smoke: A report of the surgeon general.* Atlanta, GA: U.S. Department of Health and Human Services, Centers for Disease Control and Prevention, Coordinating Center for Health Promotion, National Center for Chronic Disease Prevention and Health Promotion, Office on Smoking and Health.

Clarifying Family as Context of Care and Family as Focus of Care in Family Health

Families are intricately involved in health-related care. In fact, one of the primary purposes of family is to ensure the health and well-being of its members. A study of 138 family physicians and 4,454 directly observed visits found that a family member was present in nearly one third of visits. Seventy-two percent of established patients reported that multiple family members see that same doctor. There are at least two health care approaches that focus on families: A family history approach uses family information as a background in care of the patient but does not delve into family problems and issues; in contrast, a family orientation style views the family as the unit of care, includes multiple family members, and addresses family issues during health care visits.

However, families are diverse, encompassing a wide range of forms and living arrangements. Recognition and appreciation of the diversity of families is essential in order to effectively assist with the health of the group, as well as its members. Diversity also exists in a family's role in health care; it is often the major source of caregiving, but the family itself may also be in need of care.

This entry first discusses the various definitions of *family* and the challenges for diverse families. Next, this entry focuses on the family and the central unit in care and as context of care. Last, this entry examines the dyadic process of caregiving and care receiving and the family as the focus of care in illness or disability.

Defining "Families" for Care

Health-related professionals need to be attuned to the definition and meaning of *family* not only held by the institutional systems involved (e.g., hospitals, insurance companies, welfare departments) but by the families themselves. Although an institution may define the boundaries of family in a narrow or inflexible manner for the purpose of allocating resources (e.g., such as eligibility for health insurance coverage or hospital visitation), the actual family may define itself differently. Institutions may define family based on biological or legal criteria (e.g., marriage, birth, or adoption), whereas members may define their family based on affection, shared responsibilities, roles, or interactional processes. Definition of who is in the family can also be based on beliefs and values of cultural and religious groups that exist within the larger society. The definition of who is in (or not in) a family can differ among family members, based on varied individual experiences. When family members' own definitions and the external definitions used in the operation of institutions are in conflict, this inconsistency can pose challenges to providing adequate and effective health care. Definitions that underlie rules established by institutions may exclude participation of family members defined as critical by those receiving care; therefore, definitions need to be assessed as to the extent they may inhibit or facilitate high-quality care.

The term *family* is not synonymous with the term *nuclear family*, a family unit that consists of a mother, father, and children. The constitution of families can include the *family of origin*, referring to the family in which one grew up (which also may have changed at various points in one's childhood and adolescence), as well as the *extended family*, including those such as grandparents, aunts, uncles, and cousins who may or may not reside with the rest of the family. For most families their cherished pet is also considered a family member and may be given roles associated with care (e.g., cuddling with the care receiver, alerting others in time of emergency, fetching essential items, and providing a loving relationship that promotes healing). Acknowledging and working with the family's definition of its membership is essential in determining who is available and able to assist with care and provide support, as well as who should be involved in health-related decisions.

Structure and composition of those sharing a household may reflect a sense of family that changes not only in response to life-span development (e.g., growing up and launching young adults) but in response to economic situations. Various poverty trajectories can also influence what one views as family, with the effects of chronic poverty, intermittent poverty, and early or late poverty creating different demands on a household and caregivers. As economic situations change, household composition may change in response to economic pressures and job loss, with adult children returning in response to unemployment, underemployment, or need for a home that can accommodate grandchildren following a divorce or other life event. The U.S. Census Bureau reports that in 2006, approximately 2.5 million grandparents were the primary caregivers for their grandchildren. Members of these households may play multiple roles as caregivers to a range of individuals.

Health care considerations need to extend beyond the expectation of a nuclear family as the norm and recognize that a range of family forms can all provide effective care and well-being. The U.S. Census Bureau collects data on various family forms. It reported that in 2009, 10% of opposite-sex couples (6.7 million couples) that lived together were not married. Nearly 8% of married couples were of different races or consisted of one spouse who was Hispanic and the other non-Hispanic. In addition, there were 25.8 million married couples with children, 1.5 million unmarried couples with children, 1.7 million families with a single-parent father and minor children, and 9.9 million families with a single-parent mother and minor children. Many children and adults also live in stepfamilies, or they may live in households characterized by multipartner fertility (i.e., children from more than one father); the care-related stressors in these various families may differ from those where children share the same biological parents.

Family may also be based upon a shared gender/sexual orientation. In 2000, gay and lesbian couples comprised more than 600,000 households. With the legal status of same-sex marriages in flux across the United States, some couples may be legally recognized as married, whereas others have not been given these same rights. Diversity of gender and sexual orientation can also include transsexual individuals (those who transition from one gender to the other). In a study of couples that were established as heterosexual relationships, Christine Aramburu Alegría found that the transition of an individual from one gender to the other could be successfully negotiated within a couple's relationship. The couples were able to reestablish as same-sex relationships after the gender transition of one partner.

Potential Challenges for Diverse Families

Although diversity within families is increasingly recognized, many diverse families are still marginalized. For example, gay and lesbian couples cannot marry in most states, homeless families lack medical resources, and interracial families experience discrimination. Potential consequences of social marginalization that may impact availability and quality of health care include (a) decrease in self-regard, (b) selective disclosure of stigmatizing information, and (c) avoidance of situations that may make a family's diversity uncomfortably salient. Further, families that face the additional challenge of poverty are at increased risk for asthma and learning disabilities among children, and decreased psychological health and increased violence among adults. It is not the family form that creates these health risks, but the poverty and marginalization that are underlying factors in creating an unhealthy environment that impacts family health and well-being.

Many types of diverse families coexist within society. All have their unique challenges, resources, and strengths. In order for health professionals to work effectively with diverse families dealing with health issues, the following strategies can be effective: (a) assess families' challenges, resources, and strengths; (b) cultivate rapport and interviewing strategies that allow open disclosure of family members, health concerns, and concerns about family care; and (c) advocate for support through association with similar others or other supportive venues. Effective change within family dynamics, regardless of family form, must be based on the family's perceptions of their challenges, resources, and strengths (e.g., the approach found in the McGill model of nursing). What may appear to be a challenge to outside observers may in actuality be a perceived strength by the family. Further, families are less likely to commit to modifications in their interactions if they do not believe that they are at risk, that the modifications are likely to be effective, that they are capable of meeting the demands of the situation, or that the efforts required are likely to have the desired outcome.

Additional validation and support can come through socialization with others who are experiencing similar concerns. They can share information, experiences, and attitudes regarding how to create a healthy environment and enhance well-being of family members; how to deal with caregiving demands and challenges; and how to handle those (both inside and outside the family) whose actions and words add stress or complicate efforts to maintain or enhance family health. Couples that include gay, lesbian, and transsexual individuals have benefitted from support groups, as have stepfamilies and single-parent families. Effective support groups may be face-to-face, or they can take place online.

Family as Central Unit in Care

Many of the traditional intervention models in behavioral medicine, psychiatry, and psychotherapy focus on the patient as the unit of care. Families may be marginalized or seen as negative, pathological influences on the patient's adjustment. John Rolland, Froma Walsh, Thomas Campbell, and Susan McDaniel have argued, however, that it is often more productive to view the family, rather than the ill individual, as the unit of care. Using biopsychosocial systems models, with developmentally based family-centered interventions, they have addressed the mutual influence of the family's functioning and the physical or mental illness of a member. Viewing the family as a potential resource, as well as recognizing the challenges and suffering of all the family members, enhances the treatment process. For example, diet regimens following heart surgery are more effective if the family members are included in the behavior modification efforts.

Family as Context of Care

Most caregiving is provided by families, and much of the research published about "family" is based on the responses of an individual caregiver, not the overall family caregiving network. However, Rolland's family systems-illness model (FSIM) provides a useful strengths-based framework for understanding and designing interventions with family systems that are dealing with chronic illness or disability. In this model, family relationships are viewed as resources that can contribute to resilience, not just to risk. The model integrates family system dynamics, life-cycle stage of members, and belief systems with the demands of a particular health condition; it looks at the fit between the demands of the disease and the characteristics of a particular family and seeks to design interventions that work with that "fit." The model focuses on three dimensions important to families dealing with health concerns.

The first dimension examines the psychosocial type of disability or illness. Rather than focus exclusively on disease classification based on biological criteria, the FSIM examines the relationship between biological characteristics and psychosocial demands placed on the affected family member and family. The FSIM clusters health problems together in terms of their patterns of onset, course, outcome, incapacitation, and degree of predictability in the trajectory. *Onset* can be acute (e.g., strokes), which requires rapid mobilization of crisis management skills, utilization of outside resources, and adopting practical changes, or it can be a gradual onset (e.g., Huntington's disease). *Course* can take three forms. In a progressive course (e.g., multiple sclerosis) there are growing demands and challenges; in a constant course (e.g., spinal cord injury or single heart attack), where there is an initial event followed by a stable and predictable time period, there is the potential for family exhaustion even without changing role demands; and in a relapsing or episodic course (e.g., asthma) there are stable periods with low levels of symptoms interspersed with periods of exacerbation requiring family flexibility and alternating between two forms of family organization, with the uncertainty of when a recurrence will appear. *Outcome* involves the family's expectation of a condition in terms of the extent to which it will lead to death or shorten one's life span, ranging from some conditions that do not typically impact life span (e.g., osteoarthritis) to those that may shorten it (e.g., HIV or heart disease) to progressive and often fatal illnesses (e.g., metastatic cancer), or those that can lead to sudden death (e.g., hemophilia). The degree, kind, and timing of *incapacitation* of cognitive, sensory, stamina and/or motor areas influence family stress and role performance, as does level of disfigurement or social stigma. The *degree of uncertainty* of an illness or disability is related to family coping and planning for the future. Some health situations

inherently involve long-term uncertainty and can contribute to family dysfunction and exhaustion, unless the family can find a way to create a meaning of the situation that recognizes uncertainty and works with it.

Because health conditions are dynamic and unfold in a process over time, the second dimension in the FSIM involves the major developmental phases in the illness. Each of the three major phases on an illness involves developmental tasks; at the same time, there are ongoing developmental stages of each family member. The *crisis phase* of the illness ranges from prediagnosis through the initial readjustment and treatment plan period. It involves the task of socialization to the illness during which the family members create a meaning that allows them to retain some sense of mastery; they also grieve the loss of the family and individual as they were before the illness arrived, reorganize their family life and roles, and develop relationships with health care professionals and institutions. It is at this time that professionals need to be very sensitive to whom the family defines as its members, making sure they are included in the process. If the professional meets with the family separately from the ill member to discuss the situation, the family may assume they should not discuss the situation with the ill member. If the illness has a prolonged *chronic stage*, the family may be challenged by burnout, redefining their roles and relationships, and maintaining autonomy for the individual, as well as for all those involved in caring activities. If the illness is such that there is a *terminal phase*, then families grapple with the inevitable death, meaning reconstruction, and family reorganization that goes with it. The third dimension involves characteristics of the family system, including family process and interaction characteristics, the life-cycle stages of the family system and its individual members, multigenerational patterns and legacies in dealing with loss, and belief systems, including elements related to gender, culture, and ethnicity.

Rolland has developed an extension of the FSIM, called a family systems genetic illness model (FSGI), which is tailored to the physical and mental health disorders that are shown to have a genetic component. The FSGI addresses additional concerns, including multicultural issues in genetic screening and testing, the likelihood of developing a disorder based on specific genetic mutations, the timing of the onset compared to the individual's life-cycle stage, clinical severity, and the existence of effective interventions that can alter the onset or progression of the disease. Given the dynamic nature of genomic research, the model has been designed with flexibility to accommodate future discoveries.

Dyadic Process of Family Caregiving and Care Receiving

Although caregiving is often viewed as being provided by families, it is typically single caregivers, generally women (i.e., mothers, wives, sisters, grandmothers, daughters, and daughters-in-law), who provide the bulk of direct care. At a time when many women are holding down employment outside of the home, the average caregiver provides at least 18 hours of care a week, and 20% provide more than 40 hours per week. Studies in the United States and Canada report economic implications of the cost of care and to the occupational situation of the caregiver. Most studies of caregiving focus on the burden associated with care, suggesting that caregivers have lower levels of physical health and psychological well-being, as well as higher rates of stress, isolation, and depression than others (especially in situations involving a care recipient who exhibits behavior problems). Caregivers may simultaneously report stress and satisfaction or a sense of worth in their activities. Diane Feeney Mahoney has suggested that caregiver burden and stress be replaced with the concept of vigilance, a continual oversight of the care receiver's activities, as vigilant caregivers are "on duty" even when they are not "doing things"; this involves more neutral terminology and reflects caregivers' self-perceptions. In addition, an often-reported frustration of family members (especially spouses) is that health professionals do not value or acknowledge the firsthand information they try to provide on their observations of the ill family member; professionals who recognize this vigilant role are better positioned to take advantage of the information provided.

Reports about family caregiving typically are based on perceptions of the primary caregiving member rather than the overall family system. Not only are other caregivers missing in this approach, but the views and opinions of care receivers are generally absent. Caregiving, by its nature, is a dyadic relationship. The change in roles and sense of loss can be experienced by both members of the dyad. The giver and receiver can each experience strain on the relationship, and they may differ in their perception of the situation. Their interactions may change over time, in response to the progress of the illness. Unfortunately, most measures of care receivers have been limited to their physical functioning and severity of impairment. Even in cases where there is a lack of cognitive impairment, it is severity of illness that is used to explain caregiver well-being. Rarely are receivers given a voice in describing the situation and their needs.

Family as Focus of Care in Illness or Disability

During the illness or disability of a member, families often face the challenge of simultaneously managing the immediate, intense emotions and threats to their existing view of the world and their family, as well as the practical demands that accompany the health-related situation. They deal with multiple losses, including the loss of the family as they knew it, of the individual's role performance, and of the way relationships had been. Unfortunately, the needs of families are often overlooked by health care systems, often because professionals lack training in understanding the relationship between family systems and health. This lack of attention can result in serious short-term and long-term complications for both the progress of the patient and the well-being of the family. Some outstanding training programs have arisen in attempts to close this gap (e.g., Chicago Center for Family Health and University of Rochester Family Medicine programs).

For those unable to attend such training, some general principles (beyond those already mentioned) may be helpful in contributing to the growth and well-being of families. For example, the combination of effective formal support from health professionals (e.g., information sharing and collaborative interactions) and informal support from family members, support group participation, and employer cooperation can contribute to a positive caregiving experience. In addition, professionals need to recognize that the role of family caregiver does not end when the care receiver is placed in a nursing home or hospice facility. Most families continue their commitment to a vigilant caregiver role and have concerns for their loved one. Recent variations of Reuben Hill's ABC-X model (e.g., McCubbin's double ABC-X) may be helpful in assessing the factors that mediate the family's (and its members') ability to cope with (and adapt to) a stressful health condition, such as nursing home placement. This model examines the interrelationship between the stressor event, structural factors in the environment, family and extra-familial resources, resource strains, and family members' perceptions of the situation, as well as how this situation changes as families adjust and adapt to conditions. Although many studies speak to the psychosocial aspects of health, the ABC-X directly addresses the "elephant on the table" in many health-related situations, or the additional stress that arises from the direct and indirect economic impact of the situation.

*Colleen I. Murray and
Christine M. Aramburu Alegría*

See also Chronic Illness and Family Management Styles; Constructionist Family Theoretical Perspectives; Coping Management Styles in Families; Defining Family: An Overview of Family Definitions From a Historical Perspective; Economics as It Relates to Family Health; Family Caregiving: Caring for Children, Adults, and Elders With Developmental Disabilities; Family Pediatric Adherence to Health Care Regimen; Genetics and Family Health; Homeless Families; Resilience in Families With Health Challenges

Further Readings

Aramburu Alegría, C. (2008). Relational maintenance and schema renegotiation following disclosure of transsexualism: An examination of sustaining male-to-female transsexual and natal female couples (Doctoral dissertation, University of Nevada, Reno) *Dissertations Abstracts International: Section B, 69* (08). (UMI No. 3316374)

Feeley, N., & Gottlieb, L. N. (2000). Nursing approaches for working with family strengths and resources. *Journal of Family Nursing, 6*(1), 9–24.

Gotler, R. S., Medalie, J. H., Zyzanski, S. J., Kikano, G. E., & Stange, K. C. (2001, April). Focus on the family, part II: Does a family focus affect patient outcomes? *Family Practice Management, 8,* 45–46.

Grzywacz, J. G., & Ganong, L. (2009). A note from the guest editors: Issues in families and health research. *Family Relations, 58,* 373–378.

Lyons, K. S., Zarit, S. H., Sayer, A. G., & Whitlatch, C. J. (2002). Caregiving as a dyadic process: Perspectives from caregiver and receiver. *Journal of Gerontology: Psychological Sciences, 57B,* 195–204.

Mahoney, D. F. (2003, August). Vigilance: Evolution and definition for caregivers of family members with Alzheimer's disease. *Journal of Gerontological Nursing, 29,* 24–30.

McCubbin, H. I., & McCubbin, M. A. (1996). Resiliency in families: A conceptual model of family adjustment and adaptation in responses to stress and crises. In H. I. McCubbin, A. Thompson, & M. McCubbin (Eds.), *Family assessment: Resiliency, coping, and adaptation* (pp. 1–64). Madison: University of Wisconsin.

McDaniel, S. H., Hepworth, J., & Doherty, W. J. (1997). *The shared experience of illness.* New York: Basic Books.

Rolland, J. S. (1994). *Families, illness, & disability.* New York: Basic Books.

Rolland, J. S. (2006). Genetics, family systems, and multicultural influences. *Families, Systems, & Health, 24,* 425–441.

Tornatore, J. B., & Grant, L. A. (2002). Burden among family caregivers of persons with Alzheimer's disease in nursing homes. *The Gerontologist, 42,* 497–506.

Cocaine Exposure and the Neonate

Maternal cocaine use during pregnancy is associated with several medical complications for the mother and her fetus. The sequelae of in utero cocaine exposure extends into childhood and affects not only the child but also the child's family. Women who use cocaine during pregnancy are more likely to live in poverty and in lone-female households. Intimate partner violence and multiple sexual partners are also more common in cocaine users than in nonusers. In this entry, the epidemiology, diagnosis, and biopsychosocial impact of cocaine use during pregnancy are reviewed, as well as options for treatment and follow-up and family support.

Maternal Cocaine Use

According to several studies, cocaine intake among women of childbearing age has increased greatly. It has been estimated that in the United States the prevalence of illicit cocaine use by pregnant women has increased from 2.4% to 4%, with prevalence peaking during the first trimester and declining during subsequent trimesters. There appear to be no racial or ethnic predispositions to maternal cocaine use, although lack of stable housing and lack of resources are associated with illicit drug use in general.

Cocaine can be absorbed rapidly from a variety of sites, including mucous membranes and the gastrointestinal tract. The metabolites (breakdown products) of cocaine are water soluble and are excreted in urine; infants may be exposed to cocaine and its metabolites perinatally either via placental transfer or via accumulation in breast milk.

Diagnosis of Cocaine Exposure

Verbal screening criteria for illicit drug use in pregnancy have not been developed. It has therefore been suggested that open-ended, nonjudgmental questions be used in cases where drug use (including cocaine) is suspected. When mothers are told that the information is important to the well-being of their infant, they are often quite candid about their drug use.

Several methods exist for detection of cocaine metabolites in the adult, including analysis of plasma, urine, and hair. In the newborn, hair, urine, and meconium analyses have been used. During pregnancy, urine toxicology is the analytical method of choice, with metabolites detected up to 72 hours postexposure. In comparison, serum metabolites can be detected up to 8 hours after cocaine use.

Obstetrical Complications Associated With Cocaine Use

Ingestion of cocaine leads to vasoconstriction, hypertension, and tachycardia. Symptoms of acute cocaine use during pregnancy range from hypertension, arrhythmias and myocardial infarctions, pulmonary edema, seizures, psychosis, and intestinal ischemia. Obstetrically, cocaine use is associated with placental vasoconstriction, which decreases uteroplacental blood flow, in turn resulting in intrauterine growth retardation. Cocaine can also stimulate uterine contractions, which can precipitate premature delivery, placental abruption, or both.

Maternal Consequences of Cocaine Exposure

Migraines headaches, which are more prevalent during pregnancy, are even more frequently reported in cocaine users. This in turn may further exacerbate "jitteriness" often reported in individuals "coming down" from a cocaine dose. Cocaine is often used in conjunction with other illicit substances, nicotine, and alcohol. Cocaine addiction may supersede the need for food, leading to cases of malnutrition. In some cases the money to pay for cocaine may come from activities such as prostitution, which may expose the mother to risks of sexually transmitted diseases. The use of cocaine by the mother's partner may increase the risk for violence in the home.

Developmental Consequences of Cocaine Exposure

It has been postulated that the use of cocaine around the time of conception causes cardiovascular abnormalities, as well as gastroschisis, limb defects, and genitourinary malformations. However, there is only limited evidence that perinatal cocaine use is associated with birth defects; the most significant association is with cocaine use and the incidence of cleft palate. Part of the difficulty in discerning true associations between cocaine use and developmental defects is the concomitance of factors that can affect pregnancy outcome, such as poly drug use, smoking, alcohol ingestion, and poor prenatal care.

Neurobehavioral Consequences for the Newborn

Neurobehavioral disturbances, including irritability, tremulousness, lethargy, somnolence, labile state, decreased habituation, and visual tracking difficulties, have been described in cocaine-exposed newborns, although these are usually short term and do not require treatment. Investigators have not been able to demonstrate a direct effect of prenatal cocaine exposure on preschool development (up to the age of 3 years), although newer data suggest that cocaine exerts an indirect effect on development. There is mounting evidence that children with prenatal cocaine exposure are at increased risk for learning disabilities compared to their non–cocaine-exposed peers. While there is no indication that children exposed prenatally to cocaine have lower intelligence quotient (IQ) scores, they have been shown to have lower language abilities and lower verbal IQ than nonexposed infants.

Family Implications of Maternal Cocaine Use

In addition to the biological effects of perinatal cocaine abuse, several studies have shown adverse effects of a maternal or paternal cocaine use on a child's nurturing environment. Parents who use cocaine have difficulties interacting with their infants and, in particular, demonstrate more intrusive and hostile behaviors toward their infants. Additionally, a mother's use of cocaine is a marker of increased maltreatment or placement of an offspring in a foster environment. Taken together, such results suggest that women who use cocaine during pregnancy are at increased risk of serious parenting failure.

Treatment

During delivery and the postpartum period, treatment of the mother for cocaine exposure is generally via supportive care. The mother may be treated with short-acting benzodiazepines to mitigate mood swings, or with serotonin-selective reuptake inhibitors and tricyclic antidepressants for treatment of depression and instability.

Treatment of the newborn for cocaine exposure in utero is also supportive and should include heightened assessment. An optimal nursery environment is recommended and should include features such as avoidance of light and noise stimuli, and gentle handling by as few different caregivers as possible. Promotion of developmentally sensitive positioning, optimal nutrition, and temperature control are also part of the continuum of supportive care. Assessment with the Brazelton Neonatal Behavioral Assessment score can be used to monitor a variety of neonatal parameters, including neurological and motor development.

Beyond the immediate neonatal period, children born to mothers who take cocaine during pregnancy are at increased situational risk. Prenatal drug exposure should be viewed as a marker for family risks of social isolation, poverty, child maltreatment, domestic violence, and inadequate caretaking. Community outreach programs have been shown to be more effective than more formal, office-based programs. Programs that address the broader burden of risk may be more effective than those that address single-risk factors. Supports that assist families to continue to provide care to their infant are important in reducing the overall burden of risk to the family and society.

Debbie Fraser

See also Alcohol Addictions in the Family; Developmental Care of Preterm Infants and the Childbearing Family; Drug Addictions in the Family; Nonmarital Childbearing; Poverty, Children in, and Health Care

Further Readings

Behnke, M., Eyler, F. D., Duckworth, T. W., Garvan, C. W., Hou, W., & Wobie, K. (2005). Outcome from a prospective, longitudinal study of prenatal cocaine use: Preschool development at 3 years of age. *Journal of Pediatric Psychology, 31*(1), 41–49.

Gaither, K. (2008). Cocaine abuse in pregnancy: An evolution from panacea to pandemonium. *Southern Medical Journal, 101*(8), 783–784.

Lee, C.-T., Chen, J., Hayashi, T., Tsai, S.-Y., Sanchez, J. F., Errico, S. L., et al. (2008). A mechanism responsible for the inhibition of neural progenitor cell proliferation by cocaine. *PLoS Medicine, 5*(6), e117.

Leventhal, J. M., Forsyth, B. W. C., Qi, K., Johnson, L., Schroeder, D., & Voota, N. (1997). Maltreatment of children born to women who used cocaine during pregnancy: A population-based study. *Pediatrics, 100*(7), 1–6.

Morrow, C. R., Cuthbertson, J. L., Accornero, V. H., Xu, L., Anthony, J. C., & Bandstra, E. L. (2006). Learning disabilities and intellectual functioning in school-aged children with prenatal cocaine exposure. *Developmental Neuropsychology, 30*(3), 905–931.

van Gelder, M. M., Reefhuis, J., Caton, A. R., Werler, M. M., Drusche, C. M., & Roeleveld, N. (2009). Maternal periconceptional illicit drug use and the risk of congenital malformations. *Epidemiology, 20,* 60–66.

COLLEGE TRANSITION FOR FAMILIES

Each year, millions of families face the challenges and excitement of sending their children off to college, whether it involves moving away from home or not. According to the Institute of Education Sciences, in 2008 nearly 20 million students were enrolled as undergraduates in postsecondary programs. Sixty-two percent were enrolled in 4-year institutions, 26% in 2-year institutions, and 2% in other programs. The number of students enrolled in undergraduate college education has risen dramatically since 1970, up 72%. Today's undergraduate students are different than those from the past with higher percentages of women, ethnically and racially diverse students, and older students. The increases in postsecondary enrollment can be explained in part by the job market demands, as Patricia McDonough reports that 6 of 10 jobs require skills that can only be obtained in postsecondary training and education settings.

The changes observed in the undergraduate student population are reflective of the contemporary societal changes. The median age of marriage for young men and women is now delayed to the mid to late 20s compared to the early 20s in 1950. Likewise, the same pattern is noted for the average age of first-time mothers. The majority of high school graduates enroll in postsecondary programs as compared to a small minority of high school students a century ago. Today's young adults are more mobile, as evidenced by frequent residential moves and job changes. Jess P. Shatkin reports that for young adults between 18 and 34 years of age, the average number of job changes they have is 9.2. The dramatic changes have led to reconsideration of the developmental expectations and characteristics of college-aged students, and this time of life is now labeled as the period of emerging adulthood.

Five main attributes characterize emerging adulthood and hence the undergraduate population, which are age of identity, age of instability, the self-focused age, the age of feeling in-between, and the age of possibilities. Students have opportunities to explore life options related to every aspect of their future employment, housing, and relationships (age of identity). For college students, these explorations involve the learning of new knowledge and skills, the development of new friendships, and the discussion, debate, and testing of new ideas (age of possibilities). Participation in college environments facilitates students' focus on personal growth, self-understanding, and insights in a manner considerably different from their family life (self-focused age). Furthermore, it is not uncommon for students to engage in frequent residential and job changes until they are able to settle into more stable situations as their economic and social situations permit. Lastly, the status of being a college student consigns them to not feeling ready to assume the full responsibilities of adulthood until they are employed and earning the income needed to be self-sufficient (age of feeling in-between).

The extent to which families are prepared and supportive of their youth's transition to college will have important consequences for the college student. The college experience of parents has an important role modeling effect upon students' transition to college. According to McDonough, 82% of students whose parents are college educated enroll in college, whereas 54% of students whose parents are high school graduates enroll in college. Lastly, 36% of students whose parents did not complete high school enroll in college. It is apparent that students whose parents attended college are in a better position to assist their children in the important preparatory steps for enrolling in college by encouraging their children's aspiration for college, developing a college plan, and selecting a college choice.

The transition to college reflects a period of actual and symbolic separation from parents and family members. The transition to college represents moving out of the parents' home into a college dormitory or off-campus housing far from their communities where they grew up. This move brings about many new opportunities and daily choices that college students now make without parental oversight or influence. College students are now free to make their own choices about their meals, friends, purchases for school, and daily schedule of activities, to name a few. For many college students, this is the first opportunity to learn how and to make decisions.

One of the primary skills that students must learn to acquire is academic self-discipline. Although many students have the study skills and motivation that have enabled them to be accepted into college, the self-discipline needed for college is different and more demanding. College students are now responsible for monitoring their own academic performance for meeting course requirements. Unlike their secondary teachers, college educators do not regularly remind or prompt students of the need to study or work on course assignments. The college learning tempo is fast paced compared to that of secondary education, with less time allowed for the length of the instructional program. Classroom credit differs as well, with less dependence on frequent tests and assignments; the college course grade may be predicated on the submission of papers only.

Research has found that freshman students experience increased stress, as demonstrated by their survey responses and reports of students seeking counseling assistance. For some students, the adjustment can be very difficult, and they will have difficulty in coping with this major transition. Some of the symptoms students demonstrate that are indicative of adjustment difficulties are feelings of depression, angry outbursts, and social isolation from family and friends. Other behaviors manifested by students who have adjustment difficulties are trouble sleeping, untoward changes in their behaviors, and worsening of their grades.

For parents, the transition to college is a loss as well. Experts have described the consequences of this loss as creating for many parents the *empty nest syndrome*. The empty nest syndrome refers to the feelings of sadness and loss parents feel when their children have left home to attend college, get married, or live independently, to name a few reasons for their adult children leaving home. For parents, the challenge for them is to learn to redirect their energies to new activities and assume new role responsibilities as parents. For parents, their new challenge is to learn the balance between providing reassurance and support in their new role as parents to a college student as compared to their role when their children were dependent upon them.

Experts have offered a number of suggestions to assist both families and their children who are transitioning to college. These recommendations include fostering open communication between parents and the college student so concerns can be expressed regarding separation from the family, familiar surroundings, and their network of friends. Parents can be encouraged to initiate conversations with their children that include exploration of forthcoming social pressures that are associated with at-risk behaviors of sex, alcohol, and illicit drugs and their consequences; selections of friends; and the differences between high school and college. It is important for parents to encourage their college-age children to seek extracurricular campus and leadership activities as they provide opportunities for learning and expanding their social network and for dealing positively with the transition adjustment to college. The availability of parents to provide ongoing contact support to their children during this stressful transition can be made easier with the use of more affordable technology that enables less expensive phone calls, e-mailing, and texting.

Cecily Lynn Betz

See also Changing Family and Health Demographics; Drinking by Underage Family Members; Families Experiencing Chronic Physical and Mental Health Conditions; Family Experiencing Transitions; Partnering With Families: Family-Centered Care; Rituals, Routines, and Their Influence on Health in Families; Theoretical Perspectives Related to the Family

Further Readings

Betz, C. L., & Nehring, W. M. (2007). *Promoting health care transition planning for adolescents with special health care needs and disabilities.* Towson, MD: Brookes.

Cloitre, M., & Kamboukos, D. (n.d.). *Making the transition to college: A guide for parents.* New York: NYU Child Study Center. Retrieved April 6, 2010, from http://www.aboutourkids.org/articles/making_transition_college_guide_parents_0#

College Board. (2010). *College survival tips.* Retrieved April 6, 2010, from http://www.collegeboard.com/student/plan/college-success/963.html

Gordon, C. (2009, August 19). Tips for making the transition to college. *U.S. News & World Report.* Retrieved April 6, 2010, from http://www.usnews.com/articles/education/best-colleges/2009/08/19/4-tips-for-making-the-transition-to-college_print.htm

Knapp, L. G., Kelly-Reid, J. E., & Ginder, S. A. (2010). *Enrollment in postsecondary institutions, fall 2008; graduation rates, 2002 and 2005 cohorts; and financial statistics, fiscal year 2008* (Publication No. NCES 2010–152). Washington, DC: National Center on Education Science. Retrieved April 29, 2010, from http://nces.ed.gov/pubs2010/2010152rev.pdf

McDonough, P. M. (2004, December). *The school-to-college transition.* Washington, DC: American Council on Education, Center for Policy Analysis. Retrieved on April 6, 2010, from http://www.acenet.edu/bookstore/pdf/2004_IPtransitions.pdf

Minnesota State University. (2010). *The college transition.* Retrieved April 6, 2010, from http://www.mnsu.edu/fye/parents/familyguidebook/collegetransition.html

Reder, S. (2007). *Adult education and postsecondary success* (Policy brief for National Commission on Adult Literacy). New York: Council for Advancement of Adult Literacy. http://www.caalusa.org/content/rederpolicybriefrev10807.pdf

Schmeling, J., Schartz, H., Morris, M., & Blanck, P. (2006). Tax credits and asset accumulation: Findings from the 2004 N.O.D./Harris Survey of Americans with disabilities. *Disability Studies Quarterly, 26*(1). Retrieved July 12, 2010, from http://www.dsq-sds.org/article/view/654/831

Seixas, J., & Youcha, G. (n.d.). *Drugs, alcohol and your kid.* New York: NYU Child Study Center. Retrieved April 6, 2010, from http://www.aboutourkids.org/articles/drugs_alcohol_your_kid

Shatkin, J. K. (2002). *Transition to college: Separation and change for parents and students.* New York: NYU Child Study Center. Retrieved April 6, 2010, from http://www.aboutourkids.org/articles/transition_college_separation_change_parents_students#

University of Montana. (n.d.). *Making the transition from high school to college.* Retrieved April 6, 2010, from http://www.umt.edu/freshman/transition.htm

COMMUNICABLE DISEASE: ADULT AND ELDERLY

One of the most important health concerns is the spread of infectious diseases. An infectious disease is a clinically evident illness resulting from the presence of pathogenic microbial agents, including pathogenic viruses, pathogenic bacteria, fungi, protozoa, and multicellular parasites. Infectious pathologies are also called *communicable diseases* because of their potential of transmission from one person or species to another, either directly or via a vector (e.g., malaria which is transmitted from one person to another via a mosquito vector). During modern history, communicable diseases, although always present, have decreased in incidence and prevalence in developed countries. This situation is not the case in developing countries, where communicable diseases remain one of the most important public health concerns.

The reasons for the decrease of communicable diseases in developed countries are society-wide improvement of hygiene, housing systems, vaccination policy, decrease in average number of persons per dwelling, and better nutrition. However, there are still many groups of individuals who are more susceptible to communicable diseases, including children, adults suffering from chronic illnesses, and the elderly. This entry focuses on communicable diseases in adults and in the elderly. Over the past century agents such as AIDS, SARS (severe acute respiratory syndrome), and Influenza A/H1N1 have been promoted through changes in human behavior, such as increased frequency of traveling and changes in sexual habits. Environmental changes can also influence communicable diseases.

In addition to considering the epidemiology of some of the most important communicable diseases in adults and in the elderly, this entry also discusses the reasons why they are susceptible and what can be done by the individual or the family either for prevention or treatment, as well as the relationship between the family attitudes and practices on the probability of family members being vaccinated.

Epidemiology

The World Health Organization reports that infections cause 14 million deaths annually around the world, and infectious diseases of the respiratory tract alone cause 3 million deaths every year. In adults and the elderly, the types of infectious agent implicated in infectious disease are different from those in children. The most important communicable diseases of adults and the elderly are HIV/AIDS, tuberculosis, and malaria. Moreover, in the elderly other infectious diseases are also prevalent, such as bacterial pneumonia and influenza.

The incidence and severity of infectious diseases increase in the elderly, resulting in a large number of deaths. The most important causes are respiratory problems due to influenza and the pneumococcus (*Streptococcus pneumoniae*) and urinary infections due to gram-negative bacteria. Elderly subjects are much more susceptible to gram-negative bacterial colonization and sepsis than are younger subjects. The reactivation of some latent infections is also more common in the elderly, such as *Mycobacterium tuberculosis* and herpes zoster. One of the most significant public health problems is influenza virus infection, which causes between 10,000 and 40,000 deaths in the United States, of which 90% are in persons over 65 years, as reported by W. H. Chen and colleagues. Infections either in adults or the elderly cause an enormous burden for the person and may also disrupt the family. The care of an elderly parent with recurrent infections places a great burden on the family member in charge of the elderly. There is a direct relationship between immunosenescence (i.e., dysregulation of the immune response with aging) and the increased incidence of infections with aging.

The Host Defense: Innate and Adaptive Immunity

Most microbial infections do not result in death but are controlled with the help of the immune system. Thus, microbial infections activate the host immune response, which aims at eliminating the incoming pathogen through a controlled inflammation. Each microbial organism will elicit a distinct immune response involving different cells of the immune system. The early immune response is termed the *innate response* and is activated through receptors called *pattern recognition receptors*, such as the *Toll-like receptors* (TLRs), which recognize molecular patterns conserved through evolution in a wide range of pathogens. This process is almost an immediate reaction involving mostly polymorphonuclear granulocytes and monocytes/macrophages. Particular molecules on pathogens, called *pathogen-associated molecular patterns*, stimulate intracellular signaling, gene expression, and hence activation of antimicrobial and inflammatory activities. The innate response therefore exerts a rapid first line of defense against the infection, but at the same time also initiates the process leading to eventual development of an adaptive immune response and establishment of immunological memory. The adaptive immune system includes the humoral (e.g., antibody) response and the cellular immune response (e.g., via cytotoxicity and cytokine production). An efficiently functioning immune system will eradicate virtually any infection, be it bacterial, viral, fungal, or protozoan.

Immunosenescence

Immunosenescence affects all parts of the immune response. It has various clinical consequences in the elderly, such as more frequent infection, chronic low-grade inflammation, autoimmune diseases, and cancer. Alteration in the innate immune response may result in an altered activation of the adaptive immune response when altered activation of TLRs impacts antigen presentation. Furthermore, as the number of naive CD4+ T-cells decreases with aging, the possibility of mounting an effective adaptive immune response against a new pathogen also decreases. The dysregulation of the immune system leads to a general alteration of the T-cell response, a decrease in specificity, and loss of memory T-cells. Nevertheless, the direct relationship between the dysregulated immune system and the increased susceptibility to infections with aging is still under intense scrutiny. Susceptibility is also influenced by concomitant illnesses (chronic diseases), medications, psychological status, nutritional status, and altered homeostasis. The susceptibility to infections of the elderly population, independently of immunosenescence, is very heterogeneous as home-dwelling elderly are less susceptible to infection than their frail or nursing home counterparts. In elderly nursing home patients, protein-energy malnutrition, as well as micronutrient malnutrition, is highly prevalent, enhancing immunosenescence. Chronic diseases also contribute to immunosenescence and the consequent susceptibility to infections. Communicable diseases create a huge individual and public health problem. Solutions for their prevention and treatment are urgently needed and should be implemented.

Vaccines and Antibiotics

The fact that an infectious disease has emerged or reemerged indicates immune naïveté in the infected population, or reduced immunity or altered virulence potential, or an increase in antibiotic/antiviral resistance in the pathogen population. The rapid development of vaccines and therapeutics that target these pathogens is therefore essential to limit their spread. By controlling debilitating and often-lethal infectious diseases, vaccines and antibiotics have had an enormous impact on world health.

The market of antibiotics is flourishing. However, the use of antibiotics is limited by the emergence of new strains of resistant microorganisms. Therefore, the discovery of new antibiotics is constantly necessary to win the battle against the invasion of pathogens.

Thus, in this context it is vital to recognize the role of acute infections that can further exhaust a declining immune system and attempt to reduce them by vaccination strategies. It could be even more important to recognize the existence of chronic latent infections, particularly herpes viruses, that provide a continuous antigenic load and chronic stimulation resulting in exhaustion of the T-cells involved.

Vaccinations are critically important to maintain good health in the elderly, in the face of their declining immune competence. Even in the immunocompromised elderly, vaccinations can be beneficial in preventing pneumococcal pneumonia, influenza, and tetanus. The elderly may not achieve an adequate antibody response, but most are able to mount some level of response. The problem with the present form of conventional split or subunit vaccines is that they are not optimal for stimulation of cell-mediated immunity. There are ongoing research efforts to develop strategies for enhancing antibody production in the elderly by vaccines targeting both the humoral and the cellular immune response. An increased frequency of vaccination has also been suggested as a way of improving outcome in the elderly. A positive attitude of families toward adult vaccination—and an even more positive attitude toward elderly vaccination—is essential to achieve vaccination goals.

According to the Advisory Committee on Immunization Practice, infections caused by *Streptococcus pneumoniae* account for 25% to 35% of bacterial pneumonias resulting in hospitalization and thus remain a significant cause of morbidity and mortality in the elderly. The current pneumococcal polysaccharide vaccine is recommended for all individuals aged more than 65 years and those 18 to 64 years of age at risk of pneumococcal infection. The efficacy is still not completely proven in the elderly, but the vaccines are effective against invasive pneumococcal disease.

Influenza is one of the most devastating infectious diseases occurring in the elderly, and this underlies the urgent need for an effective vaccine preventing primary influenza infection. The current vaccine approved in the elderly consists of trivalent inactivated subvirions. Annual vaccination is recommended during fall for all persons over the age of 50 years. Recently in the United States, vaccination of the entire population without age distinction was recommended for the H1N1 pandemic. Even if immunological effectiveness is still controversial in the elderly (increase in protective antibodies), clinical effectiveness is proven; thus annual vaccination remains of critical importance for public health as well as for individuals and families. Nevertheless, the development of newer generations of more effective influenza vaccines is needed.

An efficacious vaccine exists not only in children but also in adults for tetanus, diphtheria, and pertussis. The elderly represent an important risk group both in terms of contracting these diseases and dying from their complications. Combination vaccines are available and should be given at 10-year intervals throughout life, regardless of age.

A large clinical trial on the utilization of a vaccine to prevent herpes zoster and post-herpetic neuralgia in older adults was recently carried out. Vaccination of adults cannot eradicate latent herpes zoster (VZV) but was aimed to significantly decrease zoster clinical infections, including the burden of disease and post-herpetic neuropathy. The effectiveness of the high potency VZV vaccine probably results from the restoration, to some extent, of VZV-specific T-cells to a level above the threshold for herpes zoster clinical manifestations. This implies that immunization against VZV, even if it cannot boost the immune system sufficiently to eradicate the virus, could still be strong enough to enhance acquired immunity to control the clinical manifestations of a persistent pathogen. The vaccine is now recommended once for adults over the age of 50.

Moreover, in the future it would be desirable that a vaccine could be developed against other chronic, nondirectly lethal viral infections that can cause persisting antigenic stimulation, thereby exhausting the immune repertoire. These viruses are mainly cytomegalovirus, herpes simplex virus, Epstein-Barr virus, and, although to a lesser extent in the elderly, perhaps HIV. The possibility of using these vaccines might dramatically increase the immunocompetence of elderly subjects. Identification and treatment of subclinical bacterial infections could be valuable targets for clinical interventions with potential beneficial effects on immunity, for example, the very common urinary tract infections in the elderly. The search for and eradication of these continuous sources of antigenic stimulation could also have an impact on maintenance of immune response with aging.

Communicable diseases are important causes of morbidity and mortality in adults, and especially in the elderly, affecting not only the individuals but also the lives of their families. Progress in society has reduced communicable diseases, at least in the developed countries. However, strategies should be pursued, including antibiotics but mainly by vaccination strategies to prevent these diseases. Globalization and environmental changes are favoring the emergence of new infective agents. A vigorous response from society as well as from families will be important to prevent the appearance of new pandemics.

Tamas Fulop and Eric Frost

See also Access to Health Care: Elderly; Caregiving: Elderly; Case Management for Chronic Illness/ Disability and the Family; Chronic Health Problems and Interventions for the Elderly Family; Community Services Supporting Health; Family Health Maintenance; Immunizations and Vaccinations; Role of Families in Health Promotion

Further Readings

Advisory Committee on Immunization Practice. (1997). Prevention of pneumococcal disease: Recommendations of the Advisory Committee on Immunization Practice (ACIP). *MMWR Recommendations and Reports, 46,* 1–24.
Campos-Outcalt, D. (2010). ACIP immunization update. *Journal of Family Practice, 59*(3), 155–158.
Castle, S. C., Uyemura, K., Fulop, T., & Makinodan, T. (2007). Host resistance and immune responses in advanced age. *Clinics in Geriatric Medicine, 23*(3), 463–479.
Chen, W. H., Kozlovsky, B. F., Effros, R. B., Grubeck-Loebenstein, B., Edelman, R., et al. (2009). Vaccination in the elderly: An immunological perspective. *Trends in Immunology, 30*(7), 361–359.
Derhovanessian, E., Larbi, A., & Pawelec, G. (2009). Biomarkers of human immunosenescence: Impact of Cytomegalovirus infection. *Current Opinion in Immunology, 21*(4), 440–445.
Ippolito, G., Fusco, F. M., Di Caro, A., Nisii, C., Pompa, M. G., Thinus, G., et al. (2009). Facing the threat of highly infectious diseases in Europe: The need for a networking approach. *Clinical Microbiology and Infection, 15*(8), 706–710.
Mossad, S. B. (2009). Influenza in long-term care facilities: Preventable, detectable, treatable. *Cleveland Clinic Journal of Medicine, 76*(9), 513–521.

Websites

Centers for Disease Control and Prevention: http://www.cdc.gov
European Center for Disease Prevention and Control: http://ecdc.europa.eu/en/Pages/home.aspx
Medscape Medical News: http://www.medscape.com
World Health Organization: http://www.who.int

COMMUNICABLE DISEASE: CHILDREN

Communicable or infectious diseases are responsible for killing millions of people every year. At this time in history they take their greatest toll on individuals in impoverished and developing countries. Young children are often the most susceptible members of any population group in part due to their immature immune systems and poor hygienic practices.

To become a communicable disease, an infectious agent must be capable of successful transmission from person to person. Disease results from the presence of pathogenic (disease-causing) microbial agents: viruses, bacteria, fungi, protozoa, and multicellular parasites or their toxins within human tissues. Transmission of infections can occur through direct or physical contact, indirect contact with nonliving objects, or droplet transmission such as sneezing or coughing. The incubation period, or the time interval between the initial infection and first appearance of any signs or symptoms, will vary based on the infectious agent. Fortunately only a small minority of all the microorganisms in the world are pathogenic; the majority are harmless or beneficial.

Prior to the understanding that microscopic organisms were capable of causing disease, individuals with infections were often met with misunderstanding and superstition. Robert Koch, one of the founding fathers of medical microbiology, developed the germ theory of disease and a sequence of experimental steps known as Koch's postulates in the 19th century. These postulates enabled scientists to correctly identify pathogenic agents responsible for causing disease. Modified versions of the postulates are still used today primarily in the identification of unknown or new pathogens. Control and prevention of communicable diseases within human populations involve numerous scientific fields: etiology, the science of pathogen identification; pathology, the study of pathogenic life cycles and their impact on the human body; and epidemiology, the study of how pathogens spread through populations. The study of epidemiology includes investigation of factors and patterns concerning people affected, such as age, sex, occupation, and common history. The medical community then uses this information to better contain, treat, and hopefully prevent future outbreaks.

This entry begins with a description of the immune system and its role in fighting infections. Next, this entry discusses the role of nutrition in fighting communicable diseases. Lastly, this entry discusses some common communicable diseases in children.

The Immune System

For a pathogenic agent to cause disease, it must first overwhelm the immune system. The human immune system is composed of organs and cells responsible for defending the body against foreign substances and pathogenic organisms. It includes the thymus, spleen, bone marrow, lymphoid tissues, and cells produced by them, which patrol the blood and other body tissues.

The cells in the immune system responsible for an individual's immunity to an infectious agent are known as B cells; these cells produce antibodies and later can become memory cells. B cells, which develop in the bone marrow, are capable of remembering an infectious agent if it has been

encountered before and can stimulate a rapid immune response. A more rapid response often helps the immune system to be successful at thwarting a pathogen's attempt to establish an infection. Over time this acquired immunity to various infectious agents builds up in an individual. Children, however, because they have no previous exposure, do not have this immunity and consequently are susceptible to multiple infections early in life during critical periods of development. Newborn children have a form of passive immunity that is an impermanent form of acquired immunity. Antibodies against diseases are acquired naturally from the mother via the placenta to the unborn child. Passive immunity fades over time and generally is gone after six months. Sustained breast-feeding can enhance this immunity and lengthen its duration somewhat.

There is growing awareness of the potential for long-term effects on children caused by repeated early childhood infections. Efforts to control many infectious diseases focus on nutrition, sanitation, and immunization programs. Vaccines are used to help the immune system develop immunity to infectious diseases by introducing pathogenic agents in dead or living but attenuated forms. A vaccination causes antibodies to form, and subsequent immunity to the infection can occur. To confer sustained full immunity, vaccines may need to be repeated at different times in an individual's life. When a large portion of a population is vaccinated against an infectious disease, herd immunity (also called community immunity) is established within the population. Herd immunity is based on a high proportion of individual members being resistant to a particular infection. These high numbers provide resistance to unvaccinated individuals by greatly reducing the chance of an unvaccinated person coming into contract with a person contagious for the infection. If there is concern by parents about multiple vaccinations of their children, then discussion of those concerns with medical personnel is encouraged. Encouraging families to research the subject themselves also can be helpful.

Nutritional Issues

Another issue that affects the ability to successfully thwart or fight off an infection is nutrition. Communicable diseases can have significant impacts on children and cause growth retardation and malnutrition. This can then lead to lasting impacts on the physical and cognitive development of those afflicted. Adequate nutrition is essential to the successful development of children. Nutritional deficiencies are known to be the most profound in poor and developing countries, but they can also impact children in industrialized countries. Any nutrient deficiency, if sufficiently severe, will impair resistance to infection. The relation between infection and malnutrition is known to be synergistic and double-edged. Each worsens the other, and the biological effects of malnutrition and infection combined are greater than the sum of the two. Infections cause adverse effects on an individual's nutritional status, and malnourished individuals are more susceptible to infection.

There have been numerous studies documenting the decrease in infectious disease morbidity in children with additional nutritional supplementation. There have also been studies demonstrating that many infections were increased in prevalence or severity by specific nutritional deficiencies, such as iron deficiency and protein malnutrition. Families that voluntarily limit their protein intake and consume a diet primarily limited to plants can also suffer from protein deficiency if they are not careful, because proteins cannot be synthesized by the body without a balance of all the essential amino acids, and few plants actually contain all of these.

In individuals with any infection, even a subclinical one, a catabolic response occurs that results in the decrease of intestinal absorption of nutrients. The range of infections associated with malabsorption is wide and include bacterial, viral, protozoans, and intestinal helminthes. For instance, protein, fat, and carbohydrate absorption are reduced in children with diarrhea caused by infections such as rotavirus, *Escherichia coli*, and *Shigella*. Also children with acute diarrhea and respiratory infections have been found to be inhibited in their absorption of multiple vitamins, particularly vitamin A. Vitamin A malabsorption commonly occurs with systemic febrile illnesses and has been shown to be particularly severe in children with measles and chicken pox. Other vitamins that have been shown to lower the immune response to infections if children are deficient in them or experience malabsorption leading to a deficiency in them during an infection are ascorbic acid, B vitamins, copper, zinc, and selenium. Families with children

who have had prolonged infections or limited or poor diets may need to be referred to a family nutritionist.

Communicable Diseases in Children

The types of infectious diseases children are exposed to vary based on where they live or travel in the world. Many pathogenic agents or their vectors are endemic to certain geographical regions and thus do not have a global impact, but are still highly significant in their mortality rates. Rates of infection also vary greatly due to the economic capability of the region. Illness and death from infectious disease overall is much lower in developed countries such as the United States. The use of antibiotics and vaccinations and the availability of medical personnel and services have greatly lowered the number of common communicable diseases impacting children in industrialized countries. Additional reasons for this lower rate are geographical location, nutrient availability, and the country's infrastructural sanitation capabilities. Industrialized and developing countries, however, still have potential sources of infectious outbreaks and need to continually inform and educate their populace to remain vigilant.

Families require continued education about proper hygiene methods and sanitation procedures, especially those concerning fresh imported foods and the sanitation of toys and other objects routinely handled by young children. Infants and toddlers who attend day care or who accompany parents to shelters are often exposed to a myriad of infections due to close proximity and poor hygiene skills. Children in diapers present multiple opportunities for fecal-oral disease transmission, causing other children and adults attending to those children to be at high risk for transmitting enteric diseases. Investigation into the role of fomites in the transmission of diarrhea in day care centers has shown widespread fecal coliform contamination of environmental surfaces. Families also may wish to limit children's exposure to hospitals for two reasons: (1) the presence of typically high numbers of immunocompromised patients in the hospital who are more susceptible to childhood infections, and (2) the rising number of nosocomial infections. Because of their lack of hygiene understanding, children may be at higher risk for transmitting infections or becoming infected. Other potential sources of infection to the general public arise from worldwide travel of citizens, visitors from other countries, adoptees, and imported foods, goods, and equipment, all of which conceivably could have come into contact with or contain infectious agents. Before traveling to foreign countries, families need to research what pathogens are common to the region and update their vaccinations if necessary. Families should inform their physicians before they travel internationally and should consult their family physician if an illness from an infectious agent occurs post-travel. Treatment without this information will be made under the assumption that the pathogen is endemic to the region. Numerous pathogens are endemic to tropical and subtropical regions and not temperate.

Whereas some of the most common communicable diseases in children worldwide are listed here, some of these diseases an individual will only come into contact with if they travel internationally:

Viral—chickenpox; rotavirus; respiratory syncytial virus (RSV); cold sores (Herpes simplex); hand, foot, and mouth disease; impetigo; measles; mumps; rubella (German measles); slapped cheek syndrome (parvovirus); common cold; influenza (seasonal flu); meningitis; glandular fever (infectious mononucleosis); hepatitis A; and AIDS

Bacterial—tuberculosis (TB), whooping cough (pertussis), diphtheria, scarlet fever, shigella, conjunctivitis, typhoid, and cholera

Protozoan—African sleeping sickness, malaria, and leishmaniasis

Multicellular parasites—scabies, head lice, threadworm (pin worms), and helminths

Many infectious diseases that are responsible for killing millions in poor and developing countries are uncommon in the United States, either because they are not endemic or because they have been successfully controlled through sanitation methods or through the use of antibiotics or vaccines. For example, children in the United States and other industrialized countries are vaccinated for rotavirus; however, in poor countries this virus can still cause death in children. Rotavirus is spread through respiratory secretions, person-to-person contact, and contaminated environmental surfaces.

Dehydration from diarrhea frequently occurs, and death can result if medical treatment is not available. Also major epidemic infections such as cholera and typhoid fever have been controlled through sanitation efforts.

In the United States many of these diseases are proactively treated against through the use of childhood immunization programs. The Centers for Disease Control and Prevention's recommended vaccination schedule for children 0 to 6 years of age for 2010 includes vaccinations for the following infections: hepatitis A, hepatitis B, rotavirus, diphtheria, tetanus, pertussis, Haemophilus influenzae type b, pneumococcal disease, inactivated poliovirus, influenza, measles, mumps, rubella, varicella, and meningococcal infection.

Mary Ruth Griffin

See also Access to Health Care: Child Health; Adults With Childhood-Acquired Conditions

Further Readings

Abbas, A. K., & Lichtman, A. H. (2006). *Basic immunology: Functions and disorders of the immune system* (3rd ed.). Philadelphia: Saunders.

Behrman, R. E., Kliegman, R., & Jensen, H. B. (2007). *Nelson textbook of pediatrics* (18th ed.). Philadelphia: Saunders.

Centers for Disease Control and Prevention. *Recommended immunization schedule for persons aged 0 through 6 years—United States 2010.* Retrieved March 25, 2010, from http://www.cdc.gov/vaccines/recs/schedules/downloads/child/2010/10_0-6yrs-schedule-pr.pdf

Parashar, U. D., Hummelman, E. G., Bresee, J. S., Miller, M. A., & Glass, R. I. (2003). Global illness and deaths caused by rotavirus disease in children. *Emerging Infectious Diseases, 9,* 565–572.

Scrimshaw, N. S., & SanGiovanni, J. P. (1997). Synergism of nutrition, infection, and immunity: An overview. *American Journal of Clinical Nutrition, 66,* 464S–477S.

Shors, T. (2009). *Understanding viruses.* Sudbury, MA: Jones & Bartlett.

Totora, G. J., Funke, B. R., & Case, C. L. (2007). *Microbiology: An introduction* (9th ed.). San Francisco: Benjamin Cummings.

World Health Organization. (1993). *The management and prevention of acute diarrhoea: Practical guidelines* (3rd ed.). Geneva, Switzerland: Author.

COMMUNICATION IN FAMILIES RELATED TO HEALTH AND ILLNESS

Families play a significant role in a patient's response to illness and in the process of both physical and emotional healing. Communication within families and between the family and health care professionals can greatly affect health outcomes, both for the patient and for the family as a whole. Often during the course of an illness, the family is confronted with changes in the patient's condition that warrant decision making, negotiation of caregiving tasks, and changes in the day-to-day function and communications within the family. Families may experience stress in multiple relationships, affecting the quality of patient care. As during other times of crisis, difficult family systems patterns, perhaps going back generations, can resurface. Unresolved loss issues may become salient. The good news is that there is then the opportunity to heal old wounds and create new interaction and communication patterns. Meanings created to understand and cope with a health crisis can significantly affect the outcomes for the patient and the family as a whole.

During times of illness, uncertainty and expectations can instigate conflict between families and health care providers. Expectations and desires of families may differ with the treatment, care, and outcomes targeted by health care providers. Moreover, health care providers may differ in their emphasis or values. Inadequate information and preparation regarding changes in care, communication problems with providers, and providers' enforcement of institutional policies and procedures can be sources of confusion, conflict, and frustration. Additionally, when the family's care expectations are not met, they may question or doubt providers' genuine interest and concern for the patient, the patient's family, or both. However, when family members experience empathy from hospital staff, when they feel listened to, and when time is taken to solicit their questions, concerns, and insights, the health care process is more comfortable and more effective. Family members praise nurses and doctors who listen to them, who seem to respect them, who share openly and explain

procedures and options in a way they can understand. This entry discusses the involvement of the family and community during health crises and provides recommendations for both families and health care providers to enhance the health care process.

Family Healing

Facing a crisis together can make families aware of their strengths. As they try to maintain their equilibrium, they may call on previously underused talents or resources, or they may turn to spiritual values that enrich their lives. People who have been avoiding painful issues within the family may be pushed or empowered to revisit them, with the potential for forgiveness, increased understanding, the healing of old wounds, and the strengthening of relationships. New communication skills are learned, and increased mutual respect and support can ensue.

Community Involvement

Friends, neighbors, and faith communities can provide much needed support for a family. To stay close to family, a patient may choose local care rather than be referred to a specialist at a large medical facility, and may choose a doctor he or she already knows. Parents of another patient may chose care at a metropolitan university hospital some distance from home, with the parents accompanying the child. For this family, extended family and community support (coworkers, church members) may make a crucial difference by providing meals or looking after other children. Community support in this case might also involve volunteers or support groups in the city where the hospital is located, contacted through hospital staff. Generally, then, it is a good idea for family members to talk with others, to give them the opportunity to help.

Sometimes, however, the community can be a stress rather than a support, for instance if a child is teased and isolated from friends because of the nature of the child's disease. In a situation like this, it is helpful for someone, perhaps a social worker, to talk with school officials to raise awareness and limit bullying.

Recommendations

In this section, fourteen suggestions are provided for both families and health care providers that can facilitate communication and support healing, and thus make the health care process more effective.

Families

1. Meet, shake hands, and make eye contact with each health care provider.

2. Stay available; be involved; keep lines of communication open.

3. Speak up. You have a right to ask questions and to understand. Your insight can be very valuable to successful patient care.

4. Help the patient (and others) stay calm. Learn breathing or mindfulness practices that can help everyone stay calm and clear. This supports healing.

5. Activate your support system: Consider talking to extended family, friends, neighbors, and your faith community, as well as hospital staff (e.g., clergy, family therapists, social workers) and volunteers. You do not have to do it alone.

6. Take care of yourself; share responsibilities and take turns; get some rest.

7. Remember to include and care for all of the children (both sick and well). Take time to talk with them and hear their concerns.

Health Care Providers

1. Conduct a brief initial interview to get an overview of the family system. Include a simple genogram in the chart. Remember that there is a wide variety of family structures across and within cultures; ask, do not assume, who is regarded as family.

2. Include the family from the time the patient first enters the health care system. Keep them informed and actively consult them, especially during times of anticipated transition.

3. Think of everyone involved as a team—nurses, doctors, family members, social workers, family therapists, clergy, and any future home care professionals.

4. Think about the whole family, including those you don't see. Dad or Grandmother may be home taking care of the other children but still is an important participant.

5. Remember the power of mindfulness. Teach patients how to calm themselves; teach parents how to calm themselves and their children. These practices can enhance the experience of a hospital stay, shorten its length, and also reduce the level of required medication.

6. Encourage family members to activate their support networks; help them identify potential helpers from within the extended family system, their friends, and other community members.

7. Connect families with additional sources of information and support (support groups, Internet, volunteers, others who are going through similar experiences). This is especially valuable for families and individuals far from home and those dealing with a chronic illness.

Linda G. Bell

See also Factors Influencing Family Health Values, Beliefs, and Priorities; Family Adherence to Health Care Regimen; Family Emotional Climate and Mental Health; Family Experiencing Transitions; Family Therapy; HIPAA: Privacy Laws and the Family

Further Readings

Broome, M. E., & Stuart, W. P. (2006). Interventions with families of an acutely or critically ill child. In D. R. Crane & E. S. Marshall (Eds.), *Handbook of families and health: Interdisciplinary perspectives* (pp. 451–456). Thousand Oaks, CA: Sage.

McDaniel, S., Hepworth, J., & Doherty, W. (1992). *Medical family therapy: A biopsychosocial approach to families with health problems.* New York: Basic Books.

McGoldrick, M., Gerson, R., & Petry, S. (2008). *Genograms: Assessment and intervention* (3rd ed.). New York: Norton.

Patterson, J. (2005). Weaving gold out of straw: Meaning-making in families who have children with chronic illness. In W. M. Pinsof & J. L. Lebow (Eds.). *Family psychology* (2nd ed., pp. 521–548). New York: Oxford University Press.

Wanzer, M. B., Booth-Butterfield, M., & Gruber, K. (2004). Perceptions of health care providers' communication: Relationships between patient-centered communication and satisfaction. *Health Communication, 16,* 363–383.

COMMUNITY RESOURCES FOR FAMILIES RELATED TO HEALTH

Having symbolic and tangible influences on families, communities offer various types of resources for families in need. These resources, defined broadly, include natural, economic, social, and human resources available in the community. More specifically related to family health, community resources indicate any agencies, organizations, programs, or individuals that deliver health services to the family as well as social support and social capital. Community resources that are available to families have the potential for being helpful when families are in need. These resources contribute to prevent, maintain, and promote the health of families. Families who access and utilize community resources are better able to prevent and cope with life stressors and have positive health outcomes. Following a brief introduction for emerging importance of community resources in family health, this entry discusses various types of community resources and focuses on the roles of community resources in relation to the health of the family.

Emerging Importance of Community Resources

For the past few decades, the roles of community resources in shaping the lives of family have been of interest to researchers in the fields of health, nursing, family studies, and social sciences. The increased attention to community resources related to family health stemmed from an understanding of the complex etiology of health problems and a sense of frustration that the health needs of the family are unable to be effectively met in the health care system. At the same time, the limitations in individual oriented health interventions for health behavioral change among public health professionals and the importance of the interaction between humans and their environments have led to an adapted ecological approach to address family health issues and provide interventions. Human ecology theory emphasizes the importance of social context and the larger social systems as influences on human development in the family. The roles of community resources on family health draw on the perspective of this theory, which considers the interrelationship between individuals within the family as well as between the family and the community.

Community Resources

Despite its common use in the literature, the concept of community resources has been defined and applied differently by researchers. Broadly defined, community resources include natural, economic, social, and human resources in the community. On the basis of specific interest for families related to health, community resources can be defined as sources of supplies or supports in the community that enable the family to meet and handle its health-related situations. These resources can be tangible as well as intangible. Tangible community resources include physical and organizational structures, services, and facilities for education, health, recreation, leisure, welfare, religion, transportation, and housing. They also encompass other entities such as funds, laws, and policies, and individuals that deliver those services (e.g., community workers and community nurses) within the community. Intangible community resources include norms and values, social capital, emotional social support, and a sense of solidarity.

Growing attention has been paid to social support and social capital as important community resources. Social support affects the health and well-being of the family by providing a sense of belonging and approval with the family as well as preventing and buffering life stresses. In particular, social capital (i.e., nonmonetary social resources inherent in the social networks and relationships) is considered a potential source of positive health outcome and well-being for individuals, families, and communities. Ichiro Kawachi and Lisa Berkman suggest three plausible pathways by which community social capital may affect health. First, social capital promotes rapid distribution of health information, increases adoption of healthy norms of behavior, and exerts social control over deviant health-related behavior. Second, social capital creates organizational processes to ensure access to local services and amenities such as transportation and community health clinics that are directly relevant to health. Finally, social capital could influence the health of individuals through psychosocial processes such as coping and adaptation as well as providing emotional and instrumental support.

Family Needs and Community Resources

Families have different structures (e.g., extended, nuclear, single-parent, stepparent, single adult living alone), sizes, and compositions of members who are in different stages of the life cycle (i.e., newborns, children, adolescents, nonelderly adults, and elderly). The needs and the problems that each family has vary. Some families experience illness, loss, or disturbances in internal family dynamics. Some families have lack of financial resources to seek adequate health care. Some families experience multiple problems simultaneously, such as poverty and illness, as well as problems in physical, psychological, and social functioning. Often, one type of resource that may be suitable for one family may be inappropriate for others. That is, all the community resources are not uniformly important to all the families. Specific community resources have special importance to different families. For example, families that experience financial difficulty are more likely to meet their needs from vouchers or reimbursements for allowable expenses. Families with schoolchildren would meet more of their needs through school policies. These policies ensure students' healthy diet by offering more fruits and vegetables at lunch and reducing fat food items in vending machines and other competitive food outlets at school. For families with preschoolers and elderly members, community-based resources for child day care and elder care as well as transportation would be more important to meet their needs.

The beneficial effects of community resources on families are derived not only by their availability but also by utilization of those resources for specific purposes. For effective and appropriate utilization of community resources, it is important that the family identify and access resources that they need. The community/public health nurse, as a provider of information and health care, referral agent, liaison, or resource coordinator, has played a critical role in assisting families to identify and utilize community resources. Currently emerging nongovernment-based community workers such as *community navigators* and *community guides* also play roles in assisting families to mobilize and utilize community resources. Appropriate utilization of community resources may not only provide much needed family care and services to meet their needs but also can reduce adverse health outcomes and promote health and well-being of the family.

Conclusion

Tangible and intangible community resources have the potential to reduce adverse health outcomes and promote the health and well-being of the family. These resources provide adequate preventive measures, treatment interventions, and support for families who are in need, especially poor and marginalized families. To successfully help families meet their needs, it is important to understand the family's circumstances, identify their needs, and locate resources in the community that fit their unique concerns. Moreover, the development and mobilization of a network of community resources would meet the diverse and unique needs and improve the health of the family.

Jin Young Choi

See also Community Services Supporting Health; Resources for Families During Life-Threatening Illnesses; Systems Supporting Family Health

Further Readings

Diclemente, R., Crosby, R. A., & Kegler, M. C. (Eds.). (2002). *Emerging theories in health promotion practice and research: Strategies for improving public health.* San Francisco: Jossey-Bass.

Kawachi, I., & Berkman, L. F. (2000). Social cohesion, social capital, and health. In L. F. Berkman & I. Kawachi (Eds.), *Social epidemiology* (pp. 174–190). New York: Oxford University Press.

Maurer, F. A., & Smith, C. M. (2009). *Community/public health nursing practice: Health for families and populations.* St. Louis, MO: Saunders.

COMMUNITY SERVICES SUPPORTING HEALTH

Community services supporting health can be defined as the network of systems and structures that correspondingly facilitate their comprehensive design, implementation, and evaluation while assisting communities enhance the health and well-being of families. When these systems and structures are designed and maintained with a view toward meeting the needs of those that use them, an essential public health function can be attained on behalf of all families. Implicit in the existence of well-integrated systems and structures contributing not only to the health but also the well-being of families is the recognition that health promotion can help families lead healthier lives. This entry reviews the conditions needed to facilitate the emergence of a continuum of community services likely to enhance the health and well-being of families, why and how these services can support family health, as well as how these might be structured and integrated to meet the evolving needs of families in the 21st century.

According to the World Health Organization's (WHO) *Ottawa Charter for Health Promotion*, health promotion can also contribute to the social, economic, and environmental conditions needed to achieve positive individual and population health outcomes. The charter's three essential principles are equally relevant today as they were at its inception in 1986. These include (1) advocacy for health so that it will be achieved, (2) enabling populations to reach their full health potential, and (3) mediating between stakeholders in the pursuit of health. According to the WHO, societies successful in advancing health promotion have done so by working across sectors, such as (1) enacting public policy predicated on public health, (2) creating supportive environments for health, (3) strengthening community action for health, (4) developing the personal skills of individuals to enhance their health, and (5) reorienting health services in support of populations. These streams are equally significant in the 21st century given their potential to advance prevention services and promote systems integration, as well as to ensure access to families and facilitate their participation.

In 1997, the *Jakarta Declaration* on Leading Health Promotion into the 21st Century provided a blueprint for health promotion to be advanced worldwide despite persistent challenges. The precursor conditions upon which people's ability achieving health are predicated upon, as well as the attainment of commensurate levels of social and economic integration for the larger society,

continue to be an ideal sought by many countries worldwide. According to Maurice Mittelmark, the *Jakarta Declaration* recognized the need for nations to increase their levels of societal responsibility for health as well as equity in health. Recommendations advanced were generated in response to challenges still evident today: (a) poverty (still the greatest threat to health), (b) rapid urbanization, (c) demographic shifts pointing to sizable increases in older adults, (d) high prevalence of chronic diseases, (e) prevalence of drug and substance use, (f) sedentary life patterns, (g) civil strife, (h) domestic violence, (i) high incidence of mental health disorders, and (j) environmental degradation. In addition, new and emerging infectious diseases, often resistant to antibiotics, as well as increasing levels of international migration and increasing international travel, continue exacerbating the health of populations and families globally. Moreover, the global presence of multinational corporations, continued degradation of the environment, and the imperative for people to earn a living have also contributed to alienate and stigmatize migrants, while precipitating internal conflict within host nations as well as international rifts. These factors have ultimately contributed to making the health of many families much more vulnerable.

More than three decades since the founding of the WHO's Health for All movement, and more than a quarter of a century since the addition of the "equity in health" phrase into its language, the systems and structures linked to the design, implementation, and evaluation of community services supporting health still fall short in many nations, especially poorer ones. The adoption of the *Declaration of Alma-Ata* in 1978 is also worth noting in that it was another milestone in the Health for All movement launched by the WHO's World Health Assembly. Building on the recognition of health as a fundamental social goal, the declaration provided a slightly different paradigm for health policy by emphasizing people's involvement, cooperation between sectors, and primary health care as key elements. Unfortunately, today there are persistent limitations imposed on the poor and uninsured's ability to access community services supporting health across many nations. Despite significant improvements relative to medical discovery and technology, the socioeconomic profile, health status, and morbidity patterns of millions, especially those living in nations with developing economies, continue to fall short of achieving health and well-being as defined by the WHO.

Community Conditions That Facilitate Health Services

Extant systems and structures designed within communities in support of health and health promotion can succeed when there is a high level of local autonomy and effective policy making. Independent of the systems and structures in support of family health or a comprehensive complement of community-based services to be made available, it is essential that both local needs and context inform their design, implementation, and evaluation. Policy making at the national level must always account for refinements that are warranted locally to accommodate diverse conditions. Furthermore, health-related planning, policy making, and action that are well integrated often reflect the assets as well as the local needs.

The incorporation of participatory processes is also crucial in mobilizing families to adopt a population perspective responsive to their local trends and needs. Policies and programs that respond to concrete community needs generally include everyday people in their identification as well as encouraging their continuous engagement during the development of specific policies. Participation not only enhances the capacity-building ability of those involved, but also generates the design of indigenous solutions. Similarly, the continuous collective experience often enables participants to tackle more complex issues in the future. Moreover, as people enhance their abilities identifying local conditions and needs as well as potential solutions, the more likelihood that community-level policy making supportive of health promotion can be realized.

Taking into account local culture and context (history, values, ethics, etc.) is also equally critical before designing and implementing community services intended to support families. Designing and implementing services in the community always call for intersector collaboration and thus the need for representation of key stakeholders as active participants, who can ensure both breadth and depth, and a proposed course of action. Thus, inclusion of all community stakeholders, as well as achieving consensus regarding an action plan, is equally vital when there is the need for intersector collaboration. Wide representation and a high level of consensus regarding next steps can also enhance the likelihood that future programs will continue to be responsive to identified local needs.

Equally important is the process of articulating to the public at large what is needed, that is, the use of effective dissemination strategies likely to increase the public's understanding of the community's identified needs as well as key determinants of health that must be tackled. Empowering families engaged in identifying the key determinants of health within a community and in refining decisions that will likely influence their health are probably two of the most important steps in planning responsive local community services. These processes also require wide inclusion, carefully identifying special needs, recognizing extant social and economic inequities, maximizing opportunities to enhance the health of families, soliciting wide public input, providing leadership development locally, effectively disseminating findings to the public at large, and identifying the essential elements to help build and sustain a healthy community.

Promoting social responsibility for health inclusive of wide participation across a community can also help lay the groundwork for enhancing both the formulation of responsive health policymaking and the participation of public and private sector stakeholders and the public at large. Moreover, the promotion of social responsibility for health that is inclusive also has the potential to expand the partnerships needed to advance health promotion, while growing local indigenous capacity through self-empowerment and leadership development. Communities with the self-direction, leadership, and inclusiveness to collectively articulate a vision for all families to attain health and well-being also have the potential to secure an infrastructure for health promotion.

Community Services That Support Health

In the 21st century, health and well-being are increasingly linked with prevention and population health. Implicit in the attainment of well-being are factors such as social status, income, education, employment, working conditions, access to health services, and the quality of one's physical and ecological environment. All of these dimensions are observable and can be made tangible within neighborhoods and communities worldwide.

Adam Wagstaff has documented that poverty and poor health outcomes are clearly intertwined and that poorer countries tend to report worse health outcomes than those that are better off. Within nations, the poor tend to have worse health outcomes than the rest of the population. According to Wagstaff's line of reasoning, poverty gives rise to ill health and, simultaneously, ill health keeps the poor at the bottom of the economic strata. Collectively, these factors tend to foster segmentation and disenfranchisement among certain subgroups and create different living conditions—each with significant impact on health status. More often than not, these subgroups include ethnic minorities, people of color, newly arrived immigrants, and those who are marginalized because of their lifestyle. Tackling inequities across and within groups continues to be one of the most serious dilemmas in rich and poor nations alike.

In this regard, Waqar Ahmad and Hannah Bradby's writings on the role of ethnic identity on health inequity serve as a vivid reminder of its impact and, especially, the contribution of socioeconomic position and racism to group expeiences. Similarly is Simon Dein's notion that the role of social class and gender, as well as the structure of social relationships within and across different ethnicities also needs to be taken into account in studying the relationship between ethnicity and health. Specifically, Dein identifies the need for discerning risk and protective factors as well as the effects of context. Thus, in thinking about the influence of family and social networks on health behavior, it is imperative that both the role of context and culturally defined constructs for the family be incorporated into the analytic framework.

Structuring Community Services to Meet the Needs of Families

A trend that is self-evident is the increasing provision of more services outside of hospitals and their availability closer to one's community. Most communities are committed to a vision that aims to improve the quality of life of each of its residents and to promoting their independence while also fostering support and cohesion among them and their families and other support systems.

Independent of the need for ensuring that family health and well-being will be maximized, community services represent an important asset within the local infrastructure. This situation makes it imperative for community stakeholders to jointly assess service development within the context of the local environment to ascertain that the priorities of those in need of assistance can be met close to their neighborhood. This determination is likely to capitalize on extant support systems and family and social networks, especially during an illness or when one is in need of care services.

On the other hand, the needs of families and their members span well beyond health. Equally important are, for example, services through participation in daily exercise, sports, education, volunteering, the arts, reading groups, music, advocacy, and so forth, as venues that fulfill and foster self-enhancement. How people view and feel about themselves is determined, in part, by their everyday lives and those they engage. Thus, the cultural and ethnic background and needs of families, as well as the local culture of communities, are likely to influence the design, structure, and composition of services.

This is why it is important to note at the outset the need for identifying locally indigenous approaches tailored to local circumstances that capitalize on the community culture, context, and assets. Those who are proactive in the decision making regarding their health tend to exhibit higher levels of self-efficacy and therefore are more likely to attain a clearer sense of well-being.

No one prescription of an array of community services in support of health constitutes perfection and therefore should not be replicated unless it is responsive to the needs of its prospective users. Rather, a complement of community services supportive of health must be founded on findings derived from a comprehensive needs assessment of the families it will serve, including all identified local resources and assets. Moreover, it will be critical to determine plans for subgroups that are particularly vulnerable, including clusters that may be invisible to many. The more the differences and the level of stigmatization are evident in a particular subpopulation, the greater likelihood it will require special attention.

Following is a discussion of the major components likely to provide a complement of community services supporting health, with a particular focus on the families to be served as well as to the most effective integration of complementary services. Therefore, the emphasis must be on developing simple approaches tailored to local circumstances, especially the needs of vulnerable families. In thinking about the needs of those to be served, there are several themes worth noting. These include (a) options, (b) access, (c) autonomy regarding families' health and care, and (d) independence.

What Constitutes Community Health?

The array of services to be provided across societies may vary depending on the context and prevailing level of advancement attained. On the other hand, access to *primary care* is an essential feature of one's health care, as is receiving *specialty care* when appropriate. The span of health professionals may include nurses, nurse practitioners, physician assistants, licensed vocational nurses, speech therapists, as well as physiotherapists among others. There is every reason to consider a close working relationship between these two levels of care as a means of service improvement and integration.

The role of pharmacists is critical in that they are often the first health professional contacted by community residents for consultation. This is especially evident among the elderly as well as those who are homebound. Pharmacists can have substantial knowledge of patients to whom they dispense medications and can provide information as well as support and care. Therefore, they have the ability to educate people diagnosed with common conditions, such as diabetes or hypertension, and to disseminate appropriate information relative to other important health and social services.

Access to treat minor emergencies is another important feature supporting health given that oftentimes one requires immediate attention outside of a hospital's emergency department. In fact, the likelihood is that if one seeks attention for a minor ailment in a hospital's emergency department, the delay in receiving treatment will be substantial as well as the high cost associated with it. Ensuring access enables patients to be assessed by a health care provider and to be directed to appropriate service for further treatment.

Access to sexual health services is critical given the need to improve prevention to treatment of sexually transmitted infections, human immunodeficiency virus, and reproductive health. Services provided in communities are warranted given that it is not economical to deliver these in hospital-based settings under the care of specialists. Moreover, there is every reason to include nurses and nurse practitioners in the delivery of this type of care, including backup by specialists for at-risk cases. Locally based care would also likely draw particularly vulnerable subgroups, such as teenagers.

Access to mental health services is another crucial component given what can occur when people are faced with stress and crisis. By having mental health professionals working closely with the emergency care and primary care staffs, appropriate referrals can direct attention and care early on. These services are especially critical to the most vulnerable—young children and adolescents—and particularly ethnic minorities, those with learning disabilities, sexual minorities, the homeless, and truant and adjudicated youngsters. Similarly, there is the need to attend to the mental health needs of the elderly who suffer from mental health disorders but who are otherwise healthy and living independently. In this regard, the existence of 24-hour crisis intervention teams committed to serving vulnerable populations is critical.

Access to cancer prevention is another crucial component. Breast, cervical, prostate, and skin cancer screening, for example, can be offered in community primary care settings, including timely feedback of test results. Colon cancer is another screening program worthy of inclusion aimed at men and women.

Direct *access to physical therapy and occupational therapy (as well as other allied health professionals)* offers the potential to increase patient satisfaction while saving primary care physicians time.

Reaching out to hard-to-reach populations (e.g., substance and intravenous drug users; the homeless and people living in shelters; people living in residential homes or transitional housing; ethnic minorities, newly arrived immigrants, and migrant farmworkers; people with disabilities; lesbian, gay, bisexual, and transgendered populations; sex workers; etc.) is another needed service, given that these groups may not necessarily initiate access to traditional services (health, social services, welfare, housing, etc.) on their own. In fact, these groups may altogether avoid entering traditional systems of care for a whole host of reasons. Outreach to each of these groups needs to be specifically tailored and may warrant inclusion of wraparound services—the integration of health, housing, primary care, mental health care, substance misuse, case management, and recovery, among others.

Women's health services that are women focused and family centered and that are available to them and their partners/spouses, including how and where to give birth, are also needed (access to midwives, delivering babies at birthing centers or at home, access to prenatal and postnatal care, options regarding pain relief). Attention must also be given to domestic violence, as pregnant women are at an increased risk.

Access to immunization services, especially for disadvantaged children, the elderly, newly arrived immigrants, people whose lives are transitory, and adults who may not have been vaccinated as children, is also critical. Opening access to immunizations requires a paradigm change relative to location (schools, housing developments, walk-in centers, etc.). It is also important that access to immunization services occurs in the evenings and on weekends.

Access to health care and support services for teenagers is another critically important aspect of any array of community services. Teens do not always use traditional care services. Options for service provision within school settings, recreation centers, and the like, while ensuring their acceptability and, especially, the teens' comfort, accessing sexual health and/or mental health services will be essential.

People with learning disabilities also deserve consideration and inclusion within the planning of community services supporting health. This may be with regard to enhancing access to additional local educational facilities, as well as independent, residential, or transitional living or other suitable arrangements.

Truant and adjudicated youths are also a vulnerable subgroup that could benefit from access to needed mental health services, for example, to address problems with substance use, including drugs and/or alcohol abuse. These youths are often under the care of the state as a result of having witnessed violence at home, and they may have faced physical and/or sexual abuse, as well as

dysfunction. Correctional facilities are generally not equipped to deliver the care some of these youngsters require (crisis intervention, ongoing psychiatric services, specialty care, etc.). Juvenile facilities could also partner with community-based agencies with the capacity to provide, for example, sexual health education, general education equivalency courses, and the like. This population also is in need of receiving job training that will enable them to learn skills that will make them more competitive for employment when released.

Honoring the needs of elders relative to their choice of care, being active, and living independently as long as possible will require early consultation with their service providers. This will ensure that providers have clarity regarding their patients' wishes as their need for assisted living and care change across the life span.

Responding to the wishes and needs of the terminally ill, including end-of-life care, focuses attention on providing people the opportunity to be at home when they are close to death. Services that would be integrated include primary care, social services, hospice, palliative care, and hospital services.

Conclusion

People value local services in their own community whether these are related to health, social services, or any other program with an impact on their day-to-day lives. They also value the integration of services that are closely related, especially when one is ill or in need of additional support. When people need support in carrying out activities of daily living that extend beyond what family or friends are able to lend, society makes services available either through public or private auspices or a combination thereof. The same is true when accessing discrete entitlement programs designed to provide necessary assistance. Ensuring that an appropriate array of community services to enhance a person's health and well-being has been effectively integrated should be the norm whether these are in medical care, social services, or social security benefits, and regardless of one's socioeconomic status. What is most important in doing so is to provide each person the highest level of dignity, independence, choice, and well-being. Each human being is deserving of access to comprehensive health services, as well as the support of their family—regardless of whether it is comprised by an only child, single-parent, blended, lesbian, gay, bisexual, transgendered, adoptive, grandparent, extended, or nonbiological family. For now, the changing dimensions of contemporary family life are increasingly related to demographic changes, an ever-expanding presence of people from varied cultures and ethnicities, population shifts resulting from the disproportion between aging baby boomers and younger workers, and severe global economic fluctuations. These and other shifts will continue exerting influence on the capacity of families to prevent disease while promoting their health and that of their communities.

Augusta M. Villanueva

See also Access to Health Care: Uninsured; Advocacy for Families; Community Resources for Families Related to Health; Cultural Attitudes Toward Help Seeking and Beliefs About Illness in Families; Decision Making in the Context of Health and Illness; Ethnic/Racial Influences in Families; Factors Influencing Access to Health Care for Families

Further Readings

Ahmad, W. I., & Bradby, H. (2007). Locating ethnicity and health: Exploring concepts and contexts. *Sociology of Health and Illness, 29,* 795–810.

Beckmann, M. R., Proctor, Z. J., & Yakimo, R. (2008). *Health promotion strategies through the life span* (8th ed.). Upper Saddle River, NJ: Prentice Hall.

Davies, J. K., & MacDonald, G. (Eds.). (1998). *Quality, evidence and effectiveness in health promotion.* New York: Routledge.

Dein, S. (2006). Race, culture and ethnicity in minority research: A critical discussion. *Journal of Cultural Diversity, 13,* 68–75.

Mittelmark, M. B. (2001). Promoting social responsibility for health: Health impact assessment and healthy public policy at the community level. *Health Promotion International, 16,* 269–274.

Polan, E. U., & Taylor, D. (2007). *Journey across the life span: Human development and health promotion* (3rd ed.). Philadelphia: F. A. Davis.

Wagstaff, A. (2002). Poverty and health sector inequalities. *Bulletin of the World Health Organization, 80,* 97–105.

World Health Organization. (1998). *Health promotion glossary.* (Rep. No. WHO/HPR/HEP/981).

Geneva, Switzerland: Author. Retrieved from http://www.who.int/hpr/NPH/docs/hp_glossary_en.pdf

World Health Organization. (2007). *Global age-friendly cities: A guide.* Geneva, Switzerland: Author. Retrieved from http://www.who.int/ageing/publications/Global_age_friendly_cities_Guide_English.pdf

COMMUNITY VIOLENCE EXPOSURE AND FAMILY HEALTH

Community violence exposure is a public health problem with devastating consequences for children and their families. Community violence encompasses violence experienced and witnessed by children, youths, and their families in their community, as distinguished from family and partner violence (i.e., violence occurring within the family, such as child physical and sexual abuse, adolescent relationship abuse, and domestic violence). Community violence includes use of weapons, school fighting, muggings, witnessing and hearing guns used, sexual assault, burglary, muggings, and gang activity. For recent immigrants fleeing political violence, this violence exposure also includes witnessing military gun fighting, explosions, rape, and torture.

Despite trends toward decreases in violence victimization, the United States continues to have the highest prevalence of community violence among developed countries, with a homicide rate of 6 per 100,000. Homicide is the second leading cause of death for young men ages 15 to 24 years and the leading cause of death for young African American men, according to the Centers for Disease Control and Prevention (CDC). The American Academy of Pediatrics and the American Academy of Family Physicians, among other major health professional organizations, have advocated for violence prevention programs in communities and have underscored the critical importance of provider counseling regarding guns, bullying, fighting, and gang involvement. This entry reviews the prevalence of community violence, intersections of community violence with other forms of violence, the impact of community violence on children's health, and the role of family health providers in addressing community violence.

Prevalence

Multiple studies since the early 1990s have underscored the prevalence of community violence. A 1993 study in Washington, D.C., for example, documented 19% of first and second graders had been victimized by violence, which included stabbings, shootings, muggings, and forced entry into their homes; 61% of those younger children reported witnessing such violence. In the same study, 32% of fifth and sixth graders reported violence victimization, and 72% reported witnessing violence. In a nationally representative study of adolescents, almost 20% reported being victimized by at least one type of community violence—jumped, stabbed, shot, or had a knife or gun pulled on them. While such reports of violence victimization and witnessing of community violence appear to be more prevalent in urban neighborhoods, rural and suburban communities are also affected.

Regarding school safety, many children report experiences of being bullied as well as witnessing bullying. Bullying includes a range of abusive behaviors, including threats with weapons. In a national survey, 13% of students in Grades 6 through 10 reported bullying others, 11% reported being victimized by bullies, and 6% reported both. The increased use of social media by children and youths has increased use of abusive behaviors in cyberspace.

Participation in gang activity remains a challenge in communities where few positive opportunities for youths exist, in particular for youths chronically exposed to family and community violence. The 2001 National Youth Gang Survey by the Office of Juvenile Justice and Delinquency Prevention highlights that 100% of cities with a population more than 250,000 report gang activity; 11% of rural and 35% of suburban counties report gang activity. Of the homicides reported in major cities such as Los Angeles and Chicago, more than half are related to gang violence. While gang members are overwhelmingly male, an increasing number of females are being recruited to join gangs, often accompanied by sexual violence.

Intersections of Exposure to Violence

Studies examining the prevalence of violence victimization and witnessing of community violence have documented the intersection with family violence. Specifically, a recent national study underscored the extent to which many children and youths in the United States experience multiple forms of violence victimization ("polyvictimization"). Almost two thirds of respondents were exposed to more than one type of victimization; 30% reported five or more types in their lifetime. Trauma symptoms were particularly pronounced for the 10% reporting 11 or more different forms of lifetime violence victimization. If a child has been exposed to one form of violence, other exposure to violence victimization (including witnessing of family and community violence) is likely and should be considered in assessment and treatment planning. In addition, violence exposure may be associated with additional adverse childhood experiences, such as poverty, parent mental illness, and lack of access to health care, which can exacerbate the effects of violence exposure. For new immigrant families, this exposure may also include histories of exposure to armed conflict.

Impact on Family Health

Myriad studies have documented the associations of witnessing and experiencing community violence on mental health, physical health, and social functioning. Trauma symptoms, suicidality, mental disorders such as depression and anxiety, emotional distress and aggressive behaviors, and substance abuse are all significant consequences of violence exposure. Exposure to multiple forms of victimization is not uncommon and increases risk for these poor mental health outcomes and social functioning, including poor academic outcomes and school failure. Studies indicate that those who are multiply victimized may not be receiving the mental health support they need.

The most consistent finding in the literature regarding protective factors to mitigate the negative effects of exposure to community violence is family stability and connectedness to family and neighborhood.

Role of Family Health Providers

Family health providers should receive training to increase skills in assessing for lifetime exposure to violence and in offering culturally relevant support and resources to clients and their families affected by violence. Promising interventions in the primary care setting include training primary care residents to assess for and offer anticipatory guidance for reducing exposure to community violence. Early intervention efforts with children exposed to violence appear to reduce traumatic symptoms. Innovative programs for youth violence prevention include intervening with injured youths in emergency departments and connecting them to community-based resources.

Family health providers can serve as powerful advocates for the families they serve by advocating for strengthening supports for families (including home visitation programs to reduce domestic violence and child abuse), increasing school and community-based youth violence prevention programs, and participating in community-wide efforts to keep guns out of the hands of children and youths.

Elizabeth Miller

See also Bullying and the Family; Verbal Abuse in Families

Websites

Centers for Disease Control and Prevention: Leading Causes of Death in Males: http://www.cdc.gov/men/lcod
Family Violence Prevention Fund: http://www.endabuse.org
National Center for Children Exposed to Violence: http://www.nccev.org
STRYVE: National Youth Violence Prevention Resource Center: http://www.safeyouth.org

COMPLEMENTARY AND ALTERNATIVE MEDICINE

The definition of complementary and alternative medicine (CAM) is relatively new, complex, and evolving. According to the National Center for Complementary and Alternative Medicine (NCCAM), CAM is a group of diverse medical and health care systems, practices, and products that are not presently considered to be part of conventional, mainstream medicine. Terms that are important to distinguish within this definition include *conventional medicine*—practiced by doctors of allopathic (MD) or osteopathic (DO) medicine and other health professionals, including

nurses and physical therapists; *complementary medicine*—used together with conventional medicine; and *alternative medicine*—used in place of conventional medicine. Although CAM encompasses an extremely broad group of practices, it is usually divided into four major domains, as described by NCCAM: (1) biologically based practices, (2) manipulative and body-based practices, (3) mind–body medicine, and (4) energy medicine. In addition, NCCAM recognizes *whole medical systems* that cut across all four domains, such as traditional Chinese medicine. Other terms often used to describe this wide range of health and healing practices include *unconventional, natural, holistic, whole-person, integrative, and integral medicine*. Many of these terms imply the combined use of both CAM and conventional medicine, using the best of both to create an integrative approach to health care delivery. They often embody concepts of treating the whole person: mind, body, and spirit. Currently the term *integrative medicine* has emerged as the most commonly used term to describe this blended approach and is defined by NCCAM as that which combines mainstream medical therapies and CAM therapies for which there is some high-quality scientific evidence of safety and effectiveness.

Given that population studies over the past several decades show that a growing number of people are using, and continue to use, some form of CAM, this topic has emerged as an important dimension and a new field of study within our health care system, as well as many others around the world. This entry describes the historical evolution, growth, and development of the field of CAM, including statistics regarding the populations that use CAM in the United States and recommendations from leading health care organizations as to future directions.

History, Growth, and Development

The use of diverse health interventions and health practices is not necessarily new to health care in the United States. Indeed medical pluralism has always existed in that the healthy as well as the ill have traditionally used a variety of therapies, from chicken soup and spices to herbal teas and baths, to care for themselves and their families. In addition to such home remedies, practitioners from the fields of homeopathy and osteopathy were more commonly consulted in the past. An arrest in the growth of medical pluralism and corresponding professional societies and organizations is cited to have occurred with the publication of the Flexner report in 1910. The report established a gold standard for the training of medical professionals, and its charge to focus on a biomedical, scientific curriculum closed down many "alternative" schools of healing. The standardization of medical education allowed allopathic medicine to emerge as the dominant paradigm for the county's health care delivery system.

From the 1960s to 1980s, a growing interest in more "natural" and "holistic" lifestyles and health approaches, as well as the opening of international relations with Eastern countries, such as the China delegation journalist reports on acupuncture, increased the public's awareness and curiosity regarding CAM. With more public exposure and growing interest in CAM, modalities such as yoga, meditation, and herbal remedies experienced accelerated growth through the 1990s. During this time, conventional medicine experienced its first wake-up call regarding CAM when in 1993 the *New England Journal of Medicine* published a lead article showing data from a 1990 national survey estimating that approximately one third of the U.S. population was using CAM and spending billions of dollars out of pocket for these products and services. The findings marked the time that mainstream medicine began to turn its attention and interest toward CAM, leading to further research and investigation into this new and uncharted field.

U.S. Populations That Use CAM

Following the 1990 landmark survey of U.S. adults' use of CAM came several other larger population studies, the first of which was conducted in 1997. Results showed an increase in adults' use of CAM, from 34% (1990) to 42% (1997) of the population.

More recently data have been collected as part of the National Health Interview Survey (NHIS), an annual study that reaches tens of thousands of Americans, to ask about their overall health and illness status. As part of this comprehensive survey, the NCCAM, together with the National Center for Health Statistics, developed specific questions about CAM. The 2007 study interviews reached more than 75,000 persons in 30,000 families with a household response rate of 87%. In 2002, interviews were completed with more than 93,000 persons in 37,000 families for a 90% household response rate. The 2002, and 2007 data show that overall use of CAM among U.S. adults has remained relatively stable at 36% (2002) and 38% (2007), or almost 4 out of 10 adults, using CAM in the past 12 months. The 2007 study showed that the most commonly used CAM therapies included nonvitamin, nonmineral natural products (18%), deep breathing exercises (13%), meditation (9%), chiropractic or osteopathic manipulation (9%), massage (8%), and yoga (6%). CAM was most often used to treat musculoskeletal conditions such as back, neck, or joint pain and problems. Of note, areas of CAM showing significant increases in use from 2002 included deep breathing, meditation, massage therapy, and yoga. Between 2002 and 2007, increases were seen for acupuncture, massage therapy, and naturopathy. Consistent with prior studies, CAM use was found to be greater in those who were women (43% vs. 34% men), aged 30 to 69 years, with higher levels of education (master's degree, doctorate, or professional 55%), not poor, and living in the Western United States (45%).

For the first time, the 2007 NHIS investigated children's use of CAM (aged 0–17 years) via interviews with adults. The survey revealed almost 1 in 9 children (12%) used a CAM therapy in the prior 12 months, the most common including nonvitamin, nonmineral, natural products (4%), chiropractic or osteopathic manipulation (3%), deep breathing exercise (2%), yoga (2%), and homeopathic treatment (1%). The most common conditions for which CAM therapies were used by children included back or neck pain, head or chest colds, anxiety or stress, other musculoskeletal problems, and attention deficit/hyperactivity disorder. Of note, children whose parent or relative used CAM were five times more likely to use CAM as well. Additional important economic findings showed that when families were unable to afford conventional medical care, they were more likely to use CAM than when the cost of conventional care was deemed affordable.

Another important study explored CAM use in adults 50 years or older. Through the collaborative efforts of the AARP (formally the American

Association of Retired Persons) and NCCAM, a 2006 survey revealed that 63% of the nearly 1,600 people polled used CAM. The most common forms included massage therapy, chiropractic manipulation, or other bodywork (45%) and herbal products or dietary supplements (42%). Older adults' top reasons for using CAM included treating a specific health condition (66%) as well as for overall wellness (65%). An important finding was that of those using CAM, almost 70% had not discussed the use of such therapies with their doctor. Top reasons why CAM use was not disclosed included that the doctor never asked (42%) and not knowing to tell (30%). This finding was consistent with earlier studies (1990, 1997), which showed that approximately 60% of adults had not discussed their use of CAM with their physician. As a result of this chronic and concerning gap in communication between physicians and patients using CAM, NCCAM launched a national education campaign, "Ask, Tell, Talk," which encourages both patients and health professionals to openly discuss CAM use or intended use as part of any health care visit. The aim of using these nonjudgmental communication skills is to facilitate dialogue that may discover potential CAM applications or contraindications and side effects.

All of these major, national studies indicate that CAM use spans the entire life cycle (children, adults and older adults) and that within families an adult's use of CAM leads to a much higher likelihood of children in that family also using CAM. Overall it is important to note that most patients seek CAM as a complement to their regular, conventional care rather than as an absolute alternative.

National Recommendations

In response to the findings that there is growing use of CAM in the United States, leading health and government organizations have published some important guidelines and recommendations. In 2002, the White House Commission on Complementary and Alternative Medicine Policy, a committee charged by the President and Secretary of Health and Human Services to inform public policy regarding the use of CAM, submitted specific recommendations and action steps. The guiding principles that informed their process included the following: a wholeness orientation in health care delivery, evidence of safety and efficacy, the healing capacity of the person, respect for individuality, the right to choose treatment, an emphasis on health promotion and self-care, partnerships as essential for integrated health care, education as a fundamental health care service, dissemination of comprehensive and timely information, and integral public involvement. In 2005, the Institute of Medicine (IOM) of the National Academy of Sciences, a private nonprofit society of scientific scholars that serves as an advisor to the federal government, published an extensive report, "Complementary and Alternative Medicine in the United States." The report made a number of recommendations in the areas of research, education, and clinical care, calling for further and more innovative scientific study, expansion of education across all health professions, and the development of health policy and models of care to inform and guide clinical practice. In 2009, the IOM once again addressed this growing and important dimension of health care by holding a Summit on Integrative Medicine and the Health of the Public. The meeting included diverse representation of thought leaders and organizations from both the conventional medicine and CAM communities. Spanning several days, the meeting covered a broad range of issues examining the role and value integrative medicine may serve in meeting the health needs of the public, especially given the current state and mounting crisis of our fragmented health care system. Overall the summit highlighted the following important factors to be considered in health care reform: The progression of many chronic diseases can be reversed and even healed through lifestyle modifications; genetics is not destiny; our environment influences our health; improving our primary care and chronic disease care systems is paramount; the reimbursement system must be changed; changes in education will fuel changes in practice; evidence-based medicine is the only acceptable standard; and a large demonstration project is needed.

Future Directions

CAM, and its evolution into integrative medicine, is an important aspect of health care for individual patients and families, as well as the overall health of the population. With an emphasis on prevention and wellness, and a general focus on less expensive and least invasive interventions, CAM has become an important and promising part of our health care delivery system. As the field continues to grow and evolve, further research, education, and clinical applications will be needed to better understand CAM's potential and possibly critical role in creating a health care delivery system that will optimize health and healing.

Mary P. Guerrera

See also Changing Family and Health Demographics; Cultural Attitudes Toward Help Seeking and Beliefs About Illness in Families; Factors Influencing Family Health Values, Beliefs, and Priorities; Health Management in Families; Health System Options for Families; Integrative Medicine and Health Care Settings; Optimal Healing Environments for Families

Further Readings

AARP (formally American Association of Retired Persons), National Center for Complementary and Alternative Medicine. (2007, January). *Complementary and alternative medicine: What people 50 and older are using and discussing with their physicians.* Retrieved from http://assets.aarp.org/rgcenter/health/cam_2007.pdf

Barnes P. M., Bloom, B., & Nahin, R. L. (2008). *Complementary and alternative medicine use among adults and children: United States, 2007* (National Health Statistics Rep. No. 12). Hyattsville, MD: National Center of Health Statistics. Available from http://nccam.nih.gov/news/camstats/2007

Institute of Medicine, Committee on the Use of Complementary and Alternative Medicine by the American Public. (2005). *Complementary and alternative medicine in the United States.* Washington, DC: National Academies Press. Available from http://www.nap.edu/catalog.php?record_id=11182

Jacobs, B. P., & Gundling, K. (Eds.). (2009). *The ACP evidence-based guide to complementary & alternative medicine.* Philadelphia: American College of Physicians.

Kligler, B., & Lee, R. (Eds.). (2004). *Integrative medicine: Principles for practice.* New York: McGraw-Hill.

Rakel, D. (Ed.). (2007). *Integrative medicine.* Philadelphia: Saunders.

Ruggie, M. (2004). *Marginal to mainstream: Alternative medicine in America.* Cambridge, UK: Cambridge University Press.

White House Commission on Complementary and Alternative Medicine Policy. (2002, March). *Final report.* Available from http://www.whccamp.hhs.gov/finalreport.html

Wisneski, L. A., & Anderson, L. (2009). *The scientific basis of integrative medicine.* Boca Raton, FL: CRC Press.

Websites

American Holistic Medical Association: http://www.holisticmedicine.org

American Holistic Nurses Association: http://www.ahna.org

Consortium of Academic Health Centers for Integrative Medicine: http://www.imconsortium.org

National Center for Complementary and Alternative Medicine: http://www.nccam.nih.gov

Summit on Integrative Medicine and the Health of the Public, Institute of Medicine of the National Academies 2009: http://iom.edu/Activities/Quality/IntegrativeMed/2009-FEB-25.aspx

COMPLICATED GRIEF

Complicated grief (CG) is an emotional reaction to loss that falls outside of the expected norms for the culture in which it incurs; it differs from "normal grief" in the length of time or intensity of the symptoms experienced, and/or the extent of impairment to functioning in social, domestic, or occupational activities. Approximately 10% to 20% of the bereaved experience CG, and prevalence is higher in cases of sudden or violent loss. CG is being considered for inclusion in the *Diagnostic and Statistical Manual of Mental Disorders* (5th ed.; *DSM-V*), the first disorder specific to bereavement. Its application to diverse populations has been limited, but a variety of therapeutic approaches have been advocated.

Defining Complicated Grief

CG is not defined by a single set of characteristics, and although it may overlap with major depression, anxiety, or posttraumatic distress, it is a distinct bereavement-related cluster of symptoms. The most commonly discussed types of CG are chronic or prolonged grief (which involves the lengthy presence of intense grief symptoms) and absent or delayed grief, in which there may be limited or no signs of grief soon after the loss, but signs may (although not always) appear later.

However, the absence of grief symptoms does not necessarily indicate pathology, and scholars have argued that in some cases it may reflect lack of attachment or reason to grieve, or resilience. Although CG can exist following a range of losses, it has been most frequently studied following death of a loved one.

Researchers and clinicians have argued whether the concept of CG (also called prolonged grief) should be included in the forthcoming fifth edition of the *Diagnostic and Statistical Manual of Mental Disorders,* to be published by the American Psychiatric Association. In 2006, an issue of *Omega: The Journal of Death and Dying* was dedicated to this debate. Although there is agreement that pathological grief exists, there is disagreement in whether it is a disorder and, if it is, what its classification or characteristics are. Many view it as a psychological disorder, but others have argued that CG could represent other things, such as a cultural concept, a way for bereavement agencies to determine clients, a label families use to control deviants, a label for those who resist cultural norms, or a reflection of the Western medicalization of grief, such that either CG must be viewed as distinct from normal grief or else all grief would eventually be seen as a mental illness.

Debate Over Classification of CG as a Disorder

Holly Prigerson and colleagues have argued the term *prolonged grief disorder* (PGD) provides greater clarity than CG and that their research validates PGD as meeting criteria for a mental disorder, distinct from any other disorder in the *DSM-IV.* They have proposed the following criteria for PGD: that it (a) follows the death of a significant person; (b) contains elements of separation distress (at least one of the following symptoms daily, or to a disruptive level: intrusive thoughts related to the deceased, intense separation distress, or strong yearnings); (c) includes cognitive, emotional, and behavioral symptoms that have occurred since (and in relation to) the loss (at least five of the following nine on a daily basis, or to a disruptive level: loss-related anger or bitterness, numbness, difficulty moving ahead with life, feeling shocked or stunned, feeling life is empty or lacks meaning, avoiding reminders, confusion about one's role in life or sense of self, difficulty accepting

the loss, inability to trust others); (d) has a duration of at least six months; (e) impairs functioning in important domains, such as work or family responsibilities; and (f) is not the result of substance abuse, medical condition, or other disorder.

Others have argued for a diagnostic spectrum that could be relevant to many forms of bereavement. Current criteria have been criticized as too focused on the individual, ignoring the multidimensional complexity of response to loss. In particular, current CG/PGD criteria ignore the nature of the continuing relationship to the deceased, ignore the relief and ambivalence at death in negative relationships, or limit inclusion to the traditional family (missing issues such as survivor guilt for military personnel who lose their "other family" during battle). In such cases, CG/PGD criteria may result in interventions that assume suppression of the relationship is adaptive. Others are concerned that there is limited research on cognitive processes underlying CG, or that the criteria need greater emphasis on the search for meaning reconstruction. Some have advocated the addition of neuroimaging (MRI) to better understand unique brain activation elements of CG versus normal grief and similarities between CG and other psychiatric disorders.

Applicability to Others

Understanding of CG in diverse groups is limited. Some researchers assume the same conditions (separation distress and yearning) exist in adults and children, and utilize the Inventory of Complicated Grief (ICG or ICG-R) for both groups. Studies with adolescent survivors of parent suicide suggest that different elements of the ICG may be emphasized for younger versus older adolescents. In contrast, some conceptualize a separate childhood traumatic grief, derived from child development and child trauma treatment research and associated with caregivers' emotional state. In addition, CG among people with intellectual disabilities has not been well studied, with studies often relying on retrospective reports from caregivers.

Treatments and the Future

Various treatments for CG include antidepressants alone or in conjunction with psychotherapy. Cognitive-behavioral therapy has been associated with greater improvement in CG than has supportive counseling. Innovative methods also have utilized virtual reality environment (EMMA's World) to encourage expression and processing of emotions. An online standardized treatment for pathological grief and posttraumatic stress, known as Interapy, may be effective. Another promising Internet approach utilized a 5-week treatment of cognitive-behavioral therapy techniques with online writing tasks and reported the intervention was effective at the 3-month follow-up. Overall, research and treatment advances are likely to emphasize understanding and treating CG; they will be influenced by whether CG enters the *DSM-V*, and if so, its inclusion will dictate research directions.

Colleen I. Murray

See also Death: Ambiguous Feelings Related to Loss; Death and the Grieving Process in Families; Death From Unnatural Causes: Homicides, Drive-By Shootings; Depression in the Family; Sibling Death/ Loss; War and Families

Further Readings

Bonanno, G. A. (2004). Loss, trauma, and human resilience: Have we underestimated the human capacity to thrive after extremely aversive events? *American Psychologist, 59,* 20–28.

Complicated grief [Special issue]. (2007). *European Archives of Psychiatry & Clinical Neuroscience, 257*(8).

Murray, C. I., Toth, K., & Clinkinbeard, S. S. (2005). Death, dying, and grief in families. In P. C. Mckenry & S. J. Price (Eds.), *Families & change: Coping with stressful events and transitions* (3rd ed., pp. 75–102). Thousand Oaks, CA: Sage.

O'Connor, M.-F. (2005). Bereavement and the brain: Invitation to a conversation between bereavement researchers and neuroscientists. *Death Studies, 29,* 905–922.

Parkes, C. M. (Ed.). (2006). Complicated grief [Special issue]. *Omega: The Journal of Death and Dying, 52*(1).

Prigerson, H. G., Vanderwerker, L. C., & Maciejewski, P. K. (2008). The case for inclusion of prolonged grief disorder in *DSM-V*. In M. S. Stroebe, R. O. Hansson, H. Schut, & W. Stroebe (Eds.), *Handbook of bereavement research and practice: Advances in theory and intervention* (pp. 165–186). Washington, DC: American Psychological Association.

Stroebe, M. S., Hansson, R. O., Schut, H., & Stroebe, W. (Eds.). (2008). *Handbook of bereavement research and practice: Advances in theory and intervention.* Washington, DC: American Psychological Association.

COMPUTERIZED RECORDS AND FAMILY HEALTH CARE INFORMATION

National disasters, such as Hurricane Katrina, revealed the fragile nature of our medical record system. Many of the hurricane victims were without their most basic health information, such as their current prescriptions, immunization records, and hospital histories. This experience has heightened the need to automate our health care system. Technology is being targeted as a strategy to solve the problem of storing and retrieving personal and medical health information. The personal health record (PHR) and the electronic health record (EHR) are two efforts that strengthen the medical record system, improving health data storage and data retrieval. The PHR is maintained by individual family members and is designed to detail health information throughout the individual's life span. On the other hand, the EHR is maintained by members of the health care team. This entry reviews the influence of technology on family health information through the use of the PHR and EHR.

The Personal Health Record

The PHR is an electronic application used by families to manage and share their individual health information using a computer. Although useful for any individual to manage their health information, a PHR is especially useful for individuals with chronic illnesses who have been prescribed several medications and have experienced frequent hospital admissions, tests, and therapies. The typical PHR contains health information such as current medications, past medications, health history, hospitalizations, surgeries, treatments, and allergies.

There are several PHR options for families, and the complexity of a PHR varies. A PHR can be as complex as one that links with the health provider office, or it can be as basic as a spreadsheet. A PHR that connects with the health provider office is part of the health care provider's electronic health record. With this connectivity, the PHR can then be used as a communication tool as well as a means of maintaining health information. For example, when the PHR is connected to the physician office via the EHR, the health care client has immediate access to the provider office, enabling individuals to e-mail the health care provider, schedule appointments, and seek additional information regarding health issues. Interested health care clients should check with their provider to learn what options are available. PHRs of this type can be offered by the health care provider and may include a subscription cost.

Another type of PHR is an independent or stand-alone PHR, which the family can gain access for free or pay an annual subscription from a company, such as insurance or entrepreneurial companies. For example, Google Health is free and is part of a suite of applications provided by Google. A SmartPHR, by comparison, can cost up to $40 per year. These PHRs can vary in their complexity. Some include additional features such as reminders and cards with added information encoded for emergencies. It is important that the health care client read each condition within the contract to ensure that privacy and security of their health information are guaranteed. The website myPHR is very helpful for those interested in starting a PHR. It contains information about how to start a PHR and provides lists of companies that provide this service and their fees, including web-based or stand-alone systems.

The final example of a PHR is one created by the family member using a spreadsheet. These are inexpensive and tailored to meet the personal needs of the family members. These PHRs lack preset links to the web. However, the family member can insert links within the cells of the spreadsheet.

Although anyone can benefit from maintaining their own PHR, some categories of individuals are especially well suited to assume this project. One category is family members who want to be more involved in their health care. These individuals assume a role of self-advocate in decision making with their provider. The second category is individuals who have experienced chronic illnesses and need to take an active role in noting their health histories. The third category of individuals who might benefit from using a PHR is elderly persons

who may have difficulty remembering aspects of their prescribed care.

Despite the advantages of using a PHR, some barriers to adoption have been identified. As stated before, adopting a PHR puts the family member in a more responsible role in their health care. A PHR requires the family member to commit to adding relevant health information on a regular basis. Some family members might have difficulty maintaining the PHR and find it challenging to record and maintain their own health histories. Second, it has yet to be determined who should assume the cost of the PHR. Although computers have become quite affordable in recent years, the cost of the PHR from the practitioner's office or a company may potentially be beyond the scope of a family's household budget. Finally, the PHR may be uncomfortable for the provider. A family committed to using a PHR has gained some control over their health care, removing some autonomy and control from the provider. The provider, once perceived as "owning" the health information and determining the path of treatment, now shares that role with the family.

Security and privacy of health information have emerged as concerns using the PHR linked with the provider's office or purchased on the Internet with links to the web throughout the application. A family's medical information is considered safe with updated antiviral software and a firewall or software barrier designed to prevent unwanted intrusion into someone's computer.

In summary, adopting the PHR has advantages and disadvantages for a family. A family who can weigh the options and adopt a PHR has taken a position of actively joining and participating with the health care team. Regardless of the type of PHR chosen, maintaining health information electronically may be invaluable at times when information may be difficult to recover.

The Electronic Health Record

In response to the challenge set forth by the U.S. Institute of Medicine (IOM), health care providers have begun implementing EHRs. The EHR is designed to replace the paper charting system. The EHR has several components, and any or all may be implemented by a health care organization. Within the EHR, nurses, physicians, social workers, respiratory therapists and physical therapists, for example, can read the entries made by colleagues and contribute to the record. Results from the laboratory and radiology departments can also be linked and appear on the EHR. The EHR also includes a mechanism for entering provider orders into the system (order entry function). The orders can then be communicated via the network, to the laboratory, radiology, or dietary systems for action. EHR can assist administrators in generating reports using data to illustrate cost comparisons, capture workload, or show quality markers for health care consumers.

The initial goal of the EHR, as set forth by the IOM, is to reduce error and facilitate timely documentation by health care providers. This challenge has been met through several advances in technologies. First, health care organizations and hospitals have placed computers throughout the nursing units and have increased portability by putting computers on wheels. Second, handheld and related technologies have been adopted for rapid data entry and retrieval. Handheld devices are smaller and fit in a pocket, thus making the EHR even more accessible. Other technologies designed to increase accessibility of the EHR include smartphones and tablets.

There are several advantages to using the EHR when compared to the paper medical record system. Consistent with the challenge from the IOM, the EHR assists in reducing error, as the EHR is legible and has an alert system. In addition, the EHR has a high degree of accessibility. When using an EHR, all data are legible. One known cause of medical errors is the result of not being able to read someone's handwriting. Alert systems are used to remind health care professionals of scheduled medications and therapies, as well as possible medication incompatibilities. For example, reminders can be generated to inform the provider of the need for recurring treatment such as the flu vaccine or mammogram. Furthermore, alert systems are also used as a reminder system to reduce errors of omission; for example, an alert could remind the nurse to give a medication or take an individual to a scheduled test or treatment. Unlike the paper medical record, with one copy per patient for all members of the health care team to share, the EHR is readily accessible throughout the health care system, thus supporting frequent entries and rapid access to health care information.

Despite these advantages, the EHR does have some limitations. Information can be easily entered for the wrong patient. For example, medication orders can be entered for the wrong patient and then administered in error. Alerts and alarms can be easily ignored, and levels of security or having to enter multiple passwords may be a barrier to frequent documentation entries. The EHR will accept an order from a provider for a health care client. It will not prevent the wrong order being entered for the wrong health care client. The ramifications of this error can be staggering. Furthermore, levels of security designed to protect private health care client information can be difficult to navigate, promoting infrequent documentation. For example, to enter the system, a health care team member may have to log on several times to get through the different levels of security from the system network to health care client's medical record.

In summary, the recent surge in EHR usage is in response to the challenge from the IOM. The EHR is designed to capture information and be available to the entire health care team. Accessibility to the health care client's medical record is increased through computer stations and the use of handheld devices. Although the EHR assists to reduce medical error through legibility, alerts, and alarms, some unresolved issues remain that may risk medical error.

Conclusion

The PHR and EHR are two ways in which computer technology has influenced family health information. Both applications use computers to enter, store, and retrieve health information. The PHR is maintained by the family, whereas the provider enters data in the EHR. In some cases, this information can be shared between applications. With the adoption of the PHR and EHR, there may be fewer challenges in storing and retrieving health information for individuals on a routine basis and, importantly, in the event of another national disaster.

Jane M. Carrington

See also Family Pediatric Adherence to Health Care Regimen; Family Self-Management; HIPAA: Privacy Laws and the Family; Selecting Health Care for Families With Children and Youth

Further Readings

Ash, J., Berg, M., & Coiera, E. (2004). Some unintended consequences of information technology in health care: The nature of patient care information system-related errors. *Journal of the American Medical Informatics Association, 11,* 104–112.

Denton, I. (2001). Will patients use electronic personal health records? Responses from a real-life experience. *Journal of Healthcare Information Management, 15*(3), 251–258.

Institute of Medicine. (2001). *Crossing the quality chasm.* Washington, DC: National Academies Press.

Kim, M., & Johnson, K. (2002). Personal health records. *Journal of the American Medical Informatics Association, 9,* 171–180.

Nahm, R., & Poston, I. (2000). Measurement of the effects of an integrated, point-of-care computer system on quality of nursing documentation and patient satisfaction. *Computers in Nursing, 18*(5), 220–229.

Tang, P., Ash, J., Bates, D., Overhage, J., & Sands, D. (2006). Personal health records: Definitions, benefits, and strategies for overcoming barriers to adoption. *Journal of the American Medical Informatics Association, 13,* 121–126.

Websites

Medline Plus, Personal Medical Records: http://www.nlm.nih.gov/medlineplus/personalmedicalrecords.html
myPHR: http://www.myphr.com

Conflict in Family Life, Role and Management of

At the core of healthy family functioning is conflict and how it is managed. Conflict occurs whenever two or more parties in the family disagree over a difference in wants, values, beliefs, or perceptions and then mutually contest that difference through words or actions in an effort to achieve resolution.

Despite the popular misconception that conflict shows something "wrong" going on because people are not getting along, conflict is actually a normal and necessary process through which people broker inevitable human differences in their relationships. Conflict is how family members sometimes learn to get along. It simply means that at least one party is discontent with what is happening or not happening, is willing to confront the issue, and at least wants to communicate about it and maybe wants to make a change. For example, the adolescent pushes for more freedom than parents want to allow.

Because everyone is unique, human differences do not always match or harmoniously mesh in relationships. And because changes in life are continually upsetting and resetting the terms of everyone's existence, conflicts between what was and what is, and what is and what will be, continually cause discord within people, between people, and in people's response to altered circumstances.

A common belief is that in "good" relationships there is no conflict, but this is a falsehood. This truth is that in family relationships where there is no conflict, differences are avoided or ignored, dissatisfaction is suppressed, dishonesty rules, and disaffection grows. In some families, conflict is treated as a point of difference they cannot or must not talk about; however, conflict usually means there is something they *need* to talk about. In creating a chance to discuss a difference between them, conflict creates an *opportunity for intimacy* between family members from becoming better known and from coming to better know each other. Conflict also creates an *opportunity for unity* between family members from bridging a difference with agreement that all sides commit to honor, thereby strengthening trust in the relationship.

What usually gives conflict a bad name in families is not that it occurs but how it is conducted. In families, the primary rule for conducting conflict that parents must model and supervise is *safety*. Conflict must never be used as an excuse to do intentional verbal or physical injury to anyone. In families, differences are inevitable, conflict is necessary, but violence is neither inevitable nor necessary.

The first priority in managing any family conflict is *not* resolving the issue at difference. The first priority is each party taking responsibility for monitoring its own emotional arousal (impatience, frustration, anger, or fear) so that it does not dictate words or actions that anyone will have later cause to regret. In family conflict, people's emotions must never be allowed to do anyone's "thinking" for them.

Whenever anyone feels in danger of their emotions taking over their conduct, they need to declare the need for a temporary time out and then return to the difference under discussion when they have cooled down and reason can once again prevail. The helpful role of emotions in conflict is to create sensitivity—awareness in oneself and empathy toward each other.

There is a competitive model for managing conflict that many fathers learn from having grown up with their male peers: arguing differences to win and beat the other person. And there is a communication model for managing conflict that many mothers learn from having grown up with their female peers: discussing differences to better understand each other. In general, the female model often works better in family conflict because more intimacy and unity tend to result.

There are four steps in dealing with family conflict that often produce the most beneficial results for all concerned. First, discuss to understand each other's perception and self-interest in the matter and to express one's own. Second, empathize with the other person's feelings to show concern for his or her emotional well-being. Third, propose possible arrangements that might work the disagreement out. And fourth, agree on a resolution that all are committed to support.

Language that family members use in conflict is extremely important because it influences both the conduct and outcome of disagreement. In general, it is more productive when contesting an issue to stick to specific behaviors and events that are objected to or wanted rather than to resort to abstract and evaluative terms to represent what is going on or what one needs to have happen. For example, instead of parents demanding, in frustration, that their child act more "considerately and responsibly around the home," they are better served by specifying that they need the young person to "wash, dry, and put away dirty dishes after making a snack."

Engaging in an exchange of blame is a losing effort because it is usually inflammatory, putting the other person on the defensive. In addition, it shifts all responsibility for the conflict to the person blamed, thereby leaving the blamer without any power to resolve it.

Finally, there needs to be no mind reading in conflict. Mind reading occurs when one imagines what the other person is "really" feeling, thinking, or intending. It is guessing, and it is usually guessing wrong. It leads a person to speculate the worst and then overreact in response. Therefore, in conflict, whenever one family member supposes that the other must be feeling, thinking, or intending something of a threatening or upsetting nature, before reacting to this supposition, the family member should ask if it is so. False assumptions make conflict harder to realistically discuss and to readily resolve.

Because family is the original classroom for learning how to manage conflict in caring relationships, it is the parents' job—by instruction, example, and interaction—to teach children how this is done. Because conflict creates resemblance, contestants tempted to imitate the other's influential tactics, parents must model the kinds of communication and behavior they want the child to learn. Imitation needs to come in their direction. For example, the child needs to learn how to stay on topic and stick to specifics from copying the parents; the parents must not copy the child who keeps interrupting and changing the subject when things do not go his or her way.

Learning to conduct conflict well is the work of a lifetime. It begins within the family, where the child, who is an adult in training, learns from parents how to do so constructively and well.

Carl Pickhardt

See also Family Self-Management; Parenting; Sibling Conflict; Verbal Abuse in the Family; Youth Violence Prevention in the Family

Further Readings

Canary, D. J., Cupach, W. R., & Messman, S. J. (1995). *Relationship conflict: Conflict in parent-child, friendship, and romantic relationships.* Thousand Oaks, CA: Sage.

Hall, D. C. (2001). *Stop arguing and start understanding: Eight steps to solving family conflicts.* Seattle, WA: Montlake Family Press.

Pickhardt, C. E. (2007). *The connected father: Understanding your unique role and responsibilities during your child's adolescence.* New York: Palgrave Macmillan.

Pickhardt, C. E. (2009). *Stop the screaming: How to turn angry conflict with your child into positive communication.* New York: Palgrave Macmillan.

CONSTRUCTIONIST FAMILY THEORETICAL PERSPECTIVES

Constructionist-oriented practice is distinguished by an emphasis on the communal construction of social reality, specifically the development of knowledge and truth through relationships and the influence of language and society. This emphasis on communal construction informs a medical family therapy and psychotherapy practice that is a partnership model in which patient/client and practitioner engage in a shared inquiry about the presenting problem and mutually design its solution.

The description and discussion of a constructionist family theoretical perspective in this entry presents the concept and associated practice in a general manner. The ideas and their translation to practice may be found in medical and mental health contexts, across health care disciplines, and with individuals, families, and groups of patients/clients and with colleagues.

Construction of Social Reality

Key to the concept of the construction of social reality is the notion of knowledge and language as relational and generative. This notion contests the associated traditions of knowledge as fundamental and definitive, an independent individual as the maker and holder of knowledge, and language as descriptive and representational. It challenges people to rethink how they describe and understand their worlds and provides a contemporary alternative to the positivist tradition of objective knowledge and universal truth on which health and mental health practices are often based. It also challenges the associated traditions of knowledge as fundamental and definitive, an independent individual as the maker and holder of knowledge, and language as descriptive and representational.

Alternatively, constructionist theory privileges the creation of local knowledge (i.e., the expertise, truths, values, conventions, narratives, etc.) that is created within the social system (i.e., therapy system, medical team–patient staffing) that has firsthand knowledge (i.e., unique meanings and understandings from personal experience) of their situation and need. Translated to constructionist

family health and mental health practices, though constructionists acknowledge that preformed knowledge (i.e., theoretical scripts, predetermined rules, diagnostic categories) can be useful, they maintain a cautious attitude regarding categorizing and typing (i.e., people, problems, solutions). They are mindful that categorizing and typing, for instance, risk treating a diagnosis rather than the person, prematurely filling information gaps that might inhibit learning about the uniqueness of each person and family and their circumstances and needs, and relying on mechanistic and formulaic speech and actions that likewise might risk missing the uniqueness. Constructionists remain aware, however, that local knowledge develops against a background of dominant discourses, meta-narratives, and universal truths and is influenced by these conditions.

A constructionist practitioner, for instance, is interested in the uniqueness and nuance of an individual's and his or her family members' perspectives about health and illness and working with them within that framework. The underlying premise is that when the practitioner works within the reality of the patient/client, local knowledge (i.e., resolution and management of mental health problems and treatment and management of disease) will develop that is more individually tailored, relevant, and practical, and therefore outcomes are more successful. This focus on patient/client reality contrasts with focus on the truth or correctness of a person's perspective: The latter is grounded in a positivist tradition that reality exists independent of the observer and can be objectively known. In medical family therapy and psychotherapy practice, the emphasis on the social construction of reality, and working within and with this reality, translates to the cornerstone of such practices: collaborative relationships and dialogical conversations.

Collaboration

Collaboration between practitioner and patient/client and among colleagues is paramount to constructionist practice. All members of the treatment system are viewed as forming a partnership in which each member develops a sense of participation, belonging, and ownership. With this comes a sense of commitment and shared responsibility for the task at hand and its outcome. Kenneth Gergen has referred to this process as collaborative means to therapeutic ends.

Equity is an important aspect of collaboration with an accent on mutual respect, trust, and curiosity as critical to dialogue and the kinds of relationships that it demands. Equity emphasizes de-centering the professional and de-conserving the hierarchy. Professionals are thought to have culturally a designated role of power and authority; given this role, they can exercise choice as to how to situate themselves in the relationship.

The practitioner is the catalyst for this partnership. The manner in which the professional orients himself or herself to be, act, and respond with the client/patient is an important aspect of collaboration. The professional's responses to the patient/client are critical to the development and quality of the relationship. Their responses partly create the framework, the parameter, and the opportunity for how the relationship will and will not be.

Constructionist-oriented medical family therapists and psychotherapists practice collaboratively in multiple cultures. Successful collaboration depends on an awareness of cultural differences and learning about the patient/client's culture from him or her rather than assuming knowledge of it.

Dialogue

Dialogue refers to conversation and talk in which new understanding and meaning occur. Dialogue is not limited to spoken words. It includes the many silent ways in which people communicate, express, and articulate, such as their use of signs, symbols, and gestures.

Dialogical understanding and meaning-making are not a search for facts or details but an orientation. It is a dynamic and relational process that requires its participants, according to Mikhail Bakhtin, to have a sense of mutuality, genuine respect, and sincere interest regarding the other. To set this tone, the constructionist health care provider maintains a position of curiosity and tries to understand the other person from the other's perspective rather than, for instance, from a theory or diagnosis. The provider's learning position naturally invites the patient/client into a shared inquiry in which the patient/client develops a new curiosity about his or her condition and circumstances,

and as a consequence new local knowledge (i.e., resolutions, solutions, and treatment protocols) is developed.

From a constructionist perspective, collaborative relationships and dialogical conversations are inherently transforming. That is, when people have a space and process for collaborative relationships and dialogic conversations, possibilities begin to emerge as they begin to talk with themselves, each other, and others in new ways; begin to see and experience themselves and others in new ways; and begin to behave in new ways. The newness can be expressed in an infinite variety of forms, such as enhanced self-agency, freeing self-identities, and different ways to deal with life events such as chronic illness, divorce, and death of a child.

Individuals and Families

Constructionist-oriented practitioners focus on a relational perspective and approach to medical and mental health services. Relational refers to the individual as a person-in-relationship or, as Kenneth Gergen suggests, the individual as a relational being. The treatment target or method is not distinguished by designations such as individual, family, or larger systems. Whether an individual or a family is the focus of care and regardless of the number of people in a system or their relationship with each other, each person, each member is conceptualized and approached as an individual-in-relationship. The professional assumes a similar relational stance and undertakes the same dialogical process regardless of the designated system or number of people in it.

Constructionist-oriented practitioners do not adhere to a single definition of family. The system called a family can have multiple designs in terms of membership, relationships, and values. Practitioners are aware that these dimensions in any one family system can change over time and that changing cultural and societal factors will influence the definitions of family and its members' roles.

Problems and Solutions

The formation of problems and their solutions is viewed as a relational, collaborative process that is constructed in language. This means that the focus is not on, for instance, whether the act of child abuse occurred or not, or in breast cancer whether the disease is present or not, but in the socially created understandings and meanings that are attributed to these life circumstances and how these permit or limit possibilities for treatment and recovery. The desired outcome for constructionist-oriented practitioners is to help people construct realities (i.e., problem definitions or solution options) that have possibility potential: to help people be able to have conversations with themselves (inner) and with others (outer) that permit new ways of talking about, for instance, an illness or a problem, in fresh ways that lead to new meanings and actions.

Interventions and Treatment Recommendations

Constructionist-oriented practice is not based on practitioner-predetermined, scripted interventions and treatment recommendations in the traditional sense. The development of each intervention and treatment recommendation is collaboratively tailored to each patient/client's specific needs and desires.

History

Constructionist-oriented practices, also referred to as collaborative, collaborative health care, conversational, dialogical, narrative, open dialogue, postmodern, relational, and solution-focused practices, reflect the global and local shifts in a fast-changing world with increasing attention on the decentralization of information, knowledge, and expertise and on the significance of social justice, human rights, and the people's voice. Constructionist-oriented practices are a response to people's increased demand to have input into what affects their lives and to the need for collaboration.

Constructionist theory and the practices based upon it emerged over the past 4 decades, influenced by the broader discourses of the postmodern ideological critique of modern traditions of knowledge, the social basis of scientific knowledge, and the fallacy of reason and rationality. The orienting assumptions about knowledge and language present in these discourses, however, have been present within philosophical discourses since the 18th century, beginning with the historian Giambattista Vico's notion that the observer is part of the description. No one theory of constructionism or one constructionist-based practice has developed. Multiple philosophers and social scientists whose works have significantly contributed to the movement include Mikhail Bakhtin, Jerome Bruner, Jacques Derrida, Michel Foucault, Hans-George Gadamer, Nelson Goodman, Erving Goffman, Jean François Lyotard, Maurice Merleau-Ponty, Richard Rorty, Lev Vygotsky, and Ludwig Wittgenstein.

In the medical and mental health fields, practice based on similar disclaims of objective truth and tangible, external reality have primarily emerged independently of each other in psychology and family therapy, and as such there is no one definition or model of constructionist practice. Constructionist-oriented practice has no geographical borders or cultural boundaries and is increasingly found in numerous countries and contexts around the world.

Practitioners and scholars who share common ground with a constructionist orientation include Tom Andersen, Harlene Anderson, Vivien Burr, John Cromby, Kenneth Gergen, Mary Gergen, Harold Goolishian, Lynn Hoffman, Lois Holzman, George Kelly, Imelda McCarthy, Susan McDaniel, Sheila McNamee, Robert Neimeyer, David Nightingale, Peggy Penn, Sallyann Roth, Jaakko Seikkula, John Shotter, Lois Shawver, Karl Tomm, and Michael White. Their shared goal is transformation through collaboration and dialogue, though they vary regarding the emphasis they place on any one assumption of constructionist practice as delineated in this entry or their performance of it.

Constructionist theory and practice are sometimes associated with a constructivist orientation. The focal point of each is the construction of reality. The extent varies, however, as to degree that a constructivist-oriented practitioner will focus on the importance for the constructionist-oriented practitioner of intersubjective knowing and meaning-making as a social, dialogical process making the practitioner less of an expert.

The Constructionist Practitioner Stance

The constructionist practitioner's stance is the core of each practice orientation mentioned earlier.

Stance refers to a way of being with people, including ways of orienting with, thinking with, talking with, acting with, and responding with them. The emphasis is on "with" or a withness thinking and practice, as John Shotter calls it. Withness relationships and conversations become more participatory and mutual and less hierarchical and dualistic, inviting the patient/client to participate on a more equitable basis.

The stance reflects an attitude, posture, and tone that communicate to the patient/client the special importance that the patient/client holds for the practitioner: that he or she is a unique human being and not a category of person, that he or she is recognized and appreciated, and that his or her voice is worthy of hearing without judgment. It refers to the practitioner's freshly meeting each person and his or her circumstances as if they had not met before.

The stance has interrelated characteristics considered crucial to encouraging and sustaining collaboration and dialogue. This entry highlights seven characteristics: conversational partnership, relational expertise, not-knowing, openness, uncertainty, mutual transformation, and strengths and resources. Though constructionist-oriented medical and psychotherapy practices share these characteristics, the degree to which each characteristic is present and its form of implementation will vary across practices.

Conversational Partnership

A conversational partnership is characterized by a joint activity referred to as shared or mutual inquiry. Shared inquiry is an in-there-together process in which two or more people put their heads together to puzzle over and address something. Through the inquiry patients/clients begin to develop fresh understandings and meanings that permit them to successfully address the circumstances in their lives for which they sought consultation. Constructionists trust that newness will develop through the inquiry and may take forms that neither party would have separately imagined or created.

Relational Expertise

Relational expertise refers to the cocreation of knowledge, for instance, truth, reality and expertise,

and ideas and solutions. Patient/client and practitioner form a knowledge-generating community with each bringing expertise to the encounter. Patients and clients are experts on their own lives, and practitioners are experts on a creating and facilitating a space and process for collaboration and dialogue. This calls attention to the patients' or clients' wealth of know-how and cautions practitioners to neither value nor privilege their knowledge over that of the patients and clients. Practitioner expertise is always present but not in a hierarchical way. For instance, practitioners may hold theories about substance abuse or the psychosocial components of diabetes, and they consider these theories as grounded in particular professional discourses and serving as starting points for conversation and exploration rather than guiding the direction and outcome of treatment.

Not-Knowing

Not-knowing refers to the humble attitude that practitioners hold toward their knowledge and the intent and manner with which it is introduced. Constructionist practitioners emphasize knowing with patients/clients. Not-knowing does not mean practitioners do not know anything, can discard what they know, or should not use what they know (i.e., theoretical knowledge, clinical experience, life experience). Practitioners introduce their knowledge as a consideration to be talked about. As such, practitioners are open to their knowledge being challenged by patients/clients and by colleagues.

Openness

Practitioners believe that it is important to be forthright and open about their inner thoughts so that patients/clients have a sense of what is behind, for instance, their questions and recommendations. Being open is believed to safeguard unduly steering patients/clients and to avoid unwittingly influencing patients/client noncompliance.

Uncertainty

Relationships and conversations based in a constructionist perspective are like ordinary ones that are spontaneous and in which there is natural uncertainty. Constructionist practitioners, for instance, prefer to not use prestructured questions that serve as guides toward a predetermined outcome. In embracing uncertainty, practitioners take a risk and live with the associated tension of ambiguity and unpredictability.

Mutual Transformation

An implication of the constructionist view of knowledge as socially created is that transformation, likewise, is a mutual process. Each member of the treatment system is influenced and changed through the relationship and the dialogical process.

Strengths and Resources

What is common among people regardless of their life circumstance is, as Wittgenstein (1953) says, the primary concern of being able to "go on" with each other and the search for how to know our "way about." In therapy, client and therapist join in the effort to find ways for clients to move forward and carry on with their lives.

To enhance this possibility, collaborative therapists find it helpful to have a positive outlook regarding the people who consult them regardless of their histories and circumstances. This includes a belief that the human species is naturally resilient and desires healthy relationships and qualities of life. They also find it helpful not to be constrained by discourses of pathology and dysfunction that have often already imprisoned clients and their ability to go on. Rather, they consider that each person, regardless of life circumstances, intellectual capacity, and so forth, has strengths and resources unique to him or her. Collaborative therapists would notice, be curious about, respect, and encourage a client's resources, while at the same time being sensitive to the client's reality and careful not to impose theirs on the client.

In taking this perspective, descriptions and distinctions, such as big and small problems, chronic or acute, minimize the opportunity for future possibilities best befitting the person and his or her circumstances and the ability to go on. As mentioned earlier, collaborative therapists do not think in terms of categories of people or kinds of problems, though of course similarities across the board could be found. Instead, they find it helpful to create more conventional frameworks of understanding *with* their clients that are less confining, more likely to yield an increased sense of personal agency, and more likely to hold the promise of different futures.

Conclusion

Through the constructionist-informed collaborative relationship and dialogical conversation, each member of the treatment system—individual, family members, and professional colleagues—will have a sense of participation, belonging, ownership, and responsibility. When constructionist-oriented practitioners assume a philosophical stance as described in this entry, they naturally and spontaneously create a space that invites and encourages conversations and relationships in which patients/clients and practitioners connect, collaborate, and construct with each other. Together they create possibilities and outcomes that are beyond the creativity or imagination of any one member of the system. When patients/clients contribute to the creation of the recommendation and the product, these are more uniquely fitting and their sustainability is increased. The benefit is that all combine to promote effective and efficient treatment plans, interventions, health and illness management, solutions and resolutions, and improved well-being. A constructionist-oriented perspective is equally applicable whether the individual or the family is the focus of care and when the family is viewed as the context of individual care.

The Further Readings provide an in-depth description of social construction theory for readers who want to delve more into the subject. They also provide numerous examples of the application of constructionist-oriented practice in a variety of contexts such as therapy, education, research, and medicine and in a variety of settings such as hospitals, universities, therapy rooms, and community agencies.

Harlene Anderson

See also Clarifying Family as Context of Care and Family as Focus of Care in Family Health; Family Therapy; Mental Health Assessment for Families; Psychological Theories Related to Family Health; Types of Family Provider Relationships

Further Readings

Anderson, H. (1997). *Conversation, language and possibilities: A postmodern approach to practice.* New York: Basic Books.

Freedman, J., & Combs, G. (1996). *Narrative therapy: The social construction of preferred realities.* New York: Norton.

Gergen, K. J. (2009). *An invitation to social construction* (2nd ed.). Thousand Oaks, CA: Sage.

McDaniel, S., Hepworth, J., & Doherty, W. (1992). *Medical family therapy: A biopsychosocial approach to families with health problems.* New York: Basic Books.

McNamee, S., & Gergen, K. J. (1992). *Therapy as social construction.* London: Sage.

Neimeyer, R. A. (2009). *Constructivist therapy: Distinctive features.* New York: Routledge.

Shotter, J. (2008). *Conversational realities revisited: Life, language, body and world.* Chagrin Falls, OH: Taos Institute Publishing.

White, M., & Epston, D. (1990). *Therapeutic means to therapeutic ends.* New York: Norton.

CONTRACEPTION IN CHILDBEARING COUPLES

Contraception refers to preventing conception and includes techniques that prevent fertilization of the egg or implantation of the fertilized egg in the uterus. *Birth control* is the act of preventing birth and comprises techniques to avoid birth, including pregnancy termination. Religious and ethical concerns may limit contraception to methods based on the calculation of women's fertility (natural family planning). Permanent surgical methods, including bilateral tubal ligation (cutting the woman's fallopian tubes) or vasectomy (cutting the man's vas deferens), are nearly 100% effective. In the following discussion, first-year estimated failure rates, reported by the Guttmacher Institute, are presented as percentages of pregnancy occurrence despite contraceptive use under conditions of perfect use and of typical use. Pregnancy rates for intercourse without contraception are estimated as 85%.

Two male dependent techniques are withdrawal (*coitus interruptus*) and male condoms. Withdrawal is the removal of the penis from the vagina prior to ejaculation. Estimated failure rates for withdrawal are 4% for perfect use and 18.4% for typical use. Failure rates for male condoms are 2.0% for perfect and 17.4% for typical use. Male condoms, used once only, are available with or without

lubrication. Prelubricated condoms are unlikely to rupture during use, but using petroleum or oil-based lubricants leads to rapid deterioration and breakage. Condoms are inexpensive, $.50 to $1.00 each, and prevent most sexually transmitted infections.

Male condoms belong to a group of methods called barrier methods. Barrier methods prevent sperm from entering the cervix by inserting mechanical and chemical obstructions into the vagina. The female condom is a polyurethane shield roughly in the shape of a penis. One end of the female condom is closed and has a flexible ring that is inserted over the cervix with the open end extending from the vagina. Perfect and typical use failure rates are 5% and 27%, respectively. Male and female condoms should not be used together. The cervical sponge is a soft disc placed over the cervix that is pretreated with spermicides. Used only once, it is available without prescription and retails for approximately $2.50. For women who have not borne children, failure rates are 9% for perfect and 16% for typical use. For childbearing women, failure rates are 20% and 32%, respectively.

Cervical diaphragms are rubber caps that are filled with a spermicidal product and inserted over the cervix prior to intercourse. Diaphragms are fitted by a health provider and refitted after a pregnancy or with a 10-pound weight change. Perfect use estimated failure rate is 6% and typical use 16%. Cervical caps, also used with spermicide, must be fitted by a health professional. Cervical caps are smaller and fit more snugly over the cervix than the diaphragm. Failure rates are 9% for perfect and 16% for typical use in women who have not given birth and 20% and 32% in women who have had children. Diaphragms and cervical caps should remain in place for 6 to 8 hours postcoitus. Prolonged retention is not recommended due to the risk of toxic shock syndrome. Diaphragms cost about $30 and caps range from $60 to $75, but there are added costs of provider visits and recurrent costs of spermicidal products (about $0.25 per use).

Hormonal methods of contraception have been available by prescription since the 1960s and are delivered in numerous ways. Oral contraceptives (the pill) come in a variety of combinations of the two major female hormones, estrogen and progesterone (progestin) or as progestin only. The pill costs from $5 to $50 per monthly pack. The pill is the most frequently used contraceptive in the country. Pills are taken for 3 weeks with the 4th week using placebos or no pill. The combined pill has less than a 1% failure rate for perfect use and an 8.7% failure rate with typical use. Hormonal contraceptives also are available in an injection form, usually progestin only, with a shot required every 3 months. Injections have a less than 1% failure rate with perfect and a 6.7% failure rate with typical use. Hormones are delivered through a flexible ring that is inserted into the vagina for 3 weeks and removed for the 4th week. The contraceptive patch is applied once weekly for 3 weeks and omitted the 4th week. The ring and the patch have less than a 1% failure rate with perfect and a 8% failure rate with typical use. Women who smoke or who have cardiac risk factors may not be able to use products with estrogen. Progestin-only contraceptives may reduce or stop menstrual bleeding altogether and may lead to weight gain, acne, and initial bone loss, whereas estrogen may decrease bone loss.

The intrauterine device (IUD), a small plastic device inserted by a care provider into the cervix, slowly releases progestin (5-year limit) or copper (10-year limit). Both types of IUD have less than a 1% failure for any use. Contraceptive implants are small progestin-filled rods that are surgically implanted, usually in the upper arm, for up to 3 years. Failure rates are similar to the IUD but anecdotally more failures are seen in women who weigh over 200 pounds. IUDs range in cost from $175 to $400, and the implant ranges from $300 to $700 depending on the provider cost. Implant removal costs between $100 and $200.

Emergency contraception, the "morning after pill," is hormonal and must be used within 72 hours of unprotected intercourse. Women take 2 tablets of a combination birth control pill twice, 12 hours apart. This product price ranges from $30 to $60 plus the costs of a health provider visit. The second type of emergency contraception is a progestin-only pill that requires two doses, 12 hours apart; it is available to women over 18 without a prescription. The progestin-only pill costs between $10 and $70. Both of these preparations are estimated to be 90% effective in preventing pregnancy if taken within 72 hours and 95% effective if taken within 24 hours.

Natural family planning is a group of strategies that require periodic abstinence during a woman's fertile time. They include the calendar method, the mucus method, and the temperature method. Failure rates for all use are over 25%.

M. Kay Libbus

See also Birth Order of Children in Families; Childbirth by Childbearing Couples: Reported Meanings; Childlessness

Further Readings

Guttmacher Institute. (2010, June). *Facts on contraceptive use in the United States.* Retrieved from http://www.guttmacher.org/pubs/fb_contr_use.html

Mishell, D. R. (2007). Contraception. *The Merck Manuals Online Medical Library.* Retrieved from http://www.merck.com/mmhe/sec22/ch255/ch255b.html

Schwartz, J. L., & Gabelnik, H. L. (2002). Current contraceptive research. *Perspectives on Sexual and Reproductive Health, 34*(6). Retrieved from http://www.guttmacher.org/pubs/journals/3431002.html

COPARENTING: CHILDREN

Between the time they are born and their entry into adulthood, nearly all children are parented, socialized, and acculturated by two or more different individuals who, as a collaborating unit, bear responsibility for the child's care and upbringing. Together, these accountable individuals serve as the child's coparents, that is, the collective of adults who guide the child to adulthood, shape the child's skills and sensibilities, and provide him or her with a sense of safety and security in the world. In the majority of families around the world, this coparental unit includes the child's biological mother, working in tandem with the child's father and/or with grandparents and other relative caregivers to provide the child's core family base. In cases where both biological mother and father are absent, coparenting of the child occurs within the substitute system that materializes to support the child. In these circumstances, the unit can come to involve blood and fictive kin and/or foster or adoptive parents who step forward to make a temporary or permanent commitment to the child. While a child's coparents are sometimes defined by legal arrangements, legal standing is not the principal consideration. Rather, the essential coparental unit for any child will include any and all of those individuals who collectively parent, provide for, and commit to ensuring the child's enduring safety and well-being.

Within the coparenting systems that develop within families, an important consideration for children is the extent to which the different coparenting adults are able to create a mutually supportive alliance with one another that facilitates shared and considered decision making about the child and his or her needs. Nearly all parenting adults maintain at least somewhat different notions about what is best for children, and their individual parenting practices are guided by these conscious or unconscious beliefs. When parents operate with very different ideas about what is in a child's best interests, as is not uncommon in many Western cultures, their propensity and inclination to talk together about the child and to consult and make important decisions together can be critically important. When parents understand and respect one another's perspectives and work together so as to provide a reasonably consistent and coordinated set of rules and standards for the child, they communicate solidarity to the child. This, in turn, helps the child feel safe and secure in a stable, predictable family climate. By contrast, when the adults work in opposition; ignore, disrespect, or dismiss the parenting decisions made by the child's other parenting figures; derogate or disparage one another to the child; or in other ways undermine joint parenting efforts, this confuses and sometimes disorganizes children and can lead, in more severe circumstances, to problems with behavioral adjustment.

In nuclear family systems, the dynamics of each family's coparenting system are influenced by a variety of factors, including the parents' own psychodynamics and the nature of their relationship with one another. Adults with insecure states of mind with respect to attachment or with pessimistic attitudes about coparenting are at greater risk to develop problematic coparenting alliances during their child's infancy. Marital strain preceding the birth of a child also places the coparenting alliance at risk, and numerous studies have established linkages between marital distress and problems in coparenting during infancy, childhood, and adolescence. Problems with coparenting also often continue post-divorce; ample evidence indicates that children whose parents continue high-conflict coparenting relationships after they have divorced show especially problematic adjustment, with problems of boys more pronounced early on and problems of girls surfacing later. By contrast, if parents are able to establish positive working alliances as coparents post-divorce, these same behavioral problems are seen much less frequently. Coparenting alliances also evolve in families where the parents never marry. Again, the main predictor of whether a positive coparenting alliance will materialize and be sustained through time in families where the child's mother and father never marry or live together is the nature of the relationship between them. Friendship and rapport increase the likelihood that there will be a sustained coparental alliance across developmental time. Less is currently known about factors that shape positive or negative coparenting alliances in extended kinship or multigenerational family systems, though the historical interpersonal relationship between the coparenting individuals predating the child's arrival likely plays a formative role.

While coparenting alliances owe in part to dyadic relationship quality between the coparenting adults, they are also a distinctive relationship system within the family that transcends such dyadic relationships. A fundamental tenet of family systems theories is that the whole is greater than the sum of its parts, and research studies of coparenting have supported this tenet. Proper understanding of coparental alliances necessitates taking a triadic or family group level of analysis, one in which the relationship between the adults with respect to a *particular* child is considered. First, the nature and dynamics of the same two people's coparenting alliance may differ for different children in the family. Second, even children as young as 3 months of age contribute to the relationship dynamic that evolves between them and their coparents. Third, coparenting dynamics are not simply an extension of the parenting behaviors of each parent, considered individually. When a parent or caregiver tends to a child one-on-one, it is possible, even common, for the adult's manner of working with the child to be reasonable and effective. However, when parental consistency has been studied across settings, the adult's parenting style when alone with the child is not always a good prognosticator of that same parent's behavior when coparenting together with the child's other parent. In particular, there are more pronounced shifts in important parental behaviors such as sensitivity and engagement as the adults move from parenting in dyadic settings to triadic settings in those families where the adults' marital union is strained. Fourth, in studies that have separately assessed marital adjustment, parenting style, and coparenting dynamics, coparenting indicators predict unique variance in child outcomes, after variability owing to the marital or parenting measures have been taken into consideration. Finally, longitudinal studies indicate that coparenting dynamics are stable across developmental time. Whereas most of these findings have been obtained in studies of Western nuclear family systems, numerous innovative investigations of coparenting in diverse family systems are currently under way, and new, relevant data on coparenting in such families will be forthcoming during the next decade.

James P. McHale

See also Nonmarital Childbearing; Parental Abandonment; Parental Attachment; Parenting

Further Readings

McHale, J. (2007). *Charting the bumpy road of coparenthood: Understanding the challenges of family life.* Washington, DC: Zero to Three Press.

McHale, J. (2009). Shared child-rearing in nuclear, fragile, and kinship family systems: Evolution, dilemmas, and promise of a coparenting framework. In M. Schulz, M. Pruett, P. Kerig, & R. Parke (Eds.), *Strengthening couple relationships for optimal child development: Lessons from research and intervention.* Washington, DC: American Psychological Association.

McHale, J., & Lindahl, K. (2010). *Coparenting: Theory, research and clinical applications.* Washington, DC: American Psychological Association.

COPING MANAGEMENT STYLES IN FAMILIES

Coping management styles in families have been examined in a variety of contexts. The necessity to adapt to change within the family system may be precipitated by occurrences outside of the family, such as a house fire or earthquake, or from within the family when divorce, illness, or death of a family member occurs. When a child within the family is diagnosed with a chronic illness, the family needs to change in order to meet the new demands the illness creates. The family management styles (FMS) framework was developed to describe how the child's treatment regimen is incorporated into everyday family life.

Considerable research has been conducted to increase our understanding regarding both the individual child who is experiencing chronic health problems and their families. The FMS framework complements other family frameworks and contributes to a comprehensive understanding of the family response to having a child with a chronic condition. It is more focused, for instance, than family stress and coping frameworks because it describes key aspects of how the condition is incorporated into everyday life. The goal of the framework is to identify not only the components or variables (such as child adaptation) related to family management but also to analyze how they might form patterns or typologies (such as family management style, child adaptation, and diabetes control).

In order to incorporate parents from a variety of family contexts who contribute to the management of children's chronic conditions, a household definition of family is used that includes people living with them who they think of as family. Therefore, family is defined conceptually as a group of intimates living together with strong emotional bonds and with a history and a future. In addition, a noncategorical approach is often used to select samples for studies of family management. In doing so, common psychosocial challenges are used to conceptualize the nature of chronic illness instead of biomedical diagnosis. Finally, according to Ruth Stein, children of all ages can be used to generate knowledge that spans the developmental trajectory in order to facilitate a longitudinal understanding of chronic illness and the family.

Because the focus of the family management is on everyday management, the framework has been developed primarily with child populations who have been diagnosed for more than 6 months and who have not experienced recent hospitalizations. Families of children with cancer or conditions associated with significant developmental delays were originally excluded, so that the FMS framework could be systematically developed and tested in these populations in the next stages of the research. Recent research has extended established preliminary evidence of validity for families of children with cancer.

The framework has been developed through a series of conceptual projects and empirical studies. Most recently a 53-item measure (Family Management Measure [FaMM]) of parents' perceptions of family's management was validated. A closer look at the FaMM will clarify how the FaMM was developed.

Family Management Measure

The 53-item FaMM instrument is composed of 6 scales focused on parental perception of family management. There are 45 items for all parents and 8 additional items for partnered parents only. Items are scored from 1, strongly disagree, to 5, strongly agree. Five summated scales for all parents measure the dimensions of Child's Daily Life, View of Condition Impact, Family's Life Difficulty, Condition Management Effort, and Condition Management Ability. A sixth scale for partnered parents only measures the dimension of Parental Mutuality. Higher scores on three of the scales (Child Identity, Management Ability, Parental Mutuality) indicate greater ease in managing the child's condition. Higher scores on the other three scales (Condition Impact, Difficulty, Effort) indicate greater difficulty in managing the condition. Validation with 579 parents of children with a chronic condition (349 partnered mothers, 165 partners, 65 single mothers) addressed reliability, factor structure, and construct validity.

Development and Details

The FMS framework was developed in the late 1980s, based on a program of research by Kathleen Knafl, Agatha Gallo, and Janet Deatrick, in order to understand how the family as a unit responds to childhood chronic conditions. Although originally interested in the FMS of normalization, Knafl and colleagues identified the need for a broader conceptualization of family response. Toward that end, FMS was selected to communicate the researchers' focus on a consistent pattern of active, behavioral, family unit response reflected in how the family "defines" and "manages" their situation. The researchers' work continued with various conceptual, empirical (relatively small scale), and clinical applications of the concept.

A larger scale, qualitative, longitudinal study with 63 families in which the child had a chronic condition was undertaken in order to more fully elaborate specific FMSs, explore their stability over time (at two points 12 months apart), as well as to begin to link them to child health outcomes. Five FMSs were identified: thriving, accommodating, enduring, struggling, and floundering. Each style was inductively derived within the context of the family system from interviews with individual family members. A typological format was used to present the styles, underscoring both similarities and differences between the styles that may have key clinical significance. A continuum of difficulty is represented in these styles as well as evidence about the extent to which experiences of individual family members were similar or discrepant. For instance, Thriving FMS is composed of a "Normal" Child Identity; "Accom-modative" Parenting Philosophy; and "Confident" Management Mindset. On the other hand, an Enduring FMS is composed of a "Normal, Tragic" Child Identity; "Accommodative, Protective" Paren-ting Philosophy; and, "Confident, Burden some" Management Mindset. Finally, the FMS framework was refined, adding the dimensions for each of the "Defining" and "Managing" components as well as adding a third component, "Perceived Consequences."

The FMS framework and its three components were then further elaborated into eight components based on a review of 55 studies of family management of childhood chronic conditions (excluding studies of families of children whose condition resulted in significant developmental delays). These components were identified as important aspects of family management that span multiple chronic conditions and family life cycle phases and provided the conceptual underpinnings for development of the FaMM: Child Identity (views of the child and the extent to which those views focus on illness and vulnerabilities or normalcy and capabilities); Illness View (beliefs about the seriousness and course of the illness); Management Mindset (views about the ease or difficulty of carrying out the treatment regimen); Parenting Philosophy (goals and values that guide condition management); Management Approach (assessment of the extent to which the family has developed a routine for managing the condition); Parental Mutuality (beliefs about the extent to which partners have shared views of their situation and approach to condition management); Family Focus (assessment of the balance between condition management and other aspects of family life); and Future Expectations (assessment of the implications of the condition for the child's and family's future).

According to current evidence, family management is composed of six components: the Child's Daily Life, or the parents' perceptions of the child and his or her everyday life, with higher values indicating a more normal life for the child despite the condition; the View of Condition Impact, or the parents' perceptions of the seriousness of the condition and its implications for their child and family, with higher values indicating that parents view the condition as more serious; the Family Life Difficulty, or the parents' perceptions of the extent to which having a child with a chronic condition makes life more difficult, with higher values indicating greater difficulty; the Condition Management Effort, or the parents' perceptions of the work needed to manage the condition, with higher values signifying greater effort; the Condition Management Ability, or the parents' perceptions of their competence to take care of the child's condition, with higher values signifying that parents view themselves as more capable of managing the condition; the Parental Mutuality, for partnered parents, or the partners' satisfaction with how they work together to manage the child's condition, with higher values indicating greater satisfaction. Each of the scales is related to measures of family functioning, child functional status, and child behavior, with directions of relationships as expected.

Examples

The six components or factors of the FaMM describe and measure parents' perceptions of managing their children's conditions and how they incorporate the condition into everyday family life. When used by clinicians or researchers, the FaMM can be used to identify key components of family management from the point of view of the parents and facilitate interventions to assist families. For instance, if the parents View the Condition as relatively serious but the Child's Daily Life as essentially normal, then potential interventions (i.e., changes in treatment) need to be presented in a way that preserves parental beliefs about the "normality" of their child's life. If parents View the Condition as relatively serious, the Child's Daily Life is essentially abnormal, but Family Life is difficult, then concentrating on decreasing the difficulty of Family Life may be helpful before trying to reframe beliefs about the "normality" of the Child's Daily Life. Finally, if parents perceive that they are competent (Condition Management Ability) and have to expend a great deal of effort (Condition Management Effort), then they may experience burden (effort) that is undetected by health care providers.

Interventions tailored to these six areas of family management will potentially be more effective than interventions created with a "one size fits all" philosophy. Interventions can be focused on caregiver, child, or the family issues and may include the entire family or various subsystems of the family in the actual intervention (parents, siblings, affected child, and extended family). Examples include the following:

Caregiver—Competency and effort–focused interventions can focus on how to reframe the caregiver's beliefs, attitudes, and skills that are found to be most problematic for a population of caregivers or for individual caregivers.

Child—Problem-solving skills can focus on how to identify and manage issues secondary to the emotional, physical, or social quality of life of the affected child.

Family—Family roles and relationship building can focus on reassessing family functioning in light of Parental Mutuality or Family Life Difficulty.

Various individuals can be included in such interventions as are clinically relevant and practically possible, including the caregiver, one or both parents, siblings, the affected child, and the extended family.

Future research also has the potential to refine our ideas about patterns of family management of childhood chronic conditions. While the present literature describes five FMSs that were inductively derived from qualitative research, future research grounded in the newly developed factor structure for the FaMM, using partnered parent data, and sophisticated analytic techniques will enable refining the FMSs. These styles will be intuitively helpful for the clinician and vital to the researcher in development of intervention studies that are sensitive to how the family incorporates illness management.

Janet A. Deatrick and Barbara Beacham

See also Assessing Family Health; Cancer Survivorship and the Family; Chronic Health Problems and Interventions for the Childrearing Family; Family Caregiving: Caring for Children, Adults, and Elders With Developmental Disabilities; Parenting

Further Readings

Deatrick, J. A., Mullaney, E., & Mooney-Doyle, K. (2009). Exploring family management of childhood brain tumor survivors. *Journal of Pediatric Oncology Nursing, 6*(5), 303–311.

Gallo, A. (1990). Family management style in juvenile diabetes: A case illustration. *Journal of Pediatric Nursing, 5*(1), 23–32.

Knafl, K., & Deatrick, J. (2002). The challenge of normalization for families of children with chronic conditions. *Pediatric Nursing, 28*(1), 48–53, 56.

Knafl, K., Deatrick, J., Gallo, A., Dixon, J., Grey, M., Knafl, G., et al. (2009, May 18). Assessment of the psychometric properties of the Family Management Measure. *Journal of Pediatric Psychology.* Advance online publication.

Stein, R., & Jessop, D. J. (1982). A noncategorical approach to childhood chronic illness. *Public Health Reports, 97*(4), 354–362.

Thibodeaux, A., & Deatrick, J. A. (2007). Cultural influence of family management of children with cancer. *Journal of Pediatric Oncology Nursing, 24*(4), 227–233.

Websites

Family Management Measure (FaMM): http://nursing.unc.edu/research/famm

Mothers as Caregivers for Survivors of Pediatric Brain Tumors: http://caregiverproject.securespsites.com

CORD BLOOD BANKING AND THE CHILDBEARING FAMILY

Once considered a waste product that was discarded with the placenta after birth, umbilical cord blood is now known to contain stem cells that can be used in the treatment of many life-threatening illnesses. These stem cells can be given to patients undergoing treatment for some diseases of the blood and immune system and certain inherited metabolic diseases in order to reconstitute the bone marrow. Because of this, banking of cord blood has become an option for pregnant patients at the time of delivery. Public banking involves the donation of the cord blood, free of charge. The cord blood would then be available for anyone to use. The National Marrow Donor Program oversees the cord blood stored and provides a searchable database for physicians who care for patients with diseases amenable to cord blood therapy. Alternatively, some patients arrange during their pregnancy to have their infant's cord blood stored with a private/commercial collection company for an initial processing fee followed by annual maintenance fees. In these cases, the cord blood is stored for possible future use by the child, a sibling, or other family member. After providing a brief history of cord blood transplant, this entry discusses the health effects of cord blood collection and the controversy surrounding public versus private banking and then presents recommendations from professional organizations.

History

Traditionally, all hematopoietic transplants were performed using bone marrow, which requires the donor to undergo a painful, invasive procedure. However, since the first successful umbilical cord blood transplant in 1988, thousands of cord blood transplants have been performed in children and adults undergoing treatment for certain cancers and for the correction of certain metabolic and genetic disorders.

Health Effects

Umbilical cord blood collection, whether public or private, has few, if any known risks to the mother or her newborn. The cord blood is collected after the baby is delivered and is not needed by the mother or newborn. While not a medical risk, there is a significant monetary cost to the patient to store cord blood privately. There is no social risk from either private or public cord blood banking, provided that both have rigorous and effective policies and procedures for maintaining confidentiality.

The benefits of cord blood banking are well known. In many cases of life-threatening illness, cord blood can be used as an alternative to bone marrow donation. This can reduce the need for bone marrow retrieval, a procedure that has associated risks to the donor and involves significant discomfort.

Public Versus Private Banking

The controversy regarding the benefits of cord blood donation lies in the supposed *incremental* benefit in storing the cord blood privately over donating it to a public bank or, in cases where public donation is not available, discarding the blood and relying on the public banking system for possible future needs. The incremental benefits are thought to be two: (1) Should the need arise for cord blood transplantation in this child or a sibling, there may not be a suitable or optimal match found from a public bank. (2) If cord blood were found in the future to cure other medical conditions, donating the blood to a public bank or discarding the blood may cause the newborn to miss a "once in a lifetime" opportunity to store this cord blood for future use.

These two potential benefits of private banking seem logical. However, they are not supported by current evidence. First, the chance that a particular child or sibling will develop a condition requiring cord blood transplantation is very small. Also, most of these patients would not be eligible for autologous (a patient receiving one's own) cord blood, including those with leukemia and genetic conditions. Additionally, even if the need were to arise, if the cord blood was donated to a public bank, it would likely still be available for that child. In the New York Blood Center, for example, approximately 80% of cord blood units are still available for use after 10 years of storage.

Regarding transplantation for a sibling, if at the time of delivery there is already an affected sibling or other close family member, there is a compelling reason to collect cord blood (directed donation) on the chance (about 25% for a sibling) that it would be suitable for a future transplant. However, private storage on pure speculation that a sibling may develop a condition is less compelling for the same argument that it is very unlikely it will ever be needed.

Regarding the possibility of finding a suitable match from the public banking system, a July 2005 statement from the National Marrow Donor Program (NMDP) indicates that "nearly all (>95%) patients are able to find at least one potential 4 of 6 HLA matched cord blood units on the NMDP Registry, the largest in the United States, and the majority will find a potential 5 of 6 match." The New York Blood Center, the first established cord blood bank, could find a 4 of 6 match for 99% of patients seeking a transplant, 65% found a 5 of 6 match, and 11% found a 6 of 6 match. Most cord blood transplants to date have been with a 4 out of 6 match. Additionally, recent evidence suggests that outcomes may be similar with related and nonrelated donors.

Some argue for the discovery of other important uses for cord blood in the future. However, this argument is posited typically by the private cord blood companies, who have significant financial interest in the consumer storing blood privately. While cord blood may one day be used to treat other medical conditions, it is also equally possible that cord blood therapy may one day be replaced by other modalities, such as stem cells retrieved directly from adult blood or genetically engineered stem cells.

Recommendations From Professional Organizations

The American Academy of Pediatrics discourages private cord blood storage. The American College of Obstetricians and Gynecologists recommends that patients should be provided with balanced and accurate information about cord blood banking options, including the remote possibility of needing cord blood stored privately for personal use.

Nathan S. Fox

See also Cancer in the Family; Childbirth by Childbearing Couples: Reported Meanings; Oncological Radiation Process in the Family

Further Readings

American College of Obstetricians and Gynecologists. (2008). Umbilical cord blood banking (ACOG Committee Opinion 399). *Obstetrics & Gynecology, 111*(2), 475–477.

Ecker, J. L., & Greene, M. F. (2005). The case against private umbilical cord blood banking. *Obstetrics & Gynecology, 6*, 1282–1284.

Fox, N. S., Chervenak, F. A., & McCullough, L. B. (2008). Ethical considerations in umbilical cord blood banking. *Obstetrics & Gynecology, 111*, 178–182.

Lubin, B. H., & Shearer, W. T. (2007). Cord blood banking for potential future transplantation. *Pediatrics, 119*, 165–170.

Websites

National Marrow Donor Program: http://www.marrow.org

Costs of Medical Care and Existing National, State, and Private Pay Avenues for Families

Health care costs are projected to account for 19.3% of gross domestic product in the United States in 2019, and rising health care costs are causing greater financial burdens on families. Health insurance protects families from high medical costs in case of illness. There is concern that rising health care costs are leading to high burdens even among families with health insurance. This discussion summarizes the private and public health insurance options available for nonelderly families, presents the increase in health insurance premium costs since the year 2000, and discusses current medical care costs by family insurance status, family size, and family structure. It concludes with a presentation of the burden of medical care costs on the family, defined as the share of family income spent on medical care and health insurance.

It is important to examine medical care costs within the context of the family because family members share financial resources to pay for medical care. Furthermore, expenditures for health care and insurance premiums are often incurred at the family level. For example, health plans sometimes set family-level deductibles and out-of-pocket spending limits. Moreover, many proposals to expand insurance coverage and slow the growth of health care costs are applied at the family level, and their impact varies with the level of family spending on health care. For example, proposals changing the tax treatment of health care spending are relevant at the family level.

All estimates are based on the Medical Expenditure Panel Survey (MEPS), a stratified and clustered random sample of households designed to yield nationally representative estimates of health care expenditures for the civilian, noninstitutionalized population, sponsored by the Agency for Healthcare Research & Quality (AHRQ).

Definitions

Family

The AHRQ's definition of *family* includes all persons who would typically be eligible for coverage under a private insurance family plan. This definition includes adults, spouses, and natural or adoptive children under 18 years of age, as well as children under 24 years of age who are full-time students. Consequently, the family definition used in this analysis aligns more closely with a "health insurance eligibility unit" (HIEU) rather than a standard family definition. Note that one-person families are also included in this analysis. Nonelderly families include families in which at least one person is under age 65. Elderly families, in which all persons are aged 65 or above, are not included in this analysis.

Expenditures on Health Care Services

Total expenses include payments from all sources (including third-party payers and other miscellaneous sources) to hospitals, physicians, other health care providers (including dental care), and pharmacies for services. Out-of-pocket expenses comprise the portion of total payments made by individuals for services received during the year.

Based on the HIEU definition of family unit, the total expenditures on health care services are summed across all members of the family to calculate family-level total expenditures on health care services. Family-level out-of-pocket expenses are constructed similarly. Note that while the discussion that follows focuses on mean expenditures, both mean and median expenditures are reported in the tables since the distribution of health care expenditures are highly skewed.

Family-Level Insurance Status

Family-level insurance status is constructed based on the insurance status of all nonelderly (individuals under age 65) family members during the year. Families are classified into the following five mutually exclusive insurance categories:

1. *Uninsured:* Families in which all nonelderly persons are uninsured all year.

2. *Private Insurance:* Families in which all nonelderly persons are covered by private insurance all year. In addition to all nonelderly members having private coverage all year, some members may also have concurrent public insurance during all or part of the year. Private insurance provides coverage for hospital and physician care.

3. *Partial Private Insurance:* Families in which at least one nonelderly person has private coverage for part of the year. In addition, some members may also have public insurance during all or part of the year.

4. *Public Insurance:* Families in which (1) all nonelderly persons are covered by public insurance all year, and (2) no nonelderly member has private coverage anytime during the year. Public insurance includes Medicaid/SCHIP and Medicare coverage.

5. *Partial Public Insurance:* Families in which (1) at least one nonelderly person has public coverage for part of the year, and (2) no nonelderly person has private coverage during the year.

Family Type

The AHRQ classifies two-person families into two family types: (1) adult-couple families and (2) one-adult-one-child families. Three or more person families are classified into two subcategories: (1) families with one adult and at least two children and (2) families with two adults and at least one child. Children not living with their biological parent(s) are assigned to one-parent or two-parent families depending on whether there are one or two adults in the family unit.

Health Insurance Options and Status

Private Health Insurance Options

For the nonelderly population, the most common source of private health insurance coverage is employer-sponsored insurance. Most workers purchase health insurance through their employer. About 5% of the nonelderly population purchase insurance in the individual market. Individual (nongroup) health insurance is coverage that is purchased directly from health insurers, rather than coverage through a group such as employers.

Roughly 70% of nonelderly families have access to employer coverage, and the remaining 30% are potentially eligible to purchase insurance in the individual market.

Among families with access to employer coverage, 96% have private insurance. In contrast, among families without access to employer coverage, only 11% have private coverage.

Employer-sponsored insurance tends to have more generous benefits and because employers pay a share of the premium, this leads to lower out-of-pocket costs. On average, employers pay 75% of health insurance premiums and employees pay the remainder out-of-pocket.

Because the individual market for health insurance is small, the medical spending by high-risk people who purchase individual insurance is difficult to spread broadly. If allowed by state law, insurers in the individual market manage costs by not enrolling very high risks and by charging different premiums by predicted risk. But this practice may prevent some people from getting a policy at all, or they might receive an offer with a higher premium. Some states regulate the individual market by requiring guaranteed issue and community rating. However, this can lead to low-risk people leaving the market, which can lead to higher premiums for those remaining. Higher administrative costs of selling individual insurance also cause premiums to be higher compared to employer coverage. Problems with the individual market include coverage exclusions due to medical underwriting, less generous benefits, and higher premiums.

Public Health Insurance Options

Medicaid is the health program for eligible individuals and families with low income and few resources. It is a means-tested program that is jointly funded by the states and federal government and is managed by the states.

The State Children's Health Insurance Program (SCHIP) is also managed by state governments and funded jointly by the states and federal government. The program was designed to cover uninsured children in families whose incomes are modest but too high to qualify for Medicaid.

States are given flexibility in designing their SCHIP eligibility requirements and policies within broad federal guidelines. Some states have received authority through waivers of statutory provisions to use SCHIP funds to cover the parents of children receiving benefits from both SCHIP and Medicaid, pregnant women, and other adults.

Medicare is a health insurance program for people age 65 and over, people under age 65 with certain disabilities, and people of all ages with end-stage renal disease. It is an entitlement program funded entirely at the federal level. The Medicare program has several different components: Medicare Part A covers hospital bills; Medicare Part B covers outpatient health care expenses, including doctor fees; and Medicare Part D covers prescription drugs.

Health Insurance Status of Families

In 2006, there were approximately 124 million nonelderly families in the U.S. civilian noninstitutionalized population. Among these families, 54.3% had private coverage all year (67.1 million), 7.1% had public coverage all year (8.8 million), and 14.8% were uninsured all year (18.3 million). In addition, 17.0% of families had partial private coverage (21.0 million), that is, at least one family member had private coverage for part of the year. The remaining 6.8% of families had partial public coverage (8.3 million), that is, no family member had any private coverage during the year, but at least one family member had public coverage for part of the year.

Increasing Medical Costs and Rising Premiums

Health Insurance Premiums for Employer-Sponsored Insurance

As the cost of medical care rises, health insurance premiums rise. From 1996 to 2006, total insurance premiums for employer-sponsored coverage more than doubled in nominal terms. Average total premiums for single coverage increased from $1,992 to $4,118, and average total premiums for family coverage increased from $4,954 to $11,381. Similarly, the average employee share of premiums for single coverage increased from $342 to $788, and the average employee share of premiums for family coverage increased from $1,275 to $2,890. In real terms, both total premiums and the employee share increased by 28% over this period (Table 1).

Table 1   Average Total and Out-of-Pocket (Employee Share) Premiums for Employer-Sponsored Health Insurance Policies: 1996 and 2006

	1996	2006
Single Policies		
Total premium	$1,992	$4,118
	(14)	(25)
Out-of-pocket	$342	$788
	(7)	(16)
Family Policies		
Total premium	$4,954	$11,381
	(36)	(32)
Out-of-pocket	$1,275	$2,890
	(24)	(34)

Source: Medical Expenditure Panel Survey, Insurance Component, 1996 and 2006. http://www.meps.ahrq.gov/mepsweb/data_stats/quick_tables_results.jsp

Note: Standard errors are in parentheses.

Health Insurance Premiums for Nongroup Insurance

From 1996 to 2006, total insurance premiums for individual coverage increased by 73% for single coverage and 85% for family coverage in nominal terms. Average total premiums for single coverage increased from $1,665 to $2,882, and average total premiums for family coverage increased from $3,329 to $6,160. In real terms, total premiums increased by 28% over this period. Note that benefit generosity may have changed over this period both for employer-sponsored and individual coverage, with less generous benefits and higher cost-sharing (Table 2).

Table 2   Average Premiums and Number of Policyholders for Individual Health Insurance Policies: 1996 and 2006

	1996	2006
All Policies		
Premium	$2,159	$3,801
	(101)	(187)
Number		
of policyholders	6.946	5.610
(Millions)	(.449)	(.359)
Single Policies		
Premium	$1,665	$2,882
	(108)	(175)
Number		
of policyholders	4.884	4.036
(Millions)	(.344)	(.306)
Family Policies		
Premium	$3,329	$6,160
	(241)	(338)
Number		
of policyholders	2.062	1.574
(Millions)	(.217)	(.166)

Source: Bernard, D. M. Premiums in the Individual Health Insurance Market for Policyholders under Age 65, 1996 and 2002. Statistical Brief #72. March 2005. Agency for Healthcare Research and Quality, Rockville, MD. http://meps.ahrq.gov/data_files/publications/st72/stat72.pdf and http://www.meps.ahrq.gov/mepsweb/data_stats/summ_tables/hc/hlth_insr/2006/t6_f06.htm

Note: Standard errors are in parentheses.

Family-Level Medical Care Expenditures by Insurance Status

In 2006, mean total expenditures were $5,718 over all nonelderly families. Mean total expenditures were highest among families with public insurance and lowest among uninsured families. Mean total expenditures were $8,831 among families with public coverage, $6,785 among families with private coverage, and $1,425 among uninsured families. Mean total expenditures among families with partial private coverage ($5,237) and among families with partial public coverage ($4,467) were lower than mean total expenditures among families with private coverage all year (Table 3, next page).

In 2006, mean out-of-pocket expenditures were $1,161 over all families. Family-level mean out-of-pocket expenditures on health care services were highest among families with private insurance ($1,410). Mean out-of-pocket expenditures were $643 among families with public insurance and $663 among the uninsured. The difference in mean out-of-pocket expenditures between families with public insurance and uninsured families was not statistically significant. Mean out-of-pocket expenditures among families with partial private coverage ($1,102), and among families with partial public coverage ($949) were lower than mean out-of-pocket expenditures among families with private insurance (Table 3, p. 252).

Medical Care Expenditures by Family Size and Family Structure

Among nonelderly families in 2006, 46.2% were one-person families (57.1 million), 24.2% were two-person families (29.9 million), and 29.6% were families with three or more persons (36.5 million).

Among one-person families, mean total expenditures were $3,141 and mean out-of-pocket expenditures were $622. Among two-person families, mean total expenditures were $8,190 and mean out-of-pocket expenditures were $1,735. Among families with three or more persons, family-level mean total expenditures were $7,726 and mean out-of-pocket expenditures were $1,536 (Table 4, p. 253).

Since age is positively correlated with health care expenditures, it is important to note that differences in family structure lead to different levels

Table 3a   Family-Level Total and Out-of-Pocket Expenditures on Health Care Services for Nonelderly Familiesby Insurance Status, United States, 2006

Insurance Status	Number of Families (x1000)	Percentage of Total Population	Mean Total Expenditures	Mean Out-of-Pocket Expenditures	Median Total Expenditures	Median Out-of-Pocket Expenditures
Total	123,564	100.0%	$5,718	$1,161	$1,965	$442
Private insurance[1]	67,127	54.3%	6,785	1,410	2,802	701
Public insurance[2]	8,812	7.1%	8831**	643**	4168**	147**
Uninsured[3]	18,272	14.8%	1425**	663**	99**	49**
Partial private insurance[4]	21,013	17.0%	5237**	1102**	1721**	401**
Partial public insurance[5]	8,340	6.8%	4467**	949**	1695**	188**

Source: Bernard D., Banthin J. Family-Level Expenditures on Health Care and Insurance Premiums among the Nonelderly Population, 2006. Research Findings No. 29. March 2009. Agency for Healthcare Research and Quality, Rockville, MD. http://www.meps.ahrq.gov/mepsweb/data_files/publications/rf29/rf29.pdf

Notes: ** [*] Difference from the reference category (private insurance) is significant at 1 [5] percent level.

[1]Private insurance: Families in which all nonelderly persons are covered by private insurance all year. In addition to all nonelderly members having private coverage all year, some members may also have concurrent public insurance during all or part of the year.

[2]Public insurance: Families in which (1) all nonelderly persons are covered by public insurance all year, and (2) no nonelderly member has private coverage anytime during the year.

[3]Uninsured: Families in which all nonelderly persons are uninsured all year.

[4]Partial private insurance: Families in which at least one nonelderly person has private coverage for part of the year. In addition, some members may also have public insurance during all or part of the year.

[5]Partial public insurance: Families in which (1) at least one nonelderly person has public coverage for part of the year, and (2) no nonelderly person has private coverage during the year.

Table 3b   Standard Errors for Family-Level Total and Out-of-Pocket Expenditures on Health Care Services for Nonelderly Families by Insurance Status, United States, 2006

Insurance Status	Number of Families (x1000)	Percentage of Total Population	Mean Total Expenditures	Mean Out-of-Pocket Expenditures	Median Total Expenditures	Median Out-of-Pocket Expenditures
Total	3,058		127	34	66	16
Private insurance[1]	1,876	0.70	196	52	94	21
Public insurance[2]	428	0.33	479	45	388	16
Uninsured[3]	693	0.43	117	47	17	13
Partial private insurance[4]	780	0.42	320	60	120	28
Partial public insurance[5]	363	0.24	265	78	141	19

Source: Bernard D., Banthin J. Family-Level Expenditures on Health Care and Insurance Premiums among the NonelderlyPopulation, 2006. Research Findings No. 29. March 2009. Agency for Healthcare Research and Quality, Rockville, MD. http://www.meps.ahrq.gov/mepsweb/data_files/publications/rf29/rf29.pdf

Notes: See Table 3a.

of health care spending. For example, among two-person families, mean total expenditures were $4,374 among one-adult-one-child families and $9,603 among adult-couple families. Similarly, among families with three or more persons, mean total expenditures were $5,430 among families with one adult and at least two children and $8,140 among families with two adults and at least one child (Table 4).

Share of Family Income Spent on Medical Care and Health Insurance

The burden of medical care costs on the family is defined as the share of family income spent on medical care and health insurance. In 2006, among nonelderly families with employer-sponsored coverage, single-person families and multiperson families spent, on average, 7% of their income on health insurance premiums and medical care. On average, among nonelderly families with nongroup coverage, single-person families spent 23% of their

family income while multiperson families spent 19% on health insurance premiums and medical care. On average, among nonelderly families with public insurance, single-person families spent 16% of family income while multiperson families spent 9% of income on medical care. On average, among nonelderly uninsured families, single-person families spent 9% of family income while multiperson families spent 7% of income on medical care.

However, it is important to note that the distribution of health care expenditures is skewed, with a small proportion of persons with very high health care expenditures. Therefore, examining the share of population who spend a high percentage of family income on health care is a better indicator of high burdens. Financial burden of health care expenditures on nonelderly families has been rising in recent years. Table 5 (p. 254) shows that from 2001 to 2006, the share of nonelderly persons living in families that spent over 10% of the family income on health care and health insurance premiums increased from 13.4% to 17.5%. During

Table 4a   Family-Level Total and Out-of-Pocket Expenditures on Health Care Services Among Nonelderly Families by Family Size and by Family Type, United States, 2006

Family Size and Family Structure	Number of Families (x1000)	Mean Total Expenditures	Mean Out-of-Pocket Expenditures	Median Total Expenditures	Median Out-of-Pocket Expenditures
One-person families	57,133	$3,141	$622	$545	$149
Two-person families	29,887	8,190	1,735	3,554	853
One adult and one child families	7,646	4,374	789	1,604	265
Adult couple families	21,372	9,603	1,977	4,613	1,165
Families with three or more persons	36,544	7,726	1,536	4,254	826
One adult and at least two children	6,573	5,430	800	2,639	232
Two adults and at least one child	29,954	8,140	1,616	4,500	939

Source: Bernard D., Banthin J. Family-Level Expenditures on Health Care and Insurance Premiums among the Nonelderly Population, 2006. Research Findings No. 29. March 2009. Agency for Healthcare Research and Quality, Rockville, MD. http://www.meps.ahrq.gov/mepsweb/data_files/publications/rf29/rf29.pdf

Table 4b   Standard Errors for Family-Level Total and Out-of-Pocket Expenditures on Health Care Services Among Nonelderly Families by Family Size and Family Type, United States, 2006

Family Size and Family Structure	Number of Families (x1000)	Mean Total Expenditures	Mean Out-of-Pocket Expenditures	Median Total Expenditures	Median Out-of-Pocket Expenditures
One-person families	1,703	157	34	33	11
Two-person families	872	337	99	159	39
One adult and one child families	292	212	67	89	20
Adult couple families	597	291	61	137	28
Families with three or more persons	1,130	214	42	130	30
One adult and at least two children	243	229	43	109	20
Two adults and at least one child	827	210	30	95	24

Source: Bernard D., Banthin J. Family-Level Expenditures on Health Care and Insurance Premiums among the Nonelderly Population, 2006. Research Findings No. 29. March 2009. Agency for Healthcare Research and Quality, Rockville, MD. http://www.meps.ahrq.gov/mepsweb/data_files/publications/rf29/rf29.pdf

Table 5   Prevalence of High Family Out-of-Pocket Burdens Among the Nonelderly Population by Insurance Status: 2001 and 2006

Insurance Status	Population (Thousands)		Percent Living in Family With Financial Burden >10% of Family Income[1]	
	2001	2006	2001	2006
All nonelderly	248,412	261,287	13.4 (0.4)	17.5 (0.4)
Private insurance	182,075	181,898	12.5 (0.5)	18.0 (0.6)
Public insurance	33,332	41,972	18.2 (0.9)	18.3 (0.9)
Uninsured	33,005	37,416	13.5 (0.8)	14.2 (0.9)

Source: Author's calculations using MEPS data.

Note: [1]Financial burden includes out-of-pocket health care expenditures and health insurance premiums for all family members.

this period, the share of nonelderly persons with private insurance living in families that spent over 10% of family income on health care and health insurance premiums increased from 12.5% to 18.0%. During this period, the change in the share of persons with public insurance and the uninsured with high burdens was not statistically significant (18.2% to 18.3% and 13.5% to 14.2%, respectively.)

Didem Bernard

Disclaimer: The views expressed in this article are those of the author, and no official endorsement by the U.S. Department of Health and Human Services or the AHRQ is intended or should be inferred.

See also Medicaid and Family Health; Medicare and Family Health

Further Readings

Banthin, J. S., Cunningham, P., & Bernard, D. M. (2008). Financial burden of health care, 2001–2004. *Health Affairs, 27,* 188–195.

Bernard, D. M. (2005, March). *Premiums in the individual health insurance market for policyholders under age 65, 1996 and 2002* (Statistical Brief No. 72). Rockville, MD: Agency for Healthcare Research and Quality. Retrieved from http://meps.ahrq.gov/data_files/publications/st72/stat72.pdf

Bernard D. M., & Banthin J. S. (2009, March). *Family-level expenditures on health care and insurance premiums among the nonelderly population, 2006* (Research Findings No. 29). Rockville, MD: Agency for Healthcare Research and Quality. Retrieved from http://www.meps.ahrq.gov/mepsweb/data_files/publications/rf29/rf29.pdf

Bernard, D. M., Banthin, J. S., & Encinosa, W. E. (2009). Wealth, income, and the affordability of health insurance. *Health Affairs, 28,* 887–896.

CRITICAL THEORY AND FAMILY HEALTH

The label of critical theory has been applied to several perspectives, including feminism, Marxism, some psychoanalytic approaches, and Frankfurt School Critical Theory (CT). While all of these perspectives are concerned with liberation from social inequality and domination, this entry focuses on CT. In contrast to orthodox Marxist approaches, CT stresses the importance of ideological beliefs as well as socioeconomic sources of inequality. In contrast to many feminist theorists, Frankfurt School theorists have commonly viewed the modern family as a (potential) source of protection and liberation as well as domination. Although psychoanalysis was a major source of ideas for the first generation of Frankfurt School theorists, subsequent CT scholars have stressed societal over personal psychological sources of oppression. This entry begins with a brief sketch of the Frankfurt School's history and key ideas. It then considers how those ideas have been applied to family and health issues, respectively. It concludes by suggesting some implications of CT for family health.

Frankfurt School Critical Theory

The Institute for Social Research, whose scholars came to be known as the Frankfurt School, was founded in 1923 as an adjunct to the University of Frankfurt in Germany. Prominent among the first generation of Frankfurt scholars was Max Horkheimer, who became the institute's director in 1930 and recruited many of the school's most important theorists, including Theodor Adorno, Erich Fromm, and Herbert Marcuse. Concerned about what they saw as the dogmatic structural determinism of orthodox Marxism on the one hand and the widespread acceptance of fascism on the other, Frankfurt School scholars developed their own perspective on and critique of modern social science and modern society.

Pioneering Frankfurt theorists drew on ideas from Sigmund Freud and Max Weber, as well as the early writings of Karl Marx, to critique the adequacy of a *positivist* science of human beings modeled after contemporary understandings of "natural science" and focused on prediction and control. They drew on Freud's assertions about human irrationality to try to explain the self-defeating choice by so many in their day of fascism over revolutionary action in pursuit of a more free and just society. Early Frankfurt theorists embraced Weber's rejection of the inevitability of human progress, and his critique of the modern reduction of all rationality to a mere *instrumental rationality* aimed at efficiency of means without reference to higher human ends or values. They also incorporated key insights found in Marx's early writings, including his critique of *reification* (in which "man-made" social arrangements come to be misperceived as "natural" or "necessary") and his insistence on *praxis* (i.e., that theory should be combined with action aimed at emancipatory social transformation).

Building on this work, the most prominent second-generation Frankfurt theorist, Jürgen Habermas, developed a theory of modern societies centered on the relationship between *system* and *lifeworld*. Modern societies are often defined in terms of their *system* of economic and political institutions. Expanding on Weber, Habermas sees the modern separation of the system from the *lifeworld*—the context of everyday life and its traditions, substantive values, and practices—as enabling the appropriately *instrumental* rationalization of system processes to achieve tremendous material progress. However, Habermas warns that this can also result in the "colonization of the lifeworld" such that the lifeworld becomes governed, inappropriately, by *instrumental rationality* and thus loses its ability to provide higher values and critical guidance to systemic institutions and practices.

Habermas argues that such colonization distorts the *communicative rationality* needed by the lifeworld to provide guidance to systemic institutions and practices and thus produces serious societal problems. Primary sources of communicative distortion emerge from economic and cultural inequities and forms of domination that inhibit active expression of the lifeworlds of participants in a society. For Habermas, only through the free and active exchange of ideas and values embedded in the lifeworld can a society become fully and appropriately communicatively rational. For it is only through free and active exchanges that human dialogue can be moved by the force of the better argument alone. It is on the basis of this communicative rationality that Habermas proposes to evaluate systemic institutions and practices such as the family and health care.

Critical Theorists on Family

The first-generation Frankfurt theorists rejected the *reification* of the bourgeois family as something natural and independent of history or society, but they also rejected the orthodox Marxist idea that family forms simply reflect prevailing economic structures. Horkheimer and his colleagues saw the modern patriarchal family as not simply reflecting but also reinforcing capitalism. In their earliest writings on the family, they argued that the Freudian struggle of dependent children with a dominating patriarch and sole breadwinner produced calculating, competitive individuals well suited to serve the socially destructive priorities of capitalism. Yet, they also came to stress the role of the modern family as a source of resistance to capitalism through its ability to sustain anticapitalistic (i.e., non–self-interested) social forms and relationships. Hence, they came to lament the fact that the authority of modern family forms was being undermined by capitalism's powerful and direct appeals to, and effects on, individual family members. Detailed accounts of capitalism's undermining of families' relative autonomy, with and without the Freudian overtones, have been presented by Christopher Lasch and Stuart Ewen, respectively. Thus CT can offer an important corrective to functionalist perspectives that portray the modern family and modern capitalism as mutually harmonious and beneficial on the one hand, and to much orthodox Marxist and feminist theorists of the modern family form as wholly detrimental and disposable on the other.

The tensions between modern families and modern societal forms are further theorized by Habermas. Habermas downplays his predecessors' Freudian concerns about the importance of the father as an implacable authority figure that young selves must internalize to thrive, and also their ultimate pessimism about the loss of the family as a potential source of resistance to instrumental rationalization (i.e., colonization). For Habermas, the modern family remains an important potential source of the communicative rationality and defense of the lifeworld that he too sees as essential to emancipatory social change. Habermas seems to suggest that the potential for communicative rationality is especially present in the middle-class nuclear family with its egalitarian patterns of relationship, individuated forms of interaction, and liberalized childrearing practices. Thus, Habermas sees the democratic family as an improvement over the authoritarian family in terms of its potential for fostering autonomous individuals capable of pursuing emancipating social change. Yet, Habermas also acknowledges that the emancipating potential of family life is undermined insofar as the lifeworld of family relations is colonized by instrumental rationality in the form, for example, of individualistic attitudes, bureaucratic intervention, or judicial control.

Critical Theorists and Health

As with their views on family, critical theorists offer an important corrective to views of health and health care that simply reflect the priorities of the system. As Priscilla Alderson has pointed out, CT views of health reject functionalist views of society as a sort of organism in which parts automatically function to benefit each other and the whole. For example, Howard Waitzkin has criticized functionalist definitions of health, such as those associated with the physician-verified "sick role," for reducing conceptions of health to the ability to engage in paid employment and for encouraging narrow and short-term approaches to health problems. Of course, as Waitzkin also notes, placing system priorities over concerns and understandings emerging from the lifeworld can result not only from the prioritization of profits (as in capitalist societies) but also from the prioritization of production (as in communist societies). In contrast to approaches that privilege the system, CT focuses on understanding health in ways more broadly conceived and in ways more sensitive to the normative concerns of individuals, families, and social groups. In this way, CT facilitates finding and reducing sources of health problems that may result from the system rather than merely alleviating health issues that reduce the usefulness of individuals or groups to the system.

CT has also been applied at the interactional level to pursue processes or conditions that can help make health care decisions more rational and just. Examples of this kind of application rest on the critical recognition of the tension between autonomy and authority arising from the specialization of knowledge in modern societies. Critical theorists have criticized systemic thinking for elevating the authority of medical professionals to the point where certified medical expertise becomes the sole legitimate source for improving health care. CT suggests that this can result in the practice and internalization of unequal social relations such that it results in the systematic distortion of communication processes (as when doctors or even patients themselves dismiss patients' perceptions of their health as invalid presumptuously). For example, studies have found that whereas many nurses view patient consent procedures as an essential two-way deliberation, many doctors see medical consent as a polite formality and essentially one-way dispensing of information by benign experts who simply serve the harmonious health needs of the social system and its members. Within the latter view of medical expertise, instances of patient refusal or noncompliance are dismissed as "irrational." In contrast, from a CT perspective consent may be seen as a necessary protection for patients against useless, harmful, and unwanted interventions, a constraint on the power difference in exchanges of knowledge between doctor and patient, and a possible means for opening up communication practices by showing greater respect for sick or disabled persons as valuable sources of knowledge.

Medical practitioners and researchers can also use CT to guide examinations of how oppressive structural factors (e.g., poverty, inadequate housing, food scarcity, discrimination) or cultural factors (e.g., egoistic individualism) can adversely affect people's health. For example, Selina Mohammed has suggested that pediatric nurses can assess whether or not children have ready access to healthy types of food and shelter, school programs that provide nutritious lunches and physical education classes, and affordable fitness centers or programs to facilitate exercise, as well as adequate health care services. Although positivist approaches to medicine that isolate individual factors can certainly help reduce certain health problems, CT can support research and practice that also looks more broadly at how such problems may be linked to societal factors. Functionalist approaches that focus on system priorities may increase a society's average health narrowly defined, but a CT perspective can help reveal how systemic priorities may prevent the kind of social action necessary for greater amelioration, reduction, and prevention of health problems as, for example, when the sale of the latest generation of antihistamines or antidepressants takes precedence over societal measures to reduce environmental or economic sources of health problems.

Critical theorists have warned against the widespread assumption that positivist science offers the best source of solutions for all human questions and problems. Recent critical theorists have criticized the popular understanding and acceptance of positivist science as resembling a religion. Modern men and women have come to look to positivist science to reveal the truth, to heal the sick, and even to aid in the quest for immortality. Critical theorists have also pointed out that positivist science rests on faith-like assumptions (e.g., that human beings are nothing more than natural organisms, that nature is entirely uniform and law-like, and that change always ultimately moves humanity in the direction of beneficial progress), which cannot be scientifically proven. On the other hand, critical theorists have noted that this new religion lacks any notion, like those found in older religious traditions, of natural or moral limits to the material benefits that individuals should seek from positive science.

CT highlights how modern faith in the authority and benevolence of positivist science can create contradictions and problems in modern health care. For example, Zygmunt Bauman suggests that this faith in positivist science has led to a situation in which technological developments are taken to be simple responses to "real needs" rather than critically assessing just how the medical industry itself may be involved in the actual creation of new "needs." In relation to health care, this suggests that society needs to consider how the desire for medical treatments and technologies is constructed and examine just how such desires come to impact health care. This analysis might include such considerations as examining at what point the desire for increased individual physical performance, longevity, or the latest definitions of attractiveness that new medical technologies promise to provide becomes excessive. Yet, more fundamentally, CT can encourage and enable us to question the extent to which the constructed demand for more and more health care is itself an important threat to health, increasing costs to such a point that a larger and larger share of the gross domestic product is diverted from more important means of securing the health and safety of the people.

Critical Theory and Family Health Interactions

There is abundant empirical evidence that families are important participants in the prevention and treatment, as well as the genesis and exacerbation, of health problems. Families are a primary source not only of caregiving but also of health-related behavior patterns, health beliefs and attitudes, initial assessments of members' health problems, access to professional medical care, compliance with prescribed medical regimens, and social support for chronic health problems. CT also stresses that modern families rarely operate in total isolation from the health care system or from the rest of society.

Recent applications of CT have stressed the ill effects of societal arrangements characterized by inequality and domination on family members' health. Employment, community, and living conditions that are largely beyond family members' control have been found to be crucial determinants of health outcomes for both juvenile and adult family members. Studies have found that problems such as poor or shifting labor markets have contributed to the loss of ameliorative family supports and that this, along with inadequate public supports, often leaves family members suffering from diseases that might be cheaply and easily prevented. CT is not alone in emphasizing the connection between social inequality and health problems, but what CT offers that other approaches often fail to emphasize is how a positivist medical and social science can both greatly increase the means for ameliorating health problems through its focus on isolating and treating specific aspects of health and narrow understandings of and approaches to individual and family health such that the social context of family and health connections become obscured.

While CT acknowledges the potential problems of older family forms and family authority, it also stresses that contemporary societal inequalities are more important sources of problems for families and health than family life itself. Perspectives such as psychoanalysis, feminism, and postmodernism often stress the importance of individual independence from family constraints and the right to dissolve or decrease one's family ties whenever they are seen to conflict with one's presumed needs.

However, studies have found that strong, stable, and extended family forms are positively associated with health benefits for adults and, especially, children. CT recognizes that sources of inequalities in family health can be internal (as, e.g., when a family member internalizes the belief that age, gender, or lack of "productivity" means that he or she "deserves" to be neglected or abused), but they are often, most significantly, external (as when inadequate pay or benefits, poor or shifting job markets, or lack of access to good day care or health care undermines the ability of families to look after their members' health).

CT can help health researchers, practitioners, and policymakers understand how societal factors can promote institutions, policies, traditions, and meanings that contribute to family health problems that are not natural, inevitable, or attributable simply to individual decisions or behavior. CT also suggests that such understanding is but a vital first step that must be followed by effective social action.

Stan Knapp and Bruce Lott

See also Access to Health Care: Child Health; Access to Health Care: Elderly; Access to Health Care: Uninsured; Clarifying Family as Context of Care and Family as Focus of Care in Family Health; Defining Family: An Overview of Family Definitions From a Historical Perspective; Economics as It Relates to Family Health; Kinship Care; Role of Families in Health Promotion; Theoretical Perspectives Related to the Family

Further Readings

Alderson, P. (1998). Theories in health care and research: The importance of theories in health care. *British Medical Journal, 317*(7164), 1007–1010.

Allen, D. (1989). Critical social theory as a model for analyzing ethical issues in family and community health. *Family and Community Health, 10*(1), 63–72.

Bauman, Z., & May, T. (2001). The business in everyday life: Consumption, technology and lifestyles." In Z. Bauman & T. May (Eds.), *Thinking sociologically* (2nd ed., pp. 147–162). Malden, MA: Blackwell.

Ewen, S. (2001). Mom, Dad, and the kids: Toward a modern architecture of daily life. In S. Ewen (Ed.), *Captains of consciousness: Advertising and the social roots of the consumer culture* (pp. 111–184). New York: McGraw-Hill. (Original work published 1976)

How, A. (2003). *Critical theory.* New York: Palgrave Macmillan.

Lasch, C. (1977). *Haven in a heartless world: The family besieged.* New York: Basic Books.

Mohammed, S. A. (2006). (Re)examining health disparities: Critical social theory in pediatric nursing. *Journal for Specialists in Pediatric Nursing, 11*(1), 68–70.

Waitzkin, H. (1989). A critical theory of medical discourse: Ideology, social control, and the processing of social context in medical encounters. *Journal of Health and Social Behavior, 30*(2), 220–239.

Waitzkin, H. (2000). *The second sickness: Contradictions of capitalist health care.* Lanham, MD: Rowman & Littlefield.

CULTURAGRAM USE WITH CULTURALLY DIVERSE FAMILIES

Because of the increasing diversity of the U.S. population, health care providers in inpatient, outpatient, and community settings increasingly work with immigrants. As culturally competent practice is seen as an important goal in work with culturally diverse families, the culturagram provides a useful means to help health care clinicians move toward culturally competent practice.

There have been other family assessment tools, such as the ecomap and genogram, used to assess the family. These tools look at the external resources available to the family (ecomap) or internal family relations (genogram), but do not emphasize the important role of culture in understanding the family. The culturagram has been seen as making a contribution to family theory and development. After a brief description of the history of the culturagram, this entry discusses the 10 areas culturagrams address and future directions for the culturagrams.

History

First developed in 1994 and then revised in 2000 and 2008, the culturagram looks at 10 specific areas related to understanding the family's cultural background. This family assessment instrument has been used in work with people of color, battered women, children, older people, and families in crisis, families with health problems, and Latino and Asian families.

The culturagram grew out of the recognition that families are becoming increasingly culturally diverse and that health care professionals must be able to understand cultural differences between families and within families to address more effectively the health care needs of their patients.

To characterize a family only in terms of a generic cultural identity, however, can lead to overgeneralization and stereotyping. For example, although both families are considered Hispanic/Latino, a Puerto Rican family comprising U.S. citizens who have lived in the United States for 40 years is very different from an undocumented Mexican family that emigrated last month. Even within the same ethnic group, each family has had a different immigration and acculturation experience.

Culturagram

The 10 areas that the culturagram addresses are (1) reasons for relocation, (2) legal status, (3) time in community, (4) language spoken at home and in the community, (5) health beliefs, health care access and utilization, (6) impact of trauma and crisis events, (7) contact with cultural and religious institutions, holidays, food, and clothing, (8) oppression, discrimination, bias,

and racism, (9) values about education and work, (10) values about family—structure, power, myths, and rules (Figure 1).

While health care providers may be most interested in health beliefs, health care access and utilization, a knowledge and understanding of all areas is important in engaging and planning appropriate interventions for culturally diverse families.

Reasons for Relocation

Reasons for relocating vary among families. There may be push factors (political and religious discrimination, poverty, climate change) and/or pull factors (greater economic opportunities in the United States, relatives who have immigrated previously) that contribute to families' decisions to immigrate. Families often do not emigrate together, as one parent may come first to earn money in the United States before being joined by other family members. Some immigrants are transnational, as they live in both cultures and frequently travel back and forth between their home countries and the United States, whereas others, especially refugees, may never be able to go home again.

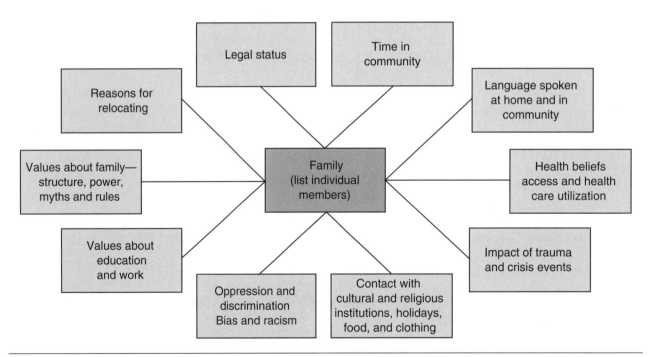

Figure 1   Culturagram

Source: Congress (2008, p. 971)

Legal Status

The legal status of a family may have an effect on individual members, as well as the family as a whole. Often members of the same family may have different legal status with one undocumented parent, another parent with a green card, and children who are born here and thus are U.S. citizens. Legal status often detrimentally affects health care access, as children who are U.S. citizens may be able to receive health care services, while those who are undocumented and even those who are legal residents are barred from all but emergency health care services. If a family member is undocumented and fears deportation, other members may become secretive and socially isolated. Parents may delay seeking health care for themselves or their children until absolutely necessary because of economic reasons or fear of exposure.

Length of Time in the Community

The length of time in the community may differ for individual family members. Family members who have arrived earlier may be more acculturated than other members. A current phenomenon involves mothers' immigrating first to the United States and then sending for their children. These circumstances can certainly have an impact on individual and family development. A young infant left in the care of relatives in the country of origin may have difficulties developing trust because of the lack of continuity in parenting during this crucial early period. Also, the family with young children that is disrupted when the mother emigrates may face challenges in reuniting as a family, especially after the children have become adolescents. Another key factor is that family members are different ages at the time they relocate. Because of attending U.S. schools and developing peer relationships, children are often more quickly acculturated than their parents. This difference may lead to conflictual role reversals in which children assume a leadership role, especially when they are used by their parents as interpreters.

Language

Language is the mechanism by which families communicate with each other. Often families may use their own native language at home but may begin to use English to communicate with those in the outside community. Sometimes children may prefer English, as knowledge of this language is seen as important for success in the United States. Children that are asked to interpret for health providers may miss school or be exposed to inappropriate topics. This points to the need for bilingual and bicultural health care providers to provide services to non-English-speaking patients.

Health Beliefs

Health issues may negatively impact on culturally diverse families, as for example when the primary wage earner with a serious illness is no longer able to work, a family member has HIV/AIDS, or a child has a chronic health condition such as asthma or diabetes. Families from different cultures have varying beliefs about health, disease, and treatment and may use health care methods other than traditional Western European medical care involving prevention, diagnosis, pharmacology, X-rays, and surgery. Health care providers need to be sensitive to differing cultural beliefs that impact on immigrants' understanding of health problems and use of health care.

Although mental health problems in a family member may have a negative impact, families from different cultural backgrounds may be reluctant to seek mental health care because of the stigma associated with mental illness. Families from different cultures may encounter barriers in accessing and utilizing medical and psychiatric treatment. Both legal and undocumented immigrants may lack health insurance and not have financial resources to pay for needed health care.

Impact of Trauma and Crisis Events

Families can encounter developmental crises as well as unexpected crises. Developmental crises occur when a family moves from one life stage to another. Stages in the life cycle for culturally diverse families may be quite different from those for traditional Anglo middle-class families. For example, for many culturally diverse families, the "launching children" stage may not occur at all, as single and even married children may continue to live in close proximity to the parents. If separation is forced, this developmental crisis might be especially traumatic. Families from different cultural backgrounds frequently care for older relatives when they develop health problems. In current times, however, families are more geographically separated and all members of the household are frequently engaged in outside employment. Thus the care of an older family member with serious health problems may be particularly challenging. Health care providers may need to help families with exploring alternative methods of care for immigrant families with a seriously ill member.

Families cope with unexpected crises in different ways. A family's reaction to crisis events is often related to its cultural values. For example, a father's accident and subsequent inability to work may be especially traumatic for an immigrant family in which the father's providing for the family is an important family value. Although rape is certainly traumatic for any family, the rape of a teenage girl may be especially traumatic for a family from a cultural background that values virginity before marriage.

Health care providers need to consider the lives of their clients in three stages, including their experience before immigrating, their transit to the United States, as well as the current situation. Immigrant individuals and families may have experienced traumatic events in their country of origin or while traveling to the United States, as well as poverty and discrimination as they try to access needed health, educational, vocational, and social services in the United States. Current policies about undocumented immigrants certainly may retraumatize immigrant families as they seek needed services.

Contact With Cultural and Religious Institutions, Holidays, Food, and Clothing

Cultural institutions providing ongoing support for immigrant families may be used differently by family members. For example, a father may belong to a social club, the mother might attend a church where her native language is spoken, and adolescent children could refuse to participate in either because they wish to become more Americanized. Religion may provide much support to culturally diverse families, so the health care provider will want to explore the family's contact with religious institutions. Churches, temples, and mosques often provide a mechanism for educating immigrant families about health care issues.

Every family celebrates particular holidays and special events. Some events mark transitions from one developmental stage to another—for example, a christening, a bar mitzvah, a wedding, or a funeral. It is important for the health care provider to learn about the cultural significance of important holidays for the family, as they are indicative of what families see as major transition points within their family. In scheduling appointments, health care providers must be sensitive to these different holidays. Those involved in inpatient hospitals or nursing homes must be aware of cultural differences in food and how cultural differences influence residents with diverse cultural backgrounds. As many immigrants come from southern climates, they may not be prepared for the cold conditions of northern winters and lack appropriate clothing.

Oppression, Discrimination, Bias, and Racism

In some countries immigrants may have experienced oppression and discrimination, which has led to their departure from their homelands and migration to the United States. In other countries those who emigrate may have been the majority population and thus never experienced prejudice until their arrival in the United States. In the United States immigrants may be the victims of discrimination and racism based on language, cultural, and racial differences. Health care administrators must continually strive to promote health care access and utilization that is fair and open to all who need it.

Values About Education and Work

All families have differing values about work and education, and culture is an important influence on such values. Economic and social differences that immigrants experience between the country of origin and the United States can affect immigrant families. For example, employment in a low-status position may be denigrating to the male breadwinner. It may be especially traumatic for the immigrant family when the father cannot find work or only work of a menial nature. Immigrants have a much higher rate of accidents than native-born individuals; this may lead to a need for acute care and then long-term rehabilitation that is not readily available.

Immigrant parents may look to teachers as the experts in educating their children and may not question educational plans for their children. The same may be true in health care when immigrant families look to doctors, nurses, and other health care providers as absolute authority figures and do not question any health care plan or seek a second opinion. Health care providers need to ensure that informed consent is a reality for immigrants who may not understand their rights. Health Insurance Portability and Accountability Act (HIPAA) regulations emphasize the importance of confidentiality and sharing of medical information only with the identified patient, not family and friends. Many immigrants coming from a more collective, community background may believe that confidential health care information may be readily shared with others in their family and community networks.

Values About Family Structure, Power, Myths, and Rules

Each family has its unique structure, its beliefs about power relationships, myths, and rules. Some of these may be unique to the cultural background of the family. The clinician needs to explore these family characteristics individually, but also to understand them in the context of the family's cultural background. Family members may have changing beliefs about male–female relationships, especially within marriage. Those with traditional beliefs about power and gender relationships within families may experience conflict in U.S. society with its more egalitarian gender relationships within the family. This difference in experience may lead to an increase in domestic violence and subsequent visits to emergency rooms. Health care providers who work with immigrant women who have been affected by domestic violence need to be sensitive to cultural issues that may have contributed to the situation and need to develop culturally sensitive interventions in working with these families. Also, childrearing practices, especially in regard to discipline, may differ in culturally

diverse families. This may result in increased reporting to Child Protective Services, and often health care providers must help immigrant families negotiate with child protection workers.

Future Directions for the Culturagram

The culturagram has been seen as an essential tool in helping social workers work more effectively with families from many different cultures. Not only does the culturagram help the health care practitioner achieve greater understanding of the culture of a family, but it also points the way toward future treatment planning and intervention.

Current practice looks to evidence that specific interventions are effective. Students and practitioners have used the culturagram in their professional practice with families and reported that it is helpful in engaging families in a nonthreatening way. Culture is seen through a multidimensional lens rather than as a monolithic entity. Initial evaluation of the culturagram has been positive, and there are further plans to assess the effectiveness of the culturagram in promoting culturally competent health care practice.

Elaine P. Congress

See also Access to Health Care: Uninsured; Cultural Attitudes Toward Help Seeking and Beliefs About Illness in Families; Illegal Alien Status and Family Health; Immigrant Families; Immigration Status and Family Health; Refugees and Family Health

Further Readings

Chang-Muy, F., & Congress, E. P. (2009). *Social work with immigrants and refugees: Legal issues, clinical skills, and advocacy.* New York: Springer.

Congress, E. (2004). Crisis intervention and diversity: Emphasis on a Mexican immigrant family's acculturation conflicts. In P. Meyer (Ed.), *Paradigms of clinical social work: Vol. 3. Emphasis on diversity* (pp. 125–144). New York: Brunner-Routledge.

Congress, E. (2004). Cultural and ethnic issues in working with culturally diverse patients and their families: Use of the culturagram to promote cultural competency in health care settings. *Social Work in Health Care, 39*(3/4), 249–262.

Congress, E. (2008). The culturagram. In A. R. Roberts (Ed.), *Social work desk reference* (2nd ed., pp. 969–975). New York: Oxford University Press.

Congress, E., & Brownell, P. (2007). Application of the culturagram with culturally and ethnically diverse battered women. In A. R. Roberts (Ed.), *Battered women and their families* (3rd ed.). New York: Springer.

Congress, E., & González, M. (2005). *Multicultural perspectives in working with families* (2nd ed.). New York: Springer.

Singer, J. B. (Host). (2008, December 1). Visual assessment tools: The Culturagram—interview with Dr. Elaine Congress [Episode 46]. *Social Work Podcast*. Podcast retrieved April 20, 2009, from http://socialworkpodcast.com/2008/12/visual-assessment-tools-culturagram.html

Webb, N. B. (2001). *Culturally diverse parent-child and family relationships*. New York: Columbia University Press.

Cultural Attitudes Toward Help Seeking and Beliefs About Illness in Families

Ethnic minority clients have been shown to experience disparities in health care as described in the Institute of Medicine's report, *Unequal Treatment: Confronting Racial and Ethnic Disparities in Health Care*. Many of these minority clients have structural barriers to obtaining the health care that they require, such as the inability to speak English; a lack of insurance, such as private insurance, Medicaid, or Medicare; and/or a lack of transportation, child care, or legal documentation. If all of these barriers were removed by providing adequate translation, as required by Executive Order 13166, "Improving Access to Services for Persons With Limited English Proficiency (LEP)," and enforced by the Office of Civil Rights, and these individuals were offered free health care, transportation, and child care, as well as care provided regardless of legal status, minorities would likely still experience disparities in health care due to cultural barriers. These barriers would manifest themselves by low utilization of services by minorities as the result of a decision to not seek help because of shame or

stigma, termination of treatment due to a mismatch between cultural values and health beliefs between the clinician and the client, the inability to find a ethnic matched provider, a poor therapeutic alliance due to racism, or even misdiagnosis as a result of stereotyping or a lack of understanding of cultural norms.

A discussion of cultural attitudes toward help seeking and beliefs about illness is crucial to understanding how the client and his or her family see the client's illness and what kind of care that they will seek. The family is included in the discussion, as the client is part of a social network that determines the client's health behaviors. Culture shapes how clients and their families experience an illness in a loved one and what type of care that they will seek out, otherwise known as the process of help-seeking behavior. In this entry, cultural attitudes toward help seeking in the context of health beliefs are explored. The approach of this entry is to not characterize every culture's health beliefs but to give examples of various categories of causation and treatment and to suggest ways for clinicians to involve clients and their families in their treatment by encouraging them to explain their health beliefs, their expectations of healers, and their attitudes about seeking help. Without this important exchange of information, health professionals may be frustrated by a client's lack of adherence, when in fact it is the client's and his or her family's lack of understanding of the health professional's beliefs in what will work with the client. It is beyond the scope of this entry to describe all explanatory models for all cultures that clinicians may encounter, and thus the approach is to describe tools that may help clinicians gain an understanding of clients that will not only enhance the therapeutic alliance but also improve adherence to treatment recommendations.

Historical Background

Throughout history, mankind has always sought explanations for the maladies of life. In many cultures, this meant a magico-religious or supernatural explanation such as evil spirits. An illness thought to be caused by evil spirits would require the services of shaman, medicine man, or witch doctor, who would perform some sort of ritual involving singing, chanting, or the beating of drums. If the cause of illness was thought to be of a physical nature, then natural traditions such as herbs, teas, a hot or cold diet, or treatments such as bleeding, coining, cupping, acupuncture, spinal manipulation, or enemas were used. Other causes may be psychological pertaining to emotional causes, or environmental, involving social causes or stress. The terms that clients and their families use to describe their suffering are known as *idioms of distress*, or physical, emotional, and interpersonal experiences seen by the individual or family members as abnormal. Behind the idioms of distress are culturally determined explanatory models that explain the cause of the illness, as the clients and their family sees it. Help seeking is defined as an attempt to alleviate distress by removing symptoms that are identified as sickness.

Being ill or sick has social consequences, usually preventing the sick individual from performing his or her role in the individual's social system, which often is the compelling reason for that person to either seek help or be compelled to seek help from his or her family, community, or health care providers. Several explanatory models, including moral, spiritual, religious, magical, medical, and psychosocial stress, may explain the individual's symptom. The *moral model* is best exemplified by saying that the client's condition is caused by a moral failing, such as laziness, selfishness, or having a weak will. The *spiritual/religious model* explains that the breaking of a religious taboo or sin causes illness. The gods or spirits then punish the client. The treatment in this case would be a consultation with a religious leader, and some act of restitution or request for forgiveness may be appropriate. A person believing in the *magical explanatory model* would feel that sorcery or witchcraft causes illness, and a shaman may be needed to perform a ritual to counteract the spell. Clients who attribute a physical etiology to the illness learn to use a *medical model*. Many non-Western cultures have their own medical models, such as traditional Chinese medicine, ayurvedic medicine, homeopathy, osteopathy, and various herbal medicine traditions. In a national survey, Leon Eisenberg and colleagues estimated that 1 of every 3 Americans used non-Western allopathic medicine remedies. A later study by Patricia Barnes and colleagues showed that 62% of adults use complementary practices. When ethnicity was explored, it was found that African Americans use complementary practices at a rate of 71.3%, and Hispanics are also high users when prayer is considered a complementary practice. Finally, the psychological stress model explains that stressful events may cause illnesses. In this case, once the stress has been alleviated, the illness should improve. Clients may use one, some, or all of these models at the same time. Once a client has been identified by himself or herself or the client's social network to be ill, which could be defined as not being able to do the tasks that the client would normally do, then the individual or family would arrange for the individual to be cared for or, as defined here, to engage in help-seeking behavior.

Help Seeking

Help seeking can be both formal and informal. Examples of informal help seeking include the family or social network, pastor or minister, or the use of traditional folk medicine. In a group-oriented society, such as seen in most non-Western cultures, the family may band together to support the sick individual, as that individual may prevent the family from fulfilling its responsibilities. Such help is often freely given with the expectation that the ill family member will repay in kind when needed to help other members of the group. For some non-Western cultures, the cause of the illness is an external force. In contrast, in most Western societies the emphasis is on the individual, and he or she is responsible for wellness or sickness, based on his or her actions or inactions. If the individual is to receive help from someone, then the individual is expected to pay back the assistance in kind to that individual. Westerner clients tend to believe that they did something as an individual to cause their illness.

Formal help seeking would occur when consultation of an outsider is needed, such as a professional counselor, community leader, or a Western doctor. The success or failure of the formal consultation will determine if other systems need to be engaged. One disadvantage of the formal help-seeking networks are that they expose the family and the client to the stigma of having an illness, a stigma that could be worse if the illness were perceived as a mental illness, so they are avoided unless other methods have failed.

Examples of Explanatory Models

The Chinese have several disease models that have been used over time and are still in use today. A key concept is Qi, or the vital energy, which is believed to flow through the body along meridians. The Chinese view of illness is that it represents an imbalance in the body. Therefore a treatment could be a diet of hot foods to balance out cold illnesses and vice versa. Other imbalances may be treated by herbs, acupuncture, cupping, or coining, or Qi Gong meditation, a combination of breathing and slow movements, similar to Tai Chi. A Western doctor is consulted only if the illness is seen to be life threatening or unmanageable by traditional methods, as described previously. Even after a Western doctor has been consulted, some less acculturated patients may see the medications as too strong and may reduce their doses. Ironically, there may be a genetic explanation for this observation, as some patients have slow metabolism, and a small dose is as effective as an average dose in a typical mainstream patient.

Examples of traditional healers can be described in the five categories of spiritual and psychological, nutritional, drug and biological, physical, or other. Religious faith healers, psychics, and mystics are included in the spiritual and psychological category, while nutritional healers use herbal remedies and special diets. Drug and biological specialists use chemicals, drugs, or vaccines to prevent or cure disease. Examples of physical healers include chiropractors and physical therapists, while the last category (i.e., "other") includes aroma therapists or iridologists.

Assessment Methods

In assessing a client, the clinician should perform a thorough developmental history, including country of origin, identified ethnicity, and family relationships. Some families are immigrant families with multiple generations living together. A typical example would be that the first generation is from the home country, monolingual, and minimally acculturated, and has children that were born in the United States. In working with first-generation immigrants, it is imperative to have the sons or daughters coordinate their health care and bridge the cultural gap between first-generation immigrants and the host culture, as well as the gap between their cultural health beliefs and that of the host culture. They also might be uninsured because of a lack of work history in this country or work skills, or they may be undocumented. Any religious or spiritual beliefs should be elicited, as well as the client's sexual orientation, which can create more barriers or might be a source of community support, depending on the community in which the client resides. If the patient is a child, then the parents' illness beliefs must be fully explored. Finally, gender may be an issue, as culturally determined gender roles and concepts of masculinity/femininity may create barriers to staying in treatment.

Culturally appropriate health care delivery can be achieved without breaking a taboo or creating a conflict with a health belief incompatible with clients' practices, such as prescribing alcohol-containing medications to a Muslim or giving non-kosher medications to an orthodox Jew. As knowledge about particular groups' cultural beliefs and customs increases, and modifications are made to the therapeutic relationship or the prescribed treatment, adherence to treatment recommendations is likely to improve. The use of a cultural consultant may help clinicians avoid stereotyping by learning about culturally normative behavior and norms as well as the assumptions made in the Western-dominated medical culture.

Illness Narratives

Eliciting an illness narrative can be facilitated by the use of nine questions first suggested by Arthur Kleinman, Leon Eisenberg, and Byron Good in 1978 (Table 1). The clinician can incorporate these into his or her standard history taking by pausing to ask the client what the client thinks is making the client sick and what should be done about it. Not only does the inquiry improve the therapeutic alliance by showing interest in the client's point

Table 1   Questions to Elicit an Explanatory Model; Kleinman's Questions to Create an Illness Narrative

1. What do you call your illness? (What do you think has caused your illness?)
2. Why did it start?
3. What do you think the illness does?
4. How severe is it?
5. How long will it last?
6. What kind of treatment should you receive?
7. What are the most important results you hope to receive from it?
8. What are the problems your illness has caused?
9. What do you fear most about your illness?

Source: Adapted from Kleinman, A., Isenberg, L., Good, B. (1978). Culture, Illness and Care: Clinical Lessons from Anthropologic and Cross-Cultural Research. *Annals of Internal Medicine* 88:251-258.

- **L**isten with sympathy and understanding to the client's perception of the problem.
- **E**xplain your perceptions of the problem and the client's as well.
- **A**cknowledge and discuss the differences and similarities between the two viewpoints.
- **R**ecommend treatment that is accepting of the client's explanatory models.
- **N**egotiate agreement with mutually agreed upon goals and therapies.

Figure 1   LEARN Model

Source: Adapted from Berlin, E. A., Fowkes, W. C. (1983). A teaching framework for cross-cultural health care: Application in family practice, *Western Journal of Medicine, 12,* 93-98.

of view, but the clinician may also uncover some illness belief that may help to improve adherence to the suggested treatment regimen by using some of the client's concepts to explain the clinician's recommendations, or to show that the expected treatments did not work, and that is why a new method should be tried. A cultural consultation from a trusted member of the client's community may be needed for complete understanding as to if the client's experience is within cultural norms and normal, or outside them and thus considered abnormal.

The LEARN Model

LEARN is a five-step model designed to improve the therapeutic alliance and outline how clinicians should work with clients who have differing cultural backgrounds than their own (Figure 1). First, clinicians listen to their client from the client's cultural perspective, using a client-centered interview. Then, clinicians explain their reasons for asking for personal information such as who does the client lives with, who administers the medications, and who makes the decisions for the family. Next, clinicians acknowledge the client's concerns by reflecting back to the client a summary of what they think the illness means to the client. Finally, clinicians recommend a course of action that includes the client's explanatory model in some way, thus negotiating a plan that takes into consideration the client's cultural norms and personal lifestyle, as opposed to dictating the course of treatment. These principles should enhance adherence and improve the clinician's understanding of the client's situation.

The Client-Centered Approach

The client-centered approach is yet another framework to develop a working therapeutic alliance with a client. First, the clinician demonstrates a genuine interest in the client's health beliefs and attitudes. Second, the clinician recognizes and understands how the client's cultural and individual perspectives affect the client's decisions on health care and preventive behaviors. Next, the clinician enlists the client's cooperation in formulating service plans and focuses more on the client's needs and perspectives rather than on the disease. Reframing the client's beliefs might be necessary to bridge to the Western model. In formulating a treatment plan the clinician should incorporate client-centered care practices, such as sending reminder notices for appointments, providing information from referring clinicians promptly, and making medical records and test results readily available to clients. Also, if the clinician is sensitive to the economic and social barriers encountered by the client and understands how they may affect the client's help-seeking behavior, the client may be more likely to return for follow-up. An educational approach on health maintenance and disease management techniques can be very effective in teaching the client how to accomplish certain health care goals and even prevent hospitalization or disability. The clinician must be aware of differing levels of health literacy of clients and must explain medical information clearly to clients without jargon or technical terms. In this way, clinicians can empower clients to partner with the clinician in actively maintaining and improving health and increase clients' feelings of competence in their ability to manage their disease.

Conclusion

Western trained counselors, nurses, physicians, and other clinicians need to understand the role of the family and culture in the health or sickness of the individual and learn how to elicit explanatory models of those clients who seek care in whatever setting help seeking is initiated to ensure proper engagement and referral to appropriate resources, to obtain the cooperation and support of family and/or community members, and to respect differing beliefs systems that may not match those of the care provider, rather than focusing only on the individual client.

Russell F. Lim

See also African American Families: Perspectives of Health; American Indian Families: Perspectives of Health; Asian Families: Perspectives of Health; Christianity's Influence on Health in the Family; Culturagram Use With Culturally Diverse Families; Ethnic/Racial Influences in Families; Factors Influencing Family Health Values, Beliefs, and Priorities; Hinduism's Influence on Health in the Family; Hispanic/Latino Families: Perspectives of Health; Islam's Influence on Health in the Family; Judaism's Influence on Health in the Family; Religious/Spiritual Influences on Health in the Family

Further Readings

Barnes, P., Powell-Griner, E., McFann, K., & Nahin, R. (2004, May 27). *Complementary and alternative medicine use among adults: United States, 2002* (CDC Advance Data Rep. No. 343). Hyattsville, MD: National Center for Health Statistics.

Bateman, W. B., Abesamis-Mendoza, N. F., Ho-Asjoe, H. (2009). *Praeger Handbook of Asian American health: Taking notice and taking action.* Santa Barbara, CA: ABC-CLIO.

Berlin, E. A., & Fowkes, W. C. (1983). A teaching framework for cross-cultural health care. *Western Journal of Medicine, 139*(6), 934–938.

Kleinman, A., Eisenberg, L., & Good, B. (1978). Culture, illness, and care: Clinical lessons from anthropologic and cross-cultural research. *Annals of Internal Medicine, 88,* 251–258.

Kline, M. V., & Huff, R. M. (2007). *Health promotion in multicultural populations: A handbook for practitioners and students.* Thousand Oaks, CA: Sage.

Lim, R. F. (Ed.). (2006). *Clinical manual of cultural psychiatry.* Arlington, VA: American Psychiatric Press.

Saint Arnault, D. (2009). Cultural determinants of help seeking: A model for research and practice. *Research and Theory for Nursing Practice: An International Journal, 23*(4), 259–278.

Smedly, B. D., Stith, A. Y., & Nelson, A. R. (Eds.). (2003). *Unequal treatment: Confronting racial and ethnic disparities in health care.* Washington, DC: National Academy Press.

Spector, R. E. (2000). *Cultural diversity in health and illness* (5th ed.). Upper Saddle River, NJ: Prentice Hall.

Tseng, W. S., & Streltzer, J. (2009). *Cultural competence in health care*. New York: Springer.

CYSTIC FIBROSIS AND THE FAMILY

Cystic fibrosis (CF) is a highly heterogeneous, life-shortening, multisystem genetic disease that involves daily management activities over the course of the disease. Once a disease that primarily affected children, today the median predicted survival is beyond 37 years of age and more than 40% of those affected with CF are adults, according to the Cystic Fibrosis Foundation.

CF merits important consideration within the context of the family not only because of its impact on individuals and families, and its extending presence across the individual and family life cycle, but because of its genetic implications for the immediate and extended family. This entry provides an overview of CF and its treatment, as well as family management and family considerations. CF is discussed in terms of the affected individual within the family context.

Background

Research has shown that CF is a common, lethal, genetic disease, affecting approximately 1 in 3,500 births in Caucasians and less so in Hispanic (1:9,000), African American (1:15,000), and Asian (1:31,000) populations. CF involves dysfunction of many organs, including the lungs, sweat glands, pancreas, bile ducts, intestines, and vas deferens. Pamela Davis reports that more than 90% of CF mortality is related to lung dysfunction, characterized by a destructive cycle of chronic infection, inflammation, bronchiectasis, and eventual respiratory failure and death. Pancreatic insufficiency is present in approximately 85% of those with CF, and CF-related diabetes has become more common, affecting 35% to 40% of adults with CF.

Genetic Aspects

CF is an autosomal recessive disorder caused by mutations in a single gene on chromosome 7. The CF gene encodes the cystic fibrosis transmembrane conductance regulator (CFTR), which primarily functions as a chloride channel. To date, more than 1,600 mutations in the CF gene have been identified, with the vast majority being highly rare. The most common mutation, ΔF508, accounts for approximately 70% of CF alleles.

The identification of varied CFTR mutations has directed much attention at exploring relationships between CF genotype and phenotype. Although several studies have demonstrated some relationships, there is great variability among individuals with the same mutation, and genotype–phenotype correlations have proven weakest for predicting the severity of CF lung disease. The weak correlation between CFTR genotype and CF lung disease suggests other factors exert influence, including the environment, medical and nutritional therapies, adherence to treatments, and CF modifier genes.

Diagnosis and Carrier Testing

Early diagnosis of CF is important because of its association with improved health outcomes and survival. In most of the United States and in many other countries, CF is included in newborn screening panels. When screening is positive, further confirmatory testing is performed via a sweat test with additional genetic and other testing as needed. Carriers of the CF gene can be identified through newborn screening, testing in families or partners of affected individuals, screening of at-risk populations, and preconception and prenatal screening.

Current Treatment Strategies

For individuals with CF and their families, treatment involves a daily, demanding regimen whose goals center on slowing the progression of lung disease, optimizing nutrition, and treating exacerbations and complications. The central treatments include oral pancreatic enzymes, vitamins, antibiotic therapies (inhaled, oral, intravenous [IV]), inhaled medications (e.g., mucolytics, bronchodilators), airway clearance techniques (e.g., chest physiotherapy, percussive vest), and nutritional interventions (i.e., a high-energy, high-fat diet; nutritional supplements). With the onset of exacerbations, individuals with CF are treated more aggressively, in the hospital or at home, with IV antibiotics and intensified airway clearance and nutritional therapies. These "tune-ups," as they are often called, are expected occurrences among CF health care providers, but often bring about significant stress and anxiety for the family, as they think about whether this occurrence may be the first sign of illness progression. Lung transplantation is a carefully considered treatment option. It is reserved for those with significant end-stage lung disease, and because of organ shortages, many who are listed do not survive to transplantation.

Family Management of Cystic Fibrosis

The daily treatment requirements for CF are costly for the individual and the family in terms of time, energy, and emotional and financial resources. Individuals and families must often make significant adjustment in their routines, roles, and responsibilities to accommodate the care required. Not surprisingly, adherence to prescribed therapies is challenging for both families and health care providers. Adherence varies with time and the type of therapy. It generally declines with increasing age and is lowest for those therapies that are most time-consuming. Similar to other chronic conditions, poor adherence is common and many therapies are performed 50% of the time or less, according to Michael Rapoff. Family functioning has been shown to influence adherence, being higher in families with greater cohesion and flexibility. Strategies that enhance adherence include helping individuals and families develop care routines, open communication between individuals/families and health care providers, and cognitive-behavioral techniques such as motivational interviewing and interventions around meal-time behaviors.

In many ways, CF places considerable demands on the family; however, research indicates that most families of individuals with CF do not show patterns of deterioration or dysfunction. Consistent with other childhood chronic illnesses, families report stress around the time of diagnosis and during exacerbations, but with time, understanding, and enhanced competence, families of individuals with CF demonstrate considerable resiliency in adapting to the illness. Those families that do best are able to strike a balance between illness management and quality of life. It is increasingly recognized that quality of life is an important consideration in both evaluating the therapies and in understanding its influence on views of the illness and management behaviors. Parent and family variables that are associated with poorer CF outcomes include single caregiver families, maternal mental health problems, lower income, and limited education.

Conclusion

The outlook for individuals with CF and their families is increasingly bright as care continues to improve and promising new treatments populate the drug development pipeline. However, increased life expectancy and additional therapies, along with many competing life demands, bring new challenges. Health care providers are challenged to focus on optimizing not only physical well-being but quality of life and individual and family functioning.

Denise B. Angst

See also Adults with Childhood-Acquired Conditions; Case Management for Chronic Illness/Disability and the Family; Changes in Family Structure, Roles; Chronic Health Problems and Interventions for the Childrearing Family; Educating the Family Regarding Chronic Physical Illness

Further Readings

Balmer, D. F., Schall, J. L., & Stallings, V. A. (2008). Social disadvantage predicts growth outcomes in preadolescent children with cystic fibrosis. *Journal of Cystic Fibrosis, 7,* 543–550.

Berge, J. M., & Patterson, J. M. (2004). Cystic fibrosis and the family: A review and critique of the literature. *Families, Systems, & Health, 22*(1), 74–100.

Bluebond-Langner, M., Lask, B., & Angst, D. B. (Eds.). (2001). *Psychosocial aspects of cystic fibrosis.* London: Arnold.

Davis, P. B. (1993). Pathophysiology of the lung disease in cystic fibrosis. In P. B. Davis (Ed.), *Cystic fibrosis* (pp. 193–218). New York: Marcel Dekker.

Erickson, S. J., Gerstle, B. A., & Gelstein, S. W. (2005). Brief intervention and motivational interviewing with children, adolescents, and their parents in pediatric health settings. *Archives in Pediatric and Adolescent Medicine, 15,* 1173–1180.

Glasscoe, C. A., & Quittner, A. L. (2008). Psychological interventions for people with cystic fibrosis and their families. Cochrane *Database of Systematic Reviews, 3.*

Grebe, T. A., Seltzer, W. K., DeMarchi, J., Silva, D. K., & Doane, W. W. (1994). Genetic analysis of Hispanic individuals with cystic fibrosis. *American Journal of Medical Genetics, 54,* 443–446.

Hamosh, A., Fitz-Simmons, S. C., Macek, M., Jr., Knowles, M. R., Rosenstein, B. J., & Cutting G. R. (1998). Comparison of the clinical manifestations of cystic fibrosis in black and white patients. *Journal of Pediatrics, 132*(2), 255–259.

Moskowitz, S. M., Chmiel, J. F., Sternen, D. L., Cheng, E., Gibson, R. L., Marshall, S. G., et al. (2008). Clinical practice and genetic counseling for cystic fibrosis and CFTR-related disorders. *Genetics in Medicine, 10*(12), 851–868.

O'Sullivan, B. P., & Freedman, S. D. (2009). Cystic fibrosis. *Lancet, 373,* 1891–1904.

Rapoff, M. A. (1999). *Adherence to pediatric medical regimens.* New York: Kluwer Academic/Plenum.

Stark, L. J., & Powers, S. W. (2005). Behavioral aspects of nutrition in children with cystic fibrosis. *Current Opinion in Pulmonary Medicine, 11,* 539–542.

White, T., Miller, J., Smith, G. L., & McMahon, W. M. (2009). Adherence and psychopathology in children and adolescents with cystic fibrosis. *European Child & Adolescent Psychiatry, 18*(2), 96–104.

Websites

Cystic Fibrosis Foundation: http://www.cff.org

Medline Plus, Cystic Fibrosis: http://www.nlm.nih.gov/medlineplus/cysticfibrosis.html

National Library of Medicine, Genetics Home Reference, Cystic Fibrosis: http://ghr.nlm.nih.gov/condition=cysticfibrosis

Deaf and Hearing Families

Families who are "deaf and hearing" are a diverse subset of families who are like other families yet share unique characteristics that set them apart from families in which everyone can hear. A *deaf and hearing family* is one in which one or more family members are deaf or hard of hearing. The family systems model and the ecological systems framework are useful models for understanding how the dynamics and experiences of families are influenced not only by all individual family members and their interactions with each other, but also by the experiences, institutions, and even the policies that affect their lives and the paths they choose. A life-span perspective is helpful for families as they pursue quality-of-life issues and developmental transitions.

Being Deaf

While some parents/caregivers have prior experience with what it means to be deaf, many report that their own child was their first exposure to hearing loss. Ross E. Mitchell and Michael A. Karchmer report that approximately 92% to 95% of all children with a hearing loss have parents/caregivers who are hearing. These families' experiences are typically very different from families in which there are other deaf family members or families who have experienced multiple generations of a deaf way of life.

Adding richness to this picture is both the diversity of families as well as the heterogeneity of the deaf experience. Hearing loss is prevalent among families of all cultural, ethnic, racial, and linguistic groups, as well as those who are rich or poor, well educated or not, urban or rural. Hearing levels vary from mild to profound and may affect one or both ears. Approximately 30% to 40% of people who are deaf or hard of hearing have a physical disability or condition that may influence their development and opportunities, according to Donald Moores.

American Sign Language, Deaf Culture, and Technologies

Hearing parents/caregivers are generally surprised to learn that their child has a hearing loss except in situations in which being deaf is a condition that is prevalent from one generation to the next. These families are often unaware that many deaf people share a common language (American Sign Language) and a culture of understanding by virtue of their life experiences as "seeing" rather than "hearing" persons.

Hearing technologies, such as hearing aids and cochlear implants, provide access to information from sound, but they do not fully restore hearing. Whereas hearing technologies are extremely beneficial to some, others find these technologies not helpful or choose not to use them. Visual technologies are an important resource for deaf and hard of hearing persons and their families. Visual alerting systems, pagers, text and e-mail messaging, videophones, and video relay phone systems open avenues for information, communication, socialization, and career opportunities.

Language and Communication

Establishing language and communication is the central issue for a child who has a hearing loss. Communication, language, and educational opportunities for deaf and hard of hearing people include a variety of choices and opportunities. Deaf and hearing families report challenges finding ways to communicate so that everyone has access to information and families can develop meaningful relationships with each other. Hearing parents/caregivers need information, support, and skills to learn how to communicate effectively. Parents/caregivers need a working knowledge of many issues, including communication and language, social-emotional development, educational programming, and decision making. Additionally, families need to understand the range of perspectives about being deaf. Two perspectives dominate: the medical-pathological perspective and the cultural-linguistic perspective. Those adhering to a medical-pathological perspective, for example, most physicians, tend to view hearing loss as an impediment to normal development and therefore consider it a condition that needs treatment or habilitation to "normalize." Those who view deafness from a cultural-linguistic viewpoint, for example, most deaf adults and others who are familiar with deafness, tend to think of being deaf more as a difference than a deficit and are less concerned with treatment options; a shared culture and language are the hallmarks of this perspective. A major challenge for families is the differences and controversies about the best way to raise a deaf child. The additional costs of raising a child who is deaf or hard of hearing can also be a challenge. Many families struggle to find funds to pay for hearing aids, speech therapy, genetic testing and counseling, sign language classes, or special services for a child with developmental challenges. According to Kathryn P. Meadow-Orlans and Marilyn A. Sass-Lehrer, in addition to financial demands, many families report limited time and resources available to adequately meet the needs of their families.

Newborn hearing screening and early identification provide families with an early start for understanding what it means to be deaf or hard of hearing and about the challenges and opportunities for their families. Researchers agree that the outcomes for children who have had early and effective early intervention are, in general, superior to those who have not had this opportunity.

Family Support and Role Models

Families develop positive and healthy concepts of being deaf through interaction and support from a variety of sources, including other families who have children who are deaf or hard of hearing, professionals with training and knowledge about deafness, adults who are deaf or hard of hearing, and websites, articles, and books. Input from multiple sources allows the family to obtain a diversity of perspectives, expertise, and values to create a balanced, viable system of support to attain successful outcomes. Manfred Hintermair and Susan Watkins, Paula Pittman, and Beth Walden have suggested that deaf and hard of hearing adults can provide hearing family members with an understanding of what it means to be deaf, offer emotional support, and model visual communication skills that can enhance the quality of family life.

The key to linguistic, communicative, cognitive, and social-emotional success for a child who is deaf or hard of hearing is meaningful parental involvement. Mary Pat Moeller and Rosemary Calderon found that young deaf children who have demonstrated strengths in both linguistic and early reading skills typically have strong family support and effective parent–child communication. According to John Luckner and Ann Velaski, families report that factors contributing to being a healthy family include commitment to the family learning to sign with their child; support from extended family, friends, and community; and support from professionals. Families provide children (whether hearing or deaf) with the social and communicative context for optimizing their life experiences as well as transmitting their individual family values, traditions, and beliefs.

Marilyn Sass-Lehrer and Janet DesGeorges

See also Americans with Disabilities Act and the Family; Caregiving: Infants; Disabilities and Family Management

Further Readings

Bodner-Johnson, B., & Sass-Lehrer, M. (2003). *The young deaf or hard of hearing child: A family-centered approach to early education.* Baltimore: Brookes.

DesGeorges, J. (2003). Families' perceptions of early hearing detection and intervention: Listening to and learning from families. *Mental Retardation and Developmental Disabilities Reviews, 9,* 89–93.

Hintermair, M. (2000). Hearing impairment, social networks, and coping: The need for families with hearing-impaired children to relate to other parents and to hearing-impaired adults. *American Annals of the Deaf, 145,* 41–51.

Marschark, M. (2007). *Raising and educating a deaf child: A comprehensive guide to choices, controversies, and decisions faced by parents and educators* (2nd ed.). New York: Oxford University Press.

Marschark, M., & Spencer, P. (Eds.). *Oxford handbook of deaf studies, language and education* (pp. 232–246). New York: Oxford University Press.

Meadow-Orlans, K., Mertens, D., & Sass-Lehrer, M. (2003). *Parents and their deaf children: The early years.* Washington, DC: Gallaudet University Press.

Meadow-Orlans, K., & Sass-Lehrer, M. (1995). Support services for families with children who are deaf: Challenges for professionals. *Topics in Early Childhood Special Education, 15*(3), 314–334.

Mitchell, R. E., & Karchmer, M. A. (2006). Demographics of deaf education: More students in more places. *American Annals of the Deaf, 151*(2), 95–104.

Moores, D. (2001). *Educating the deaf: Psychology, principles, and practices.* Boston: Houghton Mifflin.

Nussbaum, D. (2003). *Cochlear implants: Navigating a forest of information . . . one tree at a time.* Washington, DC: Gallaudet University, Laurent Clerc Deaf Education Center. Retrieved from http://clerccenter.gallaudet.edu/Documents/Clerc/CI.pdf

Schwartz, S. (Ed.). (2007). *Choices in deafness: A parent's guide to communication options.* Bethesda, MD: Woodbine House.

Watkins, S., Pittman, P., & Walden, B. (1998). The deaf mentor experimental project for young children who are deaf and their families. *American Annals of the Deaf, 143*(1), 29–34.

Yoshinaga-Itano, C. (2003). From screening to early identification and intervention: Discovering predictors to successful outcomes for children with significant hearing loss. *Journal of Deaf Studies and Deaf Education, 8*(1), 11–30.

DEATH: AMBIGUOUS FEELINGS RELATED TO LOSS

After a death, survivors typically proceed through a series of cultural, faith-based mourning rituals that mark death and honor the deceased's life. Family, friends, and community usually participate in these rituals, whose purpose is to provide comfort and closure. Closure involves restructuring the family's roles and responsibilities. However, this process is interrupted if death is ignored or minimized or there is no body verifying death. Some examples where there is no body but probable death include deaths from war (missing in action), natural disasters (e.g., floods), plane crashes, kidnappings, and fires. Deaths that the family or community does not acknowledge or minimizes include spontaneous abortions, stillbirths, death of an estranged spouse, and death of a pet. Based on Pauline Boss's theory of ambiguous loss, these are situations of unclear losses. The theory's basis is that this lack of clear loss is traumatizing to individuals, families, and communities, and it freezes grieving.

Ambiguous loss theory, built on the family stress model, provides the foundation for interventions. It is cyclical in that three factors both influence and are influenced by the other factors. The "A factor" is the ambiguous loss; the "B factor" refers to individual, family, and community resources; and the "C factor" includes the individual and community perceptions of the ambiguous loss and boundary ambiguity. Collectively, these factors impact the degree of family stress, which is on a continuum from high to low. Boss clearly states that ambiguity is not synonymous with "uncertainty" or "ambivalence."

Ambiguous losses, characterized for the physical absence but psychological presence of the loved one, can result in freezing grief processes. It is one of the most stressful types of losses because there is no clarity for family boundaries or closure. Boundary ambiguity is seen on a continuum ranging from high to low. Without a body to verify death, families tend not to acknowledge death and continue to act as if the deceased individual will return eventually. Boss defines *family boundary ambiguity* as a state in which family members are uncertain in their perception of who is part of the family and who is performing certain roles and tasks within family systems. Subsequently, family members experience role confusion, delay family decisions, and eliminate family celebrations and rituals. This is unlike a death where there is a body that proves death occurred and allows for normal grief work. Ambiguous loss is a problem when families experience high boundary ambiguity and hopelessness.

The Boundary Ambiguity Scale measures the family's perceptions about family boundaries. Boss lists six theoretical propositions as the scale's basis. The higher the family system boundary ambiguity is, the higher the family's stress and dysfunction will be. Over the short term, family boundary ambiguity may not be dysfunctional. If a high degree of family ambiguity persists over time, the family system will become highly stressed and subsequently dysfunctional. Families with varying belief systems will differ in how they perceive family boundaries. A family's value orientation influences the length of time a family can tolerate a high degree of boundary ambiguity. Larger community context influences a family's perception of events.

Many families find ways to cope with ambiguous loss. Boss provides empirically based guidelines for health care providers and families to foster resiliency with ambiguous loss. They include (a) finding meaning, (b) tempering mastery, (c) reconstructing identity, (d) normalizing ambivalence, (e) revising attachment, and (f) discovering hope.

Boss advises practitioners first to diagnose the situation as ambiguous loss. Families find comfort learning that their distress is normal. Once they understand the distress source, grieving and reconstructing rules, roles, and rituals can begin. Practitioners should encourage families to share stories and perceptions about the missing person in groups. Families' perceptions are influenced by the community and, in turn, influence the community. Meetings can serve as a mechanism to establish connections with others experiencing similar losses.

It is essential that families find meaning for the loss or accept a lack of meaning. Terrorism victims' families report that they had to discuss and adjust their family celebrations and rituals to maintain the family. Some report "presumed death" certificates or funerals allowed their own grieving to begin. Not all families dealing with ambiguous loss demonstrate similar effects. Some are able to tolerate ambiguity secondary to previous successful loss experiences, personality traits, continued trust in a supreme being, or the ability to accept two opposing ideas. They recognize that their loved one is probably dead but hope the person is not. Individuals demonstrating the most difficulty with ambiguous loss are those who typically have power and mastery in their daily life. To live with ambiguous loss, these individuals need to relinquish striving for perfect solutions.

Studies on ambiguous loss should include all family members with a focus on strengths and not pathology. They should be longitudinal and cross-cultural and include resilient and symptomatic individuals. Practitioners should treat ambiguous loss in a group setting. Practitioners who address ambiguous loss early can prevent unresolved grief, depression, relational conflicts, and long-term family dynamics problems. Finally, Boss encourages multicultural collaborations between researchers and practitioners so work on ambiguous loss can expand.

Jane M. Kurz

See also Bereavement and Perinatal Loss in Childbearing Families; Death and the Grieving Process in Families; Death Rituals in Families; Grief Work Facilitation

Further Readings

Boss, P. (1999). *Ambiguous loss: Learning to live with unresolved grief*. Cambridge, MA: Harvard University Press.

Boss, P. (2004). Ambiguous loss research, theory, and practice reflections after 9/11. *Journal of Marriage and Family, 66*, 551–566.

Boss, P. (2007). Ambiguous loss theory: Challenges for scholars and practitioners. *Family Relations, 56*, 105–111.

Boss, P. (n.d.). *Ambiguous loss*. Retrieved from http://ambiguousloss.com/about_ambiguous_loss.php

Boss, P., & Couden, B. (2002). Ambiguous loss from chronic illness: Clinical interventions with individuals, couples and families. *Journal of Clinical Psychology/In Session: Psychotherapy in Practice, 58*, 1351–1360.

Boss, P., & Greenberg, J. (1984). Family stress theory. *Family Process, 23*, 535–546.

Boss, P., Greenberg, J., & Pearce-McCall, D. (1990). *Measurement of boundary ambiguity in families* (Minnesota Agricultural Experiment Station Bulletin

No. 593–1990, item no. Ad-SB 3763) St. Paul: University of Minnesota.

Huebner, A., Mancini, J., Wilcox, R., Grass, S., & Grass, G. (2007). Parental deployment and youth in military families: Exploring uncertainly and ambiguous loss. *Family Relations, 56,* 112–122.

Websites

Pauline Boss, Ambiguous Loss:
    http://www.ambiguousloss.com

Death and the Grieving Process in Families

When death occurs, the grieving process in families is influenced by the way it arrives, the cause and timing of the death, and the various relationships involved. Additional family-related factors include past experiences with death, patterns of grieving, developmental stages of individuals and the family, ethnicity, spiritual/religious orientation, and belief systems. Also significant is lack of preparation given a societal reluctance to deal with death and related issues until faced with them as a reality. After a brief discussion of the historical context of grief process theories, this entry discusses the various influences on the grieving process, desired health outcomes, and recommended interventions and support for survivors.

Historical Context

Increased professional interest in death and dying was sparked during the late 1960s by Elisabeth Kübler-Ross, who focused her research and writing on people with terminal illnesses. About the same time, the hospice movement began in England. Subsequently, scholarly journals and professional societies devoted to the study of death-related issues marked emergence of the field of thanatology. There soon followed a wealth of research that reversed previous theories about the grief process.

Classical models of grieving were derived from the psychoanalytic perspectives of Sigmund Freud and Erich Lindemann, as well as from the attachment theory described by John Bowlby. According

to these approaches, all relationships involve the investment of energy. When a person dies, the energy previously invested in the relationship with him or her must be withdrawn so new attachments may be formed. Failing to do so in an appropriate manner indicates problems and perhaps pathology. According to these approaches, the grief process is time-limited, involving 2 weeks of intense emotion, 2 months of strong but less intense grieving, and completion of the process by the end of 2 years. Deviations from this format indicate a maladaptive mourning process.

Although the classical model is still adhered to by some, its fundamental assumptions were challenged severely by a variety of studies conducted in the 1980s. The conclusions derived from this research may be summarized as follows:

1. The grieving process may have no fixed end point and may even last a lifetime.

2. Complete detachment from the deceased is neither possible nor desirable.

3. Bereaved persons may remain involved and connected to the person who has died, often through an inner representation of him or her.

4. Bereavement may take many forms.

5. The degree to which grief is maladaptive must be decided on an individual basis.

The Many Faces of Death

When death comes unexpectedly, the person who has died may have made no provisions and may not have expressed his or her wishes regarding organ donation, funeral arrangements, burial preferences, and so forth. Survivors may have to deal with a lack of closure, as they were given no time for farewells or resolution of conflicts. Acute feelings of unreality, disbelief, shock, and many loose ends are typical, as is dissonance in terms of beliefs and meaning systems, particularly if the death occurred under tragic circumstances or involved the loss of a child. With accidental death, survivors tend to second-guess themselves, feel guilty for not having done things differently, or see themselves as somehow involved in causing the fatality. Following violent or wrongful death, survivors often worry about the suffering their loved one experienced, feel rage about injustice, and have to deal with disfigurement of the body. For survivors of a completed suicide, desire for privacy, guilt, and an inability to speak about the death (because of the social stigma involved) may be complicating factors. Even when death results from a physical condition, survivors often look for someone or something to blame.

When death is anticipated, the dying person may put his or her affairs in order, participate in funeral arrangements and burial decisions, and achieve closure in significant relationships. He or she also has opportunities to assimilate what is happening and realign beliefs and meaning systems. However, foreknowledge also tends to initiate a period of anticipatory mourning for everyone involved. Further, in an extended dying process, significant stress may be placed on caretakers, and the dying person may feel remorseful about being a burden. When death comes, a sense of relief may trigger guilt feelings about what is a normal, if mixed, reaction.

Each relationship type also creates differences in the death experience and the grieving process. Loss of a child generally includes loss of hopes and dreams as well as shattered belief systems given "a death out of time." Sibling death may create a double loss, as appropriate parental support may not be forthcoming and children's sense of security is threatened as parents behave differently. Further stress may be created as others deny or ignore what siblings may be feeling. Loss of a parent is enormous at any time, having various behavioral and emotional ramifications depending on the ages of the surviving children. Finally, spousal loss may shatter survivors' sense of security, creating feelings of being lost and out of control.

Desired Health Outcomes

Grief may last a lifetime, and family members may never "get over" the loss of a loved one. Thus, the goal is to learn how to accommodate grief and to also once again be able to experience joy. Survivors may need to understand that each person will grieve in a way appropriate for that person; revise their belief systems as they search for meaning and attempt to make peace with their loss; and be patient with themselves and others, recognizing that the grieving process takes as long as it takes.

Interventions to Facilitate Healing

The first, most important intervention involves inviting family members to tell their stories, being willing to just listen while recognizing that there is no quick fix. Survivors must be allowed to cry and to express all of their feelings. So-called irrational thoughts, feelings, behaviors, and guilt need to be normalized. Healing may be facilitated through the process of forgiveness. Helping survivors replace painful images and recognizing that perceived loose ends in need of tying up deserve time and attention also may be important. Helping with funeral planning or the creation of ceremonies may be appropriate.

Healing also may be facilitated by the following activities: (a) maintaining or transforming rooms and/or furniture; (b) journaling, meditating, praying, listening; (c) planning time to grieve; (d) wearing an article of clothing or jewelry that belonged to the deceased; (e) creating new holiday traditions; (f) acknowledging birthdays and anniversaries; (g) lighting candles; (h) creating scrapbooks, albums, and/or videos; (i) writing letters to the deceased; and (j) volunteering and/or supporting a cause.

Suggestions for assisting with the search for meaning include (a) assessing the role of religion/spirituality as a resource for hope and strength or a source of disappointment; (b) offering questions or reflections that test the logic of various lines of reasoning; (c) referring to or recommending additional resources; (d) utilizing bibliotherapy; (e) suggesting explorations of death in other cultures; (f) helping to integrate information and rewrite personal stories; and (g) confirming the possibility of reclaiming joy.

The Importance of Support for the Grief Process

Those losing a loved one often are ill prepared. Those around them, although well intentioned, often don't know how to help meaningfully, even saying or doing things that survivors find offensive. When a child, sibling, parent, or spouse dies, surviving family members also may be unable to provide necessary support. In worst case scenarios, families may never recover even a semblance of what they once had, and the challenges of grief may lead to physical illness. Survivors need appropriate support so that in the best case scenario they can emerge stronger than they were at the outset.

Dorothy S. Becvar

See also Bereavement and Perinatal Loss in Childbearing Families; Death: Ambiguous Feelings Related to Loss; Death Rituals in Families; Grief Work Facilitation

Further Readings

Becvar, D. S. (2000). Families experiencing death, dying and bereavement. In W. C. Nichols, M. A. Nichols, D. S. Becvar, & A. Y. Napier (Eds.), *The handbook of family development and intervention* (pp. 453–470). New York: Wiley.

Becvar, D. S. (2001). *In the presence of grief: Helping family members resolve death, dying and bereavement issues.* New York: Guilford Press.

Kastenbaum, R. J. (1986). *Death, society and human experience* (3rd ed.). Columbus, OH: Merrill.

DEATH FROM UNNATURAL CAUSES: DRUG OVERDOSE

Illicit drug and prescription drug use is the primary cause of unintentional overdose death. This entry describes symptoms of drug overdose, epidemiology, risk factors, societal cost, and prevention strategies for drug overdose death. Recommendations on how family can help prevent overdose death are outlined as related to these areas.

Symptoms of Overdose

Swift recognition of overdose by family members of a victim is crucial in order to immediately contact medical personnel, especially because most overdoses occur in the home. Overdose can happen to anyone who uses drugs and occurs when an amount of a drug or combination of drugs overwhelms the body—brain, heart, liver, lungs, and kidneys. Symptoms that may indicate overdose from depressant drugs like opioids (such as heroin, synthetic opioid analgesics) and sedatives (such as benzodiazepines, alcohol) include the following: slow or absent pulse; slow, shallow, erratic breathing or cessation of breathing; limp body/muscles; pale face; blue lips and/or fingernails; contracted pupils; choking or gurgling sounds; vomiting; consciousness with inability to speak; and unconsciousness or unresponsiveness. Overdose from stimulants (such as cocaine, methamphetamine) may present with the following symptoms: difficulty breathing, foaming at the mouth, pressure or pain in chest area, heart attack, stroke, shaking or seizure, racing pulse, dilated pupils, muscle cramps, vomiting, and unconsciousness.

Epidemiology

Illicit Drugs

The mortality rate among illicit drug users is estimated at roughly 10 times that of the general population, and unintentional drug overdose is a primary cause of death. It is estimated that up to 70% of illicit drug users have reported at least one nonfatal overdose during their lifetime. Up to 90% of injection drug users have witnessed an overdose. Annual overdose death rates among this population are estimated between 1% and 4% of total overdose events.

Heroin and cocaine users are at greatest risk of overdose death because of the use of multiple substances (such as mixing heroin with central nervous system depressants), reported by up to 80% of users. Mixing drugs carries high overdose death risk because of a possible increase in the overall pharmacological effect. Overdose death from amphetamine-type drugs is not as common but does occur. Cannabis does not cause overdose death but may be indirectly involved in other causes of death, such as motor vehicle crash.

Prescription Drugs

From 1999 to 2006, the number of drug overdose deaths involving prescription opioids (such as methadone, oxycodone, or hydrocodone) roughly tripled in the United States. In 2006, prescription opioid overdose death was most common among males, non-Hispanic whites, and persons between 35 and 54 years of age. Benzodiazepines were most commonly found causing death in combination with opioids. Available opioid doses are extremely potent and may result in overdose death when misused, and even when used for therapeutic purposes if not appropriately monitored by the prescribing provider.

One should be aware of the recent trend of prescription drug abuse among youth because of the potential for overdose among initiates and those who transition to use of more potent drugs. Parents may discover their child abuses prescription drugs long after initiation, so awareness of this trend is important to quickly recognize and address the problem. Young children who die of overdose most often accidentally ingest a nonillicit drug, though the death rate among this population is low compared to adults.

Risk Factors

The following are examples of drug overdose risk factors as characterized into demographic or individual, environmental, and drug-specific domains.

Demographic or Individual

Males are overrepresented in fatal drug overdoses and account for the majority of deaths. The mean age of illicit drug overdose decedents is mid-30s, with a younger profile for those who use party drugs such as ecstasy (MDMA). Research has shown that overdose risk increases with duration of use: Older, more experienced users have higher overdose death rates than younger, less experienced users.

In addition, the lowering of tolerance can occur after periods of abstinence or a short-term reduction in drug use. Increased risk of overdose death is shown, for instance, among individuals released from prison or detoxification programs as a result of lowered tolerance and misjudgment of dose when reinitiating use. Finally, high levels of depressive symptoms have been observed among drug users who experience overdose. Family members are often the first to detect signs of mental illness and can play a preventive role by taking appropriate action.

Environment

Overdose situations that occur in the presence of family less often result in death because using drugs alone eliminates the possibility of help from others. Delay or lack of medical assistance in the event of overdose can occur when the victim is distant from services (such as a rural setting) or when a bystander does not seek medical attention. In the United States, a common reason for the latter is fear of police involvement. Laws exist in the United States to encourage bystanders to call 911 in an overdose situation by providing limited immunity if fear of arrest is an issue.

Easy-to-reach medications in the home can be accidentally ingested or diverted, resulting in overdose death. Medications should be stored safely, where only people who were prescribed the drug or need to give the drug to a patient can gain access.

Drug Characteristics and Route of Administration

As mentioned, multiple drug use is a primary risk factor for overdose death. Regarding drug purity, research does not conclusively support the notion that high purity is a major cause of overdose, specifically with heroin. Purity can fluctuate depending on the source and whether the drug has been adulterated or cut for retail sale. Purity may be a factor contributing to death, although multiple drug use (a more typical situation as opposed to single drug use) is a stronger predictor of overdose death.

Drug injection is the most common and dangerous route of administration among those who die from overdose. It should be noted that both illicit drugs and prescription drugs can be injected.

Drug characteristics differ by locality and subpopulation, and they may migrate. Such factors are important, as they directly affect individual choice of drug, rates of abuse and dependence, community use patterns, route of administration, and, ultimately, overdose death risk.

Societal Cost

The World Health Organization developed a technique to measure disease burden called Disability Adjusted Life Years (DALYs), a summary measure of lost life due to premature death and lost years of productivity due to disability. In 2000, illicit drug use contributed to 0.8% of all global DALYs, or nearly 200,000 deaths worldwide.

In the United States, drug overdose is the second leading cause of unintentional injury death (behind motor vehicle crashes) but is the leading cause of injury death among persons between 35 and 54 years of age. According to the Centers for Disease Control and Prevention, in 2006, among all causes of death in the United States, unintentional drug overdose accounted for 5.6% of lost life due to premature death.

Prevention Strategies

The most effective strategy to reduce overdose death is treatment for drug dependence. Methadone is the longest standing, proven medication-assisted therapy for opioid dependence, and there is mounting evidence for the effectiveness of buprenorphine. Efforts are under way to identify effective pharmacotherapies for cocaine and methamphetamine dependence. Families can be influential in facilitating treatment entry for drug-dependent family members and an important source of support thereafter. They should understand the remitting and relapsing nature of addiction and help a family member find his or her most suitable treatment option as needed over time.

Abstinence from drug use is ideal. However, drug users and their families should be familiar with the strategy of harm reduction: a collective, practical approach to reduce the negative effects of drug use and serve as a conduit to services and communication for drug users. The intent is not to legitimize drug use but prioritize the clinical and ethical need to reduce overdose death. Overdose prevention education is delivered via outreach, syringe exchange, and treatment programs. Research shows that laypeople in the community can recognize a heroin overdose, successfully administer naloxone (an antidote to opioid overdose), and perform rescue breathing techniques during an event. This intervention should be viewed as stabilization of the victim while awaiting emergency medical care, as the victim may fall back into coma after naloxone administration.

Medical providers play a pivotal role in preventing drug overdose as more physicians are prescribing opioids. It is increasingly important to promulgate evidence-based practice guidelines for the clinical management of chronic noncancer pain, opioid prescribing and dosing. There is high risk for dependence and overdose among chronic pain patients with history of substance abuse. People in need of multiple medications to treat comorbid conditions, such as the elderly population, are also vulnerable because of potential drug interactions. It is sensible that family members of high-risk patients be educated about the drugs being taken and degree of potential overdose risk.

Other strategies to reduce overdose death that involve family, some of which are undergoing evaluation, include (a) the provision of naloxone and training to all opioid users and their families, not only heroin users; (b) proper disposal of prescription drugs to reduce diversion or abuse of unused drugs; and (c) professional standards for overdose survivors treated in the hospital, considered a window of opportunity to provide treatment referral and overdose education material at discharge. Family members should know that a person who survives an overdose is at greater risk of another event and has greater risk for subsequent fatal overdose.

It is paramount to raise overdose awareness, provide education, and increase the visibility of the problem so that families are poised to identify underlying and direct overdose risk factors, jointly develop long-term preventive routines, and respond appropriately in the event of a drug overdose.

Nina G. Shah

See also Death From Unnatural Causes: Poisoning; Drug Addictions in the Family

Further Readings

Centers for Disease Control and Prevention. (2008). Nonpharmaceutical fentanyl-related deaths—Multiple states, April 2005–March 2007. *Morbidity and Mortality Weekly Report, 57*(29), 793–796.

Darke, S., Degenhardt, L., & Mattick, R. (2007). *Mortality amongst illicit drug users: Epidemiology, causes and intervention.* New York: Cambridge University Press.

Green, T. C., Heimer, R., & Grau, L. E. (2008). Distinguishing signs of opioid overdose and indication for naloxone: An evaluation of six overdose training and naloxone distribution programs in the United States. *Addiction, 103*(6), 979–989.

McLellan, A. T., & Turner, B. (2008). Prescription opioids, overdose deaths, and physician responsibility. *Journal of the American Medical Association, 300*(22), 2672–2673.

Office of National Drug Control Policy. (2004). *The economic costs of drug abuse in the United States, 1992–2002* (Publication No. 207303). Washington, DC: Executive Office of the President.

Strang, J., Manning, V., Mayet, S., Best, D., Titherington, E., Santana L., et al. (2008). Overdose training and take-home naloxone for opiate users: Prospective cohort study of impact on knowledge and attitudes and subsequent management of overdoses. *Addiction, 103*(10), 1648–1657.

Warner M., Chen, L. H., & Makuc, D. M. (2009). *Increase in fatal poisonings involving opioid analgesics in the United States, 1999–2006* (NCHS Data Brief No. 22). Hyattsville, MD: National Center for Health Statistics.

Websites

Centers for Disease Control and Prevention: http://www.cdc.gov

Harm Reduction Coalition: http://www.harmreduction.org

National Institute on Drug Abuse: http://www.nida.nih.gov

Substance Abuse and Mental Health Services Administration, Office of Applied Studies, National Survey on Drug Use & Health: http://oas.samhsa.gov/nsduh.htm

Death From Unnatural Causes: Homicides, Drive-By Shootings

Reducing violence-related morbidity and mortality among adolescents and young adults is an urgent public health priority that is strongly related to the availability of firearms. Homicide disproportionately impacts adolescents and young adults. In 2007, homicide was the second leading cause of death among those 12 to 24 years of age, and more than 83% of all homicides were the result of a firearm injury. According to the Centers for Disease Control and Prevention, homicide among youth accounted for more than 605,000 years of potential life lost (YPLL), representing significant social and economic loss. Police records provide additional information on the burden of homicide

among those under the age of 25 years. According to figures released by the Department of Justice, persons age 24 years and younger accounted for nearly 35% of all victims of homicide in 2008. This entry first describes the characteristics of youth who die from homicide and then discusses drive-by shootings, homicides involving firearms, and the prevention of death due to homicide.

Characteristics of Youth Who Die From Homicide

Overall, youth who die as a result of homicide are more likely to live in a metropolitan area, be a member of a minority group, and have parents who did not finish high school. Younger victims of homicide are also more likely to have been exposed to family violence and are less likely to have had contact with social services before the time of their death. Moreover, early, violent death is more common among delinquent or previously incarcerated youth than among other youth, and these deaths occur disproportionately among members of minority groups. The relationship between perpetrator and homicide victim and manner of death tends to vary with age. Among younger children, the perpetrator is more likely to be a relative of the victim, and the manner of death is more likely to be physical assault. Among older adolescents and younger adults, the perpetrator is most likely to be an acquaintance of the victim, and death is most likely caused by a firearm injury.

Drive-By Shootings

Drive-by shootings are a comparatively rare form of homicide that has been strongly linked with gang activity. Previous research suggests that the vast majority of all drive-by shootings are perpetrated by, or otherwise involve, members of street gangs. However, fatalities resulting from drive-by shootings may not be limited to gang members. Results from analyses of records of drive-by shootings in Los Angeles suggest that nearly 25% of all homicide victims are innocent bystanders. Unlike patterns of victimization among those who die from any form of homicide, victims of drive-by shootings are more likely to be a minority and male. In a separate review of the characteristics of injuries resulting from drive-by shootings, it was determined that the majority of victims (69%) die from a single gunshot wound and nearly 75% occur on public streets. Gang members, a small proportion of youth, commit the majority of serious violence, and gang membership has also been associated with other individual and contextual factors that may increase risk of victimization through involvement in delinquency, substance use, and interaction with delinquent peers. Despite recent estimates that gang activity increased by as much as 12% in urban areas between the years 2002 and 2007, there is a scarcity of evaluated gang prevention programs. However, researchers have recognized the need for the evaluation of interventions as well as other prevention strategies to support the development of gang prevention programs and policies. The increased prevalence of gang activity, as well as subsequent risk for victimization among those who are not affiliated with youth gangs, emphasize the need for a continued awareness of risk for homicide associated with gang violence regardless of membership status.

Homicide and Firearms

An overwhelming majority of U.S. homicides, including those resulting from gang-related violence, involve firearms. There are documented racial disparities in firearm-related violence, and previous analyses have reported substantial increases in firearm-related mortality among high-risk populations. In terms of geography, a recent study of firearm deaths in persons 0 to 19 years of age found that, while the most urban counties had significantly more homicides, there was no difference between the most rural and most urban areas in overall firearm-related mortality. In response to the increased risk for morbidity and mortality associated with access to firearms, the National Academy of Pediatrics has recommended a multifaceted approach to reduce access to firearms among adolescents and young adults. Recommended strategies include support for legislation that would reduce the availability of firearms in homes of adolescents, routine inquiries about the presence of guns in the home, community-based coalitions to enhance public education, and the development and implementation of prevention programs designed to increase awareness of risk and enhance coping skills and conflict management.

Prevention of Violent Death

The existing violence prevention literature has concentrated disproportionately on the identification and co-occurrence of youth violence perpetration, and there is comparatively little information on the identification of factors that may uniquely contribute to an increased risk of death from homicide. However, there is evidence that risk for victimization among those who perpetrate violence is high, and some prevention programs are predicated on the assumption that reductions in violence perpetration among members of high-risk populations will correspondingly reduce rates of victimization among these same groups. This approach, consistent with current guidelines for preventing high-risk behaviors, utilizes a socioecological framework, which allows for the identification of risk characteristics and relationships at multiple levels. Using this approach, a number of individual (e.g., early expression of aggression, substance abuse), family (e.g., poor parental monitoring, low emotional attachment, exposure to violence), peer and school (e.g., peer delinquency, low academic achievement), and neighborhood factors (e.g., neighborhood poverty, access to firearms, low community participation) can be modified to reduce risk for violence and aggression.

Robert M. Bossarte, Monica H. Swahn,
and John Blosnich

See also Family Emotional Climate and Mental Health; Injury Prevention for Infants and Children Family Members; Youth Violence Prevention in the Family

Further Readings

Chew, K., McLeary, R., Lew, M., & Wang, J. (1999). The epidemiology of child homicide in California, 1981 through 1990. *Homicide Studies, 3,* 151–169.

Committee on Adolescence. (1992). Firearms and adolescents. *Pediatrics, 89,* 784–787.

Dahlberg, L. (1998). Youth violence in the United States: Major trends, risk factors, and prevention approaches. *American Journal of Preventive Medicine, 14*(4), 259–271.

Howell, J. (1999). Youth gang homicides: A literature review. *Crime & Delinquency, 45,* 208–241.

Swahn, M., Simon, T., Hertz, M., Arias, I., Bossarte, R., Ross, J., et al. (2008). Linking dating violence, peer violence, and suicidal behaviors among high-risk youth. *American Journal of Preventive Medicine, 34*(1), 30–38.

Websites

Centers for Disease Control and Prevention. Injury Prevention & Control, Data & Statistics, Web-Based Injury Statistics Query and Reporting System (WISQARS): http://www.cdc.gov/injury/wisqars

DEATH FROM UNNATURAL CAUSES: INJURIES

Death caused by accidents has been part of the human experience since the beginning of mankind. The term *accident*, with its fatalistic implication of bad luck, is now called *unintentional injury* and is recognized as a major public health issue. The terminology reflects a complete change in how societies, institutions, families, and individuals can approach injuries as diseases that can be treated as well as prevented. Prevention measures can diminish the potentially devastating effects of unintentional injuries on families.

Traditionally restricted to traumatic injuries, lethal unintentional injuries include poisoning, strangulation, suffocation, drowning, and burns. In 2006, the Centers for Disease Control and Prevention (CDC) reported that unintentional injury was the leading cause of *all* deaths in the United States for the ages 1 to 44 years. In that year, there were more than 120,000 unintentional injury deaths, compared to 56,000 deaths from influenza and pneumonia, and 18,000 deaths from homicide. The National Safety Council reported that injuries cost $684.4 billion in 2007, and the top four causes of unintentional death were (1) motor vehicle crashes, (2) poisonings, (3) falls, and (4) drowning. Outcome analysis shows that lethal injuries cause massive medical and nonmedical costs, with long-lasting economic, productivity, and mental effects on families and society.

Death from unintentional injury represents only the tip of the injury problem. The CDC reported 40 deaths per 100,000 people from unintentional injuries in 2006, compared with 9,300 nonfatal injuries per 100,000 people. The likelihood of dying from an injury varies with the type. For instance, drowning is particularly lethal, whereas falls are less so. After a brief discussion of the history of injury research, this entry focuses on common fatal injuries and strategies to prevent them.

History

The approach to injury changed in the 1960s when William Haddon, a physician, became the commissioner of the National Highway Traffic Safety Administration. Haddon developed an approach to motor vehicle crashes (MVCs) as a disease process, not an accident. He created a tool, Haddon's Matrix, for assessing the causes of injuries. Haddon's Matrix defines the contributors to the event as the host (i.e., the driver), the agent (i.e., energy transfer from the car), and the physical and social environment (i.e., the road), then divides the injury into three phases: pre-event, event, and post-event. By examining the injury contributors in the context of phases, Haddon's Matrix allows investigators to examine risk factors and preventive factors for lethal injuries.

The development of injury research has led to the systematic examination of interventions that treat or prevent injuries. Injury coding is now utilized on hospital records and death certificates. A national focus on post-event modification of injury severity prompted the development of pre-hospital care and trauma systems.

Common Fatal Injuries

In the United States and a variety of other countries, MVCs cause the highest number of unintentional deaths. According to the CDC, in 2006 in the United States, MVCs caused 14.5 deaths per 100,000 people, involving 43,000 fatalities. The death rates for MVCs have dropped over past decades as research has identified contributing factors (e.g., vehicle and road design, alcohol consumption, safety belt use, and speed) and found effective ways to address them.

Age is a risk factor for lethal injuries, and the top causes of unintentional fatalities vary by age. In 2006, MVCs were the leading cause of unintentional deaths for children aged 1 to 14 years; drowning ranked second. In adults aged 35 to 54, poisoning ranked first while in the elderly, unintentional falls were the leading cause of death, with MVCs the second leading cause.

Other risk factors for lethal injuries related to the host include gender, socioeconomic status, ethnicity, and alcohol use. Event factors usually relate to the mechanism of injury, which can be quantified, such as the speed of a car. Environmental risk factors include unsafe or unsupervised settings. The complexity of unintentional death underscores the need to identify the risk factors for each injury type using a systematic approach. Moreover, prevention strategies need to be tailored to specific risk groups.

Prevention Strategies

Research has identified effective strategies to prevent deaths from a variety of injuries. In keeping with Haddon's Matrix, injury prevention strategies can be systematically aimed at three areas: the host, the agent, and the environment. Speed limits help to slow down drivers and prevent MVCs, while enforcing safety belt use decreases injury severity resulting from MVCs. Improving strength and balance in the elderly can prevent falls. Teaching young children to swim may prevent drowning deaths. Families are integral to the implementation of such prevention measures.

Addressing the agent can also decrease injury rates and severity. Airbags in cars and effective brakes can decrease MVC severity and frequency. Proper management of medications in the elderly reduces the number of medication-induced falls.

The environment, both physical and social, can be modified to prevent unintentional injuries and deaths. Highway dividers physically separate cars traveling in opposite directions, thereby preventing MVCs. Four-sided fencing around swimming pools can prevent drowning. Efforts at the societal level, such as graduated driver's licensing, limiting alcohol levels while driving, or wearing life jackets while boating, can decrease injuries.

Prevention efforts require education, technology, and societal will. Educating families and individuals about hazards and ways to minimize them can occur in a variety of settings, including schools, media, and doctors' offices. Improving the availability of low-cost technologies, such as smoke alarms, can make a difference in preventing injuries. Enacting and enforcing legislation that promotes safe products and practices, such as requiring proper child safety seats in cars and forbidding alcohol while driving or boating, can impact the number of injuries and deaths from injuries.

Conclusion

Unintentional injuries and fatalities are no longer classified as accidental. They inflict tremendous costs on families as well as on communities and nations. Research can identify their specific causes or modifiable factors, such as environmental hazards or risky behaviors. Many lethal injuries are preventable; however, more effort is needed to continue to develop, prove, and institute prevention measures. Unquestionably, an ounce of prevention is well worth it.

Linda Quan and S. Heath Ackley

See also Death and the Grieving Process in Families; Death From Unnatural Causes: Drug Overdose; Death From Unnatural Causes: Homicides, Drive-By Shootings; Injury Prevention for Infants and Children Family Members; Injury Prevention for the Elderly Family Member; Life-Threatening Experiences, Support for the Family

Further Readings

Doll, L. S., Bonzo, S. E., Mercy, J. A., & Sleet, D. A. (Eds.). (2007). *Handbook of injury and violence prevention.* New York: Springer.

Haddon, W. (1999). The changing approach to the epidemiology, descriptively based prevention, and amelioration of trauma: The transition to approaches etiologically rather than descriptively based. *Injury Prevention, 5,* 231–235.

Liller, K. D. (Ed.). (2006). *Injury prevention for children and adolescents.* Washington, DC: American Public Health Association.

National Center for Injury Prevention and Control. (2006). *CDC injury fact book.* Atlanta, GA: Centers for Disease Control and Prevention.

National Safety Council. (2009). *Injury facts, 2009 edition.* Itasca, IL: Author.

Websites

Centers for Disease Control and Prevention. Injury Prevention & Control, Data & Statistics, Web-Based Injury Statistics Query and Reporting System (WISQARS): http://www.cdc.gov/injury/wisqars

DEATH FROM UNNATURAL CAUSES: POISONING

Poisonings are a problem that many families encounter in their lifetime. The definition of family in this context may include members of the immediate family, relatives, friends, and neighbors. Poison centers provide poison prevention material and educate families on how to poison proof their homes and make a safer home environment for all family members. Because more than 90% of all poisoning exposures called to poison centers occur in the family home, parents need to be educated on how to poison proof their homes and to call 1-800-222-1222 (toll-free poison center number) if a poisoning occurs. Poison centers are a valuable resource for families: They assist the family in a time of crisis by providing proper treatment recommendations and referring families to obtain a higher level of care if needed. Consulting with a poison center when an exposure occurs can result in a more positive outcome and minimize death and disability from serious exposures. Early intervention and prevention are key aspects of this family issue.

Background

There are 60 regional poison centers in the United States that serve all 50 states, Puerto Rico, the U.S. Virgin Islands, and three Pacific Jurisdictions. The centers are staffed 24 hours a day, year-round, by registered nurses, pharmacists, and physicians specially trained in clinical toxicology. The centers can be accessed toll-free by calling 1-800-222-1222. All of the centers are members of the American Association of Poison Control Centers (AAPCC). The AAPCC maintains the National Poison Data System (NPDS). The NPDS database started in 1983 and contains, as of July 2010, more than 50 million cases. The median time for case upload is 24 minutes, creating a real-time national exposure and information database and surveillance system.

Definitions

Cases are defined as either exposure or information calls. An *exposure* is actual or suspected contact with any substance that has been ingested, inhaled, absorbed, applied to, or injected into the body of a human or animal. This definition includes prescription drugs, nonprescription drugs, and ethanol. Exposure calls can be about exposures to seemingly nontoxic or toxic substances or adverse reactions associated with inappropriate or appropriate product use. Exposures may be classified into two broad categories: unintentional or intentional. *Unintentional* replaces the common term *accidental* as a more precise description as nothing is really accidental. *Information* calls lack an identifiable exposed person or animal. Sometimes information calls begin as information request, and additional history reveals that someone really was exposed to the substance.

Distribution of Poison Exposures by Age and Substance in the United States

In 2008, there were 2,491,049 human exposures reported to the 60 U.S. poison centers. Of these, 82.8% (2,062,385) were unintentional. Pediatric exposures (≤5 years of age) comprised 62.3% of the unintentional exposures. Table 1 lists the top 10 substance categories most frequently involved in human exposures.

Pediatric exposures were similar but show some distinct differences (Table 2). Adults 20 years of age or older were exposed to the top 10 substances shown in Table 3 (p. 288).

In 2008, there were 1,315 poison-related fatalities. Most (76.2%) of the fatalities occurred in the 20 to 59 age group. Pediatric fatalities involved less than 2% of the total fatalities. The top 10 categories associated with the largest number of fatalities (all ages) are shown in Table 4 (p. 288).

Information Calls

In 2008, there were 1,703,762 information calls made to poison centers. These ranged from questions on drug effects to carcinogenicity. More than two thirds of these calls were for medication identification. This is a growing area of public data requests. Some centers are using enhanced automated technologies to respond to these calls.

Risk Factors

Age and gender have been shown to be risk factors for exposures. In 2008, children younger than 3 years were involved in 38.7% of exposures,

Table 1   Top 10 Substance Categories Most Frequently Involved in Human Exposures

	Substance Category	Number	%
1	Analgesics	331,123	13.3
2	Cosmetics/Personal Care Products	224,884	9.0
3	Cleaning Substances (Household)	213,595	8.6
4	Sedatives/Hypnotics/Antipsychotics	165,539	6.6
5	Foreign Bodies/Toys/Miscellaneous	130,244	5.2
6	Topical Preparations	114,024	4.6
7	Antidepressants	102,510	4.1
8	Cold and Cough Preparations	98,636	4.0
9	Pesticides	93,998	3.8
10	Cardiovascular Drugs	91,421	3.7

Source: Bronstein et al. (2009).

Table 2   Top 10 Substance Categories Most Frequently Involved in Pediatric (≤5 Years) Exposures

	Substance Category	Number	%
1	Cosmetics/Personal Care Products	173,945	13.5
2	Analgesics	125,454	9.7
3	Cleaning Substances (Household)	124,934	9.7
4	Foreign Bodies/Toys/Miscellaneous	96,806	7.5
5	Topical Preparations	89,730	6.9
6	Cold and Cough Preparations	52,723	4.1
7	Vitamins	50,836	3.9
8	Antihistamines	44,649	3.5
9	Pesticides	43,526	3.4
10	Plants	43,398	3.4

Source: Bronstein et al. (2009).

and children younger than 6 years accounted for half of all human exposures. This proportion is consistently reported over time. There is a male predominance in cases involving children younger than 13 years, but this gender distribution is reversed in teenagers and adults, with females comprising the majority of reported poison exposure victims. In 16.8% of exposures that involved pharmaceutical substances, the reason for exposure was intentional, compared to only 2.9% when the exposure involved a nonpharmaceutical product. Overall unintentional exposures (62.3%) predominate in children 5 years and younger, but this ratio reverses in adults 20 years and older, with unintentional exposures at 26.7%. More than 90% of all exposures called to the poison centers occur in the family home. More than 8% of all exposures are suspected suicides; these usually occur in adults.

In addition to the aforementioned risk factors, therapeutic errors—including taking or giving the wrong medication or taking a prescribed medication dose twice—predominate in adults, whereas children are frequently given an incorrect formulation of medication or their caregivers confuse units of measure or route. Dispensing cup errors often result in 10-fold dosing errors.

Table 3   Top 10 Substance Categories Most Frequently Involved in Adult (≥20 Years) Exposures

	Substance Category	Number	%
1	Analgesics	147,052	17.2
2	Sedatives/Hypnotics/Antipsychotics	126,003	14.7
3	Cleaning Substances (Household)	70,336	8.2
4	Antidepressants	70,081	8.2
5	Cardiovascular Drugs	57,791	6.7
6	Alcohols	52,940	6.2
7	Bites and Envenomations	47,416	5.5
8	Pesticides	41,040	4.8
9	Cosmetics/Personal Care Products	32,631	3.8
10	Anticonvulsants	31,330	3.7

Source: Bronstein et al. (2009).

Table 4   Top 10 Substance Categories Associated With the Largest Number of Human Fatalities

1   Sedatives/Hypnotics/Antipsychotics
2   Opioids
3   Antidepressants
4   Cardiovascular Drugs
5   Acetaminophen Combinations
6   Alcohols
7   Stimulants and Street Drugs
8   Acetaminophen Alone
9   Antihistamines
10 Anticonvulsants

Source: Bronstein et al. (2009).

Prevention and Education

Poison centers offer a variety of poison prevention materials. These materials are available in more than 10 languages. Most centers have full-time educators who participate in community events such as health fairs. National Poison Prevention Week is held every March. It is intended to raise public awareness of proper medication use, proper medication storage, and the importance of reading and following product labeling, highlighting progress in poison prevention.

Cost Savings

Many studies have attempted to quantify the health care dollar savings created by poison centers. The most frequently quoted figure is that for every dollar spent on poison centers, more than 7 dollars are saved in health care cost. Because poison center staff are skilled in telephone triage and make follow-up calls, centers can help callers avoid unnecessary use of hospital emergency departments and other medical facilities when indicated. Typically, more than 70% of the cases reported to poison centers are managed in a non–health care facility (72.6%), usually at the site of exposure, which is usually the caller's home. Approximately 16% of calls originate from a health care facility and consist of questions about how to manage a poisoning exposure.

Conclusion

U.S. poison centers have been making a difference since 1953, when the first poison center was started in Illinois. Since then, not only the ability of poison centers to manage cases but also the field of clinical toxicology has evolved from treatment recommendations of burnt toast and ipecac (no longer recommended) to a more evidence-based practice. Poison centers are a 24/7 resource for health care professionals treating exposed patients, as their medical toxicologists are available 24 hours,

7 days a week, for consultation. Poison centers are an important part of the nation's public health infrastructure.

Alvin C. Bronstein

See also Education of Medical Health Care Providers in Family Health; Emergency Care Use by Families; First Aid and the Family; Home Environments and Their Relationship to Safety; Partnering With Families: Family-Centered Care

Further Readings

Bronstein, A. C., Spyker, D. A., Cantilena, L. R., Jr., Green, J., Rumack, B. H., & Giffin, S. L. (2009). 2008 Annual Report of the American Association of Poison Control Centers' National Poison Data System (NPDS): 26th Annual Report. *Clinical Toxicology, 47*(10), 911–1084.

Institute of Medicine, Committee on Poison Prevention and Control, Board on Health Promotion and Disease Prevention. (2004). *Forging a poison prevention and control system.* Washington, DC: National Academies Press. Available from http://www.nap.edu/catalog/10971.html

Miller, T. R., & Lestina, D. C. (1997). Costs of poisoning in the United States and savings from poison control centers: A benefit-cost analysis. *Annals of Emergency Medicine, 29*(2), 239–245.

Websites

American Association of Poison Control Centers: http://www.aapcc.org/dnn/default.aspx

DEATH RITUALS IN FAMILIES

Rituals are powerful cultural devices and organizers of family life that are intended to stabilize and support families during times of stress and transition. They vary across cultures and take place during the dying process as well as after death. Rituals can be religious and spiritual or secular in nature, and they have both public and private elements. Rituals may follow prescribed formats: They are reflections of the rules of grieving in a particular society, as well as reflectors that communicate the significance of the death and guide survivors' responses to loss. After a discussion of the purpose of death rituals and their historical context, this entry focuses on contemporary death rituals and disenfranchised grief and concludes with a discussion of rituals and worldview.

Meaning and Purpose of Death Rituals

Anthropologists have defined rituals as prescribed formal behavior, and they often view symbols as the building blocks of rituals. However, their definitions may be influenced by the fact that societies they study often consider there to be strong religious and magical aspects in all of their existence. Some aspects of rituals are not necessarily limited to religious practices. According to Roy Rappaport these include (a) repetition of actions, content, or form; (b) acting, not just thinking or saying something; (c) stylized or special behavior that differs from typical common uses of behavior; (d) an order, including a beginning and end, as well as the containment of spontaneous words or actions; (e) an evocative style of presentation, with staging and keeping the participants' attention; and (f) a collective dimension that reflects the social meaning of the ritual. Rituals do not just involve a ceremony of activity; they also appear to occur in three stages: (1) a *separation* from normal life activity and time for making special preparations for the upcoming ritual; (2) the *transitional* stage, when people participate in the ritual, take on new roles, and experience themselves in different ways; and (3) the *reintegration* stage, when people return to everyday life but take with them their new status (e.g., widow, bereaved parent, new head of the family).

Émile Durkheim, a European sociologist, studied the processes that hold a society together and reported that threats to societal cohesiveness (e.g., the death of a member) result in processes that develop *integration* (integrating the dead into the ongoing society, preserving a sense of continuity through ancestry) and *regulation* (controlling the passions of mourners by establishing norms for the behaviors and expressions of grief). He concluded that social expectations frame grieving. Rituals have also been seen by scholars as more focused on cognitive frameworks and the search for meaning, thus providing ways to address the mystery of death and the questions it raises. In general, rituals bring people together, acknowledge the significance of the loss, and create opportunities for support of grieving survivors.

Rituals also provide for a sense of meaning, making the loss more comprehensible because it fits in with a society's paradigm or system of rules. Rituals can send the message that the loss was significant because the family member was a person of value. Even in those situations where it is not possible to make sense of the loss (e.g., the murder of a child), parents seek to find meaning through the use of rituals (e.g., lighting candles, visiting the grave, doing good deeds for others in honor of their child). For others it is only through their own eventual loss of a loved one that they can begin to understand the reasoning behind the rituals of others. Anthropologist Renato Rosaldo could not understand that the grieving Ilongot (people of Northern Luzon in the Phillipines) relieved their accompanying rage through the activity of headhunting; they claimed that tossing away the head was analogous to casting away their life burdens (including eliminating the rage in their grief). He sought to find "deeper" explanations, such as the balancing of the loss of a life for the loss of another life (to which the Ilongot said he was missing the point). It was only with the death of his own wife that he came to understand the rage and physical violence that accompanies grief and its relationship to emotional relief through the ritual of headhunting.

Death Rituals in Historical Context

During some periods of history, and in some cultures, the rituals associated with death and dying have been primarily for the dying individual, whereas at other times and situations, the structure and purpose of rituals is primarily for the survivors. For example, we can follow the transitions in death rituals that occurred in Western Europe. Aries describes the deathbed scene as a primary ritual in Europe during the Middle Ages. Dying was a "great dramatic act"—a long-lasting public ceremony (given that few deaths occurred suddenly), with the dying person in charge of the timing of the rituals, as friends, family, and others simply surrounded

the bed waiting to receive the dying loved one's pardon, listening to prayers, and hearing the granting of absolution by the priest.

Around the 12th century, as a focus on destiny of the deceased gained influence, the public participants were said to be joined by a band of angels and demons who battled for possession of the person's soul. The dying individual could conduct a life review and discover his destiny by tallying the moral balance sheet of life. At this point the individual had the responsibility to make a final decision for good or evil that would seal the soul's fate.

During the Enlightenment, when scientific rationalism came to share a central place in life along with religion, the dying and grieving shifted some of their thoughts from religion to secular hopes. The potential for immortality and the hope to eventually reunite with loved ones took precedence over deciding whether to join the angels or demons. This period began a shift in focus from the dying to the survivors that continues today. Now the focus in end-of-life care is to help both the dying and the family find meaning in the actions that take place during this last period of life.

Death rituals during the Industrial Revolution and Victorian era changed in response to the new available technologies, and remnants of these changes can still be found in rituals today. The limited space that families had in their homes as a result of urban crowding contributed to the growth in the use of funeral parlors rather than the parlor for a home funeral and its accompanying wake. However, some groups, such as the Amish, still utilize home funerals. Embalming was used during the Civil War to slow the decomposition of a soldier's body so that it could be transported home for family burial. Funeral cards, which had been used to invite mourners to a funeral, today are frequently available in funeral homes as a memento of the deceased. Consistent with the overall interest in photography, postmortem photography of the deceased, especially children, lying in the coffin became quite common. These photos were given to family members, especially those who lived too far away to attend the funeral, and were also displayed in families of surviving loved ones. The use of this postmortem photography still occurs in some areas of the United States and with some cultural groups. With increased literacy and mass-produced newspapers, obituaries provided a place for the family to immortalize the deceased. Over the past 125 years these descriptions have changed from brief and somber descriptions of the deceased to longer, more expressive stories, with details of their life accomplishments and mention of close family members, as well as instructions for organizations where charitable donations can be sent.

Contemporary Death Rituals

The focus on productivity, autonomy, and technology has eroded traditional rituals across the life span. In the United States there are no nationally prescribed death rituals, and it is often unclear as to what constitutes proper behavior for the bereaved. Standard contemporary rituals have been criticized as inauthentic, rigid, and empty practices that do not provide opportunities for real social support or sufficient acknowledgment of the loss. Some have argued that death-related rituals have deteriorated in meaning to the point where they contribute to insufficient grieving, and that one-time events and rituals fail to recognize that grieving is a process that occurs over time.

However, there has been a recent renaissance of rituals, particularly those that reflect individual choices and are fashioned by survivors. Although some scholars consider rituals related to death as essential for coping with the loss and consider funerals or comparable rituals as essential for healing, Tony Walter indicates that the new rituals emerging today are typically seen as optional, not required by society. Walter discusses what he sees as the "new public mourning," which includes public mourning of celebrities and public figures as if they were family. Because this mourning of public celebrities may not be long enduring for an individual, and that person may have no experience with the death of his or her own loved ones, he or she may have unrealistic expectations of how quickly grief is resolved.

The new public mourning also includes a period when spontaneous shrines emerge (e.g., roadside shrines erected by friends shortly after the death of an adolescent) and are later permanent memorials and annual commemorations (e.g., the Vietnam Veterans Memorial Wall and annual remembrances of the Oklahoma City bombing, the Kent State massacre of students, and the September 11 terrorist attacks). Communal rituals also play an especially important role following a wide-scale disaster. They help lead to acknowledgment of the loss, making it real for people and assisting communities in constructing a new identity. An example of a communal ritual would be the prayer service for affected families held at Saint Thomas Church in New York 10 days after the September 11 attack.

Death rituals have often been used in Western societies to facilitate the relinquishing of attachments to relationships with the deceased and for transitioning into new social roles in an attempt to facilitate the resolution of grief. However, it is clear from the work of Dennis Klass that most people do not just say goodbye and let go. They maintain a sense of connection to the deceased, and although the nature of the relationship has changed, it is not perceived as dissolved or eliminated from the life and thoughts of the survivor. Rituals can be more effective if they are consistent with this continuing bond. Religious and cultural beliefs about life after death need to be considered in determining whether an expression of bereavement is problematic. For example, the belief in continuing existence of the loved one's spirit and the expectation of being reunited are not inherently problematic as long as they are consistent with the beliefs of the survivor's religion or culture. An example of this can be seen in Japan during the ceremony honoring ancestors. It involves the surviving family member transitioning from the land of living to the land of death and back again—a situation that is consistent with Japanese cultural and religious beliefs.

Rituals and Disenfranchised Grief

Ken Doka has reported that rituals (e.g., funerals) allow for structure and support, acknowledging and sanctioning grief for those who are deemed to have a right to grieve (e.g., the loving family). However, those who grieve in ways that do not conform to prescribed rituals (e.g., laughing uncontrollably during a time when somber and painful responses are expected or choosing to attend school rather than a sibling's funeral) may have grief that goes unrecognized by society. In addition, there might be some types of deaths for which sympathy is withheld and it is assumed that no rituals are necessary because there should not be any grieving. These could include deaths that are punitive, such as the execution of a murderer; death of a drug dealer, addict, or child abuser; the death of someone who "deserved it" by their risky behavior; the death of someone for whom there was a secret relationship (e.g., an adulterous partner); or the death of someone who had been a severe burden to the family. Although not recognized by others, these survivors experience grief. In such disenfranchised grief situations, therapeutic rituals could be added to an existing counseling process.

Rituals and Worldview

Death rituals are dynamic and involve process, not just a single event. They vary in form and duration, consistent with the religious and/or cultural views of those involved. Cultural groups differ in the hierarchy of value they place on the past, present, and future. Rituals will reflect those values. Although effective rituals assist with providing a meaning to the loss and a sense of social support, some rituals may not be as effective for those who experience death due to sudden, violent, or nonnormative situations. Those whose losses were related to the violation of social norms may not find much help in standardized rituals that reflect that same culture. Disenfranchised grievers also may need recognition of their loss and opportunities to experience relevant rituals in the comfort of a supportive group or professional. Given the evolving nature of rituals in the climate of new public mourning, bereaved individuals in therapeutic environments can function as co-creators of rituals that most closely meet their needs and situations. No single ritual is inherently good or bad, but each needs to be considered in the context of a specific loss and the assumptions or worldview that the survivors hold.

Colleen I. Murray

See also Bereavement and Perinatal Loss in Childbearing Families; Death and the Grieving Process in Families; Ethnic/Racial Influences in Families; Religious/Spiritual Influences on Health in the Family; Rituals, Routines, and Their Influence on Health in Families; Sibling Death/Loss; Suicide in the Family

Further Readings

DeSpelder, L. A., & Strickland, A. L. (2005). *The last dance: Encountering death and dying* (7th ed.). Boston: McGraw-Hill.

DeVries, B., & Rutherford, J. (2004). Memorializing loved ones on the World Wide Web. *Omega, 49,* 5–26.

Doka, K. (2002). The role of ritual in the treatment of disenfranchised grief. In K. Doka (Ed.), *Disenfranchised grief: New directions, challenges and strategies for practice* (pp. 135–148). Champaign, IL: Research Press.

Imber-Black, E. (2004). September 11, 2004: The third anniversary [Editorial]. *Family Process, 43,* 275–278.

Kerstens, E. K. (1999, Sept./Oct.) Victorian death rituals. *Ancestry Magazine, 19*(5). Retrieved from http://www.ancestry.com/learn/library/article.aspx?article=151

Klass, D. (2001). The inner representation of the dead child in the psychic and social narratives of bereaved parents. In R. A. Neimeyer (Ed.), *Meaning reconstruction and the experience of loss* (pp. 77–94). Washington, DC: American Psychological Association.

Murray, C. I., Toth, K., Larsen, B. L., & Moulton, S. (2010). Death, dying and grief in families. In S. J. Price, C. A. Price, & P. C. McKenry (Eds.), *Families & change: Coping with stressful events and transitions* (4th ed., pp. 73–95). Thousand Oaks, CA: Sage.

Rappaport, R. A. (1971). Ritual sanctity and cybernetics. *American Anthropologist, 73,* 59–76.

Romanoff, B. D., & Terenzio, M. (1998). Rituals and the grieving process. *Death Studies, 22,* 697–711.

Rosaldo, R. (1989). Grief and a headhunter's rage. In *Culture and truth: The remaking of social analysis* (pp. 1–21). New York: Beacon.

Rosenblatt, P. C. (2008). Grief across cultures: A review and research agenda. In M. S. Stroebe, R. O. Hansson, H. Schut, & W. Stroebe (Eds.), *Handbook of bereavement research and practice: Advances in theory and intervention* (pp. 207–222). Washington, DC: American Psychological Association.

Walter, T. (2008). The new public mourning. In M. S. Stroebe, R. O. Hansson, H. Schut, & W. Stroebe (Eds.), *Handbook of bereavement research and practice: Advances in theory and intervention* (pp. 241–262). Washington, DC: American Psychological Association.

DECISION MAKING IN THE CONTEXT OF HEALTH AND ILLNESS

Shared decision making has evolved from a traditionally paternalistic model of decision making to an approach that has been developed on a platform based on a patient-centered approach. After the development of a professional approach to medical practice in the 18th century, decision making has, to a large extent, been dominated by a paternalistic approach by which clinicians assume authority and decision-making power, oftentimes without consulting individuals about their personal preferences. Since the 1980s, individuals' right to be informed and to participate in medical care decisions has been increasingly advocated. It has also been postulated that clinical decisions (treatments, screening or diagnostic tests) should be justified by available clinical and scientific evidence and not by a clinician's assumed authority or knowledge—this development has become known as evidence-based medicine.

The combination of evidence-based medicine and the acceptance that decisions should also take individuals' preferences into account is the basis on which shared decision making has been established. This change has also been supported by a recognized need to gain informed consent for certain procedures, where there has been increasing recognition of consumer rights. The legal obligation to inform individuals prior to the risks of surgical interventions (informed consent), the consumer rights movement over the past few decades, and the evolving nature of the physician–client encounter has prepared the ground for the emergence of shared decision making, where practitioners are explicitly required to share information about uncertainties, to be open about the existence of treatment options, and to involve individuals in a process of decision making.

Individual Preferences for Involvement in Decision Making

Reviews of studies by A. Coulter, which investigated whether people wish to participate in decision making, concluded that (a) people wanted to be informed of treatment alternatives and that (b) some, depending on the circumstances, wished to be involved in making treatment decisions. However, most of the studies were based on hypothetical surveys; few studies have investigated the views of individuals after they have participated in effective, well-conducted encounters that followed the principles of shared decision making. Further evidence has suggested that people want to be informed and consulted during the medical encounter and that individual satisfaction is increased with the physician's empathy and the use of the so-called patient-centered approach.

Shared decision making is a shorthand term for a suggested approach to communication in health care encounters. Shared decision making happens when clinicians and patients communicate together using the best available evidence and patients are supported to deliberate about the possible attributes and consequences of options to arrive at informed preferences in making a determination about the best action; shared decision making implies respect for patient autonomy, whenever this is desired, ethical, and legal. This definition recognizes that there will be debate about when it is necessary to use a shared decision-making approach. Some clinical situations have very strong evidence about what is best to be done. In these situations, some clinicians argue that sharing decisions is not required. Others argue that situations of equipoise, where equally possible options exist, occur in almost all clinical situations. In addition, some ethicists hold the view that individuals should always be required to make decisions, unless they are cognitively impaired. This stance is described as supporting *mandatory autonomy*.

Others, especially clinicians, recognize that individuals often do not wish to shoulder decisional responsibility: This stance, taken by Carl Schneider, supports the notion of *optional autonomy*. It is recognized that individuals, if left unsupported when faced with difficult complex health care decisions, report feeling abandoned.

Individuals do not make decisions in isolation, and it needs to be recognized that family members are key sources of advice and information. There are also special situations when an individual's ability to self-determine cannot be realized—for example, when an individual has impaired mental capacity due to illness or dementia. The ability of children to determine their own health care is an area of increasing debate about the age threshold for individual autonomy.

Evidence About the Effectiveness of Shared Decision Making

There have been very few trials of shared decision making as a skill-based intervention, and most randomized controlled trials have been based on the introduction of decision aids or decision support interventions (DESIs). E. A. Joosten, in a systematic review of the effects of shared decision making, noted that the quality of the 11 trials included was high, but there was no consistent pattern. Five randomized controlled trials showed no difference between shared decision making and control, one trial showed no short-term effects but showed positive longer term effects, and five trials reported a positive effect of shared decision making on outcome measures. The review concluded that despite the considerable interest in applying shared decision making to clinical settings, little research regarding its effectiveness has been done to date and further work is required. It is important to note that this is a novel approach to the clinical encounter and one that is not widely implemented in clinical medicine. K. Gravel, F. Légaré, and I. Graham note the barriers to the implementation of shared decision making and associated interventions to be time constraints, a lack of applicability due to mismatch of patient characteristics, and the lack of applicability due to the clinical situation. This review revealed that interventions to foster the implementation of shared decision making in clinical practice will need to address a broad range of factors. It also suggests that on this subject, there is very little known about any health professionals other than physicians.

In contrast, there has been substantial research performed on DESIs. A. M. O'Connor has led a Cochrane Collaboration systematic review and concludes that DESIs increased knowledge, realistic expectations, and participation in decision making and reduced scores on the decisional conflict scale and indecision post-intervention compared to usual practice. Nevertheless, despite strong evidence of benefit, there is as yet no evidence of widespread use of these interventions.

Glyn Elwyn and Marie-Anne Durand

See also Problem Solving in the Context of Health and Illness; Roles of Health Care Providers for Families, Current; Roles of Health Care Providers for Families, Emerging

Further Readings

Coulter, A. (1997). Partnerships with patients: The pros and cons of shared clinical decision-making. *Journal of Health Services Research and Policy, 2,* 112–121.

Edwards, A., & Elwyn, G. (Eds.). (2009). *Shared decision making in healthcare: Evidence-based patient choice.* Oxford, UK: Oxford University Press.

Elwyn, G. (2009, October). *The imperative for shared decision making.* Paper presented at the Ernst Strungmann Forum (G. Gigerenzer & J. Muir Gray, Chairs): Better Doctors, Better Patients, Better Decisions: Envisioning Healthcare 2020, Frankfurt, Germany.

Elwyn, G., Edwards, A., Kinnersley, P., & Grol, R. (2000). Shared decision making and the concept of equipoise: The competences of involving patients in healthcare choices. *British Journal of General Practice, 50,* 892–899.

Gravel, K., Légaré, F., & Graham, I. (2006). Barriers and facilitators to implementing shared decision-making in clinical practice: A systematic review of health professionals' perceptions. *Implementation Science, 1,* 16.

Joosten, E. A. G., DeFuentes-Merillas, L., de Weert, G. H., Sensky, T., van der Staak, C. P. F., & de Jong, C. A. J. (2008). Systematic review of the effects of shared decision-making on patient satisfaction, treatment adherence and health status. *Psychotherapy and Psychosomatics, 77,* 219–226.

Levenstein, J. H. (1984). The patient-centred general practice consultation. *South African Family Practice, 5,* 276–282.

O'Connor, A. M., Bennett, C. L., Stacey, D., Barry, M., Col, N. F., Eden, K. B., et al. (2009). Decision aids for people facing health treatment or screening decisions. *Cochrane Database of Systematic Reviews,* CD001431.

Schneider, C. E. (1998). The practice of autonomy: Patients, doctors, and medical decisions. New York: Oxford University Press.

Defining Family: An Overview of Family Definitions From a Historical Perspective

Defining families, as a conceptual problem in family research and family services, has received great attention in academic circles. Since family studies emerged as an interdisciplinary enterprise, there have been contributions from many areas of thought. Running through the various approaches has been a desire to find a single comprehensive definition when, at the same time, families have been found to be more diverse than had been recognized. Family scholars have often chosen operational family definitions for research, program, or policy analysis. Even if they do not specify what they mean by *family*, the sample description may include such language as *intact family, head of household, married couple and their children*, or *single parent*. The U.S. Census reports household composition, which then stands in for families in reporting trends and describing American families. Homemaking and caregiving usually are located in space in a household, and the members of a household share food patterns, sanitary arrangements, leisure and exercise options, air quality, and other health-related environmental variables. Use of household roles does not help in analyzing the social networks of blended families and families of divorce. Being homeless may put a great strain on a family, but families attempt to continue. In the scholarship of family studies, debates about appropriate and useful family definitions have been frequent and relate to the purpose served by conceptual clarity. For the individual and his or her family, definitions are often crucial to achieving the benefits, limits, and responsibilities that accrue in granting official family status. This consequence means that definitions are highly political, and political discourse is often emotionally charged.

Traditional Definitions in Family Science

Traditional definitions of family have been incorporated into family science as ideological abstractions and assumptions. Functionalism and positivistic constructions were found in sociology, social work, and therapy. Legal analysis also used functions as a means of justifying such events as divorce and separation and adjudicating parental rights and responsibilities. In this case a group is measured by which functions are being performed in everyday life and classified as a family if most of the functions are being met. Families were defined by whether they meet the tasks. "Good" families were those that functioned well for society. Ernest Burgess was an early family sociologist who proposed that the functions of families had changed from focusing on institutional purposes to companionship. Other scholars became interested in teaching effective family processes and preserving family values. Ernest Groves was credited with teaching the first college-level marriage and family course for credit and wrote widely on preserving American families. Both Burgess and Groves were involved in founding organizations (Family Section of the American Sociological Association, National Council on Family Relations, and the Groves Conference on Marriage and Family) to promote the study of family life and applications to policies and programs. Applied family studies in social work, home economics, and cooperative extension developed concurrently conceptions of healthy families and successful helping strategies for families. Home economics early on developed a broad definition of family, which guided curriculum development to be inclusive in the discussion of families and is further promoted by the American Association of Family and Consumer Sciences today. In sociology, Talcott Parsons wrote in the 1960s a theoretical approach in which the modern nuclear family consisting of parents and their children with roles of husband as instrumental leader and wife as expressive leader as the norm linking sociology to Freudian ideas of individual development. Marvin Sussman was an early challenger to this view of modern families and, in his dissertation research, presented modified nuclear families as living separately but being closely tied to their extended families and fictive kin. Feminist writers challenged the so-called natural or traditional gender roles within and outside of families. Jesse Bernard provided the analysis of men's and women's marriages as essentially quite different in terms of personal and health outcomes, further limiting the Parsonian ideal type of family.

When Paul Glick noted the growth of cohabitation in the census and researchers began to see college cohabitation in the 1960s and 1970s, communal families were more evident in this period. Romantic images of family continued to be important, especially in the media and advertising, because such concepts simplify the complexity of everyday life.

Current Controversies in the Use of Definitions

Defining families has been a public and political issue at odds with research findings and the realities of everyday life. Conflicting views of which family constellations benefit social and related cultural goals are debated in designing programs from taxation to eligibility and legitimacy. At the national level, immigration policies favor some types of family reunification and reject others. Parental, sibling, and spousal ties are favored, and same-sex partners and extended kinship ties are often ignored. International adoption is supported by expedited papers and the availability of immediate immigration naturalization service on arrival to the United States. Because much of family law is vested at the state level, different policies apply and similar programs may be administered quite differently from place to place. Internationally, the huge divergence in family definitions and operation has directed focus toward the individual or a dyadic role such as parent. Family law is typically local and varies for different population groups. Secular and sacred views of family may remain unresolved within societies. Comparative and cross-cultural studies have often led to typologies and classifications that are in themselves political statements and may privilege one family form over another according to dominant cultural perspectives. Understanding the meanings of different arrangements in their context remains a challenge for analysts.

Family Definitions and the History of Health Care

Defining family has become a current issue in health care as medical diagnosis, treatment, and aftercare changes have become more entwined with the patients' families and fictive kin, basically seeing the family as a social construction. As the recognition of the key role of prevention and positive health activities in overall health and reduced need for medical intervention has been more widely understood, the role of families in health and intervention is recognized in family-centered medical practice and fundamental to high-quality prevention and intervention.

In recent history, this was not the case. Doctors protected families and patients from knowing how serious their relatives' conditions were. Communication with family members was quite limited, and patients were not encouraged to discuss their condition. Even today, patient privacy policies and rights may be seen as trumping family involvement, especially when the patient is not a child. In the past, institutional settings were used to treat and shelter patients with chronic problems or intractable conditions. Families were seen as being in the way, disturbing treatment, and visits were limited to a few visiting hours on certain days to only the key family members. A pioneering hospital for the treatment of bone-related problems in children limited visits to once a month on a Sunday afternoon for children undergoing long-term treatment and repeated surgeries. Now, parents are encouraged to be available at all times, and arrangements are made for them to be in the patient's room as part of the hospital culture. Formerly, parents were encouraged in state and private facilities to leave children with special needs and not to visit at all. Mental health care and intervention organizations distanced families, as the popular theories blamed family influence for the problems.

Historically, relationships between families and medical institutions were characterized by families doing most of the nursing and caregiving. Medical professionals were found treating and advising those families, even in ancient times. The role of good health practices supporting medical treatment was seen in health resorts throughout the ancient world. The Greeks had several centers for medical care and health activities. Many of the current spas in Europe have roots as health centers dating back into prehistory. The role of folk medicine and informal healers who worked with women and their families is well documented both in Europe and around the world. The midwife came into the home to deliver her services and depended upon family to help her. In the United States, doctors worked through house calls and, in consultations with families, advised them on home care and treatment support until the middle of the 20th century. Early in the development of medicine in the United States, few places had hospitals and most interventions were done at home or in the field. The daughter of Revolutionary leader John Adams was operated on for breast cancer at home. In the 18th and 19th centuries, more group-based medical education (rather than apprenticeship) was launched, and the greater use of surgical procedures led to more hospitals and clinics to delivering more care. Nursing emerged as a formal profession. At the beginning of the 20th century, a wave of medical educational reform and medical regulation shifted even more attention to institutional care, and it became common for families to cede authority and management to the institutional medical realm.

Legal relationships between families and medical institutions have also varied greatly over history. For centuries in Europe, the Roman Catholic Church dominated the legal definitions of who was married, which children were legitimate, who could inherit, and who had authority for decision making. Many hospitals and facilities for care of children and mothers who fell outside the definitions of legal families were run by the church and staffed by nursing orders of nuns and doctors trained within religious orders. These religious definitions were reflected in legal codes and in the treatment of patients and whether their families were recognized. The recent Irish Roman Catholic Church scandals, concerning the inappropriate treatment of youth and unwed mothers in religious care, suggest that some of these views lasted until the end of the 20th century. Different political events affected how families were defined. The French Revolution and the Napoleonic rule led to major changes in how families were defined in France, especially in overturning oldest male preference in inheritance. Protestant countries such as the Netherlands also shifted the legal codes on families. In England a strong history of common law combined cultural ideas surviving from before the Norman Conquest, French concepts, Catholic and then Protestant thought, and judicial history to develop a complex set of guidelines about family matters and a view of property and inheritance rights and contracts that allowed torts and legal challenges to professional practice. A glimpse at European history suggests that the role of family,

definitions of family ties, and heritable privileges run throughout the disputes and wars back into the early Middle Ages. Currently, the European Union (EU) has been making economic and human rights policy that affects relationships between individuals and institutions, while reserving family law to each country (or state/province within) on the basis of different cultural histories. In terms of health programs, the focus is on the individual, but EU countries seek to support the network of caring and are open to individuals' and their own families' approaches.

Tension Between Sources of Regulation of Families and Programs

In the United States, states, not the federal government, have been the source of regulation of both family definitions and medical practice. Practically, it has meant that every state has a different set of tensions and challenges in relating families to medical care. Who is recognized as one's family differs widely according to setting. How medical institutions interface with families and patients and with medicine itself has many permutations. These relationships vary from service to service, and companies such as insurance providers have their own systems of defining family. In relationship to governmental and service providers, family definitions are politically charged and serve to ration service, deny access, or otherwise regulate eligibility, breadth, and continuity of support. Although many federal programs—such as Social Security, which has rules on a wife's and former wife's access to benefits based on her husband's (or former husband's) contributions—have included language to determine family ties, usually federal programs have allowed states the leadership in how families are interpreted. With the Defense of Marriage Act (DOMA) signed into law under President Clinton, the federal government was bound to recognize only heterosexual partnerships in marriage and not to recognize all forms of family that individual states condone. This legislation has ramifications for states in terms of funding streams and matching grants as well as affecting other groups that accept federal funds. Many states have laws similar to DOMA, but the years following the federal legislation have been a time of expansion of family definitions and the extension of marital status to same-sex couples in Massachusetts, Connecticut, New Hampshire, Vermont, Iowa (a law seeking to limit civil marriage to a man and a woman was struck down by the Iowa State Supreme Court on April 3, 2010), and, briefly, California (a ballot initiative overturned the court's decision to allow same-sex marriage). Many states have domestic partnerships laws, which give many family rights to same-sex or heterosexual couples and their children, without the requirement that the couple be married. President Obama's executive order on April 18, 2010, to grant same-sex couples hospital visitation rights also moves in the direction of recognition of same-sex couples as families. Other issues such as custody, foster care, and guardianship of adults and elders with diminished capacity are still primarily vested in the states, and often states are quite locally centered, often refusing relatives from other states as appropriate representatives in these matters. Some states require that a person qualifying for the federal program of Medicaid for nursing home support to consent that he or she will not be moved to another state. Custody arrangements may limit out-of-state residence. Because there are 50 states with their own codes, a multitude of laws and regulations, and many social services and providers, this review is limited to a few illustrations of the uses of definitions and boundaries versus the on-the-ground, real-life experiences of many groups of people who see themselves as families over time.

Many concerns about finances, privacy, access, consent, advocacy, and continuing responsibility have components that focus on the definition of family at all levels. Some areas of prevention and promoting health practices require a broad range of targets and suggest that families be considered in the context of communities and social networks. Other medical situations may require a highly focused and narrow definition of family and support networks. The basic responsibility for financial support and paying bills is founded around family composition, structure, age, dependency status, and ability to pay. Each insurance company may define who is covered in family policies, unless there are regulations that set standards for policies. For example, a baby conceived before an insurance policy is issued could be considered a preexisting condition. The federal Patient Protection and Affordable Care Act, passed in March 2010,

is designed to reduce the use of this exclusion for many other conditions as well. Accompanying a patient in treatment, testing, or other medical situation has become more expected, but still has some limits that often focus on family relationships and whether fictive kin can be designated in the same way by the patient. Visitation may be limited for various reasons in hospitals and treatment facilities, but often the list is limited to recognized relationships, with some priorities being set especially for intensive care and off hours for visiting. Actual participation in support has become more common in such situations as childbirth and in caring for children and the elderly, but when the socially or legally preferred person is not available, the problem becomes one of how substitutes are vetted. Difficult treatment such as bone marrow or heart transplants may not be readily available to patients who have difficulty securing a support person(s) who will be available throughout the procedures and recovery. Some treatments, such as family therapy and substance abuse counseling, not only are required to define who should be included but also try to recruit the important members' participation. Support groups are now more commonly used as a major component of the overall health plan and face many of the same challenges in defining who and in what capacity they should be included. With diminished capability or coma or minor status, legal issues over custody and guardianship may be key to decision making and consent procedures. Privacy may be narrowly defined as the individual's arena, but certainly as issues of aftercare, advocacy, and social support become important, some guidelines for answering questions, sharing information, and developing plans require that a family and even a community context be recognized. Permission to stop treatment, move to palliative care, and simple discharge planning usually include major familial interactions. There are some situations in which the presence of some family members and friends who are serving as kin should or must be excluded, and the basis for such exclusion must be defensible. Much of treatment and prevention that goes on at home and in the community—with relationships among family support networks, community agencies and services, and home services—must deal with the previous issues in situations where policy is often unclear and may be contradictory.

Family conflict among the various players and nuclear families may be a major concern, especially with adults and the elderly. Many hospitals have solved this controversy by requiring a single point of contact; this may regulate the situation in the short term but often leads to deeper conflicts and even ligation. Family members may have conflicts of interest and personal vesting in decisions to be made and cannot be assumed to be representing only the patient's best interest. Advocacy and representation may be areas of conflict because of uncertainty in terms of best practice as applied to a specific case and competing schools of thought or judgment in the field itself. The state-versus-federal theme runs through many of these concerns, and in any particular area of health care prevention and intervention, several of these issues will be interacting. Most families have many problems and activities going on all the time and may have multiple health and medical concerns for any of the family members, so attention, coordination, and collaboration may be quite complex.

Illustrations of the Impact of Family Definitions on Health Care

Seven illustrations of how family definitions affect specific health care strategies and outcomes are used to exemplify some of these complexities and conflicts. As family-centered medicine has become a vital part of best practice, these cases are discussed to show how families operate in different situations, how definitions have shifted historically, how families have impacted on health, and how health care has shifted in its appreciation of family involvement and support.

Many events and factors foment change in legal, social, and practical definitions of family. It has been a major area of study and theoretical discussion, especially since the late 20th century, in the disciplines of family studies, sociology, psychology, women's studies, family therapy, social work, nursing, and law. Some concepts have focused on whose definitions are paramount in which decisions or situations. Others have noted ethical and conflicts of interest in prioritizing such definitions and acting upon them. These discussions addressed many institutions including education, work, governmental services, religion, and access to leisure,

the community, and transportation. Medical and health research findings began to support the strategic importance of family and support systems in better health outcomes, lower costs, and recovery from critical care. This massive data accumulation has also demanded a better handle on mobilizing and fostering family and social support within the health provision system. Other advances in medical care and intervention have had dramatic interplay with such systems. When old assumptions are confronted, new institutional responses may result.

HIV/AIDS

HIV/AIDS provides a complex and interesting illustration of change in policy and practice, with diverse and conflicting family definitions, as the understanding of the disease and better treatment became available both in the United States and abroad. The emergence of HIV/AIDS as first a disease noticed among the gay population and then in certain heterosexual sectors provided an immediate challenge to how family had been defined in medical settings and governmental agencies. In the 1980s, few same-sex couples had identified themselves socially as families although their partnerships might be known to their close friends and relatives. In the early years, the symptoms of HIV/AIDS may have been overlooked in early stages, so that the full-blown AIDS might have been in place when a diagnosis was made. Treatments were not standardized, and many secondary infections and cancers needed treatment. Same-sex couples were often estranged from some of their biological or legal families, many of whom rejected their lifestyle, but they did not have any other legal ties that might make them appear to be families in the eyes of the medical establishment. Stories of siblings or parents being admitted to intensive care units while partners were excluded were documented. Frequent hospitalization, discharge, and readmittance, as well as the reality that partners and friends were actually doing a lot of the caregiving, facilitated shifts in policies and definitions to accommodate the patient's definition of whom the patient's family members were. Later, when women with AIDS began to be very ill and die and left infants and young children who were infected, the role of grandparents as caregivers who managed care was recognized. As the treatment of AIDS evolved to include a spectrum of drugs that successfully prolonged and improved the quality of life, the ongoing chronic care became somewhat easier. Early AIDS patients' interactions with agencies involved eligibility for medical assistance. The patient's functioning family and support network were not within governmental definitions. This exclusion was helpful if the individual had to spend down, in order to be eligible for Medicaid, because the informal partner's income and assets did not count against financial eligibility as a spouse's might. Medicaid is the single largest source of coverage for HIV/AIDS patients in the United States; each state interprets the program in a different way. Some AIDS patients moved to accommodating states whose services were better, took full medical disability, and left their jobs or were pushed out of work. Many patients distributed their belongings and any savings. Then, the improvement in drug effectiveness and management brought many patients back to a quality of life that gave them a future and required new employment and medical coverage. Many companies and governmental employers began to offer medical insurance to partners, not just conventional families. The later explosion of AIDS cases in African American communities (a trend that was seen in these communities originally partially because of the number of men who had served time in prisons) brought forth another conflict between the individual's rights and the actual risks in families.

A pattern of husbands or cohabitants going on the "down low" (heterosexual men who are also having sex with men and keeping it a secret), not telling their wives or meaningful others and not using condoms infected many women without their knowledge. One could make a case for tracing contacts even if they are in the patient's family. Abroad, the epidemic in Africa first increased the rates of morbidity and then resulted in high mortality in the productive adult population, leaving grandparents and grandchildren first to nurse the dying and then to struggle to supply each other with food and shelter and maintain health. The new drug regimens are slowing the loss of people in midlife and infected children but do not yet address the long-term care and quality of life of survivors and their families. Definitions and priorities continue to be refined in just this one disease as it requires changes in attitude and policy.

Cystic Fibrosis

The longer survival for patients with cystic fibrosis (CF) in the 1970s caused much consternation about roles of the family of orientation in young adult life. CF, like many other relatively rare and complex maladies, requires much cooperation among patients, families, and a rigorously coordinated medical team. CF has a major impact on family functioning and represents major investments of families and society to provide excellent care.

CF, a genetically transmitted condition, had resulted in childhood death, often from respiratory infections that were complicated by heavy mucus in the lungs. A cocktail of preventive drugs and better treatment options changed the pattern of care and expectations. In the 1970s, the pattern changed from fulfilling a dream, such as a trip to Disneyland, to youth going on to college or other vocational training and considering marriage. In a study for the Cystic Fibrosis Foundation, done at that time, parents had difficulty in dealing with the "good news." They felt guilty for following recommended practices, like mist tents, when it was later found that the intervention increased problems or had side effects. They were undone by the new expectations and financial demands. Several parents asked the researchers if the study was truly confidential and anonymous, because there was only one clinic in their community and they could not afford for the medical staff to get angry with the family or the patient. Clinics at that time made it clear they were treating the child, not the whole family. Improvements have continued for these families and patients, but the underlying genetic problem does not appear to have yielded easily to intervention. Genetic counseling and testing and choices around pregnancy and carrying to term such children are areas where the family and institutional boundaries are uncertain. Individuals with CF often function very well intellectually and socially, and many are living well into middle age so the choices are extremely difficult. Families, as process, and medicine, as evolving, interact in treating many serious diseases as major innovations occur, resulting in stress for both systems.

Mental Illness

Mental illness has been the least understood area of how family members should be viewed. The dramatic changes in treatment over the 20th century meant that most individuals who are mentally ill are living in the community and mostly with their families. The hope that community mental health services would be developed has not been realized across the country. Because of the tenuous linkage among recovery, continued drug therapy, and independence, without community or family support, mental health patients are prone to readmission or dropping through the safety nets and becoming homeless or otherwise dysfunctional. Achieving adult status without necessarily being able to be independent is typical of young adults with schizophrenia or bipolar disorder. The individual and his or her family members find legal and medical approaches often not responding to their needs and practical problem solving. The transition from status as a minor to legal majority has been particularly difficult for both the medical facilities and families. Long-term institutional treatment for individuals with mental conditions was common until the mid-20th century. Families participated by visiting a few times a year and chatting with the hospital staff. Legal commitment was straightforward, and young people might continue in treatment into adulthood. Medication improved, and the maladies became chronic diseases amenable to ongoing medication and psychological support. As reforms in institutional treatment were made, it was expected that community mental health centers would provide support. At about the same period a stronger stance on personal privacy of adults in medical and agency settings was instituted. It became difficult for parents or other relatives to discover how the patient was faring. While paying for services for the young adult might be welcome, inquiries were not. Few mental health services were actually developed, and patients were discharged into the community without adequate support being arranged. Families tried to provide shelter, but they were uninformed about maintaining the treatment. Frequently the adult with mental illness was left without support, resulting in reinstitutionalization. A discharge plan for individuals who are mentally ill without recognizing family may be seen as a high-risk venture.

Childbirth

Childbirth reforms have been one area of health care in which changing approaches have been seen in the past century that radically altered the ideas of best practice, especially as far as the participation of families was concerned. In the later years of the 19th and early part of the 20th centuries, childbirth moved dramatically from the home to the hospital after antiseptic methods and anesthesia were adopted. As the childbirth medicalization became institutionalized, family members were marginalized and relegated to waiting rooms. Long hospitalizations and fewer nursing mothers were part of the process. Reform in the later part of the 20th century brought families and patient control back into childbirth. Now the entire approach is based on family involvement, and childbirth education has become a standard component of the care of expectant mothers and their families. Fathers were given a role in supporting their wives and were allowed into the delivery room if they were willing to take a preparatory course. The success of this reform was immediately followed by expanding the pool of potential players. Friends, partners, parents, all were potential supporters. Some saw the opportunity to return childbirth to home or birthing centers outside of hospitals. These options allowed all of these players and children in the family access to the birthing process. Many hospitals adopted a more welcoming posture to whomever the patient defined as family and even redecorated birthing suites to look more homelike in order to attract clients. The issue of access to quick intervention in terms of complications in pregnancy remains in controversy, as does the high number of cesarean sections in U.S. hospitals. In this case, health and medical professionals have accepted the patient's definition of family for involvement, but the hospital administration must still deal with legal and insurance definitions of financial and professional responsibility and family.

Medical Interventions and Decision Making for Infants and Children

Medical decision making is compounded by the challenges of treating infants and children in religiously or emotionally charged decision making with parents and child welfare services. Selecting who can consent and what is in the best interests of children are perennial health care challenges. Most state laws select parents to decide for their children on medical intervention, but conflict arises when parents object to a proposed intervention that will likely improve the child's quality of life or even save the child's life. Religious views may lead parents to reject interventions such as transfusion, removing intestinal blockages, or heart surgery, vaccination, or reconstructive surgery. Emotional and esthetic factors may also lead to rejection of body casting for congenital hip defect, braces, vision or hearing correction, or chemotherapy. Child welfare agencies can intervene and lift parental rights either temporarily or permanently, often at the request of medical staff on their assessment of the child's best interest. Children in foster care or families in prevention or remediation services may have a third-party involvement. With the temporary lifting of parental rights for the intervention and the speedy return of custody to parents, ethical issues of counseling, education, and follow-up arise. Strongly felt values may cause rejection or sabotage of the child's recovery, or guilt and despair may affect the parents' functioning. The health care provider is limited in time line to service or educational action. Although the hope is a long-term benefit, the actual capability for long-term coordination and follow-up is limited. Families have a life course investment in their members, and even as divorce and other instabilities threaten the continuity, the family is concerned about long-term outcomes and quality of life. Stepping in to replace family members as advocates is a weighty decision to be seriously considered and requires greater diligence in monitoring.

State-Provided Care

Conflicts are intensified when families and children are in state care either due to medical assistance or child welfare supervision. When children or elders are protected by guardians or direct supervision of governmental agencies, their families may be marginalized. When the government is a third party to decision making about children's welfare or family participation, medical decisions may be shifted to other criteria than the family's preferences. Foster parents have very limited capacity to act as advocates for the children in their care and must rely on their case workers to pursue the

child's needs in the bureaucratic system. Because the situation of foster care is viewed as temporary, health needs may not be attended to promptly and parents have already been marginalized. Dental care and prevention are especially vulnerable to postponement or never even being noticed. Records of children's past treatment and events may be lost and never reconstituted. Follow-up may be complicated by changes in placements, return to home, or other institutionalization. Children's lost families and childhoods include lost health care. It was only in the 1980s when President Reagan was apprised of the fact that families had to surrender parental rights for their physically and medically handicapped children to receive government assistance that those national rules were altered.

Similarly, elder patients who have spent down their resources to qualify for Medicaid nursing home care may be isolated from their families, or their families may be pursued for financial support. The process of spending down requires depleting available assets to the point of impoverishment and then enrolling in Medicaid. Even though there are some protections for spouses, the process is likely to alienate family members. States have flexibility in determining entitlements in Medicaid, and the majority of states have some sort of filial responsibility that allows them to seek retrieval of costs already borne by the states. Some changes have been secured by families in governmental programs by advocacy. The Americans with Disabilities Act promoted access and accommodation for everyone with disabilities in public places, housing, schools, and the workplace. Families have joined politically to advocate for change. Having a seat at the table for educational plans is a first step that has been expanded to include how people relate to work, health care, and community services for their families.

Assisted Reproductive Technology

The last example to be examined is the impact of assisted reproductive technologies in creating new family configurations and transitions, providing ethical and medical conundrums and requiring understanding of the complexities of privacy and transparency in health care and policy. The technology of overcoming fertility and reproductive problems has been far ahead of the ramifications in terms of families and their futures. Paralleling the expansion of options in having children has been the explosion of information and potential applications of genetic science. When technology requires the use of genetic materials outside the prospective parents' DNA, the issues of the knowledge of the donors' genetic contribution and health become more important, as they have long-term health implications for offspring. Secrecy and anonymity have characterized the development of interventions. Privacy is thought to protect both the donor and the new family, but it has caused problems and disputes. Artificial insemination has especially depended on anonymous donors often found in the medical sphere. The Jacobson conviction on a doctor's use of his own sperm, in Fairfax, Virginia, in 1992 and other cases where a large number of children appear to have been fathered by a single donor have shaken that tradition. Each of the other assistance interventions has its own idiosyncratic twists and turns in terms of legal and ethical issues, but all have a family component in deciding who has a stake in the child's identity and what responsibilities and rights accrue to each person and their reproductive products. Some years may go by, but a divorce or separation in either heterosexual or same-sex partners may require court settlement. Whether or not a lesbian or gay or heterosexual partner supports or has joint custody may be decided variously in different jurisdictions. A health problem of a child may spur a desire to find the blood parent or at least his or her medical records. Whose privacy and whose access to information has priority is still an unsettled issue.

Conclusion

A shift in the appreciation of family involvement and support in family-centered care has challenged assumptions about the "good" family, and how it is defined or addressed has become critical. Resolving these perceptions and deciding how to manage recognizing family members as appropriate to different health and medical situations are the keys to better outcomes and long-term health and quality care. Certainly, public health programs might best be generous in addressing messages as if all varieties of families were good targets. There is a distinct possibility that families cannot handle everything that larger institutions fail to do in ensuring their health and well-being. Defining families will likely continue to be an issue for health care and the larger community.

Barbara H. Settles

See also Addition of Family Members Through Marriage; Changes in Family Structure; Changes in Family Structure, Roles; Constructionist Family Theoretical Perspectives; Sociological Theories of Families; Theoretical Perspectives Related to the Family

Further Readings

Bogenschneider, K. (2002). *Family policy matters: How policymaking affects families and what professionals can do.* Mahwah, NJ: Erlbaum.

Caro, F. G. (Ed.). (2006). *Family and aging policy.* New York: Haworth Press.

Clarke, A. E., Shim, J. K., Mamo, L., Fosket, J. R., & Fishman, J. R. (2003). Biomedicalization: Technoscientific transformation of health, illness and U.S. biomedicine. *American Sociological Review, 68*(2), 161–194.

Coontz, S. (2000). Historical perspectives on family studies. *Journal of Marriage and Family, 62*(2), 283–297.

Flexman, R., Berke, D. L., & Settles, B. H. (1999). Negotiating family: The interface between family and support groups. In B. H. Settles, S. K. Steinmetz, G. W. Peterson, & M. B. Sussman (Eds.), *Concepts and definition of family for the 21st century* (pp. 173–190). New York: Haworth Press.

Gubrium, J. F., & Holstein, J. A. (1990). *What is family?* Mountain View, CA: Mayfield.

Hareven, T. K. (2000). *Families, history, and social change: Life-course and cross-cultural perspectives.* Boulder, CO: Westview Press.

Keefe, J., & Fancey, P. (2000). The care continues: Responsibility for elderly relatives before and after admission to a long term care facility. *Family Relations, 49*(3), 235–244.

Lumpkin, J. R. (2008). Grandparents in parental or near parental role: Sources of stress and coping mechanisms. *Journal of Family Issues, 29*(3), 357–373.

Ross, S. E., & Lin, C.-T. (2003). The effects of promoting patient access to medical records: A review. *Journal of the Medical Informatics/Association, 10,* 129–138. Retrieved July 14, 2010, from http://www.ncbi.nlm.nih.gov/pmc/articles/PMC150366/pdf/0100129.pdf

Schwartz, S. (2002). Outcomes for the sociology of mental health: Are we meeting our goals? *Journal of Health and Social Behavior, 43*(2), 223–235.

Settles, B. H. (1986). A perspective on tomorrow's families. In M. B. Sussman & S. K. Steinmetz (Eds.), *Handbook of marriage and the family* (pp. 157–180). New York: Plenum Press.

Settles, B. H. (1999). The future of families. In M. B. Sussman, S. K. Steinmetz, & G. W. Peterson (Eds.), *Handbook of marriage and the family* (2nd ed., pp. 143–176). New York: Plenum.

Settles, B. H. (2005). USA families. In B. Adams & J. Trost (Eds.), *Handbook of world families* (pp. 560–601). Thousand Oaks, CA: Sage.

Settles, B. H., Steinmetz, S. K., Peterson, G. W., & Sussman, M. B. (Eds.). (1999). *Concepts and definition of family for the 21st century.* New York: Haworth Press.

Skinner, D. A., & Kohler, J. K. (2002). Parental rights in diverse family contexts: Current legal developments. *Family Relations, 51*(4), 293–300.

DEPRESSION IN THE FAMILY

Depression, or *major depressive disorder*, is a psychiatric disorder characterized by persistent sadness or anhedonia (i.e., lack of interest or pleasure in nearly all activities) lasting 2 weeks or longer, which is accompanied by other symptoms, including changes in appetite and/or sleep, lack of energy, feeling guilty or worthless, difficulty concentrating or making decisions, and thoughts of death or suicide. Depression is a major stressor for families: It interferes with relationships between spouses and between parents and their children. At the same time, dysfunctional family relationships contribute to the development and persistence of depression in individual family members. After briefly describing the prevalence and societal costs of depression, this entry describes the bidirectional links between family relationship quality and depression, emphasizing the implications of these links for best addressing the needs of depressed individuals and their families.

Prevalence and Costs of Depression

Depression is a major public health problem, affecting 15% to 20% of people at some point in their lifetime. According to data from the National Comorbidity Survey, women are around twice as likely as men to experience depression. Children and adolescents are also affected; around 1% of children and 6% of teens meet diagnostic criteria for a depression. Depression causes significant disability and impairment across multiple life domains, including work, school, and home. In fact, it is ranked as the fourth most globally burdensome disease by the World Health Organization.

Depression and Family Relationships

Overall, being married and being part of a family are associated with better mental health. However, distress in marital and family relationships puts individuals at risk for psychological disorders, including depression. Depressed individuals frequently report family and marital problems as prominent concerns in their lives and, often, as the perceived cause of their depression. In the other direction, adults and children who are depressed tend to act and think in ways that have a negative impact on their families.

Looking specifically at the marital relationship, there is a robust association between marital distress and depression. Effects are bidirectional, with marital distress increasing the chances of developing depression and depression predicting declines in marital quality. Within individuals, periods of increased marital conflict and distress tend to co-occur with periods of elevated depression symptoms. There appears to be a cyclical relationship between marital distress and depression, in which depressed persons behave in interpersonally negative ways that create increased stress in their marriage, which then serves to exacerbate depression, and so on, in a negative spiral.

Parent–child relationships also show clear associations with depression. Much research in this area has focused on how depression in parents impacts the well-being of their children. Maternal depression is associated with numerous negative outcomes in children, including mood and anxiety disorders, behavior problems, cognitive deficits, and interpersonal difficulties such as insecure attachment and exclusion by peers. Although less well studied, depression in fathers also predicts more child psychopathology. Because genes account for about half of individuals' susceptibility to depression, some of this effect is explained by parents passing their genetic predisposition toward depression on to their children. However, depression in parents also is linked with parenting deficits that raise children's risk for depression and other problems. Depressed mothers express more negative affect toward their children, exhibit fewer positive parenting behaviors, and are more disengaged and withdrawn as parents, all of which contribute to poor child outcomes, including depression. Similarly, depression in fathers is associated with less positive parenting, more negative parenting, and greater father–child conflict, which in turn are linked with more child emotional and behavioral problems. More generally, dysfunction in parent–child relationships appears to play a key role in the onset and maintenance of depression in individual family members. Family environments characterized by high conflict, low warmth, and low cohesion raise children's risk for depression. Similarly, strained parent–child relations and family stress contribute to depression in mothers.

Clinical Implications

The robust, bidirectional associations between family relationships and depression mandate that efforts to prevent and treat depression take into account the family context of depressed adults or children. To support lasting improvement in an individual's depression, positive changes in the family, such as increased warmth and reduced hostile conflict, are important. Indeed, a growing number of studies suggest that family-focused treatments are effective in reducing depression. Several variations of parent management training, a well-established program designed to improve parenting skills and parent–child relationships, have shown promise in reducing maternal depression. Similarly, growing evidence supports the use of couples therapy, which typically focuses on improving couple communication and reducing marital distress, to treat depression. For individuals experiencing both depression and a distressed marriage, couples therapy has been shown to be as effective or superior to traditional individual psychotherapy in reducing depression. Importantly, in contrast to individual treatment, couples therapy also shows benefits to the marital relationship that are likely to help sustain the recovery from depression.

Conclusion

It is clear that depression influences, and is influenced by, family relationships. Additional research is needed to determine which individuals may benefit most from marital or parenting interventions to ameliorate depression, as well as to identify the treatment components most likely to promote lasting improvements in depressive symptoms. However, at this point, those interested in helping individuals and families struggling with depression can confidently conclude that a consideration of family and couple relationships must be an important component of any intervention.

Sarah W. Whitton

See also Access to Health Care: Child Health; Access to Health Care: Elderly; Access to Health Care: Uninsured; Bipolar Disorders and the Family; Family Emotional Climate and Mental Health; Marriage and Family Therapy for Families; Mental Health Assessment for Families; Parenting

Further Readings

Beach, S. R. H., Jones, D. J., Franklin, K. J., Gotlib, I. H., & Hammen, C. L. (2009). Marital, family, and interpersonal therapies for depression in adults. In I. H. Gotlib & C. L. Hammen (Eds.), *Handbook of depression* (2nd ed., pp. 624–641). New York: Guilford Press.

Davila, J., Stroud, C. B., Starr, L. R., Gotlib, I. H., & Hammen, C. L. (2009). Depression in couples and families. In I. H. Gotlib & C. L. Hammen (Eds.), *Handbook of depression* (2nd ed., pp. 467–491). New York: Guilford Press.

Kaslow, N. J., Deering, C. G., & Racusin, G. R. (1994). Depressed children and their families. *Clinical Psychology Review, 14*(1), 39–59.

DEVELOPMENTAL ASSESSMENT SCALES

Developmental assessment scales are screening instruments used to identify children at risk for developmental delay. Areas of development most commonly assessed with these tools include fine and gross motor abilities, language and communication proficiency, and personal and social skills. It is estimated that less than one third of children with developmental or behavioral disabilities are identified before they begin school. Because early intervention is considered vital to the treatment of children with developmental delay, the aim of most screening tools is to identify children at risk as early in life as possible.

In the earliest months and years of life, the family plays a key role in both facilitating childhood development and monitoring its progression. A comprehensive assessment of a child's development is difficult to obtain in a fixed time or setting, and therefore developmental assessment scales must often rely on the input and feedback of the family for a more complete evaluation. This entry discusses examples of developmental assessment scales and the integral role of the family in a child's developmental evaluation. Implications of the results of developmental assessment for the family are also discussed.

History

One of the first widely used developmental assessment scales was the Denver Developmental Screening Test, created in the late 1960s by William K. Frankenberg and then modified to the Denver II version in the early 1990s. The Denver tests measure the abilities of children ages 0 to 6 years to perform tasks in a variety of developmental areas and then compare their performance to expected standards relative to age (e.g., 90% of 7-month-olds should sit without support). Health professionals, educators, and other professionals use the standardized screening form and tool kit to perform the test, which takes approximately 15 to 20 minutes to administer.

Aside from lengthy administration time, limited standardization, and the need for special equipment, the Denver tests were also often criticized for not being reliable as a measure for specific developmental problems or other, less severe differences in development. Over the past 20 years several well-validated developmental scales have been developed, including many to address more specific areas of development or to target different age groups or diagnoses. In general, however, basic developmental screening tools are still used to identify children at risk for delay so that they can be referred to specialists for a more detailed evaluation.

Developmental Assessment and the Family

In recent years the role of the parents and family in a child's developmental assessment has gained greater attention. Parents and family have the advantage of spending greater time with a child in a variety of activities and observing him or her in comparison with peers of the same age group. The family may therefore be the first to identify that their child may be at risk for developmental problems. However, research has shown that only a small percentage of families will actually bring these concerns to their child's health care provider. For this reason developmental assessment has been emphasized as an integral part of each child's routine pediatric health visit.

Family Participation in Developmental Assessment

In addition to observing a child's behavior during the well-child visit, the health practitioner will also elicit information from the family about the child's daily activities and interactions. This process can be done either by a written questionnaire, interview, or both, and helps the provider develop a comprehensive assessment of a child's skills and milestone achievement. Several general developmental assessment scales exist that rely heavily on family report, including the Parents' Evaluation of Developmental Status and the Ages and Stages Questionnaire. Through these brief questions and exercises, families are encouraged to think about interactions with their child in terms of expected developmental progress (e.g., "Do you have any concerns about how your child talks and makes speech sounds?"). Eliciting parents' concerns about their child's development is essential to help guide the health practitioner in determining whether these concerns are predictive of developmental problems or not. There are also various other assessment scales, such as the Language Development Survey and the Modified Checklist for Autism in Toddlers, which rely on parent report and target specific developmental areas or diagnoses.

Developmental Assessment Results: Implications for the Family

Whether normal or abnormal, the results of developmental screening provide important information to the family. If a child appears to be within the normal expected range for development, the family is often reassured and encouraged to continue to promote activities that foster further development. Reading together and engaging in different types of play are just some examples of ways that families can promote developmental progress in their child. Families are also often given anticipatory guidance in watching for developmental milestones as their child grows.

The families of children with concerning results from developmental assessment may face more challenges. Children determined to be at risk for developmental problems are often referred to specialists in development and behavior for more thorough evaluation and diagnosis. Once completed, a thorough developmental evaluation may indicate the need for additional interventions and services that aim toward maximizing the child's achievement potential. Special school programs, behavioral therapy, or parent training are examples of such interventions. A family's ability to access resources through the community, schools, or health agencies is essential to appropriate developmental evaluation and intervention.

Many families also require assistance in coping with a child with developmental delay. Guilt and frustration are common feelings reported by parents of children with developmental disabilities. Siblings of these children may also struggle with issues of jealousy for the extra attention the child receives, or embarrassment in having a family member who is "different." Counseling and support groups are often instrumental in helping families through the difficulties of coping with a child with developmental delay.

Conclusion

Developmental assessment scales are vital to the early identification and referral of children at risk for developmental delay, and the family plays a key role in this process. Family health professionals can help elicit concerns about child development and also provide families with the resources and support necessary for further evaluation and treatment.

Christine Kennedy and Victoria Floriani Keeton

See also Access to Health Care: Child Health; Chronic Health Problems and Interventions for the Childrearing Family; Developmental Care of Preterm Infants and the Childbearing Family; Intellectual Disability in the Family; Life Span: Care Coordination for Chronic Illness/Disabilities and the Family; Psychoeducational Interventions for Families

Further Readings

Council on Children with Disabilities, Section on Developmental Behavioral Pediatrics, Bright Futures Steering Committee, & Medical Home Initiatives for Children with Special Needs Project Advisory Committee. (2006). Identifying infants and young children with developmental disorders in the medical home: An algorithm for developmental surveillance and screening. *Pediatrics, 118*(1), 405–420.

Ellingson, K. D., Briggs-Gowan, M. J., Carter, A. S., & Horwitz, S. M. (2004). Parent identification of early emerging child behavior problems. *Archives of Pediatric and Adolescent Medicine, 158*, 766–772.

Glascoe, F. P. (2005). Screening for developmental and behavioral problems. *Mental Retardation and Developmental Disabilities Research Reviews, 11*(3), 173–179.

Squires, J., Bricker, D., & Potter, L. (1997). Revision of a parent-completed development screening tool: Ages and stages questionnaires. *Journal of Pediatric Psychology, 22*(3), 313–328.

DEVELOPMENTAL CARE OF PRETERM INFANTS AND THE CHILDBEARING FAMILY

The care of premature infants within childbearing families has become a significant challenge with the global increase in prematurity rates to 12% of all births, or 16 million premature infants born each year. There is variation around the world, including an 18% rate of prematurity in the African American population of the United States. These premature infants are less well developed to handle the environment outside of their mother's womb. Increasingly these early born and low birth weight infants survive their intensive care nursery experience. However, there remains a strong likelihood of their having some type of a neurosensory impairment, which will have lifelong effects on their learning ability and social emotional health. Nearly half of all children born prematurely show later learning disabilities, attention deficits, behavior problems, adverse emotional issues, and school failure, according to H. Gerry Taylor and colleagues. The entire field of neonatology grew from the vision that perhaps an infant born too soon could survive with intensive care. For the past 6 decades the specialty of neonatology within the field of pediatric medicine has been increasingly successful in ensuring the survival of early born infants as young as 23 weeks post-conception through the intensive care provided in newborn intensive care units.

For the past 30 years there has been a slow and steady progression toward a more humane approach to the care of premature infants that is designed to protect their developing brains and central nervous systems while simultaneously integrating the high degree of technology necessary for their survival. Each infant is born into a family, and only the mother who has given birth can define that family for the professionals in the newborn intensive care unit. Family members are acknowledged and recognized as primary caregivers and long-term advocates. They are an integral part of the health care team. This individualized, relationship-based, family-centered approach to care has grown from its theoretical basis with increasing evidence in research findings and gradual implementation in clinical practice toward new policies and standards in neonatal intensive care of premature infants.

Theoretical Perspective

Preterm infants are unprepared for the extrauterine environment and are at risk for adverse effects on their brains and central nervous systems. The one sensory system that is fully developed in the most premature infant is that of pain. Pain is also the one sensation that does not require stimulation for development. The preterm infant's brain is in continuous interaction with the environment. Any and all sensory experience has an impact on the developing brain. The consequence of this is especially harmful when the brain is in a critical stage of rapid development. For the preterm infant the crucial brain and central nervous system development—including migration of neurons, lamination involving the proper alignment of cortical neurons, proliferation and interconnections of the neurons, and maturation of these brain cells—now occurs

within the context of an intensive care nursery rather than a healthy womb. The brain is therefore vulnerable for alterations in development as well as injury due to bleeding within the brains of the most immature infants and inadequate oxygen supply for the most critically ill infants.

Synactive Theory

In 1982, Heidelise Als created the model of synactive organization of behavioral development, which provides the context for the meaning of infant behavior. Within this synactive model the infant has three major subsystems of functioning, which are maturing simultaneously and affecting each other. The autonomic or physiological subsystem is observed through the infant's color, breathing, and visceral or gut functioning. The motoric subsystem is viewed through the infant's posture, muscle tone, and quality of movements from the most jittery uncoordinated to the smoother, better coordinated movements. The third major subsystem is that of the infant's states of consciousness, including deep sleep, light sleep, drowsiness, quiet alert, fussy, and irritable robust crying. The observed behavior includes the range of states available, how clear or well defined any state may be, and how the infant transitions from one state to another, such as awakening. Within the infants' alertness they show emerging ability to attend to, and interact with, surroundings. Across these subsystems, infants attempt to maintain balance or to regulate themselves. It is important for caregivers of preterm infants to facilitate normal growth and development by building on infants' emerging strengths and competences while simultaneously protecting them from overwhelming stress in the environment.

Newborn Individualized Developmental Care and Assessment Program

The challenge facing health care professionals in the newborn intensive care unit is in caring for preterm infants and their families in a manner that optimizes their developmental course and outcome. Integrating the individualized and family-centered approach to care with the intensive technology and procedures necessary for survival within a supportive environment requires a great deal of reflection and awareness of one's own actions. The Newborn Individualized Developmental Care and Assessment Program (NIDCAP) is a family-centered program that provides a systematic, neurobehavioral observation methodology in which to accomplish this goal. The infant is observed in a formal manner before, during, and after active caregiving in order to evaluate emerging strengths as well as vulnerabilities. When the infant's behavior is perceived as being meaningful, then it informs all aspects of caregiving. From this behavioral observation, the NIDCAP observer is able to identify the infant's own goals and to integrate these goals into an individualized plan of care for the infant and family.

These systematic observations, or NIDCAP reports, provide the basis for the appropriate structuring of the infant's bed-space and environment for the infant and family within the newborn intensive care unit. The timing and organization of the medical and nursing interventions are individualized to meet the needs of the infant and the infant's family. Parents and family members are supported in gaining a strong understanding of their infant's behavior and how best to support the infant in further maturation and development. Parents who are welcomed as equal members of the health care team are able to feel pleasure and pride as they support and cherish their infant.

This coordination and orchestration of all aspects of care from the infant's observed behavior must include all members of the health care team. Even young preterm infants requiring ventilator support for immature lungs and being fed by stomach tubes may demonstrate behavior that shows some effort at breathing beyond the ventilator, an interest in bracing feet into the bedding, and a beginning interest in looking at surroundings. When professional caregivers understand and acknowledge the apparent goals of infants, they not only modify their own approach to caregiving but facilitate the family in understanding and supporting the efforts of infants to achieve these goals.

Research

To date there have been nearly 50 empirical research studies that have examined the effect of an individualized, developmentally supportive, family-centered (NIDCAP) approach to care of premature

infants. The earliest studies done in the early 1980s were historical controlled trials of small sample sizes that demonstrated significantly positive results in favor of the infants to which an NIDCAP approach was applied over those provided standard care. For the NIDCAP infants, behavioral outcomes shortly after leaving the newborn intensive care unit were better, and there were fewer complications and less ventilator and oxygen support during their hospitalization. These early studies were followed by randomized controlled trials further testing the hypothesis that NIDCAP could enhance and optimize the medical and behavioral outcome of premature infants in the newborn intensive care unit and following discharge of the infants. The landmark study published in the *Journal of the American Medical Association* in 1994 by Als and her colleagues demonstrated improved lung function, better feeding ability, reduction in medical complications (including bleeding in the brain), decreased hospitalization and decreased hospital costs, as well as improved neurobehavioral outcome. The significantly better lung function and reduction in medical complications were somewhat replicated in a subsequent study after the integration of surfactant, which revolutionized the respiratory care of premature infants in the early 1990s. Several studies of older and healthier premature infants who did not require critical medical intervention and the infants cared for with the NIDCAP approach show improved neurobehavioral organization. In one study by Als and Frank Duffy, premature infants cared for in the NIDCAP manner were shown to have improved neurobehavioral functioning with actual changes in the infants' brain structure and function as measured neuroelectrophysiologically through brain imaging.

Further research investigating developmental care of the premature infant and family has been done throughout the United States, Canada, Sweden, the Netherlands, and France, as this NIDCAP approach has spread throughout the world. A three-center randomized controlled study published in 2003 showed that the NIDCAP care could be reliably replicated and achieved in different newborn intensive care units across the United States. The three-center study included nearly 100 premature infants and demonstrated significant improvements in feeding ability, daily weight gain, decreased hospitalization, decreased hospital charges, better neurobehavioral functioning, and decreased parental stress. These studies have reinforced the earliest dramatic findings and included a reduction in the incidence of apnea of prematurity as well as the need for sedation in the earliest born infants. Increasingly investigators have been able to do longer term follow-up of those infants cared for with NIDCAP in their newborn intensive care units, showing promise that the significant improvements in function last well into adolescence. The most difficult aspect to conducting research on developmental care is the complexity of both the comprehensive approach to care as well as the degree of human variables in relationship-based care. These behavioral intervention studies are cannot be blind, as in the classic "drug study" model, and those who do not understand the complexity of maintaining the integrity of the treatment intervention may fail to appreciate that significant results have surpassed the caregiving variables that tend to cross over to the control population. Behavioral intervention studies with premature infants and families is labor intensive and requires strict adherence to details of intervention as well as expertise with complex data analysis. Although there has been an occasional research study that does not show a significant improvement in premature infants, there has never been a study to show any harmful or untoward effect on preterm infants with the NIDCAP care.

Implementation in the Newborn Intensive Care Unit

The provision of developmental care for preterm infants and families in the newborn intensive care unit requires developmental specialists, specific training and education, and the full support of multidisciplinary leadership. NIDCAP is essentially requesting a complete shift in the traditional medical paradigm and is based on the acknowledgment and support of emerging competence in individual infants, family members, and professionals. In order for the degree of awareness and individualization to be maintained, there must be at least one full-time NIDCAP professional championing this approach to care. Newborn intensive care units began in the 1970s as well-lit, noisy, busy, and hectic intensive care arenas. The care was designed to be most convenient and expedient for the professional

caregivers, and family members were not welcome in the unit until the premature infant was nearly ready for discharge home. Wearing no clothing, infants were cared for on open radiant warmers and oftentimes were restrained flat on their backs without postural support. Little thought went into the comfort of the infant or the inclusion or collaboration with parents in providing clinical care to premature infants. This well-intended yet limited approach to care was based on a model that excluded any possibility that the premature infant might have emerging self-regulatory ability and would benefit from a nurturing relationship with his or her family.

Developmental care as defined by NIDCAP was born of the collaboration of psychology, nursing, and medicine with a commitment to view the infant and family in the light of their strengths and the infant's emerging competences. The evolution from traditional care to NIDCAP has required tremendous changes in philosophy and clinical practice. The shift in paradigm involves moving away from the fast-paced, reactive, task-oriented care to a more reflective relationship-based approach that acknowledges the human experience of the other and strives to facilitate emerging competence through a thorough adaptation to the environment as well as handling techniques. The NIDCAP professional caregiver strives to provide care to the premature infant that is in synchrony with the infant's own rhythms of sleep and wakefulness as well as responding in a developmentally oriented manner rather than in a crisis mode. The developmentally individualized and family-supportive newborn intensive care environment is soothing, with a calming atmosphere that demonstrates respect for the privacy of the childbearing family and their premature infant now developing outside of the womb. There is a growing body of evidence that supports the parent's body as the more optimal bed-space for the infant rather than the incubator. Newer intensive care nurseries are being designed for individual family space that allows the family to remain with their premature infant in order to comfort and nurture their infant during the newborn intensive care hospitalization.

In addition to the NIDCAP philosophy being demonstrated in the environments of newborn intensive care units, there is a clear difference in the educated hands of the NIDCAP professional providing care to premature infants. In general, there is much slower timing for interventions. Infants are understood and respected as collaborators in their own care, no matter how early born they are. Behavior guides each interaction as caregivers adjust their approach in response to infant experience and reaction to the intervention. Caregiving is no longer being done to the infant, but rather caregiving is done as an engagement process with the premature infant. There is much thought and energy in assessing, preventing, and managing the potential experience of pain, especially with the more intensive interventions required. The infant is continually assessed and supported to gradually be more successful in self-regulation. Care is taken to respect the preterm infants' ability to sleep and rest as well as to acknowledge and support their efforts to look around and interact with their environment when awake and interested. Premature infants are evaluated and treated as individuals in terms of their early interest in sucking and feeding. Whether at breast or by bottle, feedings are under the control of the awake and actively participating premature infant. Care of infants is planned and coordinated with the family to maximize their involvement and participation in caring for their infant. By the time a premature infant has reached the level of maturity and development required for discharge home, the family has gained an adequate level of competence and confidence in their ability to care for their infant and ideally experiences pleasure and pride as they make the transition from the newborn intensive care unit to home and community.

Summary

The provision of developmental care for preterm infants and the childbearing family is an evolving process from the beginning of neonatology during which it was envisioned that the fetus surviving outside of the womb might be cared for while bedded on a parent's body in newborn intensive care units designed for the intimacy of families. With the integration of protection for the developing brain and central nervous system and the respect and perception of the meaning of the infant's behavior within the context of a nurturing, softly lit, quiet, calm environment, these infants and their families may be supported in their maturation and development while simultaneously receiving the highly technological and intensive care necessary for survival. This type of developmental support will not only continue to promote the high rate of survival, but will ensure the security, protection, and intimacy needed by childbearing families. The brain and central nervous system of the premature infant is of the utmost priority in an effort to support each infant in reaching his or her optimal development.

gretchen Lawhon

See also Acute Care/Hospitalization of Family Members; Caregiving: Infants; Families Experiencing a Child's Illness; Family Experiencing Transitions; Health Needs of Childbearing Families; Parenting; Partnering With Families: Family-Centered Care

Further Readings

Als, H. (1982). Toward a synactive theory of development: Promise for the assessment of infant individuality. *Infant Mental Health Journal, 3,* 229–243.

Als, H., Duffy, F. H., McAnulty, G. B., Rivkin, M. J., Vajapeyam, S., Mulkern, R. V., et al. (2004). Early experience alters brain function and structure. *Pediatrics, 113*(4), 846–857.

Als, H., Gilkerson, L., Duffy, F. H., McAnulty, G. B., Buehler, D. M., VandenBerg, K. A., et al. (2003). A three-center randomized controlled trial of individualized developmental care for very low birth weight preterm infants: Medical, neurodevelopmental, parenting and care-giving effects. *Journal of Developmental and Behavior Pediatrics, 24*(6), 399–408.

Als, H., Lawhon, g., Duffy, F. H., McAnulty, G. B., Gibes-Grossman, R., & Blickman, J. G. (1994). Individualized developmental care for the very low birthweight preterm infant: Medical and neurofunctional effects. *Journal of the American Medical Association, 272,* 853–858.

Beck, S., Wojdyala, D., Say, L., Betran, A. P., Meraldi, M., Harris Requejo, J., et al. (2010). The worldwide incidence of preterm birth: A systematic review of maternal mortality and morbidity. *Bulletin of the World Health Organization, 88,* 31–38.

Lawhon, g. (1997). Providing developmentally supportive care in the newborn intensive care unit: An evolving challenge. *Journal of Perinatal & Neonatal Nursing, 10,* 48–61.

Lawhon, g. (2002). Facilitation of parenting the premature infant within the newborn intensive care unit. *Journal of Perinatal & Neonatal Nursing, 16*(1), 71–82.

Lawhon, g., & Hedlund, R. (2008). Newborn individualized developmental care and assessment program training and education. *Journal of Perinatal & Neonatal Nursing, 22*(2), 133–144.

Martin, J. A., Hamilton, B. E., Ventura, S. J., Menacker, F., Park, M. M., & Sutton P. D. (2002). Births: Final data for 2001. *National Vital Statistics Reports, 51*(2), 1–102.

Symington, A., & Pinelli, J. (2006). Developmental care for promoting development and preventing morbidity in preterm infants. *Cochrane Database of Systematic Reviews, 2,* 1–44.

Taylor, H. G., Klein, N. M., Minich, N., & Hack, M. (2000). Middle-school-age outcomes in children with very low birthweight. *Child Development, 71*(6), 69–82.

Websites

NIDCAP Federation International: http://www.nidcap.org

DEVELOPMENTAL TRANSITIONS IN FAMILIES

Developmental transitions in families refer to the stages and changes that occur over the life span of families. A theoretical grounding opens doors to different ways of understanding and offers varying options for assessment and intervention. By understanding theories, health care providers are better prepared to think creatively and critically about how health and illness affect families. Shirley May Harmon Hanson writes that a reciprocal relationship exists among theory, practice, and research; each informs the other, thus expanding knowledge and interventions that help individuals and families. This entry utilizes family development and transition theories to provide structure for health care providers who assess, intervene, and evaluate individual and family health care. The developmental and transition theories are intended to provide health care providers with one lens with which to provide care to families within the health care system.

Family Development Theory

The individual growth and development theory specified by Evelyn Duvall and Brent Miller serves as the foundation for family development theory or the family life cycle. Family developmental tasks are growth responsibilities rising at various stages in the lives of families, the successful achievement of which leads to satisfaction, societal approval, and success with later tasks. Failure to achieve these developmental milestones leads to unhappiness in families, disapproval by society, and difficulties with later family developmental tasks. This social sequence of events is repeated by successive generations of families.

The eight stages of the family life cycle are summarized here, and their respective developmental tasks are discussed in detail elsewhere (see Further Readings). These predictable stages and transitions are determined by family events over time, driven by the age of the oldest child:

1. Married couples (without children)

2. Childbearing families (oldest child, birth–30 months)

3. Families with preschool children (oldest child, 2½–6 years)

4. Families with school-age children (oldest child, 6–13 years)

5. Families with adolescents (oldest child, 13–20 years)

6. Families with young adults—launching (first child gone to last child leaving home)

7. Middle-age parents ("empty nest" to retirement)

8. Aging families (retirement to death of both spouses)

Across all family life cycle stages, basic family functions and tasks are essential for survival and continuity: (a) secure shelter, food, and clothing; (b) develop emotionally healthy individuals who can manage crises and experience nonmonetary achievement; (c) ensure each individual's socialization in school, work, spiritual, and community life; (d) contribute to the next generation by giving birth, adopting, or providing foster care; and (e) promote the health of family members and care for them during illness.

This family life cycle perspective emerged and prospered in the 1930–1960s, a time in history when traditional nuclear families were taken for granted: two monogamous heterosexual parents and their children. The model assumed that all families follow certain conventional and linear patterns.

Over time, it was recognized that many families do not proceed predictably along these delineated stages. Two families in the same life cycle stage could be very different from each other. Family scholars began to question this rigid model but continued to see the model as useful. Family scholars started to incorporate more diversity and broader time frames into their thinking. The original stages of the family development theory still help clinicians to anticipate important family health care transitions and challenges.

Family Careers

The concept of "family careers" moved family development theory to another level in the 1990s. Joan Aldrous, Vivian Gedaly-Duff, and colleagues define *Family Career* as the dynamic process of changes and transitions that occur during the life span of families. The concept of family careers takes into account the diverse experiences of American families and includes both the expected developmental changes and transitions of the family life cycle, including birth of child and child entering school, as well as unexpected situational events, such as divorce, remarriage, adoption, and death. Family careers involve the many variations and paths that families can take during their life span.

Changes in families do not necessarily occur in a linear fashion. Family development theory assumes that families raising more than one child have already experienced the stages of birthing and resulting family developmental tasks. Family careers takes into account the possibility that a person without children may marry a partner who already has adolescent children, resulting in parenthood starting at adolescence. Remarriage and stepparenting are common, and couples may be married or cohabiting. Family careers helps to explain the many interactions in families where adults are married or unmarried, in overlapping stages, cohabitating, single, divorced, widowed, remarried, adoptive, childless/childfree, or homosexual. The concept of family careers underscores the diversity of families and that families are dynamic in modern society.

Family Transitions

Al Meleis and colleagues have noted that an understanding of transitions is central for clinicians working with families. *Family transitions* are events that signal a reorganization of family roles and tasks. *Developmental or normative transitions* are typical and predictable changes occurring at expected time lines congruent with movement through the eight stages of the family life cycle. This includes birth, leaving home, marriage, and death. *Situational or nonnormative transitions,* such as divorce, adoption, environmental catastrophe, or critical health events, may not occur in all families. All these events involve changes in personal relationships, roles and status, environment, and physical and mental capabilities. Families experiencing either developmental or situational transitions may end up in crisis and have subsequent contact with legal, social, or health agencies.

Transitions from one family life cycle stage to another can be periods of potential crisis for families. Stages are viewed as relatively stable and calm periods of family development. During these stages of stability, family members' roles have already been clarified and preferred family strategies established. Only minor variations in roles or strategies are expected during these developmental stages. In contrast, transitions are viewed as periods of instability, disorganization, stress, and potential change. Critical family transitions, generally marked by the arrival of family members (marriage, birth, adoption) or departure of family members (children entering school, launching, death) demand adaptations and modifications within family systems. During these times of structural reorganization, tasks must be realigned, roles redefined, and strategies revised, as described by both Meleis and Sharon Price and their colleagues.

Transition models are more process oriented than family development stage models. Although family transitions are critical times of change, they are not necessarily perceived as stressful when they are expected or planned. Families can anticipate task realignments and start experimenting gradually with new strategies, while still retaining their comfort and familiarity with old strategies.

Normative events offer families useful guidelines and a repertoire of available role models, coping strategies, and sources of social support from which to draw.

Family Health Outcomes

According to Hanson, the goals of working with families using the family developmental and transition perspective are aimed toward achieving optimal family health. *Family health* refers to the biological, psychological, sociological, cultural, and spiritual dimensions of individuals and the family as a whole. Family health care is the process of providing for the health care needs of individuals and families that are within the scope of practice by clinicians. This care and subsequent outcomes should be aimed toward the family as context, the family as a whole, the family as a system, the family as a component of society, or all of these.

Much is written describing "healthy families," which is the goal of interventions by family professionals. Healthy families are both an ideal and a reality. Health is more than the absence of pathology; rather it is an interactive process associated with positive relationships and outcomes. Healthy families have a number of characteristics in common, and families require help in achieving these outcomes of families who (a) have a legitimate clear source of authority and roles established and supported over time and are able to change with time; (b) have a stable rule system that is established and consistent over time; (c) display stability and consistency in sharing nurturing behavior; (d) practice effective and stable childrearing and marriage maintenance practices; (e) establish a set of goals toward which individuals and the whole family work; (f) develop flexibility and adaptability to accommodate normal developmental challenges as well the ability to deal with unexpected crises in a positive manner; (g) display commitment and encouragement to individual members and the family as a whole; (h) spend time together and appreciate each other using communication patterns that work for all; (i) teach tolerance of other individuals and family groups who are different from themselves; (j) have a spiritual/religious foundation on which to build; (k) are able to learn skills to deal with a family member's health problems; (l) have members who are clear, open, and spontaneous in their expression of feelings, beliefs, and differences; (m) are respectful of family members' feelings; (n) encourage autonomy of their members; (o) have members who take personal responsibility for their actions; (p) have members who demonstrate closeness and warmth toward each other, with parents taking the lead; and (q) express optimism and enjoyment with each other.

Interventions That Improve Family Health

There are many interventions based on the concepts of developmental transitions in families that support the multivariate and interactive nature of relationships among family health as a whole and the health of individual members. What follows here is a list of thirteen interventions and strategies selected by Hanson that appear in the literature about care of families, regardless of which theoretical model is being used.

1. Family health care is concerned with experiences of families over time: the past, present, and future of family groups. Excellent family health care considers stages of the family life cycle and family careers patterns. Three-generational family genograms are essential strategies for family assessment and provide visual clues as to patterns, associations, and predictions when working with families.

2. Families should be understood within the cultural and community contexts of their group. Family ecomaps are essential tools for understanding how families fit into larger community or environment. Ecomaps provide graphic portrayals of support systems that serve as either support or stressors to families.

3. Family health care providers determine who constitutes the "family" in each situation: In one setting, it may be the biological family of origin; in another setting it may be the family as defined by the client/patient.

4. Families are encouraged to receive from and give to communities to which they participate and belong.

5. Family health care providers consider relationships among family members and

understand that not all members of families achieve maximum health at the same time. The focal point for the care of families changes over time. One person may be symptomatic at the present, but this focus may shift over time.

6. Family health care is directed at families whose members are healthy or ill. Family health is measured by each individual's health status as well as family health as a whole.

7. Family health care is delivered in a variety of settings by a variety of family professionals.

8. Family members may present with physical, social, cultural, psychological, cultural, or spiritual problems. All problems should be addressed by health care professionals.

9. Family care providers acknowledge how both individual health and collective family health are intertwined and how intervention at any level will impact the family system as a whole.

10. Family care providers orchestrate environments to improve family interaction. They offer care to individuals and families as a whole.

11. Optimal family health care focuses on family strengths (individual and family as a whole).

12. Family health care providers draw from family's historical ways of coping and connecting and use these strengths to cope with current health care problems.

13. Family health care providers collaborate with families during the assessment and intervention stages of the process and make families full partners of their own health destiny.

The developmental and transitions theories and interventions summarized in the previous list provide one theoretical foundation to provide care to families who experience developmental transitions that relate to family health care.

Shirley May Harmon Hanson

See also Family Experiencing Transitions; Family Health Perspectives; Family Interventions Across the Life Span; Theoretical Perspectives Related to the Family

Further Readings

Aldous, J. (1996). *Family careers: Rethinking the developmental perspective.* Thousand Oaks, CA: Sage.

Duvall, E. M., & Miller, B. C. (1985). *Marriage and family development* (6th ed.). New York: Harper & Row.

Gedaly-Duff, V., Nielsen, A., Heims, M. L., & Pate, M. F. D. (2010). Family child health nursing. In J. R. Kaakinen, V. Gedaly-Duff, D. P. Coehlo, & S. M. H. Hanson (Eds.), *Family health care nursing: Theory, practice & research* (4th ed., pp. 332–378). Philadelphia: F. A. Davis.

Hanson, S. M. H., Kaakinen, J. R., & Gedaly-Duff, V. (2006). *Family health care nursing: Theory, practice & research* (3rd ed.). Philadelphia: F. A. Davis.

Meleis, A. I., Sawyer, L. M., Im, E. O., Hilfinger Messias, D. K., & Schumacher, K. (2000). Experiencing transitions: An emerging middle-range theory. *Advances in Nursing Science, 23*(1), 12–38.

Price, S. J., Price, C. A., & McKenry, P. C. (2009). *Families & change: Coping with stressful events and transitions.* Thousand Oaks, CA: Sage.

DIABETES, TYPE 1, AND THE FAMILY

The diagnosis of Type 1 diabetes mellitus (T1DM) in a child is overwhelming for most families, requiring a major adjustment in family life. Family roles and responsibilities are adapted to incorporate the child's illness regime into the family's daily activities. The purpose of this discussion is to describe family management when a child or adolescent is diagnosed with T1DM, the newer technologies for assisting families in pediatric T1DM care, and the leading research evidence for delivering family-centered interventions. The primary goal of such interventions is to improve both physiological and psychosocial outcomes for the affected youth, including optimal glycemic control, fewer diabetes-related complications, and improved quality of life. Ultimately, the aim of interventions for the families is to facilitate appropriate management styles whereby family members and youth benefit in achieving a state of wellness for the entire family unit.

Definition and Epidemiology of Type 1 Diabetes

Diabetes is the seventh leading cause of death in the United States, and T1DM is one of the most common chronic diseases in youth, affecting approximately 1 out of 500 youth. The complexity of daily care for youth with T1DM presents ongoing challenges and adaptations for families, varying with the developmental level of the child. Although T1DM can occur at any age, the incidence increases with age, peaking at puberty. For youth diagnosed when they are under 10 years old, most diabetes is T1DM, regardless of race or ethnicity. In youth 10 to 19 years, T1DM is the major type of diabetes in non-Hispanic whites (85%), with a smaller proportion noted in minority populations: 53.9% in Hispanics, 42.2% in African Americans, 30.3% in Asian/Pacific Islanders, and 13.8% of American Indians. Recent prospective national and international registries (DIAMOND and EURODIAB) report a steep rise in T1DM in youth less than 5 years of age. Epidemiological studies have identified environmental risk factors that may be contributing to this rising trend in early onset pediatric T1DM. These factors include older maternal age, increased birth weight, early introduction of cow's milk proteins, and an increased rate of postnatal growth. Higher birth weight and early child growth in height, weight, and body mass index have been associated with a greater risk for T1DM.

The diagnosis of T1DM is usually associated with an acute illness in the child with manifestations of the classic symptoms of polyuria (frequent urination), polydipsia (excessive thirst), polyphagia (increased appetite), and weight loss, with or without ketoacidosis (accumulation of ketones in the blood). The etiology of the disease is the autoimmune destruction of the insulin-producing cells of the pancreatic islets of Langerhans. Confirmation of the diagnosis is made by a fasting blood sugar at or above 126 mg/dl or a random glucose at or above 200 mg/dl along with classic symptoms. Further evaluation with positive results for islet cell antibodies, insulin autoantibodies, or anti-GAD (glutamic acid decarboxylase) antibodies can delineate the diagnosis of T1DM versus other types of diabetes, such as Type 2 diabetes mellitus or hybrid (mixed) diabetes.

Family Management and Type 1 Diabetes

Learning that a child has a diagnosis of T1DM can be devastating to families. Adapting to the daily regime for insulin, diet modification, and physical activity requirements is often initially overwhelming. Since the seminal publication of Barbara Anderson and Wendy Auslander in 1980, which provided a critique of current knowledge on diabetes management and the family, there has been a continuing emphasis on a family systems approach to understanding family management and T1DM. Earlier research focused on a linear view of the influence of parental attitudes toward diabetes on the youth's adjustment and glycemic control. Scholars of family behavior and theory recognize that having a child member with T1DM affects the overall family functioning of all members. How effective family members are at negotiating roles and responsibilities to achieve the necessary balance for family life once a child is diagnosed with T1DM is determined by the level of stability and types of communications that occur within the family system.

Although the majority of research with T1DM youth has addressed educational and psychosocial or behavioral interventions to improve treatment adherence and improved glucose control for the child or adolescent, the past decade produced substantive scientific evidence of the effects of family management and decision making on these outcomes. One common finding regarding family strategies to promote adjustment and adherence to treatment regimes is the importance of family members to remain active in the shared responsibility of diabetes care. Fathers, as well as mothers, are assuming an increasingly greater role in the day-to-day care of a child with T1DM. As the child's developmental needs change and more self-management responsibilities are gained in later childhood and early adolescence, parents, older siblings, and other adult family members still need to be involved in insulin administration, blood testing, healthy dietary practice, and regular exercise. The ebb and flow of involvement of family members may change as the level of responsibility waxes and wanes, as commonly witnessed during the emotional upheaval of the adolescent years. Just as the structure and functions of a family vary, so does the necessary balance of communication among family members and the child with diabetes. Regardless of the style of communication, the pattern should be one of openness, patience, and flexibility in order to facilitate optimal health outcomes. Opportunities to discuss and resolve family conflicts in diabetes management can avert difficulties in treatment adherence and glucose control. In contrast to this more flexible, shared approach to family management, overprotective or permissive parenting styles can lead to maladjustment and poor adherence by the child. Additionally, a controlling parental style can result in good diabetes control but resentment and rebellion from the child, with more serious consequences such as anxiety and depression during adolescence.

Although family communication is a strong predictor of diabetes outcomes, family factors related to family structure, economics, race and culture, and geographical locale contribute to the overall family milieu for diabetes management. Both clinical evidence and well-devised scientific inquiry reveal the negative effect of single-parent families, lower socioeconomic status, and parental education, as well as poor parental problem-solving skill, on adherence and glycemic control. Despite limited studies of minority families with children who have T1DM, some evidence exists that African American youth tend to have more difficulty in achieving the American Diabetes Association's recommended levels of glycosylated hemoglobin (A1c) of less than 7% for children and less than 7.5% for adolescents. Recent normative data on nondiabetic African American youth derived from NHANES (National Health and Nutrition Evaluation Study) III, 1988–1994, indicate that A1c values are higher than in nondiabetic white youth. Thus, careful consideration is warranted when evaluating glycemic control of these minority youth and counseling families about diabetes management. Higher levels of A1c for African American children may be related to norms for them and may not be a reflection of family management issues and poor adherence. Even fewer studies have included Hispanic families of youth with T1DM. Therefore, little is known regarding family management and outcomes in Hispanic populations.

Culture and geographical locale potentially can impact family management. Both of these factors directly affect the family's decisions about dietary selections and practices, as well as the availability of healthy foods. The level of acculturation of a family can influence food choices and the meaning and frequency of food intake at social gatherings and celebrations. Families residing in communities where fruits and vegetables are locally grown or readily accessible and affordable versus those who must resort to the food products stocked on the shelves of inner-city corner markets and convenience stores have a distinct advantage on their children's health outcomes.

Technologies Used in Type 1 Diabetes Care

Continuous subcutaneous insulin infusion (CSII) pump therapy has become a predominant technological advance in the treatment of children and adolescents with T1DM. Although CSII technology has been available for several decades, it is now more readily accepted and available due to the improvement in the size and cost of the pump devices.

The landmark Diabetes Control and Complications Trial (DCCT) in the mid-1990s reported significant improvements in glycemic control with intensive insulin therapy (multiple injections per day) versus conventional two-injection regimes. The findings of this multisite, randomized clinical trial revolutionized insulin therapy and provided evidence for decreasing complications related to better A1c levels. Although adolescents were included in this trial, increasingly younger children began to be placed on multiple injections per day with blood glucose testing with a goal of achieving near-normal glucose levels. This use of intensive treatment led the way for treatment by CSII for even better glycemic control.

A major initial concern of families and clinicians related to intensive therapy or CSII was the risk for hypoglycemia. Studies show that CSII is safe and effective in improving glucose levels in children, minimizing hypoglycemia, and improving quality of life. Achieving optimal glucose control using new technologies may delay or prevent future complications. There are numerous high-tech glucose meters and pumps available with computer download capabilities for tracking and monitoring glucose response to diet, insulin, and activity levels. Families of children as young as infants and toddlers, as well as older children and teens, have the option of managing their children's diabetes with either multiple injections or pump therapy.

Evidence-Based Family-Focused Interventions

Family management for pediatric Type 1 diabetes management is an all-encompassing responsibility and involves complex, technological care. Along with the challenges posed at differing developmental levels of children, families are ever evolving in their adaptation to care for their children.

Family-focused studies demonstrate the importance of developmentally appropriate family engagement in diabetes management for optimizing glucose control, ultimately averting acute and chronic complications in youth with diabetes. Family interventions that include greater parental involvement and sharing of responsibilities, improved communication, and conflict resolution through problem-solving approaches result in improved glucose control and no adverse effects on quality of life. For adolescents who have a high risk for poor diabetes management, behavioral family system therapy specific to diabetes management assists in realistic goal setting with behavioral contracting, along with psychoeducational counseling to reveal improvements in self-management, lower family conflict, and better glycemic control.

Evidence-based family-focused interventions provide valuable knowledge for initial and continuing health care services for families of youth with T1DM. Sharing the responsibilities for diabetes management involves a mutual interchange of understanding disease effects and the emotional impact of difficulties in glucose control during certain stages of growth and development. Strong evidence from family-focused interventions supports the value of multidisciplinary teams to address the medical, social, psychological, nutritional, and educational needs for optimal family management of youth with T1DM.

Melissa Spezia Faulkner

See also Case Management for Chronic Illness/Disability and the Family; Changes in Family Structure; Changes in Family Structure, Roles; Dietary and Exercise Patterns in Families; Educating the Family Regarding Chronic Physical Illness; School Nursing and the Health of Families

Further Readings

Butler, D. A., Zuehlke, J. B., Tovar, A., Volkening, L. K., Anderson, B. J., & Laffel, L. M. B. (2008). The impact of modifiable family factors on glycemic control among youth with Type 1 diabetes. *Pediatric Diabetes, 9*(Pt. 2), 373–381.

Dabelea, D., & Klingensmith, G. J. (Eds.)., (2008). *Epidemiology of pediatric and adolescent diabetes.* New York: Informa Healthcare USA.

Eldeirawl, K., & Lipton, R. B. (2003). Predictors of hemoglobin A1c in a national sample of nondiabetic children: The third National Health and Nutrition Examination Survey, 1988–1994. *American Journal of Epidemiology, 157,* 624–632.

Helgeson, V. S., Reynolds, K. A., Siminerio, L., Escobar, O., & Becker, D. (2008). Parent and adolescent distribution of responsibility for diabetes self-care: Links to health outcomes. *Journal of Pediatric Psychology, 3*(5), 497–508.

Nansel, T. R., Anderson, B. J., Laffel, L.M. B., Simons-Morton, B. G., Weissberg-Benchell, J., Wysocki, T., et al. (2008, August 20). A multisite trial of a clinic-integrated intervention for promoting family management of pediatric Type 1 diabetes: Feasibility and design. *Pediatric Diabetes,10*(2), 105–115. Advance online publication.

Soltesz, G., Patterson, C. C., & Dahlquist, G. (2007). Worldwide childhood Type 1 diabetes incidence: What can we learn from epidemiology. *Pediatric Diabetes, 8*(Suppl. 6), 6–14.

Tamborlane, W. V., Swan, K., Sikes, K. A., Steffen, A. T., & Weinzimer, S. A. (2006). The renaissance of insulin pump therapy in childhood Type 1 diabetes. *Reviews in Endocrine & Metabolic Disorders, 7,* 205–213.

Wysocki, T., Harris, M. A., Buckloh, L. M., Mertlich, D., Lochrie, A. S., Taylor, A., et al. (2008). Randomized, controlled trial of behavioral family systems therapy for diabetes: Maintenance and generalization of effects on parent-adolescent communication. *Behavior Therapy, 39,* 33–46.

Websites

American Diabetes Foundation, For Parents & Kids: http://www.diabetes.org/living-with-diabetes/parents-and-kids

Centers for Disease Control and Prevention, Diabetes Projects: http://www.cdc.gov/diabetes/projects/index.htm

Family Support Network, Children With Diabetes: http://www.childrenwithdiabetes.com

Junior Diabetes Research Foundation International: http://www.jdrf.org

National Diabetes Education Program, Resources on
  Children and Adolescents:
    http://ndep.nih.gov/diabetes/youth/youth.htm

DIABETES, TYPE 2, AND THE FAMILY

Type 2 diabetes, also called adult-onset, late-onset, or non–insulin-dependent diabetes, is a chronic health condition in which one's body does not adequately make or use insulin, resulting in high blood sugar levels. A current problem linked to the prevalence of Type 2 diabetes nationwide is diabetes self-management. Risk factors linked with obesity and sedentary lifestyles are a growing problem for today's families. Diabetes self-management involves a lifelong, complex care regimen, and treatment decisions are challenged by self-care abilities. Although diabetes self-management is largely the responsibility of the person with the disease, it is continuously influenced by routines and behaviors of others in the family household and the larger community context.

The challenges presented in living with diabetes for many years of life are enormous for the person diagnosed and living with the disease. While the diagnosis often rests with a single member of the family, the knowledge, attitudes, beliefs, values, and behaviors of multiple family members greatly alter the ways self-management occurs. It might be argued that this disease is truly a family matter due to family inheritance factors and shared behavioral patterns. Family members' roles are of great consequence, whether the diagnosis is Type 1 or Type 2 diabetes. Therefore, whenever the topic is self-management, the family should be considered the focus of care.

Overview of the Literature

A review of the adherence literature completed 2 decades ago suggested that persons with diabetes are largely nonadherent. In fact, persons with diabetes and their health care providers agree that diabetes management is difficult, and there is substantial evidence that outcomes are frequently less than optimal. Literature about diabetes management largely concentrates on improving diabetes self-management and self-efficacy; however, focus on the individual has largely obscured the fact that families are involved. Diabetes management largely occurs in home settings; thus, family members play critical roles, as they influence chronic disease management.

Diabetes self-management is predominately behavioral and outside health professionals' observation. Lifestyle behaviors are often habituated in ways that makes them difficult to modify, and modifications may be hard to maintain for long time periods. Education is important, but it is often difficult to transfer knowledge into transformed behaviors. Research indicates that knowledge alone will not improve behaviors or increase therapeutic adherence. Self-management involves incorporation of new information or care standards into daily health routines, active participation of the person with the disease, personal motivation, abilities to engage in self-care, and access to needed resources.

Family Routines

Families use patterned behaviors or daily routines to arrange ordinary life and cope with health or illness events. Routines are aspects of families' cultural and ecological context and highlight ways to focus on family processes, individuals, and family dynamics. Sharon A. Denham's family health model suggests that routines are multiple-member activities associated with health, wellness, individual care processes, and disease management. In fact, families use health routines to (a) support health processes; (b) avoid illness, disease, and injuries; (c) attain, sustain, and regain health; (d) communicate with health experts; (e) obtain and distribute family health resources; and (f) construct family health paradigms. A diagnosis of diabetes impacts previously constructed health routines, behaviors that often need to be deconstructed and new ones constructed in accord with best practices for care management and uniquely situated family needs.

A literature review concluded that family interventions targeting illnesses like diabetes require substantial lifestyle changes, and routine activities need family support. Family-focused studies on those with Type 1 diabetes have shown that interventions can be cost-effective, improve hemoglobin A1c results, and produce positive quality of life. Even small lifestyle modifications can delay disease onset, have important implications for therapeutic management, and are important steps in preventing complications that are often life-threatening. Social support has been identified as a critical factor associated with diabetes management and, along with family context, may facilitate or threaten self-care behaviors in Type 2 diabetes. For example, more needs to be known about the ways family members support or threaten dietary routines and constructive ways to agree upon and transform needed behaviors within the family.

Family Support

Many years of literature indicate that investigators have frequently studied ways families support and interact therapeutically with those persons diagnosed with Type 1 diabetes. However, far less attention has been given to those with Type 2 diabetes, and only a paucity of information exists about the ways family members can effectively provide support for self-care regimens. In the past, research largely ignored the influence of family processes on Type 2 diabetes self-management, but studies in the 21st century have focused on the ways marital relationships, family characteristics and family context, and gender influence quality of life and diabetes self-management outcomes. In adults with Type 1 diabetes or Type 2 diabetes, spouses use various forms of support, and these can positively influence nutritional health, food procurement, meal preparation, and shared meal plans. However, negative forms of support, such as critical comments and inabilities to effectively communicate concerns and support, can result in less therapeutic outcomes. Studies of Appalachian families with a member diagnosed with Type 2 diabetes found that gender, culture, family routines, and intergenerational linkages also influenced self-management behaviors.

Diabetes is managed within the context of a family household; thus, it seems imperative that family members know the optimal ways to support and cooperate with members diagnosed with diabetes. Diabetes educators and others are challenged to reframe their practices and teaching methods so that they empower individuals to meet stated concerns, clarify authentic priorities, and operate within the limits of family resources. The need to balance the structure and rigor of complex self-care behaviors and a desire to be autonomous or unencumbered

by self-management tasks are struggles faced by those living with diabetes. Use of an empowerment model that includes several components (e.g., is patient-centered, problem-based, using empirical evidence, culturally relevant, geared toward low health literacy) and uses an integrative process to respond to unique diabetes-related needs has been shown to be successful. More evidence about empowerment interventions is still needed to show how they most effectively work to address individual needs. Empowerment acknowledges that the person with diabetes is central to its management. However, more needs to be learned about the ways empowerment can be used to strengthen family abilities to effectively self-manage the diabetes and, equally important, develop lifestyle patterns that prevent diabetes onset.

Desired Family Health Outcomes

When the problem is diabetes self-management, family members also need knowledge about therapeutic activities. Given that self-management activities occur within a family household and in conjunction with people often sharing similar habits and resources, greater attention needs to be given by care providers to the multilevel member interactions that occur within family households. Developing healthier lifestyles and wellness attitudes not only supports persons with diabetes but also prevents or delays diabetes onset for other family members.

Conclusion

Additional research is needed to answer questions about the ways family supports can enhance the quality of life and self-management outcomes of those living with Type 2 diabetes. Greater attention needs to be given to identification of the factors that characterize supportive family behaviors, the best ways to empower family units to be supportive, and the most cost-effective ways to implement interventions that facilitate family support for self-management activities. Studies also need to explore which family interventions are most efficacious. More needs to be known about the ways families construct, use, and modify family health routines in the family household to address specific self-management. Finally, care providers need to gain a new sensitivity to shift their focus from patient care to a practice of family care if they are going to better address diabetes self-management needs.

Sharon A. Denham

See also Chronic Health Problems and Interventions for the Childrearing Family; Chronic Health Problems and Interventions for the Elderly Family; Chronic Health Problems and Interventions for the Midlife Family; Family Health Maintenance; Family Pediatric Adherence to Health Care Regimen; Family Self-Management

Further Readings

Anderson, R. M., & Funnell, M. M. (2005). Patient empowerment: Reflections on the challenge of fostering the adoption of a new paradigm. *Patient Education and Counseling, 57,* 153–157.

Chesla, C. A., Fisher, L., Skaff, M. M., Mullan, J. T., Gilliss, C. A., & Kanter, R. (2003). Family predictors of disease management over one year in Latino and European American patients with Type 2 diabetes. *Family Process, 42*(3), 375–390.

Denham, S. A. (2003). *Family health: A framework for nursing.* Philadelphia: F. A. Davis.

Denham, S. A., Manoogian, M., & Schuster, L. (2007). Managing family support and dietary routines: Type 2 diabetes in rural Appalachian families. *Families, Systems, & Health, 25*(1), 36–52.

Fiese, B., & Wambolt, F. (2000). Family routines and asthma management: A proposal for family-based strategies to increase treatment adherence. *Family, Systems, & Health, 18,* 405–418.

Fiese, B. H., Tomcho, T. J., Douglas, M., Josephs, K., Poltrock, S., & Baker, T. (2002). A review of 50 years of research on naturally occurring family routines and rituals: Cause for celebration? *Journal of Family Psychology, 16,* 381–390.

Fisher, L., Chesla, C. A., Bartz, R. J., Gilliss, C., Skaff, M. A., Sabogal, F., et al. (1998). The family and Type 2 diabetes: A framework for intervention. *Diabetes Educator, 24,* 599–607.

Fisher, L., Mullen, J. T., Chesla, C. A., Bartz, R. J., Gilliss, C., Skaff, M. A., et al. (2000). The family and disease management in Hispanic and European-American patients with Type 2 diabetes. *Diabetes Care, 23,* 267–272.

Hanson, C. L., DeGuire, M. J., Schinkel, A. M., & Kolterman, O. G. (1995). Empirical validation for a family-centered model of care. *Diabetes Care, 18*(10), 1347–1356.

Manoogian, M. M., Harter, L. M., & Denham, S. A. (2010). The storied nature of health legacies in the familial experience of Type 2 diabetes. *Journal of Family Communication, 10,* 1–17.

Savoka, M., & Miller, C. (2001). Food selection and eating patterns: Themes found among people with Type 2 diabetes. *Journal of Nutrition Education, 33,* 224–233.

Trief, P. M., Britton, K. D., Wade, M. J., & Weinstock, R. S. (2002). A prospective analysis of marital relationship factors and quality of life in diabetes. *Diabetes Care, 25*(7), 1154–1158.

Trief, P. M., Sandberg, J., Greenberg, R. P., Graff, K., Castronova, N., Yoon, M., et al. (2003). Describing support: A qualitative study of couples living with diabetes. *Families, Systems, & Health, 21,* 57–67.

Websites

American Diabetes Association: http://www.diabetes.org

Centers for Disease Control and Prevention, Diabetes Public Health Resource: http://www.cdc.gov/diabetes

DIETARY AND EXERCISE PATTERNS IN FAMILIES

Dietary and exercise patterns in families have become increasingly important to control, as the incidence of overweight and obesity has increased in both adults and children over the past 4 decades. Overweight and obesity are risk factors for the development of Type 2 diabetes and, consequently, cardiovascular disease later in life. Lower income minority families are disproportionately affected. Dietary pattern changes in families include an increased consumption of fast food, calorie-dense foods, sugared beverages, and increased portion sizes. Family exercise patterns have also changed, with decreased exercise and increased sedentary behavior, such as television viewing and computer usage. Improving family dietary and exercise patterns to manage and prevent the development of overweight and obesity—and in turn the development of Type 2 diabetes and cardiovascular disease—is an important public health goal.

The family as the focus of care must be inclusive of all members who are invested in the immediate environment and may include either one or both parents, children, grandparents, aunts, uncles, stepmothers, stepfathers, or stepchildren. It is difficult for individual family members to implement dietary and exercise changes by themselves. The support of the whole family group toward eating healthier and exercising more provides a team approach toward improved health and prevention of disease.

Overview of Current Literature

Family dietary and exercise patterns have worsened over time. Consumption of fast food that is high in calories and saturated fat, coupled with larger portions and sugared drinks, has increased. It is important for adult family members to role model healthy dietary patterns and partner together with their children to eat healthier. Adults have the potential to influence family meals, the type of food provided, and where the food is provided (e.g., at home or in a restaurant).

Decreased exercise and increased sedentary behavior have increased in communities that lack adequate sidewalks or open communal green spaces that are safe for families to gather. It is important that future communities be built to encourage families to walk and play as a part of their everyday activities. Adults have the potential to role model exercise to their children and introduce exercise to children at a young age as part of their daily lives.

Family Health Outcomes

Dietary and exercise patterns in relation to family health outcomes can be examined on several levels. Overall the family is viewed as a single unit working together toward improved health outcomes. Families can include a wide variety of individuals, a fact that brings to light the importance of knowing which family members are participating and the developmental stage of the children within the family. The relationships among family members must be assessed and the impact of nutrition and exercise patterns evaluated individually and as a family. Single-parent families will have different needs than families with two parents. Adolescents, middle school age, elementary age, preschoolers, and infants all have different developmental needs, dietary intake, and exercise patterns, and all must be approached with a program that will meet their needs.

A step toward improvement in family dietary patterns includes assessment and measurement of dietary intake, including caloric density, saturated fat intake, sugared beverage intake, portions of fruits and vegetables per day, and number of fast food meals eaten per week. Measurements may include food diaries and various food frequency intake questionnaires.

Improvement in family exercise patterns includes assessment of increased exercise and decreased sedentary behaviors. Adults and children should be encouraged to get 60 minutes of exercise each day. Children enjoy exercise that is introduced in the context of play. Therefore, families should be encouraged to work together to increase exercise and play. Measurements may include pedometer readings and logbooks, Actical measurement, and various questionnaires that measure the frequency, intensity, time, and type of exercise.

Recommendations for Intervention Programs

Families can improve dietary patterns by preparing and eating more meals at home, limiting consumption of sugared beverages, and providing appropriate portion sizes. Preparing more meals at home allows families to offer a variety of vegetables and fruit and establish healthy habits of eating at least five servings a day. If families eat out, the following may help them improve their dietary patterns: Choose those restaurants that offer healthy choices and limit eating outside the home to once a week, avoid all-you-can-eat buffets and large portion meals, and share meals or take home part of the meal for lunch. Families can also offer water as a standard beverage and limit sugared beverages to an occasional moderate portion size serving. All family members above 2 years of age should drink low-fat milk; fruit juice should be limited to one serving a day. Portion sizes should be appropriate for the family member's age and activity level. Second servings of vegetables and fruit are encouraged. Family members should only eat when hungry and stop eating when full. Families should turn off the television while eating meals and sit at the table together.

Families can improve exercise patterns by encouraging all family members to increase exercise and decrease sedentary behaviors. Planning special weekend activities such as walking, hiking, biking, or swimming provides a strong foundation for all family members to participate in activities that are fun and enjoyable. Encouraging family members to get involved in active community events provides another way to increase exercise behaviors. Limiting television and computers to common areas of the home decreases usage.

The ultimate goal of improved family dietary and exercise patterns is to prevent the development of overweight and obesity, thereby decreasing the incidence and prevalence of Type 2 diabetes and, consequently, cardiovascular disease later in life.

Diane Berry

See also Diabetes, Type 2, and the Family; Exercise Promotion and Fitness; Obesity, Weight Problems, and Healthy Weight for Families

Further Readings

American Diabetes Association. (2008). Clinical practice recommendations 2008. *Diabetes Care, 31,* S1–S110.

American Heart Association. (2008). *Heart disease and stroke statistics, 2008 update.* Dallas, TX: American Heart Association.

Harper, M. G. (2006). Childhood obesity: Strategies for prevention. *Family and Community Health, 29,* 288–298.

DISABILITIES AND FAMILY MANAGEMENT

Disability can be understood as the experience of a limitation in one's ability to do the things other people of the same age can do. The 2000 U.S. Census counted more than 41 million children and adults in the United States as chronically disabled. These individuals are limited by the way their bodies function, the way they are able to carry out activities, or in the way they are able to fulfill social roles and participate in life events. The medical model of disability highlights the importance of diseases and individual consequences. In contrast, the social model rejects the idea that disability is an individual characteristic and postulates that if the physical world was fully accessible and society's attitudes were accepting, the experience of disability would not exist. Most scholars, health professionals, and people with disabilities understand disability to be an interaction between the individual and his or her environment. This biopsychosocial model of disability is used by the World Health Organization (WHO) and is the basis of their International Classification of Functioning. Because each person's and every family's experience with disability is unique, the biopsychosocial model of disability is an appropriate framework for understanding how families experience disability. This entry provides historical and current perspectives of disability and the family.

History

The number of people living with disabilities is on the rise. This situation can be attributed to major improvements in public health and medical treatment. The social history of disability has also changed over time. Up until the late 19th century, childhood disability was believed to be related to the sins of the parents. A disabled child was the burden to bear for breaking social and moral codes. Acquired disability later in life was thought to be the punishment for not leading a good and moral life. As medical science blossomed, the etiologies of the conditions associated with disability were described. Still, the stigma of disability was quite pronounced. Until the disability rights movement took hold in the mid to late 20th century, families were encouraged to institutionalize their children with disabilities. In general, individuals with disabilities were excluded from daily life and felt to be a burden on society. In recent decades, policies and social views about disability have shifted. There are now expressed goals and policies to foster community living and participation for all individuals with disabilities. The shift from institutionalization to community living has served to increase demands on families. Now essentially all children with disabilities are living with their families, and a majority of adults live with their families of origin or with spouses.

Family Functioning and Management

The ways in which families function after a baby is born with a disabling condition or someone in the family develops a disability vary considerably. Families report both positive and negative impacts of caring for a family member with a disability. Some of the typically identified positive impacts are improved self-esteem, resilience, and enhanced advocacy skills. Some of the negative consequences include caregiver stress, loss of employment, financial burden, and social isolation. Many studies identify the added work of caring for someone with a disability. This work includes daily care and assistance; advocating for and arranging health, school, and community services; balancing the needs of the family; and planning for the long-term needs of the individual with the disability.

There are a multitude of factors that can contribute to how families function. Just as disability is understood as the interaction of the individual with his or her environment, the effects on families should be understood as the interaction of the family with factors in their environment. These factors can be conceptualized as occurring at the levels of the individual with the disability, the family, the community, and society. For example, at the level of the individual, the type and severity of the disability contribute to how families are affected. At the family level, a family's cohesiveness and stability affect how they are able to adapt and function with increased care needs. Research investigating the importance of community-based supports clearly indicates that access to community resources positively affects how families function by providing external sources of support. At the society level, laws, policies, and social acceptance all interact with families' experiences and contribute to how families provide care.

Families manage their lives in a variety of different ways. Dealing with stressful situations and unexpected events is a normal part of family life. For many families caring for a child or an adult with a disability, the dominant way of managing and understanding their lives is through a process of normalization. Families see their daily routines and experiences through a lens of normalcy and therefore engage in activities that are consistent with their assessment of themselves as normal. Families incorporate the extra caregiving activities into their lives and adapt to challenges as they arise. Kathleen Knafl and colleagues described five basic family management styles of families raising a child with chronic health problems: thriving, accommodating, enduring, struggling, and floundering. These patterns of family management reflect a continuum of difficulty. Families who are thriving or accommodating tend to see the world through a normalcy lens. On the other end of the

spectrum, families who are struggling or floundering tend to experience their situations as burdensome and tragic and identify them as such. In all cases, family management techniques may become more or less successful as situations and impacting factors change over time. Families also adjust and alter their management styles in response to various influences.

Families of children with disabilities want for their children to be as happy and healthy as possible. In addition, other family members should be able to enjoy life to the fullest. Participation in life events is a goal for children with disabilities and their families. Families should actively work toward balancing their lives to incorporate all aspects of life that help them to be successful, happy, and healthy. Families may need to get assistance from community agencies, mental health professionals, and support groups to optimize their situations. Some families may need financial assistance, whereas others might need respite care or emotional support. Needing extra help or assistance is common because raising a child with disabilities is often more complex and time-consuming than raising typically developing children. If a family is struggling, they should express their concerns to their physician, social worker, or community agency representative. Once a problem is identified, the family and health and community support agencies can work together to improve the situation. Identifying resources in the community can often offset some of the negative impacts associated with caring for a child with a disability.

Conclusion

Disability is a universal experience. How individuals and families function depends on a wide array of factors. Some of these factors are intrinsic to the individual with the disability and his or her family, whereas other factors are extrinsic. When working with families, it is important to remember that they are providing extraordinary amounts of care that make it possible for individuals with disabilities to live successfully at home. Providing services that address the needs of the individuals with disabilities and their families is essential to promote the well-being of families.

Amy Houtrow

See also Adult Child With Disability: Planning for by Parents; Adult With Disability Living at Home; Americans with Disabilities Act and the Family; Birth Defects and the Family; Caregiving: Adults With Developmental Disabilities; Community Resources for Families Related to Health; Coping Management Styles in Families; Families Experiencing Chronic Physical and Mental Health Conditions; Health Management in Families

Further Readings

Deatrick, J. A., Knafl, K. A., & Murphy-Moore, C. (1999). Clarifying the concept of normalization. *Journal of Nursing Scholarship, 31,* 209–214.

Knafl, K. A., & Deatrick, J. A. (2003). Further refinement of the family management style framework. *Journal of Family Nursing, 9,* 232–256.

Simeonsson, R. J., Scarborough, A. A., & Hebbeler, K. M. (2006). ICF and ICD codes provide a standard language of disability in young children. *Journal of Clinical Epidemiology, 59,* 365–373.

Discharge Teaching for Families Taking a Family Member Home From an Acute Care Setting

The discharge of an individual from an acute care setting concludes a teaching process that begins early in the individual's hospital visit. Evolving technology and health care cost containment have resulted in many patients receiving only stabilization of their health care need within an acute care setting. Health care needs are subsequently continued in either a subacute setting (e.g., a skilled nursing facility or a rehabilitation facility) or a home setting with assistance from home health nurses, other caregivers, or both. Due to shorter lengths of stay in acute care, the patient's ability to participate in discharge teaching may be compromised. The family assumes an increasingly important role as the individual leaves the support of the acute setting. Family members placed in the role of caregivers must be carefully educated prior to assuming the extended role of health care provider; otherwise, the care of the individual may be at risk. Such education of the family member often requires extensive prior planning and preparation.

This entry begins with a description of the concerns the family of the discharged patient may have. Next, the entry examines the background, current literature, and desired family outcomes. The entry ends with a discussion of future interventions for effective discharge teaching.

Concerns of the Discharged Family Following a Period of Acute Care

The discharge of a patient from an acute setting removes the support provided by many health care disciplines and may be accompanied by life-changing events in the family. The term *discharge* suggests an "end" to treatment when, in reality, the discharge is part of a continuum of health care. The individual may no longer be able to function in the same roles previously maintained in the family and may transition, oftentimes with minimal warning, from an independent to a dependent family member. The discharge may also begin an exciting journey for the family with the addition of a new family member; however, this also may represent significant redefinition of family roles and present unanticipated stressors. As the complexity of each patient need increases, so does the time and subject matter for discharge teaching. Families of patients discharged from acute care are taught a wide range of skills, from simple activities of daily living to suctioning of tracheostomies, enteral feeding management, or care of a patient with a home ventilator. The family may be preparing for a lifetime of care of a special needs infant or end-of-life care for a dying family member or for any type of health care need in between. The opportunities to work with the family and prepare them for the health care needs of the individual, and for changes to the family roles, will occur throughout the acute treatment period. Effective preparation of the family for the discharge from acute care requires planning to begin at the time of admission. The effectiveness of their preparation not only facilitates a smooth transition to the home setting but may also prevent serious health risks in the future.

Background

Discharge planning from inpatient acute care is mandated in the United States for all patients treated in hospitals that receive Medicare or Medicaid funding. The discharge plan requirement includes counseling of the patient and family members or interested persons to ensure they are prepared for the provision of care after the discharge. Discharge teaching is a key component of an effective discharge plan, which prepares the patient and their caregiver to safely meet the psychosocial and physical needs of the patient as they transition from acute care. Although discharge planning is required in most U.S. hospitals, the absence of a standardized approach to discharge teaching results in wide variations of the process and outcomes. Discharge teaching is also affected by shortages of health care professionals, shorter hospital stays, and the hurried pace of the staff providing care to the patient. The critically important role of preparing the patient and the family for care in the next setting is easily pushed aside as other urgent acute care needs are addressed. Consequently, patients and their families may fail to receive the levels of preparation needed to ensure a smooth transition of care.

Overview of the Current Literature

Theoretical frameworks for discharge teaching interventions are interdisciplinary, with foundations in clinical psychology, developmental psychology, sociology, social psychology, change theory, and adult learning theories. An updated Cochrane Review of discharge planning from hospital to home for the year 2010 identified that individualized discharge planning does reduce hospital length of stay or readmissions, and the impact on mortality, health outcomes, and cost were not clear. A 2003 Cochrane Review compared verbal and written instructions for patients at discharge with verbal instructions only. The findings from this review recommended the combined method of written and verbal instruction with parents of discharged children; however, there were not adequate studies comparing the two methods with adults to reach a conclusion for all ages.

Readmissions

The cost for inpatient care in the United States represents the largest area of health care spending for the elderly. The lack of consistency in discharge processes creates knowledge gaps relating to the continuum of care for patients, which contribute to emergency department visits, unplanned readmissions, and adverse events such as errors with taking home medications. Readmissions to acute care within 30 days of discharge are estimated to cost $17.4 billion in the United States annually. Standardized approaches to discharge assessment and teaching, both with individuals and their family caregivers, reduce emergency department visits and readmissions to acute care. However, such interventions require approximately 2 hours per discharge in preparation and teaching time and often become an area of shortcuts for an already stressed health care delivery system. The Patient Protection and Affordable Care Act, signed into law by President Barack Obama on March 23, 2010, addresses the issues of readmissions by enacting penalties for early readmissions for the same diagnosis, which is anticipated to place an increased focus (and incentive) on the need to adequately prepare patients and their family members to provide care following discharge.

The American College of Cardiology and the Institute for Healthcare Improvement introduced a targeted national joint initiative, Hospital to Home (H2H), to reduce readmission rates of patients discharged with heart failure or acute myocardial infarction by 20%. Heart failure is the most common reason for the readmission of Medicare patients within 30 days of discharge. The focus of H2H is to ensure patients understand medications and have access to them at discharge, have a follow-up appointment and have access to the appointment, and understand the signs and symptoms that require medical attention and who to contact. The nationwide initiative will develop and share best practices for improving the transition of discharge patients from acute care to their home.

Medication Reconciliation

Medications continue to create challenges for both admission and discharge in acute health care settings. An ever-increasing number of patients, both inpatient and outpatient, are now taking daily medications. Many of the daily medications require complex coordination. Medication reconciliation, a balancing of the medications the patient was taking when they were admitted for acute care with the medications ordered at discharge, continues to elude physicians, pharmacists, and nurses across the country. Many patients are unable to identify the medications they take at home, provide incorrect or incomplete medication records when admitted for acute care, and are further confused with new prescriptions and directions to add or discontinue medications at discharge. Further contributing to the challenge of ensuring safe medication administration after discharge is the difficulty an estimated 20% of patients have obtaining the discharge medications within 48 hours of discharge. Unfortunately, such confusion contributes to emergency visits as well as readmissions for adverse events secondary to failed or mismanaged treatment plans. Several facilities have successfully utilized pharmacy contact with the patient or their family member within 1 to 4 days of discharge to review medications and ensure medications were obtained and were being taken appropriately. Patient understanding was also enhanced at one facility by using a card with space for the patient to attach a pill with the instructions and side effects for each medication. The card provided a three-dimensional example of the directions for home medication administration.

Family Caregiver Burden

It is estimated in the United States that 46 million informal family caregivers provide assistance to those with chronic health care needs, including the provision of 80% of the long-term care. Caregivers often continue to stay with the patient during periods of acute hospitalization. Satisfaction with discharge teaching may be lower with the longer involved family caregiver than with the family member of the newly diagnosed patient. Although the reason for the satisfaction difference was not measured, differences were thought to relate to perceptions of experienced caregivers that their instruction was incomplete because of an assumption of prior knowledge. Caregiver burden can be associated with fatigue, depression, and lifestyle disruption.

Targeted Disease Teaching

As individualized discharge teaching plans are developed, a need evolves to focus beyond general categories such as caregiver needs and medication administration to areas that are disease specific. With continued evolution of national disease management guidelines, health care providers responsible for patient education at discharge are challenged to ensure the education provided is current and complete. There are multiple evidence-based disease-specific resources available from professional organizations that may be utilized for discharge teaching. A few of the unique findings related to discharge teaching are discussed in this section.

The transfer of stroke patients from the hospital to the home is stressful and creates fear for the patient and their family members. The National Stroke Association reports only 55% of stroke patients understand the information they receive in the hospital, 43% are not given information about dietary changes, 1 in 3 are not given information about physical activity, and 21% do not receive information about the purpose of their home medications.

Although wide variance is found in asthmatic individuals' understanding of their disease processes, barriers can be diminished with patient education that identifies the patient's level of understanding and targets education to begin at the appropriate level. With chronic diseases such as asthma, an incorrect assumption is sometimes made that patients and caregivers have a higher level of understanding of the disease process than is present. Ensuring appropriate use of asthma medication inhalers through return demonstration, in addition to written and oral instruction, should be included in discharge teaching.

Less than half of patients who have had an acute myocardial infarction (AMI) are able to correctly name their diagnosis after hospital discharge, although most stated the treatment involved something related to their heart. When AMI patients are asked after discharge to describe a risk factor contributing to heart disease, only 10% identify physical inactivity, 14% mention obesity, 22% mention hypertension, 27% mention cholesterol, and 33% mention smoking. In a more structured approach, the importance of discharge teaching was validated with a mortality reduction of 6% for Medicare patients who completed and signed a guideline-based contract for compliance with medications, smoking cessation, diet, physician follow-up, and continuing cardiac education after treatment for AMI.

Benefits of discharge teaching are not limited to the needs of adult patients. Dramatic reduction of incidents of shaken baby syndrome (SBS), one of the tragic forms of child abuse, were found to occur with a simple combination of video education, training cards, posters, and discussion at the time of newborn discharges. Although many parents expressed prior knowledge of SBS, the program appears to provide a knowledge boost that assists in protecting infants during the high-risk period.

Desired Family Health Outcomes

Goals of discharge teaching interventions with patients and their caregiver are to reduce the fear associated with the transition from acute care to the next level of care, identify and prepare for role changes within the family, and ensure an understanding of the treatment plan and follow-up associated with ongoing health care needs. Through effective discharge teaching, emergency department visits, acute care readmissions, and adverse events will also be reduced.

A Foundation for Future Interventions

Effective discharge teaching must begin at the time of the acute care admission, reflect an assessment of the knowledge level, and be designed for the adult learner. There is significant literature available on the assumptions of adult learning, andragogy. Andragogy finds its roots in the early work of the 19th-century teacher, Alexander Kapp, and evolved over the next century. The assumptions of andragogy described by Malcolm Knowles, Elwood Holton, and Richard Swanson are that adults (a) need to know why they should learn something before they will learn it, (b) must be helped to evolve to be self-directed learners, (c) bring with them sets of experiences that provide references for learning, (d) need to have a readiness to learn, (e) need to see how learning applies to their life, and (f) respond to internal motivators such as self-esteem and improved quality of life. How the

patient or the family member learns the information necessary for a safe discharge from acute care will be influenced by subject-matter differences, situational differences, and individual differences.

The individual's literacy level must be considered in planning discharge teaching. The American Medical Association has prepared a health literacy kit, which includes information identifying the methods for assessment of patient literacy needs. Modalities such as video, web-based instruction, or computerized interactive components should be utilized for teaching, depending on how the individual most effectively learns new content. After discharge teaching has been completed, there should be planned follow-up to ensure understanding, knowledge retention, and compliance.

An estimated 20% of hospital discharges are readmitted within 30 days of discharge. The term *noncompliant patient* is used to refer to patients who failed to follow the discharge plan. There may be many reasons the plan was not followed, including failure at the time of discharge teaching to ensure the patient learned the content and understood how to acquire the needed resources to implement the plan. To enhance learning and potentially reduce the risk of noncompliance, the assumptions of adult learning must be woven into the teaching plan. Additionally, questions must be addressed during the education process to ensure the patient has the resources and capacity for compliance. It is not enough to ensure patients can demonstrate how to measure their blood glucose; do they know how to obtain the needed supplies or how they will have the supplies transported to their home if they are unable to drive? When referred to assistance programs for low-cost medications, do they have the skills needed to complete required forms? Are there language or literacy barriers that prevent them from understanding written instructions? One third of patients discharged from an emergency setting lack full comprehension of their post-discharge care instructions even though most do not perceive that they do not comprehend the instructions. Assumptions related to noncompliance may prevent health care providers from asking probing questions that reveal the true barriers to achieve compliance.

In some circumstances, during the course of discharge teaching it may become evident that the patient and his or her family caregiver will not be able to accomplish a safe discharge. The concern may evolve from the inability of the patient and family member to master needed skills or may be influenced by caregiver burnout. In the event discharge teaching reveals that the individual and family caregiver are unable to safely carry out the discharge plan, a team conference of health care providers, the patient, and the family caregiver must determine a safe discharge path, a sometimes difficult discussion of realities of individual limits and needs. An important component of discharge teaching is not only conveying information but ensuring the information is understood and within the capacity of the individuals.

In summary, effective discharge teaching of the patient and the family caregiver can reduce emergency department visits and readmissions to acute care. A systematic approach should be utilized for planning for discharge needs using assumptions from adult learning theories and based on an assessment of the individual needs of the patient and the family caregiver. The utilization of multimedia teaching approaches, including written, visual, and follow-up evaluation, is needed to ensure patient or caregiver understanding. Many national organizations provide up-to-date patient education materials, which may be used as a resource for building individualized teaching programs. Future research is needed to evaluate the effective use of technology for discharge teaching, including computerized medication reconciliation software, closed circuit patient education programs, and computerized programs for patient teaching.

Wilma Powell Stuart

See also Acute Care/Hospitalization of Family Members; Caregivers of Adults With Developmental Disabilities; Caregiving: Elderly; Caregiving: Infants; Hospitalization and Family Presence; Partnering With Families: Family-Centered Care

Further Readings

Dias, M., Smith, K., deGuehery, K., Mazur, P., Li, V., & Shaffer, M. (2005). Preventing abusive head trauma among infants and young children: A hospital-based, parent education program. *Pediatrics, 115*(4), e470–e477. Retrieved from www.pediatrics.org/cgi/doi/10.1542/peds.2004-1896

Engel, K., Heisler, M., Smith, D., Robinson, C., Forman, J., & Ubel, P. (2009). Patient comprehension of emergency department care and instructions: Are patients aware of when they do not understand? *Annals of Emergency Medicine, 53*(4), 454–461.

Fitzpatrick, M., & Dawber, S. (2008). Best practice in management of stroke: Effective transfer of care from hospital to community. *British Journal of Neuroscience Nursing, 12*(4), 582–587.

Jack, B., Chetty, V., Anthony, D., Greenwald, J., Sanchez, G., Johnson, A., et al. (2009). A reengineered hospital discharge program to decrease rehospitalization. *Annals of Internal Medicine, 150*(3), 178–187.

Johnson & Johnson Caregiver Initiative. (n.d.). *Family caregiving in America: Facts at a glance.* Retrieved April 9, 2010, from http://www.strengthforcaring.com/util/press/facts/facts-at-a-glance.html

Knowles, M., Holton, E., & Swanson, R. (2005). *The adult learner.* San Diego, CA: Elsevier.

Manning, D., O'Meara, J., Williams, A., Rahman, A., Tammel, K., Myhre, D., et al. (2007). 3D: A tool for medication discharge education. *Quality & Safety in Health Care, 16,* 71–76.

Paasche-Orlw, M., Riekert, K., Bilderback, A., Chanmugam, A., Hill, P., Rand, C., et al. (2005). Tailored education may reduce health literacy disparities in asthma self-management. *American Journal of Respiratory and Critical Care Medicine, 172,* 980–986.

Shepperd, S., McClaran J., Phillips, C., Lannin, N., Clemson, I., McCluskey, A., et al. (2010). Discharge planning from hospital to home. *Cochrane Database of Systematic Reviews, 1,* Article No. CD000313.

DIVORCE: EFFECT ON CHILDREN OR THE FAMILY

Around one third of first marriages in the United States will end in divorce within 10 years. Subsequent marriages dissolve more rapidly and at a higher rate. Consequently, roughly 1 million children experience parental divorce each year (i.e., married parents legally divorcing). In response to several decades of high divorce rates, the effect of divorce on children has emerged as a highly researched topic among social scientists. Although researchers generally have found an increased risk for negative emotional and behavioral outcomes for children whose parents have divorced, the effect of other family factors must be considered, including whether or not children whose parents divorced would have experienced the same negative outcomes had their parents remained married.

Historical Context

The legal concept of divorce can be documented as far back as the early 1100s in England and has always been present in the United States. Divorce rates in the United States remained fairly low until the early 1900s and then rose steadily from around 1910 until the 1990s, peaking at about a 50% divorce rate before stabilizing and then slightly declining (i.e., to roughly a 43% divorce rate).

In the early 1970s, scholars began to conceptualize divorce as a multicomponent process rather than an event, with most identifying the "parental divorce" as the most difficult, stressful aspect of the process. Previously, the underlying assumption was that after the divorce had been legally finalized, people healed and moved on. Conceptualizing divorce as a process, however, meant that scholars began to examine more carefully how parents and especially children fared pre- and post-divorce. These studies of divorce were traditionally valueladen, and early attempts tended to simplify and attribute outcomes to one variable explanation (e.g., divorce causes). It is now known that divorce and divorce outcomes are highly complex.

Outcomes for Children With Divorced Parents

The stress of the initial separation, pre- and post-divorce interparental conflict, environmental factors, and changes in the family system were all found to affect children's adjustment. Although researchers have disagreed on the length and severity of these effects, they have generally agreed there is a higher risk for a variety of problems among children whose parents have divorced compared to children from never-divorced families. But, even though these differences may be statistically significant, the magnitude of the differences is small. That is, most children whose parents have divorced are as well-adjusted as children with continuously married parents.

Nonetheless, experiencing their parents' divorce may heighten some children's later vulnerability to stress-related physical illnesses. Emerging research suggests that caregiving risk factors (e.g., exposure to high conflict, parental divorce) could be associated with dysregulations in children's physiological stress responses, which could contribute to later brain and body pathophysiology as well as illness (e.g., hypertension, heart disease) and perceived health (e.g., self-reported somatic symptoms, days sick, health care visits). It appears that for some adults (both those with continuously married parents and those with divorced parents), parental responsiveness and contact, as well as exposure to parental conflict, correlate with later physical health. Overall, for children with divorced parents, poor father–child relationships and higher distress associated with the divorce appear linked to poorer health status as adults. This line of research is still developing, as most of the research on divorce effects has focused on psychological and behavioral outcomes.

Divorce may heighten children's risk for internalizing problems, such as depression and anxiety. These problems, however, appear to be more related to the presence of continued parental conflict than to divorce itself. For both children and adolescents, internalizing problems tend to be greater in the initial adjustment period following divorce and then lessen or disappear within 1 or 2 years post-divorce. Children's post-divorce adjustment heavily depends on parents' ability to cooperatively coparent, and although some coparenting relationships may be difficult initially, most (80% or more) improve over time. In fact, young adult children with low-conflict divorced parents are less likely than children with high-conflict, continuously married parents to feel caught between parents or experience lower well-being.

Parental divorce has often been associated with externalizing problems, including antisocial behavior, negative school conduct, and delinquency in both children and adolescents, although the risk is diminished by parent–child closeness and nurturance. There is some evidence that divorce-related externalizing problems are more pronounced for boys than girls, though some researchers argue that boys, in general, exhibit more externalizing problems than girls. Overall, it appears that marital conflict and weakened family systems prior to divorce are more likely determinates of child externalizing problems than is divorce itself.

Finally, the experience of parental divorce seems to increase the likelihood that children whose parents have divorced will have problems in their later intimate relationships. Adolescents and young adults with divorced parents may have an increased risk of having (or perceiving to have) deficits in communication, problem-solving, and relationship skills. Some also may hold more negative views on marriage, have higher conflict in their own marriages, and be more likely to divorce than are individuals from never-divorced families of origin, but certain protective factors, such as lowered parental conflict resultant of a divorce or the occurrence of positive parental remarriage, can reduce the chances for these negative outcomes.

Clearly, there is consistent evidence that divorce increases the risk of problematic outcomes for children. The stressors associated with divorce can be many, including economic stress, diminished relationships with nonresidential parents, and complex interactions of these stressors. Other variables, such as child age at divorce, can present difficulties for children's adjustment. In general, it appears that children suffer the most psychological distress following divorce when they experience chronic interparental conflict between their mothers and fathers. Conversely, children generally have less risk when contact with both parents is maintained; children, siblings, and their parents enjoy shared activities; and parents practice positive coparenting.

It is inappropriate to minimize the pain and stress children may encounter associated with their parents' divorce. Some clearly experience long-term negative effects from their parents' divorce. However, it is important to note that resilience appears to be the normative outcome for children after divorce, and a vast majority of these children end up falling into normal ranges for psychological and cognitive functioning.

Marilyn Coleman and Graham McCaulley

See also Changes in Family Structure; Coparenting: Children; Divorce and Child Custody; Family Conflict Related to Caregiving; Roles and Functions of Families: Divorce

Further Readings

Amato, P. R. (2001). Children of divorce in the 1990s: An update of the Amato and Keith (1991) meta-analysis. *Journal of Family Psychology, 15,* 355–370.

Emery, R. E. (1999). *Marriage, divorce, and children's adjustment.* Thousand Oaks, CA: Sage.

Kelly, J. B., & Emery, R. E. (2003). Children's adjustment following divorce: Risk and resilience perspectives. *Family Relations, 52,* 352–362.

DIVORCE: LOSS OF FAMILY MEMBERS

This entry focuses on divorce within the conceptual frameworks of family systems theory and the emotional losses engendered when family members part. Emotional loss occurs as the extended family system is divided by divorce into multiple and separate family systems, each characterized by the loss of contact and relationships with members of the original extended family. Emotional loss, in turn, is viewed as a psychological stressor linked to a host of negative health and psychological outcomes—particularly pervasive sadness and depression.

Family Systems Theory and Loss

The core tenet of family systems theory is that families are an interrelated and interdependent system wherein any change in one element of the system necessarily causes changes and consequences in the balance of the system. Should one or more members leave the family system, such as in divorce, the remaining members of the system experience varying degrees of emotional loss. The losses for the principle members of the extended family system follow.

Grandparents of Divorce

In family law, grandparents in most states have no inherent rights to have contact with their grandchildren. Thus, in divorce, maternal grandparents have the least to lose as long as they maintain a good relationship with their daughters, as mothers are granted physical custody of children in about

85% of the cases. By contrast, paternal grandparents have a great deal to lose in divorce. They frequently lose contact with their grandchildren as family law and the family courts relegate their son to the peripheral position of "visitor" in their grandchildren's lives. Further, their son also may require emotional and financial support from them. Paternal grandparents thus usually have even less contact with their grandchildren than do their sons. Many paternal grandparents further view these losses as unfair and harmful both to themselves and to their grandchildren. Emotionally, they may feel that they have lost a long yearned-for relationship with their grandchildren that they have little hope of regaining. Although there are clear trends that joint legal custody has been increasing across states, physical custody—because the amount of time spent with each parent influences child support—has not followed suit.

Parents of Divorce

Divorces are initiated by wives about 70% to 80% of the time. Some divorcées are pleased with their decision. For others, however, the emotional loss of the man they chose to marry and their chosen lifestyle of a single (or cohabiting or remarried) mother turns out to be more stressful and lonely than their previous marital lifestyle.

For divorced fathers, however, the loss of their children generally has a powerful negative emotional impact. Fathers of divorce, as compared to mothers of divorce, are higher on all indices of occupational, social, and personal distress. Perhaps most telling, and as a striking index of pervasive sadness and depression, divorced fathers commit suicide 8 to 10 times more frequently than divorced mothers.

Second Wives of Divorce

Second wives are women who marry a divorced father. They also may experience loss of their own dreams and aspirations for a good, happy, and fulfilled family life due to challenges posed by family law and family courts. This unanticipated loss occurs because now the second wife, as well as the divorced father, have to deal with child emotional loss and excessive child-support financial loss. The divorced father's emotional and financial losses become the second wife's emotional and financial losses.

Children of Divorce

Family court judges are expected to rule in favor of "the best interest of the child." However, children of divorce frequently perceive judges as ruling in favor of the best interests of the mother rather than in their own best interests, according to the research of Gordon E. Finley and others.

Children of divorce predominantly see their "best interests" as being able to maintain a close emotional relationship with their fathers. In one study, more than 70% of young adults chose equal shared parenting as the best post-divorce family structure. Another national survey showed that divorce does no harm to the mother–child relationship but marginalizes or severs the father–child relationship. Finally, recent research shows that fathers have a more powerful impact on reducing high-risk behaviors in young adults than do mothers.

Conclusions on Divorce and Loss

Divorce leads to emotional losses for all members of the original extended family system. The fewest losses are experienced by mothers and maternal grandparents. The greatest losses are experienced by the children and fathers of divorce along with paternal grandparents and second wives. Emotional losses are harmful negative feelings that have real-life consequences for individuals and for society. For individuals they lead to stress and a host of high-risk behaviors. For society they lead to financial and social costs.

Social science researchers have suggested three major social changes to reduce the loss associated with divorce and its concomitant health and psychological consequences. First, divorce rates need to be reduced. Among the interventions in the literature to accomplish this are publicizing the negative consequences of divorce with the goal of changing social attitudes regarding divorce, increasing the availability of family counseling, eliminating incentives in current divorce law that advantage mothers and thus encourage them to initiate divorce, and reconceptualizing how the law and the social sciences can work together to resolve family disputes.

Second, social science research increasingly has come to support equal shared parenting and financial responsibility as the optimal post-divorce family form. Joint legal custody has been increasing, and the children of divorce would benefit further were joint physical custody also to increase.

Third and finally, to attenuate the losses of family members that exist in divorce law today, family court judges should adopt the high standards of the U.S. Supreme Court—"Equal Justice Under Law"—and rule in favor of equal justice for all members of the extended family system.

Gordon E. Finley

See also Asynchronous Development Between Partners; Changes in Family Structure, Roles; Divorce: Effect on Children or the Family; Divorce and Child Custody; Roles and Functions of Families: Divorce

Further Readings

Finley, G. E. (2006). The myth of the good divorce. [Review of the book *Between Two Worlds: The Inner Lives of the Children of Divorce*]. *PsycCRITIQUES—Contemporary Psychology: APA Review of Books, 51*(35), Article 17. Retrieved from http://psycnet.apa .org/critiques/51/35/17.html

Finley, G. E., & Schwartz, S. J. (2007). Father involvement and long-term young adult outcomes: The differential contributions of divorce and gender. *Family Court Review, 45*(4), 573–587.

Finley, G. E., & Schwartz, S. J. (2010). The divided world of the child: Divorce and long-term psychosocial adjustment. *Family Court Review, 48*(3), 516–527.

Holtzworth-Munroe, A. (Ed.). (2009). For the sake of the children: Collaborations between law and social science to advance the field of family dispute resolution [Special issue]. *Family Court Review, 47*(3).

Ng, K.-M., & Smith, S. D. (2006). The relationships between attachment theory and intergenerational systems theory. *Family Journal: Counseling and Therapy for Couples and Families, 14*, 430–440.

Divorce and Child Custody

Although the rates of divorce have remained steady in the United States for nearly 2 decades, divorce remains a relatively frequent phenomenon for American couples. According to the U.S. Census Bureau, in 2004, nearly 21% of all men and 26% of all women between 35 and 39 years old had been divorced. More than one third of Americans ages 40 to 69 years had been divorced at least once. Not all divorced adults are parents, but many are; in 2007, 25.8% of American children younger than 18 lived with one parent, and 6% lived with a parent and a stepparent. An estimated 16.8% of divorced men and 56.9% of divorced women live with their own minor children. The subsequent arrangements that families make for legal and physical custody and how family members relate to each other before and after divorce have effects on children's physical and mental well-being as well as their access to health care. As post-divorce families reorganize themselves, health professionals need to be cognizant of all participants involved in children's health care management, particularly as it applies to the consistency of care that children receive following parental divorce.

Types of Custody

When parents of minor-age children divorce, one of the major issues is custody of the children. There are two types of custody to be decided—legal and physical. Legal custody refers to the rights and responsibilities parents have to make decisions about children's upbringing. Legal custody involves decision making about children's health care, education, religious training, extracurricular activities, and other dimensions of the children's lives. Courts may assign joint or shared legal custody to both parents, or only one parent may be given the legal rights and obligations about childrearing decisions (i.e., sole legal custody).

Physical custody refers to where a child resides. In joint physical custody arrangements, children spend substantial, though not always equal, amounts of time with both parents. The children's primary residence often remains with one parent, usually the mother if children are young. Joint physical and joint legal custody are not always assigned in tandem; sometimes only one parent has legal custody, but children reside part of the time in both parents' households. In sole physical custody, the child has primary residence with one parent, who generally also has unilateral decision-making power for the child. In such cases, the nonresidential parent may have contact with the child, although the frequency of contact varies considerably.

When state statutes allow joint legal custody, 50% to 90% of parents end up with this arrangement. This is a substantial increase from the early 1990s and reflects changes in how both the legal system and parents perceive the importance of post-divorce coparenting on children's well-being. Although many more mothers than fathers seek and receive sole physical custody, there is some evidence that fathers who legally fight against sole custody for mothers are often successful because of legal biases in favor of joint legal custody. Joint physical custody is rarer than joint legal custody, but there is ample evidence from national surveys that divorced fathers see their children and are more involved with them than divorced fathers were 30 years ago. Between 35% and 60% of children have at least weekly contact with their fathers.

Mental and Physical Health Outcomes

Divorce potentially has negative effects on the health of family members as a result of increased stress surrounding separation and divorce, reductions in income, and, for children, changes in parenting. Divorce increases the stress experienced by family members in many ways: (a) Dividing households may result in relocations to new neighborhoods, new schools, and loss of family routines and rituals; (b) divorce is often accompanied by a loss of social support from friends and extended family; (c) loneliness and other emotional reactions may result, including fear, anxiety, and sadness. Underlying these changes are direct and indirect influences on the health of family members. For example, reduced incomes may result in the loss of health insurance and the inability to afford check-ups and other preventive measures. Moreover, the health of family members may be compromised even before the divorce process began if there was domestic violence, child maltreatment, child neglect, substance abuse, mental illness, or other health-related problems that led to the divorce. Mental and physical health of divorced adults and their children generally is worse than the mental and physical health of individuals in first-marriage families.

Researchers rarely have examined these connections between post-divorce custody arrangements and health. A few studies suggest there are positive effects of nonresidential fathers' involvement with children on the children's physical health and mental well-being, and investigations of cooperative coparenting and warm parental relationships with children contribute to favorable health outcomes. Post-divorce conflict between coparents appears to be a crucial element in predicting children's health and well-being. Unfortunately, despite the trend toward more parental sharing of legal and physical custody, estimates are that up to three fourths of divorced parents experience conflict during coparenting, ranging from inability to work together at all and high conflict to relatively minor differences in opinion about childrearing. Coparental conflict also can make the care of chronically ill children much more difficult.

Because the extent to which parents are able to avoid conflict and cooperate with each other in raising their children is a key factor in children's adjustment and subsequent physical and mental health, the majority of states have statutes that mandate some type of parent education for divorcing parents. These programs have been evaluated to a limited extent, but none of these evaluations had included children's health as an outcome.

Lawrence H. Ganong and Tyler B. Jamison

See also Conflict in Family Life, Role and Management of; Divorce: Effect on Children or the Family; Divorce: Loss of Family Members; Poverty, Children in, and Health Care; Remarriage and Stepfamilies; Roles and Functions of Families: Divorce

Further Readings

Bauserman, R. (2002). Child adjustment in joint-custody versus sole-custody arrangements: A meta-analytic review. *Journal of Family Psychology, 16,* 91–102.

Fabricius, W. V., & Luecken, L. J. (2007). Post-divorce living arrangements, parent conflict, and long-term physical health correlates for children of divorce. *Journal of Family Psychology, 21,* 195–205.

Gayer, D., & Ganong, L. (2006). Family structure and mothers' caregiving of children with cystic fibrosis. *Journal of Family Nursing, 12,* 390–412.

Kelly, J. B. (2006). Children's living arrangements following separation and divorce: Insights from empirical and clinical research. *Family Process, 46,* 35–52.

Kreider, R. M. (2005, February). Number, timing, and duration of marriages and divorces: 2001. *Current Population Reports* (P70–97). Washington, DC: U.S. Census Bureau.

Menning, C. L., & Stewart, S. D. (2008). Nonresident father involvement, social class, and adolescent weight. *Journal of Family Issues, 29,* 1673–1700.

U.S. Census Bureau. (2009). *Marital history for people 15 years and over, by age and sex: 2004.* Retrieved from http://www.census.gov/population/www/socdemo/marr-div/2004detailed_tables.html

U.S. Census Bureau. (2009). *Children/1 by Presence and Type of Parent(s), Race, and Hispanic Origin/2: 2007.* Retrieved from http://www.census.gov/population/www/socdemo/hh-fam/cps2007.html

Down Syndrome and the Family

Down syndrome (DS), the most common genetic cause of intellectual disabilities, affects individuals from all racial and socioeconomic backgrounds. Worldwide, there are more than 1.8 million individuals living with DS; the prevalence of DS varies from 1 out of 600 to 1 out of 1,000 live births depending on factors such as maternal age (which is a significant risk factor for DS), use of prenatal screening and diagnosis, and attitudes about pregnancy termination. DS influences not only the health of the affected individual but also the health of other family members and the family as a whole. Because of the ongoing challenges associated with raising an individual with DS (extra demands on time, effort, and resources, changes in roles and responsibilities, and social stigma), families of individuals with DS generally experience higher levels of stress than families of typically developing individuals. In prior decades it was often assumed that the increased stress would inevitably lead to negative consequences, such as stress-related illnesses, decreased psychological well-being, and family dysfunction. However, there is growing evidence that whereas some individuals and families have difficulty adapting to the increased stress, others adapt successfully and even thrive. This entry includes a brief overview of DS, a description of life with DS in the 21st century, a summary of findings from research on adaptation in families living with DS, and recommendations for how to improve health outcomes for individuals with DS and their families.

Overview of Down Syndrome

The first descriptions of what is now called DS were written in the mid-18th century, with John Langdon publishing the most in-depth physical description of DS in 1866. In 1959, Jerome Lejeune and colleagues discovered that most individuals with DS have an extra copy of chromosome 21 in all their cells. Prenatal screening for DS first became available in the 1970s. Initially it was recommended primarily for women of advanced maternal age (over the age of 35). However, in 2007, the American College of Obstetricians and Gynecologists urged that all women be offered prenatal screening for DS.

DS is a multisystem disorder that produces both structural and functional defects. Although the clinical presentation of DS is complex and variable, all individuals with DS have some level of mental retardation and many have characteristic facial features, such an upward slant to the eyes and a depressed nasal bridge. Health problems experienced by individuals with DS are the same as those that occur in the general population, but individuals with DS are affected more often and more severely with certain health problems than typically developing individuals. For example, the incidence of congenital heart disease in individuals with DS is approximately 45% to 50%, whereas the overall incidence of congenital heart disease in the general population is 0.8%. Other health problems commonly associated with DS include vision and hearing defects, sleep apnea, gastrointestinal abnormalities, leukemia, thyroid disease, and atlantoaxial instability.

Life With Down Syndrome in the 21st Century

Life with DS in the 21st century is very different than it was in prior centuries. For example, the life expectancy for individuals with DS has increased from 9 years in 1929 to at least 50 to 60 years. Moreover, the number of individuals with DS who are leading fulfilling, productive lives continues to grow at a fairly rapid pace. Prior to the 1970s, parents were often encouraged to institutionalize their children with DS because it was assumed that they would have a negative impact on their family, their community, and society. Currently, most children with DS are raised by their families. Furthermore, a waiting list exists for families interested in adopting children with DS.

In the early 1980s, only a minority of children with DS had been taught to read, and most attended segregated special classes. By the early 2000s, most children with DS were being taught to read in integrated classrooms. Many adults with DS are employed, living independently, finding partners, and marrying. Additionally, a growing number have become effective advocates for themselves and others with DS. Factors contributing to these impressive outcomes include greater family involvement in the lives of individuals with DS, changes in societal attitudes regarding the care and treatment of individuals with DS, and general advances in genetics, health care, and nutrition. Unfortunately, not all individuals with DS and their families have access to appropriate health, education, and social support services; this is especially true for minority families and those living in developing countries.

Adaptation in Families Living With Down Syndrome

Findings from existing research suggest that despite experiencing higher levels of stress than families of typically developing individuals, most families living with DS are able to adapt effectively to the ongoing challenges they face. On measures of individual, dyadic, and family functioning, families of individuals with DS are more comparable to, than different from, families of typically developing individuals. Families are more likely to be resilient and thrive if they have fewer demands; appraise the situation as a challenge rather than a tragedy; have adequate individual, family, and community resources; have adequate coping skills; and use an affirming style of problem-solving communication (one that conveys support and caring). Families are more likely to report high levels of psychological well-being and family functioning if they have positive, family-centered relationships with their health care professionals.

Improving Health Outcomes

Individuals with DS need the same age-appropriate preventative care as typically developing individuals. In addition, because of their increased risk for certain congenital abnormalities and diseases, they need additional tests and evaluations (these have been carefully outlined in health care guidelines such as those developed by a number of Down syndrome medical interest groups). Also, most individuals with DS benefit from receiving early intervention (specialized programs and resources that may include occupational, physical, and speech therapy; special education; nutritional and social work support).

Care for individuals with DS needs to be family-centered. Health care professionals need to tailor the plan of care so that it is based on the unique values, beliefs, strengths, resources, and limitations of the family. Also, it is critical that families receive up-to-date, evidence-based information in a timely manner. They also need contact information for DS support groups and community resources. Most importantly, health care professionals need to recognize and value the natural capabilities of families living with DS to endure, survive, and even thrive.

Marcia Van Riper

See also Birth Defects and the Family; Disabilities and Family Management; Family Caregiving: Caring for Children, Adults, and Elders With Developmental Disabilities; Genetics and Family Health; Intellectual Disability in the Family; Resilience in Families With Health Challenges

Further Readings

Cohen, W. I. (Ed.). (1999). Down syndrome health care guidelines. *Down Syndrome Quarterly, 4*(3). Retrieved from http://www.ds-health.com/health99.htm

Cuskelly, M., Hauser-Cram, P., & Van Riper, M. (2009). Families of children with Down syndrome: What we know and what we need to know. *Down Syndrome Research and Practice, 12,* 105–113.

Hodapp, R. M. (2007). Families of persons with Down syndrome: New perspectives, findings, and research and service needs. *Mental Retardation and Developmental Disabilities, 13,* 279–287.

Neri, G., & Opitz, J. M. (2009). Down syndrome: Comments and reflections on the 50th anniversary of Lejeune's discovery. *American Journal of Medical Genetics, Part A, 149A,* 2647–2654.

Skotko, B. G., Capone, B. T., & Kishnani, P. (2009). Postnatal diagnosis of Down syndrome: Synthesis of the evidence on how best to deliver the news. *Pediatrics, 124,* 751–758.

Van Riper, M. (2007). Families of children with Down syndrome: Responding to "a change of plans" with resilience. *Journal of Pediatric Nursing, 22,* 116–127.

Websites

Down Syndrome, Health Issues:
   http://www.ds-health.com
Down Syndrome Education International:
   http://www.downsed.org/en/gb

Drinking by Underage Family Members

Underage drinking is a major health concern. Alcohol is the most commonly used substance among adolescents. According to Monitoring the Future project, approximately 39% of eighth-grade students and 72% of adolescents by the end of high school report consuming more than a few sips of alcohol. Further, 55% of students in Grade 12 and 19% of those in Grade 8 report having been drunk at least once in their life. Although most underage drinkers will not develop a dependency on alcohol, the consequences of alcohol consumption are significant. Alcohol use is a common factor in the leading cause of morbidity and mortality for this age group, that is, accidents. This entry focuses on at-risk factors and interventions for underage drinking.

Definition and Developmental Trajectory of Underage Drinking

The developmental trajectories for alcohol use result in a complex situation for understanding and intervening in this health risk behavior. According to federal law, the minimum legal drinking age (MLDA) is 21 years. The MLDA became applicable in all states in 1998 when Wyoming became the last state to raise the drinking age to 21. Alcohol is an illegal substance for individuals under the age of 21. Thus, much of the research and interventions for school-age children and adolescents focus on prevention of alcohol use. This remains the focus through early and middle adolescence. However, toward the end of late adolescence as the legal age of alcohol use nears, the focus shifts to that of learning to drink responsibly and is aimed at the prevention of alcohol misuse, bingeing, and alcoholism once individuals are legally of age to drink alcohol.

To understand underage drinking, it is critical to be knowledgeable about the factors that place children and adolescents at risk for alcohol use and those that are protective against underage drinking. Early research and interventions focused on creating fear messages that emphasized the potential consequences of drinking. These interventions were based on the assumptions that adolescents would perceive potential threats from alcohol use. Early intervention programs were conducted primarily in school settings, as this is where children and adolescents are readily available. School-based programs emphasized changing attitudes about drinking, resisting peer pressure, not driving while drunk or with someone who is drunk, and developing refusal (saying "no") skills. The focus was on adolescents and their peers. Some of these programs had short-term effects, but few demonstrated long-term effects on underage alcohol use. Research has shown that one of the most widely implemented and well-received programs, Drug Abuse Resistance Education (D.A.R.E.), has little or no impact on alcohol use. The theoretical shift from individual-focused models to more ecological models formed the basis for additional descriptive research that identified important social environments that impacted underage drinking. Monitoring of the sale of alcohol to underage individuals has been demonstrated to be one way of limiting access to alcohol. Characteristics of schools—attendance, achievement, and truancy—are related to indicators of alcohol use and bingeing, defined as five or more drinks at one sitting. Peer factors—peer pressure to drink, own drinking—are related to underage drinking. More recent adolescent-focused interventions include the expansion of skills-based programs beyond refusal skills to social skills.

The family also is a critical environment for the initiation, amount, and duration of underage alcohol use. There is considerable evidence that children who have a parent(s) or multiple family members who have identified alcohol abuse problems are at high risk for underage drinking and potential alcohol abuse. Although specific genes for alcohol abuse have not been identified, children of families with alcohol abuse have 4 to 10 times more risk for underage drinking and subsequent alcohol abuse and related problems.

In addition to potential familial or genetic tendencies for alcohol use and misuse, family patterns and function are related to underage drinking. Considerable evidence exists that supports the following family factors that influence initiation and quantities of underage alcohol use and binge drinking: parenting/discipline style; parent and sibling alcohol approval and use of alcohol; parental monitoring of adolescents' friends, activities, and behaviors; clear and consistent family expectations and rules, especially about alcohol use; a nurturing and supportive family environment; and family involvement with children and adolescents. The foundational attitudes, beliefs, and behaviors established during adolescence within the family are challenged as the older adolescent moves to working and living independently or to continuing study in a college or university. In this phase of underage drinking, peer and social factors come more into play. However, it is important that families maintain their support, involvement, and expectations, even if the older adolescent is no longer in the family home.

Interventions

As the importance of family factors was recognized, a number of family-focused interventions were developed and evaluated. Although a number of these interventions have been found to be efficacious, there has been limited translation to "real life" implementation because of a lack of effectiveness studies, infrastructure, and funds. Thus, the challenge to move these efficacious interventions to implementation in the real world continues.

In the final phase of adolescence and transition to adulthood, the emphasis on prevention of underage alcohol use continues, but the foci of interventions shift. More attention is placed on prevention of drinking and driving and riding with drivers who have been drinking. Additionally, as adolescents approach the legal drinking age, programs have been developed that focus on drinking appropriately, avoiding binge drinking, and preventing drinking and driving/riding. These programs are often implemented in colleges and universities in response to the 1989 amendments to the Drug-Free Schools and Campuses Act. Campuses are environments where underage drinking is common and underage drinkers are available for intervention. The impact of teaching responsible drinking programs for one-on-one interventions shows some promising results, but no program has demonstrated successful results at a population level. College administrators are implementing policies and programs aimed at addressing environmental factors. These underage drinkers spend less time with families and, therefore, there is less involvement with families. However, families can continue to be an important factor in supporting underage drinkers to develop appropriate alcohol use behaviors.

Although many of the interventions to address underage drinking in families have been implemented primarily in school/college/university settings and in community settings, the role of health care providers in primary care settings has been less well studied. Given competing demands during time-limited visits, discussion of risky behaviors such as alcohol use is often limited. As children move into adolescence, they have fewer and more sporadic primary care contacts. Screening tools for children and adolescents, such as the CRAFFT, have demonstrated validity. The question remains about the availability of effective intervention once underage drinking has been identified. The U.S. Preventive Services Task Force issued an "I" recommendation for screening for alcohol use because of insufficient evidence on the potential benefits and harms of screening. The use of brief interventions have demonstrated efficacy with adults but have limited testing with adolescents.

Conclusion

Alcohol continues to be the most widely used substance among children and adolescents. Thus, underage drinking in families is a major concern.

The role of the family in the initiation, continuance, and prevention of underage drinking is critical. There are potential genetic, developmental, psychosocial, and behavioral contributions of the family for risk of underage drinking. This issue is probably best addressed at multiple levels. Families are a critical component in efforts to address underage drinking.

Carol Loveland-Cherry

See also Alcohol Addictions in the Family; Drug Addictions in the Family; Family Interventions Across the Life Span

Further Readings

Johnston, L. D., O'Malley, P. M., Bachman, J. G., & Schulenberg, J. E. (2009). *Monitoring the future: National results on adolescent drug use: Overview of key findings, 2008* (NIH Publication No. 09–7401). Bethesda, MD: National Institute on Drug Abuse. Retrieved from http://monitoringthefuture.org/pubs/monographs/overview2008.pdf

National Institute on Alcohol Abuse and Alcoholism. (2003). Underage drinking: A major public health challenge. *Alcohol Alert, 59.* Retrieved from http://pubs.niaaa.nih.gov/publications/aa59.htm

Websites

AlcoholPolicyMD.com: http://www.alcoholpolicymd.com

DRUG ADDICTIONS IN THE FAMILY

Through scientific advances, drug use has been conceptualized through different theoretical lenses. One theory deals with systems-level functioning and the role of family. Drug addiction is commonly defined as a compulsive need for and use of a habit-forming substance with the essential features of tolerance and physiological symptoms upon withdrawal. The consequences of drug addiction in the family are well documented. Not only are the substance-abusing individual's physical health, emotional well-being, and social functioning affected, but family members often also experience stress-related physical and psychological effects such as family disruption, marital discord, interpersonal conflict, financial problems, domestic violence, and child maltreatment. In this entry, the causes and correlates, assessment, and treatment of drug addiction in the family are addressed. Given the magnitude and complexity of this topic, it is important for future clinicians to have an understanding of how family environments contribute to drug addiction and treatment.

What Causes Addiction?

Research reveals multiple, interacting factors contributing to the development and maintenance of drug addiction. Just as the risk and protective framework has revolutionized prevention and treatment in medical specialties such as heart disease and AIDS, this framework has also greatly influenced the drug addiction field.

Among the various risk and protective factors researchers have identified, familial factors affect drug use in a number of ways: distant and inconsistent parenting; negative parent–child communication; unclear family rules/expectations regarding a teen's alcohol or drug use; poor parental monitoring; or a chaotic family environment. Other intrapersonal and contextual risk factors include genetic predispositions, antisocial behavior, early first use of drugs, anxiety or depression, associating with deviant peers, and low socioeconomic status. Risk factors are offset by the presence of protective factors: The more protective factors there are, the less likely is the chance of addiction.

There are numerous familial protective factors, including a caring and involved family demonstrating positive parent–child relationships, and appropriate and consistent discipline methods and supervision. Intrapersonal and contextual protective factors include healthy self-esteem, intelligence, a positive school attitude, and academic success. Advances in understanding risk and protective factors have served to further develop effective treatment strategies, which has led to a greater importance being placed on family.

The role that families play in the development, maintenance, and recovery from drug addiction cannot be underestimated. Family factors influence the onset of drug use and can exacerbate it. However, family factors are not to blame for all problems, as youth from all sorts of families can develop serious drug addiction problems.

Regardless of the parents' role in the development of their teen's drug problem, with a skillful clinician's help, parents are key to the solution. Family factors, including parental influence and a positive parent–child relationship and family environment, are among the strongest protective influences against drug taking. These findings have led to the increasing number of policy recommendations and practices involving family in the treatment for drug addiction.

Assessment

The first step in treatment is conducting an accurate and thorough assessment. Significant advances have been made in the techniques available to assess drug addiction in the context of family. In addition to providing information on actual drug use, today's assessment instruments offer an understanding of how developmental and contextual systems are involved in and affected by drug taking or drug abuse. Working from a risk and protective factor framework, clinicians consider multiple areas in their assessment process. The following are some reliable screening instruments: Addiction Severity Index, Adolescent Domain Screening Inventory, Adolescent Problem Severity Index, Drug Abuse Screening Inventory–Revised, Family Environment Scale, Multidimensional Adolescent Assessment Scale, Personal Experiences Inventory, and the Problem Oriented Screening Instrument.

Drug Abuse Treatment

Effective Treatments Incorporate the Family

Addiction is a complex, multidimensional, and multidetermined phenomenon, requiring interventions in multiple areas of functioning (the biological, behavioral, and social contexts in which substance use occurs). Integrated treatment models have proven most effective. Increasingly, family involvement is regarded as a central feature of science-based drug addiction interventions (especially in the treatment of adolescents). Although residential treatment programs are effective for those with more severe problems, family-based, outpatient behavioral treatments are also demonstrating superior outcomes with sustainability.

Adult Treatment Approaches

Because drug addiction is systemic, also affecting family members, not just the addicted individual, integrated treatment models focusing on both are recommended. These typically utilize a combination of psychopharmacological and psychosocial treatment approaches. Although still uncommon, an integration of drug abuse treatment that includes family therapy is increasingly being used. The following integrated therapeutic models are recognized, evidence-based practices: (a) Behavioral family therapy is a combination of individual interventions within a family problem-solving framework using techniques, such as contingency contracting, skills training, or cognitive restructuring, to facilitate behavioral change within a family to support abstinence. (b) Cognitive-behavioral family therapy incorporates principles and techniques of behavioral family therapy with traditional family systems therapy in which drug abuse is viewed as a conditioned behavioral response that family cues and contingencies reinforce. (c) Behavioral couples therapy is an active, couples-based intervention in which the non–substance-abusing intimate partner is involved in the treatment process. The assumptions are that intimate partners can reward abstinence, and, in reducing relationship distress, the risk for relapse is lessened. (d) Structural/strategic family therapies refer to treatments that assume that family structure determines individual behavior to a great extent and that the power of the system of the family is greater than the individual's ability to resist.

Adolescent Treatment Approaches

Adolescent drug addiction can significantly derail development, setting youth on a path toward failure in several realms of their future life. Because the conventional sequence of healthy development is bypassed—school, work, and family formation—these teens transition prematurely into adult roles without the maturity necessary to be successful in these roles.

In the past decade, research has strongly supported family-based interventions as the treatment of choice for adolescent drug abuse. Clinical practice guidelines established by federal agencies, national associations, and influential policy-making groups all stress the importance of involving caregivers and family members in the treatment of adolescent drug use. The best treatment programs are multicomponent, providing a combination of therapies and other services. The following are evidence-based family therapies widely acknowledged as being highly effective in treating adolescent drug addiction: (a) Brief strategic family therapy flows from structural/strategic family therapy and is an integrative family therapy approach that has developed culturally specific interventions for Hispanic conduct and early-stage substance-using youth. (b) Functional family therapy, both a prevention and intervention program, has been used with a wide range of youth with substance abuse or antisocial problems and, when used in juvenile justice facilities, has been shown to reduce recidivism between 25% and 60%. (c) Multidimensional family therapy is an integrative, clinically and cost-effective family-based, developmental-ecological, multiple systems approach. Combining elements from psychotherapy, family therapy, and drug counseling, multidimensional family therapy significantly reduces adolescent drug addiction, delinquent behavior, family conflict, and risk of HIV, while effectively engaging and retaining teens and parents in treatment and improving grades and family functioning. (d) Multisystemic therapy represents an approach that, depending on the particular case and assessment, selects from elements of family therapy, family preservation, parent training, and cognitive therapy methods.

Conclusion and Future Directions

The aforementioned comprehensive treatment models have been developed in light of research findings supporting family-focused interventions. While they may differ in their clinical techniques, they share a conceptual framework that acknowledges how family environments contribute to drug addiction and treatment. To this end, the challenge is expanding the focus of drug addiction treatment from the individual to the family and of preparing clinicians to implement evidence-based family interventions for drug addiction treatment.

Howard A. Liddle, Rosemarie Rodriguez,
and Lacey Teneal Greathead

See also Alcohol Addictions in the Family; Drinking by Underage Family Members; Family Therapy; Shaken Baby Syndrome in Childbearing Families

Further Readings

Center for Substance Abuse Treatment. (2004). *Substance abuse treatment and family therapy* (Treatment Improvement Protocol [TIP] Series No. 39, DHHS Publication No. [SMA] 4–3957). Rockville, MD: Substance Abuse and Mental Health Services Administration.

Copello, A. G., Velleman, R. D., & Templeton, L. J. (2005). Family interventions in the treatment of alcohol and drug problems. *Drug and Alcohol Review, 24,* 369–385.

Liddle, H. A. (2009). Treating adolescent substance abuse using multidimensional family therapy. In J. Weisz & A. Kazdin (Eds.), *Evidence-based psychotherapies for children and adolescents* (2nd ed.). New York: Guilford Press.

Rowe, C. L., & Liddle, H. A. (2003). Substance abuse. *Journal of Marital and Family Therapy, 29,* 97–120.

Assessment Tools

Corrigan, M. J., Loneck, B., & Videka, L. (2007). The development and preliminary evaluation of the Adolescent Domain Screening Inventory (ADSI): A substance use prevention tool. *Research on Social Work Practice, 17,* 348–357.

Mathiesen, S. G., Cash, S. J., & Hudson, W. W. (2002). The Multidimensional Adolescent Assessment Scale (MAAS): A validation study. *Research on Social Work Practice, 12,* 9–28.

McLellan, A. T., Luborsky, L., Woody, G. E., & O'Brien, C. (1980). An improved diagnostic evaluation instrument for substance abuse patients: The Addiction Severity Index. *Journal of Nervous and Mental Disease, 168,* 26–33.

Metzger, D. S., Kushner, H., & McLellan, A. T. (1991). *Adolescent Problem Severity Index.* Philadelphia: University of Pennsylvania.

Moos, R. H., Insel, P. M., & Humphrey, B. (1974). *Preliminary manual for Family Environment Scale, Work Environment Scale, Group Environment Scale.* Mountain View, CA: Consulting Psychologists Press.

Rahdert, E. (1991). *The Adolescent Assessment/Referral System manual* (DHHS Publication No. [ADM] 91–1735). Rockville, MD: National Institute on Drug Abuse.

Tarter, R., & Hegedus, A. (1991). The Drug Use Screening Inventory (DUSI): Its application in the evaluation and treatment of alcohol and drug abuse. *Alcohol Health and Research World, 15,* 65–75.

Winters, K. C., & Henly, G. A. (1989). *The Personal Experience Inventory and manual.* Los Angeles: Western Psychological Services.

E

Early Periodic Screening, Diagnosis, and Treatment Program for Low-Income Children

The Early Periodic Screening, Diagnosis (sometimes noted as Diagnostic), and Treatment (EPSDT) program is a component of Medicaid that aims to improve the health and well-being of all children under the age of 21 years by ensuring preventive and comprehensive health services. In 1965, the Medicaid program was enacted mandating coverage for poor children, and in 1967, EPSDT was added as a benefit to promote healthy child development and to prevent and treat conditions of childhood. Essentially, EPSDT is the child health benefit of Medicaid. In 1997, the Balanced Budget Act allowed EPSDT to be an optional benefit within State Children's Health Insurance Programs, which are operated separately from the state's Medicaid program. The program has two components: (1) ensuring the availability and accessibility of health care resources and (2) helping Medicaid beneficiaries effectively use these resources. Medicaid covers approximately a quarter of the nation's children; thus, the EPSDT benefit is a critical means of ensuring their health and well-being. Children in the Medicaid program are more likely than uninsured children, and as likely as insured children, to see a doctor and receive well-child visits, in part because of this program.

EPSDT was developed to ensure a basic level of care for low-income children, reflecting their greater need for health care services and their higher incidence of chronic health conditions and developmental concerns. A 1964 report, *One Third of a Nation,* showed widespread health problems among young military draftees that could have been avoided through adequate care in childhood. Additionally, numerous health problems among those children enrolled in Head Start were identified. These factors stimulated the development of the program in order to identify potentially disabling conditions and provide early treatment. Ideally, problems are identified and treated early, preventing further disability and unnecessary expense.

Whereas individual states are given some latitude in determining the frequency of health care visits and other program details, certain services are mandated by law. Where states can develop their own periodicity schedules for screenings or visits, they must be based on recommendations from professional organizations in the related areas. In addition, screening services must also be made available on an as-needed basis between regularly scheduled exams. There can be considerable variability in the screening schedules between states. Mandated services include (a) a comprehensive health and development history, including an assessment of physical and mental health; (b) comprehensive, unclothed physical exam; (c) immunizations based on the currently approved Advisory Committee on Immunization Practices of the Centers for Disease Control and Prevention schedule; (d) laboratory tests appropriate for the age of the child; (e) lead screening by blood test at 12 and 24 months of age, or between 36 and 72 months of age if the child has not previously been screened; (f) vision services, including assessment, diagnosis, and treatment as needed, as well as eyeglasses; (g) hearing services, including assessment, diagnosis, and treatment, and hearing aids and speech therapy as needed; (h) dental services provided through direct dental referral beginning at age 3 (or earlier if needed), including maintenance of dental health, treatment of pain and infections, and restoration of teeth; (i) health education and anticipatory guidance, including both the parent and, when appropriate, the child, on topics such as child development, healthy living, and accident and disease prevention; and (j) diagnosis and treatment, when a screening exam reveals a problem requiring further attention.

A key element of EPSDT is the requirement to provide any medically necessary health care services for the Medicaid eligible child, even if that service is not part of the state's Medicaid plan for the rest of the population, in order to correct or ameliorate physical and mental conditions discovered through screenings. These services include physician, hospital, and clinic care; family planning; home health care; physical, occupational, and respiratory therapy; medications; and case management. This provision is critical in providing an array of physical and mental health services to children in order to meet their health needs and results in much more comprehensive Medicaid coverage for children than adults. It is especially important to children with special health care needs, as EPSDT often provides more comprehensive coverage than the typical commercial plan, increasing access to key services.

Additional administrative components of the program include outreach, assistance with transportation, case management, and referrals. Referrals are made to other agencies, including the State Title V Program for Children with Special Health Care Needs; WIC—The Special Supplemental Food Program for Women, Infants, and Children; Head Start; special education; and the developmental disabilities and mental health systems. Many families are unaware of the EPSDT program and its numerous benefits, and therefore outreach is especially important to increase access and enrollment.

Children in Medicaid managed care plans are entitled to the full range of EPSDT benefits, although the child may or may not receive all of their EPSDT services through the plan. Some of the services may be "carved out" and provided through the state's regular fee-for-service Medicaid program. This, in turn, may result in challenges for families in accessing needed care, especially in the absence of adequate care coordination.

Despite the value of the program, many infants, children, and adolescents do not receive the EPSDT benefits to which they are entitled. A number of barriers prevent children from screenings; these barriers include competing family and personal issues, long waits, lengthy travel distances, limited hours of clinic operations, and poor outreach efforts. In addition, because of low Medicaid reimbursement rates in some states, the availability of Medicaid providers may be limited, thus restricting access despite the presence of insurance coverage. Parents may be unaware of the benefits afforded under the program and not realize that visits can be utilized for services such as sports or camp physicals or mental health services. Additionally, not all states address mental health issues in their EPSDT screening tools, despite requirements to do so.

During periods of state budget constraints, EPSDT has come under scrutiny due to the cost of the program and the share paid by the states, yet the cost of care for children enrolled in Medicaid is less than that of those enrolled in commercial insurance. At times, states have expressed a desire to limit the EPSDT benefit in order to reduce costs, but to date, the benefits have been spared cuts.

Kathryn Smith

See also Access to Health Care: Child Health; Medicaid and Family Health

Further Readings

Kaiser Family Foundation, Kaiser Commission on Medicaid and the Uninsured. (2005, March). *Early and periodic screening, diagnostic, and treatment services* [Fact sheet]. Washington, DC: Author. Retrieved March 15, 2010, from http://www.kff.org/medicaid/upload/Early-and-Periodic-Screening-Diagnostic-and-Treatment-Services-Fact-Sheet.pdf

Maternal and Child Health Library at Georgetown University. *Early and periodic screening, diagnostic, and treatment (EPSDT) services in Medicaid knowledge path.* Retrieved March 1, 2010, from http://www.mchlibrary.info/knowledgePaths/kp_EPSDT.html

Websites

George Washington University, School of Public Health and Health Services, Department of Health Policy: http://www.gwumc.edu/sphhs/departments/healthpolicy/index.cfm

ECOMAPS FOR FAMILIES

Individuals seeking health care and their families interact with other people and social institutions in the environment. These interactions can potentially affect the health of families, decisions about whether and from whom to seek health care, and adherence to treatment recommendations. Therefore, it is important that health care providers understand the social interactions that their patients have with other individuals and institutions in the social environment. The *ecomap* is a paper-and-pencil tool that is used to assess the quantity and quality of social relationships. The ecomap condenses complex data to form a picture of patients in their social context. This entry discusses the development and purposes of ecomaps and explains how to construct an ecomap. A case example is provided to illustrate the ecomap and how to interpret it.

Ann Hartman developed the ecomap in the 1970s to help public child welfare workers assess the needs of families. The ecomap is based on the ecological perspective, which focuses on the interactions of individuals with the social environment (hence, the word *ecomap*). The primary use of the ecomap is in clinical care, but it has recently been used in research to examine interactions of caregivers with informal and formal support systems. As a practice tool, it informs assessment, treatment planning, and evaluation. Use of the ecomap may reduce defensiveness and blaming, as its focus is on the environment rather than behaviors of the health care client. Drawing the ecomap is usually a collaborative activity between the provider and family. In this way it also contributes to the

development of the helping relationship as patients and providers work closely together to understand environmental impacts on the patient.

There are no tight and fast rules for constructing ecomaps, and providers can be flexible in how they develop and use them. For example, David Hodge described a spiritual ecogram, which integrates the traditional genogram and ecomap to focus on the individual's connections with spirituality and religion. Computer software can be purchased to draw the ecomap; alternatively, paper and pencil are adequate for the task.

Ecomaps consist of a circle in the center of a page that represents the patient or family; the circle may contain the name of the patient or a simple genogram of the family. The patient's age or other relevant information can be included in the circle. Other circles surround the patient's circle; each circle represents a relevant social system. Social systems often placed on ecomaps include the neighborhood, employment, extended family, friends, education, church, social activities, and social and health agencies. Lines connect the individual patient or family to each system. These lines depict the strength and quality of the relationship. By convention, solid lines represent a strong connection, whereas dotted lines represent weak, tenuous relationships. Hash marks show conflicted or stressful relationships. Arrows at the end of the lines show the direction in which energy and resources flow, for example, whether the relationship is reciprocal or whether one party is investing more in the relationship than is the other party. Health care providers can also write notes on the ecomap as they draw it.

It is relatively easy to learn how to construct ecomaps. Good interviewing and relationship-building skills are needed, but no formal training is required. It is recommended that providers practice or role-play with a colleague or friend prior to using ecomaps with patients. It may be more efficient to have templates available to use, with some of the common social systems already written in circles and other circles left empty to fill in for each patient's unique situation.

A simple case example illustrates how to interpret an ecomap. Linda is a 68-year-old divorced woman. From looking at her ecomap (Figure 1), it is seen that she has strong and mutual relationships with her church, adult daughter, and bowling league. She has much conflict with her neighbors.

Much energy is put into her work, but her relationship with her supervisor is tenuous. Although there is not a lot of conflict in her relationships with her mother and ex-husband, they tend to be rather one-sided, with Linda giving more to these relationships than she receives back. Some issues for further assessment arise from examining Linda's ecomap. Linda's health care provider would want to explore the extent to which her relationships with her ex-husband and mother drain her, and whether Linda has the skills or willingness to step back from them or to restructure them so they take less of her energy. Alternatively, perhaps Linda is satisfied with the nature of these relationships. The point is that the ecomap opens the door to exploring these issues with Linda. Other issues for assessment include learning more about the source of conflict with her neighbors, how long she has had a poor relationship with her supervisor, and whether she has tried to resolve these conflicts. After gathering more detailed assessment information, the next step is to identify desired outcomes and interventions to attain them. For example, perhaps Linda wants to improve her relationship with her supervisor but lacks the skills to initiate such a conversation. A possible intervention is to teach these skills to Linda and role-play with her. Linda might be determined to help her mother remain in her own home but acknowledge it is becoming more difficult to do so. The health care provider can make referrals to public health nursing, mobile meals, and other services designed to keep older adults in their own homes. Based on Linda's ecomap, the health care provider knows that Linda has a good relationship with her daughter and so could encourage Linda to ask her to share some of the responsibility for the care of her grandmother (Linda's mother).

Although Linda's ecomap is relatively simple, it shows how effectively and efficiently ecomaps shed light on the social interactions of individuals and families. The ecomap is easy to use and can help health care providers understand the social context of the lives of their clients. It enhances assessment and treatment planning, and its focus on the environment reminds both providers and clients of the multiple ways health is influenced by social context.

Marlys Staudt

See also Culturagram Use With Culturally Diverse Families; Genograms and the Family

Further Readings

Hartman, A. (1978). Diagrammatic assessment of family relationships. *Social Casework, 59,* 465–476.

Hodge, D. R. (2005). Spiritual ecograms: A new assessment instrument for identifying clients' strengths in space and across time. *Families in Society, 86,* 287–296.

Ray, R. A., & Street, A. F. (2005). Ecomapping: An innovative research tool for nurses. *Journal of Advanced Nursing, 50,* 545–552.

Rempel, G. R., Neufeld, A., & Kushner, K. E. (2007). Interactive use of genograms and ecomaps in family caregiving research. *Journal of Family Nursing, 13,* 403–419.

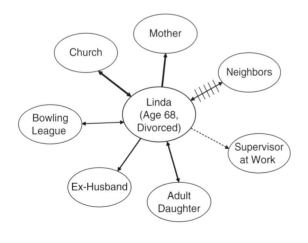

Figure 1   Ecomap for Linda, a 68-Year-Old Divorced Woman

ECONOMIC DOWNTURN AND FAMILIES

A *recession* is a sustained economic contraction. Consumers consume less, businesses invest less, the government spends less, and foreigners buy fewer U.S. products. Job losses follow for an extended time, which further erodes economic activity and directly impacts family well-being.

Family incomes used to increase when a recession ended, but that has not been the case since the early 1990s. Income continued to fall after recessions ended in 1991 and 2001. The output recovery did not translate into a labor market recovery, as was the case in recoveries before 1990. Instead, corporate profits saw a stronger-than-usual recovery.

There may be a continued disconnect between output and incomes after the 2008 downturn. Economic growth resumed in the third quarter of 2009, and nonfinancial corporate profits started to rise from their lowest point at the end of 2008, while the labor market continued to lose jobs into the first quarter of 2010.

Some families are particularly vulnerable to falling incomes. Single mothers are more likely to be unemployed or living below the poverty line than are married couples with children. Minorities have lower incomes than whites and are less able to generate savings to be used in the event of economic hardship. Women, Hispanics, and individuals who have not completed high school have more difficulty than others recovering from considerable income drops. These groups are more likely to feel the adverse effects of income losses than others. This entry focuses on the effects of economic hardships on families and sources of support for families during economic downturns.

Income and Family Hardships

Job losses create economic hardships. Families reduce spending on necessities like food and clothing to ensure that monthly bills can be paid. Also, homeowners may first deplete their savings and subsequently fall behind on their mortgage payments. The chance of foreclosure then rises. Foreclosure reduces credit scores. The combination of no savings, low incomes, and low credit scores makes it harder for former homeowners to find rental housing, resulting in increased homelessness.

Unemployed parents experience psychological stress and may develop anxiety and depression. These emotions can result in withdrawal and marital discord. There is ambiguous evidence on recessions and divorce. Greater marital stress increases the chance of divorce, whereas lower incomes reduce the chance of divorce. Economic and psychological strain contributes to heightened levels of domestic violence.

Recessions and less income adversely impact family health. The occurrence of stress-related illness increases during economic downturns. Elevated stress levels due to fear of job loss or unemployment may result in anxiety, trouble sleeping, muscle aches, and headaches. Financial strain related to unemployment and its impacts on family stability may also result in depression leading to substance abuse, somatoform disorders, and hypochondria. The decline in emotional functioning that accompanies depression may impair an individual's ability to successfully engage in a job search and obtain reemployment, thus creating a vicious mental health cycle.

Children experience both short-term and long-term adverse consequences from an economic downturn. Recessions may lead to deterioration in children's mental health, as their distracted parents become withdrawn from family life. Children who live in poverty as the result of a recession are more likely to attain lower levels of education, are less likely to achieve gainful employment, and maintain poorer health status than peers who do not enter poverty in an economic downturn.

Recessions can also delay family formation. Economic declines can lead financially burdened adult children to move back in with aging parents, and young adults may delay getting married and having children.

Income Support During Economic Downturns

Households will likely seek additional support from the government during a recession. Families may seek public housing, food, and cash assistance. They may also turn to the public for health insurance if they lose employer-sponsored health insurance coverage, either because of job loss or because of benefit reductions at struggling employers.

The growing demand for additional assistance typically arises at the level of state and local governments. These governments, though, suffer from fiscal and budgetary pressures—less revenue and balanced budget amendments—to reduce their outlays. These pressures can lead to stricter eligibility criteria for social programs as demand increases during a recession.

Nonprofit charities may provide an alternative source of income support. They suffer, though, from the same constraints of rising demand and fewer revenues as the government. Individuals have less income for donations. Corporate charitable giving also declines immediately with the onset of a recession due to lower profits. Additionally, nonprofits lose the support of state and federal governments as tax revenues decrease and contract and grant opportunities diminish. Foundation giving slows, but less dramatically than other sources of nonprofit revenue. Sustained decreases in funding make it progressively harder for nonprofits to effectively provide aid to families who are in greater need of assistance because of a recession.

Struggling families consequently may turn to friends and relatives. This could increase economic pressures on a larger circle of families, essentially spreading the initial pain of job loss and declining incomes while lowering the amount of social capital present in communities.

Christian E. Weller and Carolyn Arcand

See also Economics as It Relates to Family Health; Poverty, Children in, and Health Care

Further Readings

Acs, G., Loprest, P., & Nichols, A. (2009). *Risk and recovery: Understanding the changing risks to family incomes* (Low-Income Working Families Paper No. 14). Washington, DC: Urban Institute. Retrieved from http://www.urban.org/UploadedPDF/411971_risk_and_recovery.pdf

Dorn, S. (2008). *Health coverage in a recession* (Recession and Recovery Publication No. 6). Washington, DC: Urban Institute. Retrieved from http://www.urban.org/publications/411812.html

First Focus. (2009). *Turning point: The long term effects of recession-induced child poverty*. Washington, DC: Author. Retrieved from http://www.firstfocus.net/library/reports/turning-point-long-term-effects-recession-induced-child-poverty

Golden, S., Longhofer, W., & Winchester, D. (2009). Non profits in need. *Contexts: Understanding People in Their Social Worlds, 8*(3), 14–15.

Hegewisch, A., & Williams, C. (2010, February). *The female face of poverty and economic insecurity: The impact of the recession on women* (Briefing Paper No. IWPR R345). Washington, DC: Institute for Women's Policy Research. Retrieved from http://www.iwpr.org/pdf/R345PApoverty.pdf

Kingsley, G., Smith, R., & Price, D. (2009, May). *The impacts of foreclosures on families and communities* (Report prepared for the Open Society Institute). Washington, DC: Urban Institute. Retrieved from http://www.urban.org/UploadedPDF/411909_impact_of_forclosures.pdf

Logan, A., & Weller, C. (2009, January 16). *The state of minorities: The recession issue*. Washington, DC: Center for American Progress. Retrieved from http://www.americanprogress.org/issues/2009/01/state_of_minorities.html

Price, R., Choi, J., & Vinokur, A. (2002). Links in the chain of adversity following job loss: How financial strain and loss of personal control lead to depression, impaired functioning, and poor health. *Journal of Occupational Health Psychology, 7*(4), 302–312.

Scutella, R., & Wooden, M. (2008). The effects of household joblessness on mental health. *Social Science and Medicine, 67,* 88–100.

Solantaus, T., Leinonen, J., & Punamaki, R. (2004). Children's mental health in times of economic recession: Replication and extension of the family economic stress model in Finland. *Developmental Psychology, 40*(3), 412–429.

ECONOMICS AS IT RELATES TO FAMILY HEALTH

The interplay between health, economics, and families is complex. A solid knowledge of that interplay is critical for policymakers and practitioners alike. This entry defines the specific impact of socioeconomic status (SES)—as measured by income, education, and occupation—on health outcomes. All human beings are at risk of poor health outcomes, and indeed, all of us eventually die. However, the pace of death, the illnesses individuals have along the way, and the causes of deaths all vary depending on where one is on the SES scale. Individuals from poorer families experience higher infant mortality, more chronic conditions, and lower life expectations. That is, health varies considerably based on SES regardless of how it is measured. The reasons for this phenomenon are complex.

This entry discusses both the direct and indirect ways in which SES affects family health, including its effect on environment, health behaviors, and access to health care, while weaving in some theories that explain the context of these differences. The discussion concludes by addressing various economic interventions to improve family health based on the impact of SES on health.

Relationship Between Socioeconomic Status and Family Health

In the United States, family SES is strongly related to health status, morbidity, and mortality of individuals. Adults in low-SES families are more likely to report poorer health status and suffer from chronic conditions such as diabetes, heart disease, or cancer. Children in low-SES families are also more likely to be rated in poorer health status and are more likely to suffer negative health shocks such as accidents and chronic conditions such as diabetes. Obesity, an issue of increasing public health concern that is strongly associated with poor health outcomes, is also more prevalent among low-SES women and children. This disparity in health status translates into differential rates of mortality, with persons in the top decile of the income distribution living an average 4.5 years longer than those in the lowest decile of the income distribution.

The vast majority of information presented to consumers about health focuses on the importance of lifestyle and other daily personal choices. Sadly, knowledge and access to the "correct" choices are complicated by a person's social and economic situation. Social factors matter because they affect access to the options and opportunities that promote good health. Diana Dutton's cycle of poverty and pathology is one way of describing how being poor can both lead to, and be reinforced by, unhealthy social conditions. It details how living in poor environments and working in higher risk occupations causes stresses that, when exacerbated by a lack of sufficient coping resources, may lead to poor behavioral choices and result in a need for medical care. As individuals in poverty may have limited or inadequate access to health care, treating their health conditions may be costly both in terms of out-of-pocket expenditures and lost ability to work, leading to further poverty and the cycle repeating. All of the aforementioned factors conspire to create poorer health outcomes for those individuals trapped in the web of poverty.

More specifically, people with low SES tend to live in neighborhoods with substandard housing, which exposes individuals to pollutants, toxins, and allergens, and perhaps to inadequate sanitary or cooking facilities to take care of themselves appropriately. This housing is often located in neighborhoods that have high crime rates resulting in increased stress among residents. These neighborhoods are also generally not conducive to outside physical activity because of a lack of infrastructure or safety concerns. The neighborhoods also tend to have few grocery stores, with those that are easily accessible providing a limited assortment of nutritious foods at high prices and organized in ways that encourage poor choice. For example, grocery stores in poor neighborhoods often have soda pop showcased at the end of each aisle. All of this can lead to an unhealthy dependence on convenient, and often less nutritious, junk foods. The high levels of stress also lead to poor choices, including overeating and smoking to relieve that stress, part of the vicious cycle. All of these negative factors increase the risk of residents becoming obese.

Each of the individual components of SES—income, education, occupation—plays a role in shaping health behaviors. Availability of adequate financial resources, as measured by income, can affect health status by limiting people's access to the components needed to nourish a healthy lifestyle, such as proper nutrition and medical services, and access to stress-relieving resources. There also appears to be a negative impact on health for those of low SES living in communities with greater disparities in income. Low-SES individuals in high-disparity neighborhoods report worse health status and experience higher rates of mortality than those of similar SES living in less disparate neighborhoods.

Education can increase health status by increasing one's knowledge of healthy behaviors, ability to navigate the health care system, and ability to process and use new health information. Those with more education are likely to be exposed to useful health information, including knowledge of the negative health consequences of a variety of risky behaviors, through their greater consumption of formal news as well as through their likely more engaged and informed social networks. However, the prevalence of obesity even among persons of higher SES suggests that knowledge and opportunity may not be sufficient to translate into good choices. Those with more education navigate the health care system more adeptly and are better self-advocates, but humans are complex creatures and knowledge and opportunity alone do not guarantee consistently wise choices.

Occupation can affect health status through differential exposure to risk factors and access to health insurance. Workers in occupations requiring manual labor are more likely to develop work-related health conditions or experience a work-related disability than those in professional occupations. Moreover, as the majority of Americans under age 65 years obtain their health insurance through their employers, occupation and the quality of health insurance associated with those occupations can affect health outcomes. Occupations higher on the SES scale are more likely to come with health insurance, and that insurance tends to higher quality (lower premium and deductibles, more consumer choice) the more highly rated the job.

Access to quality health care is an important determinant of health status and health outcomes, and SES affects nearly every dimension of health care access. Those with less income and in lower rated occupations, who may need health care the most, are the least able to afford insurance. Without insurance, families typically forgo preventive care and effective chronic disease management, resulting in poor health outcomes. The poorest of the poor, of the right age, do have insurance and access to a system of health care providers (Medicare and Medicaid for those over 65, State Children's Health Program for kids 18 and under).

Understanding precisely how SES and its components affect health is difficult. Although individuals, regardless of their SES standing, may make poor choices, those of the most limited means are the ones most likely to make poorer choices because of differing values, knowledge, or opportunities and thus end up with poorer health outcomes. The social drift theory posits, however, that this may not be a unidirectional relationship. Some who find themselves in poor health may not have started out poor but lose their economic standing as a result of being ill. That is, rather than low SES causing poor health, poor health translates into being poor, as it

limits one's ability to pursue or complete higher levels of education, translating into working in worse occupations and receiving lower income. Poor health can also limit job mobility and opportunities for advancement, again suppressing income. And poor health can lead to job loss. Unpaid health bills for those inadequately insured are a major cause of bankruptcy in the United States, perhaps the strongest evidence that the relationship between SES and health status may be circular. Still, the relationship between SES and health may be driven by unobserved factors that affect both. Poor health can be a product of heritable genetic conditions or childhood environment, which can also affect one's level of cognitive functioning and thus education and income.

Family and Health in an Economic Context

The family illness model espouses the tenet that behaviors and attitudes learned in families of origin and then carried forward into our current families affect all aspects of one's health: how one defines health and illness and takes on the sick role, how one learns about and is able to pursue living a healthy lifestyle, how families help a sick member heal, and how families continue to interact with the health care system. It is within the family that food likes and dislikes are developed, members learn what and when to eat, see how people spend their time (in physical activity or not), learn how much alcohol is acceptable, and so forth.

In the context of the family illness model, the negative impact of poverty, poor choices, and poor options is seen being cycled through generations of families. This situation is further complicated by studies that have documented the importance of acknowledging cultural, racial, and ethnic factors in health care, and the family as the primary vehicle for transmission of this culture. The health care system's failure to acknowledge and understand these cultural factors leads to a less than effective health care system.

Economic Interventions to Improve Family Health

Given the aforementioned ways in which SES can affect family health, several possible public health interventions to improve family health are apparent though not necessarily easy. The risk of obesity may be significantly reduced by a nutritious diet and a regular and intensive exercise routine, but in order to pursue these behavioral changes a person needs the following: money for the purchase of nutritious food and conveniently located stores that offer food at affordable prices; opportunities to be encouraged to be physically active, including safe neighborhoods to walk, bike, and run in, and available time away from work and family obligations to participate in those activities; access to affordable health care; and a level of education or knowledge that enables one to understand the importance of each of these as a contributor to good health.

There are some mechanisms focused on the individual and families to help them make better choices around nutrition. As low-SES families are more likely to be food insecure or suffer from poor nutrition, ameliorating adverse effects requires food assistance programs such as the Women, Infants, and Children program or the Supplemental Nutrition Assistance Program. These programs increase food budgets and access to *nutritious* foods, but they are only effective if people make good nutritional choices. Therefore, expansions of these should be coupled with strong efforts at nutrition education. However, this focus may be limited by its focus on the individual or the family rather than the community.

A framework is evolving that suggests that the most effective approaches to getting people to make healthier choices are not necessarily those that solely teach the individual or even the cook to make lifestyle changes. The cycle of poverty and pathology model (itself an example of an ecological/system framework) is a reminder that it is very complicated for some individuals, especially those from low-income families, to make positive choices. Good information about how to make wise choices is not always easily understandable, and web-based information is not universally accessible—and this needs to change. But as noted earlier, knowledge is insufficient if there are no opportunities.

Those communities that appear to be most successful at behavior change are those that use an ecological rather than an individual approach. For example, having local restaurants label the nutrient content of their food helps individuals to make better choices. If the goal is to seek large numbers of people to stop smoking, it has been found to

be more cost-effective if a community passes no-smoking ordinances than if individuals go through smoking cessation programs. That is, expecting individuals, even those with sufficient knowledge, to make good choices on their own, without engaging the full support of their communities and their families, is shortsighted.

At present the ecological approach is rarely considered because society talks strongly about individual responsibility and forgets the role of communities in helping individuals to be responsible. Communities can work toward making it harder for people to make bad choices (no-smoking ordinances, "sin" taxes) at the same time they help them to make good choices (menu labeling, opening malls or gyms early for walkers), all the while continuing to work with the families to make individual changes. Housing subsidies used to move families to neighborhoods more conducive to healthy living is a possible response, as is expansion of health insurance so that the negative impacts of low SES do not impact access to needed medical care. In these ways some of the negative effects on health outcomes of low SES can be minimized while improving health outcomes for all, regardless of SES.

Roberta Riportella and Maximilian D. Schmeiser

See also Access to Health Care: Uninsured; Employment/Unemployment and Family Health Insurance Coverage; Factors Influencing Access to Health Care for Families; Medicaid and Family Health; Poverty, Children in, and Health Care; Role of Families in Health Promotion; Socioeconomic Status of Families

Further Readings

Adler, N. E., & Newman, K. (2002). Socioeconomic disparities in health: Pathways and policies. *Health Affairs, 21*(2), 60–76.

Doherty, W. J. (2002). A family-focused approach to health care. In K. Bogenschneider (Ed.), *Taking family policy seriously: How policymaking affects families and how professionals can affect policymaking* (pp. 67–76). Mahwah, NJ: Erlbaum.

Dutton, D. B. (1986). Social class, health and illness. In L. Aiken & D. Mechanic (Eds.), *Applications of social science to clinical medicine and health policy* (pp. 31–62). New Brunswick, NJ: Rutgers University Press.

Hovell, M. F., Wahlgren, D. R., & Gehrman, C. (2002). The behavioral ecological model: Integrating public health and behavioral science. In R. J. DiClemente, R. Crosby, & M. Kegler (Eds.), *Emerging theories in health promotion practice & research* (pp. 347–385). San Francisco: Jossey-Bass.

John D. and Catherine T. MacArthur Foundation Research Network on Socioeconomic Status and Health. (2009). *Reaching for a healthier life: Facts on socioeconomic status and health in the U.S.* Retrieved from http://www.macses.ucsf.edu/downloads/ Reaching_for_a_Healthier_Life.pdf

EDUCATING THE FAMILY REGARDING CHRONIC PHYSICAL ILLNESS

Recent research estimates 18% of children in the United States live with special health care needs. Most care for children with special health care needs or chronic illnesses takes place in the home and requires parents/caregivers to be prepared to meet the physical, social, and psychological needs of the child. If the child is diagnosed with a chronic physical illness such as diabetes or asthma, then this means the parents and other family members provide supportive care, maintenance of physical function care, and care that prevents further problems.

Patricia Jackson Allen and Judith A. Vessey note that much of the research about chronic physical illness in children describes the course of the illness, the necessity of child and family education, clinical interventions, and disease management models. Gail Kieckhefer and Cristine M. Trahms and Stanton Newman, Liz Steed, and Kathleen Mulligan describe a newer body of knowledge about the expanding role of the parents (and later the child) in making decisions about care, collaborative or parent–child shared management, and increased self-management as the child gets older. The evolution of the chronic disease model has resulted in the parents, family members, and child playing an active role in illness management. Chronic illness management models are programs that expect the parents, other family members, and the child to become active partners in the

care process with health care providers becoming the educators and assisting the parents and child in obtaining the knowledge and skills needed to manage the illness. The purpose of this entry is to first provide a conceptual foundation for parent education that recognizes that parent education supports the parent's development across the life span and that this education involves reorganizations of meanings, perspectives, affect, identity construction, and other qualitative changes in the parent that lead to greater integration of knowledge, self-authority, and wisdom in relationship to the self, the child with chronic illness, and the family. The second component of the conceptual foundation is that educational programs that incorporate knowledge of family life and daily routines lead to more sustainable interventions and thus better outcomes. The entry also describes the components of effective parent education programs and the use of information technology in parent education.

Conceptual Development

Parent Development

In advancing the collaborative management or parent–child shared management models, one must also examine how teaching parents to meet the needs of a child with a chronic physical illness is associated with adult development. Adult development is a trajectory of interactions that occurs over time between physiological factors and contextual (environmental) factors. Life-span developmental theorists such as Paul Baltes believe that adult development is associated with changes in context (environment). Life-span theories and system-based nursing theories maintain that development is dynamic, involving bidirectional effects between the person and the environment. All these theories propose that changes in one (person or environment) promote changes in the other. Thus, development is viewed as dynamic, interdependent, and transactional, and therefore the relationship with parents and their child with chronic illness can serve as a context of each other's development. Parenting becomes one context of multidirectional influence. In planning parent education programs, the educator needs to consider the interrelated processes of cognition, affect, valuation, and action that occur as a result of parents applying new knowledge to their caregiving and parenting practices.

The interactions that occur between a parent and a child with chronic physical illness stimulate the dialectic process in adults. For example, parents' thoughts about their own childhood experiences lead to thoughts about their parenting role. However, these thoughts conflict with the current needs of their child with a chronic illness. This contradiction within the parent system is the context for behavioral system imbalance or the need for adaptation. Using the behavioral system imbalance model, one would say that education is required to expand the parents' set, choice, and action. This education leads to multiple perspective-taking (e.g., the child's point of view) as well as to dialectical engagement of conflicting thoughts about caregiving and parenting (i.e., their old experiences versus the needs of their child with chronic illness). To develop, the parent must recognize the multiple levels of the child's needs and engage in a dialectical process that will lead to a transformation in their ways of thinking and caring.

Health care providers planning educational programs for parents with a child with a chronic physical illness must recognize that their programs have multiple purposes. On one level, they need to provide information about the disease, knowledge about new skills and treatment regimens, and techniques to carry out treatment. On the other level, the program needs to lead to new self-knowledge and ways of knowing for the parent. Recent research has shown the interconnection of cognition to emotional development. The research suggests that positive adult development involves an integration of cognitive complexity and affect. In her findings, Gisela Labouvie-Vief concludes that emotion both informs and is informed by cognition and that cognition both informs and is informed by emotion, and this relationship leads to the ability to accept change. A parent education program has the potential to move the parent from "novice" to "expert" as a caregiver and also to increase their sense of well-being as a parent.

Ecocultural Aspects of Family Education

The ecocultural theory of Ronald Gallimore posits that families construct their daily routines to reflect their goals, resources, and values. Families with a child with a chronic physical illness organize a sustainable daily routine that considers their ecology (resources and constraints), culture (values and beliefs), and the needs and abilities of the family members who carry out the routines. Therefore, the educator should assess a family's goals, resources, values, and beliefs as well as how the family puts these elements together in their daily routines. Ecocultural theory indicates that to create a routine, the family has to respond to a variety of conflicting pressures that are placed on them. The responses to these pressures are called *accommodations*. These accommodations are implemented both within the family and in response to the wider social context. When planning educational programs, it is important to consider family routines as well as how the family relates to the broader outside context that exerts an influence on them.

Gallimore, Weisner, Kaufman, and Bernheimer (1989) describe five components that comprise all family routines: "who is present, their values and goals, what tasks are being performed, why they are being performed (the motives and feelings surrounding the action), and what scripts govern the interactions including those that shape and constrain the child's participation" (p. 217). These five components exemplify the interaction between ecology and culture and provide good guidelines to use in the assessment. Health care providers planning educational programs about the child's illness and care must do so with an understanding of existing family routines in the context of parental beliefs, values, and goals. Families may not integrate a new intervention into their lives because of significant disruptions to existing sustainable family routines. To meet family goals, values, and beliefs while taking into account family resources may require the health care provider to make alterations to the intervention and in the educational program.

Effective Family Education Programs

Characteristics

Effective family education programs designed to teach family members about the child's illness, techniques of care, and strategies to increase the child's self-management skills have several components in common. First, an effective education program will consider family routines and will teach the family members how to incorporate caregiving into their daily routines.

Routines provide an ideal opportunity for parents and other family members to regularly teach the child aspects of self-care. It also lets the health care provider and family members address problems that may occur within a specific context. To provide education related to caregiving at home, health care providers must successfully collaborate with family members. Collaboration with providers allows family members to provide input on their families' values, needs, and goals, resulting in a more individualized approach to education and to designing interventions. Collaboration also enhances the parents' development as they are active participants in developing experiential learning.

Three common elements are found in effective family education programs. These elements include transference of information from the educator to the family members; modeling of techniques, behaviors, and interventions in person or through videos; and using verbal and visual tools to provide feedback. Didactic instruction refers to the transference of information through written material or discussions. Didactic instruction is an important component of family education. Didactic instruction is one of the most common education methods and can be effective when used with other educational methods. Modeling is also an effective component. Modeling techniques allow the educator to present information visually to the learner. Finally, feedback is a critical component of effective education programs. Feedback occurs when family members receive oral or written input on their implementation of the care routine or specific intervention.

Research indicates that family members' beliefs and values impact the success of an educational program. It is important to assess their perceptions about proposed interventions. Family members may be less likely to implement procedures or a program of care if they do not believe the intervention will be successful or if it does not fit with family routines. If family members believe an intervention is effective, they may be more likely to be involved with the intervention. Family involvement is a key component of successful caregiving of a child with a chronic illness. Family involvement provides parents with empowerment—the knowledge to apply an intervention on their own terms and in a way that fits with family routines. Parent empowerment increases self-confidence, and as a result parents become more competent as they develop new perspectives about caring for their child. It also builds their self-trust and insights about themselves as parents.

Educators need to consider the role an educational program plays in adult development. The educational program provides specific information about an illness as well as intervention strategies and techniques. However, the program is also helping the parents learn how to nurture their child's physical, psychosocial, and developmental needs. Along with gaining knowledge, the parent is gaining wisdom, insights, and ways of organizing the world and the relationship with their child. Parents who acquire self-knowledge begin to make new choices in caregiving and parenting that match the child's developmental and physical needs. As parents are able to create an environment that nurtures their child, parents are nurtured at the same time. Educators need to allow time for parents to reflect not only on what they "learned" from the program, but what it means to them as parents (new meaning-making), their sense of well-being, and the parent–child relationship.

There are limitations to traditional education programs that are provided in hospitals, clinics, schools, or in the home. These education programs my be cost-prohibitive and time-consuming for both educators and family members. In addition, these programs may not be feasible for parents who cannot secure child care or who have transportation problems. Finally, families who live in rural areas may not have access to such programs or may lack specialists who offer them.

To address these limitations, some educators have used technology. Family education has been successful when didactic information has been followed up with phone consultations. Family members can be given self-directed study guides and workbooks to learn about the child's illness and to learn intervention techniques. Weekly telephone consultations can be used to individualize the program and to answer questions and to provide feedback. DVD and VHS programs can also be used to provide education to family members at the hospital and at home. These can be supplemented with written materials as well as checklists of information offered in each segment of the show. The Internet also offers a method to provide family education.

Online Family Education

For families with a child with a chronic illness, the Internet offers a venue to (a) acquire knowledge about the child's illness, (b) socialize and participate in communities of others who have a child with a chronic illness, (c) seek resources that will assist them with everyday care routines, and (d) use web-based disease management tools that assist them in managing the child's care.

Disease-specific online parent networks are an example of how parents are choosing a participatory role in their child's care. There are also online sibling websites. The Internet can be used to deliver many types of family education programs. The programs should be user-friendly and easily accessed by family members with a variety of technological skills. The program can include didactic material in PowerPoint presentations and online articles, video clips, pictures, graphics, quizzes, frequently asked questions, management tools, e-mail, social networking and web links, and a discussion forum. Programs can be offered online at a lower cost as compared to traditional in-person programs. Parents can access the material at their convenience and can repeat the program as often as needed.

There is a growing body of research on the use of technology to provide information to families with children with special needs. Studies indicate that family members access online information and education sites, learn from them, and are able to implement intervention strategies. In addition, the Internet presents family members and health care providers with the opportunity to collaborate and provide feedback more frequently and effectively than over the phone. There may be disadvantages to using the Internet for education programs. Families may not have access to the Internet or may lack the computer skills to use the program. Educators may not be able to deliver the same

quality of educational programs through the Internet as they can in person. Unless the educator and the families have access to appropriate technological equipment, the educator cannot show the family members the intervention and the family members cannot provide a return demonstration. In addition, real-time feedback is not possible. Internet education programs present the information in the same fashion to everyone accessing the program. In-person programs allow the educator to individualize the program and to explain and model interventions in different ways to aid comprehension.

Successful online education programs should incorporate the following: (a) daily progress reports, (b) e-mail reminders, (c) animated materials, (d) weekly assignments, and (e) written information. These five elements should be incorporated with the elements of effective educational programs that were discussed earlier. For example, consider a web-based family education program that combines telehealth with asthma case management along with educational information and interactive planning tools. The education program includes didactic content (PowerPoint slides and video), games, experiential learning, and skill building exercises for the all family members. Daily reports of peak-flow monitoring and parent-reported symptoms about the child are used to tailor additional e-health education. The computer can also be programmed to prompt the nurse or physician when certain symptoms appear or when the parent has a question. Such programs build the parents' sense of self-efficacy and help them build their children's asthma self-management skills. Given the extensive use of the Internet to obtain health information, and the variable quality of this information, health care providers need to educate family members about strategies to evaluate e-health websites. They should also teach them how to search and recommend high-quality websites.

Conclusion

The major implication that can be drawn from the material examined in this entry is that the shaping of human lives occurs within the primary relationship between the parent and child. Educational programs offered by health care providers can have a significant impact on the relationships formed within the family system and in individual interaction between the parent and the child with a chronic physical illness. Carefully planned educational programs with a multidirectional perspective of development that considers the person and the environment (context) can enhance parent development, child development, and the quality of family life.

Bonnie Holaday

See also Chronic Health Problems and Interventions for the Childrearing Family; Chronic Illness and Family Management Styles; Coping Management Styles in Families; Ethnic/Racial Influences in Families; Parenting

Further Readings

Allen, P. J., & Vessey, J. A. (Eds.). (2004). *Primary care of the child with a chronic condition* (4th ed.). St. Louis, MO: Mosby.

Baltes, P. B. (1987). Theoretical propositions of life-span developmental psychology: On the dynamics between growth and decline. *Developmental Psychology, 23*(5), 611–626.

D'Alessandro, D. M., & Dosa, N. P. (2001). Empowering children and families with information technology. *Archives of Pediatrics and Adolescent Medicine, 155*(10), 1131–1136.

Fawcett, J. (2005). *Contemporary nursing knowledge: Analysis and evaluation of Nursing models and theories* (2nd ed.). Philadelphia: F. A. Davis.

Gallimore, R., Weisner, T. S., Kaufman, S. Z., & Bernheimer, L. P. (1989). The social construction of ecocultural niches: Family accommodation of developmentally delayed children. *American Journal of Mental Retardation, 94*(3), 216–230.

Harris, M. (2004). Program: Empowering parents of children with special health care needs: Harnessing the power of the Internet. *Health, Education & Behavior, 31*(6), 664–666.

Kieckhefer, G. M., & Trahms, C. M. (2000). Supporting development of children with chronic conditions: From compliance to shared-management. *Pediatric Nursing, 26*(4), 354–363.

Labouvie-Vief, G. (2000). Affect complexity and views of the transcendent. In P. Young-Eisendrath & M. E. Miller (Eds.), *The psychology of nature spirituality:*
Integrity, wisdom, transcendence (pp. 103–119). New York: Routledge.

Mahut, G., Scoloveno, M. A., & Donnelly, C. B. (2007). Written educational materials for families of chronically ill children. *Journal of the American Academy of Nurse Practitioners, 19*(9), 471–476.

Newman, S., Steed, L., & Mulligan, K. (2004). Self-management interventions for chronic illness. *Lancet, 364,* 1523–1537.

Scharer, K. (2005). Internet social support for parents: The state of science. *Journal of Child and Adolescent Psychiatric Nursing, 18*(1), 26–35.

Wise, M., Gustafson, D., H., Sorkness, C. A., Molfenter, T., Staresinic, A., & Meis, T. (2007). Internet telehealth for pediatric asthma case management: Integrating computerized and case manager features for tailoring a web-based asthma education program. *Health Promotion Practices, 8*(3), 282–291.

Websites

Allergy & Asthma Network: Mothers of Asthmatics: http://www.aanma.org

Children and Adults with Spina Bifida & Hydrocephalus: http://www.waisman.wisc.edu/~rowley/sb-kids

Cystic Fibrosis: http://www.cysticfibrosis.com

Pediheart.Net (Congenital Heart Disease website): http://www.pediheart.net

Sickle Cell Kids: http://www.sicklecellkids.org

EDUCATING THE FAMILY REGARDING SERIOUS MENTAL ILLNESS

An individual is judged to have a mental illness if he or she experiences a mental, behavioral, or emotional problem that meets criteria for a disorder according to the *Diagnostic and Statistical Manual of Mental Disorders, Fourth Edition* that results in functional impairment that significantly limits major life activities. Psychotic disorders, including schizophrenia and schizoaffective disorder, and major mood disorders, such as bipolar disorder and major depressive disorder, are most frequently categorized as serious mental illnesses. According to the Substance Abuse and Mental Health Services Administration, approximately 8% of adults met criteria for a serious mental illness in 2002. This entry reviews the role of the family in recovery from serious mental illness, introduces family interventions for individuals with serious mental illness and their family members, and reviews the benefits of and barriers to family involvement in the treatment of serious mental illness. The term *family* is used broadly to refer to any individual with whom the individual with serious mental illness has a close relationship and wishes to involve in his or her mental health treatment.

Serious Mental Illness and the Family

Serious mental illness is associated with a number of adverse outcomes, including increased risk for substance use; homelessness; lower levels of employment, education, and income; poorer health; and social isolation. Individuals with serious mental illness face a multitude of life stressors and challenges that increase their risk for symptom exacerbation. Subsequently, the symptoms of the illness exacerbate the individual's already precarious life circumstances. The vast majority of individuals with serious mental illness rely on family and close friends as a source of tangible and emotional support to help them more effectively cope with these adversities. Specifically, family members often provide housing and financial support to individuals with serious mental illness and are often the first to recognize changes in their loved one's functioning. In turn, individuals who have family support tend to have better outcomes. However, the life stressors and adversities that individuals with serious mental illness face not only impact their lives but can also negatively influence the lives of family and close friends. Serving in a caregiving role can be stressful for family members of individuals with serious mental illness, leading to strained interpersonal relationships and a stressful family environment.

Historical Interest in the Role of the Family in Serious Mental Illness

Historically, the family environment was conceptualized as a key factor in the development and maintenance of serious mental illness. Specifically, stressful family environments, defined as environments containing high levels of "expressed emotion" or environments in which family members are critical and emotionally overinvolved in the life of the individual with serious mental illness, have been shown to contribute to higher rates of relapse or a faster return of symptoms (among individuals with schizophrenia and bipolar disorder). Given that the experience of having a family member with serious mental illness is stressful, this stress likely contributes to distress, or depression and anxiety, and burden, including perceived stress associated with the caregiver role, for family members of individuals with serious mental illness. In turn, this stress may lead to higher levels of expressed emotion in the family. Initially, family interventions were designed to improve family communication skills in order to decrease levels of expressed emotion in the family system and, as such, were typically offered only to families with high levels of expressed emotion. These interventions were focused on modifying communication and interaction patterns between individuals with serious mental illness and their family. However, over time, the coping skills and support offered by family interventions has been recognized as beneficial to all families regardless of level of expressed emotion. Currently, family interventions are designed to be available to families regardless of level of expressed emotion, with the goal of these interventions being twofold: to educate individuals with serious mental illness and their family members and to improve the communication and problem-solving skills of both individuals with serious mental illness and their family members. There are several types of family interventions, which differ in the focus of the treatment, length of treatment, who is involved in the treatment, and expected outcomes.

Theoretical Underpinnings of Family Interventions

Family interventions can be broadly categorized as insight-oriented, systems-based, behavioral, or psychoeducational. Insight-oriented family therapies have arisen out of psychodynamic and interpersonal theories. Psychodynamic theory posits that unconscious processes and early childhood experiences impact current interpersonal interactions and relationships. According to psychodynamic theory, exploration of these unconscious processes and past experiences, in relation to emotions generated by familial interactions in the present moment, is necessary to facilitate changes in these relationship patterns. Structural and strategic family therapies represent system-level approaches. The goal of structural family therapy is to modify dysfunctional habitual patterns of interactions between family members, in turn, shifting global family interaction patterns. In a similar manner, strategic family therapy focuses on modifying specific maladaptive interpersonal behaviors in order to improve thoughts and feelings about familial relationships. Solution-focused therapy is a brief, present-focused therapy in which family members systematically work to resolve family problems. Behavioral theory suggests that changes in patterns of interaction will influence thoughts and emotions both in and about the familial relationships. According to behavioral theory, insight into past interpersonal patterns is not necessary to produce the behavioral modifications required to improve familial relationships in the present. Recent family interventions have been psychoeducational in nature, combining behavioral and problem-solving approaches with education about mental illness. The premise underlying psychoeducation is that greater knowledge about the illness and effective communication and problem solving will facilitate better self-care for the individual with serious mental illness and improved understanding and adaptive support from family members of individuals with serious mental illness.

Family Interventions

The focus of family interventions extends beyond biological relatives and caregivers to close friends and anyone who provides substantial support to the individual with serious mental illness. For the most part, family interventions include both the individual with serious mental illness and family members and are intended to improve mental health and quality-of-life outcomes for all. However, there are a minority of family interventions in which only family members attend. Desired family outcomes

include reduced subjective burden and distress, such as lower levels of negative emotion and stress associated with having a family member with serious mental illness, increased knowledge about serious mental illness, improved family relationships, and increased support. Desired outcomes of family interventions for the individual with serious mental illness include decreased symptomatology, lower rates of relapse and rehospitalization, improved family relationships, and improved social and vocational outcomes.

Family Psychoeducation Programs

Family psychoeducation (FPE) programs represent one broad class of family interventions. The goals of FPE are to provide education, skills building, and emotional support to families of individuals with serious mental illness in order to improve mental health outcomes for these individuals. Guiding principles of FPE include therapist alignment with the family, a focus on any crises in the present moment, and the provision of family support in the face of stressors. Families are encouraged to focus on helping their family member with serious mental illness to set realistic, personal goals, to facilitate social and vocational development, and to foster a positive family atmosphere. FPE programs can be administered in a multifamily format or single-family format and have been implemented with both individuals with schizophrenia and bipolar disorder and their family members.

Two of the more widely used FPE programs designed for individuals with schizophrenia are multifamily group treatment and behavioral family treatment. Multifamily group treatment lasts from 9 months to 3 years, is led by a mental health professional, and involves several families meeting as a group to receive information on mental illness and to offer mutual support and problem solving. The climate of multifamily group treatment is social and supportive in nature, and families are encouraged to establish ongoing social support networks beyond the group sessions.

Behavioral family therapy is usually conducted with an individual family and tailored to that family's individual strengths and needs. Sessions are generally held on a weekly or biweekly basis for 9 months up to 2 years. After an initial needs assessment and treatment goal identification, the intervention focuses on illness education, communication skills training, problem-solving skills, and work on individual goals. A similar family intervention adapted to address the unique needs of individuals with bipolar disorder is family-focused therapy. The format of family-focused therapy parallels that of behavioral family therapy, with both interventions placing a large emphasis on communication, structured problem solving, and out-of-session practice of skills.

Family Consultation and Brief Family Education

Briefer family services, such as family consultation and brief family education, have also been developed in an effort to educate and offer basic coping skills to families. Some established models of briefer family services permit family members to receive services even if their loved one with serious mental illness is not interested in services. Family consultation involves working with the family to address a specified need or goal identified by the individual with serious mental illness, their family members, or both. Family consultation typically involves one to five sessions with a mental health professional, with initial sessions focusing on the assessment of individual and family needs and later meetings focusing on identified goals. Thus, depending on the needs of the family, later sessions may include illness education, coping skills development, and/or referrals to community resources and programs along with a focus on resolution of particular problems as they arise. Brief family education involves a mental health professional providing families with education on mental illness and its treatment, coping strategies and skills, community resources, and other topics of importance to families of individuals with serious mental illness. Educational sessions are often conducted in a group format and can be held on a weekly or monthly basis for a specified period of time or on an ongoing basis. Peer-led family education programs, such as the Family-to-Family Education Program, are also available. In contrast to FPE, in which the focus of treatment is therapeutic and the goal is to improve outcomes for the individual with serious mental illness, the primary goal of

peer-led family education programs is the health and well-being of the family. The intervention is a 2- to 3-hour weekly class led by trained family members and designed to provide family members with education on mental illness and information on available treatments and resources, enhance family problem-solving and communication skills, and provide mutual support.

Intervention Effectiveness

The benefits of participation in programs that provide illness education, skills training, and support for both individuals with serious mental illness and family members are clear. Individuals with both schizophrenia and bipolar disorder and a recent symptom exacerbation, who participated in an FPE program that lasted 6 to 9 months or more and included illness education, problem solving, crisis intervention, and emotional support, demonstrated lower rates of relapse and rehospitalization. Moreover, individuals who received FPE reported improved treatment adherence, lower levels of perceived stress, and improved social and functional outcomes. Family members who received FPE reported decreased levels of burden and distress, improved family relationships, and greater knowledge of mental illness. The extensive evidence for the benefit of a 6- to 9-month FPE program for individuals with serious mental illness who have had a recent symptom exacerbation and their families has contributed to recommendation of its use by the Schizophrenia Patient Outcomes Research Team and the American Psychiatric Association.

There is some evidence that outcomes of family interventions vary according to the length of the intervention and the symptom profile of the individual with serious mental illness. Specifically, there is limited evidence that FPE contributes to lower rates of relapse and rehospitalization among individuals with serious mental illness who have not had a recent illness exacerbation. Likewise, family interventions that are shorter in length (less than 6 months) have not been consistently shown to contribute to lower rates of relapse or rehospitalization. However, shorter family interventions and family interventions offered to individuals without a recent symptom exacerbation contribute to other positive outcomes, including lower levels of distress, increased support, and greater knowledge of serious mental illness for family members. Participation in peer-led family education programs has evidenced a number of benefits for the family, including greater confidence in their ability to help their family member with serious mental illness, less concern about this individual, reduced subjective burden, increased knowledge of mental illness and the mental health service system, better self-care, improved family relationships, and greater satisfaction in the caregiver role.

Barriers to Implementation of Family Interventions

Despite the preponderance of evidence suggesting that family interventions are effective in improving outcomes for individuals with serious mental illness and their family members, dissemination of these interventions remains limited. When considering reasons why family interventions have not been widely adopted, there are a number of patient-, family member–, provider-, and system-level barriers that may inhibit participation. In general, providers and administrators may be unaware of the evidence base supporting the cost-effectiveness of family interventions. Moreover, lack of provider reimbursement for family services represents a considerable barrier to the provision of these services and highlights the fact that system-level changes are necessary to make the provision of family services feasible. Additional provider-level barriers include a general discomfort with family work due to lack of experience and training in working with families. Encouraging providers to consider the clinical benefits of involving family in their patients' clinical care may further motivate providers to work with families. Specifically, family members spend considerable time with the individual with serious mental illness and, because of this, may serve as a secondary source of information concerning their loved one's current health and behaviors, past illness and treatment experiences, potential stressors that lead to symptom exacerbation, and knowledge of the individual's personal strengths, resiliencies, and coping skills. This information could prove invaluable in determining appropriate treatment goals for the individual with serious mental illness. Moreover, family members can help problem solve around particular

issues or concerns and identify ways to support the individual with serious mental illness in the community, thus increasing the likelihood of progress toward and achievement of personal goals. In sum, educating providers and administrators about the cost-saving and clinical benefits associated with the inclusion of family members in the treatment of individuals with serious mental illness may lead to the erosion of system- and provider-level barriers to the provision of family interventions for serious mental illness.

When considering patient and family member barriers to the implementation of family interventions, confidentiality is a large barrier for the individual with serious mental illness. Often individuals with serious mental illness express concerns about having the clinician disclose personal information to family members, compromising their already limited autonomy. Worries about confidentiality can be dispelled by the clinician's explaining the bounds of confidentiality and ensuring that the individual with serious mental illness has control over what is shared with family members. Stigma also limits use of family interventions. Individuals with serious mental illness often worry about encountering increased stigma and judgment from family members in relation to their mental illness. Alternately, family members may have had unpleasant interactions with mental health services in the past and may fear being blamed for their relative's illness. These past experiences and anticipation of future stigmatization may contribute to family members' reluctance to pursue family services. Finally, logistical difficulties, including lack of time and transportation, also interfere with family members' involvement in family interventions. Education about the focus and potential benefits of family interventions for both the individual with serious mental illness and family may reduce family- and patient-level barriers to family interventions.

Summary and Future Directions

Family members of individuals with serious mental illness play a major role in supporting the individual with serious mental illness and thus are personally impacted by their family member's illness. This entry introduced three major types of family interventions for individuals with serious mental illness and their loved ones: FPE programs, brief family interventions, and peer-based family interventions. Whereas FPE programs aim to improve mental health and quality of life for both individuals with serious mental illness and their family members, peer and provider-led family education interventions are generally focused on improving outcomes for family members. Longer FPE programs (6 months to 2 years) have been shown to contribute to lower rates of relapse and rehospitalization, reduced symptomatology, improved treatment adherence, improved family relationships, and enhanced vocational and social outcomes for individuals with serious mental illness, and increased illness knowledge, greater satisfaction with treatment, improved family relationships, and increased support for family members. Briefer family interventions have also been shown to contribute to positive outcomes for family members, including lower levels of distress, increased support, greater knowledge of serious mental illness, and better self-care. Despite these demonstrated benefits, family interventions are not widely used; this is due to barriers at the levels of the patient, family member, provider, and system. Future research needs to further explore barriers to widespread utilization of family interventions as well as ways to facilitate dissemination of these interventions. Dissemination of family interventions for individuals with serious mental illness has the potential to improve treatment of serious mental illness and enhance quality of life and relationship satisfaction for individuals with serious mental illness and family members.

Christine Calmes, Lisa Dixon,
and Amy Drapalski

See also Bipolar Disorders and the Family; Communication in Families Related to Health and Illness; Depression in the Family; Family Emotional Climate and Mental Health; Psychoeducational Interventions for Families; Schizophrenia and the Family

Further Readings

Anderson, C. M., Hogarty, G. E., & Reiss, D. J. (1986). *Schizophrenia and the family: A practitioner's guide to psychoeducation and management.* New York: Guilford Press.

Dixon, L., Lyles, A., Scott, J., Lehman, A. L., Postrado, L., Goldman, H., et al. (1999). Services to families of adults with schizophrenia: From treatment recommendations to dissemination. *Psychiatric Services, 50,* 233–238.

Froggat, D., Fadden, G., Johnson, D. L., Leggatt, M., & Shankar, R. (2007). *Families as partners in mental health care: A guidebook for implementing family work.* Toronto, Ontario, Canada: World Fellowship for Schizophrenia and Allied Disorder.

McFarlane, W. R. (2002). *Multifamily groups in the treatment of severe psychiatric disorders.* New York: Guilford Press.

Miklowitz, D. J. (2008). *Bipolar disorder: A family-focused treatment approach.* New York: Guilford Press.

Mueser, K. T., & Glynn, S. M. (1999). *Behavioral family therapy for psychiatric disorders.* Oakland, CA: New Harbinger.

Murray-Swank, A., Dixon, L. B., & Stewart, B. (2007). Practical interviewing strategies for building an alliance with the families of patients who have severe mental illness. *Psychiatric Clinics of North America, 30,* 167–180.

EDUCATION OF CHILD LIFE PROVIDERS IN FAMILY HEALTH

Child life specialists are specially trained, college-educated professionals who care for the psychosocial needs of children and families in health care settings and related child/family psychosocial service environments. Research has demonstrated that children understand and cope with the stressors of events such as illness, hospitalization, bereavement, and trauma differently than do adults. Child life specialists are trained to encourage children's healthy coping and help them understand their experiences by utilizing play, expressive activities, education, and psychological preparation for stressful experiences. With the support of child life specialists, children and their families can learn to effectively cope with the emotionally challenging events that can threaten the normal development of children. This entry examines the education of child life providers with the intent of helping students and current health care professionals understand the unique knowledge base, skills, and abilities child life specialists bring to any team of individuals caring for a child and family in the health care environment.

History of the Child Life Profession

The child life profession is considered to be relatively new compared to other health care disciplines in North America. Research conducted in the early 1920s found that the high number of infant deaths occurring in hospitals and orphanages were due largely to minimal human contact and lack of sensory stimulation. As a specialty, pediatric medicine had only begun to evolve in the mid- to late 19th century. The medical community's answer to controlling rampant infectious diseases (e.g., measles, diphtheria, polio, and meningitis) in children during that time was to increase isolation and strictly limit physical contact between ill children and caregivers. Subsequent observation of older children who were hospitalized for long periods of time (a common occurrence in the early 20th century) revealed the significant emotional distress and social isolation that children experienced. This distress and isolation was later found to have significantly interrupted the normal developmental growth of these children. Early pioneers in the child life profession recognized children's need for sensory stimulation through play activities and schooling, as well as the need for social and emotional support.

The programs now referred to as child life programs were first conceived in the 1920s by a handful of individuals who believed in and promoted the hospitalized child's continuing need to develop and cope through play. These individuals provided play and educational activities as well as emotional support. In addition, their work often included teaching other health care staff about caring for the needs of children beyond their physical health, such as how to communicate with children in a child-friendly manner. Despite the fact that many physicians and administrators felt that play was a superfluous activity in hospitals, by the 1950s play programs had begun to spread across the United States. Over time, play programs were gradually accepted as a necessary element of pediatric care.

Throughout the 1960s, child life providers began to collaborate and advocate for children in health care settings. As the number of hospital play programs grew, so did the demand for child life specialist training programs. A number of academic programs were established at colleges and universities in the 1970s and 1980s. During this period, child life providers came together to further define theoretical foundations, practice standards, responsibilities, and requirements for education (both academic and clinical) and certification. A landmark study in Phoenix, Arizona, was conducted in the early 1980s examining the effect of a hospital-based child life program in lessening the negative effects of hospitalization and health care experiences for children. The results substantiated a need for child life providers in health care settings. Today, the educational and clinical preparation of child life specialists provides a foundation for utilizing clinical skills not only in inpatient and outpatient pediatric health care units but also in settings such as hospice and bereavement centers, children's camps, dental offices, and early intervention programs in North America and around the world.

Educational Preparation

The Child Life Council, an organization comprised of clinical child life specialists, educators, allied health workers, administrators, and students, has established standards for both academic and clinical preparation components for individuals wishing to become child life specialists. Entry-level competencies are achieved through the completion of a bachelor's degree, although many students choose to further their education by completing a master's degree program as well. Recommended educational elements include a broad spectrum of theoretical and applied coursework with a strong foundation in child development. Courses and experiences that address clinical practice issues and a clinical internship experience are necessary components. Shortly after finishing the academic and clinical education experiences, one may apply to sit for the Child Life Certification Exam, presented by the Child Life Certifying Committee under the auspices of the Child Life Council. The credential of Certified Child Life Specialist signifies that the individual has achieved a level of knowledge and performance requisite to becoming a competent child life specialist.

Academic Preparation

Individuals who wish to enter the child life profession should begin with an undergraduate academic program that provides a strong general education in writing, math, science, social and behavioral science, and the humanities. From there, students should focus on the theoretical foundations for understanding human and/or child development and families, as well as opportunities for applying theory to real-world experiences.

General Education

Students desiring to become child life specialists must have strong written and verbal communication skills. Therefore, it is essential that students take courses such as college composition, public speaking, and/or group processes. To prepare for future research participation and for understanding evidence-based practice as a professional, it is highly recommended that a student prove competent in college algebra, undergraduate-level statistics, and research methods in the social sciences. In the sciences, courses such as anatomy and biology are helpful in preparing individuals to teach children about their bodies. A strong foundation in understanding general psychology and sociology principles is recommended. Courses in the humanities, such as general, professional, or medical ethics, will provide a basis for understanding and dealing with professional ethical dilemmas.

Theoretical Foundations

At the heart of child life work is the goal of supporting children in maximizing their otherwise normal developmental potential despite the stressors that they experience while undergoing tests, procedures, and therapies to improve their physical health. To recognize delayed development, one must first understand the processes of children's typical growth. Child life specialists must be well versed in all areas of child development (cognitive, emotional, social, and physical/motor) from birth through adolescence.

To begin, child life specialists must have a working understanding of cognitive development. Individuals such as Jean Piaget and Lev Vygotsky developed theories of how children's thinking develops from infancy onward, and other scholars have developed theories of how individuals process information. Knowing how children's thinking and language change as they grow helps one understand how a child could have a misconception that

treatment of illness is a punishment for something entirely unrelated. With comprehensive knowledge of development, a child life specialist can begin to correct a child's frightening misunderstanding that one's arms and feet will be painfully pulled in opposite directions when placed on a "stretcher." Appreciating how a child thinks at different developmental stages helps a child life specialist communicate with a child on a readily understood level.

Much of the work of child life specialists is based on John Bowlby's theory of child–caregiver attachment and Mary Ainsworth's work on classifications of attachment quality. These theories are focused on the child's sense of trust in the caregiver to meet the child's basic needs, as a function of the adult's quality of ongoing care. To child life specialists, the parent–child relationship is a fundamental component in the child's coping efforts. Child life specialists continue to utilize attachment theories to assess and encourage the development and continuation of healthy parent–child relationships in the health care environment.

Another element of assessing a child's development includes an examination of social development. In the health care environment, child life specialists utilize social learning theories like that of Albert Bandura. Bandura felt strongly that children learn through observation and then change their behaviors as a result of those observations. His concept of social modeling is relied upon when teaching children coping techniques like deep breathing and relaxation for pain control, or using puppets or dolls to teach children comfortable positions for medical procedures. Erik Erikson focused on social and cultural factors as the most significant factors in a child's psychosocial development. He postulated a stage-based theory of social conflicts occurring at key points in a child's growth. A child life specialist may utilize this theory as the basis for selecting an appropriate activity for a teenager who is exploring personal identity and has a developmental need for independence, especially within the context of a chronic illness.

When meeting a child for the first time, a child life specialist attends to cues that provide some understanding of the child's temperament. Alexander Thomas and Stella Chess's important work on children's temperament gives psychosocial professionals a framework from which one can begin to understand how a child's innate characteristics of temperament will interface with the immediate environment to produce a desirable (or undesirable) climate for coping. Child life specialists can adjust some elements of the environment to better fit the child's temperament, which usually increases the child's ability to cope. For example, when working with a child who needs more time than others to adjust to new people and new situations ("slow-to-warm"), the child life specialist might take a more sensitive approach in establishing rapport and provide information about hospitalization and procedures in smaller "chunks."

Although determining a child's temperament is helpful, understanding the child's coping style is just as important in assisting the child in managing the emotional aspects of the health care experience. Child life specialists frequently rely on the stress and coping theory of Richard Lazarus and Susan Folkman. When attempting to cope, some children focus on controlling or changing the situations that cause the stress (problem-based coping), whereas others focus on controlling their emotional reactions to stressors (emotion-based coping). Understanding a child's coping style allows the child life specialist to determine which interventions will be most helpful in minimizing a child's stress in the health care environment. For instance, children who naturally utilize emotion-based coping often benefit from activities that afford them emotional expression opportunities. Interventions focused on preparation, education, and opportunities for control can be of great benefit to those children who have problem-based coping styles.

Although child life specialists aim to minimize the stressors and negative emotional reactions of children in the health care setting, the child's family system must be taken into account. It is necessary to understand the interaction among the child, the family, and the health care environment, as no one element exists in isolation. Therefore, a clear comprehension of theories such as family systems theory and Urie Bronfenbrenner's ecological theory is essential to understanding how the child and the child's illness affects the family and, conversely, how the family affects the child both in and outside of the health care environment.

In addition to building a strong conceptual foundation of child and family development, it is also important for child life specialists to understand children's play. Both Piaget and Vygotsky viewed play as crucial to children's learning and socialization. Mildred Parten characterized children's play as occurring in stages, becoming more social as children grow. The research of these scholars gives one a clear understanding that children do indeed learn through play. Play is an essential element of child life work, as it is a tool used in developing rapport, observing and assessing children's coping, and implementing interventions that decrease stress and increase children's mastery of distressing situations.

Applied Areas of Study

It is not enough to have a solid understanding of the development of children and families. Child life specialists must also be able to *apply* theoretical knowledge to their work with children and their families in the health care setting. Students should begin to build skills in application of theory during undergraduate coursework.

During the student's coursework, there are a variety of topics and issues specific to the work of child life specialists that are typically addressed. Students are introduced to the process of clinical service provision—assessment, planning, implementation, and evaluation. To assess the needs of the child and family, students must understand the possible emotional reactions of children and families to the stressors of the health care environment, particularly in regard to specific care environments (i.e., intensive care unit, emergent, outpatient, surgical, etc.) as well as the type of illness (short-term vs. chronic illness). They must also understand typical pediatric medical conditions and treatments (including medical terminology), children's conceptualization of illness, how multicultural factors affect children's and families' actions and reactions in health care, and the nature and process of building therapeutic relationships. In planning, it is also necessary to be familiar with resources, the roles and available therapies of other interdisciplinary health care providers, and the most effective methods of communicating with other health care team members.

To implement effective interventions that will reduce a child's stress and anxiety and increase coping and mastery, students are introduced to topics and methods of providing therapeutic play, expressive therapies, guided imagery, relaxation, non-pharmacological pain management techniques, as well as developmentally appropriate stress-point preparation, support, and teaching (including the use of developmentally appropriate nonthreatening language). It is also important that students have a solid understanding of death and bereavement issues and support provision techniques, patient rights and advocacy concepts, and the philosophy and practices of family-centered care. Students are typically introduced to methods of interdisciplinary communication and documentation prior to beginning their clinical internships.

Time and attention should be given to a variety of professional topics, including administration (record keeping, budgets, supervision of others, etc.), time management, and professional responsibility prioritization issues. Students should also have the opportunity to examine professional ethics, boundaries, and confidentiality; limitations/scope of clinical practice; and techniques of self-reflective and evaluative practice. Any discussion of professional issues in child life education would not be complete without a thorough review of the history of the profession, orientation to the Child Life Council, and familiarization with the child life professional certification process.

Prior to working with ill and injured children, students must build skills in working with healthy, typically developing children. This work generally occurs in educational early-childhood laboratory settings, school settings, camps, and tutoring programs. It is essential that students have the opportunity to apply their theoretical knowledge in these settings while building and honing skills in building rapport, observing and assessing children, and developing programming and activities that stimulate normal development, as well as building and nurturing professional relationships with parents and staff.

Direct contact with hospitalized children is as important to the educational preparation of would-be child life specialists as building competencies in working with healthy children. Initial contact with ill, injured, and disabled children commonly occurs in a volunteer capacity. Additional experiences in special needs and early intervention settings for children are valuable as well, regardless of academic level.

All of the theoretical and applied elements mentioned earlier should be provided in both bachelor's and master's degree programs. However, one can expect that the examination of issues will be more in depth at the graduate level. Master's programs may also allow students to extensively explore topics such as administrative and supervisory issues, program development, grant writing, and research design and implementation.

Clinical Preparation

Practicum

After the initial contact experiences, most child life students complete a practicum during which they work closely with a child life specialist engaging in observation or direct work with hospitalized children and their families. This experience is intended to prepare the student for a clinical internship. During the practicum, students learn a great deal about the health care setting, the needs of children and families, and the role and methods of child life specialists on a precursory level. It is at this juncture that a student receives feedback in regard to whether or not he or she demonstrates the ability to apply theory to practice and the interpersonal skills necessary to become competent through a clinical internship experience.

Clinical Internship

Completing a practicum-level experience in a child life program allows a student to develop some confidence in the ability to further build clinical practice skills. However, the most plentiful opportunities for building clinical practice skills and making the transition from student to professional are found during the child life internship experience. During this experience, individuals complete a minimum of 480 clock-hours (the current clinical experience minimum required to establish certification exam eligibility) of direct work with children and families in the health care setting, under the supervision of a certified child life specialist. This experience allows aspiring child life specialists exposure to a variety of patient care environments, families, and children with a variety of developmental levels, illnesses, and disabilities, as well as the opportunity to increase competency in independently providing psychosocial services. Interns receive direct supervision and feedback from their clinical preceptors with the goal of achieving entry-level professional competence by the conclusion of the experience.

Fellowship

Although not a readily available opportunity at this time, a child life fellowship is a temporary, post-internship experience pursued by some individuals. This experience allows young professionals opportunities to further build clinical skills under the guidance of a professional mentor, often while focusing in on a particular setting (e.g., intensive care) or patient diagnostic specialty area (e.g., oncology). These experiences are not mandatory for entry-level employment and can be difficult to find because of a lack of funding for fellowship positions.

Nora Hager

See also Acute Health Problems and Interventions for the Childrearing Family; Chronic Health Problems and Interventions for the Childrearing Family; Cystic Fibrosis and the Family; Parental Attachment; Partnering With Families: Family-Centered Care; Sibling Death/Loss; Siblings of Ill Children; Therapeutic Play and the Family

Further Readings

American Academy of Pediatrics, Child Life Council and Committee on Hospital Care. (2006). Child life services. *Pediatrics, 118*(4), 1757–1763.

Gaynard, L., Wolfer, J., Goldberger, J., Thompson, R., Redburn, L., & Laidley, L. (1990). *Psychosocial care of children in hospitals: A clinical practice manual.* Bethesda, MD: Association for the Care of Children's Health.

Hicks, M. (Ed.). (2008). *Child life beyond the hospital.* Rockville, MD: Child Life Council.

Rollins, J. A., Bolig, R., & Mahan, C. C. (2005). *Meeting children's psychosocial needs across the health-care continuum.* Austin, TX: PRO-ED.

Thompson, R. (1985). *Psychosocial research on pediatric hospitalization.* Springfield, IL: Charles C Thomas.

Thompson, R. (Ed.). (2009). *The handbook of child life: A guide for pediatric psychosocial care.* Springfield, IL: Charles C Thomas.

Thompson, R., & Stanford, G. (1981). *Child life in hospitals: Theory and practice.* Springfield, IL: Charles C Thomas.

Websites

Child Life Council: http://www.childlife.org

Initiative for Pediatric Palliative Care: http://www.ippcweb.org

Institute for Patient- and Family-Centered Care: http://www.familycenteredcare.org

EDUCATION OF HEALTH CARE PROVIDERS: WHO FAMILY HEALTH NURSES

In 1998 the World Health Organization (WHO) Regional Office for Europe produced Health 21, the Health for All policy framework for the WHO European Region, which resulted in the production of 21 targets on health for the 21st century. In response, WHO Europe fashioned a new role titled the *family health nurse* (FHN) and determined that this new type of nurse would make a key contribution within the multidisciplinary health care team. WHO Europe consists of 53 nations ranging from the United Kingdom and Portugal in the West to the Russian Federation in the East and Israel in the South; it also includes many of the former Soviet States as well as all of the Scandinavian countries. The curriculum that emerged prepared qualified and experienced nurses for the new role and was subsequently piloted across a number of European countries, one of those being Scotland. Community nursing roles within some remote and rural parts of Scotland at the time of the pilot were proving unsustainable, and the FHN pilot offered an opportunity to introduce the FHN role within a rural health care context. The students involved in the pilot undertook a learning journey characterized by a range of transformations whereby they experienced dramatic changes in their approaches to working with families.

Community Nursing Roles in Scotland

Health Visitors

The community nursing workforce in Scotland at the time of the pilot consisted of a number of discrete roles, all involved in the delivery of care in people's homes. Health visitors, more latterly titled public health nurses, mainly focus on reducing health inequalities by working with individuals, families, and communities to promote health and prevent ill health, with emphasis on partnership that cuts across disciplinary, professional, and organizational boundaries. What often happens, despite an emphasis on a life-span approach within the statutory standards and the educational preparation, is that health visitors largely work with children under the age of 5 years and their families, with a major emphasis on child protection. Policy in the United Kingdom over the past decade has highlighted the importance of the health visitor role in working with children from the birth to 18 years, recognizing the importance of addressing health behaviors in the school-age population, particularly with regard to smoking, exercise, diet, and sexual behavior. The reality is that very few health visitors work with schoolchildren and adult age groups, and with the exception of families with children under 5 years old, very few practitioners engage with the families of the clients/patients.

District Nurses

District nurses, in contrast, care for sick people within their own homes. The majority of patients seen by district nurses are over the age of 65 and likely to suffer from long-term conditions such as chronic leg ulcers, diabetes, multiple sclerosis, and stroke. Thus, the focus of care is largely physical

in nature. Over recent years, care has become increasingly more acute in nature; the length of time spent by patients in hospitals has reduced, and more people are discharged home with high-level complex care needs. In addition to the key roles of health visitor and district nurse, there is the community midwife, a discrete professional who cares for pregnant women and newborn children, who normally pass responsibility for care to the health visitor at around 4 weeks postpartum. In most urban settings these three roles are fulfilled by separate professionals, all of whom undertake separate educational preparations for the roles; they tend to be experienced nurses, often 5 to 10 years post qualification, and thus the time taken to prepare for these roles can be quite lengthy.

Community Nursing in the Scottish Highlands and Islands

The Highlands and Islands of Scotland are a land mass of 4 million hectares and larger than the size of Belgium. Out of a population of 440,000, there are six major urban centers of population ranging from 10,000 to 50,000 people. This is a widely dispersed population who are both rural and, more importantly, very often remote from centers of health care. In urban settings, discrete health professionals, as described, provide community health care. Quite often, in the more remote and rural communities and in particular island communities, health professionals fulfill double and triple duties in that they are both health visitors and district nurses and, in some settings, midwives as well. To be a double- or triple-duty nurse, nurses may well have trained for 3 years for their initial nurse qualification and then anything up to 3½ more years to become a triple-duty nurse. Because this training can easily take up to 10 years, it is extremely expensive and poses huge challenges for succession planning. In the late 1990s the Scottish Highlands and Islands health authorities found it increasingly more difficult to recruit nurses to fill these roles. In addition, government policy papers identified, despite protestations from the health visitor fraternity, that the majority of community nurses were not adopting a family-focused approach to care. It was not uncommon in urban settings, particularly with extended family units, to have several different health professionals engaging with one family at the same time. At times, access to a single, shared assessment and common patient record was limited. The academic preparation for these discrete roles failed to address areas such as family assessment and the family as a unit of care; there was a minimal focus on interpersonal skills development. Therefore, engagement was often determined by the main priority of care (e.g., developmental aspects of a young child in the case of a health visitor or wound care needs of an elderly grandmother in the case of a district nurse). Intergenerational aspects of health and illness rarely formed part of the care scenario. The workloads of the health visitor or district nurse meant that managers placed low priority on family-oriented approaches to care. Many community nurses argued they did adopt a family approach, but when explored in depth it became clear they were often caring for more than one family member, but they were doing this individually and not adopting a family unit approach. In areas where triple- or double-duty nurses worked, they were often attending a household for more than one member, but the visits were very often focused on a single condition, without any real acknowledgment of the family dimension. One could argue that this is not surprising, as their academic preparation focused on the discrete roles; their managers expected them to address patient/ client needs through the specific lens of the single roles. In other words, nurses were neither trained to adopt a family-centered approach nor expected to by their managers. The main activities of community nurses were often focused on conditions and illnesses, with minimal evidence of searching for unmet health needs or implementing active health promotion strategies.

Family Health Nurse Pilot

Enlightened nurse leaders at both government and local levels in Scotland seized upon the WHO Family Health Nurse initiative as an opportunity to address the workforce challenges by replacing the traditional double- and triple-duty role by nurses trained much more quickly. In essence, it was an amalgamation of the district nurse and health visitor roles; statutory restriction meant that the service still required community midwives. To describe it as an amalgamation is a gross oversimplification, as evidenced by the new curriculum. The "new" FHNs were not only going to address the areas covered by health visitors and district nurses, but they were also going to bring benefits to the individual, the family, and the community. The challenge was to shift the emphasis from an illness focus to a health focus; from a passive recipient of care to one of an active participant in care; from an individual focus to a family focus.

Family Health Nurse Role

The FHN role, as envisaged by WHO, focused on a number of key concepts. The curriculum-planning group drew on developmental theory, systems theory, and interaction theory. Developmental theory was important in promoting an understanding of both the individual and the family in the context of the major life course events that all people encounter and that vary in intensity and impact, depending on many complex factors.

Interaction theory underpins the concept of the nurse–patient relationship and the nurse–family relationship, along with the partnership and teamwork that are central to the philosophy of community health care. Systems theory is fundamental to representing and analyzing the complexities of family situations and health care. FHNs are encouraged to view the families they work with as systems that operate within the context of environments (e.g., home, work, community, school) and the way factors within that environment impact the lives and experiences of the family members. These factors, often referred to as stressors, can be perceived both positively and negatively, leading to a strengthening or weakening of resistance within the family unit. These stressors can be environmental, psychological, social, and physical in nature (e.g., genetic, bacterial infection, housing, noise). Health is a dynamic variable that operates across systems, such as the individual, the family, and the environment. Health, as a variable, changes over time just as the systems themselves change; it is the complex interchange that influences the reaction of individuals and families to health and illness. The role of the FHN is an interactive activity, in which nurse and family are partners. The goal of the nurse's activity is to maintain and, if possible, improve the family's equilibrium or health status by helping the family to avoid or to cope with stressors or threats to health.

The WHO family health nurse curriculum describes the FHN as a nurse who functions as a care provider, decision maker, communicator, community leader, and manager. Many practitioners working in the community in Scotland as either health visitors or district nurses would claim most of these roles. It is the particular way that the FHN role embraces the family as the central element of care that sets the FHN apart from other roles.

The role that emerged is that of a skilled generalist encompassing a broad range of duties, dealing, as the first point of contact, with any issues that present themselves, referring on to specialists where a greater degree of expertise is required; practitioners who based their practice on a model based on health rather than illness. The FHN takes a lead role in preventing illness and promoting health as well as caring for those people who are ill and require nursing care. This role is founded on the principle of caring for families rather than just individuals within them, and is firmly based on the concept of the nurse as a first point of contact.

The definition of *family* generates much discussion: Does the FHN work only with families constructed along traditional lines, described in terms such as *nuclear* or *extended*? In the communities served by FHNs there are many family types but, given its rural nature, there is certainly a significant percentage of extended family units. Of course, "family" is a wide-ranging concept when it comes to undertaking family assessments using genograms and ecomaps (discussed later). A family unit is more than a group of people living within a home or within a given radius of an individual or family home. In the Highlands and Islands there is a mix of family types, with extended families often spanning three or four generations all living within relative close vicinity of each other. This area is an attractive location for people looking for a lifestyle change, and there are many nuclear families living remotely from other members of their family. Socioeconomic factors, such as lack of employment, have also influenced the significant migration of younger people away from remote and rural areas, which has resulted in an increase in "older" family units, which in the past would have relied on local family members for support but now are more dependent on statutory services. The FHN works across this wide spectrum of family units as well as working with individuals living alone and, in certain urban contexts, homeless people. The "family" is what the patients or clients say it is; it is who they have determined to be the significant people in their lives, including their pets. However, there are professional and ethical constraints on the FHN's relationship with the individual patient—constraints that may conflict with the FHN's role as a systems analyst and change agent. Mobilizing the family system to bear on the health-related problems of a particular family member can raise issues related to privacy and confidentiality that may not sit comfortably with all individuals, or families for that matter.

In systems terms, the family is a health care resource caring for the patient, a vehicle for health promotion and education, and a socioeconomic environment that embodies health risks. In getting the family to see itself as a health unit, the FHN is applying the theory of family systems into his or her practice. Thus, the FHN's input to the family unit is such that it enhances the ability for self-care within both the individual and the family unit.

Family Health Nurse Practice

The following two examples may assist the understanding of the role in action.

An FHN visited a family that consisted of a married couple in their 30s. Janice was 35, had suffered from multiple sclerosis for 10 years, and was in a relapse phase with relapses becoming more frequent and longer lasting. She was experiencing significant mobility problems with below the waist numbness and spasms and urinary incontinence. Alex was 37, the senior manager within a local bank. The couple lived in the main town on one of the main islands off the north coast of Scotland; they had no family living on the island. Alex was Janice's main carer. He spent a significant amount of his time attending to Janice and felt extremely guilty if he ever arrived home late from work or if he left Janice for too long on her own or if she was incontinent; this obviously upset Janice as well. Janice's general practitioner asked the FHN to visit the home because Janice was having difficulty managing her continence and she was experiencing increasing pain from muscle spasms.

Traditionally a nurse entering such a home would carry out an assessment largely focused on addressing Janice's needs. Through the process of carrying out a comprehensive family assessment, it became clear that both Janice and Alex were suffering from increasing levels of stress emanating largely from Janice's feeling herself to be a burden on Alex and Alex's feeling that he lets his wife down at times. The initial "problem," which was largely physical in nature, became less significant when the focus was directed at the family as a unit or system. The assessment highlighted that the system was failing to help itself. The FHN arranged to meet with the couple together and separately and encouraged open discussion about their feelings. The FHN was able to organize respite cover for Janice, which meant that Alex did not have to come home at lunchtime every day, and he was able to return to play squash, which he had given up over the past few years. He was able to do this once a week because of the additional care provided for Janice.

This provides an example of how the family assessment brought out issues over and above that indicated within the initial referral. Both Alex and Janice were unaware of their right to have a carer attend the house, and both felt less stressed as a result. There were obviously other elements to emerge from the assessment, which resulted in other interventions, but this single intervention had a major impact on the family as a system.

In another family, the FHN was able to identify a significant amount of social security benefit that the family members were unaware of their right to claim. This family consisted of a mother, father, and two early teenage girls with all family members overweight. Gail, age 13, weighed 85 kg (187 lbs), and Mary, age 14, weighed 90 kg (198 lbs). On further exploration, it became clear that the girls were overly keen on sweets and soft drinks and generally had poor diets with very little in the way of vegetables. This diet was much the same for all the family members. They lived on a remote small farm with sheepherding the main activity; the ground was unsuitable for arable use. The parents drove the girls to the end of the farm road to meet the school bus and picked them at the end of the school day. Essentially, this family's diet and exercise level were poor, and as a result, all four family members were significantly obese. Family assessment was able to highlight grandparents within the family who experienced obesity as well as a family history of myocardial infarction. An important aspect of a family assessment is the exploration of intergenerational factors in an open and inclusive manner that enables all family members to understand the links between their lifestyle and health status and to see how this link tracks across generations. This can be a powerful tool for change. Because of a comprehensive exploration and discussion of the family's situation, it became clear that the family believed they could not afford "good" food. They had become used to using sweets as a reward for the children. Through discussion, the FHN was able to get the family to recognize the need for change in their health-related lifestyle behaviors and to get the children to recognize the importance of increased exercise. Probably more importantly with this family, the FHN helped identify a significant amount of unclaimed social security benefit to enable the family to buy low-fat foods, fruits and vegetables, and fewer sweets. The girls walked to and from the school bus, and sweets became a treat as opposed to a norm in the household. In this situation the FHN was not only a nurse but also a dietician, social worker, and personal trainer. Compared to nurses in urban settings, nurses in remote and rural settings do not always have the range of health professionals available to call upon. The FHN role is aptly suited to these settings.

Curriculum

WHO determined from the onset that the curriculum would be both competency and evidenced based. A pan-European working group with the explicit remit of addressing the targets established within Health 21 devised the curriculum. The group established that the program would be modular in nature, spanning a full academic year with students undertaking the program as full-time students. The rationale was linked to the need for students to immerse themselves in this new role and challenge the preconceived notions of community practice that may have become embedded through previous education and practice. Whereas the WHO determined that part-time options could apply, this was not taken up within the Scottish model. Online or distance learning was identified as an option by WHO and one that became a central feature of the

Scottish model. Curriculum planners reviewed the role of the family physician in considering whether a nurse on completion of initial training would possess sufficient competence to undertake the role. Currently family physicians across most European countries undertake additional training to fulfill that role. It is possible to draw many parallels between the two roles with both seen as first points of contact and often described as the lynchpin to other services.

A key question considered by the working group was whether the key concepts associated with family health nursing should be subsumed into basic nurse preparation, thus allowing nurses to practice in this way at point of qualification. Ultimately, the conclusion reached was to advocate a postqualifying program targeted at nurses currently working within community nursing settings. It is worth noting that a small number of the 52 countries that make up the WHO European region do not have established primary care nursing services. In some of these countries, the response to Health 21 has been a radical remodeling of undergraduate nurse education by adopting many of the FHN concepts to enable nurses to fulfill the role at point of graduation from nursing school. Family consent for involvement with the pilot was essential, as this role was testing new theoretical concepts; thus, families were able to opt out with no detriment to their care.

Central to the FHN curriculum are three key concepts: systems theory, interaction theory, and developmental theory. Understanding the complexity of the various ways health can influence family situations is aided by an appreciation of systems theory. Relationships are central to health care; the nurse–patient relationship, the nurse–family relationship, and the relationship between family members are where interaction theory plays a major role within the curriculum. The key importance of partnership working is central to primary health care delivery, another area where interaction theory plays an illuminating role. Underpinning family health care is developmental theory; the program adopts a life course approach, sometimes loosely referred to as "cradle to grave." A comprehensive understanding of developmental theory is crucial for effective family health nursing. The complex interactions within and across these theoretical concepts make the FHN curriculum unique. Key

to the FHN's role is the understanding of such complexities, that is, understanding how major life events, health, and illness influence the effective functioning of individuals and families. FHNs working with families can be viewed as systems operating together within a complex environment. Ill health can be viewed as a factor that unbalances the equilibrium of the family. The role of the FHN is to work with the family to identify both strengths and weaknesses and to help the family retain and maintain its equilibrium, to mobilize its strengths and to minimize its weaknesses. Central to the FHN role is the ability to work with families to enhance its understanding of its dynamics: to recognize stressors, to understand complex concepts such as genetics, and to create a more informed self-motivated family unit.

The curriculum conceptualizes the care provided by FHNs into four distinct categories: primary, secondary, tertiary, and crisis intervention/direct care. Primary interventions relate to identifying potential stressors and assisting families to manage said stressors by the use of health education. Secondary interventions operate at the level of health screening, vaccination programs, and surveillance of health risk. The FHNs' detailed knowledge of the family will assist them in the early detection of ill health and the rapid mobilization of additional health care professionals should the need arise. This again is about restoring equilibrium, limiting delays in access to care, and encouraging families to identify its weaknesses and utilize its strengths. Tertiary care relates to rehabilitation in cases where ill health has been an issue and where the FHN directs interventions at rebuilding a family's resistance, often through health promotion activities. Crisis intervention/direct care applies to those episodes of care where direct care provision is required as a result of an illness of any description. This may be an acute episode or a chronic condition such as wound care for a chronic leg ulcer. Regardless of the cause, this is the traditional role of the nurse in the patient's home. The FHN enables the family to muster its resources as a partner in care.

Family Assessment

Key tools in assisting FHNs to work collaboratively with families are the *genogram* and the *ecomap*. Developed by Monica McGoldrick and

Randy Gerson, the genogram is a widely used assessment tool that enables the FHN to work with the family to develop a pictorial representation of a family's health status across the generations. It enables the identification of areas of strength and areas of conflict; it identifies genetic links by highlighting causes of deaths and incidence of pathology among family members and enables patterns of disease to emerge and thus aid greater understanding by both the FHN and the family. The genogram uses a range of symbols to enable the identification of physical, psychological, and social factors that influence the family system. The ecomap, developed by Ann Hartman, is a tool similar to the genogram and is used by FHNs to identify the systems at play in an individual's life. Again, the ecomap produces a pictorial representation of family relationships; the individual is located at the center with all the key individuals represented in a hub and spoke manner with lines used to highlight the nature of the individual relationships across all the family members. It identifies lines of influence, areas of stressful relationships, and the strengths of relationships. The ecomap, along with the genogram, provides the FHN and the family a comprehensive overview of the family's resources, strengths, weaknesses, assets, and deficits that enables clarity of focus to emerge.

Student Learning

Student learning on the Scottish pilot was supported by the use of WebCT: an e-learning platform that enables teachers to deliver learning material to students who can engage with the material, and each other, at a distance. The goal to develop a distributed learning community, given the geography of the area concerned, proved to be ideal in enabling students to keep in touch. The program covered three 15-week terms over one academic year. The program consisted of four modules spread across the three terms: Communication; Working With Families in the Community; Principles and Practice of Family Health Nursing; and Research, Decision Making, and Evaluation in Clinical Practice, the latter two being double-weighted modules. All modules consisted of theory and practice with 3 weeks face-to-face theory followed by online learning while students engaged in clinical placement supported

by designated FHN mentors. Students used the communication tools of WebCT extensively with the more remote students and found it invaluable. Each module of the program had a dedicated virtual area where learning resources were located and used to support learning in practice and to bridge the theory–practice experiences throughout the program. Designated discussion boards facilitated both student–tutor and student–student learning. In the classroom, extensive use of video facilities aided the development of communication skills; a video recording of a family assessment formed the student's assessment in the communication module. Assessment across the program was competency based, and the overall achievement of the FHN outcomes was dependent upon completion of a portfolio of evidence.

Transformative Learning

Many students undertaking this program engaged in a journey of exploration; many described feelings of inadequacy during the early parts of the program. The detailed focus on communication skills, interpersonal skills, counseling, and family assessment was alien to many of the students. Much of the students' previous learning barely addressed these concepts; some had undertaken further training, but for most, the FHN program was a de-skilling experience. These students recognized the deficits in their skills across these key areas and actively questioned their previous learning experiences and expressed feelings of vulnerability. This process of deconstruction was disarming, and students sought support from both peers and tutors alike. Tutors were quick to recognize these experiences and introduced one-to-one and group sessions to provide forums for discussion of students' feelings. Also, many students found engaging with evidence extremely challenging: this is not to say their practice to date was not evidence based; they were unfamiliar with accessing databases and using evidence in the way the program demanded when they were writing up family case studies. The exact nature of student journey became apparent: from being deconstructed, de-skilled, and dependent learners, they moved toward being independent learners, active participants in their own learning communities, and acutely aware of the value of their own skills and the utility of these skills in carrying out their family assessments and supporting their families toward more independent lives.

The learning described here is reminiscent of transformative learning; the program of study fundamentally challenged the students' current knowledge base. Their understanding of current conventions about the role of the nurse in the community was challenged at every turn. The students recognized the deficits in their previous practice and acknowledged the need for new skills in family assessment, but they found this threatening. Transformative learning, as described by Jack Mezirow, encompasses a more imaginative approach to learning, involving critical self-reflection. It relies upon students suspending their existing belief systems and engaging in critical analysis of the professional practices that they and their colleagues take for granted. It requires students to challenge the basic assumptions of their profession. In this environment, the tutors were facilitators of learning—a concept that some of these "mature" learners found challenging in the extreme. The goal was to encourage students to abandon their current belief systems and to challenge current perceived wisdoms. This meant that everything they stood for was on an unstable foundation; students had to go back to basics, to engage with the literature, and to reconstruct their understanding within the context of family health nursing. Toward the end of the 1-year program, the emerging evidence from the students' online discussion demonstrated vastly improved confidence in their own knowledge and ability. Observers would see a learning community in action: sharing resources, supporting each other, and engaging with, and creating, the evidence base that is family health nursing. The evidence was reconstruction where there once had been deconstruction, or transformation.

Ian Murray

See also Assessing Family Health; Developmental Transitions in Families; Ecomaps for Families; Education of Nursing Health Care Providers in Family Health; Families: The Basic Unit of Societies; Family Adherence to Health Care Regimen; Genograms and the Family; Roles of Health Care Providers for Families, Emerging

Further Readings

Christopher, S., Dunnagan, T., Duncan, S. F., & Paul, L. (2001). Education for self-support: Evaluating outcomes using transformative learning theory. *Family Relations, 50,* 134–142.

Hartrick, G. (2000). Developing health-promoting practice with families: One pedagogical experience. *Journal of Advanced Nursing, 31*(1), 27–34.

International Council of Nurses. (2003). *Framework and core competencies for the family nurse.* Geneva, Switzerland: Author. Available from http://www.icn .ch/English/ICN-Framework-and-Core-Competencies-for-the-Family-Nurse.html

Macduff, C., & West, B. (2003). *Evaluating family health nursing through education and practice.* Edinburgh, UK: Scottish Executive Social Research.

MacIntosh, J., & Wiggins, N. (1998). Venturing through the looking glass: An instance of transformative learning in adult education. *Canadian Journal of University Continuing Education, 24,* 11–19.

Mezirow, J. (1991). *Transformative dimensions of adult learning.* San Francisco: Jossey-Bass.

NHS Education for Scotland. (2004). *Partnerships in education: Guidelines for the design and delivery of family health nurse education programmes in Scotland.* Edinburgh, UK: Author.

Nursing & Midwifery Council. (2004, August). *Standards of proficiency for specialist community public health nurses.* Available from http://www .nmc-uk.org/Educators/Standards-for-education/ Standards-of-proficiency-for-specialist-community-public-health-nurses/

Reushle, S. (2008). A practitioner's journey exploring transformative approaches to the professional development of online educators. *International Journal of Pedagogies and Learning, 4,* 15–28.

Reushle, S., & Mitchell, M. (2009). Sharing the journey of facilitator and learner: Online pedagogy in practice. *Journal of Learning Design, 3,* 11–20.

Scottish Executive Health Department. (2001). *Nursing for health: A review of the contribution of nurses, midwives and health visitors to improving the public's health in Scotland.* Edinburgh, UK: Author.

Scottish Executive Health Department. (2006). *Visible, accessible and integrated care: Report of the review of nursing in the community in Scotland.* Edinburgh, UK: Author. Retrieved from http://www.scotland.gov.uk/ Publications/2007/07/16091605/0

Scottish Executive Health Department. (2006). *The WHO Europe Family Health Nursing Pilot in Scotland: Final report.* Edinburgh, UK: Author.

Scottish Government. (2007). *Better health, better care: Action plan*. Edinburgh, UK: Author. Retrieved from http://www.scotland.gov.uk/Publications/2007/12/11103453/9

Scottish Office. (1999). *Towards a healthier Scotland: A white paper on health*. Edinburgh, UK: Author.

World Health Organization. (1998). *Health for All policy framework for the European region for the 21st century* (Rep. No. EUR/RC48/R5). Copenhagen, Denmark: Author.

World Health Organization. (2000). *The family health nurse context, conceptual framework and definitive curriculum* (Rep. No. EUR/OO/5019309/1300074). Copenhagen, Denmark: Author.

World Health Organization. (2006). *Report on the evaluation of the WHO Multi-country Family Health Nurse Pilot Study* (Rep. No. EUR/05/5065397). Copenhagen, Denmark: Author.

Wright, L. M., & Leahey, M. (2005). *Nurses and families: A guide to assessment and intervention* (4th ed.). Philadelphia: F. A. Davis.

Websites

International Council of Nurses: http://www.icn.ch
WHO European Regional Office: http://www.euro.who.int

Education of Medical Health Care Providers in Family Health

Throughout most of the 20th century, the family physician was actually a general practitioner. In the late 1960s family practice evolved as a specialty and grew rapidly in the 1970s. In addition to physicians, physician assistants and nurse practitioners are also involved in providing health care for the family. Family medicine must be distinguished from primary care, which simply implies a practitioner whom the patient would see first for any given complaint. Primary care includes the specialties of pediatrics, internal medicine, obstetrics and gynecology, and emergency medicine, as well as family practice. This entry focuses on the education of family practice professionals, including educational requirements, important attributes for those entering the field, and continuing education.

Family Practice Professionals

Physicians

Requirements for entrance to medical school are fairly standard. Students will study general biology, inorganic and organic chemistry, psychology, anatomy and physiology, physics, and mathematics as an undergraduate. Most medical schools require students to have a bachelor's degree; however, there are schools that have early admissions programs and do not require a bachelor's degree for entrance. Most premedical students are either biology or chemistry majors. However, medical schools do not require a specific degree; a student may enter medical school with a degree in English literature, for example. Medical schools only require completion of the prerequisites. In addition to the undergraduate course work, students must take the Medical College Admissions Test (MCAT) and provide letters of recommendation. Successful students generally have some experience in the health care field either with actual work experience or a job shadowing a physician. Students with high grade point averages and MCAT scores are then awarded an interview. As a general rule, the grade point average and MCAT determine who is interviewed, and the interview, letters of recommendation, and personal statement determine who is accepted to medical school.

There are two types of medicine: allopathic and osteopathic. Allopathic physicians earn a medical doctorate (MD). Osteopaths earn a doctor of osteopathy (DO). Osteopaths emphasize holistic medicine and utilize manipulation of the musculoskeletal system to treat disease. Otherwise, both allopathic and osteopathic physicians utilize both medications and surgery to treat patients. Previously there were separate allopathic and osteopathic hospitals. In today's hospitals, allopathic and osteopathic physicians work side by side. In many states the same medical board licenses both allopathic physicians and osteopathic physicians. There are, however, other states in which allopaths and osteopaths are licensed under separate boards.

For both fields of medicine, there is a typical format used by medical schools. Students spend the first two years in the classroom learning anatomy and physiology, histology, biochemistry, pathology, pharmacy, and microbiology. Historically, relatively little patient interaction occurred during the first two years. Newer trends have medical students interacting more with patients in the first two years. Osteopathic schools usually offer more patient interaction than allopathic schools during this period. At the end of the first two years, medical students take Part 1 of the United States Medical Licensure Exam (USMLE). During the last two years of medical school, students do clinical clerkships in the hospital. Students will do rotations in internal medicine, surgery, family medicine, emergency medicine, and obstetrics and gynecology. Students may do electives in orthopedics, dermatology, ophthalmology, and so forth. At the end of medical school, students take Part 2 of the USMLE.

Upon graduation, medical students take a 1-year internship and then enter a 2- to 3-year residency to become a specialist. The intern has a provisional license and must practice under the supervision of a licensed physician. A resident is fully licensed to practice medicine. Currently internships have been incorporated into the residency. At the end of the first-year internship, physicians take the final part of the USMLE. The physician having successfully passed the USMLE and successfully finished the internship is allowed to go into practice without entering residency. Those physicians going into practice without doing a residency are then known as general practitioners. It is very rare to find physicians who do not go on and complete a residency.

The family practice residency is a total of 3 years: 1 year of internship and 2 years of residency. During the first two years the intern/resident spends time in the hospital rotating through various services, including internal medicine, surgery, emergency medicine, pediatrics, obstetrics and gynecology, and of course, family practice. During this time they also have office hours in which they see patients in a family practice outpatient setting. During the third year the resident spends most of the time in the outpatient setting and also spends time on electives following specialists such as ophthalmologists, orthopedists, or dermatologists. After residency the physician may become board certified by the American Board of Family Medicine by successfully passing a written test. The family practice physician must then be recertified every 6 to 7 years by the American Board of Family Medicine.

Family practice physicians believe in treating the patient in the context of how medical problems affect the whole family, and stresses within the family will affect a medical problem. Family practice physicians emphasize preventive medicine as well. Family physicians treat patients from the cradle to the grave. Obstetrics also was a large part of family practice; however, today most family physicians do not deliver babies because the cost of malpractice insurance does not make it economically feasible.

Since the advent of the establishment of family practice as a specialty, a new specialty has been developed to treat both children and adults. Physicians can now be board certified in both internal medicine and pediatrics. Both internal medicine and pediatrics are 3-year residencies. However, under this program physicians spend a total of 4 years in residency and are double boarded in both internal medicine and pediatrics. The major difference between the family practice physician and the double boarded internist/pediatrician is obstetrics.

There is a very important distinction in being a specialist and being board certified. To be board certified a physician must finish an approved residency and pass a written test from their certifying board. However, state medical license boards grant licenses to practice medicine and surgery. Physicians with a state license can advertise being any type of specialty regardless of their training. Physicians may only advertise themselves as a board-certified physician if they have completed their residency and passed their boards.

Physician Assistants

Physician assistants have a similar role to that of physicians. They see, diagnose, and treat patients just as physicians do. It is commonplace to see primary care practices with one or more physician assistants. Not only does the physician assistant see patients, but most in the primary care field are allowed to build their own practice, that is, have their own specific group of patients that they care for on a long-term basis. The physician assistant does, however, work under the supervision of a physician, although the physician does not need to be physically present in the clinic. The role of the physician assistant will vary from state to state. In certain states the physician assistant is able to write any prescription; in other states their prescription privileges are limited.

To enter a physician assistant program, a student only needs 2 years of undergraduate training, completing required course work. The course requirements are similar to the requirements for medical school. The only substantial difference is that physician assistant programs usually do not have as a prerequisite organic chemistry. Although not required, most physician assistant students obtain their bachelor's degree. Students may be required to spend time with a practicing physician assistant prior to entering the program. Like medical school, the first half of the training is in the classroom and the second half is accomplished in the clinics. Physician assistants graduate with a master's degree. Although there are postgraduate opportunities for physician assistants similar to the residencies physicians do, most enter practice immediately after graduation and are trained by the physician for whom they work.

Nurse Practitioners

Predating by only several years the start of the family practice as a specialty and physician assistant programs was the inception of nurse practitioners programs. The nurse practitioner is a registered nurse. Upon completing the degree requirements, nurses must pass the National Council Licensure Examination (NCLEX). Many nurse practitioner programs require registered nurses to have a 4-year bachelor's degree. Nurse practitioner programs also require that nurses have experience in both acute and chronic health care. The typical nurse practitioner program is a 2-year program basically divided between the classroom and clinic.

The role of the nurse practitioner varies from state to state. In some states nurse practitioners work independently of a physician. In most states nurse practitioners see patients, order tests, make diagnoses, and prescribe treatment. Nurse practitioners can also specialize in a variety of areas, including family practice, pediatrics, geriatrics, emergency medicine, and so on. Before becoming licensed in a state, the nurse practitioner must be certified by a national body. There are two credentialing bodies: the American Nurses Credentialing Center and the American Academy of Nurse Practitioners.

Important Attributes for Those Entering the Family Health Care Profession

Anyone entering the family health care profession as a physician, physician assistant, or family nurse practitioner should have the same attributes. Intelligence is of the utmost importance. Intelligence goes beyond the ability to make good grades in college. Students need to be able to retain the material they have studied. They need to be able to take what they have learned and practically apply the information to real-life situations. Students should have a grade point average of at least 3.25; however, they are best advised to have a grade point average of 3.5 or higher.

Students should be strongly motivated. This is crucial for professional schools. These schools are expected to graduate all the students they accept. Furthermore, it is extremely rare for professional students to transfer to a different school. It is almost impossible for these schools to replace a student who has dropped out of school. A truly motivated student is obviously more likely to reach his or her goal. One of the greatest indications of motivation is hard work. Other indicators of motivation include keeping up with current events. During the interview for acceptance, students may be asked questions about what has recently been in the news. Students should understand exactly what is entailed in becoming a health professional. Again, during the interview, students may be asked questions regarding what they will be facing. Another important indication of motivation is having a strong work ethic. Classes in professional school last 8 hours per day, and students are expected to study 4 hours each night and 8 hours per day over the weekend. Given a student with an exceptionally high grade point average and poor work ethic and a student with simply a good grade point average and strong work ethic, professional schools would prefer the latter. One of the best ways to document a strong work ethic is in the letter of recommendations written by one of the student's undergraduate professors. Descriptions of a student's work ethic, such as being to class on time, attending class regularly, and being prepared, are often included in a letter of recommendation.

Students should have some work experience in medicine. Obviously, anyone wishing to be a family nurse practitioner will have clinical experience.

Some schools will require that the nurse have subsequent experience working in such settings as an intensive care unit. Having experience does not necessarily mean having a job, however. Job shadowing is considered experience. There is also a practical aspect for those students wishing to become an osteopathic physician. Osteopathic schools require a letter of recommendation from an established practicing osteopathic physician. Job shadowing is one of the best ways for a physician to get to know the student.

Students must be articulate. Educating the patient in preventive medicine and detailed plans to treat current medical problems is crucial. Diagnosing the problem is meaningless if the practitioner cannot make the patient understand what is wrong and what needs to be done. Practitioners also must be able to explain clearly and concisely what is taking place with a patient to another practitioner. The student's ability to articulate is tested during the interview.

Other important characteristics include maturity, leadership ability, the ability to think logically, and the stamina to be a lifelong learner. Maturity and leadership can be demonstrated by how the student handles extracurricular activities. Holding office in an organization always looks good on a résumé. Being able to balance extracurricular activity with the classroom is a mark of maturity. The ability to think logically is demonstrated through solving ethical dilemmas. This is usually part of the interviewing process. To stay current in the field, every provider needs to be a lifelong learner.

The issue of altruism has for a long period of time been ironic. Obviously, we want the provider taking care of our family to have entered the profession because they want to help patients and not just for monetary gain. However, students wishing to become a health care provider are often advised to avoid stating that helping people is the sole reason for pursing their respective field, as it may be seen as being too superficial a reason for entering the health care profession. The successful applicant will have several strong reasons for wanting to become a health care provider.

Continuing Education

The education of health care providers does not end with obtaining the degree, certification, or license.

This is why it is crucial that all health care providers are lifelong learners. All health care providers must stay current in the profession by obtaining continuing medical education (CME) credit or continuing education units (CEUs). CME credit can be derived from a large variety of activities. There are also numerous ways to classify these credits.

Typically Category 1 or Division I credit is obtained by the traditional methods of a conference sponsored by a hospital, residency program, or medical school. This includes correspondence courses as well. With modern technology this now may include web-based programs. Category 2 or Division II credit is usually derived from professional activities such as teaching. Prescribed credit is derived from a program that is approved by a sanctioning body such as the American Academy of Family Practice.

The board-certified family physician is required to complete 300 credit hours over a 6-year period or 150 hours over a 3-year period. Providers can document their hours through the American Academy of Family Physicians or document their credit with an online application from the American Board of Family Practice; the board divides the credits into Division I and Division II.

Division I activities are the standard conferences that have been approved or prescribed CME credit by the American Medical Association or American Academy of Family Practice. Family practice physicians are required to obtain 180 of the 300 required credits with Division I credits. This activity can be completed via the Internet, by correspondence course, or by attending a conference in person. This also includes such activities as grand rounds and local hospital or medical society meetings that have been sanctioned. The training obtained during internship and residency is considered Division I credit as well. Finally, educational programs at a medical school or university can also fulfill Division I credits.

Division II activities include reviewing manuscripts and publishing original research. Division II credit is also given for teaching in medical school. Any education experience using a wide variety of media but not approved by a sanctioning body may also qualify for Division II credit.

Physician assistants are required to complete 100 hours of continuing medical education every 2 years. Fifty hours must be Category I, and the remainder can be either Category I or Category II. Category I hours are achieved by completing CME opportunities that have been approved by a number of different sanctioning boards. As a general rule, if the provider receives a certificate at the end of the program, it was probably a Category I event. Category II includes teaching and reading journal articles. Here the physician assistant only needs to document how many hours were spent on each activity.

Nurse practitioners do not use continuing medical education hours but rather contact hours and CEUs. Contact hours are the hours spent in the clinic seeing patients. Continuing education can be the traditional methods of attending conferences, doing web-based studies, and other activities. Contact hours can be converted into CEUs. Ten contact hours is the equivalent of one CEU. The requirements vary from state to state.

Opportunities for continuing education abound. Previously providers found conferences from mailings, ads in medical journals, and by word of mouth. Now with the Internet, family health providers have an unprecedented ability to find the conference that suits them best. Many conferences are approved by multiple boards; therefore, family practitioners, physician assistants, and nurse practitioners may attend the same conferences. This is extremely important because it means all health care providers are learning the same things. In medicine, family health care providers are held to the same standard. This ensures patients are treated appropriately and in the same manner by nurse practitioners, physician assistants, and family practice physicians.

Broader Issues

Nurse practitioners, physician assistants, and family practice all started about the same time, which coincided with the advent of the Medicaid/ Medicare system. The prediction at that time was for a shortage of primary health care providers. In 2010 the first major reform in health care since the start of Medicaid/Medicare was passed. Once again the United States is experiencing a critical shortage in primary health care. The previous shortage was largely due to an increase in patient population. The current shortage can be attributed to a loss of primary care providers. Primary care practitioners

work long hours with the lowest reimbursement from Medicaid/Medicare and private insurance. Primary care practitioners are taught how to practice medicine but not the reality of practice. This is because there is so much these practitioners must learn in a short period of time, there is little room for this important aspect of practice.

John C. Robinson

See also Education of Child Life Providers in Family Health; Education of Nursing Health Care Providers in Family Health; Education of Occupational Health Providers in Family Health; Education of Physical Therapists in Family Health; Roles of Health Care Providers for Families, Current

Websites

American Academy of Family Physicians: http://www.aafp.org

American Academy of Nurse Practitioners: http://www.aanp.org

American Academy of Physician Assistants: http://www.aapa.org

American Association of Colleges of Osteopathic Medicine: http://www.aacom.org

American Board of Family Medicine: http://www.theabfm.org

American College of Nurse Practitioners: http://www.acnpweb.org

American Medical College Application Service: http://aamc.org/students/amcas

Medical College Admissions Test: http://aamc.org/students/mcat

EDUCATION OF NURSING HEALTH CARE PROVIDERS IN FAMILY HEALTH

Nursing is a very visible and valued health profession. At a workforce of 2.5 million, registered nurses are the largest health care occupation. Each year, in Gallup's annual Honesty and Ethics of Professions poll, nursing is voted as the most respected profession in the United States. The impact of nurses on health care and the care of individuals and their families is wide-reaching. Nurses coordinate and provide care in nearly every aspect of the health care arena, and the impact that the nurse has on the family is immense. Some examples of nurse–family interaction include inpatient hospital care, nursing homes, outpatient primary care clinics, specialty practice, schools, prisons, homeless shelters, public health, and home health care.

Educational preparation for nursing is variable. This entry provides a description of the different types of nursing health care providers. An overview of the general education and philosophical perspectives of nursing health care providers is given. Last, family nursing theory and the preparation of nursing health care providers in family health are highlighted.

The Nursing Workforce: An Overview

Nursing education exists at many different levels in the United States, ranging from the most basic 75 hours of education for a nursing assistant to the doctorally prepared registered nurse with up to, or exceeding, 8 years of education following high school graduation. The wide variety and range for entry into nursing provides for a rich diversity of the workforce and unending opportunities within the profession. However, an unintended consequence to the public and indeed to other health care professionals is confusion over the wide array of certifications, licenses, and educational preparations for nurses. Although there is a common ground, a nurse is not always just a nurse.

The registered nurse (RN) license is granted by a state once an individual has graduated from an approved program and successfully passed the national nursing board examination. There are three educational pathways for entry into practice as an RN. The 4-year bachelor's degree (BSN) and the 2-year associate's degree (ADN) from a community college are the two most common educational preparations.

In 1965, an American Nurses Association position statement stated that professional nursing education begins with a bachelor's degree. In a 2004 survey of RNs in the United States, 34.2% were BSN graduates and 33.7% were ADN graduates. Hospital-based diploma program graduates comprised 17%, and 13% of RNs were prepared at the master's or doctorate level. A baccalaureate nursing education provides the RN with a well-rounded liberal arts education as well as the science, theoretical, and clinical coursework needed to begin a professional nurse career. One distinction between the BSN and ADN preparations is the amount of time spent in community health or public health rotations and the amount of time devoted to understanding family health care theory and practice. The BSN education requires students to have content in community health and family health theory and practice. These experiences are not required for the ADN graduate.

The licensed practical nurse (LPN) is a license granted by the state to a graduate of a technical nursing program who successfully passed the LPN board examination. There are approximately 700,000 LPNs in the United States. The LPN educational program is generally 1 year with a combination of classroom and clinical education. The preparation is more basic and abbreviated than that of an RN. LPNs work in all types of health care settings, and the tasks include personal care, medication administration, and patient care supervision. Their activities are directed by physicians or RNs as stipulated in their scope of practice statement. The nursing assistant (NA) has 75 hours of education and training to be a direct assistant to the nurse. NAs who are certified are referred to as certified nursing assistants (CNAs). NAs work in all areas where nursing care is given, and their tasks include activities such as taking vital signs, assisting with personal care (such as bathing, grooming, and toileting), and feeding. Actions of an NA are directed and supervised by either an RN or LPN and guided by the nursing plan of care.

The advanced practice registered nurse (APRN) is an RN who is prepared at the graduate level with either a master's or doctoral degree to provide advanced nursing care. The APRN role preparations include the nurse practitioner (NP), the certified nurse midwife (CNM), the certified registered nurse anesthetist (CRNA), and the clinical nurse specialist (CNS). APRNs are nationally board certified in their specialty and provide functions similar to that of a doctor, including diagnosing and treating common acute and chronic illnesses, focusing on health promotion and disease prevention, ordering and interpreting diagnostic tests, and prescribing medication and other treatments. APRNs receive reimbursement from insurance companies for their direct patient care activities. APRNs practice in a variety of settings depending on their preparation. CRNAs are mainly found in hospitals and outpatient surgical settings where anesthesia and pain control are provided. The CNS usually works in a hospital and provides nursing care and specialty education needs to patients and nursing staff. The CNM is educated to provide expert care for women, particularly childbearing women, and newborns up to 1 month of age. Within the APRN role preparation of NP, there are six population foci: family, pediatric, women's health, adult and geriatric, psychiatric–mental health, and neonatal. The NP provides direct health care to individuals and families within a population focus. The NP is found in many different settings, generally ambulatory and usually primary care. NPs are able to prescribe medications, though the degree of physician involvement varies from state to state.

Nurses are also prepared at the doctoral level. The educational level for NP preparation has shifted from a master's degree to a doctor of nursing practice (DNP) degree with an implementation goal date of 2015. In addition, there are nurses prepared with a doctor of philosophy (PhD) in nursing. The PhD RN is educated with a focus on generating and testing nursing knowledge. The PhD nurse is an expert researcher and is a professor in a university setting conducting research and teaching students.

Nursing Philosophy and Nursing Family Theory

Nursing's Theoretical Foundation

Nursing health care providers have a unique philosophical base and perspective, which forms the basis of their care. The first nursing theorist and founder of professional nursing was Florence Nightingale. During the mid-1800s, Nightingale felt a divine call to forgo her privileged life and serve humankind. After extensive travel and study of religious order nursing care facilities, she began the first professional school of nursing for laywomen in 1853 in London, England.

Nightingale is most widely known for her prompt response to a call to lead a contingent of nurses to the Crimea, where England was ensconced in a battle. When the nurses arrived, they found that the battlefield was strewn with seriously ill and injured soldiers and the conditions were beyond filthy. Men were lying in crowded conditions, covered in lice, with human waste covering the floors. Nightingale led her nurses to restore the environment into a setting where a person could heal and where further disease would be prevented. It was Nightingale's observance of the patient–environment interaction and the importance of the environment in healing that form the basis of her theoretical framework. In fact, the patient–environment relationship continues to be a foundational theoretical pillar in nursing theory. In the most basic of terms, nursing is concerned with the lived experience of the human–environment interaction in relation to health.

Environment is a major nursing philosophical concept and can be defined to include things such as pollution, quality drinking water, and safe city streets. One's immediate surroundings can also be included in this definition, for example, the physical location of the person, such as their home or hospital room. Nurses also consider the family, work setting, or even the internal milieu of the person in the assessment of the environment.

Human/person or patient/client under nursing care is another important nursing philosophical concept. Nursing views the person as a holistic, multidimensional being. Only addressing the physiological or biological or psychological component of the person would not be consistent with a holistic nursing perspective. A holistic view of the person includes consideration of the person as a member of a family. In addition, the family unit itself may be the patient/client in need of nursing care.

Family Nursing Theory

Family nursing theory is a blend of nursing conceptual frameworks with theories from social science and family therapy. Nurses gain valuable perspectives through the incorporation of family nursing theory into their practice. Family nursing theory provides the nurse a lens through which to understand the family as a system with inherent structure, the role of family in society, the impact of society/environment on the family, developmental tasks of the family, and family communication styles. Incorporating these perspectives enables nurses to care for families and/ or to better understand and care for the person as a member of a family.

Integrated nursing family theory models, largely informed by nursing theory, social science theory, and family therapy theory, have been developed that assist nurse clinicians and researchers. The integration of several different theories allows for a wide perspective with which to frame the family health problem and from which to develop a comprehensive and creative treatment plan. Three nursing family assessment models that have been developed by family nurses will be described: (1) the Calgary Family Assessment Model, (2) the Friedman Family Assessment Model and Form, and (3) the Family Assessment and Intervention Model and the Family Systems Stressor-Strength Inventory. The nursing family assessments overlap to a certain degree, but each has different strengths for assessing families and guiding care.

The Calgary Family Assessment Model was developed by Lorraine Wright and Maureen Leahey. The model has a foundation in nursing and family therapy theories, systems theory, cybernetics theory, and communication theory. This model offers a strong assessment of the family communication, especially the emotional content.

The Friedman Family Assessment Model and Form has a strong grounding in three social sciences: structural-functional, developmental, and systems theory. The assessment looks at family values; family functions in the domains of affective, social health care; and stress and coping. The Friedman model also looks at the environmental aspects of the family and is useful when the nurse is assessing the family from a public health or community-based perspective.

The Family Assessment and Intervention Model is grounded in Betty Neuman's health care systems model. Neuman is a nursing theorist, and her nursing theory was adapted from individuals to families by Karen Berkey and Shirley Hanson. The theory is grounded in a systems perspective in which the family is seen as a system with subparts in interaction with each other. An assessment tool, the Family Systems Stressor-Strength Inventory (FS³I) was developed from the Neuman model and assesses general and specific family stressors as well as the family system strengths.

Family Health: Nursing Care and Practice

Historically, family nursing was thought to be a specialty of nursing that took place in the context of maternal–child nursing and was meant to view the child only in the context of his or her family. A more recent view of family health nursing is that of a specialty that cuts across all areas of nursing practice. Family health nursing is defined as the process of providing nursing care to families, and it includes viewing the family as context, the family as a unit/system, or the family as a segment of society.

Every member of the nursing health care team, from a nursing assistant implementing the nursing plan of care to the PhD prepared nurse researcher evaluating the effectiveness of the nursing care on the outcome of a population of individuals, has a role in the care of the family. Different educational levels prepare graduates to care for the family in a unique manner that complements the nursing team and that individual's background.

Nursing care of the family as context involves caring for the individual in the context of his or her family. This model is seen as a beginning-level view of family nursing care, and it is a competency met by a nursing generalist prepared with a BSN. The individual receiving care, the care recipient, is at the forefront of the care, and the family is assessed as part of the care recipient's environment and as context for understanding the care recipient and his or her health concerns. For example, "You tell me that your mother, who is in frail health and requires much care, lives with you. Have you thought about getting help with her care while you are recovering from surgery?"

Competencies with nursing care of the family increase as nurses gain more education and experience. Thus, the master's prepared nurse is competent in the care of the family as context and also is educated in the family as a unit or system. This nurse views the family as a unit in the foreground and each individual as a component of the family unit. The family nurse practitioner (FNP) is an example of the nurse prepared to assess the family as a unit or system. Typically the FNP is employed in a family practice setting where there is the opportunity to care for many members of the same family. These expert nurses view the family as a system whose parts are in constant interaction with one another and in constant interaction with the larger world. For example, if the main wage earner for the family is seriously ill, the FNP understands this impact and its ripple effect through the family. The FNP would include the family system in the assessment and might ask questions such as "How will the family provide food for the members?" and "How will health services be paid for?" The FNP would also consider the impact that the loss of occupational identity and associated stress might have on each family member.

The family nursing care competencies build upon one another, so doctorally prepared nurses, both PhD and DNP, are skilled in care of the family as context and the family as unit/system. The PhD and DNP prepared nurses are expert nurses who are able to care for the family as a system located within a larger community system. The family is a unit of a larger system of society. Examples of units of society include religious, education, and economic institutions. The nurse addressing the health care needs of the family at this systemic level functions in community health, with social services, or in the policy arenas. The PhD prepared nurse conducts family nursing research and develops and tests family nursing theory. The hallmark of the DNP prepared nurse would be in the implementation of and translation of family nursing research into practice.

Family nursing theory is integrated into nursing curriculums in a variety of ways. Some nursing schools may adopt family nursing as a major theoretical perspective that guides the school's curriculum. Other schools offer a required course on family nursing theories while most schools integrate the concepts of family nursing into existing courses. This pattern has historically been the case for courses dealing with maternal–child health, community, and psychiatric–mental health content. All specialties within nursing view the family as a partner in care, however, and so increasingly family nursing theory is embedded across the nursing curriculum. It is emphasized that nursing has a philosophical tradition, starting with Nightingale, of including families in the care of the person and in viewing the nurse and family as a team for care. This perspective has become even more of a reality now that hospital stays are shorter and patients are sicker and require more care when they leave the hospital.

The roles that the family nurse assumes depend in part on the health care setting, and these roles are evolving. The nurse in family health uses the holistic nursing background, expertise, and creativity to engage with the family as advocate, educator, technical expert, counselor, consultant, health interpreter, health care provider, coordinator/liaison, role model, and researcher.

Tess Judge-Ellis

See also Changing Family and Health Demographics; Defining Family: An Overview of Family Definitions From a Historical Perspective; Roles of Health Care Providers for Families, Current; Roles of Health Care Providers for Families, Emerging; School Nursing and the Health of Families; Socioeconomic Status of Families; Systems Supporting Family Health

Further Readings

Bomar, P. J. (2004). *Promoting health in families: Applying family research and theory to nursing practice* (3rd ed.). Philadelphia: Saunders.

Denham, S. (2003). *Family health: A framework for nursing*. Philadelphia: F. A. Davis.

Doane, G. H., & Varcoe, C. (2005). *Family nursing as relational inquiry: Developing health-promoting practice*. Philadelphia: Lippincott Williams & Wilkins.

Friedman, M. M., Bowden, V. R., & Jones, E. G. (2003). *Family nursing: Research, theory and practice* (5th ed.). Upper Saddle River, NJ: Prentice Hall.

Kaakinen, J. R., Gedaly-Duff, V., Coehlo, D. P., & Harmon Hanson, S. M. (2010). *Family health care nursing: Theory, practice and research* (4th ed.). Philadelphia: F. A. Davis.

Wright, L. M., & Leahey, M. (2005). *Nurses and families: A guide to family assessment and intervention* (4th ed.). Philadelphia: F. A. Davis.

EDUCATION OF OCCUPATIONAL HEALTH PROVIDERS IN FAMILY HEALTH

Occupational therapy professionals focus on the occupational health of individuals, families, and populations. Occupational therapy is an evidence-based health discipline that maximizes health and well-being through engagement in occupation despite illness, injury, disability, or economic or social circumstances. Family health is an essential aspect of occupational therapy practice. Occupational therapists work with individuals of all ages across the life span as well as families, organizations, and populations to promote health, functioning, and participation in life activities.

This entry provides a brief historical context of occupational therapy practice and an overview of the centrality of occupation in the lives of individuals and families. Further, the focus of family care and current trends in working with families in occupational therapy are described in terms of how these trends impact occupational therapy education. Family and individual health outcomes related to occupation-based goals and interventions using a family-centered approach in the context of current global economic and social stressors are highlighted. Education for competent and compassionate occupational therapy professionals is discussed, with recommendations for developing professionals who can design interventions targeting individuals, caregivers, and family members to promote and improve health and well-being. Finally, this entry describes broader societal issues of family health and health care that are relevant to the education of occupational therapy professionals.

Historical Context

Occupational therapy as a health profession emerged in the early 20th century in the United States in response to the need for therapeutic activities related to work, play, and rest to address the personal, emotional, spiritual, physical, and social needs of persons experiencing mental and physical illnesses or injury. Occupations are actions, habits, routines, or rituals that we engage in as part of our lives that give us meaning and purpose. Occupations can involve diverse activities that are part of our work, play, or how we care for ourselves and family members or significant others (activities of daily living). Occupations can also be leisure or play activities or how we engage socially in our communities. Occupations are defined as acts of doing and being in the world that are subjectively, culturally, and socially defined by the person(s) who engages in them. Occupations are considered

necessary for survival. The purpose of occupational therapy is to promote health and well-being as well as work with individuals, families, organizations, and populations to problem-solve ways to enhance functioning in order to fully participate in meaningful life activities.

The profession continues to grow in the United States and throughout the world. It remains closely connected to its early holistic view of clients as human beings who benefit from occupational therapy intervention attuned to the physical, mental, spiritual, and social aspects of the individual in the contexts of families and the community. Currently, occupational therapists and occupational therapy assistants work in a variety of practice settings across the globe, including homes, schools, workplaces, hospitals, health centers, community housing, rehabilitation centers, and educational institutions. There are approximately 55 countries that are members of the World Federation of Occupational Therapists. Broad areas of practice focus in the United States include health and wellness, children and youth, productive aging, mental health, work and industry, and rehabilitation, disability, and participation. Currently there are 376 accredited occupational therapy programs in the United States: 5 are doctoral-level programs, 142 are master's programs, and 129 are occupational therapy assistant programs.

Meeting the Health Needs of Families

Occupational therapy professionals work with families as an occupational system and also work with individuals within a family to enhance occupational performance. Family systems theory and understanding of typical development of a family, as well as that of individuals within a family, are essential for occupational therapy students to gain an appreciation of families as occupational systems. Students in occupational therapy programs gain knowledge and skills in courses such as human development, psychology, sociology, and anthropology as well as anatomy and physiology, mental health, health promotion, occupations across the life span, and fieldwork experiences in family health settings to prepare them for working with families in practice.

Family is defined within the discipline of occupational therapy as an occupational entity with a unique social network involving dynamic patterns of doing and being that develop from individual family member interaction with each other and their physical, cultural, and social environment. Furthermore, each family member has a distinctive identity as an occupational being with personal, physical, emotional, spiritual, and social attributes and potential to live, work, play, and participate in society. Occupational therapy addresses both the family and the individual together in therapy to focus on goals that are important to the individual within the family network to live life to the fullest of one's potential, regardless of illness, injury, disability, or social circumstances.

Current trends in working with families demonstrate that occupational therapy professionals engage with family members in focusing on family-centered care or the collaboration with family members and significant others in the occupational therapy process. This process involves supporting health and participation in life through engagement in occupation. Examples of interventions as part of this process may include the following: establish or restore functioning in order to perform activities of daily living, such as caring for one's children; modify leisure and play environments for a child with a disability to promote community participation and shared family outings; or create a routine of energy conservation with a client caring for an ailing spouse.

The focus of care in occupational therapy is both the family and the individual in the context of the family. An understanding of family functioning and how the families participate in routines and activities that hinder or help advance healthy lifestyles is a focus of therapy. Occupational therapy students need to be skilled in therapeutic use of self to adapt to the changing needs of families over time and throughout the family life cycle. For example, skills in interpersonal communication and clinical reasoning as well as analyzing tasks and activities can facilitate a client's ability to prepare a healthy meal as part of a treasured family gathering or to facilitate family routines broken by a catastrophic illness or injury.

Education of occupational therapy professionals involves coursework in interpersonal communication; cultural competency; occupations of children, youth, adults, and older adults; health promotion

and mental and physical disabilities; and health management and others to prepare students for a variety of family health issues. Some families and individuals enter the health care environment with limited health literacy and scarce access to supportive services. Health care professionals often need to serve as advocates for families to obtain services and help families cope with an overload of information to digest about their diagnoses, health options, prospects for recovery, and payment of services. Currently, occupational therapists in the United States have developed specialized knowledge and skills in family health issues related to advocacy, health management, obesity, health promotion, prevention of disability, violence and abuse prevention, feeding, eating and swallowing, caregivers, disaster preparedness and response, hospice and families, facilitating work performance, and school-based family health programs.

These trends impact occupational therapy education in terms of the course offerings, length of education, and types of clinical internship fieldwork experiences. In the United States, occupational therapy assistants must graduate with an associate's degree from an accredited educational institution, and occupational therapists must graduate with at least a master's degree from an accredited educational institution, including supervised clinical internships in a variety of settings, and pass a national certification examination. Additionally, most states have laws that regulate occupational therapy scope of practice.

Family Health Outcomes and Occupational Therapy Education

To support individuals and families to live meaningful and healthy lives, occupational therapy professionals address a variety of family health outcomes related to redundant instrumental activities of daily living, work, play or leisure, education, rest or sleep, and social participation. Improvement or enhancement of an individual family member's ability to perform daily living tasks through compensation, remediation, adaptation, and modification of the physical or social environment are outcomes of occupational therapy intervention. Prevention of disease and disability and health promotion through fostering engagement of healthy lifestyles are also individual and family health outcomes addressed through occupational therapy intervention. Further, improving family member body structures, functioning and performance skills, patterns and routines of healthy and restorative activities, and creating or adapting healthy environments for doing needed or desired activities is an essential goal of occupational therapists in working with families. Occupational therapists work to meet the health outcomes related to physical, emotional, and social needs of individuals and families through occupational therapy intervention that targets the client's health issues in the occupations and activities that are currently enhancing health and well-being and those that are limiting the individual's abilities to participate in healthy life activities.

Frequently the family is the target of occupational therapy intervention, as occupations are learned and performed within the family context and environment. Families influence individual performance skills, routines, and patterns in which activities of daily living occur. Disruptions in individual occupational performance due to an injury, illness, or disability influence family functioning. In turn, family disruption in daily living patterns can influence an individual's participation in occupation. For example, if a family is struggling with the care of a family member with a disability, this impacts another member's ability to balance areas of work, leisure, and self-care and restoration. This situation may lead to stressors and unhealthy behaviors that can lead to illness or chronic health conditions. Occupational therapy practitioners need to be prepared to intervene with all family members and be knowledgeable about family dynamics and family systems as families adapt to typical life transitions in routines and daily activities and those thrust on them as a result of traumatic events.

Official concept and position papers developed by the American Occupational Association reflect a variety of current family health topics and issues, including the following: family caregivers, youth violence, hospice, aging in place, obesity, nutrition, health promotion, stress and stress disorders, community mobility, access to health resources, domestic violence, chronic diseases, health disparities, work performance, depression, and creating safe, healthy communities. Occupational therapy educators and educational accreditation agencies have responded to current and projected family health needs and issues by creating standards of education that require occupational therapy professionals to demonstrate competencies as direct providers of occupational therapy services, educators, and advocates for individuals and families.

Students entering the profession as either occupational therapy assistants or occupational therapists need to have a background in liberal arts and sciences prior to their professional coursework, including health-related subject matter such as biology, anatomy, human development, diversity, psychology, and health promotion. During professional academic training, students are educated as occupational therapy generalists with a breadth of experiential fieldwork experiences across diverse practice settings and client age groups. Experiential fieldwork occurs throughout student education, and the type and length of fieldwork experiences are dependent on the professional degree sought (i.e., associate's, master's, or doctoral degree).

Didactic coursework includes developing knowledge and skills in occupational therapy theory—which includes understanding the role of occupational therapy in health and health promotion, theories of human development, mental health, physical health, and adaptation—as well as developing skills in analyzing the effects of physical and mental health, disease, and disability within the context of family and the effects of socio-cultural factors on occupational performance. Additionally, students gain expertise in the use of assistive technology, technology for screening, evaluation and documentation, evaluation of occupational performance and intervention planning, and implementation and evaluation of outcomes based on evidence of occupational therapy practice and research. Clinical reasoning and professional judgment in addressing occupational needs of individuals, families, and populations is developed throughout student education through practical and written competencies. Critical analysis of the cultural, social, economic, and political climate of service delivery is accentuated in order to understand the lived experience of clients and families and to advocate for needed health services.

Moreover, students in many programs have an opportunity to take elective coursework in clinical practice and program development in family-related health in areas such as early intervention (infants and children), youth at risk for occupational problems, youth in school settings, youth and health promotion, young adults and mental health issues, chronic health conditions and health promotion, aging well in place in the community, and working with families and caregivers. Students may also participate with faculty in research initiatives related to family health.

Recommendations for Intervention and Occupational Therapy Education

Family health, a right to health, and health promotion are part of the focus for occupational therapy intervention in the 21st century to maximize occupational engagement for all persons. In the United States and globally, occupational therapy organizations purport the human right to engage in a range of healthful, meaningful occupations and participate as valued members of families, communities, and societies. Recommendations for future occupational therapy interventions in family health include (a) advocacy for occupational therapy services for those who are unserved or underserved because of lack of reimbursement or referral; (b) preventive and health promotion intervention programming in community-based settings; (c) family-based interprofessional infant and childhood mental health team approaches for families at risk; and (d) caregiving and caregiver interventions for chronic conditions and those caring for family members with multiple disabilities.

To meet the needs for family health in the future, occupational therapy professional students will need to develop knowledge and skills in working with families as part of interprofessional teams and understand the roles and skills of health care professionals from other disciplines who work with families in health settings. Educational coursework will also likely include additional emphasis on skills in cultural competency, cultural sensitivity, and working with families from diverse backgrounds; sophisticated skills in collaboration with families and caregivers in meeting occupational outcomes; skills in evidence-based practice that includes evidence from a client and family perspective; knowledge and skills in modification of home and work environments to meet family desired occupations and maximum occupational engagement; skills in

use and adaptation of technology for evaluation; and intervention and documentation of outcomes.

The primary goal of family health from an occupational therapy perspective is a family in which all members have an opportunity to participate in valued and needed occupations to the best of their potential and are supported as a family to promote their overall health and well-being through occupation. Across the life span, occupational therapy works with individuals to optimize health, life satisfaction, and quality of living. Occupational therapy professionals also play a key role as part of interprofessional teams to enhance individual and family health within their professional roles and responsibilities based on their scope of practice. The profession of occupational therapy is expected to grow as the health of individuals and families continue to be improved through occupational therapy intervention.

Kathleen Flecky

See also Clarifying Family as Context of Care and Family as Focus of Care in Family Health; Educating the Family Regarding Serious Mental Illness; Educating the Family Regarding Chronic Physical Illness; Education of Health Care Providers: WHO Family Health Nurses; Education of Medical Health Care Providers in Family Health; Men's Health; Women's Health

Further Readings

American Council for Occupational Therapy Education. (2009). *Standards and interpretive guidelines.* Retrieved from February 28, 2010, from http://www.aota.org/Educate/Accredit/StandardsReview/guide/42369.aspx

American Occupational Therapy Association. (2007). AOTA's *Centennial Vision* and executive summary. *American Journal of Occupational Therapy, 61,* 613–614.

American Occupational Therapy Association. (2008). Occupational therapy practice framework: Domain and process (2nd ed.). *American Journal of Occupational Therapy, 62,* 625–683.

Scaffa, M. E., Van Slyke, N., & Brownson, C. A. (2008). Occupational therapy services in the promotion of health and the prevention of disease and disability.

American Journal of Occupational Therapy, 62, 694–703.

Sladyk, K., Jacobs, K., & MacRae, N. (2010). *Occupational therapy essentials for clinical competence.* Thorofare, NJ: SLACK.

Websites

American Occupational Therapy Association: http://www.aota.org
World Federation of Occupational Therapists: http://www.wfot.org

EDUCATION OF PHYSICAL THERAPISTS IN FAMILY HEALTH

Physical therapists are experts in the field of movement and mobility and provide services to those who have changes in their physical function due to injury, illness, or other causes. Physical therapists undergo specialized training to practice in a variety of settings, including hospitals, outpatient clinics, school health centers, athletic facilities, and occupational environments. When an individual undergoes changes in his or her function, it impacts the whole family unit. For example, an injured father may not be able to work and provide for his family. Similarly, an elderly person may need to rely on his or her children for support. A family is influenced by the illness of their child and may need to rely on extended family to help. Therefore, a physical therapist works not only directly with individuals who are ill or injured but also within the context of the family.

Family-centered care is a philosophy recognizing that the family plays a vital role in ensuring the health and well-being of its members. Being family centered means respecting each affected individual and his or her family. It also means honoring racial, ethnic, cultural, and socioeconomic diversity and its effect on the family's health care experience and perception of care.

Family-centered care also empowers the family to participate fully in the planning, delivery, and evaluation of health care services. It supports families in this role by building on family members' individual strengths. Family-centered care involves empowering each patient and family to discover their own strengths and to build confidence in their decisions.

The definition of family, in today's society, respects the notion that each family has unique characteristics and variables. Families come in all shapes and sizes. In today's society, family members extend beyond the "nuclear" family. By being family centered, a physical therapist recognizes, facilitates, and supports the choices made by all types of families even in difficult and challenging situations.

Patient- and family-centered care, as described, is the foundation for the physical therapy profession and is emphasized in physical therapy educational programs. Physical therapists receive training at the master's or doctorate level. There are also licensure requirements for all states in the United States. Physical therapists may also undergo additional training and receive a certificate in their specialty area. All educational programs must be accredited by an agency recognized by the U.S. Department of Education and the Council for Higher Education Accreditation. In the United States, this organization is the Commission for the Accreditation of Physical Therapy Education (CAPTE). As a requirement for accreditation, and as outlined by CAPTE, there are universal standards for universities and colleges, and these must be demonstrated in their curriculum content. Principles of family health, wellness, and respect are woven throughout these requirements. Physical therapy students learn these skills through the didactic portion of their education in the physical, biological, and behavioral sciences as well as during the clinical (hands-on) portions of their educational requirement. These concepts are integral to the entry-level physical therapist's competencies. This entry examines these competences as they relate to the individual being treated within the context of the family. It also demonstrates the partnership that exists between physical therapists, the care recipients, and their families.

The American Physical Therapy Association and the World Confederation for Physical Therapists have provided the framework for expectations of how a professional physical therapist practices.

These standards are required as part of the accreditation process for physical therapy programs. Central to these expectations is the relationship between a physical therapist and his or her patient and family. These expectations include professional values, culturally competent care, communication, and promotion of health and wellness.

Professional Practice Expectations: Core Values

Accountability includes a therapist's adhering to legal standards as well as being fiscally responsible. Being accountable as a physical therapist also includes the expectation that a physical therapist participates in organizations that promote the health and wellness of the public.

Altruism is the concept of placing the needs of individuals receiving care above his or her own. This is especially evident when a family's needs require consideration.

Care and compassion involve not only showing empathy to one's patient but also promoting involvement of care recipients and their families in their own treatment.

Integrity is the process of demonstrating forthrightness, honesty, and sincerity in all interactions with care recipients, families, and colleagues. It also involves conducting oneself in an ethical way and adhering to the codes of professional conduct.

Clinical reasoning is the use of clinical judgment and the application of current theory and knowledge to minimize therapist errors and enhance patient outcomes. This also involves the use of evidence-based practice, technology, research, and continued education to ensure the highest possible positive outcome for a patient and his or her family.

Education involves the education and training of the patient and family by whatever means maximize learning. Educational strategies may include written information, photographs, videos, or hands-on demonstration, based on one's particular learning style.

Professional duty involves demonstrating professional behavior in all interactions. It also involves undergoing processes of peer and self-assessment to ensure that one is maintaining one's professional duty.

Social responsibility refers to being an advocate for the community and for the profession of physical therapy.

Providing Culturally Competent Care

Various definitions of culture include descriptions of the changing values, traditions, and social and political relationships shared by a group of people bound together by a number of factors. These can include a common history, geographic location, language, social class, and/or religion. Various studies of culture conclude that culture is not innate or biologically inherited but learned patterns of behavior. Additionally, culture is transmitted from the older people to the young, from generation to generation. It serves as a group identity and is shared by other members of the group. Culture provides the individual or the members of a group with an effective mechanism for interacting with each other and their environment. Cultural sensitivity and effectiveness is the process of becoming "culturally competent" and striving toward the ability and availability to work effectively within the cultural context of a client, individual, family, or community, regardless of the cultural background. Culturally competent intervention includes one's developing knowledge about various cultures and learning how to conduct oneself sensitively with relevant cultural assessments. Being culturally competent also involves communicating in a way that is respectful of one's client's and family's differences, values, and preferences. To be culturally competent one must genuinely want to be culturally competent. This ability includes being aware of personal biases or prejudices toward any cultural group and avoiding a tendency to stereotype.

Communication

As already mentioned, communication is the most important tool for understanding the patient and his or her family situation. Communication not only involves understanding of verbal communication but also of nonverbal, written, and electronic information. From a physical therapist's standpoint, communication becomes most important upon the first meeting, when the therapist takes the patient's history. No matter the age of the patient or the needs of the family, information should be gathered in a way that is sensitive and respectful to the patient. One must also remember that it is a developmental skill to ask questions in a way that does not offend the patient or family. There are many tools available to help collect this information via questions. Listening while remaining nonjudgmental is one way to effectively and sensitively obtain information.

Communication must also be tailored to meet the needs of the audience. In health care, linguistic assessment is also necessary to facilitate accurate communication. It is documented that people who have limited English proficiency may experience obstacles when accessing health care. The use of specifically medically trained interpreters is important to the assessment process. Using untrained interpreters, family members, and specifically children and siblings may pose a problem due to a lack of medical knowledge. Similarly, care recipients with low literacy skills may experience delays in making appointments and may be more likely to have misunderstandings regarding time, place, date, and location of appointment. People with low literacy skills may have difficulty communicating with the health care professional and employees in the health care institution. These issues are more likely to exacerbate medical problems that require timely treatment or follow-up. Additionally, adults who have literacy deficiencies face many problems in understanding written and verbal materials that are provided to them.

One can identify people with low literacy skills by looking for clues. An example is someone who gives excuses for not being able to read something or who cannot read back information that is provided. It is important to remember that whereas some people readily admit their limitations regarding understanding verbal and written information, others may feel shame and use strategies to hide their limitations. In these situations, one can use oral explanation and demonstration. Pictures, photographs, and visual cues also help to reinforce the information. When working with clients and families with low literacy, it is important to remain nonjudgmental. Asking patients simple questions, keeping instructions simple, and repeating information many times can also be beneficial. It is also important to involve the patient and family in the learning process. Some people will also use family members to assist them with reading, and these family members can be important in the education process. It is important to involve family and friends in the learning and reinforcing of information. Empowering these individuals and families fosters independence in their physical therapy programs.

Health care professionals and physical therapists should promote the sharing of information and collaboration among patients, families, and health care staff. Additionally, one must support family caregiving and decision making and help give clients and families the tools to do so, even if one doesn't agree with the decision that is made. Institutions must involve patients and families in the planning, delivery, and evaluation of health care services. They should also consider the family's needs, as well as the patient's needs, and incorporate feedback from families into program planning. Some institutions offer places such as a family resource center, which can give patients and families opportunities to educate themselves about their needs. Some institutions have instituted family faculty. These are families who have been in similar situations and can act to encourage and facilitate support via parent-to-parent or spouse-to-spouse programs. They also provide a network for families. The development of programs that provide support to families in the community is an important related activity for the institutions.

Promotion of Health and Wellness

Physical therapists are trained and involved in the promotion of health and wellness. At the primary level this includes the prevention of an illness or disability. The secondary level of promotion a therapist is involved with is decreasing the severity of a condition. At the tertiary level, therapists limit the degree of disability. Physical therapists accomplish this goal by conducting screenings to identify factors related to the home, school, workplace, or community. Physical therapists can then define programs to address the prevention with programs in the same area. These programs can include exercise programs, ergonomic modifications, and widely based education through literature and advocacy programs. Through appropriate screening, examination, diagnosis, prognosis, and intervention, impairments may be minimized and health maintained to prevent further disability.

Principles of Family-Centered Care Applied to Physical Therapy Practice

According to the "Guide to Physical Therapy Practice" outlined by the American Physical Therapy

Association, a physical therapist is involved in screening, examination, intervention, prognostication, and discharge planning. Being family centered and maintaining the core values put forth by the profession are central to the therapist's responsibility.

Screening

A physical therapist should consider cultural influences when performing a screening assessment. Sometimes specific illnesses are common within cultural groups. Cultural characteristics may influence the presentation or the seeking of medical opinion of a condition within a specific group of people. Culture may dictate whether someone seeks medical attention on early presentation of signs and symptoms. Finally, a group's culture may influence the follow-up for a medical condition.

Examination

Throughout the examination process, communication is integral to gathering information. This is evident when a child or teen is accompanied to the clinic by his or her parent. Communication must be tailored to the age or cognitive level of the child. Teenagers may be more comfortable speaking with a parent outside the room. This may also apply to spouses. Open-ended questions can elicit how people feel about their needs. The interview process is also the time to ascertain how much or how little a family knows about the family member's illness, injury, or disability. Requests like "Tell me what brought you here" or "Tell me about why you need physical therapy" can be useful in ascertaining a family's knowledge. Professionals must also avoid using medical terminology or language that is too technical for patients and families to easily comprehend.

Intervention

Developing an intervention plan must be collaborative and tailored to the patient's and family's needs. The environment where physical therapy interventions are provided should be considered based on a family's need. For a small child, using community resources that provide service in the natural environment of the home may be more useful than services provided in an outpatient or ambulatory setting. The intervention plan needs to be agreed upon by the patient and family. If this is achieved, then there is a greater chance for compliance.

Prognosis

Goals should be centered on the client's and family's needs. It is the responsibility of the physical therapist to provide realistic information about the expectations for treatment, but this should be within the framework of the client's and family's understanding. All efforts should be made to find out what is important to them and to use that information to plan for the outcomes expected for the patient. Again, if clients and families feel their priorities are being met, there will be a greater sense of ownership and higher likelihood of successful outcomes.

Discharge Planning

Physical therapists are responsible for helping patients and families find resources in the community that will assist them. This assistance may be equipment related, educationally related, or even work related. Additionally, there are times when respite care may be needed for a family who is caring for a family member, and providing the links to agencies or resources may be valuable.

Case Example

These concepts can be best demonstrated with the following case example.

Mac is a 10-year-old boy with cerebral palsy. He lives with his mother, father, two sisters, grandmother, aunt, and four cousins in a small home in an urban environment. Mac's parents and grandmother speak minimal English. Mac is completely dependent on caregivers for his daily needs as he cannot walk as a result of his disability.

The professionals have recommended a special educational setting for Mac, where he could receive all his educational needs and therapies. The family has declined such a placement and prefer to homeschool him. For many years, the professionals who have seen Mac have tried to convince the family to get outside help to teach Mac to be able to do more for himself. The family has not followed through with any of the team's recommendations. Mac's health has been great, and there have never been any issues of neglect.

A new physical therapist offered to make a visit to the family's home to assess the situation. When she arrived, she found a very crowded living arrangement in a very small home. As she stayed to "visit," she observed a typical day in the life of Mac. She was amazed to see the whole family involved. One family member bathed and dressed him. Another family member fed him at the same time the rest of the family ate. When the other children went off to school, a cousin came into the home and taught Mac math and reading in English. Mac's mom did exercises with him to make him strong. After dinner, Mac was carried outside and taken for a walk around the neighborhood and accompanied his father to the store for some items in a homemade wagon. The children in the neighborhood even included Mac in their games.

When the physical therapist returned from her visit, she shared with the professionals that Mac's family and neighbors had embraced his care as a team. All agreed that Mac was being cared for but that perhaps they were going about helping him the wrong way. They decided to have a social worker, who was of the same ethnic group, work with the family on changing their understanding of the disability. Instead of focusing on changing what the family was doing, the team worked to support the family in what they were doing. Very soon, the family accepted some help from the team, and the team was able to give the family suggestions to make it easier for them to care for Mac. They were also able to give them suggestions for how he could play a more active role in the family and the community.

Conclusion

It is well documented that family-centered care can improve patient and family outcomes, increase satisfaction, build on patient and family strengths, increase professional satisfaction, decrease health care costs, and lead to more effective use of health care resources. Educational programs in physical

therapy continue to teach principles of professionalism, cultural competency, and communication. Entry-level therapists are educated to support families with information, education, and resources and are able to monitor the effectiveness of their efforts. Training programs should be in place to educate all health care workers both pre- and postprofessionally about their role in fostering family-centered care. These would include developing culturally appropriate observation and interviewing skills and reflective practices. The federal government will continue to look at funding systems for health programs and enact legislation to ensure that these principles are being respected.

Elena McKeogh Spearing

See also Community Resources for Families Related to Health; Cultural Attitudes Toward Help Seeking and Beliefs About Illness in Families; Disabilities and Family Management; Education of Health Care Providers: WHO Family Health Nurses; Partnering With Families: Family-Centered Care

Further Readings

American Physical Therapy Association. (2001). The guide to physical therapy practice. *Physical Therapy, 81*, 9–744.

American Physical Therapy Association. (2004). *Evaluative criteria for accreditation of education programs for the preparation of physical therapists*. Washington, DC: Author. Retrieved from http://www.apta.org

American Physical Therapy Association. (2004). *A normative model of physical therapist professional education: Version 2004*. Alexandria, VA: Author.

Camphina-Bacote, J. (1999). A model and instrument for addressing cultural competence in health care. *Journal of Nursing Education, 38*, 203–207.

Sparling, J. W., & Sekarek, D. K. (1992). Embedding the family perspective in an entry level physical therapy curriculum. *Pediatric Physical Therapy, 4*, 116–122.

Spearing, E. (2008). Providing family centered care in pediatric physical therapy. In J. Tecklin (Ed.), *Pediatric physical therapy* (4th ed.). Philadelphia: Lippincott Williams & Wilkins.

World Confederation for Physical Therapists. (2007). *WCPT guidelines for physical therapists professional education*. London: Author.

EDUCATION OF RECREATIONAL THERAPY PROVIDERS IN FAMILY HEALTH

Recreational therapy refers to the use of recreation to restore, remediate, or rehabilitate in order to improve functioning and independence as well as to reduce or eliminate the effects of illness or disability. The purpose of this entry is to provide the reader with an understanding of the profession of recreational therapy as part of today's health care system. Specifically this entry will enable the reader to understand the roles of a recreational therapist, the education and training of a recreational therapist, the credentialing requirements, the future trends, the professional organizations, and advice from outstanding professionals.

Recreational Therapy

History

Recreation as therapy first emerged in the 1850s when Florence Nightingale encouraged recreation to enhance recovery for patients in military hospitals. In the late 1800s, Jane Addams, a social worker and founder of the Hull-House settlement in Chicago, pioneered work in the therapeutic use of recreation through her use of recreation and leisure to improve the health and well-being of persons with special needs (poverty-stricken, homeless, immigrants, and those with addiction problems). During World War I, the American Red Cross provided wounded soldiers with recreational opportunities during their convalescence. As a result of World War II, the profession gained status when the Red Cross hired and trained college-educated women to work in hospital recreation.

Growth of the Profession

The National Council for Therapeutic Recreation Certification (NCTRC) states that there are currently 27,000 recreational therapy professionals with 16,000 active certified therapeutic recreation specialists (CTRSs) in the United States. According to the Bureau of Labor Statistics, employment for recreational therapists is projected to grow faster than average. This growth is due to an aging population and their anticipated therapeutic needs.

Job Skills

Recreational therapists assess the client's level of functioning and leisure interests and then provide services based on these assessments for individuals with disabilities or illnesses using a variety of recreation interventions. Interventions such as animal-assisted therapy, aquatics, adventure-based counseling, community integration, cooking, expressive arts, dance and movement, sports and games, physical activity, and relaxation techniques are often used to intervene and work on the assessed clinical problems or needs. The recreational therapist provides evidence-based practice using a holistic approach to care that emphasizes the biopsychosocial needs of the person receiving care. Furthermore, recreational therapists provide wellness and leisure education services to help clients acquire skills, awareness, attitudes, knowledge, and resources. Additionally, recreational therapists provide health promotion and prevention interventions aimed at maintaining and improving health outcomes. Health outcomes from recreational therapy interventions include, but are not limited to, decreasing depression, anxiety, agitation, negative affect, and stress, in addition to increasing mobility, physical function, satisfaction with life, well-being, positive affect, self-determination, socialization, and self-efficacy.

Recreational therapists have a strong desire to work with people. They provide services to a variety of age groups across the life span and populations, including behavioral medicine, physical disabilities, and geriatrics in a variety of agencies including hospitals, skilled nursing facilities, residential and transitional services, community parks and recreation agencies, outpatient and day services, and related human service organizations. The majority of work is in nongovernmental agencies, followed by local and federal government jobs. Some recreational therapists provide services in private practice or consultant/contractual employment.

Traditionally the recreational therapist works as part of an interdisciplinary health care team that could include physical, occupational, and speech and language therapists, nurses, social workers, educators, psychologists, and physicians. An interdisciplinary treatment team works together to develop treatment plans to meet the biopsychosocial needs of the clients.

The majority of recreational therapists report that they work full-time and are very satisfied with their jobs. Other positions within the field of recreational therapy include leader/programmers, supervisor/administrators, educator/researchers, and consultants.

Education and Training

Most recreational therapists enter the profession using the academic path, which means they have completed a bachelor's degree in therapeutic recreation or in recreation with a concentration in therapeutic recreation. However, NCTRC provides an alternative path to obtain the credential of a certified therapeutic recreation specialist. This alternative path is a combination of education, training, and work experience.

Despite which path is chosen, students are expected to have a specific body of professional knowledge before they enter the profession. The expectations include completing recreation and therapeutic recreation courses on the topics of therapeutic recreation process, assessment, and advancing the profession. Other therapeutic recreation courses may include facilitating interventions, professional ethics, and assistive devices and technology. In addition, students are expected to take supportive courses, including anatomy and physiology, abnormal psychology, and human growth and development across the life span. Students may take other supportive coursework such as medical terminology, pharmacology for health care professionals, and characteristics of illness and disability. In addition, students need the core values and beliefs that recreation and leisure experience enhance the mind, body, and spirit and that everyone has a right to these experiences.

The academic path requires a full-time, semester-long therapeutic recreation field placement experience under a certified therapeutic recreation specialist. Many universities also require additional hands-on opportunities such as volunteering, service-learning, and practicum experiences. Currently there are more than 100 colleges and universities offering degrees in recreation with a concentration in therapeutic recreation or degrees in therapeutic recreation.

Certification, Licensure, Registration, and Other Requirements

Certification

The NCTRC is the credentialing body for recreational therapists. The NCTRC website states that NCTRC was founded in 1981 as a nonprofit organization dedicated to the protection of consumers through professional certification. NCTRC is dedicated to improving the quality of human service and health care standards and maintains a relationship with the Joint Commission and the Commission on Accreditation of Rehabilitation Facilities. NCTRC is a charter member of the National Organization for Competency Assurance. Lastly, NCTRC is accredited by the National Commission for Certifying Agencies.

Most employers prefer to hire recreational therapists who are certified, many clinical settings require or expect certification, and the majority of recreational therapists choose to become certified to enhance their professional status. Professionals who are interested in becoming certified must meet the educational requirements, pass a certification exam, and complete a full-time, semester-long internship placement under CTRS. Additionally, to maintain the CTRS credential, the recreational therapist must maintain his or her certification annually. The CTRS must apply for recertification every 5 years after having completed a series of requirements, including continuing education.

Continuing education requirements are important to maintaining the knowledge and skills within the profession. A recreational therapist must be committed to professional development. Continuing education can occur through attending professional conferences, workshops, and reading and reporting research findings in professional journals. There are currently three professional journals: *American Journal of Recreation Therapy*, *Annual in Therapeutic Recreation*, and *Therapeutic Recreation Journal*. These journals provide articles on the latest research and practice methods and often offer continuing education opportunities. The two national professional organizations (American Therapeutic Recreation Association and National

Therapeutic Recreation Society) and numerous regional, state, and local recreational therapy professional groups also offer opportunities for continuing education.

As of 2010, there are four states that require a licensure to practice recreational therapy: Oklahoma, North Carolina, Utah, and New Hampshire. Each state has specific requirements and regulations, so it is best to contact the state licensing boards for more information. For example, some states require both the state license and the national certification, while others do not. In addition, some states require additional requirements beyond what is required by the national certification.

Registration

As of 2010, there are two states that require registration: California and Washington. Registration provides an official directory of recreational therapists who practice in the state. State registration recognizes and protects the title of recreational therapy as a health care profession. A person cannot represent himself or herself as a recreational therapist or represent the services he or she performs as recreational therapy unless the person meets certain educational requirements. One should check the recreational therapy title protection in each state for specific details.

Other Requirements

Some recreational therapists may have chosen to advance their careers by pursuing additional certifications, certificates, or licenses to enhance their clinical skills. Examples could be aquatic therapy, animal-assisted therapy, equine therapy, massage therapy, personal training, gerontology, special education, counseling, child life specialist, expressive arts therapy, Reiki, and therapeutic touch.

Professional Organizations

Terry Robertson and Terry Long state that professional organizations support professional growth and development, improve professional practice, and promote the advancement of the profession. There are national, regional, state, and local recreational therapy professional organizations. Belonging to a professional organization provides many benefits, including educational opportunities that support professional credentials, publication of research, definition of ethical behavior, and moving the profession forward. Two national professional organizations are highlighted here.

American Therapeutic Recreation Association

The American Therapeutic Recreation Association (ATRA) is a national membership organization representing the interests and needs of recreational therapists. The ATRA website states that ATRA was incorporated in the District of Columbia in 1984 as a nonprofit, grassroots organization in response to growing concern about the dramatic changes in the health care industry. The mission of ATRA is to serve as a member-driven association that collectively supports the recreational therapy profession. The ATRA is led by an elected board of directors and is staffed by a professional management company. ATRA hosts annual and mid-year conferences, which provide opportunities for continuing education units. ATRA publishes *Annual in Therapeutic Recreation,* offering up-to-date research and practice articles.

National Therapeutic Recreation Society

According to its website, the National Therapeutic Recreation Society (NTRS) is a branch of the National Recreation and Park Association (NRPA), which specializes in the provision of therapeutic recreation services for persons with disabilities in clinical and community settings. NTRS's vision is to advance the belief that leisure and recreation are basic human rights and are critical to health, quality of life, and happiness. As basic rights, leisure and recreation must be available to all people, including those with illnesses, disabilities, or other conditions that may restrict health, independence, and quality of life. NTRS provides an annual membership meeting in conjunction with the NRPA national meeting, providing opportunities for continuing educational units. The *Therapeutic Recreation Journal* is the research publication sponsored by NTRS.

Advice From Outstanding Professionals

Recreational therapists have the knowledge base, skills, and attitudes to contribute to the health and well-being of a variety of people dealing with numerous physical, mental, emotional, and social issues. They enhance the quality of the lives of the people they provide services to. They do this by using recreation and leisure to intervene on a problem, meet a need, and/or provide purpose and meaning in the lives of the people they serve.

A few outstanding professionals have offered their advice to those interested in pursuing a career in recreational therapy: Listen to the clients you serve; get involved in professional projects; join a professional organization; volunteer; find work that you love; be daring, flexible, and adaptable; believe in what you do; advocate for those you serve; embrace your profession; and live what you preach—a balanced and engaged life filled with meaningful activity.

Future Trends for Recreational Therapy in Health Care

To practice in today's health care environments and expand the role of the recreational therapist within the interdisciplinary health care team, recreational therapy must continue to provide research that supports their clinical practice and advanced clinical skills to meet the needs of the clients they serve. Continuing educational opportunities must be based on practice-based research and include competency testing. Time must be given to practice and fine-tune these advanced clinical skills. Education on how to collect and analyze outcome data from recreational therapy interventions needs to be part of the recreational therapy curriculum, and recreational therapists need to continue to write and publish these results. The recreational therapy profession is moving toward evidence and clinical practice guidelines that support its basic practices, such as understanding what the best recreational therapy interventions are for an older adult with a stroke or for a child with autism. Health care is rapidly changing, and the profession of recreational therapy is positioned to be a valuable part of the health care team.

Conclusion

This entry provides an overview of recreational therapy as a health care profession. It highlights the history, educational and credentialing requirements, occupational outlook, professional organizations, and future trends for recreational therapy in health care. Advice from outstanding professionals was provided, which included living a balanced and engaged life filled with work that one loves and meaningful activity that contributes to one's health and happiness.

Nancy Ellen Richeson

See also Education of Health Care Providers: WHO Family Health Nurses; Education of Medical Health Care Providers in Family Health; Education of Nursing Health Care Providers in Family Health; Education of Occupational Health Providers in Family Health; Education of Physical Therapists in Family Health

Further Readings

Bureau of Labor Statistics. *Occupational outlook handbook, 2010–11 edition: Recreational therapists.* Retrieved from http://www.bls.gov/oco/ocos082.htm

Robertson, T., & Long T. (2008). *Foundations of therapeutic recreation.* Champaign, IL: Human Kinetics.

Websites

American Therapeutic Recreation Association: http://www.atra-online.com

National Council for Therapeutic Recreation Certification: http://www.nctrc.org

National Therapeutic Recreation Society: http://www.nrpa.org/ntrs

Therapeutic Recreation Directory: http://www.recreationtherapy.com

ELDER CARE OPTIONS FOR FAMILIES: LONG-TERM CARE

An increasing proportion of elders in the population is projected for the next few decades. An increase of 76% is expected by 2030. Because the incidence of chronic illness and disability is correlated with advancing age, the demand for long-term care will correspondingly increase. Older persons will also be more ethnically and racially diverse. These circumstances cause concerns about the adequacy of long-term care services to assist culturally dissimilar elders with the management of chronic illnesses, functional impairment, and promotion of health to forestall institutionalization, maintain safety, and enhance quality of life. Although there are a number of options with specific advantages available for long-term care, these vary by state jurisdiction, have specific disadvantages, and typically present a difficult decision for older persons and their families. Many family members report that finding the best long-term care option for a loved one is challenging and that placing a parent or relative in a nursing home is a very difficult decision. This entry describes the variety of long-term care options, along with the advantages and disadvantages of each, to promote the understanding of each, to assist persons to make the best choice of long-term care options, and to encourage thoughtful consideration of options before a crisis of need occurs. Currently available long-term care options are compared and evaluated by what is most desirable, and the evidence support for the options is presented.

Long-Term Care Issues

Long-term care refers to assisting persons with health care and activities of daily living over an extended period of time. Long-term care takes place in the home and in a variety of community-based facilities. Mainly older people need long-term care, but younger persons with disabilities and chronic illnesses may also require the services. There is a continuum of long-term care options, ranging from home without services, home with services, adult day care and respite, board and room homes, elder group homes, residential facilities, assisting living facilities, and nursing homes.

There are a number of issues associated with currently available long-term care options. A number of these issues are exacerbated by a strong institutional bias in the provision of long-term care with many facilities operated by for-profit corporations. The average size of nursing homes in the United States is 93.3 beds, with each resident receiving less than 45 minutes of care over a 24-hour period, mostly by minimally prepared nursing assistants. Meridean Maas and colleagues argue that the substandard quality of care provided by inadequately prepared staff and substandard staffing, especially of registered

nurses, clearly hinders equitable access of many persons to the quality of care that is deserved. Examples of substandard care include undiagnosed and untreated pain and rampant, preventable, or treatable incontinence. Additional results of institutional bias are that (a) there is a disproportionate number of older persons living in institutions than is desirable or needed, and (b) there are fewer options for consumers that are developed and available based on need or from innovative models of care, such as options for "aging in place" or for persons with dementia or other illnesses that have associated difficult-to-manage behaviors.

The piecework and patchwork nature of long-term care options has long been noted by Rosalie Kane to seriously constrain equal access to long-term care that is appropriate and needed by many. Equity of access is a serious issue for persons living in rural areas and impoverished urban areas, where the availability of the range of options is often limited. Public third-party payment for options other than for nursing home care is mostly not authorized or is quite limited, such as for home care. Because many options require private payment, access by lower income persons is restricted. Finally, lack of sufficient culturally sensitive options in many geographic areas limits the equitable access of ethnic and racial minority persons. The unavailability of in-home care services in many areas and limited third-party payment for many needed services constitute inequity of access to a long-term care option that is preferred by many.

Advantages and Disadvantages of Current Long-Term Options

Nursing Homes

Most of the advantages of nursing homes are well known. Nursing homes provide 24-hour care, providing relief and reassurance for families. Nursing homes are regulated and required to meet certain standards, including the employment of staff with at least minimal training, even though these standards are often very low. Lastly, the care of older persons in nursing homes is reimbursed by Medicare or Medicaid, although the latter is often limited. The disadvantages are that (a) 95% of persons report that they do not ever want to go to a nursing home, (b) most are based on a medical-custodial model of care that does not emphasize quality of life, (c) there is a lack of registered nurse leadership and direction despite the fact that the preponderance of care received is nursing care, (d) the average nursing home resident spends an average of 17 hours per day in bed, (e) nursing homes are often understaffed, (f) residents may not receive enough help with eating and many are malnourished and dehydrated, and (g) many problems that affect health, function, and quality of life, such as pain, incontinence, mobility, nutrition and hydration, and boredom, may be underaddressed or not addressed at all.

Assisted Living

Assisted living is the fastest growing long-term care option, primarily developed and owned by for-profit corporations. The facilities are usually quite large, with 60 to 200 rooms or apartments, and most are private pay. The marketing appeal is to persons who are looking for some structure and assistance alternative to a nursing home, including many persons with early dementia and other mental health problems. Although assisted living varies substantially among states, in general, housing and services are provided in a physical structure that provides a home-like environment. Services may include, but are not limited to, health-related care, personal care, and assistance with instrumental activities of daily living. Assisted living may include encouragement of family involvement and resident self-direction, shared risk, and independence, emphasizing privacy, dignity, and choice. The advantages are that the facilities are more attractive, more privacy and autonomy are provided, good food is emphasized, there is opportunity to socialize with others with similar abilities and disabilities, and there is usually assistance available with medication, room maintenance, and often with hygiene. Disadvantages include that assisted living is minimally regulated and expensive. A social model is claimed, but it is easy for persons to become isolated in their room or apartment, and health concerns tend to be neglected. There is limited attention to mental health problems, especially for those with dementia, but also to prevention and management of physical health problems, contributing to the short average length of stay of 2 years. The unaddressed gap between consumer expectations and services provided is reinforced by profit

motive and marketing that resist providing needed health and function promotion and maintenance services by qualified staff led by registered nurses.

Elder Group Homes

Elder group homes are owner-operated or non-profit single-family residences with a resident manager. Room, board, and personal care are provided for three to five residents. The group home providers of services cannot be related to the residents. Personal assistance may include assistance with bathing, personal hygiene, dressing, grooming, and the supervision of self-administered medications. Medication administration, however, is not allowed. The advantages of elder group homes are that a family-like setting can be provided for persons who can no longer live alone at home, it is less costly than some other options, and it is a more normalized living environment. The disadvantages are that elder group homes tend to be few, compared to other options; the prohibition of medication administration eliminates the option for many; there are no health care services; reimbursement is poor; and group homes are usually not cost-effective to operate. The lack of cost-effectiveness means that there will likely never be many group homes, and thus they will remain a limited option for long-term care.

Residential Facilities

Residential facilities are licensed facilities but are prohibited from providing nursing care. There are also strict rules for transfer of residents to other facilities if there is a change in condition. This, combined with the fact that there are few residential facilities that are available, makes residential facilities a limited option. The main advantages are that cost is relatively low and persons can maintain largely independent living in the facilities. In addition to the disadvantage of limited availability, the main disadvantage is the lack of nursing care to promote and maintain health and function and to assist residents with the management of illnesses.

Board and Room Homes

Board and room homes are not regulated by states but must meet local fire and safety codes.

These facilities, like elder group homes, provide a more family-like environment, and a larger number of residents can be accommodated. Because they are unregulated, there is no listing of those that are available, so it is often difficult to locate the homes if they are available. Board and room homes are to provide only board and room and cannot provide nursing care. Families or the resident can, however, contract with another agency or provider to bring nursing care services into the home to care for individuals. A disadvantage can be the cost of contracting for nursing care services. Another potential disadvantage is that these homes are not regulated and do not have to meet standards required of other long-term care options for staffing, cleanliness, safety, quality and nutrient value of meals, and other aspects of health and function promotion and maintenance.

Adult Day Service

An adult day service is an organized program providing a variety of health, social, and related support services for 16 hours or less in a 24-hour day to persons with functional impairments on a regularly scheduled contractual basis. These programs have many advantages for the clients and for their family members: They allow the clients to live at home and they provide enriched activities, health care services, and safety for the clients and respite and reassurance to family members at a lower cost than other options. Adult day service programs are regulated and surveyed by states, and there is an increasing emphasis on health promotion and maintenance. Unfortunately, many adult day service programs do not serve many persons with dementia, which is a considerable disadvantage for these clients and their families. Other disadvantages are that they are underused, and thus they are difficult to sustain in smaller and more rural communities. Transportation to and from adult day care is also often a barrier to the use of this care option.

Home Care

Home care is nursing care and assistance with instrumental activities of daily living in the home. Most home care services are offered by not-for-profit county public health agencies and hospitals, and by for-profit private home care agencies. All home care agencies that receive Medicare or Medicaid reimbursement must be certified by an approved accrediting agency. The advantages of home care are that the client can continue to live a relatively normal life at home with caregiving support provided to family caregivers. If reimbursed, home care can be relatively low cost for the individual and family. The fact, however, that only certain, mostly medical, tasks and care provided in the home are reimbursed is a disadvantage, because many persons require assistance with activities of daily living and assistance with the prevention or management of disease and disability to remain at home and avoid institutionalization. Many also need daily care, help with activities, and surveillance, which are not reimbursed. Lack of this kind of assistance and attention to health promotion and prevention of disability make it difficult to maintain many persons in their own homes.

Recommendations

There is substantial evidence to support the need for a variety of options and for the improvement of care that is provided to address the problems often experienced by older persons and others who require long-term care. Most older persons want to remain optimally functional and healthy for as long as possible and thus want their function and health supported and promoted. If persons cannot stay in their own homes, they want to live in settings that are home-like, where their control and functional abilities—social, psychological, physical, and spiritual—are supported and maintained. Persons want there to be as much attention paid to their quality of life as to their diseases. Fundamentally, for options currently available and yet to be developed, there needs to be a shift in emphasis from institutional care to in-home care and community-based services. Policy makers need to support this shift by revising the standards of care and reimbursement policies so that providers are reimbursed to promote health, prevent and restore disabilities, and emphasize quality of life. Family members should be reimbursed for care and assistance provided for loved ones with oversight by qualified nurses to enable them to remain in the home. More innovations need to be developed and tested, such as alternative nursing care facilities for persons with dementia, nurse case management of older persons in their homes, and smaller, home-like settings for persons needing institutional care. Finally, a holistic nursing model that addresses the social, psychological, physical, and spiritual needs of persons, therapeutic environments, and evidence-based practices should replace the false and limiting dichotomy of social versus medical-custodial models of care.

Janet K. Pringle Specht

See also Access to Health Care: Elderly; Alzheimer's Disease: Caregiver Burden; Assisted Living Placement; Caregiving: Elderly; Chronic Health Problems and Interventions for the Elderly Family; Decision Making in the Context of Health and Illness; Family Interventions Across the Life Span; Hospice Care; Influence of Policy on Health Care for Families

Further Readings

Grabowski, D. C. (2001). Does an increase in the Medicaid reimbursement rate improve nursing home quality? *Journal of Gerontology: Social Sciences, 56B*(2), S84–S93.

Harrington, C., Zimmerman, D., Karon, S. L., Robinson, J., & Beutel, P. (2000). Nursing home staffing and its relationship to deficiencies. *Journal of Gerontology: Social Sciences, 55B*(5), S278–S287.

Hernandez, M., & Newcomer, R. (2007). Assisted living and special populations: What do we know about differences in use and potential access barriers? *The Gerontologist, 47*(3), 110–117.

Kane, R. A. (2001). Long-term care and a good quality of life: Bringing them closer together. *The Gerontologist, 41*(3), 293–304.

Kelley-Gillespie, N., & Farley, O. W. (2007). The effect of housing on perceptions of quality of life of older adults participating in a Medicaid long-term care demonstration project. *Journal of Gerontological Social Work, 49*(3), 205–228.

Maas, M. L., Specht, J. P., Buckwalter, K. C., Gittler, J., & Bechen, K. (2008). Nursing home staffing and training recommendations for promoting older adults' quality of care and life. Part 1. Deficits in the quality of care due to understaffing and undertraining. *Research in Gerontological Nursing, 1*(2), 1–13.

Maas, M. L., & Specht, J. P., Buckwalter, K. C., Gittler, J., & Bechen, K. (2008). Nursing home staffing and training recommendations for promoting older adults' quality of care and life. Part 2. Increasing nurse staffing and training. *Research in Gerontological Nursing, 1*(2), 14–24.

Marek, K. D., Popejoy, L., Petroski, G., Mehr, D., Rantz, M., & Lin, W.-C. (2005). Clinical outcomes of aging in place. *Nursing Research, 54*(3), 202–211.

ELDER EMOTIONAL ABUSE AND THE FAMILY

The term *elder emotional abuse* is often used interchangeably with the terms *elder psychological abuse* and *elder verbal abuse*. The behaviors encompassed within each such term vary across authors, increasing the difficulty of arriving at accurate measures of incidence and prevalence. In general, however, emotional abuse includes verbal assaults, such as yelling, name calling, swearing, and insults; rejection and rejecting statements; humiliation; expressions of disgust or disregard; threats of punishment, institutionalization, or abandonment; verbal harassment, fear-inducing threats; and lack of attention. The abuse may be committed intentionally or unintentionally by a family member, a friend, a professional or nonprofessional caregiver, or a health care worker. The emotional abuse may occur in a domestic setting, such as the elder's home, or in an institutional setting, such as a hospital or nursing home.

Emotional abuse is thought to be the most common form of abuse experienced by elderly persons. Depending upon the definition used for emotional abuse, the location of the study, the nature of the sample, and the questions asked, the prevalence of emotional abuse internationally has been found to range from approximately 1% in Canada to 82% in a sample of older persons in Detroit, Michigan. This entry focuses on the identification of elder emotional abuse and possible interventions.

Screening for Emotional Abuse

Research suggests that the majority of primary care physicians believe that elder abuse is a problem in which a physician can intervene and one that is most easily detected by primary care physicians. Nevertheless, many physicians never ask their elderly patients whether they are experiencing any form of maltreatment or abuse. Many of those who do encounter a patient who is being emotionally abused are unsure how to proceed, particularly when the signs of emotional abuse are subtle or the individual does not describe his or her experience as abuse, perhaps due to cultural factors. As an example, raising one's voice to a parent may be seen as disrespectful and abusive in some cultures or families and reported to a physician as such, whereas in other families or cultures such behavior reflects family members' typical style of engagement. Perceptions of abuse may also vary by age; as an example, older women from traditional patriarchal heritages may be less likely than younger individuals to classify being yelled at by their adult daughter as abusive behavior.

A review of the factors that have been found to be associated with elder emotional abuse may be helpful to physicians and other health care professionals in identifying instances of emotional abuse among their patients and clients. Characteristics of the elder that have been found to be associated with being emotionally abused in a family setting include lower age, lower cognitive functioning, lower educational level, previous experience of a traumatic event such as domestic violence, co-occurring chronic disease, a need for assistance with activities of daily living, and a history of emotional or mental problems. Rural elderly women are more likely to be the targets of emotional abuse than are their urban counterparts, perhaps as a result of increased isolation and decreased access to resources.

Elderly persons are more likely to be emotionally abused by an adult child or child-in-law, particularly if they are residing together, such as an elderly parent with his or her adult son or daughter. Research suggests that emotional abuse of an elder by an adult child is often preceded by a poor relationship of long-standing duration; the nature of the earlier relationship between the elder and the adult child is one of the most important factors in the (non)occurrence of emotional abuse. Often, the abusive adult children suffer from depression, anxiety, or both. The relationship between the sex of the abuser and the abused elder is unclear; some studies report that elderly men are more likely to suffer emotional abuse at the hands of their adult children, and other studies suggest that elderly women are more likely to be emotionally abused, particularly by their adult sons and daughters-in-law. Emotional abuse by a spouse may be a continuation of spousal abuse that has been occurring over time. In most cases, emotional abuse is most likely to be triggered by the presence of multiple factors rather than by a single factor.

Elders who are being emotionally abused may appear depressed, anxious, helpless, angry, withdrawn, confused, forgetful, hesitant, frightened, or secretive. They may be reluctant to speak about their families at all or may voice fear of one or more persons in their family or household. Abused elders may deal with the related stress by sucking or biting behaviors or may develop seemingly unrelated phobias quite suddenly.

The following questions can be asked of patients or clients to assist in screening them for emotional abuse:

Has anyone ever scolded you?

Are you afraid of anyone at home/where you are living?

Has anyone ever humiliated you?

Has anyone ever threatened to abandon you or to put you in an institution?

Has anyone ever threatened to hurt you?

However, some individuals who are abused may be reluctant to respond to such questions out of fear of retaliation or further punishment. For this reason, it is critical that the health care provider interview the elder individual out of the presence of caregivers and others.

Possible Interventions

To the extent possible, the first course of action should be to discuss the situation with the individual who is suspected of being emotionally abused. This interview can be used to assess not only the nature and extent of the abuse, but also potential courses of action and the individual's preferred ultimate resolution to the situation.

All health care workers are mandated by state laws to report suspected elder abuse. However, state laws vary in their definition of who is an elder, the types of abuse that must be reported, and the procedures for reporting the abuse. Health care providers should become familiar with the legal reporting requirements of the state(s) in which they practice. This needed knowledge also suggests the recommendation for continuing education courses for health professionals that include a focus on the recognition of emotional abuse, the requirements of the relevant state reporting laws, and the availability of supportive resources within the relevant community.

Sana Loue

See also Elder Neglect and the Family; Elder Physical Abuse and the Family; Elder Sexual Abuse and the Family; Family Conflict Related to Caregiving; Family Experiencing Transitions; Verbal Abuse in Families

Further Readings

National Research Council & Panel to Review Risk and Prevalence of Elder Abuse and Neglect. (2003). *Elder mistreatment: Abuse, neglect, and exploitation in an aging America* (R. J. Bonnie & R. B. Wallace, Eds.). Washington, DC: National Academies Press.

Nerenberg, L. (2008). *Elder abuse prevention: Emerging trends and promising strategies.* New York: Springer.

ELDER NEGLECT
AND THE FAMILY

Caregiver neglect is the failure to provide basic necessities to an older adult by an individual who has assumed responsibility to do so. It is the second most common allegation (23.7%) reported to Adult Protective Services in persons 60 years of age and older, according the 2004 survey of State Adult Protective Services. Dementia and depression are risk factors for neglect among other chronic diseases leading to functional decline and the inability for self-care and protection. Caring for persons with dementia is steadily increasing; it can lead to stress, depression, burden, anger, physical illness, and death among caregivers as well as early institutionalization of demented persons. Approximately 75% of in-home caregivers are family members or friends for the estimated three million Americans suffering from dementia of the Alzheimer's type. By the year 2050, it is estimated that 16 million individuals will suffer from Alzheimer's dementia; this will create a larger burden to families, friends, and society in general.

The purpose of this entry is to provide an overview of victim and perpetrator risk factor profiles, the identification and treatment of vulnerable elders experiencing caregiver neglect, and support for caregivers.

Duty to Report

Most states mandate health care professionals to report suspected cases of elder abuse; six states have voluntary reporting laws: Colorado, Illinois, Kentucky, North Dakota, South Dakota, and Wisconsin. The Joint Commission (formerly The Joint Commission on Accreditation of Health Organizations) mandates elder abuse protocols in all ambulatory care settings. Up to 30% of reports of elder abuse are from health professionals, while physicians make up 2% of those, according to the 2004 Survey of State Adult Protective Services. Low physician reporting rates may be due to the physician's delegation of this task to other providers; inadequate training in screening, identification, and interventions for caregiver neglect; desire to avoid legal involvement; and fear of loss of relationship with the patient and family; it may also be due to the patient's denial of abuse. Older adults are unlikely to self-report abusive situations for fear of retaliation or being relocated to a long-term care facility. Therefore, it is the duty of health care professionals to recognize potential caregiver neglect and to follow through with reporting suspected cases.

Risk Factors

Several risk factors exist for neglect of older adults. These include advanced age, functional decline, dependency on others for basic and instrumental activities of daily living, underlying psychiatric disorders, alcohol and substance abuse, living in isolation, aggressiveness toward the caregiver, and dementia with behavior problems. Likewise, the following are perpetrator risk factors: psychiatric disorders, dependency on the elder (i.e., elder's income), living with the elder, inadequate education or training in managing chronic medical conditions, being overwhelmed or burned out, and having external stressors such as working full-time and caring for his or her own children.

Identification

The American Medical Association recommends screening all older adults for abuse, including caregiver neglect. When elders and their caregivers present to physicians, each individual needs to be interviewed separately. Members of the health care team must observe the interaction between the elder and caregiver and concentrate on different explanations for suspicious injuries or poorly managed medical conditions. It is recommended that these questions be asked of the elderly individual: (a) Do you feel safe at home? (b) Who prepares your meals? (c) Who handles your finances?

If the elderly individual is unsure or reticent to answer these questions, further investigation may be warranted. At this point, if caregiver neglect is suspected, mandated reporters should notify Adult Protective Services to investigate the allegations in the home environment.

A more thorough approach to identifying caregiver neglect is the comprehensive geriatric assessment. This approach utilizes an interdisciplinary team consisting of geriatricians, nurses, social workers, nurse case managers, physical and occupational therapists, and other health care professionals. The following battery of assessment tools has been used in comprehensive geriatric assessment performed in victims of neglect: Confusion Assessment Method, Mini-Mental State Examination, CLOX Drawing Test, Geriatric Depression Scale, and the Kohlman Evaluation of Living Skills. These tools screen for delirium, dementia, depression, executive impairment, and whether the individual is capable of living independently.

The following physical examination findings, not necessarily in isolation but rather collectively, should raise suspicion: malnutrition, dehydration, suspicious lacerations (i.e., bite marks), multiple decubiti (sores from lying in one position too long), inappropriate medications, and the elder is fearful of the caregiver. It is important to distinguish self-neglect from caregiver neglect. Self-neglect is the refusal to provide self-sustaining services to oneself. The absence of a caregiver distinguishes self-neglect from caregiver neglect. Short- and long-term interdisciplinary care plans are created for victims of neglect.

Management

An interdisciplinary care plan may include hospitalization to stabilize potential life-threatening medical conditions (i.e., delirium, urinary tract infections, or poorly treated medical conditions such as diabetes mellitus or hypertension). Health care providers must determine if the victim is safe to return home. If not, transfer to a long-term care facility may be necessary unless other family members or friends can be identified to provide care. The goal would be to transfer to the least restrictive alternative.

When aiding the caregiver, it is important to identify the following: lack of education or skills in caring for the elder, available respite services, intentional neglect that requires referral for prosecution, the capacity for the caregiver to care for the elder (i.e., psychiatric illnesses in the caregiver). Prior caregiver research has focused on interventions addressing the burden and distress faced by these individuals. Examples include psychoeducational intervention, cognitive-behavioral therapy, anger and stress management, educational sessions for addressing agitated behaviors exhibited by demented individuals, respite and adult day care, and multicomponent approaches to effective caregiving. Telephone support groups and the involvement of both the caregiver and care recipient in planning care have been two of the most successful interventions.

Conclusion

Members of the health care team must routinely screen for caregiver neglect. Providing care to dependent elders with multiple chronic conditions has many challenges that require a multicomponent approach for successful management. Future research should focus on the long-term management of caregiver distress, burden, and depression, and approaches to overcoming the deteriorating and deleterious effects of the disease processes associated with chronic medical conditions to prevent caregiver neglect. Comprehensive geriatric assessment with an interdisciplinary care plan should address all aspects of managing multiple chronic health conditions by caregivers to reduce the potential strain experienced by caregivers.

Carmel B. Dyer and Sabrina Pickens

See also Alzheimer's Disease: Caregiver Burden; Caregiving: Elderly

Further Readings

Brandl, B., Dyer, C. B., Heisler, C. J., Otto, J. M., Steigel, L. A., & Thomas, R. W. (2007). *Elder abuse detection and intervention—A collaborative approach.* New York: Springer.

Dyer, C. B., Pavlik, V. N., Murphy, K. P., & Hyman, D. J. (2000). The high prevalence of depression and dementia in elder abuse or neglect. *Journal of the American Geriatrics Society, 48,* 205–208.

Dyer, C. B., Pickens, S., & Burnett, J. (2007). Vulnerable elders when it is no longer safe to live alone. *Journal of the American Medical Association, 298*(12), 1448–1450.

Lachs, M. S., Williams, C., O'Brien, S., Hurst, L., & Horwitz, R. (1997). Risk factors for reported elder abuse and neglect: A nine-year observational cohort study. *The Gerontologist, 37*(4), 469–474.

Lachs, M. S., Williams, C. S., O'Brien, S., Pillemer, K. A., & Charlson, M. E. (1998). The mortality of elder mistreatment. *Journal of the American Medical Association, 280*(5), 428–432.

Naik, A. D., Teal, C. R., Pavlik, V. N., Dyer, C. B., & McCullough, L. B. (2008). Conceptual challenges and practical approaches to screening for capacity for self-care and protection in vulnerable older adults. *Journal of the American Geriatrics Society, 56,* S266–S270.

National Center on Elder Abuse. (1998). *National elder abuse incidence study.* Available from http://www .ncea.aoa.gov/ncearoot/main_site/Library/Statistics_ Research/National_Incident.aspx

National Committee for the Prevention of Elder Abuse & National Adult Protective Services. (2006). *The 2004 Survey of State Adult Protective Services: Abuse of adults 60 years of age and older.* Retrieved from http://www.ncea.aoa.gov/ncearoot/main_site/pdf/2– 14–06%20final%2060+report.pdf

Royall, D. R., Cordes, J. A., & Polk, M. (1998). CLOX: An executive clock drawing task. *Journal of Neurology, Neurosurgery, and Psychiatry, 64,* 588–594.

Royall, D. R., Lauterbach, E. C., Cummings, J. L., Reeve, A., Rummans, T. A., Kaufer, D., et al. (2002). Executive control function: A review of its promise and challenges for clinical research. *Journal of Neuropsychiatry and Clinical Neurosciences, 14*(4), 377–405.

Royall, D. R., Mahurin, R. K., & Gray, K. F. (1992). Bedside assessment of executive cognitive impairment: The executive interview. *Journal of the American Geriatrics Society, 40,* 1221–1226.

Royall, D. R., Palmer, R., Chiodo, L. K., & Polk, M. J. (2004). Declining executive control in normal aging predicts change in functional status: The freedom house study. *Journal of the American Geriatrics Society, 52*(3), 346–352.

Royall, D. R., Palmer, R., Chiodo, L. K., & Polk, M. J. (2005). Executive control mediates memory's association with change in instrumental activities of daily living: The freedom house study. *Journal of the American Geriatrics Society, 53*(1), 11–17.

Schillerstrom, J. E., Horton, M. S., & Royall, D. R. (2005). The impact of medical illness on executive function. *Psychosomatics, 46*(6), 508–516.

Websites

National Center on Elder Abuse: http://www.ncea.aoa.gov

U.S. Administration on Aging: http://www.aoa.gov

ELDER PHYSICAL ABUSE AND THE FAMILY

Physical abuse of older adults in the family is becoming an area of increasing concern and has been the focus of a recent chapter in the World Health Organization's *World Report on Violence in Health.* This report highlighted the fact that elder physical abuse (along with other types of elder abuse) is the concern of many nations. There is now general agreement that physical abuse in older adults is defined as hitting, slapping, pushing, kicking, burning, locking an older person in a room, inappropriate use of medication and restraint, and other physical acts with the intention of causing physical pain or injury. Unfortunately, practitioners working with physical and other types of abuse are still unsure when it is occurring, how to intervene, and how to evaluate the success of therapeutic outcomes. This entry discusses several aspects of elder physical abuse, including prevalence, risk factors, prevention, assessments, and intervention.

Prevalence

A Kings Fund research study in the United Kingdom suggested prevalence rates for physical abuse of older adults living in the community was around 2.6%. Although international rates vary, this is broadly in line with international research.

Risk Factors

A review of six studies identified five risk factors that should be considered when assessing whether physical abuse is likely to occur in the family. They are (1) dependency, (2) intraindividual dynamics (psychopathology of the abuser), (3) intergenerational transmission of violence, (4) external stress, and (5) social isolation.

Dependency

Dependency occurs when an older adult victim of physical abuse is living with, and dependent on, a carer who may be inexperienced or unwilling to provide the care that is needed. Furthermore, the carer may believe the older adult is more able than the older adult actually is, and the lack of understanding of all of these issues may have also been evident earlier in the relationship.

Intraindividual Dynamics

There is substantial evidence that people who physically abuse those in their care have a history of mental health problems, most notably depression, anxiety, and/or alcohol and drug misuse.

Intergenerational Transmission of Violence

This risk factor is derived from the concept of "victim to offender," often quoted in research on child maltreatment and domestic violence, where there is a higher probability of becoming an abusive or neglectful adult carer if one has been maltreated as a child. When an older adult is the victim of physical abuse, the concept is reversed and exists as "offender to victim." This situation occurs when the older relative may have used violence in the past as a

punishment on the adult carer as a child or teenager, and now the older relative is the recipient of violent behavior. This reversal of power between parent and child over a generation should not be confused with spouse abuse between older partners.

External Stress

Stress as a risk factor has long been associated with elder physical abuse (and other types of abuse). A report in 1984 in the United Kingdom reported that 80% of social services staff believed stress to be the cause of the problem. Poor physical health of the carer, unemployment, poor housing, and other caring demands from the caregiver's spouse and children are likely to increase the probability of elder physical abuse.

Social Isolation

Social isolation has been observed in 88% of abusive carers; however, from a victim perspective, elderly people who live alone are at the lowest risk.

Prevention of Physical Abuse in Older Adults

When elderly people come into contact with either health or social care professionals, these professionals have an opportunity to screen for the risk of elder physical abuse and deal with the needs of the elderly individual, the carers, and the family. Where there is evidence of increasing dependency through disability or degenerative illness in the older adult client, family members should be encouraged to take an active role in planning for future care in partnership with health and social care professionals.

Assessment of Physical Abuse

Where physical abuse has been identified, a comprehensive assessment is clearly required. This assessment should be tailored to the individual client's needs and should engage the client as much as the client is able. The assessment process may require more care and time than usual, as victims are often reluctant to discuss the problem. There should also be a clear understanding from the outset that the physical abuse must stop.

Interventions

Psychological approaches to treatment need to focus on the needs of both the victim and the family; thus family-oriented approaches to treatment are useful as they aim to keep the relationship together. One of the goals of therapy is strengthening the family's functioning; therefore the family, and not the elderly victim, becomes the focus for assessment and intervention.

A second psychological approach is anger management, which focuses on the offender. The ability to regulate and manage anger has important implications for well-being. It has been applied to perpetrators of physical abuse of older adults using a format of individual sessions that include (a) self-report monitoring by means of diary keeping; (b) educational content—understanding reasons for anger and the nature of the older person's illness; (c) teaching self-statements for use in anticipation of, during, and after anger situations; (d) teaching the use of relaxation in coping with physical tension, and (e) dealing with the anger behavior, such as assertion skills or time out.

Conclusion

Overall management of suspected cases involving physical abuse is essential to the welfare of the older person and his or her family. Professionals should be involved in a number of decisions in order to construct a care plan with the older person that upholds his or her rights, future welfare, and quality of life, preferably in partnership with carers and other family members. Furthermore, in order to ensure the continued cessation of physical abuse, a program of support, community care, and continuing education is essential.

Alice Campbell Reay

See also Alzheimer's Disease: Caregiver Burden; Alzheimer's Disease and Communication; Elder Emotional Abuse and the Family; Elder Neglect and the Family; Family Therapy; Verbal Abuse in Families

Further Readings

Browne, K. D., & Herbert, M. (1997). *Preventing family violence*. Chichester, UK: Wiley.

Campbell Reay, A. M., & Browne, K. D. (2001). Risk factor characteristics in carers who physically abuse and neglect their elderly dependents. *Aging and Mental Health, 5*(1), 56–62.

Campbell Reay, A. M., & Browne, K. D. (2002). The effectiveness of psychological interventions with individuals who physically abuse or neglect their elderly dependents. *Journal of Interpersonal Violence, 17*(4), 416–431.

Edinberg, B. (1986). Developing and integrating family orientated approaches in care of the elderly. In K. Pillemer & R. S. Wolf (Eds.). *Elder abuse: Conflict in the family*. Dover, MA: Auburn House.

Websites

Action on Elder Abuse: http://www.elderabuse.org.uk

U.S. Administration on Aging, National Center on Elder Abuse: http://www.ncea.aoa.gov/NCEAroot/Main_Site/Index.aspx

Elder Sexual Abuse and the Family

Despite its potential negative impact on not only older persons who are victims of abuse but also their families, the topic of elder abuse has generated comparatively little scientific attention relative to child abuse. Rather than use the preferred term *elder mistreatment*, in the present case, in this discussion the term *elder sexual abuse* is used. As with most forms of elder mistreatment, it is likely that available estimates are inaccurate for sexual abuse (it is widely cited as being the least common form of elder mistreatment), in part because of the differing criteria that professionals use to define elder mistreatment as well as older persons' reluctance in reporting sexual abuse, especially if it is intrafamilial in nature. The myth of a lack of sexuality among older adults may also undermine the reporting of likely cases. Yet, elder sexual abuse is a purposeful act and a physically and emotionally traumatic experience for both the victim and the victim's family. When sexual abuse occurs at the hands of a family member, its potential to be ignored or distorted is greater. When such abuse occurs in an institutional setting, family members need to be proactive about identifying the perpetrator and, if necessary, making alternative arrangements for an older family member's care.

If the abused elder (who is likely to be female, over the age of 75, and residing in a health care facility) is physically or cognitive impaired, dependent upon the abuser (who is almost always a male), fearful of retribution or being abandoned, sexual abuse, as with other forms of elder mistreatment, is more likely. Such abused persons may have difficulty in explaining or understanding what has happened or be more behaviorally fearful. Such cues might be being quiet in the presence of the abuser, becoming more difficult to care for, or displaying more emotional ambivalence when being cared for, all of which indicate fear or distress, in contrast to being capable of confronting his or her abuser verbally. Especially if the abused elder is suffering from dementia, perpetrators on whom the elder has become emotionally, physically, or financially dependent can confuse or manipulate the victim, making disclosure, arrest, and prosecution difficult. Any indication that any form of sexual abuse has occurred involving an older adult with dementia should be taken seriously, as such persons indeed experience pain and trauma despite being cognitively impaired.

If the abuse of an older woman has been committed by a family member, available data suggest that it is a son and thus is incestual in nature. If the victim is male, the abuser is more likely to be a friend, and in such cases, fondling is the most common form of sexual abuse, especially by facility staff in long-term care institutions. Though it is perhaps less common, spousal abuse is not unheard of and may represent a long-standing pattern of domestic violence. In some cases, after someone marries again, after having been widowed, sexual abuse may also occur. When the family member is the abuser, it becomes increasingly difficult to convince the elder that it is best to separate from a son or husband, or have that person arrested. In such cases, feelings of profound betrayal and a loss of trust are accompanied by fears of abandonment, vulnerability, and uncertainty about the future. Despite the often violent and intrusive nature of elder sexual abuse, abusers are indeed seeking sexual gratification, and identifying someone who is frail or cognitively impaired offers an opportunity to impose oneself on someone who is incapable of physical resistance or of even understanding what has happened. These characteristics differentiate sexual abuse and other forms of elder mistreatment. Even when sexual abuse is long-standing in nature, older victims may not be fully examined by physicians. Moreover, their complaints and concerns may not be taken seriously not only by health care professionals but also, in some cases, by family members themselves. Importantly, the elder may have more physical and emotional difficulty in recovering from an attack, assault, or rape. Infection or breaking of bones may accompany such abuse, complicating matters further for both the elder and the family.

Because acknowledging that one's parents or grandparents are sexual beings may be difficult, family members may feel shame that such abuse has taken place or feel guilty over having not prevented it. Clearly, knowing that a family member may have sexually abused a parent or grandparent has the potential to fracture the family system, creating resentment, guilt, and hostility toward the potential abuser as well as among other family members who may disagree about disclosing this "secret" to others or to authorities.

It is important that elder sexual abuse be reported. Fortunately in this respect, other forms of elder mistreatment often accompany the sexual abuse of an older person, and those who abuse older persons may also have a history of having abused children. Abuse committed in health care facilities (nursing homes) is more likely to be reported than that which occurs in the elder's home. Perpetrators are more likely to be prosecuted and the abuse is more likely to be reported if there are obvious signs of physical trauma (i.e., bleeding, bruising, or difficulty in walking).

Bert Hayslip, Jr., and Kyle S. Page

See also Elder Care Options for Families: Long-Term Care; Elder Physical Abuse and the Family

Further Readings

Aciemo, R., Hernandez, M., Amstadter, A., Resnick, H., Steve, K., Muzzy, W., et al. (2010). Prevalence and correlates of emotional, physical, sexual, and financial abuse and potential neglect in the United States: The National Elder Mistreatment Study. *American Journal of Public Health, 100,* 292–297.

Baker, M., Sugar, N., & Eckert, L. (2009). Sexual assault of older women: Risk and vulnerability by living arrangement. *Sexuality research and Social Policy, 6,* 79–87.

Burgess, A. W. (2006). Sexual abuse, trauma and dementia in the elderly: A retrospective study of 294 cases. *Victims and Offenders, 1,* 193–204.

Connidis, I. A. (2010). *Family ties and aging.* Thousand Oaks, CA: Pine Forge Press.

Ramsey-Klawsnik, H. (2003). Elder sexual abuse within the family. *Journal of Elder Abuse and Neglect, 15,* 43–58.

ELECTRONIC HEALTH RECORD AND FAMILY HEALTH INFORMATION

National initiatives are pushing the U.S. health care industry to embrace electronic health records (EHRs) and make them available for all Americans by the year 2014. The term *electronic health record* is an umbrella term encompassing both electronic medical records (EMRs), used and maintained by health care providers, and personal health records (PHRs) maintained by consumers. Google Health and Microsoft HealthVault are examples of PHR tools, enabling lay persons to maintain an electronic record of their personal health.

Family health information is an important component of EHRs, including family history, next of kin, living situation, whom to notify in case of emergency, and support persons. Family health history information in particular has become of increasing interest in recent years as a result of the expansion of genomic knowledge and the realization that most if not all disease, especially common and chronic disease, arises from a combination of multiple genetic and environmental factors. Because family members generally share genetic and environmental factors (including behaviors) related to health, family health history provides insight into how these factors interact to result in health and disease states. EHRs hold the promise of making that information easier to maintain, analyze, and apply.

The usefulness of family health history in clinical practice is limited by the time required to collect and to analyze family health history information. EHRs may eventually address these concerns. Collecting the information may be facilitated by enabling consumers and multiple providers to directly contribute information to an electronic record of one's family health history. Additionally, a family health history could be assembled from a variety of existing sources by an EHR system. EHR systems may also facilitate automated analysis of family health history or computer-based scanning of family health histories for provocative patterns. This entry describes the current state of family health information in EHRs and explores possible forthcoming innovations.

Electronic Medical Records and Family Health Information

A group of stakeholders from federal health service agencies and the private sector recently convened to define a family health history minimum data set, the core elements of family health history that should be included in EMRs used in primary care settings. The group envisioned that standardizing representation, including the creation of a minimum data set, will facilitate communication and reuse of family health history data to improve personal health and to build knowledge. The core data elements identified by the group include common elements of family history, such as information pertaining to first- and second-degree relatives, consanguinity, adoptive status, diagnoses and causes of death, and presence or known absence of genetic mutations.

Most EMRs are equipped to maintain most if not all of the information identified in the family health history minimum data set. EMR systems often include specialized online forms for collection and maintenance of family health history information. These forms are generally to be completed by providers, often while interviewing a patient. The EMR system may prompt the provider for specific information, such as history of heart disease in a first- or second-degree relative, or number of siblings and any health concerns experienced by them. EMR systems often include smart text or drop-down menus to support the use of controlled vocabularies in documentation of family health history information, which facilitates analysis and reuse of the information in ways that would be impossible with paper-based records. The family health history maintained in an EHR may also be easily updated as new information becomes available, and a record of changes may be archived.

Some EMR systems may generate pedigrees, visual aids for analysis of family health history information, while some present the information only in a chart format.

Personal Health Records and Family Health Information

PHRs present opportunities for lay persons to maintain and manage their own health information. Google Health and Microsoft HealthVault are two free PHR systems currently available to the public. Google Health includes no specific forms, guidance, or sections for family health history information. However, a motivated user could maintain a record of family health data by entering family health information as free-text personal health conditions, for example, "history of asthma in my father's family." In contrast, Microsoft HealthVault includes a section for family history. If the user chooses to add family history information, he or she is prompted with a form asking for the relative's condition and relationship. Smart text auto-completion for relationships and condition is offered, and free text entry is also supported. At this time, HealthVault maintains a record of family history information but does not generate a pedigree or offer any analysis of the information.

Although it may not fully fit the definition of PHR, My Family Health Portrait, a web application provided by the U.S. Surgeon General, deserves special mention. This resource enables consumers to enter and maintain personal family health history information as a file on their own personal computer (or memory device if they are using a public computer). Consumers are then able to print a chart and a pedigree depicting their family health history. Although no analysis of the family health history is provided by the tool, the My Family Health Portrait website encourages users to take a printout of their family health history to their providers for review and discussion. The latest updates to My Family Health Portrait have made the resource available to organizations for adoption, customization, and incorporation into EHR systems. This may be an important step toward creating an infrastructure that would facilitate the exchange of family health history information among multiple EMR and PHR systems, increasing the usefulness of the information for personal health and knowledge building.

The Potential Impact of Family Health Information in Electronic Health Records

EHR systems present an opportunity to radically increase the accuracy and usefulness of information about family health. For example, freedom from the limitations imposed by paper-based records and reliance of visual analysis may enable us to extend the definition of family beyond biologically related individuals to embrace real contemporary family structures, which increasingly include persons related by adoption, step relationships, and emotional ties. Inclusion of information about these family members may enable us to better understand patterns of health and illness in families as well as address information that is important to nurses and other health care professionals, such as family members available to provide care during an illness or who have impact on the patient's lifestyle and health-related behaviors.

In the future, EHR systems may be able to assemble family health histories from a variety of sources, such as birth and death records or the health records of family members. Such a strategy has the potential to greatly increase the accuracy of family health history information and therefore improve personal health care and knowledge about health and illness.

Jane Peace

See also Genetic Discoveries, New: Health Information in Families Derived Through; Genetic Family Histories; Genetics: The Family Pedigree

Further Readings

Glaser, J., Henley, D. E., Downing, G., & Brinner, K. M. (2008). Advancing personalized health care through health information technology: An update from the American Health Information Community's Personalized Health Care Workgroup. *Journal of the American Medical Informatics Association, 15*(4), 391–396.

Guttmacher, A. E., & Collins, F. S. (2005). Realizing the promise of genomics in biomedical research. *Journal of the American Medical Association, 294*(11), 1399–1402.

Peace, J., & Lutz, K. F. (2009). Nursing conceptualizations of research and practice. *Nursing Outlook, 57*(1), 42–49.

Websites

Google Health: http://www.google.com/health
Microsoft HealthVault: http://www.healthvault.com
U.S. Surgeon General, My Family Health Portrait:
    https://familyhistory.hhs.gov

EMERGENCY CARE USE BY FAMILIES

Emergency care use by families involves the utilization of emergency or urgent care services by one or more family members. A family in this context includes a group of individuals living in the same household who are related by blood, marriage, and/or shared goals. Emergency care includes episodic or short-term care aimed at the diagnosis and stabilization or treatment of an immediate health problem, also known as a chief complaint. This entry details the use of emergency care services by families and suggests ways in which families can more efficiently utilize this aspect of health care.

Emergency Care Services

Emergency care services may begin in the home or community when the emergency medical system (EMS) is activated and continue through transport to, and treatment in, an emergency department (ED) at a local hospital. Emergency care services also may begin when an ill or injured family member enters the ED. Upon entry into the emergency care system, the individual is triaged, or medically sorted, based on the chief complaint and apparent urgency of the health problem. Patients not triaged as urgent or emergent may be referred to a primary health care provider or clinic for care, may be sent home for self-management of their health problem, or may be expected to wait for their care in the ED until those with more urgent needs are treated first. Immediate health problems requiring urgent or emergency care might include chest pain or sudden shortness of breath, profuse bleeding, injuries from a motor vehicle accident, loss of consciousness, injuries from a fall or other traumatic event, or imminent childbirth. The National Center for Healthcare Statistics (NCHS) noted there were 119.2 million ED visits in the United States in 2006, averaging 40.5 visits per 100 persons.

Emergency care services usually are provided by teams of specialty physicians, nurses, therapists, and technicians, and often include hightech and extensive diagnostic and treatment procedures. Emergency care services usually include focused examinations by ED physicians and nurses; collection of samples for laboratory analysis; noninvasive and/or invasive monitoring of vital functions; radiologic imaging; provision of pain relief and/or other symptom management; administration of medications and fluids to treat the underlying problem; preparation for emergency admission, transfer, and/or surgery; referral for further evaluation and/or treatment; provision for follow-up care; and instructions concerning home and follow-up care. Emergency care excludes routine health maintenance and health promotion activities. The NCHS indicated the median length of visit in the ED in 2006 was 2.6 hours, with a range of less than 1 hour to more than 24 hours. Discharge from emergency care occurs when the patient is admitted for in-patient care and/or surgery; admitted for extended observation; referred for higher level or specialty care; sent to another facility for continued monitoring and care; or discharged to home for self-care and maintenance (preferred disposition).

Family Involvement in Emergency Care

Ideally, primary health care services directed at health promotion and health maintenance activities for chronic health conditions are delivered by a family's primary care provider(s) or other community resource(s). However, families without a primary health care provider often turn to the emergency care system for routine health care needs. Family members without primary health care services tend to be more acutely ill when they do access the emergency care system.

Family members usually accompany an ill or injured family member to the ED. Their presence can facilitate as well as impede care. A noninvolved family member may be able to translate for the ill or injured family member who speaks a different language from that of the care providers, to clarify or amplify the information provided by the patient, to interpret medical or nursing instructions for the patient, and/or to gain better understanding of the follow-up care the family member will need upon discharge from the emergency care system.

Because space for visitors in treatment rooms often is limited and to facilitate the care of the family member, one person should be designated as the spokesperson responsible for conveying information to family and friends at home or away, or in the waiting room. Because waiting room times can be long and because waiting room experiences can include exposure to extreme distress, undesirable language, communicable diseases, and other unhealthy situations, children and other vulnerable individuals should not accompany an ill or injured family member to the ED.

Family-centered care is the delivery of care (in this instance, emergency care services) in the context of the family. Whether a person is the patient receiving care or an accompanying family member, individuals are members of a unique family system with its own customs, decision-making hierarchy, past experiences, and views on health care. The family therefore can influence the responses of the individual to the health care crisis and resulting care, and at the same time the experiences of the ill or injured family member may influence the functioning of the family system.

Family presence during invasive procedures or resuscitation is a current topic of interest in today's emergency care system. Evidence-based practice resources reveal that family presence can be a positive experience for families, patients, and ED staffs, while it also can be a source of stress for those same stakeholders. Inclusion of families during invasive procedures or resuscitation efforts must be a planned and coordinated activity reserved for families who are willing and able to participate effectively in patient care.

Efficient Use of Emergency Care

Emergency care services can be costly. Charges/fees for emergency care services are the patient's/family's responsibility but usually are covered by insurance, health maintenance organizations (HMOs), or other third-party payers. Families who are underinsured or uninsured often have difficulty paying for emergency care services, and the expense may result in a financial drain on the family and/or in those services being provided by the facility on an indigent basis with the facility writing off the charges. Families are encouraged to obtain routine health promotion and health maintenance services from a primary health care provider or other community resources rather

than from the emergency care system and to maintain adequate insurance on all family members.

Telephone triage may be performed by physicians, ED nurses, or other nurses with special training and consists of the family member explaining their chief complaint in detail and obtaining medical or nursing advice prior to entry into the emergency care system. Telephone triage may facilitate a family member's treatment at home prior to initiating the emergency care system, may speed that person's visit to and through the ED, or may eliminate the need for calling EMS or visiting the ED entirely. Families are encouraged to utilize telephone triage as one strategy for minimizing costly ED visits and for facilitating more effective use of the emergency care system.

Betsy M. McDowell

See also Community Resources for Families Related to Health; Family Health Maintenance; Health System Options for Families; Outpatient Mental Health Care for Families; Resuscitation, Family Presence During

Further Readings

Lewandowski, L. A., & Tesler, M. D. (Eds.). (2003). *Family-centered care: Putting it into action: The SPN/ANA guide to family-centered care.* Washington, DC: American Nurses Publishing.

Pitts, S. R., Niska, R. W., Xu, J., & Burt, C. W. (2008). National Hospital Ambulatory Medical Care Survey: 2006 emergency department summary. *National Health Statistics Reports,* No 7. Hyattsville, MD: National Center for Health Statistics.

Websites

Centers for Disease Control and Prevention, FastStats, Emergency Department Visits: http://www.cdc.gov/nchs/FASTATS/ervisits.htm

Employment/Unemployment and Family Health Insurance Coverage

As a fundamental element in people's lives, employment provides the means by which they achieve a good quality of life for their families, but the decline in family health insurance is threatening the well-being of the family. Traditionally, people who are engaged in the labor market have enjoyed a stable salary and employer-sponsored health insurance. Global market competition and an economic recession, however, have sent the unemployment rate to record heights, and correspondingly employment has drastically changed from conventional full-time work to flexible types of employment, such as part-time, on-call, contract, and informal labor. Furthermore, the power relations and marketplace organizational policies that underpin these new forms of employment have forced the employed to lower their salaries and limit their health insurance coverage. Consequently, many workers and their families fall through the health care safety net into being at risk of having poor health.

Employment, Families, and Health Insurance Coverage

Amid this dynamic change in the marketplace, employer-sponsored health insurance for workers and their families is gradually eroding away in industrialized countries. Furthermore, this erosion generates an enormous public health concern in those countries where universal health insurance coverage is nonexistent. In developing countries, public or private health insurance is very limited, with most precarious and informal workers as well as their families being excluded. The United States does not have universal health insurance, and its employer-sponsored coverage for employees and their families continues to recede; low-income workers, the unemployed, and their families (children, spouse, and the elderly) are most at risk. Unemployed workers can retain their health coverage through a subsidized program established under the Consolidated Omnibus Budget Reconciliation Act (COBRA, 1986), but almost half of the unemployed and their families fall through the cracks of COBRA because they cannot meet its qualifications or financial burden. Many women, with spouses employed in low-income full- or part-time work, do not have any health insurance. Even though Medicaid or the Children's Health Insurance Program provides health care for children whose parents have an extremely low income, the 2008 National Health Interview Survey estimates that 8.9% of U.S. children under

18 years of age (even disabled children) still have no health insurance. In most developing countries, out-of-pocket health care creates an enormous financial burden on employees and their families. Some high-income employees or employers in these countries can afford private insurance, whereas many middle- and low-income workers and their families face financial challenges and barriers of accessibility to urgently needed health services.

Health Risks for Uninsured Employees and Their Families

The decline in employer-sponsored health insurance has generated excessive health problems for employees and their families in the United States. Unemployment and precarious work are well known to be risk factors for depression, physical ailments, and mortality and thus exert a great influence on family life. At the same time, limited accessibility to necessary health services has serious repercussions for the health of workers and their families. For example, due to the financial strain of medical expenditures, uninsured workers and their spouses are more likely to delay essential preventive health care, such as dental examinations, mammograms, pap tests, and prenatal services (which can also affect the health of newborns). Even intermittent lapses in insurance coverage for workers and their families can be related to failure of timely diagnosis of diseases. To make matters worse, uninsured families are likely to forgo urgently needed health care. Accordingly, these workers and their families have a higher risk of developing chronic diseases, disability, and even mortality, and this can place a serious burden on families that have to provide home care for sick family members, especially children.

The health effect on uninsured children is more crucial because low-income parents cannot afford appropriate medical services. Uninsured children not only encounter serious barriers to accessing preventive health care but also are at high risk of unmet medical care and unfilled prescriptions. In the United States, higher health risks for children in low-income, uninsured families are reportedly found in otitis media, asthma, kidney problems, and attention deficit/hyperactivity disorder; the failure of timely diagnoses and treatments can seriously exacerbate these conditions. Furthermore, uninsured families with children who have special needs experience substantial challenges to providing appropriate health care. Young adults with disabling chronic conditions are blocked from accessing necessary health care when they are not covered by private or public health insurance. Being without employer-sponsored health coverage can create a vicious cycle for families: Not only can parents fall into having poor health, but also the burden of caring for sick children can hamper them from reentering the labor market.

Health Equity for Uninsured Families

Despite the adverse health effects of declining employees and family health insurance, very few studies have researched this area. An urgent need exists to implement research, evaluation, and monitoring of how a lack of health care services affects uninsured workers and their families, especially for the unemployed and low-income workers in private, small-sized companies. A crucial issue to consider is the protection of uninsured families and their children who face great health risks from being unable to access preventive and urgently needed health services. To achieve health equity for uninsured employees and their families, advocates propose extending publicly supported health insurance that grants universal access to health services to these families, and most especially to children.

Conclusion

Improving health insurance for workers and their families could buffer the progression of serious diseases and reinforce family health and well-being. However, most uninsured workers and their families suffer from having inadequate health services, especially in a time of economic recession. Enacting universal health coverage might seem to be insurmountable, but advocates believe public health care services should provide for all uninsured workers and their families, regardless of employment status and financial ability.

Il-Ho Kim and Carles Muntaner

See also Access to Health Care: Child Health; Access to Health Care: Uninsured; Adult Child With Disability: Planning for by Parents; Americans with Disabilities Act and the Family; Attention Deficit/Hyperactivity Disorder: Family Involvement and Management

Further Readings

Cawley, J., & Simon, K. I. (2005). Health insurance coverage and the macroeconomy. *Journal of Health Economics, 24*(2), 299–315.

Cohen, R. A., & Martinez, M. E. (2009). *Health insurance coverage: Early release of estimates from the National Health Interview Survey, 2008.* Atlanta, GA: National Center for Health Statistics. Retrieved April 8, 2010, from http://www.cdc.gov/nchs/data/nhis/earlyrelease/insur200906.pdf

Committee of the Consequences of Uninsurance. (2002). *Health insurance is a family matter.* Washington, DC: National Academies Press.

Pauly, M. V., Zweifel, P., Scheffler, R. M., Preker, A. S., & Bassett, M. (2006). Private health insurance in developing countries. *Health Affairs, 25*(2), 369–380.

ETHNIC/RACIAL INFLUENCES IN FAMILIES

Race refers to a group into which a population is divided on the basis of physical characteristics such as skin color. Ethnicity refers to family origin or culture. People of an ethnic group can share a national, linguistic, or religious heritage. Data from the U.S. Census is self-reported with citizens identifying with one of the racial or ethnic categories listed. Although many studies describe the prevalence of family health problems by racial and ethnic group, the interaction among the predictors of health problems dilutes the unique contribution of race and ethnicity. For example, multiple studies find that ethnic minority parents report higher scores on reports of child behavior problems than their non-Hispanic white peers, yet the findings are difficult to interpret because the ethnic minority families are often from less educated, low-income, and highly stressed groups. Interpretation of studies focused on one racial or ethnic group also presents problems without comparison across other groups. This entry focuses on providing culturally appropriate and culturally competent health care to improve family health outcomes across racial and ethnic minority groups.

Support for Racial and Ethnic Focus on Family Health

Public health professionals have long recognized the uniqueness of racial and ethnic groups and used approaches to partner with community clients in providing services. The literature reports epidemiologic evidence that race and ethnicity are associated either directly or indirectly with a number of outcomes, including higher rates of depression and suicide ideation among children, poorer quality health care, and increased child behavior problems. However, families that are cohesive and have strong communication often survive multiple problems. For this reason, health care providers and researchers need to avoid stereotypical assumptions in family care.

Ethnocentric and Race-Specific Family Interventions

The approach to developing culturally appropriate interventions is to use various methods—including focus groups, pilot testing, and instrument validation—to ensure the validity of approaches. Julia Cowell and her team used such an approach in tailoring a problem-solving intervention to promote mental health in a school-based population of Mexican immigrant mothers and their fourth- and fifth-grade children. The researchers teamed with school nurses and social workers as well as teachers and parents to address high rates of depressive symptoms among children and mothers. Assuming that the Mexican immigrant group would benefit from group interventions, mothers surprised the researchers with a desire to work individually on family problems rather than in peer groups. Further, mothers surprised researchers with the recommendation that the ethnicity of nurses was not important and, in fact, they preferred professionals of any ethnic group to culturally matched community health workers. Mothers did require professionals be fluent in Spanish. A subsequent clinical trial tested the effects of the Rush University Mexican American Problem Solving (MAPS) program among a sample of 302 mother and child dyads randomly assigned to treatment or control. Bilingual nurses delivered the problem-solving intervention to mothers during home visits and to groups of up to five children. Mothers practiced using a simplified problem-solving approach (STOP, THINK, ACT) on problems that were relevant or current for them. Children practiced the STOP, THINK, and ACT steps in the small groups with nurses. There were statistically significant improvements in the children's reports of schoolwork, health conceptions, and family problem-solving communication, factors predictive of mental health. Improvements in children's depression symptoms in the intervention group approached statistical significance ($p = 0.055$).

An intervention titled Mission Possible: Parents and Kids Who Listen (MP) was developed by Susan Riesch and colleagues to reduce behavior problems among young adolescents. MP was designed to promote family cohesiveness, communication, and problem solving among Caucasian and African American parents and their young adolescents and ultimately reduce youth behavior problems. The program was based on the concepts of family functioning, including cohesiveness, adaptability, and good communication. The outcomes of a clinical trial showed that family communication could be improved and that MP was effective in increasing significant satisfaction with family functioning, increased open communication, and skill in problem solving.

Similarly, the Chicago Parent Program (CPP) provided empirical evidence that group-based interventions with urban, low-income African American and Latino parents of toddlers were effective in reducing child behavior problems, increasing positive discipline and warmth, and increasing parenting self-efficacy. The group classes were delivered to groups of parents using video vignettes showing good communication and communication that could be improved between parents and toddlers. Trained group leaders guided group discussion and focused on developing parents' skills in positive communication strategies and effective methods for managing their children's misbehavior and reducing stress. Further, alternatives to harsh discipline strategies were practiced. The CPP was developed by partnering with parents of young children. Materials are at a 5th-grade reading level, and the program is typically delivered over 11 weeks. A 12th group meeting was delivered 1 to 2 months after the last group session to support parents' use of learned skills. Selected Head Start programs across the country are now using the CPP.

Assessment Tools for Diverse Families

The conceptualization of family health behavior is integral to framing an approach to working with families across racial and ethnic minority groups.

A conceptually sound approach provides a basis for selecting tools or instruments to use in working with families in practice or research. Marilyn McCubbin and Hamilton McCubbin have framed a conceptualization of the resilient family that includes predictive variables for adjustment with supporting measures to operationalize the concepts of the model. The resiliency model of family adjustment and adaptation posits that all families have stress and can apply levels of family problem solving and coping. These actions are done within the interpersonal relationships of the family at their current developmental level, drawing on their own well-being. Further, the family community relationships are influenced by their structure and level of functioning. Measures developed by the McCubbins and team include the Family Hardiness Index, Family Problem Solving Communication, Family Inventory of Life Events, and the Family Pressures Scale-Ethnic (FPRES_E). FPRES_E is a tool adapted from the Family Inventory of Life Events as a more culturally sensitive measure of family life stresses. Many of the measures have been used in conceptualizations studying a range of family health problems, including depression among immigrants from the former Soviet Union and from Mexico. Specifically, Family Problem Solving Communication was either an indirectly significant variable or a directly significant variable influencing depression symptoms in the immigrant study populations as reported by Arlene Michaels Miller and colleagues.

A growing body of research shows the validity and reliability of select measures, but many measures remain limited to the dominant culture. Further, where validity and reliability are reported, the link to lower socioeconomic status may not be clear. For example, widely used measures of child behavior, such as the Child Behavior Checklist 1½ to 5 (CBCL) and the Eyberg Child Behavior Inventory (ECBI), were based on studies in which race and ethnicity were frequently confounded with income. Deborah Gross and her team reported a study designed to separate the confounding factors by sampling across African American, Latino, and non-Latino white and language groups (Spanish vs. English) in families in low- to middle-upper-income levels. With respect to the CBCL, differential item analyses and the confirmatory factor analysis supported the use of the CBCL 1½ to 5 across African American and Latino groups. Similarly, the reliability and validity of the ECBI for 2- to 4-year-olds across African American, Latino, and non-Latino whites ($N = 682$) were acceptable.

A widely used measure of family function, the Feetham Family Function Survey (FFFS), was developed in the study of American two-parent families with children who had chronic health problems. The FFFS assesses functioning in (a) the family's relationships within the family and its subsystems, (b) the division of labor, and (c) reciprocal relationships within the family and each individual family member. Recent research has demonstrated that with some adjustment in the tool, the reliability and validity of the measure hold up for Mexican immigrant families who may be partnered or single-parent families. The study included 302 mother–child dyads, with 245 (81%) partnered and 57 (19%) single-parent families. The adjustment tested the addition of a statement defining the spouse: "The term spouse refers to your husband or the person who assumes the functions of a spouse. If you do not have a person in the spouse role, answer the questions based on how much you want the function met." Mean discrepancy scores on the FFFS for the partnered (30.5, SD 19.0) and single women (27.4, SD 18.0) were not significantly different. The FFFS also includes an importance measure for each item, and the importance scores for partnered women (5.8, SD 0.8) and single women (5.9, SD 0.7) were not different. Validity of the adapted measure, taking into account partnered single status of mothers, is suggested in the significant correlations of higher FFFS discrepancy scores, maternal depression measured by the Hopkins Symptom Checklist ($r = 0.13$, $p = 0.05$), and the Everyday Stress Index ($r = 0.19$, $p = 0.01$). The reliability of the adapted measure was reflected in the Cronbach's Alpha coefficient $r = 0.77$.

Changing Dimensions of Contemporary Family Life Among Racial and Ethnic Minorities

Changing family structure (two parents vs. single parent) is among the changing dimensions of family life and needs special attention when providing care to racial and ethnic minority families. Among

African American families, 65% of families are headed by single mothers. Current policy is focused on fathers' financial support of families, which creates a void in the emotional connectedness of African American fathers and their children. A large qualitative study using seven focus groups with 69 fathers representing a cross-section of fathers from support groups, drug treatment, church outreach, workforce reentry, and prison release revealed that fathers wanted to share in family experiences and provide guidance and support in the traditional role of father. Changes impacting families of racial and ethnic minorities include the immigration patterns of groups seeking economic security or refuge from war. In addition to language barriers among these groups, there are risks of stereotyping populations from a specific region as homogeneous when the differences are usually vast. For example, a commonly held belief is that the population of Arab immigrants is Muslim, yet many are Christian. Further, variations include different sects within the Muslim and Christian communities coming from 15 different countries. For immigrant families, including Arab, Mexican, and Asian, traditional family structure, values, and roles are based on respect rather than on equality and are challenged during adjustment in the United States. For example, the traditional family gender roles dictate that women marry and care for children and fathers provide financially for the family. Yet in many immigrant communities those gender roles are difficult to maintain when immigrant women enter the workforce to contribute to the financial stability of the family.

Policy and Practice Implications

Access to health care for children has been addressed by the federal government for many years, with the most recent effort reflected in the federally funded State Children's Health Insurance Program (SCHIP). Federal funding demands, however, have often put SCHIP at risk. Many families who are not covered because of a tradition of poverty, citizenship issues, or lack of insurance remain on their own. The financial issues, while powerful, should not prevent health care professionals from striving to develop family care that is culturally competent and assessable. To maintain ethical and culturally competent health care, providers draw on current research, partner with their constituencies, and communicate openly with communities to validate approaches to care.

Julia Muennich Cowell

See also African American Families: Perspectives of Health; American Indian Families: Perspectives of Health; Asian Families: Perspectives of Health; Factors Influencing Family Health Values, Beliefs, and Priorities; Hispanic/Latino Families: Perspectives of Health

Further Readings

Achenbach, T., & Rescorla, L. (2000). *Manual for the ASEBA preschool forms and profiles.* Burlington: University of Vermont, Research Center for Children, Youth and Families.

Aroian, K., Katz, A., & Kulwicki, A. (2006). Recruiting and retaining Arab Muslim mothers and children for research. *Journal of Nursing Scholarship, 38*(3), 255–261.

Cowell, J. M., McNaughton, D. B., & Ailey, S. H. (2000). Development and evaluation of a Mexican immigrant family support program. *Journal of School Nursing, 16*(5), 32–39.

Cowell, J. M., McNaughton, D., Ailey, S., Gross, D., & Fogg, L. (2005). Depression and suicidal ideation among Mexican American school-aged children. *Research and Theory for Nursing Practice: An International Journal, 19*(1), 77–94.

Eyberg, S., & Pincus, D., (1999). *Eyberg Child Behavior Inventory and Sutter-Eyberg Student Behavior Inventory-Revised: Professional manual.* Odessa, FL: Psychological Assessment Resources.

Gross, D., Garvey, C., Julion, W., Fogg, L., Tucker, S., & Mokros, H. (2009). Efficacy of the Chicago Parent Program with low-income African American and Latino parents of young children. *Prevention Science, 10*(1), 54–65.

Julion, W., Gross, D., Barclay-McLaughlin, G., & Fogg, L. (2007). "It's not just about MOMMAS": African-American non-resident fathers' views of paternal involvement. *Research in Nursing & Health, 30,* 595–610.

McCubbin, M. A., & McCubbin, H. I. (1995). Resiliency in families: A conceptual model of family adjustment and adaptation in response to stress and coping. In H. I. McCubbin, A. I. Thompson, & M. A. McCubbin (Eds.), *Family assessment: Resiliency, coping and adaptation* (pp. 1–65). Madison: University of Wisconsin System.

McNaughton, D., Cowell, J. M., Fogg, L., Ailey, S., & Gross, D. (2005). *Predictors of depression: Evidence to guide health promotion services for Mexican immigrant women and children.* Paper presented at the American Public Health Association annual meeting, Philadelphia.

Miller, A. M., Sorokin, O., Wang, E., Feetham, S., Choi, M., & Wilbur, J. (2006). Acculturation, social alienation, & depressed mood in midlife women from the former Soviet Union. *Research in Nursing & Health, 29,* 134–146.

Riesch, S. K., Tosi, C. B., Thurston, C. A., Forsyth, D. M., Kuenning, T. S., & Kestly, J. (1993). Effects of communication training on parents and young adolescents. *Nursing Research, 42*(1), 10–16.

Roberts, C. S., & Feetham, S. L. (1982). Assessing family functioning across three areas of relationships. *Nursing Research, 31*(4), 231–235.

Willgerodt, M. (2003). Using focus groups to develop culturally relevant instruments. *Western Journal of Nursing, 25*(7), 798–814.

EXERCISE PROMOTION AND FITNESS

According to the nursing interventions classification system, exercise promotion is defined as the facilitation of regular physical exercise to maintain or advance to a higher level of fitness and health. Fitness can be categorized as performance related or health related. In family health, the aim of fitness is on the latter within the context of the family unit. Health-related fitness focuses on achieving optimal health through physical activity while preventing disease associated with a sedentary lifestyle: It is comprised of cardiovascular fitness, muscular fitness—including endurance, strength, and flexibility—and body composition. Physical activity is defined as any bodily movement that increases energy expenditure above the baseline. Exercise, on the other hand, is a form of physical activity that is planned, structured, and repetitive. Although exercise is a type of physical activity, not all physical activity is classified as exercise.

In family health, the goal of exercise promotion and fitness is to engage in age-appropriate physical activity to achieve energy balance. The purpose of this encyclopedic entry is to discuss the epidemiology, benefits, levels, types, safety measures, recommendations, and relevance of physical activity in family health.

Epidemiology

According to the 2007 Behavioral Risk Factor Surveillance System survey using the *2008 Physical Activity Guidelines for Americans,* 64.5% of U.S. adults were classified as physically active, including 68.9% of men and 60.4% of women: Physical activity declines with age from 74.0% in 18- to 24-year-olds to 51.2% in those greater than 64 years of age. Physical inactivity is an independent risk factor for many chronic diseases. According to the World Health Organization, physical inactivity is estimated to cause 1.9 million deaths globally.

Benefits

Research has documented the health benefits associated with regular physical activity. According to the *2008 Physical Activity Guidelines for Americans,* regular physical activity is defined as 150 minutes per week of moderate-intensity aerobic activity. In children and adolescents, strong evidence supports physical activity improves cardiovascular and muscular fitness, bone health, and favorable body composition. In adults and older adults who are physically active, strong evidence supports lower risk of early death, coronary heart disease, stroke, hypertension, adverse blood lipid profile, Type 2 diabetes, metabolic syndrome, colon and breast cancers, and depression. Strong evidence also supports physical activity prevents weight gain and falls and promotes weight loss, cardiorespiratory and muscular fitness, and cognitive function in adults and older adults.

Levels

According to the *2008 Physical Activity Guidelines for Americans,* physical activity is classified by total weekly amounts of aerobic activity and is categorized into the following four levels: inactive, low, medium, and high. Inactivity is defined as no activity beyond baseline. Low level of physical activity is defined as activity beyond baseline but less than 150 minutes per week. Medium level of physical activity is defined as 150 to 300 minutes per week, and a high level of physical activity is defined as more than 300 minutes per week.

Types

Physical activity is categorized into three different types: aerobic activity, muscle-strengthening activity, and bone-strengthening activity. Aerobic activities use the body's large muscles to move for a sustained period of time. Aerobic activity can be subcategorized into light, moderate, and vigorous. Light activities include daily household chores and are not sufficient to meet the body's aerobic physical activity needs. Moderate physical activity is characterized by an increased heart rate and diaphoresis while being able to continue talking but not singing. Moderate activities include brisk walking, doubles tennis, riding a bike, or mowing the lawn. Vigorous activity is characterized by an increased heart rate and respiratory rate with limited ability to carry on a conversation without pausing to take a breath. Vigorous physical activities include running, swimming, singles tennis, and bicycling fast or on hills.

Muscle-strengthening activities involve the body's muscles working against resistance of weight or applied force. These activities include lifting weights, using elastic bands, or doing push-ups.

Bone-strengthening activities promote bone growth and strength by producing a force on the bones through impact with the ground. These activities include brisk walking, running, tennis, and jumping rope. Bone-strengthening activities can be considered aerobic or muscle-strengthening activities as well.

Safety Measures

In maintaining physical activity, it is important to promote safety measures to reduce the risk of injury and adverse outcomes. Prior to engaging in physical activity, families should understand the benefits and risks of physical activity. Activities should be age-appropriate and appropriate to the individual's current level of fitness. Families engaging in physical activity as a unit should do so according to the fitness level of the least common denominator. Families should increase the intensity, frequency, and duration of physical activity over time.

Families must protect themselves from injury by wearing appropriate gear and using appropriate equipment. They should follow the rules and policies associated with the activity and engage in the activity in a safe environment.

Recommendations

In the *2008 Physical Activity Guidelines for Americans*, recommendations were delineated for children and adolescents, adults, healthy pregnant or postpartum women, and older adults. Children and adolescents should engage in at least 60 minutes per day of a variety of physical activities that are age-appropriate and enjoyable.

Adults should do at least 150 minutes of moderate-intensity or 75 minutes of vigorous aerobic physical activity per week. Additional health benefits are gained by doubling these recommendations. Adults should also do moderate- or high-intensity muscle-strengthening activities involving all major muscle groups 2 or more days per week.

Healthy pregnant or postpartum women should get 150 minutes of moderate-intensity aerobic activity per week. According to research, moderate-intensity aerobic activity does not increase the risk for pregnancy loss, preterm delivery, or low birth weight.

For older adults, the recommended number of minutes and types of physical activity are consistent with that of adults. Older adults should focus on additional activities to maintain or improve balance to decrease the risk of falls.

Relevance

Physical activity is important to the health and well-being of families. Parents and adult caregivers play an important part in role-modeling healthy behaviors and providing age-appropriate physical activities for their children. Physical activity is a key component of maintaining an energy balance in the prevention of chronic disease in family health promotion.

Amy C. Cory

See also Assessing Family Health; Family Health Maintenance; Family Interventions Across the Life Span; Heart Disease and the Family; Hypertension and the Family; Lifestyle Changes and Family Health;

Nutrition and Nutrition Promotion for Families; Obesity, Weight Problems, and Healthy Weight for Families; Recreation in Family Health; Role of Families in Health Promotion

Further Readings

Bouchard, C., Blair, S. N., & Haskell, W. L. (Eds.). (2007). *Physical activity and health*. Champaign, IL: Human Kinetics.

Bulechek, G. M., Butcher, H. K., & Dochterman, J. M. (2007). *Nursing interventions classification (NIC)*. Philadelphia: Mosby.

Centers for Disease Control and Prevention. (2009, January). *Physical activity resources for health professionals*. Retrieved February 10, 2008, from http://www.cdc.gov/nccdphp/dnpa/physical/health_professionals/index.htm

U.S. Department of Health and Human Services. (2008, October). 2008 *Physical activity guidelines for Americans*. Retrieved February 10, 2008, from http://www.health.gov/PAGuidelines/guidelines/default.aspx

Factors Influencing Access to Health Care for Families

In response to the pressing need for eliminating health disparities, improving access to care in the United States has been a critical policy issue since the early 1980s. Numerous studies about the differential health service accessibility and utilization have contributed to the development of conceptual frameworks identifying the individual and societal determinants of access to care. The behavioral system model of health services use, initially developed by Ronald M. Andersen to study factors affecting health services utilization for families, encompasses three core components: predisposing factors, enabling factors, and need-for-care factors. Similarly, this framework is helpful for classifying pertinent factors that influence the variation in access to health care for families. This entry discusses this framework, the core components' effects on health care access, and reforms to improve access to care.

Framework

Predisposing Factors

Demographic characteristics such as age, gender, and race/ethnicity are generally found to contribute to differential access to care. Racial and ethnic disparities have permeated health care in the United States despite many efforts to reduce them. Several studies have found that insurance status among ethnic populations explain a significant part of the disparities. The Kaiser Family Foundation reports that as of 2008, nonelderly Hispanics have disproportionately higher uninsured rates than other ethnic groups at 32.2%, comparing to 12.7% of whites, 20.6% of African Americans, and 18.5% of other racial/ethnic groups. Further, a nearly threefold difference in disparities between uninsured Hispanic and white children has been found. Nevertheless, differential access to health services utilization also exists among different racial/ethnic groups with insurance or Medicaid coverage. The evidence has shown that although insurance increases access levels, it does not narrow racial/ethnic disparities. Minority children under Medicaid coverage still exhibit poorer quality of health.

At the contextual level, neighborhood racial and ethnic composition could lead to differential access to health services utilization. Individuals who are members of racial/ethnic minority groups are likely to have lower socioeconomic status. Moreover, they are more likely to reside in racially and economically segregated and stressful neighborhoods that lack resources and lack safety. Such neighborhood disadvantages also link to poor access to care. In addition, social class, family environment, and family structure are found to determine the discrepancy of access to health care for children. Children in families headed by single mothers, compared with children living in two-parent families, are more likely to have unmet health care needs. Interestingly, at a higher level of maternal education, the difference in access to care between children of single mothers and children of two parents is not significant; nevertheless, at a lower level of maternal education, children of single mothers appear to have better access to health care than do children of two-parent families.

In terms of psychological predisposition, patient preferences can reflect people's health beliefs and attitudes toward utilization of health services. Individuals' or families' deeply held beliefs are based on codified cultural or religious traditions, particularly among racial/ethnic groups. The use of home remedies and folk medicine by some cultures may delay or complicate conventional medical care. For example, some Latino parents might not contact a medical provider until perceived severe symptoms, such as vomiting, occur.

Enabling Factors

The lack of insurance coverage or underinsurance, poor access to services, and unaffordable costs are reported as major barriers to health care for low-income families. Being uninsured results not only in serious financial consequences but also in serious health consequences, including death, cancer, trauma, and morbidity. Those uninsured who obtain care are likely to receive inferior care: fewer needed services and a greater risk of death. For many health care reform advocates, expanding health insurance coverage is important. According to a study by a group advocating universal health insurance, the average worker and average family with employer-sponsored health coverage will pay on average excesses of $341 and $922, respectively, to cover the unpaid costs of health care for the uninsured. Thus, the care of the uninsured raises the cost of care for the insured. It is generally known that uncompensated care shifts the cost from the uninsured to the insured. Families USA reports that in 2004, the costs for uncompensated care were estimated to be $40.7 billion nationwide. On the other hand, the "healthy uninsured" and "wealthy uninsured" raise the insurance premiums for the people who purchase health care coverage, because one third of the medical expenses for the uninsured are uncompensated.

Medicaid has initiated some innovative strategies to increase insurance coverage, yet the uninsured rate is still growing. Reform advocates have called for a new way to fundamentally expand health insurance coverage. According to the comprehensive health reform law signed by President Obama on March 23, 2010, U.S. citizens and legal residents are required to have qualifying health coverage. Those without coverage will have to pay a tax penalty; however, some exemptions are granted for those with financial hardship. In addition, Medicaid coverage will be expanded to all non-Medicare-eligible individuals under age 65, including children, pregnant women, parents, and adults without dependent children, who have income up to 133% of the federal poverty level. Thus, the healthy uninsured and wealthy uninsured would be included under mandatory coverage, making it easier to manage subsidizing the people most unable to afford health insurance. People with less education and low incomes or who are unemployed have a greater risk of being uninsured; so are those not in marriages and those in poor health.

In conjunction with health insurance, physician-enabling characteristics are used as the measures reflecting a community's ability to provide physician services. Individuals with access to only a small number of primary care providers may encounter a variety of obstacles in the process of getting care, such as problems contacting providers' offices for appointments or having limited access to only a small number of providers that may not have weekend or evening hours. Moreover, Medicare beneficiaries in rural areas are more likely to face geographical barriers to access to health care because of longer travel distance and time, and a different mix of generalists and specialists for their care, compared with patients in urban areas. Besides, the application of enabling components in most studies of health services utilization has been limited to identifying a population's insurance coverage and the availability of a regular source of care. This approach does not fully capture all possible barriers to access to care, particularly among those with lower socioeconomic attributes. For example, linguistic disparities are also found accountable for variation in access to health services utilization. Limited-English-proficient or non-English-primary-language adults were found to be significantly worse off in access to care and health status of them and their children than those who did not identify a language problem.

Need-for-Care Factor

Health-related measures of physical environment, such as quality of housing, water, and air, as well as how healthy the environment might be, such as rate of occupational injury and disease and related deaths, are used to identify contextual need characteristics. An individual's need-for-care characteristics may include personal experience and emotional responses to symptoms of illness, pain, and concern about one's health condition. Those who suffer from depression have a stronger belief about biological etiologies and medication treatments than do healthy people.

The literature suggests that both self-reported and objectively assessed health indicators are important predictors of health services use although they are moderately correlated with each other. A study comparing the relative influences of predisposing, enabling, and need-for-care factors on physician services use by families residing in selected New York–Pennsylvania counties found that the need-for-care factors accounted for the most variance in physician visits. As well, the need for service, as exhibited by poor physical and psychological functioning, was the most important predictor of the use of physician services and hospitalization among elderly. Because need-for-care factors are measured or assessed differently in these studies, it is imperative to gather comprehensively designed instruments for evaluating both subjectively and objectively assessed indicators of health status.

Interaction Effects of the Three Factors on Access to Care

Predisposing and enabling factors could concurrently determine family's perception of necessity of receiving care and perceived health status. Incorrect beliefs about health care and treatment due to lack of health education (e.g., the belief that a cough is only the result of a rapid change in temperature) often prevent individuals and families from promptly seeking medical care. Lack of financial resources, insurance coverage, physician availability, and proximity to services could also lead to a family delaying medical visits. Further studies are needed of how interaction effects between predisposing, enabling, and need-for-care factors could determine variations in access to care among subpopulation groups; such studies could provide a basis for formulating comprehensive policies to increase access to care and eliminate health disparities.

Health Care Reform Agendas for Improving Access to Care for Families

Both personal and societal factors should be considered in constructing the health care safety net. The Geographic Information System (GIS) could be employed to identify disadvantaged and high-risk groups in terms of health care coverage, so that safety-net providers could be located to make better access possible. Providers of the health care safety net include public hospitals, community health centers, federally qualified health centers, and rural health clinics. GIS systems could guide the development of efficient and effective primary care networks that could improve the access of the uninsured or seasonal migrants in the community. The establishment of a health care federated information network for digital and electronic retrieval system (called Healthfinder system, at www.healthfinder.gov) could facilitate coordinated and patient-centric care management for families at risk for experiencing ambulatory care–sensitive conditions and help families prevent emergency room visits as well as hospitalization. Improvement of health literacy or information sharing for families who are in need of primary care through telehealth or health education mechanisms could help remove barriers to care. For instance, people could gain access to Healthy Tutor website and learn how to enhance self-care and compress morbidities. Lastly, the interplay between individual and societal factors influencing the barriers to care should be further explored in longitudinal prospective studies so that the causes of health problems of varying families in a heterogeneous society could be better detected and treated.

Thomas T. H. Wan and Natthani Meemon

See also Access to Health Care: Uninsured; Changes in Family Structure; Ethnic/Racial Influences in Families; Medicaid and Family Health; Sociological Theories of Families; Theoretical Perspectives Related to the Family

Further Readings

Andersen, R. M. (1968). *Behavioral model of families' use of health services*. Chicago: Center for Health Administration Studies.

Andersen, R. M., Rice, T. H., & Kominsky, G. F. (Eds.). (2007). *Changing the U.S. health system: Key issues in health services policy and management.* San Francisco: Jossey-Bass.

DeVoe, J. E., Baez, A., Angier, H., Krois, L., Edlund, C., & Carney, P. (2007). Insurance + access ≠ health care: Typology of barriers to health care access for low-income families. *Annals of Family Medicine, 5*(6), 511–518.

Fairbrother, G., Kenney, G., Hanson, K., & Dubay, L. (2005). How do stressful family environments relate to reported access and use of health care by low-income children? *Medical Care Research and Review, 62*(2), 205–230.

Heck, K., & Parker, J. D. (2002). Family structure, socioeconomic status, and access to health care for children. *Health Service Research, 37*(1), 171 184.

Websites

Families USA: http://www.FamiliesUSA.org

Healthy Tutor: http://healthytutor.com

Kaiser Family Foundation, Statehealthfacts.org: http://www.statehealthfacts.org

FACTORS INFLUENCING FAMILY HEALTH VALUES, BELIEFS, AND PRIORITIES

Family health values, beliefs, and priorities are established through family traditions and culture and are dependent on resources available to support healthy living and accessibility of health care. Family health beliefs are based on shared definitions of health and include informal guidelines for promoting and sustaining health as well as caring for family members who are sick or injured. Family health values relate to the overall importance of health in daily life. Family health priorities are based on available resources (time, money, food, health care services, etc.) needed to sustain health and are often balanced with other family needs. This entry examines family health values, beliefs, and priorities through an ecological perspective beginning with the family unit and expanding to influences in the larger community and society. Family is considered the unit of care and is represented as a group of people who rely on one another for care, guidance, and fulfilling expected familial roles necessary to sustain and support the goals of the family. Family health beliefs, values, and priorities are unique and dependent on factors such as culture, religion, education, and resources. The ability to engage families in health-promoting behavior is set on a foundation of a long-term relationship with families in which trust and respect are shared between health care providers and the families they work with. For the purposes of this entry, examples and application of concepts related to health are provided in reference to food preferences and exercise.

Health and the Family Unit

Family Definitions of Health

Health conceptions are rooted in family traditions and culture, are shared within the family unit, and dictate the roles and responsibilities of family members in preventing health problems and caring for each other during illness. For example, families who define health as the ability to function within an expected role may view individual responsibilities to fulfill role obligations to the family (or place of employment) as paramount to attending to the discomforts of illness experienced by self and others. Individual health concerns may take a backseat to needs of the family unit. Such views are often rooted in cultural beliefs regarding the importance of work and responsibility to fulfill one's role in the family. In contrast, other families choose to regard a sick member as the center of attention and deserving of care from others. Family members will focus their priorities on monitoring the health status of the person who is sick and take care of the person's needs for rest, fluid, nutrition, and medications. This gathering around an ill family member may be considered a sign of caring or recognition that unwell persons deserve and require extra attention.

Whereas some families view health as the absence of illness, others regard health from a perspective that considers emotional, social, and personal growth as components of healthy living. Families with the latter view may work together to support individual goals for education, contributing to society, and reaching the highest level of health possible. Definitions of health form the foundation for behavior that supports (or promotes) health, prevents illness, and determines the type of behavior and special considerations (or care) expected when health is compromised. Within families, rules (whether spoken or unspoken) determine when it is okay to stay home from work or school, times in which family members need to seek health care, and strategies for health promotion and illness prevention.

Beliefs and practices surrounding childbirth, childrearing, and care for family members during illness, as well as strategies for maintaining health, are all learned within the family unit. Although some general beliefs and values about health are expressed in specific ethnic groups, there is great variability within cultures as well as across cultures. Therefore, when working with families, it is essential that health care providers carefully assess each family's cultural beliefs and values regarding health.

Health Behaviors

Family health beliefs, values, and priorities are learned in the home environment and shared within the family and passed on from one generation to the next. Beginning in early childhood, children learn from older family members which foods and activities are considered healthy and which are not. In addition, children learn customary behavior regarding when and whether to seek formal health care services, the type of health care providers that are most trusted, reliable sources of health information, and traditions for caring for sick family members.

Food Preferences

Beliefs about food begin in early childhood. As infants, children learn that food satisfies hunger and is necessary to sustain life. Food preferences are also established in early life and are influenced by the frequency of eating certain foods, amount of certain foods, and types of foods parents eat and provide for their children. Family views on the role of food in everyday life are shared with children and often passed on to subsequent generations through beliefs of what is healthy and "normal" to eat. Children who grow up eating fresh produce and home-cooked (rather than processed) food will consider this "normal" eating practice. The same is true for children whose families consider processed foods and fast food as the foundation for a "normal" diet. In addition to food preferences, views regarding the purpose and role of food in everyday life are learned within the family. Practices such as snacking between meals or eating as a source of comfort or as a reward for hard work are established early in life. In many families, certain foods become associated with care, warmth, and feelings of acceptance and security. Within families, certain foods are seen as appropriate for promoting or maintaining health, and others are believed to be beneficial during illness. Traditional, home-cooked and warm meals that include meat, potatoes, or rice with vegetable side dishes (regardless of the number of calories) are considered healthy and essential for some. If persons are feeling tired or unwell, a meal such as this may be seen as the most important step to begin the path toward wellness.

Conceptions of ideal or "normal" body size are influenced by parental beliefs and body images of family members. Definitions of ideal body size are also influenced by general cultural beliefs and media portrayal of normal body size. Some families and cultures will tolerate larger body sizes and consider them to be the image of health and a reflection of access to an abundant diet. Whereas some families are very concerned about maintaining what they perceive as a healthy weight, others will see variations in weight as unimportant. Cultural values regarding food and body size are learned early in life and may be difficult to change in adulthood—even when change is desired (e.g., weight loss programs or prescribed diets during illness).

Exercise

The value of recreational activity and efforts to enhance physical fitness are learned in families. Whereas some families prefer sharing physical activity (such as team sports, individual competitive sports, biking, running, swimming, or dancing) for enjoyment, others consider ideal recreational activities to center on watching TV, seeing movies, and playing electronic games. In the majority of families, the ability to engage in physical activity is dependent on personal resources, such as time, money, and availability of places to exercise. In many families, adults may be working long hours and consider providing for the family as the first priority and care of self through exercise and nutrition as a lower-level priority. In addition, lower-income neighborhoods often lack health clubs that are easily accessible and affordable.

Gender Roles

Customs of care for family during illness are influenced by beliefs regarding gender roles of caring and nurturing as well as roles related to providing for the family economically. Traditionally, in many cultures, mothers (or other women) were responsible for supporting the health of the family by cooking healthy foods, caring for sick or injured family members, and deciding when and where to seek health care services. Women traditionally took on the role of family comforter and a reliable source of emotional support. Similarly, the traditional roles for men have been considered the source of financial support and responsibility for the well-being and success of the family in society. Thus men were responsible for deciding whether or not to access health care considering the family resources. In recent years, traditional gender roles have become less clear as more families require income from both parents for adequate financial support. Although gender roles are slowly becoming less restrictive in the United States, there is great variation between families, and health care providers need to assess the importance of these roles within individual families.

Family Decisions to Seek Health Care

The use of wellness or preventive care is rooted in family views of health and traditional family practices. In some families, health care systems are only accessed at times of illness or injury when immediate help is needed to solve a problem. Some families pride themselves on their ability to manage their own health problems, taking care of minor health issues at home or seeking the advice of a respected family member or friend. Health promotion or non–life-threatening health risks may go unnoticed when families do not perceive the need for conventional health care.

Children learn when and where to access health care through family traditions and patterns of behavior when a family member gets sick or makes a decision to obtain screening for a health condition.

Within these family patterns of behavior, decisions are often influenced by accessibility and affordability of health care providers, family beliefs about the value and need for preventive services, and customary response to illness. Some families believe that illness is a sign of weakness and those who complain may be teased, ignored, or belittled. Others believe that health care should only be accessed during severe illness or injury (defined as a broken bone, bleeding, or excruciating pain). Families who access health care resources infrequently might do so because of their belief that these resources should only be used for emergencies. Others might not obtain health care because they do not have the resources to pay for it. On the other side of the continuum are families who need reassurance when minor symptoms occur and who access the health care system frequently. Whereas some families will value preventive care, others will see it as unnecessary.

Home and Herbal Remedies

The use of home and herbal remedies is likely based on family cultural beliefs and traditions. Home and herbal remedies may be used for their own inherent value, possibly stemming from a long history of successful use across generations. Rationale for using home remedies can include cost, availability, and confidence in the efficacy of their use as well as trust in family traditions over the advice of health care providers who might not know the family or its culture.

Time Orientation

Time orientation is an expression of cultural beliefs that provides direction for behavior from the viewpoint of the past, present, or future. In general, the dominant American culture is future oriented, with a belief that the future can be controlled through current actions and decisions. In relation to health, a future orientation guides people to consider behavior changes that can influence a positive health status in the future (e.g., exercising, eating a diet that includes multiple fruits and vegetables each day, or quitting smoking). Persons with a present time orientation tend to act based on daily responsibilities and enjoyment experienced today. Persons with a present time orientation might believe that future events are controlled by God and are not able to be changed. Lastly, time orientation centered on the past considers the value of culture and family traditions in shaping decision making. An example might be family decision making based on long-held family practices such as rules regarding how to care for loved ones during sickness.

Religious Beliefs

The influence of religion on family health beliefs and behavior varies by family and religious traditions. Assessment of religious beliefs needs to extend beyond designation of a religious affiliation to include specific health beliefs and practices that are important to families. Religious beliefs influencing health behaviors can take the form of dietary preferences and restrictions, as well as the practice of fasting. Faith traditions may have definitions of health and illness that differ from those of the scientific health care community. For example, families practicing certain faiths find it necessary to visit with a health care practitioner within their religious circle. Religious traditions can also dictate the preferred gender of health care practitioners; for example, some traditions prohibit male health care providers from examining and treating women and female health care providers from treating men. As children grow older and approach adulthood, they will evaluate their religious beliefs and decide which beliefs to retain and which beliefs to dismiss.

Health Literacy

The U.S. Department of Health and Humans Services defines *health literacy* as "the degree to which individuals have the capacity to obtain, process, and understand basic health information and services needed to make appropriate health decisions." Health literacy encompasses a wide range of skills, including basic understanding of science and the research process, human anatomy and physiology (e.g., basic organs in the body and their function), reading, and math skills.

Health literacy is needed to understand information provided by health care providers, instructions and inserts for medications, and health insurance policies and medical bills. It is also necessary to distinguish sources of health information that are reliable and applicable to the needs of the family from those that are not. As health care has become more complex and persons with chronic illness are living longer, the involvement of family in making health care decisions has become essential along with the need to ensure accuracy and understanding of health information in families. Health care providers are responsible for explaining choices to families and thus must be aware that many families lack basic understanding of how the human body "works" and how medication used to treat health problems works. Health literacy is also necessary to read and understand health information provided by health care providers.

Findings from recent studies show that health information written on prescription and over-the-counter medication bottles is presented in complex language and at literacy levels often exceeding the 12th grade, which may explain why these instructions are commonly misunderstood. Health literacy extends beyond the ability to read basic health information to the ability to read and understand health insurance policies and health insurance bills. These documents are often written in complex language at a level that may best be understood by the persons writing them rather than by those who are meant to receive the information.

Health literacy is an essential tool for understanding and acting on any type of health information, whether it is based on media reports, health insurance documents, or handouts obtained from health care providers. Responsibility for improving health literacy in the United States is shared by schools, which teach children basic information about health, health risks, and human anatomy and physiology, as well as health care insurers and providers who must present information at a level so it can be understood.

Americans are exposed to health information from a variety of sources on a daily basis. Newscasts, newspapers, and magazines frequently dedicate space and time to reporting research and health news such as the latest trends in health promotion and illness prevention practices. With a constant exposure to multiple sources of advice, which may be conflicting, families have to decide for themselves which sources are most accurate and reliable. Health literacy is also related to cultural beliefs and practices as well as the advice received by friends, family, and social contacts. Ideally, health information should be presented in simple language using visual materials and translated into the receiver's native language.

Community Influences

Schools

Inclusion of health education in kindergarten through 12th grade is important for the upcoming generation of adults to learn and understand strategies for healthy living. Key elements of comprehensive health education programs in schools are recommended by the Centers for Disease Control and Prevention (CDC). These guidelines present a standard for health curricula in schools and apply to students from kindergarten to 12th grade. Primary components include a curriculum covering multiple health issues taught by qualified teachers or school nurses. Content should be appropriate for the developmental age of the students. The CDC presents guidelines for recommended health information at each developmental stage for youth.

Components of these programs should address helping students to develop skills they need to avoid tobacco use; dietary patterns that contribute to disease; consequences of sedentary lifestyle; sexual behaviors that may result in HIV, other sexually transmitted infections, and unintended pregnancy; and alcohol and other drug use behaviors. The extent to which schools adhere to these guidelines is dependent on many factors, such as funding for teachers specialized in health education content and time within the overall curriculum dedicated to health. As obesity and chronic illness rates in the United States continue to rise, it is essential that schools adhere to national and state standards for health education in schools. Adherence to provision of comprehensive school health programs has the potential to improve health knowledge, health status, and healthy behaviors.

Accessibility of Food

In a 2009 report by the U.S. Department of Agriculture, over 23.5 million families in the United States live in regions designated as food deserts. Food deserts are communities that have reduced access to nutritious and affordable foods as assessed by distance from home to a full-service grocery store, time required to travel to access food, and safe, reliable transportation. Food deserts are most likely to be found in low-income and rural neighborhoods where food is most readily found in convenience stores, corner grocery stores, liquor stores, and fast food restaurants. The quality of foods and their nutritious value are limited, as many choices are processed and packaged foods that are meant to be eaten on occasion, not as a primary source of nutrition for a family.

Another factor influencing food choices is the amount of time necessary to prepare and cook healthy foods. As many families require two incomes to meet basic needs, time may not always be available in families experiencing long hours at work, long commutes, or both, while juggling other needs of the family such as caring for multiple people at home. When time, energy, and finances are short, families may rely on processed or fast food as a quick and easy option.

Societal Influences

Media

In the United States, media (television, radio, print advertisements, etc.) are often used to promote health messages and products. Television is common in U.S. households and is the primary source of news and entertainment for many families. Daily exposure to media messages regarding health products, food, pharmaceuticals, and health care providers is common and frequently based on sophisticated marketing techniques tailored to specific demographics and cultural groups. Newscasts often include segments highlighting the newest research about successful treatments and correlates of healthy behavior or predictors of good or poor health. As these messages reach American homes, families are exposed to new information that can inform or confuse their health- and diet-related decisions. Although, in general, there is a degree of skepticism regarding the veracity of the health-promoting claims made by advertisers, other media sources (e.g., movies, television, and music), which may portray risky health behavior as the norm without the consequences of endangered health, may not receive the same level of examination and skepticism. To avoid potentially harmful behavior by youth who are exposed to messages that risky health behaviors are common or normal, comprehensive and accurate health education presenting the long-term consequences of endangered health is essential in schools and in families.

Health Care and Health Insurance Access

Family income is positively related to access to health care and health insurance. The 2009 report from the U.S. Census Bureau indicates that 13.2% of the American population lives in poverty, with the highest rates of poverty experienced by African American (24%) and Hispanic populations (23%). Since 1974, children 18 years and younger have become the largest group in the United States to live in poverty. Poverty distribution across age groups show that children under age 18 years are more likely to live in poverty (19%) than adults aged 19 to 64 years (11.7%) and adults aged 65 years and older (9.7%). In 2008, 10.3% of two-parent families lived in poverty while rates remained highest for single female heads of household (28.7%) and single male heads of household (13.8%).

The 2009 U.S. Census Bureau report showed that 15.4% of the U.S. population does not have health insurance. Most Americans who are insured obtain it through their employers (58.5%). It is estimated that 14.2% of families lack health insurance, and 20.8% of unrelated persons living together do not have health insurance. Racial groups most likely to be uninsured mirror those who live in poverty, with Hispanic and African American families having the highest uninsurance rates. Health care can be difficult to obtain for families without insurance. Options include paying out of pocket or seeking care at a not-for-profit, community-based health center if one is located within traveling distance from home.

Needs and Resources

As stated earlier, family health priorities are determined by numerous factors including health beliefs, cultural and family traditions, and health literacy. In addition, health priorities are often based on resources (e.g., time, finances, and availability of health care services) and the immediacy of health concerns. Health care providers should be aware that each family is unique, and individual assessment and tailoring to families are essential

for any intervention to be effective in meeting health-related goals. In considering family health, Abraham Maslow's hierarchy of needs suggests that people act to meet their most basic needs for survival with warmth, shelter, sleep, and nourishment being the most fundamental needs. When these needs are met, attention can turn to higher-level needs such as employment, education, and caring for one's health. In multiproblem families (those with many risks and needs and inadequate resources to meet them), members will strive to meet their most basic needs as a strategy to survive, and health care and other needs will often come second.

Interventions

Culturally Relevant Health Care Services

Generally, people consider previous encounters with health care providers in their decisions to access health care and consider the advice of professionals to be reliable. As the United States has become more diverse, health literacy and culture have become priorities for planning and delivering health care services that are relevant for all people. Families who encounter the health care system and perceive health care providers as rushed, cold, indifferent, or rude will be less likely to turn to formalized health care in the future. It is necessary to educate health care providers on ways to communicate and adapt health care provision to persons of diverse cultural backgrounds. The U.S. Department of Health and Human Services has developed standards for Culturally and Linguistically Appropriate Services (CLAS) for adaptation of health care services for a multicultural society as a foundation for provision of culturally acceptable health care for all persons. Families are less likely to access health care services when they don't feel respected or are unable to understand the instructions of health care providers.

Progress is being made in adapting health care services to local communities and cultural groups. Robert Huff and Michael Kline conceptualize adaptation strategies on a continuum ranging from surface to deep structure adaptation. Surface-level strategies consist of translation of written materials and display of visual materials using ethnic photographs or icons. Deep-structure approaches are developed based on community partnerships, which involve community members in planning and revising health care services that respect their cultural values, communicate in a language and literacy level that can be understood, and address community health needs.

In a similar way, health care providers need to tailor services to families by listening to their concerns, asking questions about their health beliefs and priorities, and working in partnerships with them to meet their goals. Evidence suggests that development of consistent and long-term relationships with families provides a foundation of trust that is needed to engage in health-promoting behaviors.

Desired Family Health Outcomes

In general, all families need access to food, water, shelter, and a safe and healthy environment as a foundation for healthy living. Public health services and access to preventive and acute health care play a key role in reducing the burden of chronic and preventable illness. Evidence demonstrates a significant relationship between income level and health, with those living in poverty having the worst health outcomes. Professionals who work with families need to be aware that many families do not have resources to sustain healthy living and might need referral to resources as well as advocacy support.

On a national level, Healthy People 2010 has identified 10 leading health indicators. These indicators serve as focus areas for health promotion and disease and injury prevention for the United States. Six of the indicators involve individual and family health behaviors and practices while the remaining four address the larger community. Priorities for individual and family behaviors are decreased substance abuse, responsible sexual behavior, decreased tobacco use, less obesity, more physical activity, and mental health promotion. Community- and society-level factors influencing family health include access to health care, immunizations, environmental quality, and low rates of injury and violence.

Conclusion

Family health beliefs, values, and priorities are unique for each family and are formed within

the context of family culture. With the constant stream of health information on television and radio and in newspapers and magazines, health literacy is essential to determine reliable sources of information and to understand it. Public schools and health care providers play a role in promoting and supporting health literacy efforts. Finally, access to affordable health care and a trusting relationship with a health care provider are important tools for ensuring family health.

Diane McNaughton

See also Assessing Family Health; Costs of Medical Care and Existing National, State, and Private Pay Avenues for Families; Cultural Attitudes Toward Help Seeking and Beliefs About Illness in Families; Economics as It Relates to Family Health; Rituals, Routines, and Their Influence on Health in Families

Further Readings

Black, K., & Lobo, M. (2008). A conceptual view of family resilience factors. *Journal of Family Nursing, 14*(1), 33–55.

Bomar, P. J. (2004). *Promoting health in families: Applying family research and theory to nursing practice* (3rd ed.). Philadelphia: Saunders.

Braveman, P. A., Cubbin, C., Egerter S., Williams, D. R., & Pamuk, E. (2010). Socioeconomic disparities in health in the United States: What the patterns tell us. *American Journal of Public Health, 100*(S1), S186–S196.

DeNavas-Walt, C., Proctor, B. D., & Smith, J. C. (2009). Income, poverty, and health insurance coverage in the United States: 2008 *(U.S. Census Bureau Current Population Rep. No. P60–236)*. Washington, DC: U.S. Government Printing Office.

Giger, J. N., & Davidhizar, R. E. (2007). *Transcultural nursing: Assessment and intervention* (5th ed.). St. Louis, MO: Elsevier.

Hodge, J. G., Jr., Mair, J. S., & Gable, L. A. (2008). A CDC review of school laws and policies concerning child and adolescent health [Special issue]. *Journal of School Health, 78*(2).

Huff, R. M., & Kline, M. V. (1999). *Promoting health in multicultural populations: A handbook for practitioners*. Thousand Oaks, CA: Sage.

Maslow, A. (1943). A theory of human motivation. *Psychological Review, 50*(4), 370–396.

National Center for Chronic Disease Prevention and Health Promotion, Division of Adolescent and School

Health. (n. d.). *Healthy youth. Comprehensive health education.* Retrieved April 29, 2010, from http://www.cdc.gov/HealthyYouth/CSHP/comprehensive_ed.htm

U.S. Department of Agriculture. (2009, June). *Access to affordable and nutritious food: measuring and understanding food deserts and their consequences.* Retrieved from http://www.ers.usda.gov/Publications/AP/AP036/AP036.pdf

U.S. Department of Health and Human Services. (2000). *Healthy People 2010.* Washington, DC: U.S. Government Printing Office. Retrieved from http://www.healthypeople.gov

Zarcadoolas, C., Pleasant, A. F., & Greer, D. S (2006). *Advancing health literacy: A framework for understanding and action.* San Francisco: Jossey-Bass.

Families: The Basic Unit of Societies

What is meant by the term *family* varies across the world, and a range of family types can be identified in various cultures and societies. Definitions of the family emphasize a common identity, coresidence, economic cooperation, reproduction, emotional connectedness, care work, and domestic labor. For some commentators the core of a family is a heterosexual couple who have children that they raise to adulthood—the so-called nuclear family. Other types of families provide a context in which children grow up, and these include single-parent, same-sex, and stepparent families. Solo living and the choice to remain childless do not exclude people from family membership. Families offer more than procreation of the next generation, the nurturing of the young, sick, and old. Familial relationships and networks provide intimacy and support. They can also be the source of tensions and conflict that can, on occasion, lead to abuse, violence, and death. Regardless of the type of family, families offer ways in which we learn about hygiene and health, and physical and emotional care and support.

Worldwide, health and social service policies and providers often assume that families can offer physical care, psychological support, financial and practical resources. Lively debates have taken place on what is the "normal" or "proper" family and how families should operate and, where necessary, engage with service providers. Individual, familial, and policy responses illustrate continuities and change in political, social, and religious ideas on relationships and families. Although images of heterosexual couples at the core of the nuclear family have dominated representations of families and policy provision, changes in attitudes and practices about employment, gender, childhood, and sexuality have resulted in notable changes in how health and social services view families. Welfare policies and services have broadened the scope of provision to accommodate many more types of families, although heated debates have ensued about, for example, same-sex families.

The terms *household* and *family* are distinct but may be used interchangeably. A household consists of a person or group of people living together in a specific dwelling who may or may not consider themselves a family. A household of two generations, generally parents and children, is commonly referred to as the *nuclear family*. An extended family incorporates three or more generations vertically—children, parents, grandparents, great-grandparents—and may also incorporate members who occupy horizontal positions such as aunts and uncles. Because families can be viewed as units through which societies care for and socialize their members and provide psychological and physical support, this entry discusses family membership and kinship, approaches for explaining families, and the roles families play in health care and health issues.

Family Members

Family members engage in activities with each other and often do so in preference to friends, colleagues, or neighbors. They may talk of "our family" and communicate on a regular basis, or for specific events or life stages such as birthdays, religious festivals, illness, and death. The family is the basic unit in which the physical and emotional needs of individuals are addressed. The membership of families constantly changes with births, deaths, and the development or cessation of relationships that offer various forms of sexual, emotional, and economic support. Biological membership, although not critical to family membership, is relevant to medical history and diseases that may be inherited. Recalling family events, including births, marriages, relationship breakups, and deaths, as well as other less momentous shared experiences, evokes a sense of membership. So too do memories of historical and religious events, such as civil conflicts, economic changes, festivals, and rituals (some of which may be highly idiosyncratic and thus contribute to a sense of distinct identity).

A notable feature of families in the 21st century is the increased legitimacy of varied types of families in many societies. There is less stigma attached to those who live in diverse family arrangements such as single or same-sex parents, or important alternatives to families, for example, a kibbutz or an orphanage. Nevertheless, families are often, but not exclusively, formed around a married or cohabiting adult couple with other members—children or parents—linked through biological descent or adoption. Extended family members such as aunts, uncles, and cousins may not live with, or close to, immediate members and may not see one another on a regular basis, if at all, although in some cultures close residential proximity is the norm. Nevertheless, the sense of a family identity outweighs other relationships. Family members have a sense of connectedness that provides a metaphorical boundary around their family. This notion of belonging involves the priority that members give to each other. Responsibilities and obligations to other family members, often unspoken, sometimes negotiated, remain distinctive.

Family members are generally, but not exclusively, linked through blood or intimate relationships. Immediate family members—most often parents and children and, in some cultures, grandparents and grandchildren—are likely to live together or nearby. The conjugal family of parents and their dependent children is often referred to as a nuclear family. The consanguineal family consists of a parent, his or her children, and other people usually related by blood. This type of family can often be found in societies where one parent has to travel to undertake work, for example, construction work or domestic service, or the care for a relative or friend, for example, an elderly, sick relative who lives some distance away and requires dedicated care.

A matrifocal family comprises a mother and her children. This type of family is not uncommon in a number of cultures where, for example, it is acceptable for women to raise children without cohabiting fathers, such as when men migrate for work or are engaged in military action, or there is a separation or divorce between parents. Family members also extend beyond blood relationships with, for example, neighbors and family friends, and can include people with whom we have little or no contact, such as the cousin who has lived abroad all her life.

Family Kinship

Patterns of kinship and associated terminology vary among cultures. Consider two contrasting approaches in Sudanese and Eskimo cultures. In Sudanese culture, no two relatives share the same term; by contrast, in Eskimo culture, relatives are distinguished by sex and generation and according to whether the kinship is lineal or collateral. Descriptive kinship terms employed in most Western societies are similar to Eskimo culture and include the following:

Mother: a female parent
Daughter: a female child of the parent
Sister: a female child of the same parent
Grandmother: mother of a father or mother

The pattern is the same for the male line: father, son, brother, and grandfather. A common assumption in this system is that biological lines are adhered to and a lineal format follows; descent from one person to another is in a direct line. In some families, however, a woman may have children with more than one man, and siblings may be referred to as *half-brother* or *half-sister*. Children who do not share biological or adoptive parents but whose biological parent marries one of their parents are referred to as *stepbrother* or *stepsister*.

Affinal kinship describes the relationship that a person has to the blood relatives of a spouse by virtue of the marriage. The core relationship is the legal one established between a husband and wife, albeit in many societies cohabitation can offer a similar basis to kinship where there is social recognition that there is a durable relationship. There are three types of affinity. Direct affinity exists between a husband's and wife's relations by blood. Secondary affinity is between a spouse and the other spouse's relatives by marriage. Collateral affinity exists between a spouse and the relatives of the other spouse's relatives. Affinity is important in various legal matters, such as deciding whether to prosecute a person for incest or whether to disqualify a person from jury service given there may be bias due to familial relationships and obligations.

Collateral relatives form an important grouping in many families and members, include the following:

Uncle: father's brother, mother's brother, father's/ mother's sister's husband

Nephew: sister's son, brother's son, wife's brother's son, wife's sister's son, husband's sister's son

Additional generations can be identified with prefixes that vary across cultures and languages. In North America and the United Kingdom the prefixes are *great* or *grand*; in French the prefix is *beau*. In most societies cousins may be classified as first, second, or third cousins. Two people of the same generation who share a grandparent are related by one degree of collaterality: first cousins. If they share a great-grandparent they are second cousins, and so on. Marriage can be denoted by the term *in-law*; on marriage the mother of a spouse becomes known as mother-in-law. The terms *half-brother* and *half-sister* indicate siblings with one biological or adoptive parent in common. Close family friends may be referred to as aunts or uncles or sisters or brothers, and this common practice is referred to as *fictive kinship*.

Although the language of kinship varies across cultures and languages, horizontally the extended family can include in-laws, aunts, uncles, and cousins. Societies with families strongly associated with conjugal relationships favor leaving the family of orientation—the household of childhood—and setting up a new household and potentially a family of procreation.

Explaining Families

Explanations demonstrate assumptions about the role of families and family members that have implications for care and health issues. Explanations also inform the development of policies and the organization of services. Explanations that offer insights to families and health include functionalism, domestic division of labor, psychoanalytical accounts, and family practices.

Functionalism

This approach starts from the premise that social institutions, of which the family is a major one, change to meet the needs of a society or culture. In most societies the major requirements are the following:

Primary socialization of children: This is so that children acquire the values and acceptable behaviors of society. They also learn about personal care, hygiene, and how to consider and care for others. Thus the family is the starting point for ideas and skills in health and self-care.

Personality development: Families provide emotional as well as physical support; combined, these enhance personality development.

When families do not or cannot provide socialization and personality development, the state may have legitimacy to intervene. The potential for, and level of, intervention varies according to political, economic, and welfare regimes. Assumptions about the need for, and provision of, nonparental care differ across societies and welfare regimes. Social services and the police can intervene in families when concerns are raised. In most countries legislation underpins intervention. The ways in which intervention manifests itself can make alternatives to families appear more benign than is borne out by the evidence. Growing up in a children's home or orphanage may be preferable to life in an abusive family, but in some societies, such as the United Kingdom, it is associated with lower educational attainment, increased risk of unemployment, substance misuse, and criminal activity. Intensive help may, however, help young people to achieve more in education and training, and there is evidence that this is the case in some countries, such as Finland. Families, services, and societies struggle to balance what is considered acceptable in some families.

This explanation of families and family life evolved alongside economic changes. Functionalism appeared to make sense of the effects of industrialization and urbanization. Many functions of families moved outside the household, such as the production of food and education of children, with the home becoming the focus for family activities. Family functions and roles concentrated on facilitating access to, and participation in, the labor market, including socialization and personality development. This model of the family appeared to suit postindustrial societies, and it remains a favored one by some politicians and commentators. The original explanation ascribed roles to members: the male breadwinner, the female homemaker and mother working part-time if at all, children growing up and preparing for employment, and grandparents helping with socialization, offering a sense of stability and care.

Domestic Division of Labor Based on Gender

This explanation argues that the family evolved alongside capitalist economies and in gendered ways to promote the role of a male breadwinner who is unencumbered by home life to freely participate in paid work. Procreation, childrearing, elder care, care for the sick or vulnerable, and domestic labor are critical to civilized societies. These are tasks that in contemporary societies take place outside the workplace and in ways have no or limited impact on the capacity of adults to engage in employment, especially adult males. These arrangements are premised on the continued association of care work with women. In this explanation women are primarily perceived as homemakers promoting the health and well-being of the current worker and children as future workers. The variation in state provision of care reflects differing historical, demographic, economic, and cultural presumptions about the role of the state in the provision or regulation of services. In addition to services provided, the contribution of the partner, grandparents of children, or other unpaid carers is critical to the emotional and physical health of the worker. Many women work, but their primary role is at home; this constrains their availability to work in many occupations. Often work is part-time and in areas that draw on caring skills such as nursing, teaching, retail, and cleaning work. Much of this is low paid and can be insecure, thus reinforcing dependency on the full-time male worker although variant models are becoming evident at different points on the socioeconomic spectrum. It is not uncommon for both middle-class parents in a family to choose to work part-time to share child care or for lower-paid couples to work different shifts to the same end, a practice referred to as *shift* or *serial parenting*.

Some commentators have argued that many men, and male-dominated labor organizations (unions), wished to exclude women from paid employment and potential independence as female labor might lower wage rates. Thus the familial gendered domestic division of labor results from, rather than causes, it the exclusion of women from labor markets. This explanation may have some resonance when it comes to the gender segregation of employment and the lower pay rates for women, but there are a number of changes that have taken place in recent decades. In most societies and communities, women's experiences of domestic labor and employment are now based on the requirement that all those who can, are engaged in employment. Further, the changing relationship between men and women, including increased male involvement in domestic labor, illuminates the development of legislative and welfare rights for women. Supranational organizations such as the United Nations, World Health Organization, and International Monetary Fund recognize that the education of girls promotes health and well-being for all family members. Women and girls are likely to give health skills and issues a high priority and allocate basic household resources (food, money, clothes) with greater equity.

Psychoanalytical Approaches

Psychoanalytical accounts focus on the relationships offered by families and how these are critical to emotional development and long-term well-being. The word *psyche* originates from ancient Greek and means breath, spirit, or soul; this definition draws attention to intimate and parenting relationships that can offer or deny emotional support. Psychoanalytical approaches to families tend to emphasize the parent–child relationship. Rapid brain development in early years makes adult–child interaction imperative, and this can affect the long-term workings and chemical balance of a child's brain. Foundation systems for the regulation of emotions such as kindness, empathy, and concern develop and mature in certain types of parent–child relations. Feelings and emotions may also be denied, and stress response systems can be activated. A child may grow up unable to recognize the feelings of others and with a limited capacity for awareness of others.

The family also acts as an outlet for discontentment with the day-to-day frustrations of work and the many pressures of life outside the home. The potential for the family to ameliorate tensions and pressures has resulted in the notion of the family as a haven. Mental health services recognize the role of families in offering support but also recognize families as a source of emotional trauma. Families and households can be the contexts in which tensions are created and reinforced with physical, emotional, and economic forms of abuse. Women and children are much more likely to experience violence at the hands of those with whom they have an intimate or familial relationship.

Anxiety, depression, and anger are among the emotions experienced, and at times these may be negative and destructive. Human beings have core relational needs for secure attachment and emotional responses, including praise, encouragement, approval, and the setting of boundaries in relationships and friendships. If these needs are not met, individuals and families may become dysfunctional. The focus on childhood has led to increased services for children in psychiatry, psychology, and therapy. Commentators have expressed concern over the tendency of this approach to focus on the mother–child relationship, placing further pressures on women whose multiple roles shape opportunities alongside restrictions—for example, childrearing while engaged in paid employment. The increase in activity among fathers as parents and family members cannot be ignored, although women continue to undertake more than an equal share of domestic and care labor than men. Further, if middle-class ideas dominate what is considered acceptable in families (e.g., aspirations for children to achieve a career through education, high levels of labor market activity, consumption patterns that include two or more holidays a year), then policies and services tend to concentrate on those who do not attain or aspire to this lifestyle. Such class-shaped ideologies create a policy and service environment in which lower income households, alternative families, and families of different ethnic and religious origins are considered unusual or different. Disproportionate levels of intervention in some families may be contrasted with abuses in middle-class families that become or are rendered invisible.

Family Practices

One way to explain how people engage in and interpret family membership is through family practices. *Family practices* refer to what people do together that results in their talking and thinking of themselves as a family. Examples include eating together, respecting others' right to privacy in their bedroom, taking children to the dentist, and organizing long-term health treatments. Special events are critical for family practices and include religious and public festivals, weddings, christenings and funerals, birthdays and holidays. Further, the notion of displaying families, namely, where forms of direct social interaction are used to convey the meaning that there is a family-like relationship, recognizes the relevance of illustrating and illuminating family links and relationships. These ideas about how we might explain family workings offers insights relevant to families across the world, regardless of the environmental or social context, and economic or welfare regime.

The explanations offered in this section are not mutually exclusive. They can be drawn on interchangeably to describe and analyze changes in the way people live their lives through families, and in multiple or solo households.

Demography and Disease

In societies that have experienced stability, a narrowing of inequalities, and relative peace, mortality rates—particularly those of infants—have decreased markedly over the past century. Assumptions can now be made in these societies about common patterns of parenting and child care responsibilities as well as what is associated with the expectations of age-related illness. Eurostat, the Statistical Office of the European Communities, reports that life expectancy in the European Union continues to increase. Someone born in 2007 can expect to live to 78.5 years. The United States shows a similar trend. Regional averages, however, tend to mask variations in life expectancy; for example, in 2005 the highest life expectancy in Europe was in Spain (80.7) and Sweden (80.6), although health improvements and concomitantly longer life expectancies are distributed unevenly across the classes and subcultures of individual countries. In contrast, the lowest was in Latvia and Lithuania (65 for men and 77 for women). Indeed, the majority of the lowest life expectancies in the European Union were found within the 12 countries that joined the European Union in 2004. Although this variation is significant, the European Union is a success story for longevity in all countries. In 2007 sub-Saharan Africa had a life expectancy at birth of 50 for women and 48 for men; five countries (Swaziland, Botswana, Lesotho, Zimbabwe, Zambia) within this geographical zone had the lowest life expectancies of any country in the world, with a range of 33 to 38 years.

Life expectancy differences manifest themselves in the age of the populations and families. Populations in the European Union and the United States have increasing proportions of individuals over 65 years of age, whereas in Africa, especially sub-Saharan Africa, the child population (younger than 14 years) is twice that of the European Union and United States. Despite evidence of improved survival rates in some African countries, only 3% of the population survives to reach 65 plus years. The frequency of dying young affects the care perspectives of those left to cope, as does prolonged or improving life expectancy. Longevity is also associated with limited quality of life in final years due to the onset of chronic conditions and mobility problems.

Globally, the rate of growth in population is slowing in some countries to a level that is below that needed for population replacement. By contrast sub-Saharan Africa's natural rate of increase stands at 2.5% in 2007, with both birth and death rates considerably higher than in any other world population zones. However, the infant mortality rate (96 per 1,000 live births in 2007) and HIV/AIDS infection rate (6.1 per 1,000 population in 2007) are much higher than either the European Union or United States. Deaths from AIDS in sub-Saharan Africa represent 72% of global AIDS deaths, according to the United Nations. The recognition of HIV/AIDs in the 1980s provides evidence of the ever-changing nature of disease and illness. Infectious diseases and malnutrition are evident in societies with limited or no infrastructure resultant from poverty, natural disaster, or war and conflicts. So-called lifestyle diseases such as diabetes and circulatory conditions are more prevalent in poorer groups in societies where there is relative economic prosperity. Conditions linked to climate

and the environment, for example, malaria and dysentery, continue to have a major impact on poor communities and countries. Many of these illnesses could be treated with the aid of families but limited health care services, access to drugs, clean water, and sanitation make local treatment difficult and costly. The number of preventable deaths runs into millions and is the cause for much concern on the part of international economic aid and development organizations.

Over half of the world's population lives in urban areas. Growth in the overall world population has slowed down in the past decade. Population growth, however, remains higher in countries that are often termed *developing countries*. The contrast between countries is stark. A third (34%) of the population in sub-Saharan Africa lives in urban areas, while the comparable figure in the European Union is 80%. Almost half of those who live in urban areas, regardless of their country of residence, live in cities of 500,000 or fewer inhabitants, and cities vary not just in size but in socioeconomic composition. Moreover, their history, environment, economic, migration, and demographic trends differ. Life for low-income families in California may share some broad similarities to a family in a shanty town on the outskirts of Durban, South Africa, but the experience of everyday living is quite different. For example, the availability of infrastructure in California (water, sewage systems, education, and health care services) offers a different experience of poverty to that of the family in Durban. The experience of poverty, however, may be felt just as keenly by each family as their everyday living contrasts markedly with other groups.

The impact of HIV/AIDS, and the ever-shifting trends in infectious diseases, combined with subsistence-level resources, has placed particular pressures on both young and old in large parts of Africa, Asia, Russia, and Central America. In many communities young and old become mutually dependent when economically active adults become ill or die. These experiences differ from the common expectation that when a child is born, caring needs will be met through "natural" and "normal" social relationships of "family," "gender relations" and "mothering." As a consequence of diseases, accidents, wars, and disasters, what might be viewed as the "natural" and "normal" social relationships of families, gender relations, and parenting have undergone more or less severe modification when significant proportions of progenitors are unable to look after their offspring.

Patterns of increasing urbanization continue, but to varying degrees across the world. The implications for the organization of families, family health, and health services are notable. Across the globe remote and sparsely populated localities face specific pressures related to the costs of transport and communication, which can affect support for individuals, families, and social networks, and access to services. In poor urban areas residents face a range of barriers and pressures not dissimilar to those that rural populations face. They have, for example, limited transport, higher food costs, and limited health and welfare services but live at higher densities that facilitate the spread of disease and often among a more diverse population than in the rural areas. Further, patterns of migration, driven by economic concerns, natural disasters, war, and conflict place specific pressures on families, and they become subject to separation, seek asylum, or become refugees.

Violence and Violation

Across the world there are striking similarities in the patterns of abuse and violence that take place in and around families. Emotional, economic, physical, and psychological abuses take a heavy toll on family members. Welfare services and social policies are often driven by the need to prevent these abuses or manage the consequences. Women and children face a disproportionate toll as a result of abuses in families. They are more likely to be killed by those they know, often immediate and the most intimate members of the family, whereas a larger proportion of men are killed by strangers. The U.S. Department of Health reports that 70% of female murder victims are killed by their partner or other family member, and a parent murders 90% of child victims. By contrast, a relative commits only 20% of the murders of adult men. Whereas intimacy seems to frame this violence, the threat of violence is a very obvious expression of power, oppression, and, in the majority of cases, aggressive forms of masculinity.

One specific example, namely, domestic or partner abuse, has led to much pain and suffering in families. Researchers and practitioners have debated the cause and effect of various abuses, although much of the research has concentrated on the physical dimension of abuse, as it is easier to identify than other forms of abuse. Men and women may use physical violence to achieve domination in a relationship or to express frustration. Women, however, fear violence more and experience greater physical, psychological, and economic injuries. Women earn less than men and have lower incomes in all societies. Abusive relationships have a disproportionate impact on women who are less able to leave a failing relationship. This may be due to the combination of limited income, breaking up social and educational networks for children, social and family stigma, and fear of not finding safety. Further, pressures to maintain family cohesion also lead to the toleration of abuses, sometimes over decades.

Families, relationships, and communities can be powerful forces in forging identities, sometimes constructed around grievances, and these that may be powerful forces in family-based vendettas are also prevalent in some cultures and groups, wars, conflicts, and ethnic violence. In ethnic conflicts, for example, violence becomes embedded in social relations, erupting when historical grievances are reprised through rituals and other forms of public remembrance. The role and positioning of women can become symbolic for ethnic identity, making rape, and the systematic use of gang rape, a weapon against both the individual woman and the ethnic group to which she is deemed to belong. Not only can families become places for the engendering of ethnic violence, they also constitute spaces and places in which violence takes place. Violence against women reflects their positioning as moral symbols, and this can place them in a double jeopardy of violence from men known and unknown to them—for example, in the case of honor killings, deaths resulting from the practice of dowries from a women's family considered inadequate, or exclusion from communities following rape. The physical health implications are obvious, but these also present challenges for psychological and family health services more generally.

Conclusion

The pace of change appears to increase and to lead to ever more complex living arrangements.

There are, however, continuities as well as change. In times of crisis it is not uncommon for people to look to their family for practical, financial, and emotional support. Often the presumption that support will be forthcoming is borne out. Further, the continued and strong association of all forms of nurturing and care with families serves to reinforce familial obligations and duties. Even with a growth in men taking part in formal and informal types of care, in most societies social and gendered presumptions about the centrality of family relationships in caring remain strong. The greater freedom that is often found within conjugal relationships still tends to conflict with the constraints and decisions bound up in parenthood. Thus families can be viewed as units in which, and through which, members, friends, and sometimes neighbors receive various forms of psychological and physical support and care. Where there are not welfare or health care regimes, the family is the basic unit of health care, and where these regimes exist, presumptions about the role of the family and family members ensue.

Linda McKie and Samantha Callan

See also Defining Family: An Overview of Family Definitions From a Historical Perspective; Family Experiencing Transitions; Grandparenting; History of Families; Men's Health; Parenting; Resilience in Families With Health Challenges; Women's Health

Further Readings

Barrio, L. del. (2008). *The life of women and men in Europe: A statistical portrait*. Luxembourg: Office for Official Publications of the European Communities.

Bernardes, J. (1997). *Family studies: An introduction*. London: Routledge.

Cheal, D. (2008). *Families in today's world*. London: Routledge.

Central Intelligence Unit. (2008). *World fact book*. Washington DC: Author.

Department of Health. (2005). *Responding to domestic violence: A handbook for professionals*. London: Author.

Egelman, W. (2003). *Understanding families: Critical thinking and analysis*. London: Allyn & Bacon.

Finch, J., & Mason, J. (1993). *Negotiating family responsibilities*. London: Routledge.

Morgan, D. H. J. (1996). *Family connections*. Cambridge, UK: Polity Press.

United Nations. (2006). *Sub-Saharan Africa AIDS epidemic update*. New York: Author.

White, J. (2007). *Family theories*. London: Sage.

Families Experiencing a Child's Illness

Historically, families are the basic unit of our society. When a member of a family is sick, the rest of the family is affected. When planning health care for children who are ill or have a chronic or long-term condition, because the whole family is affected, then the whole family—however perceived by that family itself—must be the unit around which care is planned. Until about the 1960s, when a child was ill and admitted to hospital, the family was given little consideration, but changes around the world in health policy and ideas in the 1950s and 1960s led to an evolution in caring for children in which the family became the unit of care rather than the individual child. From this evolution, various models of nursing care were developed, some of which are described in this entry.

Definitions of the family abound, but for the purposes of this discussion, the family is defined as whatever that family says it is. It may be a nuclear family of mother, father, and two to three children; a single family; or a large extended family; it may even contain the family pets. Whenever one family member becomes ill, the whole family unit suffers, and this is particularly so when the ill person is a child.

Parents are usually those who have responsibility for the care of children; and again, in this entry, the parent is whoever that family says it is. Parental responsibility is different across cultures. In many Western societies, parents legally take responsibility for their children until a child is 18 years of age. In other countries, a child will live with his or her parents until the child marries and leaves home. In some societies, the definition of a parent is much broader; for example, in Australian Aboriginal societies, the parent may be the child's aunt or uncle, and in fact, a child may have several parents—its natural parents, plus several members of the extended family group—and all would have equal responsibility for the child as the natural parents.

Every child in the world has a parent of some kind. A parent can be the biological mother or father, stepmother or stepfather, foster mother or foster father, guardian, or the primary caregiver of a child. Even orphans are cared for by the state. Every child who is admitted to a hospital, for whatever reason, has a parent who must be considered. Parents are important to health professionals because they provide a biological framework for the child for whom they are caring; they are the main caregivers to that child, the main psychological support for him or her, and the ones who know their child better than anyone else. When one delivers health care to a family, child, or parent, all this must be taken into consideration.

No matter how a family defines itself, when a child is ill the family experiences a range of emotions and problems that are unique to that situation. Commonly, fear plays an important role—if the child is gravely ill, there is fear that the child will die. Any acute illness may provoke a feeling of fear in the parent (and, if old enough, perhaps the child too). There is uncertainty about what is going to happen and what the illness means to the family; whether the treatment will be effective, painful, or debilitating; and what the long- and short-term outcomes will be. There is concern about how a child's illness will affect the family as a whole, the family functioning, parents' work, children's schooling, the grandparents, and other family members. All such factors are important to consider when planning care for a child who is sick and his or her family.

There is a large body of literature showing that parents are important to caregiving for a child in the hospital. Also, much research has been done that shows that not only should the parents be able to rely on the health professionals in the hospital to care for the child, but also that the parents want to be relied on to be part of the caregiving, and they want to be able to do so at the level at which they feel most comfortable. However, now that involvement of parents and family members in the care of a child who is ill has become accepted practice, some evidence is emerging that in some cases, parents may resent being made to do what they see as nurses' work. It seems that philosophies about the care of children in health care have come full circle from the times when parents were excluded completely from the hospital when their child was admitted, through various evolutionary stages of parental involvement, led by lobby and consumer groups of parents who wanted to be an integral part of the delivery of care to their children, to ideas that some parents might feel that too much involvement is expected of them.

In the past 40 years, society has changed a great deal. In Western countries now, the majority of mothers work outside the home. Consequently, having a sick child can mean financial and emotional hardship for families. Whereas in Sweden, parents are allowed 60 days per year on 80% of their salary to care for sick children, and the United States has a law protecting families from losing their jobs when they wish to be with their children, most countries do not have such benefits. A hospital admission of a child, or a child who needs care at home, may mean a parent has to take unpaid time off work, thus diminishing the family finances, or has to use holiday allowances, which may mean no rest for the parent during the year. It is not considered good pediatric practice to put pressure on parents to stay and be involved in their child's care if they cannot or do not want to.

A Child's Hospital Admission

Children come into hospitals for a wide range of illnesses, conditions, and problems, from accidental trauma to psychological problems. A walk through a children's hospital will show the wide range of children's illnesses and conditions. The most important thing to remember about children in hospitals is that their care will be very different from that given to an adult. It is usually not possible to transfer knowledge about adult care into pediatrics. For example, both children and adults get pneumonia, but a tiny infant will experience this in very different ways than will a large adult. A child's metabolism is different from that of an adult, depending on the age and developmental stage of the child. Consequently, planning care for a child who is sick requires a different set of skills, knowledge, and experience than that required for planning care for an adult. Children should never be admitted to hospital unnecessarily, because a hospital admission, with its unfamiliar setting, odd noises and smells, and painful experiences, can be traumatic. There is a large literature on diseases of children, with many textbooks dedicated to pediatric illnesses. Children may be admitted to hospitals for a wide range of conditions; these conditions can be divided into acute and chronic. *Acute* illnesses include medical and surgical conditions, and these will be either emergency admissions (e.g., injuries or asthma) or routine admissions (e.g., planned surgical procedures). Regardless of the condition for which a child has been admitted, the hospital will use one model, or perhaps several models, of pediatric care as a way to deliver care to the child and family.

Models of Care in Children's Hospitals

Hospital care for children is organized in ways that affect the whole health team, but most of the literature describing models of care is in the nursing literature, as nurses make up the majority of the hospital workforce and attend to the patients (children and parents) 24 hours of the day. They are the professional group who have constant contact with children in hospitals and are most likely to be in contact with the parents, and they have a great deal of influence on the way care is delivered. This section focuses on models of nursing care, their development, and their use in pediatrics.

Until about the 1970s and 1980s, the so-called medical model was predominant in hospitals. Nurses perceived that although the medical model might be relevant for medicine, it was only partly relevant to nurses, who dealt with the whole patient and family. Nursing models emerged, and some were particularly for the care of children and their families. Various models and theories have been tried in pediatrics, including care-by-parent, partnership in care, and family-centered care.

Care-by-Parent

During the 1960s care-by-parent units, in which the parents (and family) lived in with the sick child were first developed in the United States. A care-by-parent unit has rooms with a bed for the parent and en-suite facilities, furnished in a comfortable, home-like style. There are kitchen and laundry facilities, dining and play areas, and a treatment room. Parents live with the children and provide care in conjunction with the nurses. The role of the parent is outlined and expectations negotiated on admission. Such units are particularly

beneficial for babies who are being breastfed or for children with serious chronic diseases such as cystic fibrosis or cancer, when the treatment can be particularly threatening and privacy is of prime importance. They are equally suitable for other, short-term illnesses or surgery. Previously, the child had been the responsibility of the nurse and doctor. With the new concept, the parents retain responsibility for the child while in the care of the health professionals. Such innovations grew from a desire to include the parent in decision making about the child's care, to involve the parents in the care, thereby alleviating the anxiety of both child and parent. Included in the care-by-parent concept are members of the extended family, siblings, grandparents, and others.

Partnership in Care

A well-known model of care was devised in the United Kingdom in the 1990s. Partnership in care is based on the principles that (a) nursing care for a child in hospital can be given by the child or parents with support and education from the nurse, and (b) family or parental care can be given by the nurse if the family is absent. The role of the family, or parent, is to take on the everyday care of the child, while the role of the nurse is to teach, support, and, if necessary, refer the family to others.

Parents' views of partnership in care centered on the idea that their participation is necessary for the child's well-being, and a nonnegotiable part of parenthood, but nurses were seen as too busy to provide consistent care. Parents were prepared to learn more complex care, but only when necessary, preferring to leave it to the nurses because of the anxiety it caused the parents. The most important part of ensuring successful partnerships with nurses was giving information and using effective communication and negotiation. Parental involvement in care in partnership with the health professionals led to the development of family-centered care.

Family-Centered Care

Family-centered care (FCC) has evolved from the previous models and has come to be a cornerstone in pediatric practice, though it has never been formally evaluated. FCC is a way of caring for children and their families within health services in which care is planned around the whole family and all the family members are the care recipients. The Institute of Family-Centered Care in the United States lists several elements of FCC, including recognizing the family as a constant in the child's life; facilitating parent–professional collaboration; honoring racial, ethnic, cultural, and socioeconomic diversity of families; recognizing family strengths and different methods of coping; sharing information with families; responding to child and family developmental needs; providing families with emotional and financial support; and designing health care that is flexible, culturally competent, and responsive to family needs.

FCC is a ubiquitous model in the delivery of health care to children and families across the world. In some countries, hospitals have invested heavily in implementing FCC, but there is no rigorous evidence about whether it works or whether it makes a real difference to the families' use of services. There is, however, a growing body of qualitative research that shows that fundamental problems exist with this approach. Philip Darbyshire suggested that FCC is a wonderful ideal but is, in reality, extremely difficult to implement because of the judgmental attitudes of some health professionals toward parents, resulting in the feeling that they are "parenting in public." Similarly, the health professionals feel they are giving care in public. For FCC to succeed, a high level of understanding and empathetic communication between parents and health professionals is necessary, and this can come about only through extensive education both for health professionals who deliver the care and for the families who are receiving it. FCC is well known in developed countries and is widely used in developing nations, with similar problems in its implementation and effectiveness. However, a systematic review of studies about FCC has shown that there have been no studies to evaluate the effectiveness of FCC, and a large randomized clinical trial is needed to determine whether or not FCC makes a real difference to the well-being of children and families in hospitals.

The promotion of FCC as a model of care will continue to be examined. While it is known that rigorous studies using quantitative methods to measure the influence of FCC have not been completed yet, qualitative research is suggesting concerns with the FCC model that need solid investigation. Parents are often not equal partners when their child is admitted to the hospital; in fact, some parents have to use strategies to ensure that their needs are met. Also, some nurses use a punishing style of communication with parents to try to impose their own values as to what constituted a "good" parent when accompanying their child in the hospital.

Various models involving parents and family in the hospitalized child's care have evolved and have been embraced, at least in theory, by children's hospitals in developed countries. Research indicates that in practice, they are not so widely accepted, and further education is needed to convince health professionals of their worth. Perhaps parental involvement is often only an ideal, not easily reached, because it is difficult to remove judgmental attitudes from practice.

While models for delivery of care for all children are under development and scrutiny, other factors come into consideration for children having surgery and for their families.

Children Having Surgery

The operating room looks very different to a child than to an adult, and what adults can see and rationalize as necessary pieces of equipment can look very frightening to small children. Consequently, children who are having an operation need special consideration. To start with, they probably are hungry and thirsty because of the fasting times required before anesthetic induction. This may make them irritable and upset, and this, in turn, can upset the parents, who are probably already anxious. A child needs sound preparation before having surgery (as do the parents). Consideration of the needs of the family members is just as important in the operating room as it is anywhere else in pediatrics, and parents and family members must be advised of what is happening at all times.

Parental presence during anesthetic induction, which has been shown to relieve the anxiety of parents, is most often at the discretion of the anesthetist, whereas presence in the recovery room, where the child will be placed until he or she regains consciousness following an anesthetic, is most often dependent on the nursing staff. Reasons for excluding parents from the recovery room often include the argument that too much can go wrong postanesthesia; in addition, physical factors such as the bed area and availability of staff are sometimes cited as reasons for excluding parents from the postoperative recovery room. Hospital recovery rooms should be constructed to ensure that parents can accompany their children without compromising either the safety or privacy of child patients.

Though in some places, parental presence in the operating room is widely accepted, it remains a contentious issue. Many hospitals and anesthetists now encourage parental presence during anesthetic induction, and this is beneficial to the child, and parents' and children's anxiety is decreased. However, parents must be well prepared by the nursing staff, by ensuring they understand that their child will drop into sleep very quickly, may be floppy, and may not breathe for the 1 minute it takes to transfer the child from the parents' arms to the operating table. This is perfectly normal, but unless a parent knows what to expect, she or he can be frightened by the rapidity at which it happens.

Preparation for surgery can make a child and his or her family much less anxious. Hospital play centers have areas set up with hospital beds and equipment so children can act out their own experiences. Through play, teachers, nurses, and other health staff can handle a child's distress and help children prepare for impending situations such as operations. Clowns, puppet shows, and entertainers are sometimes used to make hospitals more enjoyable places for children, and they can be used in the operating room. Music therapy offers opportunities for structured social interaction, for enhancement of education, for decreasing fear and anxiety, as distraction from painful procedures, as relaxation therapy, and for pain control. The family remains the unit of care, and family members (e.g., parents, siblings, and grandparents) can be an integral part of the preparation of children for surgery.

Conclusion

Families play a large role in a child's admission to the hospital, and all care has to be planned around the whole family, not just the individual child. Family-centered care is a cornerstone of pediatric practice, although it has never been formally tested to see if it really does make a difference. Families with a sick child are cared for in hospitals using a variety of models of care, and three have been discussed here: care-by-parent, partnership in care, and family-centered care. Because these are based on the premise that the parents are the most important people in a child's life, know the child best, and always work in the best interest of the child, it seems obvious that the parents should be welcomed as active contributors to the care of their hospitalized child. This does not always occur.

Children having surgery are at risk of emotional trauma unless the surroundings are as child- and family-friendly as possible and the staff members are cognizant of the special needs of the child in that situation. Operating rooms can be as frightening for the family members as for the child, and family members, too, need care and support.

Linda Shields

See also Communication in Families Related to Health and Illness; Education of Nursing Health Care Providers in Family Health; Hospitalization and Family Presence; Partnering With Families: Family-Centered Care

Further Readings

Casey, A. (1995). Partnership nursing: Influences on involvement of informal carers. *Journal of Advanced Nursing, 22,* 1058–1062.

Chorney, J. M., & Kain, Z. N. (2010). Family-centered pediatric perioperative care. *Anesthesiology, 112,* 751–755.

Coyne, I. (2008). Disruption of parent participation: Nurses' strategies to manage parents on children's wards. *Journal of Clinical Nursing, 17,* 3150–3158.

Coyne, I. T. (1995). Partnership in care: Parents' views of participation in their hospitalized children's care. *Journal of Clinical Nursing, 4,* 71–79.

Darbyshire, P. (1994). *Living with a sick child in hospital: The experiences of parents and nurses.* London: Chapman & Hall.

Goodband, S., & Jennings, K. (1992). Parent care: A US experience in Indianapolis. In J. Cleary (Ed.), *Caring for children in hospital: Parents and nurses in partnership* (pp. 114–126). London: Scutari Press.

Institute for Patient- and Family-Centered Care. (2005). *Frequently asked questions.* Retrieved May 4, 2010, from http://www.familycenteredcare.org/faq.html

Kain, Z. N., & MacLaren, J. E. (2009). Healthcare provider–child–parent communication in the preoperative surgical setting. *Paediatric Anaesthesia, 19,* 376–384.

Kristensson-Hallström, I., & Elander, G. (1997). Parents' experience of hospitalization: Different strategies for feeling secure. *Pediatric Nursing, 23,* 361–376.

O'Haire, S., & Blackford, J. C. (2005). Nurses' moral agency in negotiating parental participation in care. *International Journal of Nursing Research, 11,* 250–256.

Roden, J. (2005). The involvement of parents and nurses in the care of acutely-ill children in a non-specialist pediatric setting. *Journal of Child Health Care, 9,* 222–240.

Shields, L., Pratt, J., Davis, L., & Hunter, J. (2007). Family-centred care for children in hospital. *Cochrane Database of Systematic Reviews, 24*(1), CD004811.

Shields, L., Pratt, J., & Hunter, J. (2006). Family-centered care: A review of qualitative studies. *Journal of Clinical Nursing, 15,* 1317–1323.

FAMILIES EXPERIENCING CHRONIC PHYSICAL AND MENTAL HEALTH CONDITIONS

Americans are living longer than ever before, primarily as a result of improved medical care, enhanced public health services, and increased use of preventive health practices. However, living longer does not necessarily mean living life without illness and disease. According to the National Center for Health Statistics, more than 80% of adults aged 65 and older have at least one chronic health condition, conditions that are long term, often permanent, and result in disabilities that require daily management. Further, coping with multiple health problems is common in late life. Older persons with chronic health problems become increasingly vulnerable to the physical and mental limitations associated with these conditions. They often require help performing personal care tasks and home management activities. Personal care tasks are activities such as bathing, grooming, toileting, dressing, and eating. Home management activities include tasks like shopping, preparing meals, doing housework, and handling personal finances.

Nearly three fourths of older adults who need assistance because of chronic physically or mentally debilitating conditions rely solely on family members for care. This entry addresses chronic health conditions of older adults within the context of family care and support. It describes common physical and mental health conditions experienced by individuals in late life, examines the type of care and support provided by family members, explores the influence of providing care to older adults on the health and well-being of family caregivers, and discusses intervention programs aimed at supporting aging families with chronic physical and mental health conditions.

Physical Health Conditions in Late Life

As people approach late life they often encounter changes in their physical health that disrupt their daily lives and the lives of those close to them. Some of the most troublesome health problems are due to chronic disease. Three chronic conditions are among the leading causes of disability and dependency among older adults: cardiovascular disease, musculoskeletal disorders, and diabetes.

Approximately 27 million older adults have one or more types of cardiovascular disease. Cardiovascular disease refers to a group of disorders related to the heart and circulatory system, including coronary heart disease, which includes myocardial infarctions (heart attack), angina pectoris (chest pain), heart failure, stroke, and hypertension (high blood pressure). Although cardiovascular disease is the number-one cause of death among people over the age of 65, it is not always fatal. Depending on its severity, cardiovascular disease may result in long-term disability and limitations in daily functioning due to fatigue, weakness, shortness of breath, and inability to complete simple daily activities.

Two primary disorders of the musculoskeletal system that affect older adults are arthritis and osteoporosis. Arthritis affects the joints and surrounding tissues, often causing pain, stiffness, or swelling. One half of persons over the age of 65 have some form of arthritis, according to the Centers for Disease Control and Prevention. Degenerative joint disease, or osteoarthritis, is the most common type of arthritis experienced by older adults. It affects the joints most vulnerable to physical stress, including hands, knees, hips, and shoulders. The pervasive and unpredictable nature of osteoarthritis pain can dominate the lives of older adults, limiting their daily activities and abilities to care for themselves. Osteoporosis is characterized by low bone mass to the point where the bone becomes fragile and easily fractures. It is a chronic, progressive disease that affects more than 25 million Americans, 80% of whom are older women. In the early stages of osteoporosis, most people experience unnoticeable or minimal symptoms. As the disease progresses, however, nontraumatic fractures occur (e.g., vertebral, hip, wrist). Many older women also experience pain; physical changes, including deformity; and functional limitations.

Diabetes is a metabolic disorder characterized by a deficiency in either the production or use of insulin. This disease afflicts approximately 7 million people over the age of 65 and is associated with complications in almost every body system; these complications include nerve damage, blindness, renal disorders, harm to the heart, skin problems, and poor circulation. Management of diabetes often requires older adults to make major changes in their diet and care regimes. The interaction of diabetes with other physical health problems can also result in serious health complications that place limitations on daily activities.

Gender, Race/Ethnic, and Age Differences

The presence of chronic physical health conditions varies across subpopulations of older adults. For example, older women are more likely than older men to suffer from arthritis, osteoporosis, hypertension, incontinence, and most types of orthopedic problems. As a result of these conditions, older women are also more likely than older men to have one or more physical limitations, and this gap widens with increasing age. Specifically, women are more likely to have trouble doing many daily activities in late life, including housework, shopping, walking, getting in and out of bed, and bathing.

Similar disparities in chronic health conditions exist between white and nonwhite elders. Older adults of most nonwhite/racial and ethnic groups suffer from chronic conditions at rates twice those of white older adults. African American older adults, for example, experience hypertension, stroke, and diabetes more frequently than white older adults. Onset of chronic disease often occurs at a much younger age among minority elders than for white elders. Older Hispanics experience arthritis and heart disease at rates similar to those of non-Hispanic whites. Their prevalence rate for diabetes,

however, is estimated to be 2 to 4 times higher. Older Native Americans are more likely to have arthritis, congestive heart failure, stroke, asthma, high blood pressure, and diabetes than the general population aged 55 and older.

Mental Health Conditions in Late Life

Approximately 7 million people aged 65 and older in the United States have mental health problems, and that number is expected to double by 2030. Some older adults have had serious mental illnesses (e.g., schizophrenia) most of their adult lives; others have had periodic episodes of mental illness (e.g., depression) throughout their lives or develop mental health problems in late life (e.g., alcoholism). Among the most common mental health problems in late life are depression, anxiety disorders, and dementia.

Depression is a mood disorder typically characterized by feelings of sadness, low energy, and changes in sleep or eating patterns. There are many types of depressive disorders that vary by intensity and duration. Although only about 1% of older adults are diagnosed with a major depressive disorder (e.g., bipolar disorder), 8% to 20% of older adults living in the community report troublesome symptoms of mild or minor depression that do not improve over time. A phenomenon known as late-onset depression is mild or moderate depression that first appears after the age of 60. It typically results from a major life loss (e.g., death of a spouse, change in physical functioning) or life transition (e.g., retirement) with which the person is having difficulty coping. In addition, the onset of depressive symptoms may be a side effect associated with chronic health conditions (e.g., heart disease, diabetes, cancer) or medications that alter brain chemistry. Depressive symptoms are not a normal part of aging and warrant appropriate attention from family members and professionals.

Older adults with anxiety disorders appear more tense and nervous about the future than is warranted by actual circumstances. Late life prevalence rates range from 6% to 33%, the most common type of anxiety disorder among older adults being generalized anxiety disorder. Older persons with generalized anxiety feel an overall, unfocused sense of apprehension and excessively worry about minor problems. Other types of anxiety disorders include panic disorders, phobias, and obsessive-compulsive disorders. Characterized by recurrent episodes of severe anxiety, panic disorders are evidenced by physical and emotional symptoms such as shortness of breath, increased heart rate, and fear. Phobias are irrational and persistent fears of a particular object or situation. A person with obsessive-compulsive disorder has fixated or repetitive thoughts and compulsions, which are repetitive behaviors performed in response to fears (e.g., excessive, repeated hand washing to ward off contamination by germs). Anxiety disorders are particularly difficult to identify among older adults because anxiety related to normative age-related changes (e.g. fears of losing friends or of losing control) may be very real and justifiable in late life. A constant state of worry and anxiousness, however, may seriously affect older people's quality of life, disrupting sleep and causing them to limit daily activities. If untreated, generalized anxiety may also lead to depression.

Dementia represents significant cognitive impairment (e.g., problems with memory, difficulty learning, or decline in problem-solving skills) that interferes with everyday functioning and social relationships. A prominent mental health condition in late life, dementia includes a variety of conditions caused by, or associated with, damage of brain tissue and resulting in changed cognitive functioning, behavior, or personality. According to the Alzheimer's Association, the most frequent type of dementia, Alzheimer's disease, accounts for 60% to 80% of all dementia cases. About 13% or 5.1 million adults aged 65 and older have Alzheimer's disease. Persons with Alzheimer's disease experience gradually worsening trouble remembering new information. As the disease progresses, individuals experience confusion, impaired judgment, trouble expressing themselves, and disorientation. The majority of older adults in the early and mid-stages of Alzheimer's disease remain living in the community with family members providing care and support. In the advanced stages of Alzheimer's disease, older adults need help with bathing, dressing, using the bathroom, eating, and other daily activities, and their ability to communicate significantly declines. These changes often require more intense care than families are able to provide, thus requiring that they move elderly relatives to a nursing home.

Gender, Race/Ethnic, and Age Differences

Older women report a higher prevalence of depressive symptoms and anxiety disorders than older men. More women also have Alzheimer's disease and other dementias, but this is primarily because women typically live longer than men, and their longer life expectancy increases the time during which they can develop dementia.

Some research suggests that African American and Hispanic elders have higher rates of depression and anxiety than their white counterparts, possibly due to greater health burdens, long-term health inequalities, and issues associated with acculturation. Racial and ethnic differences in rates of Alzheimer's disease and other dementias have also been reported, although differences have not been consistently found. Researchers suggest socioeconomic advantages, including greater access to education among white older adults compared to most elders from nonwhite groups, are important factors in explaining this difference.

The prevalence of dementia increases with age. Dementia is found in approximately 5% to 8% of persons aged 65 and older, 15% to 20% of those aged 75 and older, and 25% to 50% of persons aged 85 and older. Some evidence exists that older nonwhite elders have higher rates of Alzheimer's disease than white older adults. Ethnic and cultural barriers hinder the diagnosis of Alzheimer's disease and other dementias, including bias in cognitive screening tests, differences in knowledge and perceptions about Alzheimer's disease, language, and religious beliefs. These factors not only delay access to care but may also lead to misdiagnosis of dementia.

Family Care of Older Adults With Chronic Health Conditions

Family members are a vital source of support and care for older adults with physical and mental health problems. In some families, caregiving for an older relative occurs gradually over time. For others, it can happen overnight. Caregivers may be full- or part-time; they may live with their older relative or provide care from a distance. They provide a wide range of services, from simple help such as grocery shopping, to complex medical procedures, to 24-hour supervision and care.

According to John Rowlands, the nature and expected course of chronic conditions influence the type and amount of care families provide. Progressive chronic diseases, such as Alzheimer's disease, tend to be continually symptomatic and increase in severity. These conditions often cause increasing stress and strain for family members as the demands of caring for their older relatives escalates, requiring more time and attention. In comparison to progressive conditions, constant conditions have an initial event, but then stabilize over time, such as for an older person who has successful bypass surgery to increase the blood flow to his or her heart. Families of elders with these types of conditions typically have a clearer understanding of the type and amount of daily support the older adult needs. The third course of chronic illness, episodic, alternates between relatively stable periods (i.e., mild or no symptoms) and periods of flare-ups. Such conditions often are associated with chronic pain and fatigue and are psychologically stressful for both older adults and their family members; their unpredictability undermines efforts to normalize daily routines and determine care needs.

Along with the nature of the health condition, family norms and relationships strongly influence care situations. Older adults' preferences for family care follow a well-established pattern known as the "hierarchical compensatory" model of care. Spouses are most preferred and most likely to provide care. There are differences, though, in the ways older spouses approach caregiving. Wives are more likely than husbands to be solely responsible for providing hands-on care and support to their ill spouses. Husbands, in contrast, are more likely than wives to receive supplemental assistance from other family members and incorporate formal services. Given the more traditional division of labor among older couples of today, wife-caregivers find themselves assuming new and greater responsibility for male-stereotypic tasks such as yard work, household repairs, and financial management, whereas husband-caregivers are faced with assuming new responsibilities such as household chores. These new tasks present challenges for older wives and husbands that may be viewed as positive when mastered but can increase stress if the ill spouse is reluctant to give up responsibilities or is critical of a partner's performance. Most spouses with limiting physical health conditions are satisfied with the amount and type of support they receive from their partners. If they believe they are receiving more assistance than they really need, however, seemingly helpful behaviors may trigger psychological distress and relationship unhappiness.

If a spouse is unavailable or unable to provide care, help typically comes from adult children or children-in-law. Although a sense of filial responsibility often motivates adult children to help their parents, the pathways to caregiving differ within families. In families with multiple children, one child may become the de facto caregiver because she or he lives closest to the parent, is available, or is perceived by other family members as having the skills and resources necessary to provide the amount and type of care needed. Other families make a conscious choice either for one child to provide the day-to-day care or to share caregiving responsibilities equally. Some adult children report that caring for an aging parent "just happened," evolving over time as their parent experienced changes related to declines in their physical health and the need for support intensified. Although both women and men provide a wide range of help to parents, daughters and daughters-in-law, rather than sons, tend to provide more day-to-day assistance and be involved in more time-consuming tasks such as talking to doctors, arranging for home care, and helping with personal care. However, with smaller families and more women working full-time, more and more men are assuming a greater range of caregiving responsibilities.

Some families include extended kin in the care and support of older relatives. In addition to spouses and adult children, family caregivers to elders with chronic health problems may include grandchildren, siblings, nieces, and nephews. Grandchildren, for example, may initially provide periodic assistance to their grandparents and their caregivers (e.g., driving a grandparent to a doctor's appointment, helping with household chores), eventually stepping in as full-time caregivers after the declining health or death of spouses or adult children who had provided the majority of support for the older family member.

Almost 1 in 4 caregivers specifically provides assistance to a family member with dementia, Alzheimer's disease, mental confusion, or forgetfulness. According to a 2009 report issued by the national Alzheimer's

Association, about 10 million family members provide care for someone with dementia, giving over 8 billion hours of unpaid care and averaging over 16 hours per week. The number of family care hours increases as dementia becomes more severe, with some caregivers providing around-the-clock care. About 60% of family caregivers of elders with dementia are middle-aged daughters or daughters-in-law, but many elderly spouses as well as adult sons also provide care. Some of the most challenging and unique care issues facing family members arise from the impaired memory, cognition, and judgment of the elder with dementia. Nearly one third of Alzheimer's caregivers say they need help managing challenging behaviors, including wandering, a need that is rarely mentioned by caregivers of older adults without dementia. In addition, older persons with dementia are likely to have other chronic physical health conditions that complicate the job of caregiving. Because dementia is a progressive condition, the number of years spent as a caregiver can be lengthy. More than one third of family caregivers for dementia sufferers provide care from 1 to 4 years; in about one third of families, care is provided for 5 years or more.

Bidirectionality of Chronic Health Problems Within Families

Family members who care for older relatives with chronic health problems fulfill an important role not only for the elders they assist but for society as a whole. Family care, typically unpaid, has an estimated economic value of $375 billion annually, which is how much it would cost to replace that care with paid services. Being a family caregiver, however, may take a personal toll on a person's health and well-being.

Studies of the effects of caregiving on the physical health of care providers present mixed results. Some researchers suggest that caregivers and noncaregivers are comparable in their physical well-being, whereas others report significantly poorer health among caregivers. Caregiving may affect health by physically straining and exhausting the caregiver or by influencing adverse caregiver health behaviors (e.g., by interfering with sleep, limiting exercise, or not going to the doctor when sick). This is particularly true for spouse caregivers, who often jeopardize their own health in the process of caring for their partners. Indicators of poor mental health,

including depression, anger, and anxiety, are also frequently found among relatives providing care to older adults. Evidence strongly indicates that rates of depression are higher among caregivers than noncaregivers. The type of health condition facing the elder helps determine caregiver outcomes. Typically, caregivers of relatives with cognitive impairments experience higher levels of stress than those caring for family members with physical impairment.

The strains experienced by caregivers are not strictly internal but carry over to other roles and relationships. Conflict among roles is a common source of distress for family caregivers who report forfeiting other activities and relationships to satisfy their relative's care demands. Caregivers typically report feeling they have no time for themselves or others. They may feel isolated and alone as a result of lost social contacts or, perhaps more devastating, the loss of normative roles and relationships (e.g., husband–wife, mother–daughter). This sense of loss or deprivation is greater among caregivers of persons who exhibit a loss of cognitive functioning and is associated with higher levels of depression among caregivers and poorer assessment of the quality of the caregiver and elder's relationship.

Many family caregivers juggle work with caregiving responsibilities. Adult children in particular often get caught in the middle as they try to balance family care and career. They frequently wind up distracted at work, emotionally drained, and physically exhausted. Although many employers are sympathetic to the demands of caring for elderly relatives, employed caregivers are often reluctant to inform supervisors about caregiving obligations, fearing disclosure will affect job security or career prospects.

Financial strain among caregivers interacts with role strain, as caregivers find they are challenged to meet the financial demands necessitated by their family member's care. Concerns about financial resources may result from caregivers reducing work hours or leaving work to provide full-time care and incurring additional expenses associated with the care of their older relatives (e.g., special foods, respite care). Not counting spouse caregivers, family caregivers spend an average of about $600 of their own money on the care of elderly relatives in a typical month. Caregivers often report spending money they saved for their own retirement, reducing their contributions to savings, and even going into debt to be able to manage care responsibilities.

Although there is still a tendency for scholars to focus on the negative outcomes of family care of older adults with chronic physical and mental health conditions, more recent research has identified positive dimensions of the family caregiving experience. Family caregivers frequently report that caregiving makes them feel needed, useful, and good about themselves. Providing care enables them to appreciate life more and strengthens, their relationships with elderly relatives. The development of a sense of competence as a caregiver and effective coping skills that promote self-efficacy also enhances the well-being of family caregivers.

Support for Families With Chronic Physical and Mental Health Conditions

Programs designed to meet the mental health needs of family caregivers include education programs, individual and family counseling, support groups, and respite care services. Successful education, prevention, and intervention efforts to reach caregivers require culturally competent leaders who recognize and reinforce the basic family infrastructure and acknowledge the family's desire to remain self-reliant. Evaluations of caregiver intervention strategies suggest positive outcomes for the caregivers who participate. Unfortunately, a limited number of family caregivers take advantage of these programs or use services that may enhance their ability to provide care.

Education Programs

Community educational programs are a common, low-cost means of providing information to individuals faced with the challenges of providing care for aging relatives. Most programs are designed for spouses and adult children who have assumed primary responsibility for a family member experiencing physical or cognitive problems. Programs typically focus on a variety of topics, such as normal aging, chronic illness management, communication skills, coping and problem solving, living arrangements, and community resources.

Caregivers of older adults with severe physical conditions or cognitive impairment often find it difficult to attend community programs. With the widespread availability of technology, many caregivers now have the opportunity to participate in programs delivered in their homes by teleconferencing and the Internet. For example, the Alzheimer's Association offers multiple publications with information, tips, and resources for family caregivers on their website. In addition to print material, the Family Care Alliance offers teleconference seminars as an educational alternative for caregivers.

Individual Counseling and Family Counseling

Family members are often reluctant to admit they are having difficulties managing the stress associated with their caregiving responsibilities. Individual counseling can be an effective intervention that helps caregivers express their thoughts, feelings, and concerns in a safe setting. One of the goals of individual counseling is to help the person develop coping strategies to manage caregiving strain. Caregivers participating in counseling demonstrate more effective coping skills, improved psychological well-being, and improved relationships with their older relatives as compared to family caregivers who do not receive counseling.

Many caregivers need counseling services that will work with multiple family members who are involved in either the direct care of elders or whose relationships with the caregivers are altered (e.g., spouse and children of an adult child caregiver). Family interventions emphasize the educational, relational, and personal needs of all family members. Participating in family interventions improves caregiver well-being, access to social support, and use of community resources. In addition, when families collectively learn to manage the stress of their situation, they are often able to provide in-home care for their elderly relatives for a longer period of time.

Family interventions can take a variety of forms. Psychoeducational programs provide information about how disease management affects family relationships, decision making, and problem solving among family members over time. These efforts are directed at increasing disease comprehension to improve personal and relational coping. A second type of intervention focuses on improving the quality of relationships among family members with respect to the disease. A variety of group-based strategies are used to foster emotional expressiveness, reduce social isolation, prevent the disease from dominating family life, promote collaboration and problem solving among family members, enhance conflict resolution, and reduce stigma. The third type of intervention is family therapy. The approach often benefits families with problematic preexisting or disease-induced dysfunctional relationships.

One promising approach designed specifically for families of older adults with memory problems is known as caregiver family therapy (CFT). Developed by Sara Honn Qualls and her colleagues, CFT has the goals of helping families support independence for their elder members, aiding caregivers in developing supportive relationships with other family members, evaluating the needs of all family members, and assisting families in reorganizing their relationships in ways that support and sustain one another. In CFT, families participate in three sessions in which counselors assess the elder's ability to manage personal care, family member medical histories, family values, degree of family involvement, and what solutions the client has tried to cope with the problem. Sessions may involve individual counseling as well as family counseling, and sometimes include persons outside the family, such as doctors or clergy who are involved in the older adult's care.

CFT works to identify the problem in the family and restructure the family so that members meet the elder's needs and support each other in caregiving. Well-functioning families typically require first-order change, where the entire family is made aware of the problem and works together to find solutions. Other families are incapable of responding to interventions directed at first-order change because of family dynamics that make needed change impossible. For instance in families where no one is willing or able to provide care, members disagree about the elder's condition, individuals are unwilling to restructure family roles, or the family has ineffective communication patterns, the therapist may have to address long-standing family dysfunction.

Support Groups

Support groups, a popular form of caregiver education and intervention, also are widely available and generally well attended by white individuals caring for older relatives. They usually are not well attended by nonwhite individuals caring for older relatives, perhaps because of caregivers' reliance on other family members for caregiving assistance and strong cultural norms of family responsibility.

The typical support group is composed of predominantly middle-class women, mostly the wives and daughters of individuals with some form of cognitive impairment. In some communities, support groups are ongoing; in others they are time limited (e.g., six to eight sessions). Support groups typically provide both education and support and are built around seven major themes: information about the care receiver's situation, the group and its members as a mutual support system, the emotional impact of caregiving, self-care, interpersonal relationships, the use of support systems outside the group, and home care skills.

Respite Services

Respite programs provide temporary, short-term supervisory, personal, and nursing care to older adults with physical and mental impairments. Programs offer respite services in the older person's home or at a specific site in the community. Adult day services (ADS), a structured, community-based, comprehensive respite program, have received the greatest amount of attention from the research community. ADS provide a variety of health, social, and related support services in a protective setting during any part of a day (not 24-hour care). These programs typically offer some combination of health and therapeutic services for participants while meeting their socialization needs through the provision of individual and group activities and shared meals. The National Association of Adult Day Services reports that typical adult day care participants are women in their early 70s, white, living with a spouse, adult child, or other family member, and needing help with personal care tasks and/or suffering cognitive limitations.

Reports of caregivers' satisfaction with ADS are uniformly high, but analysis of benefits for the caregivers have had mixed results. Some investigators have reported that day programs have little or no effect on caregiver burden or well-being, but these studies often included caregivers who had very low rates of utilization. Research examining consistent, adequate levels of ADS present more promising results, suggesting that ADS use results in reduced time spent caregiving, reduced care-related stressors (e.g., feelings of overload and strain), improved physical and mental health, better relationships, and increased confidence in caregiving abilities.

Conclusion

When older adults are faced with chronic physical and mental health conditions, they most often rely on immediate family members for help and support. Family roles and expectations repeatedly change as a result of the elder's need for care. Relationships intensify and interactions may be strained as family members take on, or have thrust upon them, caregiving responsibilities. A decline in an older spouse's health almost inevitably places his or her partner in the role of primary caregiver. Adult children and children-in-law frequently provide long-term care for their parents with physical or cognitive limitations. Most family caregivers live either with, or in close proximity to, the older relative for whom they provide care. Regardless of age, sex, and race and ethnicity, a great deal of evidence has accumulated indicating that family caregiving often has a negative impact on caregivers' health and well-being. Although caregiving can be stressful, its effects can be mitigated at least partially by participation in educational and support programs, individual and family counseling, and use of respite services. As individuals are living longer and more family members occupy the role of caregiver, services and interventions for family caregivers will be in greater demand.

Karen A. Roberto

See also Aging and Shifting Roles in Families; Alzheimer's Disease: An Overview of Family Issues in; Alzheimer's Disease: Caregiver Burden; Caregiving: Elderly; Chronic Health Problems and Interventions for the Elderly Family

Further Readings

Qualls, S. H., & Zarit, S. H. (Eds.). (2009). *Aging families and caregiving.* Hoboken, NJ: Wiley.
Roberto, K. A., & Jarrott, S. E. (2008). Family caregivers of older adults: A life span perspective. *Family Relations, 57,* 100–111.

Rollands, J. S. (1994). *Families, illness, & disabilities: An integrated treatment model.* New York: Basic Books.
Smyer, M. A., & Qualls, S. H. (1999). *Aging and mental health.* Malden, MA: Blackwell.
Vierck, E., & Hodges, K. (2003). *Aging: Demographics, health, and health services.* Westport, CT: Greenwood Press.

Websites

Agency for Healthcare Research and Quality: http://www.ahrq.gov/research/elderdis.htm
Alzheimer's Association: http://www.alz.org/index.asp
Centers for Disease Control and Prevention: http://www.cdc.gov
Family Caregiver Alliance: http://www.caregiver.org/caregiver/jsp/home.jsp
National Alliance for Caregiving: http://www.caregiving.org

FAMILY ADHERENCE TO HEALTH CARE REGIMEN

Fostering healthy behaviors and managing chronic medical conditions are essential family actions. In 2009 nearly half of all Americans had a chronic medical condition, according to the Robert Wood Johnson Foundation. Effective management of chronic conditions may require adherence to a variety of health behaviors, including exercise, dietary modification, daily disease monitoring, keeping medical appointments, and taking prescription medications. Adherence can be essential to good health outcomes.

Adherence to Medical Treatment

The term *adherence* (also called compliance) involves accurately implementing a health care recommendation or treatment prescribed by a health care professional. Faithful adherence for many chronic disease conditions is remarkably low. Based on a meta-analysis of 569 studies of adherence conducted by M. Robin DiMatteo, at least 1 in 4 patients is nonadherent to their physician's advice. For some conditions and treatment recommendations, nonadherence is much higher.

Nonadherence has many serious implications for health outcomes and medical expenses. Symptoms can be exacerbated, unexplained relapses can occur, and functioning and well-being can be impaired. Subsequently, medical decisions may be misinformed and result in improper changes to the medical treatment or unnecessary tests. For example, a physician who is unaware of patient nonadherence may increase or change medication in light of an ineffective clinical response, not realizing that the initial dosing was never followed. Michael Sokol and colleagues note that nonadherence contributes to an increase in emergency room visits, a greater risk of hospitalization, and higher medical costs. The New England Healthcare Institute estimates the yearly cost of drug-related problems, including nonadherence to medications, to be approximately $290 billion in the United States.

The likelihood of adhering to a health care regimen varies based on a number of factors, according to the DiMatteo meta-analysis. For instance, the average rate of adherence ranges from 65% for sleep disorders to over 88% for HIV. Age is also associated with adherence: the average adherence rate for adults is higher than for children (77% vs. 71%). Further, people are more likely to adhere to medication regimens than to regimens that require health behavior changes (such as diet, exercise, glucose monitoring, and physical therapy).

Families can help, or hinder, the achievement of members' health behaviors and adherence to treatment. This entry discusses the social and psychological factors in families that can affect an individual's adherence to medical recommendations. Here, family is defined as a household unit that includes parents or guardians, adult and pediatric children, relatives, and other individuals living in the home. A family shares norms, habits, and experiences that can influence and shape the health of its members.

Family Psychosocial Factors Affecting Adherence

Adhering to a medical regimen is rarely an individual matter. Family members are often required to communicate with medical professionals, understand and accept treatment, monitor health status, and perform essential activities to implement a prescribed regimen. When children experience acute or chronic illnesses, their parents, siblings, and extended family members frequently assume significant responsibility for their care. As individuals enter adolescence, complex developmental challenges affect adherence. Among adults, family responsibilities, pressures, and interpersonal dynamics can either support health-promoting efforts or provide numerous opportunities for intentional and unintentional nonadherence.

Family Dynamics

Managing an illness can be psychologically and physically demanding. Thus, positive family interactions and supportive family attitudes are conducive to adherence. Patients in cohesive families (i.e., warm, accepting, and emotionally healthy) are more likely to be adherent; those in conflict-ridden families with negative emotional interactions tend to be less adherent. In pediatric diabetes, for example, high stress contributes to poor glycemic control both directly, by affecting metabolic functioning, and indirectly, by leading to poor adherence and ineffective regimen management.

Family size can affect adherence. For adults, being married or living with others promotes adherence, perhaps due to the support, reminders, and accountability from a household member. Larger households, however, place greater demands on parents; they are often required to balance limited energy, resources, and time between an ill child and those who are well. Research suggests that the more people there are living in a household, the lower a child's adherence will be. Moreover, the attitudes and behaviors of siblings may have a profound impact on a chronically ill child's treatment adherence.

Social Support

Support from family and friends can promote adherence in all age groups by enhancing the health care recipient's optimism and self-esteem, ameliorating depression, and reducing stress. Although emotional support is important for adherence, practical social support—such as reminders about medical appointments and assistance with the regimen itself—has a slightly stronger impact. Family members are more likely to provide practical support to health care consumers, whereas peers tend to provide emotional support and companionship. Overprotective families may socially isolate the patient and thus inadvertently contribute to poor adherence; companionship from peers can protect against social isolation.

Perceived Severity

Parents' perceptions of the severity of their children's conditions affect their willingness and ability to adhere to required care, according to M. Robin DiMatteo, Kelly Haskard, and Summer Williams. For less serious conditions (e.g., sore throat, middle ear infection), parents are more adherent when they believe their children are in poorer health. Conversely, for more serious diseases (e.g., cancer, end-stage renal disease, diabetes), children judged by their parents to be in poorer health have worse adherence. When a child is severely ill with a serious disease, parents may be less adherent; this situation may be due to denial, doubts about treatment efficacy, or a desire to protect the child from uncomfortable medical interventions. Adult health care recipients show a similar pattern: Among those diagnosed with more serious diseases, individuals in poorer health are less adherent than those in better health.

Parental and Child Beliefs

Parents' beliefs about their children's medical conditions and treatments are vital to adherence. For many chronic illnesses, mothers and children who perceive relatively greater benefits and fewer barriers to treatment are more adherent. Parents and adolescents who have high perceived self-efficacy (i.e., believe they are capable of completing the regimen tasks) are more adherent than those with low self-efficacy. However, parents of a sick child are less likely to be adherent if they do not agree on the treatment strategy or if their beliefs are not congruent with those of the physician. Parents are less adherent when they question the diagnosis, when they are unfamiliar with the physician, or when they distrust the physician. Further, some parents believe that their child will "outgrow" a chronic illness (such as asthma) and may stop adhering when the child is asymptomatic.

Communication With Health Professionals

Effective communication between health professionals and care recipients (and caregivers) involves information sharing, question asking and answering, collaborative decision making, shared treatment planning, empathy, and understanding. Effective interactions and communication with the child's physician lead parents to be more adherent to their child's treatment. Psychosocial concerns associated with health (such as family norms and attitudes that conflict with the prescribed regimen) must be raised for discussion during the medical visit. Although many parents believe that such discussion with their child's physician is important, they are often reluctant to raise these concerns. Observations of the family's situation and frank discussion of psychosocial issues are essential to meeting their needs for support and care.

Decades of research show that interactions between physicians (and other health professionals) and their adult patients are generally not effective enough to promote adequate adherence. Physicians often fail to provide sufficient medical information and tend to be vague in their instructions and recommendations. Many adults leave their physicians' offices without understanding the regimen and its purpose well enough to be adherent.

Age-Specific Adherence Problems

Adolescents

Compared to younger pediatric patients, adolescents are at a greater risk of nonadherence. An adolescent may not have yet developed the expected skills and maturity to assume responsibility for managing a chronic illness. Parents and health professionals must carefully evaluate an adolescent's competence because premature transition of regimen responsibilities from parent to child can lead to nonadherence. Adolescents are also more likely than younger children to test the boundaries of their health and to be skeptical of the long-term benefits of treatment that is unpleasant in the short term. Some may refuse to take medication in front of peers and abandon treatments that threaten their ability to "fit in." Adolescents facing multiple risk factors may be particularly vulnerable to nonadherence. For example, one study showed that adolescents with end-stage renal disease who were nonadherent to immunosuppressive treatment tended to be depressed, lacked social support, had low self-esteem, and had difficulty communicating to family members and medical professionals.

Older Adults

Older adults face special challenges that affect their willingness and ability to adhere to medical recommendations. Older adults are more likely than younger adults to be socially isolated, limited in mobility, lacking adequate financial resources, and struggling with sensory and cognitive impairments (e.g., poor hearing, eyesight, memory) that affect adherence. Mental health problems, particularly depression, are also more prevalent among older adults. Research indicates that the pessimism, social isolation, and cognitive deficits that accompany depression can contribute significantly to poor adherence.

Physicians communicate differently to older people than to younger ones. They give older patients relatively less information, less choice in their care, and less guidance about the procedures of the physical examination. Due to time limitations or the constraints of the physician–patient interaction, older patients fail to discuss as many as half of their medical and psychosocial symptoms. Some older individuals rely on caregivers and family members to help with their medical visits and treatment regimens, but the presence of a third person (such as a spouse, adult child, friend, or hired caregiver) can dramatically alter the dynamics of the medical visit. When a companion is present in the examination room, older patients raise fewer topics, are less responsive on the topics they do raise, are less expressive and assertive, and are less likely to engage in joint decision making. Physicians tend to speak to the third person, excluding the health care recipient from the conversation. Under some circumstances, a companion can facilitate the medical interaction, such as by asking the individual questions, prompting the individual to speak, and encouraging the individual to be active in medical decision making.

Recommendations

Families can exert a powerful influence on a person's health behaviors, treatment adherence, and chronic disease management. The process of medical care should take into account each patient's family context when providing information to patients. Treatment recommendations and their purpose should be clearly understood, and participation of relevant family members in medical decisions should be encouraged. The concerns of family members should be addressed, including fears, beliefs about the treatment, and family norms and attitudes about the disease and the treatment regimen. Providers should address patient and caregiver commitment (such as by asking the patient, "How will you take your medication?") and ask how the family is managing the chronic illness of its member. Input from chronically ill children and their well siblings can be very important to the care process, and adolescents should be assisted in their transition to independent care of their illnesses. Adults' challenges in coping with the added responsibilities of chronic illness in the family should be assessed, and providers should listen carefully for signs of family stress and conflict. Potential depression in family members should be assessed and treated, and guidance in obtaining resources for coping (such as community support groups) should be offered. Attention should be paid to the experience of potentially vulnerable older health care recipients.

Conclusion

An individual's health outcomes are strongly influenced by his or her family context. Families can have a powerful effect on the management of chronic illness by influencing a person's commitment, motivation, and ability to follow recommended medical treatments. To ensure optimal health behavior and adherence to medical regimens, health professionals should be aware of, and address, issues of concern for patients and their families.

M. Robin DiMatteo and Nancy L. Sin

See also Chronic Illness and Family Management Styles; Communication in Families Related to Health and Illness; Partnering With Families: Family-Centered Care; Role of Families in Health Promotion

Further Readings

Anderson, G. (2010, February). *Chronic care: Making the case for ongoing care.* Princeton, NJ: Robert Wood Johnson Foundation. Retrieved from http://www.rwjf.org/pr/product.jsp?id=50968

DiMatteo, M. R. (2004). Variations in patients' adherence to medical recommendations: A quantitative review of 50 years of research. *Medical Care, 42,* 200–209.

DiMatteo, M. R., Haskard, K. B., & Williams, S. L. (2007). Health beliefs, disease severity, and patient adherence: A meta-analysis. *Medical Care, 45,* 521–528.

DiMatteo, M. R., & Martin, L. R. (2002). *Health psychology.* Boston: Allyn & Bacon.

Drotar, D. (Ed.). (2000). *Promoting adherence to medical treatment in childhood chronic illness: Concepts, methods, and interventions.* Mahwah, NJ: Erlbaum.

Johnson, S. B., Perry, N. W., & Rozensky, R. (Eds.). (2002). *Handbook of clinical health psychology,* vol.1: *Medical disorders and behavioral applications.* Washington, DC: APA Press.

Martin, L. R., Haskard-Zolnierek, K. B., & DiMatteo, M. R. (2010). *Health behavior change and treatment adherence: Evidence-based guidelines for improving healthcare.* New York: Oxford University Press.

New England Healthcare Institute. (2009, August). *Thinking outside the pillbox: A system-wide approach to improving patient medication adherence for chronic disease.* Retrieved from http://www.nehi.net/uploads/full_report/pa_issue_brief__final.pdf

Roter, D. L., & Hall, J. A. (2006). *Doctors talking to patients/patients talking to doctors: Improving communication in medical visits* (2nd ed.). Westport, CT: Praeger.

Sokol, M. C., McGuigan, K. A., Verbrugge, R. R., & Epstein, R. S. (2005). Impact of medication adherence on hospitalization risk and healthcare cost. *Medical Care, 43,* 521–530.

Family Caregiving: Caring for Children, Adults, and Elders With Developmental Disabilities

The Centers for Disease Control and Prevention report that *developmental disabilities* are severe chronic conditions involving physical and/or mental impairments that begin before 22 years of age. People with developmental disabilities (PWDD) often have problems with language, mobility, learning, self-care, and independent living. Caring for children, adults, and elders with developmental disorders often extends over a lifetime, and family caregivers describe caregiving demands in the home as challenging and even overwhelming at times. This entry describes stressors commonly encountered by family caregivers in caring for children, adults, and elders with developmental disabilities. Emphasis is on interventions or support services to lessen these stressors and improve the physiological and psychosocial well-being of these family caregivers.

Historical Context

The majority of PWDD live with their family. The remaining live either independently or in long-term care community settings. Community-based long-term care settings include group homes, foster care, supervised apartments, and supported living. Unique needs of PWDD dictate the assistance they receive, such as help with budgeting, shopping, and household and personal care tasks. Family caregivers often provide partial or complete care in their home or assist with these tasks in community based long-term care settings, including coordinating services between health care providers and service agencies, administering medications, serving as a liaison between the person with developmental disabilities and health providers during medical visits, and delivering other care.

Definition of Family Caregiving and Associated Stressors

Family caregiving involves assisting individuals who are chronically ill or disabled, such as children, adults, and elders with developmental disabilities who are no longer able to care for themselves. Family caregivers provide the majority of long-term care services in the United States, and according to the National Family Caregivers Association, these services are conservatively valued at $375 billion a year.

Several stressors mark the lives of family caregivers of PWDD, including receiving inadequate information about, and assistance in, accessing support services and adjuncts that are a necessity in caring for someone with developmental disabilities. According to Ya-Mei Chen, Susan C. Hedrick, and Heather M. Young, these support services and adjuncts include caregiver counseling, caregiver training and education, financial assistance, respite services, case coordination, housework assistance, delivered meals, and transportation.

This information often comes from other people who have a family member with a developmental disability, other family members, and friends.

Families who care for a child, adult, or elder with challenging behaviors also experience additional stressors. Parents, in particular, report problems with accessing appropriate, high-quality services and obtaining relevant information. For example, respite often is either inadequate or unavailable to caregivers who need an occasional rest from caregiving while ensuring their family member is well cared for. Other concerns are insufficient input by caregivers into their family member's care and exclusion of the child, adult, or elder with challenging behaviors from support services.

Desirable Outcomes for Family Caregivers

Empirical data concerning family caregivers show desirable outcomes, such as less depression and better quality of life and life satisfaction. Several studies examining the health status of parents of adults with developmental disabilities report that their health status is similar to that of the general population, suggesting that these parents may be motivated to stay healthy. Family caregivers of children with developmental disabilities commonly experience more depression, whereas those with adult children may not experience depression, perhaps because they provide companionship as they age. Older caregivers tend to have a lower quality of life, less family support, and greater worries about future care arrangements of adults with developmental disabilities.

Several factors influence the physical and psychosocial well-being of these family caregivers, including characteristics of PWDD, socioeconomic status, cultural context, and extent of social participation. Families who have more social support, family cohesion, and active coping have lower burden and depression. Unsurprisingy, fewer maladaptive behaviors, better health, and less social impairment of PWDD are associated with fewer caregiving strains.

Some families, including cultural minorities and families of adults with challenging behaviors, are at risk for poorer physical and psychosocial outcomes. However, African Americans have better outcomes than whites when exposed to the stress of providing care to a disabled family member.

Interventions to Improve the Physical and Psychosocial Well-Being of Family Caregivers

Most often, caregiving is unpaid. Managing multiple roles besides that of a caregiver to a child, adult, or elder with developmental disabilities can be challenging. This section contains general caregiving strategies as well as interventions or programs that studies suggest may be useful. General caregiving strategies include encouraging caregivers to obtain caregiver support, gain power through knowledge and achievements, and balance time for family caregiving and others.

Obtain Caregiver Support

Suggestions to obtain caregiving support include the following: (a) Identify people who can provide different types of support (e.g., spouses, friends, siblings) and accept when they offer their assistance in caregiving. (b) Make a list of tasks and responsibilities that other people can assist with when they offer but are unsure how they can best help. (c) Talk with friends and share with them how beneficial their help is when they do things, such as eating together socially, shopping, and watching movies. (d) Talk with friends and share with them how beneficial their help is when they assist with caregiving responsibilities that are challenging, such as providing transportation to medical and therapy appointments or providing respite. (e) Join a local or online support group that includes people who are having similar experiences. (f) Talk with social workers and other health professionals about services and support services that are available to caregivers.

Gain Power Through Knowledge and Achievements

Suggestions to gain power through knowledge and achievements include the following: (a) Learn about PWDD and their condition from a variety of people, including health care providers and other family caregivers, and share caregiving problems and discuss possible solutions with them. (b) Encourage independence of family members with developmental disabilities. (c) Identify caregiving problems and challenges and establish goals and potential solutions for solving them. Write down goals and solutions and post them in a visible place (e.g., write them on a board on the wall) where PWDD and others will see them daily. Establish goals for both PWDD and caregivers (e.g., at least 1 hour each day for health and enjoyment activities, such as a brisk walk or reading). (d) Recognize it may be hard for PWDD and caregivers to recognize significant achievements.

Keep a diary or post on a wall about family members with developmental disabilities regarding their activities of daily living, instrumental activities of daily living, behavior, or motivation. Also identify feelings and activities (physical, emotional, social, etc.) experienced as caregivers. Review these activities and abilities every 3 months to see what achievements have been gained. Celebrate achievements of both caregivers and PWDD.

Balance Time for Family Caregiving and Others

Caregivers take care of PWDD by first taking care of themselves. It is important to balance family caregiving and other roles. Both caregivers and PWDD are valuable and deserve time and attention. Family members can learn to balance these responsibilities by allocating time for family caregiving, themselves as caregivers, other family members, and friends. Adequate attention should be devoted to friendships and social activities. Family caregivers can also arrange for regular respite, both short and long. They can schedule short breaks such as reading a book, walking, or taking a relaxing bath. Long breaks also are essential. Caregivers could arrange for a vacation or trip with family and friends.

Better caregiver support services and adjuncts are essential. For example, using consulting and education services is associated with less subjective caregiver burden and tends to improve caregivers' relationships with PWDD. Talking with another person or attending a support group or counseling class lessens negative caregiver emotions and prevents caregiver burnout. What is unclear is whether these services are useful to caregivers who provide care to children, adults, and elders with developmental disabilities with severe deficits. Caregivers with family members who have severe deficits have more difficulty using resources because the affected family member cannot be left unattended.

A significant gap in the literature is information or programs that would assist caregivers to access available services in a more efficient manner. These services include those discussed previously, as well as environmental adaptations, assistive devices, mental health care, crisis intervention, and behavior management. Family caregiving for PWDD often occurs with little warning, and family members have no time to prepare themselves as caregivers. They experience uncertainty and fail to know what services are available to them. Accessing services takes time and effort and adds to caregiver stress and burden.

Implications for Future Family Health Care

One of the priorities of family caregivers is to be assured their loved one with developmental disabilities will be well cared for when they die. Children often live significant distances from their parents, and working adults have less time to care for siblings with disabilities when their parents become unable to provide care. Aging parents who care for their child with a developmental disability need to develop plans to ensure their children receive necessary supports when they are unable to continue to provide care. Plans for guardianship, living arrangements, health care, advance directives, and financial planning for the child, adult, or elder with developmental disabilities are essential. Although siblings commonly assume care for PWDD, they often are not included in discussions of future plans for their siblings.

Given the long waiting lists for long-term care services, barriers to implementing such services are significant. The expansion of the elderly population, both those providing care as well as PWDD, necessitates funding to provide adequate support services. As family caregivers age, this increased need for support services will require adequately trained staff to implement these programs. This area is especially valuable for family caregivers of people with challenging behaviors who are often excluded from respite care. Health care professionals, therefore, need a more proactive approach to developing supportive services and programs that meet the needs of family caregivers of PWDD.

Joan S. Grant and Norman Lee Keltner

See also Caregivers of Adults With Developmental Disabilities; Caregiving: Adults With Developmental Disabilities; Caregiving: Elderly

Further Readings

Chen, Y. M., Hedrick, S. C., & Young, H. M. (2010). A pilot evaluation of the Family Caregiver Support Program. *Evaluation and Program Planning, 33*(2), 113–119.

Chou, Y. C., Lee, Y. C., Lin, L. C., Kröger, T., & Chang, A. N. (2009). Older and younger family caregivers of adults with intellectual disability: Factors associated with future plans. *Intellectual and Developmental Disabilities, 47*, 282–294.

Eisenhower, A. S., Baker, B. L., & Blacher, J. (2009). Children's delayed development and behavior problems: Impact on mothers' perceived physical health across early childhood. *Social Science & Medicine, 68*(1), 89–99.

Heller, T., Caldwell, J., & Factor, A. (2007). Aging family caregivers: Policies and practices. *Mental Retardation and Developmental Disabilities Research Reviews, 13*(2), 136–142.

Hsieh, R. L., Huang, H. Y., Lin, M. I., Wu, C. W., & Lee, W. C. (2009). Quality of life, health satisfaction and family impact on caregivers of children with developmental delays. *Child: Care, Health, and Development, 35*, 243–249.

McGill, P., Papachristoforou, E., & Cooper, V. (2006). Support for family carers of children and young people with developmental disabilities and challenging behaviour. *Child: Care, Health, and Development, 32*(2), 159–165.

Orsmond, G. I., Seltzer, M. M., Greenberg, J. S., Krauss M. W. (2006). Mother–child relationship quality among adolescents and adults with autism. *American Journal of Mental Retardation, 111*(2), 121–137.

Paczkowski, E., & Baker, B. L. (2007). Parenting children with and without developmental delay: The role of self-mastery. *Journal of Intellectual Disability Research, 51*(Pt. 6), 435–446.

Parish, S. L., & Lutwick, Z. E. (2005). A critical analysis of the emerging crisis in long-term care for people with developmental disabilities. *Social Work, 50*, 345–354.

Singer, G. H. (2006). Meta-analysis of comparative studies of depression in mothers of children with and without developmental disabilities. *American Journal of Mental Retardation, 111*(3), 155–169.

Wodehouse, G., & McGill, P. (2009). Support for family carers of children and young people with developmental disabilities and challenging behaviour: What stops it being helpful? *Journal of Intellectual Disability Research, 53*, 644–653.

Websites

Centers for Disease Control and Prevention, Developmental Disabilities: http://www.cdc.gov/ncbddd/dd/default.htm

Centers for Disease Control and Prevention, Families With Special Needs, Caregiving Tips: http://www.cdc.gov/family/specialneeds

National Family Caregivers Association: http://www.thefamilycaregiver.org

Family Conflict Related to Caregiving

Family conflict can be defined as a disagreement or differences in the beliefs, ideals, or goals between two or more members of a family or kinship network. Disagreements may involve people, groups, or systems outside of the immediate social sphere. In families in which one or more of the members has a chronic illness or disability, assistance with care is often provided by relatives. In many families, one person assumes the responsibility for the majority of the assistance given to the care recipient. In other situations, the primary provider may be assisted by a secondary person and/or other caregivers who provide supplemental care for specific tasks and offer respite, financial assistance, or other help. In a few families, caregiving responsibilities are distributed among various family members and friends. Conflicts frequently arise among family members because of the emotional connections between them, their concern about the care recipient, the closeness and frequency of their interactions, long-term family ties, and historical patterns.

The focus of this entry is on family conflict when providing care for a family member with a chronic illness or disability. It provides an overview of the context of caregiving, reviews the theoretical foundations in the family conflict literature, discusses causes of conflict, reviews recommendations for prevention and management of caregiving conflict, and concludes with societal implications. The content is presented from a broad perspective of the overall problem rather than from an age- or disease-specific perspective.

Context of Care

There are approximately 50 million people who provide care for a chronically ill or disabled family member or friend. The age range of the care recipient extends across the life span from infants and children to the very old. Causes of illness and disability are varied as well. The amount, extent, duration, type, physical and mental strain, and other social and economic factors influence the effect that caregiving has on the family. For example, the types of conflicts related to parenting an adolescent with insulin-dependent diabetes are very different from those experienced by a daughter caring for an elderly parent with dementia. The average family caregiver is 47 years old. Almost 34 million adults provide care to someone 50 years or older. Of those, 9 million care for someone with dementia. The number of unpaid family caregivers is expected to increase to 37 million by the year 2050, according to the Family Caregiver Alliance. Most of the caregiving literature focuses on the stress and burden of caring for an elderly family member with dementia; thus the evidence related to caregiving and family conflict is predominantly concentrated in this group.

Theories in Family Conflict

A variety of theories have been applied to advance the understanding of conflict in families. Family conflict theory states that families seek to resolve conflict and maintain order by agreeing on solutions through confrontation, compromise, and influence over others, often based on power, wealth, advantage, and even aggression. Conflicts about roles may occur when one person interferes or disagrees with the behavior or role that is assumed by another person within the family. Studies that have applied this theory in caregiving research have found that type of conflict in the family. In addition, conflict occurs related to expectations about who should take on the role of primary caregiver and decision maker, the types of duties assumed by the men and women in the family, rivalry among siblings about who stands to gain or lose the most in the situation, and inequalities in the duties or tasks. Role conflict may also occur when one person assumes several roles (e.g., mother, daughter, caregiver), when there is disagreement over how a person in a specific role should behave and what they should do, and when a person is forced to take on a role that he or she does not want.

In general, the larger the family is, the greater is the risk for conflict about caregiving issues. Using conflict theory, examples of conflict among family members that have been identified include situations in which an adult child who is not directly involved in caregiving becomes critical about the amount or type of care provided to the parent ("She'll never get better if you don't make her do it herself"), or an adult child attempting to override a parent's end-of-life decisions because of his or her own wishes rather than those of the parent. In addition, power struggles between adult children over who has the capacity to make decisions about health care for their elderly parent are common. In times of conflict, it is not unusual for previous resentments and animosities between various family members to surface when attempting to work through disagreements about caregiving.

In looking at families from the perspective of resilience, the ability of a family to remain or become stable in challenging situations is examined. An example of a challenging situation is that of providing care for a dependent member of the family. Characteristics of a resilient family include shared beliefs and values, a sense of unity or solidarity, ability to communicate openly with each other, ability to work through dilemmas together, and being open to change and willing to adapt. Families who are successful with caring for an ill family member are able to (a) identify the positive aspects, (b) adapt using environmental resources, and (c) discover strengths from within the family. For example, in some families one person is selected to be the decision maker while all other members agree to accept it. It is also suggested that when family members communicate clearly and discuss openly the reason for the conflict, misunderstandings can be resolved. In 20% to 30% of families, caregivers realigned their work schedules, reduced their working hours, or changed jobs to alleviate stress and role conflicts.

Another model evaluates the degree of investment that a person has in a relationship. Responses to tension and conflict vary depending on the amount of personal value assigned to the relationship. A person with a high regard for the relationship would be predisposed to look for positive solutions that would not be a detractor. Strategies used to resolve or manage conflicts in highly valued relationships are verbal communication, loyalty, and avoidance. These methods are used out of fear and the desire to protect. Fear is related to not wanting to hurt the other person(s), and protection is related to shielding others from potential harm and not wanting them to feel overwhelmed or criticized. In addition, because of historical roles and patterns of obedience and respect, adult children may prefer not to interfere with a parent's decision about his or her spouse. Conflict in the family has the potential for repercussions that can affect the overall health and well-being of the primary caregiver, the care recipient, and the overall functioning of the extended family long after the conflict has resolved and caregiving has ceased. Thus, family members may be hesitant to interfere, criticize, or intervene when the relationships are highly valued.

Sources of Conflict

Within families, most of the time disagreements occur between adult children and the caregiving parent, or between the adult children themselves. In particular, sisters are the most likely to experience conflict about the care provided for an elderly parent. Parent–child conflict can occur as well, particularly with adolescents with chronic illness, as disagreements and power struggles occur over management of the disease or disability. Caregivers of adults with dementia report more conflict among family members than caregivers of individuals with any other illness; this is likely due to difficulties in managing the disturbing behaviors and personality changes of the care recipient. Approximately 45% to 55% of families report experiencing conflict during caregiving. There are many causes of conflict for family caregivers, which include decisions about health care and end-of-life care, financial issues, roles, living arrangements, safety, respite care, and other family members' needs and wishes.

Health Care Decisions

It is not unusual for differences of opinion to occur among family members about health care for a dependent family member. Determining the best care or the optimal solution to a given health situation usually varies depending on individual past experiences, beliefs, and values. For example, one person may want to follow the recommendations of the physician and other health providers regarding treatment and care, whereas another family member may believe in complementary medications and treatments such as herbal remedies and nutritional products.

Discussions about end-of-life care are often difficult and prone to conflict. In a study by Betty Kramer, Amy Boelk, and Casey Auer, 55% of the participants did not agree on specific types of life-sustaining support and when to withdraw support. Another area of discord is when to institutionalize a relative. A common example of this situation is when the adult child or children pressure one parent, the care provider (usually the elderly mother), to institutionalize the care recipient (the elderly father) to protect the mother from the detrimental effects of caregiving.

Financial

The financial consequences of caregiving can be tremendous, often exhausting family resources. From a child with disabilities to an elderly person who is frail, a significant portion of the cost of care may not be covered by insurance. Out-of-pocket medical expenses are close to 3 times greater for a family with a member who requires assistance with daily activities than for families without a person with a disability in residence. Costs include medical equipment, treatments and therapies, specialists, medications, nutritional items, and more. Conflict occurs regarding perceptions of inequality related to sharing the cost of care for the care recipient. There may be hidden costs, such as additional household expenses for food, home maintenance, and utilities, which may become a source of conflict if the care recipient is living with one family member who is shouldering those costs. At times, conflicts escalate to the point that legal actions are sought to establish guardianship, power of attorney, and assistance with distribution of assets. In some cases, financial hardship has resulted in abandonment of the elderly relative.

Role Conflict

There are many sources of role conflict for caregivers. Primarily, working caregivers have difficulty balancing their obligations to their employer with those to their dependent family member. According to the Family Caregiver Alliance, approximately 20% of working caregivers experience work-related conflict. They attempt to manage the imbalance by reducing hours worked, changing their work schedule, taking unpaid leave time, or retiring prematurely. As a result of these changes, caregivers experience role strain, which can lead to depression and other emotional and physical effects. As well, strain may occur because of restrictions in social and leisure activities that leave the caregiver feeling isolated.

Living Arrangements

Depending on where the care recipient resides, unless all family members are in agreement about the optimal location, conflict can ensue over details such as which person is the most qualified, or has the most financial resources, or is not employed and has the most time, and so forth. Other sources of conflict include paid home care workers who provide in-home assistance. Misunderstandings about job duties and expectations about housekeeping tasks versus socialization with the dependent family member, as well as misunderstandings about the quality and quantity of work, often appear. Other sources of conflict in caregiving surround the type and quantity of in-home care. For example, for distant relatives there may be concerns about the treatment and care of their family member, whether enough time is spent with the family member, or whether enough assistance is given. Frequent emergency room visits and hospitalizations are not uncommon among people who are chronically ill. In particular, the elderly with dementia have one of the highest rates of hospitalizations compared with those with other chronic illnesses, many times due to injuries and falls. As a result, family concerns about negligence often arise.

Assistance and Respite

Conflict related to quantity of care is often because there are perceptions by one relative that another is not providing adequate help with the caregiving duties. As many as 60% of caregivers report that family conflicts are because of perceived inequalities in the distribution of the workload. A caregiver may assume the role of the martyr, feeling proud initially but becoming angry and depressed later. Another source of conflict that is common comes from relatives who reside at a distance who are not aware of the extent of care that is needed, undervalue it, and disagree over decisions about institutionalization, assistance with care, day care, or respite care. These conflicts are often due to reluctance over financial expenses or denial about the seriousness of the illness.

Family Needs

In many caregiving families, the needs of the other members may be neglected because of competing demands. Children living in a household where one of their parents is caring for an elderly parent may become resentful and unhappy. Often a spouse is neglected because of caring for the family member who is ill or disabled. In these cases, intrafamilial relationships may suffer.

Cultural Aspects of Family Conflict

There are indications that African American caregivers experience more family conflict than other caregivers. One explanation is that African American caregivers provide more care and report that their own health is worse than Caucasian caregivers, thus placing them at greater risk for conflict with other family members and friends as a result of the extensive demands on their time, energy, and health. In addition, African Americans are more likely to share the caregiving among several family members and friends; interaction among a greater number of people can increase the risk for conflict. In spite of experiencing greater family conflict, African Americans feel less depressed and report more positive aspects of caregiving than Caucasian caregivers.

In contrast, Hispanic and Asian American caregivers exhibit more depression than Caucasian caregivers and are more likely to be adult children. Similar to African American families, however, they are more likely to have several family members sharing the care. Very little is known about family conflict related to caregiving in minorities, and further research is needed.

Management of Conflict

Although some theorists and scientists believe that conflict is unavoidable and may be helpful, the generally accepted approach in the caregiving literature relates to preventing and managing conflict. Methods to prevent conflict include the following: Communicate openly and honestly early in the caregiving process, involve all family members, have regular family meetings, make plans for the future, keep out-of-town relatives updated, recognize each other's weaknesses and strengths, and be open to each other's ideas. Items suggested for family discussions are agreeing on a primary decision maker and caregiver; any legal preparations, such as advanced directives, living wills, or power of attorney; finances; living arrangements or institutionalization; respite care, day care, sharing care; and the need for additional education, support, counseling, or training. It is important to be aware that many of the topics that need to be discussed may cause emotional distress; some family members will be in denial, and others may refuse to participate. When families are large, it is especially important for as many members as possible to be involved to avoid the potential for later conflict.

Strategies for solving conflict in families can be approached within different frameworks. A structural approach proposes that there are specific interventions or activities that promote family solidarity, alleviate stress, and change communication patterns. These activities might include a planned family trip that would require the members to work together to prepare and plan, could include the care recipient, and would encourage cooperation. An interpersonal resolution framework can also be used to manage family conflict. Within this framework, participants are trained to use a social competency skill in which they learn to view conflict from the vantage point of the other person. This constructive approach encourages families to focus on the perceptions of the people involved instead of the problems.

Some families with persistent disputes become entrenched in patterns of blame and use destructive methods such as intimidation and aggression to solve conflicts. When this pattern is observed, it may be necessary to enlist the assistance of a trained counselor or mediator to help resolve the issues. In health care and hospital settings, social workers and case managers may be helpful. In extreme cases, ethics committees, adult protective services, guardian ad litem programs (legal guardians appointed by a court to represent the vulnerable person), and legal recourse may be required if there are concerns about family violence, abuse, or neglect.

Implications for Society

Changes in society are reflected in the types of conflicts faced by caregivers. Because the number of elderly in the United States and in many other parts of the world is increasing, there is a concomitant increase in the number of people with chronic illnesses and disabilities who require assistance to manage daily activities. In addition, because more women are employed outside of the home, it is anticipated that men will be participating in caregiving activities in greater numbers than previously. Caregivers who fulfill many different roles are more likely to experience anxiety, stress, depression, poorer physical health, and a greater risk for mortality.

Many people would benefit from policies that protect caregivers who experience role conflict when balancing multiple demands from employers and work with family and caregiving responsibilities. Currently most states do not provide paid family leave for family caregivers. Family-friendly policies that encourage employers to allow for flexible scheduling and hours, respite care or adult day care, paid leave for caregiving, and other employee assistance programs are needed. According to Maximiliane Szinovacz and Adam Davey, 77% of caregivers agreed that they would share the cost of such assistance. A tiered approach to family caregiving assistance has been suggested in which different levels of benefits are offered depending on individual needs.

Conflict in caregiving families is an important topic that needs further research to fully understand the contexts, correlates, and consequences, particularly among minority families. Families as caregivers will undoubtedly become a significant source of assistance for the increasing numbers of baby boomers who will reach old age in the next few decades. Greater attention to managing conflict in families will improve outcomes for the care recipient as well as the caregivers and other family members. In addition, a focus on the family as the care provider rather than a single individual is also needed as it is anticipated that more families will share the responsibility for caregiving in the future because of the substantial limitations placed on work, finances, sociallife, leisure, and personal resources.

Susan M. McLennon

See also Affect Management and the Family; Caregiving: Adults With Developmental Disabilities; Caregiving: Elderly; Conflict in Family Life, Role and Management of; Coping Management Styles in Families; Disabilities and Family Management; Factors Influencing Family Health Values, Beliefs, and Priorities; Problem Solving in the Context of Health and Illness

Further Readings

Family Caregiver Alliance. (2000). *Helping families make everyday care choices (for providers)* [Fact sheet]. Retrieved from http://www.caregiver.org/caregiver/jsp/content_node.jsp?nodeid=405

Hendershott, A. (2000). *The reluctant caregivers: Learning to care for a loved one with Alzheimer's.* Westport, CT: Greenwood.

Kramer, B. J., Boelk, A. Z., & Auer, C. (2006). Family conflict at the end of life: Lessons learned in a model program for vulnerable older adults. *Journal of Palliative Medicine, 9*(3), 791–801.

Levine, C., & Murray, T. H. (Eds.). (2004). *The cultures of caregiving: Conflict and common ground among families, health professionals, and policy makers.* Baltimore: Johns Hopkins University Press.

Szinovacz, M. E., & Davey, A. (Eds.). (2008). *Caregiving contexts: Cultural, familial, and societal implications.* New York: Springer.

Websites

Family Caregiver Alliance: http://www.caregiver.org

FAMILY EMOTIONAL CLIMATE AND MENTAL HEALTH

Just as climate is a summary of weather patterns, so the *emotional climate* of a household is a summary of patterns of interactions between members. These interactions have long been known to have an impact on the mental health of members. Among the most vulnerable to these effects are people with mental disorders. Mental disorders involve problems with thinking, emotions, or behaviors that have a significant impact on one's ability to function and can cause distress. Criteria to define mental disorders are in the World Health Organization's International Statistical Classification of Diseases and Related Health Problems and in the American Psychiatric Association's Diagnostic and Statistical Manual of Mental Disorders. Mental disorders are very common—around 1 in 5 people in Western communities fulfill criteria for a current mental disorder, and many more have subclinical problems.

Mental health is not equivalent to an absence of disorders; rather it is a sense of well-being, hope, and purpose. Some people with mental disorders can retain a sense of well-being in the face of chronic or recurring problems. Conversely, many without disorders lack these positive features. This entry discusses several models employed in the study of emotional climate and mental health.

Expressed Emotion

Some of the most influential research on the impact of emotional climate has been on expressed emotion. This concept was first advanced in the late 1950s by George Brown and colleagues, who noticed that some people who were discharged to parents or spouses after a long period in a psychiatric hospital often did worse than those discharged to siblings or friends. They suggested that an optimal level of emotional stimulation in the environment was needed. The group developed a semi-structured interview, the Camberwell Family Interview (CFI), which was administered individually to patients' relatives, to identify whether one or more showed features of high expressed emotion (EE). High EE was characterized by the frequency of comments about the patient with critical content and tone, one or more statements reflecting rejection or global criticism (i.e. about the person's character or typical behavior) or a high rated level of emotional overinvolvement (EOI). The latter concept comprised excessive anxiety about the patient (or other exaggerated emotional responses), self-sacrifice or devoted behaviors, or extremely overprotective behavior. Warmth and positive responses were also assessed but were not found to add to the predictive utility of the measure. The CFI was typically administered during a symptomatic crisis, when responses tended to be more extreme. Subsequent research has shown that the predictive utility of the CFI is much lower when used at other times.

High EE (based on the CFI) predicts relapse in a range of mental disorders. In some cases, the effect is substantial. For example, the size of the effect in schizophrenia (a severe mental disorder with features such as hallucinations, delusions, cognitive difficulties, blunted emotions, and motivational deficits) is as large as the preventive effect of antipsychotic medications (approximately doubling the risk over 12 months). It appears that other potential explanations for this effect (e.g., the severity or chronicity of problems or differential adherence to medication) can be discounted. Mechanisms appear to include the induction of distress in the affected household member.

Relatively weak associations are typically seen between EE components. The predictive success of EE may be partly due to this heterogeneity, which may allow it to capture multiple potential risk factors in a single index. Different components may be important in different disorder contexts. Depression appears especially sensitive to criticism and hostility, and those factors may also be important in eating disorders and substance misuse. On the other hand, they appear less important in some anxiety disorders. In contrast, overprotective behavior, if it supports avoidance of feared situations, might impede recovery from anxiety disorders, although further evidence of this is needed. There is some evidence that EOI may actually be protective in borderline personality disorder, which is characterized by extreme expressions of emotion and self-destructive behavior. It is possible that this group may need a more structured interpersonal environment to help them maintain stability.

Critical and hostile responses are more likely when household members have less knowledge about the disorder and less empathy concerning the difficulties the person is facing, when they believe that the person could control his or her problems with greater investment of effort, and when they attribute negative behaviors to the person's character rather than to the disorder. This suggests that an intervention that focuses on greater knowledge of mental disorder, increased empathy for the affected person's experience and more flexible and less intrusive responses to the person may improve outcomes.

Accordingly, relapse risks from high EE disappear when affected households receive a supportive intervention that gives a better understanding of the disorder and their relative's experience, and helps them develop more effective strategies to support their relative's recovery and maintain their own well-being. Consistent with EE having a causal role, reductions in relapse risk are associated with reductions in EE.

A number of similar concepts to EE have since been advanced by other research groups, using different assessment methodologies. These include affective style (from observed interactions) and parental bonding (warmth or care and overprotection or control, assessed using a questionnaire about acceptance of parenting). A number of other assessment instruments for EE have also been developed. These competing concepts and methodologies have varying relationships with the CFI, and varying predictive utility.

EE research focused on the effects of household members on the outcomes of an individual patient. While the research was generalized to other social settings, the concept remained focused on that single direction of influence. As a result, some commentators have seen EE as part of a long history of blaming psychiatric disorder on parents or family functioning.

Research on EE highlights aspects of family functioning that have wider implications. For example, overly protective parenting restricts opportunities to build confidence and skills in dealing with difficult or potentially dangerous situations, feeding into development of anxiety. A focus on disciplining or controlling negative behaviors, accompanied by low levels of affection and reward, undermine self-worth and confidence and feed negative moods. While children are particularly sensitive to the responses of their parents and adults with depression, anxiety, or suspicion retain a high sensitivity to the responses of others, these are features of relationships that affect everyone.

Communication Deviance

Another influential model of relapse, specifically in schizophrenia, has been communication deviance

(CD). Classically elicited in relatives' descriptions of inkblots or other pictures, CD is indexed by features such as odd reasoning or use of words. In verbal interactions, there is a loss of mutual understanding and of shared attentional focus. For someone with attentional and other cognitive problems (such as someone with schizophrenia), this communication may present significant difficulties. Some research has shown an association with high EE, suggesting that CD may sometimes create difficulties in forming appropriate, noncritical responses. CD also contributes to risk of relapse in schizophrenia. However, it remains unclear whether that effect is due to the communication itself or to the possibility that it reflects the presence of genetic risk. Support for the latter idea is found in associations between CD and a family history of schizophrenia.

Interactional Models

Negative interactions between members of a household are a function of both the behaviors of other members and psychological factors affecting the ways that those behaviors are interpreted and responded to (e.g., emotional context, beliefs and attitudes about the other person, cognitive functioning, social skills). Behaviors of any individual can escalate confrontations (e.g., by highly emotive behavior or generalized attacks on others), and patterns of negative interaction can emerge over time, as members recall past instances.

Stress reactions or depression related to parenting can increase the risk of inconsistent and ineffective parenting behaviors, including inadequate monitoring or attention, empty threats, and explosive episodes. Similarly, children that are more active, demanding, or anxious may trigger parental responses to these behaviors that inadvertently exacerbate these tendencies.

In the same way, adult mental disorders not only make people more vulnerable to negative interactions, but they can also trigger them. Irritability can occur in depression or mania, and mania or schizophrenia can make people impulsive and suspicious. Sadness, disappointment, and frustration at their own lives can make them lash out at others. Depressed mood and self-preoccupation can make people less empathetic and responsive, and neither humor nor shared pleasure is as effective at restoring positive interactions. People with mental

disorders are also more likely to use substances, and intoxication may exaggerate effects of their disorder. Responses of frustration by others are understandable, as is vicarious distress over losses the affected person sustains and the problems the person experiences.

The emotional, practical, and financial challenges of supporting someone with severe mental disorder are considerable. A sense of burden is experienced when the support role taxes carers' personal resources and becomes emotionally draining or distressing. Carers may themselves experience significant depression or anxiety, and physical symptoms or disorders may worsen. High levels of burden are associated with a higher risk of criticism and hostility: Both the personal distress and resentment can be seen as reactions to a highly stressful situation. People displaying high EE reactions also have perceptions that the disorder is more chronic or severe than do those showing low EE, even though these may not reflect actual differences. Interestingly, at least one study found that the high-EE group was more accurate, suggesting that a "normalizing" bias may have benefits, if EE and related relapse risks remain low.

Significant effects of mental disorder in a parent or sibling can also be seen in children and adolescents. Depression, anxiety, and impacts on sleep, appetite, play, and attention at school may occur. Maintaining a stable nurturing environment and an age-appropriate role for the child is challenging when one or more family members are struggling with mental disorder.

A Positive Model

Some families and friends manage to support affected people through mental health crises by calming their distress, avoiding defensive reactions, and nonintrusively providing a resource of assistance with problem solving and with practical tasks. They look for nondisordered or "normal" explanations for the person's behavior and foster positive goals. They understand that people with a chronic or recurring mental disorder may retain sensitivity to stress and a need for medication or other treatment. They focus on the challenges of the day, retaining their own lives while helping the person to retain a sense of dignity and worth, and they live a satisfying life. Parents provide appropriate monitoring of child behaviors while restricting control to essential matters. They are consistent and measured in response to inappropriate behavior but primarily focus on encouraging positive behaviors and recognizing achievements.

These are features of relationships that promote mental health and well-being in any context. Although it is much harder to retain them in the context of severe mental disorder, it is even more imperative to do so.

David J. Kavanagh

See also Family Experiencing Transitions; Family Secrets in Family Therapy; Family Therapy; Mental Health Assessment for Families

Further Readings

Hooley, J. M. (2007). Expressed emotion and relapse of psychopathology. *Annual Review of Clinical Psychology, 3,* 329–352.

Kavanagh, D. J. (1992). Recent developments in expressed emotion and schizophrenia. *British Journal of Psychiatry, 160,* 601–620.

Pharoah, F., Mari, J., Rathbone, J., & Wong, W. (2006). Family intervention for schizophrenia. *Cochrane Database of Systematic Reviews, 4,* Art. No. CD000088.

Steele, A., Maruyama, N., & Galynker, I. (2010). Psychiatric symptoms in caregivers of patients with bipolar disorder: A review. *Journal of Affective Disorders, 121,* 10–21.

Zabala, M. J., Macdonald, P., & Treasure, J. (2009). Appraisal of caregiving burden, expressed emotion and psychological distress in families of people with eating disorders: A systematic review. *European Eating Disorders Review, 17,* 338–349.

FAMILY EXPERIENCING TRANSITIONS

The traditional American family has experienced dramatic changes in structure and dynamic patterns of functioning over the past 60 years. Developmental patterns related to love, intimacy, and relationship have shifted significantly. This entry explores the impact of environmental, economic, and social shifts on the family and examines how families can successfully adapt to change. The

relationship to the field of life transitions counseling is explored, and theories and interventions useful to those working in the field of families in life transitions are discussed.

Entrance into a committed relationship, marriage, and first parenting have been delayed for both genders, and increased numbers of individuals remain single by choice. Most striking of all recent U.S. Census statistics is the 22% increase in one-parent families with children under 18 years if age. Patterns related to work have also shifted. For instance, fewer young adults enter a single career and remain there until retirement. People are retiring later, and many believe they will be unable to afford to stop working. Many adults have multiple career experiences throughout their work lives, and some are entering second careers at what may be considered retirement age. More young people remain in educational settings longer, and more return to the parental home, at least once, for additional financial and emotional support.

Whereas the size of the family has decreased, the life span of those within the family has increased. With advances in medicine and technology come longer life expectancies. As a result, individuals living in families are dealing with the dual opportunities and challenges of engaging in processes of healthy aging as well as potentially supporting oneself and loved ones through lives with chronic illness.

Major shifts in individual decision making around love, work, and health in one's life interact with, and are influenced by, current changes in social climate, economy, and environment. Normal individual and family development is being redefined, and current conditions are dramatically impacting the way today's families navigate the systemic life challenges they face. A recent Gallup poll indicates that adults are reporting insufficient money, high health care costs, and high debt as the most significant financial problems currently facing their families. High levels of subjective stress and lower levels of happiness and feelings of connection are also reported. Whereas the role of the traditional family has been to serve as the primary unit from which individuals gain support and share guidance and nurturance, an affirmative definition of *family* is lacking consensus, and the future role of the family and how that might contribute to the mental and physical health of its members is unclear.

What seems clear, however, is that contemporary family units are experiencing increased stress related to the intensity and duration of the levels of change being experienced. As a result, an ever-increasing number of transitions are influencing families and challenging both the physical and psychological well-being of each individual member and the family unit as a whole.

Much of what is currently written regarding life transitions has focused on individuals. Little is written about applying the principles of life transitions counseling to family systems. At present, life transitions counselors are engaged in utilizing a wide variety of approaches to assist families as well as individuals in developing greater flexibility, a willingness to try new and alternative behaviors, and the ability to adapt to and cope with rapid change and transition. Currently, much of the relevant transitions literature focuses on how to manage a specific transitional event. Families need more guidance on how to cope with those aspects generic to transitions, in general, and how to develop the human skills required for coping (managing an event) and adaptation (growth and change) so that they can better anticipate and navigate life events.

History

Life transitions counseling has evolved as a branch within the larger field of psychotherapy and mental health counseling. The theories underlying psychotherapy were initially based on what is known as the *medical model*. This model proposed that mental illness, or any emotional problem, is biological in nature and can be alleviated through medication or some biological alteration. Any problem that a person displayed was understood as purely the symptom of a problem within that individual. The goal was to identify the symptom and cure or fix it. People who sought treatment for psychotherapy were thought of as sick or defective in some way; this perception continues to be culturally and situation bound. The *Diagnostic and Statistical Manual of Mental Disorders*, Fourth Edition, Text Revision (DSM-IV-TR) is a primary criterion measure used to assess and diagnose clients. Although the DSM-IV-TR is a valuable tool when a common language is needed to describe clients, its reliability and validity have consistently been quite low.

While staunch proponents of a medical model ideology remain, many practitioners do not adhere to a model that cannot take into account a person's complete biopsychosocial system. Thus, models of therapy have evolved from a number of theoretical orientations that address a more collaborative and active therapeutic relationship and that includes prevention, healthy coping, and growth.

Life transitions counseling as a recent offshoot of traditional psychotherapy is based on the premise that all individuals encounter changes, both developmentally and experientially, that require an ability to navigate through the transition process that follows significant turns in the road. Although people frequently do this successfully, using their own resources or support of family and friends, certain transitions impact a person in such a significant way that the aid of life transitions counseling is useful. It is a counseling model designed to assist people who are coping with normal and quite often inevitable environmental change; as such, the emphasis is not on disorder within the person but on changing conditions in the life of the person and their skills for adjusting and adapting. For clinicians using a DSM-IV-TR diagnostic model, the diagnoses of adjustment disorders and the V-Codes provide some means for specifying and diagnosing transitional issues in a clinically relevant way. The model is a collaborative one, based on the normalizing tenet that change and transition are inevitable.

Change can be broadly defined as some type of event which, through its occurrence, creates an impact on a person's life that requires a response. Some typical developmental examples include being married, having a baby, moving out of a parental home, or graduating from high school. Other more traumatic change events include a family death, divorce, a stroke, the new diagnosis of an illness, and environmental disasters like Hurricane Katrina or the earthquake in Haiti. The changes signaling transition can be planned or unexpected, wanted or unwanted, viewed as emotionally positive or negative. Developmentally, nonevents can also signal transition, such as having anticipated being married or having children and finally acknowledging that this might never happen.

A transition, on the other hand, is typically considered the process of coping with the change that has occurred. It begins with the acknowledgment of the change and continues as a process across time. Simply put, change is an event, and *transition* is the process of managing that change.

Relevant Life Transitions Theories

Although the transitions theory literature is quite recent, there seems to be a relatively cohesive integration overall, regarding the assessment of people in transition, the understanding of the transition process, and ideas about how counselors can best assist clients who are in a life transition.

Nancy Schlossberg's contributions to transitions theory include the conceptualization of the transition assessment through the use of the 4 S's. As part of the assessment of how a person will cope with a life transition, the 4 S's, as they have come to be known, are utilized. This useful tool addresses a person's (1) situation (assessment of the transition and how the person perceives it), (2) self (personal demographics, health, strengths, belief system), (3) support (what the person's support system is like and how it helps or hinders how he or she copes with the transition), and (4) strategies (how the person copes with, and derives meaning from, the transition). The process by which a person goes through the transition includes moving in, moving through, and moving out. Schlossberg emphasized that all transitions need to be understood contextually, taking into consideration the multiple layers of a person's life.

William Bridges focused on the dynamics of transition, using unique language and metaphor as a way to describe the process. In his model, each transition begins with a change event that signals an "ending"—a job is lost or an illness is diagnosed, and one acknowledges the change and notices that the sense of the old and familiar has ended. Once a person has processed this ending, it is his or her time spent in the "neutral zone," as uncomfortable as it may be, where the coping and adaptation occur. Ultimately, the person steps into a "new beginning," and the transition comes to a conclusion.

J. P. Avis and M. F. Connelly have pointed to the importance of viewing transitions counseling as collaborative. Contrary to many other counseling models, the client remains the expert on his or her life and the counselor is a guide, companion, support, and bridge to new and needed resources.

Chaos theory has been presented as a useful model for conceptualizing life transitions. Whereas the linear strategies of empirical reductionistic models are useful for changing behaviors and solving problems in the short term, the nonlinear dynamics of chaos theory are more useful in explaining how a human life unfolds across time. According to chaos theory, periods of chaos and unpredictability are normal and signal an opportunity for growth. Human beings, as complex adaptive systems, are capable of emerging out of chaos into a higher level of organization and adaptation.

For the most part, transitions theory addresses the transitional impact on an individual and does not specifically focus on the family system. At the same time, transitions theorists are clear that in order to understand how a person copes, one must always understand his or her context, which primarily includes the family system.

The Family System and Transition

From a contextual standpoint, many family therapy theorists have long accepted the idea that intervention at the family level is a crucial part of facilitating change and growth. In the days of René Descartes, the components of all systems were thought to work independently and were explained and examined as separate entities. Ludwig von Bertalanffy was the first to challenge the linear and mechanistic tenets of general systems theory and apply them to biological systems. Specifically, any system is much more than just the sum of its parts, and by addressing the parts of the system independently, one can miss the essential nuances of how each reacts to and acts on each other. Family systems theory takes systems theory one step further as it applies it to the workings of a family. Similar to the nonlinear tenets of a chaos theory model, family functioning is a dynamic process; thus, a change in one part of the system will most definitely impact the remaining parts of the system, for only through change does growth occur. From a family systems counseling perspective, the emotional, physical, and health-related outcomes for an individual are greatly enhanced if, when possible, the entire family can be the focus of care. The interventions associated with individual life transitions theory can also be used effectively with a family system in transition.

The paradox of transition, especially in light of current rapid changes facing individuals, is that growth is precipitated by change, and with change come feelings of disorder that can temporarily disrupt and immobilize family functioning. It is in working with this paradox that life transitions therapists are able to facilitate growth and adaptation in the family system.

Life Transitions Counseling and Family Interventions

Given the rapid changes that are occurring at the first part of the 21st century, the old linear paradigms that have guided personal and family decision making are less likely to work as they have in the past. Individual and family destabilization is partly due to these changing realities. The challenges currently facing life transitions counselors include a shift in his or her theoretical frameworks to include increasingly complex models of mental health delivery that integrate individual and family treatment as well as incorporate components of repair with recovery and growth. This is especially necessary in an ever-changing, culturally pluralistic society.

From a nonlinear systems perspective, a change and transition in one part of the system will always affect the remaining components. Thus, the unpredictable realities of the changing economy, environment, and lifestyles will most certainly impact client mental and physical health and well-being across the life span. Clinicians should have tools and strategies that will assist individuals and families in learning skills for coping with instability and rapid change. In order for people to navigate increasingly unpredictable terrain, they will need to become more flexible in the way they anticipate and approach change and transition. This flexibility can be facilitated through working with clients at four different levels: shifts in meaning making, problem solving, behavioral change, and strengthening of attributes aligned with positive psychology. Therapists assist families in shifts of meaning making. They support the learning of improved problem-solving and behavior change skills. They facilitate the strengthening of personal attributes among members of the family that are aligned with positive emotional affect.

Postmodern Family Interventions and Meaning Making

Humans have long been described as meaning-making creatures, striving to derive significance from life events. This process can become extremely challenging during periods of highly unpredictable or traumatic change. The ideal of the American Dream has enhanced a linear view of a life event trajectory where sequentially planned actions will yield specific outcomes. Although this may happen at times, it is not the way in which all life unfolds. The unexpected happens whether desired or not. Although cause-and-effect thinking may help people manage events in the short term, an allegiance to a solely reductionistic view may create difficulty, especially when behaviors do not precipitate anticipated results. In addition to incorporating a broad cross-cultural counseling stance, a postmodern view of change takes into consideration a person's perception of an event and assists him or her in shifting this perspective so that new, more positive stories can be constructed. Simply put, there is no single "truth" but rather many possibilities that can be created.

Narrative therapy is one such form of family intervention, built on the belief that problems are created through a personal lens and that each family member creates his or her own meaning of the shared story. Thus, if a problem can be created and become embedded in the family's dynamic, then it can also be changed to a narrative that breeds more positive actions and flexible conclusions. This intervention is collaborative in its approach, as the counselor is not the "expert" but rather someone who assists family members in cocreating or reauthoring stories that shift from ones that are highly problem saturated to ones that are filled with hope and optimism.

Solution-focused therapy is another meaning-making intervention, one that fits well with the principles of nonlinear change and growth. Change is perceived as constant, and family members are seen as having the strength and resources to resolve difficulties in their lives. At times, clients perceive their problems as so large, they become incapacitated and unable to make any change at all. From a solution-focused perspective, a small change (especially as made by an individual) will reverberate throughout the system. Similar to narrative therapy, reality can be changed through shifts in meaning making, which are never permanent, and can be co-constructed to align more with the possibilities of positive change and hope.

Problem-Solving Family Interventions

Teaching families problem-solving skills and assisting them in implementing those skills is an essential part of counseling individuals and families through change and transition. At times family members simply cannot construct a problem-solving plan and are therefore unable to move forward in their transition experience. Faced with a plethora of possible decisions, choice seems impossible. Given work-related, economic, and educational flux, making the "right" choice may seem so crucial that no options seem viable, and fear around making a possible mistake can immobilize family decision makers. From a systems perspective, helping an individual see that the problem is one that affects the entire family (including partners, parents, siblings, children, or extended family) is important as it incorporates the strategic view that problems are not created in isolation but rather are part of social contexts created by the entire system.

From a nonlinear perspective, this process opens the door for alternative possibilities that might not have been thought of before. Specifically, families are encouraged to choose their most pressing problem. They are asked to think about how they are affected by this problem, what they would like it to look like when the problem disappears, and what they might be doing to contribute to keeping the problem active. A universal problem-solving model is used in which the problem is identified, multiple options are brainstormed, and a first preference is selected, implemented, and evaluated. Based on that outcome, other options may then be implemented as necessary. Most important is that counselors work collaboratively with the family in a way that generates effective solutions that family members might never have thought would work. Lastly, families are assisted in implementing their solutions, testing them out, and altering their behavior as needed.

Behavioral Interventions

Implementing the skills associated with constructing new meaning and with solving specific problems can assist family members in moving through transitions. At times, a third avenue of intervention, behavior change, is also needed for adjustment or adaptation to occur. When the transitions assessment indicates that individual behaviors need to be modified or relearned, the transitions counselor can assist with this process. Standard interventions useful for increasing or decreasing behaviors in a personal repertoire are incorporated in the transition planning. Behavior modification strategies, functional analysis of behavior assessments, and other behavior management strategies familiar to counselors are incorporated as part of the overall plan.

Positive Family Therapy Interventions

The literature has consistently demonstrated that interventions that increase positive affect may also significantly benefit overall mental and physical well-being, especially during times of extreme duress. Shifting away from reliance solely on pathology based models, Martin Seligman's groundbreaking work in positive psychology (Linley, Joseph, & Seligman, 2004) resulted in a therapeutic focus on strengths and character attributes, positive subjective experiences, and rebuilding rather than fixing. Negative emotions remain essential for human functioning, acting as a signal when some aspect of one's system is out of balance. Increased positive emotional experiences, however, provide the physical and mental health benefits that contribute to a better quality of life. Although the majority of the initial research into positive psychology has focused on individuals, most recently, the constructs of positive psychology are being applied to other constellations such as couples, groups, and families.

Among the few authors integrating positive psychology with family therapy, Collie Wyatt Conoley and Jane Close Conoley have developed a series of interventions based on outcome research in the field, with varying empirical support. The ideals of systems change are presented to the family with the understanding that each member can make a difference in working through a problem or enriching family functioning. By increasing positive family functioning, sustaining change is an ongoing process. Using the skills to amplify positive feelings, families may access increased positive emotions, even when a problem—for example, coping with a life-threatening illness—does not necessarily resolve. From a life transitions counseling perspective, change and transition are normalized, and difficulties, no matter how significant, are constructed as potential avenues for growth.

Conclusion

The initial years of the 21st century have been marked by rapid change; current predictions suggest these patterns will continue. Given that high levels of stress tend to accompany high rates of change, these shifts are likely to take a toll on the physical and mental health and well-being of individuals and their families. Rather than continuing a focus centering on pathology-based assessment and treatment, an increasing number of life transitions practitioners have begun to conceptualize "disorder" as the beginning of a transition process out of which growth and adaptation are possible. Chaos and disruption serve as a signal that change has occurred and that patterns of adjustment and possible growth will follow. Recent research has consistently pointed to the need for counseling approaches that draw on family strengths and foster resiliency by increasing positive emotions that have protective medical and psychological effects, as well as by addressing the impact of negative emotions.

By addressing individual life transitions issues from a family systems perspective, the chance is increased that more significant and long-standing changes will occur. All transitions differ in terms of the impact on the system and the depth of adjustments required. At times, events that happen in life are so traumatic that an immediate crisis response is necessary, and adaptation and growth at that time seem unattainable. History has demonstrated, however, that humans are extremely resilient and that, with time and support, families are capable of making monumental changes in adaptation and growth after periods of duress.

From a life transitions perspective, counselors can intervene at differing levels, depending on the type of transition and need of the family. Four levels of intervention allow the life transitions counselor to work effectively with family systems in transition. Counselors work collaboratively to assist families in shifting meaning making through narrative work, clients are taught improved problem-solving skills and behavior change strategies, and counselors work with families to strengthen the character attributes that are associated with positive affect and emotion. Whereas some issues may require a substantial amount of work around behavioral change or problem solving, other transitions, such as a death or significant loss, can be resolved only through shifts in meaning making. Life transitions counseling with families accords respect to the uniqueness of each transition experience, while taking a path that normalizes the natural difficulties that accompany the changes people experience in all aspects of life.

Cori Bussolari and Judith Goodell

See also Developmental Transitions in Families; Divorce: Effect on Children or the Family; Families: The Basic Unit of Societies; Family Interventions Across the Life Span; Family Therapy; Grief Work Facilitation; Job Loss Transition for Families; Resilience in Families With Health Challenges

Further Readings

American Psychiatric Association. (2000). *Diagnostic and statistical manual of mental disorders* (4th ed., text rev.). Washington, DC: Author.

Avis, J. P. (1987). Collaborative counseling: A conceptual framework and approach for counselors of adults in transition. *Counselor Education and Supervision, 27,* 15–30.

Avis, J. P., & Connelly, M. F. (2003). Positive mental health counseling across the lifespan: A preventative approach to achieving later life satisfaction. Paper presented at the World Federation for Mental Health biennial congress, Melbourne, Australia.

Borden, W. (1992). Narrative perspectives in psychosocial intervention following adverse life events. *Social Work, 37,* 135–141.

Brack, C., & Brack, G. (1995). How chaos and complexity theory can help counselors to be more effective. *Counseling and Values, 39,* 200–208.

Bridges, W. (2001). *The way of transition: Embracing life's most difficult moments.* New York: HarperCollins.

Bussolari, C., & Goodell, J. (2009). Chaos theory as a model for life transitions counseling: Nonlinear dynamics and life's changes. *Journal of Counseling & Development, 87,* 98–107.

Conoley, C. W., & Conoley, J. C. (2009). *Positive psychology and family therapy: Creative techniques and practical tools for guiding change and enhancing growth.* Hoboken, NJ: Wiley.

Corey, G. (2009). *Theory & practice of counseling & psychotherapy* (8th ed.). Belmont, CA: Brooks/Cole.

Elliot, T. R., Berry, J. W., & Grant, J. S. (2009). Problem-solving training for family caregivers of women with disabilities: A randomized clinical trial. *Behaviour Research and Therapy, 47*(7), 548–558.

Goldenberg, I., & Goldenberg, H. (2008). *Family therapy: An overview* (7th ed.). Belmont, CA: Brooks/Cole.

Hargrave, T. (2006). Case studies, failure to launch: The struggle to leave home in the 21st century. *Psychotherapy Networker, 30,* 79–86.

Linley, P. A., Joseph, S., & Seligman, M. E. P. (2004). *Positive psychology in practice.* Hoboken, NJ: Wiley.

Parker, R. M., Schaller, J., & Hansmann, S. (2003). Catastrophe, chaos, and complexity models and psychosocial adjustment to disability. *Rehabilitation Counseling Bulletin, 46,* 234–241.

Schlossberg, N. K. (1984). *Counseling adults in transition: Linking practice with theory.* New York: Springer.

Skar, P. (2004). Chaos and self-organization: Emergent patterns at critical life transitions. *Journal of Analytical Psychology, 49,* 243–263.

Skolnick, A. S., & Skolnick, J. H. (2009). *Family in transition* (15th ed.). Boston: Pearson.

von Bertalanffy, L. (1968). *General systems theory.* New York: Braziller.

Websites

Gallup Poll: http://www.gallup.com

U.S. Census Bureau: http://www.census.gov

FAMILY HEALTH MAINTENANCE

In promoting positive well-being and maintaining healthy lifestyles, families must work together to ensure that the needs of all family members are met accordingly. In general, *well-being* refers to a sense of contentment, good quality of life, and overall good physical and mental health. For families, maintaining health and well-being is a collective effort whereby routines are established, relationships are formed that foster health in others, and quality of life is promoted when better health is experienced by multiple members of the household. This entry focuses on ways that families are collectively responsible for maintaining health for multiple members of the household rather than for their own personal health only. Families are able to maintain collective health through deliberate behaviors, routines, and emotional investments in the well-being of others.

Healthy Family Behaviors

In thinking about family health, it is first important to identify what is meant by healthy behaviors. Families organize their lives and make healthy decisions across multiple domains of functioning. For instance, families must make daily choices about what foods they choose to make available at home and how they decide to prepare those foods. Healthy diets include a variety of fruits and vegetables and food that are low in sugar and fats. Often, however, healthy foods such as fresh produce are more costly and not readily available to all families, which can affect the family's overall diet. Researchers have found that the decisions families make related to food choices and preparation are made within a cultural and economic context. In addition to eating well, families also work together to make healthy decisions related to physical activity levels. This might include a family walk after dinner, baseball games on the weekends, or limited television viewing to promote shared family activity time.

Another indicator of healthy family behavior is sleep hygiene. It is important that all family members are receiving the proper amount of sleep and that families recognize how important sleep is to their daily functioning (e.g., psychological state, academic performance). Inadequate sleep has been found to be associated with poor brain development, weight gain, and increased levels of stress. Healthy behaviors among families also include taking vitamins, practicing good oral hygiene, and attending scheduled medical appointments.

Routines

Families that work together and set goals related to accomplishing positive health behaviors are more likely to adopt these behaviors into their daily lives and make lasting changes when there is predictability in their daily lives. Although all families experience stress at some point in their lives, being able to manage disruptions and challenges through planning and creating a sense of belonging can protect individual family members from the risks associated with chronic health conditions and can promote well-being in general. Much of this daily protection comes from the creation of family routines.

Family routines are collective events that occur on a daily, weekly, or annual basis. They typically include a set time and place, assignment of roles, and an element of planning ahead. Daily routines are created around mealtimes, taking medications, and sleep. Families that are able to plan ahead and provide a sense of stability to daily routines evidence lower levels of stress, find it easier to take prescribed medications, and report better sleep habits. Routines can be disrupted for a host of reasons including foreseeable developmental transitions such as having a new baby in the house or moving to a new geographic location. Routines can also be disrupted when there is a diagnosis of a chronic health condition or economic resources are strained over time. The key preservative function of routines appears to be not only maintaining a sense of order to daily life but also staying connected as a group.

Routines carry with them the opportunity to communicate about events important to family members. On a daily basis this provides an opportunity to monitor health symptoms such as wheezing in children with asthma or glucose levels for individuals with diabetes. For less frequent affairs, such as family holiday gatherings, memories about past gatherings are shared, communicating a shared heritage and sense of belonging to a larger group. Over time, these communication patterns expressed during family gatherings come to cement relationships shown to be associated with healthy functioning and quality of life.

Family Health Connections

One of the ways that families promote health for the entire group is staying connected through daily routines and looking out for one another's health. Researchers have demonstrated that good relationships are an important part of staying healthy, sticking to an exercise regimen, and even getting a good night's sleep. The exact way that family relationships promote health is not entirely understood. However, it is apparent that children, youth, and adults who feel secure within their family unit are more likely to communicate with others when they are not feeling well and seek assistance when they are in trouble. Barbara H. Fiese and Robin S. Everhart's work has demonstrated that when family members clearly communicate during regular mealtimes, family health is better overall. This finding probably comes about for a variety of reasons, including opportunities to check in on health symptoms, monitor emotions, and solve problems that would otherwise go unnoticed. It is also apparent that when one family member becomes too controlling or intrusive, there are consequences to health. Parents who become too concerned about their child's diet are likely to see either overweight conditions or eating disorders. Similarly, a spouse who consistently expresses concern is likely to deter good habits rather than support them. Staying connected with family members is an important part of health maintenance through daily communication and responsive interactions rather than an expectation that family members are to be controlled.

Quality of Life

Families that incorporate routines around family health and maintain such positive behaviors may experience a better health-related quality of life (QOL) than families who are not as focused on maintaining family health. Broadly, QOL is thought of as a measure of an individual's overall functioning and well-being. Aspects of daily life such as physical and psychological health are conceptualized as determining a person's QOL. Often health care providers utilize QOL measures to gain a better understanding of how a person is doing on a day-to-day basis with respect to his or her health. Health care providers may use the results of such assessments to determine how well the family is maintaining a healthy lifestyle and use these assessments as a jumping-off point for discussions about changes families may need to make to live healthier lifestyles. Health care providers are likely interested in ascertaining knowledge about the QOL of all family members. By doing so, health care providers and clinicians gain critical knowledge about how burdensome maintaining family health might be to the family and can begin to work with the family to isolate any barriers to positive family health. This information is vital in treatment planning with the family and determining the best way in which the family can effectively maintain health.

QOL measures can provide feedback to health care providers and families about health maintenance and how well the family is able to incorporate medical and health advice into their daily lives. For instance, a physician might learn that a child is not sleeping well at night and is having a difficult time getting up in the morning and staying awake at school. This may lead to a discussion of sleep hygiene that centers on how much TV the child is watching before bed, the child's bedtime routine, how many caffeinated beverages the child is consuming per day, and thoughts or worries that might be making it difficult for the child to fall asleep at night. Thus, by recognizing that the child's QOL is impaired by a lack of sleep, the family and health care provider can begin to consider the family's routines regarding sleep. An agreed-on and necessary change, such as removing the TV from the child's room, might begin to pave the way for a better night's sleep and, in turn, better daytime functioning for the child.

Child Age

In considering family health, it is important to recognize the role that child age may play in family health maintenance. For instance, as a child matures and transitions into adolescence, he or she begins to desire more independence in daily activities. The child's family may be less central to the child as peer relationships begin to take on greater importance. Thus, there can often be disagreements between adolescents and their parents as the family struggles to balance the child's desire for autonomy and reliance on peers for emotional support. With respect to health maintenance, this can often lead to disagreements regarding daily routines around healthy living. The adolescent may no longer want the parent to assist or remind him or her to take a vitamin or go to sleep by a certain time. This situation may lead to a decline in family health, especially if the parent erroneously assumes that the child is able

to maintain positive health behaviors on his or her own. Disagreements about attending yearly physical appointments, the dentist, or eating health foods may all present stumbling blocks to the family as they try to maintain positive family health.

Cultural Context

Family health maintenance occurs within a cultural and economic context. The creation of daily routines, adherence to medical regimens, and beliefs about family health in general are embedded in the cultural and economic environment of the family. In some instances, cultural and economic resources can serve to protect the family from threats to health maintenance. In other instances, lack of economic resources and strains presented by cultural transitions and incongruities can derail the family's attempt at maintaining good health.

Lack of economic resources can present added burdens to the maintenance of an organized family household. Often families who reside in lower-income neighborhoods spend more time commuting to and from work, rely on public transportation, have limited access to fresh fruits and vegetables in their neighborhoods, are exposed to more noise and violence, and are more susceptible to geographic relocation. Over time chronic exposure to these environmental strains can place pressure on the maintenance of daily routines associated with more optimal health and well-being. Further, chronic stress built up in chaotic home environments can also lead to poorer physiological functioning, less sleep, and irregular eating habits. Thus, attention to the broader neighborhood in which families reside should be considered when evaluating health maintenance.

Cultural practices can promote positive health, particularly when resources are available to support families. One example is family mealtimes. Beliefs associated with the practice of family mealtimes vary considerably by culture. For some cultures, there are strict expectations for attendance and behavior during daily meals. For other cultures, expectations for attendance and behavior are less well articulated, but mealtimes are still important gatherings. In a comparison of feeding styles of Puerto Rican and Anglo American mothers, it was found that the Anglo American mothers allowed their toddlers to roam the house with a peanut and butter jelly sandwich in their hands. The Puerto Rican mothers, on the other hand, kept their toddlers in high chairs and fed them by hand. Both were healthy behaviors, and both groups of children were healthy by pediatric standards. The point is that a daily routine as simple as feeding a young child will vary by the cultural context of the family.

Often, cultural beliefs are very subtle and yet they affect health maintenance. As previously mentioned, adolescence is a time of autonomy seeking and finding a balance between independence and closeness for most American families. Research has found that for some African American families, a more effective treatment strategy for managing adolescent diabetes is a holistic approach that involves nonmedicinal approaches and builds on the family's religious belief systems. Health care providers may find it beneficial to consider cultural beliefs that all families bring to the maintenance of their health behaviors.

Cultural beliefs are especially important for health care providers to attend to in discussions about medication adherence. Regardless of cultural background, parents have concerns about the use of daily child medications; among these concerns are development of dependency, immediate side effects, and long-term consequences. In racial and ethnic minority families, these medication concerns may outweigh beliefs in the necessity of medications and lead to the underuse of prescribed medications. For instance, in pediatric asthma, cultural beliefs about medications have been associated with the underuse of daily preventive medications in African American and Latino families and to the greater use of alternative medications in Latino families (e.g., home remedies, prayer). Thus, the importance of culture in family health maintenance cannot be overlooked.

Conclusion

This entry has highlighted healthy family behaviors, as well as several ways in which positive family health is maintained. The discussions herein have focused on the importance of family routines, quality of life, and cultural beliefs in family health maintenance. Throughout these topics, it is clear that families that work together to promote positive behaviors within the family are better able to make positive decisions about health and to maintain healthy behaviors over time.

Barbara H. Fiese and Robin S. Everhart

See also Changing Family and Health Demographics; Chronic Illness and Family Management Styles; Cultural Attitudes Toward Help Seeking and Beliefs About Illness in Families; Family Pediatric Adherence to Health Care Regimen; Nutrition and Nutrition Promotion for Families; Obesity, Weight Problems, and Healthy Weight for Families; Pediatric Primary Care for the Family; Problem Solving in the Context of Health and Illness

Further Readings

Fiese, B. H. (2006). *Family routines and rituals*. New Haven, CT: Yale University Press.

Fiese, B. H., & Everhart, R. S. (2006). Medical adherence and childhood chronic illness: Family daily management skills and emotional climate as emerging contributors. *Current Opinion in Pediatrics, 18,* 551–557.

Fisher, L., & Weihs, K. L. (2000). Can addressing family relationships improve outcomes in chronic disease? *Journal of Family Practice, 49,* 561–566.

Kazak, A. E., Simms, S., & Rourke, M. T. (2002). Family systems practice in pediatric psychology. *Journal of Pediatric Psychology, 27,* 133–143.

McDaniel, S. H., Campbell, T. L., Hepworth, J., & Lorenz, A. (Eds.). (2005). *Family-oriented primary care* (2nd ed.). New York: Springer.

FAMILY HEALTH PERSPECTIVES

The concept of families and health is a universal issue that concerns the most diverse people, communities, and cultures. Across the world, the family, as the fundamental unit of society, is increasingly recognized as an important influence on or determinant of the collective and individual health of its members. The complex interactions within and outside the family circle shape behavior, lifestyle, relationships, perceptions, and ultimately, health capacities and health decisions. Given the family's primary roles of nurturing, caring, protecting, and rearing, it serves as an effective entry point and focus of health promotion and health care delivery. This entry discusses the various definitions of the family, the underlying theoretical framework and strategies of a family-based approach to health, and selected examples of family-based interventions.

The Family and Family Health

The Family

The *family* has been defined based on its size, structure, composition, patterns of authority, relationships, roles and functions, developmental phase, residence, and use of resources. Thus, there are big versus small, nuclear versus extended or multigenerational, traditional versus contemporary, patriarchal versus matriarchal, two-parent versus single-parent, and young or growing families versus empty nesters. In terms of children brought into the relationship, there are childless, biological, adopted, and mixed or blended families. Mixed or blended families are formed when children from previous marriages are brought into the relationship as partners remarry, creating the new family. An arrangement in which a parent lives with an adult partner of the same or opposite sex who may or may not be the biological parent of his or her children forms a cohabitating parent–child family. People residing together within the same dwelling constitute a household, though they may not all be related by blood or marriage.

Several definitions of the family exist. The American Academy of Family Physicians sees the family as having enduring legal, genetic, or emotional ties. Marian Zeitlin and colleagues, on discussing the international development implications of a strong family, define it as a group that takes care of the needs of its members and is managed by rules. It is bound by kinship, residence, strong emotional links, and mutual relationships characterized by intimate interdependence, selective boundary maintenance, and the capacity to adapt to change and maintain its identity. Blake Poland, Lawrence Green, and Irving Rootman define the family as an intimate social unit with a past and a future that may not necessarily follow a defined pattern or structure. Definitions based on ecclesiastical beliefs emphasize the sanctity of the marriage covenants on which the family is founded and the divine roles of the husband and wife in maintaining family unity, order, and security. Other researchers

consider the family as more than a social unit. In various disciplines such as health and medicine, the family is regarded as a framework for interventions or delivery of services and programs. In the social sciences, the family serves as a unit of analysis of relationships. In health education and promotion, it is considered as a setting of practice, that is, a place or form of continuous social interactions involving physical, mental, emotional, spiritual, cultural, economic, environmental, organizational, and personal factors that affect health and well-being. As a setting for health promotion, Hassan Soubhi and Louise Potvin consider the family as a dynamic and adaptive system established by marriage, adoption, or biological connections with shared responsibilities where individual and collective needs are met in a supportive environment. Lawrence Fisher echoes this concept by defining the family as a group of individuals with a common perspective and a way of life that ultimately affects their health and wellness. Regardless of how the family is perceived, concepts of connections, relationships, functions, responsibilities, and support define the family with expectation from society for the provision of the economic and protective needs of its members.

Family Health

The World Health Organization defines *health* as the "state of complete physical, mental, and social well-being and not merely the absence of disease or infirmity." This concept of completeness underlies a holistic approach to health that consists of wellness on three major dimensions: physical, mental, and social. It attempts to redirect the traditional one-dimensional perspective of health as the absence of disease to a more encompassing picture of wellness. Congruent with this comprehensive view on health, *family health* is the state of physical, mental, and emotional wellness of the family system and its individual members. Thus, a healthy family lives a healthy lifestyle, maintains a safe and secure environment, with adequate nutrition and access to health care services for all its members. It is essential to the normal development and well-being of both children and adults. A healthy family is also characterized by nonmedical attributes such as unity, order, supportive and nurturing relationships, the capacity to achieve its aspirations, and the resilience to respond positively to challenging circumstances.

Family health can be an outcome in interventions or the focus in care delivery. As a practice approach, it explores holistically the impact on health of various determinants, factors, and risks within and outside the family. Such determinants include personal and environmental factors, organizational characteristics (dynamics, management, conflict, level of involvement), and how the combined effects of these interacting factors bear on the family's protective capacity in addressing health risk behaviors. For instance, the manner in which the family perceives and responds to issues and pressures, and its ability to adapt to change, can influence individual and group health outcomes. These health outcomes have direct and indirect health, economic, and social consequences. For example, the lack of clear, specific, and regularly enforced family rules on smoking and drinking can be used by adolescent family members as an excuse for experimenting with these substances, which, in turn, may lead to long-term addictions that may be difficult to reverse. Likewise, predominant food choices and physical activity habits in a family setting can either exacerbate or delay the onset of genetic or familial predispositions to chronic diseases associated with obesity and sedentary behavior, such as heart disease, stroke, or diabetes.

Theoretical Framework

Models of Health and Disease

Conceptual models of health and disease largely influence how society perceives and addresses individual and population-based health issues and concerns. They shape the attitudes and belief systems of the sick and the caregiver, as well as the people around them. These conceptual tools form the basis on which the promotion of health, the practice of medicine, and the delivery of care are framed. Any of these models, a combination, or even a variant of existing ones may form the philosophical, administrative, and operational aspects of service delivery of public health and health care systems. The biomedical or disease model, illness model, sickness or sick role model, and the more contemporary biopsychosocial-ecological model are among the several theoretical representations of health and disease (see Table 1). From the biomedical to the biopsychosocial, these models

reflect the evolving process of how society views health or infirmity, thus influencing the type of intervention and delivery of service. They dictate the acceptable professional boundaries between caregivers and those receiving their care and the extent to which patients and their families are allowed to participate in health decisions.

Based on the biomedical or disease model, health and disease are seen as distinct conditions rather than as points on a continuum. *Health* and *disease* are defined based on the presence or absence of certain disease-causing agents and their effects on the body. Each exists only in the absence of the other. That is, every disease is assumed to result purely from known or unknown biological agents such as bacteria, fungi, viruses, or parasites, with the pathological process manifested through a set of clinical signs and symptoms, whereas health is considered the absence of such etiologic factors. Disease is described primarily based on physical parameters and outcomes. Professional diagnosis is largely dependent on the use of technology to provide evidence of biological causation, and treatment is directed at removing the underlying cause. This representation of health and disease stemmed from the work of Louis Pasteur and Robert Koch, which led to the establishment of the doctrine of specific etiology. Although the biomedical model provides a sound framework in the diagnosis and treatment of infectious diseases, many find it inadequate. For instance, it does not explain the absence of disease despite the presence of opportunistic bacteria in the body such as *Staphylococcus aureus* or *Streptococci*. It does not account for the multifactorial nature of chronic diseases or the behavioral and psychological problems ensuing from the interplay biological, psychological, and social determinants. Treatment rather than prevention is stressed. Further, this model has been criticized for reinforcing the view of physicians as authority figures rather than as partners in health, while individuals under their care are seen as passive recipients of treatment.

The illness model focuses predominantly on the individual's subjective perception of infirmity regardless of the absence of an outward manifestation of an ailment. This emphasis on subjective and psychological factors may cause professional judgment to be used a secondary level of importance.

The sickness or sick role model emphasizes the social environment more than the psychological

Table 1   Approaches for Defining and Understanding Health

	Disease Model	*Illness Model*	*Sickness Model*	*Family Health Perspective*
Basis	Biomedical	Psychological	Sociological	Biopsychosocial/ ecological
Orientation	Pathological symptoms	Subjective perception	Socially constructed	Ecological and family systems
Assessment and Intervention	Professional objective diagnosis of symptoms	Professional evaluations and understanding of one's self-constructed conditions	Professional assessments of psychosocial environment	Professional interventions based on the dynamics of people's subjective perspectives and changing their social environment

Source: From John T. Pardeck and Francis K. Yuen (Eds.), *Family Health: A Holistic Approach to Social Work Practice*, p. 4. Westport, CT: Auburn House (1999). Copyright 1991 by Auburn House.

factors. This model is founded on the medical sociological theory espoused by American sociologist Talcott Parsons, in which disease is considered to be a temporary deviation in behavior. As a transient digression from the norm, while ill, the "sick" individual is not held accountable for his condition or in the discharge of duties, such as work and family responsibilities. His absence from his usual social activities is likewise excused. However, he is expected to cope with his condition by seeking professional evaluation and following prescribed instructions. The doctor is seen as being in a position of authority who can detect disease, prescribe treatment, and excuse the sick individual from his duties. Although this model attempts to account for the social forces that influence sickness and wellness, it has limitations. The individual's role in the development of the disease is not accounted for, nor is the protracted nature of chronic diseases clarified. The model does not explain psychiatric disorders like Munchausen syndrome in which the individual feigns disease or injury to obtain sympathy or attention. Further, an individual need not necessarily assume the "sick role" to require medical attention or services as in receiving immunizations or prenatal care.

The biopsychosocial model came about as a challenge to the predominant health care system

that is perceived to rely heavily on the biological mechanisms of disease. In 1977, George L. Engel, a psychiatrist from the University of Rochester, articulated the need to shift to an integrated framework that admits the value of the biomedical model while accounting for the psychological and sociological dimensions of human functioning in the promotion of health and the causation of disease. Fundamental to this model is the belief that the mind and body are connected and interdependent. That is, interactions between the mind and the body plus the combined effects of intermediate factors in the environment may bring about health and disease. These factors include biological (age, sex, genetic predisposition, family history, immune status); psychological (thoughts, emotions, perceptions, attitudes, and behavior, including stress, adjustment reactions, emotional turmoil, negative thinking, lack of self-control, dependency, depression, and deviant behavior); and social factors (interpersonal relationships, education, socioeconomic status, culture, religion, work, equity and access to health care services, and others). The psychological and social dimensions explain how behavioral risk factors can hasten the development of disease and the corresponding response at the individual and family levels. From this model emerged the practice of having an interdisciplinary team of professionals in primary and advanced medical care to more effectively address the patient's needs at all three levels of functioning. Because this model attempts to understand health and disease in a comprehensive manner, it seamlessly connects with the ecological or family health perspective.

A Family Health Perspective: General System Theory and Ecological Systems Theory

The family provides its members with a context and system for seeing, interpreting, responding, and interacting with the world around them. Through recurring and often predictable patterns of interactions, attitudes and behaviors are established and reinforced among children and adult members of the family. This is demonstrated in family values, routines, practices, or traditions. The family is at the center of a network of complex interactions. At this locus, various influences from other social constructs—such as the neighborhood, school, church, workplace, and government—ultimately converge, are processed, and decided on individually and collectively. The independent and combined effects of all these internal and external variables and their interactions shape perceptions and lifestyle and the capacity to adapt to and change one's environment. The ensuing patterns of established behavior reflect the pervasive group thinking, values, and response of the family.

The family perspective to health is rooted in the general system theory and the ecological systems theory. Ludwig von Bertalanffy, an Austrian biologist, advocated for an interdisciplinary or general system approach in understanding the behavior and organization of dynamic systems. The approach is built on a framework of wholeness in which the unifying principles across the sciences are holistically applied to investigate ongoing interactions within and between systems versus looking at respective elements in isolation. In this theory, a system is defined as consisting of interrelated elementary units that are linked to their environment. The connections between individual parts in a system and to its environment explain why a change in one could affect the others. A system may be described as open or closed depending on the amount of bidirectional exchange with other social constructs. A closed system is isolated from its environment, whereas an open one maintains a continuous inflow and outflow of materials, information, or energy from its environment. All living systems are assumed to be open systems. Systems may also be functional or dysfunctional depending on their capacity to reach a steady state despite stresses and changes within themselves and to the larger ecological structure. For instance, a supportive environment within and beyond the family is considered to positively affect individual and group health, and the reverse is true where support and/or order is either lacking, fragmented, or dysfunctional.

The ecological model views the family as a system embedded in larger social systems that continually interact with each other. In the ecological model, individual elements or members make up the microlevel system as in the family, which in turn interacts with even bigger social structures, the mesosystem and the macrosystem. Individual members in the microsystem are interconnected and interdependent as exemplified by the interactions among parents, siblings, and peers. Thus, what affects a single member may also have an effect on others in the group. The family, as the center of a network of social systems, is likewise shaped by its ties, interactions, and shared experiences with the mesosystem (neighborhood, school, church, and workplace) and the macrosystem, or the bigger social, cultural, economic, and political constructs surrounding the family and the community. In turn, all these systems are indirectly influenced by the exosystem, or external environmental factors such as policies, programs, resource availability and utilization, poverty, and others. This multisystem approach, which accounts for the multilevel forces that affect human development from childhood to adulthood, came from the work of renowned American psychologist and Head Start Program cofounder Urie Brofenbrenner. A variation of this model was developed by Kenneth McLeroy and his colleagues Daniel Bibeau, Allan Steckler, and Karen Glanz in looking at health promotion from a systems perspective. In McLeroy and colleagues' variant of the ecological theory, system-level variables correspond to the concentric social systems of Brofenbrenner's: intrapersonal factors (personal characteristics such as knowledge, skills, attitudes, and behavior, and psychological factors such as self-efficacy, self-esteem, and perceived susceptibility), interpersonal factors (family, work, friendships, and other immediate social networks), institutional factors (social institutions with formal and informal rules of operation), community (norms, beliefs, values, and practices), and public policy (rights, poverty, resource allocation, and others). Health is promoted through multilevel strategies that build on the partnerships within and beyond each social system. By utilizing interventions directed at the family, health promotion measures are tailored to meet the unique needs of individuals and families within the context of multilevel interactions.

Family-Centered Approach to Health Promotion

The most proximal influences to the individual are exerted by the family. Individual–family interactions from childhood to adulthood constitute and reinforce entrenched health behaviors. Family-level influences on health are exerted not only through shared genetics but also by having a shared physical and social environment. For example, a person's vulnerability or resistance to the development of chronic diseases such as obesity, diabetes, heart disease, stroke, or cancer is rooted in genetic makeup yet nurtured by the behavior and lifestyle choices that are initiated and cultivated within a family environment. This influence becomes more pronounced when family members reside in the same household, as a result of shared environmental risks and regular interactions. For instance, similarities in body weight, lipid profiles, blood pressures and smoking behavior can be traced back to dietary habits and physical activity levels common at the family setting. Stress from illness, death, or conflicts in interpersonal relationships may also harm one's health. This is exemplified by the results of the Stockholm Coronary Risk Study in that marital stress increases the risk for future heart attacks or death as much as threefold among married or cohabiting women 40 to 65 years of age who reported a problematic spousal relationship. The elevated risk is attributed to the emotional strain and the perceived lack of social support in the relationship.

Community-level factors, in the form of social determinants, affect health at the personal and family levels. *Social determinants* are the social and economic conditions in which people grow and live that are shaped by money, policy, and the distribution of material resources and opportunities. The resulting socioeconomic differences stratify people in terms of educational attainment, quality of housing, neighborhood conditions, and access to medical care—all of which eventually shape health outcomes. For example, the Stockholm Coronary Risk Study also showed that community-level influences, such as work stress and low socioeconomic status, can worsen the prognosis for heart disease among females. Sir Michael Marmot's Whitehall Study on the prevalence of cardiorespiratory diseases and mortality rates among British civil servants confirmed the impact of socioeconomic status. His findings indicate that men in the lowest employment grades, such as doorkeepers and messengers, were three times more likely to die earlier than men in the highest grade, such as administrators. Increasing research on social determinants has shown them to be the underlying cause of poverty and health inequalities not just among nations but also within the socioeconomic strata of a country.

McLeroy and colleagues advocate an ecological approach to health promotion through multilevel interventions. This approach is based on the assumption that family-level influences can affect not only individual and group health outcomes but also those of the community and vice versa. Thus rather than designing policies and preventive strategies that solely target individual risk factors, the enabling and hindering influences in the social milieu around which individuals function are also taken into account. These enabling and hindering influences are based on the concept of risk and protective factors that underlies much of the research and practice on public health issues such as health behavior change, chronic diseases, and substance use. Protective factors include beliefs, values, knowledge, parent–child bond, attitudes, behavior, norms, practices, and social network and support that decrease the chances for disease, injury, drug abuse, or involvement in any unhealthy behavior. On the other hand, risk factors promote the likelihood of occurrence of such conditions. In essence, protective and risk factors are the established attitudes and behaviors that either safeguard one's health or increase the possibility of disease or injury. Because these factors are reinforced in a family setting, they affect children throughout their lives.

A growing number of studies show that the family, as a group setting, can also exert the capacity to change set behavior that places an individual's health at risk. For example, the Minnesota Heart Health Program utilizes school-based interventions to reduce family-level risks for heart disease. Brochures on cardiovascular disease and related health topics are sent home with the students. In the home, student-led health discussions help the family understand their risk for eventually developing heart disease. This increase in awareness strengthens the parents' and children's ability to make healthy choices. In El Paso, Texas, the Child and Adolescent Trial for Cardiovascular Health program is another school-based intervention with school- and family-based components that promote healthy eating practices, increased physical activity, and health curricula for third-, fourth-, and fifth-grade students. This resulted in sustained changes in sodium and saturated fat intake and increased engagement in physical activities at school and in the home. The Families and Schools Together program, sponsored by the Substance Abuse and Mental Health Services Administration, uses a multifamily group intervention to reduce the risk for substance use among children from 5 to 12 years of age. The schoolchildren and their respective family members, particularly those that exhibit risk factors for future substance use, are involved in the program. It aims to enhance family functioning and the ability to deal with stress while preventing school failure and substance use. The combined school and family efforts resulted in a reduction in childhood aggression and anxiety with an improvement in school performance and social skills. The mechanisms as to how families function, relate, and contribute to each other and to their social environment are increasingly utilized in designing preventive programs and health interventions that link the family with the broader public health infrastructure. As a primary stakeholder and determinant of health, the family can assist significantly in building healthy communities, as it can be part of the problem as well as the solution.

Service Delivery Through a Family Health Perspective

Various forces predominate in settings of health promotion and practice. They drive the manner in which programs, interventions, and services are delivered. These forces may be directed toward the organization, the individual, or the family. When the motivation behind programs and care is directed toward the needs and benefits of the company, the forces at play are said to be organization centered. When the needs of the person push the delivery of care, it is said to be individual centered. When the emphasis is on the choices, priorities, and strengths that the family brings in partnership with professionals, the delivery of care is said to be driven by family-centered forces.

Family-Focused Versus Family-Centered Approach

The practice approach directed at the family as the target of behavior change has led to the use of two common terminologies: *family centered* and *family focused*. Both terms refer to a type of program, intervention, or service delivery model originally directed at families with children but now widely used in various disciplines and settings.

Family-focused is distinguished from a family-centered approach in that it treats the family as a unit of intervention in a top-down style. Professionals are viewed as experts while the family serves as the passive recipient of care. In contrast, family-centered is a collaborative approach to health promotion, health care, and health decisions based on mutual trust, respect, and equal partnerships between the family and health care providers, and/or public health professionals. The entire family is considered as the client, and emphasis is placed on its strengths and ability to make fully informed decisions. Essential to this approach is recognizing the family as the basic organizational unit that defines and directs the health behaviors and practices of its members. It builds on the expertise that professionals bring into the partnership and on the strengths that enable the family to act as a contributing decision maker as well as a positive and reinforcing influence on its members. Through integrated health education strategies that encourage healthy behaviors in the home, families become more effective agents of change. The San Diego Family Health Project, Louisiana Heart Smart Family Health Program, HeartSmart Family Fun Pack in Canada, and similar programs utilize family-directed activities to help at-risk families establish and maintain a heart-healthy diet and active lifestyle.

In terms of delivery of care, a family-centered approach is considered the standard in addressing the needs of children with special health care and welfare needs. This was initiated in 1987 as part of former Surgeon General C. Everett Koop's national call for family-centered, community-based coordinated care. In 2005, the Division of Services for Children with Special Health Needs under the Maternal and Child Health Bureau of the U.S. Department of Health and Human Services refined its operating definition of family-centered care and set forth the guiding principles for care delivery and the formulation of policies for children with special health needs. *Family-centered care* is defined as a "respectful family-professional partnership" that is the "standard of practice" in ensuring "the health and well-being of children and their families." It is built on the "strengths, cultures, traditions, and expertise" that are brought into the partnership, "which results in high-quality services." It is founded on the principle that the family is a constant factor in the child's life. Hence, families and professionals work together as partners at all levels of health care that promotes a life-cycle approach. Mutual trust and respect are fostered for the skills and expertise that each partner brings. This partnership is characterized by open and objective communication, sharing of information, and the willingness to negotiate, with joint decisions made based on the best interest of the child and the family.

The manner in which care is given is considered to be as important as the provision of care. It values human interactions, such as family-to-family and peer support networks, including community-based services. Unlike the traditional delivery of care, the family-centered approach stresses collaboration rather than control. Although the expertise and opinions of professionals are recognized and welcomed, there is an open, unbiased, and ongoing exchange of information between families and professionals. Care is delivered in an adaptable and accessible manner that is responsive to the clinical and developmental needs of the child while remaining respectful of the preferences and choices of the family. Rather than focusing on weaknesses or encouraging dependence on outside support and resources, families are empowered to recognize their own strengths, capacities, and resources.

Although family-centered care was originally intended for families that have children with special health care needs, the underlying principles of this approach cross several disciplines such as health promotion and education, nursing, medicine, and the social sciences. Advocates of this approach assert that the time and cost in investing in such framework of practice is recouped many times over in terms of improved health outcomes and higher-quality delivery of care. These long-term benefits come as a result of relationship building, shared priorities and goals, effective communication, and a proactive versus reactive attitude. Conversely, when communication and trust break down between families and professionals, the result can be costly in terms of poor health outcomes, errors, dissatisfaction, wasted resources, and misunderstandings that may lead to unnecessary malpractice suits and litigations.

Challenges to the Study of Family Health

The study of families and health is an enormous area of research and practice. Its scope presents challenges in terms of its integration into the existing clinical and public health systems. As a living and dynamic unit of organization, the nature, composition, function, and evolving developmental phases of the family present a research complexity. Although the ecological approach seeks to comprehensively account for the numerous interactions that affect health at the personal and family levels, not all of these multilevel interfaces are quantifiable using existing evaluation methods and tools. From a research perspective, collecting and analyzing large data sets to accurately determine the variance contributed by each and every social and psychological element, independently and collectively, is a huge task requiring large amounts of time, labor, and resources that typical studies cannot afford. This adds to the difficulty that program designers, researchers, and even policymakers face in disentangling specific outcome measures that universally define a healthy family. Challenges remain in translating family-level health measures into corresponding public health indices that would garner political support and funding in integrating the family with health systems.

From a practice perspective, although comprehensive and collaborative in approach, challenges in family-directed interventions arise from the lack of a standard working definition of the family;

limitations in family choice due to ethical, safety, practical, and legal concerns; and from ensuing, intensified, or unresolved internal family conflicts that affect group decision making. For instance, the varying definitions of the family have not settled the programmatic dilemma of whether interventions should be delivered to the family as a single consenting unit, or separately to multiple individuals with differing opinions and desire for involvement. Critical decisions may also be hampered when the specific family member involved is either too young or is mentally or physically incapable of making an informed decision.

M. Lelinneth Beloy Novilla

See also Biopsychosocial Theoretical Perspectives of Family Systems; Cultural Attitudes Toward Help Seeking and Beliefs About Illness in Families; Family Health Maintenance; Partnering With Families: Family-Centered Care; Social Support Systems for the Family; Systems Supporting Family Health

Further Readings

Allen, R. I., & Petr, C. G. (1996). Toward developing standards and measurements for family-centered practice in family support programs. In G. H. S. Singer, L. E. Powers, & A. L. Olson (Eds.), *Redefining family support: Innovations in public-private partnerships.* Baltimore: Paul H. Brookes.

Bergmann, K. E., & Bergmann, R. L. (2003). *Health promotion and disease prevention in the family: Communicating knowledge, competence and health behavior.* New York: de Gruyter.

Deep, P. (1999). Biological and biopsychosocial models of health and disease in dentistry. *Journal of the Canadian Dental Association, 65,* 496–497.

Engel, G. L. (1977). The need for a new medical model: A challenge for biomedicine. *Science, 196*(4286), 129–136.

Ferrer, R. L., Palmer, R., & Burge, S. (2005). The family contribution to health status: A population-level estimate. *Annals of Family Medicine, 3*(2), 102–108.

Fisher, L. (2000). Homes and families as health promotion settings: Commentary. In B. D. Poland, L. W. Green, & I. Rootman (Eds.), *Settings for health promotion: Linking theory and practice* (pp. 67–76). Thousand Oaks, CA: Sage.

How families matter in health: Challenges of the evolving 21st century family[Special issue]. (2003). *Pfizer Journal, 7*(1).

Johnson, B., Abraham, M., Conway, J., Simmons, L., Edgman-Levitan, S., Sodomka, P., et al. (2008, April). *Partnering with patients and families to design a patient- and family-centered health care system: Recommendations and practices.* Bethesda, MD: Institute for Family-Centered Care. Retrieved April 8, 2009, from http://www.familycenteredcare.org/pdf/PartneringwithPatientsandFamilies.pdf

McLeroy, K. R., Bibeau, D., Steckler, A., & Glanz, K. (1988). An ecological perspective on health promotion programs. *Health Education Quarterly, 15*(4), 351–377.

Novilla, M. L. B., Barnes, M. D., De La Cruz, N. G., Williams, P., & Rogers, J. (2006). Public health perspectives on the family: An ecological approach to health promotion in the family and community. *Family and Community Health, 29*(1), 28–42.

Orth-Gomer, K., Wamala, S. P., Horsten, M., Schenck-Gustaffson, K., Schneiderman, N., & Mittleman, M. A. (2000). Marital stress worsens prognosis in women with coronary heart disease: The Stockholm Female Coronary Risk Study. *Journal of the American Medical Association, 284*(23), 3008–3014.

Pardeck, J. T., & Yuen, F. K. O. (Eds.). (1999). *Family health: A holistic approach to social work practice.* Westport, CT: Auburn House.

Poland, B. D., Green, L. W., & Rootman, I. (Eds.). (2000). *Settings for health promotion: Linking theory and practice.* Thousand Oaks, CA: Sage.

Soubhi, H., & Potvin, L. (2000). Homes and families as health promotion settings. In B. D. Poland, L. W. Green, & I. Rootman (Eds.), *Settings for health promotion: Linking theory and practice* (pp. 44–66). Thousand Oaks, CA: Sage.

World Health Organization. (1948). *WHO definition of health.* Retrieved April 8, 2009, from http://www.who.int/about/definition/en/print.html

Zeitlin, M. F., Megawangi, R., Kramer, E. M., Colleta, N. D., Babatunde, E. D., & Garman, D. (1995). *Strengthening the family: Implications for international development.* Tokyo: United Nations University Press.

Websites

American Academy of Family Physicians: http://www.aafp.org/x6799.xml

Institute for Patient- and Family-Centered Care: http://www.familycenteredcare.org

Massachusetts Community Gateway: http://www.communitygateway.org

Maternal and Child Health Bureau, Division of Services for Children With Special Health Needs, Department of Health and Human Services on Cultural Competence in Family-Centered Care: http://www .familyvoices.org/pub/general/FCCare.pdf

FAMILY INTERVENTIONS ACROSS THE LIFE SPAN

The significance of attending to the psychosocial impact of illness on individuals and family members is described in this entry as a means to alleviate psychosocial distress and perhaps to improve the medical condition. Critical issues are discussed, such as effective communication (including empathic effectiveness), the primacy of patients' mental representations of illness, and patients' coping abilities. Family health intervention researchers are still in the process of determining or refining intervention efforts to address the psychosocial impact of illness and to discover who might benefit from which type of intervention. Nonetheless, this entry provides some information or guidance for practice and for clinically relevant research. Much research is still needed to develop the foundational knowledge for family practice, though the preliminary results of this body of research suggest that attention to family health when addressing psychosocial distress is a logical undertaking.

As a note to readers, *clinician* in this entry broadly refers to medical and allied health professionals, including nurses and social workers. Reference is made to *illness* in a generic sense rather than focusing on any one type of illness; however, examples of practice research are provided that refer to specific illnesses. That is, this entry is focused on broad issues important to the patient–family–systems interactions apart from the illness group to which the patient belongs. Finally, the focus is on family health interventions in acute care settings (including treatment for chronic disease) as opposed to community or public health and long-term care. The focus is also on interventions to address psychosocial distress associated with medical illness rather than the medical illness itself. Finally, an inclusive or broad definition of family relationships is employed. These relationships are considered to have three main characteristics: continual and emotional connection and intimate knowledge of daily activities.

Family Health Theory, Research, and Practice

The families of ill people, regardless of age, benefit from assistance with their attempts to comprehend the hospitalization and illness processes. Navigating the health care system can be arduous and confusing. Moreover, understanding complex terminology used to describe illness or prognoses can further complicate matters and elevate the stress levels of the family members. It is a curious human phenomenon to protect oneself from harmful information, such that stress can interfere with the ability to absorb the weight of the diagnosis and prognosis. Comprehending the definition of the illness is one matter; understanding the potential impact on one's life is another. The experience of illness can be characterized as stressful. Many people face a number of challenges from the primary illness, such as pain, fatigue, and unpleasant side effects from pharmacological treatment. Illness can also affect a wide range of psychosocial functions, such as one's mental health; in particular, individuals who are ill may experience distress, anxiety, and depression. The impact of illness on one's identity, occupational status, and the ability to function in family and social roles can be devastating. Illness can interrupt or even terminate occupational, personal, and social roles; interfere with one's identity; and affect family relationships.

Family life-span intervention can be crucial for addressing distress arising from these two aspects of illness: the actual illness and its psychosocial impact. Interventions have been developed to address distress arising from the diagnosis and reality of illness. Individuals with illness or injury often embark on a journey of information gathering. Information about the etiology and prognosis can be helpful to people who are trying to understand why they are ill, what the illness is, and what it means for them and their children or other family members. This information is often derived from knowledge developed in research, though the research is often quite sophisticated and the terminology used by clinicians may render it inaccessible to many people. Also, the distress associated with illness can interfere with comprehension of complicated data or complex treatment regimes. In this instance of uncertainty, educational interventions may improve the quality of life for patients and their families. Information about the illness, the course or various courses it can take, the types of treatment available, the side effects, and the availability of community resources can be delivered in patient- and family-friendly formats that also allow questions to be asked and answered at a time that is useful to those needing the information. In acute care settings, many strategies are used in attempts at arming patients and families with the various types of information related to their illness. Common interventions or strategies have taken the form of individual or family counseling, group informational or psychoeducational sessions, and pamphlets or informational brochures. Many interventions are delivered in person or via the Internet.

Family health interventions have been developed from multiple disciplines, such as nursing, social work, psychology, family sociology, and family therapy, to enhance health and the management of disease. Family interventions include psychoeducational intervention and patient- and family-centered counseling. They can also be used to teach family members how to support each other. Family functioning is associated with health and illness across the life span, and family factors influence disease management. Treatment regimes such as changes in lifestyle can affect family relationships. Further, successful treatment regimes, such as changes in lifestyle, can depend on support from family members. Often adherence to complex regimes can prove onerous. Motivation may need to be nurtured to complete regimes and alter behaviors. The family environment is the context in which people learn how to cope with distress (e.g., parents model responses to distress for their children). Family members can facilitate coping strategies such as regulating emotional distress so that the ill person can engage in problem-focused coping. Healthy family relationships can optimize psychosocial functioning. For example, protective factors include closeness and mutually supportive relationships, coping skills of individual members, effective communication, and an organized yet flexible family system. Risk factors include unsupportive family relationships (including conflict), psychological trauma, external stress, and few resources (including low socioeconomic status). Conflictual or unhealthy family relationships can interfere with coping and can even heighten the distress. Protective factors can be enhanced and risk factors addressed in family intervention. The quality of family functioning influences psychological and self-care adjustment to disease. Indeed, pre-illness psychopathology can increase the risk for maladaptive responses to illness. Disease-specific risk factors, such as high severity and invasive treatment, can affect adjustment.

Clinical practice including family health intervention has been influenced by two interconnected movements in health care: the introduction of the biopsychosocial model and evidence-based practice. Traditionally, medicine has been concerned with illness and the elimination of illness. The biomedical approach to the provision of care was considered the dominant framework influencing practice. Psychiatrist George L. Engel, among other authors, introduced the biopsychosocial framework for research and practice. This framework, like the ecological and family systems theories, is based on general systems theory, first developed in biology by Paul Weiss and Ludwig von Bertalanffy. According to this framework, the patient exists within a system of hierarchical levels of organization. The individual is at the highest level of the organismic hierarchy and simultaneously represents the lowest level of the social system. The social system includes dyadic interactions (such as between clinician and patient), family, community, culture, society, and the biosphere. Engel encouraged clinicians to approach clinical practice from the inclusive framework of the systems-oriented biopsychosocial model. For clinicians to practice within this approach, practice would begin at the level of the clinician–patient relationship, would include patients' inner experience (e.g., thoughts), and would extend to a consideration at each level of the social system (e.g., family, community resources) and the search for relevant information to patient care.

The biopsychosocial model of care is compatible with the current trend toward evidence-based practice. According to D. L. Sackett and colleagues, evidence-based practice is the "conscientious, explicit and judicious use of current best evidence in making decisions about the care of individual patients." In evidence-based practice, clinicians integrate information from three main areas: the best available evidence from systematic research, clinical expertise, and patients' perspectives (e.g., values, preferences). The concept of basing practice on high-quality evidence has been adopted by most professional associations, including those involved in family health intervention.

Theory Underlying Family Health Intervention

In cognitive theories of stress and coping, as well as theories of illness representations and uncertainty, the mental processes and abilities of affected individuals and their families to comprehend and adapt to this significant life stressor are described. Ecological and social support theories concern the influence and pattern of interactions between an individual and the environment and how these influence the psychological and social well-being of health care recipients and families. Together these theories can help individuals and clinicians alike understand the illness process and help mediate coping and adjustment.

In the theory of stress and coping proposed by Richard Lazarus and Susan Folkman, stress is viewed as relational (arising from the interaction of people and their environments) and process oriented (dynamic and bidirectional relationship between the person and the environment). Psychological stress occurs when people evaluate illness-related events as taxing or exceeding their resources and endangering their well-being. Cognitive appraisal and coping efforts are viewed as mediators of stress and adaptational outcomes. The cognitive appraisal of illness events occurs in two major forms. In primary appraisal the personal relevance of an event to well-being is evaluated as irrelevant, benign, or stressful. In the secondary appraisal, coping resources and strategies are evaluated. The significance of a stressful appraisal is shaped by general beliefs about control and commitments. The degree of control people believe they have can influence perceptions of well-being, and stress may increase when beliefs are incongruent with the medical situation. *Commitments* refer to aspects of life that are considered important, such as values, ideals, and goals. An illness encounter that interacts with a person's significant commitments may increase stress. Coping resources can be physical, psychological, social, or material, and illness may be appraised as taxing or exceeding resources of personal stamina, energy, social support, self-esteem, and finances. Together, primary and secondary appraisals shape the meaning

of each illness-related event, determine the stress associated with that encounter, and may elicit certain coping efforts.

Coping refers to cognitive and behavioral efforts to reduce or manage the external and internal demands arising from an appraisal of stress. Coping efforts serve two major functions. Problem-focused coping relies on strategies to manage the stress. Emotion-focused strategies are employed to reduce or regulate the emotions arising from stress. From this perspective, it is important to note that coping refers to efforts and does not confer the notion that some coping strategies are more effective than others. That is, coping refers to efforts and has nothing to do with outcomes. Specific coping strategies, for example, denial, are not considered more adaptive than any other type. Both emotion- and problem-focused forms of coping strategies are often used in highly stressful situations. For example, seeking social support from friends and family as a coping strategy can provide informational or instructive support as well as important emotional support. Many types of coping strategies are often used, and the proportion of each form of coping is dependent on appraisal of the situation and the available resources. Interestingly, people tend to employ strategies they have previously used; that is, individuals often restrict themselves to a small repertoire of strategies no matter the situation. The interpretation of one's illness and coping capacities are considered mediators of psychosocial outcomes or adjustment. However, it is conceivable that psychological adjustment influences one's capacity to cope. Therefore, it is the fit between interpretation of illness and capacities for dealing with it that appears relevant for well-being.

The theory of illness representations described by Howard Leventhal and colleagues is a cognitively oriented theory that concerns perceived threats to health and the emotional reactions to these threats. People engage in parallel cognitive processes of how they are to think or interpret the threat of illness, and of regulating their emotional responses. Active problem solving is used to seek information about the meaning of illness symptoms in order to manage the threat. Illness representations are formed by information from previous social and cultural knowledge of the illness; the external environment of clinicians, family, friends, and the media; previous and current personal experiences of illness; and health-related stimuli, such as somatic symptoms. Mental representations also reflect characteristic attributes, including the label, etiology, timeline, controllability, and consequences of an illness threat. Mental representations shape and guide coping efforts and appraisal of the success or failure of coping efforts. Representations of emotion are important determinants of emotional outcome and shape coping efforts and appraisal of the coping effort. However, problems may arise when patients have difficulty integrating knowledge and emotions from their own illness experiences with information delivered by clinicians, and mental representations may not be congruent with actual medical information.

According to the theory of uncertainty in illness, as health care recipients process health-related stimuli, they form cognitive schema of their illness and may experience feelings of uncertainty. Uncertainty is generated when the experience of illness is complex, unpredictable, and ambiguous. Insufficient information makes it difficult to develop meaning of illness or make predictions about outcomes, and coping strategies are employed to reduce this uncertainty. Uncertainty is not inherently good or bad but instead is appraised by the patient as danger or opportunity and drives coping efforts and adjustment. Managing uncertainty is essential for adaptation.

Although these are cognitive theories, they are not inconsistent with ecological or social support theories, that is, mental representation or cognitive appraisals of environmental factors, such as quality of social support. According to the ecological theory, there is a reciprocal relationship between person and environment. Transactions between person and environment are mutually influential, interactive events that occur over time, such that the person affects the environment and the environment affects the person. From this point of view, the person and environment are inseparable and must be considered as a unitary system. A central element of this system is *goodness-of-fit*, which refers to the extent to which the qualities of the environment match the adaptive needs of a person. Goodness-of-fit is established through transactions between person and environment and determine whether an environment is either supportive or stress producing. A person experiences stress when there is an imbalance or lack of fit between the

perceived demands of a particular event and the perceived capability to use resources to meet the demands of the event. In the case of illness, the perception of the physical, social, and psychological aspects of one's illness and the ability to deal with these aspects may be unbalanced, and this unbalance can lead to distress. Adaptation occurs when goodness-of-fit is achieved between the person and environment and is more likely when the environment supports family well-being and people act with competence.

Research and Practice Across the Life Span

Illness during infancy appears to be especially difficult for families. Medically ill infants are perceived as fragile. It is often difficult to maintain normalcy in the parent–infant relationship; for example, parents may experience interruption in their role as parent. Research suggests that when an infant is hospitalized in a neonatal intensive care unit (NICU), parents experience considerable stress, predominantly from the characteristics and symptoms of the infant (e.g., difficulty breathing), the interruption in role as parent, the sights and sounds (such as alarms and monitors) of the NICU, and the interactions with medical or hospital personnel.

For parents, children and adolescents coping with illness can raise some of the same stress responses as an infant. Children with various illnesses have been found to use a variety of coping strategies, none of which is related to positive psychological adjustment. Children experience challenges with pain and physical symptoms, treatment side effects, separation from family while hospitalized, and reduced school and leisure activities. Avoidance and distraction are commonly used coping strategies, whereas seeking social support is less commonly used by children. Further, many children with illness or injury experience elevated levels of stress posthospitalization. Consideration of children's level of cognitive and social development is an essential component of assessment of psychosocial distress and intervention needs.

Many of these practices and concepts apply to the elderly population. Elderly patients discharged from acute care settings have been shown to experience multiple challenges, including readmission, psychological distress, and difficulty with personal care and household activities. These patients appear to be most vulnerable within the first month postdischarge. Screening tools (e.g., Identification of Seniors at Risk) for adverse outcomes, as well as discharge assessment, may prevent or minimize these challenges.

Preparation for discharge has become a critical component of care, including the accessibility of information and linkage to community resources. For some populations this is especially crucial. People are being discharged "quicker and sicker" than in earlier times. Their readiness for discharge is tenuous; this is particularly important for fragile patients. For example, in an examination of adverse outcomes following discharge to their homes (as opposed to a long-term care facility), 25% of elderly patients were readmitted within 1 month of discharge. Place of discharge is also important. Some elderly in this study were living with their adult children; others were released into the care of their elderly and often frail spouses— and these individuals may be considered as having an advantage over those who were living alone. One can refer individuals needing health care to community resources, but this strategy requires the individual to initiate contact. It is not uncommon for people with medical illness to also experience moderate or even severe levels of depression, which can impede their ability to contact community resources. For frail individuals living alone, where does the responsibility lie for ensuring a successful discharge? These situations illustrate a need for careful and comprehensive discharge planning. There is some evidence for comprehensive discharge planning that involves a thorough assessment and follows patients after discharge. Many discharge tools only contain items for the assessment of medical needs post-discharge, and tests of cognitive abilities (e.g., Mini-Mental State Examination) are commonly utilized in hospital. However, psychological health and social and family variables have important implications for successful discharge.

Research and Practice in Family Intervention

Illness can be a stressful time for families. The psychosocial impact of illness is considerable for many people. Whereas some families bond together and strengthen their relationships in this time of distress, others experience considerable problems in coping. The distress can intensify or magnify any preexisting family problems and wreak havoc with family relationships. Families with problems in functioning are at increased need for psychosocial supports.

It cannot be assumed that everyone needs psychosocial intervention to address the impact of illness, and in fact, it might not be the best use of scarce resources. It seems appropriate to identify distress and to offer psychosocial intervention for those who indicate clinical levels of distress or for adversity. However, research suggests that physicians do not often discern distress in patients or family members though it is possible that it is observed but not addressed for various reasons; for example, distress is not their area of expertise, they have an unrelenting schedule, or the hospital cultural environment may not permit or support such actions. Thus, there is a need to routinely involve a psychosocial clinician (e.g., nurse or social worker) in the care of patients.

Clinical practice guidelines (e.g., National Comprehensive Cancer Network) for distress include the identification (i.e., screening) and treatment of distress, followed by reevaluation. A wide range of psychosocial interventions have been developed in attempts at addressing distress, though the field could benefit from the addition of strong evidence of effectiveness. Family intervention for psychosocial distress can be addressed with a wide range of supports and services. Interventions are designed to help patients and family members utilize the health care system and community resources, as well as enhance their coping and adjustment and alleviate distress. Interventions can include psychoeducation, counseling, linkages to peer support (individual or group), cognitive behavioral intervention and stress management, and coping skills training. Psychosocial interventions with a focus on stress and coping appear most promising for alleviating psychosocial distress.

Offering multiple formats of educational intervention may be optimal for some conditions. This approach can be appealing because it can be used to address a broad range of diverse situations within the population and may be easier for those living in remote areas or for those too ill to travel. However, many people and family members would prefer one-on-one sessions with a nurse, social worker, or other allied health professional who can tailor the information to the specific needs of the family; others benefit from both group informational sessions and individual or family counseling.

Delivery of psychosocial care, and in some instances health care, is being adapted to accommodate the growing reliance on electronic media for knowledge transfer or education. Increased reliance on the Internet suggests that it may be beneficial for some family members. Psychoeducational efforts can be provided through an electronic link or take-home DVD, for example. Information and support services, including educational programs, health assessments, disease management support, and psychosocial interventions, can be provided in a quick and up-to-date medium to meet specific health needs. Patients and their families may be more comfortable with Internet support groups, as they remain anonymous and can contribute or obtain information from the security of their own home and without the concern of being evaluated. It allows for private access to information about sensitive health issues, and individuals can review the information repeatedly. Family members who are providing at-home care to an ill spouse or relative may not be able to leave the home to receive support, and Internet resources allow individuals from diverse communities to access support without traveling and at times that are convenient for them. However, it does require the requisite technological savvy and access to equipment (e.g., computer).

Uncertainty in illness is described as problematic, and psychoeducational intervention is often provided to help people deal with this uncertainty. Psychoeducational support has been viewed favorably by patients. However, there is another kind of uncertainty that often remains even after informational and educational needs have been addressed, that is, uncertainty of one's personal outcomes. Often people have no control over the outcome of their medical condition; thus fostering acceptance may be warranted.

Dealing with an illness is a time when good communication and interpersonal skills are needed, but many do not know what or how to provide verbal support or comfort. Efforts to minimize the situation (e.g., "You'll be okay" or "Don't worry, the treatment will work") isolates the person, or the person gets the sense that the speaker does not understand the situation or the experience of illness. Often when people do not know what to say, nothing is said, and the individual or family is left feeling even more isolated. Clinicians can help family members learn how to communicate effectively. Patients and family members can also be coached to improve communication skills to enhance their family relationships and support for one another. Further, health care roles are becoming increasingly specialized, and there can be several professionals involved in a person's care. These multiple interactions with different professionals can foster confusion, especially if patients receive contradictory information from different sources. Effective communication is highly critical between clinicians and patients and among the various clinicians. Medical and allied health professionals are often busy and may not have time to evaluate the impact of their communication with families. Effective communication between clinicians and patients (e.g., fully describing all treatment options, discharge options) is critical. Effective communication among health sectors enhances continuity of care (within hospitals) and the transfer of care (between hospitals, from hospital to home or community, e.g., nursing home). Effective communication is essential for empathic effectiveness, which can validate patients' experiences of illness and distress.

Effective communication and interpersonal skills are important for patient care. In addition to the involvement of a greater number of specialized professionals and greater involvement of patients in decision making, it can also be beneficial to involve family members. Family involvement in medical decisions and in provision of care (e.g., personal care) and psychosocial care can be advantageous for patients and clinicians. Communication skills in small groups of family members can present a challenge for some clinicians.

Effective communication is a major component in interventions based on social support theory. For example, for individual peer support (support given by trained, experienced peer to recipient with no prior experience of illness event), research suggests that matching is key; this includes similarity in not only ethnicity, language spoken, and characteristics of disorder but also personality and communication or interactional styles. Some mechanisms through which the intervention appears to exert an effect are empathic understanding and validation of the stressful experience. Validation can be offered by sharing common experience (i.e., with someone who understands or has had a similar experience), acknowledging the difficulty, and recognizing that stress is normal under these circumstances. Effective communication from a person who shares the illness experience can convey empathic understanding, validate emotions, and help to alleviate distress. Another critical component of the intervention is the influence of social interactions on cognitive appraisals. That is, alleviating psychosocial distress requires a change in perceptions.

The Primacy of Cognitive Appraisal

In cognitive theories and ecological theories that describe the theoretical processes through which patients and families attempt to cope with illness, the mental representation of the illness and its impact are highlighted as critical. Indeed, the cognitive appraisals have more to do with adjustment than the actual severity of illness or prognosis. For many patients (and family members) their mental representation of the illness undergoes continual change as the cognitive schema is continually updated or adapted to accommodate new information, such as fluctuations in biomedical markers or perceived successfulness of coping efforts. Clinicians' understanding of the relevance of patients' appraisal is paramount. It is highly important for clinicians to appreciate the primacy of cognitive representations of illness, the multiple levels at which they operate, and how they guide patients' decisions about treatment options, compliance with behavioral interventions, and, most importantly, patients' adjustment to illness (or overall mental well-being). Clinicians may ask patients about their perceptions and interpretations (e.g., What are you thinking about the illness? How you are coping?). This dialogue offers the opportunity to validate patients' experiences. Guidance and education can have a powerfully positive influence on patients' revision of their mental representations such that useful representations are constructed. What seems to be an important contribution to patients' adjustment to illness is their perception of the illness and their coping abilities, and in some cases, their acceptance of not knowing their personal outcomes. Knowledge of the way mental representations and cognitions (e.g., acceptance) affect patients can guide the development of psychosocial interventions.

Michèle Preyde and Gillian Marit

See also Families Experiencing Chronic Physical and Mental Health Conditions; Family Adherence to Health Care Regimen

Further Readings

Engel, G. L. (1980). The clinical application of the biopsychosocial model. *American Journal of Psychiatry, 137,* 535–544.

Lazarus, R. S., & Folkman, S. (1984). *Stress, appraisal, and coping.* New York: Springer.

Leventhal, H., Meyer, D., & Nerenz, D. (1980). The common sense representation of illness danger. In S. Rachman (Ed.), *Contributions to medical psychology* (vol. 2, pp. 7–30). New York: Pergamon Press.

Mishel, M. H. (1988). Uncertainty in illness. *Image: Journal of Nursing Scholarship, 22,* 256–262.

Preyde, M., & Ardal, F. (2003). Effectiveness of the parent buddy program for parents of very preterm infants in the neonatal intensive care unit. *Canadian Medical Association Journal, 168*(8), 969–973.

Preyde, M., & Chapman, T. (2007). Psychosocial profile of elderly patients discharged from a community hospital. *Social Work in Health Care, 45*(2), 77–95.

Preyde, M., MacAulay, C., & Dingwall, T. (2009). Discharge planning from hospital to home for elderly patients: A meta-analysis. *Journal of Evidence-Based Social Work, 6*(2), 198–216.

Preyde, M., & Synnott, E. (2009). Psychosocial intervention for adults with cancer: A meta-analysis. *Journal of Evidence-Based Social Work, 6*(4), 321–347.

Sackett, D. L., Rosenberg, W., Gray, J. A., Haynes, R. B., & Richardson, W. S. (1996). Evidence-based medicine: What it is and what it isn't. *British Medical Journal, 312,* 71–72.

Sollner, W., DeVries, A., Steixner, E., Lukas, P., Sprinzl, G., & Rumpold, G. (2001). How successful are oncologists in identifying patient distress, perceived social support, and need for psychosocial counseling? *British Journal of Cancer, 84,* 179–185.

Weihs, K., Fisher, L., & Baird, M. (2002). Families, health and behaviour. *Families, Systems, & Health, 20*(1), 7–46.

FAMILY INTERVIEWS

There are many definitions of *family*. The essential feature of a family consists of at least two or more persons in a relationship by birth, by marriage, by adoption, or acquired by mutual consent. Family members may physically live together or be emotionally connected to each other, share goods and services, and manifest intimacy, protection, care, and love for one another. Health care workers and professionals interview individual family members and the family as a whole in order to understand and assess the health of the family. When people experience difficulties in the family, the interview helps the professional detect the possible origin and factors contributing to the problem. At the end of the interview, the professional should have some idea as how to correct the dysfunction and how to strengthen the family so that it can work toward wellness. This entry describes the history and goals of family interviews, discusses different methods of conducting interviews, and provides the steps following an interview.

History

Health care professionals have been involved in talking to individual persons since the development of psychology and counseling in the early 20th century. However, in the second half of the 20th century they began to see the importance of also talking to family members in order to understand the family dynamics and how such interactions affect both the family life and the individual life. Psychodynamic theories raise the issue that a person's personality is determined and affected by early childhood experiences with the primary caregivers, be it psychosexually or psychosocially. Later psychological theories also see the importance of how other people affect individuals, resulting in how people process their thoughts and emotions, or how one's resultant behavior can influence or reinforce subsequent behaviors. The family therapy theories subscribe to the importance of a systems way of looking at things, basically emphasizing the interrelatedness of one another. In medicine, particularly in family medicine, the biological linear understanding of disease is now replaced with a circular bio-psycho-socio-cultural-spiritual understanding. Such a paradigm shift is now well accepted and adopted in the health care field.

Family Interview Goals

There are many ways of carrying out a family interview. They all try to accomplish one or more of the following goals: The first goal is to have a better understanding of the individual, by exploring that person's early life and upbringing, and how the home and social environment influenced that person's life. Both the professional and the person being interviewed may be able to obtain useful information as to how the present state of the person is affected by that upbringing, be it positive or negative. A second goal is to have an opportunity where family members have a chance to understand the other members by listening to these members' retelling of their life stories. This process will result in more mutual understanding and acceptance and less criticism and discontent. The third goal is to discern if there are processes or issues that are passed on from one generation to the next. This is particularly important if diseases like cancer, diabetes, and hypertension, or relational dynamics between different members, are passed on between generations. Having such an understanding may facilitate preventive measures. For example, if there is a first-degree relative who has contracted colon cancer, earlier colorectal cancer detection procedures can be performed; or when there is physical abuse in the previous generation, one will have a heightened alertness whether the present generation will learn from such practice. A fourth goal is to understand how the resultant relational dynamics are affecting present relationships, particularly in terms of personality, behaviors, thinking, and emotions of family members. Because a person's character is influenced by both the genetic predisposition and the environment, knowing the family's interactional dynamics may explain the alliances and disengagement of different family members. A fifth goal is to see if there are ways to improve family relationships after the assessment and possible formulation of family dynamics. At this point, the health care professional may decide whether to pursue more therapy and counseling or refer the family to other experts in dealing with the different issues raised. The sixth goal is to provide an opportunity where family members can sit together to discuss certain issues and resolve conflicts. Finally, the last goal is to form the basis of carrying out more intensive counseling or therapy for the individuals and family.

Different Methods of Conducting Family Interviews

Understanding About Individuals

The basic premise is that the present state of the mind and behavior patterns of the person are affected by the past. Thus elucidating the past will help that person gain insight as to how the present comes into being. There are different ways to carry out such an interview. The common ones are working with family-of-origin issues and using different personality theories to try to understand the personality of that individual. The key determinants include whether the person has an overall positive or negative upbringing and whether the person's attachment experience during childhood was secure, ambivalent, or avoidant, resulting in secure relationships, anxious relationships, or disengaged and narcissistic relationships, respectively, in adult life.

Understanding About Each Other

When the interview is carried out, the remaining family members will listen and try to understand about that person. With the new information, perhaps other family members will be able to realize the underlying reasons why a person behaves, thinks, or feels in a certain way. It is hoped that, at the end of the process, there will be more acceptance of one another. In such family interviews, after finishing with one person, the professional will work with the other person(s) in the family, and the process is repeated until every member has had a chance to share his or her inner world with the others. Following this process, there is often more mutual understanding and acceptance and less animosity among family members.

Understanding About Intergenerational Issues

Health care professionals in the past have used various methodologies to look at intergenerational issues. Among these, the genogram is the most widely used. The *genogram* is a graphic representation of the family tree, providing medical and psychosocial information about a person's family members and their relationships over at least three generations. With the genogram, family members and health care professionals are able to visualize illnesses and relational dynamics and how they are transmitted from one generation to the next. It may even alert the professional to look for potential problems in health and relationships, including physical or emotional abuse, cancers, hereditary illnesses, and drug and alcohol use.

Understanding About Interpersonal Dynamics

Different family therapy theorists have used different ways to understand interpersonal dynamics. These interviews help the professional to explore how a particular person thinks, feels, and behaves in different situations, while at the same time to understand how that person interacts with different people. Some of the common parameters about the dynamics include how a person is connected to or enmeshed with the other person(s), how flexible or rigid that person is in dealing with others, and whether the person has a better way of interacting with others through a permeable clear boundary. Through such family therapy interviews, the professional can understand the interactional pattern among individuals; for example, whether one person is pursuing and the other is withdrawing, or if a person functions incongruently toward another person through placating, blaming, computing (logical without any affective expression), or distracting.

Opportunities for Family Meetings

Family practitioners and clinicians have used family meetings or conferences as a means to make family members sit together to resolve differences and to make decisions that are acceptable to all. In such a meeting, every member participates and contributes to the issue, and ultimately they come up with joint decisions. Usually in such meetings, even children play a role. Meetings provide family members a way to communicate and listen to each other and a positive family environment to foster collaboration.

Steps Following a Family Interview

The family interview provides an understanding of how individuals and relationships behave and interact with each other. After the interview, the professional will have a working hypothesis to explain the family's behavioral and interactional patterns. In individuals and families that present with dysfunction or dissatisfaction with themselves and their relationships, such an assessment can provide the professional a way to move on to the next phase of therapy. The goals of this phase are to rephrase, reframe, rescript, and help the family members make better changes and adjustments in their lives.

Vincent H. K. Poon

See also Families: The Basic Unit of Societies; Family Health Perspectives; Family Interventions Across the Life Span

Further Readings

Murdock, N. L. (2009). *Theories of counseling and psychotherapy.* Upper Saddle River, NJ: Pearson.

Nichols, M. P., & Schwartz, R. C. (2007). *The essentials of family therapy* (3rd ed.). Boston: Pearson.

Poon, V. H. K. (2007). Model of counseling for family doctors. *Canadian Family Physician, 53,* 1013–1014.

Poon, V. H. K. (2008). Love matters: A counseling tool to assess couple relationships. *Canadian Family Physician, 54,* 858–869.

Watson, W. J., Poon, V. H. K., & Waters, I. A. (2003). Genograms: Seeing the patient through another window. In W. J. Watson & M. McCaffery (Eds.), *Working with families: Case-based modules on common problems in family medicine.* Toronto, Ontario, Canada: University of Toronto, Working With Families Institute.

FAMILY PEDIATRIC ADHERENCE TO HEALTH CARE REGIMEN

David Sackett, one of the early pioneers in adherence research, defined *adherence* as the degree to which a person's behavior corresponds with medical or health advice. This includes adherence to recommendations for general health promotion (e.g., obtaining vaccinations on schedule), adherence to regimens prescribed for treatment of acute conditions (e.g., antibiotics for otitis media, or ear

infections) as well as adherence to the more challenging daily care tasks faced by children with chronic medical conditions. Poor adherence is common in the pediatric population and results in wasted medical expenditures and decreased quality of life for children and families. For children, the family context has a crucial influence on adherence. Caregivers administer medical care to younger children and play a major role in facilitating successful regimen completion even for older adolescents. This entry provides an overview of historical issues in the study of pediatric adherence, describes family influences on children's adherence, and briefly reviews family-based interventions to improve adherence in the pediatric population.

History

In the past, the term *compliance* was commonly used in preference to adherence when describing the degree to which patients followed medical advice. However, compliance suggests that the youth and family should passively conform to health care recommendations given by their physician. Use of the term *adherence* reflects a change to a more collaborative mind-set in health care delivery, with family members viewed as active care partners. However, the term *adherence* still assumes that all medical advice is accurate or good and that health care recipients should therefore follow medical advice as given.

Research on the causes of pediatric nonadherence has been hampered by a number of factors, including difficulties with the measurement of adherence. Some adherence behaviors can be easily measured due to the need to use medical devices with monitoring software in order to complete the self-care behavior. However, assessment of adherence to other care tasks requires reliance on self-report. Self-report is often influenced by self-presentational biases or recall factors that reduce its utility. Techniques such as pill counts or medication assays are also subject to bias, as they can be manipulated immediately before medical visits. Conversely, measures of health outcomes are an inadequate proxy for adherence because they are influenced by the child's individual physiology and do not directly measure behavior. Newer technologies, such as the use of electronic diaries, should help to inform future work in this area.

Models for understanding adherence behavior have been developed primarily for adults and include social cognitive models (e.g., theory of planned behavior), the health beliefs model, and the transtheoretical model. These models emphasize motivation, beliefs, and judgments and are not easily applicable to children because of their immature cognitive status and dependence on others for care. Social-ecological frameworks are a better fit for understanding pediatric adherence. Social-ecological theory proposes that complex problem behaviors, such as poor adherence, are multiply determined and reflect difficulties within many systems in which the child and family are embedded. Extrafamilial systems, such as the health care system, school, work, peers, and even community and cultural institutions, are seen as interconnected with the child and family and must be understood in order to predict adherence to treatment recommendations.

Family Influences on Adherence

It is important to acknowledge that the child's developmental status will have a significant impact on the role other family members play in the child's health care. For young children, caregivers typically carry out health care tasks on behalf of the child. As children approach adolescence, caregivers typically become increasingly disengaged, despite evidence that such decreased involvement is detrimental. Youth and caregiver knowledge of how to carry out the recommended health care is clearly a prerequisite for adequate adherence. However, knowledge is a necessary but insufficient condition for ensuring adequate adherence.

Single-parent and low-income families are at higher risk for poor adherence. Such demographic factors are difficult to disentangle, as single-parent families are likely to have lower incomes and families with limited financial resources may encounter substantial barriers to adherence due to the costs often associated with implementing health care recommendations. However, single-parent status appears to be independently associated with poor adherence, demonstrating the importance of social support for health care completion.

Parenting style and family relationships are strongly related to the degree of youth adherence. Children whose caregivers more closely supervise their completion of health care tasks have better adherence than those whose caregivers are uninvolved in care. Overall family warmth and instrumental support for completion of specific care tasks are also related to adherence outcomes. Conversely, in families with high rates of conflict and poor problem-solving skills, youth are less likely to complete necessary care. Family organizational skills, particularly ability to integrate medical care tasks into daily routines, are also important.

Family relationships with children's medical care providers are critical to the prediction of youth adherence. Youth and caregiver reports of better interpersonal relationships with their physician are associated with higher adherence. Consistent with this, family reports that medical care providers use a participatory decision-making style where opinions are solicited from family while making recommendations and decisions about care are also related to better adherence.

Family Interventions to Promote Pediatric Adherence

Overall, the goal of family-based adherence interventions is to optimize health outcomes for the child while decreasing family stress associated with caring for the medical condition. Interventions with the most evidence supporting them include (a) interventions that improve family interactions with health care providers by changing information provision style, increasing frequency of contact, or both; (b) interventions that target family interactions or parenting by increasing collaboration and teamwork between caregivers and youth or by improving family problem-solving and communication skills; and (c) interventions that use contingency management to reward the youth for improvements in adherence behavior. Serious and chronic adherence problems in youth typically reflect more seriously disrupted family relations, extensive family stressors, or both, and require multicomponent family-based interventions.

Conclusion

Given the prevalence of poor adherence, it is crucial that professionals attend to the degree to which children and families follow health care advice. Caregivers have a substantial influence on children's adherence. Therefore it is important to ensure that families have the needed resources to carry out care recommendations. Interventions to support adherence to treatment recommendations can reduce health care costs and improve quality of life for children and their families.

Deborah Ellis

See also Asthma Family Issues: Prevention and Control; Case Management for Chronic Illness/Disability and the Family; Chronic Illness and Family Management Styles; Cystic Fibrosis and the Family; Diabetes, Type 1, and the Family; Family Adherence to Health Care Regimen

Further Readings

Drotar, D. (Ed.). (2000). *Promoting adherence to medical treatment in chronic childhood illness: Concepts, methods and interventions.* Mahwah, NJ: Erlbaum.

Rapoff, M. A. (2009). Adherence issues among adolescents with chronic illnesses. In S. A. Schumaker, J. K. Ockene, & K. A. Riekert (Eds.), *The handbook of health behavior change* (3rd ed., pp. 545–583). New York: Springer.

Lemanek, K. (2004). Adherence. In R. T. Brown (Ed.), *Handbook of pediatric psychology in school settings* (pp. 129–148). Mahwah, NJ: Erlbaum.

Lemanek, K. L., Kamps, J., & Chung, N. B. (2001). Empirically supported treatments in pediatric psychology: Regimen adherence. *Journal of Pediatric Psychology, 26,* 253–275.

FAMILY SECRETS IN FAMILY THERAPY

Families often do not have models for necessary instrumental, problem-solving, and emotional conversations required when confronted with serious illness. This lack leads easily to anxiety, silence, distance, and secrecy at the very time when people most need one another. Family therapy focused on the place of illness in family relationships and the impact of secrets can provide direction for openness and the recovery of closeness, warmth, and mutual support.

Overview

Secrets are relational. They are born, flourish, maintain, and, perhaps, dissolve within networks of our most important relationships—between spouses, parent and children, siblings. They may cascade down generations and across boundaries. Secrets may be shaped within larger institutions, such as a medical system, and directly impact patients and families. Or they may be created at the highest levels of government and affect our intimate lives.

To assess and intervene effectively in secrets requires a multisystemic lens. Such a lens may focus on a single individual, a couple, a household, multiple generations, institutions, or nations, examining how a secret is generated and how individual and relational well-being is affected by the presence of a secret. No individual or family abruptly decides to keep a secret. Rather, secrets are shaped by societal stigma and shame, and reenforced by cultural, ethnic, gender, religious, social class, family-of-origin, and current family beliefs. For instance, in some cultures, cancer is considered shameful. A cancer diagnosis may be kept secret from the patient by medical professionals, while other family members may be told. A secret is thus created not only between patient and doctor but also between patient and family members. Imagine that same cancer diagnosis in the United States. The patient will be told his or her diagnosis. However, if this patient comes from a culture where cancer is stigmatized, he or she may not tell his or her adolescent children, and a secret is born within the family.

Certain secrets are located at multiple levels of interacting systems. For instance, in the so-called Tuskegee experiment of the 20th century, the secret of a syphilis diagnosis was kept by the U.S. Public Health Service from nearly 400 poor and illiterate African American men. Treatment was denied in order to study the effects of untreated syphilis, even after penicillin was discovered and the men could have been treated. Instead, they went blind, insane, or died of a disease kept secret from them and their families by both the government and the medical system. Such a secret has had a profound multigenerational and community impact on African American families and their relationship with health care systems. When the HIV/AIDS epidemic began, the prior secrecy, lies, and deceptions of Tuskegee were a specter creating distrust among patients, their families, and the health care system.

Secrets need to be understood from several perspectives, including the actual content of the secret, the meaning attributed to such content, the relationships shaped by secrets, and the emotional cost of maintaining or opening a secret. For example, a young woman receives a diagnosis of multiple sclerosis and decides to keep this a secret from her father. This secret only begins to make sense when one learns that this woman's mother had multiple sclerosis and spent many years in bed before dying in her 40s. Soon, however, this young woman stops her several-times-a-year visits to her father, who lives a short plane ride away. She grows more and more anxious that he will discover her secret, while he grows more and more sad that his daughter has stopped visiting him. She lies to him, telling him her work is keeping her away. They grow distant, unhappy, and confused. A previously close relationship has been spoiled by the presence of a secret.

Secrets may protect individuals and families, but more often they prevent access to necessary information, raise anxiety, and distort relationships. When a family is tied in relational knots by the presence of one or more secrets, family therapy or therapy with an individual from a family systems perspective can be an effective treatment. The young woman with multiple sclerosis consulted a family therapist. The therapist gently challenged her belief that her father could not bear hearing that she had this illness. Asked to examine the advantages and disadvantages of opening this secret to her father, the young woman realized that maintaining the secret was making their relationship impossible and creating deep sadness in both father and daughter. She traveled home and told her father her diagnosis, reopening this important relationship. Together they were able to mourn again the loss of her mother, while simultaneously discussing ways that the daughter's illness and treatment 3 decades later were different and far more hopeful.

Secrets When Illness Persists

A single mother and her 10-year-old son came for family therapy, concerned with their angry relationship and the boy's poor school performance. Their mutually battling relationship made no sense to them or to their family therapist, as their arguments seemed triggered by nonsense.

Utilizing Time Lines

To illuminate the genesis of a secret, it is helpful for therapist and family to construct a time line, looking at significant developmental transitions, including marriage, births, stages of child development, divorce, deaths, and critical events, such as illness, migration, job or financial changes. The therapist is looking for both facts of family life over time and emotional responses.

The therapist created a time line with this family in order to discern the nature of their relationship over time and when it had become so unhappy. During this process, the mother revealed that the anger between them began a year ago, coincidental in time with some "medical problems." When the therapist tried to inquire about the medical problems, the mother changed the subject and the boy quickly escalated, yelling at his mother about his homework. Clearly, the mother was keeping a secret from her son about an illness. Angry interaction had become a convenient distraction. Sensing that something was seriously wrong, the boy became more and more frightened and unable to concentrate at school. The family therapist met alone with the mother and learned that she had breast cancer, now in remission. Extended family and friends had all counseled her to keep her cancer diagnosis and treatments a secret from her son. During her treatments, the boy spent lots of time at his aunt's house, with no explanation given to him for this change in routine. His grades plummeted. He and his mother began arguing in ways they had never done before.

Using Genograms

Early in family therapy, the therapist constructs a genogram, a diagram of three or more generations of the family. This enables therapist and family to see repeating intergenerational patterns and themes over time.

The therapist constructed a genogram with the mother, focusing in particular on illnesses across generations and how these were handled. Quickly, the mother and therapist discerned patterns of secrecy where illness pertained. In particular, several generations of women had breast cancer. Children only learned of these illnesses once they became adults. The mother also recalled how anger and fighting had replaced warm and loving relationships between parents and children during these illnesses. The therapist told the mother that children would usually rather have a mad mom than a sad mom.

Examining these intergenerational patterns and illness beliefs enabled this mother to confront the secrecy. She opened the secret of her breast cancer to her son and apologized to him for the secrecy. With their therapist, they looked at the genogram in order to contextualize family attitudes and behavior toward illness and secrets. As the boy was able to learn the facts of his mother's illness, her treatments, and her very positive prognosis, his schoolwork improved, as did their relationship.

Areas of Illness Secrets

This clinical story is a common one when illness enters a family. Families all too quickly adopt the unexamined position that "talking about the illness will make it worse," as one father remarked. Families proceed to create secrets in four areas: (1) the diagnosis, especially if an illness is considered shameful; (2) the prognosis, especially when an illness is progressive or life-shortening; (3) treatments, especially if these are disfiguring; and (4) emotional responses to the illness, such as fear, sadness, and anger.

When working with families with medical illness, the family therapist seeks to discover the meanings various family members give to the illness. Using the genogram, the therapist helps the family to retell stories passed from one generation to the next regarding ways to handle illness, both medically and interpersonally. The impact of illness secrets in previous generations and in the present is examined. With the guidance of the therapist, family members readily discover troubling triangles shaped by secrets; rigid boundaries between the family and the outside world that prevent new information from entering the family and keep potentially supportive relationships at bay; distance and cut-offs from relational resources; and a high degree of anxiety driven by secret keeping. Focus is placed on taboo issues. What are the

family's beliefs about what can be discussed and with whom? What are children allowed to know and at what ages? What is the emotional price for maintaining silence? As family members contextualize the current illness with which they are dealing by examining family-of-origin beliefs, themes, and taboos, challenging secrecy becomes more possible for both therapist and family. Throughout this process, the therapist looks for strengths and resiliencies that may be called on in the present. The family therapist helps family members to examine the cost of secrecy to healthy relationships, mutual support, and individual well-being. Using questions that pose future scenarios focused on relationships and change, the therapist enables family members to envision new possibilities. For instance, asking "If you were to tell your 16-year-old daughter about your diabetes, do you think this would make you closer or create more distance between you?" allows a father who has grown mysteriously sullen since his diagnosis to recall his earlier emotional connectedness with his daughter and to begin to imagine opening his secret.

Distinguishing Healthy Privacy From Secrecy With Illness

Drawing a distinction between privacy and secrecy with medical matters is both critical and difficult. A couple, pregnant through egg donation may be told by their doctor that this matter is "private" and that they do not need to tell anyone, including their child. Twenty-five years later, this child develops a genetic illness, needs an organ transplant, needs a blood transfusion, or is struggling emotionally with matters of identity—suddenly what was private is transformed to that which is secret. Private matters do not impact another person's right to information or their emotional or physical well-being, whereas secrets do. Shame does not adhere to private matters but rather to secrets. Disclosing a medical diagnosis to one's intimates does not require that same disclosure to one's neighbors or coworkers. Medical privacy laws are extremely important, but these can sometimes confuse families regarding privacy and secrecy. In effective family therapy with medical illness, it is important to help families discuss and distinguish privacy from secrecy. When family members open an illness secret, they do so in the confines of close and meaningful relationships, and not out on the front lawn or on a talk show. Following such disclosure, a new boundary is drawn: a boundary of privacy.

Using Family Therapy to Open Complex Illness Secrets

Opening illness secrets in family therapy may be just the beginning of the work. Over the course of an illness or after a death, new secrets may emerge. A father's death from a heart attack may be related to his never-spoken-about alcoholism. Or everyone in a family may believe that a mother's lung cancer is directly related to her secretive smoking that all have known about but none has dared mention. For a family to grieve well and move on with life may require creating a context of openness where blame and guilt can be properly weighed, acknowledged, and transcended.

When a spouse has a life-shortening illness, it is not unusual for each member of the couple to be harboring unspoken feelings and beliefs about the illness, fault, guilt, and the future. A wife may be imagining her life after her husband has died, while he is hoping for a new treatment. They become more out of sync and more distant at the very time when they most need each other. Helping couples to speak the unspeakable becomes the work of the family therapist. Often such work will emerge in spontaneous and unexpected ways. In a couple's therapy session, a dying husband praised his wife for the care she took of him. She suddenly stopped him, insisting that she had not taken good care of him. She revealed her enormous guilt and sense of responsibility for pushing him to change doctors for his colitis, resulting in a misdiagnosis of his colon cancer. As often happens when one secret is revealed, this revelation was followed by the husband stating openly for the first time that he knew he was dying. These mutual unveilings of deeper emotional truths melted what had been a frozen distance in this couple, enabling a renewal of warmth and connection for the husband's final weeks of life.

Evan Imber-Black

See also Families Experiencing Chronic Physical and Mental Health Conditions; Family Interviews; Family Therapy; Family Transitions and Ambiguous Loss; Genograms and the Family

Further Readings

Black, L. W. (1993). AIDS and secrets. In E. Imber-Black (Ed.), *Secrets in families and family therapy* (pp. 355–371). New York: Norton.

Imber-Black, E. (1993). Secrets in families and family therapy: An overview. In E. Imber-Black (Ed.), *Secrets in families and family therapy* (pp. 3–28). New York: Norton.

Imber-Black, E. (1998). *The secret life of families: Truth-telling, privacy and reconciliation in a tell-all society.* New York: Bantam.

McGoldrick, M., Gerson, R., & Petry, S. (2008). *Genograms: Assessment and intervention* (3rd ed.). New York: Norton.

Roberts, J. (2003). Rituals and serious illness: Marking the path. In E. Imber-Black, J. Roberts, & R. Whiting (Eds.), *Rituals in families and family therapy* (pp. 237–252). New York: Norton.

Rolland, J. (1994). *Families, illness and disability: An integrative treatment model.* New York: Basic Books.

FAMILY SELF-MANAGEMENT

Families are assuming increasing responsibility to manage their own and their family members' chronic conditions, prevent or delay the onset of secondary conditions, and actively engage in lifestyles that foster health. To effect the achievement of improved outcomes, health care providers need to better understand the escalating demands placed on individuals and families to self-manage, develop sensitive measures of the dimensions of self-management, and identify strategies that optimize individual and family self-management behaviors. After providing a brief background, this entry defines self-management and its common uses and discusses self-management theory and outcome measures.

Background

Individuals and families take responsibility for self-management of chronic conditions or for implementing healthy behaviors by intentionally performing a group of learned behaviors. Historically, individual and family self-management have been studied as separate entities, with individuals self-managing independently of their families and families not accounting for the impact of family self-management on each individual. This dichotomy is being rethought, and current work is beginning to focus on the synchrony of individual and family self-management. Individuals assume different roles over time. For example, parents often play a major role in the management of the health care needs of a child with a chronic condition. However, roles may change when the child transitions into adolescence or young adulthood, when adults experience new illness and disability, or when older adults experience diminishing mental or physical functional status. Individuals and families continually change, and an ability to balance demands on a day-to-day basis reflects an understanding of self-management as dynamic and fluid across the individual and families. Combining individual and family perspectives of family self-management enhances the understanding of this dynamic process.

Definition

The term *self-management* (SM) is used differently in the health care literature than in everyday language. Common uses include SM as processes, SM as outcomes, and SM as interventions. The process of SM refers to the processes or ways individuals and families manage chronic conditions or risk factors. SM outcomes are the health care outcomes achieved as a result of engaging in the SM process. Finally, SM interventions are interventions or programs delivered by health care professionals to foster a person's engagement in SM behaviors.

Numerous scholars have made substantive contributions to the current understandings of SM, and a more complete discussion can be found by consulting the list of Further Readings at the end of this entry. The work of two groups will be highlighted. In a program of research that has spanned over 20 years, Kate Lorig and colleagues in the Stanford Patient Education Research Center have developed and tested disease self-management programs aimed at the individual. These programs focus uniquely on patient concerns and self-management challenges and have demonstrated improved outcomes for persons with HIV, arthritis, back pain, and diabetes, and have been translated into eight languages. The Stanford Patient Education Research Center website, funded by grants from the National Institute of Nursing Research,

contains details on multiple self-management assessment instruments and their psychometric properties.

Margret Grey and colleagues at the Center for Self and Family Management at Yale University have developed a framework for self and family management, primarily delineating the risk and protective factors and associated outcomes. This framework has been used as the basis of intervention studies focusing on a variety of conditions, including teen mothers, diabetes and cancer in children, HIV, Tourette's syndrome, and acute coronary syndrome.

Details of Individual and Family Self-Management Theory

The individual and family self-management theory is a newly developed mid-range descriptive theory. This theory integrates both individual and family self-management and organizes relevant concepts of SM in three overall categories: context, process and outcomes. Context includes concepts in several domains that challenge or protect individuals' and families' engagement in SM. Specifically included are (a) condition-specific factors (e.g., physiological, structural, or functional characteristics of the condition, its treatment, or prevention), (b) physical and social environment factors (e.g., access to health care, transition in health care provider or setting, transportation, neighborhoods, schools, work, culture, and social capital), and (c) individual and family factors (e.g., cognitive status, perspectives, information processing, developmental stages, individual and family capabilities and cohesion, literacy, and resourcefulness).

Processes are based on the dynamic interaction among the following: (a) condition-specific knowledge and beliefs (e.g., self-efficacy, outcome expectancy, goal congruence), (b) acquisition and use of self-regulation skills and abilities (e.g., goal setting, self-monitoring and reflective thinking, decision making, planning and action, self-evaluation and management of responses) and (c) social facilitation that occurs within relationships and enhances an individual's capacity to change (e.g., social influence, support, and negotiated collaboration).

Outcomes include proximal or short-term outcomes leading to attainment of distal outcomes. The theory's proposed proximal outcomes are individual and family self-management behaviors, including engagement in activities and treatment regimens, symptom management, or use of recommended pharmacological therapies. Engagement in health behaviors may or may not impact cost of health care services. The more distal outcomes then become (a) health status (indicating prevention, attenuation, stabilization, or worsening of the condition), (b) quality of life and perceived well-being, and (c) costs, including both direct and indirect costs.

Self-management interventions are aimed at context or process factors and generally yield enhanced SM behaviors. These behaviors then impact the distal outcomes. Interventions impact SM behaviors used in a wide range of chronic health conditions (e.g., arthritis) as well as health promotion.

Measurement of Family Self-Management Outcomes

Measures of both individual and family SM outcome behaviors are emerging and include those specific to a condition (asthma or diabetes SM behaviors), a single behavior (exercise or nutrition behavior), or a specific age (Adolescent/Young Adult Self-Management and Independence Scale II). Measures of individual health status are more established (see the Stanford Patient Education Research Center website), whereas there are still controversies around the measurement of quality of life, especially family quality of life. Advanced techniques for cost measurement need to be developed. One emerging measure, the Family Management Measure, captures parents' perceptions of family management of a child's chronic health condition, including daily life, the child's future, difficulties of family life, efforts needed, and parents' perception of how well they are managing.

Self-management is a complex topic understood from numerous perspectives. There is strong evidence that engagement in SM results in better positive outcomes. Progress is currently being made with respect to theoretical development, measurement, and testing of effective strategies.

Kathleen J. Sawin and Polly Ryan

See also Chronic Illness and Family Management Styles; Family Adherence to Health Care Regimen; Health Management in Families; Theoretical Perspectives Related to the Family

Further Readings

Grey, M., Knafl, K., & McCorkle, R. (2006). A framework for the study of self- and family management of chronic conditions. *Nursing Outlook.*, 54(5), 278–286.

Lorig, K. R., & Holman, H. R. (2003) Self-management and education: History, definition, outcomes, and mechanisms. *Annals of Behavioral Medicine, 26*(1), 1–7.

Ryan, P. (2009). Integrated theory of health behavior change: Background and intervention development. *Clinical Nurse Specialist, 23*(3), 161–170.

Ryan, P., & Sawin, K. (2009). The individual and family self-management theory: Background and perspectives on context, process, and outcomes. *Nursing Outlook, 57*(4), 217–225.

Websites

Stanford Patient Education Research Center: http://patienteducation.stanford.edu/programs/cdsmp.html

University of Wisconsin–Milwaukee, Self-Management Science Center: http://www4.uwm.edu/smsc

Yale University School of Nursing, Center for Self and Family Management of Vulnerable Populations: http://nursing.yale.edu/Centers/ECSMI/P30

FAMILY THERAPY

Family therapy is a relative newcomer to the mental health arena. Like the services provided by others in this arena, it is a form of treatment provided to individuals, couples, families, and larger systems by licensed professionals whose goal is to help clients resolve whatever problems they may be experiencing. However, the field of family therapy is unique in its use of a systemic perspective, or an orientation that is relational and contextual. In other words, family therapists focus on understanding individuals in the context of their relationships, and they focus on understanding families in the context of the society of which they are a part. More important than who is in the therapy room (individual or family) is how the family therapist thinks about the particular client or client system. Rather than assessing individuals in isolation, the therapist assumes interdependence and interconnectedness. Rather than searching for the causes of problems, the therapist is more interested in what is going on in the here and now in terms of how the problem is being maintained and what the client's desired goals or solutions are. Although the history of family therapy is relatively brief, licensure for family therapists is now available in all 50 U.S. states, and family therapy is available not only throughout the United States and Canada but also in many other parts of the world. This entry discusses several aspects of family therapy, including historical context, issues amenable to family therapy, effectiveness, with an emphasis on facilitating resilience, training, process, and desired outcomes.

Historical Context

Family therapy emerged in the late 1940s and early 1950s as professionals in various parts of the country began to consider such phenomena as mutual influence, patterns of interaction, and feedback loops between individuals and within systems. Shifting away from an emphasis on the internal states or minds of individuals to a consideration of the dynamics of relationships in families, therapists soon began to develop a variety of family therapy theories and models. The most prominent of the original, or classic, family therapy models include contextual family therapy, created by Ivan Boszormenyi-Nagy; natural systems theory, created by Murray Bowen; the symbolic/experiential approach of Carl Whitaker; the dynamic process model, created by Virginia Satir; strategic family therapy, created by Jay Haley; the brief therapy/communications approach created by the Mental Research Institute in Palo Alto, California; and various behavioral and behavioral/cognitive family therapy approaches.

Although in the early days of the field, professionals tended to align themselves with a particular model or school, by the 1980s there was recognition of the need to be knowledgeable about, and have the ability to integrate information from, all of the family therapy theories. As a postmodern consciousness began to impact the field, several additional approaches to working with individuals and families evolved. These include the reflecting team approach of Tom Anderson; the solution-oriented therapy of Bill O'Hanlon; the solution-focused approach of Steve de Shazer and Insoo

Kim Berg; the narrative therapy of Michael White and David Epston; and the therapeutic conversations approach of Harlene Anderson and Harry Goolishian. Each of these approaches attempts to build on lessons learned over the years and to incorporate recent trends emerging across many disciplines. They therefore include an emphasis on recognizing the expertise of both clients and clinicians as well as awareness of the importance of facilitating an ethical and respectful process aimed at the achievement of client-defined goals. Many family therapists today use a combination of classic and postmodern approaches. Perhaps most important, a great deal of research has demonstrated the effectiveness of family therapy for dealing with, and resolving, a variety of mental and physical health challenges.

Issues Amenable to Family Therapy

Research on the effectiveness of family therapy shows that the outcomes of this modality are as good as, or better than, those for other psychotherapeutic approaches. Studies have focused on therapy for addictions, childhood conduct disorders, emotional problems, juvenile delinquency, marital problems, relationship enhancement, psychosomatic disorders, physical problems, psycho-education for families with a member diagnosed with schizophrenia, anxiety, depression, child abuse, and spouse abuse. Within each of these categories family therapists have continued to refine their approaches and demonstrate the effectiveness of their work.

Some general conclusions relative to family therapy include the fact that for marital problems, conjoint therapy is twice as likely to be effective than is individual therapy. Further, conjoint therapy is particularly preferred for marriages in which alcohol is a problem. In all cases, improving the ability to communicate effectively has been found to be a significant contributor to successful outcomes in therapy for marital problems.

In addition, research studies have indicated that a variety of family therapy approaches may be effective when working with childhood or adolescent behavior problems. The success rate for family therapy in this realm is approximately 70%. For these, as well as many other problems, a relatively brief approach, meaning 20 sessions or less, has proved to be sufficient for the resolution of problems.

Family therapy for clients dealing with physical problems is based on the awareness that when one family member is ill, all members of the family are affected. In addition, the health of the patient may be influenced by what is going on in the family. Thus the ability of family members to work together to shift roles as needed and provide appropriate support for the patient may facilitate his or her healing process. The same also may be said for various emotional and relationship problems. To do effective family therapy, therefore, specialized training is required.

Family Therapy Training

To become a family therapist, students are required to become proficient and demonstrate competence in a variety of areas. These areas include the theoretical foundations of family therapy, with a specific focus on a systems perspective; human development and family studies, with an emphasis on such areas as individual and family development, sexual functioning, and psychopathology; the therapeutic models and approaches noted earlier; values and ethics relative to family therapy; and a specified number of hours of practicum experiences that focus on working with clients—individuals, couples, and families—utilizing a systems perspective. Having completed their studies, trainees then need to engage in supervised clinical experiences for a minimum of 2 years, successfully pass a licensure examination, and then apply for a license. Only then are they able to call themselves family therapists and to practice independently.

Overseeing the training of family therapists are licensed professionals who have been certified by their state or province to provide supervision. Many of these professionals also have earned the Approved Supervisor designation from the American Association for Marriage and Family Therapy (AAMFT). Becoming a supervisor requires specialized training as well as experience as both a family therapist and as a supervisor. For AAMFT Approved Supervisors, a refresher course taken every 5 years also is required.

Facilitating Resilience

Once out in the field, one of the most effective ways that family therapists may help their clients is through a focus on strengths as well as on facilitating resilience for both the family as a whole and for the individual members. *Resilience* refers to the ability of individuals and families to deal successfully with whatever challenges and crises life presents to them and to emerge from the process stronger than they were prior to this period in their lives. Facilitating resilience requires knowledge in a variety of areas, many of which are part of the initial training to become a family therapist. These include knowledge about expected developmental challenges (e.g., physical, cognitive, psychological, psychosocial, moral, spiritual, family); unexpected developmental challenges (e.g., loss of a relationship, job, home, physical capacity, or something of value; denial of membership in a valued group; loss of respect or experience of betrayal; loss of self-esteem; death of someone important; parent being called to active duty, going to war, or taking a job away from home; a grandparent moving in with the family; winning a large sum of money); structural variations in families (e.g., divorced families with young children, blended/reconstituted families, single-parent families, multigenerational families, adoptive families, lesbian and gay families); ethnic and cultural variations in families (e.g., African American, Asian American, Hispanic American, Native American), with a particular emphasis on perception of, and behavior in, therapy; and the processes characterizing successful families.

Although no family demonstrates all of the processes found to characterize successful families, and there may be differences relative to culture and ethnicity, those that can be described as having healthy functioning tend to have a majority of the following: a legitimate source of authority; a stable rule system consistently followed; stable, consistent nurturing behavior; stable childrearing patterns; stable couple maintenance behavior; a sense of family nationality or belonging; respect for individual differences; flexibility and adaptability; initiative and creativity; clear generational boundaries; a balance between separateness and togetherness; clear and congruent communication; spontaneity and humor; mutuality, cooperation, and collaboration; shared roles and responsibilities; permission to express all feelings; friendliness, good will, and optimism; belief in a larger force; an ethical sense of values; shared rituals and celebrations; a natural network of relationships outside the family; shared goals; and the ability to negotiate without intimidation.

Facilitating resilience also involves being aware of both the risk and protective factors that various research studies have identified relative to specific emotional, physical, and relationship problems and challenges. Risk factors are those areas of family life and dynamics that are particularly vulnerable in specific situations. Protective factors are those aspects of family life and dynamics that enable particular challenges and crises to be dealt with effectively. For example, the risk factors for chronic illness include anxiety and/or depression both for the affected individual and other family members; economic issues, given the high cost of care as well as decreased ability to work; lack of availability to other family members; and irritability related to caregiving and care receiving. The protective factors for chronic illness include coherent illness narratives on the part of all family members; an accurate understanding of the situation and what is happening; effective communication; the ability to deal with larger systems; and the utilization of individual, family, and community resources. In family therapy the focus would therefore be on the latter, protective factors.

For families of children with disabilities, the risk factors include anxiety, depression, and reductions in self-esteem; high levels of frustration; decreases in both marital and personal satisfaction; feelings of guilt and confusion; significant grief and loss issues; and the need to process a great deal of new information, often in short periods of time. In family therapy the following protective factors would be the focus: balancing the illness with other family needs; maintaining clear family boundaries as well as family flexibility; developing communication competence; attributing positive meaning to the situation; maintaining commitment to the family and to social integration; engaging in active coping efforts; and developing collaborative relationships with professionals.

The risk factors for severe mental illness include grief for the one afflicted and for personal losses; grief related to the loss of hopes, dreams, and expectations; chronic sorrow related to losses and challenges; an emotional roller coaster related to the typical relapse/remission cycle; empathic pain for the afflicted one's losses; energy drain related to coping and caregiving; disruption in family routines; obstacles in the service delivery system; and the stigma associated with mental illness. The following protective factors would be a main focus of family therapy: sensitive understanding and an emphasis on normalizing what the family is experiencing; a focus on the strengths and skills of everyone involved; education regarding the illness, the mental health system, and potential resources; effective communication and problem-solving skills; the ability to manage stress and resolve feelings of grief and loss; and a supportive family environment.

When the problem is alcohol abuse, the family risk factors include rigid roles, an individualistic perspective, and poor communication; little understanding of life-cycle developmental processes and issues; a present focus at the expense of past connections and future directions; chaotic daily life and a sense of being overwhelmed; blaming and scapegoating; a fatalistic rather than an optimistic outlook; lack of coherence in values and behaviors; and decreased flexibility and use of social or economic resources. The protective factors on which family therapy would focus would include knowledge related to substance abuse; skills relative to family management and family relationships; supportive parent–child involvement in community activities; the use of community resources and the creation of safe, supportive contexts; and family ritual observance.

Families who have experienced the murder of a child are characterized by the following risk factors: shock and being traumatized; numbness and disbelief; guilt; loss of systems of meaning making; and despair and depression. However, even for these families, there are protective factors that family therapy would seek to encourage. These include acceptance of what has occurred; finding new meaning in the events; making a decision to avoid allowing the event to ruin one's life; reaching out to others in compassion; personal independence, determination, self-confidence, and optimism; spirituality; the sense of a continuing bond with the victim; social support; previous successful coping experience; and self-care.

Finally, the risk factors for lesbian families have been found to include the following: rejection by the couples' families of origin; stigmatization by the heterosexual majority; lack of legal sanction for committed relationships; disputes over parental rights; and in some cases, racism and economic inequality. The family therapy focus on protective factors would include intentionality (e.g., choosing kin, including perceiving friends as family members; becoming parents either naturally or by adoption; integrating heterosexual individuals into their lives; managing disclosure carefully; developing a supportive community; designing rituals to foster identity and solidify relationships; creating innovative strategies to achieve legalization, e.g., by filing a power of attorney or mingling finances) and redefinition (e.g., politicizing, becoming activists, educating children regarding the management of stigma, naming, integrating homosexuality with other aspects of identity shared by all regardless of sexual orientation, envisioning family).

The Process of Family Therapy

When individuals, couples, or family members go for family therapy, it is likely that they first will be asked to sign an informed consent agreement. The form generally describes what clients can expect as well as the limits of confidentiality. Having agreed to participate, the clients then meet with the therapist, who will begin by becoming acquainted with each person in order to establish a relationship of trust. The therapist will want to know what the clients would like help with and what they would like family therapy to help them achieve.

A tool often used by family therapists is a genogram. This visual mapping of a family over time, including at least three generations, enables both clients and therapist to view patterns and trends that otherwise might be overlooked. Such information may be helpful in understanding the logic of the current problem with which clients are dealing. The family therapist also may create an ecomap, which allows everyone to get a better understanding of other systems—such as work or school—with which clients may be involved that have an impact on the life of the family. Beyond the use of these rather standard tools, the process primarily involves conversations that are consistent with the particular therapist's theoretical orientation. Family therapists may make suggestions for new behaviors or new ways of thinking and perhaps even provide homework assignments. However, the choice to accept or reject what the therapist offers always resides with the client.

Reasons for Family Therapy

Family therapy may be helpful in many situations because of its relational, rather than individual, focus. Clients are encouraged to understand that mutual influence is inevitable and that although one person may be showing symptoms, everyone participates in the creation of, as well as the solution to, problems. Rather than judging a person as good or bad, right or wrong, the emphasis is on empathic understanding of the way the problem somehow "makes sense" in that person's context. Keeping in mind previous efforts by the client to solve the problem, the family therapist then can look for and suggest new ways to deal with it, ways that hopefully will be more effective. Such an approach not only accomplishes the client-defined goal but takes the burden off of the so-called identified patient.

Recent research has indicated that there are several common factors that cut across all the family therapy approaches that influence a successful outcome in family therapy. That is, therapists tend to be most effective when, among other behaviors, they are able to build alliances and engage with clients, generate a sense of hope and the expectation of positive outcomes, understand problems relationally, focus on changes in meaning, and meet clients where they are. This speaks volumes about the context of family therapy.

Indeed, family therapy is powerful partly because it is based on a way of thinking that is different from that of Western society in general. For example, a focus on individuals and individualism is one of the most highly cherished values in the United States. Not surprisingly, the strategies Americans generally use to solve problems are logical to this way of thinking. They thus tend to look for a cause and blame the other without considering the possibility that the person pointing a finger or doing the blaming may be participating in both the creation and the maintenance of the problem. When such strategies work, that is wonderful. When they don't work, then something new and different may be exactly what is needed. That is exactly what family therapy has to offer.

Dorothy S. Becvar

See also Ecomaps for Families; Genograms and the Family; Marriage and Family Therapy for Families; Resilience in Families With Health Challenges

Further Readings

Becvar, D. S. (2007.) *Families that flourish: Facilitating resilience in clinical practice.* New York: Norton.

Becvar, D. S., & Becvar, R. J. (2009). *Family therapy: A systemic integration* (7th ed.). Boston: Allyn & Bacon.

Sprenkle, D. H. (Ed.). (2002). *Effectiveness research in marriage and family therapy.* Alexandria, VA: American Association for Marriage and Family Therapy.

Walsh, F. (2007). *Strengthening family resilience* (2nd ed.). New York: Guilford.

FAMILY TRANSITIONS AND AMBIGUOUS LOSS

Family transitions include situations in which there are additions or exits of members, as well as events that require changes of the roles, behaviors, expectations, and interactions among members. Although some transitions are clear-cut, others involve events that result in doubt as to how the family should proceed. An *ambiguous loss* is a stressor situation in which the loss remains unclear, clouded by insufficient information or confusion. It occurs during transitions during which a family member is concurrently present and absent. Ambiguous losses involve both the psychological family that we socially construct and to which we give meaning and the physical or legal family structure that exists. This discussion presents two forms of ambiguous loss. The first form is situations in which an individual is physically present in the family but psychologically absent or unavailable. Examples of this form include when a family member has Alzheimer's disease or other illness that leads to dementia, traumatic brain injury, coma, stroke, depression, chronic mental illness, autism, addiction, or an excessive preoccupation with work or an activity. The second form is situations in which an individual is physically absent but psychologically present. Examples of this second form include instances in which a profoundly disabled child is placed in out-of-home care, a catastrophic disaster after which no body is located, and in cases of kidnapping, divorce, adoption, a soldier missing in action, and experiences of migration or immigration.

Etiology of Ambiguous Loss

Concreteness of a loss helps family members cognitively process and cope with the stress associated with a loss, grieve the change, renegotiate family boundaries, and gain some closure on the situation. Although the transition may be painful, there is clarity to the event and family members can construct a meaning of the loss. In the case of ambiguous loss, there is no official verification of death and no clear ending; family members are frozen in grief, immobilized, and traumatized. Closure is impossible, and the situation requires that they continue to live with the paradox of absence and presence. Coping and decision-making processes are blocked. Their relationship with the person who is "there, but not there" is not clear; expectations, behaviors, and interactions no longer fit the rules and structures under which they previously existed. The ambiguous situation contributes to ambivalent feelings and behaviors.

The meaning of the loss or transition is not clear, and previous meanings and definitions held within the family no longer fit the circumstances. Individual family members struggle to make sense of the situation and to construct their own meaning of the current status of a person who is both present and absent. That person may no longer be able to meet emotional needs of the family and cannot participate in renegotiation of individual roles in areas of finances, household management, and caretaking.

Family members dealing with ambiguous loss may exhibit symptoms that resemble complicated grief, as well as depression and anxiety. They may exhibit ambivalence toward the affected family member, as well as toward other loved ones, and engage in escalated levels of family conflict. Unlike post-traumatic stress disorder, the traumatizing ambiguous experience exists in the present and often continues for many years. According to Pauline Boss, the leading scholar on ambiguous loss, it is a relational disorder, not a psychic dysfunction.

Ambiguous loss is exacerbated by common conditions in the outside environment, creating a situation where the family is isolated from usual forms of support. In a society focused on finding solutions, unresolved situations can be viewed as a sign of failure. Friends lose patience at the family's inability to resolve the matter, and they avoid the suffering individuals. When there has been an institutionalization of the family member, the remaining family may stop visiting their loved one and consider the individual as already dead. This process can be a means of coping as they attempt to deal with their level of discomfort with being unable to extinguish the ambiguity and resolve the loss. Other support systems may be ineffective; religious groups that have rituals to aid with death often have no comparable activities to give meaning to an ongoing loss. Because closure is the usual goal of grief therapy, traditional therapies are also insufficient in situations of ambiguous loss where closure is not a realistic goal.

Ambiguous loss often coexists with a sense of boundary ambiguity (i.e., a perceptual response reflected in the degree of ambiguity as to who is considered "in" or "out" of the family). Ambiguity as to the extent to which the loved one is still a member of the family can be reflected in decisions of who is included in family activities, rituals, and traditions. Professional help and professional caregivers who live in the home to care for a chronically ill family member may raise issues of boundary ambiguity for themselves and for the family. In addition, family members may struggle with reassigning roles and tasks, perceiving it as a disloyalty to the loved one or a giving up of hope. Cultural beliefs influence family tolerance for ambiguity and how loss is perceived.

Resiliency

Resiliency and coping in families dealing with ambiguous loss is not measured in stages or linear recovery but in their learning to tolerate the stress of ambiguity. Boss has suggested six guidelines for resiliency where there is physical presence and psychological absence. The first of these is the importance of using a dialectical process to find meaning or make sense out of what is happening, for there is no hope without meaning. Families are challenged to find meaning in the situation in spite of an absence of information or attainable truth, and in the presence of ambiguity and unanswered questions. The second involves tempering mastery by learning to hold two opposing ideas at the same time, which allows for a synthesis between the status quo and desire for closure, balancing the need for some control with the loss situation.

Family members also benefit from reconstructing their identity to include more flexible gender and generational roles, normalizing ambivalence by recognizing that conflicting emotions are a normal reaction to abnormal loss, revising attachments to accept the ambiguity, and discovering hope.

Colleen I. Murray and Angela D. Broadus

See also Death: Ambiguous Feelings Related to Loss; Family Caregiving: Caring for Children, Adults, and Elders With Developmental Disabilities; Family Experiencing Transitions; Problem Solving in the Context of Health and Illness; Resilience in Families With Health Challenges

Further Readings

Boss, P. (2006). *Loss, trauma, and resilience: Therapeutic work with ambiguous loss.* New York: Norton.

Boss, P. (2007). Ambiguous loss theory: Challenges for scholars and practitioners. *Family Relations, 56,* 105–111.

Boss, P., & Couden, B. A. (2002). Ambiguous loss from chronic physical illness: Clinical interventions with individuals, couples, and families. *JCLP/In Session: Psychotherapy in Practice, 58,* 1351–1360.

Cacciatore, J., DeFrain, J., & Jones, K. L. C. (2008). When a baby dies: Ambiguity and stillbirth. *Marriage & Family Review, 44,* 439–454.

Collins, R. C., & Kennedy, M. C. (2008). Serving families who have served: Providing family therapy and support in interdisciplinary polytrauma rehabilitation. *Journal of Clinical Psychology, 64,* 993–1003.

Murray, C. I., Toth, K., Larsen, B. L., & Moulton, S. (2010). Death, dying, and grief in families. In S. J. Price, C. A. Price, & P. C. McKenry (Eds.), *Families & change: Coping with stressful events and transitions* (4th ed., pp. 73–95). Thousand Oaks, CA: Sage.

Roper, S. O., & Jackson, J. B. (2007). The ambiguities of out-of-home care: Children with severe or profound disabilities. *Family Relations, 56,* 147–161.

FETAL ALCOHOL EXPOSURE AND FAMILY HEALTH

Ingestion of alcohol during pregnancy has been shown to interfere with normal fetal development, leading to life long consequences for the child, the child's family, and society. Fetal alcohol exposure is one of the leading causes of mental retardation in developed countries, and the resulting cost of lost productivity, medical intervention, and educational efforts has been estimated to be upward of $5.4 billion annually in the United States and $5.3 billion in Canada, according to the U.S. Department of Health and Human Services and Brenda Stade and colleagues.

This entry reviews the current nomenclature used to classify infants and children who demonstrate the effects of fetal alcohol exposure, identifies risk factors for and features of fetal alcohol spectrum disorder, and discusses interventions to decrease the impact of this disorder on the child and family. Finally, maternal screening tools and strategies for preventing damage to the developing fetus are described.

Terminology

First described in the 1970s, the group of characteristic features of *fetal alcohol exposure* was referred to as fetal alcohol syndrome (FAS). Characteristics of FAS include intrauterine growth restriction (length and/or weight) that continues after birth, neurobehavioral deficits and specific facial features (short palpebral fissures, a smooth philtrum, and a thin upper lip), all of which must be present for a confirmed history of maternal alcohol use during pregnancy. Today it is recognized that the effects of maternal alcohol ingestion occur across a continuum ranging from children who have normal facial features and growth but have neurodevelopmental deficits to the full-blown FAS as originally described. The term *fetal alcohol spectrum disorder* (FASD) is used to describe the variety of clinical presentations ascribed to fetal alcohol exposure. Debate continues regarding the nomenclature of the subsets of FASD. In 1996 the Institute of Medicine proposed the following subcategories of FASD: FAS with confirmed maternal alcohol exposure; FAS without confirmed exposure; partial FAS with confirmed exposure; alcohol related birth defects; and alcohol-related neurodevelopmental disorder. In the late 1990s the subcategories of FASD were further described with the use of a four-digit diagnostic code representing the severity of the four important diagnostic criteria of FAS: growth deficiency, facial features, neurologic deficits, and intrauterine alcohol exposure.

Incidence and Epidemiology

The diagnosis of FASD is clinically difficult even in the face of full-blown FAS. The characteristic facial features most commonly appear around 8 months of age and become less apparent after 8 years of age. Other findings such as neurologic deficits may not be apparent until childhood. Diagnosis is also complicated by inaccurate parental recall or underreporting of drinking during pregnancy. Given the difficulty in making an accurate diagnosis of FASD and geographic and population variances, accurate rates of FAS and FASD are elusive. In the United States the incidence of FAS is thought to be about 1 to 3 per 1,000 live births, and the incidence of FASD 9.1 per 1,000 live births. The reported incidence is much higher in certain at-risk populations. For example FASD rates of 7 to 100 per 1,000 live births have been reported in various Canadian First Nations communities. The incidence of FAS among the offspring of heavy drinkers is estimated to be 43 per 1,000 live births.

Risk Factors

Despite extensive research examining the effects of alcohol exposure on the developing fetus there is no consensus on safe levels of alcohol ingestion in pregnancy. The most significant risk factor for the development of FASD is high concentrations of blood alcohol. Factors that affect the degree of expression of fetal alcohol effects are related to the timing of exposure, the pattern and frequency of consumption, maternal age, and the mother's genetic ability to metabolize alcohol.

Clinical Features of Fetal Alcohol Spectrum Disorder

As previously discussed, the clinical features of intrauterine alcohol exposure vary widely across the spectrum from fully expressed FAS to subtle behavioral or learning deficits.

Newborn

Facial features in the newborn may be absent or very subtle. Growth restriction (weight and head circumference) is the most prevalent feature of FAS seen in the newborn. Symptoms of acute alcohol withdrawal may be present if heavy maternal alcohol ingestion occurred near the time of delivery.

A variety of congenital anomalies, including renal, cardiac, and skeletal defects, have been attributed to fetal alcohol exposure and may be noted at birth.

Infancy/Early Childhood

Alcohol-affected infants and young children often experience delays in attaining speech and motor developmental milestones as well as attention deficit disorder with hyperactivity and impulsivity. Hearing loss and olfactory deficits have also been noted in these children.

School-Age Children

The intelligence quotient in children with FAS has been shown to range between 50 and 115. Even with IQs in the higher end of the range, children with FAS perform poorly in school, have problems with short-term and spatial memory, and have poor retention of learning. Speech and language delays persist, as do attention deficits. Children with FAS have difficulty maintaining friendships and often have low self-esteem. The use of poor judgment, as well as difficulty in the process of distinguishing right from wrong, results in an increase in conflicts in school, work, and society.

Diagnosis and Intervention

Infants or children suspected of having FASD should be referred to a multidisciplinary team that has specialized knowledge in the diagnosis of alcohol-related effects.

Early diagnosis of the affected infant is critical so that interventions can be initiated with the goal of minimizing the secondary problems experienced by individuals affected by alcohol. Accurate diagnosis of an affected infant will also facilitate timely intervention for the mother to reduce the risk for subsequent pregnancies. The diagnosis of FASD in a child should also prompt care providers to examine other siblings in the family who may have undiagnosed alcohol-related problems.

It is also important that a diagnosis of FASD not be made incorrectly. The label of FASD may result in stigmatization of both the mother and the child in addition to ineffective treatment for the labeled child. Other potential causes for the child's disabilities may be overlooked.

Management of the infant or child with FASD is aimed at maximizing the child's potential and preventing secondary morbidities and begins with support and guidance for the family. Behavioral issues may prove taxing for care providers and may lead to high levels of tension and frustration. Anticipatory guidance directed toward behavioral management is important in preventing situations of abuse. Educational resources will be required to support FAS children in school.

Screening and Prevention

Efforts at preventing FASD should begin with educating adolescents and young adults about the effects of alcohol in pregnancy. Primary preventive strategies aimed at identifying at-risk women prior to their becoming pregnant should also be emphasized.

Screening of all pregnant women should be undertaken using a validated screening tool. Ethel Burns, Ron Gray, and Leslie A. Smith provide several such screening tools in their review "Brief Screening Questionnaires to Identify Problem Drinking During Pregnancy." The letters used in these screening tool titles each stand for a question in the screening tool. The T-ACE or TWEAK tools are used commonly. For pregnant adolescents the CRAFFT tool may be used. When a pregnant woman is found to be at risk for heavy alcohol use, the care provider should ascertain the quantity and frequency of alcohol use to validate the screening. Support and counseling by a trained practitioner or referral for services should be initiated when risk is identified. According to the National Institute on Alcohol Abuse and Alcoholism, any woman who drinks more than three drinks on one occasion in the past month or anyone drinking more than seven drinks per week should be assessed for alcohol-related problems.

Abstinence from alcohol during pregnancy should be recommended to all women of childbearing age. Women who are concerned that they may have consumed some alcohol prior to being aware of their pregnancy can take some comfort from two meta-analyses that found no adverse fetal effects after small quantities of alcohol consumption. Other studies have shown, however, that behavioral changes may be seen in children whose mothers consumed as little as one drink per week compared to children whose mothers did not consume alcohol during pregnancy.

Debbie Fraser

See also Alcohol Addictions in the Family; Birth Defects and the Family; Drug Addictions in the Family

Further Readings

Astley, S. J., & Clarren, S. K. (2000). Diagnosing the full spectrum of fetal alcohol exposed individuals: Introducing the 4-digit diagnostic code. *Alcohol, 35,* 400–410.

Burns, E., Gray, R., & Smith, L. A. (2010). Brief screening questionnaires to identify problem drinking during pregnancy: A systematic review. *Addiction, 105*(4), 601–614.

Chudley, A. E. (2008). Fetal alcohol spectrum disorder: Counting the invisible—mission impossible? *Archives of Disease in Childhood, 93,* 721–722.

Chudley, A. E., Conry, J., Cook, J. L., Loock, C., Rosales, T., LeBlanc, N., et al. (2005). Fetal alcohol spectrum disorder: Canadian guidelines for diagnosis. *Canadian Medical Association Journal, 172,* S1–S21.

Canadian Pediatric Society First Nations and Inuit Health Committee. (2002). Fetal alcohol syndrome. *Paediatrics & Child Health, 7*(3), 161–174.

Green, J. H. (2007). Fetal alcohol spectrum disorders: Understanding the effects of prenatal alcohol exposure and supporting students. *Journal of School Health, 77*(3), 103–108.

Harwood, H. (n.d.). *Economic costs of fetal alcohol exposure.* Rockville, MD: Substance Abuse & Mental Health Services Administration. Retrieved from http://www.fasdcenter.samhsa.gov/documents/RickHarwoodPresentation.pdf

Hoyme, H. E., May, P. A., & Kalberg, W. O., Kodituwakku, P., Gossage, J. P., Trujillo, P. M., et al. (2005). A practical clinical approach to diagnosis of fetal alcohol spectrum disorders: Clarification of the 1996 Institute of Medicine Criteria. *Pediatrics, 115*(1), 39–48.

Koren, K., Nulman, I., Chudley, A. E., & Loock, C. (2003). Fetal alcohol spectrum disorder. *Canadian Medical Association Journal, 169*(11), 1181–1185.

Loock, C., Conry, J., Cook, J. L., Chudley, A. E., Rosales, T. (2005). Identifying fetal alcohol spectrum disorder in primary care. *Canadian Medical Association Journal, 172*(5), 628–630.

Stade, B., Ali, A., Bennett, D., Campbell, D., Johnston, M., Lens, C., et al. (2009). The burden of prenatal exposure to alcohol: Revised measurement of cost. *Canadian Journal of Clinical Pharmacology, 16*(1), 91–102.

FICTIVE KIN RELATIONSHIPS

Fictive kin relationships are those in which an individual or group is accorded the status of a family member in the absence of a biological or legal relationship. Fictive kin are generally incorporated into existing family structures although there are reports of groups of unrelated individuals who self-identify as family. Racial/ethnic minority families, particularly those with limited economic resources, are more likely than Caucasian families to assign family status to nonbiologically related persons. However, fictive kin relationships have been reported for gays and lesbians of all races and ethnicities. Persons assigned fictive kin status are expected to assume all of the rights and responsibilities of biological family members, such as the right to participate in family decision making and the responsibility to assist the family in meeting their needs. This entry discusses the history of fictive kin relationships, how one attains such status, and the implications of fictive kin relationships for family health.

History

Fictive kin relationships have been identified among African American, Puerto Rican, Latino, and Chinese families as an adaptive strategy to assist with providing care to dependent family members, such as their children and the aged. Fictive kin relationships are most common among African American families regardless of the family income level. The greater prevalence of fictive kin among African American families is believed to be an adaptive response that began during slavery in response to the separation of family members. More recently the greater prevalence of fictive kin among low-income African American families has been attributed to a need to obtain greater access to resources for their families by expanding the number of family members.

Any family member, most commonly an adult, may grant fictive kin status to another person outside of the family. The family status of that person may be acknowledged by only the family member granting the fictive kin status or by all members of the family. Examples of families granting fictive kin status to entire families or groups rather than to individuals are rare.

Fictive Kin Status

Attaining fictive kin status requires that a person have prolonged physical proximity to a family member in order to develop a relationship that is both interdependent and mutually beneficial. Persons generally attain fictive kin status by consistently contributing to the emotional or material needs of an individual over time. This relationship is reciprocal, wherein each person contributes to the emotional and material sustenance of the other over time. An important difference between reciprocal relationships observed in friendships and those observed for fictive kin is the longer time lag for fictive kin between incurring obligation due to meeting emotional or material needs and repayment of that obligation that results in a pattern of repeated sharing. This pattern of reciprocal sharing over time leads to a sense of confidence in each person that the other will consistently be available to assist with emotional or material needs as they arise.

The term *fictive kin* is sometimes used interchangeably with the term *extended family* although there are important differences. Fictive kin attain their status through behaviors rather than biology or marriage. Extended family members are related through biology or marriage and extend the family beyond the boundaries of the nuclear family members of father, mother, and children. Examples of extended family members include grandparents, uncles, aunts, or cousins.

Implications for Family Health Care

How a family is defined and whether family members are given permission to define the structure and boundaries of their own family have important implications for health service delivery, research, and policy. Health professionals who include all relevant family members can significantly increase the efficacy of their health care interventions and the family's satisfaction with health care decision making. Researchers examining family processes will benefit by assessing the presence and roles of fictive kin in order to better understand the strategies families use to obtain and allocate needed resources. Finally, policymakers who fail to recognize fictive kin relationships may condone policies that permit traumatic separation of children from their long-term caregivers because they lack biological or legal affiliations.

Currently health professionals assess biological and legally related family members by requesting the names of persons in specific family roles, such as spouse, mother, or son. Fictive kin relationships are easily overlooked when this form of assessment is used to identify family members. Health professionals can better assess fictive kin by asking individuals and family members to provide the names of persons considered to be important family members. Health professionals, who work with racial/ethnic families or with gays and lesbians of any racial or ethnic group, should routinely inquire about fictive kin *or play relatives,* a term used frequently by African Americans to describe fictive kin relationships.

Fictive kin make important contributions to the family or to family members over time regardless of their biological or legal affinity. Fictive kin are important sources of both emotional and material support for family members and should be included in health care decision making.

Constance Dallas

See also Defining Family: An Overview of Family Definitions From a Historical Perspective; Families: The Basic Unit of Societies; Kinship Care; Research Perspectives Used for the Study of Families; Same-Sex Partner Rights; Social Support Systems for the Family

Further Readings

Bould, S. (2003). Caring neighborhoods: Bringing up the kids together. *Journal of Family Issues, 24,* 427–447.

Chatters, L. M., Taylor, R. J., & Jayakody, R. (1994). Fictive kin relationships in black extended families. *Journal of Comparative Family Studies, 25,* 297–312.

Dill, B. T. (1998). Fictive kin, paper sons and compadrazgo: Women of color and the struggle for family survival. In K. V. Hansen & A. I. Garey (Eds.), *Families in the U.S.: Kinship and domestic politics* (pp. 431–448). Philadelphia: Temple University Press.

Gutman, H. G. (1976). *The black family in slavery and freedom: 1750–1925.* New York: Vintage.

Lan, P. (2002). Subcontracting filial piety: Elder care in ethnic Chinese immigrant families in California. *Journal of Family Issues, 23,* 812–835.

Muraco, A. (2006). Intentional families: Fictive kin ties between cross-gender, different sexual orientation friends. *Journal of Marriage and Family, 68,* 1313–1325.

Stack, C. B. (1974). *All our kin: Strategies for survival in a black community*. New York: Harper & Row.

Stewart, P. (2007). Who is kin? Family definition and African American families. *Journal of Human Behavior in the Social Environment, 15*(2/3), 163–181.

First Aid and the Family

First aid is the immediate care by laypersons for humans or animals suffering from acute injury or illness. Simple first aid measures can be performed by anyone. First aid given by laypersons is an important factor in saving human lives.

History

Throughout history, humans have been caring for others, and people have given help to others in need. First aid is connected to the Red Cross movement, which was started by Henri Dunant after the battle of Solferino in 1859. First aid started as taking care of wounded people, especially soldiers. In the 1960s cardiopulmonary resuscitation and the A (airway control)–B (mouth-to-mouth breathing)–C (chest or cardiac compressions) of life were introduced.

Data from Seattle have shown that teaching resuscitation to the public can lead to more survivors of cardiac arrest. The rate of survival for cardiac arrest is 46% in Seattle and King County compared to 6–10% in the rest of the U.S. This has lead to the slogan:

If you have to have a heart attack, have it in Seattle. (www.mediconefoundation.org)

In Seattle, 771,000 people have been taught CPR (cardiopulmonary resuscitation) since 1971, and each year 12000–13000 are trained by the Medic II program.

Sudden Cardiac Death and Resuscitation

Sudden cardiac death is one of the leading causes of death in European countries. Although Emergency Medical Services in Western societies are well-trained and -equipped, bystanders are needed because brain damage can occur within 3–5 minutes without breathing and circulation. Early combined chest compressions and rescue breathing (CPR) by bystanders and early defibrillation are strategies which have led to many saved lives. Without bystander CPR, the chances of surviving a sudden cardiac death are low. Today automated external defibrillators (AEDs) are located in public areas and can be operated by layrescuers. After CPR and defibrillation the patient must be stabilized by advanced life support provided by paramedics or physicians. This is known as the concept of the "Chain of Survival," which consists of four steps:

1. Early recognition of an emergency and call for help

2. Early bystander CPR

3. Early defibrillation

4. Early advanced life support

Importance of First Aid Education for the Whole Family

It is important that everybody in the family can provide first aid in an emergency situation. Emergency situations and the need to give first aid can occur anywhere and at any time. There have been reports in the media about young children being able to save a parent's life with an emergency call or other basic first aid measures. First aid knowledge can also lead to early recognition of possible life-threatening situations such as heart attack or stroke. Early recognition can help reduce the time to medical treatment and by this reduce negative consequences for the victim.

Recommendations for First Aid Education

Life-supporting first aid (LSFA) should be simple to learn and to recall and should be part of basic health education for all people. Eisenburger and Safar introduced a simplified content of what to teach laypersons, which includes 6 items (Eisenburger and Safar 1999, modified by Georg Bollig): If unconscious: TILT the head back; if not breathing: BLOW (breath slowly into the person's mouth); if no pulse (or in doubt): **PUMP** (give chest compressions of the center of the person's breastbone); if bleeding: **COMPRESS** (until bleeding stops); if unconscious and breathing: Turn the person into stable side position, keep the head tilted back; if conscious and foreign body in airway is suspected: Apply abdominal thrusts.

According to Eisenburger and Safar, fewer than 30% of out-of-hospital resuscitation attempts are started by lay bystanders. More people should start resuscitation attempts. Motivation is a crucial factor in applying first aid and CPR. Therefore teaching first aid to the public and getting people to use their knowledge in a real emergency situation is needed. In order to motivate people to apply first aid knowledge, first aid education should start early in life, measures must be simple and easy to remember, and repetition throughout life is needed. Basic first aid training can be started in kindergarten and primary school. Children who are 6–7 years of age are able to perform basic, life-saving first aid measures such as assessment of consciousness and breathing, calling for help, establishing a recovery position, and airway management. CPR can be introduced to children from the age of 10–12 years, although they might not be able to provide CPR as effectively as adults.

First aid should be part of lifelong learning, starting early in kindergarten and repetition should be given in regular intervals. This has lead to a Four-Step Model of First Aid Education (see Figure 1). Today a wide range of educational efforts is used, including web-based learning, peer-training, and courses for kindergarten children and nursing home residents. Hopefully these efforts can spread first aid knowledge throughout the whole society.

The adult basic life-support algorithms in the new guidelines 2010 of the American Heart Association (AHA) and the European Resuscitation Council (ERC) do show some minor differences. The most important steps of adult basic life support according to both guidelines are:

1. Person unresponsive and not breathing?

2. Call for help/activate the Emergency Medical Service (telephone number 911 in the U.S., 112 in many European countries, or the national emergency number)

3. Start chest compressions ("push hard and push fast")

4. Attach a defibrillator if available (and follow the advice of the automated external defibrillator [AED])

5. 2 rescue breaths and 30 chest compressions

6. Continue CPR 30:2 (30 chest compressions and 2 rescue breaths)

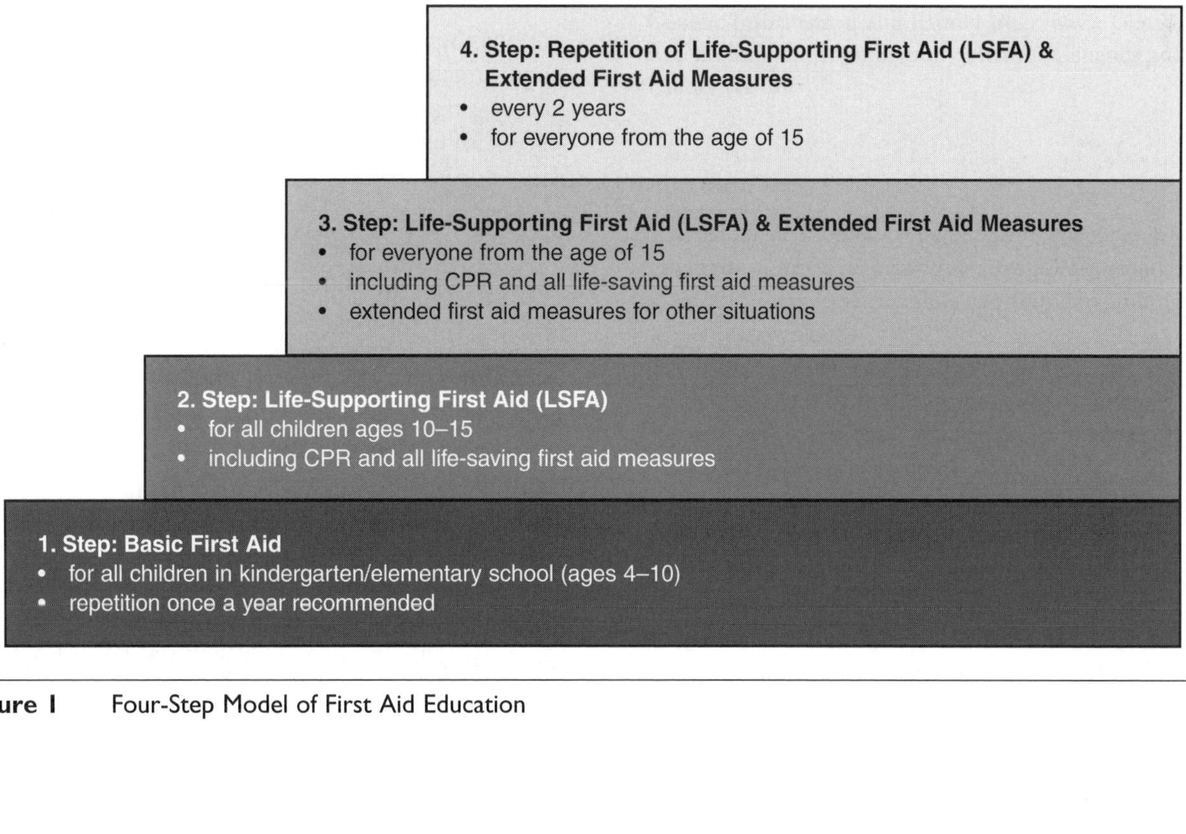

4. Step: Repetition of Life-Supporting First Aid (LSFA) & Extended First Aid Measures
- every 2 years
- for everyone from the age of 15

3. Step: Life-Supporting First Aid (LSFA) & Extended First Aid Measures
- for everyone from the age of 15
- including CPR and all life-saving first aid measures
- extended first aid measures for other situations

2. Step: Life-Supporting First Aid (LSFA)
- for all children ages 10–15
- including CPR and all life-saving first aid measures

1. Step: Basic First Aid
- for all children in kindergarten/elementary school (ages 4–10)
- repetition once a year recommended

Figure 1   Four-Step Model of First Aid Education

According to the new guidelines 2010, there is no need to check the pulse before starting CPR. Laypersons who are not trained to provide or who are reluctant to perform mouth-to-mouth ventilation (rescue breaths) should give compression-only CPR. That means to provide chest compressions without rescue breaths and without interruption of the chest compressions.

Conclusion

First aid given by laypersons is an important factor of survival. Everyone should learn and apply life-saving first aid. Education should start in the kindergarten, and repetitions throughout life are important. Actual guidelines for first aid and resuscitation change over time and are adapted to new scientific evidence in consensus meetings. Guidelines are presented by Koster and colleagues as well as Berg and colleagues, cited in the Further Readings and can be retrieved from the web (see websites of the European Resuscitation Council and the American Heart Association).

Georg Bollig

See also Acute Care/Hospitalization of Family Members; Acute Health Problems and Interventions for the Childbearing Family; Acute Health Problems and Interventions for the Elderly Family Resuscitation; Acute Health Problems and Interventions for the Midlife Family; Resuscitation, Family Presence During; Sudden Infant Death Syndrome in Childrearing Families

Further Readings

Berg, R. A., Hemphill, R., Abella, B. S., Aufderheide, T. P., Cave, D. M., Hazinski, M. F., et al. (2010). Part 5: Adult Basic Life Support: 2010 American Heart Association Guidelines for Cardiopulmonary Resuscitation and Emergency Cardiovascular Care. *Circulation, 122*, S685–S705.

Bollig, G., Wahl, H. A., & Svendsen, M.V. (2009). Primary school children are able to perform basic life-saving first aid measures. *Resuscitation, 80*, 689–692.

Eisenburger, P., & Safar, P. (1999). Life supporting first aid training of the public-review and recommendations. *Resuscitation, 41*, 3–18.

Koster, R. W., Baubin, M. A., Bossaert, L. L., Cabalero, A., Cassan, P., Castren, M., et al. (2010). European Resuscitation Council Guidelines for Resuscitation 2010. Section 2. Adult basic life support and use of automated external defibrillators. *Resuscitation, 81*, 1277–1292.

Websites

American Heart Association: http://www.americanheart.org
European Resuscitation Council: http://www.erc.edu
Fire Department Seattle: http://www.seattle.gov/fire/medics/medicOne.htm and http://www.seattle.gov/fire/medics/medicTwo.htm
International Red Cross: http://www.ifrc.org

Food Allergies and Family Experiences

A food allergy is a serious chronic health condition that can be life threatening. More than 12 million Americans have food allergies, and about 3 million of them are children. Severefood allergies account for 150 to 200 fatalities each year. After first defining a food allergy, this entry discusses the causes, symptoms, and treatments. Then, anaphylaxis, a severe reaction, is discussed, along with peanut allergies. Lastly, the impact of food allergies is examined.

Food Allergy Defined

A *food allergy* is an immune system response to a food that the human body has mistakenly identified as a harmful substance. Once the immune system decides that a particular food is harmful to the body, it creates specific antibodies (immunoglobulin E) to defy the perceived enemy. Because of the perceived invasion, the immune system releases massive amounts of chemicals, including histamine, to protect the body. These chemicals trigger a surge of symptoms that can affect the skin, respiratory system, gastrointestinal tract, or cardiovascular system.

Food Allergy Causes, Symptoms, and Treatments

Although several risk factors have been identified, the exact causes of food allergies are yet to be discovered. Common diagnostic methods include skin and blood tests. Ninety percent of all food allergies are related to eight common foods: dairy products, eggs, peanuts, tree nuts, fish, shellfish, soy, and wheat. Symptoms of food allergies usually occur immediately or within 1 to 2 hours after contact with the food allergen. Some of the common symptoms of an allergic reaction include skin symptoms (itching, hives, flushing, etc.), gastrointestinal symptoms (tingling and burning of the mouth/throat, vomiting, etc.), and respiratory symptoms (nasal congestion, sneezing, etc.). Medications such as epinephrine (EpiPen, for anaphylaxis), diphenhydramine (antihistamine, for allergy), and corticosteroid (for inflammatory skin) are frequently prescribed to alleviate allergic reactions. Reactions can range from slight to severe and should be dealt with immediately.

Anaphylaxis

Anaphylaxis is a severe allergic reaction affecting the entire body that can develop rapidly and even be fatal. The symptoms of anaphylaxis include itching lips, tongue, and palate; swollen throat and eyes; increased heartbeat; itching and/or hives; difficulty breathing; abdominal cramps, nausea, vomiting, and/or diarrhea; and dizziness, lightheadedness, or loss of consciousness. Emergency treatment is critical, and untreated anaphylaxis can result in a coma or fatality. The sooner anaphylaxis is treated, the less severe it will be. If a physician has previously prescribed an epinephrine injection kit, it should be administered into a muscle immediately while the ambulance is awaited. If there is no improvement after several minutes, a second injection should be given.

Peanut Allergy

Peanuts and tree nuts are the leading causes of fatal and severe reactions. Peanut dust is a unique concern for people with a severe peanut allergy. For some, accidental skin contact with, or inhalation of, peanut dust can trigger severe allergic reactions. Air travel can be particularly challenging because some airlines continue to serve peanut products. Foods for special events, such as candy and bakery goods, frequently contain or are in contact with peanuts and tree nuts. Not being allowed to eat treats and candies for special events can be difficult for young children, and the alternative treat is frequently

not an equally attractive option. Although some schools have completely banned the use of peanut products on school property, most educational settings continue to permit the use and consumption of such products.

Impact of Food Allergies

Although breast-feeding and gradual introduction of solid foods during infancy have been recommended for high-risk children, there are no definite cures for food allergies. Avoiding specific foods has been the primary coping mechanism for most people with food allergies. To have a nutrient-rich and balanced diet while avoiding trigger foods, food preparation and meal planning are crucial. Accidental cross contamination via preparation surface, utensils, and kitchen appliances can be fatal. When using packaged or canned foods, it is important to read labels containing information about ingredients and manufacture facilities. Dining out is a leap of faith, as most states do not require food allergy awareness training within the food service industry. The daily stress of ensuring food safety can cause frustration and put great financial burden on families. Food allergies can also take a toll on other aspects of life, such as vacation and work, as access to safe food and adequate medical facilities are important concerns for people with food allergies.

Family advocacy plays a vital role for children with food allergies. Policies on handling food allergies vary by state and school district. Parents or guardians should inquire about specific food-related policies and activities, as alternative cafeteria seating arrangements may be needed. Before a child is admitted to any setting that serves food, a proactive individualized Food Allergy Action Plan must be established. Because severe food allergies can substantially limit students' activities, students with hidden disabilities are protected from discrimination under Section 504 of the Rehabilitation Act of 1973. Ultimately, it is the parents or guardians of children with food allergies who must be the strongest advocates for the safety of their children.

Severe anaphylaxis and death are more likely to occur in adolescents and young adults than in any other age group. Physical intimacy, even an innocent kiss from someone who has eaten an allergen, can be potentially harmful. Increased autonomy, along with the tendency to underestimate risk, may place adolescents in grave danger. Communicating with adolescents about the importance of carrying medication, inquiring about the ingredients of foods, handling intimate relationships appropriately, and combating peer pressure, are crucial for keeping them safe.

Conclusion

The key component of ensuring a safe environment for individuals with food allergies is the genuine compassion and support from every family member, teacher, friend, classmate, coworker, and neighbor. Some children outgrow their food allergies, while others discover new food allergies later in life. Most individuals and families cope effectively with food allergies and have gained greater awareness of healthy foods and a better lifestyle. Food allergies are manageable, and food allergy–related fatalities are 100% preventable. A brighter future is anticipated with increased food allergy awareness and continued advocacy for policies that better ensure the safety of many food allergy sufferers.

I. Joyce Chang

See also Access to Health Care: Child Health; Adolescent Counseling; Advocacy for Families; Allergies and the Family; Asthma Family Issues: Prevention and Control; Disabilities and Family Management; Rehabilitation Act; Selecting Child Care for Children

Further Readings

Braly, J. (with Thompson, J.). (2000). *Food allergy relief.* Lincolnwood, IL: Keats.

Dozor, A. J., & Kelly, K. (2004). *The asthma and allergy action plan for kids.* New York: Fireside.

Tsai, H. J., Kumar, R., Pongracic, J., Liu, X., Story, R., Yu, Y., et al. (2009). Familial aggregation of food allergy and sensitization to food allergens: A family-based study. *Clinical and Experimental Allergy, 39*(1), 101–109.

Websites

Food Allergy & Anaphylaxis Network: http://www .foodallergy.org

Healthy Childcare, No for Nuts: http://www .healthychild.net/NutritionAction.php?article_id=262

Mayo Clinic, Peanut Allergy: http://www.mayoclinic .com/health/peanut-allergy/DS00710

National Institute of Allergy and Infectious Diseases, Food Allergy: http://www3.niaid.nih.gov/topics/ foodAllergy

FOSTER CARE EMANCIPATION

Foster care emancipation describes the process by which a youth in foster care is "freed" from or "ages out" of the public child welfare system. The term *aging out of foster care* is beginning to replace *emancipation* because it is becoming increasingly clear that there is very little "freedom" associated with leaving the foster care system. Reaching the age of adulthood means that the young person is no longer eligible for financial support by the governmental institutions that are responsible for the safety and care of dependent and neglected children. In the United States and most Western countries, this age is 18 years.

When parents are not able to care for a child because of substance abuse, mental illness, incarceration, and myriad other reasons resulting in parental neglect, the public child welfare system may remove that child from the home. In addition, a child who is experiencing emotional, physical, or sexual abuse may also be removed from the home. That child may be placed in foster care with another family who will foster (care for and look after) him or her until reunification with the family of origin can be achieved. If family reunification does not take place, the child may remain in foster care until he or she reaches the legal age of adulthood (age of emancipation).

If a young person is likely to remain in a foster home from the age of 16 years until the age of 18 years, then he or she is known today as a transitional aged youth. This transition can be abrupt and these youth often find themselves without a home, a job, or their family. This transition to adulthood is fraught with enormous challenges that are not typically experienced by the vast majority of non-foster youth. These youth who age out of care are at a significantly higher risk for homelessness, unemployment, educational deficits, unplanned pregnancies, welfare dependency, and health and mental health problems. This entry discusses some of these concerns as well as the disproportionate representation of minority youth, particularly African American youth, in the foster care system.

Correlates of Health Disparities: Education and Employment

Some of these emerging adults reconnect with their families of origin only to find that many of the problems that required removal from their homes and foster care placement still remain. In these situations, there is little institutional response to, or support for, their plight. Many of these young adults are disproportionately faced with the need for additional social services and supports after they have endured placement instability (multiple foster care placements).

Placement instability is also associated with poor health and mental health outcomes. Physical examinations might not occur as needed, and chronic health problems may not be properly monitored. A change in placement can also result in needed medication not following the youth to the next foster home. Separation from family, for whatever reason, may lead to anxiety and depression. Multiple placements can dampen a youth's ability and desire to forge close, trusting relationships with adults and peers. This lack of attachment may follow the youth into adulthood.

Foster care instability is associated with educational disruption (changing schools frequently) that adversely affects academic achievement. About 50% of foster youth complete high school before they leave foster care. Many go on to complete a general equivalency diploma (GED) at a later date. Although a GED is better than no high school certificate, there are differences in the career pathways available to high school diploma completers versus the GED completers. A very small proportion of emancipating youth enter postsecondary education and of those who do, the completion rate is very low, about 10%. Consequently, most emancipating youth have a limited career trajectory and face a future with fewer resources for housing, food, and medical care, especially in a world in which some postsecondary education is needed.

Former foster youth, like most vulnerable youth, are at risk for unemployment or minimum wage employment because of the few marketable skills they possess. Clearly, their prospects are dimmed because of limited education or vocational training. Another factor is the lack of support and encouragement former foster youth receive from family and kin networks. The Independent Living Programs (ILPs) are designed to prepare youth (while they are in foster care) for life after aging out of foster care. Studies show that many of these ILPs have limited utility for these youth because the programs often fail to provide hands-on experiences and may occur well in advance of emancipation. Because the programs are voluntary, youth may decide not to participate in them or think they do not need them.

Health and Mental Health: Behaviors and Access

According to public policy, emancipating youth should leave the foster care system with a high school diploma, documentation such as a birth certificate and social security number, and enrollment in Medicaid, for which they are eligible until the age of 21. However, numerous young people leave foster care with none or only one or two of these documents. Those youth without a birth certificate are unable to obtain a social security card, enroll in various educational programs, apply for driver's license, or prove who they are.

These former foster care youth are more likely than their nonfoster care peers to be involved in risky behaviors such as unprotected sexual encounters, drug and alcohol abuse, and criminal activities. They have higher rates of health issues such as HIV/AIDS, unplanned pregnancies, sexually transmitted diseases, and other infectious diseases. They leave the child welfare system with little knowledge of how to access or navigate the health care system. Their health care needs are often greater than their peers, but they do not have the resources to pay for treatment and they do not have the knowledge of how to access services. Because a high percentage of these youth lack health insurance and are unaware of their eligibility for Medicaid or any other resources, any health or mental health condition is likely to receive delayed or no treatment.

It is estimated that as high as 70% of youth transitioning out of the foster care system suffer from one or more mental health problems severe enough to justify mental health care. The most common disorders are depression, anxiety disorders, substance abuse, and post-traumatic stress disorder. When these disorders go untreated, they often result in disruptive or criminal behavior that places these young people at risk for incarceration. Some researchers estimate that 50% of all individuals who are incarcerated are former foster care youth.

Minority Groups

There are approximately 500,000 children across the United States who are currently in the foster care system. Of this group, about 20,000 age out of care annually and are expected to transition to adult independence. African American and Hispanic children are disproportionately represented in the child welfare system. It is estimated that 30% of foster children are African American, even though African American children represent about 15% of all children under the age of 18 years in the country. In some states, this is similarly true for Hispanic and American Indian children. Children of color represent nearly half of all children in the foster care system. Additionally, virtually all the children in the system are from poor or low-income families. Overall, public child welfare is a system for poor and nonwhite children. For these reasons, it is critical that young people age out of foster care equipped with the skills, knowledge, and resources necessary for self-sufficiency.

Assisting Youth to Transition Out of Foster Care: Policies

Although Title IV-E of the Social Security Act added the ILPs to address the needs of emancipating youth, the majority of public policy efforts were aimed at youth in foster care, and little attention was directed toward the aging out process. Policymakers recognized that former foster youth in general were not realizing a healthy and productive life compared to their same-aged peers. In 1999 Congress passed the Foster Care Independence Act (FCIA) to replace Title IV-E. This act provided the states with a dedicated funding stream for programs for foster youth and increased funds for ILPs. The act established the John H. Chafee Foster Care Independent Living Program, commonly referred to as the Chafee Act. This act provides flexible funding to states to develop and implement independent living services to all foster care children who are expected to remain in care until the age of 18 years. It allows Medicare

coverage, as well as room and board, for former foster youth until the age of 21. These provisions are to be carried out by the states so they can tailor the programs to meet the needs of their foster youth population. The implementation of state programs designed to help emancipated youth are uneven in their effectiveness. In 2001, the FCIA was amended to include the Promoting Safe and Stable Families Act to help states pay postsecondary education and training and related costs as one means to support those former foster youth to attend college if they were academically able.

The states may also access other programs, such as Temporary Assistance for Needy Families, the Workforce Investment Act, and Medicaid. Although these programs do not specifically target youth transitioning out of foster care, they meet other eligibility requirements such as unemployment, homelessness, and single parenthood. These youth are also eligible for programs in other systems such as the mental health system. However, this situation still leaves the youth to try to navigate various systems and unconnected services by themselves.

The Fostering Connections to Success and Increasing Adoptions Act of 2008 (H.R. 6893) recognizes that former foster youth might not be ready for independent living at the age of 18 years. This act permits states to extend foster care supports and services, under certain conditions, up to the age of 21. Thus, leaving the foster care system becomes an option for the young person rather than a policy requirement. State child welfare and state Medicaid agencies are expected to work together to forge a plan to improve the mental and physical health outcomes of this population. This option provides additional time for ensuring the youth learn the life skills needed to support a successful transition to adulthood. Extending Medicaid and other entitlements to youth beyond this age of 18 years is now open to states, and many are moving in this direction. This flexibility in policy can provide the safety net that these youth need to move more incrementally into adulthood. The 20,000 youth who age out of the foster care system annually need public support to assist them to become healthy, productive, and contributing members of society.

Alfreda P. Iglehart and Rosina M. Becerra

See also Access to Health Care: Child Health; Child Emotional Abuse and the Family; Child Neglect and the Family; Child Physical Abuse and the Family; Child Sexual Abuse and the Family; Foster Care for Minors; Homeless Families; Kinship Care; Parental Abandonment; Poverty, Children in, and Health Care

Further Readings

Courtney, M., Dworsky, A., Ruth, G., Keller, T., Havlicek, J., & Bost, N. (2005). *Midwest evaluation of the adult functioning of former foster youth: Outcomes at age 19*. University of Chicago: Chapin Hall Center for Children. Retrieved from http://www .chapinhall.org/sites/default/files/ChapinHall Document_4.pdf

Iglehart, A. P., & Becerra, R. M. (2002). Latino and African-American youth: Transition to adulthood and life after foster care emancipation. *Journal of Ethnic and Cultural Diversity in Social Work, 11*(1/2), 79–107.

Landsverk, J., Burns, B. J., Stambaugh, L. F., & Rolls Reutz, J. (2006, February). *Mental health care for children and adolescents in foster care: Review of research literature*. Seattle, WA: Casey Family Programs. Retrieved from http://www.casey.org/ resources/publications/MentalHealthCareChildren.htm

Pecora, P. J., Kessler, R. C., Williams, J., O'Brien, K., Downs, A. C., English, D., et al. (2005). *Improving family foster care: Findings from the Northwest Foster Care Alumni Study*. Seattle, WA: Casey Family Programs. Retrieved from http://www.casey .org/Resources/Publications/ImprovingFamily FosterCare.htm

Websites

Casey Family Programs: http://www.casey.org

Chapin Hall Center for Children: http://www.chapinhall .org

Child Trends: http://www.childtrends.org

University of California, San Francisco, Public Policy Analysis & Education Center: http://policy.ucsf.edu

FOSTER CARE FOR MINORS

Foster care refers to the system of federal, state, and local laws and practices pursuant to which children are removed from their home due to allegations of abuse or neglect and placed under the jurisdiction of both a child welfare agency and a juvenile court. The overriding objective of the U.S. child welfare system is to protect children who are not safe in their own homes. Although foster care was intended to be an interim solution until children could return to their birth families or find adoptive homes, the U.S. Department of Health and Human Services reports that almost half of foster children spend at least 2 years in the child welfare system and nearly 20% wait 5 or more years for a safe, permanent family.

As a result of numerous funding streams and myriad laws, the U.S. child welfare system includes federal, state, and local government agencies; juvenile and family courts; and community-based, as well as public and private, social service agencies. Although states have primary responsibility for establishing the legal and administrative structure for child welfare services, federal funding, legislation, and regulations establish a framework for state programmatic and fiscal decisions. In some states, child welfare services are subject to local as well as state funding and administration.

This entry discusses the current state of the U.S. foster care system and the challenges facing foster youth—including health and mental health concerns, outcomes for foster children and youth "aging out" of foster care, and trends associated with youth who "cross over" from foster care into the justice system.

Foster Care Overview

As the challenges facing struggling families and the ranks of children below the poverty line have grown, so too has the number of children in our nation's foster care system. Today there are approximately 500,000 children in foster care, almost double the number from the 1980s.

Although foster care provides many children with a necessary safe haven, courts and child welfare agencies are charged—first and foremost—with endeavoring to reunite the family unit. Some children remain under child welfare agency and court jurisdiction for only a few months while their parents get their lives back on track. Thousands of others, however, cannot safely be returned home and spend many years in foster care until they age out (also referred to as *emancipation*), generally at the age of 18. For these children, what is intended as a short-term way station can extend into years of instability.

Foster children often drift from placement to placement, community to community, and school to school, moving on average through three different foster care residences. Over time, these youngsters find themselves separated not only from their biological parents but also from siblings and other key supports. This constant movement inhibits the ability to provide foster youth with the most basic of health, and psychological treatment and support. Half of the youth in foster care do not receive appropriate mental health services, and many lack timely and basic medical care.

With this backdrop, it is not surprising that foster youth find it difficult to keep up. That is, 75% of children in foster care are working below grade level in school, 50% do not complete high school, and as few as 15% attend college, as reported by Miriam Aroni Krinsky. Youth who leave foster care face tremendous challenges and disheartening outcomes as they transition into adulthood.

The Role of the Courts and Legal Process

Every child who enters or leaves foster care must come before a dependency judge. Courts and the legal process oversee critical and often life-changing decisions in the lives of the children and parents under their jurisdiction. It is the court that determines whether a child should remain in foster care or can safely return home, whether reunification will occur or parental rights will be terminated, where foster children will live and how often they will move, whether they will have contact with their siblings and other family members, and when and how they will leave the system.

Often, however, courts are understaffed, caseloads are exceedingly high, and court dockets are overcrowded. These conditions can result in the conduct of hearings and rendering of significant decisions in a matter of minutes. Children (including teens) often have no legal representation and are not present in court. Parents similarly are not always adequately represented or supported through the complex legal process that will determine their parental rights. Moreover, communication among child welfare agencies, other professionals involved in the child and parent's life, and court officials tends to be constrained, and judges do not always receive key information pertaining to the decisions they render.

National reforms have urged enhanced support for the court and legal process and improved data and information sharing among judges, child welfare agencies, and other departments and agencies involved in the lives of foster youth and their parents. There have also been calls for more open and accountable dependency and child welfare systems and an enhanced voice (including effective legal representation) for both children and parents.

Foster Care Funding

The federal government spends $7 billion annually to help protect children from abuse and neglect. Yet the largest source of federal child welfare funds (funds that flow under Title IV-E of the Social Security Act) can be accessed only after a child has been removed from the home and brought into foster care. As a result, child welfare has little or no resources to provide in-home or other preventive services that could keep more families intact. Indeed, there is a disincentive to serve children within their home under these existing federal funding eligibility requirements that tie monetary allocations to the placement of children in out-of-home care and the length of time a child spends in care.

Even absent new resources, many experts have argued that federal funding streams should be reformed to provide child welfare officials with flexibility to offer preventive services and supports that could give troubled but still functioning families a fighting chance to stay together. By allowing child welfare agencies to implement services aimed at serving families before tragedy strikes, the U.S. child welfare system could develop differential responses at the front end of the foster care system, thus serving more families with greater success. This approach would also enable court-supervised interventions to focus on children and families with the greatest need.

Challenges Facing Foster Youth

Health and Mental Health Issues

In 2004, Krinsky reported that when youth enter the dependency court system, approximately 80% have a chronic medical condition, and 25% have three or more chronic problems. These conditions include failure to grow, asthma, anemia, neurological conditions, and visual, hearing, or dental problems. Further, many have significant developmental and mental health concerns. Older youth have significantly increased risk for drug abuse, early sexual activity, sexually transmitted diseases, and pregnancy.

Although these youth have extensive medical needs, there are many hurdles associated with prompt and effective delivery of essential medical treatment to children in care. Doctors and caregivers often lack access to critical medical information. A comprehensive medical history is rare when children enter care. Many children have had only erratic contact with health care providers prior to placement, and social workers seldom have an opportunity to review the children's health history with birth parents. Thereafter, as children move from placement to placement, their medical records often are missing or poorly maintained. Thus, children living in foster care commonly experience problems including under- or overimmunization, lack of continuity in medication, inadequate attention to basic health needs (including dental and eye care, yearly exams, and tracking of developmental milestones), and potentially life-threatening misdiagnoses.

Although efforts are under way in some states to create a foster youth health and education "passport" that travels with the child, implementation of this process nationwide has yet to occur, and concerns about sharing records have slowed an already challenging endeavor. Moreover, when youth in care move across county or state lines, difficulties associated with transferring not simply medical records but also health care coverage and benefits can create further barriers to medical care.

Children who drift from placement to placement experience a range of additional concerns stemming from discontinuity of health care. Confronted with a different physician on every visit, these youth have little opportunity to develop a doctor–patient relationship. Adolescents in particular do not view their physician as a trusted confidant or source of information regarding physical development, birth control, or other personal and confidential matters.

Foster children similarly face a wide array of untreated mental health concerns. Experts estimate that 40% to 85% of youth in out-of-home care suffer significant emotional disturbance and that adolescents living with foster parents or in group homes have a four times higher rate of serious psychiatric

disorders than youth living with their own families. The mental health needs of foster children frequently are overlooked until the child exhibits extreme and harmful behavior. Even then, the lack of coordination between the child welfare, mental health, and school systems results in fragmented provision of services. Children are not properly assessed, no one is given the clear responsibility of monitoring the mental health needs of these children, and when mental health services are finally made available, they are often either inadequate or too late to be of meaningful benefit to the child.

Teens and Youth Transitioning From Care

Whereas the total number of children in foster care nationally has been on the decline, the number of youth aging out of care has increased. According to the Pew Charitable Trusts, in 2005, more than 24,000 youth left care at the age of 18 with no family to support or guide them. These data show a 41% increase since 1998. Further, more than 165,000 youth aged out of the child welfare system between 1998 and 2005.

The average age of financial independence in the United States is 26 years of age, and many parents support their children both financially and emotionally beyond that age. Yet foster care policies and practices are premised on the presumption that foster youth somehow can attain independence by age 18. These adolescents are unprepared for independent adult life: They earn, on average, $6,000 per year (well below the national poverty level), only one third have a driver's license, and less than one quarter have the basic tools or skills to set up a household.

Youth who age out of care face tremendous challenges and dismal outcomes. One third of youth who leave the foster care system evidence mental health problems, alcohol or substance abuse, and major depression; over a third of foster youth earn neither a high school diploma nor a GED; and fewer than half of these young adults are employed 12 to 18 months after aging out of the system.

According to Mark Courtney and colleagues, within the first couple of years after young people emancipate from foster care, (a) 51% will be unemployed, (b) one third will be on public assistance, (c) 25% become homeless, and (d) 25% will be incarcerated.

Recent federal legislation seeks to address these concerns and create new opportunities to support foster youth beyond the age of 18. Pursuant to the Fostering Connections to Success and Increasing Adoptions Act (P.L. 110-351), effective October 1, 2010, federal funds will for the first time support state extension of foster care services and oversight up to age 21. With these new resources, however, come new challenges, as professionals in the court and child welfare systems seek to identify successful approaches and best practices to address the unique needs of these young adults.

Crossover Youth

Foster youth commonly lack a consistent and positive adult role model, tend to feel socially isolated, and are deprived of the opportunity to participate in activities that are a fundamental part of development. As a result, foster youth are at an elevated risk of entry into the justice system.

Studies confirm that the risk of delinquent behavior is nearly 50% higher for victims of abuse and neglect. Many of these youth enter the justice system as a result of "placement crimes" stemming from their residence in group home facilities where adolescent misbehavior is addressed differently than it would be in a family setting.

Once they come into contact with law enforcement, foster youth often find themselves battling the justice system with little support. As a result, they are more likely to end up arrested, detained, charged with a crime, and sentenced to longer terms of imprisonment than nonfoster youth. Thereafter, given the lack of child welfare services for the child or family once the youth has crossed into juvenile justice, foster youth have no home to return to on exiting custody and may as a result spend longer periods of time incarcerated or under probation supervision. These disheartening outcomes confirm the need to develop and promote effective prevention and intervention strategies and enhanced approaches on behalf of society's most vulnerable children and youth.

Miriam Aroni Krinsky

See also Adolescent Counseling; Foster Care Emancipation; Mental Health Assessment for Families; Poverty, Children in, and Health Care

Further Readings

Courtney, M., Dworsky, A., Ruth, G., Keller, T., Havlicek, J., & Bost, N. (2005). *Midwest evaluation of the adult functioning of former foster youth: Outcomes at age 19.* Chicago: Chapin Hall Center for Children. Retrieved from http://www.chapinhall.org/sites/default/files/ChapinHallDocument_4.pdf

Herz, D., Krinsky, M., & Ryan, J. P. (2006). Improving system responses to crossover youth: The role of research and practice partnerships. *The Link, 5*

Krinsky, M. (2004, September 28). Foster care system must do more to heal its ailing children. *California Daily Journal.* Available at http://www.dailyjournal.com

Krinsky, M. (2010). Disrupting the pathway from foster care to the justice system. *Family Court Review, 28,* 324.

Pew Charitable Trusts. (2007). *Time for reform: Aging out and on their own.* Philadelphia: Pew Charitable Trusts. Available at http://kidsarewaiting.org/tools/reports/files/0006.pdf

Pew Charitable Trusts. (2007). *Time for reform: Investing in prevention: Keeping children safe at home.* Philadelphia: Pew Charitable Trusts. Available at http://www.preventchildabuse.org/about_us/media_releases/pew_kaw_prevention_report_final.pdf

Pew Commission on Children in Foster Care. (2004). *Fostering the future: Safety, permanence and well-being for children in foster care.* Available at http://www.pewfostercare.org

Fragile X Syndrome and the Family

Fragile X syndrome (FXS) is the most common inherited form of intellectual disability. Families of children with FXS must deal with all of the usual challenges of raising a child with a disability. In addition, the fact that FXS is inherited means that parents need to consider their own reproductive risk, determine whether other children are carriers, and inform extended family members. New research suggesting that carriers may also be affected adds further to the experience of fragile X for the family. This entry presents an overview of FXS and its consequences for families.

Overview

History

Fragile X syndrome was initially known as Martin-Bell syndrome, based on clinical observations of a family with multiple affected family members. In 1974 Herbert Lubs discovered that many individuals who had the clinical symptoms of Martin-Bell had an abnormality on the X chromosome, leading him to name it "fragile X syndrome." In 1991 several teams of researchers from around the world identified the fragile X gene and described the molecular basis for this condition.

FXS is caused by a mutation or alteration on a single gene on the X chromosome. The cause of these mutations is not known. Relatively small mutations mean that an individual is a carrier of fragile X. Carriers are at increased risk of having a child with FXS. Once mutations expand to a certain size, the gene is not able to produce a protein known to be necessary for normal brain development, resulting in FXS.

Inheritance

Because females have two X chromosomes (XX) and males have one (XY), anyone can have FXS or be a carrier. The children of carrier females have a 50% chance of inheriting the altered FX gene. All daughters of carrier males will inherit the altered gene; none of their sons will inherit the gene because males do not pass on an X chromosome to their male offspring.

The FX gene can be transmitted in a carrier state or in the "full mutation" state. The odds of the gene expanding to the full mutation increase across generations.

Effects

Males with FXS typically have a moderate intellectual disability (IQ scores in the 50–55 range). They often also have attention and anxiety problems, and as many as 40% may also have autism. Females are less severely affected, typically having a learning disability and milder problems with attention and anxiety.

Originally carriers were not thought to be affected. However, it is now known that female carriers are at risk for early menopause and male carriers are at risk for tremors and other neurological problems that can emerge in middle age. Carriers may also be at risk for other cognitive and emotional problems. As a result, the term *fragile X associated disorders* is now used to encompass the full range of possible effects of the gene mutation.

Family Consequences

Getting a Diagnosis

Fragile X is not obvious at birth and so must be discovered as symptoms emerge. Developmental delays and language problems gradually become apparent near the end of the first year of life. But these problems are not specific to fragile X, and research shows that often children do not get diagnosed until 3 years of age. This causes tremendous frustration for parents, and children miss the opportunity to participate in early intervention programs that could provide special education and therapy. Because FXS is inherited from carrier parents, many families will have a second child with FXS before the first child is diagnosed.

Telling Others

Once one child has been identified with FXS, parents must be tested to determine the carrier. This knowledge forces families to consider risk for FXS when deciding whether to have additional children. Other children in the family may need testing to determine carrier status. Many parents are surprised to learn that other children in the family have FXS or are carriers, and they may worry about when and how to tell them. Also, parents are faced with the challenge of telling their own parents, siblings, or other extended family members about the possibility that they too might be affected by fragile X. For some families this can be a difficult process.

Getting Services

Children with FXS are eligible for special education services, but many professionals are not familiar with FXS. Parents may be frustrated with the lack of awareness in the medical and education community and may feel that their children are not receiving services tailored to their individual needs. As children become adults, the transition to independent living and employment pose additional challenges. Many adult children with FXS still live with their parents.

Dealing With Effects on Carriers

For many families, the possibility that carriers are affected adds to the perceived and real burden of raising a child with FXS. Carrier daughters are faced with the problem of early menopause, raising questions about how and when to tell potential partners and decisions about the possibility of having children earlier than they would have chosen. Carrier males may experience a debilitating tremor disorder. And all carriers are at risk (though the odds are not known) for other emotional and cognitive problems.

The Hope for a Cure

The fact that FXS and associated disorders are all caused by a change in a single gene leads to hope for a possible treatment or cure. Research in the past 5 years has led to discoveries about the underlying mechanisms affected by fragile X and new treatments. Animal trials have proved to be successful, and parents anxiously await the onset of human trials that are needed to prove safety and efficacy.

Don Bailey

See also Genetic Discoveries, New: Health Information in Families Derived Through; Genetic Family Histories; Genetic Information and Family Interviews; Genetic Research Findings and Disease Management for Families

Further Readings

Bailey, D. B., Raspa, M., Bishop, E., & Olmsted, M. (2009). The functional skills of individuals with fragile X syndrome: A lifespan, cross-sectional analysis. *American Journal on Intellectual and Developmental Disabilities, 114,* 289–303.

Hagerman, R. J., & Hagerman P. J. (Eds.). (2002). *Fragile X syndrome: Diagnosis, treatment, and research*. Baltimore: Johns Hopkins University Press.

Websites

eMedicine, Fragile X Syndrome: http://emedicine .medscape.com/article/943776-overview

Medline Plus, Fragile X Syndrome: http://www.nlm.nih .gov/medlineplus/fragilexsyndrome.html

National Fragile X Foundation: http://www.fragilex.org

GAMBLING ADDICTIONS IN THE FAMILY

Pathological gambling is a serious health concern that can have negative consequences on marriages, families, and children. Pathological gambling contributes to chaos and dysfunction within the family; disrupts marriages, thereby leading to high rates of separation and divorce; and is associated with child abuse and neglect.

Family of Origin and the Pathological Gambler

Families of pathological gamblers are filled with members who gamble excessively; suffer from depressive and anxiety disorders; and misuse alcohol, drugs, or both. Data from family studies provide insight into the makeup of the gambler's family of origin. For example, Donald W. Black, Patrick O. Monahan, M'Hamed Temkit, and Martha Shaw compared pathological gamblers to controls and assessed their first-degree relatives. The prevalence of problematic gambling was significantly greater in the relatives of those with pathological gambling than in the comparison relatives (12.4% vs. 3.5%). Pathological gambling relatives were also at greater risk for alcohol disorders, antisocial personality disorder, and mental disorders in general. Others have shown that major mood and anxiety disorders also run in these families. Of interest, the families of pathological gamblers also are significantly larger than control families; this is important because large

family size is independently related to delinquency, crime, and violence.

The parents of pathological gamblers have been described as falling into a *hard parent/soft parent* dichotomy, with fathers being the hard parent much of the time. In this scheme, the hard parent takes a firm line on helping the gambler ("I am not willing to bail you out anymore"), whereas the soft parent is emotionally closer to the gambler and feels an obligation to help him or her ("I cannot desert you"). The dichotomy in the parental approach brings more stress and discord into the family unit, more so as the gambler tends to manipulate and side with the soft parent.

Effects of Pathological Gambling on the Spouse or Partner

For each problem gambler, it has been estimated that there are 10 to 15 other people whose lives are adversely affected by the gambler's activities. None are more greatly affected than the gambler's immediate family.

One of the most robust findings to emerge from studies of pathological gamblers is their high divorce rate. Clinical studies and surveys show that the divorce rate is consistently higher than that in comparison groups. As reported by Dean Gerstein and colleagues, the National Gambling Impact Study revealed the lifetime divorce rates for problem and pathological gamblers were 40%2 and 53%, respectively; the rate for nongamblers was 18%.

High divorce rates are not hard to understand when, as Henry Lesieur observed, the partners of persons with pathological gambling are put at serious financial risk, which may include huge credit card debts, multiple mortgages, illegal loans, formal and/or informal loans, loss of rent or mortgage funds resulting in homelessness or eviction, or misuse of irreplaceable retirement funds or savings. Economic control, such as limiting or blocking access to family funds, can be a form of abuse that is used to conceal and maintain a family member's disordered gambling.

Domestic violence is also frequent in couples in which one member demonstrates pathological gambling. Robert L. Muelleman, Tami DenOtter, Michael C. Wadman, T. Paul Tran, and James Anderson interviewed women admitted to an emergency department and found that of those reporting violence, 23% had partners with pathological gambling, and most of these also had an alcohol disorder. They concluded that a woman whose partner had problem gambling was more than 10 times as likely to be a victim of partner violence than if the partner did not have problem gambling. If the gambler was also a problem drinker, that likelihood was increased over 50-fold. These findings are partially consistent with research in which gamblers retrospectively described their parents as neglectful.

Valerie C. Lorenz and Robert A. Yaffee surveyed women belonging to GamAnon, an organization designed to support and educate families and friends of pathological gamblers, about their medical health, emotional health, and the health of their marital relationship. They were asked to recall the emotions and symptoms they experienced when the partner's gambling was at its worst. The emotions most frequently identified by spouses were anger or resentment, depression, isolation, and feeling guilty about contributing to the gambling. Physical complaints included chronic or severe headaches and stomach and bowel ailments; sexual relations were reported to be seriously disturbed as well. Most spouses contemplated leaving their gambling spouses, and nearly one third did so.

Effects of Pathological Gambling on Offspring

The parents' gambling behavior affects their children as well. In one study, women pathological gamblers reported that their gambling resulted in stress, guilt, mood swings, a sense of isolation, and neglectful behavior, all of which negatively impacted their children. Durand F. Jacobs and colleagues. also surveyed youth who reported that one or both parents had problem gambling and compared them to students who reported no gambling among their parents. Offspring of gambling parents were at much greater risk for smoking and alcohol or drug use; psychosocial problems such as an unhappy childhood, or having a "broken home"; educational difficulties; and emotional disorders, including dysphoria and suicidal behavior. Adolescent gambling behavior itself was strongly associated with parental gambling.

Lesieur and Jerome Rothschild developed a questionnaire and surveyed children of married Gamblers Anonymous (GA) members in the United States and Canada. They found that, when compared with nationally normed samples from intact families, the GA offspring were more likely to have been subjected to parental physical violence and abuse.

Treatment for Spouses of Partners

Research on methods for helping families better cope with the stress of living with a pathological gambler is ongoing. This work has involved teaching the partner better coping skills and attempting to engage the gambler in treatment. In one study, partners were randomly assigned to either coping skills training or to a delayed treatment condition. Partners assigned to the training received education about gambling and learned special coping skills that included cognitive behavioral techniques, problem solving, and communication skills. At the end of treatment, the researchers found the partners who learned new coping skills were less anxious and depressed than those in the control group.

Conclusion

Pathological gambling has serious repercussions for families, marriages, and offspring. One source of family dysfunction comes from the excess burden of mental illness and addictive disorders found in the families of origin of the individuals with pathological gambling. Spouses of gamblers and their offspring bear the brunt of the stress within the family, experiencing emotional and physical turmoil. Research on the collateral effects of pathological gambling and its treatment is in its infancy, yet it is an area that demands greater attention.

Donald W. Black and Martha C. Shaw

See also Alcohol Addictions in the Family; Drug Addictions in the Family

Further Readings

Black, D. W., Monahan, P. O., Temkit, M., & Shaw, M. (2006). A family study of pathological gambling. *Psychiatry Research, 141,* 295–303.

Gerstein, D., Hoffmann, J., Larison, C., Engelman, L., Murphy, S., Palmer, A., et al. (1999). *Gambling impact and behavior study: Report to the National Gambling Impact Study Commission.* Chicago: National Opinion Research Center at the University of Chicago.

Heineman, M. (1989). The parents of male compulsive gamblers: Clinical issues/treatment approaches. *Journal of Gambling Behavior, 5,* 321–332.

Jacobs, D. F., Marston, A. R., Singer, R. D., Widaman, K., Little, T., & Veizades, J. (1989). Children of problem gamblers. *Journal of Gambling Behavior, 5,* 261–268.

Lesieur, H. R. (1998). Costs and treatment of pathological gambling. *Annals of the American Academy of Political and Social Science, 556,* 153–171.

Lesieur, H. R., & Rothschild, J. (1989). Children of Gamblers Anonymous members. *Journal of Gambling Behavior, 5,* 269–281.

Lorenz, V. C., & Yaffee, R. A. (1988). Pathological gambling: Psychosomatic, emotional and marital difficulties as reported by the spouse. *Journal of Gambling Behavior, 4,* 13–26.

Muelleman, R. L., DenOtter, T., Wadman, M. C., Tran, T. P., & Anderson, J. (2002). Problem gambling in the partner of the emergency department patient as a risk factor for intimate partner violence. *Journal of Emergency Medicine, 23,* 307–312.

Rychtarik, R. G., & McGillicuddy, N. B. (2006). Preliminary evaluation of a coping skills training program for those with a pathological-gambling partner. *Journal of Gambling Studies, 22,* 165–178.

Shaw, M. C., Forbush, K. T., Schlinder, J., & Rosenman, E. (2007). The effect of pathological gambling on families, marriages, and children. *CNS Spectrums, 12,* 615–622.

GENETIC CONDITIONS, COMMUNICATION IN FAMILIES

The definition of *family communication* is complex and depends on what is meant by *family* and *communication*. In this entry communication is seen as a verbal and nonverbal process made up of different signs and symbols, not just language and talking. The definition of family is also complex. In sociology families are viewed as a group of people whose structure is governed by the rules and beliefs of a particular society, not biological relationships alone. In Western societies families generally have two forms: nuclear and extended. The nuclear family is a small group of relatives, most commonly a mother, father, and their children. Extended family are more distant and do not usually live in the same household.

Genetic conditions are important to families and individuals because they carry information about disease that can be passed on through generations from parents to children. Knowing (or not knowing) about a family history of genetic illness may be important for an individual's health, lifestyle, and psychological well-being. Those affected by genetic disorders frequently experience feelings of guilt and shame about the potential of passing on illness to their children. Research suggests that communication in families about genetic conditions is not always straightforward, with some relatives being poorly informed or even ignorant about their family history of disease. This is an important issue because genetic testing and knowledge about genetic susceptibility have become more widely available and will be relevant to more and more people. This entry discusses some of the concerns for families and health professionals with regard to the passing on of genetic knowledge to at-risk relatives. It begins by discussing whose responsibility it is to pass on such information and the issue of nondisclosure. It moves on to outline the role of health professionals in this area and provides a summary of empirical evidence. The entry concludes by discussing the difficulties in determining and assessing successful family communication about genetic risk.

Who Is Responsible?

In the United States and the United Kingdom it is a family's responsibility to pass on information about genetic conditions. Health providers keep such information confidential except in exceptional circumstances. For example, if an adult child who is at 25% risk for Huntington's disease wants to take the predictive test to know if he or she carries the mutated gene, then a parent's right not to know their carrier status may be sacrificed. (Huntington's disease is an incurable autosomal dominant neurodegenerative disorder for which predictive genetic testing is available.) Several studies have explored individual views about who should tell, and these generally found that people want genetic information to be passed on by their family, although health professionals may be needed for support.

Nondisclosure of Genetic Information

In cases of nondisclosure health professionals may decide to break confidentiality in order to alert at-risk relatives, particularly if preventive action is available and/or people could make more informed reproductive decisions. Nondisclosure occurs when an individual does not pass on genetic information to an at-risk family member which is relevant for their health and reproductive choices. For example, if a woman (or man) knows she or he is a BRCA gene carrier (a gene mutation associated with a high risk of developing breast or ovarian cancer), this situation may have important implications for close and extended relatives. Three different forms of nondisclosure have been identified: positive (not telling in order to prevent harm, or from the psychological burden of knowing one's risk), negative (refusing to overcome communication barriers, such as family rifts), or neutral (perceiving there is nothing to be done). Although nondisclosure may raise difficult ethical dilemmas, particularly the negative form, several studies suggest it is not a frequent concern for clinicians. Given this infrequency and the existence of confidentiality guidelines, researchers suggest that such dilemmas be assessed on a case-by-case basis. The duty to warn at-risk relatives must also be balanced against wider implications of breaking confidentiality or damaging public trust in the doctor–patient relationship.

Role of Health Professionals

In the United States and the United Kingdom the genetic counseling profession is guided by the principle of nondirectiveness. Individuals are provided with information about a genetic condition so that they can make informed decisions without any undue influence or coercion. Nevertheless, one area where genetic professionals are encouraged to be directive is family communication about hereditary illness. National and international guidelines vary about the extent to which health professionals should be directive in this area. For example, in France doctors must do everything they can to persuade an individual to pass on genetic information, whereas in the United Kingdom guidelines are not so strong; genetic counselors are encouraged to give advice about how and when information can be passed on and to whom it is most relevant. In most circumstances health professionals hope to persuade individuals to alert relatives and offer them support to do so. This communication is generally achieved through identifying those at risk, scenario-based counseling, and writing information letters to be disseminated. In order to provide effective support, health professionals should also know about how families communicate about genetic risk.

Disclosure of Genetic Information in Families

The disclosure of genetic risk information means that an "unknowing" individual is informed about his or her risk by a "knowing" party. This communication can be a one-off event (i.e., an individual is told on one occasion only) or a lengthy and incremental process influenced by a multitude of factors. Individuals have consistently been shown to have concerns about what, when, and how to tell relatives about genetic risk across a range of disorders.

When to Tell

The issue of when to tell relatives is a dilemma. For example, parents generally want to put off telling for as long as possible in order to protect their children, but they need to tell them in time so that informed decisions can be made, including any preventive/disease management options, genetic testing, reproduction, careers, and insurance.

In general the "right time" will depend on the recipient's life stage, his or her perceived emotional readiness, and the right opportunity. Several studies also draw attention to parents who have told children about a genetic condition in childhood or adolescence because of feeling they were old enough to understand or needed to know how to manage the treatment of their condition, as with cystic fibrosis. Thus, decisions about when to tell family members are related to the medical course of the illness and availability of treatment. In adult-onset genetic conditions such as hereditary breast or ovarian cancer, parents might put off alerting children about their risk until they approach screening age.

How and What to Tell

Studies suggest there are different patterns of family communication depending on the nature of the disease and the availability of treatment. For example, in families affected by Lynch syndrome (hereditary nonpolyposis colorectal cancer), for which treatment is available, it is more common to follow a matter-of-fact approach to telling relatives and to talk about the illness in normal social interaction. More varied patterns of disclosure have been observed in families affected by adult-onset genetic diseases such as Huntington's disease and hereditary breast or ovarian cancer, ranging along a continuum from open/supportive styles, to selective/limited disclosure, to total secrecy. Styles of communication may also vary within and between families, which can lead to different views and tensions between relatives. Several studies also provide examples of unplanned and spontaneous disclosures where strong emotions, or the impact of a devastating disease like Huntington's, may lead to unpredictable and ill-considered disclosure behavior. The timing and style in which parents found out themselves may influence how they go on to tell others. Individuals may also draw on these two types of disclosure: alerting, where an individual's risk is announced, and educating, where an explanation about the illness is given. There remains little empirical evidence on the nature of information passed on to relatives and recipients' understanding of what they have been told.

Other Issues

Studies suggest that individuals need to make sense of their own personal risk before disseminating any knowledge to relatives. Further, recipients may begin to understand such information only when it becomes relevant to them, demonstrating the importance of "checking back" on someone's understanding of what they have been told.

Ideas about "who is family" are likely to influence disclosure decisions. This is important because views may differ from those of a geneticist about who is seen as family and which relatives are important to inform. Studies show that people generally disclose to first-degree relatives and family members they feel emotionally close to. Alerting geographically and emotionally distant relatives is more selective. Family rifts, divorce, separation, adoption, and large age gaps between siblings can be significant barriers, although some individuals feel a duty to inform as many close and extended relatives as they can.

Implicit rules based on social constructions of family and kinship also influence disclosure patterns. For example, several studies draw attention to those who have wanted to pass on risk information to unknowing nieces and nephews but did not feel they had the authority to do so because this was viewed as a parent's responsibility. Cultural differences are likely to impact such authority "rules."

Several studies report instances of family messengers or pivotal relatives who take on responsibility for telling (or not telling), absolving others of the role. Research also draws attention to the use of intermediaries when passing on risk information; men, in particular, may adopt this strategy. For example, if a grandparent tells his or her grown-up child, then that child would be expected to tell his or her own children, although the adult child may not necessarily do so.

In families it is generally the women who are the gatekeepers of genetic information, but some fathers have been found to take responsibility for telling, and the opinions of male relatives can strongly influence women's disclosure decisions and styles of communication. In some circumstances disclosure is more gender neutral, as with families affected by Lynch syndrome and hereditary pancreatitis; this suggests it is not always women who take on the telling role.

What Is Successful Family Communication About Genetic Risk?

"Successful" family communication about genetic risk seems hard to evaluate because of the complexity of the issues outlined earlier. Nevertheless, from a clinical perspective the use of three outcome measures has been suggested: (1) whether individuals choose to partake in genetic testing or attend genetic counseling, (2) recipients' knowledge and understanding, and (3) the impact on individuals and families.

Overall, communication regarding genetic conditions is a relatively new area of research with studies only beginning to explore how families tell each other about genetic risk. There is a lack of empirical data about the process of disclosure and its outcomes, as well as how health professionals can most effectively advise and support patients, particularly with regard to telling children. There is continued debate about the extent to which it is a family or professional responsibility to pass on genetic information to at-risk relatives.

Karen Forrest Keenan

See also Conflict in Family Life, Role and Management of; Family Secrets in Family Therapy; Genetic Research Findings and Family Health; Genetics and Family Health

Further Readings

Clarke, A., Richards, A., Kerzin-Storrar, L., Halliday, J., Young, M. A., Simpson, S. A., et al. (2005). Genetic professionals' reports of nondisclosure of genetic risk information in families. *European Journal of Human Genetics, 13,* 556–562.

Forrest, K., Simpson, S. A., Wilson, B. J., van Teijlingen, E. R., McKee, L., Haites, N., et al. (2003). To tell or not to tell: Barriers and facilitators in family communication about genetic risk. *Clinical Genetics, 64,* 317–326.

Forrest, L. E., Delatycki, M. B., Skene, L., & Aitken, M. (2007). Communicating genetic information in families: A review of guidelines and position papers. *European Journal of Human Genetics, 15,* 612–618.

Gaff, C. L., Clarke, A. J., Atkinson, P., Sivelle, S., Elwyn, G., Iredale, R., et al. (2007). Process and outcome in communication of genetic information within families: A systematic review. *European Journal of Human Genetics, 15,* 999–1011.

Metcalfe, A., Coad, J., Plumridge, G., Gill, P., & Farndon, P. (2008). Family communication between children and their parents about inherited genetic conditions: A meta-synthesis of the research. *European Journal of Human Genetics, 16,* 1193–2000.

GENETIC CONDITIONS, EXPERIENCES OF FAMILIES DURING THE PREDIAGNOSIS AND DIAGNOSIS PHASES OF

Genetic testing is both an individual and a family experience. Even though genetic testing is performed on genetic material obtained from individuals, the decision of a family member to undergo genetic testing, as well as the family member's test result, can have profound and long-term implications on the immediate and extended family. For example, if a young adult male with a family history of Huntington's disease (a progressive neurodegenerative disorder inherited in an autosomal dominant pattern) decides to undergo predictive or presymptomatic testing (testing used to detect gene mutations associated with diseases that typically appear later in life), even though his parents and siblings have asked him not to, his decision will most likely have a powerful impact that will reverberate throughout both his immediate and his extended family, especially if the results are positive (indicating that he will eventually develop Huntington's disease).

This entry begins with an overview of past, present, and future trends in genetic testing. Then, there is a brief description of four nonsymptomatic time phases to help explain why individual and family experiences may differ depending on where family members are in terms of testing and diagnosis. This is followed by a discussion of how family experiences in each phase might vary depending on the type of condition. In this entry, genetic conditions include both single gene disorders and multifactorial or genomic conditions resulting from complex interactions between genetic and environmental factors.

Genetic Testing: Past, Present, and Future Trends

Advances in genetics and genomics have radically altered the genetic testing landscape. Not only have there been dramatic increases in the number of diseases for which genetic testing is offered, the number of laboratories offering genetic testing has increased appreciably. In addition, there have been noteworthy changes in the types of genetic testing being offered, as well as the types of diseases for which genetic testing exists.

In 1993, genetic testing was available for about 100 diseases and there were approximately 100 laboratories offering genetic testing. The main types of testing being offered in the 1990s were prenatal screening for Down syndrome and other chromosomal disorders, newborn screening and diagnostic testing for relatively rare single gene (Mendelian) disorders such as phenylketonuria and sickle cell disease, and predictive testing for adult-onset conditions like Huntington's disease.

As of May 2010, the number of diseases for which genetic testing is available has increased to 2,062 diseases, and there are over 600 laboratories offering genetic testing. The types of genetic testing now being offered include preimplantation genetic testing of embryos, predispositional testing for hereditary forms of cancer, pharmacogenetic testing or genotype-guided drug therapy, and whole genome sequencing for a wide variety of diseases such as diabetes and heart disease. Moreover, a growing number of companies (e.g., 23andMe, DNAdirect, Navigenics, and Pathway Genomics) are offering direct-to-consumer testing (genetic tests that are marketed directly to consumers via television, print advertisements, or the Internet).

One company offering direct-to-consumer testing has begun marketing a genetic testing kit in drugstores. Although the cost of the kit is generally under $30, the cost of having the DNA analyzed can be as high as $500 if the customer orders all the different types of testing offered (ancestry testing, predispositional testing for over 70 conditions, testing for drug responses and adverse drug reactions, and carrier testing). Although it is too early to speculate how marketing genetic testing in drugstores will ultimately impact how genetic services are provided worldwide, it is not too early to consider the impact this may have on the family experience of being tested for and living with a genetic condition. Clearly, easy access to genetic testing kits will increase the number of individuals and families who believe they are at greater risk for developing one or more genetic conditions. Awareness of increased risk for developing genetic conditions may have positive consequences if it results in individuals and families engaging in activities designed to improve their health outcomes, but it may also result in negative consequences if the results are incorrect or misleading. For example, the findings could give family members a false sense of security or, conversely, they could be needlessly alarmed by the findings and this could ultimately result in family members undergoing inappropriate, unnecessary, and expensive examination and treatment.

In the future, there will most likely be a dramatic increase in whole genome sequencing. Current estimates suggest that by 2013, one or more companies will have the technology needed to map an individual's entire genome in 15 minutes for less than $1,000. If this does become a reality, there will undoubtedly be ramifications for families. Families who have access to the testing will have a greater chance of obtaining personalized health care (health care that utilizes gene-based information to understand each family member's individual requirements for health maintenance, disease prevention, and therapy tailored to their genetic uniqueness). However, there is concern that many families will not be able to afford this type of genetic testing and because of this, the gap between the "haves" and the "have-nots" will widen. That is, families who have the resources needed to get personalized health care are likely to become healthier than those who do not.

Nonsymptomatic Time Phases of Genetic/Genomic Conditions

There is growing recognition that the number of individuals and families considered at increased risk for genetic conditions is much greater than was once thought. Additionally, the boundary between health and chronic illness is becoming increasingly blurred by the designation of "genetically at risk." Because of these changes, greater attention needs to be devoted to understanding how individual and family experiences vary depending on where family members are in terms of testing and diagnosis. A framework that may help clinicians and researchers to gain a deeper understanding of this is the family systems genetic illness model, developed by John Rolland and Janet Williams.

The family systems genetic illness model includes four nonsymptomatic time phases: (1) awareness, (2) crisis I pretesting, (3) crisis II test/posttesting, and (4) long-term adaptation. In addition, Rolland and Williams have identified key individual and family developmental tasks associated with each of the nonsymptomatic phases. The awareness phase begins with some knowledge of genetic risk, but family members are not actively considering testing or testing is not currently available. In the crisis I pretesting phase, one or more family members are actively considering testing and there is some understanding of possible implications for not only the individual being tested but other family members. The crisis II phase includes both the testing experience and the early posttest period. The long-term adaptation phase begins following awareness of positive test results and ends with the onset of symptoms. The four phases are linked by critical transition periods, during which family members consider the fit of their life structure, plans, and dreams in the face of the developing challenges they will be facing in the next time phase.

Experiences of Families During the Prediagnosis and Diagnosis Phases

Prediagnosis Phase

Based on the four nonsymptomatic time phases included in the family systems genetic illness model, the prediagnosis phase can be divided into three different phases: awareness, crisis I pretesting, and crisis II test/posttesting. Family experiences during these phases may vary depending on the type of condition for which testing is being considered. The next few paragraphs include examples to illustrate this.

Awareness Phase

An expectant couple in their 40s may have some knowledge that they are at increased risk for having a child with Down syndrome, but they may not have given much thought to whether they are interested in undergoing prenatal testing or what type of testing they would want to undergo (e.g., maternal serum screening, chorionic villi sampling, diagnostic ultrasounds, or amniocentesis). In contrast, if the expectant mother has a strong family history of Huntington's disease, she may have already been dealing with a lengthy, multigenerational history of anticipatory loss (the experience of living with the possibility or inevitability of future loss). In addition, in her family, genetic testing may be viewed as a necessity rather than an option. This view of genetic testing may be especially problematic for the couple if they want a child and have been experiencing problems with infertility. They may find it too stressful to even discuss prenatal testing and the choices they would need to make if their fetus was diagnosed with Down syndrome or found to carry the genetic mutation associated with Huntington's disease. Further, the woman would most likely be encouraged to find out her own mutation status first. Or, if she is unwilling to do this, her health

care provider might suggest that there is always the option of nondisclosure preimplantation diagnosis with future pregnancies.

Preimplantation diagnosis is a procedure that makes it possible for a couple with a family history of conditions like Huntington's disease to ensure that their offspring will not develop Huntington's disease. In nondisclosure preimplantation, only the lab knows if any of the embryos had the mutation associated with Huntington's disease; this is not disclosed to the couple. For some families, preimplantation diagnosis is not an option, either because of financial constraints or the fact that some individuals and families consider the act of discarding embryos as unacceptable.

Crisis I Pretesting Phase

During the crisis I phase, one or more family members are actively considering testing. This can be a very stressful time for families, especially if family members do not agree about the right of family members to make their own decisions about testing. In a family with a strong history of breast and ovarian cancer, there may be a push for family members to undergo genetic testing for mutations associated with hereditary breast and ovarian cancer (i.e., BRCA1 and BRCA2). However, some family members may choose not to undergo testing, and this may result in negative consequences at multiple levels. A young woman who has been strongly encouraged to undergo testing by her mother may choose to actively defy her mother's wishes. Siblings who disagree about the need to undergo testing may decide to go their separate ways even after one of them has been diagnosed with breast cancer. Both of these are unfortunate outcomes because not only do they increase the level of distress in the family, they often occur at a time when support by family members could serve a critical role in improving individual and family outcomes.

Crisis II Test/Posttesting

Women who choose to undergo BRCA1 and BRCA2 testing often state that their main reason for undergoing testing is to gain information that could be shared with others, for example, offspring, siblings, and cousins. Yet those who get a positive result often find it difficult to share their results with the family members they were hoping to help. Many women report feeling torn between the responsibility to inform at-risk relatives and the desire not to harm or cause distress in other family members.

In some cases, testing negative can be even more stressful than testing positive. For example, if an individual grows up thinking he or she will inevitably develop Huntington's disease because the majority of family members in the previous generation had Huntington's disease, testing negative (which indicates that they do not have the mutation or that they do not have the condition) may actually precipitate a crisis for not only the individual who tested negative but also the individual's spouse or partner and other members of his or her family. The development of a crisis situation may be due in part to the fact that the individual and possibly other family members made life choices thinking that the individual would not live a long life. However, now that the individual might live a long life, the choices that were made may have profound negative consequences at the individual, dyadic, and family level.

Postdiagnosis Phase

The postdiagnosis phase may be short or it may extend for decades in the case of individuals who have undergone genetic testing for adult-onset disorders. The ability of family members to live as fully as possible, in spite of their heightened genetic risk, is one of the major challenges of this phase. Another challenge is figuring out how to minimize relationship skews between those who tested positive and those who tested negative.

In some cases, finding out that a family member has a genetic condition may be viewed as a positive event. This is especially true for families who have been searching for a diagnosis for a long period of time. Recent advances in technology have resulted in a growing number of families of children with rare conditions using Internet search engines to obtain a diagnosis for their child. Clearly, advances in genetics and technologies will continue to alter many aspects of the family experience of being tested for and living with a genetic condition.

Marcia Van Riper

See also Genetic Conditions, Communication in Families; Genetic Information and Family Interviews; Genetic Research Findings and Disease Management for Families; Genetic Research Findings and Family Health; Genetics and Family Health

Further Readings

Bouwman, M. G., Teunissen, Q. G. A., Wijburg, F. A., & Linthorst, G. E. (2010). "Doctor Google" ending the diagnostic odyssey in lysosomal storage disorders: Parents using Internet search engines as an efficient diagnostic strategy in rare diseases. *Archives of Disease in Children, 95*(8), 642–644.

Rolland, J. S., & Williams, J. K. (2006). Toward a psychosocial model for the new era of genetics. In S. M. Miller, S. H. McDaniel, J. S. Rolland, & S. L. Feetham (Eds.), *Individuals, families, and the new era of genetics: Biopsychosocial perspectives* (pp. 3–35). New York: Norton.

Seymour, K. C., Addington-Hall, J., Lucassen, A. M., & Foster, C. L. (2010). What facilitates or impedes family communication following genetic testing for cancer risk? A systematic review and meta-synthesis of primary qualitative research. *Journal of Genetic Counseling, 19*(4), 330–342.

Sobel, S. K., & Cowan, D. B. (2000). Impact of genetic testing for Huntington's disease on the family system. *American Journal of Medical Genetics, 90,* 45–59.

Van Riper, M. (2005). Genetic testing and the family. *Journal of Midwifery & Women's Health, 50,* 227–233.

Van Riper, M., & Gallo, A. (2005). Family, health, and genomics. In D. R. Crane & E. S. Marshall (Eds.), *Handbook of families and health: Interdisciplinary perspectives* (pp. 195–217). Thousand Oaks, CA: Sage.

Websites

GeneTests: http://www.genetests.org

Genetic Alliance: http://www.geneticalliance.org

National Human Genome Research Institute, Frequently Asked Questions About Genetic Testing: http://www.genome.gov/pfv.cfm?pageID=19516567

GENETIC DISCOVERIES, NEW: HEALTH INFORMATION IN FAMILIES DERIVED THROUGH

Clinical genetics is a specialty of medicine that focuses on the diagnosis, prevention, and management of genetic disorders. The family is an important part of a clinical genetics visit in that results of genetic testing may have relevance to the health of not only the patient but also their extended family members. The family history is of critical importance as well, because the health history of others in the extended family tree may give clues to the underlying diagnosis by pointing toward a mode of inheritance that can have a significant role in narrowing down possible diagnoses. Clinical genetics in its present-day form is a relatively new specialty of medicine. The correct chromosome number in humans was described in 1956. Developments in the science of genetics have made progress at amazing speed and currently have increasing relevance in the clinical care and counseling of patients and their families with a range of rare and commonly occurring disorders. A draft sequence of the human genome was developed in 2001 and the completed sequence was published in 2003, greatly aiding international efforts in disease gene discovery. This entry focuses on the individual with congenital malformations or intellectual disability and the role that recent genetic discoveries have in the diagnosis and management of a patient and family in this situation.

Background

With the publication of the sequence of the human genome in 2003, it was found that instead of the predicted 50,000 to 150,000 genes, humans only have about 35,000 genes to account for the variability in human complexity compared with that of animal models. Only about 7% of human genes appear to be vertebrate specific. Efforts have been under way to explain how genetic structure influences function and disease given the surprisingly small number of overall genes present. Generally the mantra of how genetic information is interpreted into information that dictates structure and function of the human body is as follows:

$$DNA \rightarrow RNA \rightarrow Protein$$

The details of microbiology that describe each of the processes represented by the arrows are beyond the scope of this text and should be reviewed elsewhere if the reader is unfamiliar with these concepts.

Human DNA is approximately 3 billion base pairs long and is packaged into chromosomes. There are 22 pairs numbered by convention 1–22 and X

and Y chromosomes that determine gender, making a total of 46 chromosomes in a normal human. Deviation from the total number of 46 chromosomes is poorly tolerated in embryology, typically resulting in miscarriage early in gestation. New findings suggest that it is not only required to have the correct number of chromosomes, but in the chromosome pair one set from each parent is required. Changes in the base pair sequence of a gene, termed a *mutation*, have been shown to cause disease. Historically the search for a single disease-causing gene for a given disorder was the focus of research. There are many syndromes that have been catalogued in this fashion. Currently there is increased appreciation for the role proteins may have in cellular dysfunction as well as the impact multiple genes acting together may exhibit. Thus the normal functioning of a human genetic sequence is complex on multiple levels.

New Developments

Microarray

Chromosome structure and function are of much interest in that chromosomes may be visualized under a light microscope and examined. The discipline that has evolved to study chromosomes and their behavior is called cytogenetics. In the past, chromosome examination of individuals with obvious physical or intellectual deficits was completed using a light microscope by specially trained cytogeneticists to diagnose disorders of chromosome number or structure (e.g., Down syndrome that results from three copies of chromosome 21). In that there were many individuals with obvious phenotypic abnormalities in whom no chromosomal defect could be identified, efforts have been focused on increasingly detailed analysis of chromosomes beyond that of light microscopy. The most recent addition to cytogenetic technology is comparative genomic hybridization, or microarray.

The technique of microarray is clinically available and performed at multiple laboratories across the United States and also used internationally. In this approach DNA clones that span chromosomes at specific intervals are dyed and compared to a normal test DNA sample dyed a different color. The fluorescent dye will result in a signal that differs in intensity if the copy number of the target sequence of the two DNA samples varies. Results are usually reported using computer-assisted analysis to give an overview of copy number alterations. This technique displays microduplications and microdeletions that were not previously observed using light microscopy techniques alone. The use of computer-assisted analysis speeds turnaround time, making this a highly effective technique to rapidly examine DNA copy number variations across the entire complement of a person's DNA.

Disadvantages to microarray are that rearrangements in chromosomal material not associated with an addition or deletion are missed. In addition, the sensitivity of this technique is dependent on the number of DNA clones used in the test sample. Most laboratory platforms use targeted DNA clones that detect known disease locations. Thus it is possible that deletion or duplication that is not covered by the clones used in that particular laboratory protocol may be missed. In addition, due to the rapidly increasing number of DNA clones that are being incorporated into most laboratory protocols, it is possible that microdeletions and microduplications that have not been reported previously may be found. Interpreting these results is the subject of much international collaboration and interest but may prove confusing for a family.

Epigenetics

Epigenetics is the study of the control mechanisms which are layered onto the primary nucleotide sequence to produce signals that turn gene expression on and off. It is now understood that certain genes are expressed only when inherited by a particular parent. The addition of methyl groups to the structure of chromatin usually silences gene expression. Whereas this is a normal and desirable function in a typical individual, methylation errors have been shown to cause disease when important genes are turned off (e.g., Rett syndrome). When an epigenetically regulated gene is imprinted as being from a given parent, the signals for expression or silencing of the gene are specific to which parent the allele was inherited from. Of note, although the epigenetic marks are acquired by the DNA and chromatin early in embryological development, they may be used throughout the lifetime of the person. The best-studied epigenetic phenomenon is genomic imprinting.

It is not enough to have the full complement of 46 chromosomes; for a viable offspring to exist, genetic material from the mother and the father is essential. Genomic imprinting refers to the mark, or imprint, placed on certain genes early in embryogenesis designating that allele as being from the mother or the father. A small number of genes have been shown to be expressed only from one parent. Clinical disease has been demonstrated when two copies of an imprinted gene come from the same parent; this is called *uniparental disomy* (UPD). Prader-Willi syndrome and Angelman syndrome are frequently cited examples. It should be noted that other genetic mechanisms also cause both syndromes, with UPD mechanisms making up the minority of causes. Both syndromes arise from the same chromosomal loci, 15q11–13. Angelman syndrome is caused by an excess of paternal genetic material and Prader-Willi is caused by an excess of maternal genetic material. Even though both disease entities are from the same locus, their phenotypic expression is very different. Angelman syndrome is characterized by significant developmental delays, intellectual disability, seizure activity, and paroxysms of inappropriate laughter. Speech is profoundly affected, making communication difficult. Ataxia and jerky arm movements are common. Prader-Willi syndrome is characterized by hypotonia with significant feeding problems in infancy. Patients with Prader-Willi syndrome frequently outgrow the early failure to thrive and become morbidly obese if appetites are left uncurbed. The degree of intellectual impairment is less pronounced than what is seen in Angelman syndrome. UPD is not the only mechanism that yields these phenotypes, but it is an important factor to keep in mind when considering a differential diagnosis in an intellectually impaired child. More information on specific syndromes is found at the GeneTests website.

Importance of Genetic Testing

In order to efficiently and effectively manage the patient with congenital malformations, intellectual disability, or both, an accurate diagnosis is required. The provision of accurate information, including natural history and recurrence risks, for the family hinges on identification of the underlying cause. Screening for commonly co-occurring comorbidities is directed by knowing the genetic syndrome involved. The family can also be directed to a support group specific to the disorder. Many times services available in the community for early intervention and subsequent services through the educational system can be tailored to the diagnosis of the child. Early eligibility may be facilitated by a diagnosis as well. Families can also be offered research participation, as available, for further understanding and treatment for the particular disorder.

Recommendations for Intervention in the Special Needs Patient

As stated earlier, many of the medical interventions for a child with congenital malformations and/or intellectual disability hinge on arriving at a correct diagnosis. Consultation with a clinical geneticist will facilitate testing and diagnosis. The testing available has rapidly evolved with the field of clinical genetics. For many rare conditions a geneticist is a resource for accurate information not readily available elsewhere. After a diagnosis is made, periodic consultation with a geneticist will help guide efficient medical management specific to the disorder. The role of the health care system extends far beyond the initial evaluation and diagnosis. A medical home approach to care is essential in the management of a child or adult with special health care needs because of the complexity that arises when multiple medical and community resources are involved. A medical home will be the key to coordinate multiple specialty evaluations and subsequent care.

The birth of a child with malformations or developmental disabilities places a great deal of stress on families. Support of the family through the grieving process is essential. Community early intervention services play a major role in the day-to-day contact with families. Knowing how early intervention services are coordinated in the community is key for any health professional involved with children who have the potential for developmental delays. Contact with the Title V office at the state or local health department may be helpful. The need for accurate information to be passed along to the therapist(s) and subsequent educational team members is also important. It is readily accepted that the majority of children with special health care needs will reach adulthood. Information obtained

from the clinical genetics team will assist the patient and their family members in obtaining future help with appropriate disability benefits, employment, and housing.

Laura Pickler

See also Disabilities and Family Management; Genetic Family Histories; Guardianship/Conservatorship; Life-Threatening Illness and the Family; Roles of Health Care Providers for Families, Emerging; Social Security; Social Support Systems for the Family

Further Readings

Albertson, D. G., & Pinkel, D. (2003). Genomic microarrays in human genetic disease and cancer. *Human Molecular Genetics, 12*, R145–R152.

Bejjani, B. A., Theisen, A. P., Ballif, B. C., & Shaffer, L. G. (2005). Array-based comparative genomic hybridization in clinical diagnosis. *Expert Review of Molecular Diagnostics, 5*(3), 421–429.

Butler, M. G. (2002). Imprinting disorders: Non-Mendelian mechanisms affecting growth. *Journal of Pediatric Endocrinology and Metabolism, 15*(Suppl. 5), 1279–1288.

Jones, K. L. (2005). *Smith's recognizable patterns of human malformation* (6th ed.). Philadelphia: Saunders.

Peltonen, L. (2007). Genome structure and gene expression. In D. L. Rimoin, J. M. Connor, R. E. Pyeritz, B. R. Korf (Eds.), *Emery and Rimoin's principles and practice of medical genetics* (pp. 61–80). Philadelphia: Elsevier.

Websites

GeneTests: http://www.genetests.org

National Center for Medical Home Implementation: http://www.medicalhomeinfo.org

GENETIC FAMILY HISTORIES

A widespread and cost-effective method to determine whether a health condition has an inherited component is through the family history interview. The family history interview is commonly the critical factor for identifying individuals at risk for hereditary syndromes. Family history information can lead to referrals for genetic consultation and genetic testing. Clinicians will often recommend disease-screening interventions, lifestyle changes, and prophylactic medications and procedures based on one's family history. Within the context of the genetic family history, the collection of family history information takes the form of a pedigree or genogram. A *pedigree* is a diagram that details familial relationships and health status. The benefit of recording the family history in the form of a pedigree is that this representation helps to facilitate the identification of specific patterns of genetic inheritance, such as autosomal dominant, autosomal recessive, and X-linked. This entry discusses the relationship between family histories and genetic testing, describes how to collect a pedigree, and discusses the limitations of the family history interview.

Family Histories and Genetic Testing

An individual's family history can often lead to referrals for genetic counseling and testing. In some health conditions, predictive models have been developed that can predict one's likelihood of harboring a deleterious gene mutation based on family history characteristics. For colon cancer, specific criteria have been developed, called the Amsterdam criteria, which, based on family history information, can be used to determine the likelihood that an individual may have Lynch syndrome. Lynch syndrome, or hereditary nonpolyposis colorectal cancer, is a hereditary cancer syndrome caused by an inherited mutation in proteins related to the repair of damaged DNA. To meet Amsterdam criteria a family history must include three or more family members with a confirmed diagnosis of colorectal cancer, one of whom is a first-degree (parent, child, sibling) relative of the other two; there must be two successive affected generations; and there must be one or more colon cancers diagnosed under age 50 years. Similar family history–based criteria have been developed to guide decisions regarding genetic testing for hereditary breast and ovarian cancer syndromes.

How to Construct a Pedigree

The pedigree begins with the *consultand*, or the individual giving the family history. A consultand can be affected with the disease of interest or not. If the consultand is affected with the medical condition of interest or has a known genetic mutation, he or she is sometimes referred to as the *proband*. In constructing the pedigree, males are represented by open squares and females by open circles. Horizontal lines between two partners are called *relationship lines*. Horizontal lines connecting brothers and sisters are called *sibship lines*. Descending from the sibship line is a vertical line that connects the individual sibling to the sibship line. Finally, a vertical line connecting a relationship line to a sibship line is called a *line of descent*. To cover all of the complexities of extended families and relationships, there are dozens of described symbols. Symbols have been created to represent twins, adoption, divorce, stillbirth, or a consanguineous relationship, among others. Relatives identified as affected with a certain condition have their square or circle shaded in. In general, the pedigree includes three generations.

When constructing a pedigree, it is vital to collect detailed information on relative health status. For each identified relative, his or her age, year of birth, age of death, and cause of death (if expired) should be collected and recorded on the pedigree. For relatives affected with any health condition, the age at which they were diagnosed should be collected. If any individual has undergone genetic testing, this testing should be documented within the pedigree. Another important data element is the race/ethnicity of the consultand's grandparents. This information can be important, as certain genetic mutations have been found more commonly in individuals with specific ethnic backgrounds.

In interpreting a pedigree, it is helpful to remember that first-degree relatives are mothers, fathers, full siblings, and children and share 50% of their genetic information with the consultand. Second-degree relatives include grandparents, grandchildren, half-siblings, aunts, uncles, nephews, and nieces and share 25% of their genetic information with the consultand. Third-degree relatives such as first cousins share 12.5% of their genetic information with the consultand. Increasing number of relatives identified as affected, particularly those who share a greater percentage of genetic information with the consultand, is suggestive of a greater risk of developing the disease in question. Additionally, when relatives are identified who have been diagnosed with a certain condition at a young age, or at least significantly younger than the typical age of diagnosis, an individual's disease risk is increased. Finally, the pattern of health conditions within the family can suggest potential hereditary syndrome for which there are known genetic mutations for testing. For example, relatives within the same lineage being diagnosed with colon cancer and uterine cancer might suggest Lynch syndrome (hereditary nonpolyposis colorectal cancer).

Accuracy of the Family History Interview

Family history information can result in referrals for genetic counseling and testing as well as the early initiation of invasive screening procedures. Because a positive family history can alter medical management, it is important to determine how accurately an individual reports his or her family history. Several studies have explored this question for multiple diagnoses. In general, a report of a family history of breast, colorectal, or prostate cancer in first-degree relatives tends to be moderately to highly accurate; however, other tumors such as uterine, lung, and melanoma suffer from much lower sensitivities and specificities. In addition, family cancer histories are much less accurate when referring to a second-degree relative. Studies on psychiatric diseases have tended to demonstrate more accurate reporting for clinically severe diseases, such as schizophrenia or mania, and less accuracy for conditions such as anxiety, personality disorders, and depression. However, the sensitivities for family psychiatric history are still far below those of breast or colon cancer. For other adult-onset chronic diseases, sensitivities for family histories of coronary artery disease, diabetes, and hypercholesterolemia can reach as high as 85% to 90%; however, this is limited to a very small sample of applicable studies. The accuracy of family history reports for conditions such as birth defects, neurological diseases, and hypertension tend to be very poor.

Factors Influencing the Accuracy of the Family History Interview

Numerous factors may influence the accuracy of family history information: factors such as communication patterns within families, knowledge of medical terminology, characteristics of the informant, and the method of family history collection. The most frequently investigated patient characteristic is informant age. Accuracy in reporting a family history of myocardial infarction, diabetes mellitus, stroke, and any cancer is similar in all age groups. In adolescents, correct knowledge of medical terminology does not influence the accuracy of reported family history information. This finding might explain why education level generally does not affect reporting accuracy. For cancer family history, no clear trends exist between consultand age and reporter accuracy. However, for family psychiatric health history, older consultands tend to be more accurate than younger consultands.

The most consistently reported factor associated with family history accuracy is degree of relatedness of the individual identified by the consultand. In general, family history reports for second- and third-degree relatives appear less accurate compared to those for first-degree relatives, and this trend seems stable across different disease states. Another important factor that influences family history accuracy is the disease status of the consultand. In most studies, affected probands tend to report more accurately compared to disease-free consultands. Rarely have studies evaluated how family dynamics might influence the accuracy of family history reports although the limited number of published studies suggest that family psychosocial issues might affect family history accuracy.

The clinical setting in which the family history is collected may also affect the accuracy of family history information and subsequently influence patient management. For most studies conducted within the primary care setting, when compared to patient-completed family history questionnaires, family history information recorded within medical charts tends to underestimate the number of affected relatives, with the clinical consequences being under surveillance. When directly compared to patient-completed questionnaires, primary care medical records can underdocument cancer risk by as much as 20% to 50%. Conversely, studies conducted in high-risk cancer clinics or genetic clinics have typically found that after family history verification, most patients require reduced clinical surveillance. Often verification of a reported family history resulted in a change in management of families, with most cases being assigned a decreased level of genetic risk.

Family history ascertainment is a critical component of determined genetic risk and the likelihood that an individual may harbor a disease-causing genetic variant. The careful collection and construction of a pedigree can assist the health care provider in identifying specific features, which might suggest a hereditary component within a family. There are several limitations regarding the accuracy of family history information and verification, though the direct contact of identified affected relatives is sometimes necessary to ensure an accurately collected pedigree.

Harvey J. Murff

See also Cancer in the Family; Family Health Maintenance; Genetic Information and Family Interviews; Genetic Research Findings and Disease Management for Families; Genograms and the Family

Further Readings

Bennett, R. L. (2010). *The practical guide to the genetic family history* (2nd ed.). New York: Wiley-Liss.

Guttmacher, A. E., Collins, F. S., & Carmona, R. H. (2004). The family history, more important than ever. *New England Journal of Medicine, 351,* 2333–2336.

Wilson, B., Qureshi, N., Little, J., Santaguida, P., Carroll, J., Allanson, J., et al. (2009). *Clinical utility of cancer family history collection in primary care* (Evidence Report/Technology Assessment No. 170, AHRQ Publication No. 09-E007). Rockville, MD: Agency for Healthcare Research and Quality.

Yoon, P. W., Scheuner, M. T., Peterson-Oehlke, K., Gwinn, M., Faucett, A., & Khoury, M. J. (2002). Can family history be used as a tool for public health and preventive medicine? *Genetics in Medicine, 4,* 304–310.

Websites

Centers for Disease Control and Prevention, Family Health History: http://www.cdc.gov/genomics/famhistory/index.htm

Information for Genetic Professionals: http://www.kumc.edu/gec/geneinfo.html

National Human Genome Research Institute: http://www.genome.gov

U.S. Surgeon General, My Family Health Portrait: http://familyhistory.hhs.gov/fhh-web/home.action

GENETIC INFORMATION AND FAMILY INTERVIEWS

As far back in the history of medicine as Hippocrates, astute clinicians have observed that one's family history influences disease risk. Although collecting information on the disease status of relatives has long been a fixed part of the medical interview, only over the past few decades has medical science begun to unravel the genetic underpinnings of the family history. This discussion describes the genetic information obtainable from the family interview, comments on how this information influences health care, and discusses the limitations of the family history interview for disease risk assessment. For some chronic diseases and cancers, individuals with positive family histories often have lifetime disease risks that are two- to fourfold greater than the general population. As such, multiple clinical guidelines for disease prevention have been "personalized" based on family medical history.

Within this discussion, the focus of care is on the individual who presents to a health care provider with a relative affected with a medical or psychiatric condition. In the setting of the genetic interview, this individual is the consultand. If this individual is affected with the condition of interest, an alternative name is *proband*. The consultand reports the health history of his or her relatives. Relatives are categorized based on the amount of genetic information they share with the consultand. First-degree relatives are mothers, fathers, full siblings, and children. First-degree relatives share 50% of their genetic information with the consultand. Second-degree relatives include grandparents, grandchildren, half-siblings, aunts, uncles, nephews, and nieces. Second-degree relatives share 25% of their genetic information with the consultand. Finally, third-degree relatives, which include first cousins, share 12.5% of their genetic information with the consultand.

Why Collect a Family History

Collecting family history information within the context of a medical encounter is time intensive. Obtaining a formal, three-generation family pedigree may require a 1- to 2-hour interview with a genetic counselor. Studies using direct observation have demonstrated that in clinical practice, family practitioners are generally able to spend only 2 minutes or less discussing the family history. The single largest barrier to the collection of family history information within clinical medicine is time constraints. Despite these barriers to comprehensive collection of family history information in clinical care, family health information is a vital component of high-quality health care.

In the "genomics age," collection of family history has been utilized for identifying individuals who may be at increased risk for certain medical conditions. In addition, the family history can be used to risk-stratify individuals toward appropriate screening interventions to minimize disease risk. Prior to the relatively recent increase in molecular biology knowledge, the family history interview focused more on the social environment of the consultand. The family history interview was also seen primarily as a way to begin to develop a therapeutic bond between patient and provider.

Genetic Information Obtained From Family Interviews

Although the family history interview is a critical component of the genetic interview and the primary driver for genetic testing, it is important to remember that the family history interview represents both shared genetic and shared environmental exposures among a family. Family members are more likely to share similar environments and similar dietary habits than are nonrelated individuals. As such, teasing out the environmental versus the genetic component of a condition is quite challenging; however, some have argued that this distinction is irrelevant to clinical care.

The family interview can provide a practitioner with useful genetic information regarding the consultand. First, based on the distribution of reported diseases within a family, the practitioner can determine if a condition might represent a Mendelian or single gene disorder. A Mendelian pattern refers to the work of Gregor Mendel, an Austrian monk who first described many of the models of discrete trait transmission including what is now known as the law of segregation and the law of independent assortment. The chromosomal location of a gene is known as its *locus*. Humans have two sets of chromosomes, one from their mother and one from their

father, and alternative forms of a gene on these chromosomes are called *alleles*. When the presence of a condition is determined by a single locus, it is called a *Mendelian trait*. Some inheritance patterns of Mendelian traits include autosomal dominant, autosomal recessive, and X-linked transmission patterns.

Despite the importance of detecting a Mendelian trait through examination of the consultand's pedigree, most common medical conditions, which have a genetic component, do not follow simple Mendelian inheritance. These conditions, sometimes referred to as *polygenetic*, result from the combination of multiple genes or the interaction of one's genes and one or more environmental exposures. As such, sometimes a distinction is made between a *hereditary* condition, one that is likely a single gene disorder following a Mendelian transmission pattern, and a *familial* condition, one in which one or more family members are affected but there does not appear to be Mendelian inheritance.

Other elements of the family history interview can clue the provider toward a possible genetic (or inherited) condition. For cancers, these include diagnoses at young ages, multiple primary tumors, and bilateral tumors in paired organs. The pattern of diseases within the family could even suggest potential hereditary syndrome for which there are known genetic mutations for testing. For example, relatives diagnosed with both breast and ovarian cancer might suggest a hereditary breast-ovarian syndrome.

Medical Interventions Based on Family History Information

A family history of a condition can increase one's risk of disease substantially. This risk generally increases as the number of affected relatives increase and as the age at which the individuals were diagnosed decreases. As such, family history information has become increasingly incorporated into clinical guidelines. Disease screening and prevention guidelines can be altered based on a positive family history. Multiple cancer guidelines have been published which recommend the early initiation of screening for breast, colorectal, and prostate cancer in individuals with a family history of disease.

For colorectal cancer, clinical screening guidelines have been tailored to specific family history patterns. For example, individuals who report a first-degree relative affected with colorectal cancer after the age of 60 years are considered to be at the same level of risk for colorectal cancer as individuals without a family history. Individuals who report either two or more first-degree relatives affected with colorectal cancer and/or a single first-degree relative diagnosed before the age of 60 years are recommended to initiate colorectal cancer screening at the age of 40 years or 10 years earlier than the earliest affected relatives did. For colorectal cancer, family history information also plays a role in determining what type of screening modality is appropriate. Individuals with strong family histories are advised to undergo colonoscopy examinations, whereas individuals with low-risk family histories could also consider less invasive screening modalities such as fecal occult blood testing. Finally, individuals with multiple relatives affected with colorectal cancer may have a pedigree suggestive of Lynch syndrome (hereditary nonpolyposis colorectal cancer). Individuals with family histories suggestive of Lynch syndrome may be appropriate for genetic testing and more intensive disease surveillance. For both breast and colorectal cancer, clinical algorithms have been constructed which, based on family history information, can predict the probability that an individual is harboring a potentially deleterious genetic mutation and might benefit from genetic counseling and genetic testing.

Limitations of the Family History Interview for Capturing Genetic Information

Although family history information can change medical management for several conditions, the family history interview is frequently poorly conducted in clinical practice. As such, important information such as lineage and age at diagnosis is often not obtained. This limits the value of the family history for genetic risk assessment. Several studies have suggested that individuals who may be at higher genetic risk for certain conditions are not being identified by their providers because of inadequate family history collection. Multiple methods are being developed to try to facilitate family history collection including computer-based collection tools and telephone-based tools. These tools will allow individuals to complete their family history information while at home and after contact with specific relatives and later transmit this information

to their health care provider. Currently these new tools are investigational.

Another limitation of using the family interview for genetic information is related to the inaccuracy of the family history. Several studies have indicated that the family history is often inaccurate. Reporting of relatives affected with hypertension is very poor. Some cancers are reported with moderate to high accuracy, such as breast and colorectal, whereas others are often misreported. It is unclear why these inaccuracies occur. Social factors might influence the accuracy as well as specific family dynamics. In addition, some of the limitation of family medical history could be related to a relative's lack of knowledge regarding their personal medical history.

Although the family interview is not a perfect tool for capturing genetic information, it remains a powerful and clinically useful component of medical care. Individuals with positive family histories are often screened more intensively for medical conditions and may be candidates for genetic testing based on the familial pattern of disease. Family history is often poorly collected, but current work with nontraditional medical encounters might help to improve the collection of this information.

Harvey J. Murff

See also Cancer in the Family; Family Health Maintenance; Genetic Family Histories; Genetic Research Findings and Disease Management for Families; Genograms and the Family

Further Readings

Bennett, R. L. (1999). *The practical guide to the genetic family history*. New York: Wiley-Liss.

Berg, A. O., Baird, M. A., Botkin, J. R., Driscoll, D. A., Fishman, P. A., Guarino, P. D., et al. (2009). National Institutes of Health State-of-the-Science Conference statement: Family history and improving health. *Annals of Internal Medicine, 151*, 872–877.

Guttmacher, A. E., Collins, F. S., Carmona, R. H. (2004). The family history, more important than ever. *New England Journal of Medicine, 351*, 2333–2336.

Qureshi, N., Wilson, B., Santaguida, P., Carroll, J., Allanson, J., Ruiz Culebro, C., et al. (2007). Collection and use of cancer family history in primary care (Evidence Report/Technology Assessment No. 159, AHRQ Publication No. 08-E001). Rockville, MD: Agency for Healthcare Research and Quality.

Wilson, B. J., Qureshi, N., Santaguidea, P., Little, J., Carroll, J. C., Allanson, J., et al. (2009). Systematic review: Family history in risk assessment for common diseases. *Annals of Internal Medicine, 151,* 878–885.

Websites

American Cancer Society, American Cancer Society Guidelines for the Early Detection of Cancer: http://www.cancer.org/docroot/PED/content/PED_2_3X_ACS _Cancer_Detection_Guidelines_36 asp?sitearea=PED
Centers for Disease Control and Prevention, Family Health History: http://www.cdc.gov/genomics/famhistory/index.htm
United States Surgeon General, My Family Health Portrait: http://familyhistory.hhs.gov/fhh-web/home.action

GENETIC RESEARCH FINDINGS AND DISEASE MANAGEMENT FOR FAMILIES

Genetics research has led to an expanded view of health care and a different way of thinking about the meaning of the word *patient.* Our knowledge of the heritability of some diseases mandates a shift in the focus of care. A new perspective must consider the care of the individual along with the care of the family. In the context of genetics and genomics, these are interdependent. As a consequence, the sequence of disease assessment and management may alternate. It may begin with diagnosis of disease in an individual and follow to the diagnosis of similarly affected family member, or it may begin with family assessment and lead to predictive predisposition testing in unaffected individuals. This flexibility in perspective has been one of the principal conceptual outcomes of genetics research and disease management for families. In effect this perspective eliminated the health care provider's need to wait for symptoms.

This new perspective applies to all disorders that are associated with changes to human genetic material. This includes heritable disorders caused by germline (transmitted to offspring) or *de novo* (new) mutations to protein coding and other regions of genomic and mitochondrial DNA. Some disorders are cancer predisposition syndromes, such as breast and ovarian cancer, multiple endocrine neoplasia, and familial adenomatous polyposes, or single gene disorders, such as cystic fibrosis, Marfan syndrome, and polycystic kidney disease. Other disorders are caused by chromosomal abnormalities in which whole segments of chromosome are lost, translocated, or do not replicate normally. Some of the chromosomal abnormalities are Down syndrome, Turner's, Fragile X, and Klinefelter syndrome, to name just a few.

Genetic research using genome-wide association studies of uncommon and common chronic disorders such as heart disease, diabetes, allergies and asthma have uncovered an element of heritability in all of them. Scientists now believe that all disease has a genetic or epigenetic component, such that genetic defects may cause disease, contribute to the development of disease, change the way the body responds to or adapts to environmental exposures, or modify the body's ability to prevent disease. Genetic propensities may be modified by environmental factors, and environmental factors may trigger genetic propensities. These findings have led to the popular and technically true idea that "all disease is genetic."

This entry begins with a definition of the patient and the historical context of genetic research. Next, the entry provides an overview of the current approach to genetic research. The entry concludes with a discussion of policies that help protect families.

Definition of the Patient: Person or Family

The chronology of health care may begin with the patient and expand to the family or begin with the family and focus in on individuals. The definition of a *patient* will depend on the desired outcome of care as treatment or prevention of disease. Treatment of a genetic disorder will situate initial care with the affected individual while prevention will consider all individuals who are at risk. The focus of disease management must never be stationary but rather must shift and respond to emerging health needs. Through diagnosis of genetic disease one automatically gains information about the genetic status of some or many family members. This information regards at least the affected person's parents and possibly most relatives. Moreover, because heritable diseases are, by nature, multigenerational, the boundaries of health care services need to be expanded. Genetic counseling for family planning is a main venue for expanding such boundaries. Future parents are advised on the probability of future generations being affected by a known heritable disease. In such a case the "patient" is yet unborn. When disease has genetic determinants, different language is needed. One term derived from genetic research is *proband,* or the first member of the family seeking genetic health services. In the context of family disease management, this term may be more appropriate than the term *patient.*

Historical Context

The Human Genome Project was conceived in the late 1980s and began in 1990 as an international endeavor. Among the accomplishments was the inception of the Ethical, Legal, and Social Implications (ELSI) program. This new and unique program in research and health care generated questions that continue to guide genetics research. The most significant product is the idea that research should take into account how findings might translate to practice and, in particular, affect humanity. The overarching questions that became newly relevant were "Who is the subject?" and "What is the nature and use of genetic information derived from this research?"

It soon became clear that the subject is not only the individual but also all genetically related individuals (i.e., the family, both nuclear and extended). Moreover, genetic information has meaning and is relevant to both the source (i.e., affected person) and to associated others (possibly affected relatives). Genetic information derived from an individual may also have relevance to cultural and racial groups.

The ELSI issues are highly complex. Early family disease management research was shadowed by fears of loss of employment, loss of health or life insurance, and anticipated risk of uninsurability if genetic risk for disease was exposed. This fear posed a barrier to families who wished to learn of familial diseases but feared negative outcomes or economic consequences.

Overview of Current Approaches to Research

There are hundreds of specific health disorders under investigation that are directly caused by, or associated with, genetic defects such as mutations or chromosomal abnormalities. The mutations or chromosomal defects may be acquired at the time of conception or inherited from an affected parent. Screening, diagnostic, and lifelong management depends on the type of genetic defect and inheritance pattern. Some disorders have immediate physical and health outcomes such as Tay-Sachs disease, hemophilia, and Down syndrome. Research of these disorders addresses the earliest age of diagnosis (sometimes preimplantation and prenatally) and the best form of medical management that may begin at birth and continue for life. There is evidence that these conditions take a great toll on the family as a unit and strain emotional, financial, and social resources.

Other genetic disorders caused by different kinds of molecular changes to the genome or epigenome have been shown to impose an increased risk for later, or adult-onset, disease, and symptoms may manifest variably over time and differently according to the specific genetic defect. There is considerable study being conducted on late-onset disorders, including cancer predisposition syndromes (e.g., breast and ovarian cancer), colorectal cancers, and Huntington's disease. Research has shown us that these disorders require a different, more future-oriented, and preventive approach to management. Care is dominated by hypervigilance and medical monitoring for years before symptoms are manifested. In addition, family counseling and education are used for prophylactic treatments.

Regardless of the approach to care, families affected with genetic disorders must attend to the lifelong psychosocial issues. Scientific evidence is equivocal on the negative psychosocial effects of genetic diagnoses. Some individuals experience relief on receiving a diagnosis, but others experience distress. Many individuals anticipate and fear negative financial and social consequences even though no data exist to substantiate such fears.

State of the Science

The state of the science of genetic research and disease management for families is limited, primarily because research often exposes more uncertainties and raises more questions than answers. Scientists are continually learning more about the biochemical nature of disease and concluding that no disease is simple. Disease management was more easily directed when a single cause could be identified. In the case of genetic diseases, sometimes a single gene defect is causative. More often, multiple genetic changes are implicated and increasingly the complexity of the gene–environment interaction is at the root of complex (and once thought to be simple) disease.

Although not yet available, perhaps the single most important research finding will be the development of a process for accurately and consistently measuring and weighing the contributions of genetic and environmental factors. This one goal drives much contemporary clinical genetic and genomic research efforts.

Current research is taking a careful look at identifying biomarkers of disease. Such markers may be the protein products of gene transcription and translation. Abnormal biological products are the result of abnormal genetic activity. Abnormal biomarkers may be identified in blood or other tissue in which the disease manifests. New genetic markers may be able to predict whether a person is likely to have coronary artery disease (CAD) or other types of disease in the future. For example, research shows that people who are prediabetic or who have Type 2 diabetes have much shorter telomeres. Because these people are prone to CAD, an early test could indicate their susceptibility and help them to alter their lifestyle to avoid or delay the onset of the disease. This type of predictive testing holds great promise and informs translational research efforts.

Impact on Families: Knowing One's Risk for Disease

Genetic testing is available to assess one's risk for a number of diseases that are caused by mutations to one or more genes. Single gene disorders are easier to diagnose when there is an affected family member and situation has led to the increased availability of genetic tests that are available direct to the consumer or through one's health provider.

Considerable research has been conducted on psychosocial implications of genetic risk assessment. Primarily studies have been done with families affected with cancer predisposition syndromes, such as breast and ovarian cancer (BRCA1), familial adenomatous polyposis, and uncommon single gene disorders such as multiple endocrine neoplasia.

Studies of families affected with Huntington's disease have found similar findings. The research shows that there are complex psychosocial implications for individuals who seek to find out their genetic risk of disease and for their close relatives, such as spouses, children, and parents.

The very process of undergoing risk assessment creates fears, uncertainty, and emotional distress in some individuals. There have been reports of family members refusing to undergo testing because of fear of the outcome. Emotional distress has occurred among affected and unaffected (mutation-free) family members. Knowing one's genetic risk for disease creates personal feelings of fear, worry, and hopelessness. The certainty of known risk is offset with the uncertainty of expression and penetrance. In other words, a person may know he or she has a genetic mutation associated with disease but does not know and cannot predict when or how it will manifest as illness. Among unaffected family members who find out they do not carry the disease-causing mutation, there have been reports of feeling relief along with guilt that they are spared the future suffering that awaits a loved one. Health care providers and clinical researchers' predictions of a high uptake of genetic testing services have not been realized. Fear of knowing one's risk has been hypothesized as the reason.

Genetic Testing for Children

Parents hold responsibility for ensuring the health and welfare of their offspring. When a family has a known genetic mutation associated with disease, such as Huntington's or BRCA1, parents are faced with the difficult task of deciding when to test children and, if testing is conducted, what to do with the results, especially if carrier status is confirmed. There are no recommendations, backed up by research, to assist parents in the process of decision making regarding genetic testing. General counseling guidelines dictate that genetic testing be performed if results can inform medical monitoring and treatment. To date, follow-up care for a child diagnosed with a genetic disorder is fragmented and inconsistent across service providers.

Desired Family Health Outcomes

Disease management for families must be comprehensive and multigenerational. It must take a different approach to conceptualizing the patient and the "fact of illness." The absolute good to be achieved is the prevention of disease through modification of genetic, environmental, or both factors, simultaneously. As a matter of routine, health care providers should construct a family pedigree of three generations and include all diseases, exposures, birth defects, pregnancies and miscarriages, deaths and causes, ethnicity, and race, along with other needed information.

Policy and Protection of the Family

Genetic Information Nondiscrimination Act

On May 21, 2008, President George W. Bush signed into law the Genetic Information Nondiscrimination Act that will protect Americans against discrimination based on their genetic information when applied to health insurance and employment. The bill had passed the Senate unanimously and the House by a vote of 414 to 1. The long-awaited measure, which was debated in Congress for more than a decade, will pave the way for people to take full advantage of the promise of personalized medicine without fear of discrimination.

Secretary's Advisory Committee on Genetics, Health, and Society

Advances in biological sciences, human genetics, and genomics have quickly led to new technologies that have the potential to predict, diagnose, and treat rare and common diseases. The new technologies, however, have practical implications with respect to quality assurance of the testing process and the clinical value and their applications. In December of 2002, Health and Human Services Secretary Tommy G. Thompson formed the Secretary's Advisory Committee on Genetics, Health, and Society (SACGHS) and appointed 13 experts in medicine, nursing, ethics, and bench science. A fundamental and ongoing task of the committee is to assess the state of the science on genetic and genomic information and monitor how technology is being integrated with health care and public health initiatives.

Since its inception, SACGHS has provided oversight of the technical aspects of test development and the clinical utility of tests once these tests are determined to be valid, accurate, and reliable. SACGHS advises the Secretary of Health and Human Services on the broad range of human health and societal issues raised by the development and use and potential misuse of genetic technologies. SACGHS solicits public and private sector input and makes recommendations, as appropriate.

Conclusion

Only through multigenerational research can health care providers truly understand the complexity of the genetic disease, its impact on health, and the long-term implications of gene penetrance, gene expression, and disease phenotype. Further research is needed to explore ways to effectively and equitably integrate genetic technology into health care and public health; evaluate access to genetic technologies and use of genetic information in education, employment, insurance, and law; and track public opinion of the absolute values. Ultimately, genetic research will improve nurses' ability to increase the family's understanding about a genetic disease, discuss options regarding disease management, advise on the risks and benefits of possible testing, and make sense of the trends in genetic research.

Ellen Giarelli

See also Genetic Conditions, Communication in Families; Genetic Information and Family Interviews; Genetic Research Findings and Family Health; Genetics and Family Health

Further Readings

Genetic Alliance. (2007). *Understanding genetics: A guide for patients and health professionals.* Available from http://www.geneticalliance.org/understanding .genetics.download

Miller, S. M., McDaniel, S. H., Rolland, J. S., & Feetham, S. L. (Eds.). (2006). *Individuals, families and the new era of genetics: Biopsychosocial perspectives.* New York: Norton.

Monsen, R. B. (Ed.). (2008). *Genetics and ethics in health care: New questions in the age of genomic health.* Silver Spring, MD: American Nurses Association.

Street, E., & Soldan, J. (1998). A conceptual framework for the psychosocial issues faced by families with genetic conditions. *Families, Systems, & Health, 16*(3), 217–233.

Woods, C. R. (2005). *Focus on DNA research*. New York: Nova Biomedical.

Websites

National Human Genome Research Institute: http://www.genome.gov

Secretary's Advisory Committee on Genetics, Health, and Society (SACGHS): http://oba.od.nih.gov/SACGHS/sacghs_home.html

GENETIC RESEARCH FINDINGS AND FAMILY HEALTH

Recent advances in genetic research have emphasized that each individual should be considered in the context of the family, as biological family members have many genes in common. At least 50% of our genes are shared between first-degree relatives. In addition, family members share common environments and cultures. Genetic and genomic information has taken on new importance as health care providers have embraced genomic and personalized health care for individuals and families. Genomic health care is the use of information from genomes and their derivatives (RNA, proteins, and metabolites) to guide health care decision making and is a key component of personalized health care. For providers, this means the ability to determine the risk of disease related to genetic factors, new approaches to disease prevention or risk reduction, and a better understanding of prognosis, progression, and response to treatment. For families, this means learning how to manage the knowledge related to genetically influenced conditions, proactive planning, and possibly living with uncertainty, threatened loss, and anxiety. The new era of genetic and genomic health care means that families will move through their life cycle with increasing information available to them regarding genetically influenced risk for traits (e.g., learning disabilities, hearing loss), specific disorders (e.g., colorectal cancer, schizophrenia), or conditions (e.g., Huntington's disease). The purpose of this entry is to focus on the research related to the impact of genetic information (family history and genetic testing) and the associated health benefits and risks for the family.

Families and the Genomic Era

Family Focus

A developmental family systems perspective is useful when considering the impact of genetic information for a family. John Rolland's family systems genetic illness model is a family-centered model that helps to explain how a family copes and adapts to genetic information and what the relationships are between individual and family dynamics with genomic disorders. The model is intended for use with conditions for which genetic alterations contribute to the cause of a disease, and when predictive, presymptomatic, or carrier testing is or may become available. Family systems theory focuses on the interaction among family members and draws attention to family functioning. Rolland's model is useful because it incorporates the psychosocial demands of being genetically at risk and/or diagnosed with a genetic condition along with the biomedical orientation.

The developmental component of the model draws attention to the dimension of time. In the era of genomic health, the dimension of time takes on new importance. The timing of the news of being genetically at risk, the diagnosis of genetic mutation that will lead to illness, and the onset of the disorder will have a profound impact on the individual and family life cycles. Individual and family life-cycle stages have specific developmental tasks, and by considering the timing of the information and/or diagnosis, the major life cycle tasks that will be challenged and future developmental tasks that will be affected are apparent.

The conceptual time also allows health care providers and families to think longitudinally about the course of an illness. Genetic testing permits families and providers to expand their thinking about the phases of an illness to include the time before a genetic disease appears. John Rolland and Janet Williams conceptualize the phases before the clinical onset of a genomic disease as (1) awareness phase, (2) crisis I pretesting phase, (3) crisis II test/posttesting phase, and (4) long-term adaptation phase. Those identified as genetically at risk will live with uncertainty and live as the "worried-well."

This developmental systems model shifts from a focus on intervention after disease onset to more preventive approaches before symptoms appear. Individuals and families will be challenged to make decisions about the use of genetic information that identifies genomic aspects of disease or disease risk and will find that the genomic era has blurred the boundary between health and illness.

Familial Risk Assessment

The family health history is the first step in establishing genetic risk and is one part of a comprehensive genetic assessment. The purpose of a genetic family history assessment is to identify specific genetic conditions or patterns of inheritance that suggest a genetic factor or condition in which further genetic testing or counseling would be useful. Family history is a significant and prevalent risk factor for many common diseases. For the common chronic diseases, such as cardiovascular disease, that are usually multifactorial in nature, family history of disease reflects the effects of genetic and nongenetic risk factors (e.g., culture, behavior, environmental exposure) shared by family members.

The person with the condition in question is called the *proband*. If the person seeking genetic consultation is healthy, he or she may be called the *consultand*. Family members are ranked into primary or first-degree relatives, second-degree relatives, tertiary relatives, and so on. Primary relatives are parents, siblings, and children of the proband or consultand. They share one half of their genetic material with the proband.

Secondary relatives share one fourth of their genetic material and include grandparents, aunts, uncles, and grandchildren. Tertiary relatives share one eighth of the genetic material and are first cousins, and great-grandchildren. Health care providers construct a pictorial representation called a *family pedigree* or *genogram* that helps to clarify the relationships. Families can now develop their own family history using online programs from the U.S. Surgeon General (My Family Health Portrait) and the Centers for Disease Control and Prevention (Family Healthware). Research has demonstrated they are an effective means of developing a family health history.

The results of the family health history should be discussed with care by a knowledgeable health care provider or genetic counselor. Some families may have a multigenerational history of a genomic disorder and have been living with the uncertainty of onset while others have no such history and are unaware of any genetic risks. The latter group may have the strongest reaction to indications of genetic risk of disease.

Family members need to discuss whether they want to proceed with genetic testing. They need to understand what tests are available, their reliability and validity, and what the tests can and cannot do. They also need to discuss the potential impact of genetic testing for self and the family. Family members need to understand there are uncertainties surrounding test interpretation (including the potential for false positives) and must be informed about the cost of the genetic testing. According to research, a pertinent component of these discussions is the impact that the decision to pursue genetic testing will have on various family members and family dynamics in response to positive results. Research indicates that the intensity of these discussions varies with family history and experience with genetic disorders. Genetic testing should be the decision of each family member; there should be no coercion involved.

Genetic Testing

Genetic testing involves laboratory analyses of chromosomes, genes, or gene products (enzymes or proteins) to detect a genetic alternation that can cause, or is likely to cause, a specific genetic disorder or condition. Genetic testing can be DNA or RNA based, chromosomal or biochemical. Biochemical tests analyze for the presence or absence of key proteins, which may indicate altered genes or cause malfunctioning of specific genes. DNA-based tests are to test for genetic traits, predispositions, and conditions. These tests involve the direct examination of the DNA molecule itself. DNA microarray analysis can be used to measure changes in expression levels, to detect single nucleotide polymorphisms (SNPs), and to genotype mutant genomes. The creation of a high-density map of SNPs is a tool that is helping health care providers and scientists pinpoint genetic differences that predispose some individuals to disease or that are the basis of variable responses to treatment. Microarray analysis offers the possibility of predicting which clients will and will not benefit from therapy such as chemotherapy. The advent of genomics in which the whole genome is the unit of analysis, rather than individual genes, is revolutionizing the study of complex diseases such as cancer and diabetes.

Genetic tests performed for clinical purposes are those tests where specimens are analyzed and results reported to a health care provider, or to the client, for the purposes of diagnosis, prevention, or treatment. The indications for genetic testing include the following: *carrier testing* (to determine if an individual or couple carries a recessive allele for an inherited disorder); *preimplantation diagnosis* (to diagnose a genetic disorder in the developing embryo prior to implantation); *newborn screening* (part of a state public health program to identify specific genetic conditions for early treatment); *diagnostic testing* (to diagnose or confirm the diagnosis of a genetic condition in an individual); *predictive testing* (to determine the probability of a healthy individual, without a known history, of developing a disease); and *presymptomatic testing* (to determine whether or not individuals who have a family history, but are asymptomatic, have a specific gene mutation).

Research studies indicate that the results of genetic testing can have a profound impact on family life. If the tests are positive, families must accept the results of the test and its implications, grieve losses or changes in individual or family identity, and develop a family plan in response to the genetic knowledge. As an example, consider a man found to have Machado-Joseph disease, an inherited neuromuscular disease. He is married and has two late adolescent children, one of whom also tested positive and is highly likely to develop the disease. This family needs to discuss the meaning of the test results for all family members and develop future goals and discuss changes in family roles with a counselor.

Genetic testing can also identify family members in terms of predisposition to a variety of serious illnesses such as breast and ovarian cancer. Family members will know who is at risk because they have the BRCA1 and BRCA2 mutation or they do not have it. Once a mutation is identified in a family, those who choose not to undergo the genetic testing must still live with the awareness of their risk. Research indicates that the results of the testing can alter family dynamics and realign relationships within the family unit.

As the use of genetic testing becomes more widely available for a broad range of illnesses, more people will be screened for conditions that have identifiable genetic risk factors. Family-centered education before and after genetic testing will be needed to explain the meaning of the results and to help family members make decisions and plan for the future.

Enabling Family Health

The use of genomic technologies for risk assessment along with the family health history is improving health care decision making so as to achieve the goal of personalized health care. It is also permitting individuals and families to take a more active role in prospective health care activities. The new knowledge obtained from the study of genomes and their by-products has permitted the development of predictors of family disease predisposition (who is at risk), prognosis (who to treat), and therapeutic response (how to treat). Families know who is at risk within their families, are aware of the prognosis if preventive actions are not taken, and can take an active role in decreasing risk by making lifestyle changes (smoking cessation, physical activity, diet modifications, etc.). Thus, for many families the results of genetic testing create many new opportunities for preventive health care. The core of prospective health care is the personalized health risk assessment (family history, genetic testing, and predictive modeling). A predictive model uses statistical algorithms to identify factors and predict events. The model can be used to forecast events based on biomarkers that are most likely to correlate with, or be causative of, a future diagnosis of a genetic condition. Developing an accurate baseline risk assessment has been greatly facilitated by clinical research, the HapMap Project, and the Genetic Association Information Network.

Knowledge of familial risk level can guide the formation of personalized health planning for individual family members. Such a plan would include a health provider, a description of each family member's health status, a health risk analysis (genetic, environmental, and lifestyle) and prevention strategies to be employed over a 1-year period and those to be employed over a longer interval. Prevention strategies for those with significantly increased familial risk could be targeted for intensive lifestyle changes, screening at early ages, more frequent and with more intense methods, use of preventive medications, and, for those at the highest risk, prophylactic procedures and surgeries.

Cardiovascular disease is the leading cause of death in most industrialized countries and provides a useful example of the use of genomic knowledge and preventive health care. Studies have found that coronary artery disease is associated with single gene mutations, chromosomal defects, and multigene and environmental factors. A family history of coronary artery disease, lifestyle, lipid and nonlipid risk factors, plus a genetic predisposition for the disease, places an individual at risk. Whereas genetic factors cannot be altered, modifications in lifestyle and lipid and nonlipid risk factors can influence gene expression and reduce an individual's risk for developing the disease. The Third National Health and Nutrition Examination Survey found that modifiable risk factors for common chronic diseases aggregate in families, and modifying risk factors within a family rather than focusing on the individual is an effective strategy. However, health care providers need to help family members understand the practical and emotional demands of living with the risk of a condition over time in the nonsymptomatic phase. Preventive consultations over the life span will help family members maintain their preventive activities.

The family systems genetic illness model indicates the value of regular assessment and reevaluation of individuals, couples, and families in both the nonsymptomatic and symptomatic phases of a genetic condition. Research indicates that life-cycle changes and transition points in the life cycle are good points for reevaluation and counseling.

Preventive checkups help the family maintain their health promotion and prevention activities, and anticipatory guidance is useful to prepare the family members for future challenges.

Conclusion

Genetic research enables individuals and families to use their family genetic health history and genetic testing results for health promotion and disease prevention. Recent research advances in the field of genomics have helped to explain the modifiable and nonmodifiable risk factors that contribute to diseases within the context of shared genes, behaviors, and the environment. The familiar risk assessment serves as an important tool for health care providers and families to promote a healthy lifestyle and modify risk.

Bonnie Holaday

See also Assessing Family Health; Coping Management Styles in Families; Genetic Research Findings and Disease Management; Genetics: The Family Pedigree; Genograms and the Family

Further Readings

Amundadottir, L. T., Thorvaldsson, S., & Gudbjartsson, D. F. (2004). Cancer as a complex phenotype: Pattern distribution within and beyond the nuclear family. *PLoS Medicine, 4*(1), e65–e71.

Carter, E. A., & McGoldrick, M. (1999). *The evolving family life cycle: Individual family and social perspective* (3rd ed.). New York: Allyn & Bacon.

Cuzick, J. (2000). Future possibilities in the prevention of breast cancer. *Breast Cancer Research, 2*(4), 258–263.

Feetham, S. L. (1999). Families and the genetic revolution: Implications for primary care, education, research and policy. *Families, Systems, & Health, 17*(1), 27–43.

Forrest, K., Simpson, S. A., & Wilson, B. J. (2003). To tell or not to tell: Barriers and facilitators in family communication about genetic risk. *Clinical Genetics, 64*, 317–326.

Hadley, D. W., Jenkins, J., Diamond, E., & Nakahara, K. (2003). Genetic counseling and testing in families with hereditary nonpolyposis colorectal cancer. *Archives of Internal Medicine, 163*, 573–582.

Kupfer, S. S., McGaffrey, S., & Kim, K. E. (2006). Racial and gender disparities in hereditary colorectal cancer risk assessment: The role of family history. *Journal of Cancer Education, 21*, S32–S36.

Miller, S. M., Roussi, P., Daly, M. B., & Buzalglo, J. S. (2005). Enhanced counseling for women undergoing BRCA1/2 testing: Impact on subsequent decision making about risk prevention behaviors. *Health, Education and Behavior, 32*(5), 654–667.

O'Neill, S. M., Rubinstein, W. S., Wang, C., Yoon, P. W., Acheson, L. S., Rothrock, N., et al. (2009). Familial risk for common diseases in primary care: The Family Healthware Impact Trial. *American Journal of Preventive Medicine, 36*(5), 654–667.

Rolland, J. S., & Williams, J. (2005). Towards a biopsychosocial model for 21st-century genetics. *Family Process, 44*(1), 3–24.

Stephens, J. W., & Humphries, S. E. (2003). The molecular genetics of cardiovascular disease: Clinical implications. *Journal of Internal Medicine, 253*(1), 120–127.

Websites

Family Healthware: http://www.cdc.gov/genomics/famhistory/famhx.htm

GeneTests: http://www.genetests.org

My Family Health Portrait: https://familyhistory.hhs.gov

National Health and Nutrition Examination Survey:
    http://www.cdc.gov/nchs/nhanes
Understanding Gene Testing:
    http://www.accessexcellence.org/AE/AEPC/NIH

GENETICS: THE FAMILY PEDIGREE

A *pedigree* is a graphic diagram of a family's medical history. It is commonly called a *family tree*. Using a combination of symbols, it concisely records the family medical history, thereby helping families, individuals, and health providers identify inherited conditions along with biological and social relationships. According to Robin Bennett and Patricia Bender, a comprehensive pedigree analyzes at least three generations of blood relatives to identify and calculate the risk of transmitting inherited conditions, establish a pattern of inheritance, provide a medical diagnosis and treatment, plan testing strategies, determine reproductive options, and educate the family. According to Sharon Olsen, Sharon Dudley-Brown, and Patricia McMullen, an estimated 45% to 79% of families have at least one chronic disease that may be inherited.

The pedigree or family tree allows multiple disciplines to quickly and concisely communicate family histories to other members of the health care team. The inexpensive timesaving pedigree is the first step in the genetic screening process. Using the pedigree, the genetic counselor or advanced practice nurse with a genetics specialty (APNG) can identify the pattern of inheritance, discuss the risk for inheriting genetic conditions for future offspring, and diagnose health problems using genetic testing if indicated. Lifestyle changes can be made based on the family tree to optimize longevity. This entry describes the process of creating a pedigree and provides a case study as an example.

Creating a Pedigree

In 1995 a task force was created to standardize the pedigree nomenclature. The pedigree diagram is constructed in a personal face-to-face private interview and is a "living" document, maturing as the family's lives progress through time. The 30-minute interview assesses at least three family generations, including aunts, uncles, and cousins, for both maternal and paternal lineages. It addresses medical conditions and age of diagnosis, present age or age of death, lifestyle behaviors that affect disease states (such as smoking), inherited genetic disorders, and birth defects, according to Olsen and colleagues.

Pedigree Symbols

Family Member Symbols

Symbols are used to concisely document a family history and to encourage the use of the pedigree across the health care disciplines in a uniform fashion. There are four groups of symbols representing family members, relationships, assisted reproductive technology, and diagnostic evaluations. In the family pedigree (Figure 1, p. 548), the males are represented by squares, females by circles, and diamonds when gender is unknown. Deaths are denoted with a diagonal line across the pedigree symbol, and the age of death is listed following a "d." Stillbirths are denoted by a diagonal line and have the initials "SB" with the age of gestation listed. Terminated pregnancies and spontaneous abortions (i.e., ectopic pregnancies or miscarriages) are small triangles with a shortened individual line. Terminated pregnancies also have a diagonal line across the symbol. Family members with a genetic or health condition are shaded. If the family member has two or more genetic conditions, they are shaded with a pattern. Carrier states are indicated with a solid dot and an asymptomatic/presymptomatic carrier has a vertical line across the symbol. A current pregnancy is denoted with a "P," and an adopted child is enclosed in parentheses.

Relationship Symbols

The second group of symbols represents relationships through the use of lines (Figure 2, p. 549). Marriage or mating has a horizontal relationship line. Offspring are suspended from the vertical generation line. The proband, designated with an arrow pointing toward the gender symbol, is the family member with the genetic condition of concern (i.e., a cousin with cystic fibrosis). For family planning the consultand is the focus of the consultation (i.e., parent of an expected baby).

Assisted Reproductive Technology Symbols

The next group of symbols responds to advanced technology associated with the human genome project and advances in assisted reproductive technology. The symbols are written inside the pedigree symbol: A "D" is used to indicate donor (sperm or ovum), and an "S" is used to indicate a surrogate who has not donated an ovum. If the woman is both a surrogate and an ovum donor, a "D" for donor is used. The line descends from the pregnant women to the pregnancy or child directly below the symbol, as in Figure 3 (p. 549).

Diagnostic Evaluation Symbols

The last group of pedigree symbols is for diagnostic evaluations such as karyotyping or DNA analysis, which may be performed in conjunction with amniocentesis or chorionic villus sampling during the pregnancy or after birth. Preimplantation genetic diagnosis may be used before conception with in vitro fertilization. The symbols for diagnostic evaluation are listed in Figure 4 (p. 549).

The Pedigree Guidelines

To begin constructing a pedigree, start near the bottom center of a piece of paper for young families. Start higher on the paper if the proband is older and has many offspring, nieces, or nephews. The paternal side of the family is on the left side and the maternal side is kept on the right. Siblings are listed from oldest to youngest starting on the left if possible. Unaffected siblings can be grouped by placing the number of siblings in the pedigree symbol. The letter "n" is written in the pedigree symbol if the number of siblings is unknown. Roman numerals indicate generations and are listed on the left with the oldest generation designated as "I." The Arabic numbers identify each person within that generation from left to right. Identify each person with initials, names, and date of birth or age of death. Ethnicity is listed above each family. Record the name and title of the individual constructing the family tree, the historian's name, and the date. Indicate if the historian is unsure of a portion of the family's past medical history on the pedigree per Bender. The pedigree is only as useful as the historian is accurate.

The Interview

The interview process is best conducted in a quiet, private location because of the confidential nature of the questions such as divorce, mental illness, HIV status, or suicide. The age of onset is listed beneath the pedigree symbol. The questions should also address the health conditions listed in Figures 5, 6, and 7, labeled family history, review of systems, and abnormal tests (pp. 550-551).

Inheritance Patterns

The comprehensive pedigree diagram captures many family diagnoses simultaneously to calculate disease risk, confirm a suspected disease, or offer additional genetic testing, according to Olsen and colleagues. The patterns of inheritance are assessed by a genetic counselor or APNG, and probability of inheriting a genetic condition is calculated. The four patterns include autosomal dominant (which affects 50% of the offspring if one parent is affected); autosomal recessive (which affects 25% of the offspring with the phenotypic condition—50% will be a carrier of the mutated gene and 25% will have normal genes if both parents are carriers); X-linked recessive (the gene is carried by the female parent—the male children express the phenotypic condition, and the female's expression may vary because it may only affect half of the X chromosomes); X-linked dominant (which affects all genders because only one copy of the gene is necessary for the expression of the condition).

Case Study

The family pedigree depicted in Figure 8 (p. 552) is a graphic representation of this case study using the symbols described in Figures 1 and 2. Graham and Kristian (identified in the lower left corner of the pedigree in Figure 8) are newly married and expecting their first child. Graham's father mentioned that there was a family history of cystic fibrosis on the paternal side of the family. Graham and Kristian want to verify that their new baby won't inherit the disease. They were referred to a genetic counselor for their first of three visits.

The proband family member affected by cystic fibrosis is Graham's paternal grandfather's niece. She died at age 25 years of pneumonia. Her sister is a carrier of the cystic fibrosis gene. Their parents were first cousins (consanguineous) and both carried the recessive cystic fibrosis gene. Graham's paternal grandfather died at age 64 years of lung cancer after smoking for over half of his life. He

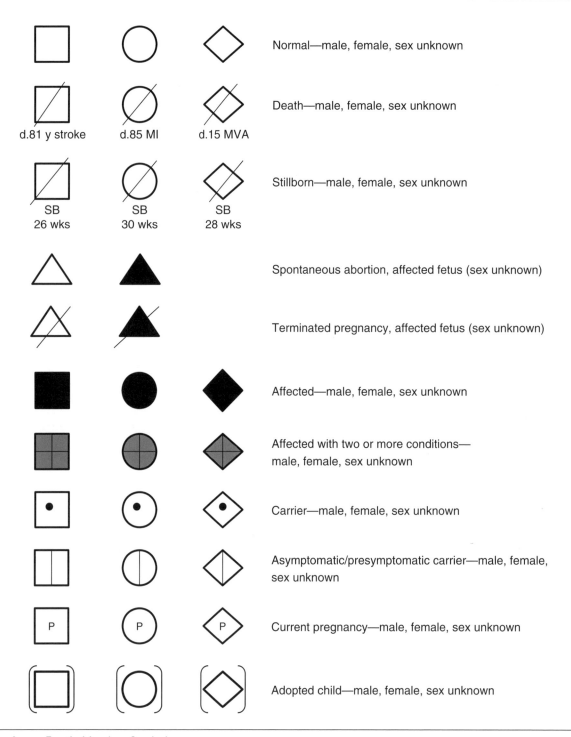

Figure 1   Family Member Symbols

also had emphysema and arthritis. Graham's paternal grandmother died at age 81 of a stroke and had a past medical history of migraine headaches, hypothyroidism, hypertension, obesity, and diabetes mellitus, which was diagnosed at age 75. She had two sisters, both deceased. One sister died at

85 years and had Alzheimer's disease and was hypertensive. The other sister died at 82 years of a myocardial infarction and was hypertensive and obese. Graham's father is 56 years old and has hypertension and hypercholesterolemia. Graham's mother is 46 years old with hypercholesterolemia

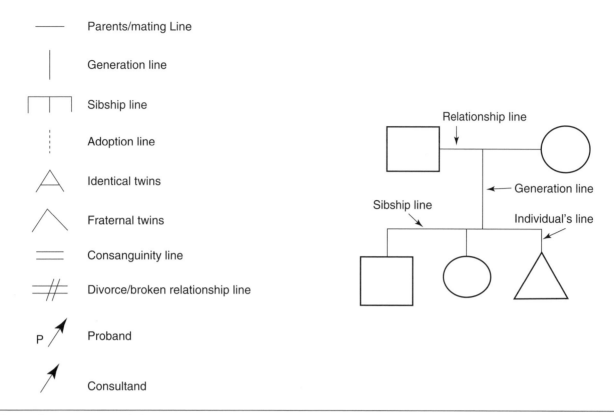

Parents/mating Line

Generation line

Sibship line

Adoption line

Identical twins

Fraternal twins

Consanguinity line

Divorce/broken relationship line

P   Proband

Consultand

Relationship line

Generation line

Sibship line

Individual's line

Figure 2   Relationship Symbols

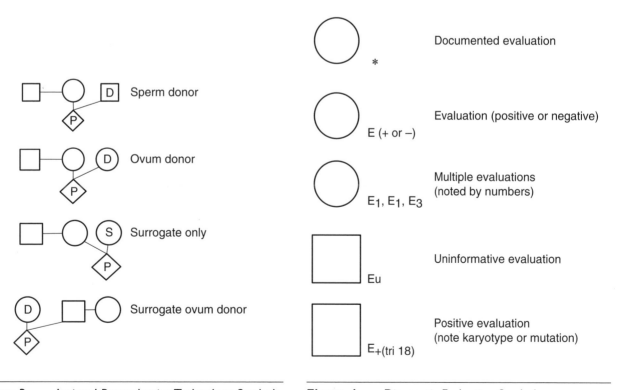

Sperm donor

Ovum donor

Surrogate only

Surrogate ovum donor

Documented evaluation

*

Evaluation (positive or negative)

E (+ or −)

Multiple evaluations
(noted by numbers)

E_1, E_1, E_3

Uninformative evaluation

Eu

Positive evaluation
(note karyotype or mutation)

$E_{+(tri\ 18)}$

Figure 3   Assisted Reproductive Technology Symbols

Figure 4   Diagnostic Evaluation Symbols

Figure 5   Family History Examples

Family History:	Examples:
Birth defects	Cleft palate, spina bifida
Genetic conditions	Cystic fibrosis, Huntington's disease, Tay-Sachs disease
Mental retardation	Down syndrome
Psychiatric problems	Bipolar, depression, obsessive-compulsive disorder
Alzheimer's disease	Before 60 years
Cancer	Ovarian, breast, endometrial, thyroid, colon before 45 to 50 years, prostate before 45 years
Cholesterol	Elevated
Triglyceride	Elevated
Cardiovascular	Hypertension, myocardial infarction, stroke before 60 years, deep vein thrombosis before 40 years of age
Miscarriages	Three or more
Stillbirths	Three or more
Unexplained infertility	

Sources: American Medical Association (2010); Bender (1998); Gaff (2005).

Figure 6   Review of Systems Examples

Review of Systems:	Examples:
Neurological	Essential tremor, developmental delay, learning difficulties, neurofibromatosis, seizure disorder
Muscular	Duchenne muscular dystrophy, unexplained movement disorder
Skeletal	Extra fingers or toes, dysmorphic facial features, abnormal head size
Gastrointestinal	Gallbladder, liver, intestinal, hemochromatosis
Genitourinary	Kidney, bladder conditions
Cardiac	Marfan syndrome, congenital heart disease
Dermatological	Birthmarks, hyperpigmentation of lower lip
Endocrine	Unusual growth patterns, early-onset diabetes
Hematological	Hemophilia, sickle cell
Vision loss	Before 55 years, early cataracts
Hearing loss	Before 50 to 60 years

Sources: American Medical Association (2010); Bender (1998); Gaff (2005).

and essential tremor. Graham's mother had three sons, including Graham. Graham has essential tremors and obsessive-compulsive disorder (OCD). Graham's 15-year-old brother is healthy, and his 12-year-old brother has OCD. Graham has four maternal aunts and one unborn (termination of unknown sex). The oldest is 60 years of age and was diagnosed with schizophrenia at age 41 years. She has a past medical history of alcoholism and is a smoker. The next maternal aunt is 59 years and has essential tremors. They have four children: two healthy daughters and a 25-year-old son with essential tremor and OCD and an adopted son

with attention deficit/hyperactivity disorder. The last two aunts are identical twins. The 54-year-old aunt is married and has three sons: The oldest has spina bifida, the middle son has essential tremor, and the youngest has OCD. The last aunt is married and has three daughters: The older two are healthy, and the youngest daughter has OCD. Graham's maternal grandfather died at 81 years of a stroke and was diagnosed with diabetes at 78 years of age and had a past medical history of essential tremor, hypertension, and obesity. He was an only child. Graham's maternal grandmother is 81 years and has a history of migraine headaches and hypercholesterolemia. She has one sister and a brother. Her sister was a smoker and died at 65 years of lung cancer. Her only brother is 70 years old

```
┌─────────────────────────────┐
│     Abnormal Testing:       │
│                             │
│    Prenatal ultrasound      │
│                             │
│     Newborn screening       │
└─────────────────────────────┘
```

Figure 7   Abnormal Testing

and has OCD. The paternal side of the family is English-German and Scottish-Irish and the maternal side of the family is Swedish and German.

The three generations are listed with Roman numerals from the oldest to the youngest. The person conducting the interview, along with their credentials, is listed on the pedigree, as is the identity of the historian giving the information and the date of the interview.

Outcome

The couple returned for their second visit with the genetic counselor, and she recommended mutation analysis for cystic fibrosis. Because Kristian is 20 weeks pregnant, she opted for an amniocentesis. The fetus was positive for carrying the recessive cystic fibrosis gene, but the child will not have the disease. If the baby eventually marries a spouse with the recessive cystic fibrosis gene, they will have a 25% chance of having a child with the disease, a 25% chance of having a healthy child without carrying the affected gene, and a 50% chance that the offspring will carry the affected gene but remain asymptomatic. Graham and Kristian's offspring is at risk for hypertension, migraine headaches, essential tremor, and OCD. The older family members with hypertension and obesity had cardiovascular events late in life. Early treatment of hypertension and maintaining a healthy weight were emphasized for Graham and the new baby based on the family history. The essential tremor and OCD both followed an autosomal recessive inheritance pattern, and 25% of their future children may have either OCD or essential tremor. The baby is also at a higher risk for alcoholism and smoking addiction with resulting lung cancer. Additional education in that area is needed to avoid addiction.

Julia Eggert and Heide S. Temples

See also Birth Defects and the Family; Genetic Family Histories; Genetic Information and Family Interviews; Genetic Research Findings and Disease Management for Families; Newborn Screening for Families; Preconceptual Counseling for Childbearing Couples; Prediction of Genetic Health Problems in Family Members

Further Readings

American Medical Association. (2010). *Family medical history*. Retrieved from http://www.ama-assn.org/ama/pub/physician-resources/medical-science/genetics-molecular-medicine/family-history.shtml

Bender, P. L. (1998). Genetic family history assessment. *AACN Clinical Issues, 9*(4), 483–490.

Bennett, R. L. (2010). *The practical guide to the genetic family history*. Hoboken, NJ: Wiley.

Bennett, R. L., Steinhaus, K. L., Uhrich, S. B., O'Sullivan, C. K., Resta, R. G., Lochner-Doyle, D., et al. (1995). Recommendations for standardized human pedigree nomenclature. *American Journal of Human Genetics, 45*, 745–752.

Berry, T. A., & Shooner, K. A. (2004). Family history: The first genetic screen. *The Nurse Practitioner, 29*(11), 14–25.

Case, D. O. (2008). Collection of family health histories: The link between genealogy and public health. *Journal of the American Society for Information Science and Technology, 59*(14), 2312–2319.

Gaff, C. L. (2005). Identifying clients who might benefit from genetic services and information. *Nursing Standard, 20, 1*, 49–53.

Lea, D. L. (2003). How genetics changes daily practice. *Nursing Management, 34*(11), 19–25.

Olsen, S., Dudley-Brown, S., & McMullen, P. (2004). Case for blending pedigrees, genograms and ecomaps: Nursing's contribution to the "big picture." *Nursing and Health Sciences, 6*, 295–308.

Qureshi, N., Bethea, J., Modell, B., Brennan, P., Papageorgiou, A., Raeburn, S., et al. (2005). Collecting genetic information in primary care: Evaluating a new family history tool. *Family Practice, 10*, 663–669.

Websites

National Society of Genetic Counselors: http://www.nsgc.org

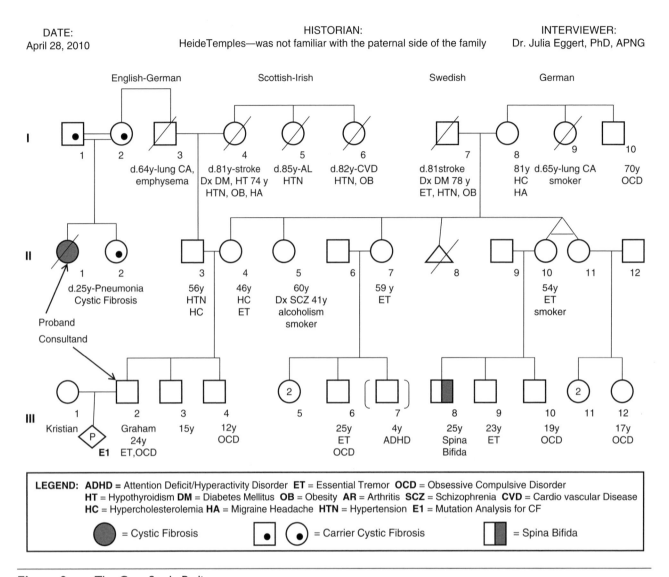

DATE:
April 28, 2010

HISTORIAN:
HeideTemples—was not familiar with the paternal side of the family

INTERVIEWER:
Dr. Julia Eggert, PhD, APNG

Figure 8   The Case Study Pedigree

GENETICS AND FAMILY HEALTH

The Human Genome Project marked a new beginning toward understanding the genetic basis of an increasing number of medical conditions. In addition to many gene–disease associations that were unveiled and characterized, significant attention was captured by the 0.1% of the genome that represents interindividual variability. Over 3 million interindividual differences at the nucleotide level, known as *single nucleotide polymorphisms*, were catalogued, and many of them shape predispositions to medical conditions, adverse reactions in response to therapeutic agents, or sensitivity to environmental

chemicals. More recently, an additional source of interindividual genetic variability—the deletion or duplication in varying numbers of genes or chromosomal regions as large as 3 million bases—became known as *copy number variation* (CNV). CNVs were linked to medical conditions such as autism spectrum disorders, schizophrenia, infectious disease susceptibility, and autoimmune diseases, but they were also described in apparently healthy individuals.

At the same time, recent years witnessed a new generation of DNA sequencing methodologies, which rely on increasingly sophisticated platforms, software, and bioinformatics tools and provide sequences with higher accuracy, at lower costs, and faster than before. Some instruments can sequence between 10 and 80 million base pairs within an hour. This marks an important step toward the $1,000 human genome, a much-anticipated milestone in the transition toward the era of personalized medicine, in which the sequencing of a human genome could be performed for $1,000, allowing individual genetic profiles to become part of prophylactic and therapeutic clinical decisions.

As a result of these advances, genetic testing has undergone a considerable expansion, and over 1,200 different tests have become available. Some genetic tests predict the risk to develop specific medical conditions, whereas others are informative about the response to a therapeutic agent, the risk to develop adverse reactions during treatment, or the sensitivity to occupational and environmental chemicals. This entry focuses on genetic testing and its implications for families.

Genetic Testing and the Nature of Genetic Information

Genetic testing opened an unexplored area, and brought challenges that were never before encountered by medical, legal, and social professionals. Several categories of genetic tests were described, with certain degrees of overlap. Diagnostic testing, such as the one performed for Duchenne muscular dystrophy, is usually conducted to confirm a diagnosis that is suspected based on medical tests, clinical presentation, and family history. Carrier testing is of particular importance for recessive conditions, such as cystic fibrosis, in which two copies of the mutation are necessary to develop clinical disease. Individuals with only one copy are known as healthy carriers and are usually asymptomatic, but they can transmit the mutation to their offspring. A child may inherit two copies of the mutation, one from each parent, and develop clinical disease, even though both parents are asymptomatic, because they both are healthy carriers harboring one copy of the mutation each. Genetic testing for recessive conditions can identify healthy carriers and is particularly important when making reproductive decisions, but its value is controversial in individuals who have not reached reproductive age, which represents the life stage when learning about one's carrier status becomes most relevant.

Predictive testing unveils mutations in healthy individuals who are at risk for future disease. One type of predictive testing, presymptomatic testing, is most frequently exemplified by Huntington's disease, a condition with autosomal dominant inheritance: A single copy of the mutation is sufficient to cause disease, despite a nonmutated copy of the same gene that exists on the other chromosome. Thus, a child has a 50% chance of harboring the mutation and developing the disease if only one parent has this condition. In this case, the presence of the mutation indicates with certainty that an individual will develop this progressive neurodegenerative condition, usually during the 4th or 5th decade of life. However, testing cannot predict the exact age when clinical symptoms will appear, and differences in the age at onset and clinical presentation have been reported even among monozygotic twins, suggesting that even for conditions with a strong genetic component, nongenetic influences are important. Particularly as no treatments are currently available, the benefits of predicting such a debilitating condition with onset during adulthood are highly debated and controversial.

A second type of presymptomatic genetic testing, predispositional genetic testing, is exemplified by testing for BRCA1 and BRCA2, the genes linked to breast and ovarian cancer. Women learning about their carrier status benefit from certain options, such as increased surveillance, lifestyle changes, or prophylactic surgeries. Although the BRCA1 and BRCA2 mutations confer a higher lifetime risk to develop breast and ovarian cancer, a positive genetic test does not indicate with certainty that disease will develop, and 20% to 30% of women carrying BRCA mutations never develop cancer. Similarly, because many breast and ovarian cancers are not inherited, a negative genetic test does not mean that the person will never develop cancer. Only 7% to 15% of breast and ovarian cancer patients have mutations in cancer susceptibility genes, and most women with breast and ovarian cancer do not have BRCA mutations. One study revealed that women with a significant family history of breast cancer, despite not harboring BRCA mutations, have a fourfold higher risk of breast cancer. Learning about the carrier status has to be balanced against the fact that positive genetic tests may cause anxiety, while negative tests might create a false sense of security that could lead to less frequent screenings and decreased surveillance.

Another type of genetic testing, newborn screening, is illustrated by the test for phenylketonuria

(PKU), which also exemplifies the benefits that genetic testing provides for treatable conditions. PKU, an autosomal recessive metabolic disease, affects approximately 1 in 10,000–13,000 newborn babies and is caused by a mutation that leads to an enzymatic deficiency resulting in the inability to metabolize phenylalanine, an essential dietary amino acid. When phenylalanine conversion to tyrosine is impaired, the toxic levels of blood phenylalanine that accumulate cause severe behavioral and physical delay. Newborn screening programs virtually eliminated the developmental delay caused by this condition.

Additional types of genetic testing are preimplantation testing, performed on embryos conceived by in vitro fertilization, and prenatal testing, performed on the fetus during pregnancy.

As genetic testing is becoming widely available for an increasing number of medical conditions, important questions are focusing on how to define genetic information and how to best characterize its position with regard to results generated by medical tests in general. Questions arise as to whether the results of the two types of tests should be equally private, or whether genetic information deserves enhanced privacy and protection over other medical information. This issue has important implications with regard to how genetic information is collected and stored, for how long it is stored and to whom it becomes available, and under what circumstances it can be accessed. Definitions of *genetic information* and *genetic test* vary significantly. Whereas some authors envision genetic information specifically as DNA mutations, others view this term more broadly and include even tests that measure compounds such as metabolites and proteins, which for a long time have been used in clinical medicine and are informative of genetic conditions. Certain medical tests can reveal genetic risks without examining DNA mutations—for example, the ultrasonographic detection of cysts in the kidney, spleen, and liver, most likely points toward polycystic kidney disease. Yet other authors urge for an even broader definition that would include family history, a powerful and well-established predictor of genetic predispositions. Historically, a patient's family history has been very informative about diseases affecting other family members, and this piece of information is often more powerful than any single genetic test that is currently available. Learning about an individual's family history, and about the age at which the parents,

grand-parents, or siblings have died, can point toward genetic conditions to which the patient is also predisposed.

Mark Rothstein points out that, in addition to genetic tests, medical tests and family history are additional sources of genetic information and, as a result, the line between what constitutes genetic versus nongenetic information, or the distinction between genetic and other medical tests, is becoming increasingly blurred. Other authors, such as George Annas, argue that genetic information is different and should be considered more private than other types of medical information. He points out that genetic information is not only about the individual but also about family members, and he emphasizes that it may open several concerns in addition to those surrounding medical tests, such as how to store not only the highly confidential test results but also the original DNA sample. DNA can be amplified with the polymerase chain reaction technology and new tests may be conducted, sometimes centuries after an initial sample was collected. For example, a group of researchers was recently planning to test DNA from Tutankhamun's body, and from several of his family members, to establish the exact kinship relations. A study that analyzed remains found in a grave from Russia revealed that they belonged to two of Tsar Nicholas II and Tsarina Alexandra's children, solving one of the greatest mysteries of the past century, the fate of the Romanov family.

Genetics and Family Dynamics

Genetic testing has significant emotional and psychological consequences, both for the individual being tested and for family members. Some studies found little psychological and emotional impact after testing, whereas others pointed to increased levels of anxiety both in individuals being tested and in their partners. Several studies reported that distress levels decrease in the months subsequent to genetic testing, more quickly for noncarriers than for carriers, whereas other studies did not detect differences between the two groups.

Whereas many studies focus on individuals with positive genetic tests, relatively little research has been conducted to understand the impact of receiving negative test results, yet this aspect of genetic testing seems equally important. Even the news of not being a carrier for a mutation can sometimes lead to distress. A study that enrolled first-degree relatives of ovarian cancer patients revealed that, even though most participants anticipated a sense of relief, 25% anticipated feeling guilty after testing negative. The phenomenon of "survivor guilt" subsequent to receiving genetic test results has been described for several conditions and is characterized by the fact that individuals, despite feeling a certain sense of relief, question the reasons why they are the ones to test negative and express concern for the well-being of family members who tested positive or who already have cancer. In a study that examined genetic testing for Huntington's disease, Susan Sobel and C. Brookes Cowan reported that the four individuals exhibiting the most pronounced depression were the ones who tested negative. Based on their family history, these individuals initially assumed that they were carriers and, after learning otherwise, they experienced grief for opportunities that they did not pursue. The authors described suicide attempts both among individuals who learned about being carriers and among those who learned that they did not harbor the mutation. For example, a young woman attempted suicide after testing negative, because she felt disconnected from her siblings who had the disease. In addition to positive and negative results, genetic test result can sometimes be ambiguous. One study reported that up to 10% of the individuals tested for BRCA1 and BRCA2 mutations had results of uncertain significance and, as a result, experienced anxiety. These examples reveal that depression, anxiety, and grief can be expected not only in people testing positive for a genetic condition but also in those who are not carriers, thus underscoring the need to provide counseling to all individuals receiving genetic testing.

In addition to the complex psychoemotional implications, genetic testing is also at the forefront of an important decision-making process: that of communicating the information to relatives who might be at risk. Communication about genetic risk opens very specific concerns, depending on the disease being tested for, and ample differences exist among families, even when testing for the same condition. While some studies report a strengthening in the family relationship between relatives who test positive and who identify common concerns to address together, other studies reveal conflicts or weakening of the relationships (particularly among

family members with different coping styles) or no changes at all.

One of the controversies surrounding the communication of genetic test results within families revolves around how to reach a balance between an individual's right to privacy and other family members' rights to learn about information that might benefit their health. In addition to the conflict between an individual's desire for confidentiality and family members' right to learn about genetic conditions that might affect them, another conflict emerges, between an individual's desire to share genetic information with family members and their wishes, and rights, not to know. Anneke Lucassen points out that genetic information should be available to all family members involved, to ensure that all those at risk have access to the information. Under these circumstances, the concept of family confidentiality would replace that of individual confidentiality. At the same time, Angus Clarke argues, even though genetic information is shared among relatives, certain items belong more strongly to particular individuals within the family, and even though family members have mutual obligations to share important medical information, in most cases, genetic information is private.

Additional dilemmas gravitate around what to tell relatives at risk, and when to tell them. Studies that addressed the communication of genetic test results within families found that disclosure of genetic risk to family members represents a complex topic, shaped by many variables. Close social relationships with relatives, the feeling of responsibility toward children, and the need for support often emerged as factors associated with the decision to discuss genetic tests with relatives. Family disagreements, the lack of close relationships, a desire to protect others from distressing information, and negative or inconclusive test results were often mentioned as reasons for not discussing the issue with other family members.

A survey conducted in the United States in 2001–2002 found that 60% of the medical geneticists interviewed had seen patients who did not want to inform at-risk relatives, and most participants reported that this had occurred on several occasions. Thus, health care professionals will most likely be faced with many patients who were not informed about the test results by relatives undergoing genetic testing. This issue promises to open significant challenges for the patient–health professional relationship.

Genetic Testing and Patient–Physician Confidentiality

Genetic medicine, by definition, is informative about predispositions that are relevant for entire families and could impact the health and lifestyle of several family members. At the same time, the patient–physician relationship in modern medicine is rooted in the concept of confidentiality. Reaching a balance between the respect for patients' confidentiality and privacy, and the responsibility of notifying relatives at risk about disease predispositions relevant for their health, represents a dilemma for health professionals and has major legal, medical, social, and ethical implications. David John Doukas and Jessica W. Berg talk about "tensions between the physician's individual and family obligations." To address the competing interests that a physician has toward the patient as well as toward the patient's family members, they propose the "family covenant," a model of patient care in which individual genetic testing and health care are considered within the context of families and the physician's responsibilities extend to the entire family. However, the situation is more complex. Various authors point out that even the definition of a family, for the purpose of genetic counseling, is challenging, because genetic relatedness and genetic risk extend beyond the nuclear family and different physicians may treat different members of extended families. In addition, individuals' increasing mobility in the current society, when adult children and their own nuclear families often reside in different geographical regions, creates challenges to sharing the same health care provider.

Gayun Chan-Smutko, Devanshi Patel, Kristen M. Shannon, and Paula D. Ryan provide an interesting case study, in which a female patient without a personal history of cancer developed endometrial polyps, her sister was recently diagnosed with endometrial cancer, and one of their grandfathers died of colon cancer at an early age. MSH2 mutations predispose to both colon and endometrial cancer. The physician encourages the sister with the cancer diagnosis to undergo genetic testing but cannot divulge the test results to the other sister; in addition, the sisters are not speaking to one another. Even if one sister undergoes genetic testing, the results cannot be placed in the other sister's chart without a signed release form. This opens a challenge about how to provide the best medical care to the unaffected sister and, in more general terms, an ethical dilemma about defining the duties that a health care professional has toward each family member. The authors recommend that issues related to nondisclosure between family members be solved during appropriate precounseling steps.

Medical professionals' obligation to inform people at risk, known as the "duty to warn," has emerged in several instances, such as communicable infectious diseases or when someone's safety is jeopardized. *Tarasoff v. Regents of the University of California* provides a relevant legal precedent in this respect. In October 1969, a student undergoing counseling confided in the counselor that he intended to kill a female student he had been stalking, who was attending the same university. The counselor subsequently notified the campus police but did not directly inform the woman, who was later murdered. In 1976 the California Supreme Court ruled that a mental health professional is required to breach patient confidentiality and take reasonable actions to warn identifiable third parties about serious or imminent threats. Under these circumstances, health professionals have an obligation that extends not only toward the patient or client but also toward people who are threatened.

In the case of genetic diseases, it is still unclear whether medical professionals are required to notify at-risk relatives, and courts have rendered opposing decisions. In one case, *Pate v. Threlkel*, a woman sued her mother's physician arguing that he did not inform her mother, who was previously treated for medullary thyroid carcinoma, about the risk of transmitting this condition to descendants. The daughter was diagnosed with advanced thyroid cancer several years later and, in her lawsuit, argued that had the physician warned her mother about the genetic risk, she could have detected the cancer at an early stage. In 1995 the Florida Supreme Court decided that a physician has a duty to warn patients that their genetic conditions might be transmissible to children and that this duty is fulfilled by warning the patient, as health professionals cannot be expected to find and inform all individual family members. The court also pointed out that notification about genetic predispositions differs from notification for infectious diseases, because in the case of genetic conditions, a mutation is already present and the development of disease is neither preventable nor imminent.

In another case, *Safer v. Estate of Pack*, the New Jersey Supreme Court decided that a physician has a duty to warn individuals at risk for genetic conditions and that this burden is on the physician. However, the court did not address whether warning family members at risk is practical and whether it would not impose an unrealistic burden. In this case, a physician initially treated a patient diagnosed with colon cancer in 1956. The patient died in 1964, and in 1990 the patient's daughter, Donna Safer, was also diagnosed with colon cancer. She subsequently sued the physician's estate, claiming that the physician, who by then was deceased, had a duty to warn her of the genetic nature of the disease and of her higher risk. In this case, the New Jersey Supreme Court rejected the idea that notifying only the patient satisfies the duty to warn those at risk and argued that a physician has to take "reasonable steps" to inform family members at risk. It is important to remark that both of these cases pointed out that medical professionals have a duty to warn about genetic risk, but the standards to accomplish this obligation were different.

Genetic Testing in Minors and in People Who Cannot Consent

A special situation with respect to privacy and confidentiality in genetic testing is encountered in minors. Because parents will always find out about the results of genetic tests, children do not enjoy the same level of confidentiality as adults undergoing testing. This establishes a conflict between the parental interest to perform a genetic test in a child and the child's interest for privacy.

Four broad types of genetic tests have been described in children: diagnostic testing for childhood-onset conditions, predictive testing for adolescence-onset conditions, predictive testing for adult-onset conditions, and carrier testing; complex ethical and legal issues surround each of these categories. Whereas newborn screening for treatable metabolic conditions, such as PKU, provides significant and well-established benefits, childhood genetic testing for adult-onset conditions, such as

Huntington's disease or retinitis pigmentosa (a progressive retinal dystrophy leading to variable degrees of blindness), is highly debated and controversial.

Several guidelines emphasize that with certain exceptions (such as overwhelming parental anxiety, which sometimes exerts a more negative impact than testing itself and can lead to psychological, immunological, neurological, and endocrine consequences), genetic tests should not be conducted in children, and testing should instead be deferred until they can give informed consent. M. Bloch and M. R. Hayden emphasize that the only instance justifying genetic testing in childhood is when a clearly demonstrated advantage exists for the child. However, this issue is shaped by several variables, including the specific condition tested for and unique circumstances characterizing individual families, and it appears that no simple solution exists.

R. E. Duncan and M. B. Delatycki argue that cognitive and psychosocial considerations justify separating the discussions about predictive genetic testing between children and adults. From a cognitive standpoint children are more vulnerable. The impact of genetic testing during adolescence, a special developmental stage when self-identity is being shaped and the first intimate relationships are established, is very different than in adults, providing a good reason to postpone genetic testing until adulthood.

Alan Fryer points out that even defining the age at which a child could give consent is difficult, because this is related not simply to biological age but also to maturity. Moreover, he emphasizes that an additional concern, besides confidentiality, is that genetic test results are released directly to the parents, a practice that breaches the policy of providing the patient with counseling before, during, and after the test.

Other authors recommend that pediatricians encourage genetic testing in children at a young age. One consideration is that parents, when requesting genetic testing for their children, do not violate the principles of confidentiality, because they are the ones who often authorize other medical procedures that their children require. Further, as some authors argue, parents need this piece of information to make decisions about their children's health, well-being, and future, and because they (and not practitioners) bear the emotional and moral burdens and make the financial decisions, the decisions should be theirs.

Genetic testing in minors can be associated with a variety of problems, including the feeling of worthlessness in those who test positive or the development of "survivor guilt" in patients who test negative, as also described in adults. In addition, in many families, a negative genetic test in one child was linked to the perception of increased risk in the other siblings and was reported to change the dynamics of family relationships.

Pascal Borry and colleagues emphasize that children often have difficulties processing the news that they might become sick later in life. The authors further underscore that even though an often-reported belief is that genetic testing might psychologically prepare children for the future, only 10% to 15% of adults with a family history of Huntington's disease eventually undergo genetic testing. This represents an important reason to postpone genetic testing until adulthood, particularly because it is impossible to later "undo" the knowledge, and children undergoing testing lose the opportunity, later in life, to exercise their right "not to know."

Direct-to-Consumer Genetic Testing

Genetic testing should always be offered under the direct supervision of health professionals, who provide counseling before, during, and after the test, and interpret the results in the context of additional medical information and family history. However, a phenomenon that increasingly started to emerge during recent years is the availability of genetic testing directly to consumers, which became known as *direct-to-consumer* (DTC) marketing of genetic testing. There are two major aspects related to DTC genetic testing. One of them refers to the practice of advertising the availability of the genetic test directly to consumers, who subsequently can perform testing in health care facilities. The second aspect refers to the situation when not only is the availability of the genetic test marketed, but the test itself is also commercialized directly to consumers, who subsequently also receive the test results directly. DTC genetic testing is often performed without pretesting and posttesting counseling, and health care professionals are not always involved. Further, as some companies provide genetic testing over the Internet and have physical locations in a country other than where the test is sold, regulation is challenging, if possible at all.

There are many arguments favoring or opposing DTC genetic testing. By revealing predispositions, genetic tests can increase awareness, lead to more frequent screenings, or encourage lifestyle interventions, ultimately improving health. When offered directly to consumers, genetic tests provide increased convenience, as individuals do not require appointments to undergo testing or receive the test results. In addition, testing outside of the medical establishment can ease some people's fears about the results becoming part of their medical record. However, the fact that genetic counseling is often not part of the DTC genetic testing raises serious concerns. In addition, a study revealed that two thirds of DTC genetic tests used emotional appeals rather than accurately describing the benefits and limitations of testing. Sara Chandros Hull and Kiran Prasad report about an advertisement for BRCA testing, during the moments preceding a theater play depicting a woman's fight against ovarian cancer. The authors underscore several troubling aspects related to this approach and analyze why the practice is manipulating, misleading, and misguiding.

The availability of DTC genetic testing is even more important with respect to minors. To examine protections that are available for children in context of DTC genetic testing, Borry and colleagues examined several websites that provide health-related genetic tests directly to consumers and found several companies that did not address the protection offered to minors and others that agreed to provide genetic testing for minors, an aspect that is worrisome to some health professionals who believe more regulatory attention is warranted.

As genetic testing assumes an increasingly important role in many medical specialties, it is essential to implement educational initiatives targeting both consumers and health professionals, to dispel the widespread myths about genetic determinism, and to emphasize the complex interactions between genetic and environmental factors that shape most medical conditions. A consumer survey conducted in Australia revealed serious misconceptions with regard to understanding genetic risk. Most participants thought that an increased genetic risk meant that they would develop the disease irrespective of what they did and indicated that a healthy lifestyle would not make a difference. In addition, 80% incorrectly believed that being a carrier meant that they had the disease. Educational initiatives should particularly emphasize the need to perform genetic testing only in health care settings, where health care professionals are available and involved, and should increase consumers' and professionals' awareness about potential false-positive and false-negative test results.

With new gene–disease associations being constantly unveiled, more genetic tests are expected to become available in the health care and direct-to-consumer settings. Understanding the strengths and limitations of genetic testing and the particular challenges that each individual test opens for the individual, the family, and the patient–physician relationship is becoming increasingly important for health care providers, irrespective of their specific field, to routinely address during their interaction with patients and their families.

Richard Albert Stein

See also Genetic Conditions, Communication in Families; Genetic Family Histories; Genetic Research Findings and Disease Management for Families; Genetic Research Findings and Family Health

Further Readings

Annas, G. J. (1999). Genetic privacy: There ought to be a law. *Texas Review of Law and Politics, 4*(1), 9–15.

Bloch, M., & Hayden, M. R. (1990). Opinion: Predictive testing for Huntington's disease in childhood: Challenges and implications. *American Journal of Human Genetics, 46*(1), 1–4.

Borry, P., Goffin, T., Nys, H., & Dierickx, K. (2008). Predictive genetic testing in minors for adult-onset genetic diseases. *Mount Sinai Journal of Medicine, 75*(3), 287–296.

Borry, P., Howard, H. C., Sénécal, K., & Avard, D. (2010). Health-related direct-to-consumer genetic testing: A review of companies' policies with regard to genetic testing in minors. *Familial Cancer, 9*(1), 51–59.

Chan-Smutko, G., Patel, D., Shannon, K.M., Ryan, P.D. (2008). Professional challenges in cancer genetic testing: Who is the patient? *The Oncologist, 13*(3), 232–238.

Clarke, A. (2007). Should families own genetic information? No. *British Medical Journal, 335*(7609), 23.

Coble, M. D., Loreille, O. M., Wadhams, M. J., Edson, S. M., Maynard, K., Meyer, C. E., et al. (2009). Mystery solved: The identification of the two missing Romanov children using DNA analysis. *PLoS ONE, 4*(3), e4838.

Douglas, H. A., Hamilton, R. J., & Grubs, R. E. (2009). The effect of BRCA gene testing on family relationships: A thematic analysis of qualitative interviews. *Journal of Genetic Counseling, 18*(5), 418–435.

Doukas, D. J., & Berg, J. W. (2001). The family covenant and genetic testing. *American Journal of Bioethics, 1*(3), 3–10.

Duncan, R. E., & Delatycki, M. B. (2006). Predictive genetic testing in young people for adult-onset conditions: Where is the empirical evidence? *Clinical Genetics, 69*(1), 8–16.

Falk, M. J., Dugan, R. B., O'Riordan, M. A., Matthews, A. L., & Robin, N. H. (2003). Medical geneticists' duty to warn at-risk relatives for genetic disease. *American Journal of Medical Genetics A, 120A*(3), 374–380.

Fryer, A. (2000). Inappropriate genetic testing of children. *Archives of Diseases in Childhood, 83*(4), 283–285.

Gallo, A. M., Angst, D. B., & Knafl, K. A. (2009). Disclosure of genetic information within families. *American Journal of Nursing, 109*(4), 65–69.

Holm, S. (2001). The privacy of Tutankhamen—utilising the genetic information in stored tissue samples. *Theoretical Medicine and Bioethics, 22*(5), 437–449.

Hull, S. C., & Prasad, K. (2001). Reading between the lines: Direct-to-consumer advertising of genetic testing. *Hastings Center Report, 31*(3), 33–35.

Lerman, C., Daly, M., Masny, A., & Balshem, A. (1994). Attitudes about genetic testing for breast-ovarian cancer susceptibility. *Journal of Clinical Oncology, 12*(4), 843–850.

Liang, A. (1998). The argument against a physician's duty to warn for genetic diseases: The conflicts created by *Safer v. Estate of Pack. Journal of Health Care Law and Policy, 1*(2), 437–453.

Lucassen, A. (2007). Should families own genetic information? Yes. *British Medical Journal, 335*(7609), 22.

Offit, K., Groeger, E., Turner, S., Wadsworth, E. A., & Weiser, M. A. (2004). The "duty to warn" a patient's family members about hereditary disease risks. *Journal of the American Medical Association, 292*(12), 1469–1473.

Pate v. Threlkel, 640 So.2d 183, 186 (Fla. 1st DCA 1994).

Pelias, M. K. (2006). Genetic testing of children for adult-onset diseases: Is testing in the child's best interests? *Mount Sinai Journal of Medicine, 73*(3), 605–608.

Peshkin, B. N., DeMarco, T. A., Brogan, B. M., Lerman, C., & Isaacs, C. (2001). BRCA1/2 testing: Complex themes in result interpretation. *Journal of Clinical Oncology, 19*(9), 2555–2565.

Rhodes, R. (2006). Why test children for adult-onset genetic diseases? *Mount Sinai Journal of Medicine, 73*(3), 609–616.

Rothstein, M. A. (1999). Why treating genetic information separately is a bad idea. *Texas Review of Law and Politics, 4*(1), 33–37.

Sobel, S., & Cowan, C. B. (2003). Ambiguous loss and disenfranchised grief: The impact of DNA predictive testing on the family as a system. *Family Process, 42*(1), 47–57.

Storm, C., Agarwal, R., & Offit, K. (2008). Ethical and legal implications of cancer genetic testing: Do physicians have a duty to warn patient's relatives about possible genetic risks? *Journal of Oncology Practice, 4*(5), 229–230.

Tarasoff v. Regents of the University of California, 17 Cal.3d 425, 551 P.2d 334, 131 Cal. Rptr. 14 (1976).

Wertz, D. C., Fanos, J. H., & Reilly, P. R. (1994). Genetic testing for children and adolescents. Who decides? *Journal of the American Medical Association, 272*(11), 875–881.

Genograms and the Family

A *genogram* is an assessment tool that diagrams select aspects of family structure and history. Using symbols that represent each member of a family, it is a visual representation of family patterns, family definitions, and family issues across multiple generations. Genograms have been used in many different social service settings by social workers, nurse practitioners, psychologists, other mental health professionals, and medical practitioners. This entry describes their use in health care settings.

Guidelines, Uses, and Development

Ann Hartman suggests the following guidelines for conducting a genogram assessment. Starting with the presenting problem, talk about the problem in the larger context of what else is going on with the family. Assess the immediate household first, and then the current extended family, followed by previous generations. The practitioner should evaluate the present family situation and then the historical chronology of family events. Begin with easy, nonthreatening questions, and then move to more difficult, anxiety-provoking ones. Record obvious, concrete facts, and as you conduct the interview, begin to make clinical judgments about family functioning and relationships and hypotheses about family patterns.

Genograms are used to explore family health patterns of illness and disease as well as mental health, substance abuse, and family violence history. There is growing evidence that genetics plays some part in health, so understanding the family intergenerational patterns is necessary for diagnosing health problems. A family paradigm is the family's view of the world and health problems; illness and treatment must be understood in the context of family traditions, rituals, and myths. Two family issues relevant to the use of genograms in health care settings are the coinciding of life events with the presenting health problem and the impact of life changes, transitions, and trauma on the current presenting problem.

The development of a genogram is a collaborative process between the assessor and family member and his or her family. It is effective for children as well as adults. Using genograms is useful in building rapport with a member of a health care team to improve communication and foster disclosure of medical concerns. As a tool in assessment and intervention, genograms may be limited by the client's capacity to remember aspects of their family of origin and by the client's knowledge of family events and history. Some families may transfer very little information regarding family events and history from one family member to another. In these instances, family members may possess little information with which to complete a genogram. More problematic are constructing genograms for adoptees who are in closed adoptions; a closed adoption means there is no detailed information shared about the birth family history. According to Victor Groza, Daniela Ileana, and Ivor Irwin, this situation occurs in infant adoptions in the United States and continues in international adoption, where health information is often unknown or inaccurate.

Genograms With Special Populations

Genograms have been adapted for use with special populations. J. Curtis McMillen and Groza use a modification of genograms to map foster care placements and changes in placements that occur for children in the child welfare system; they demonstrate how to use genograms to assist families in integrating foster and adoptive children into the family system. Catherine Bannerman suggests that practitioners working with the elderly use genograms to identify important social network resources and facilitate life review.

Other Health Care Uses of Genograms

Health record keeping, management, and preventive medicine are all areas in which genograms can be useful. Practitioners may use a genogram to gather family history of medical illnesses across multiple generations, in this way creating a record of illnesses prevalent in a patient's family history. Practitioners may also use the genogram to document the history of illness for one patient, dating each illness in the genogram or examining the interactions between the onset of one family member's illness and another member's illness. One example occurs when a child in a family experiences a significant illness. Caretakers might then experience significant stress in response to a child's illness, particularly if it becomes a chronic condition. Caretakers may develop physical symptoms and complaints as a result of the ongoing stress of caring for a sick child. Using a genogram for medical record keeping that includes the illnesses of all family members can assist the practitioner in identifying the relationship between one family member's illness and another member's symptoms.

Genograms may also assist patients with managing health issues by identifying important social supports such as family members, extended family members, or nonfamily members of social networks. These individuals may assist patients in regaining and maintaining physical health. One example might be identifying a family member who may assist the patient in getting to the pharmacy to refill medications or who can remind the patient to consistently take medication for the management of illness. For patients whose illnesses require lifestyle changes such as dietary changes, smoking cessation, or increased exercise, a genogram may help practitioners identify family members who can support such changes in the patient's life.

Genograms may also be used for prevention and early diagnosis of illnesses for which patients have a predisposition to developing. A gathering of family history of medical conditions through a genogram assists in identification of multigenerational development of specific illnesses. For example, the visual cue of a genogram in which a patient's mother, aunt, and grandmother have died of breast cancer is a powerful way of identifying a patient's physical vulnerability to the disease and a signal to question her about her own thoughts, concerns, and self-care in relation to the illness. A further example is the use of genograms in diagnosing women at risk for heart attack when experiencing diffuse symptoms. A genogram illustrating a family history of heart disease might assist practitioners in making such diagnoses in instances when a patient's symptoms are ambiguous.

Genograms and Family Stress

Family stressors may significantly affect a patient's capacity to get well when ill or to remain well. Monica McGoldrick, Randy Gerson, and Sylvia Shellenberger note that family functioning may affect the course of chronic medical conditions such as diabetes, mental health problems, and substance abuse over time. Using a genogram to assess family functioning for patients with serious and chronic medical conditions allows medical practitioners to identify family stressors and patterns of functioning that can exacerbate illness or limit a patient's capacity to regain and maintain physical health. Identifying barriers to health embodied in dysfunctional family patterns allows practitioners to intervene or refer patients for assistance in managing family difficulties.

Victor Groza and Suzanne Brown

See also Culturagram Use With Culturally Diverse Families; Factors Influencing Family Health Values, Beliefs, and Priorities; Families Experiencing Chronic Physical and Mental Health Conditions; Health Management in Families; Partnering With Families: Family-Centered Care

Further Readings

Bannerman, C. (1986). Genograms and elderly patients. *Journal of Family Practice, 23*(5), 426–428.

Groza, V., Ileana, D., & Irwin, I. (1999). *A peacock or a crow? Stories, interviews and commentaries on Romanian adoptions.* Brunswick, OH: Crown Custom Publishing.

Hartman, A. (1978). Diagrammatic assessment of family relationships. *Social Casework, 59*(8), 465–476.

Hartman, A., & Laird, J. (1983). *Family-centered social work practice*. New York: The Free Press.

McGoldrick, M., Gerson, R., & Shellenberger, S. 1999. *Genograms: Assessment and intervention* (2nd ed.). London: Norton.

McMillen, J. C., & Groza, V. (1994). Using placement genograms in child welfare practice. *Child Welfare, 73*(4), 307–318.

GRANDPARENTING

Demographic change and changing family values have profoundly altered the nature of grandparenting. Grandparents and grandchildren spend more time with each other over extended periods of their life courses as a consequence of rising life expectancy. Whereas grandparenting in the past was often restricted by early onset of ill health or frailness when grandchildren were still young, today's grandparents see their grandchildren growing up to have children of their own (great-grandparenthood). On the other hand, today's grandparents have fewer grandchildren than previous generations as a result of declining fertility levels. Increasing popularity of liberal family values has challenged the dominance of family formation based on marriage, with the outcome of greater variability of family forms (cohabitation, single parents, etc.). Greater ease of dissolving marriage and remarrying has caused the emergence of reconstituted or "patchwork families," resulting in the loss of old and the creation of new grandparent–grandchild relationships.

Further, grandparenting styles are beginning to change as birth cohorts socialized to comply with more liberal family values are beginning the passage into grandparenthood. These "new" grandmothers and grandfathers also interpreted their roles as mothers and fathers differently from previous generations, with both sexes sharing responsibility for child care to a greater extent and both increasingly combining child care with paid work. Particularly noteworthy is the changed role of grandfathers, who are much more actively engaged with their grandchildren than previous generations, regardless of the grandchild's sex. Nevertheless,

grandmothers continue playing a pivotal role as "kin-keepers."

Challenges Faced by Grandparents

A problem many grandparents face is that they are only indirectly affected by family conflicts and as such not part of the (institutional) solution. Whereas the child's best interest is increasingly recognized and safeguarded in divorce settlements, the interest of grandparents in continuing to maintain close relationships with their grandchildren is considered to a much lesser extent. However, this is beginning to change. The legal position of grandparents has seen some improvements in recent years in the United States as well as in Germany and Italy, whereas British grandparents still have very limited legal rights following divorce.

This lack of recognition is in marked contrast to grandparents' contribution to solving family problems. Grandparents have always been a valuable source of support for their adult children and grandchildren, a finding well-documented in the research literature. There is clear evidence that divorce results in more involvement of the maternal grandparents, while the paternal grandparents are getting less involved or cease maintaining the relationship with their grandchildren altogether. Less clear is to what extent this withdrawal is voluntary or forced on them.

Moreover, grandparental child care is often precondition for a single parent's employment. Providing regular child care can be challenging for a grandparent, particularly for older grandparents and grandparents not in good health. Some grandparents switch from full-time to part-time employment to enable their children to work, thus losing part of their income. Particularly challenging is the situation for grandparents with simultaneous caregiving responsibilities for grandchildren and for older family members ("sandwich situation"). An even higher level of grandparental involvement is required in cases of custodial grandparenting. Ana Beltran reported in 2000 that 3.7 million custodian grandparents were raising about 3.9 million grandchildren in the United States.

But even in the absence of parental conflict, grandparents can be prevented from seeing their grandchildren frequently when their children do not live geographically close—a trend increasingly observed in line with greater demands for labor mobility. Advances in communication technology (cell phones, e-mail, Skype) may have created new ways of communicating between grandparents and grandchildren across long distances, but they cannot fully compensate for face-to-face contact.

Health Outcomes of Grandparenting

Grandparenting can have positive and negative health outcomes. There is compelling research evidence of positive effects of grandparenting on well-being in old age. Recent research has shown that interaction with grandchildren can significantly improve the condition of older people suffering from dementia or Alzheimer's disease. In contrast, family conflicts not only affect grandparents' relationships with grandchildren; they can also have a detrimental effect on their physical and psychological well-being. Moreover, stress associated with child care is a strong predictor of negative health outcomes. Particularly severe are negative health outcomes for custodial grandparents, especially single custodian grandparents. Research found that they are much more likely to develop depressive symptoms and to have activities-of-daily-living limitations than grandparents without child care obligations.

Intervention Programs

Grandparents play an immensely important role in maintaining stability and continuity for children at times of family crisis. Thus, a forward-looking family policy would recognize and protect grandparents' rights in divorce settlements. Continued contact with the absent parent (usually the child's father) has proved to be beneficial for children affected by divorce—the same line of reasoning could be applied to maintaining close grandparent–grandchild relationships.

Many working parents—and single parents in particular—rely on grandparents for child care. However, it is imperative that they are supported in doing so for maintaining their health and well-being. One-stop information centers could be a way of helping grandparents find information and support, such as counseling services tailored to meet grandparents' needs or temporary respite services. Sufficient provision of affordable, flexible, and good-quality institutional child care could

relieve grandparents from this "duty" and enable them and their children to combine paid work with family care and manage healthy work–life balances. Some may regard this as an expensive luxury. However, such institutional solutions may become a necessity for our aging societies, which increasingly rely on aging workforces for generating their wealth.

Andreas Hoff

See also Grandparents Parenting

Further Readings

Beltran A. (2000). Grandparents and other relatives raising children: Supportive public policies. *Public Policy and Aging Report, 11*(1), 1, 3–7.

Drew, L. M., & Smith, P. K. (1999). The impact of parental separation/divorce on grandparent–grandchild relationships. *International Journal of Aging and Human Development, 48,* 191–215.

Ferguson, N. (2004). *Grandparenting in divorced families.* Bristol, UK: Policy Press.

Mann, R., Leeson, G. W., & Khan, H. A. (in press). Grandfathers in contemporary families in Britain: Evidence from qualitative research. *Journal of Intergenerational Relationships, 8(3).*

Marx, J., & Solomon, J. C. (2000). Physical health of custodial grandparents. In C. B. Cox (Ed.), *To grandmother's house we go and stay: Perspectives on custodial grandparents* (pp. 37–55). New York: Springer.

Minkler, M., & Fuller-Thomsen, E. (1999). The health of grandparents raising grandchildren: Results of a national study. *American Journal of Public Health, 89*(9), 1384–1389.

Szinovcz, M. E., De Viney, S., & Atkinson, M. P. (1999). Effects of surrogate parenting on grandparents' well-being. *Journal of Gerontology: Social Sciences, 54B*(6), S376–S388.

GRANDPARENTS PARENTING

Increasingly grandparents are parenting their grandchildren as a result of problems in the parent generation, such as drug addiction, incarceration, and AIDS. Parenting of grandchildren (often referred to as *custodial grandparenting*) goes beyond simple babysitting; it involves taking primary responsibility for the care of one or more grandchildren for 6 months or more without the parents present. In most cases, such grandparents do not have legal authority over their grandchildren (through adoption, legal custody, or guardianship); consequently, they often encounter obstacles in registering their grandchildren for school and getting them health insurance.

In addition to skipped-generation households where parents are not present, grandparents are also increasingly coparenting grandchildren in three-generational households largely as a result of divorce, financial difficulties, or both, in the parent generation. Although coparenting grandparents share equally in the caregiving and financial support of grandchildren, they usually fare better than custodial grandparents on most outcome measures.

Shifts in family roles from grandparent to parent or coparent can complicate family structure and compromise the health and well-being of grandparents and possibly grandchildren. Following a brief history of this social phenomenon, the repercussions of this role for grandparents' health and well-being are described, as well as social programs aimed at mitigating these problems.

History

According to the U.S. Census Bureau, 2.4 million grandparents were raising their grandchildren in 2000—a 30% increase since 1990—and 5.7 million grandparents were living with, and thus most likely coparenting, their grandchildren. This increase in the number of custodial grandparents has been attributed to public health epidemics of drug abuse, teen pregnancy, HIV/AIDS, and violence, as well as a concomitant rise in incarceration and death among the parent generation.

According to the U.S. Census Bureau, of the grandparents who were parenting their grandchildren in 2000, 72% were 65 years of age or less, 77% were female, and 54% were married. With regard to racial/ethnic composition, 51% were white non-Hispanic, 38% were African American, and 13% were white Hispanic. Although a greater number of custodial grandparents were white non-Hispanic, proportionately, African Americans (4.3%) and

white Hispanics (2.9%) were more likely than white non-Hispanics (1%) to be parenting grandchildren. One fifth of grandparent caregivers live below the poverty line, a proportion that is greater than for other types of families with children.

Effects on Family Health

Effects on Grandparents' Health

Researchers have been concerned with the toll that caregiving for grandchildren may take on grandparents, despite the fact that grandparents report that aspects of caregiving are rewarding. The parenting of grandchildren has been found to have negative effects on grandparents' social, financial, psychological, and physical well-being. Compared to noncaregiving grandparents, caregiving grandparents report higher rates of depression, diabetes, hypertension, and insomnia. Compared to their age counterparts, custodial grandparents have more difficulty performing activities of daily living.

The parenting of grandchildren also indirectly affects the health of grandparents through changes in lifestyle, relationships with others, and social roles. Custodial grandparents have less time for exercise and doctor visits. Further, the stress of caregiving may contribute to poor health behaviors such as smoking, limited social activities with a spouse or friend, and a reduced number of hours in paid employment. Consequently, grandparents may suffer declines in health, become socially isolated, and become financially strapped.

Although most of the research on caregiving grandparents is based on data collected from small convenience samples using cross-sectional methods, a few long-term longitudinal studies have corroborated the finding that caregiving grandparents are more likely than their noncaregiving counterparts to experience poorer psychological and physical well-being over time. However, a recent longitudinal study based on a large nationally representative sample suggests that the ill health effects of caregiving may be not the result of provision of care to grandchildren but rather a logical extension of preexisting health problems. Future research needs to replicate this finding with other nationally representative data sets.

Effects on Grandchildren's Health

Research on the effects of custodial grandparenting on the health and well-being of grandchildren is scarce to nonexistent; however, it is assumed that grandchildren benefit from this caregiving arrangement, especially compared to foster care or remaining in the care of a drug-abusing or physically abusive parent. One study examining academic success found that children raised by grandparents were less likely than those raised in a nuclear family, and equally likely as those raised in a single-parent family, to excel in school. However, more research is needed to determine the health and well-being of grandchildren raised by grandparents.

Programs

Grandparents who take on the responsibility of parenting their grandchildren may need assistance so that they do not suffer ill effects. Although custodial grandparents (and their grandchildren) have been targeted for services, they often do not know about these services or how to access them. Those who do know often face barriers, including lack of child care or free time, which prevent them from accessing these services. Most commonly custodial grandparents have difficulty gaining access to medical care, health insurance, and legal services. In 2000 the National Family Caregiver Support Program was established to help states disseminate information about support services and how to access them. Support services include programs to meet the physical, psychological, financial, legal, and social needs of grandparents and their grandchildren. Custodial grandparents also have access to public benefit programs such as Supplemental Security Income that provide financial assistance and medical insurance. Further, social support groups, some of which have been created through Generations United, have also been found to be an effective way to help custodial grandparents maintain the health and well-being of themselves and their grandchildren.

Roseann Giarrusso

See also Coparenting: Children; Factors Influencing Access to Health Care for Families; Family Caregiving: Caring for Children, Adults, and Elders With Developmental Disabilities; Grandparenting

Further Readings

Baker, L. A., & Silverstein, M. (2008). Preventive health behaviors among grandmothers raising grandchildren. *Journal of Gerontology: Social Sciences, 63B*(5), S304–S311.

Hayslip, B., Jr., & Kaminski, P. L. (2005). Grandparents raising their grandchildren: A review of the literature and suggestions for practice. *The Gerontologist, 45*(2), 262–269.

Hughes, M. E., Waite, L. J., LaPierre, T. A., & Luo, Y. (2007). All in the family: The impact of caring for grandchildren on grandparents' health. *Journal of Gerontology: Social Sciences, 62B*, S108–S119.

Minkler, M., & Fuller-Thomson, E. (2005). African American grandparents raising grandchildren: A national study using the Census 2000 American Community Survey. *Journal of Gerontology: Social Sciences, 60B*, S82–S92.

Websites

Generations United: http://www.gu.org

GRIEF WORK FACILITATION

Grief is the human response to a significant loss. Often the loss is the death of a family member or close friend, but it may be the loss of a job, or a part of one's body, or loss of self-esteem. This entry primarily addresses the loss of a family member and various approaches to grief work facilitation.

Background

At times *grief* is used interchangeably with the terms *bereavement* or *mourning*. However, others try to distinguish between grief and bereavement, usually referring to the death of someone, and mourning, the outward manifestations of sorrow such as crying, lamenting, or wearing black as a sign of the death of a family member.

Although grief associated with death and other significant losses is a fairly common experience, the adjustment to loss can have a range and variety of responses, including both positive and negative responses. Some people are able to adjust to a loss with continued or increased purpose in life and increased functionality in personal relationships and occupation; this is often labeled *resiliency*. However, for other individuals, grief seems to interfere with family and other relationships, work performance, and personal mental health. These powerful dysfunctional behaviors are usually temporary but can become long term and therefore pose serious concerns for individuals adjusting to loss.

Potentially problematic responses to significant loss include anxiety, depression, substance abuse, physical health problems, family strife, divorce, job loss, increased accidents, suicide, and other mental disorders. These responses not only increase societal burden by early death but also by increasing susceptibility to health problems. Family members carry the burden of each family member's grief.

Grief work facilitation is a term applied to a systematic approach to helping a person, family, or group of people adjust to the death of a family member or other loss. The goals of grief work facilitation are to decrease suffering, increase understanding of the human experience of bereavement, and improve social and psychological functioning. In some instances there may be a goal to increase spirituality and spiritual functioning. *Grief work* is a term often applied to the psychological and neuroprocessing effort to adjust to the loss of a significant person or other loss. The bereaved often describe the fatigue and exhaustion they experience in making sense of the loss and adjusting to life without their loved one. Thus, *grief work* is a good term for this arduous journey.

The experience of grief and bereavement is as old as human existence. In Sigmund Freud's *Mourning and Melancholia*, he tried to distinguish between the normal course of adjustment to grief and a form of adjustment that was more psychologically complicated and dysfunctional. Freud coined the word *grief work* to describe the psychological effort needed to readjust to life after the loss of a significant person. René Spitz's studies of pathologic infant development when children were removed from their mothers during the WWII Blitz of London and John Bowlby's research and three-volume treatise on attachment and loss have laid out the distress and anguish behaviors associated with bereavement. Margaret Stroebe, Robert Hansson, Henk Schut, and Wolfgang Stroebe have authored three books on bereavement research and practice, which clearly reflect the development of the knowledge in this field.

Grief in Families

Most of the literature on grief and bereavement is addressed from an individual point of view. The powerful psychological and physiological impact on individuals is compelling, yet few people live isolated from family members. Families can be traditional, nuclear or extended families, or selected individuals or groups identified as family.

Beth Vaughan-Cole identified three contexts for viewing families for research, but the three frames of reference could be considered for clinical use as well. One context is viewing the family from an individual family member's perspective. The second context is from a dyadic perspective, such as parents, parent–child, or siblings' views of the family. The third perspective is a view of the family as a whole. Although all three can have a family focus, the three different perspectives suggest different approaches to grief work facilitation.

Grief Work Facilitation

At the time of a loss, it is often not clear who is vulnerable to serious adjustment problems even though there are some variables that suggest greater vulnerability, such as the loss of a child, a child's loss of a parent, death due to sudden and unexpected events (including accidents, suicide, homicide, and other traumatic events), and multiple losses.

The bereaved often do not want to seek professional mental health services because they feel grief is a normal experience. They are more often drawn to self-help groups, for example, parents of children who have died from SIDS (sudden infant death syndrome), Compassionate Friends (national grief support organization for families who have lost a child), or loss of spouse groups. Also, they are drawn to educational approaches such as psychoeducation courses or programs on loss and short-term grief groups.

Aside from hospice programs, health care providers and the agencies or institutions that employ them generally do not have specific programs for the bereaved. Often it is only when the bereaved become seriously impaired that they seek help with bereavement adjustment.

Because personal responses to loss can vary from mild to severe, the goals and approaches to assisting the bereaved may vary as well. However, in nearly all situations the two most serious goals are to reduce debilitating psychic pain and foster functional behavior. The formal clinical approaches to grief work facilitation are (a) individual therapy or counseling, (b) group approaches (support groups, group therapy, or group counseling), and (c) family therapy or counseling. Informal approaches to grief support are often offered by clergy and by self-help grief programs.

Individual Grief Facilitation

Many grief adjustment issues can be a focus for individual mental health counseling. Anxiety, depression, and substance abuse are central to a great deal of therapy and counseling. Other issues, such as guilt and loneliness, can be explored with great benefit to clients in therapy. Mourning behaviors have a strong impact on family interactions and family life. Grief-focused individual psychotherapy would include addressing the implications of grief and mourning on family members and the family as a whole. Because death of a loved one is relatively common, adjustment to loss may be added to other ongoing mental health problems in therapy. Supportive individual grief facilitation may also be offered by people who are not mental health professionals, for example, first responders, police, firefighters, victim advocates, and laypeople who are trained and employed by churches or health care agencies.

Grief Group Facilitation

Even though there are a wide variety of group approaches to loss and bereavement, group therapy/counseling offers some of the best interventions for grief work facilitation. Irvin Yalom researched and wrote extensively about the importance of groups in helping the bereaved. Of his 11 curative factors unique to groups, the concepts of universality, instillation of hope, and existential factors are especially healing in groups organized around a single focus such as loss.

Most group therapy techniques foster effective problem solving, good health, and well-being through group member interaction. Group leaders are knowledgeable mental health professionals, well educated in mental illness and in group leadership and group therapy skills. They carefully balance significant issues and continually monitor the effects of interventions on the health and well-being

of the group members. The group leader selects group members from applicants who wish to be in such a group. The group leader may have additional criteria for admission to the group. Due to the high value placed on confidentiality, other members from the same family generally would not be in the same group. Family relationships and issues are commonly the focus of discussion in grief groups as members struggle to improve their lived experiences.

A popular and effective method of grief work facilitation is the psychoeducational group. Whereas many groups are led by mental health professionals, others are often led by people who have experienced grief themselves. For example, a person who has had a family member or close friend die by suicide may attend a group led by someone who has lost someone to suicide. This strong affinity to attend groups led by someone "who has been through it like I have" is a very potent engaging and healing factor. Group selection is generally open to people who have had similar experiences. Sometimes these groups will have couples or more than one family member in the same group. The added dynamic of family interaction within a group requires careful group management, for a couple can dominate the group process.

These psychoeducational groups often have an organized curriculum that emphasizes common grief adjustment issues and open discussion. If the groups are taught and led by experienced group professionals, the curriculum and the group dynamics are managed within a professional framework. Lay leaders of grief groups are encouraged to seek additional training in group leadership and seek professional consultation.

Facilitation of Family Grief

Family therapy/counseling is a unique form of therapeutic intervention. Generally, the entire nuclear family, and sometimes the extended family, is present. It is a dynamic and effective strategy for improving family problem-solving issues and relationships. It is often fast paced with multiple issues being introduced and addressed in a single session. Family therapy/counseling is an excellent venue for addressing the loss of a family member and the repercussions of that loss on each family member and the family as a whole. The loss of a family member often requires that a family restructure their roles and responsibilities, as well as interfamily relationships, at the same time that family members are grieving. Some churches may have a systematic supportive approach to helping grieving families. Although not a structured approach, there are reports of one family helping another family around issues of loss, but little is known about what contributes to a successful outcome for the receiving family.

Types of Grief Work Facilitators

The list of mental health professionals educated in grief work facilitation generally includes psychologists, licensed clinical social workers, psychiatric nurse practitioners, psychiatrists, marriage and family therapists, chaplains, and clergy. There are some health educators who receive additional instruction in grief group facilitation. There are other professionals also prepared in some aspects of grief work facilitation, and they are firefighters, police, victim advocates, first responders, nurses, nurse practitioners, physicians, and physician assistants.

Conclusion

Grief and bereavement are serious though common lived experiences. Loss of a significant family member or friend can dramatically impact individual and family functioning. Some people are resilient, and a significant loss can enhance their meaning of life and increase their efforts to contribute to the lives of their family and others. However, for some, a significant loss interferes with purposeful engagement with others, affects cognitive functioning, and seriously impairs personal and professional functioning.

This entry of grief work facilitation has focused on a background of grief in individuals and families, with a discussion of grief work facilitation modalities and a brief description of professionals educated to facilitate grief work.

Beth Vaughan-Cole

See also Death and the Grieving Process in Families; Death From Unnatural Causes: Drug Overdose; Death From Unnatural Causes: Homicides, Drive-By Shootings; Death From Unnatural Causes: Injuries; Death From Unnatural Causes: Poisoning; Sibling Death/Loss; Social Support Systems for the Family; Types of Family Provider Relationships

Further Readings

Stroebe, M. S., Hansson, R. O., Schut, H., & Stroebe, W. (Eds.). (2008). *Handbook of bereavement research and practice: Advances in theory and intervention*. Washington, DC: American Psychological Association.

Stroebe, M. S., Hansson, R. O., Stroebe, W., & Schut, H. (Eds.). (2001). *Handbook of bereavement research: Consequences, coping, and care*. Washington, DC: American Psychological Association.

Vaughan-Cole, B. (2006). Death, grief, and bereavement in families. In D. R. Crane & E. S. Marshall (Eds.), *Handbook of families and health: Interdisciplinary perspectives* (pp. 244–268). Thousand Oaks, CA: Sage.

Yalom, I. D., & Leszcz, M. (2005). *Theory and practice of group psychotherapy* (5th ed.). New York: Basic Books.

GUARDIANSHIP/CONSERVATORSHIP

The terms *guardianship* and *conservatorship* in the United States differ from state to state and may have different meanings. A guardian in one state may refer only to the care of a minor, whereas in another state it may refer to both minors and adults. This entry contains basic information about guardianship and conservatorship from the perspective of family members trying to provide for a loved one who lacks the capacity to care for his or her own health, seek treatment, or manage day-to-day living needs because of a debilitating physical or mental illness. Because most minors (younger than 18 years of age) are under the care of their parents (or become dependents or wards of the state), this entry focuses on disabled adults in need of conservatorship. Some states do not distinguish between conservatorship and guardianship and refer to the care of all incapacitated persons, including minors and adults in need of protection, as a guardianship. Some states refer to a guardian of the person and a conservator of the estate, whereas other states have conservators of both the person and the estate. For purposes of this entry, the term *conservatorship* will be used, noting this may refer to guardianship in some states. Additionally, some forms of conservatorship cannot be instituted by a private party and must be filed by a governmental agency. Those types of conservatorship petitions will be touched on, because family and friends can still play a vital role in the care of the conservator through coordination with the agency filing the petition.

Definition

Both guardianship and conservatorship processes are formal legal proceedings intended to protect a person who cannot properly provide for one or more of his or her personal needs, including physical health, medical care, food, clothing, shelter; or for a person who is substantially unable to manage his or her own financial resources or to resist fraud or undue influence. The court-appointed conservator becomes the fiduciary or responsible party, who makes various decisions in the best interest of the conservatee. Petitioning for a conservatorship is an intricate process requiring expert opinions, court investigations, and strict notification requirements, as the granting of a petition allows the conservator to make decisions involving fundamentally protected rights for another person.

Conservators (and guardians) are individuals empowered with court authority to care for a person unable to care for himself or herself, his or her estate, or both. *Authority of the person* refers to decisions regarding direct care of the individual, such as medical care and housing. *Authority of the estate* refers to decisions about finances, such as investment accounts and property.

There are several types of conservatorships, and each has different requirements and legal mandates. Indications for conservatorship can be divided into two major categories: one for progressive, degenerative neurological conditions (e.g., Alzheimer's disease and other related dementias) and another for persistent severe mental illness (e.g., schizophrenia). Due to the age of onset of the two categories of diseases, people with dementia tend to be older and have multiple co-occurring medical disorders, whereas people with mental illness tend to be younger and more physically healthy.

For example, in California, the least invasive type of conservatorship is a probate conservatorship, followed by a probate conservatorship with dementia powers, then a Lanterman-Petris-Short (LPS) conservatorship, and finally a Murphy's conservatorship. A probate conservatorship is generally initiated for an individual with dementia. An LPS conservatorship is initiated for a person with a mental illness, and Murphy's conservatorship is for an individual with mental illness who has committed certain dangerous felonies and is incompetent to stand trial for those crimes. The last two types of conservatorship have the potential of curtailing a person's liberty interests, allowing involuntary placement in a locked facility, and therefore require stringent constitutional safeguards and standards of proof. Only the "public conservator" may petition the court for these two types of conservatorships, although if granted, a family member may be appointed conservator.

The person seeking a conservatorship must first determine the benefits of this time-intensive and sometimes costly process. Before initiating a conservatorship, it is important to consider less restrictive options. Many incapacitated individuals will accept voluntary assistance from capable family or friends or fiduciary payees. Others have made plans for their incapacity through advanced planning, including the use of trusts, advanced health care directives, durable power of attorney, or a multitude of other advanced plans. Therefore, it is important to check to see if the incapacitated person has planned for advance directives before filing a petition for conservatorship.

A conservatorship referral can come from a number of sources including family members, social services (Adult Protective Services), health care professionals, banks, and others who have a statutory fiduciary duty to report a potentially incapacitated person to a public agency. This application (or petition) process often requires statements and evaluations from the conservator, physicians, court investigator, conservatorship investigative officer, and attorneys. The final decision to grant or deny a conservatorship lies with the judge, sometime after a jury's verdict. Because this process is involuntary, the nature of guardianships and conservatorships characteristically restricts autonomy and can give control of a conservatee's assets and property to another person. In addition, other civil liberties may be taken from an individual, including the right to make health care decisions, vote, drive a car, enter into contracts, or own a gun.

History

Historically, individuals with mental illness, dementia, or other medical issues that impair their ability to care for themselves were either cared for by family or were stripped of their constitutional freedoms and locked in state institutions and suffered social stigmas. Starting in the late 1960s, societal views on restricting individual freedoms evolved (in part due to the cost of "institutionalizing" mentally ill people) and so did the laws on conservatorship and guardianship. State legislatures aimed to put an end to the inappropriate, indefinite, and involuntary commitment of mentally disordered persons by changing the laws, and the courts, in landmark legal decisions, followed a similar course. As a result, incapacitated individuals unable to care for their basic needs, unable to manage their financial resources, and vulnerable to fraud or undue influence were given greater rights, more oversight by the courts, court-appointed attorneys, and conservators. They also were given greater freedoms and placed in less restrictive environments.

From the late 1980s through the end of the century, increased research, along with more accepting societal views on mental illness and dementia, brought about further changes to the laws, adding specific provisions for the elderly and demented individuals. Recently, the laws on fiduciary duties have become more restrictive, with even greater court oversight, in an attempt to further protect the assets of incapacitated individuals. Due to restrictions, initially aimed at protecting civil liberties, family and friends of individuals who need conservatorship are also experiencing more barriers to the conservatorship process.

Role of Conservator

Any competent person willing and able to provide appropriately for the needs of the conservatee can act as the conservator. If no qualified person petitions and is appointed by the court, the court can appoint a "public guardian" to act as the conservator. A person can be the conservator of the "person," a conservator of the "estate," or a conservator of both the "person and estate."

The role of the conservator of the person is to provide for the conservatee's basic necessities of food, clothing, and shelter, as well as physical and mental health, in a safe and comfortable environment in the conservatee's home or an alternate placement as close to the standard of living as the conservatee enjoyed prior to being placed on conservatorship. The conservator has a duty to

place the conservatee in the least restrictive appropriate setting to meet the needs of the conservatee. In many cases the court will grant exclusive medical authority to the conservator. The job of conservator of the person can be time consuming and difficult, but there are a number of publications that can help make it a manageable process.

The role as the conservator of the estate is that of a financial planner and accountant. The conservator is responsible for the assets of the conservatee and therefore responsible for the estate assets, income, and management. This person, who does not have to be the same person as the conservator of the person, also has to pay bills, file tax returns, and care for the personal and real property of the conservatee. The conservator of the estate is also accountable for any losses to the estate and, as such, may have to be bonded for any loss. Because bond companies insure loss by the conservator, they almost always require a conservator to be represented by an attorney before they issue a bond. Therefore, if a request is made to become the conservator of the estate, it is prudent and cost effective to hire an attorney to help in all aspects of the case. Depending on the size of the estate, it is common for the conservator of the estate to hire financial managers, tax advisors, accountants, real estate managers, and other professionals to help manage the estate.

Medical and Psychiatric Evaluations

A medical or psychiatric evaluation is usually required in the conservatorship application. If the individual is not currently receiving treatment in a hospital setting by a physician, then a personal physician or psychiatrist will need to perform a full history and physical examination of the proposed conservatee to determine the medical and psychiatric diagnoses. Given the assumptions that conservatorship is of relatively long duration (e.g., several months with need for renewals in California), reversible medical conditions or conditions with a limited time course will unlikely be approved. For example, having a severe central nervous system infection may place an individual in a state unable to make decisions about health care needs but may not meet the requirements requiring an appointment of a conservator. However, in such cases, either a family member, or preferably the stated health care attorney-in-fact, will make those decisions through the power of attorney. In the case of psychotic depression, while the individual may have limited insight into his or her illness and decline treatment, a time-limited involuntary treatment can be sought in the hospital setting, and conservatorship would only be required if the person does not recover sufficiently.

During the evaluation process, the physician will examine an individual's clinical decision-making capacity by examining cognitive and psychiatric functioning. In terms of cognitive functioning, the physician will evaluate and make conclusions about sensory acuity, motor skills, attention span, domains of memory (working, short-term, long-term), comprehension, communication, arithmetic, verbal reasoning, visual-spatial skills, and abstract thinking. As for psychiatric functioning, the physician (usually a psychiatrist) will examine for the presence of thought disorder (disorganized or incoherent thinking), hallucinations (usually seeing or hearing things that are not there), delusions (believing in events that are not true or has not occurred), thoughts of hurting oneself or others, insight (or understanding about illness and the treatments needed), and rational judgment (about living arrangements, finances, and treatments). Depending on the type of petition filed, two independent evaluations may be required, especially for the application process. For psychiatric disorders, usually a psychiatric evaluation is needed.

Legal Considerations

Depending on the type of conservatorship, there may be no attorneys to multiple attorneys involved in the matter. Most often there are at least two attorneys involved: One represents the petitioner (the person requesting to become the conservator) and the other represents the proposed conservatee. Anytime a petition proposes to limit substantial liberty interests of an allegedly incompetent person, such as removing that person from his or her home, requesting locked or secure perimeter housing, or requesting the use of antipsychotic medications, the court will appoint an attorney to represent the proposed conservatee.

The attorney representing a client with diminished capacity has a difficult task of balancing ethical duties with what he or she and possibly all the experts believe are in the client's best interest against the expressed views of the client. Generally, the attorney is advised to represent the client in the same manner as he or she would any competent client. The attorney must consider the expressed and implied intentions of the client when he or she was competent to help guide the representation. Sources of information may include past lifestyle, written instruments such as advance directives, power of attorney, wills and trusts, or statements to family and friends. The American Bar Association states the following in its Model Rules of Professional Conduct: "When a lawyer reasonably believes that the client has diminished capacity, is at risk of substantial physical, financial or other harm unless action is taken and cannot adequately act in the client's own interest, the lawyer may take reasonably necessary protective action, including consulting with individuals or entities that have the ability to take action to protect the client and, in appropriate cases, seeking the appointment of a guardian ad litem, conservator or guardian" (rule 1.14(b)).

Applying for Guardianship/Conservatorship

Family members have preference over every other individual or entity for appointment as the conservator. Nonetheless, some family members with a criminal background may not be able to act as a conservator. Also, family members cannot petition for all forms of conservatorship; these family members include a person who is gravely disabled (defined as a person with a mental disorder who is unable to provide for the necessities of food, clothing, or shelter) or a conservatee who is facing certain felonies charges, such as someone who meets criteria of a Murphy's conservatorship in California.

The easiest, fastest, and most stress-free method of applying for conservatorship is to hire an attorney well-versed in the law of conservatorship. A local attorney association or a private fiduciary can provide referrals to an attorney competent in this area of law. If a public agency has initiated the petition, a family member should work closely with them and may seek appointment as the conservator from their petition. In many instances, with court approval, the estate of the conservatee can pay for the cost of the attorney.

A person who seeks to file a petition without the aid of an attorney (filing In Pro Per) will need to consult legal form books and, if available, the court's website for the proper forms. There may be many complicated steps in preparing and filing a petition, which are beyond the scope of this entry, including the filing of a temporary conservatorship, removing a conservatee from his or her home, filing on a veteran or someone on social security, and petitions requiring the appointment of an attorney for a conservatee.

Typically, when filing a petition for conservatorship, a doctor's declaration stating that the proposed conservatee is incapacitated and in need of a conservator is needed. The petition must be filed with the appropriate court, at which time the clerk will set a hearing on the petition. Notice must be given to the proposed conservatee and his or her relatives, as specified by law, as to the date, time, and place of the court hearing. Once all parties and individuals have been served, a proof of service must be filed with the court. Prior to the hearing, a court investigator will talk to all parties to determine the appropriateness of the petition and the suitability of the proposed conservator and will file a report with the court regarding the findings. If an attorney was appointed for the conservatee, that person will also file a report with the court. If the petitioner seeks to become the conservator of the estate, an inventory of the property must be collected and given to a probate referee for appraisal. Assuming all the paperwork is completed properly and there is a need for conservatorship, the court will make a decision on the merits of the petition. Once a conservatorship is in place, it may have to be renewed yearly, and periodically the conservator will have to file accountings on the assets of the estate.

Dilemmas: Family Members/ Parents as Conservators

There are obvious benefits to having a family member as the conservator. Families know the likes and dislikes and can spend more time with the conservatee than a private or public fiduciary. They may not charge the conservatee as much for caring for the person and estate and therefore may be more cost effective than hiring a private fiduciary. Family members can be more flexible and take more risks in caring for the conservatee than an outside fiduciary, even though the legal and ethical standards are the same.

On the downside, some families have internal disputes, which may cause further tension and possible conflicts among the family members regarding the care and management of the person and estate. These disputes can lead to costly legal battles and break up families. Further, private and public fiduciaries have expertise in caring for individuals and their estates. They know funding sources and how to work with bureaucratic systems such as Social Security, Medicare, the Department of Veterans Affairs, and health insurers. Fiduciaries also are experts on the laws of conservatorship and know when and how to file those petitions with the court. They also have attorneys, doctors, accountants, tax professionals, and real estate advisors at their disposal, all knowledgeable about the laws on conservatorship. Further, it can be very difficult for family and friends to make the tough decisions for their loved one with mental illness. Often they will have to make decisions the conservatee is opposed to, such as involuntary antipsychotic medication treatments and placements in locked facilities. This can lead to resentment of the family or friend by the conservatee.

Therefore, in making the decision to become a conservator, a person should consider many factors, including the makeup of the family, the condition and demeanor of the proposed conservatee, the time commitment, expertise or willingness to learn about mental disorder, and the possible complications of the estate. Finally, the person must consider the implications and personal costs if the conservatorship is not managed correctly.

Conclusion

The terms, definitions, and usage of *guardianship* and *conservatorship* differ from state to state but are uniformly formal requests to the court to restrict the liberty rights of individuals. Therefore, an alternative, less formal means of protecting an incapacitated person with dementia or mental illness is often a desirable approach. Depending on the underlying medical or psychiatric disorder, the terms and the legal requirement of the conservatorship may differ. If a formal petition is necessary, then the proposed conservator should contact the state court for forms and procedures and the local attorney association for recommendations of attorneys who practice in this area. The conservator should look to sources that explain the conservatorship process and fiduciary duties, such as the *Handbook for Conservators*, so that he or she can competently care for the conservatee.

Glen L. Xiong and Denis Zilaff

See also Advocacy for Families; Alzheimer's Disease: An Overview of Family Issues; Caregiving: Adults With Developmental Disabilities; Caregiving: Elderly; Parental Abandonment

Further Readings

American Bar Association. (n.d.). *Model rules of professional conduct*. Available at http://www.abanet.org/cpr/mrpc/mrpc_toc.html

Judicial Council of California. (2002). *Handbook for conservators*. San Francisco: Author. Available at http://www.courtinfo.ca.gov/selfhelp/seniors/handbook.htm

Leatherman, M. E., & Goethe, K. E. (2009). Substituted decision making: Elder guardianship. *Journal of Psychiatric Practice*,15(6), 470–476.

Moye, J., Butz, S. W., Marson, D. C., Wood, E., & ABA-APA Capacity Assessment of Older Adults Working Group. (2007). A Conceptual Model and Assessment Template for Capacity Evaluation in Adult Guardianship. *The Gerontologist, 47*(5), 591–603.